American Prisoners of War
Held at Chatham
During the War of 1812

American Prisoners of War
Held at
Chatham during the War of 1812

Transcribed by
Eric Eugene Johnson

Society of the War of 1812
in the
State of Ohio

HERITAGE BOOKS
2019

HERITAGE BOOKS
AN IMPRINT OF HERITAGE BOOKS, INC.

Books, CDs, and more—Worldwide

For our listing of thousands of titles see our website
at
www.HeritageBooks.com

Published 2019 by
HERITAGE BOOKS, INC.
Publishing Division
5810 Ruatan Street
Berwyn Heights, Md. 20740

Copyright © 2019 Society of the War of 1812 in the State of Ohio

All rights reserved. No part of this book may be reproduced or transmitted in any form or by any means, electronic or mechanical, including photocopying, recording or by any information storage and retrieval system without written permission from the author, except for the inclusion of brief quotations in a review.

International Standard Book Number
Paperbound: 978-0-7884-5769-2

- Table of Contents -

Introduction	1
The Honored Dead	5
Abbreviations	6
Alphabetical listing of names	7
Numeric listing by prisoner number	295
Prisoner listing by ship or regiment	323
Definitions	367
Bibliography	373

Introduction

This is a transcription of American prisoner of war records from the U.S. Navy, privateers and merchant vessels (plus some civilians) who were captured, and then interned by the British Empire at Chatham, England during the War of 1812. There are also many U.S. Army soldiers included in these transcriptions who had been transferred from Montreal and Halifax, Canada to Chatham.

This volume was compiled from copies of the *General Entry Book of American Prisoners of War* ledgers of the British Admiralty made by the Public Records Office in London, Great Britain (ADM 103 series). The *General Entry Book* (GEB) records are composed of lines for the recording of names and personal information of those incarcerated. The record of each prisoner is found on two facing pages. The clerk making the entries wrote the page number on the upper right-side corner of each page. The names and information of nine men can be found on each double page for the Americans interned at the Chatham.

Microfilm	POW facilities	Dates	Number of prisoners
ADM 103/56	Chatham	Oct 1812 – Mar 1813	1,053
ADM 103/57	Chatham	Mar 1813 – Aug 1813	1,034
ADM 103/58	Chatham	Aug 1813 – Jan 1814	1,088
ADM 103/59	Chatham	Jan 1814 – Oct 1814	777
Total			3,955

Below are the column headers from the GEB ledgers used at Chatham. Titles in brackets, "[" and "]", indicates that the transcriber has changed the column headers from the original to a more meaningful header. Some of the columns have been eliminated in this book while other columns have been combined.

Column 1 – Number
   Each prisoner of war arriving at a prisoner facility was assigned a number.

Column 2 – By what Ship or how taken [How taken]
   This column lists the Royal Naval ship or privateer which captured the prisoner. Also included in this column are the men who gave themselves up as a prisoner, who were impressed by the Royal Navy, taken ashore or captured by the Royal Army.

Column 3 – Time when [When Taken]
   The date the prisoner was taken into custody.

Column 4 – Where Taken
   This column lists the location of capture which could indicate latitudes and longitudes if at sea, a port, or a geographic region or location.

Column 5 – Name of Prize [Prize Name]
   The name of the ship or vessel of the prisoner of war, or if from land forces, the name of the regiment or service.

Column 6 - Whether Man of War, Privateer, or Merchant Vessel [Ship Type]
   The type of ship or vessel, that is: man of war (warship), revenue cutter, privateer, letter of marque, merchant vessel, or prize of a privateer. Land forces indicate regular army, volunteers or militia.

Column 7 – Prisoner's Names [title not used]
   The prisoner names given in the GEB are first name then last name, e.g. John Smith, but in this book the last name is given first then the first name.

Column 8 – Quality [Rank]
   This column gives the rank of the prisoner. In addition to naval, privateer and merchant vessel ranks, there are also civilians, merchants, supercargoes and passengers found in these records.

Column 9 – Time when received into custody [Date Received]
   The date when a prisoner arrived at a prisoner facility.

Column 10 – From what ship, or whence received [From what ship]
   The location of the prisoner before being received at the current prisoner of war facility. This could be the capturing ship, the ship that transported the prisoner to England, a hospital, another prison facility or parole location.

Column 11 – Place of Nativity [Born]
   Lists the birth place of a prisoner.

Column 12 – Age
   The age of the prisoner in years, most likely, from his last birthday.

Columns 13 through 18 are not used in this book [Race]
   These columns indicate the height, hair color, color of eyes, type of complexion and body marks (including tattoos) or wounds of a prisoner. Included in these physical descriptions are the races of non-Caucasians, which are Black, Negro, Mulatto, Creole or Chinese. The author has created a new column entitled Race to indicate non-Caucasians.

Columns 19 through 32 are not used in this book
   The personal items of a prisoner were inventoried upon arrival at a prisoner of war facility and the required missing items were replaced. These items include hammocks, beds, straw mattresses, cushions, blankets, hats, jackets, waistcoats, trousers, shirts, shoes, stockings and handkerchiefs.

Columns 33 through 35 have been combined into a single entry [titles not used]
   This new column indicates when a prisoner died at a prisoner facility, when he escaped from a prisoner facility, when he was discharged to another prison facility, or when he was released and sent back to the United States.

   Column 33 – Exchanged, Discharged, Died or Escaped [field not used]
      "E" or "R" indicates that the prisoner escaped from the parole location while "D" indicates that he was discharged. "DD" indicates that he died while assigned to a parole location.

   Column 34 – Time When [field not used]
      Contains the date of the event from column 33.

   Column 35 - Whither, and by what order if discharged. [field not used]
      This column shows the place or ship that the prisoner was sent when he was discharged from the prison facility. Orders were given by the His Majesty's Transport Board.

The Royal Navy's Chatham Dockyards was the home of one of the three prisoner of war prison ship facilities in England which were used during the War of 1812 to house American prisoners of war. The facility had been used since 1796 to intern French prisoners of war (and their allies) during the Napoleonic Wars. The other two prison ship facilities were located at Portsmouth and at Plymouth.

A total of 3,955 Americans were interned at Chatham between 11 August 1812 and 22 October 1814. The name of a Frenchman, John Sanssuillon, was placed in the ledger between prisoner numbers 1809 and 1810. He is listed as prisoner number 1809a in this book. No reason is given for this insertion, and no personal information was recorded for him. He was released and sent to Calais, France.

One American, James Johnson, has two prisoner numbers, 3725 and 3794. He was released and then appears again in the ledger without a explantation. It is noted in the ledger that this is the same man.

A total of forty-five men escaped from the prison hulks and it appears that those who were recaptured, were not sent back to Chatham. There were 124 recorded deaths at Chatham and there appears to be 543 African Americans listed on the ledger rolls.

Chatham received prisoners directly from the prison facilities at Halifax, Plymouth and Portsmouth. A large number of men were captured at the ports in Great Britain at the beginning of the war and sent to Chatham. The majority of the prisoners were sent to Dartmoor before the end of October 1814 when the prison facility was closed. With the end of the Napoleonic Wars, the English sent all of the French prisoners home, and moved all of the American prisoners in England to Dartmoor.

Senior officers from the captured American ships and officers from the U.S. Army were first sent to Chatham and within days they were sent to either Reading or Ashburton on parole. These men were free to live in these English villages instead of being interned on the prison ships.

The penmanship in the first two ledgers was very good, and from poor to good in the remaining two ledgers. The spelling of non-familiar names was done phonetically.

Any errors or omissions are regretted and are the fault of the transcriber.

Eric Eugene Johnson

President (2008-2011)
Society of the War of 1812 in the State of Ohio

Registrar General (2017-   )
General Society of the War of 1812

- In memory of those who did not return -
The Honored Dead

Abbott, Samuel
Adams, Leonard
Allen, William
Andrews, Joseph
Antoine, John
Baddrige, Charles
Bakeman, Ely
Baptist, Michael
Barber, Major
Basset, Edward S.
Beach, John
Billings, Thomas
Blackman, Moses
Brower, Frederick
Brown, Edward
Brown, Jesse
Brown, John
Bump, Henry
Bunker, Nicholas
Butcher, James
Butler, William
Carson, Robert
Chase, Welcom
Christie, John
Clough, Isaac
Collins, Sylvester
Cook, William
Copland, Thomas
Coston, Thomas
Crosy, S. M.
Cunningham, Caleb
Curry, William
Dempsey, Daniel
Devereux, John
Dougherty, Hamilton
Dow, John
Downey, John
Ellingwood, William H.
Elsworth, John
Evans, John
Forman, William
Forseyth, Alexander

Freeman, John
Gibson, Samuel
Gordon, Sperrin
Grandy, Amos
Gray, Thomas
Green, James Beckwith
Green, John
Green, William
Hall, Henry
Handerson, Hans
Hardward, Isaac
Harvey, Peter
Head, James
Holt, Jacob L.
House, Snow
Hubart, Joseph
Hubbard, Christian
Hubbard, George
Hutchinson, Thomas
Ireland, John
Jackson, Samuel
Johnson, John
Johnson, Peter
Jones, James
Jones, John
Kennard, Joseph
Lant, Henry
Lathrum, William
Ledlowe, John
Lewis, Job
Light, John
Limon, Andrew
Ludlow, Reuben
Malony, Robert
Malvern, Lanis
Manley, Randolph
Mansfield, Elijah
McEver, William
Miles, John
Miller, Ezekiel
Mills, Samuel
Moore, Benjamin

Morgan, John R.
Mossland, Reuben
Nash, William
Nelson, Samuel A.
Newby, John
Newell, Benjamin
Nickels, Hugh
Norton, David
Paine, Clement
Pinkham, Daniel
Pollet, William
Pollett, Edward
Porter, William
Pousland, William
Randson, John
Read, Major
Richards, George
Rooter, John
Ropes, Daniel
Ryan, Thomas
Saunders, Charles
Sawyer, Jonathan
Scott, Henry
Selby, Hans
Silver, Samuel
Simonds, Proctor
Skinner, Ebenezer
Smith, John
Tardy, Anthony
Thompson, George
Warren, James
Watson, John
Webber, Stephen
Wicks, James
Williams, Edward
Williams, Frederick
Williams, George
Winchester, Richard
Witney, Samuel
Worthing, Isaac

- Those who die in service to the United States should not be forgotten –

Abbreviations

HM – His Majesty
HMS – His Majesty's Ship
HMT – His Majesty's Transport
U.S. – United States
U.S.M.C. – United States Marine Corps
U.S.R.M. – United States Revenue Marine
War – Warship
MV – Merchant Vessel
P – Privateer
LM – Letter of Marque
WI – West Indies

Also, standard state name abbreviations were used

The locations in Maine are listed as MA and not ME. During the War of 1812, Maine was still a part of Massachusetts.

(1), (2), etc. – Different men with the same names assigned to a single ship or a number of ships with the same name.

Alphabetical listing of names

Abbot, William F. - Seaman - Number: 353 - Prize name: Postsea, prize to the Privateer Thrasher - Ship type: P - How taken: HM Sloop Helena - When taken: 31 Dec 1813 - Where taken: off Azores - Date received: 19 Jan 1813 - From what ship: HMS Raisonnable - Born: Cape Ann - Age: 25 - Discharged on 24 Jul 1813 and released to Cartel Hoffminy.

Abbott, Daniel - Seaman - Number: 3290 - Prize name: Vivid - Ship type: P - How taken: HM Frigate Nymphe - When taken: 20 Apr 1813 - Where taken: off Cape Cod - Date received: 23 Feb 1814 - From what ship: Halifax via HMT Malabar - Born: Billerica - Age: 17 - Discharged on 21 Jul 1814 and sent to Dartmoor on HMS Portia.

Abbott, Samuel - Seaman - Number: 2583 - How taken: Impressed at London - When taken: 19 Oct 1813 - Date received: 1 Nov 1813 - From what ship: HMS Raisonnable - Born: Andover, MA - Age: 27 - Died on 17 Feb 1814.

Abbott, William - Steward - Number: 3313 - Prize name: Enterprise - Ship type: P - How taken: HM Frigate Tenedos - When taken: 21 May 1813 - Where taken: off Cape Cod - Date received: 23 Feb 1814 - From what ship: Halifax via HMT Malabar - Born: Ipswich - Age: 22 - Discharged on 10 Oct 1814 and sent to Dartmoor on the Mermaid.

Abraham, Joseph - Seaman - Number: 2330 - How taken: Impressed at Gravesend, England - When taken: 24 Sep 1813 - Date received: 12 Oct 1813 - From what ship: HMS Raisonnable - Born: Hamilton - Age: 22 - Discharged on 21 Jan 1814 and released to HMS Ceres.

Abraham, William - 2nd Mate - Number: 1415 - Prize name: Mariner - Ship type: MV - How taken: HM Brig Lyra - When taken: 15 Dec 1812 - Where taken: off Bilboa, Spain - Date received: 5 Apr 1813 - From what ship: Plymouth via HMS Dwarf - Born: Nantucket - Age: 28 - Discharged on 2 Jul 1813 and released to Cartel Moses Brown.

Adams, Abijah - Seaman - Number: 3948 - Prize name: Rattlesnake - Ship type: LM - How taken: HM Frigate Rhin - When taken: 17 Mar 1814 - Where taken: off Bermuda - Date received: 18 Oct 1813 - From what ship: London - Born: Boston - Age: 27 - Discharged on 22 Oct 1814 and sent to Dartmoor on HMS Leyden.

Adams, Henry - Mate - Number: 3356 - Prize name: Rolla - Ship type: P - How taken: HM Ship-of-the-Line Victorious - When taken: 8 Jan 1813 - Where taken: off Halifax - Date received: 23 Feb 1814 - From what ship: Halifax via HMT Malabar - Born: Hardwick - Age: 22 - Discharged on 10 Oct 1814 and sent to Dartmoor on the Mermaid.

Adams, Leonard - Seaman - Number: 750 - Prize name: Quebec of London, prize of the Privateer Paul Jones - Ship type: P - How taken: HM Brig Derwent - When taken: 29 Jan 1813 - Where taken: off Lisbon - Date received: 25 Feb 1813 - From what ship: HMS Brazen - Born: New York - Age: 26 - Died on 31 Mar 1813 from debility (feeble).

Adams, Robert - Seaman - Number: 256 - How taken: Gave himself up at London - When taken: 28 Nov 1812 - Date received: 7 Dec 1812 - From what ship: HMS Raisonnable - Born: Newburyport - Age: 33 - Discharged on 4 Mar 1813 to the Wailey.

Adams, Thomas - Seaman - Number: 177 - How taken: Stopped at London - When taken: 29 Oct 1812 - Date received: 5 Nov 1812 - From what ship: HMS Namur - Born: Long Island - Age: 27 - Discharged in Jul 1813 and released to Cartel Moses Brown.

Adams, Thomas - Seaman - Number: 2293 - How taken: Gave himself up from HM Frigate Ganymede - When taken: 1 Apr 1813 - Date received: 17 Sep 1813 - From what ship: HMS Raisonnable - Born: New York - Age: 48 - Discharged on 4 Sep 1814 and sent to Dartmoor on HMS Freya.

Adams, Thomas - Seaman - Number: 2601 - How taken: Gave himself up from HM Ship-of-the-Line Tremendous - When taken: 27 May 1813 - Date received: 5 Nov 1813 - From what ship: HMS Hindostan - Born: Charleston - Age: 48 - Race: Blackman - Discharged on 12 Aug 1814 and sent to Dartmoor on HMS Alpheus.

Adams, William - Seaman - Number: 3856 - How taken: Gave himself up from HM Ship-of-the-Line Africa - When taken: 4 Oct 1813 - Date received: 24 Aug 1814 - From what ship: London - Born: Colchester - Age: 23 - Race: Black - Discharged on 26 Sep 1814 and sent to Dartmoor on HMS Leyden.

Adivoe, Henry - Seaman - Number: 1788 - How taken: Taken up at London - When taken: 11 Jun 1813 - Date received: 1 Jul 1813 - From what ship: HMS Raisonnable - Born: New York - Age: 34 - Discharged on 25 Jul 1814 and sent to Dartmoor on HMS Bittern.

Albert, Hezekiah - Seaman - Number: 1442 - Prize name: Orbit - Ship type: MV - How taken: HM Brig Achates - When taken: 29 Jan 1813 - Where taken: Lat 49 N Long 13 W - Date received: 6 Apr 1813 - From what ship: Plymouth via HMS Decoy - Born: Rhode Island - Age: 20 - Discharged on 25 Sep 1814 and sent to Dartmoor on HMS Leyden.

Albert, John - Seaman - Number: 1295 - How taken: Gave himself up from HM Guardship Royal William - When taken: 3 Feb 1813 - Date received: 16 Mar 1813 - From what ship: Portsmouth, via HMS Abundance - Born: New Jersey - Age: 22 - Race: Black - Discharged on 23 Jul 1814 and sent to Dartmoor.

Albro, George - Seaman - Number: 1509 - How taken: Gave himself up from HM Ship-of-the-Line Blake - When taken: 10 Dec 1812 - Date received: 8 Apr 1813 - From what ship: Portsmouth, via an admiral's tender - Born: Newport - Age: 33 - Discharged on 4 Aug 1814 and sent to Dartmoor on HMS Alpheus.

Aldor, Robert (alias Robert Lucas) - Seaman - Number: 2306 - How taken: Gave himself up from HM Sloop Acorn - When taken: 27 Jul 1813 - Date received: 8 Oct 1813 - From what ship: Portsmouth, via an admiral's tender - Born: Philadelphia - Age: 22 - Discharged on 8 Sep 1814 and sent to Dartmoor on HMS Niobe.

Aldridge, Richard - Seaman - Number: 2726 - Prize name: Mary, prize to the Privateer True Blooded Yankee - Ship type: P - How taken: HM Ship of-the-Line Bellerophon - When taken: 16 Dec 1813 - Where taken: off Land's End, England - Date received: 7 Jan 1814 - From what ship: Portsmouth - Born: Pennsylvania - Age: 26 - Discharged on 8 Sep 1814 and sent to Dartmoor on HMS Niobe.

Alexander, George - Seaman - Number: 2084 - How taken: Gave himself up from HM Brig Scorpion - When taken: 27 May 1813 - Date received: 9 Aug 1813 - From what ship: HMS Thames - Born: Philadelphia - Age: 26 - Discharged on 12 Aug 1814 and sent to Dartmoor on HMS Alpheus.

Alexander, James - Cook - Number: 378 - Prize name: Union American - Ship type: MV - How taken: Impressed at London - When taken: 23 Jan 1813 - Date received: 31 Jan 1813 - From what ship: HMS Raisonnable - Born: Cambridge, MA - Age: 31 - Race: Black man - Discharged on 24 Jul 1813 and released to Cartel Hoffminy.

Alexander, John - Seaman - Number: 154 - Prize name: Urbana - Ship type: MV - How taken: Stopped at London - When taken: 28 Oct 1812 - Date received: 5 Nov 1812 - From what ship: HMS Namur - Born: Newcastle, DE - Age: 33 - Discharged in Jul 1813 and released to Cartel Moses Brown.

Alexander, Richard - Seaman - Number: 3178 - Prize name: Wolf Cove - Ship type: MV - How taken: HM Frigate Briton - When taken: 1 Dec 1813 - Where taken: off Brest, France - Date received: 7 Jan 1813 - From what ship: Halifax - Born: Massachusetts - Age: 22 - Discharged on 25 Sep 1814 and sent to Dartmoor on HMS Leyden.

Alexander, Robert - Seaman - Number: 1776 - How taken: Gave himself up from HMS Dapper - When taken: 7 Jan 1813 - Date received: 14 Jun 1813 - From what ship: HMS Arethusa - Born: Salem - Age: 28 - Discharged on 24 Jul 1813 and released to Cartel Hoffminy.

Allen, Andrew - Seaman - Number: 293 - Prize name: Dido - Ship type: MV - How taken: Detained off Faco - When taken: 12 Aug 1812 - Date received: 23 Dec 1812 - From what ship: Greenlaw Depot - Born: Manchester - Age: 45 - Discharged on 10 May 1813 and released to Cartel Admittance.

Allen, Barnes - Seaman - Number: 532 - Prize name: Baltimore - Ship type: P - How taken: HM Transport Diadem - When taken: 7 Oct 1812 - Where taken: S. Andres - Date received: 23 Feb 1813 - From what ship: Portsmouth via HMS Dromedary - Born: Baltimore - Age: 33 - Discharged on 8 Jun 1813 and released to Cartel Rodrigo.

Allen, Daniel - Boy - Number: 131 - Prize name: Eliza Ann - Ship type: MV - How taken: Stopped at London - When taken: 26 Oct 1812 - Date received: 5 Nov 1812 - From what ship: HMS Namur - Born: Beverly, MA

- Age: 12 - Discharged on 23 Mar 1813 and released to the Cartel Robinson Potter.

Allen, David - Seaman - Number: 2854 - Prize name: Fire Fly - Ship type: LM - How taken: HM Frigate Revolutionnaire - When taken: 19 Oct 1813 - Where taken: off Cape Ortegal, Spain - Date received: 7 Jan 1814 - From what ship: Portsmouth - Born: Massachusetts - Age: 20 - Discharged on 26 Sep 1814 and sent to Dartmoor on HMS Leyden.

Allen, E. T. - Seaman - Number: 2236 - How taken: Apprehended at London off MV Castle Huntley - When taken: 13 Aug 1813 - Date received: 7 Sep 1813 - From what ship: HMS Raisonnable - Born: New Bedford - Age: 22 - Escaped on 16 May 1814 from HM Prison Ship Crown Prince.

Allen, Edward - 2nd Mate - Number: 1330 - Prize name: Sea Nymph - Ship type: MV - How taken: HM Brig Thrasher - When taken: 4 Mar 1813 - Where taken: off River Jade (Germany) - Date received: 22 Mar 1813 - From what ship: HMS Thrasher - Born: Nantucket - Age: 19 - Discharged on 23 Jul 1814 and sent to Dartmoor.

Allen, Edward D. - Prize Master - Number: 3008 - Prize name: Yankee - Ship type: P - How taken: HM Frigate Shannon - When taken: 20 Aug 1813 - Where taken: at sea - Date received: 7 Jan 1814 - From what ship: Halifax - Born: Connecticut - Age: 23 - Discharged on 25 Sep 1814 and sent to Dartmoor on HMS Leyden.

Allen, Elijah - Seaman - Number: 1039 - Prize name: Catharine - Ship type: MV - How taken: HM Frigate Leonidas - When taken: 31 Jul 1812 - Where taken: off Ireland - Date received: 11 Mar 1813 - From what ship: Yarmouth via HMS Tenders - Born: New Bedford - Age: 18 - Discharged on 26 Jul 1813 and released to Cartel Hoffminy.

Allen, George - Seaman - Number: 3327 - Prize name: Porcupine - Ship type: LM - How taken: HM Frigate Acasta - When taken: 18 Jul 1813 - Where taken: off Cape Sable, Florida - Date received: 23 Feb 1814 - From what ship: Halifax via HMT Malabar - Born: New York - Age: 19 - Race: Black - Discharged on 10 Oct 1814 and sent to Dartmoor on the Mermaid.

Allen, Henry - Seaman - Number: 1324 - Prize name: Sword Fish - Ship type: P - How taken: HM Ship-of-the-Line Elephant - When taken: 28 Dec 1812 - Where taken: off Azores - Date received: 16 Mar 1813 - From what ship: Portsmouth, via HMS Abundance - Born: Salem - Age: 23 - Discharged on 24 Jul 1813 and released to Cartel Hoffminy.

Allen, Isaac - Seaman - Number: 1750 - How taken: Gave himself up from HMS Impeteux - When taken: 2 Dec 1812 - Date received: 30 May 1813 - From what ship: HMS Impetius - Born: Philadelphia - Age: 28 - Discharged on 24 Jul 1814 and sent to Dartmoor on HMS Liffey.

Allen, Jacob - Seaman - Number: 1471 - Prize name: Union - Ship type: MV - How taken: HM Frigate Iris - When taken: 17 Jan 1813 - Where taken: at sea - Date received: 6 Apr 1813 - From what ship: Portsmouth via Tender Eliza - Born: Lancaster - Age: 32 - Discharged on 28 Apr 1813 and released to the David Scott.

Allen, John - Seaman - Number: 3893 - How taken: Gave himself up from HM Frigate Astrea - When taken: 13 Apr 1813 - Date received: 30 Aug 1814 - From what ship: Transport Office - Born: Delaware - Age: 36 - Discharged on 2 Sep 1814 and sent to Dartmoor on HMS Leyden.

Allen, John - Seaman - Number: 294 - Prize name: Dido - Ship type: MV - How taken: Detained off Faco - When taken: 12 Aug 1812 - Date received: 23 Dec 1812 - From what ship: Greenlaw Depot - Born: Boston - Age: 25 - Race: Black man - Discharged on 10 May 1813 and released to Cartel Admittance.

Allen, John - Seaman - Number: 1340 - How taken: Gave himself up from HM Ship-of-the-Line Cornwall - When taken: 21 Mar 1813 - Date received: 26 Mar 1813 - From what ship: HMS Raisonnable - Born: Barnstable - Age: 23 - Discharged on 23 Jul 1814 and sent to Dartmoor.

Allen, John - Boy - Number: 1898 - Prize name: Prompt - Ship type: MV - How taken: Chance, British privateer - When taken: 28 Mar 1813 - Where taken: Bay of Biscay - Date received: 7 Jul 1813 - From what ship: Portsmouth via HMS Tribune - Born: Boston - Age: 14 - Discharged on 4 Aug 1814 and sent to Dartmoor on HMS Liverpool.

Allen, John - Seaman - Number: 2244 - Prize name: Orders in Council - Ship type: LM - How taken: HM Frigate Surveillante - When taken: 1 Jan 1813 - Where taken: off Cape Ortegal, Spain - Date received: 7 Sep 1813 - From what ship: HMS Raisonnable - Born: New York - Age: 24 - Race: Mulatto - Discharged on 11 Aug

1814 and sent to Dartmoor on HMS Freya.

Allen, John D. - Seaman - Number: 1923 - How taken: Impressed at London - When taken: 7 Jul 1813 - Date received: 11 Jul 1813 - From what ship: HMS Raisonnable - Born: New York - Age: 29 - Discharged on 4 Aug 1814 and sent to Dartmoor on HMS Liverpool.

Allen, Peter - Seaman - Number: 612 - Prize name: King of Rome - Ship type: P - How taken: HM Brig Wolverine - When taken: 13 Dec 1812 - Where taken: at sea - Date received: 23 Feb 1813 - From what ship: Portsmouth via HMS Dromedary - Born: Spain - Age: 32 - Discharged on 2 Jul 1813 and released to Cartel Moses Brown.

Allen, William - Seaman - Number: 774 - Prize name: Alagana - Ship type: MV - How taken: HM Ship-of-the-Line San Juan - When taken: 8 May 1812 - Where taken: Gibraltar - Date received: 25 Feb 1813 - From what ship: HMS Brazen - Born: Westmoreland, VA - Age: 32 - Discharged on 10 May 1813 and released to Cartel Admittance.

Allen, William - Seaman - Number: 946 - Prize name: Mariner - Ship type: MV - How taken: HM Brig Lyra - When taken: 15 Dec 1812 - Where taken: off Bilboa, Spain - Date received: 10 Mar 1813 - From what ship: HMS Tigress - Born: Newbury - Age: 19 - Discharged on 2 Jul 1813 and released to Cartel Moses Brown.

Allen, William - Seaman - Number: 1827 - Prize name: tender to the Privateer True Blooded Yankee - Ship type: P - How taken: HM Brig Hope - When taken: 24 Jun 1813 - Where taken: off Brest, France - Date received: 7 Jul 1813 - From what ship: Portsmouth via HMS Scorpion - Born: Georgetown - Age: 36 - Discharged on 25 Jul 1814 and sent to Dartmoor on HMS Bittern.

Allen, William - Seaman - Number: 2591 - How taken: Gave himself up from HM Brig Scorpion - When taken: 27 May 1813 - Date received: 5 Nov 1813 - From what ship: HMS Hindostan - Born: Newport, RI - Age: 32 - Race: Blackman - Died on 16 Feb 1814 from pulmanary inflamation.

Allen, William - Seaman - Number: 3401 - Prize name: Elbridge Gerry - Ship type: P - How taken: HM Frigate Crescent - When taken: 16 Sep 1813 - Where taken: at sea - Date received: 23 Feb 1814 - From what ship: Halifax via HMT Malabar - Born: New York - Age: 22 - Race: Black - Discharged on 22 Oct 1814 and sent to Dartmoor on HMS Leyden.

Alley, Jacob - Seaman - Number: 658 - Prize name: U.S.R.M. Cutter James Madison - Ship type: War - How taken: HM Frigate Barbadoes - When taken: 22 Aug 1812 - Where taken: at sea - Date received: 24 Feb 1813 - From what ship: Portsmouth via HMS Ulysses - Born: Boston - Age: 24 - Discharged on 10 May 1813 and released to Cartel Admittance.

Allison, William R. - Seaman - Number: 3654 - Prize name: prize to the Privateer Blockade - Ship type: P - How taken: HM Sloop Sapphire - When taken: 24 Feb 1814 - Where taken: coast of America - Date received: 31 Mar 1814 - From what ship: HMS Raisonnable - Born: Alexandria - Age: 28 - Discharged on 25 Sep 1814 and sent to Dartmoor on HMS Niobe.

Allyn, David - Seaman - Number: 62 - Prize name: Laurel - Ship type: MV - How taken: From a cutter off Bermuda - When taken: 24 Jul 1812 - Date received: 3 Nov 1812 - From what ship: HMS Plover - Born: Hartford, CT - Age: 23 - Discharged on 23 Mar 1813 and released to the Cartel Robinson Potter.

Alston, Richard - Seaman - Number: 3259 - Prize name: Volante - Ship type: P - How taken: HM Brig Curlew - When taken: 25 Mar 1813 - Where taken: off Boston - Date received: 23 Feb 1814 - From what ship: Halifax via HMT Malabar - Born: Marblehead - Age: 21 - Discharged on 10 Oct 1814 and sent to Dartmoor on the Mermaid.

Amos, Isaac - Seaman - Number: 1336 - How taken: Gave himself up from HM Ship-of-the-Line Sultan - When taken: 1 Nov 1812 - Date received: 22 Mar 1813 - From what ship: HMS Raisonnable - Born: Boston - Age: 20 - Race: Mulatto - Discharged on 23 Jul 1814 and sent to Dartmoor.

Anan, John - Seaman - Number: 3950 - How taken: Impressed at London - When taken: 13 Oct 1814 - Date received: 21 Oct 1813 - From what ship: Quebec - Born: Philadelphia - Age: 22 - Race: Black - Discharged on 22 Oct 1814 and sent to Dartmoor on HMS Leyden.

Andersen, James - Seaman - Number: 464 - Prize name: Hunter - Ship type: P - How taken: HM Frigate Phoebe - When taken: 23 Dec 1812 - Where taken: off Azores - Date received: 19 Feb 1813 - From what ship: HMS

Modeste - Born: Christiansand - Age: 18 - Discharged on 24 Jul 1813 and released to Cartel Hoffminy.

Andersen, John - Seaman - Number: 2149 - Prize name: Matilda, prize of the U.S. Brig Argus - Ship type: War - How taken: HM Frigate Revolutionnaire - When taken: 25 Jul 1813 - Where taken: off Lorient, France - Date received: 9 Aug 1813 - From what ship: HMS Thames - Born: Salem - Age: 27 - Race: Black - Discharged on 1 Oct 1813 and released to HMS Ceres.

Anderson, Aaron - Seaman - Number: 1102 - Prize name: Calcutta, East Indian Ship - Ship type: MV - How taken: Two Brothers, British privateer from Guernsey - When taken: 30 Nov 1812 - Where taken: off St. Helena - Date received: 14 Mar 1813 - From what ship: Portsmouth via HMS Beagle - Born: Newburn, NY - Age: 18 - Discharged on 8 Jun 1813 and released to Cartel Rodrigo.

Anderson, Alexander - Seaman - Number: 1941 - Prize name: Criterion - Ship type: MV - How taken: HM Frigate Belle Poule - When taken: 14 Feb 1813 - Where taken: Bay of Biscay - Date received: 15 Jul 1813 - From what ship: Plymouth - Born: Connecticut - Age: 26 - Discharged on 17 Jun 1814 and sent to Dartmoor on HMS Pincher.

Anderson, Andre - Private - Number: 2634 - Prize name: 14th U.S. Infantry - Ship type: LF - How taken: British forces - When taken: 24 Jun 1813 - Where taken: Beaver Dams, Upper Canada - Date received: 5 Nov 1813 - From what ship: HMS Hindostan - Born: North Ireland - Age: 40 - Discharged on 10 Oct 1814 and sent to U.S. on Cartel St. Philip.

Anderson, Andrew - Seaman - Number: 659 - Prize name: U.S.R.M. Cutter James Madison - Ship type: War - How taken: HM Frigate Barbadoes - When taken: 22 Aug 1812 - Where taken: at sea - Date received: 24 Feb 1813 - From what ship: Portsmouth via HMS Ulysses - Born: Savannah - Age: 26 - Discharged on 10 May 1813 and released to Cartel Admittance.

Anderson, David - Cook - Number: 2826 - Prize name: Portsmouth Packet - Ship type: P - How taken: HM Brig Fantome - When taken: 5 Oct 1813 - Where taken: off Portland - Date received: 7 Jan 1814 - From what ship: Halifax - Born: New York - Age: 31 - Race: Mulatto - Discharged on 25 Sep 1814 and sent to Dartmoor on HMS Leyden.

Anderson, George - Seaman - Number: 3210 - Prize name: Volunteer - Ship type: MV - How taken: Vittoria, British privateer from Guernsey - When taken: 26 Dec 1813 - Where taken: Bay of Biscay - Date received: 13 Jan 1814 - From what ship: Portsmouth via HMS Poictiers - Born: Philadelphia - Age: 36 - Discharged on 26 Sep 1814 and sent to Dartmoor on HMS Leyden.

Anderson, Goodman - Seaman - Number: 2518 - Prize name: Yorktown - Ship type: P - How taken: HM Brig Nimrod - When taken: 17 Jul 1813 - Where taken: Grand Banks - Date received: 22 Oct 1813 - From what ship: Portsmouth via HMT Malabar - Born: Eisenburg, Sweden - Age: 33 - Released on 18 Feb 1814.

Anderson, Henry - Seaman - Number: 1718 - Prize name: Recaptured British MV - Ship type: P - How taken: HM Frigate Revolutionnaire - When taken: 10 Apr 1813 - Where taken: off the Western Isles, Scotland - Date received: 25 May 1813 - From what ship: Portsmouth via HMS Impetius - Born: Addington - Age: 20 - Discharged on 22 Oct 1814 and sent to Dartmoor on HMS Leyden.

Anderson, James - Seaman - Number: 1865 - How taken: Gave himself up from HM Frigate Leonidas - Date received: 7 Jul 1813 - From what ship: Portsmouth via HMS Tribune - Born: Long Island - Age: 39 - Discharged on 4 Aug 1814 and sent to Dartmoor on HMS Liverpool.

Anderson, James - Seaman - Number: 2292 - How taken: Gave himself up from HM Brig Scorpion - When taken: 20 Oct 1812 - Date received: 17 Sep 1813 - From what ship: HMS Raisonnable - Born: Maryland - Age: 21 - Race: Black - Released on 16 Feb 1814.

Anderson, John - Seaman - Number: 3513 - Prize name: Pilot - Ship type: LM - How taken: Vittoria, British privateer from Guernsey - When taken: 28 Jan 1814 - Where taken: off Bordeaux, France - Date received: 23 Feb 1814 - From what ship: Portsmouth via HMT Malabar - Born: Maryland - Age: 24 - Discharged on 25 Sep 1814 and sent to Dartmoor on HMS Leyden.

Anderson, John (alias Lloyd) - Mate - Number: 2437 - Prize name: Savannah - Ship type: MV - How taken: Taken up at Farhan - When taken: 10 Oct 1813 - Date received: 21 Oct 1813 - From what ship: Portsmouth via HMT Malabar - Born: Washington - Age: 29 - Discharged on Sep 1814 and released to Nore.

Anderson, Joseph - Seaman - Number: 1184 - How taken: Gave himself up from HM Ship of-the-Line Diomede - When taken: 12 Oct 1812 - Date received: 16 Mar 1813 - From what ship: Portsmouth, via HMS Abundance - Born: Baltimore - Age: 33 - Discharged on 11 Aug 1814 and sent to Dartmoor.

Anderson, Joseph - Seaman - Number: 106 - Prize name: Hope - Ship type: MV - How taken: Stopped at London - When taken: 26 Oct 1812 - Date received: 4 Nov 1812 - From what ship: HMS Namur - Born: Delaware - Age: 42 - Discharged on 12 Apr 1813 and released to HMS Carnatic.

Anderson, Niels - Seaman - Number: 232 - Prize name: Navigator - Ship type: MV - How taken: HM Ship-of-the-Line Cressy - When taken: 11 Aug 1812 - Where taken: Baltic - Date received: 25 Nov 1812 - From what ship: HMS Raisonnable - Born: Bergen, Norway - Age: 35 - Discharged on 19 Mar 1813 and released to the Navigator.

Anderson, Oliver - Seaman - Number: 660 - Prize name: U.S.R.M. Cutter James Madison - Ship type: War - How taken: HM Frigate Barbadoes - When taken: 22 Aug 1812 - Where taken: at sea - Date received: 24 Feb 1813 - From what ship: Portsmouth via HMS Ulysses - Born: Sweden - Age: 23 - Discharged on 10 May 1813 and released to Cartel Admittance.

Anderson, Robert - Seaman - Number: 2005 - How taken: Gave himself up from HM Brig Foxhound - Date received: 15 Jul 1813 - From what ship: Plymouth - Born: Rhode Island - Age: 26 - Escaped on 16 May 1814 from the HM Prison Ship Crown Prince.

Anderson, William - Seaman - Number: 850 - Prize name: Ocean, prized to the Privateer Diligent - Ship type: P - How taken: HM Frigate Surveillante - When taken: 20 Dec 1812 - Where taken: Lat 44 N, Long 6 W - Date received: 1 Mar 1813 - From what ship: Plymouth via HMS Namur - Born: New York - Age: 29 - Race: Black - Discharged on 8 Sep 1814 and sent to Dartmoor on HMS Niobe.

Anderson, William - Seaman - Number: 810 - Prize name: Leader - Ship type: MV - How taken: HM Frigate Andromach - When taken: 10 Dec 1812 - Where taken: off Bordeaux, France - Date received: 27 Feb 1813 - From what ship: Plymouth via HMS Namur - Born: Christiansted - Age: 20 - Discharged in Jul 1813 and released to Cartel Moses Brown.

Anderton, Samuel - Prize Master - Number: 1012 - Prize name: Sword Fish - Ship type: P - How taken: HM Ship-of-the-Line Elephant - When taken: 28 Dec 1812 - Where taken: off Azores - Date received: 10 Mar 1813 - From what ship: HMS Furious - Born: Marblehead - Age: 32 - Discharged on 24 Jul 1813 and released to Cartel Hoffminy.

Anderton, Thomas - Seaman - Number: 1156 - Prize name: Sword Fish - Ship type: P - How taken: HM Ship-of-the-Line Elephant - When taken: 28 Dec 1812 - Where taken: off Azores - Date received: 16 Mar 1813 - From what ship: Portsmouth, via HMS Abundance - Born: Marblehead - Age: 17 - Discharged on 24 Jul 1813 and released to Cartel Hoffminy.

Andrew, Joseph - Seaman - Number: 5 - Prize name: Cato - Ship type: MV - How taken: Detained on the Baltic - When taken: 11 Aug 1812 - Date received: 29 Oct 1812 - From what ship: HMS Raisonnable - Born: Marblehead - Age: 24 - Discharged on 10 May 1813 and released to Cartel Admittance.

Andrews, Asa - Seaman - Number: 291 - Prize name: Dido - Ship type: MV - How taken: Detained off Faco - When taken: 12 Aug 1812 - Date received: 23 Dec 1812 - From what ship: Greenlaw Depot - Born: Beverly - Age: 21 - Discharged on 10 May 1813 and released to Cartel Admittance.

Andrews, David (1) - Private - Number: 3105 - Prize name: 14th U.S. Infantry - Ship type: LF - How taken: British forces - When taken: 24 Jun 1813 - Where taken: Beaver Dams, Upper Canada - Date received: 7 Jan 1814 - From what ship: Halifax - Born: Philadelphia - Age: 23 - Discharged on 10 Oct 1814 and sent to U.S. on Cartel St. Philip.

Andrews, David (2) - Private - Number: 3110 - Prize name: 14th U.S. Infantry - Ship type: LF - How taken: British forces - When taken: 24 Jun 1813 - Where taken: Beaver Dams, Upper Canada - Date received: 7 Jan 1814 - From what ship: Halifax - Born: Philadelphia - Age: 21 - Discharged on 10 Oct 1814 and sent to U.S. on Cartel St. Philip.

Andrews, Edward - Private - Number: 3062 - Prize name: 14th U.S. Infantry - Ship type: LF - How taken: British forces - When taken: 24 Jun 1813 - Where taken: Beaver Dams, Upper Canada - Date received: 7 Jan 1814 -

From what ship: Halifax - Born: Connecticut - Age: 22 - Discharged on 10 Oct 1814 and sent to U.S. on Cartel St. Philip.

Andrews, John - Seaman - Number: 2499 - Prize name: Porcupine - Ship type: LM - How taken: HM Frigate Acasta - When taken: 3 Jun 1813 - Where taken: off Cape Sable, Florida - Date received: 22 Oct 1813 - From what ship: Portsmouth via HMT Malabar - Born: Boston - Age: 21 - Discharged on 8 Sep 1814 and sent to Dartmoor on HMS Niobe.

Andrews, John (1) - Seaman - Number: 2380 - How taken: Gave himself up from HM Ship-of-the-Line America - When taken: 26 Dec 1812 - Date received: 20 Oct 1813 - From what ship: Portsmouth, via an admiral's tender - Born: Charleston - Age: 27 - Race: Black - Discharged on 4 Sep 1814 and sent to Dartmoor on HMS Freya.

Andrews, John (2) - Seaman - Number: 2384 - How taken: Gave himself up from HM Ship-of-the-Line America - When taken: 26 Dec 1812 - Date received: 20 Oct 1813 - From what ship: Portsmouth, via an admiral's tender - Born: Alexandria - Age: 24 - Discharged on 4 Sep 1814 and sent to Dartmoor on HMS Freya.

Andrews, Joseph - Seaman - Number: 3172 - Prize name: Wolf Cove - Ship type: MV - How taken: HM Frigate Briton - When taken: 1 Dec 1813 - Where taken: off Brest, France - Date received: 7 Jan 1814 - From what ship: Halifax - Born: Massachusetts - Age: 25 - Died on 3 Jun 1814 from fever.

Andrey, Alexander - Seaman - Number: 553 - Prize name: Baltimore - Ship type: P - How taken: HM Transport Diadem - When taken: 7 Oct 1812 - Where taken: S. Andres - Date received: 23 Feb 1813 - From what ship: Portsmouth via HMS Dromedary - Born: Baltimore - Age: 23 - Discharged on 8 Jun 1813 and released to Cartel Rodrigo.

Angel, Sylvester - Seaman - Number: 3228 - How taken: Gave himself up from HM Ship-of-the-Line Illustrious - When taken: 1 Dec 1813 - Date received: 13 Jan 1814 - From what ship: Portsmouth via HMS Poictiers - Born: New London - Age: 26 - Discharged on 25 Sep 1814 and sent to Dartmoor on HMS Leyden.

Anthony, Abraham - Seaman - Number: 440 - Prize name: Hunter - Ship type: P - How taken: HM Frigate Phoebe - When taken: 23 Dec 1812 - Where taken: off Azores - Date received: 19 Feb 1813 - From what ship: HMS Modeste - Born: New Haven - Age: 24 - Race: Negro - Discharged on 2 Jul 1813 and released to Cartel Moses Brown.

Anthony, James - Seaman - Number: 2849 - Prize name: Blockade - Ship type: P - How taken: HM Brig Recruit - When taken: 17 Aug 1813 - Where taken: coast of America - Date received: 7 Jan 1814 - From what ship: Halifax - Born: Italy - Age: 21 - Discharged on 22 Oct 1814 and sent to Dartmoor on HMS Leyden.

Anthony, John - Seaman - Number: 923 - Prize name: Experiment - Ship type: MV - How taken: HM Brig Rover - When taken: 10 Nov 1812 - Where taken: off Bordeaux, France - Date received: 10 Mar 1813 - From what ship: HMS Tigress - Born: New Orleans - Age: 28 - Discharged on 8 Jun 1813 and released to Cartel Rodrigo.

Anthony, John - Seaman - Number: 3273 - Prize name: Volante - Ship type: P - How taken: HM Brig Curlew - When taken: 25 Mar 1813 - Where taken: off Boston - Date received: 23 Feb 1814 - From what ship: Halifax via HMT Malabar - Born: New Orleans - Age: 47 - Discharged on 10 Oct 1814 and sent to Dartmoor on the Mermaid.

Anthony, Luke - Seaman - Number: 530 - Prize name: Baltimore - Ship type: P - How taken: HM Transport Diadem - When taken: 7 Oct 1812 - Where taken: S. Andres - Date received: 23 Feb 1813 - From what ship: Portsmouth via HMS Dromedary - Born: New Orleans - Age: 20 - Discharged on 8 Jun 1813 and released to Cartel Rodrigo.

Antoine, John - Seaman - Number: 3238 - How taken: Gave himself up from HM Brig Bruiser - When taken: 3 Feb 1814 - Date received: 10 Feb 1814 - From what ship: HMS Cadmus - Born: Porto Rico - Age: 28 - Died on 24 Apr 1814 from fever.

Antoine, John - Seaman - Number: 700 - Prize name: Deanna, recaptured British vessel - Ship type: P - How taken: HM Ship-of-the-Line Polyphemus - When taken: 14 Sep 1812 - Where taken: at sea - Date received: 24 Feb 1813 - From what ship: Portsmouth via HMS Ulysses - Born: Bradford, MA - Age: 27 - Discharged on 8 Jun 1813 and released to Cartel Rodrigo.

Antonio, Francis - Seaman - Number: 3221 - Prize name: Volunteer - Ship type: MV - How taken: Vittoria, British privateer from Guernsey - When taken: 26 Dec 1813 - Where taken: Bay of Biscay - Date received: 13 Jan 1814 - From what ship: Portsmouth via HMS Poictiers - Born: Portugal - Age: 23 - Discharged on 22 Oct 1814 and sent to Dartmoor on HMS Leyden.

Appleton, John - Gunner - Number: 2819 - Prize name: Portsmouth Packet - Ship type: P - How taken: HM Brig Fantome - When taken: 5 Oct 1813 - Where taken: off Portland - Date received: 7 Jan 1814 - From what ship: Halifax - Born: Virginia - Age: 34 - Discharged on 25 Sep 1814 and sent to Dartmoor on HMS Leyden.

Archer, James - Seaman - Number: 3248 - Prize name: Thorn - Ship type: P - How taken: Shannon, Nova Scotia privateer - When taken: 7 Nov 1813 - Where taken: off Newfoundland - Date received: 23 Feb 1814 - From what ship: Halifax via HMT Malabar - Born: Brewster - Age: 25 - Discharged on 10 Oct 1814 and sent to Dartmoor on the Mermaid.

Armstrong, Elijah - Seaman - Number: 578 - How taken: Gave himself up from HM Ship-of-the-Line Victory - When taken: 18 Dec 1812 - Date received: 23 Feb 1813 - From what ship: Portsmouth via HMS Dromedary - Born: Harford - Age: 22 - Discharged on 26 Jul 1814 and sent to Dartmoor on HMS Raven.

Armstrong, Nicholas - Seaman - Number: 1483 - Prize name: Union - Ship type: MV - How taken: HM Frigate Iris - When taken: 17 Jan 1813 - Where taken: at sea - Date received: 6 Apr 1813 - From what ship: Portsmouth via Tender Eliza - Born: Philadelphia - Age: 17 - Discharged on 26 Jul 1813 and released to Cartel Hoffminy.

Armstrong, Thomas - Seaman - Number: 570 - Prize name: Perseverance - Ship type: MV - How taken: HM Sloop Atalante - When taken: 31 Jul 1812 - Where taken: at sea - Date received: 23 Feb 1813 - From what ship: Portsmouth via HMS Dromedary - Born: Wiscasset, MA - Age: 20 - Discharged on 23 Mar 1813 and released to the Cartel Robinson Potter.

Armstrong, Thomas - Seaman - Number: 2168 - How taken: Gave himself up from HM Ship-of-the-Line Swiftsure - When taken: 26 Dec 1812 - Date received: 16 Aug 1813 - From what ship: Portsmouth, via an admiral's tender - Born: Lancaster - Age: 26 - Discharged on 17 Jun 1814 and sent to Dartmoor on the Penebar.

Arnold, Benjamin - Marine Private - Number: 3674 - Prize name: Lord Ponsonby, prize of the Privateer Diomede - Ship type: P - How taken: HM Brig Sappho - When taken: 27 Feb 1814 - Where taken: at sea - Date received: 4 May 1814 - From what ship: Portsmouth - Born: Connecticut - Age: 23 - Discharged on 25 Sep 1814 and sent to Dartmoor on HMS Niobe.

Arnold, James - Seaman - Number: 3827 - Prize name: Rattlesnake - Ship type: LM - How taken: HM Frigate Rhin - When taken: 12 Mar 1814 - Where taken: off Bermuda - Date received: 16 Aug 1814 - From what ship: London - Born: Providence - Age: 30 - Discharged on 22 Oct 1814 and sent to Dartmoor on HMS Leyden.

Arnold, James - Master of Arms - Number: 1938 - How taken: Taken up at Plymouth - When taken: 17 Jan 1813 - Date received: 15 Jul 1813 - From what ship: Plymouth - Born: Weymouth - Age: 27 - Discharged on 17 Jun 1814 and sent to Dartmoor on HMS Pincher.

Arnold, Obadiah - Seaman - Number: 3637 - Prize name: Bunker Hill - Ship type: P - How taken: HM Frigate Pomone & HM Frigate Cydnus - When taken: 4 Mar 1814 - Where taken: Bay of Biscay - Date received: 31 Mar 1814 - From what ship: HMS Raisonnable - Born: Rhode Island - Age: 22 - Discharged on 25 Sep 1814 and sent to Dartmoor on HMS Niobe.

Arnold, William - Seaman - Number: 1111 - Prize name: Tom Thumb - Ship type: MV - How taken: Lion, British privateer - When taken: 15 Feb 1813 - Where taken: Bay of Biscay - Date received: 14 Mar 1813 - From what ship: Portsmouth via HMS Beagle - Born: Baltimore - Age: 16 - Discharged on 23 Jul 1814 and sent to Dartmoor.

Arthur, Alexander - Boy - Number: 937 - Prize name: Argus - Ship type: MV - How taken: HM Cutter Fancy - When taken: 19 Dec 1812 - Where taken: Bay of Biscay - Date received: 10 Mar 1813 - From what ship: HMS Tigress - Born: New York - Age: 15 - Discharged on 2 Jul 1813 and released to Cartel Moses Brown.

Artis, William - Seaman - Number: 3431 - Prize name: Juliana Smith - Ship type: P - How taken: HM Frigate Nymphe - When taken: 12 May 1813 - Where taken: off Cape Sable, Florida - Date received: 23 Feb 1814 - From what ship: Halifax via HMT Malabar - Born: Marblehead - Age: 22 - Discharged on 22 Oct 1814 and sent to Dartmoor on HMS Leyden.

Ashfield, Henry - Seaman - Number: 1903 - Prize name: Weasel - Ship type: MV - How taken: HM Brig Foxhound - When taken: 25 Mar 1813 - Where taken: Bay of Biscay - Date received: 7 Jul 1813 - From what ship: Portsmouth via HMS Tribune - Born: New York - Age: 19 - Discharged on 4 Aug 1814 and sent to Dartmoor on HMS Liverpool.

Asten, John - Boy - Number: 1170 - Prize name: Sword Fish - Ship type: P - How taken: HM Ship-of-the-Line Elephant - When taken: 28 Dec 1812 - Where taken: off Azores - Date received: 16 Mar 1813 - From what ship: Portsmouth, via HMS Abundance - Born: Boston - Age: 19 - Discharged on 24 Jul 1813 and released to Cartel Hoffminy.

Atkin, Robert G. - 2nd Mate - Number: 67 - Prize name: Elson - Ship type: MV - How taken: HM Frigate Ethalion - When taken: 12 Aug 1812 - Where taken: Baltic - Date received: 4 Nov 1812 - From what ship: HMS Namur - Born: Marblehead - Age: 27 - Discharged on 10 May 1813 and released to Cartel Admittance.

Atkins, Francis - Seaman - Number: 2265 - Prize name: Eliza - Ship type: MV - How taken: HMS Charles - When taken: 20 Jul 1813 - Where taken: off Petershead, Scotland - Date received: 14 Sep 1813 - From what ship: HMS Raisonnable - Born: Georgetown - Age: 35 - Escaped on 16 May 1814 from HM Prison Ship Crown Prince.

Atkinson, Charles - Seaman - Number: 3831 - Prize name: Rambler - Ship type: MV - How taken: HM Transport Morley - When taken: 10 Feb 1813 - Where taken: off Isle de France (Mauritius) - Date received: 16 Aug 1814 - From what ship: London - Born: Salem - Age: 33 - Discharged on 22 Oct 1814 and sent to Dartmoor on HMS Leyden.

Atkinson, John - Seaman - Number: 1578 - How taken: Gave himself up from HM Ship-of-the-Line Braham - When taken: 10 Dec 1812 - Date received: 16 Apr 1813 - From what ship: HMS Namur, admiral's tender - Born: Baltimore - Age: 29 - Race: Black - Discharged on 3 Aug 1813 and released to HMS Ceres.

Atwood, Edward - Seaman - Number: 1293 - How taken: Gave himself up from HM Guardship Royal William - When taken: 3 Feb 1813 - Date received: 16 Mar 1813 - From what ship: Portsmouth, via HMS Abundance - Born: Putney - Age: 25 - Race: Mulatto - Discharged on 23 Jul 1814 and sent to Dartmoor.

Atwood, John - Seaman - Number: 3472 - Prize name: Yankee - Ship type: P - How taken: HM Frigate Shannon - When taken: 20 Aug 1813 - Where taken: at sea - Date received: 23 Feb 1814 - From what ship: Halifax via HMT Malabar - Born: Dighton - Age: 20 - Discharged on 22 Oct 1814 and sent to Dartmoor on HMS Leyden.

Atwood, Nathaniel - Seaman - Number: 2922 - Prize name: Juliana Smith - Ship type: P - How taken: HM Frigate Nymphe - When taken: 12 May 1813 - Where taken: off Cape Sable, Florida - Date received: 7 Jan 1814 - From what ship: Halifax - Born: Massachusetts - Age: 24 - Discharged on 25 Sep 1814 and sent to Dartmoor on HMS Leyden.

Atwood, Thomas - Seaman - Number: 1896 - Prize name: Prompt - Ship type: MV - How taken: Chance, British privateer - When taken: 28 Mar 1813 - Where taken: Bay of Biscay - Date received: 7 Jul 1813 - From what ship: Portsmouth via HMS Tribune - Born: Wilmington - Age: 29 - Discharged on 12 Aug 1814 and sent to Dartmoor on HMS Alpheus.

Augustus, Benjamin - Seaman - Number: 2073 - How taken: Gave himself up from HM Guardship Royal William - When taken: 29 Oct 1812 - Date received: 9 Aug 1813 - From what ship: HMS Thames - Born: Philadelphia - Age: 22 - Race: Mulatto - Discharged on 4 Aug 1814 and sent to Dartmoor on HMS Liverpool.

Aulajo, Thomas - Seaman - Number: 837 - Prize name: Vengeance - Ship type: LM - How taken: HM Frigate Phoebe - When taken: 1 Jan 1813 - Where taken: Lat 44.4 Long 23 - Date received: 1 Mar 1813 - From what ship: Plymouth via HMS Namur - Born: Baltimore - Age: 28 - Discharged on 24 Jul 1813 and released to Cartel Hoffminy.

Aurel, Leonard - Seaman - Number: 1958 - Prize name: Ferox - Ship type: MV - How taken: HM Frigate Medusa & HM Brig Lyra - When taken: 28 Mar 1813 - Where taken: off Cape Ortegal, Spain - Date received: 15 Jul 1813 - From what ship: Plymouth - Born: Gothenburg, Sweden - Age: 21 - Released on 13 Sep 1813.

Austin, James - Seaman - Number: 2116 - How taken: Gave himself up from HM Ship-of-the-Line Union - When taken: 27 May 1813 - Date received: 9 Aug 1813 - From what ship: HMS Thames - Born: Long Island - Age: 22 - Race: Black - Escaped on 29 Jul 1814 from HM Prison Ship Nassau.

Austin, Jonathan - Seaman - Number: 1998 - How taken: Gave himself up from HM Ship-of-the-Line Clarence - Date received: 15 Jul 1813 - From what ship: Plymouth - Born: Massachusetts - Age: 29 - Discharged on 17 Jun 1814 and sent to Dartmoor on HMS Pincher.

Austin, William - Seaman - Number: 3879 - How taken: Gave himself up from HM Frigate Clorinde - When taken: 18 Dec 1813 - Date received: 28 Aug 1814 - From what ship: London - Born: Philadelphia - Age: 32 - Discharged on 8 Sep 1814 and sent to Dartmoor on HMS Niobe.

Averill, Samuel - Seaman - Number: 3829 - Prize name: Rattlesnake - Ship type: LM - How taken: HM Frigate Rhin - When taken: 12 Mar 1814 - Where taken: off Bermuda - Date received: 16 Aug 1814 - From what ship: London - Born: Wiscasset - Age: 21 - Discharged on 22 Oct 1814 and sent to Dartmoor on HMS Leyden.

Avery, Charles - Seaman - Number: 1858 - How taken: Gave himself up from HM Bomb Vessel Strombolo - Date received: 7 Jul 1813 - From what ship: Portsmouth via HMS Tribune - Born: New York - Age: 34 - Discharged on 25 Jul 1814 and sent to Dartmoor on HMS Bittern.

Avis, Jervis - Private - Number: 3072 - Prize name: 14th U.S. Infantry - Ship type: LF - How taken: British forces - When taken: 24 Jun 1813 - Where taken: Beaver Dams, Upper Canada - Date received: 7 Jan 1814 - From what ship: Halifax - Born: Maryland - Age: 31 - Discharged on 10 Oct 1814 and sent to U.S. on Cartel St. Philip.

Avory, John - Seaman - Number: 3288 - Prize name: Vivid - Ship type: P - How taken: HM Frigate Nymphe - When taken: 20 Apr 1813 - Where taken: off Cape Cod - Date received: 23 Feb 1814 - From what ship: Halifax via HMT Malabar - Born: Truro - Age: 18 - Discharged on 10 Oct 1814 and sent to Dartmoor on the Mermaid.

Awe, Joseph - Seaman - Number: 511 - Prize name: Josephine - Ship type: MV - How taken: HM Sloop Goree - When taken: 15 Aug 1812 - Where taken: off Bermuda - Date received: 23 Feb 1813 - From what ship: Portsmouth via HMS Dromedary - Born: New Orleans - Age: 25 - Discharged on 10 May 1813 and released to Cartel Admittance.

Awker, Edward - Seaman - Number: 2079 - How taken: Gave himself up from HM Ship-of-the-Line Armada - When taken: 8 Jun 1813 - Date received: 9 Aug 1813 - From what ship: HMS Thames - Born: Massachsetts - Age: 24 - Race: Mulatto - Discharged on 4 Aug 1814 and sent to Dartmoor on HMS Liverpool.

Ayers, John - Seaman - Number: 13 - Prize name: Eliza Ann - Ship type: MV - How taken: HM Ship-of-the-Line Vigo - When taken: 11 Aug 1812 - Where taken: Hanoi Bay - Date received: 29 Oct 1812 - From what ship: HMS Raisonnable - Born: Manchester - Age: 19 - Discharged on 10 May 1813 and released to Cartel Admittance.

Ayres, Henry - Seaman - Number: 2302 - Prize name: Dolphin - Ship type: P - How taken: HM Brig Curlew - When taken: 1 Feb 1813 - Where taken: off Barbados - Date received: 29 Sep 1813 - From what ship: HMS Raisonnable - Born: Maryland - Age: 30 - Discharged on 4 Sep 1814 and sent to Dartmoor on HMS Freya.

Ayres, William - Seaman - Number: 3846 - How taken: Gave himself up from HMS Progress at Madras, India - When taken: Jul 1813 - Date received: 21 Aug 1814 - From what ship: Gravesend - Born: Providence - Age: 33 - Discharged on 10 Oct 1814 and sent to Dartmoor on the Mermaid.

Babb, Benjamin - Seaman - Number: 1287 - How taken: Gave himself up from HM Guardship Royal William - When taken: 3 Feb 1813 - Date received: 16 Mar 1813 - From what ship: Portsmouth, via HMS Abundance - Born: Barrington, RI - Age: 33 - Discharged on 23 Jul 1814 and sent to Dartmoor.

Babbitt, Edward B. - Midshipman - Number: 2039 - Prize name: Kitty, prize of the U.S. Frigate President - Ship type: War - How taken: Dart, British privateer from Guernsey - When taken: 20 Jun 1813 - Where taken: off the Western Isles, Scotland - Date received: 4 Aug 1813 - From what ship: HMS Christian VII - Born: Brookfield - Age: 20 - Released from Chatham on 21 Sep 1813 and sent to Ashburton on parole.

Babcock, Clark - Seaman - Number: 1780 - Prize name: Moscow - Ship type: MV - How taken: Impressed at Gravesend, England - When taken: 27 Sep 1813 - Date received: 1 Jul 1813 - From what ship: HMS Raisonnable - Born: Rhode Island - Age: 45 - Discharged on 24 Jul 1814 and sent to Dartmoor on HMS Liffey.

Bacchus, John - Seaman - Number: 2757 - Prize name: Norfolk, prize to the Globe - Ship type: P - How taken: HM Brig Fantome - When taken: 29 May 1813 - Where taken: off Norfolk - Date received: 7 Jan 1814 - From what ship: Halifax - Born: New London - Age: 23 - Discharged on 25 Sep 1814 and sent to Dartmoor on HMS Leyden.

Bachelor, Nathaniel - Master - Number: 895 - Prize name: Phoenix - Ship type: MV - How taken: HM Ship-of-the-Line San Juan - When taken: 8 Aug 1812 - Where taken: Gibraltar - Date received: 1 Mar 1813 - From what ship: Plymouth via HMS Namur - Born: Beverly, MA - Age: 31 - Discharged on 27 Apr 1813 and sent to Reading on parole.

Bachelor, Nathaniel - Captain - Number: 1678 - Prize name: Phoenix - Ship type: MV - How taken: HM Ship-of-the-Line San Juan - When taken: 8 Aug 1812 - Where taken: Gibraltar - Date received: 11 May 1813 - From what ship: from Reading - Born: Beverly - Age: 31 - Discharged on 11 May 1813 and released to the Cartel Admittance.

Backman, Charles - Seaman - Number: 2602 - How taken: Gave himself up from HM Ship-of-the-Line Prince of Wales - When taken: 27 May 1813 - Date received: 5 Nov 1813 - From what ship: HMS Hindostan - Born: Philadelphia - Age: 20 - Discharged on 12 Aug 1814 and sent to Dartmoor on HMS Alpheus.

Baddrige, Charles - Seaman - Number: 2844 - Prize name: Polly - Ship type: P - How taken: HM Sloop Plover - When taken: 20 Jul 1813 - Where taken: off Halifax - Date received: 7 Jan 1814 - From what ship: Halifax - Born: Salem - Age: 28 - Died on 19 Jan 1814.

Badsse, Philip - Prize Master - Number: 1013 - Prize name: Sword Fish - Ship type: P - How taken: HM Ship-of-the-Line Elephant - When taken: 28 Dec 1812 - Where taken: off Azores - Date received: 10 Mar 1813 - From what ship: HMS Furious - Born: Marblehead - Age: 30 - Discharged on 24 Jul 1813 and released to Cartel Hoffminy.

Bagley, Moses - Surgeon - Number: 1129 - Prize name: Sword Fish - Ship type: P - How taken: HM Ship-of-the-Line Elephant - When taken: 28 Dec 1812 - Where taken: off Azores - Date received: 14 Mar 1813 - From what ship: Portsmouth, Mundane - Born: Canada - Age: 34 - Discharged on 10 May 1813 and released to Cartel Admittance.

Bailey, Charles - Seaman - Number: 129 - Prize name: Brutus - Ship type: MV - How taken: Stopped at London - When taken: 26 Oct 1812 - Date received: 5 Nov 1812 - From what ship: HMS Namur - Born: Boston - Age: 19 - Discharged in Jul 1813 and released to Cartel Moses Brown.

Bailey, Daniel - Seaman - Number: 2764 - Prize name: Thomas - Ship type: P - How taken: HM Frigate Nymphe - When taken: 24 Jun 1813 - Where taken: off Halifax - Date received: 7 Jan 1814 - From what ship: Halifax - Born: Portsmouth - Age: 24 - Discharged on 8 Sep 1814 and sent to Dartmoor on HMS Niobe.

Bailey, Isaac - Seaman - Number: 3269 - Prize name: Volante - Ship type: P - How taken: HM Brig Curlew - When taken: 25 Mar 1813 - Where taken: off Boston - Date received: 23 Feb 1814 - From what ship: Halifax via HMT Malabar - Born: Baltimore - Age: 29 - Race: Mulatto - Discharged on 10 Oct 1814 and sent to Dartmoor on the Mermaid.

Bailey, John - Seaman - Number: 1743 - How taken: Gave himself up from HMS Castilian - When taken: 17 Apr 1813 - Date received: 25 May 1813 - From what ship: Portsmouth via HMS Impetius - Born: Bristol - Age: 26 - Race: Blackman - Discharged on 24 Jul 1814 and sent to Dartmoor on HMS Liffey.

Bailey, John - Seaman - Number: 1907 - Prize name: Weasel - Ship type: MV - How taken: HM Brig Foxhound - When taken: 25 Mar 1813 - Where taken: Bay of Biscay - Date received: 7 Jul 1813 - From what ship: Portsmouth via HMS Tribune - Born: Gloucester - Age: 29 - Discharged on 4 Aug 1814 and sent to Dartmoor on HMS Liverpool.

Bailey, Joseph - Seaman - Number: 875 - Prize name: Stephen - Ship type: MV - How taken: Briton, letter of marque - When taken: 1 Jan 1813 - Where taken: off Bordeaux, France - Date received: 1 Mar 1813 - From what ship: Plymouth via HMS Namur - Born: Pennsylvania - Age: 21 - Race: Blackman - Discharged on 21 Apr 1813 and released to HMS Raisonnable.

Bailey, Peter - Seaman - Number: 2783 - Prize name: Thomas - Ship type: P - How taken: HM Frigate Nymphe - When taken: 24 Jun 1813 - Where taken: off Halifax - Date received: 7 Jan 1814 - From what ship: Halifax -

Born: Bristol - Age: 19 - Discharged on 8 Sep 1814 and sent to Dartmoor on HMS Niobe.

Bailey, Samuel - Seaman - Number: 1952 - Prize name: Ferox - Ship type: MV - How taken: HM Frigate Medusa & HM Brig Lyra - When taken: 28 Mar 1813 - Where taken: off Cape Ortegal, Spain - Date received: 15 Jul 1813 - From what ship: Plymouth - Born: Portland - Age: 32 - Discharged on 17 Jun 1814 and sent to Dartmoor on HMS Redbreast.

Bailey, William - Seaman - Number: 2118 - How taken: Gave himself up from HM Ship-of-the-Line Union - When taken: 27 May 1813 - Date received: 9 Aug 1813 - From what ship: HMS Thames - Born: Philadelphia - Age: 29 - Discharged on 12 Aug 1814 and sent to Dartmoor on HMS Alpheus.

Bain, John - Seaman - Number: 803 - Prize name: Dolphin - Ship type: MV - How taken: HM Ship-of-the-Line Colossus - When taken: 5 Jan 1813 - Where taken: off the Western Isles, Scotland - Date received: 27 Feb 1813 - From what ship: Plymouth via HMS Namur - Born: New York - Age: 40 - Race: Black - Discharged on 24 Jul 1813 and released to Cartel Hoffminy.

Baisley, Abraham - Marine Private - Number: 3667 - Prize name: Yorktown - Ship type: P - How taken: HM Frigate Maidstone - When taken: 17 Jul 1813 - Where taken: Grand Banks - Date received: 4 May 1814 - From what ship: Portsmouth - Born: New York - Age: 22 - Discharged on 25 Sep 1814 and sent to Dartmoor on HMS Niobe.

Bakeman, Ely - Seaman - Number: 2432 - Prize name: Hepsey - Ship type: MV - How taken: HM Brig Zenobia - When taken: 22 Jun 1813 - Where taken: off Lisbon - Date received: 21 Oct 1813 - From what ship: Portsmouth via HMT Malabar - Born: Massachusetts - Age: 25 - Died on 22 Dec 1813 from pneumonia.

Baker, Daniel - Seaman - Number: 2119 - How taken: Gave himself up from HM Ship-of-the-Line Union - When taken: 27 May 1813 - Date received: 9 Aug 1813 - From what ship: HMS Thames - Born: Massachusetts - Age: 21 - Discharged on 12 Aug 1814 and sent to Dartmoor on HMS Alpheus.

Baker, Henry - Seaman - Number: 668 - Prize name: U.S.R.M. Cutter James Madison - Ship type: War - How taken: HM Frigate Barbadoes - When taken: 22 Aug 1812 - Where taken: at sea - Date received: 24 Feb 1813 - From what ship: Portsmouth via HMS Ulysses - Born: Norfolk - Age: 28 - Discharged on 10 May 1813 and released to Cartel Admittance.

Baker, John - 2nd Mate - Number: 1199 - Prize name: Expectation - Ship type: MV - How taken: HM Frigate Briton - When taken: 17 Dec 1812 - Where taken: at sea - Date received: 16 Mar 1813 - From what ship: Portsmouth, via HMS Abundance - Born: Salem - Age: 26 - Discharged on 2 Jul 1813 and released to Cartel Moses Brown.

Baker, Robert - Seaman - Number: 2357 - How taken: Gave himself up from HM Ship-of-the-Line Hibernia - When taken: 25 Jun 1813 - Date received: 20 Oct 1813 - From what ship: Portsmouth, via an admiral's tender - Born: Virginia - Age: 29 - Discharged on 4 Sep 1814 and sent to Dartmoor on HMS Freya.

Bale, Charles - Seaman - Number: 2580 - How taken: Gave himself up from HM Ship-of-the-Line Colossus - When taken: 4 Oct 1812 - Date received: 23 Oct 1813 - From what ship: Portsmouth via HMS Raisonnable - Born: Hampshire - Age: 25 - Discharged on 8 Sep 1814 and sent to Dartmoor on HMS Niobe.

Baley, J. K. - Seaman - Number: 2026 - How taken: Impressed at Barbados off the MV Tiger of Liverpool - When taken: 21 Dec 1812 - Date received: 24 Jul 1813 - From what ship: HMS Raisonnable - Born: Massachusetts - Age: 45 - Discharged on 21 Jan 1814 and released to HMS Ceres.

Ball, Erastus - Seaman - Number: 107 - Prize name: Eliza Ann - Ship type: MV - How taken: Stopped at London - When taken: 26 Oct 1812 - Date received: 4 Nov 1812 - From what ship: HMS Namur - Born: Salisbury, CT - Age: 21 - Discharged on 4 Mar 1813 to the Wailey.

Ball, John - Seaman - Number: 563 - How taken: Gave himself up from HM Frigate Argo - When taken: 25 Nov 1812 - Date received: 23 Feb 1813 - From what ship: Portsmouth via HMS Dromedary - Born: Rhode Island - Age: 21 - Discharged on 19 May 1813 and released to HMS Ceres.

Ballard, John - Seaman - Number: 197 - How taken: Gave himself up from HM Brig Zenobia - When taken: 25 Aug 1812 - Date received: 6 Nov 1812 - From what ship: HMS Echo - Born: Georgetown, SC - Age: 27 - Discharged on 26 Jul 1814 and sent to Dartmoor on HMS Raven.

Ballard, Martin - Private - Number: 3127 - Prize name: 14th U.S. Infantry - Ship type: LF - How taken: British forces - When taken: 24 Jun 1813 - Where taken: Beaver Dams, Upper Canada - Date received: 7 Jan 1814 - From what ship: Halifax - Born: New York - Age: 20 - Discharged on 10 Oct 1814 and sent to U.S. on Cartel St. Philip.

Bane, Charles - Seaman - Number: 2667 - How taken: Gave himself up from HM Brig Vixen - When taken: 12 Sep 1813 - Date received: 20 Nov 1813 - From what ship: HMS Raisonnable - Born: Rhode Island - Age: 22 - Race: Blackman - Discharged on 8 Sep 1814 and sent to Dartmoor on HMS Niobe.

Banta, John - Seaman - Number: 1651 - How taken: Gave himself up from HM Ship-of-the-Line Sterling Castle - Date received: 9 May 1813 - From what ship: HMS Raisonnable - Born: New Jersey - Age: 31 - Discharged on 13 Aug 1814 and sent to Dartmoor.

Baptieste, John - Seaman - Number: 2242 - Prize name: Orders in Council - Ship type: LM - How taken: HM Frigate Surveillante - When taken: 1 Jan 1813 - Where taken: off Cape Ortegal, Spain - Date received: 7 Sep 1813 - From what ship: HMS Raisonnable - Born: New Orleans - Age: 40 - Discharged on 22 Jun 1814 and sent to Calais, France on the Simon & Mary.

Baptist, John - Seaman - Number: 801 - Prize name: Dolphin - Ship type: MV - How taken: HM Ship-of-the-Line Colossus - When taken: 5 Jan 1813 - Where taken: off the Western Isles, Scotland - Date received: 27 Feb 1813 - From what ship: Plymouth via HMS Namur - Born: New Orleans - Age: 44 - Discharged on 24 Jul 1813 and released to Cartel Hoffminy.

Baptist, Michael - Seaman - Number: 217 - Prize name: Frederick - Ship type: MV - How taken: Impressed at Gravesend, England - When taken: Oct 1812 - Date received: 15 Nov 1812 - From what ship: HMS Raisonnable - Born: Boston - Age: 30 - Died on 23 Mar 1813 from pneumonia.

Baptiste, John - Seaman - Number: 1002 - Prize name: Brunswick - Ship type: MV - How taken: HM Frigate Iris - When taken: 17 Dec 1812 - Where taken: off Spain - Date received: 10 Mar 1813 - From what ship: HMS Furious - Born: New Orleans - Age: 26 - Race: Black - Discharged on 2 Jul 1813 and released to Cartel Moses Brown.

Baptiste, John - Seaman - Number: 3402 - Prize name: Elbridge Gerry - Ship type: P - How taken: HM Frigate Crescent - When taken: 16 Sep 1813 - Where taken: at sea - Date received: 23 Feb 1814 - From what ship: Halifax via HMT Malabar - Born: Cape Elizabeth - Age: 45 - Discharged on 21 Jul 1814 and sent to Dartmoor on HMS Portia.

Barber, Henry - Seaman - Number: 42 - Prize name: Suwarrow - Ship type: MV - How taken: HM Brig Recruit - When taken: 20 Jul 1812 - Where taken: off New York - Date received: 3 Nov 1812 - From what ship: HMS Plover - Born: New Haven, CT - Age: 20 - Discharged on 23 Mar 1813 and released to the Cartel Robinson Potter.

Barber, John - Seaman - Number: 1219 - Prize name: Rossie - Ship type: MV - How taken: HM Frigate Dryand - When taken: 7 Jan 1813 - Where taken: at sea - Date received: 16 Mar 1813 - From what ship: Portsmouth, via HMS Abundance - Born: Gravesend, England - Age: 27 - Discharged on 24 Jul 1813 and released to Cartel Hoffminy.

Barber, Major - Seaman - Number: 2427 - Prize name: Maydock - Ship type: MV - How taken: HM Brig Rebuff - When taken: 16 Jun 1813 - Where taken: off Cape St. Marys, Newfoundland - Date received: 21 Oct 1813 - From what ship: Portsmouth via HMT Malabar - Born: North Carolina - Age: 22 - Race: Black - Died on 27 Jul 1814 from measles.

Barchant, George - 2nd Mate - Number: 130 - Prize name: Brutus - Ship type: MV - How taken: Stopped at London - When taken: 26 Oct 1812 - Date received: 5 Nov 1812 - From what ship: HMS Namur - Born: Boston - Age: 29 - Discharged on 4 Mar 1813 to the Wailey.

Barchman, John - Master's Mate - Number: 419 - Prize name: Hunter - Ship type: P - How taken: HM Frigate Phoebe - When taken: 23 Dec 1812 - Where taken: off Azores - Date received: 19 Feb 1813 - From what ship: HMS Modeste - Born: Dover - Age: 26 - Discharged on 2 Jul 1813 and released to Cartel Moses Brown.

Bardoe, John - Seaman - Number: 1051 - How taken: Taken up at Liverpool - When taken: 5 Nov 1812 - Date received: 11 Mar 1813 - From what ship: Yarmouth via HMS Tenders - Born: Bridges - Age: 23 - Discharged in Jul 1813 and released to Cartel Moses Brown.

Bark, David - Seaman - Number: 1296 - How taken: Gave himself up from HM Guardship Royal William - When taken: 3 Feb 1813 - Date received: 16 Mar 1813 - From what ship: Portsmouth, via HMS Abundance - Born: Providence - Age: 23 - Discharged on 23 Jul 1814 and sent to Dartmoor.

Barker, George - Seaman - Number: 3302 - Prize name: Catherine - Ship type: P - How taken: HM Ship-of-the-Line La Hogue - When taken: 2 May 1813 - Where taken: off Cape Sable, Florida - Date received: 23 Feb 1814 - From what ship: Halifax via HMT Malabar - Born: Africa - Age: 19 - Race: Black - Discharged on 10 Oct 1814 and sent to Dartmoor on the Mermaid.

Barlett, N. - Seaman - Number: 77 - Prize name: Antelope - Ship type: MV - How taken: HMS Horato - When taken: 2 Aug 1812 - Where taken: off Norway - Date received: 4 Nov 1812 - From what ship: HMS Namur - Born: Plymouth, MA - Age: 57 - Discharged on 23 Mar 1813 and released to the Cartel Robinson Potter.

Barlow, John - Private - Number: 2654 - Prize name: 5th U.S. Infantry - Ship type: LF - How taken: British forces - When taken: 8 Jun 1813 - Where taken: Beaver Dams, Upper Canada - Date received: 5 Nov 1813 - From what ship: HMS Hindostan - Born: Yorkshire - Age: 32 - Discharged on 17 Jun 1814 and sent to Dartmoor.

Barnard, John - Seaman - Number: 3811 - How taken: Gave himself up from HM Frigate Phoenix - When taken: 17 Jul 1813 - Date received: 13 Jun 1814 - From what ship: Quebec - Born: Lopus - Age: 35 - Discharged on 25 Sep 1814 and sent to Dartmoor on HMS Leyden.

Barnes, Isaac - Seaman - Number: 29 - Prize name: Arial - Ship type: MV - How taken: HM Brig Recruit - When taken: 2 Jun 1812 - Where taken: coast of America - Date received: 3 Nov 1812 - From what ship: HMS Plover - Born: Delaware - Age: 31 - Discharged on 23 Mar 1813 and released to the Cartel Robinson Potter.

Barnes, William Smith - Quartermaster - Number: 3506 - Prize name: Elbridge Gerry - Ship type: P - How taken: HM Frigate Crescent - When taken: 16 Sep 1813 - Where taken: at sea - Date received: 23 Feb 1814 - From what ship: Portsmouth via HMT Malabar - Born: Connecticut - Age: 41 - Discharged on 26 Sep 1814 and sent to Dartmoor on HMS Leyden.

Barnett, John - Seaman - Number: 1599 - How taken: Impressed at Gravesend, England - When taken: 13 Feb 1813 - Date received: 19 Apr 1813 - From what ship: HMS Raisonnable - Born: Baltimore - Age: 53 - Race: Black - Discharged on 7 Aug 1813 and released to HMS Ceres.

Barnett, John - Seaman - Number: 561 - How taken: Gave himself up from HM Guardship Royal William - When taken: 18 Nov 1812 - Date received: 23 Feb 1813 - From what ship: Portsmouth via HMS Dromedary - Born: Fairfax, VA - Age: 27 - Discharged on 26 Sep 1814 and sent to Dartmoor on HMS Leyden.

Barnsall, Lewis - Seaman - Number: 1991 - How taken: Gave himself up from HM Ship-of-the-Line Clarence - Date received: 15 Jul 1813 - From what ship: Plymouth - Born: Boston - Age: 27 - Discharged on 17 Jun 1814 and sent to Dartmoor on HMS Pincher.

Baron, Peter - Seaman - Number: 2912 - Prize name: Pomona, prize of Privateer Prince de Neuchatel - Ship type: P - How taken: HM Frigate Ethalion - When taken: 14 Dec 1813 - Where taken: at sea - Date received: 7 Jan 1814 - From what ship: Portsmouth - Born: New Orleans - Age: 26 - Released on 6 Aug 1814.

Barrett, Bias - Seaman - Number: 227 - Prize name: Hickerson - Ship type: MV - How taken: Apprehended at London - When taken: 17 Nov 1812 - Date received: 25 Nov 1812 - From what ship: HMS Raisonnable - Born: New York - Age: 23 - Discharged on 12 Apr 1813 and released to HMS Carnatic.

Barrett, George - Seaman - Number: 1671 - How taken: Gave himself up from HM Frigate Galetea - Date received: 9 May 1813 - From what ship: HMS Raisonnable - Born: Lancaster - Age: 39 - Discharged on 11 Aug 1814 and sent to Dartmoor on HMS Shamrock.

Barrett, James - Seaman - Number: 1318 - How taken: Gave himself up from HM Guardship Royal William - When taken: 3 Feb 1813 - Date received: 16 Mar 1813 - From what ship: Portsmouth, via HMS Abundance - Born: Delaware - Age: 27 - Discharged on 23 Jul 1814 and sent to Dartmoor.

Barry, John - Seaman - Number: 520 - Prize name: William - Ship type: MV - How taken: HM Brig Recruit - When taken: 29 Aug 1812 - Where taken: at sea - Date received: 23 Feb 1813 - From what ship: Portsmouth via

HMS Dromedary - Born: Savannah, GA - Age: 63 - Race: Black man - Discharged on 8 Jun 1813 and released to Cartel Rodrigo.

Barry, Peter - Seaman - Number: 2406 - How taken: Gave himself up from HM Ship-Sloop Jalouse - Date received: 21 Oct 1813 - From what ship: Portsmouth via HMT Malabar - Born: Salem - Age: 39 - Race: Black - Discharged on 4 Sep 1814 and sent to Dartmoor on HMS Freya.

Bartelett, John - Seaman - Number: 2247 - Prize name: Joseph - Ship type: MV - How taken: HM Frigate Iris - When taken: 8 Jun 1813 - Where taken: off Spain - Date received: 7 Sep 1813 - From what ship: HMS Raisonnable - Born: Marblehead - Age: 24 - Discharged on 11 Aug 1814 and sent to Dartmoor on HMS Freya.

Bartell, William - Seaman - Number: 2803 - Prize name: Industry - Ship type: P - How taken: HM Brig Heron - When taken: 3 Nov 1813 - Where taken: off Halifax - Date received: 7 Jan 1814 - From what ship: Halifax - Born: Marblehead - Age: 38 - Discharged on 8 Sep 1814 and sent to Dartmoor on HMS Niobe.

Bartholf, Nicholas - Seaman - Number: 1880 - Prize name: Tiger - Ship type: MV - How taken: HM Brig Scylla - When taken: 22 Mar 1813 - Where taken: Bay of Biscay - Date received: 7 Jul 1813 - From what ship: Portsmouth via HMS Tribune - Born: New York - Age: 20 - Released on 11 Jul 1814.

Bartis, John - Seaman - Number: 1894 - Prize name: Prompt - Ship type: MV - How taken: Chance, British privateer - When taken: 28 Mar 1813 - Where taken: Bay of Biscay - Date received: 7 Jul 1813 - From what ship: Portsmouth via HMS Tribune - Born: New Orleans - Age: 26 - Race: Black - Discharged on 12 Aug 1814 and sent to Dartmoor on HMS Alpheus.

Bartlett, George B. - Sailing Master - Number: 1182 - Prize name: Sword Fish - Ship type: P - How taken: HM Ship-of-the-Line Elephant - When taken: 28 Dec 1812 - Where taken: off Azores - Date received: 16 Mar 1813 - From what ship: Portsmouth, via HMS Abundance - Born: Marblehead - Age: 31 - Discharged on 8 Jun 1813 and released to Cartel Rodrigo.

Bartlett, John - Marine Private - Number: 3664 - Prize name: Elbridge Gerry - Ship type: P - How taken: HM Frigate Crescent - When taken: 13 Nov 1813 - Where taken: off St. Johns - Date received: 4 May 1814 - From what ship: Portsmouth - Born: Hampshire - Age: 23 - Discharged on 25 Sep 1814 and sent to Dartmoor on HMS Niobe.

Bartlett, Robert - Seaman - Number: 2687 - Prize name: Growler - Ship type: P - How taken: HM Brig Electra - When taken: 7 Jul 1813 - Where taken: off St. Johns - Date received: 7 Jan 1814 - From what ship: Portsmouth - Born: Philadelphia - Age: 26 - Discharged on 8 Sep 1814 and sent to Dartmoor on HMS Niobe.

Bartlett, Scipio - Seaman - Number: 3715 - Prize name: Requin - Ship type: LM - How taken: HM Frigate Venus - When taken: 5 Mar 1814 - Where taken: off Bordeaux, France - Date received: 18 May 1814 - From what ship: HMS Raisonnable - Born: Boston - Age: 64 - Race: Black - Discharged on 26 Sep 1814 and sent to Dartmoor on HMS Leyden.

Barton, Elijah - Seaman - Number: 493 - Prize name: Hannibal - Ship type: MV - How taken: MV Potent - When taken: 24 Sep 1812 - Where taken: off Bermuda - Date received: 23 Feb 1813 - From what ship: Portsmouth via HMS Dromedary - Born: New York - Age: 20 - Discharged on 8 Jun 1813 and released to Cartel Rodrigo.

Barton, James - Seaman - Number: 3406 - Prize name: Elbridge Gerry - Ship type: P - How taken: HM Frigate Tenedos - When taken: 21 May 1813 - Where taken: off Cape Cod - Date received: 23 Feb 1814 - From what ship: Halifax via HMT Malabar - Born: Portland - Age: 15 - Discharged on 21 Jul 1814 and sent to Dartmoor on HMS Portia.

Barton, Nathan - Seaman - Number: 867 - Prize name: Columbia - Ship type: MV - How taken: HM Frigate Briton - When taken: 17 Jan 1813 - Where taken: off Bordeaux, France - Date received: 1 Mar 1813 - From what ship: Plymouth via HMS Namur - Born: Baltimore - Age: 26 - Discharged in Jul 1813 and released to Cartel Moses Brown.

Barton, Peter - Seaman - Number: 894 - Prize name: Hannah of New York - Ship type: MV - How taken: HM Ship-of-the-Line Trident - When taken: 25 Aug 1812 - Where taken: Malta - Date received: 1 Mar 1813 - From what ship: Plymouth via HMS Namur - Born: Marblehead - Age: 29 - Discharged on 8 Jun 1813 and released to Cartel Rodrigo.

Basset, Edward S. - Seaman - Number: 181 - How taken: Stopped at London - When taken: 29 Oct 1812 - Date received: 5 Nov 1812 - From what ship: HMS Namur - Born: Philadelphia - Age: 52 - Died on 10 Jan 1813 from pneumonia.

Bassett, John - Seaman - Number: 2950 - Prize name: Enterprise - Ship type: P - How taken: HM Frigate Tenedos - When taken: 21 May 1813 - Where taken: off Cape Cod - Date received: 7 Jan 1814 - From what ship: Halifax - Born: Massachusetts - Age: 25 - Discharged on 25 Sep 1814 and sent to Dartmoor on HMS Leyden.

Bassett, William - Seaman - Number: 3669 - Prize name: Teazer - Ship type: P - How taken: HM Frigate Boreas - When taken: 15 Jun 1813 - Where taken: off Halifax - Date received: 4 May 1814 - From what ship: Portsmouth - Born: Philadelphia - Age: 20 - Race: Black - Discharged on 25 Sep 1814 and sent to Dartmoor on HMS Niobe.

Basstisto, John - Seaman - Number: 1676 - Prize name: Bonne Citoyenne - Ship type: MV - How taken: HMS Castilian - When taken: Feb 1813 - Where taken: off Aux Bound - Date received: 9 May 1813 - From what ship: HMS Raisonnable - Born: Bordeaux, France - Age: 22 - Discharged on 25 Sep 1814 and sent to Dartmoor on HMS Leyden.

Bateman, Michael - Seaman - Number: 3286 - Prize name: Vivid - Ship type: P - How taken: HM Frigate Nymphe - When taken: 20 Apr 1813 - Where taken: off Cape Cod - Date received: 23 Feb 1814 - From what ship: Halifax via HMT Malabar - Born: Salem - Age: 54 - Discharged on 10 Oct 1814 and sent to Dartmoor on the Mermaid.

Bates, Joseph - Seaman - Number: 2373 - How taken: Gave himself up from HM Ship-of-the-Line Swiftsure - When taken: 26 Dec 1812 - Date received: 20 Oct 1813 - From what ship: Portsmouth, via an admiral's tender - Born: Massachusetts - Age: 21 - Discharged on 4 Sep 1814 and sent to Dartmoor on HMS Freya.

Bates, Josiah - Seaman - Number: 3913 - Prize name: Sister - Ship type: MV - How taken: HM Frigate Unicorn - When taken: 3 Jul 1814 - Where taken: off Christian Land - Date received: 9 Sep 1814 - From what ship: HMS Namur - Born: Philadelphia - Age: 27 - Discharged on 22 Oct 1814 and sent to Dartmoor on HMS Leyden.

Battes, John - Seaman - Number: 2949 - Prize name: Enterprise - Ship type: P - How taken: HM Frigate Tenedos - When taken: 21 May 1813 - Where taken: off Cape Cod - Date received: 7 Jan 1814 - From what ship: Halifax - Born: Massachusetts - Age: 43 - Discharged on 25 Sep 1814 and sent to Dartmoor on HMS Leyden.

Baurs, Francis - Seaman - Number: 1839 - Prize name: tender to the Privateer True Blooded Yankee - Ship type: P - How taken: HM Ship-of-the-Line Fame - When taken: 24 Jun 1813 - Where taken: off Brest, France - Date received: 7 Jul 1813 - From what ship: Portsmouth via HMS Scorpion - Born: New Orleans - Age: 20 - Discharged on 22 Jun 1814 and sent to Calais, France on the Simon & Mary.

Baxter, Alexander - Seaman - Number: 194 - Prize name: Lord Hebbes - Ship type: MV - How taken: Impressed at Folkstone - When taken: 13 Sep 1812 - Date received: 6 Nov 1812 - From what ship: HMS Echo - Born: Philadelphia - Age: 38 - Discharged in Jul 1813 and released to Cartel Moses Brown.

Baxter, David - Seaman - Number: 3656 - Prize name: Caroline - Ship type: MV - How taken: HM Brig Moselle - When taken: 12 Aug 1813 - Where taken: off Charleston - Date received: 23 Apr 1814 - From what ship: HMS Raisonnable - Born: Yarmouth - Age: 22 - Discharged on 25 Sep 1814 and sent to Dartmoor on HMS Niobe.

Baxter, Franklin - Seaman - Number: 3810 - How taken: Gave himself up from HM Frigate Phoenix - When taken: 17 Jul 1813 - Date received: 13 Jun 1814 - From what ship: Quebec - Born: Barnstable - Age: 24 - Discharged on 25 Sep 1814 and sent to Dartmoor on HMS Leyden.

Bayman, James - Seaman - Number: 1242 - Prize name: Rossie - Ship type: MV - How taken: HM Frigate Dryand - When taken: 7 Jan 1813 - Where taken: at sea - Date received: 16 Mar 1813 - From what ship: Portsmouth, via HMS Abundance - Born: Vermont - Age: 21 - Discharged on 24 Jul 1813 and released to Cartel Hoffminy.

Beach, John - Seaman - Number: 3603 - Prize name: Liberty - Ship type: MV - How taken: Surrendered at Stromness, Scotland - When taken: 30 Dec 1813 - Date received: 29 Mar 1814 - From what ship: Hired tender Anna - Born: Boston - Age: 30 - Died on 30 Apr 1814 from fever.

Beals, John - Private - Number: 3109 - Prize name: 14th U.S. Infantry - Ship type: LF - How taken: British forces - When taken: 24 Jun 1813 - Where taken: Beaver Dams, Upper Canada - Date received: 7 Jan 1814 - From what ship: Halifax - Born: Maryland - Age: 23 - Discharged on 10 Oct 1814 and sent to U.S. on Cartel St. Philip.

Bean, Amos - Seaman - Number: 1264 - How taken: Gave himself up from HM Ship-of-the-Line Mars - When taken: 9 Dec 1812 - Date received: 16 Mar 1813 - From what ship: Portsmouth, via HMS Abundance - Born: Brentwood, MD - Age: 22 - Discharged on 23 Jul 1814 and sent to Dartmoor.

Bean, John - Seaman - Number: 3265 - Prize name: Volante - Ship type: P - How taken: HM Brig Curlew - When taken: 25 Mar 1813 - Where taken: off Boston - Date received: 23 Feb 1814 - From what ship: Halifax via HMT Malabar - Born: Providence - Age: 29 - Discharged on 21 Jul 1814 and sent to Dartmoor on HMS Portia.

Bean, William - Seaman - Number: 1855 - How taken: Gave himself up from HM Ship-of-the-Line Malta - Date received: 7 Jul 1813 - From what ship: Portsmouth via HMS Tribune - Born: Petersburg, VA - Age: 34 - Discharged on 25 Jul 1814 and sent to Dartmoor on HMS Bittern.

Beans, James - Seaman - Number: 1206 - Prize name: Expectation - Ship type: MV - How taken: HM Frigate Briton - When taken: 17 Dec 1812 - Where taken: at sea - Date received: 16 Mar 1813 - From what ship: Portsmouth, via HMS Abundance - Born: Virginia - Age: 34 - Discharged on 2 Jul 1813 and released to Cartel Moses Brown.

Beard, John - Private - Number: 3124 - Prize name: 14th U.S. Infantry - Ship type: LF - How taken: British forces - When taken: 24 Jun 1813 - Where taken: Beaver Dams, Upper Canada - Date received: 7 Jan 1814 - From what ship: Halifax - Born: Pennsylvania - Age: 29 - Discharged on 10 Oct 1814 and sent to U.S. on Cartel St. Philip.

Beard, Richard - Private - Number: 3098 - Prize name: 14th U.S. Infantry - Ship type: LF - How taken: British forces - When taken: 24 Jun 1813 - Where taken: Beaver Dams, Upper Canada - Date received: 7 Jan 1814 - From what ship: Halifax - Born: Maryland - Age: 19 - Discharged on 10 Oct 1814 and sent to U.S. on Cartel St. Philip.

Beasley, Edward - Seaman - Number: 1201 - Prize name: Expectation - Ship type: MV - How taken: HM Frigate Briton - When taken: 17 Dec 1812 - Where taken: at sea - Date received: 16 Mar 1813 - From what ship: Portsmouth, via HMS Abundance - Born: Maryland - Age: 22 - Discharged on 2 Jul 1813 and released to Cartel Moses Brown.

Beatty, John - Seaman - Number: 3002 - Prize name: Grand Turk - Ship type: P - How taken: HM Frigate Tenedos - When taken: 26 May 1813 - Where taken: off Cape Sable, Florida - Date received: 7 Jan 1814 - From what ship: Halifax - Born: New Jersey - Age: 24 - Discharged on 25 Sep 1814 and sent to Dartmoor on HMS Leyden.

Beaty, James - Seaman - Number: 757 - Prize name: Quebec of London, prize of the Privateer Paul Jones - Ship type: P - How taken: HM Brig Derwent - When taken: 29 Jan 1813 - Where taken: off Lisbon - Date received: 25 Feb 1813 - From what ship: HMS Brazen - Born: Fribourg, MA - Age: 36 - Discharged on 23 Jul 1814 and sent to Dartmoor on HMS Acasta.

Beauty, Edmund - Seaman - Number: 3630 - Prize name: Bunker Hill - Ship type: P - How taken: HM Frigate Pomone & HM Frigate Cydnus - When taken: 4 Mar 1814 - Where taken: Bay of Biscay - Date received: 31 Mar 1814 - From what ship: HMS Raisonnable - Born: Baltimore - Age: 17 - Discharged on 22 Oct 1814 and sent to Dartmoor on HMS Leyden.

Beck, William - Seaman - Number: 1306 - How taken: Gave himself up from HM Guardship Royal William - When taken: 3 Feb 1813 - Date received: 16 Mar 1813 - From what ship: Portsmouth, via HMS Abundance - Born: Portsmouth - Age: 49 - Discharged on 23 Jul 1814 and sent to Dartmoor.

Beckett, William - Seaman - Number: 1023 - Prize name: Hibernia - Ship type: MV - How taken: Taken up at Liverpool - When taken: 18 Oct 1812 - Date received: 11 Mar 1813 - From what ship: Yarmouth via HMS Tenders - Born: Virginia - Age: 28 - Race: Black - Discharged in Jul 1813 and released to Cartel Moses Brown.

Beckner, Henry - Seaman - Number: 610 - Prize name: Antelope - Ship type: P - How taken: HM Brig Zephyr - When taken: 10 Dec 1812 - Where taken: at sea - Date received: 23 Feb 1813 - From what ship: Portsmouth via HMS Dromedary - Born: Brunswick, NJ - Age: 26 - Discharged on 2 Jul 1813 and released to Cartel Moses Brown.

Beckwith, James - Seaman - Number: 3203 - How taken: Gave himself up from HM Transport Leopard - When taken: 25 Dec 1813 - Date received: 7 Jan 1813 - From what ship: Portsmouth - Born: Maryland - Age: 25 - Discharged on 26 Sep 1814 and sent to Dartmoor on HMS Leyden.

Beecher, William Palmer - Seaman - Number: 1897 - Prize name: Prompt - Ship type: MV - How taken: Chance, British privateer - When taken: 28 Mar 1813 - Where taken: Bay of Biscay - Date received: 7 Jul 1813 - From what ship: Portsmouth via HMS Tribune - Born: New Haven - Age: 16 - Discharged on 4 Aug 1814 and sent to Dartmoor on HMS Liverpool.

Beers, James - Seaman - Number: 33 - Prize name: Arial - Ship type: MV - How taken: HM Brig Recruit - When taken: 2 Jun 1812 - Where taken: coast of America - Date received: 3 Nov 1812 - From what ship: HMS Plover - Born: Philadelphia - Age: 29 - Discharged on 23 Mar 1813 and released to the Cartel Robinson Potter.

Behon, Simon - Seaman - Number: 2921 - Prize name: Juliana Smith - Ship type: P - How taken: HM Frigate Nymphe - When taken: 12 May 1813 - Where taken: off Cape Sable, Florida - Date received: 7 Jan 1814 - From what ship: Halifax - Born: Massachusetts - Age: 18 - Discharged on 25 Sep 1814 and sent to Dartmoor on HMS Leyden.

Belford, Isaac - Seaman - Number: 868 - Prize name: Columbia - Ship type: MV - How taken: HM Frigate Briton - When taken: 17 Jan 1813 - Where taken: off Bordeaux, France - Date received: 1 Mar 1813 - From what ship: Plymouth via HMS Namur - Born: Portland - Age: 19 - Discharged in Jul 1813 and released to Cartel Moses Brown.

Bell, George - Seaman - Number: 812 - Prize name: Leader - Ship type: MV - How taken: HM Frigate Andromach - When taken: 10 Dec 1812 - Where taken: off Bordeaux, France - Date received: 27 Feb 1813 - From what ship: Plymouth via HMS Namur - Born: Boston - Age: 20 - Discharged in Jul 1813 and released to Cartel Moses Brown.

Bell, Richard - Seaman - Number: 3423 - Prize name: Thomas - Ship type: P - How taken: HM Frigate Nymphe - When taken: 27 Jun 1813 - Where taken: at sea - Date received: 23 Feb 1814 - From what ship: Halifax via HMT Malabar - Born: Portland - Age: 19 - Race: Black - Discharged on 22 Oct 1814 and sent to Dartmoor on HMS Leyden.

Bell, Robert L. - Seaman - Number: 2045 - How taken: Gave himself up from MV Camberwell - When taken: 31 May 1813 - Date received: 4 Aug 1813 - From what ship: HMS Christian VII - Born: Danbury, CT - Age: 29 - Race: Blackman - Discharged on 3 Nov 1813 and released to HMS Ceres.

Bellas, John - Seaman - Number: 805 - Prize name: Bell - Ship type: MV - How taken: Phillis - When taken: 18 Dec 1812 - Where taken: off Cadiz, Spain - Date received: 27 Feb 1813 - From what ship: Plymouth via HMS Namur - Born: Norfolk, VA - Age: 27 - Race: Black - Discharged on 8 Jun 1813 and released to Cartel Rodrigo.

Bendionan, Vincent - Seaman - Number: 279 - How taken: Apprehended at London - When taken: 10 Dec 1812 - Date received: 23 Dec 1812 - From what ship: HMS Raisonnable - Born: Wilmington, DE - Age: 22 - Discharged on 12 Apr 1813 and released to HMS Carnatic.

Benjamin, Edward - Prize Master - Number: 2729 - Prize name: Mary, prize to the Privateer True Blooded Yankee - Ship type: P - How taken: HM Ship of-the-Line Bellerophon - When taken: 16 Dec 1813 - Where taken: off Land's End, England - Date received: 7 Jan 1814 - From what ship: Portsmouth - Born: Connecticut - Age: 25 - Discharged on 24 Sep 1814 and sent to Norway.

Benjamin, James - Seaman - Number: 1202 - Prize name: Expectation - Ship type: MV - How taken: HM Frigate Briton - When taken: 17 Dec 1812 - Where taken: at sea - Date received: 16 Mar 1813 - From what ship: Portsmouth, via HMS Abundance - Born: Philadelphia - Age: 23 - Discharged on 2 Jul 1813 and released to Cartel Moses Brown.

Benjamin, Joseph - Seaman - Number: 1128 - How taken: Gave himself up from HM Guardship Royal William - When taken: 1 Feb 1813 - Date received: 14 Mar 1813 - From what ship: Portsmouth via HMS Beagle - Born: Philadelphia - Age: 34 - Race: Black - Discharged on 11 Aug 1814 and sent to Dartmoor on HMS Freya.

Benjamin, Polasskie - Seaman - Number: 1504 - Prize name: Pallas - Ship type: MV - How taken: HM Brig Papillon - When taken: 23 Jan 1813 - Where taken: off Cadiz, Spain - Date received: 8 Apr 1813 - From what ship: Portsmouth, via an admiral's tender - Born: Stratford, CT - Age: 17 - Discharged on 14 Aug 1814 and sent to Dartmoor.

Benner, Lewis - Seaman - Number: 925 - Prize name: Experiment - Ship type: MV - How taken: HM Brig Rover - When taken: 10 Nov 1812 - Where taken: off Bordeaux, France - Date received: 10 Mar 1813 - From what ship: HMS Tigress - Born: Baltimore - Age: 22 - Race: Mulatto - Discharged on 8 Jun 1813 and released to Cartel Rodrigo.

Bennet, Andrew - Seaman - Number: 45 - Prize name: General Blake - Ship type: MV - How taken: HM Brig Recruit - When taken: 11 Jun 1812 - Where taken: off Rhode Island - Date received: 3 Nov 1812 - From what ship: HMS Plover - Born: Swanton, RI - Age: 20 - Discharged on 23 Mar 1813 and released to the Cartel Robinson Potter.

Bennet, John - Seaman - Number: 3703 - How taken: Gave himself up from the Earl Falk - When taken: 9 May 1814 - Date received: 10 May 1814 - From what ship: Eagle - Born: Shrewsbury - Age: 34 - Discharged on 26 Sep 1814 and sent to Dartmoor on HMS Leyden.

Bennet, William - Seaman - Number: 347 - Prize name: Postsea, prize to the Privateer Thrasher - Ship type: P - How taken: HM Sloop Helena - When taken: 31 Dec 1813 - Where taken: off Azores - Date received: 19 Jan 1813 - From what ship: HMS Raisonnable - Born: Cape Ann - Age: 33 - Discharged on 24 Jul 1813 and released to Cartel Hoffminy.

Bennett, Robert - Seaman - Number: 3863 - Prize name: Rose - Ship type: MV - How taken: HM Brig Racehorse - When taken: 3 Sep 1812 - Where taken: Isle de France (Mauritius) - Date received: 24 Aug 1814 - From what ship: London - Born: Nantucket - Age: 29 - Discharged on 22 Oct 1814 and sent to Dartmoor on HMS Leyden.

Benny, Malloc - Seaman - Number: 874 - Prize name: Stephen - Ship type: MV - How taken: Briton, letter of marque - When taken: 1 Jan 1813 - Where taken: off Bordeaux, France - Date received: 1 Mar 1813 - From what ship: Plymouth via HMS Namur - Born: Norwich - Age: 25 - Race: Blackman - Discharged on 24 Jul 1813 and released to Cartel Hoffminy.

Bennyman, John - Seaman - Number: 1534 - How taken: Gave himself up from HM Ship-of-the-Line Sterling Castle - When taken: 20 Sep 1812 - Date received: 8 Apr 1813 - From what ship: Portsmouth, via an admiral's tender - Born: Wilmington - Age: 29 - Released on 26 Sep 1814.

Benson, George - Seaman - Number: 1580 - How taken: Gave himself up from HM Ship-of-the-Line Colossus - When taken: 10 Dec 1812 - Date received: 16 Apr 1813 - From what ship: HMS Namur, admiral's tender - Born: Nottingham - Age: 39 - Race: Black - Discharged on 24 Jul 1814 and sent to Dartmoor.

Benson, Jonas - Seaman - Number: 1768 - How taken: Gave himself up from HM Frigate North Star - When taken: 26 May 1813 - Date received: 14 Jun 1813 - From what ship: HMS Arethusa - Born: Maryland - Age: 23 - Discharged on 24 Jul 1814 and sent to Dartmoor on HMS Liffey.

Benster, John - Seaman - Number: 991 - Prize name: Otter - Ship type: MV - How taken: HM Ship-Sloop Jalouse - When taken: 1 Dec 1812 - Where taken: off Cape St. Vincent, Portugal - Date received: 10 Mar 1813 - From what ship: HMS Tigress - Born: Virginia - Age: 23 - Released on 20 Mar 1813 to HMS Otter.

Bergen, Leven - Seaman - Number: 1763 - How taken: Gave himself up from HM Ship-of-the-Line Sterling Castle - When taken: 5 Jun 1813 - Date received: 14 Jun 1813 - From what ship: HMS Arethusa - Born: Maryland -

Age: 33 - Race: Blackman - Discharged on 24 Jul 1814 and sent to Dartmoor on HMS Liffey.

Berlew, Gibeon - Private - Number: 3082 - Prize name: 14th U.S. Infantry - Ship type: LF - How taken: British forces - When taken: 24 Jun 1813 - Where taken: Beaver Dams, Upper Canada - Date received: 7 Jan 1814 - From what ship: Halifax - Born: Jersey - Age: 24 - Discharged on 10 Oct 1814 and sent to U.S. on Cartel St. Philip.

Bernard, Zacharias - Master - Number: 2675 - Prize name: Renown, whaler - Ship type: MV - How taken: HM Brig Nimrod - When taken: 2 Apr 1813 - Where taken: Pacific Ocean - Date received: 2 Dec 1813 - From what ship: HMS Raisonnable - Born: Nantucket - Age: 33 - Discharged on 14 Dec 1813 and sent to Reading on parole.

Berry, George - Seaman - Number: 2666 - How taken: Gave up from HM Ship-of-the-Line Christian VII - When taken: 4 Aug 1813 - Date received: 13 Nov 1813 - From what ship: HMS Ceres - Born: Dover, DE - Age: 27 - Race: Blackman - Released on 26 Sep 1814.

Berry, George - Seaman - Number: 2061 - How taken: Gave up from HM Ship-of-the-Line Christian VII - When taken: 4 Aug 1813 - Date received: 4 Aug 1813 - From what ship: HMS Christian VII - Born: Dover, DE - Age: 27 - Race: Blackman - Discharged on 11 Nov 1813 and released to HMS Ceres.

Berry, John - Seaman - Number: 729 - Prize name: Eos - Ship type: MV - How taken: Detained at Portsmouth harbor - When taken: 31 Jul 1812 - Date received: 24 Feb 1813 - From what ship: Portsmouth via HMS Ulysses - Born: Kingston - Age: 18 - Race: Color Man - Discharged on 23 Mar 1813 and released to the Cartel Robinson Potter.

Berry, Joseph - Seaman - Number: 1230 - Prize name: Rossie - Ship type: MV - How taken: HM Frigate Dryand - When taken: 7 Jan 1813 - Where taken: at sea - Date received: 16 Mar 1813 - From what ship: Portsmouth, via HMS Abundance - Born: Baltimore - Age: 18 - Discharged on 24 Jul 1813 and released to Cartel Hoffminy.

Berry, Samuel - Seaman - Number: 3363 - Prize name: U.S.R.M. Cutter Surveyor - Ship type: War - How taken: HM Frigate Narcissus - When taken: 12 Jun 1813 - Where taken: York River, Virginia - Date received: 23 Feb 1814 - From what ship: Halifax via HMT Malabar - Born: Bedford - Age: 28 - Discharged on 10 Oct 1814 and sent to U.S. on Cartel St. Philip.

Berry, William - Seaman - Number: 3372 - Prize name: Yorktown - Ship type: P - How taken: HM Frigate Maidstone - When taken: 17 Jul 1813 - Where taken: Grand Banks - Date received: 23 Feb 1814 - From what ship: Halifax via HMT Malabar - Born: Long Island - Age: 24 - Discharged on 10 Oct 1814 and sent to Dartmoor on the Mermaid.

Bessom, Nicholas - Seaman - Number: 1165 - Prize name: Sword Fish - Ship type: P - How taken: HM Ship-of-the-Line Elephant - When taken: 28 Dec 1812 - Where taken: off Azores - Date received: 16 Mar 1813 - From what ship: Portsmouth, via HMS Abundance - Born: Marblehead - Age: 20 - Discharged on 24 Jul 1813 and released to Cartel Hoffminy.

Best, John - Seaman - Number: 1316 - How taken: Gave himself up from HM Guardship Royal William - When taken: 3 Feb 1813 - Date received: 16 Mar 1813 - From what ship: Portsmouth, via HMS Abundance - Born: New Jersey - Age: 29 - Discharged on 23 Jul 1814 and sent to Dartmoor.

Bevers, Clement - Seaman - Number: 841 - Prize name: Vengeance - Ship type: LM - How taken: HM Frigate Phoebe - When taken: 1 Jan 1813 - Where taken: Lat 44.4 Long 23 - Date received: 1 Mar 1813 - From what ship: Plymouth via HMS Namur - Born: Baltimore - Age: 43 - Discharged on 24 Jul 1813 and released to Cartel Hoffminy.

Bicketson, John - Seaman - Number: 288 - Prize name: Francis Ann - Ship type: MV - How taken: Apprehended at Leight, Scotland - When taken: 5 Aug 1812 - Date received: 23 Dec 1812 - From what ship: Greenlaw Depot - Born: New Bedford - Age: 18 - Discharged on 23 Mar 1813 and released to the Cartel Robinson Potter.

Bickford, Ebenezer - Master's Mate - Number: 421 - Prize name: Hunter - Ship type: P - How taken: HM Frigate Phoebe - When taken: 23 Dec 1812 - Where taken: off Azores - Date received: 19 Feb 1813 - From what ship: HMS Modeste - Born: Salem - Age: 26 - Discharged on 2 Jul 1813 and released to Cartel Moses Brown.

Bickford, William - Seaman - Number: 876 - Prize name: Hero - Ship type: MV - How taken: Cornet - When taken: 10 Feb 1813 - Where taken: off Lisbon - Date received: 1 Mar 1813 - From what ship: Plymouth via HMS Namur - Born: Charlestown - Age: 36 - Released on 27 Mar 1813.

Bids, Thomas - Seaman - Number: 3306 - Prize name: Lark - Ship type: MV - How taken: HM Schooner Bream - When taken: 12 Apr 1813 - Where taken: off Cape Sable, Florida - Date received: 23 Feb 1814 - From what ship: Halifax via HMT Malabar - Born: Topsfield - Age: 36 - Discharged on 10 Oct 1814 and sent to Dartmoor on the Mermaid.

Bienent, Edward - Seaman - Number: 836 - Prize name: Vengeance - Ship type: LM - How taken: HM Frigate Phoebe - When taken: 1 Jan 1813 - Where taken: Lat 44.4 Long 23 - Date received: 1 Mar 1813 - From what ship: Plymouth via HMS Namur - Born: Salisbury - Age: 17 - Discharged on 24 Jul 1813 and released to Cartel Hoffminy.

Billings, Richard - Seaman - Number: 2762 - Prize name: Thomas - Ship type: P - How taken: HM Frigate Nymphe - When taken: 24 Jun 1813 - Where taken: off Halifax - Date received: 7 Jan 1814 - From what ship: Halifax - Born: Massachusetts - Age: 21 - Discharged on 8 Sep 1814 and sent to Dartmoor on HMS Niobe.

Billings, Thomas - Seaman - Number: 2327 - How taken: Impressed at Gravesend, England - When taken: 1 Jun 1813 - Date received: 12 Oct 1813 - From what ship: HMS Raisonnable - Born: Connecticut - Age: 44 - Died on 24 Nov 1813 from consumption (tuberculosis).

Bin, Peter - Private - Number: 1617 - Prize name: 13th U.S. Infantry - Ship type: LF - How taken: British forces - When taken: 13 Oct 1812 - Where taken: Upper Canada - Date received: 9 May 1813 - From what ship: HMS Raisonnable - Born: Londonderry, Ireland - Age: 24 - Discharged on 22 Oct 1814 and sent to Dartmoor on HMS Leyden.

Bircham, Joseph - Shipwright - Number: 370 - How taken: Impressed at Gravesend, England - When taken: 23 Dec 1812 - Date received: 21 Jan 1813 - From what ship: HMS Raisonnable - Born: South Carolina - Age: 40 - Discharged on 24 Jul 1813 and released to Cartel Hoffminy.

Bird, Benjamin E. - 2nd Lieutenant - Number: 3044 - Prize name: U.S. Light Dragoons - Ship type: LF - How taken: British forces - When taken: 28 May 1813 - Where taken: Sackets Harbor - Date received: 7 Jan 1814 - From what ship: Halifax - Born: Pennsylvania - Age: 20 - Discharged on 14 Jan 1814 and sent to Reading on parole.

Bird, James - Seaman - Number: 2053 - How taken: Gave himself up from HM Ship-of-the-Line Fame - When taken: 4 May 1813 - Date received: 4 Aug 1813 - From what ship: HMS Christian VII - Born: Connecticut - Age: 36 - Discharged on 4 Aug 1814 and sent to Dartmoor on HMS Liverpool.

Birmingham, Thomas - Seaman - Number: 2539 - Prize name: Ulysses - Ship type: MV - How taken: HM Ship-of-the-Line Majestic - When taken: 4 Aug 1813 - Where taken: off the Western Isles, Scotland - Date received: 22 Oct 1813 - From what ship: Portsmouth via HMT Malabar - Born: Ireland - Age: 64 - Released on 27 Apr 1814.

Bisbee, Asaph - Seaman - Number: 1275 - Prize name: Sword Fish - Ship type: P - How taken: HM Ship-of-the-Line Elephant - When taken: 28 Dec 1812 - Where taken: off Azores - Date received: 16 Mar 1813 - From what ship: Portsmouth, via HMS Abundance - Born: Plymouth - Age: 24 - Discharged on 24 Jul 1813 and released to Cartel Hoffminy.

Bisbee, Elijah - Seaman - Number: 3760 - Prize name: Argus - Ship type: MV - How taken: HM Ship-of-the-Line San Domingo - When taken: 1 Mar 1814 - Where taken: off Savannah - Date received: 26 May 1814 - From what ship: HMS Hindostan - Born: Plymouth - Age: 19 - Discharged on 25 Sep 1814 and sent to Dartmoor on HMS Niobe.

Bisbee, J. D. - Seaman - Number: 3741 - Prize name: Argus - Ship type: MV - How taken: HM Ship-of-the-Line San Domingo - When taken: 1 Mar 1814 - Where taken: off Savannah - Date received: 26 May 1814 - From what ship: HMS Hindostan - Born: Middleboro - Age: 22 - Discharged on 26 Sep 1814 and sent to Dartmoor on HMS Leyden.

Bishop, Edward - Seaman - Number: 1889 - Prize name: Dick - Ship type: MV - How taken: HM Brig Dispatch - When taken: 17 Mar 1813 - Where taken: off Bordeaux, France - Date received: 7 Jul 1813 - From what ship:

Portsmouth via HMS Tribune - Born: New York - Age: 27 - Discharged on 12 Aug 1814 and sent to Dartmoor on HMS Alpheus.

Bishop, James - Seaman - Number: 316 - Prize name: Joseph Ricketsen - Ship type: MV - How taken: HM Brig Rifleman - When taken: 22 Aug 1812 - Where taken: off Scotland - Date received: 23 Dec 1812 - From what ship: Greenlaw Depot - Born: Middlesex - Age: 22 - Released on 2 Apr 1813.

Bissell, Samuel W. - Seaman - Number: 2435 - Prize name: Hepsey - Ship type: MV - How taken: HM Brig Zenobia - When taken: 22 Jun 1813 - Where taken: off Lisbon - Date received: 21 Oct 1813 - From what ship: Portsmouth via HMT Malabar - Born: Connecticut - Age: 22 - Discharged on 4 Sep 1814 and sent to Dartmoor on HMS Freya.

Bissun, Thomas - Seaman - Number: 3476 - Prize name: Yankee - Ship type: P - How taken: HM Frigate Shannon - When taken: 20 Aug 1813 - Where taken: at sea - Date received: 23 Feb 1814 - From what ship: Halifax via HMT Malabar - Born: Bordeaux - Age: 29 - Discharged on 10 Oct 1814 and sent to U.S. on Cartel St. Philip.

Bitters, John - Seaman - Number: 1203 - Prize name: Expectation - Ship type: MV - How taken: HM Frigate Briton - When taken: 17 Dec 1812 - Where taken: at sea - Date received: 16 Mar 1813 - From what ship: Portsmouth, via HMS Abundance - Born: Philadelphia - Age: 23 - Discharged on 2 Jul 1813 and released to Cartel Moses Brown.

Black, James - Seaman - Number: 3389 - Prize name: Fox - Ship type: P - How taken: HM Frigate Maidstone - When taken: 18 Jul 1813 - Where taken: Grand Banks - Date received: 23 Feb 1814 - From what ship: Halifax via HMT Malabar - Born: Briston - Age: 27 - Discharged on 22 Oct 1814 and sent to Dartmoor on HMS Leyden.

Black, John - Seaman - Number: 1141 - Prize name: Sword Fish - Ship type: P - How taken: HM Ship-of-the-Line Elephant - When taken: 28 Dec 1812 - Where taken: off Azores - Date received: 16 Mar 1813 - From what ship: Portsmouth, Mundane - Born: Salem - Age: 20 - Race: Black - Discharged on 24 Jul 1813 and released to Cartel Hoffminy.

Black, John - Private - Number: 3123 - Prize name: 14th U.S. Infantry - Ship type: LF - How taken: British forces - When taken: 24 Jun 1813 - Where taken: Beaver Dams, Upper Canada - Date received: 7 Jan 1814 - From what ship: Halifax - Born: Maryland - Age: 24 - Discharged on 10 Oct 1814 and sent to U.S. on Cartel St. Philip.

Black, Philip - Lieutenant - Number: 2788 - Prize name: Yorktown - Ship type: P - How taken: British squadron - When taken: 17 Jul 1813 - Where taken: Grand Banks - Date received: 7 Jan 1814 - From what ship: Halifax - Born: New York - Age: 22 - Discharged on 20 Aug 1814 and sent to Dartmoor on HMS Shamrock.

Black, Ruddick - Seaman - Number: 3475 - Prize name: Yankee - Ship type: P - How taken: HM Frigate Shannon - When taken: 20 Aug 1813 - Where taken: at sea - Date received: 23 Feb 1814 - From what ship: Halifax via HMT Malabar - Born: Barnstable - Age: 18 - Discharged on 22 Oct 1814 and sent to Dartmoor on HMS Leyden.

Black, Thomas - Boatswain - Number: 3629 - Prize name: Bunker Hill - Ship type: P - How taken: HM Frigate Pomone & HM Frigate Cydnus - When taken: 4 Mar 1814 - Where taken: Bay of Biscay - Date received: 31 Mar 1814 - From what ship: HMS Raisonnable - Born: Philadelphia - Age: 33 - Discharged on 20 Aug 1814 and sent to Dartmoor on HMS Shamrock.

Black, William - Seaman - Number: 3708 - How taken: Impressed at Hall - When taken: 26 Feb 1814 - Date received: 15 May 1815 - From what ship: Eagle - Born: New Hampshire - Age: 25 - Discharged on 20 Aug 1814 and sent to Dartmoor on HMS Shamrock.

Black, William - Seaman - Number: 1000 - Prize name: Brunswick - Ship type: MV - How taken: HM Frigate Iris - When taken: 17 Dec 1812 - Where taken: off Spain - Date received: 10 Mar 1813 - From what ship: HMS Tigress - Born: New Hampshire - Age: 24 - Discharged on 2 Jul 1813 and released to Cartel Moses Brown.

Blackburn, William - Seaman - Number: 44 - Prize name: General Blake - Ship type: MV - How taken: HM Brig Recruit - When taken: 11 Jun 1812 - Where taken: off Rhode Island - Date received: 3 Nov 1812 - From what ship: HMS Plover - Born: Frederick Town, MD - Age: 26 - Discharged on 23 Mar 1813 and released to the Cartel Robinson Potter.

Blackman, Moses - Seaman - Number: 1906 - Prize name: Weasel - Ship type: MV - How taken: HM Brig Foxhound - When taken: 25 Mar 1813 - Where taken: Bay of Biscay - Date received: 7 Jul 1813 - From what ship: Portsmouth via HMS Tribune - Born: Boston - Age: 40 - Died on 5 Dec 1813 from inflammation of the lungs.

Blair, Benjamin - Seaman - Number: 3433 - Prize name: Enterprise - Ship type: P - How taken: HM Frigate Tenedos - When taken: 21 May 1813 - Where taken: off Cape Cod - Date received: 23 Feb 1814 - From what ship: Halifax via HMT Malabar - Born: Marblehead - Age: 17 - Discharged on 22 Oct 1814 and sent to Dartmoor on HMS Leyden.

Blair, David - Seaman - Number: 3432 - Prize name: Juliana Smith - Ship type: P - How taken: HM Frigate Nymphe - When taken: 12 May 1813 - Where taken: off Cape Sable, Florida - Date received: 23 Feb 1814 - From what ship: Halifax via HMT Malabar - Born: Marblehead - Age: 28 - Discharged on 22 Oct 1814 and sent to Dartmoor on HMS Leyden.

Blair, Robert - Seaman - Number: 2809 - Prize name: Industry - Ship type: P - How taken: HM Brig Heron - When taken: 3 Nov 1813 - Where taken: off Halifax - Date received: 7 Jan 1814 - From what ship: Halifax - Born: Marblehead - Age: 22 - Race: Black - Discharged on 25 Sep 1814 and sent to Dartmoor on HMS Leyden.

Blaird, David - Seaman - Number: 3561 - Prize name: Hannah - Ship type: MV - How taken: HM Ship-of-the-Line Conquestador - When taken: 15 Jan 1814 - Where taken: at sea - Date received: 7 May 1814 - From what ship: Portsmouth via HMS Favorite - Born: Pelham - Age: 29 - Discharged on 25 Sep 1814 and sent to Dartmoor on HMS Leyden.

Blake, Charles - Seaman - Number: 1268 - Prize name: Sword Fish - Ship type: P - How taken: HM Ship-of-the-Line Elephant - When taken: 28 Dec 1812 - Where taken: off Azores - Date received: 16 Mar 1813 - From what ship: Portsmouth, via HMS Abundance - Born: Newburyport - Age: 16 - Discharged on 24 Jul 1813 and released to Cartel Hoffminy.

Blake, Charles - Seaman - Number: 2521 - Prize name: Yorktown - Ship type: P - How taken: HM Brig Nimrod - When taken: 17 Jul 1813 - Where taken: Grand Banks - Date received: 22 Oct 1813 - From what ship: Portsmouth via HMT Malabar - Born: Boston - Age: 21 - Discharged on 8 Sep 1814 and sent to Dartmoor on HMS Niobe.

Blake, William - Seaman - Number: 2107 - How taken: Gave himself up from HM Ship-of-the-Line Repulse - When taken: 27 May 1813 - Date received: 9 Aug 1813 - From what ship: HMS Thames - Born: Massachusetts - Age: 43 - Discharged on 12 Aug 1814 and sent to Dartmoor on HMS Alpheus.

Blanchard, John - Seaman - Number: 2989 - Prize name: America - Ship type: P - How taken: HM Frigate Shannon - When taken: 25 May 1813 - Where taken: off Cape Cod - Date received: 7 Jan 1814 - From what ship: Halifax - Born: Boston - Age: 18 - Discharged on 25 Sep 1814 and sent to Dartmoor on HMS Leyden.

Blaney, Henry - Private - Number: 1624 - Prize name: 13th U.S. Infantry - Ship type: LF - How taken: British forces - When taken: 13 Oct 1812 - Where taken: Upper Canada - Date received: 9 May 1813 - From what ship: HMS Raisonnable - Born: County Mayo, Ireland - Age: 29 - Discharged on 22 Oct 1814 and sent to Dartmoor on HMS Leyden.

Blaney, Stephen - Seaman - Number: 2983 - Prize name: Enterprise - Ship type: P - How taken: HM Frigate Tenedos - When taken: 21 May 1813 - Where taken: off Cape Cod - Date received: 7 Jan 1814 - From what ship: Halifax - Born: Portsmouth - Age: 27 - Discharged on 25 Sep 1814 and sent to Dartmoor on HMS Leyden.

Blankenship, Charles - Seaman - Number: 656 - Prize name: U.S.R.M. Cutter James Madison - Ship type: War - How taken: HM Frigate Barbadoes - When taken: 22 Aug 1812 - Where taken: at sea - Date received: 24 Feb 1813 - From what ship: Portsmouth via HMS Ulysses - Born: Rochester, MA - Age: 28 - Discharged on 10 May 1813 and released to Cartel Admittance.

Blazon, Stephen - Seaman - Number: 1109 - Prize name: Tom Thumb - Ship type: MV - How taken: Lion, British privateer - When taken: 15 Feb 1813 - Where taken: Bay of Biscay - Date received: 14 Mar 1813 - From what ship: Portsmouth via HMS Beagle - Born: Baltimore - Age: 23 - Discharged on 11 Aug 1814 and sent to Dartmoor on HMS Freya.

Bliss, Frederick - Seaman - Number: 1922 - How taken: Impressed at London - When taken: 7 Jul 1813 - Date received: 11 Jul 1813 - From what ship: HMS Raisonnable - Born: New York - Age: 26 - Discharged on 8 Sep 1814 and sent to Dartmoor on HMS Niobe.

Blood, Simon - Carpenter - Number: 186 - Prize name: Calaban - Ship type: MV - How taken: HM Battery Gorgon - When taken: 12 Aug 1812 - Where taken: Great Belt, Denmark - Date received: 5 Nov 1812 - From what ship: HMS Namur - Born: New Hampshire - Age: 36 - Discharged on 10 May 1813 and released to Cartel Admittance.

Bloomsdale, John - Seaman - Number: 3589 - Prize name: Devon, prize to the Privateer Bunker Hill - Ship type: P - How taken: HM Brig Fly - When taken: 21 Jan 1814 - Where taken: at sea - Date received: 26 Mar 1814 - From what ship: Plymouth via HMS Raleigh - Born: Albany - Age: 23 - Discharged on 25 Sep 1814 and sent to Dartmoor on HMS Niobe.

Blossom, Seth - Seaman - Number: 3409 - Prize name: Elbridge Gerry - Ship type: P - How taken: HM Frigate Tenedos - When taken: 21 May 1813 - Where taken: off Cape Cod - Date received: 23 Feb 1814 - From what ship: Halifax via HMT Malabar - Born: Wiscasset - Age: 22 - Discharged on 21 Jul 1814 and sent to Dartmoor on HMS Portia.

Blue, Peter - Carpenter - Number: 1939 - Prize name: Hope - Ship type: MV - How taken: Chance, British privateer - When taken: 15 Feb 1813 - Where taken: off Bordeaux, France - Date received: 15 Jul 1813 - From what ship: Plymouth - Born: Lisbon - Age: 46 - Discharged on 17 Jun 1814 and sent to Dartmoor on HMS Pincher.

Blumbhouser, Samuel - Seaman - Number: 2058 - How taken: Gave up from HM Ship-of-the-Line Monmouth - When taken: 15 Jul 1813 - Date received: 4 Aug 1813 - From what ship: HMS Raisonnable - Born: Marblehead - Age: 40 - Discharged on 4 Aug 1814 and sent to Dartmoor on HMS Liverpool.

Bocatt, John - Seaman - Number: 959 - How taken: Gave himself up from HM Ship-of-the-Line Salvador del Mundo - Date received: 10 Mar 1813 - From what ship: HMS Tigress - Born: Kings County - Age: 37 - Discharged on 4 Aug 1814 and sent to Dartmoor on HMS Liverpool.

Bodkin, William - Seaman - Number: 3351 - Prize name: Thomas - Ship type: P - How taken: HM Frigate Nymphe - When taken: 26 Jun 1813 - Where taken: off Halifax - Date received: 23 Feb 1814 - From what ship: Halifax via HMT Malabar - Born: Portsmouth - Age: 55 - Race: Black - Discharged on 10 Oct 1814 and sent to Dartmoor on the Mermaid.

Boger, James - Seaman - Number: 223 - How taken: Apprehended at London - When taken: 18 Nov 1812 - Date received: 25 Nov 1812 - From what ship: HMS Raisonnable - Born: Delaware - Age: 43 - Discharged on 24 Jul 1813 and released to Cartel Hoffminy.

Boggs, James - Seaman - Number: 2258 - Prize name: Governor McKane - Ship type: LM - How taken: HM Brig Rover - When taken: 26 Jan 1813 - Where taken: off Bordeaux, France - Date received: 7 Sep 1813 - From what ship: HMS Raisonnable - Born: Philadelphia - Age: 63 - Discharged on 11 Aug 1814 and sent to Dartmoor on HMS Freya.

Boillet, John - Seaman - Number: 2276 - How taken: Gave himself up from HM Brig Raven - When taken: 15 Aug 1813 - Date received: 16 Sep 1813 - From what ship: HMS Raisonnable - Born: Charlestown - Age: 29 - Discharged on 4 Sep 1814 and sent to Dartmoor on HMS Freya.

Boite, Julius Pierre - Marine Private - Number: 3691 - Prize name: Bunker Hill - Ship type: P - How taken: HM Frigate Pomone & HM Frigate Cydnus - When taken: 4 Mar 1814 - Where taken: Bay of Biscay - Date received: 4 May 1814 - From what ship: Portsmouth - Born: Nantes, France - Age: 41 - Discharged on 22 Jun 1814 and sent to Calais, France on the Simon & Mary.

Bond, Samuel - Seaman - Number: 2126 - How taken: Gave himself up from HM Ship-of-the-Line Ocean - When taken: 28 May 1813 - Date received: 9 Aug 1813 - From what ship: HMS Thames - Born: Baltimore - Age: 40 - Race: Black - Discharged on 12 Aug 1814 and sent to Dartmoor on HMS Alpheus.

Bontrous, John - Passenger - Number: 1722 - Prize name: Powhattan - Ship type: MV - How taken: HMS Horatio - When taken: 13 Dec 1812 - Where taken: Bay of Biscay - Date received: 25 May 1813 - From what ship: Portsmouth via HMS Impetius - Born: Leon, France - Age: 24 - Discharged on 24 Jul 1813 and released to

Cartel Hoffminy.

Booder, Jacob - Seaman - Number: 1138 - Prize name: Sword Fish - Ship type: P - How taken: HM Ship-of-the-Line Elephant - When taken: 28 Dec 1812 - Where taken: off Azores - Date received: 16 Mar 1813 - From what ship: Portsmouth, Mundane - Born: New York - Age: 21 - Race: Black - Discharged on 24 Jul 1813 and released to Cartel Hoffminy.

Booth, George - Private - Number: 3117 - Prize name: 14th U.S. Infantry - Ship type: LF - How taken: British forces - When taken: 24 Jun 1813 - Where taken: Beaver Dams, Upper Canada - Date received: 7 Jan 1814 - From what ship: Halifax - Born: Maryland - Age: 21 - Discharged on 10 Oct 1814 and sent to U.S. on Cartel St. Philip.

Booth, Joseph - Seaman - Number: 329 - Prize name: Thomas - Ship type: MV - How taken: Apprehended at London - When taken: 4 Jan 1813 - Date received: 11 Jan 1813 - From what ship: HMS Raisonnable - Born: Herring Bay, MD - Age: 30 - Discharged on 12 Apr 1813 and released to HMS Carnatic.

Booth, Thomas - Seaman - Number: 1297 - How taken: Gave himself up from HM Guardship Royal William - When taken: 3 Feb 1813 - Date received: 16 Mar 1813 - From what ship: Portsmouth, via HMS Abundance - Born: Maryland - Age: 29 - Race: Black - Discharged on 23 Jul 1814 and sent to Dartmoor.

Bordage, Raymond - Seaman - Number: 3854 - How taken: Gave himself up from HM Frigate Owen Glendower - When taken: 20 Jun 1813 - Date received: 24 Aug 1814 - From what ship: London - Born: New Orleans - Age: 32 - Discharged on 26 Sep 1814 and sent to Dartmoor on HMS Leyden.

Bordley, George - Seaman - Number: 2099 - How taken: Gave himself up from HM Ship-of-the-Line Barfleur - When taken: 27 May 1813 - Date received: 9 Aug 1813 - From what ship: HMS Thames - Born: Rhode Island - Age: 30 - Race: Black - Discharged on 12 Aug 1814 and sent to Dartmoor on HMS Alpheus.

Boss, Thomas - Seaman - Number: 1432 - Prize name: Louisa, prize of the Privateer Decatur - Ship type: P - How taken: HM Frigate Andromache - When taken: 11 Jan 1813 - Where taken: off Bordeaux, France - Date received: 6 Apr 1813 - From what ship: Plymouth via HMS Decoy - Born: Hampton - Age: 31 - Released on 20 Jul 1813.

Boston, John - Seaman - Number: 3680 - Prize name: Sally - Ship type: MV - How taken: HM Brig Derwent - When taken: 21 Jul 1814 - Where taken: at sea - Date received: 4 May 1814 - From what ship: Portsmouth - Born: Salem - Age: 36 - Discharged on 25 Sep 1814 and sent to Dartmoor on HMS Niobe.

Boston, Peter - Seaman - Number: 1930 - Prize name: Edward - Ship type: MV - How taken: Seringapatam, British letter of marque - When taken: 6 Jan 1813 - Where taken: South America - Date received: 11 Jul 1813 - From what ship: HMS Raisonnable - Born: Nantucket - Age: 53 - Race: Black - Discharged on 24 Jul 1813 and released to Cartel Hoffminy.

Boston, Robert - Seaman - Number: 717 - Prize name: James - Ship type: MV - How taken: Detained at Portsmouth harbor - When taken: 31 Jul 1812 - Date received: 24 Feb 1813 - From what ship: Portsmouth via HMS Ulysses - Born: Lyman, MA - Age: 22 - Discharged on 23 Mar 1813 and released to the Cartel Robinson Potter.

Boswell, Samuel - Seaman - Number: 3399 - Prize name: Yankee - Ship type: P - How taken: HM Brig Ringdove - When taken: 17 Oct 1813 - Where taken: at sea - Date received: 23 Feb 1814 - From what ship: Halifax via HMT Malabar - Born: Somerset - Age: 18 - Discharged on 22 Oct 1814 and sent to Dartmoor on HMS Leyden.

Boterol, John - Pilot - Number: 1815 - Prize name: tender to the Privateer True Blooded Yankee - Ship type: P - How taken: HM Ship-of-the-Line Fame - When taken: 24 Jun 1813 - Where taken: off Brest, France - Date received: 7 Jul 1813 - From what ship: Portsmouth via HMS Scorpion - Born: New Orleans - Age: 30 - Discharged on 22 Jun 1814 and sent to Calais, France on the Simon & Mary.

Bounty, Charles - Cook - Number: 226 - How taken: Apprehended at London - When taken: 6 Nov 1812 - Date received: 25 Nov 1812 - From what ship: HMS Raisonnable - Born: Gosham, NY - Age: 48 - Discharged in Jul 1813 and released to Cartel Moses Brown.

Bourn, James - Boy - Number: 170 - Prize name: Javen - Ship type: MV - How taken: Detained at London - When taken: 1 Aug 1812 - Date received: 5 Nov 1812 - From what ship: HMS Namur - Born: New York - Age: 18

- Discharged in Jul 1813 and released to Cartel Moses Brown.

Bourn, John - Seaman - Number: 771 - Prize name: Alagana - Ship type: MV - How taken: HM Ship-of-the-Line San Juan - When taken: 8 May 1812 - Where taken: Gibraltar - Date received: 25 Feb 1813 - From what ship: HMS Brazen - Born: Mathews County, MD - Age: 37 - Discharged on 10 May 1813 and released to Cartel Admittance.

Bourn, Oliver - Seaman - Number: 3415 - Prize name: Portsmouth Packet - Ship type: P - How taken: HM Brig Fantome - When taken: 5 Oct 1813 - Where taken: Grand Banks - Date received: 23 Feb 1814 - From what ship: Halifax via HMT Malabar - Born: Kennebunkport - Age: 17 - Discharged on 22 Oct 1814 and sent to Dartmoor on HMS Leyden.

Bourns, Solomon - Seaman - Number: 237 - How taken: Impressed at London - When taken: 17 Nov 1812 - Date received: 25 Nov 1812 - From what ship: HMS Raisonnable - Born: Kingston - Age: 19 - Discharged on 24 Jul 1813 and released to Cartel Hoffminy.

Bovey, Benjamin - Seaman - Number: 754 - Prize name: Quebec of London, prize of the Privateer Paul Jones - Ship type: P - How taken: HM Brig Derwent - When taken: 29 Jan 1813 - Where taken: off Lisbon - Date received: 25 Feb 1813 - From what ship: HMS Brazen - Born: New Orleans - Age: 18 - Race: Mulatto - Discharged on 23 Jul 1814 and sent to Dartmoor on HMS Acasta.

Bovey, Jesse - Seaman - Number: 380 - Prize name: Union American - Ship type: MV - How taken: Taken up at London - When taken: 28 Dec 1812 - Date received: 31 Jan 1813 - From what ship: HMS Raisonnable - Born: Massachusetts - Age: 32 - Discharged on 24 Jul 1813 and released to Cartel Hoffminy.

Bowden, Benjamin - Mate - Number: 2702 - Prize name: Growler - Ship type: P - How taken: HM Brig Electra - When taken: 7 Jul 1813 - Where taken: off St. Johns - Date received: 7 Jan 1814 - From what ship: Portsmouth - Born: Marblehead - Age: 25 - Discharged on 8 Sep 1814 and sent to Dartmoor on HMS Leyden.

Bowden, John - Seaman - Number: 3377 - Prize name: U.S.R.M. Cutter Surveyor - Ship type: War - How taken: HM Frigate Narcissus - When taken: 12 Jun 1813 - Where taken: York River, Virginia - Date received: 23 Feb 1814 - From what ship: Halifax via HMT Malabar - Born: Salem - Age: 21 - Discharged on 21 Jul 1814 and sent to Dartmoor on HMS Portia.

Bowden, William - Seaman - Number: 2691 - Prize name: Growler - Ship type: P - How taken: HM Brig Electra - When taken: 7 Jul 1813 - Where taken: off St. Johns - Date received: 7 Jan 1814 - From what ship: Portsmouth - Born: Marblehead - Age: 17 - Discharged on 8 Sep 1814 and sent to Dartmoor on HMS Niobe.

Bowdley, Thomas - Boy - Number: 474 - Prize name: Hunter - Ship type: P - How taken: HM Frigate Phoebe - When taken: 23 Dec 1812 - Where taken: off Azores - Date received: 19 Feb 1813 - From what ship: HMS Modeste - Born: Boston - Age: 15 - Discharged on 24 Jul 1813 and released to Cartel Hoffminy.

Bowen, Artemas - Sergeant - Number: 3094 - Prize name: 14th U.S. Infantry - Ship type: LF - How taken: British forces - When taken: 24 Jun 1813 - Where taken: Beaver Dams, Upper Canada - Date received: 7 Jan 1814 - From what ship: Halifax - Born: Massachusetts - Age: 33 - Discharged on 10 Oct 1814 and sent to U.S. on Cartel St. Philip.

Bowen, Lewis - 2nd Mate - Number: 480 - Prize name: Vengeance - Ship type: LM - How taken: HM Frigate Phoebe - When taken: 1 Jan 1813 - Where taken: Lat 44.4 Long 23 - Date received: 19 Feb 1813 - From what ship: HMS Modeste - Born: New York - Age: 20 - Discharged on 24 Jul 1813 and released to Cartel Hoffminy.

Bowen, Sylvester - Seaman - Number: 3467 - Prize name: Yankee - Ship type: P - How taken: HM Frigate Shannon - When taken: 20 Aug 1813 - Where taken: at sea - Date received: 23 Feb 1814 - From what ship: Halifax via HMT Malabar - Born: Rhode Island - Age: 26 - Discharged on 25 Sep 1814 and sent to Dartmoor on HMS Leyden.

Bowen, William - Private - Number: 3096 - Prize name: 14th U.S. Infantry - Ship type: LF - How taken: British forces - When taken: 24 Jun 1813 - Where taken: Beaver Dams, Upper Canada - Date received: 7 Jan 1814 - From what ship: Halifax - Born: Maryland - Age: 23 - Discharged on 10 Oct 1814 and sent to U.S. on Cartel St. Philip.

Bowie, Henry - 2nd Mate - Number: 629 - Prize name: Antelope - Ship type: P - How taken: HM Brig Zephyr - When taken: 10 Dec 1812 - Where taken: at sea - Date received: 23 Feb 1813 - From what ship: Portsmouth via HMS Dromedary - Born: Yorktown - Age: 25 - Discharged on 8 Jun 1813 and released to Cartel Rodrigo.

Bowins, George - Seaman - Number: 1744 - How taken: Gave himself up from HMS Impeteux - When taken: 2 Dec 1812 - Date received: 26 May 1813 - From what ship: Portsmouth via HMS Impetius - Born: Philadelphia - Age: 30 - Discharged on 24 Jul 1814 and sent to Dartmoor on HMS Liffey.

Bowman, John - Seaman - Number: 35 - Prize name: Mary - Ship type: MV - How taken: From a cutter's boat off Bermuda - When taken: 8 Aug 1812 - Date received: 3 Nov 1812 - From what ship: HMS Plover - Born: Reading, PA - Age: 39 - Discharged on 23 Mar 1813 and released to the Cartel Robinson Potter.

Boyd, Andrew - Seaman - Number: 3450 - Prize name: Elbridge Gerry - Ship type: P - How taken: HM Frigate Crescent - When taken: 16 Sep 1813 - Where taken: at sea - Date received: 23 Feb 1814 - From what ship: Halifax via HMT Malabar - Born: Providence - Age: 26 - Discharged on 22 Oct 1814 and sent to Dartmoor on HMS Leyden.

Boyd, Andrew - Seaman - Number: 2430 - Prize name: Hepsey - Ship type: MV - How taken: HM Brig Zenobia - When taken: 22 Jun 1813 - Where taken: off Lisbon - Date received: 21 Oct 1813 - From what ship: Portsmouth via HMT Malabar - Born: Maryland - Age: 22 - Discharged on 4 Sep 1814 and sent to Dartmoor on HMS Freya.

Boyd, Edward - Seaman - Number: 454 - Prize name: Hunter - Ship type: P - How taken: HM Frigate Phoebe - When taken: 23 Dec 1812 - Where taken: off Azores - Date received: 19 Feb 1813 - From what ship: HMS Modeste - Born: Salem - Age: 19 - Discharged on 24 Jul 1813 and released to Cartel Hoffminy.

Boyd, John - Seaman - Number: 577 - How taken: Gave himself up from HM Frigate Loire - When taken: 14 Dec 1812 - Date received: 23 Feb 1813 - From what ship: Portsmouth via HMS Dromedary - Born: Kennebunk - Age: 20 - Discharged on 23 Jul 1813 and released to HMS Ceres.

Boyd, John - Seaman - Number: 1226 - Prize name: Rossie - Ship type: MV - How taken: HM Frigate Dryand - When taken: 7 Jan 1813 - Where taken: at sea - Date received: 16 Mar 1813 - From what ship: Portsmouth, via HMS Abundance - Born: New York - Age: 36 - Discharged on 24 Jul 1813 and released to Cartel Hoffminy.

Boyd, John - Seaman - Number: 2152 - How taken: Gave himself up at London - When taken: 24 Jul 1813 - Date received: 14 Aug 1813 - From what ship: HMS Raisonnable - Born: New Bedford - Age: 23 - Released on 26 Sep 1814.

Boyd, John - Seaman - Number: 2557 - How taken: Gave himself up from HM Frigate Bombay - When taken: 29 Oct 1812 - Date received: 23 Oct 1813 - From what ship: Portsmouth via HMS Raisonnable - Born: North Carolina - Age: 40 - Discharged on 8 Sep 1814 and sent to Dartmoor on HMS Niobe.

Boyd, Peter - Seaman - Number: 2032 - How taken: Given up from HM Brig Furious - When taken: 25 Apr 1813 - Date received: 1 Aug 1813 - From what ship: HMS Raisonnable - Born: Georgetown, SC - Age: 29 - Discharged on 19 Oct 1813 and released to HMS Ceres.

Boyd, Stephen (alias Steffen Beale) - Seaman - Number: 2340 - Prize name: Hindostan - Ship type: MV - How taken: HM Brig Zenobia - When taken: 25 Jun 1813 - Where taken: off Lisbon - Date received: 20 Oct 1813 - From what ship: Portsmouth, via an admiral's tender - Born: Hamburg - Age: 30 - Discharged on 22 Oct 1814 and sent to Dartmoor on HMS Leyden.

Boyer, John - Seaman - Number: 2451 - Prize name: Wiley Reynard - Ship type: P - How taken: HM Frigate Shannon - When taken: 16 Aug 1812 - Where taken: off Halifax - Date received: 21 Oct 1813 - From what ship: Portsmouth via HMT Malabar - Born: Bordeaux - Age: 20 - Discharged on 22 Jun 1814 and sent to Calais, France on the Simon & Mary.

Boyle, James - Seaman - Number: 328 - How taken: Apprehended at London - When taken: 29 Dec 1812 - Date received: 11 Jan 1813 - From what ship: HMS Raisonnable - Born: Bradford - Age: 35 - Discharged on 24 Jul 1813 and released to Cartel Hoffminy.

Boyle, Joseph - Seaman - Number: 3271 - Prize name: Volante - Ship type: P - How taken: HM Brig Curlew - When taken: 25 Mar 1813 - Where taken: off Boston - Date received: 23 Feb 1814 - From what ship: Halifax via

HMT Malabar - Born: Ellenton - Age: 40 - Discharged on 10 Oct 1814 and sent to Dartmoor on the Mermaid.

Brackett, John - Seaman - Number: 3257 - Prize name: Revenge - Ship type: MV - How taken: HM Frigate Shannon - When taken: 5 Nov 1813 - Where taken: off Halifax - Date received: 23 Feb 1814 - From what ship: Halifax via HMT Malabar - Born: Portland - Age: 19 - Discharged on 10 Oct 1814 and sent to Dartmoor on the Mermaid.

Bradbury, Nathan - Seaman - Number: 63 - Prize name: Laurel - Ship type: MV - How taken: From a cutter off Bermuda - When taken: 24 Jul 1812 - Date received: 3 Nov 1812 - From what ship: HMS Plover - Born: Boston, MA - Age: 23 - Discharged on 23 Mar 1813 and released to the Cartel Robinson Potter.

Bradford, George - 2nd Lieutenant - Number: 3199 - Prize name: Elbridge Gerry - Ship type: P - How taken: HM Frigate Crescent - When taken: 16 Sep 1813 - Where taken: at sea - Date received: 7 Jan 1813 - From what ship: Portsmouth - Born: Massachusetts - Age: 30 - Discharged on 25 Sep 1814 and sent to Dartmoor on HMS Leyden.

Bradie, John - Seaman - Number: 3814 - How taken: Gave himself up from HM Frigate Hussar - When taken: 26 Jul 1813 - Date received: 13 Jun 1814 - From what ship: Quebec - Born: Boston - Age: 30 - Race: Black - Discharged on 25 Sep 1814 and sent to Dartmoor on HMS Leyden.

Brady, James - Seaman - Number: 1217 - Prize name: Rossie - Ship type: MV - How taken: HM Frigate Dryand - When taken: 7 Jan 1813 - Where taken: at sea - Date received: 16 Mar 1813 - From what ship: Portsmouth, via HMS Abundance - Born: Baltimore - Age: 23 - Discharged on 24 Jul 1813 and released to Cartel Hoffminy.

Bragden, James - Seaman - Number: 3292 - Prize name: Montgomery - Ship type: P - How taken: HM Frigate Nymphe - When taken: 5 May 1813 - Where taken: off Cape Cod - Date received: 23 Feb 1814 - From what ship: Halifax via HMT Malabar - Born: York - Age: 27 - Discharged on 10 Oct 1814 and sent to Dartmoor on the Mermaid.

Brainard, Richard - Seaman - Number: 1291 - How taken: Gave himself up from HM Guardship Royal William - When taken: 3 Feb 1813 - Date received: 16 Mar 1813 - From what ship: Portsmouth, via HMS Abundance - Born: Acton - Age: 23 - Released on 7 Oct 1813.

Braley, George - Master - Number: 2025 - Prize name: Governor Gerry - Ship type: MV - How taken: HM Brig Royalist - When taken: 31 May 1813 - Where taken: Bay of Biscay - Date received: 24 Jul 1813 - From what ship: from Ashburton - Born: New York - Age: 31 - Discharged on 24 Jul 1813 and released to Cartel Hoffminy.

Bramblecome, David - Seaman - Number: 636 - Prize name: Cornelia - Ship type: MV - How taken: HM Brig Zenobia - When taken: 14 Aug 1812 - Where taken: Western ocean - Date received: 23 Feb 1813 - From what ship: Portsmouth via HMS Dromedary - Born: Marblehead - Age: 38 - Discharged on 23 Mar 1813 and released to the Cartel Robinson Potter.

Branch, Anthony - Seaman - Number: 2349 - How taken: Gave himself up from HM Ship-of-the-Line Centaur - When taken: 25 Jun 1813 - Date received: 20 Oct 1813 - From what ship: Portsmouth, via an admiral's tender - Born: Lancaster - Age: 25 - Discharged on 4 Sep 1814 and sent to Dartmoor on HMS Freya.

Brandy, Francis - Mate - Number: 828 - Prize name: Eunice - Ship type: MV - How taken: Gave himself up at Liverpool - When taken: 7 Nov 1813 - Date received: 1 Mar 1813 - From what ship: Plymouth via HMS Namur - Born: New Orleans - Age: 25 - Discharged on 24 Jul 1813 and released to Cartel Hoffminy.

Branham, Stephen - Seaman - Number: 589 - Prize name: Antelope - Ship type: P - How taken: HM Brig Zephyr - When taken: 10 Dec 1812 - Where taken: at sea - Date received: 23 Feb 1813 - From what ship: Portsmouth via HMS Dromedary - Born: Philadelphia - Age: 30 - Discharged on 2 Jul 1813 and released to Cartel Moses Brown.

Brant, Solomon - Seaman - Number: 399 - Prize name: Maria - Ship type: MV - How taken: HM Brig Papillon - When taken: 25 Nov 1812 - Where taken: off Cadiz, Spain - Date received: 13 Feb 1813 - From what ship: HMS Raisonnable - Born: New York - Age: 31 - Discharged on 8 Jun 1813 and released to Cartel Rodrigo.

Branton, Samuel - Seaman - Number: 1190 - How taken: Gave himself up from HM Transport Romulus - When taken: 14 Aug 1812 - Date received: 16 Mar 1813 - From what ship: Portsmouth, via HMS Abundance - Born: Philadelphia - Age: 27 - Discharged on 11 Aug 1814 and sent to Dartmoor on HMS Freya.

Brassier, William - Boy - Number: 389 - Prize name: John - Ship type: MV - How taken: HM Sloop Blossom - When taken: 16 Aug 1812 - Where taken: off Gibraltar - Date received: 13 Feb 1813 - From what ship: HMS Raisonnable - Born: Plymouth, MA - Age: 18 - Discharged on 10 May 1813 and released to Cartel Admittance.

Bray, George - Carpenter - Number: 377 - Prize name: Union American - Ship type: MV - How taken: Impressed at London - When taken: 25 Jan 1813 - Date received: 31 Jan 1813 - From what ship: HMS Raisonnable - Born: Baltimore - Age: 29 - Discharged on 24 Jul 1813 and released to Cartel Hoffminy.

Bray, Zacharias - Seaman - Number: 1276 - Prize name: Sword Fish - Ship type: P - How taken: HM Ship-of-the-Line Elephant - When taken: 28 Dec 1812 - Where taken: off Azores - Date received: 16 Mar 1813 - From what ship: Portsmouth, via HMS Abundance - Born: Salem - Age: 20 - Race: Black - Discharged on 24 Jul 1813 and released to Cartel Hoffminy.

Brenton, York - Seaman - Number: 1294 - How taken: Gave himself up from HM Guardship Royal William - When taken: 3 Feb 1813 - Date received: 16 Mar 1813 - From what ship: Portsmouth, via HMS Abundance - Born: Newbury - Age: 32 - Race: Black - Discharged on 23 Jul 1814 and sent to Dartmoor.

Brewer, James - Seaman - Number: 811 - Prize name: Leader - Ship type: MV - How taken: HM Frigate Andromach - When taken: 10 Dec 1812 - Where taken: off Bordeaux, France - Date received: 27 Feb 1813 - From what ship: Plymouth via HMS Namur - Born: Boston - Age: 20 - Discharged in Jul 1813 and released to Cartel Moses Brown.

Briant, Moses - Seaman - Number: 1735 - How taken: Gave himself up from HM Guardship Royal William - When taken: Nov 1812 - Date received: 25 May 1813 - From what ship: Portsmouth via HMS Impetius - Born: Middleboy, MA - Age: 23 - Discharged on 24 Jul 1814 and sent to Dartmoor on HMS Liffey.

Brice, John - Seaman - Number: 2124 - How taken: Gave himself up from HM Ship-of-the-Line Ocean - When taken: 28 May 1813 - Date received: 9 Aug 1813 - From what ship: HMS Thames - Born: New York - Age: 31 - Discharged on 12 Aug 1814 and sent to Dartmoor on HMS Alpheus.

Brickall, William - Seaman - Number: 125 - How taken: Stopped at London - When taken: 26 Oct 1812 - Date received: 4 Nov 1812 - From what ship: HMS Namur - Born: Westfield, MA - Age: 22 - Discharged in Jul 1813 and released to Cartel Moses Brown.

Brickman, John - Carpenter - Number: 3523 - Prize name: Pilot - Ship type: LM - How taken: Vittoria, British privateer from Guernsey - When taken: 28 Jan 1814 - Where taken: off Bordeaux, France - Date received: 23 Feb 1814 - From what ship: Portsmouth via HMT Malabar - Born: Virginia - Age: 25 - Race: Mulatto - Discharged on 22 Oct 1814 and sent to Dartmoor on HMS Leyden.

Bridges, Jeremiah - Seaman - Number: 3751 - Prize name: Argus - Ship type: MV - How taken: HM Ship-of-the-Line San Domingo - When taken: 1 Mar 1814 - Where taken: off Savannah - Date received: 26 May 1814 - From what ship: HMS Hindostan - Born: Not legible - Age: 27 - Discharged on 25 Sep 1814 and sent to Dartmoor on HMS Niobe.

Bridges, John - Seaman - Number: 2744 - Prize name: Wasp - Ship type: P - How taken: HM Schooner Bream - When taken: 9 Jun 1813 - Where taken: off Halifax - Date received: 7 Jan 1814 - From what ship: Halifax - Born: Beverly - Age: 27 - Discharged on 25 Sep 1814 and sent to Dartmoor on HMS Leyden.

Briggs, Boileau - Seaman - Number: 1819 - Prize name: tender to the Privateer True Blooded Yankee - Ship type: P - How taken: HM Brig Hope - When taken: 24 Jun 1813 - Where taken: off Brest, France - Date received: 7 Jul 1813 - From what ship: Portsmouth via HMS Scorpion - Born: Virginia - Age: 31 - Race: Black - Discharged on 25 Jul 1814 and sent to Dartmoor on HMS Bittern.

Briggs, Frank - Seaman - Number: 3470 - Prize name: Yankee - Ship type: P - How taken: HM Frigate Shannon - When taken: 20 Aug 1813 - Where taken: at sea - Date received: 23 Feb 1814 - From what ship: Halifax via HMT Malabar - Born: Freetown - Age: 21 - Discharged on 22 Oct 1814 and sent to Dartmoor on HMS Leyden.

Briggs, Thomas - Seaman - Number: 2924 - Prize name: Juliana Smith - Ship type: P - How taken: HM Frigate

Nymphe - When taken: 12 May 1813 - Where taken: off Cape Sable, Florida - Date received: 7 Jan 1814 - From what ship: Halifax - Born: Massachusetts - Age: 26 - Discharged on 25 Sep 1814 and sent to Dartmoor on HMS Leyden.

Briggs, William - Boy - Number: 3294 - Prize name: Montgomery - Ship type: P - How taken: HM Frigate Nymphe - When taken: 5 May 1813 - Where taken: off Cape Cod - Date received: 23 Feb 1814 - From what ship: Halifax via HMT Malabar - Born: Salem - Age: 14 - Discharged on 10 Oct 1814 and sent to Dartmoor on the Mermaid.

Brightman, Isaac - 1st Mate - Number: 2676 - Prize name: Renown, whaler - Ship type: MV - How taken: HM Brig Nimrod - When taken: 2 Apr 1813 - Where taken: Pacific Ocean - Date received: 2 Dec 1813 - From what ship: HMS Raisonnable - Born: Nantucket - Age: 26 - Discharged on 14 Dec 1813 and sent to Reading on parole.

Brightman, Joseph - Seaman - Number: 1033 - How taken: Gave himself up from HM Ship-of-the-Line San Josef - When taken: 5 Nov 1812 - Date received: 11 Mar 1813 - From what ship: Yarmouth via HMS Tenders - Born: Boston - Age: 36 - Discharged on 4 Aug 1814 and sent to Dartmoor on HMS Liverpool.

Brill, John - Boy - Number: 1910 - Prize name: Weasel - Ship type: MV - How taken: HM Brig Foxhound - When taken: 25 Mar 1813 - Where taken: Bay of Biscay - Date received: 7 Jul 1813 - From what ship: Portsmouth via HMS Tribune - Born: New York - Age: 13 - Discharged on 4 Aug 1814 and sent to Dartmoor on HMS Liverpool.

Brimhall, Cornelius - Seaman - Number: 258 - How taken: Gave himself up at London - When taken: 27 Nov 1812 - Date received: 7 Dec 1812 - From what ship: HMS Raisonnable - Born: Portland, MA - Age: 38 - Discharged on 24 Jul 1813 and released to Cartel Hoffminy.

Brimmer, John - Seaman - Number: 1158 - Prize name: Sword Fish - Ship type: P - How taken: HM Ship-of-the-Line Elephant - When taken: 28 Dec 1812 - Where taken: off Azores - Date received: 16 Mar 1813 - From what ship: Portsmouth, via HMS Abundance - Born: New York - Age: 37 - Discharged on 24 Jul 1813 and released to Cartel Hoffminy.

Brinkman, Jan - Seaman - Number: 315 - Prize name: Joseph Ricketsen - Ship type: MV - How taken: HM Brig Rifleman - When taken: 22 Aug 1812 - Where taken: off Scotland - Date received: 23 Dec 1812 - From what ship: Greenlaw Depot - Born: Oldenburg - Age: 35 - Discharged on 10 May 1813 and released to Cartel Admittance.

Brisk, John - Seaman - Number: 2449 - Prize name: Wiley Reynard - Ship type: P - How taken: HM Frigate Shannon - When taken: 16 Aug 1812 - Where taken: off Halifax - Date received: 21 Oct 1813 - From what ship: Portsmouth via HMT Malabar - Born: Marblehead - Age: 24 - Discharged on 22 Jun 1814 and sent to Calais, France on the Simon & Mary.

Brison, James - Private - Number: 3097 - Prize name: 14th U.S. Infantry - Ship type: LF - How taken: British forces - When taken: 24 Jun 1813 - Where taken: Beaver Dams, Upper Canada - Date received: 7 Jan 1814 - From what ship: Halifax - Born: Baltimore - Age: 22 - Discharged on 10 Oct 1814 and sent to U.S. on Cartel St. Philip.

Brisons, John - Seaman - Number: 3648 - Prize name: Bunker Hill - Ship type: P - How taken: HM Frigate Pomone & HM Frigate Cydnus - When taken: 4 Mar 1814 - Where taken: Bay of Biscay - Date received: 31 Mar 1814 - From what ship: HMS Raisonnable - Born: Baltimore - Age: 32 - Race: Black - Discharged on 25 Sep 1814 and sent to Dartmoor on HMS Niobe.

Broadest, Moses - Private - Number: 3101 - Prize name: 14th U.S. Infantry - Ship type: LF - How taken: British forces - When taken: 24 Jun 1813 - Where taken: Beaver Dams, Upper Canada - Date received: 7 Jan 1814 - From what ship: Halifax - Born: Maryland - Age: 20 - Discharged on 10 Oct 1814 and sent to U.S. on Cartel St. Philip.

Broden, Norman - Seaman - Number: 1089 - Prize name: Rachael - Ship type: MV - How taken: HM Schooner Herring - When taken: 9 Feb 1813 - Where taken: at sea - Date received: 14 Mar 1813 - From what ship: Portsmouth via HMS Cornwell - Born: Marblehead - Age: 29 - Discharged on 23 Jul 1814 and sent to Dartmoor.

Brooks, Edward - Seaman - Number: 512 - Prize name: Josephine - Ship type: MV - How taken: HM Sloop Goree - When taken: 15 Aug 1812 - Where taken: off Bermuda - Date received: 23 Feb 1813 - From what ship: Portsmouth via HMS Dromedary - Born: Baltimore - Age: 22 - Discharged on 10 May 1813 and released to Cartel Admittance.

Brooks, Edward - Seaman - Number: 891 - Prize name: Print of Boston - Ship type: MV - How taken: HM Ship-of-the-Line Colossus - When taken: 21 Jan 1813 - Where taken: at sea - Date received: 1 Mar 1813 - From what ship: Plymouth via HMS Namur - Born: Marblehead, MA - Age: 21 - Discharged on 17 Jun 1814 and sent to Dartmoor on HMS Redbreast.

Brooks, John - Seaman - Number: 2174 - How taken: Gave himself up from HM Ship-of-the-Line Leviathan - When taken: 28 Oct 1812 - Date received: 16 Aug 1813 - From what ship: Portsmouth, via an admiral's tender - Born: North Carolina - Age: 34 - Discharged on 17 Jun 1814 and sent to Dartmoor on the Penebar.

Brooks, John - Seaman - Number: 3295 - Prize name: Montgomery - Ship type: P - How taken: HM Frigate Nymphe - When taken: 5 May 1813 - Where taken: off Cape Cod - Date received: 23 Feb 1814 - From what ship: Halifax via HMT Malabar - Born: Africa - Age: 21 - Race: Black - Discharged on 10 Oct 1814 and sent to Dartmoor on the Mermaid.

Brooks, Oliver - Seaman - Number: 110 - Prize name: Phoenix - Ship type: MV - How taken: Stopped at London - When taken: 26 Oct 1812 - Date received: 4 Nov 1812 - From what ship: HMS Namur - Born: Gloucester, VA - Age: 60 - Discharged in Jul 1813 and released to Cartel Moses Brown.

Broughton, John - Seaman - Number: 211 - How taken: Gave himself up from MV Perverance - When taken: 2 Nov 1812 - Date received: 15 Nov 1812 - From what ship: HMS Raisonnable - Born: Marblehead, MA - Age: 20 - Discharged in Jul 1813 and released to Cartel Moses Brown.

Brower, Frederick - Seaman - Number: 1100 - Prize name: Calcutta, East Indian Ship - Ship type: MV - How taken: Two Brothers, British privateer from Guernsey - When taken: 30 Nov 1812 - Where taken: off St. Helena - Date received: 14 Mar 1813 - From what ship: Portsmouth via HMS Beagle - Born: Albany - Age: 27 - Died on 8 May 1813 from pneumonia.

Brower, John - Gunner's Mate - Number: 3738 - Prize name: Argus - Ship type: MV - How taken: HM Ship-of-the-Line San Domingo - When taken: 1 Mar 1814 - Where taken: off Savannah - Date received: 26 May 1814 - From what ship: HMS Hindostan - Born: New York - Age: 42 - Discharged on 21 Jul 1814 and sent to Dartmoor on HMS Portia.

Brower, John - Seaman - Number: 3417 - Prize name: Globe - Ship type: P - How taken: HM Frigate Spartan - When taken: 13 Jun 1813 - Where taken: off Delaware - Date received: 23 Feb 1814 - From what ship: Halifax via HMT Malabar - Born: New York - Age: 23 - Discharged on 22 Oct 1814 and sent to Dartmoor on HMS Leyden.

Brown, Abijah - Seaman - Number: 1704 - How taken: Taken up at London - When taken: 12 May 1813 - Date received: 22 May 1813 - From what ship: HMS Raisonnable - Born: Not legible - Age: 28 - Discharged on 24 Jul 1814 and sent to Dartmoor on HMS Liffey.

Brown, Abraham - Seaman - Number: 3907 - How taken: Gave himself up from HM Ship-of-the-Line Carnatic - When taken: 13 Sep 1814 - Date received: 4 Sep 1814 - From what ship: Transport Office - Born: Massachusetts - Age: 53 - Discharged on 25 Sep 1814 and sent to Dartmoor on HMS Leyden.

Brown, Benjamin - Seaman - Number: 3334 - Prize name: Porcupine - Ship type: LM - How taken: HM Frigate Acasta - When taken: 18 Jul 1813 - Where taken: off Cape Sable, Florida - Date received: 23 Feb 1814 - From what ship: Halifax via HMT Malabar - Born: Thomastown - Age: 28 - Discharged on 10 Oct 1814 and sent to Dartmoor on the Mermaid.

Brown, Charles - Seaman - Number: 2532 - Prize name: Yorktown - Ship type: P - How taken: HM Brig Nimrod - When taken: 17 Jul 1813 - Where taken: Grand Banks - Date received: 22 Oct 1813 - From what ship: Portsmouth via HMT Malabar - Born: New York - Age: 28 - Discharged on 8 Sep 1814 and sent to Dartmoor on HMS Niobe.

Brown, David - Seaman - Number: 2295 - How taken: Impressed at London - When taken: 14 Sep 1813 - Date received: 20 Sep 1813 - From what ship: HMS Raisonnable - Born: New York - Age: 21 - Discharged on 4

Sep 1814 and sent to Dartmoor on HMS Freya.

Brown, Edward - Seaman - Number: 2979 - Prize name: Enterprise - Ship type: P - How taken: HM Frigate Tenedos - When taken: 21 May 1813 - Where taken: off Cape Cod - Date received: 7 Jan 1814 - From what ship: Halifax - Born: Marblehead - Age: 26 - Died on 3 May 1814 from fever.

Brown, Elisha - Seaman - Number: 1530 - How taken: Gave himself up from HM Frigate Franchise - When taken: 20 Sep 1812 - Date received: 8 Apr 1813 - From what ship: Portsmouth, via an admiral's tender - Born: Georgetown - Age: 25 - Discharged on 4 Aug 1814 and sent to Dartmoor on HMS Alpheus.

Brown, Francis - Seaman - Number: 2443 - How taken: Taken off of the Russian MV Neptune at Cork - When taken: 28 Sep 1812 - Date received: 21 Oct 1813 - From what ship: Portsmouth via HMT Malabar - Born: Pennsylvania - Age: 28 - Race: Mulatto - Discharged on 4 Sep 1814 and sent to Dartmoor on HMS Freya.

Brown, Frederick - Seaman - Number: 3644 - Prize name: Bunker Hill - Ship type: P - How taken: HM Frigate Pomone & HM Frigate Cydnus - When taken: 4 Mar 1814 - Where taken: Bay of Biscay - Date received: 31 Mar 1814 - From what ship: HMS Raisonnable - Born: Ballston - Age: 23 - Race: Black - Discharged on 22 Oct 1814 and sent to Dartmoor on HMS Leyden.

Brown, George - Seaman - Number: 1610 - How taken: Gave himself up from HM Frigate President at Chatham - When taken: 27 Apr 1813 - Date received: 1 May 1813 - From what ship: HMS President - Born: Baltimore - Age: 31 - Discharged on 24 Jul 1814 and sent to Dartmoor.

Brown, George - Seaman - Number: 2575 - How taken: Gave himself up from HM Ship-of-the-Line Ocean - When taken: 20 Oct 1812 - Date received: 23 Oct 1813 - From what ship: Portsmouth via HMS Raisonnable - Born: Rhode Island - Age: 35 - Discharged on 8 Sep 1814 and sent to Dartmoor on HMS Niobe.

Brown, George - Prize Master - Number: 1921 - Prize name: Margaret, prize of the Privateer True Blooded Yankee - Ship type: P - How taken: HM Brig Nimrod - When taken: 9 May 1813 - Where taken: off Morant Bay, Jamaica - Date received: 10 Jul 1813 - From what ship: Escorted from transport office - Born: Wellfleet, MA - Age: 37 - Released on 11 Jul 1814.

Brown, Isaac - Seaman - Number: 2573 - How taken: Gave himself up from HM Brig Shearwater - When taken: 24 Mar 1813 - Date received: 23 Oct 1813 - From what ship: Portsmouth via HMS Raisonnable - Born: Bucks County - Age: 30 - Race: Black - Discharged on 8 Sep 1814 and sent to Dartmoor on HMS Niobe.

Brown, Jacob - Seaman - Number: 2057 - How taken: Gave himself up from HM Brig Onyx - When taken: 23 May 1813 - Date received: 4 Aug 1813 - From what ship: HMS Christian VII - Born: Germantown - Age: 29 - Discharged on 4 Aug 1814 and sent to Dartmoor on HMS Liverpool.

Brown, James - Seaman - Number: 26 - Prize name: Navigator - Ship type: MV - How taken: Detained on the Baltic - When taken: 2 Jun 1812 - Date received: 3 Nov 1812 - From what ship: HMS Raisonnable - Born: Large Island - Age: 21 - Discharged on 19 Mar 1813 and released to the Navigator.

Brown, James - Seaman - Number: 3243 - How taken: Gave himself up from HM Store Ship Serapis - When taken: 8 Dec 1813 - Date received: 14 Feb 1814 - From what ship: HMS Raisonnable - Born: Virginia - Age: 26 - Discharged on 11 Aug 1814 and sent to Dartmoor on HMS Freya.

Brown, James - Seaman - Number: 1795 - Prize name: Jupiter - Ship type: MV - How taken: Taken up at London - When taken: 12 Jun 1813 - Date received: 1 Jul 1813 - From what ship: HMS Raisonnable - Born: Bermuda - Age: 42 - Race: Mulatto - Discharged on 2 Jul 1813 and released to HMS Ceres.

Brown, James - Private - Number: 2613 - Prize name: 14th U.S. Infantry - Ship type: LF - How taken: British forces - When taken: 24 Jun 1813 - Where taken: Beaver Dams, Upper Canada - Date received: 5 Nov 1813 - From what ship: HMS Hindostan - Born: Fifeshire, Scotland - Age: 33 - Discharged on 10 Oct 1814 and sent to U.S. on Cartel St. Philip.

Brown, James - Seaman - Number: 2196 - How taken: Gave himself up from HM Ship-of-the-Line Caledonia - When taken: 5 Dec 1812 - Date received: 18 Aug 1813 - From what ship: French Account - Born: Maryland - Age: 30 - Discharged on 11 Aug 1814 and sent to Dartmoor on HMS Freya.

Brown, Jesse - Boy - Number: 479 - Prize name: Hunter - Ship type: P - How taken: HM Frigate Phoebe - When taken: 23 Dec 1812 - Where taken: off Azores - Date received: 19 Feb 1813 - From what ship: HMS Modeste

- Born: Boston - Age: 17 - Discharged on 24 Jul 1813 and released to Cartel Hoffminy.

Brown, Jesse - Master's Mate - Number: 2986 - Prize name: America - Ship type: P - How taken: HM Frigate Shannon - When taken: 25 May 1813 - Where taken: off Cape Cod - Date received: 7 Jan 1814 - From what ship: Halifax - Born: Belfast, MA - Age: 30 - Died on 10 Jun 1814 from fever.

Brown, John - 2nd Mate - Number: 984 - Prize name: Otter - Ship type: MV - How taken: HM Ship-Sloop Jalouse - When taken: 1 Dec 1812 - Where taken: off Cape St. Vincent, Portugal - Date received: 10 Mar 1813 - From what ship: HMS Tigress - Born: Marblehead - Age: 38 - Released on 20 Mar 1813 to HMS Otter.

Brown, John - Boy - Number: 473 - Prize name: Hunter - Ship type: P - How taken: HM Frigate Phoebe - When taken: 23 Dec 1812 - Where taken: off Azores - Date received: 19 Feb 1813 - From what ship: HMS Modeste - Born: New York - Age: 15 - Discharged on 24 Jul 1813 and released to Cartel Hoffminy.

Brown, John - Seaman - Number: 913 - How taken: Gave himself up from HM Brig Goldfinch at Plymouth - When taken: 27 Nov 1812 - Date received: 10 Mar 1813 - From what ship: HMS Tigress - Born: Boston - Age: 34 - Discharged on 3 Oct 1813 and released to HMS Ceres.

Brown, John - Seaman - Number: 2128 - How taken: Gave himself up from HM Ship-of-the-Line Ocean - When taken: 28 May 1813 - Date received: 9 Aug 1813 - From what ship: HMS Thames - Born: Massachusetts - Age: 20 - Race: Black - Discharged on 12 Aug 1814 and sent to Dartmoor on HMS Alpheus.

Brown, John - Seaman - Number: 1672 - How taken: Gave himself up from HM Schooner Pioneer - When taken: 28 Apr 1813 - Date received: 9 May 1813 - From what ship: HMS Raisonnable - Born: Charleston - Age: 19 - Discharged on 8 Sep 1814 and sent to Dartmoor on HMS Niobe.

Brown, John - Seaman - Number: 3305 - Prize name: Lark - Ship type: MV - How taken: HM Schooner Bream - When taken: 12 Apr 1813 - Where taken: off Cape Sable, Florida - Date received: 23 Feb 1814 - From what ship: Halifax via HMT Malabar - Born: Salem - Age: 44 - Died on 6 Mar 1814 from fever.

Brown, John - Seaman - Number: 2737 - Prize name: Growler - Ship type: P - How taken: HM Brig Electra - When taken: 7 Jul 1813 - Where taken: off St. Johns - Date received: 7 Jan 1814 - From what ship: Halifax - Born: New York - Age: 28 - Discharged on 25 Sep 1814 and sent to Dartmoor on HMS Leyden.

Brown, John - Quarter Gunner - Number: 2872 - Prize name: Elbridge Gerry - Ship type: P - How taken: HM Frigate Crescent - When taken: 16 Sep 1813 - Where taken: at sea - Date received: 7 Jan 1814 - From what ship: Portsmouth - Born: Charlestown - Age: 20 - Discharged on 25 Sep 1814 and sent to Dartmoor on HMS Leyden.

Brown, John - Private - Number: 2622 - Prize name: 14th U.S. Infantry - Ship type: LF - How taken: British forces - When taken: 24 Jun 1813 - Where taken: Beaver Dams, Upper Canada - Date received: 5 Nov 1813 - From what ship: HMS Hindostan - Born: North Ireland - Age: 34 - Discharged on 10 Oct 1814 and sent to U.S. on Cartel St. Philip.

Brown, Joseph - Seaman - Number: 2173 - How taken: Gave himself up from HM Ship-of-the-Line Swiftsure - When taken: 26 Dec 1812 - Date received: 16 Aug 1813 - From what ship: Portsmouth, via an admiral's tender - Born: Old Providence - Age: 32 - Race: Blackman - Discharged on 17 Jun 1814 and sent to Dartmoor on the Penebar.

Brown, Joseph - Seaman - Number: 2458 - Prize name: Wiley Reynard - Ship type: P - How taken: HM Frigate Shannon - When taken: 16 Aug 1812 - Where taken: off Halifax - Date received: 21 Oct 1813 - From what ship: Portsmouth via HMT Malabar - Born: New Orleans - Age: 20 - Discharged on 22 Jun 1814 and sent to Calais, France on the Simon & Mary.

Brown, Joseph - Sailing Master - Number: 2712 - Prize name: Growler - Ship type: P - How taken: HM Brig Electra - When taken: 7 Jul 1813 - Where taken: off St. Johns - Date received: 7 Jan 1814 - From what ship: Portsmouth - Born: Marblehead - Age: 29 - Discharged on 25 Sep 1814 and sent to Dartmoor on HMS Leyden.

Brown, Mark - Seaman - Number: 2178 - How taken: Gave himself up from HM Ship-of-the-Line Leviathan - When taken: 28 Oct 1812 - Date received: 16 Aug 1813 - From what ship: Portsmouth, via an admiral's tender - Born: Maryland - Age: 28 - Discharged on 11 Aug 1814 and sent to Dartmoor on HMS Freya.

Brown, Michael - Seaman - Number: 3245 - How taken: Gave himself up from HM Ship-of-the-Line Cumberland - When taken: 16 Feb 1814 - Date received: 16 Feb 1814 - From what ship: HMS Cumberland - Born: Virginia - Age: 55 - Discharged on 26 Sep 1814 and sent to Dartmoor on HMS Leyden.

Brown, Michael - Private - Number: 3083 - Prize name: 14th U.S. Infantry - Ship type: LF - How taken: British forces - When taken: 24 Jun 1813 - Where taken: Beaver Dams, Upper Canada - Date received: 7 Jan 1814 - From what ship: Halifax - Born: New York - Age: 23 - Discharged on 10 Oct 1814 and sent to U.S. on Cartel St. Philip.

Brown, Peter - Seaman - Number: 1690 - Prize name: Governor Middleton - Ship type: MV - How taken: Thetis, British privateer - When taken: 2 May 1813 - Where taken: Bay of Biscay - Date received: 15 May 1813 - From what ship: HMS Viper - Born: Philadelphia - Age: 38 - Discharged on 4 Nov 1813 and released to HMS Ceres.

Brown, Reuben - Seaman - Number: 2066 - How taken: Gave himself up from HM Ship-of-the-Line Berwick - When taken: 29 Oct 1812 - Date received: 9 Aug 1813 - From what ship: HMS Thames - Born: Boston - Age: 32 - Race: Black - Discharged on 4 Aug 1814 and sent to Dartmoor on HMS Liverpool.

Brown, Robert - Seaman - Number: 2508 - Prize name: Globe - Ship type: P - How taken: HM Prison Ship Victorious - When taken: 8 Jun 1813 - Where taken: Chesapeake Bay - Date received: 22 Oct 1813 - From what ship: Portsmouth via HMT Malabar - Born: Baltimore - Age: 30 - Discharged on 8 Sep 1814 and sent to Dartmoor on HMS Niobe.

Brown, Samuel - Seaman - Number: 2767 - Prize name: Thomas - Ship type: P - How taken: HM Frigate Nymphe - When taken: 24 Jun 1813 - Where taken: off Halifax - Date received: 7 Jan 1814 - From what ship: Halifax - Born: Massachusetts - Age: 25 - Discharged on 8 Sep 1814 and sent to Dartmoor on HMS Niobe.

Brown, Samuel - Seaman - Number: 2046 - How taken: Gave himself up from HM Ship-of-the-Line Malta - When taken: 18 Mar 1813 - Date received: 4 Aug 1813 - From what ship: HMS Christian VII - Born: Georgetown - Age: 30 - Discharged on 4 Aug 1814 and sent to Dartmoor on HMS Liverpool.

Brown, Sawyer - Seaman - Number: 3017 - How taken: Gave himself up from HM Ship-of-the-Line Invincible - When taken: 14 Jan 1813 - Date received: 7 Jan 1814 - From what ship: Portsmouth - Born: New York - Age: 37 - Race: Black - Discharged on 4 Sep 1814 and sent to Dartmoor on HMS Freya.

Brown, Seth - Seaman - Number: 1834 - Prize name: tender to the Privateer True Blooded Yankee - Ship type: P - How taken: HM Ship-of-the-Line Fame - When taken: 24 Jun 1813 - Where taken: off Brest, France - Date received: 7 Jul 1813 - From what ship: Portsmouth via HMS Scorpion - Born: Bristol - Age: 23 - Discharged on 25 Jul 1814 and sent to Dartmoor on HMS Bittern.

Brown, Thomas - Seaman - Number: 3386 - Prize name: Polly - Ship type: P - How taken: HM Frigate Maidstone - When taken: 18 Jul 1813 - Where taken: Grand Banks - Date received: 23 Feb 1814 - From what ship: Halifax via HMT Malabar - Born: Salem - Age: 16 - Discharged on 20 Aug 1814 and sent to Dartmoor on HMS Shamrock.

Brown, Thomas - Seaman - Number: 3407 - Prize name: Elbridge Gerry - Ship type: P - How taken: HM Frigate Tenedos - When taken: 21 May 1813 - Where taken: off Cape Cod - Date received: 23 Feb 1814 - From what ship: Halifax via HMT Malabar - Born: Baltimore - Age: 15 - Race: Black - Discharged on 22 Oct 1814 and sent to Dartmoor on HMS Leyden.

Brown, Thomas - Seaman - Number: 2105 - How taken: Gave himself up from HM Frigate Bombay - When taken: 27 May 1813 - Date received: 9 Aug 1813 - From what ship: HMS Thames - Born: Rhode Island - Age: 40 - Discharged on 12 Aug 1814 and sent to Dartmoor on HMS Alpheus.

Brown, Thomas - Seaman - Number: 2669 - Prize name: Hamlett - Ship type: MV - How taken: Impressed at London - When taken: 11 Nov 1813 - Date received: 21 Nov 1813 - From what ship: HMS Raisonnable - Born: Philadelphia - Age: 30 - Escaped on 10 Jun 1814 from HM Prison Ship Crown Prince.

Brown, Thomas - Boy - Number: 2540 - Prize name: Volante - Ship type: P - How taken: British squadron - When taken: 15 May 1813 - Where taken: coast of America - Date received: 22 Oct 1813 - From what ship: Portsmouth via HMT Malabar - Born: Boston - Age: 14 - Discharged on 8 Sep 1814 and sent to Dartmoor on HMS Niobe.

Brown, Thomas - Seaman - Number: 2403 - How taken: Gave himself up from HM Frigate Orpheus - When taken: 26 Dec 1812 - Date received: 21 Oct 1813 - From what ship: Portsmouth via HMT Malabar - Born: New Jersey - Age: 31 - Discharged on 4 Sep 1814 and sent to Dartmoor on HMS Freya.

Brown, Thomas - Seaman - Number: 2794 - Prize name: Fox - Ship type: P - How taken: HM Brig Manly - When taken: 1 Aug 1813 - Where taken: off Halifax - Date received: 7 Jan 1814 - From what ship: Halifax - Born: New York - Age: 23 - Discharged on 11 Aug 1814 and sent to Dartmoor on HMS Freya.

Brown, Wheeler - Carpenter - Number: 1436 - Prize name: Orbit - Ship type: MV - How taken: HM Brig Achates - When taken: 29 Jan 1813 - Where taken: Lat 49 N Long 13 W - Date received: 6 Apr 1813 - From what ship: Plymouth via HMS Decoy - Born: New London - Age: 43 - Discharged on 24 Jul 1814 and sent to Dartmoor.

Brown, William - Seaman - Number: 105 - Prize name: Earl St. Vincent - Ship type: MV - How taken: Stopped at London - When taken: 26 Oct 1812 - Date received: 4 Nov 1812 - From what ship: HMS Namur - Born: Baltimore - Age: 34 - Discharged on 28 Apr 1813 and released to the David Scott.

Brown, William - Seaman - Number: 1068 - How taken: Gave himself up from HM Frigate Ulysses - When taken: 13 Jan 1813 - Date received: 14 Mar 1813 - From what ship: Portsmouth via HMS Cornwell - Born: New York - Age: 30 - Discharged on 11 Aug 1814 and sent to Dartmoor.

Brown, William - Seaman - Number: 2536 - Prize name: Polly - Ship type: P - How taken: HM Brig Ringdove - When taken: 27 Jul 1813 - Where taken: at sea - Date received: 22 Oct 1813 - From what ship: Portsmouth via HMT Malabar - Born: Salem - Age: 21 - Discharged on 8 Sep 1814 and sent to Dartmoor on HMS Niobe.

Brown, Zeth - Seaman - Number: 796 - Prize name: Dolphin - Ship type: MV - How taken: HM Ship-of-the-Line Colossus - When taken: 5 Jan 1813 - Where taken: off the Western Isles, Scotland - Date received: 27 Feb 1813 - From what ship: Plymouth via HMS Namur - Born: Boston - Age: 30 - Discharged on 24 Jul 1813 and released to Cartel Hoffminy.

Brush, Abel - Seaman - Number: 3373 - Prize name: Yorktown - Ship type: P - How taken: HM Frigate Maidstone - When taken: 17 Jul 1813 - Where taken: Grand Banks - Date received: 23 Feb 1814 - From what ship: Halifax via HMT Malabar - Born: New Jersey - Age: 21 - Discharged on 10 Oct 1814 and sent to Dartmoor on the Mermaid.

Brush, Thomas - Seaman - Number: 2807 - Prize name: Industry - Ship type: P - How taken: HM Brig Heron - When taken: 3 Nov 1813 - Where taken: off Halifax - Date received: 7 Jan 1814 - From what ship: Halifax - Born: Marblehead - Age: 54 - Discharged on 11 Aug 1814 and sent to Dartmoor on HMS Freya.

Bryan, Timothy - Supercargo - Number: 3801 - Prize name: Rambler - Ship type: MV - How taken: HM Transport Morley - When taken: 10 Feb 1813 - Date received: 5 Jun 1814 - From what ship: HMS Raisonnable - Born: Salem - Age: 27 - Discharged on 10 Jun 1814 and sent to Plymouth for embarkation.

Bryant, James - Seaman - Number: 2015 - Prize name: Polly - Ship type: MV - How taken: HM Frigate Surveillante - When taken: 23 Mar 1813 - Where taken: Bay of Biscay - Date received: 15 Jul 1813 - From what ship: Plymouth - Born: Beverly - Age: 18 - Discharged on 17 Jun 1814 and sent to Dartmoor on HMS Pincher.

Buddington, Asa - Seaman - Number: 1187 - How taken: Gave himself up from HM Frigate Stag - When taken: 11 Sep 1812 - Date received: 16 Mar 1813 - From what ship: Portsmouth, via HMS Abundance - Born: New London - Age: 47 - Discharged on 11 Aug 1814 and sent to Dartmoor on HMS Freya.

Buell, Jeremiah - Seaman - Number: 2722 - Prize name: U.S. Schooner Growler - Ship type: War - How taken: HM Schooner Lord Melvin - When taken: 11 Aug 1813 - Where taken: Lake Ontario - Date received: 7 Jan 1814 - From what ship: Portsmouth - Born: Connecticut - Age: 25 - Discharged on 10 Oct 1814 and sent to U.S. on Cartel St. Philip.

Buffington, James - Master & passenger - Number: 2438 - How taken: Taken off of the Russian MV Neptune at Cork - When taken: 28 Sep 1812 - Date received: 21 Oct 1813 - From what ship: Portsmouth via HMT Malabar - Born: Salem - Age: 43 - Discharged on 14 Sep 1813 and sent to Reading on parole.

Bugs, Abram - Seaman - Number: 24 - How taken: Discharged from HM Ship Sarpedo - When taken: 22 Oct 1812 - Date received: 29 Oct 1812 - From what ship: HMS Raisonnable - Born: New York - Age: 26 - Discharged on 24 Sep 1814 and sent to Dartmoor on HMS Freya.

Bull, James - Seaman - Number: 3439 - Prize name: Portsmouth Packet - Ship type: P - How taken: HM Brig Fantome - When taken: 5 Oct 1813 - Where taken: Grand Banks - Date received: 23 Feb 1814 - From what ship: Halifax via HMT Malabar - Born: Providence - Age: 19 - Discharged on 22 Jun 1814 and sent to Calais, France on the Simon & Mary.

Bump, Henry - Seaman - Number: 2523 - Prize name: Yorktown - Ship type: P - How taken: HM Brig Nimrod - When taken: 17 Jul 1813 - Where taken: Grand Banks - Date received: 22 Oct 1813 - From what ship: Portsmouth via HMT Malabar - Born: New Bedford - Age: 21 - Died on 27 Mar 1814 from fever.

Bumpus, Asa - Seaman - Number: 1665 - How taken: Gave himself up from HMS Frigate Nemesis - Date received: 9 May 1813 - From what ship: HMS Raisonnable - Born: Boston - Age: 28 - Discharged on 16 Jun 1813 and released to HMS Ceres.

Bunker, Nicholas - Seaman - Number: 2207 - Prize name: Jane, prize of the Privateer Snap Dragon - Ship type: P - How taken: HM Frigate Crescent & HM Ship-of-the-Line Bellerophon - When taken: 28 Jun 1813 - Where taken: Newfoundland Bank - Date received: 18 Aug 1813 - From what ship: Portsmouth, via an admiral's tender - Born: Massachusetts - Age: 40 - Died on 5 Jun 1814 from fever.

Bunker, Peter - Seaman - Number: 1403 - Prize name: Porcupine - Ship type: MV - How taken: HM Frigate Dryand - When taken: 8 Jan 1813 - Where taken: off Bordeaux, France - Date received: 5 Apr 1813 - From what ship: Plymouth via HMS Dwarf - Born: Nantucket - Age: 32 - Discharged on 24 Jul 1813 and released to Cartel Hoffminy.

Bunker, Thomas - Seaman - Number: 2318 - Prize name: Fame - Ship type: MV - How taken: HM Ship-of-the-Line Cressy - When taken: 20 Jul 1813 - Where taken: at sea - Date received: 8 Oct 1813 - From what ship: Portsmouth, via an admiral's tender - Born: Nantucket - Age: 19 - Discharged on 4 Sep 1814 and sent to Dartmoor on HMS Freya.

Burch, James - Seaman - Number: 1502 - Prize name: Resolution - Ship type: MV - How taken: Hibernia, British letter of marque - When taken: 21 Sep 1812 - Where taken: off Bermuda - Date received: 6 Apr 1813 - From what ship: Plymouth via an admiral's tender - Born: New Jersey - Age: 26 - Discharged on 8 Jun 1813 and released to Cartel Rodrigo.

Burdock, Enos - Seaman - Number: 2331 - How taken: Impressed at Gravesend, England - When taken: 11 Aug 1813 - Date received: 12 Oct 1813 - From what ship: HMS Raisonnable - Born: Rhode Island - Age: 22 - Discharged on 4 Sep 1814 and sent to Dartmoor on HMS Freya.

Burel, Angelo - Carpenter - Number: 403 - How taken: Gave himself up from HM Gunpowder Hulk Alexander - When taken: 1 Feb 1813 - Date received: 13 Feb 1813 - From what ship: HMS Raisonnable - Born: Lorient, France - Age: 29 - Discharged on 27 Sep 1813 and released to HMS Ceres.

Burgess, Francis - Seaman - Number: 3247 - Prize name: Thorn - Ship type: P - How taken: Shannon, Nova Scotia privateer - When taken: 7 Nov 1813 - Where taken: off Newfoundland - Date received: 23 Feb 1814 - From what ship: Halifax via HMT Malabar - Born: Marblehead - Age: 19 - Discharged on 10 Oct 1814 and sent to Dartmoor on the Mermaid.

Burham, Benjamin - Seaman - Number: 368 - How taken: Impressed at Gravesend, England - When taken: 3 Dec 1812 - Date received: 21 Jan 1813 - From what ship: HMS Raisonnable - Born: North Carolina - Age: 26 - Discharged on 24 Jul 1813 and released to Cartel Hoffminy.

Burk, John - Seaman - Number: 61 - Prize name: Salley - Ship type: MV - How taken: HM Brig Recruit - When taken: 20 Jul 1812 - Where taken: off Bermuda - Date received: 3 Nov 1812 - From what ship: HMS Plover - Born: New Bedford, MA - Age: 19 - Discharged on 24 Feb 1813 and released to HMS Ceres.

Burk, William - Seaman - Number: 2233 - How taken: Impressed at London - When taken: 23 Aug 1813 - Date received: 29 Aug 1813 - From what ship: HMS Raisonnable - Born: Falmouth - Age: 23 - Race: Blackman - Discharged on 12 Aug 1814 and sent to Dartmoor on HMS Alpheus.

Burke, J. C. - Seaman - Number: 1932 - Prize name: John - Ship type: P - How taken: HM Brig Peruvian - When taken: 6 Feb 1813 - Where taken: West Indies - Date received: 11 Jul 1813 - From what ship: HMS Raisonnable - Born: Prussia - Age: 42 - Discharged on 24 Jul 1813 and released to Cartel Hoffminy.

Burke, John - Seaman - Number: 3490 - How taken: Gave himself up from HM Ship-of-the-Line Bulwark - When taken: 28 Dec 1813 - Date received: 23 Feb 1814 - From what ship: Portsmouth via HMT Malabar - Born: Washington - Age: 23 - Discharged on 26 Sep 1814 and sent to Dartmoor on HMS Leyden.

Burke, Samuel - Seaman - Number: 623 - Prize name: King of Rome - Ship type: P - How taken: HM Brig Wolverine - When taken: 13 Dec 1812 - Where taken: at sea - Date received: 23 Feb 1813 - From what ship: Portsmouth via HMS Dromedary - Born: Boston - Age: 18 - Discharged on 2 Jul 1813 and released to Cartel Moses Brown.

Burlugh, Henry - Seaman - Number: 743 - How taken: Gave himself from MV Bennett - When taken: 5 Feb 1813 - Where taken: London - Date received: 25 Feb 1813 - From what ship: HMS Raisonnable - Born: Newmarket, NH - Age: 21 - Discharged on 4 Aug 1814 and sent to Dartmoor on HMS Liverpool.

Burne, John - Seaman - Number: 2535 - Prize name: Snap Dragon - Ship type: P - How taken: HM Brig Ringdove - When taken: 15 Jul 1813 - Where taken: at sea - Date received: 22 Oct 1813 - From what ship: Portsmouth via HMT Malabar - Born: North Carolina - Age: 17 - Discharged on 25 May 1814 and released to HMS Ceres.

Burnham, David - Seaman - Number: 1319 - How taken: Gave himself up from HM Guardship Royal William - When taken: 3 Feb 1813 - Date received: 16 Mar 1813 - From what ship: Portsmouth, via HMS Abundance - Born: Ipswich - Age: 50 - Discharged on 23 Jul 1814 and sent to Dartmoor.

Burnham, John - Seaman - Number: 1081 - How taken: Gave himself up from HM Brig Bold - When taken: 15 Feb 1813 - Date received: 14 Mar 1813 - From what ship: Portsmouth via HMS Cornwell - Born: Boothbay, MA - Age: 22 - Discharged on 11 Aug 1814 and sent to Dartmoor.

Burns, George - Seaman - Number: 962 - Prize name: Empress - Ship type: MV - How taken: HM Brig Rover - When taken: 30 Nov 1812 - Where taken: St. Andrew - Date received: 10 Mar 1813 - From what ship: HMS Tigress - Born: New York - Age: 36 - Discharged on 8 Jun 1813 and released to Cartel Rodrigo.

Burns, John - Seaman - Number: 1710 - Prize name: Decatur - Ship type: MV - How taken: HM Frigate Desiree - When taken: 7 May 1813 - Where taken: off Nantes, France - Date received: 25 May 1813 - From what ship: Portsmouth via HMS Impetius - Born: Philadelphia - Age: 28 - Discharged on 24 Jul 1814 and sent to Dartmoor on HMS Liffey.

Burrell, Jesse - Seaman - Number: 2811 - Prize name: Industry - Ship type: P - How taken: HM Brig Heron - When taken: 3 Nov 1813 - Where taken: off Halifax - Date received: 7 Jan 1814 - From what ship: Halifax - Born: Massachusetts - Age: 22 - Discharged on 25 Sep 1814 and sent to Dartmoor on HMS Leyden.

Burrell, Rial - Seaman - Number: 1346 - How taken: Gave himself up from HM Frigate Latona - When taken: 17 Mar 1813 - Date received: 30 Mar 1813 - From what ship: HMS Raisonnable - Born: Boston - Age: 24 - Discharged on 25 Jul 1814 and sent to Dartmoor on HMS Bittern.

Burridge, Robert - Gunner - Number: 2800 - Prize name: Industry - Ship type: P - How taken: HM Brig Heron - When taken: 3 Nov 1813 - Where taken: off Halifax - Date received: 7 Jan 1814 - From what ship: Halifax - Born: Marblehead - Age: 46 - Discharged on 8 Sep 1814 and sent to Dartmoor on HMS Niobe.

Burris, M. - Seaman - Number: 3621 - Prize name: Liberty - Ship type: MV - How taken: Surrendered at Stromness, Scotland - When taken: 30 Dec 1813 - Date received: 29 Mar 1814 - From what ship: Hired tender Anna - Born: Bennington - Age: 37 - Discharged on 25 Sep 1814 and sent to Dartmoor on HMS Niobe.

Burroth, Mansfield - Boy - Number: 475 - Prize name: Hunter - Ship type: P - How taken: HM Frigate Phoebe - When taken: 23 Dec 1812 - Where taken: off Azores - Date received: 19 Feb 1813 - From what ship: HMS Modeste - Born: Salem - Age: 17 - Discharged on 24 Jul 1813 and released to Cartel Hoffminy.

Burrow, Charles - Seaman - Number: 2268 - Prize name: Eliza - Ship type: MV - How taken: HMS Charles - When taken: 20 Jul 1813 - Where taken: off Petershead, Scotland - Date received: 14 Sep 1813 - From what ship: HMS Raisonnable - Born: New York - Age: 25 - Discharged on 20 Aug 1814 and sent to Dartmoor on HMS Shamrock.

Burton, William - Seaman - Number: 1510 - How taken: Gave himself up from HM Ship-of-the-Line Blake - When taken: 10 Dec 1812 - Date received: 8 Apr 1813 - From what ship: Portsmouth, via an admiral's tender - Born: Kent County - Age: 52 - Discharged on 4 Aug 1814 and sent to Dartmoor on HMS Alpheus.

Bushfield, James - 2nd Mate - Number: 3223 - Prize name: Volunteer - Ship type: MV - How taken: Vittoria, British privateer from Guernsey - When taken: 26 Dec 1813 - Where taken: Bay of Biscay - Date received: 13 Jan 1814 - From what ship: Portsmouth via HMS Poictiers - Born: New York - Age: 27 - Discharged on 25 Sep 1814 and sent to Dartmoor on HMS Leyden.

Buskell, William - Seaman - Number: 3869 - Prize name: Rattlesnake - Ship type: LM - How taken: HM Frigate Rhin - When taken: 17 Mar 1814 - Where taken: off Bermuda - Date received: 26 Aug 1814 - From what ship: London - Born: Baltimore - Age: 40 - Discharged on 26 Sep 1814 and sent to Dartmoor on HMS Leyden.

Bussey, Charles - Seaman - Number: 3887 - How taken: Gave himself up from HM Frigate Hussar - When taken: 26 Jul 1813 - Date received: 30 Aug 1814 - From what ship: Transport Office - Born: Dorchester - Age: 23 - Discharged on 25 Sep 1814 and sent to Dartmoor on HMS Leyden.

Busson, John - Seaman - Number: 1537 - Prize name: Dick - Ship type: MV - How taken: HM Brig Dispatch - When taken: 17 Mar 1813 - Where taken: off Bordeaux, France - Date received: 8 Apr 1813 - From what ship: Portsmouth, via an admiral's tender - Born: Baltimore - Age: 28 - Released on 11 Jul 1814.

Bustin, John - Seaman - Number: 1973 - Prize name: Lightning - Ship type: MV - How taken: HM Frigate Medusa - When taken: 2 Apr 1813 - Where taken: Bay of Biscay - Date received: 15 Jul 1813 - From what ship: Plymouth - Born: New York - Age: 20 - Discharged on 17 Jun 1814 and sent to Dartmoor on HMS Redbreast.

Butcher, James - Seaman - Number: 1799 - How taken: Impressed at Shields off MV Lord Wellington - When taken: 25 Jun 1813 - Date received: 3 Jul 1813 - From what ship: HMS Raisonnable - Born: New York - Age: 27 - Race: Black - Died on 17 Feb 1814 from phthisis (tuberculosis).

Butler, George - Seaman - Number: 1008 - How taken: Gave himself up from HM Frigate Ceres - When taken: 20 Dec 1812 - Date received: 10 Mar 1813 - From what ship: HMS Furious - Born: Charlestown - Age: 24 - Discharged on 4 Aug 1814 and sent to Dartmoor on HMS Liverpool.

Butler, George - Seaman - Number: 3308 - Prize name: Governor Plumer - Ship type: P - How taken: HM Brig Bold - When taken: 17 May 1813 - Date received: 23 Feb 1814 - From what ship: Halifax via HMT Malabar - Born: Berwick - Age: 16 - Discharged on 21 Jul 1814 and sent to Dartmoor on HMS Portia.

Butler, Henry - Seaman - Number: 2447 - Prize name: Wiley Reynard - Ship type: P - How taken: HM Frigate Shannon - When taken: 16 Aug 1812 - Where taken: off Halifax - Date received: 21 Oct 1813 - From what ship: Portsmouth via HMT Malabar - Born: New York - Age: 28 - Race: Mulatto - Discharged on 4 Sep 1814 and sent to Dartmoor on HMS Freya.

Butler, John - Steward - Number: 188 - Prize name: Arabella - Ship type: MV - How taken: Taken at London - When taken: 27 Oct 1812 - Date received: 5 Nov 1812 - From what ship: HMS Namur - Born: Leonards, MD - Age: 29 - Discharged in Jul 1813 and released to Cartel Moses Brown.

Butler, John - Seaman - Number: 2049 - How taken: Gave himself up from HM Ship-of-the-Line Fame - When taken: 4 May 1813 - Date received: 4 Aug 1813 - From what ship: HMS Christian VII - Born: Trallon - Age: 33 - Discharged on 4 Aug 1814 and sent to Dartmoor on HMS Liverpool.

Butler, Thomas - Seaman - Number: 3491 - How taken: Gave himself up from HM Ship-of-the-Line Bulwark - When taken: 28 Dec 1813 - Date received: 23 Feb 1814 - From what ship: Portsmouth via HMT Malabar - Born: Maryland - Age: 37 - Discharged on 26 Sep 1814 and sent to Dartmoor on HMS Leyden.

Butler, Thomas - Seaman - Number: 1663 - How taken: Gave himself up from HM Ship-of-the-Line Plantagenet - Date received: 9 May 1813 - From what ship: HMS Raisonnable - Born: Woodbury - Age: 23 - Released on 8 Oct 1814.

Butler, William - Seaman - Number: 3647 - Prize name: Bunker Hill - Ship type: P - How taken: HM Frigate Pomone & HM Frigate Cydnus - When taken: 4 Mar 1814 - Where taken: Bay of Biscay - Date received: 31 Mar 1814 - From what ship: HMS Raisonnable - Born: Newburyport - Age: 45 - Discharged on 25 Sep 1814 and sent to Dartmoor on HMS Niobe.

Butler, William - Seaman - Number: 1641 - Prize name: Henryettos - Ship type: MV - How taken: HMS Castilian - When taken: 12 Mar 1813 - Where taken: off Cape Ortegal, Spain - Date received: 9 May 1813 - From what ship: HMS Raisonnable - Born: Baltimore - Age: 40 - Discharged on 24 Jul 1814 and sent to Dartmoor.

Butler, William - Seaman - Number: 2078 - How taken: Gave himself up from HM Ship-of-the-Line Armada - When taken: 8 Jun 1813 - Date received: 9 Aug 1813 - From what ship: HMS Thames - Born: Maryland - Age: 51 - Race: Black - Died on 29 Apr 1814 from phthisis (tuberculosis).

Butterfield, Edward - Seaman - Number: 903 - Prize name: Pallas - Ship type: MV - How taken: HM Brig Papillon - When taken: 17 Aug 1812 - Where taken: off Cadiz, Spain - Date received: 1 Mar 1813 - From what ship: Plymouth via HMS Namur - Born: Boston - Age: 18 - Discharged on 23 Mar 1813 and released to the Cartel Robinson Potter.

Butts, Joseph W. - Seaman - Number: 2571 - How taken: Gave himself up from HM Ship-of-the-Line Centaur - When taken: 11 Sep 1813 - Date received: 23 Oct 1813 - From what ship: Portsmouth via HMS Raisonnable - Born: Boston - Age: 23 - Discharged on 8 Sep 1814 and sent to Dartmoor on HMS Niobe.

Byer, Peter - Seaman - Number: 1878 - Prize name: Tiger - Ship type: MV - How taken: HM Brig Scylla - When taken: 22 Mar 1813 - Where taken: Bay of Biscay - Date received: 7 Jul 1813 - From what ship: Portsmouth via HMS Tribune - Born: Boston - Age: 27 - Discharged on 22 Jun 1814 and sent to Calais, France on the Simon & Mary.

Byron, Ebenezer - Seaman - Number: 3442 - Prize name: Portsmouth Packet - Ship type: P - How taken: HM Brig Fantome - When taken: 5 Oct 1813 - Where taken: Grand Banks - Date received: 23 Feb 1814 - From what ship: Halifax via HMT Malabar - Born: Portsmouth - Age: 47 - Discharged on 22 Oct 1814 and sent to Dartmoor on HMS Leyden.

Caban, Samuel - Seaman - Number: 1103 - Prize name: Calcutta, East Indian Ship - Ship type: MV - How taken: Two Brothers, British privateer from Guernsey - When taken: 30 Nov 1812 - Where taken: off St. Helena - Date received: 14 Mar 1813 - From what ship: Portsmouth via HMS Beagle - Born: Salem - Age: 30 - Discharged on 8 Jun 1813 and released to Cartel Rodrigo.

Cadwell, Abraham - Seaman - Number: 2551 - How taken: Gave himself up from HM Brig Scorpion - When taken: 2 Dec 1812 - Date received: 23 Oct 1813 - From what ship: Portsmouth via HMS Raisonnable - Born: Pennsylvania - Age: 36 - Discharged on 8 Sep 1814 and sent to Dartmoor on HMS Niobe.

Cadwell, James - Seaman - Number: 1960 - Prize name: Ferox - Ship type: MV - How taken: HM Frigate Medusa & HM Brig Lyra - When taken: 28 Mar 1813 - Where taken: off Cape Ortegal, Spain - Date received: 15 Jul 1813 - From what ship: Plymouth - Born: Hartford - Age: 25 - Discharged on 17 Jun 1814 and sent to Dartmoor on HMS Redbreast.

Cadwell, Samuel - Seaman - Number: 1879 - Prize name: Tiger - Ship type: MV - How taken: HM Brig Scylla - When taken: 22 Mar 1813 - Where taken: Bay of Biscay - Date received: 7 Jul 1813 - From what ship: Portsmouth via HMS Tribune - Born: New York - Age: 19 - Discharged on 4 Aug 1814 and sent to Dartmoor on HMS Liverpool.

Caen, John - Seaman - Number: 208 - How taken: Gave himself up from English MV Fredericktown - When taken: 28 Oct 1812 - Date received: 15 Nov 1812 - From what ship: HMS Raisonnable - Born: Lime, CT - Age: 26 - Discharged on 26 Jul 1814 and sent to Dartmoor on HMS Raven.

Cain, Enoch - Seaman - Number: 1116 - How taken: Gave himself up from HM Ship-of-the-Line Tigre - Date received: 14 Mar 1813 - From what ship: Portsmouth via HMS Beagle - Born: Philadelphia - Age: 35 - Race: Mulatto - Discharged on 11 Aug 1814 and sent to Dartmoor on HMS Freya.

Cainmel, Jeremiah - Seaman - Number: 134 - Prize name: Leander - Ship type: MV - How taken: Stopped at London - When taken: 26 Oct 1812 - Date received: 5 Nov 1812 - From what ship: HMS Namur - Born: East Hartford - Age: 24 - Discharged in Jul 1813 and released to Cartel Moses Brown.

Calaban, Ambrose - Cook - Number: 204 - Prize name: Navigator - Ship type: MV - How taken: HM Ship-of-the-Line Cressy - When taken: 11 Aug 1812 - Where taken: Baltic - Date received: 15 Nov 1812 - From what ship: HMS Raisonnable - Born: Virginia - Age: 30 - Released on 18 Mar 1813 to HMS Navigator.

Calanan, John - Seaman - Number: 2081 - How taken: Gave himself up from HM Ship-of-the-Line Armada - When taken: 8 Jun 1813 - Date received: 9 Aug 1813 - From what ship: HMS Thames - Born: New York - Age: 33 - Discharged on 26 Sep 1814 and sent to Dartmoor on HMS Leyden.

Calder, John H. - Seaman - Number: 1869 - Prize name: Tiger - Ship type: MV - How taken: HM Brig Scylla - When taken: 22 Mar 1813 - Where taken: Bay of Biscay - Date received: 7 Jul 1813 - From what ship: Portsmouth via HMS Tribune - Born: New York - Age: 22 - Discharged on 4 Aug 1814 and sent to Dartmoor on HMS Liverpool.

Caldwell, Charles - Seaman - Number: 3712 - Prize name: Requin - Ship type: LM - How taken: HM Frigate Venus - When taken: 5 Mar 1814 - Where taken: off Bordeaux, France - Date received: 18 May 1814 - From what ship: HMS Raisonnable - Born: Boston - Age: 20 - Discharged on 26 Sep 1814 and sent to Dartmoor on HMS Leyden.

Caleb, Lewis - Seaman - Number: 3673 - How taken: Gave himself up from HMS Muros - Date received: 4 May 1814 - From what ship: Portsmouth - Born: New Orleans - Age: 25 - Race: Black - Discharged on 25 Sep 1814 and sent to Dartmoor on HMS Niobe.

Calentine, Samuel - Seaman - Number: 363 - Prize name: Namur - Ship type: MV - How taken: Gave himself up at Nore, England - When taken: 12 Dec 1812 - Date received: 21 Jan 1813 - From what ship: HMS Raisonnable - Born: New York - Age: 44 - Discharged on 26 Jul 1814 and sent to Dartmoor on HMS Raven.

Caley, Henry - Seaman - Number: 50 - Prize name: White Oak - Ship type: MV - How taken: HM Brig Recruit - When taken: 22 Jul 1812 - Where taken: off Bermuda - Date received: 3 Nov 1812 - From what ship: HMS Plover - Born: Alexandria, VA - Age: 24 - Discharged on 23 Mar 1813 and released to the Cartel Robinson Potter.

Calkings, Zera - Seaman - Number: 863 - Prize name: Brutus - Ship type: MV - How taken: Briton, letter of marque - When taken: 13 Jan 1813 - Where taken: Bay of Biscay - Date received: 1 Mar 1813 - From what ship: Plymouth via HMS Namur - Born: Connecticut - Age: 20 - Discharged on 24 Jul 1813 and released to Cartel Hoffminy.

Callam, John - Seaman - Number: 3298 - Prize name: Montgomery - Ship type: P - How taken: HM Frigate Nymphe - When taken: 5 May 1813 - Where taken: off Cape Cod - Date received: 23 Feb 1814 - From what ship: Halifax via HMT Malabar - Born: Salem - Age: 26 - Discharged on 25 Sep 1814 and sent to Dartmoor on HMS Leyden.

Callec, Samuel - Seaman - Number: 81 - Prize name: Edward - Ship type: MV - How taken: HM Frigate Ethalion - When taken: 12 Aug 1812 - Where taken: Great Belt, Denmark - Date received: 4 Nov 1812 - From what ship: HMS Namur - Born: Nobleboro, MA - Age: 20 - Discharged on 10 May 1813 and released to Cartel Admittance.

Cameron, Daniel - Seaman - Number: 2787 - Prize name: Yorktown - Ship type: P - How taken: British squadron - When taken: 17 Jul 1813 - Where taken: Grand Banks - Date received: 7 Jan 1814 - From what ship: Halifax - Born: Virginia - Age: 35 - Discharged on 26 Sep 1814 and sent to Dartmoor on HMS Leyden.

Campbell, James - Seaman - Number: 2202 - How taken: Gave himself up from HM Sloop Volentaire - When taken: 25 Oct 1812 - Date received: 18 Aug 1813 - From what ship: Portsmouth, via an admiral's tender - Born: New York - Age: 36 - Discharged on 11 Aug 1814 and sent to Dartmoor on HMS Freya.

Campbell, John - Seaman - Number: 1517 - How taken: Gave himself up from HM Transport Minerva - When taken: 14 Oct 1812 - Date received: 8 Apr 1813 - From what ship: Portsmouth, via an admiral's tender - Born: Boston - Age: 26 - Discharged on 2 Jul 1813 and released to Cartel Moses Brown.

Campbell, John - Carpenter - Number: 97 - Prize name: Julius Caesar - Ship type: MV - How taken: Stopped at London - When taken: 26 Oct 1812 - Date received: 4 Nov 1812 - From what ship: HMS Namur - Born: Philadelphia - Age: 38 - Discharged in Jul 1813 and released to Cartel Moses Brown.

Campbell, John - Seaman - Number: 3218 - Prize name: Volunteer - Ship type: MV - How taken: Vittoria, British privateer from Guernsey - When taken: 26 Dec 1813 - Where taken: Bay of Biscay - Date received: 13 Jan 1814 - From what ship: Portsmouth via HMS Poictiers - Born: Maryland - Age: 26 - Discharged on 25 Sep 1814 and sent to Dartmoor on HMS Leyden.

Campbell, Nicholas - Seaman - Number: 2558 - How taken: Gave himself up from HM Frigate Bombay - When taken: 29 Oct 1812 - Date received: 23 Oct 1813 - From what ship: Portsmouth via HMS Raisonnable - Born: Albany - Age: 30 - Discharged on 8 Sep 1814 and sent to Dartmoor on HMS Niobe.

Campbell, William - Cook - Number: 3569 - Prize name: Minerva - Ship type: MV - How taken: HM Ship-of-the-Line Conquestador - When taken: 19 Jan 1814 - Where taken: Bay of Biscay - Date received: 7 May 1814 - From what ship: Portsmouth via HMS Favorite - Born: Lorient, France - Age: 17 - Discharged on 25 Sep 1814 and sent to Dartmoor on HMS Niobe.

Camsure, Dominick - Surgeon & passenger - Number: 2899 - Prize name: Dart - Ship type: P - How taken: HM Frigate Niger & HMS Fortunee - When taken: 10 Nov 1813 - Where taken: off Cape Finisterre, Spain - Date received: 7 Jan 1814 - From what ship: Portsmouth - Born: New Orleans - Age: 28 - Released on 15 Jun 1814.

Canada, James - Seaman - Number: 3952 - How taken: Gave himself up from HM Ship-of-the-Line Blenheim - When taken: 27 Aug 1814 - Date received: 21 Oct 1813 - From what ship: Quebec - Born: Philadelphia - Age: 36 - Discharged on 22 Oct 1814 and sent to Dartmoor on HMS Leyden.

Canada, Prince - Seaman - Number: 866 - Prize name: Columbia - Ship type: MV - How taken: HM Frigate Briton - When taken: 17 Jan 1813 - Where taken: off Bordeaux, France - Date received: 1 Mar 1813 - From what ship: Plymouth via HMS Namur - Born: Providence - Age: 39 - Race: Black - Discharged in Jul 1813 and released to Cartel Moses Brown.

Canada, William - Seaman - Number: 239 - How taken: Gave himself up from HM Brig Rolla - When taken: 10 Nov 1812 - Date received: 1 Dec 1812 - From what ship: HMS Raisonnable - Born: Abbeville, SC - Age: 34 - Discharged on 26 Jul 1814 and sent to Dartmoor on HMS Raven.

Cane, Thomas - Private - Number: 3120 - Prize name: 14th U.S. Infantry - Ship type: LF - How taken: British forces - When taken: 24 Jun 1813 - Where taken: Beaver Dams, Upper Canada - Date received: 7 Jan 1814 - From what ship: Halifax - Born: Staten Island - Age: 22 - Discharged on 10 Oct 1814 and sent to U.S. on Cartel St. Philip.

Cannon, Thomas - Seaman - Number: 3488 - How taken: Gave himself up from HM Ship-of-the-Line Bulwark - When taken: 28 Dec 1813 - Date received: 23 Feb 1814 - From what ship: Portsmouth via HMT Malabar - Born: New York - Age: 30 - Discharged on 26 Sep 1814 and sent to Dartmoor on HMS Leyden.

Cannon, William - Seaman - Number: 1600 - How taken: Impressed at Yarmouth - When taken: 6 Mar 1813 - Date received: 19 Apr 1813 - From what ship: HMS Raisonnable - Born: Pennsylvania - Age: 35 - Discharged on 24 Jul 1814 and sent to Dartmoor.

Capilo, Francis - Seaman - Number: 1731 - Prize name: Powhattan - Ship type: MV - How taken: HMS Horatio - When taken: 13 Dec 1812 - Where taken: Bay of Biscay - Date received: 25 May 1813 - From what ship: Portsmouth via HMS Impetius - Born: Seckel, Austria - Age: 35 - Discharged on 24 Jul 1813 and released to Cartel Hoffminy.

Cappel, John - Seaman - Number: 1904 - Prize name: Weasel - Ship type: MV - How taken: HM Brig Foxhound - When taken: 25 Mar 1813 - Where taken: Bay of Biscay - Date received: 7 Jul 1813 - From what ship: Portsmouth via HMS Tribune - Born: Newport - Age: 18 - Discharged on 4 Aug 1814 and sent to Dartmoor on HMS Liverpool.

Capron, William - Seaman - Number: 862 - Prize name: Brutus - Ship type: MV - How taken: Briton, letter of marque - When taken: 13 Jan 1813 - Where taken: Bay of Biscay - Date received: 1 Mar 1813 - From what ship: Plymouth via HMS Namur - Born: Nantucket - Age: 20 - Discharged on 24 Jul 1813 and released to Cartel Hoffminy.

Carban, Thomas - Seaman - Number: 915 - How taken: Impressed at Belfast - When taken: 15 Sep 1812 - Date received: 10 Mar 1813 - From what ship: HMS Tigress - Born: New Orleans - Age: 29 - Discharged on 2 Jul 1813 and released to Cartel Moses Brown.

Carbody, Darby - Private - Number: 2636 - Prize name: 14th U.S. Infantry - Ship type: LF - How taken: British forces - When taken: 24 Jun 1813 - Where taken: Beaver Dams, Upper Canada - Date received: 5 Nov 1813 - From what ship: HMS Hindostan - Born: County Tipperary, Ireland - Age: 52 - Discharged on 10 Oct 1814 and sent to U.S. on Cartel St. Philip.

Card, Israel - Seaman - Number: 3898 - How taken: Gave himself up from MV Webster, East Indianman - When taken: 29 Aug 1813 - Date received: 30 Aug 1814 - From what ship: Transport Office - Born: Rhode Island -

Age: 38 - Discharged on 22 Oct 1814 and sent to Dartmoor on HMS Leyden.

Card, Nathaniel - Boatswain's Mate - Number: 431 - Prize name: Hunter - Ship type: P - How taken: HM Frigate Phoebe - When taken: 23 Dec 1812 - Where taken: off Azores - Date received: 19 Feb 1813 - From what ship: HMS Modeste - Born: Marblehead - Age: 55 - Discharged on 2 Jul 1813 and released to Cartel Moses Brown.

Card, Samuel - Seaman - Number: 3441 - Prize name: Portsmouth Packet - Ship type: P - How taken: HM Brig Fantome - When taken: 5 Oct 1813 - Where taken: Grand Banks - Date received: 23 Feb 1814 - From what ship: Halifax via HMT Malabar - Born: Raynham - Age: 25 - Discharged on 21 Jul 1814 and sent to Dartmoor on HMS Portia.

Card, Thomas - Seaman - Number: 2501 - Prize name: Thomas - Ship type: P - How taken: HM Frigate Nymphe - When taken: 28 Jun 1813 - Where taken: off Halifax - Date received: 22 Oct 1813 - From what ship: Portsmouth via HMT Malabar - Born: New Castle - Age: 18 - Discharged on 8 Sep 1814 and sent to Dartmoor on HMS Niobe.

Carebo, Henry - Seaman - Number: 677 - Prize name: U.S.R.M. Cutter James Madison - Ship type: War - How taken: HM Frigate Barbadoes - When taken: 22 Aug 1812 - Where taken: at sea - Date received: 24 Feb 1813 - From what ship: Portsmouth via HMS Ulysses - Born: Orleans - Age: 36 - Discharged on 10 May 1813 and released to Cartel Admittance.

Carey, James - Private - Number: 2657 - Prize name: 14th U.S. Infantry - Ship type: LF - How taken: British forces - When taken: 24 Jun 1813 - Where taken: Beaver Dams, Upper Canada - Date received: 5 Nov 1813 - From what ship: HMS Hindostan - Born: County Donegal, Ireland - Age: 32 - Discharged on 10 Oct 1814 and sent to U.S. on Cartel St. Philip.

Carlander, John - Seaman - Number: 766 - Prize name: Margarethe - Ship type: MV - How taken: HM Ship-of-the-Line San Juan - When taken: 8 May 1812 - Where taken: Gibraltar - Date received: 25 Feb 1813 - From what ship: HMS Brazen - Born: Finland - Age: 35 - Discharged on 10 May 1813 and released to Cartel Admittance.

Carlos, John - Seaman - Number: 2448 - Prize name: Wiley Reynard - Ship type: P - How taken: HM Frigate Shannon - When taken: 16 Aug 1812 - Where taken: off Halifax - Date received: 21 Oct 1813 - From what ship: Portsmouth via HMT Malabar - Born: New Hampshire - Age: 50 - Discharged on 4 Sep 1814 and sent to Dartmoor on HMS Freya.

Carlton, William N. - Seaman - Number: 2030 - How taken: Impressed at London off British MV Luster - When taken: 12 Jul 1812 - Date received: 24 Jul 1813 - From what ship: HMS Raisonnable - Born: Philadelphia - Age: 23 - Discharged on 4 Aug 1814 and sent to Dartmoor on HMS Liverpool.

Carman, Francis - Seaman - Number: 1558 - Prize name: Dolphin - Ship type: LM - How taken: HM Ship-of-the-Line Colossus - When taken: 5 Jan 1813 - Where taken: off the Western Isles, Scotland - Date received: 8 Apr 1813 - From what ship: Plymouth via HMS Olympia - Born: New Orleans - Age: 23 - Discharged on 27 Jul 1813 and released to Cartel Hoffminy.

Carman, George - Seaman - Number: 3532 - Prize name: Commodore Perry - Ship type: MV - How taken: Sent into custody from a cutter - When taken: 25 Feb 1814 - Where taken: off Bordeaux, France - Date received: 5 Mar 1814 - From what ship: HMS Raisonnable - Born: New Jersey - Age: 23 - Discharged on 26 Sep 1814 and sent to Dartmoor on HMS Leyden.

Carman, James - Seaman - Number: 1253 - How taken: Gave himself up from HM Frigate Ulysses - When taken: 23 Dec 1812 - Date received: 16 Mar 1813 - From what ship: Portsmouth, via HMS Abundance - Born: Philadelphia - Age: 22 - Discharged on 4 May 1813 and released to HMS Ceres.

Carnes, John - Seaman - Number: 3184 - Prize name: Wolf Cove - Ship type: MV - How taken: HM Frigate Briton - When taken: 1 Dec 1813 - Where taken: off Brest, France - Date received: 7 Jan 1813 - From what ship: Halifax - Born: Copenhagen - Age: 31 - Discharged on 25 Sep 1814 and sent to Dartmoor on HMS Leyden.

Carney, Edward - Boatswain's Mate - Number: 1555 - Prize name: Dolphin - Ship type: LM - How taken: HM Ship-of-the-Line Colossus - When taken: 5 Jan 1813 - Where taken: off the Western Isles, Scotland - Date received: 8 Apr 1813 - From what ship: Plymouth via HMS Olympia - Born: Philadelphia - Age: 39 -

Discharged on 27 Jul 1813 and released to Cartel Hoffminy.

Carney, Thomas - Prize Master - Number: 1014 - Prize name: Sword Fish - Ship type: P - How taken: HM Ship-of-the-Line Elephant - When taken: 28 Dec 1812 - Where taken: off Azores - Date received: 10 Mar 1813 - From what ship: HMS Furious - Born: Marblehead - Age: 29 - Discharged on 24 Jul 1813 and released to Cartel Hoffminy.

Carney, William - Seaman - Number: 1062 - How taken: Gave himself up from HM Guardship Royal William - When taken: 5 Feb 1813 - Date received: 14 Mar 1813 - From what ship: Portsmouth via HMS Cornwell - Born: Boston - Age: 48 - Race: Black - Discharged on 11 Aug 1814 and sent to Dartmoor.

Carns, Richard - Seaman - Number: 1479 - Prize name: Union - Ship type: MV - How taken: HM Frigate Iris - When taken: 17 Jan 1813 - Where taken: at sea - Date received: 6 Apr 1813 - From what ship: Portsmouth via Tender Eliza - Born: Philadelphia - Age: 17 - Discharged on 26 Jul 1813 and released to Cartel Hoffminy.

Caroline, Tobias - Seaman - Number: 942 - How taken: Gave himself up from HM Ship-of-the-Line Orion - When taken: 5 Sep 1812 - Date received: 10 Mar 1813 - From what ship: HMS Tigress - Born: Albany, NY - Age: 38 - Discharged on 4 Aug 1814 and sent to Dartmoor on HMS Liverpool.

Carpenter, Nathaniel - Seaman - Number: 1797 - Prize name: Henry - Ship type: MV - How taken: Impressed at Shields - When taken: 18 May 1813 - Date received: 3 Jul 1813 - From what ship: HMS Raisonnable - Born: Newport - Age: 27 - Discharged on 25 Jul 1814 and sent to Dartmoor on HMS Bittern.

Carpenter, William - Seaman - Number: 374 - How taken: Impressed at Gravesend, England - When taken: 2 Jan 1813 - Date received: 21 Jan 1813 - From what ship: HMS Raisonnable - Born: Bristol, RI - Age: 23 - Discharged on 24 Jul 1813 and released to Cartel Hoffminy.

Carr, John - Private - Number: 3060 - Prize name: 14th U.S. Infantry - Ship type: LF - How taken: British forces - When taken: 24 Jun 1813 - Where taken: Beaver Dams, Upper Canada - Date received: 7 Jan 1814 - From what ship: Halifax - Born: Maryland - Age: 26 - Discharged on 10 Oct 1814 and sent to U.S. on Cartel St. Philip.

Carr, Joseph - Seaman - Number: 205 - How taken: Gave himself up from HM Frigate Alceste - When taken: 14 Sep 1812 - Date received: 15 Nov 1812 - From what ship: HMS Raisonnable - Born: Connecticut - Age: 28 - Discharged on 26 Jul 1814 and sent to Dartmoor on HMS Raven.

Carr, Richard - Seaman - Number: 914 - How taken: HM Battery Princess - When taken: 5 Aug 1812 - Where taken: Liverpool - Date received: 10 Mar 1813 - From what ship: HMS Tigress - Born: Charlestown - Age: 29 - Discharged on 2 Jul 1813 and released to Cartel Moses Brown.

Carr, Samuel - Cook - Number: 992 - Prize name: Otter - Ship type: MV - How taken: HM Ship-Sloop Jalouse - When taken: 1 Dec 1812 - Where taken: off Cape St. Vincent, Portugal - Date received: 10 Mar 1813 - From what ship: HMS Tigress - Born: New York - Age: 30 - Released on 20 Mar 1813 to HMS Otter.

Carrel, Michael - Seaman - Number: 1174 - Prize name: Sword Fish - Ship type: P - How taken: HM Ship-of-the-Line Elephant - When taken: 28 Dec 1812 - Where taken: off Azores - Date received: 16 Mar 1813 - From what ship: Portsmouth, via HMS Abundance - Born: Marblehead - Age: 21 - Discharged on 24 Jul 1813 and released to Cartel Hoffminy.

Carrol, Robert - Seaman - Number: 462 - Prize name: Hunter - Ship type: P - How taken: HM Frigate Phoebe - When taken: 23 Dec 1812 - Where taken: off Azores - Date received: 19 Feb 1813 - From what ship: HMS Modeste - Born: Boston - Age: 16 - Discharged on 24 Jul 1813 and released to Cartel Hoffminy.

Carso, John - Seaman - Number: 55 - Prize name: Trim - Ship type: MV - How taken: From a cutter off Bermuda - When taken: 26 Jul 1812 - Date received: 3 Nov 1812 - From what ship: HMS Plover - Born: New Castle, DE - Age: 36 - Race: Black - Discharged on 23 Mar 1813 and released to the Cartel Robinson Potter.

Carson, Robert - Seaman - Number: 824 - Prize name: Columbia - Ship type: MV - How taken: HM Frigate Briton - When taken: 17 Dec 1812 - Where taken: off Bordeaux, France - Date received: 27 Feb 1813 - From what ship: Plymouth via HMS Namur - Born: New York - Age: 41 - Died on 28 Feb 1813 from apoplexy.

Carswell, William - Seaman - Number: 2987 - Prize name: America - Ship type: P - How taken: HM Frigate

Shannon - When taken: 25 May 1813 - Where taken: off Cape Cod - Date received: 7 Jan 1814 - From what ship: Halifax - Born: Massachusetts - Age: 21 - Discharged on 25 Sep 1814 and sent to Dartmoor on HMS Leyden.

Carter, Ebenezer - Seaman - Number: 1747 - How taken: Taken up at London - When taken: 24 May 1813 - Date received: 28 May 1813 - From what ship: HMS Raisonnable - Born: Portsmouth, NH - Age: 53 - Discharged on 13 Oct 1813 and released to HMS Ceres.

Carter, Enoch - Seaman - Number: 3588 - Prize name: Devon, prize to the Privateer Bunker Hill - Ship type: P - How taken: HM Brig Fly - When taken: 21 Jan 1814 - Where taken: at sea - Date received: 26 Mar 1814 - From what ship: Plymouth via HMS Raleigh - Born: Middletown - Age: 37 - Discharged on 25 Sep 1814 and sent to Dartmoor on HMS Niobe.

Carter, Henry - Seaman - Number: 3563 - Prize name: Harvest, prize of the Privateer Bunker Hill - Ship type: P - How taken: HM Brig Orestes - When taken: 21 Jan 1814 - Where taken: Bay of Biscay - Date received: 7 May 1814 - From what ship: Portsmouth via HMS Favorite - Born: New York - Age: 26 - Race: Mulatto - Discharged on 25 Sep 1814 and sent to Dartmoor on HMS Niobe.

Carter, John - Cook - Number: 1911 - Prize name: Weasel - Ship type: MV - How taken: HM Brig Foxhound - When taken: 25 Mar 1813 - Where taken: Bay of Biscay - Date received: 7 Jul 1813 - From what ship: Portsmouth via HMS Tribune - Born: New York - Age: 25 - Race: Black - Discharged on 4 Aug 1814 and sent to Dartmoor on HMS Liverpool.

Carter, Moses - Surgeon - Number: 413 - Prize name: Hunter - Ship type: P - How taken: HM Frigate Phoebe - When taken: 23 Dec 1812 - Where taken: off Azores - Date received: 19 Feb 1813 - From what ship: HMS Modeste - Born: Concord - Age: 29 - Discharged on 23 Mar 1813 and released to the Cartel Robinson Potter.

Carter, Thomas - Seaman - Number: 2160 - Prize name: tender to the Privateer True Blooded Yankee - Ship type: P - How taken: HM Ship-of-the-Line Fame - When taken: 24 Jun 1813 - Where taken: at sea - Date received: 16 Aug 1813 - From what ship: Portsmouth, via an admiral's tender - Born: New York - Age: 25 - Discharged on 17 Jun 1814 and sent to Dartmoor on the Penebar.

Cartwright, Philip - Seaman - Number: 309 - Prize name: Cuba - Ship type: MV - How taken: HM Brig Sarpedon - When taken: 12 Aug 1812 - Date received: 23 Dec 1812 - From what ship: Greenlaw Depot - Born: Philadelphia - Age: 32 - Discharged on 10 May 1813 and released to Cartel Admittance.

Carver, Abraham - Seaman - Number: 1411 - Prize name: Porcupine - Ship type: MV - How taken: HM Frigate Dryand - When taken: 8 Jan 1813 - Where taken: off Bordeaux, France - Date received: 5 Apr 1813 - From what ship: Plymouth via HMS Dwarf - Born: New Jersey - Age: 26 - Discharged on 24 Jul 1813 and released to Cartel Hoffminy.

Carves, John - Seaman - Number: 452 - Prize name: Hunter - Ship type: P - How taken: HM Frigate Phoebe - When taken: 23 Dec 1812 - Where taken: off Azores - Date received: 19 Feb 1813 - From what ship: HMS Modeste - Born: Kennebunk - Age: 29 - Discharged on 24 Jul 1813 and released to Cartel Hoffminy.

Case, Barns - Seaman - Number: 190 - Prize name: Roberson - Ship type: MV - How taken: Detained at Dover - When taken: 7 Aug 1812 - Date received: 6 Nov 1812 - From what ship: HMS Echo - Born: New York - Age: 26 - Discharged on 23 Mar 1813 and released to the Cartel Robinson Potter.

Cash, John - Seaman - Number: 2732 - Prize name: Growler - Ship type: P - How taken: HM Brig Electra - When taken: 7 Jul 1813 - Where taken: off St. Johns - Date received: 7 Jan 1814 - From what ship: Halifax - Born: New York - Age: 29 - Discharged on 25 Sep 1814 and sent to Dartmoor on HMS Leyden.

Cashinan, William - Private - Number: 3047 - Prize name: U.S. Light Dragoons - Ship type: LF - How taken: British forces - When taken: 24 Jun 1813 - Where taken: Beaver Dams, Upper Canada - Date received: 7 Jan 1814 - From what ship: Halifax - Born: Bedford - Age: 21 - Discharged on 10 Oct 1814 and sent to U.S. on Cartel St. Philip.

Castor, Charles - Seaman - Number: 1126 - Prize name: Columbia - Ship type: MV - How taken: HM Frigate Briton - When taken: 17 Dec 1812 - Where taken: off Bordeaux, France - Date received: 14 Mar 1813 - From what ship: Portsmouth via HMS Beagle - Born: Batavia - Age: 19 - Race: Mulatto - Discharged on 2 Jul 1813 and released to Cartel Moses Brown.

Catley, William - Gunner - Number: 3933 - Prize name: Hawk - Ship type: P - How taken: HM Frigate Piqua - When taken: 26 Apr 1814 - Where taken: West Indies - Date received: 25 Sep 1814 - From what ship: London - Born: Maryland - Age: 24 - Discharged on 22 Oct 1814 and sent to Dartmoor on HMS Leyden.

Caufield, Arthur - Seaman - Number: 2758 - Prize name: Norfolk, prize to the Globe - Ship type: P - How taken: HM Brig Fantome - When taken: 29 May 1813 - Where taken: off Norfolk - Date received: 7 Jan 1814 - From what ship: Halifax - Born: Middleton - Age: 23 - Discharged on 25 Sep 1814 and sent to Dartmoor on HMS Leyden.

Caughan, Patrick - Private - Number: 2620 - Prize name: 14th U.S. Infantry - Ship type: LF - How taken: British forces - When taken: 5 Jul 1813 - Where taken: Upper Canada - Date received: 5 Nov 1813 - From what ship: HMS Hindostan - Born: Wexford, Ireland - Age: 41 - Discharged on 10 Oct 1814 and sent to U.S. on Cartel St. Philip.

Caverena, Jose Maria - Seaman - Number: 3214 - Prize name: Volunteer - Ship type: MV - How taken: Vittoria, British privateer from Guernsey - When taken: 26 Dec 1813 - Where taken: Bay of Biscay - Date received: 13 Jan 1814 - From what ship: Portsmouth via HMS Poictiers - Born: Cartagena, Spain - Age: 22 - Race: Mulatto - Discharged on 25 Sep 1814 and sent to Dartmoor on HMS Leyden.

Caesar, James - Seaman - Number: 2408 - How taken: Gave himself up from HM Hospital Ship Trent - Date received: 21 Oct 1813 - From what ship: Portsmouth via HMT Malabar - Born: Charleston - Age: 28 - Race: Mulatto - Released on 26 Sep 1814.

Chace, Nathaniel - Prize Master - Number: 2817 - Prize name: Portsmouth Packet - Ship type: P - How taken: HM Brig Fantome - When taken: 5 Oct 1813 - Where taken: off Portland - Date received: 7 Jan 1814 - From what ship: Halifax - Born: Massachusetts - Age: 30 - Discharged on 25 Sep 1814 and sent to Dartmoor on HMS Leyden.

Chalk, John - Seaman - Number: 746 - Prize name: Quebec of London, prize of the Privateer Paul Jones - Ship type: P - How taken: HM Brig Derwent - When taken: 29 Jan 1813 - Where taken: off Lisbon - Date received: 25 Feb 1813 - From what ship: HMS Brazen - Born: Embden, MA - Age: 38 - Discharged on 25 Sep 1814 and sent to Dartmoor on HMS Freya.

Chambers, Charles - Seaman - Number: 999 - Prize name: Brunswick - Ship type: MV - How taken: HM Frigate Iris - When taken: 17 Dec 1812 - Where taken: off Spain - Date received: 10 Mar 1813 - From what ship: HMS Tigress - Born: Richmond - Age: 18 - Discharged on 2 Jul 1813 and released to Cartel Moses Brown.

Chambers, Henry - Private - Number: 3070 - Prize name: 14th U.S. Infantry - Ship type: LF - How taken: British forces - When taken: 24 Jun 1813 - Where taken: Beaver Dams, Upper Canada - Date received: 7 Jan 1814 - From what ship: Halifax - Born: Maryland - Age: 29 - Discharged on 10 Oct 1814 and sent to U.S. on Cartel St. Philip.

Chambers, Joseph - 2nd Mate - Number: 1246 - Prize name: Rossie - Ship type: MV - How taken: HM Frigate Dryand - When taken: 7 Jan 1813 - Where taken: at sea - Date received: 16 Mar 1813 - From what ship: Portsmouth, via HMS Abundance - Born: New Jersey - Age: 26 - Discharged on 24 Jul 1813 and released to Cartel Hoffminy.

Chandler, Enoch - Seaman - Number: 2738 - Prize name: Growler - Ship type: P - How taken: HM Brig Electra - When taken: 7 Jul 1813 - Where taken: off St. Johns - Date received: 7 Jan 1814 - From what ship: Halifax - Born: New York - Age: 30 - Discharged on 25 Sep 1814 and sent to Dartmoor on HMS Leyden.

Chandler, Ezekiel - Seaman - Number: 221 - How taken: Apprehended at London - When taken: 18 Nov 1812 - Date received: 25 Nov 1812 - From what ship: HMS Raisonnable - Born: North Yarmouth, MA - Age: 24 - Discharged on 26 Jul 1813 and released to Cartel Hoffminy.

Chandler, Henry - Seaman - Number: 965 - Prize name: Empress - Ship type: MV - How taken: HM Brig Rover - When taken: 30 Nov 1812 - Where taken: St. Andrew - Date received: 10 Mar 1813 - From what ship: HMS Tigress - Born: Pittsfield - Age: 24 - Discharged on 8 Jun 1813 and released to Cartel Rodrigo.

Chapel, Samuel - Seaman - Number: 496 - Prize name: Nancy - Ship type: MV - How taken: HM Brig Parthian - When taken: 1 Aug 1812 - Where taken: off the Needles, Isle of Wight - Date received: 23 Feb 1813 - From what ship: Portsmouth via HMS Dromedary - Born: Marblehead - Age: 27 - Discharged on 17 Nov 1813 to the Cartel Robinson Potter.

Chapel, William - Seaman - Number: 1484 - Prize name: Resolution - Ship type: MV - How taken: Hibernia, British letter of marque - When taken: 21 Sep 1812 - Where taken: off Bermuda - Date received: 6 Apr 1813 - From what ship: Portsmouth via Tender Eliza - Born: Flourtown, PA - Age: 20 - Discharged on 8 Jun 1813 and released to Cartel Rodrigo.

Chapley, John - Cook - Number: 2156 - How taken: Gave himself up at Chatham - When taken: 15 Aug 1813 - Date received: 15 Aug 1813 - From what ship: Chatham - Born: Boston - Age: 45 - Discharged on 12 Aug 1814 and sent to Dartmoor on HMS Alpheus.

Chaplin, Thomas - Passenger - Number: 3354 - Prize name: Rolla - Ship type: P - How taken: HM Ship-of-the-Line Victorious - When taken: 8 Jan 1813 - Where taken: off Halifax - Date received: 23 Feb 1814 - From what ship: Halifax via HMT Malabar - Born: Baltimore - Age: 48 - Discharged on 10 Oct 1814 and sent to Dartmoor on the Mermaid.

Chapman, John - Seaman - Number: 25 - Prize name: Cato - Ship type: MV - How taken: Detained on the Baltic - When taken: 2 Jun 1812 - Date received: 3 Nov 1812 - From what ship: HMS Raisonnable - Born: New Orleans - Age: 21 - Discharged on 10 May 1813 and released to Cartel Admittance.

Chapman, Josiah F. - Mate - Number: 386 - Prize name: Sally - Ship type: MV - How taken: HM Brig Badger - When taken: 6 Sep 1812 - Where taken: off Minorca, Spain - Date received: 13 Feb 1813 - From what ship: HMS Raisonnable - Born: Beverly, MA - Age: 45 - Discharged on 10 May 1813 and released to Cartel Admittance.

Chappel, Edward - Seaman - Number: 1781 - Prize name: Moscow - Ship type: MV - How taken: Impressed at Gravesend, England - When taken: 27 Sep 1813 - Date received: 1 Jul 1813 - From what ship: HMS Raisonnable - Born: Newport, RI - Age: 20 - Discharged on 24 Jul 1814 and sent to Dartmoor on HMS Liffey.

Chappel, John - Seaman - Number: 149 - Prize name: Country Square - Ship type: MV - How taken: Stopped at London - When taken: 28 Oct 1812 - Date received: 5 Nov 1812 - From what ship: HMS Namur - Born: Kennebunkport - Age: 24 - Discharged in Jul 1813 and released to Cartel Moses Brown.

Charles, Thomas - Seaman - Number: 1784 - How taken: Taken up at London - When taken: 14 Jun 1813 - Date received: 1 Jul 1813 - From what ship: HMS Raisonnable - Born: Eastport, MA - Age: 23 - Race: Mulatto - Discharged on 28 Oct 1813 and released to HMS Ceres.

Chase, Constant - Mate - Number: 3730 - Prize name: Argus - Ship type: MV - How taken: HM Ship-of-the-Line San Domingo - When taken: 1 Mar 1814 - Where taken: off Savannah - Date received: 26 May 1814 - From what ship: HMS Hindostan - Born: Finsbury - Age: 28 - Discharged on 25 Sep 1814 and sent to Dartmoor on HMS Niobe.

Chase, Eliphalet - Seaman - Number: 725 - Prize name: Eos - Ship type: MV - How taken: Detained at Portsmouth harbor - When taken: 31 Jul 1812 - Date received: 24 Feb 1813 - From what ship: Portsmouth via HMS Ulysses - Born: Newburyport - Age: 24 - Discharged on 23 Mar 1813 and released to the Cartel Robinson Potter.

Chase, John - Seaman - Number: 3225 - Prize name: Volunteer - Ship type: MV - How taken: Vittoria, British privateer from Guernsey - When taken: 26 Dec 1813 - Where taken: Bay of Biscay - Date received: 13 Jan 1814 - From what ship: Portsmouth via HMS Poictiers - Born: Massachusetts - Age: 23 - Discharged on 25 Sep 1814 and sent to Dartmoor on HMS Leyden.

Chase, Joseph - Seaman - Number: 2056 - How taken: Gave himself up from HM Ship-of-the-Line Fame - When taken: 4 May 1813 - Date received: 4 Aug 1813 - From what ship: HMS Christian VII - Born: Portland - Age: 29 - Discharged on 4 Aug 1814 and sent to Dartmoor on HMS Liverpool.

Chase, Mathew - Seaman - Number: 763 - Prize name: Margarethe - Ship type: MV - How taken: HM Ship-of-the-Line San Juan - When taken: 8 May 1812 - Where taken: Gibraltar - Date received: 25 Feb 1813 - From what ship: HMS Brazen - Born: Rhode Island - Age: 33 - Discharged on 23 Mar 1813 and released to the Cartel Robinson Potter.

Chase, Nathaniel - Seaman - Number: 1895 - Prize name: Prompt - Ship type: MV - How taken: Chance, British privateer - When taken: 28 Mar 1813 - Where taken: Bay of Biscay - Date received: 7 Jul 1813 - From what ship: Portsmouth via HMS Tribune - Born: Cape Cod - Age: 24 - Discharged on 12 Aug 1814 and sent to Dartmoor on HMS Alpheus.

Chase, Nathaniel - Seaman - Number: 2310 - Prize name: Kitty, prize of the U.S. Frigate President - Ship type: War - How taken: Dart, British privateer from Guernsey - When taken: 20 Jun 1813 - Where taken: off the Western Isles, Scotland - Date received: 8 Oct 1813 - From what ship: Portsmouth, via an admiral's tender - Born: Massachusetts - Age: 23 - Discharged on 8 Sep 1814 and sent to Dartmoor on HMS Niobe.

Chase, Oliver - Seaman - Number: 3031 - How taken: Gave himself up from HM Brig Racehorse - When taken: 25 Oct 1813 - Date received: 7 Jan 1814 - From what ship: Portsmouth - Born: Massachusetts - Age: 29 - Discharged on 26 Sep 1814 and sent to Dartmoor on HMS Leyden.

Chase, Samuel - Seaman - Number: 672 - Prize name: U.S.R.M. Cutter James Madison - Ship type: War - How taken: HM Frigate Barbadoes - When taken: 22 Aug 1812 - Where taken: at sea - Date received: 24 Feb 1813 - From what ship: Portsmouth via HMS Ulysses - Born: Harwich - Age: 27 - Discharged on 10 May 1813 and released to Cartel Admittance.

Chase, Welcome - Seaman - Number: 3607 - Prize name: Liberty - Ship type: MV - How taken: Surrendered at Stromness, Scotland - When taken: 30 Dec 1813 - Date received: 29 Mar 1814 - From what ship: Hired tender Anna - Born: Trois Town - Age: 23 - Died on 20 Jun 1814 from fever.

Chasses, Jacob - Seaman - Number: 2587 - How taken: Gave himself up from HM Ship-of-the-Line Union - When taken: 27 May 1813 - Date received: 5 Nov 1813 - From what ship: HMS Hindostan - Born: Rhode Island - Age: 22 - Released on 10 Jun 1814.

Chattels, John - Seaman - Number: 540 - Prize name: Baltimore - Ship type: P - How taken: HM Transport Diadem - When taken: 7 Oct 1812 - Where taken: S. Andres - Date received: 23 Feb 1813 - From what ship: Portsmouth via HMS Dromedary - Born: Baltimore - Age: 26 - Discharged on 8 Jun 1813 and released to Cartel Rodrigo.

Chauvet, Thomas - Boy - Number: 3584 - Prize name: Devon, prize to the Privateer Bunker Hill - Ship type: P - How taken: HM Brig Fly - When taken: 21 Jan 1814 - Where taken: at sea - Date received: 26 Mar 1814 - From what ship: Plymouth via HMS Raleigh - Born: Lanion, France - Age: 11 - Discharged on 11 Aug 1814 and sent to Dartmoor on HMS Liverpool.

Cheslie, Amos - Seaman - Number: 2810 - Prize name: Industry - Ship type: P - How taken: HM Brig Heron - When taken: 3 Nov 1813 - Where taken: off Halifax - Date received: 7 Jan 1814 - From what ship: Halifax - Born: Portsmouth - Age: 20 - Discharged on 25 Sep 1814 and sent to Dartmoor on HMS Leyden.

Chestly, Amos - Seaman - Number: 1434 - Prize name: Louisa, prize of the Privateer Decatur - Ship type: P - How taken: HM Frigate Andromache - When taken: 11 Jan 1813 - Where taken: off Bordeaux, France - Date received: 6 Apr 1813 - From what ship: Plymouth via HMS Decoy - Born: Dover - Age: 19 - Race: Black - Discharged on 24 Jul 1813 and released to Cartel Hoffminy.

Chew, Joseph - Seaman - Number: 1566 - Prize name: Dolphin - Ship type: LM - How taken: HM Ship-of-the-Line Colossus - When taken: 5 Jan 1813 - Where taken: off the Western Isles, Scotland - Date received: 8 Apr 1813 - From what ship: Plymouth via HMS Olympia - Born: New Castle - Age: 32 - Race: Negro - Discharged on 27 Jul 1813 and released to Cartel Hoffminy.

Chidsey, Abraham - Seaman - Number: 516 - Prize name: William - Ship type: MV - How taken: HM Brig Recruit - When taken: 29 Aug 1812 - Where taken: at sea - Date received: 23 Feb 1813 - From what ship: Portsmouth via HMS Dromedary - Born: New Haven - Age: 21 - Discharged on 10 May 1813 and released to Cartel Admittance.

Childers, Joshua - Private - Number: 3052 - Prize name: U.S. Light Dragoons - Ship type: LF - How taken: British forces - When taken: 24 Jun 1813 - Where taken: Beaver Dams, Upper Canada - Date received: 7 Jan 1814 - From what ship: Halifax - Born: Virginia - Age: 22 - Discharged on 10 Oct 1814 and sent to U.S. on Cartel St. Philip.

Childs, Samuel - Seaman - Number: 468 - Prize name: Hunter - Ship type: P - How taken: HM Frigate Phoebe - When taken: 23 Dec 1812 - Where taken: off Azores - Date received: 19 Feb 1813 - From what ship: HMS

Modeste - Born: Roxbury - Age: 26 - Discharged on 24 Jul 1813 and released to Cartel Hoffminy.

Childs, William - Seaman - Number: 3438 - Prize name: Portsmouth Packet - Ship type: P - How taken: HM Brig Fantome - When taken: 5 Oct 1813 - Where taken: Grand Banks - Date received: 23 Feb 1814 - From what ship: Halifax via HMT Malabar - Born: Rhode Island - Age: 12 - Discharged on 22 Oct 1814 and sent to Dartmoor on HMS Leyden.

Chine, Samuel - Seaman - Number: 887 - Prize name: Print of Boston - Ship type: MV - How taken: HM Ship-of-the-Line Colossus - When taken: 21 Jan 1813 - Where taken: at sea - Date received: 1 Mar 1813 - From what ship: Plymouth via HMS Namur - Born: Marblehead, MA - Age: 25 - Discharged on 11 Aug 1814 and sent to Dartmoor on HMS Freya.

Chip, Charles - Seaman - Number: 1536 - Prize name: Dick - Ship type: MV - How taken: HM Brig Dispatch - When taken: 17 Mar 1813 - Where taken: off Bordeaux, France - Date received: 8 Apr 1813 - From what ship: Portsmouth, via an admiral's tender - Born: Norfolk - Age: 27 - Discharged on 12 Aug 1814 and sent to Dartmoor on HMS Alpheus.

Chivers, Cantab - Seaman - Number: 3823 - How taken: Gave himself up from HM Frigate Andromache - When taken: 20 Jul 1814 - Date received: 23 Jun 1814 - From what ship: Quebec - Born: New Haven - Age: 31 - Race: Black - Discharged on 20 Aug 1814 and sent to Dartmoor on HMS Shamrock.

Chivers, Joseph - Seaman - Number: 3179 - Prize name: Wolf Cove - Ship type: MV - How taken: HM Frigate Briton - When taken: 1 Dec 1813 - Where taken: off Brest, France - Date received: 7 Jan 1813 - From what ship: Halifax - Born: Massachusetts - Age: 25 - Discharged on 25 Sep 1814 and sent to Dartmoor on HMS Leyden.

Choete, Thomas - Seaman - Number: 3759 - Prize name: Argus - Ship type: MV - How taken: HM Ship-of-the-Line San Domingo - When taken: 1 Mar 1814 - Where taken: off Savannah - Date received: 26 May 1814 - From what ship: HMS Hindostan - Born: Newburyport - Age: 18 - Discharged on 25 Sep 1814 and sent to Dartmoor on HMS Niobe.

Chonard, Jack - Seaman - Number: 278 - How taken: Apprehended at London - When taken: 10 Dec 1812 - Date received: 23 Dec 1812 - From what ship: HMS Raisonnable - Born: Long Island - Age: 18 - Discharged on 2 Jun 1814 and released to HMS Ceres.

Christian, John - Seaman - Number: 2965 - Prize name: Enterprise - Ship type: P - How taken: HM Frigate Tenedos - When taken: 21 May 1813 - Where taken: off Cape Cod - Date received: 7 Jan 1814 - From what ship: Halifax - Born: Massachusetts - Age: 35 - Discharged on 22 Oct 1814 and sent to Dartmoor on HMS Leyden.

Christian, Tyrel - Seaman - Number: 3845 - How taken: Gave himself up from HM Ship-of-the-Line Minden at Madras, India - When taken: 14 Oct 1813 - Date received: 21 Aug 1814 - From what ship: Gravesend - Born: Charleston - Age: 41 - Discharged on 20 Sep 1814 and sent to Dartmoor on HMS Leyden.

Christie, John - Seaman - Number: 1822 - Prize name: tender to the Privateer True Blooded Yankee - Ship type: P - How taken: HM Brig Hope - When taken: 24 Jun 1813 - Where taken: off Brest, France - Date received: 7 Jul 1813 - From what ship: Portsmouth via HMS Scorpion - Born: Philadelphia - Age: 18 - Discharged on 25 Jul 1814 and sent to Dartmoor on HMS Bittern.

Christie, John - Master's Mate - Number: 2725 - Prize name: U.S. Schooner Growler - Ship type: War - How taken: HM Schooner Lord Melvin - When taken: 11 Aug 1813 - Where taken: Lake Ontario - Date received: 7 Jan 1814 - From what ship: Portsmouth - Born: Massachusetts - Age: 42 - Died on 25 May 1814 from fever.

Christie, William - 2nd Mate - Number: 707 - Prize name: Leonidas - Ship type: MV - How taken: Detained at Portsmouth harbor - When taken: 31 Jul 1812 - Date received: 24 Feb 1813 - From what ship: Portsmouth via HMS Ulysses - Born: Situate, MA - Age: 24 - Discharged on 23 Mar 1813 and released to the Cartel Robinson Potter.

Christo, Peter - Seaman - Number: 3339 - Prize name: Porcupine - Ship type: LM - How taken: HM Frigate Acasta - When taken: 18 Jul 1813 - Where taken: off Cape Sable, Florida - Date received: 23 Feb 1814 - From what ship: Halifax via HMT Malabar - Born: New Orleans - Age: 34 - Discharged on 22 Jun 1814 and sent to Calais, France on the Simon & Mary.

Chult, David - Seaman - Number: 961 - How taken: Gave himself up from HM Ship-of-the-Line Salvador del

Mundo - Date received: 10 Mar 1813 - From what ship: HMS Tigress - Born: Salem - Age: 31 - Discharged on 4 Aug 1814 and sent to Dartmoor on HMS Liverpool.

Church, Benjamin - Seaman - Number: 1288 - How taken: Gave himself up from HM Guardship Royal William - When taken: 3 Feb 1813 - Date received: 16 Mar 1813 - From what ship: Portsmouth, via HMS Abundance - Born: Newport - Age: 38 - Discharged on 23 Jul 1814 and sent to Dartmoor.

Church, Ezekiel - Seaman - Number: 2335 - How taken: Impressed at London - When taken: 12 Aug 1813 - Date received: 12 Oct 1813 - From what ship: HMS Raisonnable - Born: Virginia - Age: 28 - Race: Blackman - Released on 8 Oct 1814.

Church, Jeremiah - Seaman - Number: 1790 - How taken: Taken up at Gravesend, England - When taken: 16 May 1813 - Date received: 1 Jul 1813 - From what ship: HMS Raisonnable - Born: Rhode Island - Age: 26 - Race: Black - Discharged on 25 Jul 1814 and sent to Dartmoor on HMS Bittern.

Church, Richard - Seaman - Number: 1066 - How taken: Gave himself up from HM Frigate Ulysses - When taken: 13 Jan 1813 - Date received: 14 Mar 1813 - From what ship: Portsmouth via HMS Cornwell - Born: Baltimore - Age: 32 - Discharged on 11 Aug 1814 and sent to Dartmoor.

Churchill, Henry - Seaman - Number: 1870 - Prize name: Tiger - Ship type: MV - How taken: HM Brig Scylla - When taken: 22 Mar 1813 - Where taken: Bay of Biscay - Date received: 7 Jul 1813 - From what ship: Portsmouth via HMS Tribune - Born: Massachusetts - Age: 27 - Discharged on 4 Aug 1814 and sent to Dartmoor on HMS Liverpool.

Cilby, Thomas - Mate - Number: 3595 - Prize name: Liberty - Ship type: MV - How taken: Surrendered at Stromness, Scotland - When taken: 30 Dec 1813 - Date received: 29 Mar 1814 - From what ship: Hired tender Anna - Born: Connecticut - Age: 24 - Discharged on 25 Sep 1814 and sent to Dartmoor on HMS Niobe.

Claby, Martin L. - Seaman - Number: 2885 - Prize name: Taken off an English whaler - How taken: HM Ship-of-the-Line Illustrious - When taken: 22 Oct 1813 - Where taken: at sea - Date received: 7 Jan 1814 - From what ship: Portsmouth - Born: Boston - Age: 24 - Discharged on 25 Sep 1814 and sent to Dartmoor on HMS Leyden.

Clark, Abraham D. - Lieutenant - Number: 2157 - Prize name: tender to the Privateer True Blooded Yankee - Ship type: P - How taken: HM Ship-of-the-Line Fame - When taken: 24 Jun 1813 - Where taken: at sea - Date received: 16 Aug 1813 - From what ship: Portsmouth, via an admiral's tender - Born: New York - Age: 29 - Discharged on 17 Jun 1814 and sent to Dartmoor on the Penebar.

Clark, Alexander - Boy - Number: 732 - Prize name: Richmond - Ship type: MV - How taken: Detained at Portsmouth harbor - When taken: 31 Jul 1812 - Date received: 24 Feb 1813 - From what ship: Portsmouth via HMS Ulysses - Born: Charlestown - Age: 18 - Discharged on 23 Mar 1813 and released to the Cartel Robinson Potter.

Clark, Elisha - Seaman - Number: 1426 - How taken: Gave himself up from HM Frigate Andromache - When taken: 24 Dec 1812 - Date received: 5 Apr 1813 - From what ship: Plymouth via HMS Dwarf - Born: New Bedford - Age: 35 - Discharged on 24 Jul 1814 and sent to Dartmoor.

Clark, John - Seaman - Number: 2548 - How taken: Taken by the guards at Gosport - When taken: 2 Oct 1813 - Date received: 23 Oct 1813 - From what ship: Portsmouth via HMS Raisonnable - Born: Boston - Age: 29 - Discharged on 25 Sep 1814 and sent to Dartmoor on HMS Leyden.

Clark, Joseph - Seaman - Number: 3445 - Prize name: Elbridge Gerry - Ship type: P - How taken: HM Frigate Crescent - When taken: 16 Sep 1813 - Where taken: at sea - Date received: 23 Feb 1814 - From what ship: Halifax via HMT Malabar - Born: Wiscasset - Age: 22 - Discharged on 21 Jul 1814 and sent to Dartmoor on HMS Portia.

Clark, Peleg - Seaman - Number: 314 - Prize name: Joseph Ricketsen - Ship type: MV - How taken: HM Brig Rifleman - When taken: 22 Aug 1812 - Where taken: off Scotland - Date received: 23 Dec 1812 - From what ship: Greenlaw Depot - Born: Rhode Island - Age: 47 - Discharged on 10 May 1813 and released to Cartel Admittance.

Clark, Samuel - Seaman - Number: 3878 - How taken: Gave himself up from HM Frigate Clorinde - When taken: 18

Dec 1813 - Date received: 28 Aug 1814 - From what ship: London - Born: Pennsylvania - Age: 32 - Discharged on 8 Sep 1814 and sent to Dartmoor on HMS Niobe.

Clark, Samuel - Seaman - Number: 1356 - Prize name: Dart - Ship type: MV - How taken: HM Brig Doterel - When taken: 5 Mar 1813 - Where taken: at sea - Date received: 3 Apr 1813 - From what ship: Portsmouth, via an admiral's tender - Born: Alfred - Age: 28 - Discharged on 25 Sep 1814 and sent to Dartmoor on HMS Leyden.

Clark, Stephen - Private - Number: 3108 - Prize name: 14th U.S. Infantry - Ship type: LF - How taken: British forces - When taken: 24 Jun 1813 - Where taken: Beaver Dams, Upper Canada - Date received: 7 Jan 1814 - From what ship: Halifax - Born: New Jersey - Age: 27 - Discharged on 10 Oct 1814 and sent to U.S. on Cartel St. Philip.

Clark, Titus - Mate - Number: 2261 - Prize name: Eliza - Ship type: MV - How taken: HMS Charles - When taken: 20 Jul 1813 - Where taken: off Petershead, Scotland - Date received: 14 Sep 1813 - From what ship: HMS Raisonnable - Born: Connecticut - Age: 22 - Discharged on 20 Aug 1814 and sent to Dartmoor on HMS Shamrock.

Clark, William - Seaman - Number: 494 - Prize name: Hannibal - Ship type: MV - How taken: MV Potent - When taken: 24 Sep 1812 - Where taken: off Bermuda - Date received: 23 Feb 1813 - From what ship: Portsmouth via HMS Dromedary - Born: New York - Age: 19 - Discharged on 8 Jun 1813 and released to Cartel Rodrigo.

Clarke, Arnold - Seaman - Number: 1196 - How taken: Gave himself up from HM Ship-of-the-Line Tigre - When taken: 15 Aug 1812 - Date received: 16 Mar 1813 - From what ship: Portsmouth, via HMS Abundance - Born: New York - Age: 23 - Discharged on 11 Aug 1814 and sent to Dartmoor on HMS Freya.

Clarke, Clarence - Seaman - Number: 522 - Prize name: Lydia - Ship type: MV - How taken: HM Frigate Orpheus - When taken: 3 Sep 1812 - Where taken: at sea - Date received: 23 Feb 1813 - From what ship: Portsmouth via HMS Dromedary - Born: Middletown - Age: 21 - Discharged on 10 May 1813 and released to Cartel Admittance.

Clarke, Isaac - Seaman - Number: 2968 - Prize name: Enterprise - Ship type: P - How taken: HM Frigate Tenedos - When taken: 21 May 1813 - Where taken: off Cape Cod - Date received: 7 Jan 1814 - From what ship: Halifax - Born: Massachusetts - Age: 22 - Discharged on 25 Sep 1814 and sent to Dartmoor on HMS Leyden.

Clarke, John - Private - Number: 1629 - Prize name: 13th U.S. Infantry - Ship type: LF - How taken: British forces - When taken: 13 Oct 1812 - Where taken: Upper Canada - Date received: 9 May 1813 - From what ship: HMS Raisonnable - Born: Galloway, Scotland - Age: 46 - Discharged on 22 Oct 1814 and sent to Dartmoor on HMS Leyden.

Clarke, William - Seaman - Number: 1767 - How taken: Gave himself up from HM Frigate North Star - When taken: 26 May 1813 - Date received: 14 Jun 1813 - From what ship: HMS Arethusa - Born: Philadelphia - Age: 33 - Discharged on 24 Jul 1814 and sent to Dartmoor on HMS Liffey.

Clarke, William - Seaman - Number: 2471 - Prize name: Montgomery - Ship type: P - How taken: HM Frigate Nymphe - When taken: 5 May 1813 - Where taken: off Cape Cod - Date received: 21 Oct 1813 - From what ship: Portsmouth via HMT Malabar - Born: Marblehead - Age: 25 - Discharged on 8 Sep 1814 and sent to Dartmoor on HMS Niobe.

Claw, Morris - Seaman - Number: 2013 - How taken: Gave himself up from HM Ship-of-the-Line Ville de Paris - Date received: 15 Jul 1813 - From what ship: Plymouth - Born: Long Island - Age: 31 - Race: Black - Discharged on 17 Jun 1814 and sent to Dartmoor on HMS Pincher.

Clawson, Henry - Seaman - Number: 2907 - Prize name: U.S. Schooner Julia - Ship type: War - How taken: HM Schooner Earl Moria - When taken: 11 Aug 1813 - Where taken: Lake Ontario - Date received: 7 Jan 1814 - From what ship: Portsmouth - Born: New York - Age: 23 - Discharged on 10 Oct 1814 and sent to U.S. on Cartel St. Philip.

Clawson, John - Seaman - Number: 2350 - How taken: Gave himself up from HM Ship-of-the-Line Centaur - When taken: 25 Jun 1813 - Date received: 20 Oct 1813 - From what ship: Portsmouth, via an admiral's tender -

Born: Vermont - Age: 19 - Discharged on 4 Sep 1814 and sent to Dartmoor on HMS Freya.

Clay, John - Seaman - Number: 1662 - How taken: Gave himself up from HM Frigate Freya - Date received: 9 May 1813 - From what ship: HMS Raisonnable - Born: Norfolk - Age: 57 - Discharged on 11 Apr 1814 and sent to Dartmoor.

Clayton, Thomas - Private - Number: 2608 - Prize name: U.S. Light Artillery - Ship type: LF - How taken: British forces - When taken: 1 Jun 1813 - Where taken: Upper Canada - Date received: 5 Nov 1813 - From what ship: HMS Hindostan - Born: Cambridge, England - Age: 46 - Discharged on 17 Jun 1814 and sent to Dartmoor.

Clements, Henry - Seaman - Number: 652 - Prize name: U.S.R.M. Cutter James Madison - Ship type: War - How taken: HM Frigate Barbadoes - When taken: 22 Aug 1812 - Where taken: at sea - Date received: 24 Feb 1813 - From what ship: Portsmouth via HMS Ulysses - Born: Albany, NY - Age: 49 - Discharged on 10 May 1813 and released to Cartel Admittance.

Clements, William - Seaman - Number: 2275 - How taken: Impressed at London - When taken: 9 Sep 1813 - Date received: 16 Sep 1813 - From what ship: HMS Raisonnable - Born: Salem - Age: 23 - Discharged on 4 Sep 1814 and sent to Dartmoor on HMS Freya.

Clements, William - Seaman - Number: 1800 - How taken: Impressed at Shields - When taken: 16 Jun 1813 - Date received: 3 Jul 1813 - From what ship: HMS Raisonnable - Born: Guilford, CT - Age: 29 - Discharged on 25 Jul 1814 and sent to Dartmoor on HMS Bittern.

Clerk, Robert - Seaman - Number: 198 - Prize name: Union - Ship type: MV - How taken: Rose, brig - When taken: Sep 1812 - Where taken: Downs - Date received: 6 Nov 1812 - From what ship: HMS Echo - Born: Philadelphia - Age: 28 - Discharged on 24 Jul 1813 and released to Cartel Hoffminy.

Cleveland, Davis - Seaman - Number: 1443 - Prize name: Orbit - Ship type: MV - How taken: HM Brig Achates - When taken: 29 Jan 1813 - Where taken: Lat 49 N Long 13 W - Date received: 6 Apr 1813 - From what ship: Plymouth via HMS Decoy - Born: Nantucket - Age: 19 - Discharged on 24 Jul 1814 and sent to Dartmoor.

Cleveland, Ebenezer - Seaman - Number: 3326 - Prize name: Porcupine - Ship type: LM - How taken: HM Frigate Acasta - When taken: 18 Jul 1813 - Where taken: off Cape Sable, Florida - Date received: 23 Feb 1814 - From what ship: Halifax via HMT Malabar - Born: Maryland - Age: 25 - Race: Black - Discharged on 21 Jul 1814 and sent to Dartmoor on HMS Portia.

Clifford, S. L. - Seaman - Number: 1522 - How taken: Gave himself up from HM Frigate Brune - When taken: 19 Jan 1813 - Date received: 8 Apr 1813 - From what ship: Portsmouth, via an admiral's tender - Born: Philadelphia - Age: 33 - Discharged on 4 Aug 1814 and sent to Dartmoor on HMS Alpheus.

Clothy, John - Seaman - Number: 2484 - Prize name: Enterprise - Ship type: P - How taken: HM Frigate Tenedos - When taken: 21 May 1813 - Where taken: off Cape Cod - Date received: 22 Oct 1813 - From what ship: Portsmouth via HMT Malabar - Born: Marblehead - Age: 41 - Discharged on 8 Sep 1814 and sent to Dartmoor on HMS Niobe.

Clothy, William - Seaman - Number: 2489 - Prize name: Enterprise - Ship type: P - How taken: HM Frigate Tenedos - When taken: 21 May 1813 - Where taken: off Cape Cod - Date received: 22 Oct 1813 - From what ship: Portsmouth via HMT Malabar - Born: Marblehead - Age: 34 - Discharged on 8 Sep 1814 and sent to Dartmoor on HMS Niobe.

Clough, Isaac - Seaman - Number: 216 - Prize name: Cato - Ship type: MV - How taken: HM Ship-of-the-Line Vigo - When taken: 11 Sep 1812 - Where taken: Hanoi - Date received: 15 Nov 1812 - From what ship: HMS Raisonnable - Born: Marblehead - Age: 26 - Discharged on 16 May 1813 and released to Admittance Cartel.

Clough, Isaac - Seaman - Number: 3171 - Prize name: Wolf Cove - Ship type: MV - How taken: HM Frigate Briton - When taken: 1 Dec 1813 - Where taken: off Brest, France - Date received: 7 Jan 1814 - From what ship: Halifax - Born: Marblehead - Age: 20 - Died on 15 Apr 1814 from fever.

Cloutman, George - Master's Mate - Number: 1020 - Prize name: Sword Fish - Ship type: P - How taken: HM Ship-of-the-Line Elephant - When taken: 28 Dec 1812 - Where taken: off Azores - Date received: 10 Mar 1813 - From what ship: HMS Furious - Born: Marblehead - Age: 22 - Discharged on 24 Jul 1813 and released to Cartel Hoffminy.

Cloutman, Joseph - Seaman - Number: 2480 - Prize name: Enterprise - Ship type: P - How taken: HM Frigate Tenedos - When taken: 21 May 1813 - Where taken: off Cape Cod - Date received: 22 Oct 1813 - From what ship: Portsmouth via HMT Malabar - Born: Massachusetts - Age: 21 - Discharged on 8 Sep 1814 and sent to Dartmoor on HMS Niobe.

Cloutman, Robert - 1st Lieutenant - Number: 1009 - Prize name: Sword Fish - Ship type: P - How taken: HM Ship-of-the-Line Elephant - When taken: 28 Dec 1812 - Where taken: off Azores - Date received: 10 Mar 1813 - From what ship: HMS Furious - Born: Marblehead - Age: 49 - Discharged on 8 Jun 1813 and released to Cartel Rodrigo.

Cloutman, Robert - Master - Number: 3168 - Prize name: Wolf Cove - Ship type: MV - How taken: HM Frigate Briton - When taken: 1 Dec 1813 - Where taken: off Brest, France - Date received: 7 Jan 1814 - From what ship: Halifax - Born: New York - Age: 30 - Discharged on 25 Sep 1814 and sent to Dartmoor on HMS Leyden.

Cloutman, Samuel - Carpenter's Mate - Number: 433 - Prize name: Hunter - Ship type: P - How taken: HM Frigate Phoebe - When taken: 23 Dec 1812 - Where taken: off Azores - Date received: 19 Feb 1813 - From what ship: HMS Modeste - Born: Salem - Age: 25 - Discharged on 2 Jul 1813 and released to Cartel Moses Brown.

Clover, Louis - Seaman - Number: 3918 - Prize name: Union - Ship type: MV - How taken: HM Transport Malabar No. 352 - When taken: 17 Jan 1814 - Where taken: Calcutta - Date received: 12 Sep 1814 - From what ship: London - Born: Jersey - Age: 23 - Discharged on 22 Oct 1814 and sent to Dartmoor on HMS Leyden.

Coaner, Peter - Mate - Number: 136 - Prize name: Frederick - Ship type: MV - How taken: Stopped at London - When taken: 28 Oct 1812 - Date received: 5 Nov 1812 - From what ship: HMS Namur - Born: Alexandria, VA - Age: 31 - Discharged on 23 Mar 1813 and released to the Cartel Robinson Potter.

Coats, John - Seaman - Number: 195 - Prize name: New Zealand - Ship type: MV - How taken: HM Frigate Inconstant - When taken: 10 May 1812 - Date received: 6 Nov 1812 - From what ship: HMS Echo - Born: Stonington, CT - Age: 29 - Discharged on 23 Mar 1813 and released to the Cartel Robinson Potter.

Cobb, Samuel - 2nd Mate - Number: 1004 - Prize name: Experiment - Ship type: MV - How taken: HM Brig Rover - When taken: 10 Nov 1812 - Where taken: off Bordeaux, France - Date received: 10 Mar 1813 - From what ship: HMS Furious - Born: Massachusetts - Age: 28 - Discharged on 8 Jun 1813 and released to Cartel Rodrigo.

Cochran, Peter - Sailing Master - Number: 1399 - Prize name: Porcupine - Ship type: MV - How taken: HM Frigate Dryand - When taken: 8 Jan 1813 - Where taken: off Bordeaux, France - Date received: 5 Apr 1813 - From what ship: Plymouth via HMS Dwarf - Born: Boston - Age: 49 - Discharged on 24 Jul 1813 and released to Cartel Hoffminy.

Cochran, Stephen - Seaman - Number: 840 - Prize name: Vengeance - Ship type: LM - How taken: HM Frigate Phoebe - When taken: 1 Jan 1813 - Where taken: Lat 44.4 Long 23 - Date received: 1 Mar 1813 - From what ship: Plymouth via HMS Namur - Born: Wiscasset - Age: 20 - Discharged on 24 Jul 1813 and released to Cartel Hoffminy.

Codding, Caleb - Seaman - Number: 2172 - How taken: Gave himself up from HM Ship-of-the-Line Swiftsure - When taken: 26 Dec 1812 - Date received: 16 Aug 1813 - From what ship: Portsmouth, via an admiral's tender - Born: Taunton - Age: 48 - Discharged on 17 Jun 1814 and sent to Dartmoor on the Penebar.

Codshell, Joseph - Seaman - Number: 2033 - Prize name: Hope & Anchor (Danish sloop) - Ship type: MV - How taken: HM Sloop Nightingale - When taken: 25 Mar 1813 - Where taken: off the Scaws (Skagen, Denmark) - Date received: 1 Aug 1813 - From what ship: HMS Raisonnable - Born: Newport, RI - Age: 31 - Discharged on 4 Aug 1814 and sent to Dartmoor on HMS Liverpool.

Cody, James - Seaman - Number: 1864 - How taken: Gave himself up from HM Frigate Leonidas - Date received: 7 Jul 1813 - From what ship: Portsmouth via HMS Tribune - Born: Boston - Age: 31 - Discharged on 4 Aug 1814 and sent to Dartmoor on HMS Liverpool.

Coffin, Abel - Seaman - Number: 3655 - Prize name: prize to the Privateer Blockade - Ship type: P - How taken: HM Sloop Sapphire - When taken: 24 Feb 1814 - Where taken: coast of America - Date received: 10 Apr

1814 - From what ship: HMS Raisonnable - Born: Newbury - Age: 22 - Discharged on 25 Sep 1814 and sent to Dartmoor on HMS Niobe.

Coffin, Charles - Seaman - Number: 128 - How taken: Stopped at London - When taken: 26 Oct 1812 - Date received: 5 Nov 1812 - From what ship: HMS Namur - Born: Boston - Age: 21 - Discharged in Jul 1813 and released to Cartel Moses Brown.

Coffin, Edward - Seaman - Number: 3514 - Prize name: Pilot - Ship type: LM - How taken: Vittoria, British privateer from Guernsey - When taken: 28 Jan 1814 - Where taken: off Bordeaux, France - Date received: 23 Feb 1814 - From what ship: Portsmouth via HMT Malabar - Born: Nantucket - Age: 24 - Discharged on 25 Sep 1814 and sent to Dartmoor on HMS Leyden.

Coffin, Frederick H. - Seaman - Number: 834 - Prize name: John Barnes - Ship type: MV - How taken: Gave himself up at Liverpool - When taken: 7 Nov 1813 - Date received: 1 Mar 1813 - From what ship: Plymouth via HMS Namur - Born: Nantucket - Age: 30 - Discharged in Jul 1813 and released to Cartel Moses Brown.

Coffin, George - Seaman - Number: 1562 - Prize name: Dolphin - Ship type: LM - How taken: HM Ship-of-the-Line Colossus - When taken: 5 Jan 1813 - Where taken: off the Western Isles, Scotland - Date received: 8 Apr 1813 - From what ship: Plymouth via HMS Olympia - Born: New York - Age: 23 - Discharged on 27 Jul 1813 and released to Cartel Hoffminy.

Coffin, James - Seaman - Number: 2419 - Prize name: Sampson - Ship type: MV - How taken: HM Brig Rebuff - When taken: 12 May 1813 - Where taken: off Cape St. Vincent, Portugal - Date received: 21 Oct 1813 - From what ship: Portsmouth via HMT Malabar - Born: Washington - Age: 28 - Discharged on 4 Sep 1814 and sent to Dartmoor on HMS Freya.

Coffin, Joseph - Seaman - Number: 3016 - How taken: Gave himself up from HM Ship-of-the-Line Invincible - When taken: 14 Jan 1813 - Date received: 7 Jan 1814 - From what ship: Portsmouth - Born: Rhode Island - Age: 29 - Discharged on 25 Sep 1814 and sent to Dartmoor on HMS Leyden.

Coffin, Valentine - 2nd Mate - Number: 3789 - Prize name: Ocean, south seaman - Ship type: MV - How taken: HM Sloop Atalante - When taken: 16 Nov 1812 - Where taken: off Cape of Good Hope - Date received: 26 May 1814 - From what ship: HMS Hindostan - Born: Nantucket - Age: 33 - Discharged on 29 Sep 1814 and sent to Dartmoor on HMS Freya.

Coggins, George - Seaman - Number: 737 - Prize name: Nancy - Ship type: MV - How taken: HM Brig Parthian - When taken: 1 Aug 1812 - Where taken: off the Needles, Isle of Wight - Date received: 24 Feb 1813 - From what ship: Portsmouth via HMS Ulysses - Born: Liory, MA - Age: 26 - Discharged on 23 Mar 1813 and released to the Cartel Robinson Potter.

Cogswell, Edward - Armorer's Mate - Number: 426 - Prize name: Hunter - Ship type: P - How taken: HM Frigate Phoebe - When taken: 23 Dec 1812 - Where taken: off Azores - Date received: 19 Feb 1813 - From what ship: HMS Modeste - Born: Concord - Age: 21 - Discharged on 2 Jul 1813 and released to Cartel Moses Brown.

Colborne, John L. - Seaman - Number: 2546 - Prize name: Prize to the U.S. Frigate President - Ship type: War - How taken: HM Transport Regulus - When taken: 4 Sep 1812 - Where taken: Newfoundland Bank - Date received: 22 Oct 1813 - From what ship: Portsmouth via HMT Malabar - Born: New Orleans - Age: 33 - Discharged on 8 Sep 1814 and sent to Dartmoor on HMS Niobe.

Cole, Andrew - Private - Number: 2653 - Prize name: 6th U.S. Infantry - Ship type: LF - How taken: British forces - When taken: 24 Jun 1813 - Where taken: Beaver Dams, Upper Canada - Date received: 5 Nov 1813 - From what ship: HMS Hindostan - Born: North Ireland - Age: 22 - Discharged on 10 Oct 1814 and sent to U.S. on Cartel St. Philip.

Cole, Hutchinson A. - 2nd Officer - Number: 1021 - Prize name: Calcutta, East Indian Ship - Ship type: MV - How taken: Two Brothers, British privateer from Guernsey - When taken: 23 Nov 1812 - Where taken: off St. Helena - Date received: 10 Mar 1813 - From what ship: HMS Furious - Born: Rhode Island - Age: 22 - Discharged on 23 Mar 1813 and released to the Cartel Robinson Potter.

Cole, John - Seaman - Number: 1913 - Prize name: Ajax, prize to the Privateer Governor Tomkins - Ship type: P - How taken: HM Frigate Revolutionnaire - When taken: 10 Apr 1813 - Where taken: at sea - Date received: 7

Jul 1813 - From what ship: Portsmouth via HMS Tribune - Born: New Orleans - Age: 27 - Discharged on 8 Sep 1814 and sent to Dartmoor on HMS Niobe.

Cole, Peter - Seaman - Number: 484 - How taken: Gave himself up at Shields - When taken: 20 Dec 1812 - Date received: 19 Feb 1813 - From what ship: HMS Raisonnable - Born: Philadelphia - Age: 22 - Discharged on 24 Jul 1813 and released to Cartel Hoffminy.

Cole, Stephen - Seaman - Number: 1811 - Prize name: William Rathbourn, prize of the Privateer Jack - Ship type: P - How taken: HM Brig Charybdis - When taken: 9 Oct 1812 - Where taken: at sea - Date received: 7 Jul 1813 - From what ship: Portsmouth via HMS Scorpion - Born: Sanford - Age: 31 - Discharged on 26 Jul 1813 and released to Cartel Hoffminy.

Cole, William - Seaman - Number: 1891 - Prize name: Prompt - Ship type: MV - How taken: Chance, British privateer - When taken: 28 Mar 1813 - Where taken: Bay of Biscay - Date received: 7 Jul 1813 - From what ship: Portsmouth via HMS Tribune - Born: Cape Cod - Age: 23 - Discharged on 4 Aug 1814 and sent to Dartmoor on HMS Liverpool.

Cole, William - Seaman - Number: 1838 - Prize name: tender to the Privateer True Blooded Yankee - Ship type: P - How taken: HM Ship-of-the-Line Fame - When taken: 24 Jun 1813 - Where taken: off Brest, France - Date received: 7 Jul 1813 - From what ship: Portsmouth via HMS Scorpion - Born: Virginia - Age: 26 - Discharged on 25 Jul 1814 and sent to Dartmoor on HMS Bittern.

Cole, Zachariah - Seaman - Number: 3362 - Prize name: U.S.R.M. Cutter Surveyor - Ship type: War - How taken: HM Frigate Narcissus - When taken: 12 Jun 1813 - Where taken: York River, Virginia - Date received: 23 Feb 1814 - From what ship: Halifax via HMT Malabar - Born: Annapolis - Age: 23 - Race: Black - Discharged on 10 Oct 1814 and sent to U.S. on Cartel St. Philip.

Coleman, Daniel - Seaman - Number: 673 - Prize name: U.S.R.M. Cutter James Madison - Ship type: War - How taken: HM Frigate Barbadoes - When taken: 22 Aug 1812 - Where taken: at sea - Date received: 24 Feb 1813 - From what ship: Portsmouth via HMS Ulysses - Born: Philadelphia - Age: 37 - Discharged on 10 May 1813 and released to Cartel Admittance.

Coleman, John - Seaman - Number: 1348 - How taken: Taken up at Dublin - When taken: 15 Nov 1812 - Date received: 3 Apr 1813 - From what ship: Portsmouth, via an admiral's tender - Born: Delaware - Age: 27 - Discharged on 2 Jul 1813 and released to Cartel Moses Brown.

Coleman, Jonathan - Seaman - Number: 943 - How taken: Gave himself up from HM Ship-of-the-Line Orion - When taken: 28 Sep 1812 - Date received: 10 Mar 1813 - From what ship: HMS Tigress - Born: New York - Age: 25 - Discharged on 24 Jul 1814 and sent to Dartmoor on HMS Liffey.

Collier, Thomas - Seaman - Number: 3910 - How taken: Gave himself up from Worley - When taken: 9 Sep 1814 - Date received: 9 Sep 1814 - From what ship: Chatham - Born: Virginia - Age: 32 - Discharged on 22 Oct 1814 and sent to Dartmoor on HMS Leyden.

Collier, Thomas - Seaman - Number: 91 - Prize name: Rising Stars - Ship type: MV - How taken: Stopped at London - When taken: 26 Nov 1812 - Date received: 4 Nov 1812 - From what ship: HMS Namur - Born: Virginia - Age: 29 - Discharged on 4 Mar 1813 to the Wailey.

Collins, George - Seaman - Number: 3042 - How taken: Gave himself up from HM Ship-of-the-Line Vigo - When taken: 8 Dec 1813 - Date received: 7 Jan 1814 - From what ship: Portsmouth - Born: Boston - Age: 28 - Race: Black - Discharged on 20 Aug 1814 and sent to Dartmoor on HMS Shamrock.

Collins, John - 3rd Lieutenant - Number: 3727 - Prize name: Argus - Ship type: MV - How taken: HM Ship-of-the-Line San Domingo - When taken: 1 Mar 1814 - Where taken: off Savannah - Date received: 26 May 1814 - From what ship: HMS Hindostan - Born: Washington - Age: 32 - Discharged on 22 Oct 1814 and sent to Dartmoor on HMS Leyden.

Collins, Sylvester - Mate - Number: 3279 - Prize name: Vivid - Ship type: P - How taken: HM Frigate Nymphe - When taken: 20 Apr 1813 - Where taken: off Cape Cod - Date received: 23 Feb 1814 - From what ship: Halifax via HMT Malabar - Born: Truro - Age: 25 - Died on 16 Mar 1814 from pulmonic complications.

Colquhoun, William - Seaman - Number: 1583 - How taken: Gave himself up from HM Ship-of-the-Line Christian VII - When taken: 21 Dec 1812 - Date received: 18 Apr 1813 - From what ship: HMS Rosario - Born:

Philadelphia - Age: 37 - Discharged on 11 Apr 1814 and sent to Dartmoor.

Colwell, John - Seaman - Number: 1205 - Prize name: Expectation - Ship type: MV - How taken: HM Frigate Briton - When taken: 17 Dec 1812 - Where taken: at sea - Date received: 16 Mar 1813 - From what ship: Portsmouth, via HMS Abundance - Born: Philadelphia - Age: 28 - Discharged on 2 Jul 1813 and released to Cartel Moses Brown.

Colwell, John - Seaman - Number: 108 - Prize name: Eliza Ann - Ship type: MV - How taken: Stopped at London - When taken: 26 Oct 1812 - Date received: 4 Nov 1812 - From what ship: HMS Namur - Born: Delaware - Age: 30 - Discharged in Jul 1813 and released to Cartel Moses Brown.

Combs, Thomas - Seaman - Number: 1235 - Prize name: Rossie - Ship type: MV - How taken: HM Frigate Dryand - When taken: 7 Jan 1813 - Where taken: at sea - Date received: 16 Mar 1813 - From what ship: Portsmouth, via HMS Abundance - Born: Maryland - Age: 37 - Discharged on 24 Jul 1813 and released to Cartel Hoffminy.

Condon, John - Seaman - Number: 784 - Prize name: Dolphin - Ship type: MV - How taken: HM Ship-of-the-Line Colossus - When taken: 5 Jan 1813 - Where taken: off the Western Isles, Scotland - Date received: 27 Feb 1813 - From what ship: Plymouth via HMS Namur - Born: Philadelphia - Age: 24 - Discharged on 24 Jul 1813 and released to Cartel Hoffminy.

Condon, Michael - Private - Number: 1625 - Prize name: 13th U.S. Infantry - Ship type: LF - How taken: British forces - When taken: 13 Oct 1812 - Where taken: Upper Canada - Date received: 9 May 1813 - From what ship: HMS Raisonnable - Born: Dublin - Age: 40 - Discharged on 22 Oct 1814 and sent to Dartmoor on HMS Leyden.

Cone, John - Seaman - Number: 2954 - Prize name: Enterprise - Ship type: P - How taken: HM Frigate Tenedos - When taken: 21 May 1813 - Where taken: off Cape Cod - Date received: 7 Jan 1814 - From what ship: Halifax - Born: Massachusetts - Age: 42 - Discharged on 25 Sep 1814 and sent to Dartmoor on HMS Leyden.

Conelly, James - Seaman - Number: 1586 - How taken: Gave himself up from HM Ship-of-the-Line Christian VII - When taken: 21 Dec 1812 - Date received: 18 Apr 1813 - From what ship: HMS Rosario - Born: Baltimore - Age: 20 - Discharged on 11 Apr 1814 and sent to Dartmoor.

Conklan, Enoch - Captain - Number: 1337 - Prize name: Antelope - Ship type: P - How taken: HM Brig Zephyr - When taken: 10 Dec 1812 - Where taken: at sea - Date received: 24 Mar 1813 - From what ship: Cartel Robinson Potter - Born: Boston - Age: 32 - Discharged on 26 Mar 1813 and sent to Reading on parole.

Conklan, Enoch - Captain - Number: 1573 - Prize name: Antelope - Ship type: P - How taken: HM Brig Zephyr - When taken: 10 Dec 1812 - Where taken: at sea - Date received: 12 Apr 1813 - From what ship: from Reading - Born: Boston - Age: 32 - Discharged on 21 Apr 1813 and sent to Reading on parole.

Conklan, Enoch - Captain - Number: 1615 - Prize name: Antelope - Ship type: P - How taken: HM Brig Zephyr - When taken: 10 Dec 1812 - Where taken: at sea - Date received: 8 May 1813 - From what ship: from Reading - Born: Boston - Age: 32 - Discharged on 10 May 1813 and released to Cartel Admittance.

Conklin, Smith - Seaman - Number: 3580 - How taken: Gave himself up from HM Ship-of-the-Line Salvador del Mundo - When taken: 29 Dec 1813 - Date received: 26 Mar 1814 - From what ship: Plymouth via HMS Raleigh - Born: New York - Age: 21 - Discharged on 26 Sep 1814 and sent to Dartmoor on HMS Leyden.

Conley, Cornelius - Seaman - Number: 3262 - Prize name: Volante - Ship type: P - How taken: HM Brig Curlew - When taken: 25 Mar 1813 - Where taken: off Boston - Date received: 23 Feb 1814 - From what ship: Halifax via HMT Malabar - Born: Boston - Age: 22 - Discharged on 10 Oct 1814 and sent to Dartmoor on the Mermaid.

Conner, Jesse - Seaman - Number: 1186 - How taken: Gave himself up from HM Sloop Partridge - When taken: 29 Sep 1812 - Date received: 16 Mar 1813 - From what ship: Portsmouth, via HMS Abundance - Born: Virginia - Age: 29 - Escaped on 16 May 1814.

Conner, Michael - Seaman - Number: 3567 - Prize name: Minerva - Ship type: MV - How taken: HM Ship-of-the-Line Conquestador - When taken: 19 Jan 1814 - Where taken: Bay of Biscay - Date received: 7 May 1814 - From what ship: Portsmouth via HMS Favorite - Born: Massachusetts - Age: 22 - Discharged on 25 Sep

1814 and sent to Dartmoor on HMS Niobe.

Connor, John - Seaman - Number: 3020 - How taken: Gave himself up from HM Ship-of-the-Line Invincible - When taken: 14 Jan 1813 - Date received: 7 Jan 1814 - From what ship: Portsmouth - Born: New York - Age: 25 - Discharged on 4 Sep 1814 and sent to Dartmoor on HMS Freya.

Connoway, James - Seaman - Number: 1262 - How taken: Gave himself up from HM Ship-of-the-Line Mars - When taken: 9 Dec 1812 - Date received: 16 Mar 1813 - From what ship: Portsmouth, via HMS Abundance - Born: North Carolina - Age: 53 - Race: Mulatto - Discharged on 23 Jul 1814 and sent to Dartmoor.

Conway, Andrew - Seaman - Number: 1074 - How taken: Gave himself up from HM Brig Electra - When taken: 20 Sep 1812 - Date received: 14 Mar 1813 - From what ship: Portsmouth via HMS Cornwell - Born: New York - Age: 26 - Discharged on 11 Aug 1814 and sent to Dartmoor.

Conway, James - Seaman - Number: 3809 - How taken: Gave himself up from HM Ship-of-the-Line Leader - When taken: 6 Jul 1813 - Date received: 13 Jun 1814 - From what ship: Quebec - Born: Washington - Age: 20 - Discharged on 26 Sep 1814 and sent to Dartmoor on HMS Leyden.

Conway, Samuel - Seaman - Number: 1053 - How taken: Taken up by Tender Elizabeth at Greenock, Scotland - When taken: 29 Oct 1812 - Date received: 11 Mar 1813 - From what ship: Yarmouth via HMS Tenders - Born: Salem - Age: 28 - Discharged in Jul 1813 and released to Cartel Moses Brown.

Cook, Hazard - Private - Number: 3152 - Prize name: 14th U.S. Infantry - Ship type: LF - How taken: British forces - When taken: 24 Jun 1813 - Where taken: Beaver Dams, Upper Canada - Date received: 7 Jan 1814 - From what ship: Halifax - Born: Massachusetts - Age: 25 - Discharged on 10 Oct 1814 and sent to U.S. on Cartel St. Philip.

Cook, Isaac - Seaman - Number: 2555 - How taken: Gave himself up from HM Ship-of-the-Line Prince of Wales - When taken: 21 May 1813 - Date received: 23 Oct 1813 - From what ship: Portsmouth via HMS Raisonnable - Born: Long Island - Age: 24 - Discharged on 8 Sep 1814 and sent to Dartmoor on HMS Niobe.

Cook, Jacob - Seaman - Number: 118 - Prize name: Urbana - Ship type: MV - How taken: Stopped at London - When taken: 26 Oct 1812 - Date received: 4 Nov 1812 - From what ship: HMS Namur - Born: Somerset, NJ - Age: 37 - Discharged on 1 Feb 1813 and released to the British MV Frederick.

Cook, John - Seaman - Number: 2093 - How taken: Gave himself up from HM Brig Scorpion - When taken: 27 May 1813 - Date received: 9 Aug 1813 - From what ship: HMS Thames - Born: Frankport, PA - Age: 25 - Discharged on 12 Aug 1814 and sent to Dartmoor on HMS Alpheus.

Cook, John - Sergeant - Number: 3074 - Prize name: 14th U.S. Infantry - Ship type: LF - How taken: British forces - When taken: 24 Jun 1813 - Where taken: Beaver Dams, Upper Canada - Date received: 7 Jan 1814 - From what ship: Halifax - Born: Maryland - Age: 20 - Discharged on 10 Oct 1814 and sent to U.S. on Cartel St. Philip.

Cook, John - Seaman - Number: 2537 - Prize name: Polly - Ship type: P - How taken: HM Brig Ringdove - When taken: 27 Jul 1813 - Where taken: at sea - Date received: 22 Oct 1813 - From what ship: Portsmouth via HMT Malabar - Born: Boston - Age: 34 - Discharged on 8 Sep 1814 and sent to Dartmoor on HMS Niobe.

Cook, Silvanus - Carpenter - Number: 2868 - Prize name: Elbridge Gerry - Ship type: P - How taken: HM Frigate Crescent - When taken: 16 Sep 1813 - Where taken: at sea - Date received: 7 Jan 1814 - From what ship: Portsmouth - Born: Massachusetts - Age: 30 - Discharged on 25 Sep 1814 and sent to Dartmoor on HMS Leyden.

Cook, Tarden - Seaman - Number: 285 - Prize name: Francis Ann - Ship type: MV - How taken: Apprehended at Leight, Scotland - When taken: 5 Aug 1812 - Date received: 23 Dec 1812 - From what ship: Greenlaw Depot - Born: Dartmouth - Age: 16 - Race: Black man - Discharged on 23 Mar 1813 and released to the Cartel Robinson Potter.

Cook, William - Private - Number: 3139 - Prize name: U.S. Artillery - Ship type: LF - How taken: British forces - When taken: 24 Jun 1813 - Where taken: Beaver Dams, Upper Canada - Date received: 7 Jan 1814 - From what ship: Halifax - Born: Boston - Age: 30 - Died on 21 Apr 1814 from fever.

Coombe, Michael - Seaman - Number: 3190 - Prize name: Growler - Ship type: P - How taken: HM Brig Electra -

When taken: 7 Jul 1813 - Where taken: off St. Johns - Date received: 7 Jan 1813 - From what ship: Portsmouth - Born: Marblehead - Age: 21 - Discharged on 25 Sep 1814 and sent to Dartmoor on HMS Leyden.

Coomes, Richard - Steward - Number: 761 - Prize name: Margarethe - Ship type: MV - How taken: HM Ship-of-the-Line San Juan - When taken: 8 May 1812 - Where taken: Gibraltar - Date received: 25 Feb 1813 - From what ship: HMS Brazen - Born: Philadelphia - Age: 26 - Discharged on 23 Mar 1813 and released to the Cartel Robinson Potter.

Coon, John (alias John Combs) - Seaman - Number: 1363 - How taken: Gave himself up from HM Guardship Royal William - When taken: 12 Mar 1813 - Date received: 3 Apr 1813 - From what ship: Portsmouth, via an admiral's tender - Born: Pennsylvania - Age: 24 - Discharged on 4 Aug 1814 and sent to Dartmoor on HMS Alpheus.

Cooper, Alfred - Seaman - Number: 1112 - Prize name: Tom Thumb - Ship type: MV - How taken: Lion, British privateer - When taken: 15 Feb 1813 - Where taken: Bay of Biscay - Date received: 14 Mar 1813 - From what ship: Portsmouth via HMS Beagle - Born: Newburyport - Age: 32 - Discharged on 11 Aug 1814 and sent to Dartmoor on HMS Freya.

Cooper, Edward - Seaman - Number: 2512 - Prize name: Wasp - Ship type: P - How taken: HM Schooner Bream - When taken: 9 Jun 1813 - Where taken: off Halifax - Date received: 22 Oct 1813 - From what ship: Portsmouth via HMT Malabar - Born: Boothbay - Age: 20 - Discharged on 8 Sep 1814 and sent to Dartmoor on HMS Niobe.

Cooper, Eleazer - Seaman - Number: 11 - Prize name: Eliza Ann - Ship type: MV - How taken: HM Ship-of-the-Line Vigo - When taken: 11 Aug 1812 - Where taken: Hanoi Bay - Date received: 29 Oct 1812 - From what ship: HMS Raisonnable - Born: Nantucket - Age: 19 - Discharged on 10 May 1813 and released to Cartel Admittance.

Cooper, James - Seaman - Number: 518 - Prize name: William - Ship type: MV - How taken: HM Brig Recruit - When taken: 29 Aug 1812 - Where taken: at sea - Date received: 23 Feb 1813 - From what ship: Portsmouth via HMS Dromedary - Born: Talbot, Maryland - Age: 22 - Race: Black man - Discharged on 8 Jun 1813 and released to Cartel Rodrigo.

Cooper, James - Seaman - Number: 1753 - How taken: Gave himself up from HMS Impeteux - When taken: 2 Dec 1812 - Date received: 30 May 1813 - From what ship: HMS Impetius - Born: Boston - Age: 24 - Discharged on 24 Jul 1814 and sent to Dartmoor on HMS Liffey.

Cooper, Thomas - Seaman - Number: 3812 - How taken: Gave himself up from HM Frigate Phoenix - When taken: 17 Jul 1813 - Date received: 13 Jun 1814 - From what ship: Quebec - Born: Maryland - Age: 26 - Discharged on 25 Sep 1814 and sent to Dartmoor on HMS Leyden.

Cooper, Thomas - Boatswain - Number: 3026 - How taken: Gave himself up from HM Frigate Nisus - When taken: 24 Apr 1813 - Date received: 7 Jan 1814 - From what ship: Portsmouth - Born: Philadelphia - Age: 33 - Discharged on 13 Aug 1814 and sent to Dartmoor on HMS Freya.

Cooper, Thomas - 2nd Mate - Number: 3227 - Prize name: Union - Ship type: P - How taken: Susan, East Indian Ship - When taken: 10 Jun 1812 - Where taken: Sago Roads - Date received: 13 Jan 1814 - From what ship: Portsmouth via HMS Poictiers - Born: Massachusetts - Age: 34 - Discharged on 25 Sep 1814 and sent to Dartmoor on HMS Leyden.

Cooper, William - Master's Mate - Number: 3874 - How taken: Gave himself up from Transport Office Assistance - When taken: 26 Aug 1814 - Date received: 28 Aug 1814 - From what ship: London - Born: New York - Age: 34 - Discharged on 25 Sep 1814 and sent to Dartmoor on HMS Leyden.

Cooper, William - Mate - Number: 159 - Prize name: Thomas - Ship type: MV - How taken: Stopped at London - When taken: 27 Oct 1812 - Date received: 5 Nov 1812 - From what ship: HMS Namur - Born: New York - Age: 35 - Discharged in Jul 1813 and released to Cartel Moses Brown.

Cooperies, Nicholas - Seaman - Number: 860 - Prize name: Brutus - Ship type: MV - How taken: Briton, letter of marque - When taken: 13 Jan 1813 - Where taken: Bay of Biscay - Date received: 1 Mar 1813 - From what ship: Plymouth via HMS Namur - Born: Bosno, Turkey - Age: 44 - Discharged on 24 Jul 1813 and released to Cartel Hoffminy.

Copasses, Matthew (alias Cabristal) - Seaman - Number: 1228 - Prize name: Rossie - Ship type: MV - How taken: HM Frigate Dryand - When taken: 7 Jan 1813 - Where taken: at sea - Date received: 16 Mar 1813 - From what ship: Portsmouth, via HMS Abundance - Born: Maryland - Age: 18 - Discharged on 24 Jul 1813 and released to Cartel Hoffminy.

Copland, Thomas - Seaman - Number: 2390 - How taken: Gave himself up from HM Ship-of-the-Line Achille - When taken: 26 Dec 1812 - Date received: 20 Oct 1813 - From what ship: Portsmouth, via an admiral's tender - Born: Massachusetts - Age: 29 - Died on 2 Mar 1814 from fever.

Corban, Daniel - Seaman - Number: 1185 - How taken: Gave himself up from HM Sloop Partridge - When taken: 12 Sep 1812 - Date received: 16 Mar 1813 - From what ship: Portsmouth, via HMS Abundance - Born: Philadelphia - Age: 29 - Discharged on 11 Aug 1814 and sent to Dartmoor.

Cord, Jacob - Private - Number: 3057 - Prize name: 14th U.S. Infantry - Ship type: LF - How taken: British forces - When taken: 24 Jun 1813 - Where taken: Beaver Dams, Upper Canada - Date received: 7 Jan 1814 - From what ship: Halifax - Born: Maryland - Age: 21 - Discharged on 10 Oct 1814 and sent to U.S. on Cartel St. Philip.

Cornelius, John - Seaman - Number: 592 - Prize name: Antelope - Ship type: P - How taken: HM Brig Zephyr - When taken: 10 Dec 1812 - Where taken: at sea - Date received: 23 Feb 1813 - From what ship: Portsmouth via HMS Dromedary - Born: Stanton, PA - Age: 38 - Discharged on 2 Jul 1813 and released to Cartel Moses Brown.

Corneille, Jacques - Boy - Number: 2189 - Prize name: True Blooded Yankee - Ship type: P - How taken: HM Frigate Hamadryad - When taken: 24 Jul 1813 - Where taken: off Norway - Date received: 17 Aug 1813 - From what ship: HMS Raisonnable - Born: Lamballe, France - Age: 16 - Discharged on 22 Jun 1814 and sent to Calais, France on the Simon & Mary.

Corvet, Isaac - Seaman - Number: 1657 - How taken: Gave himself up from HM Frigate Loire - Date received: 9 May 1813 - From what ship: HMS Raisonnable - Born: New York - Age: 31 - Discharged on 1 Oct 1813 and released to HMS Ceres.

Cosse, Francis D. - Seaman - Number: 3416 - Prize name: Teazer - Ship type: P - How taken: HM Frigate Boreas - When taken: 15 Jun 1813 - Where taken: off Halifax - Date received: 23 Feb 1814 - From what ship: Halifax via HMT Malabar - Born: New Orleans - Age: 37 - Discharged on 22 Jun 1814 and sent to Calais, France on the Simon & Mary.

Coston, Thomas - Seaman - Number: 2444 - Prize name: Wiley Reynard - Ship type: P - How taken: HM Frigate Shannon - When taken: 16 Aug 1812 - Where taken: off Halifax - Date received: 21 Oct 1813 - From what ship: Portsmouth via HMT Malabar - Born: Virginia - Age: 35 - Died on 5 Dec 1813.

Cotterill, Henry - Seaman - Number: 2398 - How taken: Gave himself up from HM Ship-of-the-Line Majestic - When taken: 26 Dec 1812 - Date received: 21 Oct 1813 - From what ship: Portsmouth via HMT Malabar - Born: New London - Age: 53 - Discharged on 4 Sep 1814 and sent to Dartmoor on HMS Freya.

Cotterill, James - Seaman - Number: 2002 - How taken: Gave himself up from HM Hospital Ship Trent - Date received: 15 Jul 1813 - From what ship: Plymouth - Born: Nobleboro - Age: 36 - Discharged on 12 Sep 1813 and released to HMS Ceres.

Cotton, Edward - Seaman - Number: 3420 - Prize name: Thomas - Ship type: P - How taken: HM Frigate Nymphe - When taken: 27 Jun 1813 - Where taken: at sea - Date received: 23 Feb 1814 - From what ship: Halifax via HMT Malabar - Born: Portsmouth - Age: 43 - Discharged on 22 Oct 1814 and sent to Dartmoor on HMS Leyden.

Couet, John - Seaman - Number: 482 - Prize name: Vengeance - Ship type: LM - How taken: HM Frigate Phoebe - When taken: 1 Jan 1813 - Where taken: Lat 44.4 Long 23 - Date received: 19 Feb 1813 - From what ship: HMS Modeste - Born: Charles County - Age: 32 - Discharged on 24 Jul 1813 and released to Cartel Hoffminy.

Couley, Andrew - Seaman - Number: 590 - Prize name: Antelope - Ship type: P - How taken: HM Brig Zephyr - When taken: 10 Dec 1812 - Where taken: at sea - Date received: 23 Feb 1813 - From what ship: Portsmouth via HMS Dromedary - Born: New York - Age: 31 - Discharged on 2 Jul 1813 and released to Cartel Moses Brown.

County, David - Private - Number: 3069 - Prize name: 14th U.S. Infantry - Ship type: LF - How taken: British forces - When taken: 24 Jun 1813 - Where taken: Beaver Dams, Upper Canada - Date received: 7 Jan 1814 - From what ship: Halifax - Born: Pennsylvania - Age: 27 - Discharged on 10 Oct 1814 and sent to U.S. on Cartel St. Philip.

Coursis, Frederick - Seaman - Number: 3209 - Prize name: Volunteer - Ship type: MV - How taken: Vittoria, British privateer from Guernsey - When taken: 26 Dec 1813 - Where taken: Bay of Biscay - Date received: 13 Jan 1814 - From what ship: Portsmouth via HMS Poictiers - Born: Memel, Prussia - Age: 26 - Released on 6 Aug 1814.

Courtis, Thomas - Seaman - Number: 1256 - How taken: Gave himself up from HM Ship-of-the-Line Mars - When taken: 9 Dec 1812 - Date received: 16 Mar 1813 - From what ship: Portsmouth, via HMS Abundance - Born: Marblehead - Age: 36 - Discharged on 23 Jul 1814 and sent to Dartmoor.

Courtney, George - Private - Number: 2626 - Prize name: 14th U.S. Infantry - Ship type: LF - How taken: British forces - When taken: 24 Jun 1813 - Where taken: Beaver Dams, Upper Canada - Date received: 5 Nov 1813 - From what ship: HMS Hindostan - Born: North Ireland - Age: 48 - Discharged on 10 Oct 1814 and sent to U.S. on Cartel St. Philip.

Courtney, John - Seaman - Number: 235 - Prize name: Isabella - Ship type: MV - How taken: Impressed at London - When taken: 15 Nov 1812 - Date received: 25 Nov 1812 - From what ship: HMS Raisonnable - Born: New York - Age: 30 - Discharged on 24 Jul 1813 and released to Cartel Hoffminy.

Cousor, Adam - Seaman - Number: 817 - Prize name: Columbia - Ship type: MV - How taken: HM Frigate Briton - When taken: 17 Dec 1812 - Where taken: off Bordeaux, France - Date received: 27 Feb 1813 - From what ship: Plymouth via HMS Namur - Born: Philadelphia - Age: 30 - Discharged in Jul 1813 and released to Cartel Moses Brown.

Covell, John - Seaman - Number: 2253 - Prize name: Joseph - Ship type: MV - How taken: HM Frigate Iris - When taken: 8 Jun 1813 - Where taken: off Spain - Date received: 7 Sep 1813 - From what ship: HMS Raisonnable - Born: Massachusetts - Age: 24 - Discharged on 11 Aug 1814 and sent to Dartmoor on HMS Freya.

Covelle, Ephraim - Seaman - Number: 1289 - How taken: Gave himself up from HM Guardship Royal William - When taken: 3 Feb 1813 - Date received: 16 Mar 1813 - From what ship: Portsmouth, via HMS Abundance - Born: Wellfleet, MA - Age: 39 - Discharged on 23 Jul 1814 and sent to Dartmoor.

Cowen, William - Seaman - Number: 3832 - How taken: Gave himself up from HM Frigate Indefatigable at Cape of Good Hope - When taken: 14 Aug 1813 - Date received: 16 Aug 1814 - From what ship: London - Born: Long Island - Age: 36 - Discharged on 22 Oct 1814 and sent to Dartmoor on HMS Leyden.

Cowen, William - Seaman - Number: 599 - Prize name: Antelope - Ship type: P - How taken: HM Brig Zephyr - When taken: 10 Dec 1812 - Where taken: at sea - Date received: 23 Feb 1813 - From what ship: Portsmouth via HMS Dromedary - Born: New York - Age: 32 - Discharged on 2 Jul 1813 and released to Cartel Moses Brown.

Cowgan, John - Private - Number: 1620 - Prize name: 13th U.S. Infantry - Ship type: LF - How taken: British forces - When taken: 13 Oct 1812 - Where taken: Upper Canada - Date received: 9 May 1813 - From what ship: HMS Raisonnable - Born: County Sligo, Ireland - Age: 49 - Discharged on 22 Oct 1814 and sent to Dartmoor on HMS Leyden.

Cox, Abraham - Seaman - Number: 2590 - How taken: Gave himself up from HM Brig Scorpion - When taken: 27 May 1813 - Date received: 5 Nov 1813 - From what ship: HMS Hindostan - Born: Maryland - Age: 25 - Race: Blackman - Discharged on 12 Aug 1814 and sent to Dartmoor on HMS Alpheus.

Cox, Daniel - Seaman - Number: 1147 - Prize name: Sword Fish - Ship type: P - How taken: HM Ship-of-the-Line Elephant - When taken: 28 Dec 1812 - Where taken: off Azores - Date received: 16 Mar 1813 - From what ship: Portsmouth, Mundane - Born: Frederick, MD - Age: 38 - Race: Black - Discharged on 24 Jul 1813 and released to Cartel Hoffminy.

Cox, Isaac - Cook - Number: 630 - Prize name: Antelope - Ship type: P - How taken: HM Brig Zephyr - When taken: 10 Dec 1812 - Where taken: at sea - Date received: 23 Feb 1813 - From what ship: Portsmouth via HMS Dromedary - Born: Not readable - Age: 36 - Race: Black - Discharged on 2 Jul 1813 and released to Cartel Moses Brown.

Crafts, William - Seaman - Number: 94 - Prize name: Eliza Ann - Ship type: MV - How taken: HM Ship-of-the-Line Vigo - When taken: 11 Aug 1812 - Where taken: Hanoi Bay - Date received: 4 Nov 1812 - From what ship: HMS Namur - Born: Massachusetts - Age: 21 - Discharged on 10 May 1813 and released to Cartel Admittance.

Craig, James - Seaman - Number: 327 - How taken: Apprehended at London - When taken: 1 Jan 1813 - Date received: 11 Jan 1813 - From what ship: HMS Raisonnable - Born: New York - Age: 32 - Released on 26 Jul 1813.Craigg, William - Seaman - Number: 398 - Prize name: Maria - Ship type: MV - How taken: HM Brig Papillon - When taken: 25 Nov 1812 - Where taken: off Cadiz, Spain - Date received: 13 Feb 1813 - From what ship: HMS Raisonnable - Born: New York - Age: 29 - Discharged on 8 Jun 1813 and released to Cartel Rodrigo.

Crandell, John - Seaman - Number: 1957 - Prize name: Ferox - Ship type: MV - How taken: HM Frigate Medusa & HM Brig Lyra - When taken: 28 Mar 1813 - Where taken: off Cape Ortegal, Spain - Date received: 15 Jul 1813 - From what ship: Plymouth - Born: Duchess County, NY - Age: 29 - Discharged on 17 Jun 1814 and sent to Dartmoor on HMS Redbreast.

Crane, Andrew - Seaman - Number: 292 - Prize name: Dido - Ship type: MV - How taken: Detained off Faco - When taken: 12 Aug 1812 - Date received: 23 Dec 1812 - From what ship: Greenlaw Depot - Born: Beverly - Age: 47 - Discharged on 10 May 1813 and released to Cartel Admittance.

Craney, Edward - Private - Number: 2651 - Prize name: 6th U.S. Infantry - Ship type: LF - How taken: British forces - When taken: 24 Jun 1813 - Where taken: Beaver Dams, Upper Canada - Date received: 5 Nov 1813 - From what ship: HMS Hindostan - Born: Leinster, Ireland - Age: 36 - Discharged on 10 Oct 1814 and sent to U.S. on Cartel St. Philip.

Crapon, George - Seaman - Number: 3792 - Prize name: Valentine - Ship type: MV - How taken: HM Ship-of-the-Line Minden - When taken: 16 Nov 1812 - Where taken: off Cape of Good Hope - Date received: 26 May 1814 - From what ship: HMS Hindostan - Born: New York - Age: 19 - Discharged on 29 Sep 1814 and sent to Dartmoor on HMS Freya.

Crapsey, James - Seaman - Number: 2027 - Prize name: Bows (British MV) - How taken: HM Brig Opossium - When taken: 16 Nov 1812 - Where taken: Barbados - Date received: 24 Jul 1813 - From what ship: HMS Raisonnable - Born: Kingston - Age: 24 - Discharged on 25 Sep 1814 and sent to Dartmoor on HMS Niobe.

Crawford, James - Seaman - Number: 2095 - How taken: Gave himself up from HM Ship-of-the-Line Barfleur - When taken: 27 May 1813 - Date received: 9 Aug 1813 - From what ship: HMS Thames - Born: New York - Age: 25 - Discharged on 3 Nov 1813 and released to HMS Ceres.

Crawford, Nelson - Seaman - Number: 1971 - Prize name: Lightning - Ship type: MV - How taken: HM Frigate Medusa - When taken: 2 Apr 1813 - Where taken: Bay of Biscay - Date received: 15 Jul 1813 - From what ship: Plymouth - Born: Richmond - Age: 26 - Discharged on 17 Jun 1814 and sent to Dartmoor on HMS Redbreast.

Cree, William - Seaman - Number: 3453 - Prize name: Elbridge Gerry - Ship type: P - How taken: HM Frigate Crescent - When taken: 16 Sep 1813 - Where taken: at sea - Date received: 23 Feb 1814 - From what ship: Halifax via HMT Malabar - Born: Bangor - Age: 21 - Discharged on 21 Jul 1814 and sent to Dartmoor on HMS Portia.

Creiger, John - Seaman - Number: 3606 - Prize name: Liberty - Ship type: MV - How taken: Surrendered at Stromness, Scotland - When taken: 30 Dec 1813 - Date received: 29 Mar 1814 - From what ship: Hired tender Anna - Born: New York - Age: 21 - Discharged on 25 Sep 1814 and sent to Dartmoor on HMS Niobe.

Crocker, Sylvester - Prize Master - Number: 2698 - Prize name: Growler - Ship type: P - How taken: HM Brig Electra - When taken: 7 Jul 1813 - Where taken: off St. Johns - Date received: 7 Jan 1814 - From what ship: Portsmouth - Born: Massachusetts - Age: 32 - Discharged on 8 Sep 1814 and sent to Dartmoor on HMS Leyden.

Crofts, William - Sailmaker - Number: 1462 - Prize name: Union - Ship type: MV - How taken: HM Frigate Iris - When taken: 17 Jan 1813 - Where taken: at sea - Date received: 6 Apr 1813 - From what ship: Portsmouth via Tender Eliza - Born: Newport - Age: 28 - Discharged on 24 Jul 1813 and released to Cartel Hoffminy.

Cromwell, Glacio - Seaman - Number: 1584 - How taken: Gave himself up from HM Ship-of-the-Line Christian VII - When taken: 21 Dec 1812 - Date received: 18 Apr 1813 - From what ship: HMS Rosario - Born: Baltimore - Age: 23 - Race: Black - Discharged on 11 Apr 1814 and sent to Dartmoor.

Crosby, Andrew - Seaman - Number: 3368 - Prize name: Yorktown - Ship type: P - How taken: HM Frigate Maidstone - When taken: 17 Jul 1813 - Where taken: Grand Banks - Date received: 23 Feb 1814 - From what ship: Halifax via HMT Malabar - Born: New York - Age: 17 - Discharged on 25 Sep 1814 and sent to Dartmoor on HMS Leyden.

Crosby, John - Seaman - Number: 3742 - Prize name: Argus - Ship type: MV - How taken: HM Ship-of-the-Line San Domingo - When taken: 1 Mar 1814 - Where taken: off Savannah - Date received: 26 May 1814 - From what ship: HMS Hindostan - Born: Boston - Age: 19 - Discharged on 25 Sep 1814 and sent to Dartmoor on HMS Niobe.

Cross, Ephraim - Seaman - Number: 2507 - Prize name: Thomas - Ship type: P - How taken: HM Frigate Nymphe - When taken: 28 Jun 1813 - Where taken: off Halifax - Date received: 22 Oct 1813 - From what ship: Portsmouth via HMT Malabar - Born: Massachusetts - Age: 42 - Discharged on 8 Sep 1814 and sent to Dartmoor on HMS Niobe.

Cross, John - Seaman - Number: 601 - Prize name: Antelope - Ship type: P - How taken: HM Brig Zephyr - When taken: 10 Dec 1812 - Where taken: at sea - Date received: 23 Feb 1813 - From what ship: Portsmouth via HMS Dromedary - Born: Boston - Age: 21 - Discharged on 2 Jul 1813 and released to Cartel Moses Brown.

Cross, Stephen - Seaman - Number: 3321 - Prize name: Porcupine - Ship type: LM - How taken: HM Frigate Acasta - When taken: 18 Jul 1813 - Where taken: off Cape Sable, Florida - Date received: 23 Feb 1814 - From what ship: Halifax via HMT Malabar - Born: Manchester - Age: 21 - Discharged on 10 Oct 1814 and sent to Dartmoor on the Mermaid.

Crosus, Richard - Seaman - Number: 3711 - Prize name: Requin - Ship type: LM - How taken: HM Frigate Venus - When taken: 5 Mar 1814 - Where taken: off Bordeaux, France - Date received: 18 May 1814 - From what ship: HMS Raisonnable - Born: Vienna - Age: 23 - Race: Black - Discharged on 25 Sep 1814 and sent to Dartmoor on HMS Leyden.

Crosy, S. M. - Private - Number: 3126 - Prize name: 14th U.S. Infantry - Ship type: LF - How taken: British forces - When taken: 24 Jun 1813 - Where taken: Beaver Dams, Upper Canada - Date received: 7 Jan 1814 - From what ship: Halifax - Born: Massachusetts - Age: 29 - Died on 25 Apr 1814 from fever.

Crow, John - Seaman - Number: 3524 - How taken: Gave himself up from HM Transport William Pitt No. 421 - When taken: 2 Dec 1813 - Date received: 23 Feb 1814 - From what ship: Portsmouth via HMT Malabar - Born: Baltimore - Age: 21 - Discharged on 21 Jul 1814 and sent to Dartmoor on HMS Portia.

Crow, Jonathan - Seaman - Number: 793 - Prize name: Dolphin - Ship type: MV - How taken: HM Ship-of-the-Line Colossus - When taken: 5 Jan 1813 - Where taken: off the Western Isles, Scotland - Date received: 27 Feb 1813 - From what ship: Plymouth via HMS Namur - Born: Philadelphia - Age: 21 - Discharged on 24 Jul 1813 and released to Cartel Hoffminy.

Crowell, Uriel - Seaman - Number: 1542 - How taken: Impressed at Greenock, Scotland - When taken: 27 Dec 1812 - Date received: 8 Apr 1813 - From what ship: Plymouth via HMS Olympia - Born: Georgetown - Age: 33 - Discharged on 27 Jul 1813 and released to Cartel Hoffminy.

Cruff, William - Seaman - Number: 687 - Prize name: Fame, prize of Privateer Decatur - Ship type: P - How taken: HM Ship-of-the-Line Polyphemus - When taken: 13 Sep 1812 - Where taken: at sea - Date received: 24 Feb 1813 - From what ship: Portsmouth via HMS Ulysses - Born: Marblehead, MA - Age: 28 - Discharged on 8 Jun 1813 and released to Cartel Rodrigo.

Crumpton, William - Seaman - Number: 2269 - Prize name: Eliza - Ship type: MV - How taken: HMS Charles - When taken: 20 Jul 1813 - Where taken: off Petershead, Scotland - Date received: 14 Sep 1813 - From what ship: HMS Raisonnable - Born: Philadelphia - Age: 19 - Discharged on 20 Aug 1814 and sent to Dartmoor on HMS Shamrock.

Cuff, Charles - Seaman - Number: 2154 - How taken: Gave himself up at London - When taken: 30 Jul 1813 - Date received: 14 Aug 1813 - From what ship: HMS Raisonnable - Born: New York - Age: 35 - Race: Blackman - Discharged on 4 Nov 1813 and released to HMS Ceres.

Cullett, William - Seaman - Number: 2672 - How taken: Impressed at London - When taken: 10 Nov 1813 - Date received: 21 Nov 1813 - From what ship: HMS Raisonnable - Born: Philadelphia - Age: 60 - Discharged on 8 Sep 1814 and sent to Dartmoor on HMS Niobe.

Cummings, Edward - Seaman - Number: 501 - How taken: Gave himself up from HM Ship-of-the-Line Ruby - When taken: 15 Aug 1812 - Date received: 23 Feb 1813 - From what ship: Portsmouth via HMS Dromedary - Born: Philadelphia - Age: 35 - Discharged on 26 Jul 1814 and sent to Dartmoor on HMS Raven.

Cummins, David - Captain - Number: 3093 - Prize name: 14th U.S. Infantry - Ship type: LF - How taken: British forces - When taken: 24 Jun 1813 - Where taken: Beaver Dams, Upper Canada - Date received: 7 Jan 1814 - From what ship: Halifax - Born: Boston - Age: 26 - Discharged on 14 Jan 1814 and sent to Reading on parole.

Cunning, James - Seaman - Number: 2586 - How taken: Gave himself up from HM Ship-of-the-Line Union - When taken: 27 May 1813 - Date received: 5 Nov 1813 - From what ship: HMS Hindostan - Born: Pennsylvania - Age: 31 - Discharged on 12 Aug 1814 and sent to Dartmoor on HMS Alpheus.

Cunningham, Caleb - Private - Number: 3144 - Prize name: 14th U.S. Infantry - Ship type: LF - How taken: British forces - When taken: 24 Jun 1813 - Where taken: Beaver Dams, Upper Canada - Date received: 7 Jan 1814 - From what ship: Halifax - Born: Virginia - Age: 32 - Died on 21 Mar 1814 from fever.

Cunningham, John - Seaman - Number: 550 - Prize name: Baltimore - Ship type: P - How taken: HM Transport Diadem - When taken: 7 Oct 1812 - Where taken: S. Andres - Date received: 23 Feb 1813 - From what ship: Portsmouth via HMS Dromedary - Born: Georgetown - Age: 22 - Discharged on 8 Jun 1813 and released to Cartel Rodrigo.

Cunningham, John - Seaman - Number: 1049 - How taken: Taken up from HM Battery Princess at Liverpool - When taken: 27 Oct 1812 - Date received: 11 Mar 1813 - From what ship: Yarmouth via HMS Tenders - Born: Charlestown - Age: 23 - Discharged in Jul 1813 and released to Cartel Moses Brown.

Cunningham, Silas - Seaman - Number: 782 - Prize name: Eliza - Ship type: MV - How taken: HM Sloop Hyacinth - When taken: 27 Aug 1812 - Where taken: off Gibraltar - Date received: 27 Feb 1813 - From what ship: Plymouth via HMS Namur - Born: Charlestown, MA - Age: 31 - Discharged on 10 May 1813 and released to Cartel Admittance.

Currin, Andrew - Mate - Number: 6 - Prize name: Eliza Ann - Ship type: MV - How taken: HM Ship-of-the-Line Vigo - When taken: 11 Aug 1812 - Where taken: Hanoi Bay - Date received: 29 Oct 1812 - From what ship: HMS Raisonnable - Born: Nantucket - Age: 31 - Discharged on 23 Mar 1813 and released to the Cartel Robinson Potter.

Curry, William - Seaman - Number: 2997 - Prize name: Grand Turk - Ship type: P - How taken: HM Frigate Tenedos - When taken: 26 May 1813 - Where taken: off Cape Sable, Florida - Date received: 7 Jan 1814 - From what ship: Halifax - Born: Boston - Age: 18 - Died on 13 Apr 1814 from fever.

Curtis, Enoch - Seaman - Number: 3483 - How taken: Gave himself up from HM Sloop Dauntless - Date received: 23 Feb 1814 - From what ship: Portsmouth via HMT Malabar - Born: Boston - Age: 35 - Discharged on 12 Aug 1814 and sent to Dartmoor on HMS Alpheus.

Curtis, Ephraim - Seaman - Number: 3614 - Prize name: Liberty - Ship type: MV - How taken: Surrendered at Stromness, Scotland - When taken: 30 Dec 1813 - Date received: 29 Mar 1814 - From what ship: Hired tender Anna - Born: Freeport - Age: 24 - Discharged on 26 Sep 1814 and sent to Dartmoor on HMS Leyden.

Curtis, George - Seaman - Number: 1500 - Prize name: Union - Ship type: MV - How taken: HM Frigate Iris - When taken: 17 Jan 1813 - Where taken: at sea - Date received: 6 Apr 1813 - From what ship: Plymouth via an admiral's tender - Born: Philadelphia - Age: 24 - Discharged on 27 Jul 1813 and released to Cartel Hoffminy.

Cushman, Orson - Seaman - Number: 1686 - How taken: Impressed from Russian MV Moscow - When taken: 27 Apr 1813 - Date received: 15 May 1813 - From what ship: HMS Raisonnable - Born: Stafford, CT - Age: 24 - Discharged on 24 Jul 1814 and sent to Dartmoor on HMS Liffey.

Cusser, John Charles - Seaman - Number: 3219 - Prize name: Volunteer - Ship type: MV - How taken: Vittoria, British privateer from Guernsey - When taken: 26 Dec 1813 - Where taken: Bay of Biscay - Date received: 13 Jan 1814 - From what ship: Portsmouth via HMS Poictiers - Born: New York - Age: 39 - Discharged on 25 Sep 1814 and sent to Dartmoor on HMS Leyden.

Cutler, Thomas - Seaman - Number: 3700 - How taken: Gave himself up from the Earl Falk - When taken: 9 May 1814 - Date received: 10 May 1814 - From what ship: Eagle - Born: Exeter - Age: 22 - Discharged on 26 Sep 1814 and sent to Dartmoor on HMS Leyden.

Daggett, Hansel - Seaman - Number: 2133 - How taken: Gave himself up from HMS Montrell - When taken: 5 Jul 1813 - Date received: 9 Aug 1813 - From what ship: HMS Thames - Born: Massachusetts - Age: 22 - Discharged on 12 Aug 1814 and sent to Dartmoor on HMS Alpheus.

Dagman, Caleb - Seaman - Number: 650 - Prize name: U.S.R.M. Cutter James Madison - Ship type: War - How taken: HM Frigate Barbadoes - When taken: 22 Aug 1812 - Where taken: at sea - Date received: 24 Feb 1813 - From what ship: Portsmouth via HMS Ulysses - Born: Situate - Age: 30 - Discharged on 10 May 1813 and released to Cartel Admittance.

Dairs, William - Seaman - Number: 1304 - How taken: Gave himself up from HM Guardship Royal William - When taken: 3 Feb 1813 - Date received: 16 Mar 1813 - From what ship: Portsmouth, via HMS Abundance - Born: Baltimore - Age: 35 - Discharged on 23 Jul 1814 and sent to Dartmoor.

Dalliber, James - Boy - Number: 1171 - Prize name: Sword Fish - Ship type: P - How taken: HM Ship-of-the-Line Elephant - When taken: 28 Dec 1812 - Where taken: off Azores - Date received: 16 Mar 1813 - From what ship: Portsmouth, via HMS Abundance - Born: Marblehead - Age: 15 - Discharged on 24 Jul 1813 and released to Cartel Hoffminy.

Dalton, John - Private - Number: 1621 - Prize name: 13th U.S. Infantry - Ship type: LF - How taken: British forces - When taken: 13 Oct 1812 - Where taken: Upper Canada - Date received: 9 May 1813 - From what ship: HMS Raisonnable - Born: Dublin, Ireland - Age: 46 - Discharged on 22 Oct 1814 and sent to Dartmoor on HMS Leyden.

Dalton, Joseph - Seaman - Number: 1791 - How taken: Taken up at London - When taken: 10 Jun 1813 - Date received: 1 Jul 1813 - From what ship: HMS Raisonnable - Born: Boston - Age: 22 - Discharged on 3 Nov 1813 and released to HMS Ceres.

Dame, John - Boy - Number: 3934 - Prize name: Hawk - Ship type: P - How taken: HM Frigate Piqua - When taken: 26 Apr 1814 - Where taken: West Indies - Date received: 28 Sep 1814 - From what ship: London - Born: Norfolk - Age: 16 - Discharged on 22 Oct 1814 and sent to Dartmoor on HMS Leyden.

Dandridge, Richard - Private - Number: 3165 - Prize name: U.S. Light Dragoons - Ship type: LF - How taken: British forces - When taken: 24 Jun 1813 - Where taken: Beaver Dams, Upper Canada - Date received: 7 Jan 1814 - From what ship: Halifax - Born: Virginia - Age: 30 - Discharged on 10 Oct 1814 and sent to U.S. on Cartel St. Philip.

Daniels, Bradley - Seaman - Number: 777 - Prize name: Eliza - Ship type: MV - How taken: HM Sloop Hyacinth - When taken: 27 Aug 1812 - Where taken: off Gibraltar - Date received: 27 Feb 1813 - From what ship: Plymouth via HMS Namur - Born: New London, CT - Age: 26 - Discharged on 10 May 1813 and released to Cartel Admittance.

Daniels, John - Mate - Number: 896 - Prize name: Phoenix - Ship type: MV - How taken: HM Ship-of-the-Line San Juan - When taken: 8 Aug 1812 - Where taken: Gibraltar - Date received: 1 Mar 1813 - From what ship: Plymouth via HMS Namur - Born: Salem - Age: 27 - Discharged on 10 May 1813 and released to Cartel Admittance.

Dannell, Edward - Seaman - Number: 3391 - Prize name: Fox - Ship type: P - How taken: HM Frigate Maidstone - When taken: 18 Jul 1813 - Where taken: Grand Banks - Date received: 23 Feb 1814 - From what ship: Halifax via HMT Malabar - Born: Charlestown - Age: 21 - Discharged on 22 Oct 1814 and sent to Dartmoor on HMS Leyden.

Darran, Duncan - Seaman - Number: 207 - How taken: Gave himself up from HM Ship-of-the-Line Namur - When taken: 1 Nov 1812 - Date received: 15 Nov 1812 - From what ship: HMS Raisonnable - Born: Stamford, CT - Age: 26 - Discharged on 26 Jul 1814 and sent to Dartmoor on HMS Raven.

Darrison, William - Boy - Number: 3378 - Prize name: Polly - Ship type: MV - How taken: Prize - When taken: 20 Jul 1813 - Where taken: Georges Bank - Date received: 23 Feb 1814 - From what ship: Halifax via HMT Malabar - Born: Salem - Age: 13 - Discharged on 22 Oct 1814 and sent to Dartmoor on HMS Leyden.

Darrow, Aaron - Seaman - Number: 2412 - How taken: Gave himself up from HM Hospital Ship Trent - Date received: 21 Oct 1813 - From what ship: Portsmouth via HMT Malabar - Born: Massachusetts - Age: 24 - Discharged on 4 Sep 1814 and sent to Dartmoor on HMS Freya.

Daumied, Edward - Private - Number: 2635 - Prize name: 14th U.S. Infantry - Ship type: LF - How taken: British forces - When taken: 24 Jun 1813 - Where taken: Beaver Dams, Upper Canada - Date received: 5 Nov 1813 - From what ship: HMS Hindostan - Born: County Limerick, Ireland - Age: 40 - Discharged on 10 Oct 1814 and sent to U.S. on Cartel St. Philip.

David, Michael - Seaman - Number: 585 - Prize name: Oaks - Ship type: MV - How taken: Royal Hill - When taken: 26 Dec 1812 - Date received: 23 Feb 1813 - From what ship: Portsmouth via HMS Dromedary - Born: Roxbury - Age: 36 - Released on 25 Mar 1813.

Davidson, John - Boy - Number: 2342 - Prize name: Hindostan - Ship type: MV - How taken: HM Brig Zenobia - When taken: 25 Jun 1813 - Where taken: off Lisbon - Date received: 20 Oct 1813 - From what ship: Portsmouth, via an admiral's tender - Born: Charlestown - Age: 17 - Discharged on 22 Jun 1814 and sent to Calais, France on the Simon & Mary.

Davidson, Thomas - Mate - Number: 1418 - Prize name: Postsea, prize to the Privateer Thrasher - Ship type: P - How taken: HM Sloop Helena - When taken: 31 Dec 1813 - Where taken: off Azores - Date received: 5 Apr 1813 - From what ship: Plymouth via HMS Dwarf - Born: Baltimore - Age: 29 - Discharged on 24 Jul 1813 and released to Cartel Hoffminy.

Davies, Charles - Seaman - Number: 768 - Prize name: Margarethe - Ship type: MV - How taken: HM Ship-of-the-Line San Juan - When taken: 8 May 1812 - Where taken: Gibraltar - Date received: 25 Feb 1813 - From what ship: HMS Brazen - Born: Philadelphia - Age: 20 - Discharged on 10 May 1813 and released to Cartel Admittance.

Davies, John - Seaman - Number: 2052 - How taken: Gave himself up from HM Ship-of-the-Line Fame - When taken: 4 May 1813 - Date received: 4 Aug 1813 - From what ship: HMS Christian VII - Born: Kennebunk - Age: 36 - Discharged on 24 Sep 1813 and released to HMS Ceres.

Davis, Andrew - Seaman - Number: 901 - Prize name: Pallas - Ship type: MV - How taken: HM Brig Papillon - When taken: 17 Aug 1812 - Where taken: off Cadiz, Spain - Date received: 1 Mar 1813 - From what ship: Plymouth via HMS Namur - Born: Eastport, MA - Age: 24 - Discharged on 23 Mar 1813 and released to the Cartel Robinson Potter.

Davis, Andrew - Seaman - Number: 2219 - How taken: Apprehended at London - When taken: 11 Aug 1813 - Date received: 22 Aug 1813 - From what ship: HMS Raisonnable - Born: Philadelphia - Age: 23 - Discharged on 11 Aug 1814 and sent to Dartmoor on HMS Freya.

Davis, Benjamin - Seaman - Number: 152 - Prize name: Country Square - Ship type: MV - How taken: Stopped at London - When taken: 28 Oct 1812 - Date received: 5 Nov 1812 - From what ship: HMS Namur - Born: Columbia, SC - Age: 24 - Discharged in Jul 1813 and released to Cartel Moses Brown.

Davis, Daniel - Seaman - Number: 582 - How taken: Gave himself up from HM Ship-of-the-Line Aboukir - When taken: 28 Oct 1812 - Date received: 23 Feb 1813 - From what ship: Portsmouth via HMS Dromedary - Born: Kennebunk - Age: 35 - Discharged on 4 Aug 1814 and sent to Dartmoor on HMS Liverpool.

Davis, Daniel - Seaman - Number: 1366 - How taken: Gave himself up from HM Guardship Royal William - When taken: 12 Mar 1813 - Date received: 3 Apr 1813 - From what ship: Portsmouth, via an admiral's tender - Born: Carolina - Age: 28 - Discharged on 24 Jul 1814 and sent to Dartmoor.

Davis, Francis - Seaman - Number: 1914 - Prize name: Ajax, prize to the Privateer Governor Tomkins - Ship type: P - How taken: HM Frigate Revolutionnaire - When taken: 10 Apr 1813 - Where taken: at sea - Date received: 7 Jul 1813 - From what ship: Portsmouth via HMS Tribune - Born: New Orleans - Age: 22 - Discharged on 22 Jun 1814 and sent to Calais, France on the Simon & Mary.

Davis, George - Seaman - Number: 203 - Prize name: Navigator - Ship type: MV - How taken: HM Ship-of-the-Line Cressy - When taken: 11 Aug 1812 - Where taken: Baltic - Date received: 15 Nov 1812 - From what ship: HMS Raisonnable - Born: New Jersey - Age: 32 - Released on 18 Mar 1813 to HMS Navigator.

Davis, George - Seaman - Number: 1313 - How taken: Gave himself up from HM Guardship Royal William - When taken: 3 Feb 1813 - Date received: 16 Mar 1813 - From what ship: Portsmouth, via HMS Abundance - Born: Albany - Age: 19 - Race: Black - Discharged on 23 Jul 1814 and sent to Dartmoor.

Davis, George - Seaman - Number: 2305 - How taken: Gave himself up from HM Sloop Sabrina - When taken: 9 Aug 1813 - Date received: 8 Oct 1813 - From what ship: Portsmouth, via an admiral's tender - Born: New Jersey - Age: 34 - Discharged on 4 Sep 1814 and sent to Dartmoor on HMS Freya.

Davis, Henry - Seaman - Number: 3723 - Prize name: Valentine - Ship type: MV - How taken: HM Ship-of-the-Line Minden - When taken: 17 Nov 1812 - Where taken: off Cape of Good Hope - Date received: 23 May 1814 - From what ship: London - Born: Providence - Age: 23 - Discharged on 25 Sep 1814 and sent to Dartmoor on HMS Leyden.

Davis, James - Seaman - Number: 3371 - Prize name: Yorktown - Ship type: P - How taken: HM Frigate Maidstone - When taken: 17 Jul 1813 - Where taken: Grand Banks - Date received: 23 Feb 1814 - From what ship: Halifax via HMT Malabar - Born: New York - Age: 20 - Race: Black - Discharged on 10 Oct 1814 and sent to Dartmoor on the Mermaid.

Davis, James - Seaman - Number: 1677 - How taken: Gave himself up from HM Tender Elizabeth - Date received: 9 May 1813 - From what ship: HMS Raisonnable - Born: New Jersey - Age: 31 - Discharged on 20 Aug 1814 and sent to Dartmoor on HMS Shamrock.

Davis, John - Seaman - Number: 3935 - Prize name: Gloucester - Ship type: P - How taken: HM Frigate Pique - When taken: 4 May 1814 - Where taken: West Indies - Date received: 29 Sep 1814 - From what ship: London - Born: New York - Age: 40 - Discharged on 22 Oct 1814 and sent to Dartmoor on HMS Leyden.

Davis, John - Seaman - Number: 265 - Prize name: Mandrel - Ship type: MV - How taken: Apprehended at London - When taken: 5 Aug 1812 - Date received: 7 Dec 1812 - From what ship: HMS Raisonnable - Born: Gosport, VA - Age: 40 - Discharged on 23 Mar 1813 and released to the Cartel Robinson Potter.

Davis, John - Seaman - Number: 845 - Prize name: Lucian, prize of the Privateer Armstrong - Ship type: P - How taken: Briton, letter of marque - When taken: 29 Nov 1812 - Where taken: off Bermuda - Date received: 1 Mar 1813 - From what ship: Plymouth via HMS Namur - Born: New York - Age: 33 - Discharged on 8 Jun 1813 and released to Cartel Rodrigo.

Davis, John - Seaman - Number: 912 - Prize name: Independence - Ship type: MV - How taken: HM Frigate Medusa - When taken: 9 Nov 1812 - Where taken: off San Sebastian, Spain - Date received: 10 Mar 1813 - From what ship: HMS Tigress - Born: New York - Age: 24 - Discharged on 8 Jun 1813 and released to Cartel Rodrigo.

Davis, John - Private - Number: 3119 - Prize name: 14th U.S. Infantry - Ship type: LF - How taken: British forces - When taken: 24 Jun 1813 - Where taken: Beaver Dams, Upper Canada - Date received: 7 Jan 1814 - From what ship: Halifax - Born: Pennsylvania - Age: 25 - Discharged on 10 Oct 1814 and sent to U.S. on Cartel St. Philip.

Davis, John - Seaman - Number: 3332 - Prize name: Porcupine - Ship type: LM - How taken: HM Frigate Acasta - When taken: 18 Jul 1813 - Where taken: off Cape Sable, Florida - Date received: 23 Feb 1814 - From what ship: Halifax via HMT Malabar - Born: Newbury - Age: 33 - Discharged on 10 Oct 1814 and sent to Dartmoor on the Mermaid.

Davis, John - Seaman - Number: 2789 - Prize name: Yorktown - Ship type: P - How taken: British squadron - When taken: 17 Jul 1813 - Where taken: Grand Banks - Date received: 7 Jan 1814 - From what ship: Halifax - Born: North Carolina - Age: 28 - Discharged on 22 Jun 1814 and sent to Calais, France on the Simon &

Mary.

Davis, John - Pilot - Number: 2875 - Prize name: Elbridge Gerry - Ship type: P - How taken: HM Frigate Crescent - When taken: 16 Sep 1813 - Where taken: at sea - Date received: 7 Jan 1814 - From what ship: Portsmouth - Born: Massachusetts - Age: 27 - Discharged on 25 Sep 1814 and sent to Dartmoor on HMS Leyden.

Davis, John - Seaman - Number: 2520 - Prize name: Yorktown - Ship type: P - How taken: HM Brig Nimrod - When taken: 17 Jul 1813 - Where taken: Grand Banks - Date received: 22 Oct 1813 - From what ship: Portsmouth via HMT Malabar - Born: Maryland - Age: 29 - Discharged on 8 Sep 1814 and sent to Dartmoor on HMS Niobe.

Davis, Joseph - Master - Number: 1638 - Prize name: Henryettos - Ship type: MV - How taken: HMS Castilian - When taken: 12 Mar 1813 - Where taken: off Cape Ortegal, Spain - Date received: 9 May 1813 - From what ship: HMS Raisonnable - Born: Philadelphia - Age: 42 - Discharged on 13 May 1814 and sent to Reading on parole.

Davis, Lot - Seaman - Number: 3465 - Prize name: Elbridge Gerry - Ship type: P - How taken: HM Frigate Crescent - When taken: 16 Sep 1813 - Where taken: at sea - Date received: 23 Feb 1814 - From what ship: Halifax via HMT Malabar - Born: Barnstable - Age: 21 - Discharged on 22 Oct 1814 and sent to Dartmoor on HMS Leyden.

Davis, Michael - Seaman - Number: 524 - Prize name: Lydia - Ship type: MV - How taken: HM Frigate Orpheus - When taken: 3 Sep 1812 - Where taken: at sea - Date received: 23 Feb 1813 - From what ship: Portsmouth via HMS Dromedary - Born: Middletown - Age: 22 - Discharged on 10 May 1813 and released to Cartel Admittance.

Davis, Moses - Seaman - Number: 2245 - Prize name: Joseph - Ship type: MV - How taken: HM Frigate Iris - When taken: 8 Jun 1813 - Where taken: off Spain - Date received: 7 Sep 1813 - From what ship: HMS Raisonnable - Born: Cape Ann - Age: 22 - Discharged on 11 Aug 1814 and sent to Dartmoor on HMS Freya.

Davis, Nathan - Seaman - Number: 663 - Prize name: U.S.R.M. Cutter James Madison - Ship type: War - How taken: HM Frigate Barbadoes - When taken: 22 Aug 1812 - Where taken: at sea - Date received: 24 Feb 1813 - From what ship: Portsmouth via HMS Ulysses - Born: Gorham, MA - Age: 22 - Discharged on 10 May 1813 and released to Cartel Admittance.

Davis, Nicholas - Seaman - Number: 251 - Prize name: Pigmy - Ship type: MV - How taken: Gave himself off at Scaur, Scotland - When taken: 28 Jul 1812 - Date received: 7 Dec 1812 - From what ship: HMS Raisonnable - Born: Altona - Age: 30 - Discharged on 23 Mar 1813 and released to the Cartel Robinson Potter.

Davis, Nicholas - Seaman - Number: 3040 - How taken: Gave himself up from HM Brig Echo - When taken: 3 Nov 1812 - Date received: 7 Jan 1814 - From what ship: Portsmouth - Born: Hudson - Age: 31 - Race: Mulatto - Discharged on 26 Sep 1814 and sent to Dartmoor on HMS Leyden.

Davis, Osborn - Seaman - Number: 2375 - How taken: Gave himself up from HM Ship-of-the-Line America - When taken: 26 Dec 1812 - Date received: 20 Oct 1813 - From what ship: Portsmouth, via an admiral's tender - Born: New Jersey - Age: 29 - Discharged on 4 Sep 1814 and sent to Dartmoor on HMS Freya.

Davis, Samuel - Seaman - Number: 3835 - How taken: Gave himself up from HM Frigate Africanus at Madeira, Portugal - When taken: 4 Oct 1813 - Date received: 19 Aug 1814 - From what ship: London - Born: Charlestown - Age: 24 - Race: Black - Discharged on 15 Sep 1814 and released to HMS Argonaut.

Davis, Solomon - Seaman - Number: 3768 - Prize name: Argus - Ship type: MV - How taken: HM Ship-of-the-Line San Domingo - When taken: 1 Mar 1814 - Where taken: off Savannah - Date received: 26 May 1814 - From what ship: HMS Hindostan - Born: Boston - Age: 17 - Discharged on 29 Sep 1814 and sent to Dartmoor on HMS Freya.

Davis, Thomas - Private - Number: 3113 - Prize name: 14th U.S. Infantry - Ship type: LF - How taken: British forces - When taken: 24 Jun 1813 - Where taken: Beaver Dams, Upper Canada - Date received: 7 Jan 1814 - From what ship: Halifax - Born: Massachusetts - Age: 22 - Discharged on 10 Oct 1814 and sent to U.S. on Cartel St. Philip.

Davis, William - Seaman - Number: 355 - Prize name: Postsea, prize to the Privateer Thrasher - Ship type: P - How taken: HM Sloop Helena - When taken: 31 Dec 1813 - Where taken: off Azores - Date received: 19 Jan 1813

- From what ship: HMS Raisonnable - Born: Cape Ann - Age: 20 - Discharged on 24 Jul 1813 and released to Cartel Hoffminy.

Davis, William - Seaman - Number: 2770 - Prize name: Thomas - Ship type: P - How taken: HM Frigate Nymphe - When taken: 24 Jun 1813 - Where taken: off Halifax - Date received: 7 Jan 1814 - From what ship: Halifax - Born: New York - Age: 29 - Discharged on 8 Sep 1814 and sent to Dartmoor on HMS Niobe.

Davis, William - Seaman - Number: 2730 - Prize name: Growler - Ship type: P - How taken: HM Brig Electra - When taken: 7 Jul 1813 - Where taken: off St. Johns - Date received: 7 Jan 1814 - From what ship: Halifax - Born: New York - Age: 28 - Discharged on 25 Sep 1814 and sent to Dartmoor on HMS Leyden.

Dawson, John - Seaman - Number: 996 - How taken: Gave himself up from HMS Trinculo - When taken: 14 Dec 1812 - Date received: 10 Mar 1813 - From what ship: HMS Tigress - Born: Philadelphia - Age: 20 - Discharged on 4 Aug 1814 and sent to Dartmoor on HMS Liverpool.

Day, Frederick - Seaman - Number: 2735 - Prize name: Growler - Ship type: P - How taken: HM Brig Electra - When taken: 7 Jul 1813 - Where taken: off St. Johns - Date received: 7 Jan 1814 - From what ship: Halifax - Born: Massachusetts - Age: 27 - Discharged on 25 Sep 1814 and sent to Dartmoor on HMS Leyden.

Day, John - Seaman - Number: 2859 - Prize name: Fire Fly - Ship type: LM - How taken: HM Frigate Revolutionnaire - When taken: 19 Oct 1813 - Where taken: off Cape Ortegal, Spain - Date received: 7 Jan 1814 - From what ship: Portsmouth - Born: Massachusetts - Age: 30 - Discharged on 26 Sep 1814 and sent to Dartmoor on HMS Leyden.

Day, Thomas - Seaman - Number: 3041 - How taken: Gave himself up from HM Brig Espoir - When taken: 8 Dec 1813 - Date received: 7 Jan 1814 - From what ship: Portsmouth - Born: Frederick County, VA - Age: 23 - Discharged on 11 Aug 1814 and sent to Dartmoor on HMS Freya.

Dayley, G. W. - Seaman - Number: 2274 - Prize name: prize to the Privateer Blockade - Ship type: P - How taken: HM Frigate Brazen - When taken: 29 Jun 1813 - Where taken: coast of Scotland - Date received: 14 Sep 1813 - From what ship: HMS Raisonnable - Born: Newport - Age: 23 - Discharged on 4 Sep 1814 and sent to Dartmoor on HMS Freya.

de Colville, Laurence - Seaman - Number: 1486 - How taken: Impressed at Belfast - When taken: 15 Nov 1812 - Date received: 6 Apr 1813 - From what ship: Portsmouth via Tender Eliza - Born: Newbury - Age: 20 - Discharged on 2 Jul 1813 and released to Cartel Moses Brown.

de Park, John - Seaman - Number: 562 - How taken: Gave himself up from HM Guardship Royal William - When taken: 18 Nov 1812 - Date received: 23 Feb 1813 - From what ship: Portsmouth via HMS Dromedary - Born: New York - Age: 30 - Discharged on 4 Aug 1814 and sent to Dartmoor on HMS Liverpool.

De Young, Richard - Seaman - Number: 393 - Prize name: Dolphin - Ship type: MV - How taken: HM Ship-of-the-Line Invincible - When taken: 24 Aug 1812 - Where taken: Mediterranean - Date received: 13 Feb 1813 - From what ship: HMS Raisonnable - Born: Waterford, CT - Age: 27 - Discharged on 8 Jun 1813 and released to Cartel Rodrigo.

Deagle, James - Seaman - Number: 2300 - Prize name: Maria - Ship type: MV - How taken: Apprehended at London - When taken: 21 Sep 1813 - Date received: 29 Sep 1813 - From what ship: HMS Raisonnable - Born: Yarmouth - Age: 24 - Discharged on 4 Sep 1814 and sent to Dartmoor on HMS Freya.

Deal, John - Seaman - Number: 1956 - Prize name: Ferox - Ship type: MV - How taken: HM Frigate Medusa & HM Brig Lyra - When taken: 28 Mar 1813 - Where taken: off Cape Ortegal, Spain - Date received: 15 Jul 1813 - From what ship: Plymouth - Born: Philadelphia - Age: 40 - Discharged on 17 Jun 1814 and sent to Dartmoor on HMS Redbreast.

Dealing, Elisha - Marine Private - Number: 3357 - Prize name: Fly - Ship type: P - How taken: HM Transport Dover - When taken: 27 Jan 1813 - Where taken: off Newfoundland - Date received: 23 Feb 1814 - From what ship: Halifax via HMT Malabar - Born: Portsmouth - Age: 20 - Discharged on 10 Oct 1814 and sent to Dartmoor on the Mermaid.

Deambo, Dom - Seaman - Number: 3341 - Prize name: Porcupine - Ship type: LM - How taken: HM Frigate Acasta - When taken: 18 Jul 1813 - Where taken: off Cape Sable, Florida - Date received: 23 Feb 1814 - From what ship: Halifax via HMT Malabar - Born: Bayonne - Age: 18 - Discharged on 22 Jun 1814 and sent to Calais,

France on the Simon & Mary.

Dean, Daniel - Gunner's Mate - Number: 423 - Prize name: Hunter - Ship type: P - How taken: HM Frigate Phoebe - When taken: 23 Dec 1812 - Where taken: off Azores - Date received: 19 Feb 1813 - From what ship: HMS Modeste - Born: New York - Age: 32 - Discharged on 2 Jul 1813 and released to Cartel Moses Brown.

Dean, Jeremiah B. - Marine Officer - Number: 3505 - Prize name: Elbridge Gerry - Ship type: P - How taken: HM Frigate Crescent - When taken: 16 Sep 1813 - Where taken: at sea - Date received: 23 Feb 1814 - From what ship: Portsmouth via HMT Malabar - Born: Boston - Age: 24 - Discharged on 26 Sep 1814 and sent to Dartmoor on HMS Leyden.

Dean, Peter - Seaman - Number: 3641 - Prize name: Bunker Hill - Ship type: P - How taken: HM Frigate Pomone & HM Frigate Cydnus - When taken: 4 Mar 1814 - Where taken: Bay of Biscay - Date received: 31 Mar 1814 - From what ship: HMS Raisonnable - Born: New Jersey - Age: 30 - Race: Black - Discharged on 22 Jun 1814 and sent to Calais, France on the Simon & Mary.

Dean, Samuel - Seaman - Number: 1702 - How taken: Taken up at London - When taken: 18 May 1813 - Date received: 22 May 1813 - From what ship: HMS Raisonnable - Born: New York - Age: 29 - Discharged on 7 Jun 1813 and released to HMS Ceres.

Debaize, Francois Jean - Seaman - Number: 3570 - Prize name: Devon, prize to the Privateer Bunker Hill - Ship type: P - How taken: HM Brig Fly - When taken: 21 Jan 1814 - Where taken: at sea - Date received: 7 May 1814 - From what ship: Portsmouth via HMS Favorite - Born: Isle de France - Age: 21 - Race: Black - Escaped from HM Prison Ship Glory.

DeBock, Cornelius - Seaman - Number: 947 - Prize name: Mariner - Ship type: MV - How taken: HM Brig Lyra - When taken: 15 Dec 1812 - Where taken: off Bilboa, Spain - Date received: 10 Mar 1813 - From what ship: HMS Tigress - Born: Russia - Age: 36 - Discharged on 2 Jul 1813 and released to Cartel Moses Brown.

Defray, Edward - Seaman - Number: 3596 - Prize name: Liberty - Ship type: MV - How taken: Surrendered at Stromness, Scotland - When taken: 30 Dec 1813 - Date received: 29 Mar 1814 - From what ship: Hired tender Anna - Born: Marblehead - Age: 26 - Discharged on 25 Sep 1814 and sent to Dartmoor on HMS Niobe.

Degars, Pedro - Seaman - Number: 1760 - Prize name: Pallas - Ship type: MV - How taken: HM Brig Rebuff - When taken: 23 Dec 1812 - Where taken: off Cadiz, Spain - Date received: 11 Jun 1813 - From what ship: HMS Raisonnable - Born: San Sebastian, Spain - Age: 35 - Discharged on 16 Jun 1813 and released to HMS Ceres.

Deistel, John - Seaman - Number: 1280 - Prize name: Sword Fish - Ship type: P - How taken: HM Ship-of-the-Line Elephant - When taken: 28 Dec 1812 - Where taken: off Azores - Date received: 16 Mar 1813 - From what ship: Portsmouth, via HMS Abundance - Born: Salem - Age: 35 - Discharged on 24 Jul 1813 and released to Cartel Hoffminy.

Delancey, William - Boy - Number: 604 - Prize name: Antelope - Ship type: P - How taken: HM Brig Zephyr - When taken: 10 Dec 1812 - Where taken: at sea - Date received: 23 Feb 1813 - From what ship: Portsmouth via HMS Dromedary - Born: Westchester - Age: 16 - Discharged on 2 Jul 1813 and released to Cartel Moses Brown.

Delaney, Mathew - Seaman - Number: 1979 - How taken: Gave himself up from HM Ship-of-the-Line Malta - Date received: 15 Jul 1813 - From what ship: Plymouth - Born: Philadelphia - Age: 22 - Discharged on 27 Aug 1813 and released to HMS Ceres.

Delenne, John - 2nd Mate - Number: 1352 - Prize name: Dart - Ship type: MV - How taken: HM Brig Doterel - When taken: 5 Mar 1813 - Where taken: at sea - Date received: 3 Apr 1813 - From what ship: Portsmouth, via an admiral's tender - Born: Hamburg, Germany - Age: 21 - Released on 24 Jul 1814.

Delignay, George - Private - Number: 3078 - Prize name: 14th U.S. Infantry - Ship type: LF - How taken: British forces - When taken: 24 Jun 1813 - Where taken: Beaver Dams, Upper Canada - Date received: 7 Jan 1814 - From what ship: Halifax - Born: Pennsylvania - Age: 26 - Discharged on 10 Oct 1814 and sent to U.S. on Cartel St. Philip.

Delosia, Samuel - Seaman - Number: 196 - Prize name: Watts - Ship type: MV - How taken: Impressed off Dover -

When taken: 18 Sep 1812 - Date received: 6 Nov 1812 - From what ship: HMS Echo - Born: Providence, RI - Age: 28 - Discharged on 23 Mar 1813 and released to the Cartel Robinson Potter.

Demarlow, Francis - Seaman - Number: 3519 - Prize name: Pilot - Ship type: LM - How taken: Vittoria, British privateer from Guernsey - When taken: 28 Jan 1814 - Where taken: off Bordeaux, France - Date received: 23 Feb 1814 - From what ship: Portsmouth via HMT Malabar - Born: Philadelphia - Age: 22 - Race: Mulatto - Discharged on 26 Sep 1814 and sent to Dartmoor on HMS Leyden.

Demerie, Etienne - Boy - Number: 3585 - Prize name: Devon, prize to the Privateer Bunker Hill - Ship type: P - How taken: HM Brig Fly - When taken: 21 Jan 1814 - Where taken: at sea - Date received: 26 Mar 1814 - From what ship: Plymouth via HMS Raleigh - Born: Paris - Age: 11 - Escaped on 20 May 1814 from HM Prison Ship Glory.

D'Emery, Adrian - Marine Private - Number: 3694 - Prize name: Bunker Hill - Ship type: P - How taken: HM Frigate Pomone & HM Frigate Cydnus - When taken: 4 Mar 1814 - Where taken: Bay of Biscay - Date received: 4 May 1814 - From what ship: Portsmouth - Born: Melun, France - Age: 17 - Escaped on 20 May 1814 from HM Prison Ship Glory.

Dempsey, Daniel - Boy - Number: 2862 - Prize name: Fire Fly - Ship type: LM - How taken: HM Frigate Revolutionnaire - When taken: 19 Oct 1813 - Where taken: off Cape Ortegal, Spain - Date received: 7 Jan 1814 - From what ship: Portsmouth - Born: Massachusetts - Age: 15 - Died on 12 Mar 1814 from fever.

Denham, William - Seaman - Number: 1298 - How taken: Gave himself up from HM Guardship Royal William - When taken: 3 Feb 1813 - Date received: 16 Mar 1813 - From what ship: Portsmouth, via HMS Abundance - Born: Maryland - Age: 29 - Discharged on 12 Oct 1813 and released to HMS Ceres.

Denishaw, Henry - Seaman - Number: 2920 - Prize name: Juliana Smith - Ship type: P - How taken: HM Frigate Nymphe - When taken: 12 May 1813 - Where taken: off Cape Sable, Florida - Date received: 7 Jan 1814 - From what ship: Halifax - Born: Boston - Age: 19 - Released on 6 Aug 1814.

Dennis, John - Seaman - Number: 614 - Prize name: King of Rome - Ship type: P - How taken: HM Brig Wolverine - When taken: 13 Dec 1812 - Where taken: at sea - Date received: 23 Feb 1813 - From what ship: Portsmouth via HMS Dromedary - Born: Rhode Island - Age: 26 - Discharged on 2 Jul 1813 and released to Cartel Moses Brown.

Dennis, Thomas - Boy - Number: 521 - Prize name: William - Ship type: MV - How taken: HM Brig Recruit - When taken: 29 Aug 1812 - Where taken: at sea - Date received: 23 Feb 1813 - From what ship: Portsmouth via HMS Dromedary - Born: Kent, MD - Age: 17 - Discharged on 8 Jun 1813 and released to Cartel Rodrigo.

Dennis, Thomas - Seaman - Number: 1816 - Prize name: tender to the Privateer True Blooded Yankee - Ship type: P - How taken: HM Ship-of-the-Line Fame - When taken: 24 Jun 1813 - Where taken: off Brest, France - Date received: 7 Jul 1813 - From what ship: Portsmouth via HMS Scorpion - Born: Newport - Age: 27 - Discharged on 9 Jul 1813 and released to HMS Ceres.

Dennis, Thomas - Boy - Number: 710 - Prize name: Bellville - Ship type: MV - How taken: Detained at Portsmouth harbor - When taken: 31 Jul 1812 - Date received: 24 Feb 1813 - From what ship: Portsmouth via HMS Ulysses - Born: Ipswich, MA - Age: 16 - Discharged on 23 Mar 1813 and released to the Cartel Robinson Potter.

Dennis, Thomas - Seaman - Number: 1917 - How taken: Impressed at London - When taken: 10 Jun 1813 - Date received: 7 Jul 1813 - From what ship: HMS Raisonnable - Born: Marblehead - Age: 23 - Discharged on 4 Aug 1814 and sent to Dartmoor on HMS Liverpool.

Dennison, Andrew - Seaman - Number: 2839 - Prize name: Portsmouth Packet - Ship type: P - How taken: HM Brig Fantome - When taken: 5 Oct 1813 - Where taken: off Portland - Date received: 7 Jan 1814 - From what ship: Halifax - Born: Massachusetts - Age: 21 - Discharged on 25 Sep 1814 and sent to Dartmoor on HMS Leyden.

Dennison, Laurence - Seaman - Number: 1120 - How taken: Gave himself up from HM Frigate Niobe - When taken: 1 Aug 1813 - Date received: 14 Mar 1813 - From what ship: Portsmouth via HMS Beagle - Born: Vermont - Age: 23 - Discharged on 11 Aug 1814 and sent to Dartmoor on HMS Freya.

Dennison, Nathaniel - Seaman - Number: 3471 - Prize name: Yankee - Ship type: P - How taken: HM Frigate

Shannon - When taken: 20 Aug 1813 - Where taken: at sea - Date received: 23 Feb 1814 - From what ship: Halifax via HMT Malabar - Born: Not legible - Age: 0 - Discharged on 11 Mar 1814 and released to HMS Thames.

Denvon, Charles - Private - Number: 2627 - Prize name: 14th U.S. Infantry - Ship type: LF - How taken: British forces - When taken: 24 Jun 1813 - Where taken: Beaver Dams, Upper Canada - Date received: 5 Nov 1813 - From what ship: HMS Hindostan - Born: Leight, Scotland - Age: 39 - Discharged on 10 Oct 1814 and sent to U.S. on Cartel St. Philip.

Deny, James - Seaman - Number: 317 - Prize name: Joseph Ricketsen - Ship type: MV - How taken: HM Brig Rifleman - When taken: 22 Aug 1812 - Where taken: off Scotland - Date received: 23 Dec 1812 - From what ship: Greenlaw Depot - Born: Maryland - Age: 28 - Race: Black man - Discharged on 10 May 1813 and released to Cartel Admittance.

Derrick, John - Seaman - Number: 1928 - Prize name: Edward - Ship type: MV - How taken: Seringapatam, British letter of marque - When taken: 6 Jan 1813 - Where taken: South America - Date received: 11 Jul 1813 - From what ship: HMS Raisonnable - Born: Dunkirk, France - Age: 47 - Discharged on 24 Jul 1813 and released to Cartel Hoffminy.

Derring, William F. - Sailmaker - Number: 2697 - Prize name: Growler - Ship type: P - How taken: HM Brig Electra - When taken: 7 Jul 1813 - Where taken: off St. Johns - Date received: 7 Jan 1814 - From what ship: Portsmouth - Born: Marblehead - Age: 22 - Discharged on 25 Sep 1814 and sent to Dartmoor on HMS Leyden.

Deselva, Manuel - Seaman - Number: 1362 - Prize name: Dart - Ship type: MV - How taken: HM Brig Doterel - When taken: 5 Mar 1813 - Where taken: at sea - Date received: 3 Apr 1813 - From what ship: Portsmouth, via an admiral's tender - Born: Madeira, Portugal - Age: 15 - Released on 25 Jun 1814.

Devereux, Benjamin - Carpenter - Number: 2710 - Prize name: Growler - Ship type: P - How taken: HM Brig Electra - When taken: 7 Jul 1813 - Where taken: off St. Johns - Date received: 7 Jan 1814 - From what ship: Portsmouth - Born: Salem - Age: 27 - Discharged on 8 Sep 1814 and sent to Dartmoor on HMS Leyden.

Devereux, John - Seaman - Number: 3000 - Prize name: Grand Turk - Ship type: P - How taken: HM Frigate Tenedos - When taken: 26 May 1813 - Where taken: off Cape Sable, Florida - Date received: 7 Jan 1814 - From what ship: Halifax - Born: Massachusetts - Age: 21 - Died on 4 Jul 1814 from fever.

Deverter, William - Seaman - Number: 1367 - How taken: Gave himself up from HM Frigate Niobe - When taken: 13 Mar 1813 - Date received: 3 Apr 1813 - From what ship: Portsmouth, via an admiral's tender - Born: Philadelphia - Age: 31 - Discharged on 24 Jul 1814 and sent to Dartmoor.

Devine, John - Seaman - Number: 3576 - Prize name: Confidence - Ship type: MV - How taken: HM Sloop Erebus - When taken: 25 Jan 1814 - Where taken: off Gothenburg, Sweden - Date received: 11 Mar 1814 - From what ship: HMS Raisonnable - Born: Germantown - Age: 27 - Released on 26 Jul 1814.

Devine, John - Seaman - Number: 2234 - Prize name: Confidence - Ship type: MV - How taken: HM Sloop Erebus - When taken: 25 Jun 1813 - Where taken: off Gothenburg, Sweden - Date received: 7 Sep 1813 - From what ship: HMS Raisonnable - Born: Germantown - Age: 26 - Discharged on 2 Mar 1813 and released to HMS Ceres.

Devol, Alexander - Seaman - Number: 3010 - Prize name: Yankee - Ship type: P - How taken: HM Frigate Shannon - When taken: 20 Aug 1813 - Where taken: at sea - Date received: 7 Jan 1814 - From what ship: Halifax - Born: Rhode Island - Age: 27 - Discharged on 25 Sep 1814 and sent to Dartmoor on HMS Leyden.

Dew, Frederick - Prize Master - Number: 2752 - Prize name: Globe - Ship type: P - How taken: HM Frigate Spartan - When taken: 13 Jun 1813 - Where taken: off Delaware - Date received: 7 Jan 1814 - From what ship: Halifax - Born: Baltimore - Age: 35 - Discharged on 25 Sep 1814 and sent to Dartmoor on HMS Leyden.

Dews, William - Seaman - Number: 1774 - How taken: Gave himself up from HM Frigate Melpomene - When taken: 8 Jan 1813 - Date received: 14 Jun 1813 - From what ship: HMS Arethusa - Born: Savannah - Age: 44 - Discharged on 24 Jul 1814 and sent to Dartmoor on HMS Liffey.

Dexter, George W. - Boy - Number: 3837 - Prize name: Derby - Ship type: MV - How taken: HM Frigate Nereus - When taken: 4 Feb 1813 - Where taken: off Cape of Good Hope - Date received: 21 Aug 1814 - From what ship: London - Born: Gloucester - Age: 15 - Discharged on 4 Sep 1814 and sent to Dartmoor on HMS Freya.

Dexter, Philip - 1st Mate - Number: 3836 - Prize name: Derby - Ship type: MV - How taken: HM Frigate Nereus - When taken: 4 Feb 1813 - Where taken: off Cape of Good Hope - Date received: 21 Aug 1814 - From what ship: London - Born: Gloucester - Age: 26 - Discharged on 4 Sep 1814 and sent to Dartmoor on HMS Freya.

Diamond, George - Seaman - Number: 3424 - Prize name: Thomas - Ship type: P - How taken: HM Frigate Nymphe - When taken: 27 Jun 1813 - Where taken: at sea - Date received: 23 Feb 1814 - From what ship: Halifax via HMT Malabar - Born: New York - Age: 20 - Race: Black - Discharged on 22 Oct 1814 and sent to Dartmoor on HMS Leyden.

Dibbins, Edward - Private - Number: 2623 - Prize name: 14th U.S. Infantry - Ship type: LF - How taken: British forces - When taken: 24 Jun 1813 - Where taken: Beaver Dams, Upper Canada - Date received: 5 Nov 1813 - From what ship: HMS Hindostan - Born: North Ireland - Age: 55 - Discharged on 10 Oct 1814 and sent to U.S. on Cartel St. Philip.

Dibble, Zachariah - Seaman - Number: 3497 - How taken: Gave himself up from HM Ship-of-the-Line Malta - When taken: 4 Feb 1814 - Date received: 23 Feb 1814 - From what ship: Portsmouth via HMT Malabar - Born: Connecticut - Age: 40 - Discharged on 21 Jul 1814 and sent to Dartmoor on HMS Portia.

Dickinson, Francis - Seaman - Number: 821 - Prize name: Columbia - Ship type: MV - How taken: HM Frigate Briton - When taken: 17 Dec 1812 - Where taken: off Bordeaux, France - Date received: 27 Feb 1813 - From what ship: Plymouth via HMS Namur - Born: Philadelphia - Age: 27 - Discharged in Jul 1813 and released to Cartel Moses Brown.

Dickson, Enos - Seaman - Number: 103 - Prize name: Liberty - Ship type: MV - How taken: Stopped at London - When taken: 26 Oct 1812 - Date received: 4 Nov 1812 - From what ship: HMS Namur - Born: Greenwood, CT - Age: 28 - Discharged in Jul 1813 and released to Cartel Moses Brown.

Dickson, Richard - Seaman - Number: 1388 - Prize name: Stephen - Ship type: MV - How taken: Briton, letter of marque - When taken: 1 Jan 1813 - Where taken: off Bordeaux, France - Date received: 5 Apr 1813 - From what ship: Plymouth via HMS Dwarf - Born: Long Island - Age: 24 - Discharged on 24 Jul 1813 and released to Cartel Hoffminy.

Didler, Henry - Seaman - Number: 3266 - Prize name: Volante - Ship type: P - How taken: HM Brig Curlew - When taken: 25 Mar 1813 - Where taken: off Boston - Date received: 23 Feb 1814 - From what ship: Halifax via HMT Malabar - Born: Baltimore - Age: 20 - Discharged on 22 Oct 1814 and sent to Dartmoor on HMS Leyden.

Dieman, John - Seaman - Number: 3549 - Prize name: General Kempt, prize of the Privateer Grand Turk - Ship type: P - How taken: HM Brig Foxhound - When taken: 18 Dec 1813 - Where taken: Lat 48.4 Long 6 - Date received: 7 May 1814 - From what ship: Portsmouth via HMS Favorite - Born: Marblehead - Age: 20 - Discharged on 21 Jul 1814 and sent to Dartmoor on HMS Portia.

Dieson, Abraham - Seaman - Number: 269 - How taken: Apprehended at London - When taken: 30 Nov 1812 - Date received: 7 Dec 1812 - From what ship: HMS Raisonnable - Born: Brownhill, CT - Age: 27 - Discharged on 24 Jul 1813 and released to Cartel Hoffminy.

Digereas, William - Seaman - Number: 3316 - Prize name: America - Ship type: P - How taken: HM Frigate Shannon - When taken: 13 Jul 1813 - Where taken: off Cape Cod - Date received: 23 Feb 1814 - From what ship: Halifax via HMT Malabar - Born: Salem - Age: 16 - Discharged on 10 Oct 1814 and sent to Dartmoor on the Mermaid.

Dildure, Samuel - Seaman - Number: 1257 - How taken: Gave himself up from HM Ship-of-the-Line Mars - When taken: 9 Dec 1812 - Date received: 16 Mar 1813 - From what ship: Portsmouth, via HMS Abundance - Born: Princeton, NJ - Age: 24 - Discharged on 23 Jul 1814 and sent to Dartmoor.

Dill, William - Seaman - Number: 3769 - Prize name: Argus - Ship type: MV - How taken: HM Ship-of-the-Line San Domingo - When taken: 1 Mar 1814 - Where taken: off Savannah - Date received: 26 May 1814 - From what ship: HMS Hindostan - Born: Boston - Age: 20 - Discharged on 25 Sep 1814 and sent to Dartmoor on HMS Niobe.

Diseveriere, Cosnery - Seaman - Number: 2227 - Prize name: Porcupine - Ship type: LM - How taken: HM Frigate

Acasta - When taken: 29 Jun 1813 - Where taken: off Cape Sable, Florida - Date received: 22 Aug 1813 - From what ship: HMS Raisonnable - Born: France - Age: 22 - Discharged on 22 Jun 1814 and sent to Calais, France on the Simon & Mary.

Dishele, Alexander - Seaman - Number: 1394 - Prize name: Blue Bird - Ship type: MV - How taken: HM Frigate Briton - When taken: 1 Jan 1813 - Where taken: off Bordeaux, France - Date received: 5 Apr 1813 - From what ship: Plymouth via HMS Dwarf - Born: Abercrombie - Age: 21 - Discharged on 24 Jul 1813 and released to Cartel Hoffminy.

Dissmore, Abraham - Mate - Number: 3884 - Prize name: Rambler - Ship type: MV - How taken: HM Transport Morley - When taken: 10 Feb 1813 - Where taken: off Isle de France (Mauritius) - Date received: 30 Aug 1814 - From what ship: Chatham - Born: Boston - Age: 31 - Discharged on 4 Sep 1814 and sent to Dartmoor on HMS Freya.

Dixey, Peter - Cook - Number: 1133 - Prize name: Sword Fish - Ship type: P - How taken: HM Ship-of-the-Line Elephant - When taken: 28 Dec 1812 - Where taken: off Azores - Date received: 16 Mar 1813 - From what ship: Portsmouth, Mundane - Born: Marblehead - Age: 44 - Discharged on 24 Jul 1813 and released to Cartel Hoffminy.

Dixey, Walston - Seaman - Number: 3858 - Prize name: Derby - Ship type: MV - How taken: HM Frigate Nereus - When taken: 4 Feb 1813 - Where taken: off Cape of Good Hope - Date received: 24 Aug 1814 - From what ship: London - Born: Marblehead - Age: 21 - Discharged on 20 Oct 1814 and released to HMS Argonaut.

Dixon, John - Pilot - Number: 3748 - Prize name: Argus - Ship type: MV - How taken: HM Ship-of-the-Line San Domingo - When taken: 1 Mar 1814 - Where taken: off Savannah - Date received: 26 May 1814 - From what ship: HMS Hindostan - Born: Savannah - Age: 26 - Discharged on 25 Sep 1814 and sent to Dartmoor on HMS Niobe.

Dixon, Peter - Seaman - Number: 3496 - How taken: Gave himself up from HM Ship-of-the-Line Malta - When taken: 4 Feb 1814 - Date received: 23 Feb 1814 - From what ship: Portsmouth via HMT Malabar - Born: New York - Age: 26 - Discharged on 26 Sep 1814 and sent to Dartmoor on HMS Leyden.

Dobbs, Jeremiah - Seaman - Number: 556 - Prize name: Felix - Ship type: MV - How taken: HM Frigate Indefatigable - When taken: 13 Nov 1812 - Where taken: Portsmouth harbor - Date received: 23 Feb 1813 - From what ship: Portsmouth via HMS Dromedary - Born: New York - Age: 24 - Discharged on 8 Jun 1813 and released to Cartel Rodrigo.

Doboll, William - Seaman - Number: 250 - Prize name: Pigmy - Ship type: MV - How taken: Gave himself off at Scaur, Scotland - When taken: 28 Jul 1812 - Date received: 7 Dec 1812 - From what ship: HMS Raisonnable - Born: Boston - Age: 26 - Discharged on 23 Mar 1813 and released to the Cartel Robinson Potter.

Dodge, John - Seaman - Number: 2734 - Prize name: Growler - Ship type: P - How taken: HM Brig Electra - When taken: 7 Jul 1813 - Where taken: off St. Johns - Date received: 7 Jan 1814 - From what ship: Halifax - Born: Massachusetts - Age: 29 - Released on 6 Aug 1814.

Dodge, Joseph - Seaman - Number: 3941 - Prize name: Hawk - Ship type: P - How taken: HM Frigate Piqua - When taken: 26 Apr 1814 - Where taken: West Indies - Date received: 10 Oct 1814 - From what ship: Quebec - Born: Charleston - Age: 19 - Discharged on 22 Oct 1814 and sent to Dartmoor on HMS Leyden.

Dodge, Joseph - 1st Mate - Number: 1687 - Prize name: Governor Middleton - Ship type: MV - How taken: Thetis, British privateer - When taken: 2 May 1813 - Where taken: Bay of Biscay - Date received: 15 May 1813 - From what ship: HMS Viper - Born: Lock Isle - Age: 26 - Discharged on 24 Jul 1814 and sent to Dartmoor on HMS Liffey.

Dodick, Mathew - Seaman - Number: 898 - Prize name: John - Ship type: MV - How taken: HM Sloop Blossom - When taken: 15 Aug 1812 - Where taken: off Gibraltar - Date received: 1 Mar 1813 - From what ship: Plymouth via HMS Namur - Born: County Antrim, Ireland - Age: 29 - Discharged on 10 May 1813 and released to Cartel Admittance.

Dodson, Thomas - Corporal - Number: 3045 - Prize name: U.S. Light Dragoons - Ship type: LF - How taken: British forces - When taken: 9 Jun 1813 - Where taken: Stoney Creek, Upper Canada - Date received: 7 Jan 1814 - From what ship: Halifax - Born: Pennsylvania - Age: 28 - Released on 17 Jun 1814.

Doe, Thomas - Seaman - Number: 7 - Prize name: Eliza Ann - Ship type: MV - How taken: HM Ship-of-the-Line Vigo - When taken: 11 Aug 1812 - Where taken: Hanoi Bay - Date received: 29 Oct 1812 - From what ship: HMS Raisonnable - Born: Nantucket - Age: 21 - Discharged on 10 May 1813 and released to Cartel Admittance.

Doer, James - Seaman - Number: 1692 - Prize name: Governor Middleton - Ship type: MV - How taken: Thetis, British privateer - When taken: 2 May 1813 - Where taken: Bay of Biscay - Date received: 15 May 1813 - From what ship: HMS Viper - Born: Kettering, MA - Age: 20 - Discharged on 24 Jul 1814 and sent to Dartmoor on HMS Liffey.

Doevall, Francis - Boatswain's Mate - Number: 1132 - Prize name: Sword Fish - Ship type: P - How taken: HM Ship-of-the-Line Elephant - When taken: 28 Dec 1812 - Where taken: off Azores - Date received: 16 Mar 1813 - From what ship: Portsmouth, Mundane - Born: Salem - Age: 35 - Discharged on 24 Jul 1813 and released to Cartel Hoffminy.

Dolabar, John - Seaman - Number: 885 - Prize name: Print of Boston - Ship type: MV - How taken: HM Ship-of-the-Line Colossus - When taken: 21 Jan 1813 - Where taken: at sea - Date received: 1 Mar 1813 - From what ship: Plymouth via HMS Namur - Born: Marblehead, MA - Age: 23 - Discharged on 17 Jun 1814 and sent to Dartmoor on HMS Redbreast.

Dole, Anthony - Private - Number: 1636 - Prize name: U.S. Light Artillery - Ship type: LF - How taken: British forces - When taken: 13 Oct 1812 - Where taken: Upper Canada - Date received: 9 May 1813 - From what ship: HMS Raisonnable - Born: St. Davids, Upper Canada - Age: 25 - Discharged on 22 Oct 1814 and sent to Dartmoor on HMS Leyden.

Dole, Henry - 1st Mate - Number: 2681 - Prize name: Liveoak - Ship type: MV - How taken: Impressed at Leight, Scotland - When taken: 4 Dec 1813 - Date received: 16 Dec 1813 - From what ship: HMS Raisonnable - Born: Newburyport - Age: 24 - Discharged on 8 Sep 1814 and sent to Dartmoor on HMS Niobe.

Doliber, Joseph - 1st Mate - Number: 1088 - Prize name: Rachael - Ship type: MV - How taken: HM Schooner Herring - When taken: 9 Feb 1813 - Where taken: at sea - Date received: 14 Mar 1813 - From what ship: Portsmouth via HMS Cornwell - Born: Marblehead - Age: 44 - Discharged on 11 Aug 1814 and sent to Dartmoor.

Doliver, Joseph - Boy - Number: 2250 - Prize name: Joseph - Ship type: MV - How taken: HM Frigate Iris - When taken: 8 Jun 1813 - Where taken: off Spain - Date received: 7 Sep 1813 - From what ship: HMS Raisonnable - Born: Gloucester - Age: 18 - Discharged on 11 Aug 1814 and sent to Dartmoor on HMS Freya.

Dolorer, John - Seaman - Number: 451 - Prize name: Hunter - Ship type: P - How taken: HM Frigate Phoebe - When taken: 23 Dec 1812 - Where taken: off Azores - Date received: 19 Feb 1813 - From what ship: HMS Modeste - Born: Marblehead - Age: 18 - Discharged on 24 Jul 1813 and released to Cartel Hoffminy.

Dominic, John - Seaman - Number: 404 - Prize name: Hope - Ship type: MV - How taken: HM Schooner Bramble - When taken: 3 Dec 1812 - Where taken: Coruna, Spain - Date received: 19 Feb 1813 - From what ship: HMS Modeste - Born: New Orleans - Age: 25 - Released on 10 Apr 1813.

Dominico, Joseph - Seaman - Number: 705 - Prize name: Deanna, recaptured British vessel - Ship type: P - How taken: HM Ship-of-the-Line Polyphemus - When taken: 14 Sep 1812 - Where taken: at sea - Date received: 24 Feb 1813 - From what ship: Portsmouth via HMS Ulysses - Born: New York - Age: 21 - Discharged on 8 Jun 1813 and released to Cartel Rodrigo.

Donaldson, Joseph - Seaman - Number: 1888 - Prize name: Dick - Ship type: MV - How taken: HM Brig Dispatch - When taken: 17 Mar 1813 - Where taken: off Bordeaux, France - Date received: 7 Jul 1813 - From what ship: Portsmouth via HMS Tribune - Born: New York - Age: 21 - Discharged on 12 Aug 1814 and sent to Dartmoor on HMS Alpheus.

Donaway, Daniel - Seaman - Number: 357 - Prize name: Postsea, prize to the Privateer Thrasher - Ship type: P - How taken: HM Sloop Helena - When taken: 31 Dec 1813 - Where taken: off Azores - Date received: 19 Jan 1813 - From what ship: HMS Raisonnable - Born: Cape Ann - Age: 24 - Discharged on 24 Jul 1813 and released to Cartel Hoffminy.

Doniner, John - Private - Number: 1623 - Prize name: 13th U.S. Infantry - Ship type: LF - How taken: British forces

- When taken: 13 Oct 1812 - Where taken: Upper Canada - Date received: 9 May 1813 - From what ship: HMS Raisonnable - Born: County Cavan, Ireland - Age: 41 - Discharged on 22 Oct 1814 and sent to Dartmoor on HMS Leyden.

Donnally, Anthony - Private - Number: 1627 - Prize name: 13th U.S. Infantry - Ship type: LF - How taken: British forces - When taken: 13 Oct 1812 - Where taken: Upper Canada - Date received: 9 May 1813 - From what ship: HMS Raisonnable - Born: Isle of Man - Age: 39 - Discharged on 22 Oct 1814 and sent to Dartmoor on HMS Leyden.

Donnell, Samuel - Seaman - Number: 3404 - Prize name: Elbridge Gerry - Ship type: P - How taken: HM Frigate Tenedos - When taken: 21 May 1813 - Where taken: off Cape Cod - Date received: 23 Feb 1814 - From what ship: Halifax via HMT Malabar - Born: Portland - Age: 19 - Discharged on 25 Sep 1814 and sent to Dartmoor on HMS Leyden.

Dooley, James - Captain - Number: 2785 - Prize name: Rolla - Ship type: P - How taken: HM Ship-of-the-Line Victorious - When taken: 8 Jun 1813 - Where taken: Chesapeake Bay - Date received: 7 Jan 1814 - From what ship: Halifax - Born: Maryland - Age: 25 - Discharged on 4 Apr 1814 and sent to Ready on parole.

Doosenberry, Richard - Seaman - Number: 3676 - Prize name: Lord Ponsonby, prize of the Privateer Diomede - Ship type: P - How taken: HM Brig Sappho - When taken: 27 Feb 1814 - Where taken: at sea - Date received: 4 May 1814 - From what ship: Portsmouth - Born: New York - Age: 32 - Discharged on 25 Sep 1814 and sent to Dartmoor on HMS Niobe.

Dorr, Edward - Prize Master - Number: 685 - Prize name: Fame, prize of Privateer Decatur - Ship type: P - How taken: HM Ship-of-the-Line Polyphemus - When taken: 13 Sep 1812 - Where taken: at sea - Date received: 24 Feb 1813 - From what ship: Portsmouth via HMS Ulysses - Born: Salisbury, MA - Age: 29 - Discharged on 8 Jun 1813 and released to Cartel Rodrigo.

Dorrick, James - Seaman - Number: 897 - Prize name: John - Ship type: MV - How taken: HM Sloop Blossom - When taken: 15 Aug 1812 - Where taken: off Gibraltar - Date received: 1 Mar 1813 - From what ship: Plymouth via HMS Namur - Born: Newport, RI - Age: 29 - Discharged on 10 May 1813 and released to Cartel Admittance.

Dotto, Cornelius - Seaman - Number: 3260 - Prize name: Volante - Ship type: P - How taken: HM Brig Curlew - When taken: 25 Mar 1813 - Where taken: off Boston - Date received: 23 Feb 1814 - From what ship: Halifax via HMT Malabar - Born: Marblehead - Age: 21 - Discharged on 10 Oct 1814 and sent to Dartmoor on the Mermaid.

Douchney, Hiram - Seaman - Number: 864 - Prize name: Columbia - Ship type: MV - How taken: HM Frigate Briton - When taken: 17 Jan 1813 - Where taken: off Bordeaux, France - Date received: 1 Mar 1813 - From what ship: Plymouth via HMS Namur - Born: Bridgetown - Age: 24 - Discharged in Jul 1813 and released to Cartel Moses Brown.

Doud, John - Private - Number: 2637 - Prize name: 14th U.S. Infantry - Ship type: LF - How taken: British forces - When taken: 24 Jun 1813 - Where taken: Beaver Dams, Upper Canada - Date received: 5 Nov 1813 - From what ship: HMS Hindostan - Born: County Mayo, Ireland - Age: 52 - Discharged on 10 Oct 1814 and sent to U.S. on Cartel St. Philip.

Dougherty, Hamilton - Private - Number: 3122 - Prize name: 14th U.S. Infantry - Ship type: LF - How taken: British forces - When taken: 24 Jun 1813 - Where taken: Beaver Dams, Upper Canada - Date received: 7 Jan 1814 - From what ship: Halifax - Born: Virginia - Age: 27 - Died on 23 May 1814 from fever.

Douglas, Charles - Seaman - Number: 1244 - Prize name: Rossie - Ship type: MV - How taken: HM Frigate Dryand - When taken: 7 Jan 1813 - Where taken: at sea - Date received: 16 Mar 1813 - From what ship: Portsmouth, via HMS Abundance - Born: Virginia - Age: 24 - Discharged on 24 Jul 1813 and released to Cartel Hoffminy.

Douglas, Thomas - Cook - Number: 1003 - Prize name: Columbia - Ship type: MV - How taken: HM Frigate Briton - When taken: 15 Nov 1812 - Where taken: off Bordeaux, France - Date received: 10 Mar 1813 - From what ship: HMS Furious - Born: Newport - Age: 25 - Race: Black - Discharged on 2 Jul 1813 and released to Cartel Moses Brown.

Douglas, Thomas - Boy - Number: 1499 - Prize name: Union - Ship type: MV - How taken: HM Frigate Iris - When taken: 17 Jan 1813 - Where taken: at sea - Date received: 6 Apr 1813 - From what ship: Plymouth via an admiral's tender - Born: Alexandria - Age: 15 - Race: Negro - Discharged on 27 Jul 1813 and released to Cartel Hoffminy.

Douglass, John - Seaman - Number: 2291 - How taken: Gave himself up from HM Ship-of-the-Line Union - When taken: 15 Nov 1812 - Date received: 17 Sep 1813 - From what ship: HMS Raisonnable - Born: New London - Age: 22 - Discharged on 4 Sep 1814 and sent to Dartmoor on HMS Freya.

Douglass, Samuel - Seaman - Number: 3447 - Prize name: Elbridge Gerry - Ship type: P - How taken: HM Frigate Crescent - When taken: 16 Sep 1813 - Where taken: at sea - Date received: 23 Feb 1814 - From what ship: Halifax via HMT Malabar - Born: Cape Elizabeth - Age: 22 - Discharged on 22 Oct 1814 and sent to Dartmoor on HMS Leyden.

Douglass, William - Seaman - Number: 3600 - Prize name: Liberty - Ship type: MV - How taken: Surrendered at Stromness, Scotland - When taken: 30 Dec 1813 - Date received: 29 Mar 1814 - From what ship: Hired tender Anna - Born: Norway - Age: 18 - Discharged on 25 Sep 1814 and sent to Dartmoor on HMS Niobe.

Dow, Henry - Seaman - Number: 3270 - Prize name: Volante - Ship type: P - How taken: HM Brig Curlew - When taken: 25 Mar 1813 - Where taken: off Boston - Date received: 23 Feb 1814 - From what ship: Halifax via HMT Malabar - Born: Hampton - Age: 25 - Discharged on 10 Oct 1814 and sent to Dartmoor on the Mermaid.

Dow, John - Seaman - Number: 1444 - Prize name: Orbit - Ship type: MV - How taken: HM Brig Achates - When taken: 29 Jan 1813 - Where taken: Lat 49 N Long 13 W - Date received: 6 Apr 1813 - From what ship: Plymouth via HMS Decoy - Born: Massachsetts - Age: 22 - Died on 6 Jul 1813 from pneumonia.

Dowling, Anthony - Seaman - Number: 848 - Prize name: Rising Sun - Ship type: MV - How taken: HM Ship-Sloop Jalouse - When taken: 6 Dec 1812 - Where taken: at sea - Date received: 1 Mar 1813 - From what ship: Plymouth via HMS Namur - Born: New York - Age: 28 - Race: Blackman - Released on 20 May 1813 to Rising Sun.

Dowling, Peter - Seaman - Number: 504 - How taken: Gave himself up from HM Ship-of-the-Line Ruby - When taken: 15 Aug 1812 - Date received: 23 Feb 1813 - From what ship: Portsmouth via HMS Dromedary - Born: Wells Town, PA - Age: 24 - Discharged on 19 May 1813 and released to HMS Ceres.

Downey, John - Seaman - Number: 2944 - Prize name: Enterprise - Ship type: P - How taken: HM Frigate Tenedos - When taken: 21 May 1813 - Where taken: off Cape Cod - Date received: 7 Jan 1814 - From what ship: Halifax - Born: Salem - Age: 33 - Died on 27 Apr 1814 from fever.

Downing, Henry - Captain - Number: 1328 - Prize name: Sea Nymph - Ship type: MV - How taken: HM Brig Thrasher - When taken: 4 Mar 1813 - Where taken: off River Jade (Germany) - Date received: 22 Mar 1813 - From what ship: HMS Thrasher - Born: Newport - Age: 33 - Discharged on 3 Jun 1813 and sent to Reading on parole.

Downs, John - Boy - Number: 3510 - Prize name: Pilot - Ship type: LM - How taken: Vittoria, British privateer from Guernsey - When taken: 28 Jan 1814 - Where taken: off Bordeaux, France - Date received: 23 Feb 1814 - From what ship: Portsmouth via HMT Malabar - Born: Philadelphia - Age: 10 - Discharged on 8 Sep 1814 and sent to Dartmoor on HMS Niobe.

Downs, William - Boy - Number: 3509 - Prize name: Pilot - Ship type: LM - How taken: Vittoria, British privateer from Guernsey - When taken: 28 Jan 1814 - Where taken: off Bordeaux, France - Date received: 23 Feb 1814 - From what ship: Portsmouth via HMT Malabar - Born: Philadelphia - Age: 16 - Discharged on 26 Sep 1814 and sent to Dartmoor on HMS Leyden.

Doyle, John - Seaman - Number: 3217 - Prize name: Volunteer - Ship type: MV - How taken: Vittoria, British privateer from Guernsey - When taken: 26 Dec 1813 - Where taken: Bay of Biscay - Date received: 13 Jan 1814 - From what ship: Portsmouth via HMS Poictiers - Born: Staghen, Prussia - Age: 26 - Released on 6 Aug 1814.

Drake, Daniel - Seaman - Number: 3405 - Prize name: Elbridge Gerry - Ship type: P - How taken: HM Frigate Tenedos - When taken: 21 May 1813 - Where taken: off Cape Cod - Date received: 23 Feb 1814 - From what ship: Halifax via HMT Malabar - Born: Boothbay - Age: 17 - Discharged on 21 Jul 1814 and sent to Dartmoor on HMS Portia.

Drake, John - Seaman - Number: 1723 - Prize name: Powhattan - Ship type: MV - How taken: HMS Horatio - When taken: 13 Dec 1812 - Where taken: Bay of Biscay - Date received: 25 May 1813 - From what ship: Portsmouth via HMS Impetius - Born: Baltimore - Age: 35 - Discharged on 24 Jul 1813 and released to Cartel Hoffminy.

Drayton, John - Seaman - Number: 3930 - How taken: Gave himself up from HM Ship-of-the-Line Queen Charlotte - When taken: 23 Sep 1814 - Date received: 24 Sep 1814 - From what ship: HMS Namur - Born: Baltimore - Age: 23 - Race: Mulatto - Discharged on 29 Sep 1814 and sent to Dartmoor on HMS Freya.

Drew, Samuel - Seaman - Number: 16 - Prize name: Lucky - Ship type: MV - How taken: Detained at Hanoi Bay - When taken: 11 Aug 1812 - Date received: 29 Oct 1812 - From what ship: HMS Raisonnable - Born: Gilmanton, NH - Age: 26 - Discharged on 10 May 1813 and released to Cartel Admittance.

Drinkwater, Andrew - Seaman - Number: 655 - Prize name: U.S.R.M. Cutter James Madison - Ship type: War - How taken: HM Frigate Barbadoes - When taken: 22 Aug 1812 - Where taken: at sea - Date received: 24 Feb 1813 - From what ship: Portsmouth via HMS Ulysses - Born: North Yarmouth, MA - Age: 23 - Discharged on 10 May 1813 and released to Cartel Admittance.

Drisco, James - Seaman - Number: 3309 - Prize name: Governor Plumer - Ship type: P - How taken: HM Brig Bold - When taken: 17 May 1813 - Date received: 23 Feb 1814 - From what ship: Halifax via HMT Malabar - Born: Portsmouth - Age: 15 - Discharged on 10 Oct 1814 and sent to Dartmoor on the Mermaid.

Driscol, Jeremiah - Seaman - Number: 2506 - Prize name: Thomas - Ship type: P - How taken: HM Frigate Nymphe - When taken: 28 Jun 1813 - Where taken: off Halifax - Date received: 22 Oct 1813 - From what ship: Portsmouth via HMT Malabar - Born: Portsmouth - Age: 29 - Discharged on 8 Sep 1814 and sent to Dartmoor on HMS Niobe.

Driver, Thomas - Seaman - Number: 1693 - Prize name: Governor Middleton - Ship type: MV - How taken: Thetis, British privateer - When taken: 2 May 1813 - Where taken: Bay of Biscay - Date received: 15 May 1813 - From what ship: HMS Viper - Born: Philadelphia - Age: 20 - Discharged on 24 Jul 1814 and sent to Dartmoor on HMS Liffey.

Drummond, John - Private - Number: 3051 - Prize name: U.S. Light Dragoons - Ship type: LF - How taken: British forces - When taken: 24 Jun 1813 - Where taken: Beaver Dams, Upper Canada - Date received: 7 Jan 1814 - From what ship: Halifax - Born: Delaware - Age: 25 - Discharged on 10 Oct 1814 and sent to U.S. on Cartel St. Philip.

Drybourgh, James - 2nd Mate - Number: 932 - Prize name: Argus - Ship type: MV - How taken: HM Cutter Fancy - When taken: 17 Dec 1812 - Where taken: Bay of Biscay - Date received: 10 Mar 1813 - From what ship: HMS Tigress - Born: Philadelphia - Age: 31 - Discharged on 2 Jul 1813 and released to Cartel Moses Brown.

Ducat, William - Seaman - Number: 2937 - Prize name: Governor Plumer - Ship type: P - How taken: HM Brig Shamrock - When taken: 26 May 1813 - Where taken: at sea - Date received: 7 Jan 1814 - From what ship: Halifax - Born: New Jersey - Age: 31 - Discharged on 25 Sep 1814 and sent to Dartmoor on HMS Leyden.

Dudes, J. B. - Seaman - Number: 3324 - Prize name: Porcupine - Ship type: LM - How taken: HM Frigate Acasta - When taken: 18 Jul 1813 - Where taken: off Cape Sable, Florida - Date received: 23 Feb 1814 - From what ship: Halifax via HMT Malabar - Born: Bayonne - Age: 21 - Discharged on 22 Jun 1814 and sent to Calais, France on the Simon & Mary.

Dudley, Ephraim - Marine Sergeant - Number: 1173 - Prize name: Sword Fish - Ship type: P - How taken: HM Ship-of-the-Line Elephant - When taken: 28 Dec 1812 - Where taken: off Azores - Date received: 16 Mar 1813 - From what ship: Portsmouth, via HMS Abundance - Born: East Sudbury - Age: 25 - Discharged on 24 Jul 1813 and released to Cartel Hoffminy.

Duffy, Nathaniel - Seaman - Number: 1407 - Prize name: Porcupine - Ship type: MV - How taken: HM Frigate Dryand - When taken: 8 Jan 1813 - Where taken: off Bordeaux, France - Date received: 5 Apr 1813 - From what ship: Plymouth via HMS Dwarf - Born: Pawtucket - Age: 21 - Discharged on 24 Jul 1813 and released to Cartel Hoffminy.

Duganeu, Charles - Private - Number: 3106 - Prize name: 14th U.S. Infantry - Ship type: LF - How taken: British forces - When taken: 24 Jun 1813 - Where taken: Beaver Dams, Upper Canada - Date received: 7 Jan 1814 - From what ship: Halifax - Born: Paris - Age: 36 - Discharged on 10 Oct 1814 and sent to U.S. on Cartel St. Philip.

Duhard, Thomas - 3rd Mate - Number: 1247 - Prize name: Rossie - Ship type: MV - How taken: HM Frigate Dryand - When taken: 7 Jan 1813 - Where taken: at sea - Date received: 16 Mar 1813 - From what ship: Portsmouth, via HMS Abundance - Born: Baltimore - Age: 21 - Discharged on 24 Jul 1813 and released to Cartel Hoffminy.

Dullivan, James - Seaman - Number: 3428 - Prize name: Industry - Ship type: P - How taken: HM Frigate Maidstone - When taken: 18 Jul 1813 - Where taken: Grand Banks - Date received: 23 Feb 1814 - From what ship: Halifax via HMT Malabar - Born: Marblehead - Age: 18 - Discharged on 22 Oct 1814 and sent to Dartmoor on HMS Leyden.

Duncan, Edward - Seaman - Number: 2356 - How taken: Gave himself up from HM Ship-of-the-Line Hibernia - When taken: 25 Jun 1813 - Date received: 20 Oct 1813 - From what ship: Portsmouth, via an admiral's tender - Born: Rhode Island - Age: 38 - Race: Mulatto - Discharged on 4 Sep 1814 and sent to Dartmoor on HMS Freya.

Duncan, George - Seaman - Number: 3526 - How taken: Impressed at London - When taken: 25 Feb 1814 - Date received: 26 Feb 1814 - From what ship: HMS Raisonnable - Born: Benedict, MD - Age: 28 - Race: Black - Discharged on 21 Jul 1814 and sent to Dartmoor on HMS Portia.

Duncan, Thomas - Seaman - Number: 2955 - Prize name: Enterprise - Ship type: P - How taken: HM Frigate Tenedos - When taken: 21 May 1813 - Where taken: off Cape Cod - Date received: 7 Jan 1814 - From what ship: Halifax - Born: Massachusetts - Age: 19 - Discharged on 25 Sep 1814 and sent to Dartmoor on HMS Leyden.

Dunchellier, Isaac - Seaman - Number: 2017 - Prize name: Eliza - Ship type: MV - How taken: HM Frigate Surveillante - When taken: 27 Apr 1813 - Where taken: Bay of Biscay - Date received: 15 Jul 1813 - From what ship: Plymouth - Born: Boston - Age: 21 - Discharged on 17 Jun 1814 and sent to Dartmoor on HMS Pincher.

Dunham, David - Seaman - Number: 2314 - Prize name: Fame - Ship type: MV - How taken: HM Ship of-the-Line Cressy - When taken: 20 Jul 1813 - Where taken: at sea - Date received: 8 Oct 1813 - From what ship: Portsmouth, via an admiral's tender - Born: Massachusetts - Age: 27 - Discharged on 4 Sep 1814 and sent to Dartmoor on HMS Freya.

Dunham, Joseph - Seaman - Number: 2550 - How taken: Gave himself up from HM Brig Scorpion - When taken: 2 Dec 1812 - Date received: 23 Oct 1813 - From what ship: Portsmouth via HMS Raisonnable - Born: Massachusetts - Age: 20 - Discharged on 8 Sep 1814 and sent to Dartmoor on HMS Niobe.

Dunn, David - Seaman - Number: 1912 - Prize name: Weasel - Ship type: MV - How taken: HM Brig Foxhound - When taken: 25 Mar 1813 - Where taken: Bay of Biscay - Date received: 7 Jul 1813 - From what ship: Portsmouth via HMS Tribune - Born: New York - Age: 27 - Discharged on 4 Aug 1814 and sent to Dartmoor on HMS Liverpool.

Dunn, Henry G. - Seaman - Number: 740 - Prize name: Emeline - Ship type: MV - How taken: Apprehended at London - When taken: 10 Feb 1813 - Date received: 25 Feb 1813 - From what ship: HMS Raisonnable - Born: Tappahannock - Age: 27 - Discharged on 25 Jul 1814 and sent to Dartmoor on HMS Raven.

Dunn, Hezekiah - Seaman - Number: 931 - Prize name: Experiment - Ship type: MV - How taken: HM Brig Rover - When taken: 10 Nov 1812 - Where taken: off Bordeaux, France - Date received: 10 Mar 1813 - From what ship: HMS Tigress - Born: Maryland - Age: 24 - Discharged on 8 Jun 1813 and released to Cartel Rodrigo.

Dunn, James - Seaman - Number: 2161 - How taken: Gave himself up from HM Frigate Unicorn - When taken: 17 Jun 1813 - Date received: 16 Aug 1813 - From what ship: Portsmouth, via an admiral's tender - Born: Boston - Age: 30 - Race: Mulatto - Discharged on 17 Jun 1814 and sent to Dartmoor on the Penebar.

Dunn, Thomas - Seaman - Number: 2232 - Prize name: Ann - Ship type: MV - How taken: Impressed at London - When taken: 1 Aug 1813 - Date received: 29 Aug 1813 - From what ship: HMS Raisonnable - Born: New

York - Age: 19 - Discharged on 17 Jun 1814 and sent to Dartmoor on the Penebar.

Dunningberg, Henry - Seaman - Number: 3007 - Prize name: Yankee - Ship type: P - How taken: HM Frigate Shannon - When taken: 20 Aug 1813 - Where taken: at sea - Date received: 7 Jan 1814 - From what ship: Halifax - Born: Maryland - Age: 25 - Discharged on 25 Sep 1814 and sent to Dartmoor on HMS Leyden.

Dunstan, John - Seaman - Number: 1255 - How taken: Gave himself up from HM Transport Diadem - When taken: 28 Oct 1812 - Date received: 16 Mar 1813 - From what ship: Portsmouth, via HMS Abundance - Born: Baltimore - Age: 23 - Released on 17 Jul 1814.

Dupre, John - Seaman - Number: 3274 - Prize name: Volante - Ship type: P - How taken: HM Brig Curlew - When taken: 25 Mar 1813 - Where taken: off Boston - Date received: 23 Feb 1814 - From what ship: Halifax via HMT Malabar - Born: Bordeaux, France - Age: 19 - Discharged on 22 Jun 1814 and sent to Calais, France on the Simon & Mary.

Durant, John - Seaman - Number: 31 - Prize name: Arial - Ship type: MV - How taken: HM Brig Recruit - When taken: 2 Jun 1812 - Where taken: coast of America - Date received: 3 Nov 1812 - From what ship: HMS Plover - Born: Martha's Vineyard, MA - Age: 35 - Discharged on 23 Mar 1813 and released to the Cartel Robinson Potter.

Durham, Charles - Seaman - Number: 1955 - Prize name: Ferox - Ship type: MV - How taken: HM Frigate Medusa & HM Brig Lyra - When taken: 28 Mar 1813 - Where taken: off Cape Ortegal, Spain - Date received: 15 Jul 1813 - From what ship: Plymouth - Born: New York - Age: 37 - Discharged on 17 Jun 1814 and sent to Dartmoor on HMS Redbreast.

Dussing, Caesar - Seaman - Number: 642 - Prize name: Purse - Ship type: MV - How taken: HM Frigate Armide - When taken: 20 May 1812 - Where taken: off Bordeaux, France - Date received: 24 Feb 1813 - From what ship: Portsmouth via HMS Ulysses - Born: Isle of France - Age: 19 - Discharged on 17 Nov 1813 to the Cartel Robinson Potter.

Duvall, N. D. - Seaman - Number: 2343 - Prize name: Hindostan - Ship type: MV - How taken: HM Brig Zenobia - When taken: 25 Jun 1813 - Where taken: off Lisbon - Date received: 20 Oct 1813 - From what ship: Portsmouth, via an admiral's tender - Born: Maryland - Age: 23 - Discharged on 4 Sep 1814 and sent to Dartmoor on HMS Freya.

Dyer, Ezekiel - Seaman - Number: 527 - Prize name: Diamond - Ship type: MV - How taken: Detained at Bermuda - When taken: 17 Sep 1812 - Date received: 23 Feb 1813 - From what ship: Portsmouth via HMS Dromedary - Born: Cape Elizabeth - Age: 43 - Discharged on 23 Mar 1813 and released to the Cartel Robinson Potter.

Dyer, Thomas - Seaman - Number: 3883 - Prize name: Derby - Ship type: MV - How taken: HM Frigate Nereus - When taken: 16 Feb 1813 - Where taken: off Cape of Good Hope - Date received: 28 Aug 1814 - From what ship: London - Born: Boston - Age: 23 - Discharged on 8 Sep 1814 and sent to Dartmoor on HMS Niobe.

Eagerly, Elijah - Seaman - Number: 3452 - Prize name: Elbridge Gerry - Ship type: P - How taken: HM Frigate Crescent - When taken: 16 Sep 1813 - Where taken: at sea - Date received: 23 Feb 1814 - From what ship: Halifax via HMT Malabar - Born: Portland - Age: 22 - Discharged on 22 Oct 1814 and sent to Dartmoor on HMS Leyden.

Eagin, John - Private - Number: 2607 - Prize name: U.S. Light Artillery - Ship type: LF - How taken: British forces - When taken: 1 Jun 1813 - Where taken: Upper Canada - Date received: 5 Nov 1813 - From what ship: HMS Hindostan - Born: County Kilkenny, Ireland - Age: 28 - Discharged on 17 Jun 1814 and sent to Dartmoor.

Earl, Maris - Seaman - Number: 1200 - Prize name: Expectation - Ship type: MV - How taken: HM Frigate Briton - When taken: 17 Dec 1812 - Where taken: at sea - Date received: 16 Mar 1813 - From what ship: Portsmouth, via HMS Abundance - Born: New York - Age: 27 - Discharged on 2 Jul 1813 and released to Cartel Moses Brown.

Ears, Ludwig - Cook - Number: 1713 - Prize name: Decatur - Ship type: MV - How taken: HM Frigate Desiree - When taken: 7 May 1813 - Where taken: off Nantes, France - Date received: 25 May 1813 - From what ship: Portsmouth via HMS Impetius - Born: Seaqaund, Prussia - Age: 29 - Released on 20 Jul 1813.

Eastlake, James - Seaman - Number: 2213 - Prize name: Jane, prize of the Privateer Snap Dragon - Ship type: P - How taken: HM Frigate Crescent & HM Ship of-the-Line Bellerophon - When taken: 28 Jun 1813 - Where taken: Newfoundland Bank - Date received: 18 Aug 1813 - From what ship: Portsmouth, via an admiral's tender - Born: North Carolina - Age: 21 - Discharged on 11 Aug 1814 and sent to Dartmoor on HMS Freya.

Eaton, Benjamin - Seaman - Number: 88 - Prize name: Calaban - Ship type: MV - How taken: HM Battery Gorgon - When taken: 12 Aug 1812 - Where taken: Great Belt, Denmark - Date received: 4 Nov 1812 - From what ship: HMS Namur - Born: Seabrook, NH - Age: 27 - Discharged on 10 May 1813 and released to Cartel Admittance.

Eaton, Israel - Lieutenant - Number: 2798 - Prize name: Industry - Ship type: P - How taken: HM Brig Heron - When taken: 3 Nov 1813 - Where taken: off Halifax - Date received: 7 Jan 1814 - From what ship: Halifax - Born: Marblehead - Age: 37 - Discharged on 8 Sep 1814 and sent to Dartmoor on HMS Niobe.

Eaton, James - Seaman - Number: 1854 - How taken: Gave himself up from HM Ship-of-the-Line Malta - Date received: 7 Jul 1813 - From what ship: Portsmouth via HMS Tribune - Born: Philadelphia - Age: 26 - Discharged on 15 Sep 1813 and released to HMS Ceres.

Eaton, John - Seaman - Number: 1224 - Prize name: Rossie - Ship type: MV - How taken: HM Frigate Dryand - When taken: 7 Jan 1813 - Where taken: at sea - Date received: 16 Mar 1813 - From what ship: Portsmouth, via HMS Abundance - Born: Baltimore - Age: 25 - Discharged on 24 Jul 1813 and released to Cartel Hoffminy.

Eaton, Joseph - Seaman - Number: 3173 - Prize name: Wolf Cove - Ship type: MV - How taken: HM Frigate Briton - When taken: 1 Dec 1813 - Where taken: off Brest, France - Date received: 7 Jan 1814 - From what ship: Halifax - Born: Massachusetts - Age: 20 - Discharged on 25 Sep 1814 and sent to Dartmoor on HMS Leyden.

Eccleston, Gardner - Seaman - Number: 371 - Prize name: Henry - Ship type: MV - How taken: Impressed at Gravesend, England - When taken: 24 Dec 1812 - Date received: 21 Jan 1813 - From what ship: HMS Raisonnable - Born: Connecticut - Age: 29 - Discharged on 24 Jul 1813 and released to Cartel Hoffminy.

Eddy, Richard - Seaman - Number: 2529 - Prize name: Yorktown - Ship type: P - How taken: HM Brig Nimrod - When taken: 17 Jul 1813 - Where taken: Grand Banks - Date received: 22 Oct 1813 - From what ship: Portsmouth via HMT Malabar - Born: Freetown - Age: 31 - Discharged on 8 Sep 1814 and sent to Dartmoor on HMS Niobe.

Edgerly, William - Seaman - Number: 2009 - How taken: Gave himself up from HM Ship-of-the-Line Royal Sovereign - Date received: 15 Jul 1813 - From what ship: Plymouth - Born: Portsmouth - Age: 22 - Escaped on 16 May 1814 from the HM Prison Ship Crown Prince.

Edmond, John - Seaman - Number: 3425 - Prize name: Wasp - Ship type: P - How taken: HM Schooner Bream - When taken: 9 Jun 1813 - Where taken: off Halifax - Date received: 23 Feb 1814 - From what ship: Halifax via HMT Malabar - Born: Newbury - Age: 18 - Discharged on 22 Oct 1814 and sent to Dartmoor on HMS Leyden.

Edmunds, Francis - Seaman - Number: 364 - Prize name: Namur - Ship type: MV - How taken: Gave himself up at Nore, England - When taken: 2 Jan 1813 - Date received: 21 Jan 1813 - From what ship: HMS Raisonnable - Born: Virginia - Age: 41 - Discharged on 26 Jul 1814 and sent to Dartmoor on HMS Raven.

Edwards, Isaac - Seaman - Number: 1660 - How taken: Gave himself up from HM Ship-of-the-Line Scepter - Date received: 9 May 1813 - From what ship: HMS Raisonnable - Born: Gorham, MA - Age: 34 - Discharged on 13 Aug 1814 and sent to Dartmoor.

Edwards, John - Seaman - Number: 3774 - Prize name: Argus - Ship type: MV - How taken: HM Ship-of-the-Line San Domingo - When taken: 1 Mar 1814 - Where taken: off Savannah - Date received: 26 May 1814 - From what ship: HMS Hindostan - Born: New York - Age: 35 - Race: Black - Discharged on 25 Sep 1814 and sent to Dartmoor on HMS Niobe.

Edwards, John - Seaman - Number: 1523 - How taken: Gave himself up from HM Frigate Brune - When taken: 19 Jan 1813 - Date received: 8 Apr 1813 - From what ship: Portsmouth, via an admiral's tender - Born: Norfolk - Age: 34 - Race: Black - Discharged on 29 Jun 1813 and released to HMS Ceres.

Edwards, Price - Seaman - Number: 228 - How taken: Apprehended at London - When taken: 12 Nov 1812 - Date received: 25 Nov 1812 - From what ship: HMS Raisonnable - Born: New York - Age: 25 - Discharged in Jul

1813 and released to Cartel Moses Brown.

Edwards, Thomas - Seaman - Number: 3701 - How taken: Gave himself up from the Earl Falk - When taken: 9 May 1814 - Date received: 10 May 1814 - From what ship: Eagle - Born: Charlestown - Age: 47 - Race: Black - Discharged on 22 Oct 1814 and sent to Dartmoor on HMS Leyden.

Edwards, William - Seaman - Number: 3537 - Prize name: Commodore Perry - Ship type: MV - How taken: Sent into custody from a cutter - When taken: 25 Feb 1814 - Where taken: off Bordeaux, France - Date received: 5 Mar 1814 - From what ship: HMS Raisonnable - Born: Sussex, MA - Age: 23 - Discharged on 26 Sep 1814 and sent to Dartmoor on HMS Leyden.

Elburn, John (alias Allen) - Seaman - Number: 3004 - Prize name: Yankee - Ship type: P - How taken: HM Frigate Shannon - When taken: 20 Aug 1813 - Where taken: at sea - Date received: 7 Jan 1814 - From what ship: Halifax - Born: New Orleans - Age: 22 - Released on 6 Aug 1814.

Eldridge, Nicholas - Seaman - Number: 1978 - How taken: Gave himself up from HM Ship-of-the-Line Malta - Date received: 15 Jul 1813 - From what ship: Plymouth - Born: Massachsetts - Age: 32 - Discharged on 25 Sep 1814 and sent to Dartmoor on HMS Leyden.

Eldridge, Samuel - Seaman - Number: 718 - Prize name: James - Ship type: MV - How taken: Detained at Portsmouth harbor - When taken: 31 Jul 1812 - Date received: 24 Feb 1813 - From what ship: Portsmouth via HMS Ulysses - Born: Lyman, MA - Age: 22 - Discharged on 23 Mar 1813 and released to the Cartel Robinson Potter.

Eldridge, William - Seaman - Number: 2294 - Prize name: Juliana Smith - Ship type: P - How taken: HM Frigate Nymphe - When taken: 12 May 1813 - Where taken: off Cape Sable, Florida - Date received: 20 Sep 1813 - From what ship: HMS Raisonnable - Born: Harwich - Age: 25 - Discharged on 4 Sep 1814 and sent to Dartmoor on HMS Freya.

Elfe, James - Boy - Number: 2346 - Prize name: Hindostan - Ship type: MV - How taken: HM Brig Zenobia - When taken: 25 Jun 1813 - Where taken: off Lisbon - Date received: 20 Oct 1813 - From what ship: Portsmouth, via an admiral's tender - Born: Charlestown - Age: 15 - Discharged on 4 Sep 1814 and sent to Dartmoor on HMS Freya.

Elisha, Thomas - Seaman - Number: 1808 - How taken: Impressed at London - When taken: 28 Jun 1813 - Date received: 3 Jul 1813 - From what ship: HMS Raisonnable - Born: Baltimore - Age: 27 - Discharged on 25 Jul 1814 and sent to Dartmoor on HMS Bittern.

Ellen, Nathaniel - Seaman - Number: 95 - Prize name: Eliza Ann - Ship type: MV - How taken: HM Ship-of-the-Line Vigo - When taken: 11 Aug 1812 - Where taken: Hanoi Bay - Date received: 4 Nov 1812 - From what ship: HMS Namur - Born: Massachusetts - Age: 22 - Discharged on 10 May 1813 and released to Cartel Admittance.

Ellingwood, William H. - Seaman - Number: 3193 - Prize name: Growler - Ship type: P - How taken: HM Brig Electra - When taken: 7 Jul 1813 - Where taken: off St. Johns - Date received: 7 Jan 1813 - From what ship: Portsmouth - Born: Massachusetts - Age: 28 - Died on 18 May 1814 from fever.

Elliott, Andrew - Seaman - Number: 3393 - Prize name: Fox - Ship type: P - How taken: HM Frigate Maidstone - When taken: 18 Jul 1813 - Where taken: Grand Banks - Date received: 23 Feb 1814 - From what ship: Halifax via HMT Malabar - Born: Portsmouth - Age: 25 - Discharged on 22 Oct 1814 and sent to Dartmoor on HMS Leyden.

Elliott, Francis - Seaman - Number: 1469 - Prize name: Union - Ship type: MV - How taken: HM Frigate Iris - When taken: 17 Jan 1813 - Where taken: at sea - Date received: 6 Apr 1813 - From what ship: Portsmouth via Tender Eliza - Born: Philadelphia - Age: 25 - Discharged on 26 Jul 1813 and released to Cartel Hoffminy.

Elliott, Robert - Seaman - Number: 2074 - How taken: Gave himself up from HM Ship-of-the-Line Armada - When taken: 8 Jun 1813 - Date received: 9 Aug 1813 - From what ship: HMS Thames - Born: Massachsetts - Age: 44 - Discharged on 4 Aug 1814 and sent to Dartmoor on HMS Liverpool.

Ellis, Cornelius - Seaman - Number: 3902 - How taken: Gave himself up from the MV Blenheim - When taken: 28 Aug 1814 - Date received: 31 Aug 1814 - From what ship: Transport Office - Born: Middleboro - Age: 26 -

Discharged on 25 Sep 1814 and sent to Dartmoor on HMS Leyden.

Ellis, John - Boatswain - Number: 20 - Prize name: Navigator - Ship type: MV - How taken: HM Ship-of-the-Line Cressy - When taken: 11 Aug 1812 - Where taken: Baltic - Date received: 29 Oct 1812 - From what ship: HMS Raisonnable - Born: Maryland - Age: 23 - Discharged on 19 Mar 1813 and released to the Navigator.

Ellis, John - Seaman - Number: 927 - Prize name: Experiment - Ship type: MV - How taken: HM Brig Rover - When taken: 10 Nov 1812 - Where taken: off Bordeaux, France - Date received: 10 Mar 1813 - From what ship: HMS Tigress - Born: New York - Age: 21 - Discharged on 8 Jun 1813 and released to Cartel Rodrigo.

Ellis, John - Seaman - Number: 648 - Prize name: U.S.R.M. Cutter James Madison - Ship type: War - How taken: HM Frigate Barbadoes - When taken: 22 Aug 1812 - Where taken: at sea - Date received: 24 Feb 1813 - From what ship: Portsmouth via HMS Ulysses - Born: Copstown, MD - Age: 33 - Discharged on 10 May 1813 and released to Cartel Admittance.

Ellis, John - Seaman - Number: 3426 - Prize name: Industry - Ship type: P - How taken: HM Frigate Maidstone - When taken: 18 Jul 1813 - Where taken: Grand Banks - Date received: 23 Feb 1814 - From what ship: Halifax via HMT Malabar - Born: Topson - Age: 17 - Discharged on 22 Oct 1814 and sent to Dartmoor on HMS Leyden.

Ellis, William - Seaman - Number: 1223 - Prize name: Rossie - Ship type: MV - How taken: HM Frigate Dryand - When taken: 7 Jan 1813 - Where taken: at sea - Date received: 16 Mar 1813 - From what ship: Portsmouth, via HMS Abundance - Born: Baltimore - Age: 15 - Discharged on 24 Jul 1813 and released to Cartel Hoffminy.

Ellwell, Jonathan - Seaman - Number: 1139 - Prize name: Sword Fish - Ship type: P - How taken: HM Ship-of-the-Line Elephant - When taken: 28 Dec 1812 - Where taken: off Azores - Date received: 16 Mar 1813 - From what ship: Portsmouth, Mundane - Born: St. George - Age: 28 - Discharged on 24 Jul 1813 and released to Cartel Hoffminy.

Elsworth, John - Private - Number: 3161 - Prize name: 14th U.S. Infantry - Ship type: LF - How taken: British forces - When taken: 24 Jun 1813 - Where taken: Beaver Dams, Upper Canada - Date received: 7 Jan 1814 - From what ship: Halifax - Born: Philadelphia - Age: 22 - Died on 6 May 1814 from fever.

Elvyn, Laurence - Seaman - Number: 3815 - How taken: Gave himself up from Chatham - When taken: 23 Jun 1814 - Date received: 23 Jun 1814 - From what ship: Chatham - Born: Boston - Age: 18 - Discharged on 22 Oct 1814 and sent to Dartmoor on HMS Leyden.

Elwell, Abraham - Seaman - Number: 354 - Prize name: Postsea, prize to the Privateer Thrasher - Ship type: P - How taken: HM Sloop Helena - When taken: 31 Dec 1813 - Where taken: off Azores - Date received: 19 Jan 1813 - From what ship: HMS Raisonnable - Born: Cape Ann - Age: 24 - Discharged on 24 Jul 1813 and released to Cartel Hoffminy.

Elwell, James - Seaman - Number: 295 - Prize name: America - Ship type: MV - How taken: HM Brig Cracker - When taken: 1 Aug 1812 - Date received: 23 Dec 1812 - From what ship: Greenlaw Depot - Born: Gloucester, VA - Age: 27 - Discharged on 23 Mar 1813 and released to the Cartel Robinson Potter.

Ely, Abraham - Seaman - Number: 2282 - How taken: Impressed at London - When taken: 8 Sep 1813 - Date received: 17 Sep 1813 - From what ship: HMS Raisonnable - Born: Baltimore - Age: 29 - Discharged on 4 Sep 1814 and sent to Dartmoor on HMS Freya.

Emerson, David - Marine Private - Number: 2716 - Prize name: Growler - Ship type: P - How taken: HM Brig Electra - When taken: 7 Jul 1813 - Where taken: off St. Johns - Date received: 7 Jan 1814 - From what ship: Portsmouth - Born: Massachusetts - Age: 22 - Discharged on 25 Sep 1814 and sent to Dartmoor on HMS Leyden.

Emlin, Edward - Seaman - Number: 234 - How taken: Apprehended at London - When taken: 13 Nov 1812 - Date received: 25 Nov 1812 - From what ship: HMS Raisonnable - Born: Brunswick, NJ - Age: 51 - Discharged in Jul 1813 and released to Cartel Moses Brown.

Emming, Thomas - Seaman - Number: 2076 - How taken: Gave himself up from HM Ship-of-the-Line Armada - When taken: 8 Jun 1813 - Date received: 9 Aug 1813 - From what ship: HMS Thames - Born: New York - Age: 42 - Race: Black - Discharged on 4 Aug 1814 and sent to Dartmoor on HMS Liverpool.

Endersen, James - Seaman - Number: 1964 - How taken: Gave himself up at Greenock, Scotland - When taken: 23 Jan 1813 - Date received: 15 Jul 1813 - From what ship: Plymouth - Born: New York - Age: 29 - Discharged on 17 Jun 1814 and sent to Dartmoor on HMS Redbreast.

English, James - Seaman - Number: 12 - Prize name: Eliza Ann - Ship type: MV - How taken: HM Ship-of-the-Line Vigo - When taken: 11 Aug 1812 - Where taken: Hanoi Bay - Date received: 29 Oct 1812 - From what ship: HMS Raisonnable - Born: New Jersey - Age: 24 - Discharged on 10 May 1813 and released to Cartel Admittance.

Erskine, George - Seaman - Number: 178 - How taken: Stopped at London - When taken: 28 Oct 1812 - Date received: 5 Nov 1812 - From what ship: HMS Namur - Born: Wiscasset, MA - Age: 49 - Discharged in Jul 1813 and released to Cartel Moses Brown.

Esperaza, Jacob - Seaman - Number: 1207 - Prize name: Expectation - Ship type: MV - How taken: HM Frigate Briton - When taken: 17 Dec 1812 - Where taken: at sea - Date received: 16 Mar 1813 - From what ship: Portsmouth, via HMS Abundance - Born: Virginia - Age: 34 - Discharged on 2 Jul 1813 and released to Cartel Moses Brown.

Estey, William - Seaman - Number: 1848 - How taken: Given up from HMS Horatio - Date received: 7 Jul 1813 - From what ship: Portsmouth via HMS Tribune - Born: New Jersey - Age: 22 - Discharged on 25 Jul 1814 and sent to Dartmoor on HMS Bittern.

Euston, Ephraim - Seaman - Number: 2715 - Prize name: Growler - Ship type: P - How taken: HM Brig Electra - When taken: 7 Jul 1813 - Where taken: off St. Johns - Date received: 7 Jan 1814 - From what ship: Portsmouth - Born: Massachusetts - Age: 20 - Discharged on 25 Sep 1814 and sent to Dartmoor on HMS Leyden.

Evans, Hale - Seaman - Number: 1412 - Prize name: Porcupine - Ship type: MV - How taken: HM Frigate Dryand - When taken: 8 Jan 1813 - Where taken: off Bordeaux, France - Date received: 5 Apr 1813 - From what ship: Plymouth via HMS Dwarf - Born: Nottingham - Age: 22 - Discharged on 24 Jul 1813 and released to Cartel Hoffminy.

Evans, Hezekiel - Seaman - Number: 3895 - How taken: Gave himself up from Progress - When taken: 15 Aug 1813 - Date received: 30 Aug 1814 - From what ship: Transport Office - Born: Newport - Age: 30 - Discharged on 2 Sep 1814 and sent to Dartmoor on HMS Leyden.

Evans, James - Private - Number: 3817 - How taken: Gave himself up from Chatham - When taken: 30 Jun 1814 - Date received: 30 Jun 1814 - From what ship: Chatham - Born: Western Ireland - Age: 50 - Discharged on 10 Oct 1814 and sent to U.S. on Cartel St. Philip.

Evans, James - Private - Number: 2647 - Prize name: 23rd U.S. Infantry - Ship type: LF - How taken: British forces - When taken: 6 Jun 1813 - Where taken: Stoney Creek, Upper Canada - Date received: 5 Nov 1813 - From what ship: HMS Hindostan - Born: Western Ireland - Age: 49 - Discharged on 17 Jun 1814 and sent to Dartmoor.

Evans, James - Seaman - Number: 2006 - How taken: Gave himself up from HM Brig Foxhound - Date received: 15 Jul 1813 - From what ship: Plymouth - Born: Charlestown - Age: 30 - Discharged on 17 Jun 1814 and sent to Dartmoor on HMS Pincher.

Evans, John - Seaman - Number: 225 - How taken: Apprehended at London - When taken: 9 Nov 1812 - Date received: 25 Nov 1812 - From what ship: HMS Raisonnable - Born: Portland, MA - Age: 30 - Discharged in Jul 1813 and released to Cartel Moses Brown.

Evans, John - Captain - Number: 1181 - Prize name: Sword Fish - Ship type: P - How taken: HM Ship-of-the-Line Elephant - When taken: 28 Dec 1812 - Where taken: off Azores - Date received: 16 Mar 1813 - From what ship: Portsmouth, via HMS Abundance - Born: Gloucester - Age: 29 - Discharged on 10 May 1813 and released to Cartel Admittance.

Evans, John - Seaman - Number: 603 - How taken: Taken up at Liverpool - When taken: 10 Dec 1812 - Date received: 23 Feb 1813 - From what ship: Portsmouth via HMS Dromedary - Born: Norfolk - Age: 28 - Discharged on 2 Jul 1813 and released to Cartel Moses Brown.

Evans, John - Seaman - Number: 2846 - Prize name: Blockade - Ship type: P - How taken: HM Brig Recruit - When taken: 17 Aug 1813 - Where taken: coast of America - Date received: 7 Jan 1814 - From what ship: Halifax - Born: Somerset - Age: 20 - Died on 5 Mar 1814 from small pox.

Evans, Jonathan - Sailmaker - Number: 162 - Prize name: Galen - Ship type: MV - How taken: HM Battery Gorgon - When taken: 12 Aug 1812 - Where taken: Great Belt, Denmark - Date received: 5 Nov 1812 - From what ship: HMS Namur - Born: Philadelphia - Age: 25 - Discharged on 10 May 1813 and released to Cartel Admittance.

Evans, Robert - Seaman - Number: 400 - Prize name: Maria - Ship type: MV - How taken: HM Brig Papillon - When taken: 25 Nov 1812 - Where taken: off Cadiz, Spain - Date received: 13 Feb 1813 - From what ship: HMS Raisonnable - Born: West Town Chester - Age: 39 - Discharged on 8 Jun 1813 and released to Cartel Rodrigo.

Evans, Thomas - Seaman - Number: 993 - Prize name: Rising - Ship type: MV - How taken: HM Ship-Sloop Jalouse - When taken: 6 Dec 1812 - Where taken: at sea - Date received: 10 Mar 1813 - From what ship: HMS Tigress - Born: Ryswick - Age: 33 - Released on 20 Mar 1813 to the Rising Sun.

Evans, Williams - Seaman - Number: 3861 - Prize name: James - Ship type: MV - How taken: HM Brig Harpy - When taken: 18 Dec 1812 - Where taken: off Isle de France (Mauritius) - Date received: 24 Aug 1814 - From what ship: London - Born: Baltimore - Age: 40 - Discharged on 22 Oct 1814 and sent to Dartmoor on HMS Leyden.

Even, Peter - Seaman - Number: 647 - Prize name: U.S.R.M. Cutter James Madison - Ship type: War - How taken: HM Frigate Barbadoes - When taken: 22 Aug 1812 - Where taken: at sea - Date received: 24 Feb 1813 - From what ship: Portsmouth via HMS Ulysses - Born: Nantes, France - Age: 45 - Discharged on 10 May 1813 and released to Cartel Admittance.

Evert, John (alias Evard) - Seaman - Number: 2542 - Prize name: Yorktown - Ship type: P - How taken: HM Brig Nimrod - When taken: 17 Jul 1813 - Where taken: Grand Banks - Date received: 22 Oct 1813 - From what ship: Portsmouth via HMT Malabar - Born: New York - Age: 26 - Discharged on 8 Sep 1814 and sent to Dartmoor on HMS Niobe.

Ewell, Edward - Seaman - Number: 3591 - Prize name: Devon, prize to the Privateer Bunker Hill - Ship type: P - How taken: HM Brig Fly - When taken: 21 Jan 1814 - Where taken: at sea - Date received: 26 Mar 1814 - From what ship: Plymouth via HMS Raleigh - Born: Norfolk - Age: 21 - Discharged on 25 Sep 1814 and sent to Dartmoor on HMS Niobe.

Fadden, Charles - Boy - Number: 2222 - Prize name: Thomas - Ship type: MV - How taken: HM Brig Frolic - When taken: 29 Jun 1813 - Where taken: off St. Thomas, WI - Date received: 22 Aug 1813 - From what ship: HMS Raisonnable - Born: New York - Age: 16 - Discharged on 25 Sep 1814 and sent to Dartmoor on HMS Leyden.

Fairweather, Robert - Gunner - Number: 1459 - Prize name: Union - Ship type: MV - How taken: HM Frigate Iris - When taken: 17 Jan 1813 - Where taken: at sea - Date received: 6 Apr 1813 - From what ship: Portsmouth via Tender Eliza - Born: Philadelphia - Age: 28 - Discharged on 24 Jul 1813 and released to Cartel Hoffminy.

Fall, James - Seaman - Number: 2930 - Prize name: Governor Plumer - Ship type: P - How taken: HM Brig Shamrock - When taken: 26 May 1813 - Where taken: at sea - Date received: 7 Jan 1814 - From what ship: Halifax - Born: Massachusetts - Age: 33 - Discharged on 25 Sep 1814 and sent to Dartmoor on HMS Leyden.

Fameroy, Ashley - Seaman - Number: 261 - Prize name: Patent - Ship type: MV - How taken: Gave himself up at Gravesend, England - When taken: 7 Nov 1812 - Date received: 7 Dec 1812 - From what ship: HMS Raisonnable - Born: Farmington, CT - Age: 23 - Discharged in Jul 1813 and released to Cartel Moses Brown.

Fangall, William - Seaman - Number: 1591 - Prize name: Dick - Ship type: MV - How taken: HM Brig Dispatch - When taken: 15 Mar 1813 - Where taken: off Bordeaux, France - Date received: 18 Apr 1813 - From what ship: HMS Rosario - Born: Philadelphia - Age: 25 - Discharged on 13 Apr 1814 and sent to Dartmoor.

Fannol, Augustus - Seaman - Number: 461 - Prize name: Hunter - Ship type: P - How taken: HM Frigate Phoebe - When taken: 23 Dec 1812 - Where taken: off Azores - Date received: 19 Feb 1813 - From what ship: HMS

Modeste - Born: New York - Age: 19 - Race: Negro - Discharged on 24 Jul 1813 and released to Cartel Hoffminy.

Far, William - Seaman - Number: 348 - Prize name: Postsea, prize to the Privateer Thrasher - Ship type: P - How taken: HM Sloop Helena - When taken: 31 Dec 1813 - Where taken: off Azores - Date received: 19 Jan 1813 - From what ship: HMS Raisonnable - Born: Camden, MA - Age: 24 - Discharged on 24 Jul 1813 and released to Cartel Hoffminy.

Fargo, Elijah - Seaman - Number: 247 - How taken: Gave himself up from HM Brig Rolla - When taken: 10 Nov 1812 - Date received: 1 Dec 1812 - From what ship: HMS Raisonnable - Born: New London, CT - Age: 25 - Discharged on 25 Jul 1814 and sent to Dartmoor on HMS Bittern.

Farman, Joseph - Private - Number: 3065 - Prize name: 14th U.S. Infantry - Ship type: LF - How taken: British forces - When taken: 24 Jun 1813 - Where taken: Beaver Dams, Upper Canada - Date received: 7 Jan 1814 - From what ship: Halifax - Born: Maryland - Age: 26 - Discharged on 10 Oct 1814 and sent to U.S. on Cartel St. Philip.

Farmer, Joseph - Seaman - Number: 2036 - How taken: Impressed at London - When taken: 23 Jul 1813 - Date received: 1 Aug 1813 - From what ship: HMS Raisonnable - Born: Salem - Age: 34 - Race: Black - Discharged on 12 Aug 1814 and sent to Dartmoor on HMS Alpheus.

Farrell, Andrew - Seaman - Number: 1997 - How taken: Gave himself up from HM Ship-of-the-Line Clarence - Date received: 15 Jul 1813 - From what ship: Plymouth - Born: Norida, NY - Age: 25 - Discharged on 25 Sep 1814 and sent to Dartmoor on HMS Leyden.

Farrell, John - Seaman - Number: 1057 - Prize name: Independence - Ship type: MV - How taken: HM Frigate Medusa - When taken: 9 Nov 1812 - Where taken: off San Sebastian, Spain - Date received: 11 Mar 1813 - From what ship: Yarmouth via HMS Tenders - Born: New Jersey - Age: 24 - Discharged on 8 Jun 1813 and released to Cartel Rodrigo.

Fate, Thomas - Seaman - Number: 922 - Prize name: Experiment - Ship type: MV - How taken: HM Brig Rover - When taken: 10 Nov 1812 - Where taken: off Bordeaux, France - Date received: 10 Mar 1813 - From what ship: HMS Tigress - Born: Maryland - Age: 34 - Discharged on 8 Jun 1813 and released to Cartel Rodrigo.

Fell, George - 2nd Mate - Number: 3800 - Prize name: Rambler - Ship type: MV - How taken: HM Transport Morley - When taken: 10 Feb 1813 - Date received: 5 Jun 1814 - From what ship: HMS Raisonnable - Born: Salem - Age: 32 - Discharged on 29 Sep 1814 and sent to Dartmoor on HMS Freya.

Fell, William - Seaman - Number: 2585 - How taken: Impressed at London - When taken: 21 Oct 1813 - Date received: 1 Nov 1813 - From what ship: HMS Raisonnable - Born: Providence - Age: 37 - Escaped on 16 May 1814 from HM Prison Ship Crown Prince.

Felt, John - Cook - Number: 158 - How taken: Stopped at London - When taken: 26 Oct 1812 - Date received: 5 Nov 1812 - From what ship: HMS Namur - Born: Salem, MA - Age: 38 - Discharged in Jul 1813 and released to Cartel Moses Brown.

Ferguson, John - Seaman - Number: 2303 - Prize name: Frances Ann - Ship type: MV - How taken: HM Brig Surinam - When taken: 19 Aug 1813 - Where taken: at sea - Date received: 29 Sep 1813 - From what ship: HMS Raisonnable - Born: North Carolina - Age: 45 - Discharged on 4 Sep 1814 and sent to Dartmoor on HMS Freya.

Ferguson, Thomas - Seaman - Number: 2509 - Prize name: Globe - Ship type: P - How taken: HM Prison Ship Victorious - When taken: 8 Jun 1813 - Where taken: Chesapeake Bay - Date received: 22 Oct 1813 - From what ship: Portsmouth via HMT Malabar - Born: Baltimore - Age: 23 - Discharged on 8 Sep 1814 and sent to Dartmoor on HMS Niobe.

Ferlecque, Augustine - Seaman - Number: 3693 - Prize name: Bunker Hill - Ship type: P - How taken: HM Frigate Pomone & HM Frigate Cydnus - When taken: 4 Mar 1814 - Where taken: Bay of Biscay - Date received: 4 May 1814 - From what ship: Portsmouth - Born: Brest, France - Age: 27 - Discharged on 22 Jun 1814 and sent to Calais, France on the Simon & Mary.

Ferley, John - Seaman - Number: 1999 - How taken: Gave himself up from HM Ship-of-the-Line Clarence - Date received: 15 Jul 1813 - From what ship: Plymouth - Born: Baltimore - Age: 33 - Discharged on 17 Jun 1814 and sent to Dartmoor on HMS Pincher.

Fernald, John - Seaman - Number: 1947 - How taken: Gave himself up from HM Ship-of-the-Line Leyden - Date received: 15 Jul 1813 - From what ship: Plymouth - Born: Massachsetts - Age: 27 - Discharged on 17 Jun 1814 and sent to Dartmoor on HMS Redbreast.

Fernald, Tobias - Seaman - Number: 48 - Prize name: White Oak - Ship type: MV - How taken: HM Brig Recruit - When taken: 22 Jul 1812 - Where taken: off Bermuda - Date received: 3 Nov 1812 - From what ship: HMS Plover - Born: York, MA - Age: 30 - Discharged on 23 Mar 1813 and released to the Cartel Robinson Potter.

Fernald, William - Seaman - Number: 2938 - Prize name: Governor Plumer - Ship type: P - How taken: HM Brig Shamrock - When taken: 26 May 1813 - Where taken: at sea - Date received: 7 Jan 1814 - From what ship: Halifax - Born: New Hampshire - Age: 26 - Discharged on 25 Sep 1814 and sent to Dartmoor on HMS Leyden.

Fernandes, Anthony - Seaman - Number: 1145 - Prize name: Sword Fish - Ship type: P - How taken: HM Ship-of-the-Line Elephant - When taken: 28 Dec 1812 - Where taken: off Azores - Date received: 16 Mar 1813 - From what ship: Portsmouth, Mundane - Born: Coruna, Spain - Age: 24 - Discharged on 24 Jul 1813 and released to Cartel Hoffminy.

Ferriere, George - Seaman - Number: 1320 - How taken: Impressed at the Hyde Rendezvous - When taken: 3 Feb 1813 - Date received: 16 Mar 1813 - From what ship: Portsmouth, via HMS Abundance - Born: Boston - Age: 36 - Discharged on 24 Jul 1813 and released to Cartel Hoffminy.

Ferris, Jacob - Seaman - Number: 1261 - How taken: Gave himself up from HM Ship-of-the-Line Mars - When taken: 9 Dec 1812 - Date received: 16 Mar 1813 - From what ship: Portsmouth, via HMS Abundance - Born: New York - Age: 32 - Discharged on 23 Jul 1814 and sent to Dartmoor.

Ferris, James - Seaman - Number: 3024 - How taken: Gave himself up from HM Ship-of-the-Line Invincible - When taken: 14 Jan 1813 - Date received: 7 Jan 1814 - From what ship: Portsmouth - Born: Cambridge - Age: 25 - Race: Black - Discharged on 20 Aug 1814 and sent to Dartmoor on HMS Shamrock.

Fethien, Thomas - Seaman - Number: 3574 - How taken: Impressed at London - When taken: 29 Jan 1814 - Date received: 11 Mar 1814 - From what ship: HMS Raisonnable - Born: Bridgetown - Age: 36 - Released on 26 Jul 1814.Fields, Alexander - Seaman - Number: 2162 - How taken: Gave himself up from HM Frigate Unicorn - When taken: 17 Jun 1813 - Date received: 16 Aug 1813 - From what ship: Portsmouth, via an admiral's tender - Born: Charlestown - Age: 28 - Discharged on 17 Jun 1814 and sent to Dartmoor on the Penebar.

Fiels, Jacob - Seaman - Number: 3284 - Prize name: Vivid - Ship type: P - How taken: HM Frigate Nymphe - When taken: 20 Apr 1813 - Where taken: off Cape Cod - Date received: 23 Feb 1814 - From what ship: Halifax via HMT Malabar - Born: Quincy - Age: 20 - Discharged on 26 Sep 1814 and sent to Dartmoor on HMS Leyden.

Fife, Thomas - Seaman - Number: 3862 - Prize name: James - Ship type: MV - How taken: HM Brig Harpy - When taken: 18 Dec 1812 - Where taken: off Isle de France (Mauritius) - Date received: 24 Aug 1814 - From what ship: London - Born: Philadelphia - Age: 25 - Discharged on 22 Oct 1814 and sent to Dartmoor on HMS Leyden.

Filch, Jonathan - Seaman - Number: 2132 - How taken: Gave himself up from HMS Montrell - When taken: 5 Jul 1813 - Date received: 9 Aug 1813 - From what ship: HMS Thames - Born: New Hampshire - Age: 22 - Discharged on 12 Aug 1814 and sent to Dartmoor on HMS Alpheus.

Findley, Thomas - Seaman - Number: 2971 - Prize name: Enterprise - Ship type: P - How taken: HM Frigate Tenedos - When taken: 21 May 1813 - Where taken: off Cape Cod - Date received: 7 Jan 1814 - From what ship: Halifax - Born: Massachusetts - Age: 16 - Discharged on 25 Sep 1814 and sent to Dartmoor on HMS Leyden.

Finey, John - Private - Number: 2649 - Prize name: 6th U.S. Infantry - Ship type: LF - How taken: British forces - When taken: 24 Jun 1813 - Where taken: Beaver Dams, Upper Canada - Date received: 5 Nov 1813 - From what ship: HMS Hindostan - Born: County Sligo, Ireland - Age: 26 - Discharged on 10 Oct 1814 and sent to U.S. on Cartel St. Philip.

Fingersen, John F. - Seaman - Number: 1197 - How taken: Gave himself up from HM Ship-of-the-Line Tigre -

When taken: 15 Aug 1812 - Date received: 16 Mar 1813 - From what ship: Portsmouth, via HMS Abundance - Born: Wiscasset - Age: 27 - Discharged on 25 Sep 1814 and sent to Dartmoor on HMS Leyden.

Finn, John - Seaman - Number: 3713 - Prize name: Requin - Ship type: LM - How taken: HM Frigate Venus - When taken: 5 Mar 1814 - Where taken: off Bordeaux, France - Date received: 18 May 1814 - From what ship: HMS Raisonnable - Born: Boston - Age: 19 - Discharged on 26 Sep 1814 and sent to Dartmoor on HMS Leyden.

Fippen, John - Mate - Number: 3169 - Prize name: Wolf Cove - Ship type: MV - How taken: HM Frigate Briton - When taken: 1 Dec 1813 - Where taken: off Brest, France - Date received: 7 Jan 1814 - From what ship: Halifax - Born: Massachusetts - Age: 27 - Discharged on 25 Sep 1814 and sent to Dartmoor on HMS Leyden.

Fisher, Francis - Mate - Number: 189 - Prize name: Roberson - Ship type: MV - How taken: Detained at Dover - When taken: 7 Aug 1812 - Date received: 6 Nov 1812 - From what ship: HMS Echo - Born: Edgar, MA - Age: 32 - Discharged on 23 Mar 1813 and released to the Cartel Robinson Potter.

Fisher, Richard D. - Carpenter - Number: 1552 - Prize name: Dolphin - Ship type: LM - How taken: HM Ship-of-the-Line Colossus - When taken: 5 Jan 1813 - Where taken: off the Western Isles, Scotland - Date received: 8 Apr 1813 - From what ship: Plymouth via HMS Olympia - Born: Philadelphia - Age: 32 - Discharged on 27 Jul 1813 and released to Cartel Hoffminy.

Fiske, Cyrus - Seaman - Number: 3498 - How taken: Gave himself up from HM Ship-of-the-Line Bulwark - Date received: 23 Feb 1814 - From what ship: Portsmouth via HMT Malabar - Born: Massachusetts - Age: 27 - Discharged on 25 Sep 1814 and sent to Dartmoor on HMS Leyden.

Fitch, Henry - Mate - Number: 139 - Prize name: George Carming - Ship type: MV - How taken: Stopped at London - When taken: 27 Oct 1812 - Date received: 5 Nov 1812 - From what ship: HMS Namur - Born: New Haven, CT - Age: 28 - Discharged in Jul 1813 and released to Cartel Moses Brown.

Fitch, John - Seaman - Number: 1344 - How taken: Gave himself up from HM Transport Malabar - When taken: 16 Mar 1813 - Date received: 30 Mar 1813 - From what ship: HMS Raisonnable - Born: New Bedford - Age: 25 - Discharged on 14 Sep 1813 and released to HMS Ceres.

Fitch, William - Seaman - Number: 1505 - Prize name: Pallas - Ship type: MV - How taken: HM Brig Rebuff - When taken: 23 Jan 1813 - Where taken: off Cadiz, Spain - Date received: 8 Apr 1813 - From what ship: Portsmouth, via an admiral's tender - Born: New York - Age: 21 - Discharged on 25 Sep 1814 and sent to Dartmoor on HMS Niobe.

Fitzgerald, John - Private - Number: 1628 - Prize name: 13th U.S. Infantry - Ship type: LF - How taken: British forces - When taken: 13 Oct 1812 - Where taken: Upper Canada - Date received: 9 May 1813 - From what ship: HMS Raisonnable - Born: Dublin, Ireland - Age: 39 - Discharged on 22 Oct 1814 and sent to Dartmoor on HMS Leyden.

Fitzpatrick, John - Private - Number: 3816 - How taken: Gave himself up from Chatham - When taken: 23 Jun 1814 - Date received: 29 Jun 1814 - From what ship: Chatham - Born: County Kilkenny, Ireland - Age: 31 - Discharged on 10 Oct 1814 and sent to U.S. on Cartel St. Philip.

Fleming, Alexander - Seaman - Number: 2428 - Prize name: Maydock - Ship type: MV - How taken: HM Brig Rebuff - When taken: 16 Jun 1813 - Where taken: off Cape St. Marys, Newfoundland - Date received: 21 Oct 1813 - From what ship: Portsmouth via HMT Malabar - Born: Massachusetts - Age: 26 - Discharged on 4 Sep 1814 and sent to Dartmoor on HMS Freya.

Fletcher, Henry - Quartermaster - Number: 429 - Prize name: Hunter - Ship type: P - How taken: HM Frigate Phoebe - When taken: 23 Dec 1812 - Where taken: off Azores - Date received: 19 Feb 1813 - From what ship: HMS Modeste - Born: Boston - Age: 29 - Discharged on 2 Jul 1813 and released to Cartel Moses Brown.

Fletcher, John - Seaman - Number: 3397 - Prize name: Growler - Ship type: P - How taken: HM Brig Electra - When taken: 7 Jul 1813 - Where taken: off St. Johns - Date received: 23 Feb 1814 - From what ship: Halifax via HMT Malabar - Born: Warren - Age: 11 - Discharged on 22 Oct 1814 and sent to Dartmoor on HMS Leyden.

Flood, John - Seaman - Number: 2065 - How taken: Gave himself up from HM Ship-of-the-Line Berwick - When taken: 29 Oct 1812 - Date received: 9 Aug 1813 - From what ship: HMS Thames - Born: Burlington, VT - Age: 27 - Discharged on 4 Aug 1814 and sent to Dartmoor on HMS Liverpool.

Flood, John - Seaman - Number: 1652 - How taken: Gave himself up from HM Ship-of-the-Line Sterling Castle - Date received: 9 May 1813 - From what ship: HMS Raisonnable - Born: Portland - Age: 22 - Discharged on 13 Aug 1814 and sent to Dartmoor.

Florence, Charles - Gunner - Number: 2707 - Prize name: Growler - Ship type: P - How taken: HM Brig Electra - When taken: 7 Jul 1813 - Where taken: off St. Johns - Date received: 7 Jan 1814 - From what ship: Portsmouth - Born: Marblehead - Age: 55 - Discharged on 7 Feb 1814 and sent to Hoxton, England.

Flower, Artemas - Seaman - Number: 934 - Prize name: Argus - Ship type: MV - How taken: HM Cutter Fancy - When taken: 17 Dec 1812 - Where taken: Bay of Biscay - Date received: 10 Mar 1813 - From what ship: HMS Tigress - Born: Connecticut - Age: 35 - Discharged on 2 Jul 1813 and released to Cartel Moses Brown.

Floyd, James - Seaman - Number: 1050 - How taken: Taken up from HM Battery Princess at Liverpool - When taken: 29 Oct 1812 - Date received: 11 Mar 1813 - From what ship: Yarmouth via HMS Tenders - Born: New York - Age: 28 - Race: Black - Discharged on 19 May 1813 and released to HMS Ceres.

Flushman, H. P. - Clerk - Number: 414 - Prize name: Hunter - Ship type: P - How taken: HM Frigate Phoebe - When taken: 23 Dec 1812 - Where taken: off Azores - Date received: 19 Feb 1813 - From what ship: HMS Modeste - Born: New Jersey - Age: 25 - Discharged on 23 Mar 1813 and released to the Cartel Robinson Potter.

Fogerty, Archibald - Seaman - Number: 1742 - How taken: Gave himself up from HMS Horatio - When taken: 16 May 1813 - Date received: 25 May 1813 - From what ship: Portsmouth via HMS Impetius - Born: Thomastown, MA - Age: 38 - Discharged on 24 Jul 1814 and sent to Dartmoor on HMS Liffey.

Fogg, Noel - Seaman - Number: 1804 - How taken: Impressed at London - When taken: 23 Jun 1813 - Date received: 3 Jul 1813 - From what ship: HMS Raisonnable - Born: New Hampshire - Age: 28 - Discharged on 25 Jul 1814 and sent to Dartmoor on HMS Bittern.

Fogust, Able - Seaman - Number: 2088 - How taken: Gave himself up from HM Ship-of-the-Line Scipion - When taken: 27 May 1813 - Date received: 9 Aug 1813 - From what ship: HMS Thames - Born: Massachsetts - Age: 25 - Race: Mulatto - Discharged on 12 Aug 1814 and sent to Dartmoor on HMS Alpheus.

Fohis, James - Seaman - Number: 1902 - Prize name: Weasel - Ship type: MV - How taken: HM Brig Foxhound - When taken: 25 Mar 1813 - Where taken: Bay of Biscay - Date received: 7 Jul 1813 - From what ship: Portsmouth via HMS Tribune - Born: New Jersey - Age: 20 - Discharged on 4 Aug 1814 and sent to Dartmoor on HMS Liverpool.

Folger, Frederick - Seaman - Number: 2368 - How taken: Gave himself up from HM Ship-of-the-Line Swiftsure - When taken: 26 Dec 1812 - Date received: 20 Oct 1813 - From what ship: Portsmouth, via an admiral's tender - Born: Baltimore - Age: 27 - Discharged on 4 Sep 1814 and sent to Dartmoor on HMS Freya.

Follinsbe, William - Seaman - Number: 1831 - Prize name: tender to the Privateer True Blooded Yankee - Ship type: P - How taken: HM Ship-of-the-Line Fame - When taken: 24 Jun 1813 - Where taken: off Brest, France - Date received: 7 Jul 1813 - From what ship: Portsmouth via HMS Scorpion - Born: Newburyport - Age: 29 - Discharged on 25 Jul 1814 and sent to Dartmoor on HMS Bittern.

Foloson, Christopher (alias Gunn) - Boy - Number: 1646 - Prize name: Henryettos - Ship type: MV - How taken: HMS Castilian - When taken: 12 Mar 1813 - Where taken: off Cape Ortegal, Spain - Date received: 9 May 1813 - From what ship: HMS Raisonnable - Born: North Carolina - Age: 10 - Discharged on 24 Jul 1814 and sent to Dartmoor.

Folsom, Abraham - Private - Number: 1637 - Prize name: 4th U.S. Infantry - Ship type: LF - How taken: British forces - When taken: 16 Aug 1812 - Where taken: Detroit - Date received: 9 May 1813 - From what ship: HMS Raisonnable - Born: New Hampshire - Age: 20 - Discharged on 24 Jun 1813 and released to HMS Ceres.

Foot, Benjamin - Seaman - Number: 3459 - Prize name: Elbridge Gerry - Ship type: P - How taken: HM Frigate Crescent - When taken: 16 Sep 1813 - Where taken: at sea - Date received: 23 Feb 1814 - From what ship:

Halifax via HMT Malabar - Born: Yarmouth - Age: 17 - Discharged on 21 Jul 1814 and sent to Dartmoor on HMS Portia.

Forbes, James - Mate - Number: 1569 - Prize name: Charles - Ship type: MV - How taken: Detained at Belfast - When taken: 8 Aug 1813 - Date received: 8 Apr 1813 - From what ship: Plymouth via HMS Olympia - Born: Philadelphia - Age: 28 - Discharged on 21 Apr 1813 and sent to Reading on parole.

Forbes, John - Seaman - Number: 2473 - Prize name: Montgomery - Ship type: P - How taken: HM Frigate Nymphe - When taken: 5 May 1813 - Where taken: off Cape Cod - Date received: 22 Oct 1813 - From what ship: Portsmouth via HMT Malabar - Born: Salem - Age: 29 - Discharged on 8 Sep 1814 and sent to Dartmoor on HMS Niobe.

Forbes, Robert - Seaman - Number: 2183 - How taken: Gave himself up from HM Ship-of-the-Line Leviathan - When taken: 28 Oct 1812 - Date received: 16 Aug 1813 - From what ship: Portsmouth, via an admiral's tender - Born: Jersey - Age: 32 - Discharged on 25 Sep 1814 and sent to Dartmoor on HMS Leyden.

Ford, M. Benjamin - Seaman - Number: 1229 - Prize name: Rossie - Ship type: MV - How taken: HM Frigate Dryand - When taken: 7 Jan 1813 - Where taken: at sea - Date received: 16 Mar 1813 - From what ship: Portsmouth, via HMS Abundance - Born: Charlestown - Age: 28 - Discharged on 24 Jul 1813 and released to Cartel Hoffminy.

Forester, Joseph - Seaman - Number: 2462 - Prize name: Thorn - Ship type: P - How taken: Shannon, Nova Scotia privateer - When taken: 2 Oct 1812 - Where taken: off Newfoundland - Date received: 21 Oct 1813 - From what ship: Portsmouth via HMT Malabar - Born: Baltimore - Age: 22 - Race: Blackman - Discharged on 4 Sep 1814 and sent to Dartmoor on HMS Freya.

Forman, William - Carpenter - Number: 3198 - Prize name: Growler - Ship type: P - How taken: HM Brig Electra - When taken: 7 Jul 1813 - Where taken: off St. Johns - Date received: 7 Jan 1813 - From what ship: Portsmouth - Born: Eaton - Age: 27 - Died on 10 Apr 1814 from fever.

Forrest, James - Seaman - Number: 1853 - How taken: Given up from HM Ship-of-the-Line Malta - Date received: 7 Jul 1813 - From what ship: Portsmouth via HMS Tribune - Born: Philadelphia - Age: 40 - Discharged on 4 Aug 1814 and sent to Dartmoor on HMS Liverpool.

Forrest, William - Seaman - Number: 1339 - How taken: Gave himself up from HM Brig Epervier - When taken: 5 Aug 1812 - Date received: 26 Mar 1813 - From what ship: HMS Raisonnable - Born: Philadelphia - Age: 32 - Discharged on 12 Aug 1814 and sent to Dartmoor on HMS Alpheus.

Forrester, Arthur - Private - Number: 3153 - Prize name: U.S. Artillery - Ship type: LF - How taken: British forces - When taken: 24 Jun 1813 - Where taken: Beaver Dams, Upper Canada - Date received: 7 Jan 1814 - From what ship: Halifax - Born: Massachusetts - Age: 34 - Discharged on 10 Oct 1814 and sent to U.S. on Cartel St. Philip.

Forsyth, Alexander - Seaman - Number: 3236 - How taken: Impressed at London - When taken: 22 Jan 1814 - Date received: 8 Feb 1814 - From what ship: HMS Raisonnable - Born: Charlestown - Age: 27 - Died on 16 Apr 1814 from fever.

Forstman, John - Seaman - Number: 3012 - Prize name: Yankee - Ship type: P - How taken: HM Frigate Shannon - When taken: 20 Aug 1813 - Where taken: at sea - Date received: 7 Jan 1814 - From what ship: Halifax - Born: Stockholm - Age: 20 - Discharged on 25 Sep 1814 and sent to Dartmoor on HMS Leyden.

Forsyth, Robert - Seaman - Number: 2511 - Prize name: Globe - Ship type: P - How taken: HM Prison Ship Victorious - When taken: 8 Jun 1813 - Where taken: Chesapeake Bay - Date received: 22 Oct 1813 - From what ship: Portsmouth via HMT Malabar - Born: Baltimore - Age: 23 - Discharged on 8 Sep 1814 and sent to Dartmoor on HMS Niobe.

Fortune, John - Seaman - Number: 881 - Prize name: Hero - Ship type: MV - How taken: Cornet - When taken: 10 Feb 1813 - Where taken: off Lisbon - Date received: 1 Mar 1813 - From what ship: Plymouth via HMS Namur - Born: Africa - Age: 33 - Race: Black - Released on 27 Mar 1813.

Fortune, John - Seaman - Number: 2743 - Prize name: Teazer - Ship type: P - How taken: HM Frigate Boreas - When taken: 15 Jun 1813 - Where taken: off Halifax - Date received: 7 Jan 1814 - From what ship: Halifax - Born: New London - Age: 29 - Race: Black - Discharged on 25 Sep 1814 and sent to Dartmoor on HMS

Leyden.

Fosset, Robert - Seaman - Number: 3953 - How taken: Gave himself up from HM Sloop Indian - When taken: 20 Aug 1814 - Date received: 21 Oct 1813 - From what ship: Quebec - Born: Burlington - Age: 28 - Race: Black - Discharged on 22 Oct 1814 and sent to Dartmoor on HMS Leyden.

Foster, George - Seaman - Number: 3191 - Prize name: Growler - Ship type: P - How taken: HM Brig Electra - When taken: 7 Jul 1813 - Where taken: off St. Johns - Date received: 7 Jan 1813 - From what ship: Portsmouth - Born: Marblehead - Age: 42 - Discharged on 25 Sep 1814 and sent to Dartmoor on HMS Leyden.

Foster, Isaiah - Seaman - Number: 456 - Prize name: Hunter - Ship type: P - How taken: HM Frigate Phoebe - When taken: 23 Dec 1812 - Where taken: off Azores - Date received: 19 Feb 1813 - From what ship: HMS Modeste - Born: Salisbury, CT - Age: 26 - Discharged on 24 Jul 1813 and released to Cartel Hoffminy.

Foster, Joseph - Seaman - Number: 1807 - How taken: Impressed at London - When taken: 25 Jun 1813 - Date received: 3 Jul 1813 - From what ship: HMS Raisonnable - Born: Dorchester - Age: 26 - Discharged on 25 Jul 1814 and sent to Dartmoor on HMS Bittern.

Foster, Samuel - Seaman - Number: 2733 - Prize name: Growler - Ship type: P - How taken: HM Brig Electra - When taken: 7 Jul 1813 - Where taken: off St. Johns - Date received: 7 Jan 1814 - From what ship: Halifax - Born: Massachusetts - Age: 40 - Discharged on 25 Sep 1814 and sent to Dartmoor on HMS Leyden.

Foster, Thomas - Seaman - Number: 2576 - How taken: Gave himself up from HM Ship-of-the-Line Scipion - When taken: 10 Dec 1812 - Date received: 23 Oct 1813 - From what ship: Portsmouth via HMS Raisonnable - Born: Plymouth - Age: 28 - Discharged on 11 Aug 1814 and sent to Dartmoor on HMS Freya.

Fountain, Isaac - Seaman - Number: 909 - Prize name: Independence - Ship type: MV - How taken: HM Frigate Medusa - When taken: 9 Nov 1812 - Where taken: off San Sebastian, Spain - Date received: 10 Mar 1813 - From what ship: HMS Tigress - Born: New York - Age: 25 - Discharged on 8 Jun 1813 and released to Cartel Rodrigo.

Fowler, John - Prize Master - Number: 337 - Prize name: Postsea, prize to the Privateer Thrasher - Ship type: P - How taken: HM Sloop Helena - When taken: 31 Dec 1813 - Where taken: off Azores - Date received: 19 Jan 1813 - From what ship: HMS Raisonnable - Born: Marblehead - Age: 26 - Discharged on 24 Jul 1813 and released to Cartel Hoffminy.

Fowler, Joshua - Seaman - Number: 3908 - How taken: Gave himself up from HM Ship-of-the-Line HM Ship-of-the-Line Carnatic - When taken: 13 Sep 1814 - Date received: 4 Sep 1814 - From what ship: Transport Office - Born: Boston - Age: 30 - Discharged on 25 Sep 1814 and sent to Dartmoor on HMS Leyden.

Fowler, Timothy - Seaman - Number: 10 - Prize name: Eliza Ann - Ship type: MV - How taken: HM Ship-of-the-Line Vigo - When taken: 11 Aug 1812 - Where taken: Hanoi Bay - Date received: 29 Oct 1812 - From what ship: HMS Raisonnable - Born: Nantucket - Age: 19 - Discharged on 10 May 1813 and released to Cartel Admittance.

Foxwell, George - Seaman - Number: 304 - Prize name: Cygnet - Ship type: MV - How taken: HM Brig Sarpedon - When taken: 12 Aug 1812 - Date received: 23 Dec 1812 - From what ship: Greenlaw Depot - Born: Maryland - Age: 28 - Discharged on 10 May 1813 and released to Cartel Admittance.

Francis, Abraham - Seaman - Number: 2496 - Prize name: Porcupine - Ship type: LM - How taken: HM Frigate Acasta - When taken: 3 Jun 1813 - Where taken: off Cape Sable, Florida - Date received: 22 Oct 1813 - From what ship: Portsmouth via HMT Malabar - Born: Marblehead - Age: 34 - Race: Mulatto - Discharged on 8 Sep 1814 and sent to Dartmoor on HMS Niobe.

Francis, Frederick - Seaman - Number: 1142 - Prize name: Sword Fish - Ship type: P - How taken: HM Ship-of-the-Line Elephant - When taken: 28 Dec 1812 - Where taken: off Azores - Date received: 16 Mar 1813 - From what ship: Portsmouth, Mundane - Born: Salem - Age: 19 - Race: Black - Discharged on 24 Jul 1813 and released to Cartel Hoffminy.

Francis, John - Seaman - Number: 3777 - Prize name: Argus - Ship type: MV - How taken: HM Ship-of-the-Line San Domingo - When taken: 1 Mar 1814 - Where taken: off Savannah - Date received: 26 May 1814 - From what ship: HMS Hindostan - Born: Newport - Age: 23 - Race: Black - Discharged on 25 Sep 1814 and sent to Dartmoor on HMS Niobe.

Francis, John - Seaman - Number: 3613 - Prize name: Liberty - Ship type: MV - How taken: Surrendered at Stromness, Scotland - When taken: 30 Dec 1813 - Date received: 29 Mar 1814 - From what ship: Hired tender Anna - Born: Boston - Age: 32 - Discharged on 25 Sep 1814 and sent to Dartmoor on HMS Leyden.

Francis, John - Seaman - Number: 1736 - How taken: Gave himself up from HM Guardship Royal William - When taken: Nov 1812 - Date received: 25 May 1813 - From what ship: Portsmouth via HMS Impetius - Born: Portsmouth, VA - Age: 32 - Race: Mulatto - Discharged on 24 Jul 1814 and sent to Dartmoor on HMS Liffey.

Francis, John - Seaman - Number: 3036 - How taken: Gave himself up from HM Sloop-of-War Bonne Citoyenne - When taken: 24 Nov 1813 - Date received: 7 Jan 1814 - From what ship: Portsmouth - Born: Nantucket - Age: 22 - Race: Black - Discharged on 20 Aug 1814 and sent to Dartmoor on HMS Shamrock.

Francis, Peter - Seaman - Number: 1055 - Prize name: Independence - Ship type: MV - How taken: HM Frigate Medusa - When taken: 9 Nov 1812 - Where taken: off San Sebastian, Spain - Date received: 11 Mar 1813 - From what ship: Yarmouth via HMS Tenders - Born: Boston - Age: 20 - Discharged on 8 Jun 1813 and released to Cartel Rodrigo.

Francis, Prince - Seaman - Number: 1317 - How taken: Gave himself up from HM Guardship Royal William - When taken: 3 Feb 1813 - Date received: 16 Mar 1813 - From what ship: Portsmouth, via HMS Abundance - Born: Connecticut - Age: 32 - Race: Black - Discharged on 23 Jul 1814 and sent to Dartmoor.

Francoise, James - Seaman - Number: 911 - Prize name: Independence - Ship type: MV - How taken: HM Frigate Medusa - When taken: 9 Nov 1812 - Where taken: off San Sebastian, Spain - Date received: 10 Mar 1813 - From what ship: HMS Tigress - Born: New Orleans - Age: 16 - Discharged on 8 Jun 1813 and released to Cartel Rodrigo.

Franklin, William - Seaman - Number: 3911 - How taken: Gave himself up from HM Frigate Daphine - When taken: 20 Jul 1814 - Date received: 8 Sep 1814 - From what ship: HMS Namur - Born: Virginia - Age: 32 - Discharged on 26 Sep 1814 and sent to Dartmoor on HMS Leyden.

Fray, James - Seaman - Number: 3374 - Prize name: Yorktown - Ship type: P - How taken: HM Frigate Maidstone - When taken: 17 Jul 1813 - Where taken: Grand Banks - Date received: 23 Feb 1814 - From what ship: Halifax via HMT Malabar - Born: Baltimore - Age: 23 - Discharged on 10 Oct 1814 and sent to Dartmoor on the Mermaid.

Frazer, Hulbert - Private - Number: 3099 - Prize name: 14th U.S. Infantry - Ship type: LF - How taken: British forces - When taken: 24 Jun 1813 - Where taken: Beaver Dams, Upper Canada - Date received: 7 Jan 1814 - From what ship: Halifax - Born: Maryland - Age: 29 - Discharged on 10 Oct 1814 and sent to U.S. on Cartel St. Philip.

Frazier, John - Seaman - Number: 1862 - How taken: Gave himself up from HM Frigate Leonidas - Date received: 7 Jul 1813 - From what ship: Portsmouth via HMS Tribune - Born: New York - Age: 29 - Discharged on 12 Aug 1814 and sent to Dartmoor on HMS Alpheus.

Frazier, William - Seaman - Number: 2442 - How taken: Taken off of the Russian MV Neptune at Cork - When taken: 28 Sep 1812 - Date received: 21 Oct 1813 - From what ship: Portsmouth via HMT Malabar - Born: Pennsylvania - Age: 31 - Race: Mulatto - Discharged on 4 Sep 1814 and sent to Dartmoor on HMS Freya.

Fredericks, John - Seaman - Number: 1516 - How taken: Gave himself up from HM Transport Minerva - When taken: 14 Oct 1812 - Date received: 8 Apr 1813 - From what ship: Portsmouth, via an admiral's tender - Born: New Orleans - Age: 20 - Race: Mulatto - Discharged on 2 Jul 1813 and released to Cartel Moses Brown.

Fredericks, John - Seaman - Number: 2263 - Prize name: Eliza - Ship type: MV - How taken: HMS Charles - When taken: 20 Jul 1813 - Where taken: off Petershead, Scotland - Date received: 14 Sep 1813 - From what ship: HMS Raisonnable - Born: Virginia - Age: 32 - Discharged on 22 Oct 1814 and sent to Dartmoor on HMS Leyden.

Fredericks, John - Seaman - Number: 2890 - Prize name: Dart - Ship type: P - How taken: HM Frigate Niger & HMS Fortunee - When taken: 10 Nov 1813 - Where taken: off Cape Finisterre, Spain - Date received: 7 Jan

1814 - From what ship: Portsmouth - Born: New Orleans - Age: 38 - Released on 6 Aug 1814.

Freeborn, John - Seaman - Number: 382 - How taken: Gave himself up from HM Ship of the Line Alfred - When taken: 26 Jan 1813 - Date received: 31 Jan 1813 - From what ship: HMS Raisonnable - Born: Philadelphia - Age: 23 - Discharged on 26 Jul 1814 and sent to Dartmoor on HMS Raven.

Freeman, Alexander - Seaman - Number: 1040 - Prize name: Catharine - Ship type: MV - How taken: HM Frigate Leonidas - When taken: 31 Jul 1812 - Where taken: off Ireland - Date received: 11 Mar 1813 - From what ship: Yarmouth via HMS Tenders - Born: Boston - Age: 17 - Discharged on 26 Jul 1813 and released to Cartel Hoffminy.

Freeman, Asa - Seaman - Number: 2298 - Prize name: Rebecca - Ship type: MV - How taken: Apprehended at London - When taken: 26 Sep 1813 - Date received: 29 Sep 1813 - From what ship: HMS Raisonnable - Born: Nantucket - Age: 23 - Race: Black - Discharged on 18 Oct 1813 and released to HMS Ceres.

Freeman, Charles - Seaman - Number: 1959 - Prize name: Ferox - Ship type: MV - How taken: HM Frigate Medusa & HM Brig Lyra - When taken: 28 Mar 1813 - Where taken: off Cape Ortegal, Spain - Date received: 15 Jul 1813 - From what ship: Plymouth - Born: Delaware - Age: 23 - Race: Black - Discharged on 17 Jun 1814 and sent to Dartmoor on HMS Redbreast.

Freeman, John - Seaman - Number: 53 - Prize name: Trim - Ship type: MV - How taken: From a cutter off Bermuda - When taken: 26 Jul 1812 - Date received: 3 Nov 1812 - From what ship: HMS Plover - Born: Suffolk, MA - Age: 24 - Discharged on 23 Mar 1813 and released to the Cartel Robinson Potter.

Freeman, John - Marine Sergeant - Number: 2874 - Prize name: Elbridge Gerry - Ship type: P - How taken: HM Frigate Crescent - When taken: 16 Sep 1813 - Where taken: at sea - Date received: 7 Jan 1814 - From what ship: Portsmouth - Born: Massachusetts - Age: 23 - Died on 28 May 1814 from fever.

Freeman, Plim - Seaman - Number: 3778 - Prize name: Argus - Ship type: MV - How taken: HM Ship-of-the-Line San Domingo - When taken: 1 Mar 1814 - Where taken: off Savannah - Date received: 26 May 1814 - From what ship: HMS Hindostan - Born: Reading - Age: 32 - Race: Black - Discharged on 25 Sep 1814 and sent to Dartmoor on HMS Niobe.

Freeman, Prince - Seaman - Number: 2004 - How taken: Gave himself up from HM Ship-of-the-Line Boyne - Date received: 15 Jul 1813 - From what ship: Plymouth - Born: Gloucester - Age: 34 - Discharged on 17 Jun 1814 and sent to Dartmoor on HMS Pincher.

Frees, James - Seaman - Number: 1439 - Prize name: Orbit - Ship type: MV - How taken: HM Brig Achates - When taken: 29 Jan 1813 - Where taken: Lat 49 N Long 13 W - Date received: 6 Apr 1813 - From what ship: Plymouth via HMS Decoy - Born: Lancaster - Age: 40 - Discharged on 25 Sep 1814 and sent to Dartmoor on HMS Niobe.

French, Dudley - Seaman - Number: 2028 - Prize name: Mary - Ship type: MV - How taken: Detained at Surinam - When taken: 17 Jun 1812 - Date received: 24 Jul 1813 - From what ship: HMS Raisonnable - Born: Newburyport - Age: 17 - Discharged on 7 Sep 1813 and released to HMS Ceres.

Fresk, Joshua - Seaman - Number: 19 - Prize name: Lucky - Ship type: MV - How taken: Detained at Hanoi Bay - When taken: 11 Aug 1812 - Date received: 29 Oct 1812 - From what ship: HMS Raisonnable - Born: Salem - Age: 18 - Discharged on 10 May 1813 and released to Cartel Admittance.

Fron, Frederick - Seaman - Number: 964 - Prize name: Empress - Ship type: MV - How taken: HM Brig Rover - When taken: 30 Nov 1812 - Where taken: St. Andrew - Date received: 10 Mar 1813 - From what ship: HMS Tigress - Born: Bremen, Germany - Age: 25 - Discharged on 8 Jun 1813 and released to Cartel Rodrigo.

Fry, Peter - Seaman - Number: 1694 - Prize name: Governor Middleton - Ship type: MV - How taken: Thetis, British privateer - When taken: 2 May 1813 - Where taken: Bay of Biscay - Date received: 15 May 1813 - From what ship: HMS Viper - Born: Alexandria - Age: 23 - Discharged on 24 Jul 1814 and sent to Dartmoor on HMS Liffey.

Fry, Thomas - Seaman - Number: 2388 - How taken: Gave himself up from HM Ship-of-the-Line Achille - When taken: 26 Dec 1812 - Date received: 20 Oct 1813 - From what ship: Portsmouth, via an admiral's tender - Born: Newport - Age: 36 - Discharged on 4 Sep 1814 and sent to Dartmoor on HMS Freya.

Fuller, John - Seaman - Number: 1820 - Prize name: tender to the Privateer True Blooded Yankee - Ship type: P - How taken: HM Brig Hope - When taken: 24 Jun 1813 - Where taken: off Brest, France - Date received: 7 Jul 1813 - From what ship: Portsmouth via HMS Scorpion - Born: Salem - Age: 27 - Discharged on 9 Jul 1813 and released to HMS Ceres.

Fuller, Nathaniel - Seaman - Number: 2483 - Prize name: Enterprise - Ship type: P - How taken: HM Frigate Tenedos - When taken: 21 May 1813 - Where taken: off Cape Cod - Date received: 22 Oct 1813 - From what ship: Portsmouth via HMT Malabar - Born: Ipswich - Age: 22 - Discharged on 8 Sep 1814 and sent to Dartmoor on HMS Niobe.

Fuller, Zachariah - Seaman - Number: 1396 - Prize name: Blue Bird - Ship type: MV - How taken: HM Frigate Briton - When taken: 1 Jan 1813 - Where taken: off Bordeaux, France - Date received: 5 Apr 1813 - From what ship: Plymouth via HMS Dwarf - Born: Pennsylvania - Age: 30 - Discharged on 24 Jul 1813 and released to Cartel Hoffminy.

Fullerton, John - Private - Number: 3140 - Prize name: U.S. Artillery - Ship type: LF - How taken: British forces - When taken: 24 Jun 1813 - Where taken: Beaver Dams, Upper Canada - Date received: 7 Jan 1814 - From what ship: Halifax - Born: Philadelphia - Age: 42 - Discharged on 10 Oct 1814 and sent to U.S. on Cartel St. Philip.

Fulton, James - Seaman - Number: 3427 - Prize name: Industry - Ship type: P - How taken: HM Frigate Maidstone - When taken: 18 Jul 1813 - Where taken: Grand Banks - Date received: 23 Feb 1814 - From what ship: Halifax via HMT Malabar - Born: Marblehead - Age: 15 - Discharged on 22 Oct 1814 and sent to Dartmoor on HMS Leyden.

Funk, Samuel - Seaman - Number: 75 - Prize name: Rachel & Ann - Ship type: MV - How taken: Stopped at London - When taken: 26 Oct 1812 - Date received: 4 Nov 1812 - From what ship: HMS Namur - Born: Haverhill - Age: 26 - Discharged on 4 Mar 1813 to the Wailey.

Furness, Jesse - Seaman - Number: 3762 - Prize name: Argus - Ship type: MV - How taken: HM Ship-of-the-Line San Domingo - When taken: 1 Mar 1814 - Where taken: off Savannah - Date received: 26 May 1814 - From what ship: HMS Hindostan - Born: New Jersey - Age: 24 - Discharged on 25 Sep 1814 and sent to Dartmoor on HMS Niobe.

Fuster, Peter - Seaman - Number: 632 - Prize name: King of Rome - Ship type: P - How taken: HM Brig Wolverine - When taken: 13 Dec 1812 - Where taken: at sea - Date received: 23 Feb 1813 - From what ship: Portsmouth via HMS Dromedary - Born: New Holland - Age: 20 - Race: Black man - Discharged on 2 Jul 1813 and released to Cartel Moses Brown.

Fyans, Joseph - Seaman - Number: 1824 - Prize name: tender to the Privateer True Blooded Yankee - Ship type: P - How taken: HM Brig Hope - When taken: 24 Jun 1813 - Where taken: off Brest, France - Date received: 7 Jul 1813 - From what ship: Portsmouth via HMS Scorpion - Born: New York - Age: 29 - Race: Mulatto - Released on 11 Jul 1814.

Gage, Lot - Seaman - Number: 3755 - Prize name: Argus - Ship type: MV - How taken: HM Ship-of-the-Line San Domingo - When taken: 1 Mar 1814 - Where taken: off Savannah - Date received: 26 May 1814 - From what ship: HMS Hindostan - Born: Barnstable - Age: 19 - Discharged on 25 Sep 1814 and sent to Dartmoor on HMS Niobe.

Gage, Thomas - Seaman - Number: 2961 - Prize name: Enterprise - Ship type: P - How taken: HM Frigate Tenedos - When taken: 21 May 1813 - Where taken: off Cape Cod - Date received: 7 Jan 1814 - From what ship: Halifax - Born: Massachusetts - Age: 23 - Discharged on 22 Oct 1814 and sent to Dartmoor on HMS Leyden.

Gale, Oliver - Seaman - Number: 680 - Prize name: U.S.R.M. Cutter James Madison - Ship type: War - How taken: HM Frigate Barbadoes - When taken: 22 Aug 1812 - Where taken: at sea - Date received: 24 Feb 1813 - From what ship: Portsmouth via HMS Ulysses - Born: New York - Age: 26 - Race: Man of color - Discharged on 10 May 1813 and released to Cartel Admittance.

Gale, Sam - Seaman - Number: 1345 - How taken: Taken up at London - When taken: 17 Mar 1813 - Date received: 30 Mar 1813 - From what ship: HMS Raisonnable - Born: Salem - Age: 29 - Discharged on 12 Apr 1813 and released to HMS Carnatic.

Gale, William - Seaman - Number: 3770 - Prize name: Argus - Ship type: MV - How taken: HM Ship-of-the-Line San Domingo - When taken: 1 Mar 1814 - Where taken: off Savannah - Date received: 26 May 1814 - From what ship: HMS Hindostan - Born: Baltimore - Age: 20 - Race: Black - Discharged on 25 Sep 1814 and sent to Dartmoor on HMS Niobe.

Gall, William - Seaman - Number: 568 - Prize name: Rising States - Ship type: MV - How taken: HM Frigate Fortunee - When taken: 28 Aug 1812 - Where taken: off the Western Isles, Scotland - Date received: 23 Feb 1813 - From what ship: Portsmouth via HMS Dromedary - Born: Long Island - Age: 35 - Race: Black man - Discharged on 8 Jun 1813 and released to Cartel Rodrigo.

Galt, Robert - Seaman - Number: 342 - Prize name: Postsea, prize to the Privateer Thrasher - Ship type: P - How taken: HM Sloop Helena - When taken: 31 Dec 1813 - Where taken: off Azores - Date received: 19 Jan 1813 - From what ship: HMS Raisonnable - Born: Baltimore - Age: 19 - Discharged on 7 Apr 1813 and released to the HMS Raisonnable.

Gammell, Samuel - Seaman - Number: 1323 - How taken: Gave himself up from HM Guardship Royal William - When taken: 3 Feb 1813 - Date received: 16 Mar 1813 - From what ship: Portsmouth, via HMS Abundance - Born: Boston - Age: 37 - Released on 16 Aug 1813.

Gamslo, Carl - Seaman - Number: 1730 - Prize name: Powhattan - Ship type: MV - How taken: HMS Horatio - When taken: 13 Dec 1812 - Where taken: Bay of Biscay - Date received: 25 May 1813 - From what ship: Portsmouth via HMS Impetius - Born: Mortif, Austria - Age: 24 - Discharged on 24 Jul 1813 and released to Cartel Hoffminy.

Ganagon, Edward - Private - Number: 1631 - Prize name: 6th U.S. Infantry - Ship type: LF - How taken: British forces - When taken: 13 Oct 1812 - Where taken: Upper Canada - Date received: 9 May 1813 - From what ship: HMS Raisonnable - Born: County Donegal, Ireland - Age: 30 - Discharged on 22 Oct 1814 and sent to Dartmoor on HMS Leyden.

Gannet, Mathew - Seaman - Number: 2231 - Prize name: Marchione of Ely - Ship type: MV - How taken: Impressed at London - When taken: 13 Aug 1813 - Date received: 29 Aug 1813 - From what ship: HMS Raisonnable - Born: Massachusetts - Age: 26 - Discharged on 12 Aug 1814 and sent to Dartmoor on HMS Alpheus.

Gard, Gulab - Seaman - Number: 661 - Prize name: U.S.R.M. Cutter James Madison - Ship type: War - How taken: HM Frigate Barbadoes - When taken: 22 Aug 1812 - Where taken: at sea - Date received: 24 Feb 1813 - From what ship: Portsmouth via HMS Ulysses - Born: Groton, CT - Age: 29 - Discharged on 10 May 1813 and released to Cartel Admittance.

Gardener, Jerry - Seaman - Number: 3579 - How taken: Gave himself up from a MV brig - When taken: 10 Dec 1812 - Date received: 26 Mar 1814 - From what ship: Plymouth via HMS Raleigh - Born: Rhode Island - Age: 27 - Race: Black - Discharged on 26 Sep 1814 and sent to Dartmoor on HMS Leyden.

Gardiner, Amboy - Seaman - Number: 1349 - Prize name: Industry - Ship type: MV - How taken: HM Frigate Dryand - When taken: 7 Jan 1813 - Where taken: at sea - Date received: 3 Apr 1813 - From what ship: Portsmouth, via an admiral's tender - Born: Middleton - Age: 29 - Race: Black - Discharged on 24 Jul 1813 and released to Cartel Hoffminy.

Gardner, Anthony - Seaman - Number: 873 - Prize name: Stephen - Ship type: MV - How taken: Briton, letter of marque - When taken: 1 Jan 1813 - Where taken: off Bordeaux, France - Date received: 1 Mar 1813 - From what ship: Plymouth via HMS Namur - Born: Londonderry, Ireland - Age: 27 - Race: Blackman - Discharged on 24 Jul 1813 and released to Cartel Hoffminy.

Gardner, George - Seaman - Number: 2389 - How taken: Gave himself up from HM Ship-of-the-Line Achille - When taken: 26 Dec 1812 - Date received: 20 Oct 1813 - From what ship: Portsmouth, via an admiral's tender - Born: New York - Age: 21 - Race: Black - Discharged on 4 Sep 1814 and sent to Dartmoor on HMS Freya.

Gardner, James - Seaman - Number: 814 - Prize name: Leader - Ship type: MV - How taken: HM Frigate Andromach - When taken: 10 Dec 1812 - Where taken: off Bordeaux, France - Date received: 27 Feb 1813 - From what ship: Plymouth via HMS Namur - Born: Newburyport - Age: 23 - Discharged on 21 Apr 1813 and released to HMS Raisonnable.

Gardner, James - Seaman - Number: 2360 - How taken: Gave himself up from HM Ship-of-the-Line Hibernia - When taken: 25 Jun 1813 - Date received: 20 Oct 1813 - From what ship: Portsmouth, via an admiral's tender - Born: Hartford - Age: 31 - Discharged on 4 Sep 1814 and sent to Dartmoor on HMS Freya.

Gardner, John - Seaman - Number: 2547 - Prize name: Prize to the U.S. Frigate President - Ship type: War - How taken: HM Transport Regulus - When taken: 4 Sep 1812 - Where taken: Newfoundland Bank - Date received: 22 Oct 1813 - From what ship: Portsmouth via HMT Malabar - Born: Salem - Age: 22 - Discharged on 8 Sep 1814 and sent to Dartmoor on HMS Niobe.

Gardner, Jonathan - Seaman - Number: 1779 - Prize name: Moscow - Ship type: MV - How taken: Impressed at Gravesend, England - When taken: 27 Sep 1813 - Date received: 1 Jul 1813 - From what ship: HMS Raisonnable - Born: Ingram - Age: 43 - Discharged on 4 Aug 1814 and sent to Dartmoor on HMS Liverpool.

Gardner, Peter - Seaman - Number: 2010 - How taken: Gave himself up from HM Ship-of-the-Line Royal Sovereign - Date received: 15 Jul 1813 - From what ship: Plymouth - Born: New York - Age: 24 - Discharged on 17 Jun 1814 and sent to Dartmoor on HMS Pincher.

Gardner, Samuel - Gunner's Mate - Number: 432 - Prize name: Hunter - Ship type: P - How taken: HM Frigate Phoebe - When taken: 23 Dec 1812 - Where taken: off Azores - Date received: 19 Feb 1813 - From what ship: HMS Modeste - Born: Salem - Age: 37 - Discharged on 2 Jul 1813 and released to Cartel Moses Brown.

Gardner, William - Seaman - Number: 2241 - Prize name: Orders in Council - Ship type: LM - How taken: HM Frigate Surveillante - When taken: 1 Jan 1813 - Where taken: off Cape Ortegal, Spain - Date received: 7 Sep 1813 - From what ship: HMS Raisonnable - Born: Boston - Age: 20 - Discharged on 11 Aug 1814 and sent to Dartmoor on HMS Freya.

Garmindia, Stephen - Seaman - Number: 2226 - Prize name: Porcupine - Ship type: LM - How taken: HM Frigate Acasta - When taken: 29 Jun 1813 - Where taken: off Cape Sable, Florida - Date received: 22 Aug 1813 - From what ship: HMS Raisonnable - Born: San Sebastian, Spain - Age: 27 - Discharged on 22 Jun 1814 and sent to Calais, France on the Simon & Mary.

Garrett, Simon T. - Mate - Number: 2703 - Prize name: Growler - Ship type: P - How taken: HM Brig Electra - When taken: 7 Jul 1813 - Where taken: off St. Johns - Date received: 7 Jan 1814 - From what ship: Portsmouth - Born: Virginia - Age: 21 - Discharged on 8 Sep 1814 and sent to Dartmoor on HMS Leyden.

Garrison, Christian - Seaman - Number: 1608 - How taken: Gave himself up from HM Frigate President at Chatham - When taken: 27 Apr 1813 - Date received: 1 May 1813 - From what ship: HMS President - Born: New Jersey - Age: 27 - Discharged on 25 Sep 1814 and sent to Dartmoor.

Garrison, John - Seaman - Number: 1059 - Prize name: Independence - Ship type: MV - How taken: HM Frigate Medusa - When taken: 9 Nov 1812 - Where taken: off San Sebastian, Spain - Date received: 11 Mar 1813 - From what ship: Yarmouth via HMS Tenders - Born: New York - Age: 22 - Discharged on 8 Jun 1813 and released to Cartel Rodrigo.

Garthon, Willey - Seaman - Number: 816 - Prize name: Columbia - Ship type: MV - How taken: HM Frigate Briton - When taken: 17 Dec 1812 - Where taken: off Bordeaux, France - Date received: 27 Feb 1813 - From what ship: Plymouth via HMS Namur - Born: Philadelphia - Age: 34 - Discharged in Jul 1813 and released to Cartel Moses Brown.

Garthy, James - Seaman - Number: 1969 - Prize name: Lightning - Ship type: MV - How taken: HM Frigate Medusa - When taken: 2 Apr 1813 - Where taken: Bay of Biscay - Date received: 15 Jul 1813 - From what ship: Plymouth - Born: Philadelphia - Age: 21 - Discharged on 17 Jun 1814 and sent to Dartmoor on HMS Redbreast.

Gase, Zachariah - Seaman - Number: 713 - Prize name: Ganges - Ship type: MV - How taken: Detained at Portsmouth harbor - When taken: 31 Jul 1812 - Date received: 24 Feb 1813 - From what ship: Portsmouth via HMS Ulysses - Born: Beverly, MA - Age: 20 - Discharged on 23 Mar 1813 and released to the Cartel Robinson Potter.

Gaskin, William - Seaman - Number: 3909 - How taken: Gave himself up from HM Ship-of-the-Line Queen Charlotte - When taken: 13 Sep 1814 - Date received: 7 Sep 1814 - From what ship: Transport Office - Born:

Norfolk - Age: 26 - Race: Black - Discharged on 10 Oct 1814 and sent to Dartmoor on the Mermaid.

Gasseyr, Zephyr - Seaman - Number: 682 - Prize name: U.S.R.M. Cutter James Madison - Ship type: War - How taken: HM Frigate Barbadoes - When taken: 22 Aug 1812 - Where taken: at sea - Date received: 24 Feb 1813 - From what ship: Portsmouth via HMS Ulysses - Born: Savannah - Age: 28 - Discharged on 10 May 1813 and released to Cartel Admittance.

Gatchell, John G. - Prize Master - Number: 2713 - Prize name: Growler - Ship type: P - How taken: HM Brig Electra - When taken: 7 Jul 1813 - Where taken: off St. Johns - Date received: 7 Jan 1814 - From what ship: Portsmouth - Born: Massachusetts - Age: 26 - Discharged on 25 Sep 1814 and sent to Dartmoor on HMS Leyden.

Gault, William - Seaman - Number: 1944 - Prize name: Cannoniere - Ship type: P - How taken: HM Ship-of-the-Line Warspite - When taken: 14 Mar 1813 - Where taken: Bay of Biscay - Date received: 15 Jul 1813 - From what ship: Plymouth - Born: New York - Age: 21 - Discharged on 17 Jun 1814 and sent to Dartmoor on HMS Redbreast.

Gavet, James - Gunner's Mate - Number: 3737 - Prize name: Argus - Ship type: MV - How taken: HM Ship-of-the-Line San Domingo - When taken: 1 Mar 1814 - Where taken: off Savannah - Date received: 26 May 1814 - From what ship: HMS Hindostan - Born: Salem - Age: 26 - Discharged on 25 Sep 1814 and sent to Dartmoor on HMS Niobe.

Gavot, Henry - Marine Private - Number: 3689 - Prize name: Bunker Hill - Ship type: P - How taken: HM Frigate Pomone & HM Frigate Cydnus - When taken: 4 Mar 1814 - Where taken: Bay of Biscay - Date received: 4 May 1814 - From what ship: Portsmouth - Born: Isle de Basse, France - Age: 28 - Discharged on 22 Jun 1814 and sent to Calais, France on the Simon & Mary.

Gebers, Henry - Seaman - Number: 675 - Prize name: U.S.R.M. Cutter James Madison - Ship type: War - How taken: HM Frigate Barbadoes - When taken: 22 Aug 1812 - Where taken: at sea - Date received: 24 Feb 1813 - From what ship: Portsmouth via HMS Ulysses - Born: Swinemunde, Prussia - Age: 31 - Discharged on 10 May 1813 and released to Cartel Admittance.

Geely, Joseph - Seaman - Number: 706 - Prize name: Deanna, recaptured British vessel - Ship type: P - How taken: HM Ship-of-the-Line Polyphemus - When taken: 14 Sep 1812 - Where taken: at sea - Date received: 24 Feb 1813 - From what ship: Portsmouth via HMS Ulysses - Born: Mountsart, MA - Age: 20 - Discharged on 8 Jun 1813 and released to Cartel Rodrigo.

Geline, John - Seaman - Number: 827 - How taken: Gave himself up from HM Hospital Ship Trent - Date received: 1 Mar 1813 - From what ship: Plymouth via HMS Namur - Born: Warrington - Age: 35 - Discharged on 17 Jun 1814 and sent to Dartmoor on HMS Redbreast.

George, Isaac - Seaman - Number: 1198 - Prize name: Columbia - Ship type: MV - How taken: HM Frigate Briton - When taken: 17 Dec 1812 - Where taken: off Bordeaux, France - Date received: 16 Mar 1813 - From what ship: Portsmouth, via HMS Abundance - Born: Philadelphia - Age: 26 - Discharged on 2 Jul 1813 and released to Cartel Moses Brown.

George, Peter - Seaman - Number: 508 - Prize name: Josephine - Ship type: MV - How taken: HM Sloop Goree - When taken: 15 Aug 1812 - Where taken: off Bermuda - Date received: 23 Feb 1813 - From what ship: Portsmouth via HMS Dromedary - Born: Charlestown - Age: 32 - Discharged on 10 May 1813 and released to Cartel Admittance.

George, Thomas - Seaman - Number: 1122 - Prize name: U.S.R.M. Cutter James Madison - Ship type: War - How taken: HM Frigate Barbadoes - When taken: 22 Aug 1812 - Where taken: at sea - Date received: 14 Mar 1813 - From what ship: Portsmouth via HMS Beagle - Born: Norfolk - Age: 23 - Discharged on 10 May 1813 and released to Cartel Admittance.

George, William Main - Seaman - Number: 1379 - How taken: Gave himself up from HM Ship-of-the-Line Colossus - When taken: 6 Mar 1813 - Date received: 3 Apr 1813 - From what ship: Portsmouth, via an admiral's tender - Born: Watertown, MA - Age: 23 - Discharged on 24 Jul 1814 and sent to Dartmoor.

George, William W. - Seaman - Number: 1092 - Prize name: Rachael - Ship type: MV - How taken: HM Schooner Herring - When taken: 9 Feb 1813 - Where taken: at sea - Date received: 14 Mar 1813 - From what ship:

Portsmouth via HMS Beagle - Born: Marblehead - Age: 20 - Discharged on 8 Sep 1814 and sent to Dartmoor on HMS Niobe.

Gibbins, Hiram - Seaman - Number: 2953 - Prize name: Enterprise - Ship type: P - How taken: HM Frigate Tenedos - When taken: 21 May 1813 - Where taken: off Cape Cod - Date received: 7 Jan 1814 - From what ship: Halifax - Born: Massachusetts - Age: 23 - Discharged on 25 Sep 1814 and sent to Dartmoor on HMS Leyden.

Gibbons, Andrew - Seaman - Number: 936 - Prize name: Argus - Ship type: MV - How taken: HM Cutter Fancy - When taken: 17 Dec 1812 - Where taken: Bay of Biscay - Date received: 10 Mar 1813 - From what ship: HMS Tigress - Born: New York - Age: 22 - Discharged on 2 Jul 1813 and released to Cartel Moses Brown.

Gibbs, Daniel - Seaman - Number: 1900 - Prize name: Weasel - Ship type: MV - How taken: HM Brig Foxhound - When taken: 25 Mar 1813 - Where taken: Bay of Biscay - Date received: 7 Jul 1813 - From what ship: Portsmouth via HMS Tribune - Born: Newport - Age: 19 - Discharged on 4 Aug 1814 and sent to Dartmoor on HMS Liverpool.

Gibbs, James - Seaman - Number: 1538 - How taken: Impressed at Belfast - When taken: Nov 1812 - Date received: 8 Apr 1813 - From what ship: Plymouth via HMS Olympia - Born: Philadelphia - Age: 32 - Race: Black - Discharged on 2 Jul 1813 and released to Cartel Moses Brown.

Gibbs, Perry - Cook - Number: 156 - How taken: Stopped at London - When taken: 28 Oct 1812 - Date received: 5 Nov 1812 - From what ship: HMS Namur - Born: Georgetown, MD - Age: 26 - Discharged in Jul 1813 and released to Cartel Moses Brown.

Gibbs, Valentine - Seaman - Number: 2417 - How taken: Gave himself up from HM Frigate Curacoa - Date received: 21 Oct 1813 - From what ship: Portsmouth via HMT Malabar - Born: North Carolina - Age: 29 - Discharged on 4 Sep 1814 and sent to Dartmoor on HMS Freya.

Gibey, John - Seaman - Number: 831 - Prize name: John Barnes - Ship type: MV - How taken: Gave himself up at Liverpool - When taken: 7 Nov 1813 - Date received: 1 Mar 1813 - From what ship: Plymouth via HMS Namur - Born: Baltimore - Age: 21 - Discharged in Jul 1813 and released to Cartel Moses Brown.

Gibson, Samuel - Seaman - Number: 3242 - How taken: Gave himself up from HM Transport Bruisor - When taken: 3 Feb 1814 - Date received: 10 Feb 1814 - From what ship: HMS Cadmus - Born: Boston - Age: 29 - Race: Black - Discharged on 25 Sep 1814 and sent to Dartmoor on HMS Leyden.

Gibson, Samuel - Seaman - Number: 3239 - How taken: Gave himself up from HM Brig Bruiser - When taken: 3 Feb 1814 - Date received: 10 Feb 1814 - From what ship: HMS Cadmus - Born: New Haven - Age: 28 - Died on 26 Apr 1814 from fever.

Gibson, William - Seaman - Number: 515 - Prize name: William - Ship type: MV - How taken: HM Brig Recruit - When taken: 29 Aug 1812 - Where taken: at sea - Date received: 23 Feb 1813 - From what ship: Portsmouth via HMS Dromedary - Born: Williamstown - Age: 21 - Discharged on 10 May 1813 and released to Cartel Admittance.

Gifford, Barry - Seaman - Number: 1034 - Prize name: Catharine - Ship type: MV - How taken: HM Frigate Leonidas - When taken: 31 Jul 1812 - Where taken: off Ireland - Date received: 11 Mar 1813 - From what ship: Yarmouth via HMS Tenders - Born: Westport - Age: 22 - Discharged on 26 Jul 1813 and released to Cartel Hoffminy.

Gifford, Francis - Seaman - Number: 606 - Prize name: Antelope - Ship type: P - How taken: HM Brig Zephyr - When taken: 10 Dec 1812 - Where taken: at sea - Date received: 23 Feb 1813 - From what ship: Portsmouth via HMS Dromedary - Born: Monmouth - Age: 26 - Discharged on 2 Jul 1813 and released to Cartel Moses Brown.

Gilbert, Elijah - Private - Number: 3089 - Prize name: 23rd U.S. Infantry - Ship type: LF - How taken: British forces - When taken: 24 Jun 1813 - Where taken: Beaver Dams, Upper Canada - Date received: 7 Jan 1814 - From what ship: Halifax - Born: York - Age: 23 - Discharged on 10 Oct 1814 and sent to U.S. on Cartel St. Philip.

Gilbert, George - Boy - Number: 1961 - Prize name: Ferox - Ship type: MV - How taken: HM Frigate Medusa & HM Brig Lyra - When taken: 28 Mar 1813 - Where taken: off Cape Ortegal, Spain - Date received: 15 Jul 1813 - From what ship: Plymouth - Born: Gloucester - Age: 16 - Discharged on 17 Jun 1814 and sent to

Dartmoor on HMS Redbreast.

Gilbert, Isaac - Seaman - Number: 2525 - Prize name: Yorktown - Ship type: P - How taken: HM Brig Nimrod - When taken: 17 Jul 1813 - Where taken: Grand Banks - Date received: 22 Oct 1813 - From what ship: Portsmouth via HMT Malabar - Born: New York - Age: 25 - Discharged on 8 Sep 1814 and sent to Dartmoor on HMS Niobe.

Gilbert, Thomas - Seaman - Number: 1286 - How taken: Gave himself up from HM Guardship Royal William - When taken: 3 Feb 1813 - Date received: 16 Mar 1813 - From what ship: Portsmouth, via HMS Abundance - Born: New York - Age: 27 - Discharged on 1 Aug 1813 and released to HMS Ceres.

Gilbert, Thomas - Seaman - Number: 1741 - How taken: Gave himself up from HM Sloop Talbot - When taken: 23 Apr 1813 - Date received: 25 May 1813 - From what ship: Portsmouth via HMS Impetius - Born: Wilmington - Age: 40 - Discharged on 24 Jul 1814 and sent to Dartmoor on HMS Liffey.

Gilbert, William A. - Seaman - Number: 145 - Prize name: Edward - Ship type: MV - How taken: HM Frigate Ethalion - When taken: 2 Aug 1812 - Where taken: Great Belt, Denmark - Date received: 5 Nov 1812 - From what ship: HMS Namur - Born: Brunswick, NJ - Age: 33 - Discharged on 10 May 1813 and released to Cartel Admittance.

Giles, John - Seaman - Number: 596 - Prize name: Antelope - Ship type: P - How taken: HM Brig Zephyr - When taken: 10 Dec 1812 - Where taken: at sea - Date received: 23 Feb 1813 - From what ship: Portsmouth via HMS Dromedary - Born: New York - Age: 48 - Discharged on 2 Jul 1813 and released to Cartel Moses Brown.

Giles, John - Seaman - Number: 3413 - Prize name: Stark (General Stark) - Ship type: P - How taken: HM Frigate Maidstone - When taken: 15 Jul 1813 - Where taken: Halifax - Date received: 23 Feb 1814 - From what ship: Halifax via HMT Malabar - Born: Boothbay - Age: 19 - Discharged on 22 Oct 1814 and sent to Dartmoor on HMS Leyden.

Gill, James - Seaman - Number: 790 - Prize name: Dolphin - Ship type: MV - How taken: HM Ship-of-the-Line Colossus - When taken: 5 Jan 1813 - Where taken: off the Western Isles, Scotland - Date received: 27 Feb 1813 - From what ship: Plymouth via HMS Namur - Born: New Jersey - Age: 31 - Discharged on 24 Jul 1813 and released to Cartel Hoffminy.

Gill, John - Private - Number: 1619 - Prize name: 13th U.S. Infantry - Ship type: LF - How taken: British forces - When taken: 13 Oct 1812 - Where taken: Upper Canada - Date received: 9 May 1813 - From what ship: HMS Raisonnable - Born: County Sligo, Ireland - Age: 21 - Discharged on 22 Oct 1814 and sent to Dartmoor on HMS Leyden.

Gilles, St. Clair - Seaman - Number: 1595 - How taken: Impressed at Gravesend, England - When taken: 4 Mar 1813 - Date received: 19 Apr 1813 - From what ship: HMS Raisonnable - Born: Long Island - Age: 27 - Discharged on 23 Nov 1813 and released to HMS Ceres.

Gilligan, William - Seaman - Number: 1472 - Prize name: Union - Ship type: MV - How taken: HM Frigate Iris - When taken: 17 Jan 1813 - Where taken: at sea - Date received: 6 Apr 1813 - From what ship: Portsmouth via Tender Eliza - Born: Limerick - Age: 31 - Released on 4 Sep 1813 and sent to Ireland.

Gilpin, John - Seaman - Number: 1527 - How taken: Gave himself up from HM Frigate Franchise - When taken: 20 Sep 1812 - Date received: 8 Apr 1813 - From what ship: Portsmouth, via an admiral's tender - Born: Philadelphia - Age: 28 - Race: Mulatto - Discharged on 29 Jun 1813 and released to HMS Ceres.

Girdler, James - Seaman - Number: 3342 - Prize name: Porcupine - Ship type: LM - How taken: HM Frigate Acasta - When taken: 18 Jul 1813 - Where taken: off Cape Sable, Florida - Date received: 23 Feb 1814 - From what ship: Halifax via HMT Malabar - Born: Manchester - Age: 18 - Discharged on 10 Oct 1814 and sent to Dartmoor on the Mermaid.

Giria, John - Seaman - Number: 3344 - Prize name: Porcupine - Ship type: LM - How taken: HM Frigate Acasta - When taken: 18 Jul 1813 - Where taken: off Cape Sable, Florida - Date received: 23 Feb 1814 - From what ship: Halifax via HMT Malabar - Born: Bayonne - Age: 21 - Discharged on 22 Jun 1814 and sent to Calais, France on the Simon & Mary.

Given, James - Private - Number: 2642 - Prize name: 14th U.S. Infantry - Ship type: LF - How taken: British forces

- When taken: 24 Jun 1813 - Where taken: Beaver Dams, Upper Canada - Date received: 5 Nov 1813 - From what ship: HMS Hindostan - Born: North Ireland - Age: 46 - Discharged on 10 Oct 1814 and sent to U.S. on Cartel St. Philip.

Glascow, John - Seaman - Number: 459 - Prize name: Hunter - Ship type: P - How taken: HM Frigate Phoebe - When taken: 23 Dec 1812 - Where taken: off Azores - Date received: 19 Feb 1813 - From what ship: HMS Modeste - Born: Boston - Age: 23 - Discharged on 24 Jul 1813 and released to Cartel Hoffminy.

Glenn, Robert - Seaman - Number: 407 - Prize name: Hope - Ship type: MV - How taken: HM Sloop Pheasant - When taken: 13 Dec 1812 - Where taken: off Azores - Date received: 19 Feb 1813 - From what ship: HMS Modeste - Born: Pennsylvania - Age: 53 - Discharged on 2 Jul 1813 and released to Cartel Moses Brown.

Glover, Benjamin - Seaman - Number: 3905 - How taken: Gave himself up from the MV John - When taken: 28 Aug 1814 - Date received: 31 Aug 1814 - From what ship: Transport Office - Born: Massachusetts - Age: 22 - Discharged on 25 Sep 1814 and sent to Dartmoor on HMS Leyden.

Glover, John - Boy - Number: 2816 - Prize name: Industry - Ship type: P - How taken: HM Brig Heron - When taken: 3 Nov 1813 - Where taken: off Halifax - Date received: 7 Jan 1814 - From what ship: Halifax - Born: Marblehead - Age: 18 - Discharged on 25 Sep 1814 and sent to Dartmoor on HMS Leyden.

Glower, Samuel - Seaman - Number: 2369 - How taken: Gave himself up from HM Ship-of-the-Line Swiftsure - When taken: 26 Dec 1812 - Date received: 20 Oct 1813 - From what ship: Portsmouth, via an admiral's tender - Born: North Carolina - Age: 21 - Discharged on 4 Sep 1814 and sent to Dartmoor on HMS Freya.

Goday, W. - Seaman - Number: 346 - Prize name: Postsea, prize to the Privateer Thrasher - Ship type: P - How taken: HM Sloop Helena - When taken: 31 Dec 1813 - Where taken: off Azores - Date received: 19 Jan 1813 - From what ship: HMS Raisonnable - Born: Cape Ann - Age: 21 - Discharged on 24 Jul 1813 and released to Cartel Hoffminy.

Godshall, John - Seaman - Number: 1490 - Prize name: Union - Ship type: MV - How taken: HM Frigate Iris - When taken: 17 Jan 1813 - Where taken: at sea - Date received: 6 Apr 1813 - From what ship: Plymouth via an admiral's tender - Born: Philadelphia - Age: 18 - Discharged on 26 Jul 1813 and released to Cartel Hoffminy.

Godsoe, William - Seaman - Number: 580 - Prize name: Perseverance - Ship type: MV - How taken: HM Sloop Atalante - When taken: 31 Jul 1812 - Where taken: at sea - Date received: 23 Feb 1813 - From what ship: Portsmouth via HMS Dromedary - Born: New Hampshire - Age: 43 - Discharged on 8 Jun 1813 and released to Cartel Rodrigo.

Godson, John - Seaman - Number: 846 - Prize name: Lucian, prize of the Privateer Armstrong - Ship type: P - How taken: Briton, letter of marque - When taken: 29 Nov 1812 - Where taken: off Bermuda - Date received: 1 Mar 1813 - From what ship: Plymouth via HMS Namur - Born: Fredericksburg - Age: 39 - Discharged on 8 Jun 1813 and released to Cartel Rodrigo.

Goff, Peter - Boatswain - Number: 2820 - Prize name: Portsmouth Packet - Ship type: P - How taken: HM Brig Fantome - When taken: 5 Oct 1813 - Where taken: off Portland - Date received: 7 Jan 1814 - From what ship: Halifax - Born: Connecticut - Age: 28 - Discharged on 25 Sep 1814 and sent to Dartmoor on HMS Leyden.

Golding, Abijah - Seaman - Number: 3659 - How taken: Impressed at London - When taken: 4 Apr 1814 - Date received: 23 Apr 1814 - From what ship: HMS Raisonnable - Born: Lancaster - Age: 27 - Race: Black - Discharged on 25 Sep 1814 and sent to Dartmoor on HMS Niobe.

Golever, William - Seaman - Number: 634 - How taken: Gave himself up from HM Ship-of-the-Line Vigo - When taken: 31 Dec 1812 - Date received: 23 Feb 1813 - From what ship: Portsmouth via HMS Dromedary - Born: Boston - Age: 40 - Discharged on 26 Jul 1814 and sent to Dartmoor on HMS Raven.

Gomerson, James - Seaman - Number: 2956 - Prize name: Enterprise - Ship type: P - How taken: HM Frigate Tenedos - When taken: 21 May 1813 - Where taken: off Cape Cod - Date received: 7 Jan 1814 - From what ship: Halifax - Born: Massachusetts - Age: 25 - Discharged on 22 Oct 1814 and sent to Dartmoor on HMS Leyden.

Gomez, Manuel - Seaman - Number: 853 - Prize name: Brutus - Ship type: MV - How taken: Briton, letter of marque - When taken: 13 Jan 1813 - Where taken: Bay of Biscay - Date received: 1 Mar 1813 - From what ship: Plymouth via HMS Namur - Born: Oporto, Portugal - Age: 24 - Released on 20 May 1813 to Rising Sun.

Goodman, James - Seaman - Number: 3369 - Prize name: Yorktown - Ship type: P - How taken: HM Frigate Maidstone - When taken: 17 Jul 1813 - Where taken: Grand Banks - Date received: 23 Feb 1814 - From what ship: Halifax via HMT Malabar - Born: New York - Age: 19 - Discharged on 21 Jul 1814 and sent to Dartmoor on HMS Portia.

Goodrich, H. C. - Private - Number: 3084 - Prize name: 14th U.S. Infantry - Ship type: LF - How taken: British forces - When taken: 24 Jun 1813 - Where taken: Beaver Dams, Upper Canada - Date received: 7 Jan 1814 - From what ship: Halifax - Born: Massachusetts - Age: 27 - Discharged on 10 Oct 1814 and sent to U.S. on Cartel St. Philip.

Goodwin, John - Seaman - Number: 3301 - Prize name: Catherine - Ship type: P - How taken: HM Ship-of-the-Line La Hogue - When taken: 2 May 1813 - Where taken: off Cape Sable, Florida - Date received: 23 Feb 1814 - From what ship: Halifax via HMT Malabar - Born: Fort George - Age: 27 - Discharged on 10 Oct 1814 and sent to Dartmoor on the Mermaid.

Goodwin, Jonas B. - Seaman - Number: 1087 - Prize name: Benjamin - Ship type: MV - How taken: HM Frigate Medusa - When taken: 31 Dec 1812 - Where taken: at sea - Date received: 14 Mar 1813 - From what ship: Portsmouth via HMS Cornwell - Born: Marblehead - Age: 17 - Discharged on 24 Jul 1813 and released to Cartel Hoffminy.

Goodwin, Joseph - Private - Number: 3055 - Prize name: 14th U.S. Infantry - Ship type: LF - How taken: British forces - When taken: 9 Jun 1813 - Where taken: Canada - Date received: 7 Jan 1814 - From what ship: Halifax - Born: Maryland - Age: 25 - Released on 17 Jun 1814.

Gordon, James - Seaman - Number: 2086 - How taken: Gave himself up from HM Ship-of-the-Line Scipion - When taken: 27 May 1813 - Date received: 9 Aug 1813 - From what ship: HMS Thames - Born: Massachsetts - Age: 25 - Discharged on 12 Aug 1814 and sent to Dartmoor on HMS Alpheus.

Gordon, John - Seaman - Number: 2332 - How taken: Gave himself up from HM Frigate Bucephalus - When taken: 20 Aug 1813 - Date received: 12 Oct 1813 - From what ship: HMS Raisonnable - Born: Baltimore - Age: 27 - Discharged on 25 Sep 1814 and sent to Dartmoor on HMS Leyden.

Gordon, Richard - Seaman - Number: 3651 - Prize name: Bunker Hill - Ship type: P - How taken: HM Frigate Pomone & HM Frigate Cydnus - When taken: 4 Mar 1814 - Where taken: Bay of Biscay - Date received: 31 Mar 1814 - From what ship: HMS Raisonnable - Born: Boston - Age: 39 - Race: Black - Discharged on 25 Sep 1814 and sent to Dartmoor on HMS Niobe.

Gordon, Sperrin - Seaman - Number: 2835 - Prize name: Portsmouth Packet - Ship type: P - How taken: HM Brig Fantome - When taken: 5 Oct 1813 - Where taken: off Portland - Date received: 7 Jan 1814 - From what ship: Halifax - Born: Massachusetts - Age: 24 - Died on 4 Mar 1814 from small pox.

Gordon, William - Seaman - Number: 2589 - How taken: Gave himself up from HM Ship-of-the-Line Union - When taken: 27 May 1813 - Date received: 5 Nov 1813 - From what ship: HMS Hindostan - Born: New York - Age: 26 - Race: Blackman - Discharged on 12 Aug 1814 and sent to Dartmoor on HMS Alpheus.

Gordon, William - Steward - Number: 1803 - How taken: Impressed at London - When taken: 29 Jun 1813 - Date received: 3 Jul 1813 - From what ship: HMS Raisonnable - Born: Wilmington - Age: 33 - Race: Mulatto - Discharged on 12 Aug 1814 and sent to Dartmoor on HMS Alpheus.

Gore, John - Seaman - Number: 772 - Prize name: Alagana - Ship type: MV - How taken: HM Ship-of-the-Line San Juan - When taken: 8 May 1812 - Where taken: Gibraltar - Date received: 25 Feb 1813 - From what ship: HMS Brazen - Born: Castine, MA - Age: 25 - Discharged on 10 May 1813 and released to Cartel Admittance.

Gorton, John - Seaman - Number: 3871 - How taken: Gave himself up from Chatham - When taken: 18 Aug 1814 - Date received: 28 Aug 1814 - From what ship: Chatham - Born: North Carolina - Age: 33 - Discharged on 22 Oct 1814 and sent to Dartmoor on HMS Leyden.

Gosling, Joseph - Seaman - Number: 3544 - Prize name: Commodore Perry - Ship type: MV - How taken: Sent into custody from a cutter - When taken: 25 Feb 1814 - Where taken: off Bordeaux, France - Date received: 5 Mar 1814 - From what ship: HMS Raisonnable - Born: Quebec - Age: 26 - Discharged on 26 Sep 1814 and sent to Dartmoor on HMS Leyden.

Goss, Jesse - Seaman - Number: 2488 - Prize name: Enterprise - Ship type: P - How taken: HM Frigate Tenedos - When taken: 21 May 1813 - Where taken: off Cape Cod - Date received: 22 Oct 1813 - From what ship: Portsmouth via HMT Malabar - Born: Marblehead - Age: 18 - Discharged on 8 Sep 1814 and sent to Dartmoor on HMS Niobe.

Goss, Joshua - Boy - Number: 2016 - Prize name: Polly - Ship type: MV - How taken: HM Frigate Surveillante - When taken: 23 Mar 1813 - Where taken: Bay of Biscay - Date received: 15 Jul 1813 - From what ship: Plymouth - Born: Marblehead - Age: 14 - Discharged on 17 Jun 1814 and sent to Dartmoor on HMS Pincher.

Goswick, William - Seaman - Number: 1758 - How taken: Gave himself up from HM Brig Cordelia - When taken: 12 Nov 1812 - Date received: 11 Jun 1813 - From what ship: HMS Raisonnable - Born: New York - Age: 38 - Race: Mulatto - Released on 11 Jul 1814.

Gotier, Charles J. - Seaman - Number: 3661 - Prize name: Pilot - Ship type: LM - How taken: Vittoria, British privateer from Guernsey - When taken: 28 Jan 1814 - Where taken: off Bordeaux, France - Date received: 4 May 1814 - From what ship: Portsmouth - Born: Salem - Age: 23 - Discharged on 25 Sep 1814 and sent to Dartmoor on HMS Niobe.

Gould, Henry - Seaman - Number: 3872 - How taken: Gave himself up from Chatham - When taken: 18 Aug 1814 - Date received: 28 Aug 1814 - From what ship: Chatham - Born: Nantucket - Age: 27 - Race: Black - Discharged on 22 Oct 1814 and sent to Dartmoor on HMS Leyden.

Gould, John - Seaman - Number: 1357 - Prize name: Dart - Ship type: MV - How taken: HM Brig Doterel - When taken: 5 Mar 1813 - Where taken: at sea - Date received: 3 Apr 1813 - From what ship: Portsmouth, via an admiral's tender - Born: Kittery, MA - Age: 25 - Discharged on 25 Jul 1814 and sent to Dartmoor on HMS Bittern.

Gould, Nicholas - Private - Number: 1680 - How taken: Gave himself up from the Royal Marines - When taken: Feb 1813 - Date received: 14 May 1813 - From what ship: Royal Marines - Born: New York - Age: 24 - Discharged on 15 Sep 1813 and released to HMS Ceres.

Goulding, Samuel - Seaman - Number: 2526 - Prize name: Yorktown - Ship type: P - How taken: HM Brig Nimrod - When taken: 17 Jul 1813 - Where taken: Grand Banks - Date received: 22 Oct 1813 - From what ship: Portsmouth via HMT Malabar - Born: New York - Age: 23 - Discharged on 8 Sep 1814 and sent to Dartmoor on HMS Niobe.

Gourley, William - Seaman - Number: 2181 - How taken: Gave himself up from HM Ship-of-the-Line Leviathan - When taken: 28 Oct 1812 - Date received: 16 Aug 1813 - From what ship: Portsmouth, via an admiral's tender - Born: Philadelphia - Age: 26 - Escaped on 10 Jun 1814 from HMS Kent.

Gowalter, John - Seaman - Number: 2812 - Prize name: Industry - Ship type: P - How taken: HM Brig Heron - When taken: 3 Nov 1813 - Where taken: off Halifax - Date received: 7 Jan 1814 - From what ship: Halifax - Born: Marblehead - Age: 41 - Discharged on 25 Sep 1814 and sent to Dartmoor on HMS Leyden.

Gowalter, John - Seaman - Number: 2802 - Prize name: Industry - Ship type: P - How taken: HM Brig Heron - When taken: 3 Nov 1813 - Where taken: off Halifax - Date received: 7 Jan 1814 - From what ship: Halifax - Born: Marblehead - Age: 22 - Discharged on 8 Sep 1814 and sent to Dartmoor on HMS Niobe.

Graham, George - Seaman - Number: 1387 - Prize name: Stephen - Ship type: MV - How taken: Briton, letter of marque - When taken: 1 Jan 1813 - Where taken: off Bordeaux, France - Date received: 5 Apr 1813 - From what ship: Plymouth via HMS Dwarf - Born: New York - Age: 19 - Discharged on 24 Jul 1813 and released to Cartel Hoffminy.

Graham, William - Seaman - Number: 1493 - Prize name: Union - Ship type: MV - How taken: HM Frigate Iris - When taken: 17 Jan 1813 - Where taken: at sea - Date received: 6 Apr 1813 - From what ship: Plymouth via an admiral's tender - Born: Delaware - Age: 18 - Discharged on 26 Jul 1813 and released to Cartel Hoffminy.

Gran, Abraham - Seaman - Number: 333 - How taken: Apprehended at Leight, Scotland - When taken: 14 Dec 1812 - Date received: 11 Jan 1813 - From what ship: HMS Raisonnable - Born: New York - Age: 22 - Discharged on 24 Jul 1813 and released to Cartel Hoffminy.

Grandy, Amos - Seaman - Number: 2957 - Prize name: Enterprise - Ship type: P - How taken: HM Frigate Tenedos - When taken: 21 May 1813 - Where taken: off Cape Cod - Date received: 7 Jan 1814 - From what ship: Halifax - Born: Massachusetts - Age: 38 - Died on 16 May 1814 from fever.

Grant, Christian - Seaman - Number: 1155 - Prize name: Sword Fish - Ship type: P - How taken: HM Ship-of-the-Line Elephant - When taken: 28 Dec 1812 - Where taken: off Azores - Date received: 16 Mar 1813 - From what ship: Portsmouth, via HMS Abundance - Born: Marblehead - Age: 22 - Discharged on 24 Jul 1813 and released to Cartel Hoffminy.

Grant, John - Seaman - Number: 72 - Prize name: Elson - Ship type: MV - How taken: HM Frigate Ethalion - When taken: 12 Aug 1812 - Where taken: Baltic - Date received: 4 Nov 1812 - From what ship: HMS Namur - Born: Marblehead - Age: 18 - Discharged on 10 May 1813 and released to Cartel Admittance.

Grant, Samuel - Seaman - Number: 2843 - Prize name: Portsmouth Packet - Ship type: P - How taken: HM Brig Fantome - When taken: 5 Oct 1813 - Where taken: off Portland - Date received: 7 Jan 1814 - From what ship: Halifax - Born: Massachusetts - Age: 21 - Discharged on 25 Sep 1814 and sent to Dartmoor on HMS Leyden.

Grant, William - Seaman - Number: 3176 - Prize name: Wolf Cove - Ship type: MV - How taken: HM Frigate Briton - When taken: 1 Dec 1813 - Where taken: off Brest, France - Date received: 7 Jan 1814 - From what ship: Halifax - Born: Massachusetts - Age: 17 - Discharged on 25 Sep 1814 and sent to Dartmoor on HMS Leyden.

Graveling, Jesse - Seaman - Number: 361 - Prize name: Postsea, prize to the Privateer Thrasher - Ship type: P - How taken: HM Sloop Helena - When taken: 31 Dec 1813 - Where taken: off Azores - Date received: 19 Jan 1813 - From what ship: HMS Raisonnable - Born: Leghorn, Italy - Age: 38 - Discharged on 24 Jul 1813 and released to Cartel Hoffminy.

Gravely, Joseph - Seaman - Number: 3583 - Prize name: Devon, prize to the Privateer Bunker Hill - Ship type: P - How taken: HM Brig Fly - When taken: 21 Jan 1814 - Where taken: at sea - Date received: 26 Mar 1814 - From what ship: Plymouth via HMS Raleigh - Born: Lorient, France - Age: 71 - Escaped on 20 May 1814 from HM Prison Ship Glory.

Graves, John - Seaman - Number: 2598 - How taken: Gave himself up from HM Ship-of-the-Line Berwick - When taken: 27 May 1813 - Date received: 5 Nov 1813 - From what ship: HMS Hindostan - Born: Marblehead - Age: 34 - Race: Blackman - Discharged on 12 Aug 1814 and sent to Dartmoor on HMS Alpheus.

Graves, Thomas - Seaman - Number: 3931 - How taken: Gave himself up from HMS Port Mahan - When taken: 20 Sep 1814 - Date received: 24 Sep 1814 - From what ship: HMS Namur - Born: Boston - Age: 28 - Race: Mulatto - Discharged on 29 Sep 1814 and sent to Dartmoor on HMS Freya.

Gray, Charles - Seaman - Number: 958 - How taken: Gave himself up from HM Ship-of-the-Line Salvador del Mundo - Date received: 10 Mar 1813 - From what ship: HMS Tigress - Born: Maryland - Age: 33 - Race: Mulatto - Discharged on 19 May 1813 and released to HMS Ceres.

Gray, John - Seaman - Number: 2070 - How taken: Gave himself up from HM Frigate Resistance - When taken: Aug 1813 - Date received: 9 Aug 1813 - From what ship: HMS Thames - Born: Haverhill, MD - Age: 29 - Discharged on 4 Aug 1814 and sent to Dartmoor on HMS Liverpool.

Gray, John - Private - Number: 3077 - Prize name: 14th U.S. Infantry - Ship type: LF - How taken: British forces - When taken: 24 Jun 1813 - Where taken: Beaver Dams, Upper Canada - Date received: 7 Jan 1814 - From what ship: Halifax - Born: Delaware - Age: 25 - Discharged on 10 Oct 1814 and sent to U.S. on Cartel St. Philip.

Gray, Samuel - Private - Number: 2615 - Prize name: 14th U.S. Infantry - Ship type: LF - How taken: British forces - When taken: 24 Jun 1813 - Where taken: Beaver Dams, Upper Canada - Date received: 5 Nov 1813 - From what ship: HMS Hindostan - Born: County Antrim, Ireland - Age: 39 - Discharged on 10 Oct 1814 and sent to U.S. on Cartel St. Philip.

Gray, Thomas - Seaman - Number: 1649 - How taken: Gave himself up from HM Brig Ringdove - Date received: 9 May 1813 - From what ship: HMS Raisonnable - Born: New York - Age: 30 - Discharged on 13 Aug 1814 and sent to Dartmoor.

Gray, Thomas - Seaman - Number: 1793 - How taken: Gave himself up from HM Transport Chatham - When taken: 10 Jun 1813 - Date received: 1 Jul 1813 - From what ship: HMS Raisonnable - Born: Baltimore - Age: 31 - Died on 4 Jan 1814 from pneumonia.

Greaves, Samuel - Seaman - Number: 890 - Prize name: Print of Boston - Ship type: MV - How taken: HM Ship-of-the-Line Colossus - When taken: 21 Jan 1813 - Where taken: at sea - Date received: 1 Mar 1813 - From what ship: Plymouth via HMS Namur - Born: Marblehead, MA - Age: 39 - Discharged on 17 Jun 1814 and sent to Dartmoor on HMS Redbreast.

Green, Charles - Seaman - Number: 2466 - Prize name: Cossack - Ship type: P - How taken: HM Frigate Amelia - When taken: 11 Apr 1813 - Where taken: off St. Johns - Date received: 21 Oct 1813 - From what ship: Portsmouth via HMT Malabar - Born: Newbury - Age: 21 - Discharged on 8 Sep 1814 and sent to Dartmoor on HMS Niobe.

Green, George - Seaman - Number: 2382 - How taken: Gave himself up from HM Ship-of-the-Line America - When taken: 26 Dec 1812 - Date received: 20 Oct 1813 - From what ship: Portsmouth, via an admiral's tender - Born: Baltimore - Age: 44 - Race: Black - Discharged on 4 Sep 1814 and sent to Dartmoor on HMS Freya.

Green, Henry - Seaman - Number: 1279 - Prize name: Sword Fish - Ship type: P - How taken: HM Ship-of-the-Line Elephant - When taken: 28 Dec 1812 - Where taken: off Azores - Date received: 16 Mar 1813 - From what ship: Portsmouth, via HMS Abundance - Born: Baltimore - Age: 27 - Race: Black - Discharged on 24 Jul 1813 and released to Cartel Hoffminy.

Green, Horace - Seaman - Number: 839 - Prize name: Vengeance - Ship type: LM - How taken: HM Frigate Phoebe - When taken: 1 Jan 1813 - Where taken: Lat 44.4 Long 23 - Date received: 1 Mar 1813 - From what ship: Plymouth via HMS Namur - Born: Hampshire County - Age: 19 - Discharged on 24 Jul 1813 and released to Cartel Hoffminy.

Green, James - Seaman - Number: 135 - Prize name: Leander - Ship type: MV - How taken: Stopped at London - When taken: 26 Oct 1812 - Date received: 5 Nov 1812 - From what ship: HMS Namur - Born: Dorset, MD - Age: 36 - Discharged on 26 Jul 1814 and sent to Dartmoor on HMS Raven.

Green, James Beckwith - Boatswain - Number: 2897 - Prize name: Dart - Ship type: P - How taken: HM Frigate Niger & HMS Fortunee - When taken: 10 Nov 1813 - Where taken: off Cape Finisterre, Spain - Date received: 7 Jan 1814 - From what ship: Portsmouth - Born: Virginia - Age: 20 - Died on 10 Jun 1814 from fever.

Green, John - Seaman - Number: 3721 - Prize name: Requin - Ship type: LM - How taken: HM Frigate Venus - When taken: 6 Mar 1814 - Where taken: off Bordeaux, France - Date received: 18 May 1814 - From what ship: HMS Raisonnable - Born: Philadelphia - Age: 18 - Discharged on 25 Sep 1814 and sent to Dartmoor on HMS Leyden.

Green, John - Seaman - Number: 1041 - Prize name: Wasp - Ship type: MV - How taken: Earl Spencer, East Indianman - When taken: 4 Aug 1812 - Where taken: off Cape Clear, Ireland - Date received: 11 Mar 1813 - From what ship: Yarmouth via HMS Tenders - Born: Albany - Age: 23 - Race: Black - Died on 8 Jun 1813 from pneumonia.

Green, John - Seaman - Number: 298 - Prize name: America - Ship type: MV - How taken: HM Brig Cracker - When taken: 1 Aug 1812 - Date received: 23 Dec 1812 - From what ship: Greenlaw Depot - Born: Not readable - Age: 29 - Discharged on 23 Mar 1813 and released to the Cartel Robinson Potter.

Green, John - Seaman - Number: 1342 - How taken: Gave himself up from HM Ship-of-the-Line Cornwall - When taken: 21 Mar 1813 - Date received: 26 Mar 1813 - From what ship: HMS Raisonnable - Born: Baltimore - Age: 23 - Race: Blackman - Discharged on 23 Jul 1814 and sent to Dartmoor.

Green, John - Seaman - Number: 3255 - Prize name: Fox - Ship type: MV - How taken: HM Frigate Shannon - When taken: 7 Nov 1813 - Where taken: Newfoundland Bank - Date received: 23 Feb 1814 - From what ship: Halifax via HMT Malabar - Born: Norfolk - Age: 25 - Race: Black - Discharged on 10 Oct 1814 and sent to Dartmoor on the Mermaid.

Green, Samuel - Seaman - Number: 935 - Prize name: Argus - Ship type: MV - How taken: HM Cutter Fancy -

When taken: 17 Dec 1812 - Where taken: Bay of Biscay - Date received: 10 Mar 1813 - From what ship: HMS Tigress - Born: Massachusetts - Age: 29 - Discharged on 2 Jul 1813 and released to Cartel Moses Brown.

Green, Thomas - Seaman - Number: 3929 - How taken: Gave himself up from HMS Rolus - When taken: 23 Sep 1814 - Date received: 24 Sep 1814 - From what ship: HMS Namur - Born: Boston - Age: 49 - Race: Mulatto - Discharged on 29 Sep 1814 and sent to Dartmoor on HMS Freya.

Green, William - Seaman - Number: 3507 - Prize name: Elbridge Gerry - Ship type: P - How taken: HM Frigate Crescent - When taken: 16 Sep 1813 - Where taken: at sea - Date received: 23 Feb 1814 - From what ship: Portsmouth via HMT Malabar - Born: Baltimore - Age: 36 - Died on 19 Aug 1814 from fever.

Greenfield, William - Seaman - Number: 594 - Prize name: Antelope - Ship type: P - How taken: HM Brig Zephyr - When taken: 10 Dec 1812 - Where taken: at sea - Date received: 23 Feb 1813 - From what ship: Portsmouth via HMS Dromedary - Born: Charlestown - Age: 40 - Discharged on 2 Jul 1813 and released to Cartel Moses Brown.

Greenleaf, James - Seaman - Number: 79 - Prize name: Edward - Ship type: MV - How taken: HM Frigate Ethalion - When taken: 12 Aug 1812 - Where taken: Great Belt, Denmark - Date received: 4 Nov 1812 - From what ship: HMS Namur - Born: Massachusetts - Age: 26 - Discharged on 10 May 1813 and released to Cartel Admittance.

Greenleaf, Thomas - Seaman - Number: 1449 - Prize name: Orbit - Ship type: MV - How taken: HM Brig Achates - When taken: 29 Jan 1813 - Where taken: Lat 49 N Long 13 W - Date received: 6 Apr 1813 - From what ship: Plymouth via HMS Decoy - Born: America - Age: 17 - Discharged on 24 Jul 1814 and sent to Dartmoor.

Gregory, George - Seaman - Number: 3551 - Prize name: Squirrel - Ship type: MV - How taken: HM Frigate Belle Poule - When taken: 14 Dec 1813 - Where taken: Bay of Biscay - Date received: 7 May 1814 - From what ship: Portsmouth via HMS Favorite - Born: Maryland - Age: 23 - Discharged on 26 Sep 1814 and sent to Dartmoor on HMS Leyden.

Gregous, William - Cook - Number: 34 - Prize name: Arial - Ship type: MV - How taken: HM Brig Recruit - When taken: 2 Jun 1812 - Where taken: coast of America - Date received: 3 Nov 1812 - From what ship: HMS Plover - Born: Montgomery, PA - Age: 32 - Race: Mulatto - Discharged on 23 Mar 1813 and released to the Cartel Robinson Potter.

Grendy, Edward - Seaman - Number: 3235 - How taken: Impressed at London - When taken: 19 Jan 1814 - Date received: 8 Feb 1814 - From what ship: HMS Raisonnable - Born: North Carolina - Age: 26 - Discharged on 25 Sep 1814 and sent to Dartmoor on HMS Leyden.

Grey, James - Seaman - Number: 1739 - How taken: Gave himself up from HM Ship-of-the-Line Cornwall - When taken: 14 May 1813 - Date received: 25 May 1813 - From what ship: Portsmouth via HMS Impetius - Born: New Jersey - Age: 25 - Discharged on 24 Jul 1814 and sent to Dartmoor on HMS Liffey.

Grey, William - Seaman - Number: 3527 - How taken: Impressed at Harwich, England - When taken: 21 Feb 1814 - Date received: 26 Feb 1814 - From what ship: HMS Raisonnable - Born: Boston - Age: 29 - Discharged on 22 Oct 1814 and sent to Dartmoor on HMS Leyden.

Griffen, John - Seaman - Number: 3928 - How taken: Gave himself up from HMS Rolus - When taken: 23 Sep 1814 - Date received: 24 Sep 1814 - From what ship: HMS Namur - Born: Providence - Age: 29 - Race: Mulatto - Discharged on 29 Sep 1814 and sent to Dartmoor on HMS Freya.

Griffen, William - Seaman - Number: 2727 - Prize name: Mary, prize to the Privateer True Blooded Yankee - Ship type: P - How taken: HM Ship of-the-Line Bellerophon - When taken: 16 Dec 1813 - Where taken: off Land's End, England - Date received: 7 Jan 1814 - From what ship: Portsmouth - Born: Philadelphia - Age: 43 - Discharged on 8 Sep 1814 and sent to Dartmoor on HMS Niobe.

Griffin, James - Seaman - Number: 146 - Prize name: Country Square - Ship type: MV - How taken: Stopped at London - When taken: 26 Oct 1812 - Date received: 5 Nov 1812 - From what ship: HMS Namur - Born: Baltimore - Age: 27 - Discharged on 19 Jan 1813 to the HMS Scipion.

Griffin, John - Seaman - Number: 3717 - Prize name: Requin - Ship type: LM - How taken: HM Frigate Venus - When taken: 5 Mar 1814 - Where taken: off Bordeaux, France - Date received: 18 May 1814 - From what ship: HMS Raisonnable - Born: Philadelphia - Age: 18 - Race: Black - Discharged on 26 Sep 1814 and sent to Dartmoor on HMS Leyden.

Griffin, John - Private - Number: 3116 - Prize name: 14th U.S. Infantry - Ship type: LF - How taken: British forces - When taken: 24 Jun 1813 - Where taken: Beaver Dams, Upper Canada - Date received: 7 Jan 1814 - From what ship: Halifax - Born: Pennsylvania - Age: 25 - Discharged on 10 Oct 1814 and sent to U.S. on Cartel St. Philip.

Griffin, Samuel - Seaman - Number: 1153 - Prize name: Sword Fish - Ship type: P - How taken: HM Ship-of-the-Line Elephant - When taken: 28 Dec 1812 - Where taken: off Azores - Date received: 16 Mar 1813 - From what ship: Portsmouth, via HMS Abundance - Born: Maryland - Age: 20 - Discharged on 24 Jul 1813 and released to Cartel Hoffminy.

Griffiths, Joseph - Mate - Number: 3796 - Prize name: Argus - Ship type: MV - How taken: HM Ship-of-the-Line San Domingo - When taken: 1 Mar 1814 - Where taken: off Savannah - Date received: 26 May 1814 - From what ship: London - Born: Philadelphia - Age: 30 - Discharged on 25 Sep 1814 and sent to Dartmoor on HMS Niobe.

Grimes, Nicholas - Private - Number: 3130 - Prize name: 14th U.S. Infantry - Ship type: LF - How taken: British forces - When taken: 24 Jun 1813 - Where taken: Beaver Dams, Upper Canada - Date received: 7 Jan 1814 - From what ship: Halifax - Born: Maryland - Age: 23 - Discharged on 10 Oct 1814 and sent to U.S. on Cartel St. Philip.

Grinnell, William - Seaman - Number: 286 - Prize name: Francis Ann - Ship type: MV - How taken: Apprehended at Leight, Scotland - When taken: 5 Aug 1812 - Date received: 23 Dec 1812 - From what ship: Greenlaw Depot - Born: New Bedford - Age: 21 - Discharged on 23 Mar 1813 and released to the Cartel Robinson Potter.

Griswold, Josiah - 2nd Lieutenant - Number: 2311 - Prize name: Blockade - Ship type: P - How taken: HM Brig Charybdis - When taken: 31 Oct 1812 - Where taken: off Virgin Islands, WI - Date received: 8 Oct 1813 - From what ship: Portsmouth, via an admiral's tender - Born: Connecticut - Age: 27 - Discharged on 8 Sep 1814 and sent to Dartmoor on HMS Niobe.

Grose, Daniel - Seaman - Number: 1001 - Prize name: Brunswick - Ship type: MV - How taken: HM Frigate Iris - When taken: 17 Dec 1812 - Where taken: off Spain - Date received: 10 Mar 1813 - From what ship: HMS Tigress - Born: New York - Age: 38 - Discharged on 2 Jul 1813 and released to Cartel Moses Brown.

Grosette, Jean Maurice - Seaman - Number: 3586 - Prize name: Devon, prize to the Privateer Bunker Hill - Ship type: P - How taken: HM Brig Fly - When taken: 21 Jan 1814 - Where taken: at sea - Date received: 26 Mar 1814 - From what ship: Plymouth via HMS Raleigh - Born: Perouse, France - Age: 15 - Escaped on 20 May 1814 from HM Prison Ship Glory.

Gross, James - Seaman - Number: 3251 - Prize name: Thorn - Ship type: P - How taken: Shannon, Nova Scotia privateer - When taken: 7 Nov 1813 - Where taken: off Newfoundland - Date received: 23 Feb 1814 - From what ship: Halifax via HMT Malabar - Born: Marblehead - Age: 35 - Discharged on 10 Oct 1814 and sent to Dartmoor on the Mermaid.

Groves, Pierce - Seaman - Number: 1642 - Prize name: Henryettos - Ship type: MV - How taken: HMS Castilian - When taken: 12 Mar 1813 - Where taken: off Cape Ortegal, Spain - Date received: 9 May 1813 - From what ship: HMS Raisonnable - Born: Talbot - Age: 23 - Race: Black - Discharged on 24 Jul 1814 and sent to Dartmoor.

Groves, Richard - Mate - Number: 2136 - Prize name: Matilda, prize of the U.S. Brig Argus - Ship type: War - How taken: HM Frigate Revolutionnaire - When taken: 25 Jul 1813 - Where taken: off Lorient, France - Date received: 9 Aug 1813 - From what ship: HMS Thames - Born: Salem - Age: 23 - Released from Chatham on 21 Sep 1813 and sent to Ashburton on parole; sent to Dartmouth on 3 Nov 1814 to embark to the United States on the San Felipe.

Groves, Thomas - Seaman - Number: 3868 - Prize name: Rattlesnake - Ship type: LM - How taken: HM Frigate Rhin - When taken: 17 Mar 1814 - Where taken: off Bermuda - Date received: 25 Aug 1814 - From what ship: London - Born: Marblehead - Age: 21 - Race: Black - Discharged on 22 Oct 1814 and sent to Dartmoor on HMS Leyden.

Grunlief, Timothy - Steward's Mate - Number: 437 - Prize name: Hunter - Ship type: P - How taken: HM Frigate Phoebe - When taken: 23 Dec 1812 - Where taken: off Azores - Date received: 19 Feb 1813 - From what ship: HMS Modeste - Born: Newburyport - Age: 35 - Discharged on 2 Jul 1813 and released to Cartel Moses Brown.

Grush, Joseph - Seaman - Number: 2218 - How taken: Apprehended at London - When taken: 13 Aug 1813 - Date received: 18 Aug 1813 - From what ship: HMS Raisonnable - Born: Marblehead - Age: 21 - Discharged on 11 Aug 1814 and sent to Dartmoor on HMS Freya.

Grush, Nathaniel - Seaman - Number: 3194 - Prize name: Growler - Ship type: P - How taken: HM Brig Electra - When taken: 7 Jul 1813 - Where taken: off St. Johns - Date received: 7 Jan 1813 - From what ship: Portsmouth - Born: Marblehead - Age: 17 - Discharged on 25 Sep 1814 and sent to Dartmoor on HMS Leyden.

Gudlers, George - Seaman - Number: 1269 - Prize name: Sword Fish - Ship type: P - How taken: HM Ship-of-the-Line Elephant - When taken: 28 Dec 1812 - Where taken: off Azores - Date received: 16 Mar 1813 - From what ship: Portsmouth, via HMS Abundance - Born: Marblehead - Age: 24 - Discharged on 24 Jul 1813 and released to Cartel Hoffminy.

Guire, Andrew - Seaman - Number: 2179 - How taken: Gave himself up from HM Ship-of-the-Line Leviathan - When taken: 28 Oct 1812 - Date received: 16 Aug 1813 - From what ship: Portsmouth, via an admiral's tender - Born: Lancaster - Age: 42 - Discharged on 25 Sep 1814 and sent to Dartmoor on HMS Leyden.

Gunnell, William - Seaman - Number: 954 - How taken: Gave himself up from HM Transport Romulus - When taken: 1 Jan 1813 - Date received: 10 Mar 1813 - From what ship: HMS Tigress - Born: New York - Age: 45 - Discharged on 4 Aug 1814 and sent to Dartmoor on HMS Liverpool.

Gyer, Henry - Seaman - Number: 3482 - How taken: Gave himself up from HM Ship-of-the-Line Invincible - When taken: 31 Jan 1814 - Date received: 23 Feb 1814 - From what ship: Portsmouth via HMT Malabar - Born: Boston - Age: 29 - Discharged on 26 Sep 1814 and sent to Dartmoor on HMS Leyden.

Hackett, Theophilus - Seaman - Number: 690 - Prize name: Fame, prize of Privateer Decatur - Ship type: P - How taken: HM Ship-of-the-Line Polyphemus - When taken: 13 Sep 1812 - Where taken: at sea - Date received: 24 Feb 1813 - From what ship: Portsmouth via HMS Ulysses - Born: Newburyport - Age: 19 - Discharged on 8 Jun 1813 and released to Cartel Rodrigo.

Haddart, Robert - Seaman - Number: 2516 - Prize name: Wasp - Ship type: P - How taken: HM Schooner Bream - When taken: 9 Jun 1813 - Where taken: off Halifax - Date received: 22 Oct 1813 - From what ship: Portsmouth via HMT Malabar - Born: Salem - Age: 29 - Discharged on 8 Sep 1814 and sent to Dartmoor on HMS Niobe.

Hadley, George - Seaman - Number: 2337 - Prize name: Falcon, prize of the U.S. Frigate President - Ship type: War - How taken: Spanish army - When taken: 2 Jul 1813 - Where taken: off Passage Harbor - Date received: 20 Oct 1813 - From what ship: Portsmouth, via an admiral's tender - Born: Chester - Age: 32 - Discharged on 4 Sep 1814 and sent to Dartmoor on HMS Freya.

Hagen, Joel - Seaman - Number: 3323 - Prize name: Porcupine - Ship type: LM - How taken: HM Frigate Acasta - When taken: 18 Jul 1813 - Where taken: off Cape Sable, Florida - Date received: 23 Feb 1814 - From what ship: Halifax via HMT Malabar - Born: Boston - Age: 18 - Discharged on 10 Oct 1814 and sent to Dartmoor on the Mermaid.

Halbrook, Benjamin - Seaman - Number: 179 - Prize name: Mary Ann Transport - How taken: Stopped at London - When taken: 28 Oct 1812 - Date received: 5 Nov 1812 - From what ship: HMS Namur - Born: Baltimore - Age: 24 - Discharged on 19 Jan 1813 to the HMS Scipion.

Hale, Robert - Seaman - Number: 56 - Prize name: Trim - Ship type: MV - How taken: From a cutter off Bermuda - When taken: 26 Jul 1812 - Date received: 3 Nov 1812 - From what ship: HMS Plover - Born: Alexandria, VA - Age: 24 - Race: Mulatto - Discharged on 23 Mar 1813 and released to the Cartel Robinson Potter.

Hale, William - Steward - Number: 1705 - Prize name: Darby - Ship type: MV - How taken: HM Frigate Narcissus - When taken: 4 Feb 1813 - Where taken: off St. Helena - Date received: 22 May 1813 - From what ship: HMS Raisonnable - Born: Boston - Age: 39 - Race: Blackman - Released on 10 Jun 1813 to attend a trial.

Haley, John - Seaman - Number: 3710 - Prize name: Requin - Ship type: LM - How taken: HM Frigate Venus - When taken: 5 Mar 1814 - Where taken: off Bordeaux, France - Date received: 18 May 1814 - From what ship: HMS Raisonnable - Born: Beaufort - Age: 34 - Discharged on 25 Sep 1814 and sent to Dartmoor on HMS Leyden.

Haley, Thomas - 1st Mate - Number: 980 - Prize name: Hope - Ship type: MV - How taken: HM Sloop Pheasant - When taken: 13 Dec 1812 - Where taken: off Azores - Date received: 10 Mar 1813 - From what ship: HMS Tigress - Born: Virginia - Age: 28 - Discharged on 2 Jul 1813 and released to Cartel Moses Brown.

Hall, Charles - Merchant - Number: 742 - How taken: Impressed at Gravesend, England - When taken: 18 Feb 1813 - Date received: 25 Feb 1813 - From what ship: HMS Raisonnable - Born: Portsmouth, NH - Age: 40 - Discharged on 23 Mar 1813 and released to the Cartel Robinson Potter.

Hall, David - Seaman - Number: 3605 - Prize name: Liberty - Ship type: MV - How taken: Surrendered at Stromness, Scotland - When taken: 30 Dec 1813 - Date received: 29 Mar 1814 - From what ship: Hired tender Anna - Born: Delaware - Age: 26 - Race: Black - Discharged on 25 Sep 1814 and sent to Dartmoor on HMS Niobe.

Hall, Ezekiel - 1st Lieutenant - Number: 3481 - Prize name: Pilot - Ship type: LM - How taken: Vittoria, British privateer from Guernsey - When taken: 1 Jan 1814 - Where taken: off Bordeaux, France - Date received: 23 Feb 1814 - From what ship: Halifax via HMT Malabar - Born: Somerset - Age: 35 - Discharged on 28 Feb 1814 and sent to Reading on parole.

Hall, George - Carpenter - Number: 30 - Prize name: Arial - Ship type: MV - How taken: HM Brig Recruit - When taken: 2 Jun 1812 - Where taken: coast of America - Date received: 3 Nov 1812 - From what ship: HMS Plover - Born: Delaware - Age: 33 - Discharged on 23 Mar 1813 and released to the Cartel Robinson Potter.

Hall, George - Seaman - Number: 2664 - How taken: Impressed at London - When taken: 20 Oct 1813 - Date received: 11 Nov 1813 - From what ship: HMS Namur, admiral's tender - Born: Bedford - Age: 22 - Discharged on 17 Jun 1814 and sent to Dartmoor.

Hall, Henry - Seaman - Number: 1338 - How taken: Gave himself up from HM Brig Echo - When taken: 1 Aug 1812 - Date received: 26 Mar 1813 - From what ship: HMS Raisonnable - Born: Baltimore - Age: 27 - Died on 18 Sep 1813 from phthisis (tuberculosis) and small pox.

Hall, James - Seaman - Number: 3001 - Prize name: Grand Turk - Ship type: P - How taken: HM Frigate Tenedos - When taken: 26 May 1813 - Where taken: off Cape Sable, Florida - Date received: 7 Jan 1814 - From what ship: Halifax - Born: Massachusetts - Age: 23 - Discharged on 25 Sep 1814 and sent to Dartmoor on HMS Leyden.

Hall, James - Seaman - Number: 1942 - Prize name: William Bayard - Ship type: MV - How taken: HM Ship-of-the-Line Warspite - When taken: 3 Mar 1813 - Where taken: Bay of Biscay - Date received: 15 Jul 1813 - From what ship: Plymouth - Born: New York - Age: 22 - Discharged on 20 Oct 1813 and released to HMS Ceres.

Hall, James - Seaman - Number: 2596 - How taken: Gave himself up from HM Ship-of-the-Line Berwick - When taken: 27 May 1813 - Date received: 5 Nov 1813 - From what ship: HMS Hindostan - Born: Connecticut - Age: 39 - Discharged on 12 Aug 1814 and sent to Dartmoor on HMS Alpheus.

Hall, John - Seaman - Number: 3005 - Prize name: Yankee - Ship type: P - How taken: HM Frigate Shannon - When taken: 20 Aug 1813 - Where taken: at sea - Date received: 7 Jan 1814 - From what ship: Halifax - Born: Maryland - Age: 22 - Discharged on 25 Sep 1814 and sent to Dartmoor on HMS Leyden.

Hall, John - Seaman - Number: 2289 - How taken: Gave himself up from HM Ship-of-the-Line Royal George - When taken: 29 Oct 1812 - Date received: 17 Sep 1813 - From what ship: HMS Raisonnable - Born: Baltimore - Age: 31 - Discharged on 11 Aug 1814 and sent to Dartmoor on HMS Freya.

Hall, Perry - Seaman - Number: 2453 - Prize name: Wiley Reynard - Ship type: P - How taken: HM Frigate Shannon - When taken: 16 Aug 1812 - Where taken: off Halifax - Date received: 21 Oct 1813 - From what ship: Portsmouth via HMT Malabar - Born: Baltimore - Age: 25 - Race: Blackman - Discharged on 4 Sep 1814 and sent to Dartmoor on HMS Freya.

Hall, Richard - Passenger - Number: 3626 - How taken: Taken off a Swedish ship bound for America - Date received: 29 Mar 1814 - From what ship: Hired tender Anna - Born: Boston - Age: 35 - Race: Black -

Discharged on 25 Sep 1814 and sent to Dartmoor on HMS Niobe.

Hall, Spencer - Master - Number: 385 - Prize name: Sally - Ship type: MV - How taken: HM Brig Badger - When taken: 6 Sep 1812 - Where taken: off Minorca, Spain - Date received: 13 Feb 1813 - From what ship: HMS Raisonnable - Born: Salem - Age: 25 - Discharged on 10 May 1813 and released to Cartel Admittance.

Hall, Sylvester - Seaman - Number: 3014 - Prize name: Yankee - Ship type: P - How taken: HM Frigate Shannon - When taken: 20 Aug 1813 - Where taken: at sea - Date received: 7 Jan 1814 - From what ship: Halifax - Born: Rhode Island - Age: 23 - Discharged on 25 Sep 1814 and sent to Dartmoor on HMS Leyden.

Hall, Thomas - Seaman - Number: 1225 - Prize name: Rossie - Ship type: MV - How taken: HM Frigate Dryand - When taken: 7 Jan 1813 - Where taken: at sea - Date received: 16 Mar 1813 - From what ship: Portsmouth, via HMS Abundance - Born: Philadelphia - Age: 23 - Discharged on 24 Jul 1813 and released to Cartel Hoffminy.

Hall, William - Prize Master - Number: 415 - Prize name: Hunter - Ship type: P - How taken: HM Frigate Phoebe - When taken: 23 Dec 1812 - Where taken: off Azores - Date received: 19 Feb 1813 - From what ship: HMS Modeste - Born: Wells - Age: 29 - Discharged on 2 Jul 1813 and released to Cartel Moses Brown.

Hall, William - Seaman - Number: 1531 - How taken: Gave himself up from HM Frigate Franchise - When taken: 20 Sep 1812 - Date received: 8 Apr 1813 - From what ship: Portsmouth, via an admiral's tender - Born: Charlestown - Age: 21 - Discharged on 4 Aug 1814 and sent to Dartmoor on HMS Alpheus.

Halbrook, D. - Seaman - Number: 2103 - How taken: Gave himself up from HM Frigate Bombay - When taken: 27 May 1813 - Date received: 9 Aug 1813 - From what ship: HMS Thames - Born: Connecticut - Age: 31 - Discharged on 8 Aug 1814 and sent to Dartmoor on HMS Alpheus.

Haller, Joseph - 2nd Mate - Number: 1640 - Prize name: Henryettos - Ship type: MV - How taken: HMS Castilian - When taken: 12 Mar 1813 - Where taken: off Cape Ortegal, Spain - Date received: 9 May 1813 - From what ship: HMS Raisonnable - Born: Connecticut - Age: 24 - Discharged on 24 Jul 1814 and sent to Dartmoor.

Hallet, William - Seaman - Number: 3763 - Prize name: Argus - Ship type: MV - How taken: HM Ship-of-the-Line San Domingo - When taken: 1 Mar 1814 - Where taken: off Savannah - Date received: 26 May 1814 - From what ship: HMS Hindostan - Born: Barnstable - Age: 24 - Discharged on 25 Sep 1814 and sent to Dartmoor on HMS Niobe.

Hallman, Anthony - Mate - Number: 142 - Prize name: Harmak & Sally - Ship type: MV - How taken: Detained in the London docks - When taken: 3 Aug 1812 - Date received: 5 Nov 1812 - From what ship: HMS Namur - Born: Philadelphia - Age: 21 - Discharged on 23 Mar 1813 and released to the Cartel Robinson Potter.

Halloo, John - Private - Number: 3133 - Prize name: 14th U.S. Infantry - Ship type: LF - How taken: British forces - When taken: 24 Jun 1813 - Where taken: Beaver Dams, Upper Canada - Date received: 7 Jan 1814 - From what ship: Halifax - Born: Amsterdam - Age: 24 - Discharged on 10 Oct 1814 and sent to U.S. on Cartel St. Philip.

Hamilton, G. W. - Seaman - Number: 2517 - Prize name: Yorktown - Ship type: P - How taken: HM Brig Nimrod - When taken: 17 Jul 1813 - Where taken: Grand Banks - Date received: 22 Oct 1813 - From what ship: Portsmouth via HMT Malabar - Born: New York - Age: 27 - Discharged on 8 Sep 1814 and sent to Dartmoor on HMS Niobe.

Hamilton, John - Seaman - Number: 3604 - Prize name: Liberty - Ship type: MV - How taken: Surrendered at Stromness, Scotland - When taken: 30 Dec 1813 - Date received: 29 Mar 1814 - From what ship: Hired tender Anna - Born: Salem - Age: 39 - Race: Black - Discharged on 25 Sep 1814 and sent to Dartmoor on HMS Niobe.

Hamilton, John - Seaman - Number: 1560 - Prize name: Dolphin - Ship type: LM - How taken: HM Ship-of-the-Line Colossus - When taken: 5 Jan 1813 - Where taken: off the Western Isles, Scotland - Date received: 8 Apr 1813 - From what ship: Plymouth via HMS Olympia - Born: New London - Age: 23 - Race: Negro - Discharged on 27 Jul 1813 and released to Cartel Hoffminy.

Hamilton, Richard - Prize Master - Number: 2191 - Prize name: True Blooded Yankee - Ship type: P - How taken: HM Frigate Hamadryad - When taken: 24 Jul 1813 - Where taken: off Norway - Date received: 17 Aug 1813 - From what ship: HMS Raisonnable - Born: New London - Age: 24 - Discharged on 17 Jun 1814 and sent to

Dartmoor on the Penebar.

Hamilton, Robert - Seaman - Number: 3541 - Prize name: Commodore Perry - Ship type: MV - How taken: Sent into custody from a cutter - When taken: 25 Feb 1814 - Where taken: off Bordeaux, France - Date received: 5 Mar 1814 - From what ship: HMS Raisonnable - Born: Philadelphia - Age: 31 - Discharged on 25 Sep 1814 and sent to Dartmoor on HMS Niobe.

Hamlet, John - Seaman - Number: 231 - How taken: Apprehended at London - When taken: 15 Nov 1812 - Date received: 25 Nov 1812 - From what ship: HMS Raisonnable - Born: Cape May - Age: 26 - Race: Mulatto - Discharged in Jul 1813 and released to Cartel Moses Brown.

Hammet, John - Seaman - Number: 441 - Prize name: Hunter - Ship type: P - How taken: HM Frigate Phoebe - When taken: 23 Dec 1812 - Where taken: off Azores - Date received: 19 Feb 1813 - From what ship: HMS Modeste - Born: Plymouth - Age: 26 - Discharged on 2 Jul 1813 and released to Cartel Moses Brown.

Hammon, John - Seaman - Number: 3249 - Prize name: Thorn - Ship type: P - How taken: Shannon, Nova Scotia privateer - When taken: 7 Nov 1813 - Where taken: off Newfoundland - Date received: 23 Feb 1814 - From what ship: Halifax via HMT Malabar - Born: Marblehead - Age: 19 - Discharged on 10 Oct 1814 and sent to Dartmoor on the Mermaid.

Hammon, William - Prize Master - Number: 3246 - Prize name: Thorn - Ship type: P - How taken: Shannon, Nova Scotia privateer - When taken: 7 Nov 1813 - Where taken: off Newfoundland - Date received: 23 Feb 1814 - From what ship: Halifax via HMT Malabar - Born: York - Age: 25 - Discharged on 22 Oct 1814 and sent to Dartmoor on HMS Leyden.

Hammond, Benjamin - Seaman - Number: 282 - Prize name: Francis Ann - Ship type: MV - How taken: Apprehended at Leight, Scotland - When taken: 5 Aug 1812 - Date received: 23 Dec 1812 - From what ship: Greenlaw Depot - Born: New Bedford - Age: 19 - Discharged on 23 Mar 1813 and released to the Cartel Robinson Potter.

Hammond, Isaac - Seaman - Number: 3702 - How taken: Gave himself up from the Earl Falk - When taken: 9 May 1814 - Date received: 10 May 1814 - From what ship: Eagle - Born: Rochester - Age: 34 - Discharged on 26 Sep 1814 and sent to Dartmoor on HMS Leyden.

Hammond, Stephen - Seaman - Number: 59 - Prize name: York - Ship type: MV - How taken: HM Sloop Rattler - When taken: 11 Jul 1812 - Where taken: off Bermuda - Date received: 3 Nov 1812 - From what ship: HMS Plover - Born: Rochester, MA - Age: 25 - Discharged on 23 Mar 1813 and released to the Cartel Robinson Potter.

Hammond, William - Seaman - Number: 4 - Prize name: Cato - Ship type: MV - How taken: Detained on the Baltic - When taken: 11 Aug 1812 - Date received: 29 Oct 1812 - From what ship: HMS Raisonnable - Born: Marblehead - Age: 26 - Discharged on 10 May 1813 and released to Cartel Admittance.

Hamson, Henry - Quartermaster - Number: 1163 - Prize name: Sword Fish - Ship type: P - How taken: HM Ship-of-the-Line Elephant - When taken: 28 Dec 1812 - Where taken: off Azores - Date received: 16 Mar 1813 - From what ship: Portsmouth, via HMS Abundance - Born: Marblehead - Age: 31 - Discharged on 24 Jul 1813 and released to Cartel Hoffminy.

Hamson, John - Seaman - Number: 2958 - Prize name: Enterprise - Ship type: P - How taken: HM Frigate Tenedos - When taken: 21 May 1813 - Where taken: off Cape Cod - Date received: 7 Jan 1814 - From what ship: Halifax - Born: Massachusetts - Age: 23 - Discharged on 25 Sep 1814 and sent to Dartmoor on HMS Leyden.

Hamson, William - Seaman - Number: 2947 - Prize name: Enterprise - Ship type: P - How taken: HM Frigate Tenedos - When taken: 21 May 1813 - Where taken: off Cape Cod - Date received: 7 Jan 1814 - From what ship: Halifax - Born: Massachusetts - Age: 21 - Discharged on 25 Sep 1814 and sent to Dartmoor on HMS Leyden.

Hand, Wilson - Seaman - Number: 99 - Prize name: Hebe - Ship type: MV - How taken: Stopped at London - When taken: 26 Oct 1812 - Date received: 4 Nov 1812 - From what ship: HMS Namur - Born: Suffolk County, NY - Age: 23 - Discharged in Jul 1813 and released to Cartel Moses Brown.

Handerson, Hans - Seaman - Number: 2137 - Prize name: Matilda, prize of the U.S. Brig Argus - Ship type: War -

How taken: HM Frigate Revolutionnaire - When taken: 25 Jul 1813 - Where taken: off Lorient, France - Date received: 9 Aug 1813 - From what ship: HMS Thames - Born: Norway - Age: 35 - Died on 5 Sep 1814 from debility (feeble).

Handley, Thomas - Seaman - Number: 2106 - How taken: Gave himself up from HM Ship-of-the-Line Repulse - When taken: 27 May 1813 - Date received: 9 Aug 1813 - From what ship: HMS Thames - Born: Massachusetts - Age: 33 - Discharged on 4 Aug 1814 and sent to Dartmoor on HMS Alpheus.

Handy, Levi - Seaman - Number: 2790 - Prize name: Yorktown - Ship type: P - How taken: British squadron - When taken: 17 Jul 1813 - Where taken: Grand Banks - Date received: 7 Jan 1814 - From what ship: Halifax - Born: Eastport - Age: 25 - Escaped on 13 May 1814 from HM Prison Ship Crown Prince.

Hanfield, Enos - Seaman - Number: 2470 - Prize name: Montgomery - Ship type: P - How taken: HM Frigate Nymphe - When taken: 5 May 1813 - Where taken: off Cape Cod - Date received: 21 Oct 1813 - From what ship: Portsmouth via HMT Malabar - Born: Salem - Age: 23 - Discharged on 8 Sep 1814 and sent to Dartmoor on HMS Niobe.

Hanscom, Thomas - Seaman - Number: 2146 - Prize name: Matilda, prize of the U.S. Brig Argus - Ship type: War - How taken: HM Frigate Revolutionnaire - When taken: 25 Jul 1813 - Where taken: off Lorient, France - Date received: 9 Aug 1813 - From what ship: HMS Thames - Born: Massachusetts - Age: 21 - Discharged on 12 Aug 1814 and sent to Dartmoor on HMS Alpheus.

Hansen, William - Seaman - Number: 545 - Prize name: Baltimore - Ship type: P - How taken: HM Transport Diadem - When taken: 7 Oct 1812 - Where taken: S. Andres - Date received: 23 Feb 1813 - From what ship: Portsmouth via HMS Dromedary - Born: Stockholm - Age: 28 - Discharged on 8 Jun 1813 and released to Cartel Rodrigo.

Hanson, Peter - Seaman - Number: 2143 - Prize name: Matilda, prize of the U.S. Brig Argus - Ship type: War - How taken: HM Frigate Revolutionnaire - When taken: 25 Jul 1813 - Where taken: off Lorient, France - Date received: 9 Aug 1813 - From what ship: HMS Thames - Born: Gothenburg, Sweden - Age: 19 - Discharged on 12 Aug 1814 and sent to Dartmoor on HMS Alpheus.

Hanson, William - Seaman - Number: 2828 - Prize name: Portsmouth Packet - Ship type: P - How taken: HM Brig Fantome - When taken: 5 Oct 1813 - Where taken: off Portland - Date received: 7 Jan 1814 - From what ship: Halifax - Born: Hampshire - Age: 20 - Discharged on 25 Sep 1814 and sent to Dartmoor on HMS Leyden.

Harbrook, Richard - Seaman - Number: 2779 - Prize name: Thomas - Ship type: P - How taken: HM Frigate Nymphe - When taken: 24 Jun 1813 - Where taken: off Halifax - Date received: 7 Jan 1814 - From what ship: Halifax - Born: New Hampshire - Age: 18 - Discharged on 8 Sep 1814 and sent to Dartmoor on HMS Niobe.

Hardiman, John - Seaman - Number: 1830 - Prize name: tender to the Privateer True Blooded Yankee - Ship type: P - How taken: HM Ship-of-the-Line Fame - When taken: 24 Jun 1813 - Where taken: off Brest, France - Date received: 7 Jul 1813 - From what ship: Portsmouth via HMS Scorpion - Born: Georgetown - Age: 28 - Discharged on 22 Jun 1814 and sent to Calais, France on the Simon & Mary.

Harding, J. Christian - Seaman - Number: 2893 - Prize name: Dart - Ship type: P - How taken: HM Frigate Niger & HMS Fortunee - When taken: 10 Nov 1813 - Where taken: off Cape Finisterre, Spain - Date received: 7 Jan 1814 - From what ship: Portsmouth - Born: Prussia - Age: 25 - Released on 6 Aug 1814.

Harding, John - Seaman - Number: 3761 - Prize name: Argus - Ship type: MV - How taken: HM Ship-of-the-Line San Domingo - When taken: 1 Mar 1814 - Where taken: off Savannah - Date received: 26 May 1814 - From what ship: HMS Hindostan - Born: Boston - Age: 18 - Discharged on 25 Sep 1814 and sent to Dartmoor on HMS Niobe.

Harding, John G. - Seaman - Number: 397 - Prize name: Maria - Ship type: MV - How taken: HM Brig Papillon - When taken: 25 Nov 1812 - Where taken: off Cadiz, Spain - Date received: 13 Feb 1813 - From what ship: HMS Raisonnable - Born: Wiscasset - Age: 20 - Discharged on 8 Jun 1813 and released to Cartel Rodrigo.

Harding, Joseph - Seaman - Number: 653 - Prize name: U.S.R.M. Cutter James Madison - Ship type: War - How taken: HM Frigate Barbadoes - When taken: 22 Aug 1812 - Where taken: at sea - Date received: 24 Feb 1813

- From what ship: Portsmouth via HMS Ulysses - Born: Savannah - Age: 35 - Discharged on 10 May 1813 and released to Cartel Admittance.

Harding, Joseph - Prize Master - Number: 3304 - Prize name: Juliana Smith - Ship type: P - How taken: HM Frigate Nymphe - When taken: 12 May 1813 - Where taken: off Cape Sable, Florida - Date received: 23 Feb 1814 - From what ship: Halifax via HMT Malabar - Born: Chatham - Age: 33 - Discharged on 10 Oct 1814 and sent to Dartmoor on the Mermaid.

Harding, William - Seaman - Number: 3671 - Prize name: Pilot - Ship type: LM - How taken: Vittoria, British privateer from Guernsey - When taken: 28 Jan 1813 - Where taken: off Bordeaux, France - Date received: 4 May 1814 - From what ship: Portsmouth - Born: South Carolina - Age: 23 - Race: Black - Discharged on 25 Sep 1814 and sent to Dartmoor on HMS Niobe.

Hardward, Isaac - Seaman - Number: 249 - Prize name: Patent - Ship type: MV - How taken: Gave himself up at Gravesend, England - When taken: 9 Nov 1812 - Date received: 7 Dec 1812 - From what ship: HMS Raisonnable - Born: Not listed - Age: 32 - Died on 5 Jan 1813 from phthisis (tuberculosis).

Hardwick, James - Seaman - Number: 776 - Prize name: Eliza - Ship type: MV - How taken: HM Sloop Hyacinth - When taken: 27 Aug 1812 - Where taken: off Gibraltar - Date received: 27 Feb 1813 - From what ship: Plymouth via HMS Namur - Born: Georgetown, SC - Age: 18 - Discharged on 10 May 1813 and released to Cartel Admittance.

Hardy, John - Seaman - Number: 1213 - Prize name: Expectation - Ship type: MV - How taken: HM Frigate Briton - When taken: 17 Dec 1812 - Where taken: at sea - Date received: 16 Mar 1813 - From what ship: Portsmouth, via HMS Abundance - Born: Philadelphia - Age: 27 - Race: Black - Discharged on 2 Jul 1813 and released to Cartel Moses Brown.

Hargood, George - Private - Number: 3059 - Prize name: 14th U.S. Infantry - Ship type: LF - How taken: British forces - When taken: 24 Jun 1813 - Where taken: Beaver Dams, Upper Canada - Date received: 7 Jan 1814 - From what ship: Halifax - Born: Maryland - Age: 29 - Discharged on 10 Oct 1814 and sent to U.S. on Cartel St. Philip.

Harlow, Sylvanus - Seaman - Number: 714 - Prize name: Ganges - Ship type: MV - How taken: Detained at Portsmouth harbor - When taken: 31 Jul 1812 - Date received: 24 Feb 1813 - From what ship: Portsmouth via HMS Ulysses - Born: Plymouth, MA - Age: 32 - Discharged on 23 Mar 1813 and released to the Cartel Robinson Potter.

Harman, Isaac - Quartermaster - Number: 2870 - Prize name: Elbridge Gerry - Ship type: P - How taken: HM Frigate Crescent - When taken: 16 Sep 1813 - Where taken: at sea - Date received: 7 Jan 1814 - From what ship: Portsmouth - Born: Massachusetts - Age: 24 - Discharged on 25 Sep 1814 and sent to Dartmoor on HMS Leyden.

Harms, John - Seaman - Number: 3220 - Prize name: Volunteer - Ship type: MV - How taken: Vittoria, British privateer from Guernsey - When taken: 26 Dec 1813 - Where taken: Bay of Biscay - Date received: 13 Jan 1814 - From what ship: Portsmouth via HMS Poictiers - Born: Memel - Age: 21 - Released on 6 Aug 1814.

Harrens, William - Seaman - Number: 1943 - Prize name: William Bayard - Ship type: MV - How taken: HM Ship-of-the-Line Warspite - When taken: 3 Mar 1813 - Where taken: Bay of Biscay - Date received: 15 Jul 1813 - From what ship: Plymouth - Born: New Jersey - Age: 27 - Escaped on 16 Mar 1814 from HM Prison Ship Crown Prince.

Harris, Abraham Harris - Seaman - Number: 686 - Prize name: Fame, prize of Privateer Decatur - Ship type: P - How taken: HM Ship-of-the-Line Polyphemus - When taken: 13 Sep 1812 - Where taken: at sea - Date received: 24 Feb 1813 - From what ship: Portsmouth via HMS Ulysses - Born: Ipswich, MA - Age: 24 - Discharged on 8 Jun 1813 and released to Cartel Rodrigo.

Harris, David - Seaman - Number: 697 - Prize name: Deanna, recaptured British vessel - Ship type: P - How taken: HM Ship-of-the-Line Polyphemus - When taken: 14 Sep 1812 - Where taken: at sea - Date received: 24 Feb 1813 - From what ship: Portsmouth via HMS Ulysses - Born: Ipswich, MA - Age: 20 - Discharged on 8 Jun 1813 and released to Cartel Rodrigo.

Harris, Ebenezer - Seaman - Number: 3565 - Prize name: Minerva - Ship type: MV - How taken: HM Ship-of-the-

Line Conquestador - When taken: 19 Jan 1814 - Where taken: Bay of Biscay - Date received: 7 May 1814 - From what ship: Portsmouth via HMS Favorite - Born: Yarmouth - Age: 25 - Discharged on 25 Sep 1814 and sent to Dartmoor on HMS Niobe.

Harris, Alpheus - Seaman - Number: 3783 - Prize name: Argus - Ship type: MV - How taken: HM Ship-of-the-Line San Domingo - When taken: 1 Mar 1814 - Where taken: off Savannah - Date received: 26 May 1814 - From what ship: HMS Hindostan - Born: Chesterfield - Age: 22 - Discharged on 25 Sep 1814 and sent to Dartmoor on HMS Niobe.

Harris, George - Seaman - Number: 3825 - Prize name: Penn, whaler - Ship type: MV - How taken: HM Sloop Acorn - When taken: 14 Oct 1813 - Where taken: South Seas - Date received: 14 Aug 1814 - From what ship: Deptford - Born: Nantucket - Age: 17 - Discharged on 22 Oct 1814 and sent to Dartmoor on HMS Leyden.

Harris, James - Seaman - Number: 930 - Prize name: Experiment - Ship type: MV - How taken: HM Brig Rover - When taken: 10 Nov 1812 - Where taken: off Bordeaux, France - Date received: 10 Mar 1813 - From what ship: HMS Tigress - Born: Maryland - Age: 28 - Discharged on 8 Jun 1813 and released to Cartel Rodrigo.

Harris, James - Seaman - Number: 1654 - How taken: Gave himself up from HM Ship-of-the-Line Sterling Castle - Date received: 9 May 1813 - From what ship: HMS Raisonnable - Born: Pennsylvania - Age: 24 - Discharged on 13 Aug 1814 and sent to Dartmoor.

Harris, John - Marine Private - Number: 3581 - How taken: Gave himself up from HMS San Salvador - When taken: 7 Jan 1814 - Date received: 26 Mar 1814 - From what ship: Plymouth via HMS Raleigh - Born: Virginia - Age: 26 - Discharged on 26 Sep 1814 and sent to Dartmoor on HMS Leyden.

Harris, Joseph - Lieutenant - Number: 2942 - Prize name: Enterprise - Ship type: P - How taken: HM Frigate Tenedos - When taken: 21 May 1813 - Where taken: off Cape Cod - Date received: 7 Jan 1814 - From what ship: Halifax - Born: Massachusetts - Age: 32 - Discharged on 22 Oct 1814 and sent to Dartmoor on HMS Leyden.

Harris, Simon - Seaman - Number: 3558 - Prize name: Zephyr, prize of Privateer Rattlesnake - Ship type: P - How taken: HM Frigate Surveillante - When taken: 6 Jan 1814 - Where taken: Bay of Biscay - Date received: 7 May 1814 - From what ship: Portsmouth via HMS Favorite - Born: Virginia - Age: 40 - Race: Black - Discharged on 25 Sep 1814 and sent to Dartmoor on HMS Niobe.

Harris, William - Seaman - Number: 1413 - Prize name: Porcupine - Ship type: MV - How taken: HM Frigate Dryand - When taken: 8 Jan 1813 - Where taken: off Bordeaux, France - Date received: 5 Apr 1813 - From what ship: Plymouth via HMS Dwarf - Born: Philadelphia - Age: 33 - Discharged on 24 Jul 1813 and released to Cartel Hoffminy.

Harris, William - Seaman - Number: 1347 - Prize name: U.S.R.M. Cutter James Madison - Ship type: War - How taken: HM Frigate Barbadoes - When taken: 22 Aug 1812 - Where taken: at sea - Date received: 3 Apr 1813 - From what ship: Portsmouth, via an admiral's tender - Born: Portland, MA - Age: 35 - Discharged on 4 May 1813 and released to HMS Raisonnable.

Harris, William - Seaman - Number: 872 - Prize name: Stephen - Ship type: MV - How taken: Briton, letter of marque - When taken: 1 Jan 1813 - Where taken: off Bordeaux, France - Date received: 1 Mar 1813 - From what ship: Plymouth via HMS Namur - Born: Pennsylvania - Age: 32 - Race: Blackman - Discharged on 24 Jul 1813 and released to Cartel Hoffminy.

Harris, William - Seaman - Number: 1974 - Prize name: Polly - Ship type: MV - How taken: HM Frigate Surveillante - When taken: 23 Mar 1813 - Where taken: Bay of Biscay - Date received: 15 Jul 1813 - From what ship: Plymouth - Born: Marblehead - Age: 43 - Discharged on 17 Jun 1814 and sent to Dartmoor on HMS Redbreast.

Harris, William - Seaman - Number: 1852 - How taken: Gave himself up from HM Ship-of-the-Line Malta - Date received: 7 Jul 1813 - From what ship: Portsmouth via HMS Tribune - Born: New York - Age: 37 - Discharged on 25 Jul 1814 and sent to Dartmoor on HMS Bittern.

Harrison, Henry - Seaman - Number: 2054 - How taken: Gave himself up from HM Ship-of-the-Line Fame - When taken: 4 May 1813 - Date received: 4 Aug 1813 - From what ship: HMS Christian VII - Born: New York -

Age: 28 - Discharged on 25 Sep 1814 and sent to Dartmoor on HMS Niobe.

Harrison, John - Seaman - Number: 1468 - Prize name: Union - Ship type: MV - How taken: HM Frigate Iris - When taken: 17 Jan 1813 - Where taken: at sea - Date received: 6 Apr 1813 - From what ship: Portsmouth via Tender Eliza - Born: Portsmouth - Age: 25 - Discharged on 26 Jul 1813 and released to Cartel Hoffminy.

Harrison, Joseph - Seaman - Number: 775 - Prize name: Eliza - Ship type: MV - How taken: HM Sloop Hyacinth - When taken: 27 Aug 1812 - Where taken: off Gibraltar - Date received: 27 Feb 1813 - From what ship: Plymouth via HMS Namur - Born: Charlestown - Age: 19 - Discharged on 10 May 1813 and released to Cartel Admittance.

Hart, Frederick - Seaman - Number: 797 - Prize name: Dolphin - Ship type: MV - How taken: HM Ship-of-the-Line Colossus - When taken: 5 Jan 1813 - Where taken: off the Western Isles, Scotland - Date received: 27 Feb 1813 - From what ship: Plymouth via HMS Namur - Born: Philadelphia - Age: 19 - Discharged on 24 Jul 1813 and released to Cartel Hoffminy.

Hart, Marquis - Seaman - Number: 1756 - How taken: Impressed at Newcastle on Tyne - When taken: 1 May 1813 - Date received: 8 Jun 1813 - From what ship: HMS Raisonnable - Born: Deptford, Kent - Age: 19 - Released on 20 Sep 1814.

Hart, Samuel - Seaman - Number: 2786 - Prize name: Montgomery - Ship type: P - How taken: HM Frigate Nymphe - When taken: 5 May 1813 - Where taken: off Cape Cod - Date received: 7 Jan 1814 - From what ship: Halifax - Born: Salem - Age: 26 - Escaped on 16 May 1814 from HM Prison Ship Crown Prince.

Hart, William - Seaman - Number: 148 - Prize name: Country Square - Ship type: MV - How taken: Stopped at London - When taken: 30 Oct 1812 - Date received: 5 Nov 1812 - From what ship: HMS Namur - Born: Bristol - Age: 18 - Discharged in Jul 1813 and released to Cartel Moses Brown.

Hart, William - Seaman - Number: 2718 - Prize name: Growler - Ship type: P - How taken: HM Brig Electra - When taken: 7 Jul 1813 - Where taken: off St. Johns - Date received: 7 Jan 1814 - From what ship: Portsmouth - Born: New York - Age: 30 - Discharged on 25 Sep 1814 and sent to Dartmoor on HMS Leyden.

Hartford, James - Seaman - Number: 997 - How taken: Impressed from HM Frigate Andromache at Cork - When taken: 6 Dec 1812 - Date received: 10 Mar 1813 - From what ship: HMS Tigress - Born: New Hampshire - Age: 30 - Discharged on 14 May 1813 and released to HMS Ceres.

Hartford, John - Seaman - Number: 865 - Prize name: Columbia - Ship type: MV - How taken: HM Frigate Briton - When taken: 17 Jan 1813 - Where taken: off Bordeaux, France - Date received: 1 Mar 1813 - From what ship: Plymouth via HMS Namur - Born: New Hampshire - Age: 22 - Discharged in Jul 1813 and released to Cartel Moses Brown.

Hartford, William - Seaman - Number: 3851 - Prize name: James - Ship type: MV - How taken: HM Brig Harpy - When taken: 16 Dec 1812 - Where taken: off Isle de France (Mauritius) - Date received: 22 Aug 1814 - From what ship: Gravesend - Born: New Hampshire - Age: 24 - Discharged on 22 Oct 1814 and sent to Dartmoor on HMS Leyden.

Harvey, Anthony - Seaman - Number: 3195 - Prize name: Growler - Ship type: P - How taken: HM Brig Electra - When taken: 7 Jul 1813 - Where taken: off St. Johns - Date received: 7 Jan 1813 - From what ship: Portsmouth - Born: Baltimore - Age: 28 - Race: Black - Discharged on 25 Sep 1814 and sent to Dartmoor on HMS Leyden.

Harvey, John - Seaman - Number: 2008 - How taken: Gave himself up from HM Brig Foxhound - Date received: 15 Jul 1813 - From what ship: Plymouth - Born: New Orleans - Age: 45 - Discharged on 17 Jun 1814 and sent to Dartmoor on HMS Pincher.

Harvey, Joseph - Seaman - Number: 3562 - Prize name: Hannah - Ship type: MV - How taken: HM Ship-of-the-Line Conquestador - When taken: 15 Jan 1814 - Where taken: at sea - Date received: 7 May 1814 - From what ship: Portsmouth via HMS Favorite - Born: Beverly - Age: 33 - Discharged on 25 Sep 1814 and sent to Dartmoor on HMS Niobe.

Harvey, Peter - Seaman - Number: 2377 - How taken: Gave himself up from HM Ship-of-the-Line America - When taken: 26 Dec 1812 - Date received: 20 Oct 1813 - From what ship: Portsmouth, via an admiral's tender - Born: Philadelphia - Age: 29 - Discharged on 16 Feb 1814 and released to HMS Ceres.

Harvey, Peter - Seaman - Number: 2908 - Prize name: U.S. Schooner Julia - Ship type: War - How taken: HM Schooner Earl Moria - When taken: 11 Aug 1813 - Where taken: Lake Ontario - Date received: 7 Jan 1814 - From what ship: Portsmouth - Born: Portland - Age: 26 - Died on 17 Mar 1814 from fever.

Harway, Samuel - Seaman - Number: 1792 - How taken: Taken up at London - When taken: 9 Jun 1813 - Date received: 1 Jul 1813 - From what ship: HMS Raisonnable - Born: North Carolina - Age: 40 - Discharged on 3 Nov 1813 and released to HMS Ceres.

Harwill, William - Seaman - Number: 2014 - How taken: Gave himself up from HM Ship-of-the-Line Clarence - Date received: 15 Jul 1813 - From what ship: Plymouth - Born: New York - Age: 22 - Discharged on 17 Jun 1814 and sent to Dartmoor on HMS Pincher.

Harwood, William - Seaman - Number: 2429 - Prize name: Maydock - Ship type: MV - How taken: HM Brig Rebuff - When taken: 16 Jun 1813 - Where taken: off Cape St. Marys, Newfoundland - Date received: 21 Oct 1813 - From what ship: Portsmouth via HMT Malabar - Born: Maryland - Age: 31 - Discharged on 4 Sep 1814 and sent to Dartmoor on HMS Freya.

Hasem, John - Seaman - Number: 1464 - Prize name: Union - Ship type: MV - How taken: HM Frigate Iris - When taken: 17 Jan 1813 - Where taken: at sea - Date received: 6 Apr 1813 - From what ship: Portsmouth via Tender Eliza - Born: Boston - Age: 30 - Race: Negro - Discharged on 24 Jul 1813 and released to Cartel Hoffminy.

Haskins, John - Seaman - Number: 2411 - How taken: Gave himself up from HM Hospital Ship Trent - Date received: 21 Oct 1813 - From what ship: Portsmouth via HMT Malabar - Born: Bedford - Age: 20 - Discharged on 4 Sep 1814 and sent to Dartmoor on HMS Freya.

Hastings, Johnson - Seaman - Number: 495 - Prize name: Hannibal - Ship type: MV - How taken: MV Potent - When taken: 24 Sep 1812 - Where taken: off Bermuda - Date received: 23 Feb 1813 - From what ship: Portsmouth via HMS Dromedary - Born: Boston - Age: 22 - Discharged on 8 Jun 1813 and released to Cartel Rodrigo.

Hathaway, William N. - Boy - Number: 1046 - Prize name: Perseverance - Ship type: MV - How taken: HM Frigate Sybille & Fortune - When taken: 12 Aug 1812 - Where taken: off Cape Clear, Ireland - Date received: 11 Mar 1813 - From what ship: Yarmouth via HMS Tenders - Born: New York - Age: 14 - Discharged on 8 Jun 1813 and released to Cartel Rodrigo.

Hatch, Abraham - Seaman - Number: 809 - Prize name: Leader - Ship type: MV - How taken: HM Frigate Andromach - When taken: 10 Dec 1812 - Where taken: off Bordeaux, France - Date received: 27 Feb 1813 - From what ship: Plymouth via HMS Namur - Born: Bristol, MA - Age: 29 - Discharged in Jul 1813 and released to Cartel Moses Brown.

Hatch, Walter - Seaman - Number: 904 - How taken: Gave himself up from HM Brig Liberty - When taken: 28 Jul 1812 - Date received: 1 Mar 1813 - From what ship: Plymouth via HMS Namur - Born: Bridgetown, MA - Age: 25 - Discharged on 23 Mar 1813 and released to the Cartel Robinson Potter.

Hatch, William - Seaman - Number: 2140 - Prize name: Matilda, prize of the U.S. Brig Argus - Ship type: War - How taken: HM Frigate Revolutionnaire - When taken: 25 Jul 1813 - Where taken: off Lorient, France - Date received: 9 Aug 1813 - From what ship: HMS Thames - Born: Connecticut - Age: 22 - Discharged on 4 Aug 1814 and sent to Dartmoor on HMS Alpheus.

Hathaway, Philip - Seaman - Number: 3013 - Prize name: Yankee - Ship type: P - How taken: HM Frigate Shannon - When taken: 20 Aug 1813 - Where taken: at sea - Date received: 7 Jan 1814 - From what ship: Halifax - Born: Massachusetts - Age: 23 - Discharged on 25 Sep 1814 and sent to Dartmoor on HMS Leyden.

Hatton, Peter - Seaman - Number: 3204 - Prize name: Fly, prize of the U.S. Frigate President - Ship type: War - How taken: HM Frigate Regulus & HM Frigate Melpomene - When taken: 4 Sep 1813 - Where taken: at sea - Date received: 7 Jan 1813 - From what ship: Portsmouth - Born: New Hampshire - Age: 40 - Discharged on 22 Oct 1814 and sent to Dartmoor on HMS Leyden.

Haushaw, George - Seaman - Number: 1752 - How taken: Gave himself up from HMS Impeteux - When taken: 2 Dec 1812 - Date received: 30 May 1813 - From what ship: HMS Impetius - Born: Salem - Age: 24 - Discharged on 24 Jul 1814 and sent to Dartmoor on HMS Liffey.

Hawkins, Isaac - Seaman - Number: 2538 - Prize name: Columbia - Ship type: MV - How taken: HM Frigate Briton - When taken: 17 Jan 1813 - Where taken: off Bordeaux, France - Date received: 22 Oct 1813 - From what ship: Portsmouth via HMT Malabar - Born: Maryland - Age: 31 - Race: Mulatto - Discharged on 8 Sep 1814 and sent to Dartmoor on HMS Niobe.

Hawkins, John - Seaman - Number: 1945 - How taken: Gave himself up from HM Ship-of-the-Line Leyden - Date received: 15 Jul 1813 - From what ship: Plymouth - Born: Philadelphia - Age: 32 - Discharged on 17 Jun 1814 and sent to Dartmoor on HMS Redbreast.

Hawley, Frederick - Seaman - Number: 1309 - How taken: Gave himself up from HM Guardship Royal William - When taken: 3 Feb 1813 - Date received: 16 Mar 1813 - From what ship: Portsmouth, via HMS Abundance - Born: Wilmington - Age: 23 - Discharged on 23 Jul 1814 and sent to Dartmoor.

Hay, John - 2nd Lieutenant - Number: 3303 - Prize name: Juliana Smith - Ship type: P - How taken: HM Frigate Nymphe - When taken: 12 May 1813 - Where taken: off Cape Sable, Florida - Date received: 23 Feb 1814 - From what ship: Halifax via HMT Malabar - Born: New Jersey - Age: 34 - Discharged on 10 Oct 1814 and sent to Dartmoor on the Mermaid.

Haywood, John - Seaman - Number: 506 - Prize name: Josephine - Ship type: MV - How taken: HM Sloop Goree - When taken: 15 Aug 1812 - Where taken: off Bermuda - Date received: 23 Feb 1813 - From what ship: Portsmouth via HMS Dromedary - Born: New York - Age: 21 - Discharged on 10 May 1813 and released to Cartel Admittance.

Haywood, John - Seaman - Number: 2286 - How taken: Gave himself up from HM Ship-of-the-Line Scipion - When taken: 20 Oct 1812 - Date received: 17 Sep 1813 - From what ship: HMS Raisonnable - Born: Maryland - Age: 25 - Race: Black - Discharged on 4 Sep 1814 and sent to Dartmoor on HMS Freya.

Haywood, Simon - Seaman - Number: 847 - Prize name: Lucian, prize of the Privateer Armstrong - Ship type: P - How taken: Briton, letter of marque - When taken: 29 Nov 1812 - Where taken: off Bermuda - Date received: 1 Mar 1813 - From what ship: Plymouth via HMS Namur - Born: Lenox - Age: 21 - Discharged on 8 Jun 1813 and released to Cartel Rodrigo.

Hazard, Charles - Seaman - Number: 3636 - Prize name: Bunker Hill - Ship type: P - How taken: HM Frigate Pomone & HM Frigate Cydnus - When taken: 4 Mar 1814 - Where taken: Bay of Biscay - Date received: 31 Mar 1814 - From what ship: HMS Raisonnable - Born: Providence - Age: 24 - Discharged on 25 Sep 1814 and sent to Dartmoor on HMS Niobe.

Hazard, Prince - Seaman - Number: 2850 - Prize name: Blockade - Ship type: P - How taken: HM Brig Recruit - When taken: 17 Aug 1813 - Where taken: coast of America - Date received: 7 Jan 1814 - From what ship: Halifax - Born: Rhode Island - Age: 22 - Race: Black - Discharged on 26 Sep 1814 and sent to Dartmoor on HMS Leyden.

Hazard, Robert - Seaman - Number: 3624 - How taken: Gave himself up from HM Sloop Stork - When taken: 24 Feb 1814 - Date received: 29 Mar 1814 - From what ship: Hired tender Anna - Born: Rhode Island - Age: 25 - Discharged on 26 Sep 1814 and sent to Dartmoor on HMS Leyden.

Hazard, Thomas - Seaman - Number: 1045 - Prize name: Warren - Ship type: MV - How taken: HM Frigate Sybille & HMS Fortunee - When taken: 3 Sep 1812 - Where taken: Lat 41.4 Long 33 - Date received: 11 Mar 1813 - From what ship: Yarmouth via HMS Tenders - Born: South Kingston - Age: 24 - Race: Black - Discharged on 8 Jun 1813 and released to Cartel Rodrigo.

Hazard, Thomas - Seaman - Number: 2364 - How taken: Gave himself up from HM Ship-of-the-Line Berwick - When taken: 25 Jun 1813 - Date received: 20 Oct 1813 - From what ship: Portsmouth, via an admiral's tender - Born: Rhode Island - Age: 22 - Race: Mulatto - Released on 8 Oct 1814.

Hazel, Thomas - Seaman - Number: 1729 - Prize name: Powhattan - Ship type: MV - How taken: HMS Horatio - When taken: 13 Dec 1812 - Where taken: Bay of Biscay - Date received: 25 May 1813 - From what ship: Portsmouth via HMS Impetius - Born: Loris, Austria - Age: 20 - Discharged on 24 Jul 1813 and released to Cartel Hoffminy.

Head, James - 1st Lieutenant - Number: 2865 - Prize name: Elbridge Gerry - Ship type: P - How taken: HM Frigate Crescent - When taken: 16 Sep 1813 - Where taken: at sea - Date received: 7 Jan 1814 - From what ship:

Portsmouth - Born: Massachusetts - Age: 28 - Died on 29 Mar 1814 from small pox.

Heady, Linsey - Seaman - Number: 2574 - How taken: Gave himself up from HM Ship-of-the-Line Union - When taken: 2 Dec 1812 - Date received: 23 Oct 1813 - From what ship: Portsmouth via HMS Raisonnable - Born: New Jersey - Age: 38 - Discharged on 8 Sep 1814 and sent to Dartmoor on HMS Niobe.

Hearins, Patrick - Private - Number: 1634 - Prize name: U.S. Light Artillery - Ship type: LF - How taken: British forces - When taken: 13 Oct 1812 - Where taken: Upper Canada - Date received: 9 May 1813 - From what ship: HMS Raisonnable - Born: Things County, Ireland - Age: 38 - Discharged on 22 Oct 1814 and sent to Dartmoor on HMS Leyden.

Hearl, Hiram - Master's Mate - Number: 2158 - Prize name: tender to the Privateer True Blooded Yankee - Ship type: P - How taken: HM Ship-of-the-Line Fame - When taken: 24 Jun 1813 - Where taken: at sea - Date received: 16 Aug 1813 - From what ship: Portsmouth, via an admiral's tender - Born: Bath - Age: 29 - Escaped on 16 May 1814 from HMS Horatio.

Heater, William - Seaman - Number: 3034 - How taken: Gave himself up from HM Schooner Charlotte - When taken: Jul 1813 - Date received: 7 Jan 1814 - From what ship: Portsmouth - Born: Hampshire - Age: 26 - Discharged on 11 Aug 1814 and sent to Dartmoor on HMS Freya.

Heaton, Henry - Seaman - Number: 2376 - How taken: Gave himself up from HM Ship-of-the-Line America - When taken: 26 Dec 1812 - Date received: 20 Oct 1813 - From what ship: Portsmouth, via an admiral's tender - Born: Lancaster - Age: 33 - Discharged on 4 Sep 1814 and sent to Dartmoor on HMS Freya.

Hebius, Jeremiah - Seaman - Number: 1787 - How taken: Taken up at London - When taken: 17 Jun 1813 - Date received: 1 Jul 1813 - From what ship: HMS Raisonnable - Born: Virginia - Age: 29 - Discharged on 25 Jul 1814 and sent to Dartmoor on HMS Bittern.

Hecox, George - Seaman - Number: 703 - Prize name: Deanna, recaptured British vessel - Ship type: P - How taken: HM Ship-of-the-Line Polyphemus - When taken: 14 Sep 1812 - Where taken: at sea - Date received: 24 Feb 1813 - From what ship: Portsmouth via HMS Ulysses - Born: New Haven - Age: 28 - Discharged on 8 Jun 1813 and released to Cartel Rodrigo.

Hedden, Amos - Private - Number: 3081 - Prize name: 14th U.S. Infantry - Ship type: LF - How taken: British forces - When taken: 24 Jun 1813 - Where taken: Beaver Dams, Upper Canada - Date received: 7 Jan 1814 - From what ship: Halifax - Born: New Jersey - Age: 23 - Discharged on 10 Oct 1814 and sent to U.S. on Cartel St. Philip.

Hedley, John - Seaman - Number: 1063 - How taken: Gave himself up from HM Guardship Royal William - When taken: 5 Feb 1813 - Date received: 14 Mar 1813 - From what ship: Portsmouth via HMS Cornwell - Born: New York - Age: 29 - Discharged on 11 Aug 1814 and sent to Dartmoor.

Heimer, Daniel - Seaman - Number: 3545 - Prize name: Commodore Perry - Ship type: MV - How taken: Sent into custody from a cutter - When taken: 25 Feb 1814 - Where taken: off Bordeaux, France - Date received: 5 Mar 1814 - From what ship: HMS Raisonnable - Born: Charlestown - Age: 29 - Discharged on 26 Sep 1814 and sent to Dartmoor on HMS Leyden.

Hellen, John P. - Seaman - Number: 3722 - Prize name: Valentine - Ship type: MV - How taken: HM Ship-of-the-Line Minden - When taken: 17 Nov 1812 - Where taken: off Cape of Good Hope - Date received: 23 May 1814 - From what ship: London - Born: Providence - Age: 21 - Discharged on 22 Oct 1814 and sent to Dartmoor on HMS Leyden.

Helm, Charles - Seaman - Number: 870 - Prize name: Columbia - Ship type: MV - How taken: HM Frigate Briton - When taken: 17 Jan 1813 - Where taken: off Bordeaux, France - Date received: 1 Mar 1813 - From what ship: Plymouth via HMS Namur - Born: Philadelphia - Age: 35 - Discharged in Jul 1813 and released to Cartel Moses Brown.

Helman, John - Seaman - Number: 654 - Prize name: U.S.R.M. Cutter James Madison - Ship type: War - How taken: HM Frigate Barbadoes - When taken: 22 Aug 1812 - Where taken: at sea - Date received: 24 Feb 1813 - From what ship: Portsmouth via HMS Ulysses - Born: Eastport, MA - Age: 18 - Discharged on 10 May 1813 and released to Cartel Admittance.

Hemonder, Peter - Seaman - Number: 3684 - Prize name: Bunker Hill - Ship type: P - How taken: HM Frigate

Pomone & HM Frigate Cydnus - When taken: 4 Mar 1814 - Where taken: Bay of Biscay - Date received: 4 May 1814 - From what ship: Portsmouth - Born: Visby, Sweden - Age: 20 - Discharged on 25 Sep 1814 and sent to Dartmoor on HMS Niobe.

Hemp, James - Seaman - Number: 1861 - How taken: Given up from HM Frigate Leonidas - Date received: 7 Jul 1813 - From what ship: Portsmouth via HMS Tribune - Born: New York - Age: 27 - Discharged on 25 Jul 1814 and sent to Dartmoor on HMS Bittern.

Henday, Thomas - Seaman - Number: 3318 - Prize name: Porcupine - Ship type: LM - How taken: HM Frigate Acasta - When taken: 18 Jul 1813 - Where taken: off Cape Sable, Florida - Date received: 23 Feb 1814 - From what ship: Halifax via HMT Malabar - Born: Boston - Age: 22 - Discharged on 10 Oct 1814 and sent to Dartmoor on the Mermaid.

Henderson, Benjamin - Seaman - Number: 724 - Prize name: Eos - Ship type: MV - How taken: Detained at Portsmouth harbor - When taken: 31 Jul 1812 - Date received: 24 Feb 1813 - From what ship: Portsmouth via HMS Ulysses - Born: Newburyport - Age: 26 - Discharged on 23 Mar 1813 and released to the Cartel Robinson Potter.

Henderson, David - Seaman - Number: 819 - Prize name: Columbia - Ship type: MV - How taken: HM Frigate Briton - When taken: 17 Dec 1812 - Where taken: off Bordeaux, France - Date received: 27 Feb 1813 - From what ship: Plymouth via HMS Namur - Born: Philadelphia - Age: 21 - Discharged in Jul 1813 and released to Cartel Moses Brown.

Hendrick, John - Seaman - Number: 3779 - Prize name: Argus - Ship type: MV - How taken: HM Ship-of-the-Line San Domingo - When taken: 1 Mar 1814 - Where taken: off Savannah - Date received: 26 May 1814 - From what ship: HMS Hindostan - Born: Rotterdam - Age: 32 - Released on 16 Jun 1814.

Hendrick, Thomas - Seaman - Number: 3780 - Prize name: Argus - Ship type: MV - How taken: HM Ship-of-the-Line San Domingo - When taken: 1 Mar 1814 - Where taken: off Savannah - Date received: 26 May 1814 - From what ship: HMS Hindostan - Born: Rotterdam - Age: 24 - Released on 16 Jun 1814.

Hendrickson, Michael - Carpenter - Number: 1644 - Prize name: Henryettos - Ship type: MV - How taken: HMS Castilian - When taken: 12 Mar 1813 - Where taken: off Cape Ortegal, Spain - Date received: 9 May 1813 - From what ship: HMS Raisonnable - Born: Finland - Age: 43 - Released on 1 Jul 1813.

Henley, John - Seaman - Number: 3299 - Prize name: Montgomery - Ship type: P - How taken: HM Frigate Nymphe - When taken: 5 May 1813 - Where taken: off Cape Cod - Date received: 23 Feb 1814 - From what ship: Halifax via HMT Malabar - Born: Marblehead - Age: 53 - Discharged on 10 Oct 1814 and sent to Dartmoor on the Mermaid.

Henney, Peter - Seaman - Number: 2198 - How taken: Gave himself up from HM Ship-of-the-Line Caledonia - When taken: 5 Dec 1812 - Date received: 18 Aug 1813 - From what ship: Portsmouth, via an admiral's tender - Born: New York - Age: 55 - Race: Black - Discharged on 11 Aug 1814 and sent to Dartmoor on HMS Freya.

Henricks, Jeremiah - Seaman - Number: 670 - Prize name: U.S.R.M. Cutter James Madison - Ship type: War - How taken: HM Frigate Barbadoes - When taken: 22 Aug 1812 - Where taken: at sea - Date received: 24 Feb 1813 - From what ship: Portsmouth via HMS Ulysses - Born: Baltimore - Age: 16 - Discharged on 10 May 1813 and released to Cartel Admittance.

Henry, Edward - Boy - Number: 478 - Prize name: Hunter - Ship type: P - How taken: HM Frigate Phoebe - When taken: 23 Dec 1812 - Where taken: off Azores - Date received: 19 Feb 1813 - From what ship: HMS Modeste - Born: Newburyport - Age: 15 - Discharged on 24 Jul 1813 and released to Cartel Hoffminy.

Henry, George - Private - Number: 3050 - Prize name: U.S. Light Dragoons - Ship type: LF - How taken: British forces - When taken: 24 Jun 1813 - Where taken: Beaver Dams, Upper Canada - Date received: 7 Jan 1814 - From what ship: Halifax - Born: Pennsylvania - Age: 26 - Discharged on 10 Oct 1814 and sent to U.S. on Cartel St. Philip.

Henry, Henry - Seaman - Number: 2336 - Prize name: Falcon, prize of the U.S. Frigate President - Ship type: War - How taken: Spanish army - When taken: 2 Jul 1813 - Where taken: off Passage Harbor - Date received: 20 Oct 1813 - From what ship: Portsmouth, via an admiral's tender - Born: Massachusetts - Age: 25 -

Discharged on 4 Sep 1814 and sent to Dartmoor on HMS Freya.

Henry, James - Private - Number: 2633 - Prize name: 14th U.S. Infantry - Ship type: LF - How taken: British forces - When taken: 24 Jun 1813 - Where taken: Beaver Dams, Upper Canada - Date received: 5 Nov 1813 - From what ship: HMS Hindostan - Born: North Ireland - Age: 32 - Discharged on 10 Oct 1814 and sent to U.S. on Cartel St. Philip.

Henry, John - Seaman - Number: 1400 - Prize name: Porcupine - Ship type: MV - How taken: HM Frigate Dryand - When taken: 8 Jan 1813 - Where taken: off Bordeaux, France - Date received: 5 Apr 1813 - From what ship: Plymouth via HMS Dwarf - Born: New Orleans - Age: 36 - Discharged on 24 Jul 1813 and released to Cartel Hoffminy.

Henry, William - Seaman - Number: 3716 - Prize name: Requin - Ship type: LM - How taken: HM Frigate Venus - When taken: 5 Mar 1814 - Where taken: off Bordeaux, France - Date received: 18 May 1814 - From what ship: HMS Raisonnable - Born: New London - Age: 22 - Race: Black - Discharged on 26 Sep 1814 and sent to Dartmoor on HMS Leyden.

Henwood, Eliza - Cook - Number: 214 - How taken: Gave himself up from MV Perverance - When taken: 2 Nov 1812 - Date received: 15 Nov 1812 - From what ship: HMS Raisonnable - Born: Maryland - Age: 26 - Discharged in Jul 1813 and released to Cartel Moses Brown.

Henzeman, Christopher - Seaman - Number: 3540 - Prize name: Commodore Perry - Ship type: MV - How taken: Sent into custody from a cutter - When taken: 25 Feb 1814 - Where taken: off Bordeaux, France - Date received: 5 Mar 1814 - From what ship: HMS Raisonnable - Born: Prussia - Age: 21 - Discharged on 25 Sep 1814 and sent to Dartmoor on HMS Niobe.

Hera, John A. - Seaman - Number: 785 - Prize name: Dolphin - Ship type: MV - How taken: HM Ship-of-the-Line Colossus - When taken: 5 Jan 1813 - Where taken: off the Western Isles, Scotland - Date received: 27 Feb 1813 - From what ship: Plymouth via HMS Namur - Born: Philadelphia - Age: 24 - Discharged on 24 Jul 1813 and released to Cartel Hoffminy.

Herdru, Charles - Seaman - Number: 140 - Prize name: Davy Dearborn - Ship type: MV - How taken: Stopped at London - When taken: 26 Oct 1812 - Date received: 5 Nov 1812 - From what ship: HMS Namur - Born: Greenwich, CT - Age: 22 - Discharged on 23 Mar 1813 and released to the Cartel Robinson Potter.

Herrington, Ezekiel - Private - Number: 3087 - Prize name: 14th U.S. Infantry - Ship type: LF - How taken: British forces - When taken: 23 Jun 1813 - Where taken: Beaver Dams, Upper Canada - Date received: 7 Jan 1814 - From what ship: Halifax - Born: Vermont - Age: 18 - Discharged on 10 Oct 1814 and sent to U.S. on Cartel St. Philip.

Herts, John Edward - Seaman - Number: 193 - Prize name: Mary Ann - Ship type: MV - How taken: HM Brig Castilian - When taken: 14 Aug 1812 - Where taken: Downs - Date received: 6 Nov 1812 - From what ship: HMS Echo - Born: Volgaards, Sweden - Age: 30 - Discharged in Jul 1813 and released to Cartel Moses Brown.

Hewet, James - Seaman - Number: 307 - Prize name: Cuba - Ship type: MV - How taken: HM Brig Sarpedon - When taken: 12 Aug 1812 - Date received: 23 Dec 1812 - From what ship: Greenlaw Depot - Born: Dover - Age: 32 - Discharged on 10 May 1813 and released to Cartel Admittance.

Heyden, William - Seaman - Number: 1378 - How taken: Gave himself up from HM Ship of-the-Line Bellerophon - When taken: 18 Mar 1813 - Date received: 3 Apr 1813 - From what ship: Portsmouth, via an admiral's tender - Born: Boston - Age: 32 - Discharged on 24 Jul 1814 and sent to Dartmoor.

Heywood, John - Seaman - Number: 1659 - How taken: Gave himself up from HM Ship-of-the-Line Scepter - Date received: 9 May 1813 - From what ship: HMS Raisonnable - Born: Baltimore - Age: 25 - Race: Mulatto - Discharged on 13 Aug 1814 and sent to Dartmoor.

Hicks, James - Seaman - Number: 3955 - How taken: Gave himself up from HM Sloop Indian - When taken: 20 Aug 1814 - Date received: 21 Oct 1813 - From what ship: HMS Namur - Born: Providence - Age: 32 - Race: Black - Discharged on 22 Oct 1814 and sent to Dartmoor on HMS Leyden.

Hicks, Ogershill - Seaman - Number: 3473 - Prize name: Yankee - Ship type: P - How taken: HM Frigate Shannon - When taken: 20 Aug 1813 - Where taken: at sea - Date received: 23 Feb 1814 - From what ship: Halifax via

HMT Malabar - Born: Tiverton - Age: 26 - Discharged on 22 Oct 1814 and sent to Dartmoor on HMS Leyden.

Higby, James - Boy - Number: 3798 - Prize name: Alligator - Ship type: MV - How taken: HM Ship-of-the-Line San Domingo - When taken: 16 May 1813 - Where taken: off Bengal - Date received: 5 Jun 1814 - From what ship: HMS Raisonnable - Born: Newport - Age: 17 - Discharged on 29 Sep 1814 and sent to Dartmoor on HMS Freya.

Higgins, Asa - Seaman - Number: 2476 - Prize name: Juliana Smith - Ship type: P - How taken: HM Frigate Nymphe - When taken: 12 May 1813 - Where taken: off Cape Sable, Florida - Date received: 22 Oct 1813 - From what ship: Portsmouth via HMT Malabar - Born: Orleans - Age: 21 - Discharged on 8 Sep 1814 and sent to Dartmoor on HMS Niobe.

Higgins, John - Seaman - Number: 3289 - Prize name: Vivid - Ship type: P - How taken: HM Frigate Nymphe - When taken: 20 Apr 1813 - Where taken: off Cape Cod - Date received: 23 Feb 1814 - From what ship: Halifax via HMT Malabar - Born: Wellfleet - Age: 19 - Discharged on 10 Oct 1814 and sent to Dartmoor on the Mermaid.

Higgins, William - Seaman - Number: 1028 - Prize name: Charles - Ship type: MV - How taken: Taken up at Liverpool - When taken: 18 Oct 1812 - Date received: 11 Mar 1813 - From what ship: Yarmouth via HMS Tenders - Born: Virginia - Age: 24 - Race: Black - Discharged in Jul 1813 and released to Cartel Moses Brown.

Hill, Benjamin - Seaman - Number: 2468 - Prize name: Cossack - Ship type: P - How taken: HM Frigate Amelia - When taken: 11 Apr 1813 - Where taken: off St. Johns - Date received: 21 Oct 1813 - From what ship: Portsmouth via HMT Malabar - Born: Salem - Age: 22 - Discharged on 8 Sep 1814 and sent to Dartmoor on HMS Niobe.

Hill, Charles - Seaman - Number: 15 - Prize name: Lucky - Ship type: MV - How taken: Detained at Hanoi Bay - When taken: 11 Aug 1812 - Date received: 29 Oct 1812 - From what ship: HMS Raisonnable - Born: Salem - Age: 20 - Discharged on 10 May 1813 and released to Cartel Admittance.

Hill, Daniel - Seaman - Number: 3568 - Prize name: Minerva - Ship type: MV - How taken: HM Ship-of-the-Line Conquestador - When taken: 19 Jan 1814 - Where taken: Bay of Biscay - Date received: 7 May 1814 - From what ship: Portsmouth via HMS Favorite - Born: Charlestown - Age: 27 - Race: Black - Discharged on 25 Sep 1814 and sent to Dartmoor on HMS Niobe.

Hill, Ephraim - Seaman - Number: 1884 - Prize name: Tiger - Ship type: MV - How taken: HM Brig Scylla - When taken: 22 Mar 1813 - Where taken: Bay of Biscay - Date received: 7 Jul 1813 - From what ship: Portsmouth via HMS Tribune - Born: Hartford - Age: 24 - Race: Black - Discharged on 4 Aug 1814 and sent to Dartmoor on HMS Liverpool.

Hill, George - Seaman - Number: 622 - Prize name: King of Rome - Ship type: P - How taken: HM Brig Wolverine - When taken: 13 Dec 1812 - Where taken: at sea - Date received: 23 Feb 1813 - From what ship: Portsmouth via HMS Dromedary - Born: New York - Age: 16 - Discharged on 2 Jul 1813 and released to Cartel Moses Brown.

Hill, James - Seaman - Number: 3019 - How taken: Gave himself up from HM Ship-of-the-Line Invincible - When taken: 14 Jan 1813 - Date received: 7 Jan 1814 - From what ship: Portsmouth - Born: Boston - Age: 31 - Discharged on 25 Sep 1814 and sent to Dartmoor on HMS Leyden.

Hill, Jeremiah - Seaman - Number: 3226 - Prize name: Watson, prize of the Privateer True Blooded Yankee - Ship type: P - How taken: Chance, British privateer from Jersey - When taken: 13 Dec 1813 - Where taken: coast of France - Date received: 13 Jan 1814 - From what ship: Portsmouth via HMS Poictiers - Born: Baltimore - Age: 27 - Discharged on 25 Sep 1814 and sent to Dartmoor on HMS Leyden.

Hill, John - Boatswain - Number: 2888 - Prize name: Taken off an English whaler - How taken: HM Ship-of-the-Line Illustrious - When taken: 22 Oct 1813 - Where taken: at sea - Date received: 7 Jan 1814 - From what ship: Portsmouth - Born: Salem - Age: 26 - Discharged on 25 Sep 1814 and sent to Dartmoor on HMS Leyden.

Hill, Josiah - Seaman - Number: 1876 - Prize name: Tiger - Ship type: MV - How taken: HM Brig Scylla - When taken: 22 Mar 1813 - Where taken: Bay of Biscay - Date received: 7 Jul 1813 - From what ship: Portsmouth via HMS Tribune - Born: New Orleans - Age: 20 - Race: Black - Discharged on 4 Aug 1814 and sent to Dartmoor on HMS Liverpool.

Hill, Justice - Seaman - Number: 3612 - Prize name: Liberty - Ship type: MV - How taken: Surrendered at Stromness, Scotland - When taken: 30 Dec 1813 - Date received: 29 Mar 1814 - From what ship: Hired tender Anna - Born: Stockbridge - Age: 27 - Discharged on 25 Sep 1814 and sent to Dartmoor on HMS Niobe.

Hill, Manuel - Seaman - Number: 3337 - Prize name: Porcupine - Ship type: LM - How taken: HM Frigate Acasta - When taken: 18 Jul 1813 - Where taken: off Cape Sable, Florida - Date received: 23 Feb 1814 - From what ship: Halifax via HMT Malabar - Born: Andover - Age: 19 - Discharged on 10 Oct 1814 and sent to Dartmoor on the Mermaid.

Hill, Pompey - Seaman - Number: 1231 - Prize name: Rossie - Ship type: MV - How taken: HM Frigate Dryand - When taken: 7 Jan 1813 - Where taken: at sea - Date received: 16 Mar 1813 - From what ship: Portsmouth, via HMS Abundance - Born: Maryland - Age: 34 - Race: Black - Discharged on 24 Jul 1813 and released to Cartel Hoffminy.

Hill, Stephen - Private - Number: 3058 - Prize name: 14th U.S. Infantry - Ship type: LF - How taken: British forces - When taken: 24 Jun 1813 - Where taken: Beaver Dams, Upper Canada - Date received: 7 Jan 1814 - From what ship: Halifax - Born: Maryland - Age: 23 - Discharged on 10 Oct 1814 and sent to U.S. on Cartel St. Philip.

Hill, Timothy - Seaman - Number: 2068 - How taken: Gave himself up from HM Frigate Resistance - When taken: 30 Nov 1812 - Date received: 9 Aug 1813 - From what ship: HMS Thames - Born: Morristown, NJ - Age: 33 - Race: Mulatto - Discharged on 4 Aug 1814 and sent to Dartmoor on HMS Liverpool.

Hill, William - Seaman - Number: 1218 - Prize name: Rossie - Ship type: MV - How taken: HM Frigate Dryand - When taken: 7 Jan 1813 - Where taken: at sea - Date received: 16 Mar 1813 - From what ship: Portsmouth, via HMS Abundance - Born: Philadelphia - Age: 25 - Discharged on 24 Jul 1813 and released to Cartel Hoffminy.

Hill, William - Seaman - Number: 1482 - Prize name: Union - Ship type: MV - How taken: HM Frigate Iris - When taken: 17 Jan 1813 - Where taken: at sea - Date received: 6 Apr 1813 - From what ship: Portsmouth via Tender Eliza - Born: Spring Mills, NJ - Age: 34 - Discharged on 26 Jul 1813 and released to Cartel Hoffminy.

Hinkle, Henry - Seaman - Number: 2680 - How taken: Gave himself up from HM Bomb Vessel Thunder - When taken: 29 Oct 1812 - Date received: 2 Dec 1813 - From what ship: HMS Raisonnable - Born: Sweden - Age: 25 - Discharged on 29 Dec 1813 and sent to France.

Hinton, John - Seaman - Number: 1670 - How taken: Gave himself up from HM Ship-of-the-Line Tigre - Date received: 9 May 1813 - From what ship: HMS Raisonnable - Born: North Carolina - Age: 25 - Discharged on 11 Aug 1814 and sent to Dartmoor on HMS Shamrock.

Hitch, Joshua - Supercargo - Number: 2024 - Prize name: Governor Gerry - Ship type: MV - How taken: HM Brig Royalist - When taken: 31 May 1813 - Where taken: Bay of Biscay - Date received: 24 Jul 1813 - From what ship: from Ashburton - Born: New York - Age: 28 - Discharged on 24 Jul 1813 and released to Cartel Hoffminy.

Hitchcock, Edward - Seaman - Number: 1508 - How taken: Gave himself up from HM Ship-of-the-Line Blake - When taken: 10 Dec 1812 - Date received: 8 Apr 1813 - From what ship: Portsmouth, via an admiral's tender - Born: Newark - Age: 46 - Race: Blackman - Discharged on 4 Sep 1814 and sent to Dartmoor on HMS Freya.

Hitchcock, Moses - Seaman - Number: 2217 - How taken: Apprehended at London - When taken: 13 Aug 1813 - Date received: 18 Aug 1813 - From what ship: HMS Raisonnable - Born: New York - Age: 30 - Race: Blackman - Discharged on 11 Aug 1814 and sent to Dartmoor on HMS Freya.

Hitchens, John - Boy - Number: 986 - Prize name: Otter - Ship type: MV - How taken: HM Ship-Sloop Jalouse - When taken: 1 Dec 1812 - Where taken: off Cape St. Vincent, Portugal - Date received: 10 Mar 1813 - From what ship: HMS Tigress - Born: Castine - Age: 15 - Race: Mulatto - Released on 20 Mar 1813 to HMS Otter.

Hitchins, William - Prize Master - Number: 2871 - Prize name: Elbridge Gerry - Ship type: P - How taken: HM Frigate Crescent - When taken: 16 Sep 1813 - Where taken: at sea - Date received: 7 Jan 1814 - From what ship: Portsmouth - Born: Massachusetts - Age: 23 - Discharged on 25 Sep 1814 and sent to Dartmoor on HMS Leyden.

Hobdyke, John - Seaman - Number: 1239 - Prize name: Rossie - Ship type: MV - How taken: HM Frigate Dryand - When taken: 7 Jan 1813 - Where taken: at sea - Date received: 16 Mar 1813 - From what ship: Portsmouth, via HMS Abundance - Born: Portsmouth - Age: 16 - Race: Black - Discharged on 18 Oct 1813 and released to HMS Ceres.

Hobert, George - Seaman - Number: 446 - Prize name: Hunter - Ship type: P - How taken: HM Frigate Phoebe - When taken: 23 Dec 1812 - Where taken: off Azores - Date received: 19 Feb 1813 - From what ship: HMS Modeste - Born: Monmouth - Age: 19 - Discharged on 24 Jul 1813 and released to Cartel Hoffminy.

Hodges, Hercules - Seaman - Number: 3767 - Prize name: Argus - Ship type: MV - How taken: HM Ship-of-the-Line San Domingo - When taken: 1 Mar 1814 - Where taken: off Savannah - Date received: 26 May 1814 - From what ship: HMS Hindostan - Born: Barnstable - Age: 18 - Discharged on 25 Sep 1814 and sent to Dartmoor on HMS Niobe.

Hoffman, Joseph - Seaman - Number: 241 - How taken: Gave himself up from HM Ship-of-the-Line Monmouth - When taken: 18 Sep 1812 - Date received: 1 Dec 1812 - From what ship: HMS Raisonnable - Born: Boston - Age: 25 - Discharged on 26 Jul 1814 and sent to Dartmoor on HMS Raven.

Hogan, William - Seaman - Number: 1322 - How taken: Gave himself up from HM Guardship Royal William - When taken: 3 Feb 1813 - Date received: 16 Mar 1813 - From what ship: Portsmouth, via HMS Abundance - Born: Portland - Age: 43 - Discharged on 26 Jul 1814 and sent to Dartmoor on HMS Raven.

Hogg, Jacob - Seaman - Number: 3531 - Prize name: Commodore Perry - Ship type: MV - How taken: Sent into custody from a cutter - When taken: 25 Feb 1814 - Where taken: off Bordeaux, France - Date received: 5 Mar 1814 - From what ship: HMS Raisonnable - Born: New Jersey - Age: 40 - Discharged on 26 Sep 1814 and sent to Dartmoor on HMS Leyden.

Holbrook, Robert - Seaman - Number: 2502 - Prize name: Thomas - Ship type: P - How taken: HM Frigate Nymphe - When taken: 28 Jun 1813 - Where taken: off Halifax - Date received: 22 Oct 1813 - From what ship: Portsmouth via HMT Malabar - Born: Boston - Age: 23 - Discharged on 8 Sep 1814 and sent to Dartmoor on HMS Niobe.

Holden, Charles - Boatswain's Mate - Number: 424 - Prize name: Hunter - Ship type: P - How taken: HM Frigate Phoebe - When taken: 23 Dec 1812 - Where taken: off Azores - Date received: 19 Feb 1813 - From what ship: HMS Modeste - Born: Salem - Age: 37 - Discharged on 2 Jul 1813 and released to Cartel Moses Brown.

Holden, John - Seaman - Number: 3252 - Prize name: Thorn - Ship type: P - How taken: Shannon, Nova Scotia privateer - When taken: 7 Nov 1813 - Where taken: off Newfoundland - Date received: 23 Feb 1814 - From what ship: Halifax via HMT Malabar - Born: Marblehead - Age: 15 - Discharged on 10 Oct 1814 and sent to Dartmoor on the Mermaid.

Holden, Nathaniel - Seaman - Number: 2459 - Prize name: Wiley Reynard - Ship type: P - How taken: HM Frigate Shannon - When taken: 16 Aug 1812 - Where taken: off Halifax - Date received: 21 Oct 1813 - From what ship: Portsmouth via HMT Malabar - Born: Charleston - Age: 18 - Discharged on 4 Sep 1814 and sent to Dartmoor on HMS Freya.

Holdridge, Hector - Seaman - Number: 2259 - Prize name: Eliza - Ship type: MV - How taken: HMS Charles - When taken: 20 Jul 1813 - Where taken: off Petershead, Scotland - Date received: 14 Sep 1813 - From what ship: HMS Raisonnable - Born: Chatham - Age: 21 - Discharged on 4 Sep 1814 and sent to Dartmoor on HMS Freya.

Holland, William - 2nd Mate - Number: 306 - Prize name: Cuba - Ship type: MV - How taken: HM Brig Sarpedon - When taken: 12 Aug 1812 - Date received: 23 Dec 1812 - From what ship: Greenlaw Depot - Born: Norfolk - Age: 31 - Discharged on 10 May 1813 and released to Cartel Admittance.

Holm, Andre - Seaman - Number: 362 - Prize name: Postsea, prize to the Privateer Thrasher - Ship type: P - How taken: HM Sloop Helena - When taken: 31 Dec 1813 - Where taken: off Azores - Date received: 19 Jan 1813 - From what ship: HMS Raisonnable - Born: Stockholm, Sweden - Age: 31 - Released on 20 May 1813.

Holmes, Abraham - Seaman - Number: 2919 - Prize name: Juliana Smith - Ship type: P - How taken: HM Frigate Nymphe - When taken: 12 May 1813 - Where taken: off Cape Sable, Florida - Date received: 7 Jan 1814 - From what ship: Halifax - Born: Massachusetts - Age: 19 - Discharged on 25 Sep 1814 and sent to Dartmoor on HMS Leyden.

Holmes, Elisha - Seaman - Number: 2766 - Prize name: Thomas - Ship type: P - How taken: HM Frigate Nymphe - When taken: 24 Jun 1813 - Where taken: off Halifax - Date received: 7 Jan 1814 - From what ship: Halifax - Born: Massachusetts - Age: 23 - Discharged on 25 Sep 1814 and sent to Dartmoor on HMS Leyden.

Holms, John - Seaman - Number: 1919 - How taken: Given up from HM Ship-of-the-Line York - When taken: 1 Jun 1813 - Date received: 8 Jul 1813 - From what ship: Cumberland - Born: New York - Age: 29 - Discharged on 4 Aug 1814 and sent to Dartmoor on HMS Liverpool.

Holstien, Richard - Seaman - Number: 2877 - Prize name: Baroness Longueville, British South Sea Whaler - Ship type: MV - How taken: HM Ship-of-the-Line Illustrious - When taken: 5 Aug 1813 - Where taken: off St. Helena - Date received: 7 Jan 1814 - From what ship: Portsmouth - Born: Virginia - Age: 33 - Discharged on 10 Oct 1814 and sent to Dartmoor on the Mermaid.

Holston, John - Seaman - Number: 87 - Prize name: Gartlen - Ship type: MV - How taken: Stopped at London - When taken: 26 Oct 1812 - Date received: 4 Nov 1812 - From what ship: HMS Namur - Born: Virginia - Age: 27 - Discharged on 28 May 1813 and released to HMS Ceres.

Holt, Jacob L. - Seaman - Number: 2948 - Prize name: Enterprise - Ship type: P - How taken: HM Frigate Tenedos - When taken: 21 May 1813 - Where taken: off Cape Cod - Date received: 7 Jan 1814 - From what ship: Halifax - Born: Massachusetts - Age: 26 - Died on 16 Apr 1814 from fever.

Holt, Simeon - Seaman - Number: 730 - Prize name: Eos - Ship type: MV - How taken: Detained at Portsmouth harbor - When taken: 31 Jul 1812 - Date received: 24 Feb 1813 - From what ship: Portsmouth via HMS Ulysses - Born: Boston - Age: 17 - Discharged on 23 Mar 1813 and released to the Cartel Robinson Potter.

Homan, John - Seaman - Number: 1090 - Prize name: Rachael - Ship type: MV - How taken: HM Schooner Herring - When taken: 9 Feb 1813 - Where taken: at sea - Date received: 14 Mar 1813 - From what ship: Portsmouth via HMS Beagle - Born: Marblehead - Age: 27 - Discharged on 11 Aug 1814 and sent to Dartmoor on HMS Freya.

Homan, Jonas - Seaman - Number: 1091 - Prize name: Rachael - Ship type: MV - How taken: HM Schooner Herring - When taken: 9 Feb 1813 - Where taken: at sea - Date received: 14 Mar 1813 - From what ship: Portsmouth via HMS Beagle - Born: Marblehead - Age: 19 - Discharged on 11 Aug 1814 and sent to Dartmoor on HMS Freya.

Homan, Joseph - Seaman - Number: 695 - Prize name: Deanna, recaptured British vessel - Ship type: P - How taken: HM Ship-of-the-Line Polyphemus - When taken: 14 Sep 1812 - Where taken: at sea - Date received: 24 Feb 1813 - From what ship: Portsmouth via HMS Ulysses - Born: Marblehead, MA - Age: 28 - Discharged on 8 Jun 1813 and released to Cartel Rodrigo.

Homer, Henry - Seaman - Number: 3444 - Prize name: Elbridge Gerry - Ship type: P - How taken: HM Frigate Crescent - When taken: 16 Sep 1813 - Where taken: at sea - Date received: 23 Feb 1814 - From what ship: Halifax via HMT Malabar - Born: Cape Elizabeth - Age: 19 - Discharged on 21 Jul 1814 and sent to Dartmoor on HMS Portia.

Homes, Thomas - Seaman - Number: 248 - How taken: Gave himself up from MV Bearings, East Indianman - When taken: 2 Nov 1812 - Date received: 1 Dec 1812 - From what ship: HMS Raisonnable - Born: Philadelphia - Age: 38 - Discharged in Jul 1813 and released to Cartel Moses Brown.

Homes, Zachariah - Seaman - Number: 390 - Prize name: John - Ship type: MV - How taken: HM Sloop Blossom - When taken: 16 Aug 1812 - Where taken: off Gibraltar - Date received: 13 Feb 1813 - From what ship: HMS Raisonnable - Born: Plymouth, MA - Age: 33 - Discharged on 10 May 1813 and released to Cartel Admittance.

Hood, Daniel - Seaman - Number: 280 - Prize name: Forester - Ship type: MV - How taken: Apprehended at London - When taken: 13 Dec 1812 - Date received: 23 Dec 1812 - From what ship: HMS Raisonnable - Born: Edgecombe, MA - Age: 20 - Discharged on 24 Jul 1813 and released to Cartel Hoffminy.

Hook, Aaron - Seaman - Number: 988 - Prize name: Otter - Ship type: MV - How taken: HM Ship-Sloop Jalouse - When taken: 1 Dec 1812 - Where taken: off Cape St. Vincent, Portugal - Date received: 10 Mar 1813 - From what ship: HMS Tigress - Born: New Hampshire - Age: 20 - Released on 20 Mar 1813 to HMS Otter.

Hool, Salmon - Seaman - Number: 1607 - Prize name: Madelina - Ship type: MV - How taken: Impressed at London - When taken: 7 Apr 1813 - Date received: 22 Apr 1813 - From what ship: HMS Raisonnable - Born: Not listed - Discharged on 12 Aug 1814 and sent to Dartmoor on HMS Alpheus.

Hooper, Joseph A. - Gunner's Mate - Number: 2708 - Prize name: Growler - Ship type: P - How taken: HM Brig Electra - When taken: 7 Jul 1813 - Where taken: off St. Johns - Date received: 7 Jan 1814 - From what ship: Portsmouth - Born: Marblehead - Age: 23 - Discharged on 8 Sep 1814 and sent to Dartmoor on HMS Leyden.

Hooper, Samuel - Seaman - Number: 3437 - Prize name: Portsmouth Packet - Ship type: P - How taken: HM Brig Fantome - When taken: 5 Oct 1813 - Where taken: Grand Banks - Date received: 23 Feb 1814 - From what ship: Halifax via HMT Malabar - Born: Warren - Age: 29 - Discharged on 22 Oct 1814 and sent to Dartmoor on HMS Leyden.

Hooseman, John - Seaman - Number: 1290 - How taken: Gave himself up from HM Guardship Royal William - When taken: 3 Feb 1813 - Date received: 16 Mar 1813 - From what ship: Portsmouth, via HMS Abundance - Born: Maryland - Age: 22 - Discharged on 23 Jul 1814 and sent to Dartmoor.

Hopkins, Robert - Seaman - Number: 299 - Prize name: America - Ship type: MV - How taken: HM Brig Cracker - When taken: 1 Aug 1812 - Date received: 23 Dec 1812 - From what ship: Greenlaw Depot - Born: Mouland - Age: 32 - Discharged on 23 Mar 1813 and released to the Cartel Robinson Potter.

Hopkins, Samuel - Seaman - Number: 96 - Prize name: Fleetwood - Ship type: MV - How taken: Stopped at London - When taken: 26 Oct 1812 - Date received: 4 Nov 1812 - From what ship: HMS Namur - Born: Baltimore - Age: 36 - Discharged on 24 Feb 1813 and released to HMS Ceres.

Hopkins, Samuel - Seaman - Number: 1674 - How taken: Gave himself up from HM Ship-of-the-Line Gloucester - When taken: 26 Dec 1812 - Date received: 9 May 1813 - From what ship: HMS Raisonnable - Born: Rhode Island - Age: 42 - Discharged on 20 Aug 1814 and sent to Dartmoor on HMS Shamrock.

Horner, John - Seaman - Number: 2338 - Prize name: Falcon, prize of the U.S. Frigate President - Ship type: War - How taken: Spanish army - When taken: 2 Jul 1813 - Where taken: off Passage Harbor - Date received: 20 Oct 1813 - From what ship: Portsmouth, via an admiral's tender - Born: Boston - Age: 27 - Discharged on 4 Sep 1814 and sent to Dartmoor on HMS Freya.

Horsefall, William - Seaman - Number: 2581 - How taken: Impressed at London - When taken: 15 Oct 1813 - Date received: 1 Nov 1813 - From what ship: HMS Raisonnable - Born: New York - Age: 26 - Discharged on 8 Sep 1814 and sent to Dartmoor on HMS Niobe.

Horsey, Thomas W. - Seaman - Number: 1684 - Prize name: Abraham Newland - Ship type: MV - How taken: Impressed at Gravesend, England - When taken: 20 Mar 1813 - Date received: 15 May 1813 - From what ship: HMS Raisonnable - Born: Boston - Age: 28 - Discharged on 24 Jul 1814 and sent to Dartmoor on HMS Liffey.

Hosmer, Joseph - Quartermaster - Number: 428 - Prize name: Hunter - Ship type: P - How taken: HM Frigate Phoebe - When taken: 23 Dec 1812 - Where taken: off Azores - Date received: 19 Feb 1813 - From what ship: HMS Modeste - Born: Salem - Age: 21 - Discharged on 2 Jul 1813 and released to Cartel Moses Brown.

Hosstidler, Jesse - Seaman - Number: 1801 - Prize name: Henry - Ship type: MV - How taken: Impressed at London - When taken: 19 May 1813 - Date received: 3 Jul 1813 - From what ship: HMS Raisonnable - Born: Pennsylvania - Age: 33 - Discharged on 25 Jul 1814 and sent to Dartmoor on HMS Bittern.

Hotchkiss, Levi - 2nd Lieutenant - Number: 410 - Prize name: Hunter - Ship type: P - How taken: HM Frigate Phoebe - When taken: 23 Dec 1812 - Where taken: off Azores - Date received: 19 Feb 1813 - From what ship: HMS Modeste - Born: Boston - Age: 25 - Discharged on 2 Jul 1813 and released to Cartel Moses Brown.

House, Frederick - Private - Number: 3054 - Prize name: U.S. Heavy Artillery - Ship type: LF - How taken: British forces - When taken: 24 Jun 1813 - Where taken: Beaver Dams, Upper Canada - Date received: 7 Jan 1814 - From what ship: Halifax - Born: New York - Age: 28 - Discharged on 10 Oct 1814 and sent to U.S. on Cartel St. Philip.

House, Snow - Seaman - Number: 2155 - How taken: Gave himself up at London - When taken: 10 Aug 1813 - Date received: 14 Aug 1813 - From what ship: HMS Raisonnable - Born: Hanover, MA - Age: 40 - Died on 17 Dec 1813 from phthisis (tuberculosis).

Hovey, Joseph - Seaman - Number: 2796 - Prize name: Fox - Ship type: P - How taken: HM Brig Manly - When taken: 1 Aug 1813 - Where taken: off Halifax - Date received: 7 Jan 1814 - From what ship: Halifax - Born: Bath - Age: 15 - Discharged on 8 Sep 1814 and sent to Dartmoor on HMS Niobe.

Howard, Henry - Seaman - Number: 1243 - Prize name: Rossie - Ship type: MV - How taken: HM Frigate Dryand - When taken: 7 Jan 1813 - Where taken: at sea - Date received: 16 Mar 1813 - From what ship: Portsmouth, via HMS Abundance - Born: Philadelphia - Age: 29 - Discharged on 24 Jul 1813 and released to Cartel Hoffminy.

Howater, Henry - Seaman - Number: 1832 - Prize name: tender to the Privateer True Blooded Yankee - Ship type: P - How taken: HM Ship-of-the-Line Fame - When taken: 24 Jun 1813 - Where taken: off Brest, France - Date received: 7 Jul 1813 - From what ship: Portsmouth via HMS Scorpion - Born: Wappen Creek, NY - Age: 24 - Race: Black - Discharged on 5 Aug 1813 and released to HMS Ceres.

Howe, Jacob - Seaman - Number: 3758 - Prize name: Argus - Ship type: MV - How taken: HM Ship-of-the-Line San Domingo - When taken: 1 Mar 1814 - Where taken: off Savannah - Date received: 26 May 1814 - From what ship: HMS Hindostan - Born: Bridgetown - Age: 24 - Discharged on 25 Sep 1814 and sent to Dartmoor on HMS Niobe.

Howe, William - Seaman - Number: 3282 - Prize name: Vivid - Ship type: P - How taken: HM Frigate Nymphe - When taken: 20 Apr 1813 - Where taken: off Cape Cod - Date received: 23 Feb 1814 - From what ship: Halifax via HMT Malabar - Born: Petersham - Age: 28 - Discharged on 21 Jul 1814 and sent to Dartmoor on HMS Portia.

Howell, Sullivan - Seaman - Number: 102 - Prize name: Liberty - Ship type: MV - How taken: Stopped at London - When taken: 26 Oct 1812 - Date received: 4 Nov 1812 - From what ship: HMS Namur - Born: North Carolina - Age: 33 - Discharged in Jul 1813 and released to Cartel Moses Brown.

Howell, John - Seaman - Number: 1661 - How taken: Gave himself up from HM Ship-of-the-Line Scepter - Date received: 9 May 1813 - From what ship: HMS Raisonnable - Born: Philadelphia - Age: 24 - Discharged on 13 Aug 1814 and sent to Dartmoor.

Howell, John - Seaman - Number: 2290 - How taken: Gave himself up from HM Brig Paulina - When taken: 30 May 1813 - Date received: 17 Sep 1813 - From what ship: HMS Raisonnable - Born: Baltimore - Age: 46 - Discharged on 4 Sep 1814 and sent to Dartmoor on HMS Freya.

Howell, William - Seaman - Number: 3508 - Prize name: Pilot - Ship type: LM - How taken: Vittoria, British privateer from Guernsey - When taken: 28 Jan 1814 - Where taken: off Bordeaux, France - Date received: 23 Feb 1814 - From what ship: Portsmouth via HMT Malabar - Born: New York - Age: 23 - Discharged on 26 Sep 1814 and sent to Dartmoor on HMS Leyden.

Howland, William - Seaman - Number: 939 - Prize name: Three Brothers - Ship type: MV - How taken: HM Brig Bermuda - When taken: 9 Dec 1812 - Where taken: off St. Valery - Date received: 10 Mar 1813 - From what ship: HMS Tigress - Born: Greenfield - Age: 24 - Discharged on 2 Jul 1813 and released to Cartel Moses Brown.

Howland, William - Seaman - Number: 287 - Prize name: Francis Ann - Ship type: MV - How taken: Apprehended at Leight, Scotland - When taken: 5 Aug 1812 - Date received: 23 Dec 1812 - From what ship: Greenlaw Depot - Born: New Bedford - Age: 20 - Discharged on 23 Mar 1813 and released to the Cartel Robinson Potter.

Howland, William - Carpenter - Number: 2087 - How taken: Gave himself up from HM Ship-of-the-Line Scipion - When taken: 27 May 1813 - Date received: 9 Aug 1813 - From what ship: HMS Thames - Born: Massachsetts - Age: 40 - Discharged on 4 Aug 1814 and sent to Dartmoor on HMS Liverpool.

Howlen, Samuel - Seaman - Number: 990 - Prize name: Otter - Ship type: MV - How taken: HM Ship-Sloop Jalouse - When taken: 1 Dec 1812 - Where taken: off Cape St. Vincent, Portugal - Date received: 10 Mar 1813 - From what ship: HMS Tigress - Born: Boston - Age: 26 - Released on 20 Mar 1813 to HMS Otter.

Hoy, Barney - Private - Number: 2646 - Prize name: 23rd U.S. Infantry - Ship type: LF - How taken: British forces - When taken: 6 Jun 1813 - Where taken: Stoney Creek, Upper Canada - Date received: 5 Nov 1813 - From what ship: HMS Hindostan - Born: Western Ireland - Age: 28 - Discharged on 10 Oct 1814 and sent to U.S. on Cartel St. Philip.

Hoy, Philip - Seaman - Number: 104 - Prize name: Dominick - Ship type: MV - How taken: Stopped at London - When taken: 26 Oct 1812 - Date received: 4 Nov 1812 - From what ship: HMS Namur - Born: Baltimore - Age: 35 - Discharged in Jul 1813 and released to Cartel Moses Brown.

Hoyt, Ichabod - Seaman - Number: 733 - Prize name: Nancy - Ship type: MV - How taken: HM Brig Parthian - When taken: 1 Aug 1812 - Where taken: off the Needles, Isle of Wight - Date received: 24 Feb 1813 - From what ship: Portsmouth via HMS Ulysses - Born: Amesburg, MA - Age: 24 - Discharged on 23 Mar 1813 and released to the Cartel Robinson Potter.

Hoyt, James M. - Seaman - Number: 40 - Prize name: Suwarrow - Ship type: MV - How taken: HM Brig Recruit - When taken: 20 Jul 1812 - Where taken: off New York - Date received: 3 Nov 1812 - From what ship: HMS Plover - Born: Hanford, MA - Age: 27 - Discharged on 23 Mar 1813 and released to the Cartel Robinson Potter.

Hoyt, Robert - Seaman - Number: 273 - How taken: Apprehended at London - When taken: 10 Dec 1812 - Date received: 23 Dec 1812 - From what ship: HMS Raisonnable - Born: Norfolk, NY - Age: 39 - Discharged on 24 Jul 1813 and released to Cartel Hoffminy.

Hronias, Henry - Seaman - Number: 1727 - Prize name: Powhattan - Ship type: MV - How taken: HMS Horatio - When taken: 13 Dec 1812 - Where taken: Bay of Biscay - Date received: 25 May 1813 - From what ship: Portsmouth via HMS Impetius - Born: Cummings County - Age: 25 - Discharged on 24 Jul 1813 and released to Cartel Hoffminy.

Hubart, Joseph - Seaman - Number: 2374 - How taken: Gave himself up from HM Ship-of-the-Line Swiftsure - When taken: 26 Dec 1812 - Date received: 20 Oct 1813 - From what ship: Portsmouth, via an admiral's tender - Born: Barlow - Age: 37 - Died on 25 Sep 1814 from catarrhal affection.

Hubbard, Alfred - 2nd Mate - Number: 1890 - Prize name: Prompt - Ship type: MV - How taken: Chance, British privateer - When taken: 28 Mar 1813 - Where taken: Bay of Biscay - Date received: 7 Jul 1813 - From what ship: Portsmouth via HMS Tribune - Born: New Haven - Age: 28 - Discharged on 4 Aug 1814 and sent to Dartmoor on HMS Liverpool.

Hubbard, Christian - Carpenter - Number: 3232 - How taken: Impressed at London - When taken: 14 Sep 1813 - Date received: 13 Jan 1814 - From what ship: Portsmouth via HMS Poictiers - Born: Virginia - Age: 41 - Died on 2 May 1814 from fever.

Hubbard, George - Seaman - Number: 1766 - How taken: Gave up from HM Sloop North Star - When taken: 26 May 1813 - Date received: 14 Jun 1813 - From what ship: HMS Arethusa - Born: Ingram, MA - Age: 20 - Died on 10 Jan 1814 from phthisis (tuberculosis).

Hubbard, John G. - Seaman - Number: 3936 - How taken: Gave himself up from HM Ship-of-the-Line Fame - When taken: 20 Sep 1814 - Date received: 28 Sep 1814 - From what ship: Fame - Born: Marblehead - Age: 25 - Discharged on 29 Sep 1814 and sent to Dartmoor on HMS Freya.

Hubbard, William - Seaman - Number: 2365 - How taken: Gave himself up from HM Ship-of-the-Line Union - When taken: 25 Jun 1813 - Date received: 20 Oct 1813 - From what ship: Portsmouth, via an admiral's tender - Born: Connecticut - Age: 24 - Discharged on 21 Jan 1814 and released to HMS Ceres.

Hubbard, William - Prize Master - Number: 2992 - Prize name: America - Ship type: P - How taken: HM Frigate Shannon - When taken: 25 May 1813 - Where taken: off Cape Cod - Date received: 7 Jan 1814 - From what ship: Halifax - Born: Rhode Island - Age: 36 - Discharged on 25 Sep 1814 and sent to Dartmoor on HMS Leyden.

Hubble, James - Seaman - Number: 3590 - Prize name: Devon, prize to the Privateer Bunker Hill - Ship type: P - How taken: HM Brig Fly - When taken: 21 Jan 1814 - Where taken: at sea - Date received: 26 Mar 1814 - From what ship: Plymouth via HMS Raleigh - Born: Fairfield - Age: 29 - Discharged on 10 Oct 1814 and sent to Dartmoor on the Mermaid.

Hubi, Pierre M. - Boy - Number: 3692 - Prize name: Bunker Hill - Ship type: P - How taken: HM Frigate Pomone & HM Frigate Cydnus - When taken: 4 Mar 1814 - Where taken: Bay of Biscay - Date received: 4 May 1814 - From what ship: Portsmouth - Born: Lorient, France - Age: 11 - Discharged on 22 Jun 1814 and sent to Calais, France on the Simon & Mary.

Hudson, Peter - Cook - Number: 1937 - Prize name: Tickler of Nantes - Ship type: MV - How taken: HM Frigate Magiciene - When taken: 5 Jun 1813 - Where taken: Bay of Biscay - Date received: 11 Jul 1813 - From what ship: HMS Raisonnable - Born: New York - Age: 23 - Race: Black - Discharged on 12 Aug 1814 and sent to Dartmoor on HMS Alpheus.

Hudson, William - 2nd Lieutenant - Number: 1540 - How taken: Impressed at Greenock, Scotland - When taken: 2 Dec 1812 - Date received: 8 Apr 1813 - From what ship: Plymouth via HMS Olympia - Born: North Carolina - Age: 38 - Discharged on 27 Jul 1813 and released to Cartel Hoffminy.

Huff, Charles - Seaman - Number: 1350 - Prize name: Sword Fish - Ship type: P - How taken: HM Ship-of-the-Line Elephant - When taken: 12 Dec 1812 - Where taken: off Azores - Date received: 3 Apr 1813 - From what ship: Portsmouth, via an admiral's tender - Born: Kennebunk - Age: 20 - Discharged on 24 Jul 1813 and released to Cartel Hoffminy.

Huff, Michael - Corporal - Number: 3075 - Prize name: 14th U.S. Infantry - Ship type: LF - How taken: British forces - When taken: 24 Jun 1813 - Where taken: Beaver Dams, Upper Canada - Date received: 7 Jan 1814 - From what ship: Halifax - Born: Frankfort, Germany - Age: 39 - Discharged on 10 Oct 1814 and sent to U.S. on Cartel St. Philip.

Hughes, John - Seaman - Number: 3788 - Prize name: Adaline - Ship type: LM - How taken: HM Frigate Magiciene - When taken: 14 Mar 1814 - Where taken: off Cape Ortegal, Spain - Date received: 26 May 1814 - From what ship: HMS Hindostan - Born: Philadelphia - Age: 20 - Discharged on 22 Oct 1814 and sent to Dartmoor on HMS Leyden.

Hughes, John - Seaman - Number: 1775 - How taken: Impressed from Lady Castburgh - When taken: May 1813 - Date received: 14 Jun 1813 - From what ship: HMS Arethusa - Born: Baltimore - Age: 24 - Discharged on 24 Jul 1814 and sent to Dartmoor on HMS Liffey.

Hughes, Peter - Seaman - Number: 1535 - Prize name: U.S.R.M. Cutter James Madison - Ship type: War - How taken: HM Frigate Barbadoes - When taken: 22 Aug 1812 - Where taken: at sea - Date received: 8 Apr 1813 - From what ship: Portsmouth, via an admiral's tender - Born: Scotch Plain, NJ - Age: 18 - Discharged on 10 May 1813 and released to Cartel Admittance.

Hules, Cyrus - Seaman - Number: 2671 - Prize name: Hamlett - Ship type: MV - How taken: Impressed at London - When taken: 11 Nov 1813 - Date received: 21 Nov 1813 - From what ship: HMS Raisonnable - Born: Boston - Age: 22 - Discharged on 8 Sep 1814 and sent to Dartmoor on HMS Niobe.

Hull, Edward - Seaman - Number: 1901 - Prize name: Weasel - Ship type: MV - How taken: HM Brig Foxhound - When taken: 25 Mar 1813 - Where taken: Bay of Biscay - Date received: 7 Jul 1813 - From what ship: Portsmouth via HMS Tribune - Born: Newport - Age: 19 - Discharged on 4 Aug 1814 and sent to Dartmoor on HMS Liverpool.

Hull, Thomas - Seaman - Number: 2541 - Prize name: Thomas - Ship type: P - How taken: HM Frigate Nymphe - When taken: 28 Jun 1813 - Where taken: off Halifax - Date received: 22 Oct 1813 - From what ship: Portsmouth via HMT Malabar - Born: Portland - Age: 26 - Race: Mulatto - Discharged on 25 Sep 1814 and sent to Dartmoor on HMS Leyden.

Humphrey, Asa - Seaman - Number: 3462 - Prize name: Elbridge Gerry - Ship type: P - How taken: HM Frigate Crescent - When taken: 16 Sep 1813 - Where taken: at sea - Date received: 23 Feb 1814 - From what ship:

Halifax via HMT Malabar - Born: Gray - Age: 22 - Discharged on 22 Oct 1814 and sent to Dartmoor on HMS Leyden.

Hunderville, John - Private - Number: 3061 - Prize name: 14th U.S. Infantry - Ship type: LF - How taken: British forces - When taken: 24 Jun 1813 - Where taken: Beaver Dams, Upper Canada - Date received: 7 Jan 1814 - From what ship: Halifax - Born: Maryland - Age: 26 - Discharged on 10 Oct 1814 and sent to U.S. on Cartel St. Philip.

Hunn, John - Seaman - Number: 3876 - How taken: Gave himself up from HM Frigate Clorinde - When taken: 18 Dec 1813 - Date received: 28 Aug 1814 - From what ship: London - Born: Delaware - Age: 36 - Race: Black - Discharged on 8 Sep 1814 and sent to Dartmoor on HMS Niobe.

Hunt, David - Seaman - Number: 1977 - How taken: Gave himself up from HMS Bustard - Date received: 15 Jul 1813 - From what ship: Plymouth - Born: Brunswick - Age: 28 - Discharged on 17 Jun 1814 and sent to Dartmoor on HMS Pincher.

Hunt, Samuel - Seaman - Number: 3502 - Prize name: Volunteer - Ship type: MV - How taken: Vittoria, British privateer from Guernsey - When taken: 26 Sep 1813 - Where taken: Bay of Biscay - Date received: 23 Feb 1814 - From what ship: Portsmouth via HMT Malabar - Born: New York - Age: 29 - Discharged on 22 Oct 1814 and sent to Dartmoor on HMS Leyden.

Hunter, Isaac - Seaman - Number: 332 - Prize name: Mountaineer - Ship type: MV - How taken: Apprehended at London - When taken: 5 Jan 1813 - Date received: 11 Jan 1813 - From what ship: HMS Raisonnable - Born: North Carolina - Age: 40 - Race: Black man - Discharged on 24 Jul 1813 and released to Cartel Hoffminy.

Hunter, Isaac - Seaman - Number: 1920 - How taken: Given up from HM Ship-of-the-Line York - When taken: 1 Jun 1813 - Date received: 8 Jul 1813 - From what ship: Cumberland - Born: Winchester, VA - Age: 24 - Race: Black - Discharged on 4 Aug 1814 and sent to Dartmoor on HMS Liverpool.

Hunter, James - Private - Number: 2650 - Prize name: 6th U.S. Infantry - Ship type: LF - How taken: British forces - When taken: 24 Jun 1813 - Where taken: Beaver Dams, Upper Canada - Date received: 5 Nov 1813 - From what ship: HMS Hindostan - Born: Londonderry, Ireland - Age: 48 - Discharged on 10 Oct 1814 and sent to U.S. on Cartel St. Philip.

Hunter, James - Seaman - Number: 2510 - Prize name: Globe - Ship type: P - How taken: HM Prison Ship Victorious - When taken: 8 Jun 1813 - Where taken: Chesapeake Bay - Date received: 22 Oct 1813 - From what ship: Portsmouth via HMT Malabar - Born: Maryland - Age: 28 - Discharged on 8 Sep 1814 and sent to Dartmoor on HMS Niobe.

Hunter, James - Private - Number: 3141 - Prize name: 14th U.S. Infantry - Ship type: LF - How taken: British forces - When taken: 24 Jun 1813 - Where taken: Beaver Dams, Upper Canada - Date received: 7 Jan 1814 - From what ship: Halifax - Born: Maryland - Age: 27 - Discharged on 10 Oct 1814 and sent to U.S. on Cartel St. Philip.

Hunter, John - Captain - Number: 127 - Prize name: Eliza - Ship type: MV - How taken: Stopped at St. Michaels - When taken: Jan 1812 - Date received: 5 Nov 1812 - From what ship: HMS Namur - Born: North Carolina - Age: 32 - Discharged on 23 Mar 1813 and released to the Cartel Robinson Potter.

Hunter, John - Seaman - Number: 3211 - Prize name: Volunteer - Ship type: MV - How taken: Vittoria, British privateer from Guernsey - When taken: 26 Dec 1813 - Where taken: Bay of Biscay - Date received: 13 Jan 1814 - From what ship: Portsmouth via HMS Poictiers - Born: St. Bartholomew - Age: 28 - Discharged on 25 Sep 1814 and sent to Dartmoor on HMS Leyden.

Huntress, Robert - Boatswain - Number: 1435 - Prize name: Orbit - Ship type: MV - How taken: HM Brig Achates - When taken: 29 Jan 1813 - Where taken: Lat 49 N Long 13 W - Date received: 6 Apr 1813 - From what ship: Plymouth via HMS Decoy - Born: Portsmouth - Age: 37 - Discharged on 24 Jul 1814 and sent to Dartmoor.

Hurd, Abel - Seaman - Number: 2410 - How taken: Gave himself up from HM Hospital Ship Trent - Date received: 21 Oct 1813 - From what ship: Portsmouth via HMT Malabar - Born: Boston - Age: 35 - Discharged on 4 Sep 1814 and sent to Dartmoor on HMS Freya.

Hurd, John - Private - Number: 3135 - Prize name: 14th U.S. Infantry - Ship type: LF - How taken: British forces - When taken: 24 Jun 1813 - Where taken: Beaver Dams, Upper Canada - Date received: 7 Jan 1814 - From what ship: Halifax - Born: New York - Age: 29 - Discharged on 10 Oct 1814 and sent to U.S. on Cartel St. Philip.

Hurst, Dudley - Seaman - Number: 507 - Prize name: Josephine - Ship type: MV - How taken: HM Sloop Goree - When taken: 15 Aug 1812 - Where taken: off Bermuda - Date received: 23 Feb 1813 - From what ship: Portsmouth via HMS Dromedary - Born: Providence - Age: 25 - Discharged on 10 May 1813 and released to Cartel Admittance.

Hurstley, Charles - Seaman - Number: 2047 - How taken: Gave himself up from HM Brig Philomel - When taken: 28 Dec 1812 - Date received: 4 Aug 1813 - From what ship: HMS Christian VII - Born: Harford - Age: 26 - Discharged on 25 Jul 1814 and sent to Dartmoor on HMS Bittern.

Hurt, Samuel - Seaman - Number: 1237 - Prize name: Rossie - Ship type: MV - How taken: HM Frigate Dryand - When taken: 7 Jan 1813 - Where taken: at sea - Date received: 16 Mar 1813 - From what ship: Portsmouth, via HMS Abundance - Born: Kent County - Age: 24 - Discharged on 24 Jul 1813 and released to Cartel Hoffminy.

Huse, Ebenezer - Seaman - Number: 2308 - Prize name: Kitty, prize of the U.S. Frigate President - Ship type: War - How taken: Dart, British privateer from Guernsey - When taken: 20 Jun 1813 - Where taken: off the Western Isles, Scotland - Date received: 8 Oct 1813 - From what ship: Portsmouth, via an admiral's tender - Born: Massachusetts - Age: 24 - Discharged on 8 Sep 1814 and sent to Dartmoor on HMS Niobe.

Hussey, Ebenezer - Seaman - Number: 2845 - Prize name: Blockade - Ship type: P - How taken: HM Brig Recruit - When taken: 17 Aug 1813 - Where taken: coast of America - Date received: 7 Jan 1814 - From what ship: Halifax - Born: Nantucket - Age: 28 - Escaped on 16 May 1814 from HM Prison Ship Crown Prince.

Hussey, Thomas - Seaman - Number: 1916 - Prize name: Regulator - Ship type: MV - How taken: Impressed at London - When taken: 5 Jul 1813 - Date received: 7 Jul 1813 - From what ship: HMS Raisonnable - Born: New York - Age: 34 - Discharged on 4 Aug 1814 and sent to Dartmoor on HMS Liverpool.

Hussy, Edward - Cooper - Number: 2317 - Prize name: Fame - Ship type: MV - How taken: HM Ship of-the-Line Cressy - When taken: 20 Jul 1813 - Where taken: at sea - Date received: 8 Oct 1813 - From what ship: Portsmouth, via an admiral's tender - Born: Nantucket - Age: 19 - Escaped on 16 May 1814 from HM Prison Ship Crown Prince.

Huston, James - Seaman - Number: 2262 - Prize name: Eliza - Ship type: MV - How taken: HMS Charles - When taken: 20 Jul 1813 - Where taken: off Petershead, Scotland - Date received: 14 Sep 1813 - From what ship: HMS Raisonnable - Born: New York - Age: 29 - Discharged on 20 Aug 1814 and sent to Dartmoor on HMS Shamrock.

Hutchins, Josiah - Boy - Number: 1123 - Prize name: Ganges - Ship type: MV - How taken: Detained at Portsmouth harbor - When taken: 31 Jul 1812 - Date received: 14 Mar 1813 - From what ship: Portsmouth via HMS Beagle - Born: Wiscasset - Age: 14 - Discharged on 8 Jun 1813 and released to Cartel Rodrigo.

Hutchins, William - Seaman - Number: 651 - Prize name: U.S.R.M. Cutter James Madison - Ship type: War - How taken: HM Frigate Barbadoes - When taken: 22 Aug 1812 - Where taken: at sea - Date received: 24 Feb 1813 - From what ship: Portsmouth via HMS Ulysses - Born: Rocketts, VA - Age: 29 - Discharged on 10 May 1813 and released to Cartel Admittance.

Hutchinson, James - Seaman - Number: 780 - Prize name: Eliza - Ship type: MV - How taken: HM Sloop Hyacinth - When taken: 27 Aug 1812 - Where taken: off Gibraltar - Date received: 27 Feb 1813 - From what ship: Plymouth via HMS Namur - Born: Charlestown - Age: 18 - Race: Black - Discharged on 10 May 1813 and released to Cartel Admittance.

Hutchinson, Thomas - Cook - Number: 242 - How taken: Gave himself up from HM Ship-of-the-Line Mulgrave - When taken: 28 Nov 1812 - Date received: 1 Dec 1812 - From what ship: HMS Raisonnable - Born: Little Britain, PA - Age: 28 - Died on 23 Nov 1813 from liver disease.

Hutchinson, Townsend - Seaman - Number: 1375 - How taken: Gave himself up from HM Ship of-the-Line Bellerophon - When taken: 18 Mar 1813 - Date received: 3 Apr 1813 - From what ship: Portsmouth, via an admiral's tender - Born: Long Island - Age: 52 - Discharged on 24 Jul 1814 and sent to Dartmoor.

Hutson, John - Seaman - Number: 2120 - How taken: Gave himself up from HM Ship-of-the-Line Union - When taken: 27 May 1813 - Date received: 9 Aug 1813 - From what ship: HMS Thames - Born: Copenhagen - Age: 28 - Discharged on 12 Aug 1814 and sent to Dartmoor on HMS Alpheus.

Hyatt, William - Seaman - Number: 627 - Prize name: King of Rome - Ship type: P - How taken: HM Brig Wolverine - When taken: 13 Dec 1812 - Where taken: at sea - Date received: 23 Feb 1813 - From what ship: Portsmouth via HMS Dromedary - Born: New York - Age: 28 - Discharged on 2 Jul 1813 and released to Cartel Moses Brown.

Idiarty, Francois - Seaman - Number: 2229 - Prize name: Porcupine - Ship type: LM - How taken: HM Frigate Acasta - When taken: 29 Jun 1813 - Where taken: off Cape Sable, Florida - Date received: 22 Aug 1813 - From what ship: HMS Raisonnable - Born: France - Age: 23 - Discharged on 22 Jun 1814 and sent to Calais, France on the Simon & Mary.

Inberg, Gabriel - Seaman - Number: 625 - Prize name: King of Rome - Ship type: P - How taken: HM Brig Wolverine - When taken: 13 Dec 1812 - Where taken: at sea - Date received: 23 Feb 1813 - From what ship: Portsmouth via HMS Dromedary - Born: Finland - Age: 27 - Released on 21 May 1813.

Ingalls, Samuel - Carpenter - Number: 1019 - Prize name: Sword Fish - Ship type: P - How taken: HM Ship-of-the-Line Elephant - When taken: 28 Dec 1812 - Where taken: off Azores - Date received: 10 Mar 1813 - From what ship: HMS Furious - Born: Marblehead - Age: 25 - Discharged on 24 Jul 1813 and released to Cartel Hoffminy.

Ingalls, Edward - Seaman - Number: 455 - Prize name: Hunter - Ship type: P - How taken: HM Frigate Phoebe - When taken: 23 Dec 1812 - Where taken: off Azores - Date received: 19 Feb 1813 - From what ship: HMS Modeste - Born: Lynn - Age: 21 - Discharged on 24 Jul 1813 and released to Cartel Hoffminy.

Ingersen, James B. - Seaman - Number: 2022 - How taken: Impressed at London - When taken: 9 Jul 1813 - Date received: 16 Jul 1813 - From what ship: HMS Raisonnable - Born: Portland, MA - Age: 19 - Discharged on 4 Aug 1814 and sent to Dartmoor on HMS Liverpool.

Ingersoll, John - Mate - Number: 3799 - Prize name: Alligator - Ship type: MV - How taken: HM Ship-of-the-Line San Domingo - When taken: 16 May 1813 - Where taken: off Bengal - Date received: 5 Jun 1814 - From what ship: HMS Raisonnable - Born: Richmond - Age: 19 - Discharged on 29 Sep 1814 and sent to Dartmoor on HMS Freya.

Ingersoll, Abraham - Seaman - Number: 1817 - Prize name: tender to the Privateer True Blooded Yankee - Ship type: P - How taken: HM Ship-of-the-Line Fame - When taken: 24 Jun 1813 - Where taken: off Brest, France - Date received: 7 Jul 1813 - From what ship: Portsmouth via HMS Scorpion - Born: Boston - Age: 33 - Discharged on 25 Jul 1814 and sent to Dartmoor on HMS Bittern.

Inglas, John - Seaman - Number: 2801 - Prize name: Industry - Ship type: P - How taken: HM Brig Heron - When taken: 3 Nov 1813 - Where taken: off Halifax - Date received: 7 Jan 1814 - From what ship: Halifax - Born: Marblehead - Age: 25 - Discharged on 8 Sep 1814 and sent to Dartmoor on HMS Niobe.

Ingraham, Peter - Seaman - Number: 1210 - Prize name: Expectation - Ship type: MV - How taken: HM Frigate Briton - When taken: 17 Dec 1812 - Where taken: at sea - Date received: 16 Mar 1813 - From what ship: Portsmouth, via HMS Abundance - Born: Lancaster - Age: 33 - Discharged on 2 Jul 1813 and released to Cartel Moses Brown.

Ingrane, John - Seaman - Number: 1716 - Prize name: Recaptured British MV - Ship type: P - How taken: HM Frigate Revolutionnaire - When taken: 10 Apr 1813 - Where taken: off the Western Isles, Scotland - Date received: 25 May 1813 - From what ship: Portsmouth via HMS Impetius - Born: New York - Age: 20 - Discharged on 24 Jul 1814 and sent to Dartmoor on HMS Liffey.

Innis, John - Boy - Number: 1168 - Prize name: Sword Fish - Ship type: P - How taken: HM Ship-of-the-Line Elephant - When taken: 28 Dec 1812 - Where taken: off Azores - Date received: 16 Mar 1813 - From what ship: Portsmouth, via HMS Abundance - Born: Boston - Age: 12 - Discharged on 24 Jul 1813 and released to Cartel Hoffminy.

Ireland, John - Private - Number: 3137 - Prize name: 6th U.S. Infantry - Ship type: LF - How taken: British forces - When taken: 24 Jun 1813 - Where taken: Beaver Dams, Upper Canada - Date received: 7 Jan 1814 - From what ship: Halifax - Born: Delaware - Age: 29 - Died on 7 May 1814 from fever.

Ireson, Robert B. - Seaman - Number: 889 - Prize name: Print of Boston - Ship type: MV - How taken: HM Ship-of-the-Line Colossus - When taken: 21 Jan 1813 - Where taken: at sea - Date received: 1 Mar 1813 - From what ship: Plymouth via HMS Namur - Born: Marblehead, MA - Age: 15 - Discharged on 17 Jun 1814 and sent to Dartmoor on HMS Redbreast.

Iriarty, Ignacio - Seaman - Number: 2228 - Prize name: Porcupine - Ship type: LM - How taken: HM Frigate Acasta - When taken: 29 Jun 1813 - Where taken: off Cape Sable, Florida - Date received: 22 Aug 1813 - From what ship: HMS Raisonnable - Born: San Sebastian, Spain - Age: 25 - Discharged on 22 Jun 1814 and sent to Calais, France on the Simon & Mary.

Irvin, John - Seaman - Number: 376 - Prize name: Union American - Ship type: MV - How taken: Impressed at London - When taken: 19 Jan 1813 - Date received: 31 Jan 1813 - From what ship: HMS Raisonnable - Born: New York - Age: 25 - Discharged on 24 Jul 1813 and released to Cartel Hoffminy.

Irwin, Andrew - Seaman - Number: 1609 - How taken: Gave himself up from HM Frigate President at Chatham - When taken: 27 Apr 1813 - Date received: 1 May 1813 - From what ship: HMS President - Born: Jenkintown, PA - Age: 29 - Discharged on 24 Jul 1814 and sent to Dartmoor.

Irwin, Magnus - Boy - Number: 1498 - Prize name: Union - Ship type: MV - How taken: HM Frigate Iris - When taken: 17 Jan 1813 - Where taken: at sea - Date received: 6 Apr 1813 - From what ship: Plymouth via an admiral's tender - Born: Philadelphia - Age: 16 - Discharged on 27 Jul 1813 and released to Cartel Hoffminy.

Istill, James - Seaman - Number: 1717 - Prize name: Recaptured British MV - Ship type: P - How taken: HM Frigate Revolutionnaire - When taken: 10 Apr 1813 - Where taken: off the Western Isles, Scotland - Date received: 25 May 1813 - From what ship: Portsmouth via HMS Impetius - Born: Philadelphia - Age: 26 - Discharged on 24 Jul 1814 and sent to Dartmoor on HMS Liffey.

Jackson, Allison - Seaman - Number: 1666 - How taken: Gave himself up from HM Frigate Hotspur - Date received: 9 May 1813 - From what ship: HMS Raisonnable - Born: Virginia - Age: 26 - Race: Mulatto - Discharged on 11 Aug 1814 and sent to Dartmoor on HMS Shamrock.

Jackson, C. L. - Mate - Number: 320 - Prize name: Amphion - Ship type: MV - How taken: Thracian - When taken: 16 Dec 1812 - Where taken: off Norway - Date received: 5 Jan 1813 - From what ship: HMS Sheldrake - Born: Plymouth, MA - Age: 27 - Discharged in Jul 1813 and released to Cartel Moses Brown.

Jackson, Charles - Seaman - Number: 3615 - Prize name: Liberty - Ship type: MV - How taken: Surrendered at Stromness, Scotland - When taken: 30 Dec 1813 - Date received: 29 Mar 1814 - From what ship: Hired tender Anna - Born: Troy - Age: 17 - Discharged on 25 Sep 1814 and sent to Dartmoor on HMS Leyden.

Jackson, Daniel - Seaman - Number: 1984 - How taken: Gave himself up from HM Ship-of-the-Line Ajax - Date received: 15 Jul 1813 - From what ship: Plymouth - Born: Connecticut - Age: 37 - Discharged on 17 Jun 1814 and sent to Dartmoor on HMS Pincher.

Jackson, Frederick - Seaman - Number: 3521 - Prize name: Pilot - Ship type: LM - How taken: Vittoria, British privateer from Guernsey - When taken: 28 Jan 1814 - Where taken: off Bordeaux, France - Date received: 23 Feb 1814 - From what ship: Portsmouth via HMT Malabar - Born: Maryland - Age: 22 - Race: Black - Discharged on 26 Sep 1814 and sent to Dartmoor on HMS Leyden.

Jackson, George - Seaman - Number: 883 - Prize name: Madisonia - Ship type: MV - How taken: HM Frigate Garland - When taken: 28 Jul 1812 - Where taken: off Martinique - Date received: 1 Mar 1813 - From what ship: Plymouth via HMS Namur - Born: New Orleans - Age: 22 - Discharged on 23 Mar 1813 and released to the Cartel Robinson Potter.

Jackson, Henry - Seaman - Number: 3622 - Prize name: Liberty - Ship type: MV - How taken: Surrendered at Stromness, Scotland - When taken: 30 Dec 1813 - Date received: 29 Mar 1814 - From what ship: Hired tender Anna - Born: New York - Age: 46 - Race: Black - Discharged on 25 Sep 1814 and sent to Dartmoor on HMS Niobe.

Jackson, Isaac - Seaman - Number: 2304 - How taken: Gave himself up from HM Brig Cadmus - When taken: 13 Aug 1813 - Date received: 29 Sep 1813 - From what ship: HMS Raisonnable - Born: New Castle - Age: 25 - Discharged on 4 Sep 1814 and sent to Dartmoor on HMS Freya.

Jackson, J. K. - Seaman - Number: 1700 - Prize name: Governor Middleton - Ship type: MV - How taken: Thetis,

British privateer - When taken: 2 May 1813 - Where taken: Bay of Biscay - Date received: 15 May 1813 - From what ship: HMS Viper - Born: Kent, MD - Age: 30 - Race: Blackman - Discharged on 2 Nov 1813 and released to HMS Ceres.

Jackson, James - Seaman - Number: 3436 - Prize name: Enterprise - Ship type: P - How taken: HM Frigate Tenedos - When taken: 21 May 1813 - Where taken: off Cape Cod - Date received: 23 Feb 1814 - From what ship: Halifax via HMT Malabar - Born: Portsmouth - Age: 17 - Discharged on 22 Oct 1814 and sent to Dartmoor on HMS Leyden.

Jackson, John - Seaman - Number: 726 - Prize name: Eos - Ship type: MV - How taken: Detained at Portsmouth harbor - When taken: 31 Jul 1812 - Date received: 24 Feb 1813 - From what ship: Portsmouth via HMS Ulysses - Born: New York - Age: 29 - Race: Man of color - Discharged on 23 Mar 1813 and released to the Cartel Robinson Potter.

Jackson, John - Seaman - Number: 126 - Prize name: Brutus - Ship type: MV - How taken: Stopped at London - When taken: 26 Oct 1812 - Date received: 5 Nov 1812 - From what ship: HMS Namur - Born: Norfolk, VA - Age: 29 - Discharged in Jul 1813 and released to Cartel Moses Brown.

Jackson, John - Seaman - Number: 871 - Prize name: Columbia - Ship type: MV - How taken: HM Frigate Briton - When taken: 17 Jan 1813 - Where taken: off Bordeaux, France - Date received: 1 Mar 1813 - From what ship: Plymouth via HMS Namur - Born: New York - Age: 27 - Race: Blackman - Discharged in Jul 1813 and released to Cartel Moses Brown.

Jackson, John - Seaman - Number: 2446 - Prize name: Wiley Reynard - Ship type: P - How taken: HM Frigate Shannon - When taken: 16 Aug 1812 - Where taken: off Halifax - Date received: 21 Oct 1813 - From what ship: Portsmouth via HMT Malabar - Born: New York - Age: 52 - Race: Black - Discharged on 4 Sep 1814 and sent to Dartmoor on HMS Freya.

Jackson, John - Seaman - Number: 1794 - How taken: Gave himself up from HM Sloop-Brig Rosario - When taken: 4 Jun 1813 - Date received: 1 Jul 1813 - From what ship: HMS Raisonnable - Born: Long Island - Age: 27 - Race: Mulatto - Discharged on 16 Sep 1813 and released to HMS Ceres.

Jackson, Samuel - Carpenter - Number: 2821 - Prize name: Portsmouth Packet - Ship type: P - How taken: HM Brig Fantome - When taken: 5 Oct 1813 - Where taken: off Portland - Date received: 7 Jan 1814 - From what ship: Halifax - Born: Portsmouth - Age: 52 - Died on 19 May 1814 from fever.

Jackson, Sidney - Seaman - Number: 2075 - How taken: Gave himself up from HM Ship-of-the-Line Armada - When taken: 8 Jun 1813 - Date received: 9 Aug 1813 - From what ship: HMS Thames - Born: Virginia - Age: 23 - Race: Black - Discharged on 4 Aug 1814 and sent to Dartmoor on HMS Liverpool.

Jackson, Thomas - Boy - Number: 1455 - Prize name: Orbit - Ship type: MV - How taken: HM Brig Achates - When taken: 29 Jan 1813 - Where taken: Lat 49 N Long 13 W - Date received: 6 Apr 1813 - From what ship: Plymouth via HMS Decoy - Born: Jersey - Age: 14 - Race: Negro - Discharged on 19 Oct 1813 and released to HMS Ceres.

Jackson, Thomas - Seaman - Number: 1571 - How taken: Impressed at Greenock, Scotland - When taken: 27 Nov 1812 - Date received: 8 Apr 1813 - From what ship: Plymouth via HMS Olympia - Born: New Jersey - Age: 27 - Race: Negro - Discharged on 27 Jul 1813 and released to Cartel Hoffminy.

Jackson, Thomas - Seaman - Number: 2044 - Prize name: Marquis of Huntley, East Indianman - Ship type: MV - How taken: Sent to prison - When taken: 27 Jul 1812 - Where taken: Nore, England - Date received: 4 Aug 1813 - From what ship: HMS Christian VII - Born: New York - Age: 22 - Race: Blackman - Discharged on 28 Oct 1813 and released to HMS Ceres.

Jackson, William - Seaman - Number: 1653 - How taken: Gave himself up from HM Ship-of-the-Line Sterling Castle - Date received: 9 May 1813 - From what ship: HMS Raisonnable - Born: New Town, Long Island - Age: 38 - Race: Black - Discharged on 13 Aug 1814 and sent to Dartmoor.

Jackson, William - Seaman - Number: 2333 - How taken: Gave himself up from HM Sloop-of-War Fawn - When taken: 8 Oct 1813 - Date received: 12 Oct 1813 - From what ship: HMS Raisonnable - Born: Salem - Age: 17 - Discharged on 11 Aug 1814 and sent to Dartmoor on HMS Freya.

Jackson, William - Seaman - Number: 2879 - Prize name: Baroness Longueville, British South Sea Whaler - Ship type: MV - How taken: HM Ship-of-the-Line Illustrious - When taken: 5 Aug 1813 - Where taken: off St. Helena - Date received: 7 Jan 1814 - From what ship: Portsmouth - Born: Long Island - Age: 28 - Race: Black - Discharged on 25 Sep 1814 and sent to Dartmoor on HMS Leyden.

Jackson, William - Seaman - Number: 2135 - How taken: Gave himself up from HM Schooner Charlotte - When taken: 28 May 1813 - Date received: 9 Aug 1813 - From what ship: HMS Thames - Born: Charlestown - Age: 53 - Race: Black - Discharged on 4 Aug 1814 and sent to Dartmoor on HMS Alpheus.

Jacob, Lewis - Seaman - Number: 3268 - Prize name: Volante - Ship type: P - How taken: HM Brig Curlew - When taken: 25 Mar 1813 - Where taken: off Boston - Date received: 23 Feb 1814 - From what ship: Halifax via HMT Malabar - Born: New Orleans - Age: 30 - Race: Black - Discharged on 10 Oct 1814 and sent to Dartmoor on the Mermaid.

Jacobs, George - Cook - Number: 157 - How taken: Stopped at London - When taken: 28 Oct 1812 - Date received: 5 Nov 1812 - From what ship: HMS Namur - Born: New York - Age: 29 - Discharged on 4 Mar 1813 to the Wailey.

Jacobs, John - Private - Number: 3149 - Prize name: 14th U.S. Infantry - Ship type: LF - How taken: British forces - When taken: 24 Jun 1813 - Where taken: Beaver Dams, Upper Canada - Date received: 7 Jan 1814 - From what ship: Halifax - Born: Washington - Age: 31 - Discharged on 10 Oct 1814 and sent to U.S. on Cartel St. Philip.

Jacobs, William - Seaman - Number: 3285 - Prize name: Vivid - Ship type: P - How taken: HM Frigate Nymphe - When taken: 20 Apr 1813 - Where taken: off Cape Cod - Date received: 23 Feb 1814 - From what ship: Halifax via HMT Malabar - Born: Norway - Age: 25 - Discharged on 22 Oct 1814 and sent to Dartmoor on HMS Leyden.

Jacobson, Jacob - Seaman - Number: 941 - Prize name: Three Brothers - Ship type: MV - How taken: HM Brig Bermuda - When taken: 9 Dec 1812 - Where taken: off St. Valery - Date received: 10 Mar 1813 - From what ship: HMS Tigress - Born: Achim, Prussia - Age: 28 - Discharged on 2 Jul 1813 and released to Cartel Moses Brown.

Jacobson, William - Seaman - Number: 313 - Prize name: Joseph Ricketsen - Ship type: MV - How taken: HM Brig Rifleman - When taken: 22 Aug 1812 - Where taken: off Scotland - Date received: 23 Dec 1812 - From what ship: Greenlaw Depot - Born: Oldenburg - Age: 39 - Discharged on 26 Jul 1814 and sent to Dartmoor on HMS Raven.

James, George - Seaman - Number: 3267 - Prize name: Volante - Ship type: P - How taken: HM Brig Curlew - When taken: 25 Mar 1813 - Where taken: off Boston - Date received: 23 Feb 1814 - From what ship: Halifax via HMT Malabar - Born: Rhode Island - Age: 35 - Discharged on 10 Oct 1814 and sent to Dartmoor on the Mermaid.

James, Isaac - Seaman - Number: 236 - How taken: Impressed at London - When taken: 12 Nov 1812 - Date received: 25 Nov 1812 - From what ship: HMS Raisonnable - Born: Nantucket - Age: 30 - Discharged in Jul 1813 and released to Cartel Moses Brown.

James, John - Seaman - Number: 3486 - How taken: Gave himself up from HMS Muros - When taken: 27 Jan 1813 - Date received: 23 Feb 1814 - From what ship: Portsmouth via HMT Malabar - Born: Philadelphia - Age: 26 - Race: Black - Discharged on 26 Sep 1814 and sent to Dartmoor on HMS Leyden.

James, John - Seaman - Number: 1565 - Prize name: Dolphin - Ship type: LM - How taken: HM Ship-of-the-Line Colossus - When taken: 5 Jan 1813 - Where taken: off the Western Isles, Scotland - Date received: 8 Apr 1813 - From what ship: Plymouth via HMS Olympia - Born: New Orleans - Age: 30 - Discharged on 27 Jul 1813 and released to Cartel Hoffminy.

James, John - Seaman - Number: 645 - Prize name: U.S.R.M. Cutter James Madison - Ship type: War - How taken: HM Frigate Barbadoes - When taken: 22 Aug 1812 - Where taken: at sea - Date received: 24 Feb 1813 - From what ship: Portsmouth via HMS Ulysses - Born: Hackettstown, NJ - Age: 26 - Discharged on 10 May 1813 and released to Cartel Admittance.

James, John - Seaman - Number: 3035 - How taken: Gave himself up from HM Brig Port Mahon - When taken: Jul 1813 - Date received: 7 Jan 1814 - From what ship: Portsmouth - Born: Chester - Age: 30 - Escaped on 16

May 1814 from HM Prison Ship Crown Prince.

James, John - Seaman - Number: 2553 - How taken: Gave himself up from HM Ship-of-the-Line Prince of Wales - When taken: 21 May 1813 - Date received: 23 Oct 1813 - From what ship: Portsmouth via HMS Raisonnable - Born: South Carolina - Age: 26 - Race: Black - Discharged on 8 Sep 1814 and sent to Dartmoor on HMS Niobe.

James, Sacket - Seaman - Number: 1982 - How taken: Gave himself up from HM Ship-of-the-Line Dublin - Date received: 15 Jul 1813 - From what ship: Plymouth - Born: Virginia - Age: 50 - Discharged on 4 Aug 1814 and sent to Dartmoor on HMS Liverpool.

Jameson, George - Seaman - Number: 975 - Prize name: Empress - Ship type: MV - How taken: HM Brig Rover - When taken: 30 Nov 1812 - Where taken: St. Andrew - Date received: 10 Mar 1813 - From what ship: HMS Tigress - Born: Charlestown - Age: 40 - Discharged on 8 Jun 1813 and released to Cartel Rodrigo.

Jameson, George - Seaman - Number: 2355 - How taken: Gave himself up from HM Ship-of-the-Line Hibernia - When taken: 25 Jun 1813 - Date received: 20 Oct 1813 - From what ship: Portsmouth, via an admiral's tender - Born: Philadelphia - Age: 53 - Race: Black - Discharged on 4 Sep 1814 and sent to Dartmoor on HMS Freya.

Jane, Joseph - Seaman - Number: 1043 - Prize name: Warren - Ship type: MV - How taken: HM Frigate Sybille & HMS Fortunee - When taken: 3 Sep 1812 - Where taken: Lat 41.4 Long 33 - Date received: 11 Mar 1813 - From what ship: Yarmouth via HMS Tenders - Born: Providence - Age: 20 - Discharged on 8 Jun 1813 and released to Cartel Rodrigo.

Jardine, Samuel - Seaman - Number: 3682 - How taken: Gave himself up from HM Transport Ceylon - Date received: 4 May 1814 - From what ship: Portsmouth - Born: Massachusetts - Age: 23 - Discharged on 20 Aug 1814 and sent to Dartmoor on HMS Shamrock.

Jarratt, Abraham - Seaman - Number: 1706 - Prize name: Darby - Ship type: MV - How taken: HM Frigate Narcissus - When taken: 4 Feb 1813 - Where taken: off St. Helena - Date received: 22 May 1813 - From what ship: HMS Raisonnable - Born: Domico, MA - Age: 22 - Discharged on 24 Jul 1814 and sent to Dartmoor on HMS Liffey.

Jarvis, George - Seaman - Number: 3822 - How taken: Gave himself up from HM Frigate Andromache - When taken: 20 Jul 1814 - Date received: 23 Jun 1814 - From what ship: Quebec - Born: Albany - Age: 40 - Race: Black - Discharged on 20 Aug 1814 and sent to Dartmoor on HMS Shamrock.

Jarvis, Thomas - Seaman - Number: 3429 - Prize name: Industry - Ship type: P - How taken: HM Frigate Maidstone - When taken: 18 Jul 1813 - Where taken: Grand Banks - Date received: 23 Feb 1814 - From what ship: Halifax via HMT Malabar - Born: Boston - Age: 19 - Race: Black - Discharged on 22 Oct 1814 and sent to Dartmoor on HMS Leyden.

Jasmine, Paul - Seaman - Number: 2147 - Prize name: Matilda, prize of the U.S. Brig Argus - Ship type: War - How taken: HM Frigate Revolutionnaire - When taken: 25 Jul 1813 - Where taken: off Lorient, France - Date received: 9 Aug 1813 - From what ship: HMS Thames - Born: Boston - Age: 18 - Race: Black - Discharged on 12 Aug 1814 and sent to Dartmoor on HMS Alpheus.

Jefferies, David - Seaman - Number: 233 - Prize name: Moses Brown - Ship type: MV - How taken: Impressed on London docks - When taken: 13 Nov 1812 - Date received: 25 Nov 1812 - From what ship: HMS Raisonnable - Born: Philadelphia - Age: 21 - Discharged in Jul 1813 and released to Cartel Moses Brown.

Jeffreys, Henry - Seaman - Number: 2863 - Prize name: Fire Fly - Ship type: LM - How taken: HM Frigate Revolutionnaire - When taken: 19 Oct 1813 - Where taken: off Cape Ortegal, Spain - Date received: 7 Jan 1814 - From what ship: Portsmouth - Born: Delaware - Age: 23 - Discharged on 25 Sep 1814 and sent to Dartmoor on HMS Leyden.

Jeffreys, Henry - Seaman - Number: 1593 - Prize name: Dick - Ship type: MV - How taken: HM Brig Dispatch - When taken: 15 Mar 1813 - Where taken: off Bordeaux, France - Date received: 18 Apr 1813 - From what ship: HMS Rosario - Born: Elizabethtown - Age: 23 - Discharged on 13 Apr 1814 and sent to Dartmoor.

Jeffreys, Philip - Seaman - Number: 503 - How taken: Gave himself up from HM Ship-of-the-Line Ruby - When taken: 15 Aug 1812 - Date received: 23 Feb 1813 - From what ship: Portsmouth via HMS Dromedary - Born:

Camptown, MA - Age: 32 - Discharged on 19 May 1813 and released to HMS Ceres.

Jenkins, Peter - Seaman - Number: 783 - Prize name: Dolphin - Ship type: MV - How taken: HM Ship-of-the-Line Colossus - When taken: 5 Jan 1813 - Where taken: off the Western Isles, Scotland - Date received: 27 Feb 1813 - From what ship: Plymouth via HMS Namur - Born: Philadelphia - Age: 27 - Discharged on 24 Jul 1813 and released to Cartel Hoffminy.

Jenkins, Richard - Seaman - Number: 439 - Prize name: Hunter - Ship type: P - How taken: HM Frigate Phoebe - When taken: 23 Dec 1812 - Where taken: off Azores - Date received: 19 Feb 1813 - From what ship: HMS Modeste - Born: Boston - Age: 26 - Discharged on 2 Jul 1813 and released to Cartel Moses Brown.

Jennings, John - Seaman - Number: 905 - How taken: Gave himself up from HM Ship-of-the-Line San Juan - When taken: 9 Aug 1812 - Date received: 1 Mar 1813 - From what ship: Plymouth via HMS Namur - Born: Annapolis - Age: 39 - Discharged on 25 Sep 1814 and sent to Dartmoor on HMS Leyden.

Jennings, Luther - Seaman - Number: 2223 - Prize name: Thomas - Ship type: MV - How taken: HM Brig Frolic - When taken: 29 Jun 1813 - Where taken: off St. Thomas, WI - Date received: 22 Aug 1813 - From what ship: HMS Raisonnable - Born: Massachusetts - Age: 24 - Discharged on 11 Aug 1814 and sent to Dartmoor on HMS Freya.

Jennings, Samuel - Seaman - Number: 1433 - Prize name: Louisa, prize of the Privateer Decatur - Ship type: P - How taken: HM Frigate Andromache - When taken: 11 Jan 1813 - Where taken: off Bordeaux, France - Date received: 6 Apr 1813 - From what ship: Plymouth via HMS Decoy - Born: Baltimore - Age: 40 - Race: Negro - Discharged on 24 Jul 1813 and released to Cartel Hoffminy.

Jenny, John - Private - Number: 3107 - Prize name: 14th U.S. Infantry - Ship type: LF - How taken: British forces - When taken: 24 Jun 1813 - Where taken: Beaver Dams, Upper Canada - Date received: 7 Jan 1814 - From what ship: Halifax - Born: Maryland - Age: 21 - Discharged on 10 Oct 1814 and sent to U.S. on Cartel St. Philip.

Jeremy, Stephen - Seaman - Number: 1152 - Prize name: Sword Fish - Ship type: P - How taken: HM Ship-of-the-Line Elephant - When taken: 28 Dec 1812 - Where taken: off Azores - Date received: 16 Mar 1813 - From what ship: Portsmouth, Mundane - Born: Baltimore - Age: 27 - Race: Mulatto - Discharged on 24 Jul 1813 and released to Cartel Hoffminy.

Jerry, Daniel - Seaman - Number: 987 - Prize name: Otter - Ship type: MV - How taken: HM Ship-Sloop Jalouse - When taken: 1 Dec 1812 - Where taken: off Cape St. Vincent, Portugal - Date received: 10 Mar 1813 - From what ship: HMS Tigress - Born: Connecticut - Age: 20 - Released on 20 Mar 1813 to HMS Otter.

Jessamine, John - Seaman - Number: 2519 - Prize name: Yorktown - Ship type: P - How taken: HM Brig Nimrod - When taken: 17 Jul 1813 - Where taken: Grand Banks - Date received: 22 Oct 1813 - From what ship: Portsmouth via HMT Malabar - Born: Bremen - Age: 22 - Discharged on 8 Sep 1814 and sent to Dartmoor on HMS Niobe.

Jeurnuseu, John - Seaman - Number: 2055 - How taken: Gave himself up from HM Ship-of-the-Line Fame - When taken: 4 May 1813 - Date received: 4 Aug 1813 - From what ship: HMS Christian VII - Born: Delaware - Age: 28 - Race: Blackman - Discharged on 4 Aug 1814 and sent to Dartmoor on HMS Liverpool.

Jewell, Samuel - Seaman - Number: 929 - Prize name: Experiment - Ship type: MV - How taken: HM Brig Rover - When taken: 10 Nov 1812 - Where taken: off Bordeaux, France - Date received: 10 Mar 1813 - From what ship: HMS Tigress - Born: Maryland - Age: 20 - Discharged on 8 Jun 1813 and released to Cartel Rodrigo.

Jewett, Jasper - Seaman - Number: 3904 - How taken: Gave himself up from the MV John - When taken: 28 Aug 1814 - Date received: 31 Aug 1814 - From what ship: Transport Office - Born: New Hampshire - Age: 23 - Discharged on 25 Sep 1814 and sent to Dartmoor on HMS Leyden.

Jilson, Samuel - Seaman - Number: 2110 - How taken: Gave himself up from HM Frigate Undaunted - When taken: 28 May 1813 - Date received: 9 Aug 1813 - From what ship: HMS Thames - Born: Rhode Island - Age: 39 - Discharged on 12 Aug 1814 and sent to Dartmoor on HMS Alpheus.

John, Richard J. - Seaman - Number: 1209 - Prize name: Expectation - Ship type: MV - How taken: HM Frigate Briton - When taken: 17 Dec 1812 - Where taken: at sea - Date received: 16 Mar 1813 - From what ship: Portsmouth, via HMS Abundance - Born: Norfolk - Age: 20 - Discharged on 2 Jul 1813 and released to

Cartel Moses Brown.

Johns, Bellona - Seaman - Number: 859 - Prize name: Brutus - Ship type: MV - How taken: Briton, letter of marque - When taken: 13 Jan 1813 - Where taken: Bay of Biscay - Date received: 1 Mar 1813 - From what ship: Plymouth via HMS Namur - Born: New Orleans - Age: 24 - Discharged on 24 Jul 1813 and released to Cartel Hoffminy.

Johnson, Alexander - Seaman - Number: 748 - Prize name: Quebec of London, prize of the Privateer Paul Jones - Ship type: P - How taken: HM Brig Derwent - When taken: 29 Jan 1813 - Where taken: off Lisbon - Date received: 25 Feb 1813 - From what ship: HMS Brazen - Born: New York - Age: 23 - Discharged on 25 Sep 1814 and sent to Dartmoor on HMS Freya.

Johnson, Andre - Seaman - Number: 542 - Prize name: Baltimore - Ship type: P - How taken: HM Transport Diadem - When taken: 7 Oct 1812 - Where taken: S. Andres - Date received: 23 Feb 1813 - From what ship: Portsmouth via HMS Dromedary - Born: Karlskrona, Sweden - Age: 30 - Discharged on 8 Jun 1813 and released to Cartel Rodrigo.

Johnson, Andrew - Boy - Number: 1159 - Prize name: Sword Fish - Ship type: P - How taken: HM Ship-of-the-Line Elephant - When taken: 28 Dec 1812 - Where taken: off Azores - Date received: 16 Mar 1813 - From what ship: Portsmouth, via HMS Abundance - Born: Norfolk - Age: 17 - Discharged on 24 Jul 1813 and released to Cartel Hoffminy.

Johnson, Andrew - Seaman - Number: 666 - Prize name: U.S.R.M. Cutter James Madison - Ship type: War - How taken: HM Frigate Barbadoes - When taken: 22 Aug 1812 - Where taken: at sea - Date received: 24 Feb 1813 - From what ship: Portsmouth via HMS Ulysses - Born: Karlskrona, Sweden - Age: 22 - Discharged on 28 Apr 1813 and released to the David Scott.

Johnson, Charles - Seaman - Number: 2524 - Prize name: Yorktown - Ship type: P - How taken: HM Brig Nimrod - When taken: 17 Jul 1813 - Where taken: Grand Banks - Date received: 22 Oct 1813 - From what ship: Portsmouth via HMT Malabar - Born: Gothenburg, Sweden - Age: 32 - Discharged on 25 Sep 1814 and sent to Dartmoor on HMS Leyden.

Johnson, David - Seaman - Number: 1124 - Prize name: Empress - Ship type: MV - How taken: HM Brig Rover - When taken: 30 Nov 1813 - Where taken: St. Andrew - Date received: 14 Mar 1813 - From what ship: Portsmouth via HMS Beagle - Born: Wilmington - Age: 22 - Discharged on 8 Jun 1813 and released to Cartel Rodrigo.

Johnson, Easton - Seaman - Number: 3037 - How taken: Gave himself up from HM Ship-of-the-Line Illustrious - When taken: 7 Sep 1813 - Date received: 7 Jan 1814 - From what ship: Portsmouth - Born: Boston - Age: 24 - Escaped on 13 May 1814 from HM Prison Ship Crown Prince.

Johnson, Edward - Seaman - Number: 1520 - How taken: Gave himself up from HM Frigate Brune - When taken: 19 Jan 1813 - Date received: 8 Apr 1813 - From what ship: Portsmouth, via an admiral's tender - Born: Kensington, CT - Age: 26 - Discharged on 4 Aug 1814 and sent to Dartmoor on HMS Alpheus.

Johnson, Francis - Seaman - Number: 2830 - Prize name: Portsmouth Packet - Ship type: P - How taken: HM Brig Fantome - When taken: 5 Oct 1813 - Where taken: off Portland - Date received: 7 Jan 1814 - From what ship: Halifax - Born: Maryland - Age: 28 - Race: Mulatto - Discharged on 27 Mar 1814 and released to HMS Ceres.

Johnson, Frederick - Seaman - Number: 1301 - How taken: Gave himself up from HM Guardship Royal William - When taken: 3 Feb 1813 - Date received: 16 Mar 1813 - From what ship: Portsmouth, via HMS Abundance - Born: Connecticut - Age: 52 - Discharged on 23 Jul 1814 and sent to Dartmoor.

Johnson, George - Seaman - Number: 3705 - How taken: Gave himself up from HM Brig Acteon - When taken: 9 May 1814 - Date received: 15 May 1815 - From what ship: Eagle - Born: Philadelphia - Age: 31 - Discharged on 26 Sep 1814 and sent to Dartmoor on HMS Leyden.

Johnson, George - Private - Number: 1633 - Prize name: 6th U.S. Infantry - Ship type: LF - How taken: British forces - When taken: 13 Oct 1812 - Where taken: Upper Canada - Date received: 9 May 1813 - From what ship: HMS Raisonnable - Born: County Armagh, Ireland - Age: 45 - Discharged on 22 Oct 1814 and sent to Dartmoor on HMS Leyden.

Johnson, George - Seaman - Number: 229 - How taken: Apprehended at London - When taken: 11 Nov 1812 - Date received: 25 Nov 1812 - From what ship: HMS Raisonnable - Born: Portsmouth, NH - Age: 26 - Discharged in Jul 1813 and released to Cartel Moses Brown.

Johnson, George - Seaman - Number: 2981 - Prize name: Enterprise - Ship type: P - How taken: HM Frigate Tenedos - When taken: 21 May 1813 - Where taken: off Cape Cod - Date received: 7 Jan 1814 - From what ship: Halifax - Born: Portsmouth - Age: 19 - Discharged on 25 Sep 1814 and sent to Dartmoor on HMS Leyden.

Johnson, Henry - Seaman - Number: 3888 - How taken: Gave himself up from HM Frigate Phoenix - When taken: 17 Jul 1813 - Date received: 30 Aug 1814 - From what ship: Transport Office - Born: New York - Age: 26 - Race: Black - Discharged on 25 Sep 1814 and sent to Dartmoor on HMS Leyden.

Johnson, Henry - Seaman - Number: 1025 - Prize name: Hannah - Ship type: MV - How taken: Taken up at Liverpool - When taken: 18 Oct 1812 - Date received: 11 Mar 1813 - From what ship: Yarmouth via HMS Tenders - Born: Philadelphia - Age: 34 - Race: Black - Discharged in Jul 1813 and released to Cartel Moses Brown.

Johnson, Hugh - Private - Number: 3155 - Prize name: 14th U.S. Infantry - Ship type: LF - How taken: British forces - When taken: 24 Jun 1813 - Where taken: Beaver Dams, Upper Canada - Date received: 7 Jan 1814 - From what ship: Halifax - Born: New Jersey - Age: 24 - Discharged on 10 Oct 1814 and sent to U.S. on Cartel St. Philip.

Johnson, Jacob - Seaman - Number: 1452 - Prize name: Orbit - Ship type: MV - How taken: HM Brig Achates - When taken: 29 Jan 1813 - Where taken: Lat 49 N Long 13 W - Date received: 6 Apr 1813 - From what ship: Plymouth via HMS Decoy - Born: Long Island - Age: 23 - Discharged on 24 Jul 1814 and sent to Dartmoor.

Johnson, Jacob - Seaman - Number: 2498 - Prize name: Porcupine - Ship type: LM - How taken: HM Frigate Acasta - When taken: 3 Jun 1813 - Where taken: off Cape Sable, Florida - Date received: 22 Oct 1813 - From what ship: Portsmouth via HMT Malabar - Born: Marblehead - Age: 22 - Race: Blackman - Discharged on 11 Aug 1814 and sent to Dartmoor on HMS Freya.

Johnson, James - Seaman - Number: 3794 - Prize name: Valentine - Ship type: MV - How taken: HM Ship-of-the-Line Minden - When taken: 16 Nov 1812 - Where taken: off Cape of Good Hope - Date received: 26 May 1814 - From what ship: HMS Hindostan - Born: Providence - Age: 27 - Same name as prisoner number 3725.

Johnson, James - Seaman - Number: 3725 - Prize name: Valentine - Ship type: MV - How taken: HM Ship-of-the-Line Minden - When taken: 17 Nov 1812 - Where taken: off Cape of Good Hope - Date received: 23 May 1814 - From what ship: London - Born: Rhode Island - Age: 27 - Discharged on 25 Sep 1814 and sent to Dartmoor on HMS Leyden.

Johnson, James - Seaman - Number: 1450 - Prize name: Orbit - Ship type: MV - How taken: HM Brig Achates - When taken: 29 Jan 1813 - Where taken: Lat 49 N Long 13 W - Date received: 6 Apr 1813 - From what ship: Plymouth via HMS Decoy - Born: Northumberland - Age: 34 - Race: Negro - Discharged on 24 Jul 1814 and sent to Dartmoor.

Johnson, John - Seaman - Number: 1076 - How taken: Gave himself up from HM Brig Electra - When taken: 20 Sep 1812 - Date received: 14 Mar 1813 - From what ship: Portsmouth via HMS Cornwell - Born: Boston - Age: 27 - Discharged on 11 Aug 1814 and sent to Dartmoor.

Johnson, John - Seaman - Number: 2891 - Prize name: Dart - Ship type: P - How taken: HM Frigate Niger & HMS Fortunee - When taken: 10 Nov 1813 - Where taken: off Cape Finisterre, Spain - Date received: 7 Jan 1814 - From what ship: Portsmouth - Born: New York - Age: 25 - Released on 17 Aug 1814.

Johnson, John - Seaman - Number: 1699 - Prize name: Governor Middleton - Ship type: MV - How taken: Thetis, British privateer - When taken: 2 May 1813 - Where taken: Bay of Biscay - Date received: 15 May 1813 - From what ship: HMS Viper - Born: Groton, CT - Age: 18 - Discharged on 24 Jul 1814 and sent to Dartmoor on HMS Liffey.

Johnson, John - Seaman - Number: 3025 - How taken: Gave himself up from HM Ship-of-the-Line Invincible - When taken: 14 Jan 1813 - Date received: 7 Jan 1814 - From what ship: Portsmouth - Born: Philadelphia -

Age: 33 - Escaped on 16 May 1814 from HM Prison Ship Crown Prince and drown.

Johnson, Joseph - Seaman - Number: 202 - How taken: Gave himself up from HM Hulk Prince William - When taken: 13 Oct 1812 - Date received: 15 Nov 1812 - From what ship: HMS Raisonnable - Born: Philadelphia - Age: 30 - Discharged on 26 Jul 1814 and sent to Dartmoor on HMS Raven.

Johnson, Mathew - Seaman - Number: 2048 - How taken: Gave himself up from HM Brig Philomel - When taken: 28 Dec 1812 - Date received: 4 Aug 1813 - From what ship: HMS Christian VII - Born: Charleston - Age: 35 - Discharged on 4 Aug 1814 and sent to Dartmoor on HMS Liverpool.

Johnson, Oliver - Seaman - Number: 1192 - How taken: Gave himself up from HM Transport Romulus - When taken: 14 Aug 1812 - Date received: 16 Mar 1813 - From what ship: Portsmouth, via HMS Abundance - Born: Connecticut - Age: 28 - Discharged on 11 Aug 1814 and sent to Dartmoor on HMS Freya.

Johnson, Peter - Seaman - Number: 3213 - Prize name: Volunteer - Ship type: MV - How taken: Vittoria, British privateer from Guernsey - When taken: 26 Dec 1813 - Where taken: Bay of Biscay - Date received: 13 Jan 1814 - From what ship: Portsmouth via HMS Poictiers - Born: New York - Age: 19 - Died on 22 Apr 1814 from fever.

Johnson, Richard - Seaman - Number: 2549 - Prize name: Fame - Ship type: MV - How taken: HM Ship-of-the-Line Cressy - When taken: 20 Jul 1813 - Where taken: at sea - Date received: 23 Oct 1813 - From what ship: Portsmouth via HMS Raisonnable - Born: New York - Age: 42 - Race: Mulatto - Discharged on 8 Sep 1814 and sent to Dartmoor on HMS Niobe.

Johnson, Richard - Seaman - Number: 2604 - How taken: Gave himself up from HM Ship-of-the-Line Ocean - When taken: 27 May 1813 - Date received: 5 Nov 1813 - From what ship: HMS Hindostan - Born: Norfolk, VA - Age: 24 - Race: Blackman - Discharged on 12 Aug 1814 and sent to Dartmoor on HMS Alpheus.

Johnson, Robert - Seaman - Number: 65 - Prize name: Canaware - Ship type: MV - How taken: HM Brig Recruit - When taken: 20 Jul 1812 - Where taken: off Delaware - Date received: 3 Nov 1812 - From what ship: HMS Plover - Born: Middlesex County, VA - Age: 38 - Discharged on 23 Mar 1813 and released to the Cartel Robinson Potter.

Johnson, Robert - Seaman - Number: 917 - Prize name: Ceres - Ship type: MV - How taken: HM Battery Princess - When taken: 3 Aug 1812 - Where taken: Liverpool - Date received: 10 Mar 1813 - From what ship: HMS Tigress - Born: New York - Age: 23 - Race: Black - Discharged on 4 Jul 1813 and sent to Downs (England) militia.

Johnson, Samuel - Seaman - Number: 109 - Prize name: Phoenix - Ship type: MV - How taken: Stopped at London - When taken: 26 Oct 1812 - Date received: 4 Nov 1812 - From what ship: HMS Namur - Born: Philadelphia - Age: 28 - Discharged on 7 Jun 1813 and released to the HMS Ceres.

Johnson, Samuel - Seaman - Number: 633 - How taken: Gave himself up from HM Ship-of-the-Line Vigo - When taken: 31 Dec 1812 - Date received: 23 Feb 1813 - From what ship: Portsmouth via HMS Dromedary - Born: Providence - Age: 59 - Discharged on 12 Aug 1814 and sent to Dartmoor on HMS Alpheus.

Johnson, Samuel B. - Seaman - Number: 3593 - How taken: Gave himself up from HM Frigate Eridanus - When taken: 15 Sep 1813 - Date received: 26 Mar 1814 - From what ship: Plymouth via HMS Raleigh - Born: Salem - Age: 39 - Discharged on 20 Aug 1814 and sent to Dartmoor on HMS Shamrock.

Johnson, Stephen - Seaman - Number: 268 - How taken: Apprehended at London - When taken: 30 Nov 1812 - Date received: 7 Dec 1812 - From what ship: HMS Raisonnable - Born: Long Island - Age: 23 - Discharged on 24 Jul 1813 and released to Cartel Hoffminy.

Johnson, Thomas - Mate - Number: 1761 - Prize name: Revenge - Ship type: MV - How taken: HM Brig Monthy - When taken: 20 May 1813 - Where taken: Bay of Biscay - Date received: 14 Jun 1813 - From what ship: HMS Raisonnable - Born: Wilmington - Age: 25 - Discharged on 10 Oct 1814 and sent to Dartmoor on the Mermaid.

Johnson, Thomas - Seaman - Number: 2774 - Prize name: Thomas - Ship type: P - How taken: HM Frigate Nymphe - When taken: 24 Jun 1813 - Where taken: off Halifax - Date received: 7 Jan 1814 - From what ship: Halifax - Born: New York - Age: 38 - Discharged on 8 Sep 1814 and sent to Dartmoor on HMS Niobe.

Johnson, Thomas - Seaman - Number: 1856 - How taken: Given up from HM Ship-of-the-Line Malta - Date received: 7 Jul 1813 - From what ship: Portsmouth via HMS Tribune - Born: Baltimore - Age: 27 - Discharged on 25 Jul 1814 and sent to Dartmoor on HMS Bittern.

Johnson, William - Seaman - Number: 1073 - How taken: Gave himself up from HM Brig Electra - When taken: 20 Sep 1812 - Date received: 14 Mar 1813 - From what ship: Portsmouth via HMS Cornwell - Born: Charlestown - Age: 32 - Discharged on 16 Jun 1813 and released to HMS Ceres.

Johnson, William - Seaman - Number: 1285 - How taken: Gave himself up from HM Guardship Royal William - When taken: 3 Feb 1813 - Date received: 16 Mar 1813 - From what ship: Portsmouth, via HMS Abundance - Born: Philadelphia - Age: 28 - Discharged on 23 Jul 1814 and sent to Dartmoor.

Johnson, William - Seaman - Number: 255 - How taken: Gave himself up at London - When taken: 24 Nov 1812 - Date received: 7 Dec 1812 - From what ship: HMS Raisonnable - Born: New York - Age: 30 - Discharged on 24 Jul 1813 and released to Cartel Hoffminy.

Johnston, Benjamin - Seaman - Number: 312 - Prize name: Cuba - Ship type: MV - How taken: HM Brig Sarpedon - When taken: 12 Aug 1812 - Date received: 23 Dec 1812 - From what ship: Greenlaw Depot - Born: Rhode Island - Age: 22 - Race: Black man - Discharged on 10 May 1813 and released to Cartel Admittance.

Johnston, Edward - Seaman - Number: 1549 - Prize name: Resolution - Ship type: MV - How taken: Hibernia, British letter of marque - When taken: 21 Sep 1812 - Where taken: off Bermuda - Date received: 8 Apr 1813 - From what ship: Plymouth via HMS Olympia - Born: Kent County - Age: 25 - Discharged on 18 Oct 1813 and released to HMS Ceres.

Johnston, Henry - Seaman - Number: 2440 - How taken: Taken off of the Russian MV Neptune at Cork - When taken: 28 Sep 1812 - Date received: 21 Oct 1813 - From what ship: Portsmouth via HMT Malabar - Born: Danvers - Age: 20 - Discharged on 4 Sep 1814 and sent to Dartmoor on HMS Freya.

Johnston, Samuel - Mate - Number: 1461 - Prize name: Union - Ship type: MV - How taken: HM Frigate Iris - When taken: 17 Jan 1813 - Where taken: at sea - Date received: 6 Apr 1813 - From what ship: Portsmouth via Tender Eliza - Born: New Jersey - Age: 23 - Discharged on 24 Jul 1813 and released to Cartel Hoffminy.

Johnston, Samuel - Seaman - Number: 1546 - Prize name: Hunter - Ship type: P - How taken: HM Frigate Phoebe - When taken: 23 Dec 1812 - Where taken: off Azores - Date received: 8 Apr 1813 - From what ship: Plymouth via HMS Olympia - Born: Boston - Age: 60 - Discharged on 27 Jul 1813 and released to Cartel Hoffminy.

Johnston, Thomas - Seaman - Number: 1940 - Prize name: Criterion - Ship type: MV - How taken: HM Frigate Belle Poule - When taken: 14 Feb 1813 - Where taken: Bay of Biscay - Date received: 15 Jul 1813 - From what ship: Plymouth - Born: Albany - Age: 22 - Discharged on 17 Jun 1814 and sent to Dartmoor on HMS Pincher.

Johnstone, Robert - Seaman - Number: 2887 - Prize name: Taken off an English whaler - How taken: HM Ship-of-the-Line Illustrious - When taken: 22 Oct 1813 - Where taken: at sea - Date received: 7 Jan 1814 - From what ship: Portsmouth - Born: Baltimore - Age: 24 - Discharged on 25 Sep 1814 and sent to Dartmoor on HMS Leyden.

Johnstone, William - Seaman - Number: 1467 - Prize name: Union - Ship type: MV - How taken: HM Frigate Iris - When taken: 17 Jan 1813 - Where taken: at sea - Date received: 6 Apr 1813 - From what ship: Portsmouth via Tender Eliza - Born: Philadelphia - Age: 23 - Discharged on 26 Jul 1813 and released to Cartel Hoffminy.

Jonathan, Jonathan - Seaman - Number: 3844 - How taken: Gave himself up from HM Ship-of-the-Line Minden at Madras, India - When taken: 14 Oct 1813 - Date received: 21 Aug 1814 - From what ship: Gravesend - Born: Portsmouth - Age: 26 - Discharged on 20 Sep 1814 and sent to Dartmoor on HMS Leyden.

Jones, Anthony - Seaman - Number: 2416 - How taken: Gave himself up from HM Frigate Astrea - When taken: 18 Oct 1813 - Date received: 21 Oct 1813 - From what ship: Portsmouth via HMT Malabar - Born: New Orleans - Age: 32 - Discharged on 26 Sep 1814 and sent to Dartmoor on HMS Leyden.

Jones, Benjamin - Seaman - Number: 1966 - Prize name: William Bayard - Ship type: MV - How taken: HM Ship-of-the-Line Warspite - When taken: 3 Mar 1813 - Where taken: Bay of Biscay - Date received: 15 Jul 1813 -

From what ship: Plymouth - Born: Medford - Age: 27 - Discharged on 17 Jun 1814 and sent to Dartmoor on HMS Redbreast.

Jones, Cabell - 2nd Mate - Number: 1216 - Prize name: Rossie - Ship type: MV - How taken: HM Frigate Dryand - When taken: 7 Jan 1813 - Where taken: at sea - Date received: 16 Mar 1813 - From what ship: Portsmouth, via HMS Abundance - Born: Chester - Age: 29 - Discharged on 2 Jul 1813 and released to Cartel Moses Brown.

Jones, Charles - Seaman - Number: 1786 - How taken: Taken up at London - When taken: 15 Jun 1813 - Date received: 1 Jul 1813 - From what ship: HMS Raisonnable - Born: Philadelphia - Age: 30 - Discharged on 15 Dec 1813 and released to HMS Ceres.

Jones, David - Seaman - Number: 175 - How taken: Stopped at London - When taken: 27 Oct 1812 - Date received: 5 Nov 1812 - From what ship: HMS Namur - Born: Baltimore - Age: 19 - Discharged in Jul 1813 and released to Cartel Moses Brown.

Jones, Henry - Mate - Number: 172 - How taken: Stopped at London - When taken: 27 Oct 1812 - Date received: 5 Nov 1812 - From what ship: HMS Namur - Born: Baltimore - Age: 27 - Discharged in Jul 1813 and released to Cartel Moses Brown.

Jones, Isaac - Seaman - Number: 3891 - How taken: Gave himself up from HM Frigate Hussar - When taken: 26 Jul 1813 - Date received: 30 Aug 1814 - From what ship: Transport Office - Born: Boston - Age: 22 - Discharged on 25 Sep 1814 and sent to Dartmoor on HMS Leyden.

Jones, James - Seaman - Number: 3886 - How taken: Gave himself up from HM Frigate Hussar - When taken: 26 Jul 1813 - Date received: 30 Aug 1814 - From what ship: Transport Office - Born: New York - Age: 27 - Discharged on 25 Sep 1814 and sent to Dartmoor on HMS Leyden.

Jones, James - Passenger - Number: 1885 - Prize name: Tiger - Ship type: MV - How taken: HM Brig Scylla - When taken: 22 Mar 1813 - Where taken: Bay of Biscay - Date received: 7 Jul 1813 - From what ship: Portsmouth via HMS Tribune - Born: Connecticut - Age: 35 - Died on 6 Jul 1814 from apoplexy.

Jones, James - Seaman - Number: 2776 - Prize name: Thomas - Ship type: P - How taken: HM Frigate Nymphe - When taken: 24 Jun 1813 - Where taken: off Halifax - Date received: 7 Jan 1814 - From what ship: Halifax - Born: Massachusetts - Age: 32 - Race: Black - Discharged on 8 Sep 1814 and sent to Dartmoor on HMS Niobe.

Jones, John - Seaman - Number: 3873 - Prize name: Venus - Ship type: MV - How taken: Gave himself up from Barbados - When taken: 14 Sep 1814 - Date received: 27 Aug 1814 - From what ship: Chatham - Born: New York - Age: 32 - Race: Black - Discharged on 26 Sep 1814 and sent to Dartmoor on HMS Leyden.

Jones, John - Seaman - Number: 1431 - Prize name: Louisa, prize of the Privateer Decatur - Ship type: P - How taken: HM Frigate Andromache - When taken: 11 Jan 1813 - Where taken: off Bordeaux, France - Date received: 6 Apr 1813 - From what ship: Plymouth via HMS Decoy - Born: Norfolk - Age: 17 - Discharged on 24 Jul 1813 and released to Cartel Hoffminy.

Jones, John - Seaman - Number: 1481 - Prize name: Union - Ship type: MV - How taken: HM Frigate Iris - When taken: 17 Jan 1813 - Where taken: at sea - Date received: 6 Apr 1813 - From what ship: Portsmouth via Tender Eliza - Born: Philadelphia - Age: 17 - Discharged on 26 Jul 1813 and released to Cartel Hoffminy.

Jones, John - Seaman - Number: 1395 - Prize name: Blue Bird - Ship type: MV - How taken: HM Frigate Briton - When taken: 1 Jan 1813 - Where taken: off Bordeaux, France - Date received: 5 Apr 1813 - From what ship: Plymouth via HMS Dwarf - Born: New Jersey - Age: 28 - Discharged on 24 Jul 1813 and released to Cartel Hoffminy.

Jones, John - Seaman - Number: 2445 - Prize name: Wiley Reynard - Ship type: P - How taken: HM Frigate Shannon - When taken: 16 Aug 1812 - Where taken: off Halifax - Date received: 21 Oct 1813 - From what ship: Portsmouth via HMT Malabar - Born: Massachusetts - Age: 31 - Discharged on 22 Jun 1814 and sent to Calais, France on the Simon & Mary.

Jones, John - Seaman - Number: 2995 - Prize name: America - Ship type: P - How taken: HM Frigate Shannon - When taken: 25 May 1813 - Where taken: off Cape Cod - Date received: 7 Jan 1814 - From what ship: Halifax - Born: Rhode Island - Age: 19 - Died on 31 Mar 1814 from fever.

Jones, Lewis - Seaman - Number: 3657 - Prize name: Caroline - Ship type: MV - How taken: HM Brig Moselle - When taken: 12 Aug 1813 - Where taken: off Charleston - Date received: 23 Apr 1814 - From what ship: HMS Raisonnable - Born: Maryland - Age: 25 - Discharged on 25 Sep 1814 and sent to Dartmoor on HMS Niobe.

Jones, Peter (alias Benjamin Jones) - Seaman - Number: 1990 - How taken: Gave himself up from HM Ship-of-the-Line Magnificent - Date received: 15 Jul 1813 - From what ship: Plymouth - Born: Maryland - Age: 24 - Race: Black - Discharged on 17 Jun 1814 and sent to Dartmoor on HMS Pincher.

Jones, Samuel - Seaman - Number: 219 - How taken: Apprehended at London - When taken: 3 Nov 1812 - Date received: 15 Nov 1812 - From what ship: HMS Raisonnable - Born: Philadelphia - Age: 30 - Discharged on 12 Apr 1813 and released to HMS Carnatic.

Jones, Samuel B. - Seaman - Number: 3795 - Prize name: Valentine - Ship type: MV - How taken: HM Ship-of-the-Line Minden - When taken: 16 Nov 1812 - Where taken: off Cape of Good Hope - Date received: 28 May 1814 - From what ship: London - Born: Providence - Age: 22 - Discharged on 29 Sep 1814 and sent to Dartmoor on HMS Freya.

Jones, Stephen - Seaman - Number: 2856 - Prize name: Fire Fly - Ship type: LM - How taken: HM Frigate Revolutionnaire - When taken: 19 Oct 1813 - Where taken: off Cape Ortegal, Spain - Date received: 7 Jan 1814 - From what ship: Portsmouth - Born: Massachusetts - Age: 18 - Discharged on 26 Sep 1814 and sent to Dartmoor on HMS Leyden.

Jones, Theodore - Seaman - Number: 3489 - How taken: Gave himself up from HM Ship-of-the-Line Bulwark - When taken: 28 Dec 1813 - Date received: 23 Feb 1814 - From what ship: Portsmouth via HMT Malabar - Born: Maryland - Age: 26 - Discharged on 26 Sep 1814 and sent to Dartmoor on HMS Leyden.

Jones, Thomas - Seaman - Number: 3926 - How taken: Gave himself up from HM Ship-of-the-Line Blenheim - When taken: 2 Sep 1814 - Date received: 24 Sep 1814 - From what ship: HMS Namur - Born: Boston - Age: 26 - Discharged on 29 Sep 1814 and sent to Dartmoor on HMS Freya.

Jones, Thomas - Seaman - Number: 787 - Prize name: Dolphin - Ship type: MV - How taken: HM Ship-of-the-Line Colossus - When taken: 5 Jan 1813 - Where taken: off the Western Isles, Scotland - Date received: 27 Feb 1813 - From what ship: Plymouth via HMS Namur - Born: Philadelphia - Age: 18 - Discharged on 24 Jul 1813 and released to Cartel Hoffminy.

Jones, Thomas - Cook - Number: 2688 - Prize name: Growler - Ship type: P - How taken: HM Brig Electra - When taken: 7 Jul 1813 - Where taken: off St. Johns - Date received: 7 Jan 1814 - From what ship: Portsmouth - Born: Baltimore - Age: 38 - Discharged on 8 Sep 1814 and sent to Dartmoor on HMS Niobe.

Jones, Thomas - Seaman - Number: 3022 - How taken: Gave himself up from HM Ship-of-the-Line Invincible - When taken: 14 Jan 1813 - Date received: 7 Jan 1814 - From what ship: Portsmouth - Born: Baltimore - Age: 25 - Discharged on 26 Sep 1814 and sent to Dartmoor on HMS Leyden.

Jones, Urigh - Cook - Number: 806 - Prize name: Bell - Ship type: MV - How taken: Phillis - When taken: 18 Dec 1812 - Where taken: off Cadiz, Spain - Date received: 27 Feb 1813 - From what ship: Plymouth via HMS Namur - Born: Philadelphia - Age: 25 - Race: Black - Discharged on 8 Jun 1813 and released to Cartel Rodrigo.

Jones, William - Boatswain's Mate - Number: 3736 - Prize name: Argus - Ship type: MV - How taken: HM Ship-of-the-Line San Domingo - When taken: 1 Mar 1814 - Where taken: off Savannah - Date received: 26 May 1814 - From what ship: HMS Hindostan - Born: Philadelphia - Age: 27 - Discharged on 25 Sep 1814 and sent to Dartmoor on HMS Niobe.

Jones, William - Seaman - Number: 598 - Prize name: Antelope - Ship type: P - How taken: HM Brig Zephyr - When taken: 10 Dec 1812 - Where taken: at sea - Date received: 23 Feb 1813 - From what ship: Portsmouth via HMS Dromedary - Born: New York - Age: 31 - Discharged on 2 Jul 1813 and released to Cartel Moses Brown.

Jones, William - Seaman - Number: 2150 - Prize name: Lyon - Ship type: MV - How taken: Impressed at Brazil - When taken: 16 May 1813 - Date received: 9 Aug 1813 - From what ship: HMS Thames - Born: New York - Age: 45 - Discharged on 12 Aug 1814 and sent to Dartmoor on HMS Alpheus.

Jones, William - Seaman - Number: 1994 - How taken: Gave himself up from HM Ship-of-the-Line Clarence - Date received: 15 Jul 1813 - From what ship: Plymouth - Born: Baltimore - Age: 28 - Race: Black - Discharged on 18 Oct 1813 and released to HMS Ceres.

Jones, William - Seaman - Number: 3224 - Prize name: Volunteer - Ship type: MV - How taken: Vittoria, British privateer from Guernsey - When taken: 26 Dec 1813 - Where taken: Bay of Biscay - Date received: 13 Jan 1814 - From what ship: Portsmouth via HMS Poictiers - Born: Baltimore - Age: 25 - Race: Mulatto - Discharged on 25 Sep 1814 and sent to Dartmoor on HMS Leyden.

Jones, William M. - Private - Number: 3151 - Prize name: 14th U.S. Infantry - Ship type: LF - How taken: British forces - When taken: 24 Jun 1813 - Where taken: Beaver Dams, Upper Canada - Date received: 7 Jan 1814 - From what ship: Halifax - Born: Virginia - Age: 20 - Discharged on 10 Oct 1814 and sent to U.S. on Cartel St. Philip.

Jordan, Artemas - Seaman - Number: 2563 - How taken: Gave himself up from HM Battery Gorgon - When taken: 1 Nov 1812 - Date received: 23 Oct 1813 - From what ship: Portsmouth via HMS Raisonnable - Born: Plymouth - Age: 28 - Discharged on 8 Sep 1814 and sent to Dartmoor on HMS Niobe.

Jordan, David - Seaman - Number: 1485 - Prize name: Resolution - Ship type: MV - How taken: Hibernia, British letter of marque - When taken: 21 Sep 1812 - Where taken: off Bermuda - Date received: 6 Apr 1813 - From what ship: Portsmouth via Tender Eliza - Born: Portland - Age: 38 - Discharged on 8 Jun 1813 and released to Cartel Rodrigo.

Jordan, Peter - Seaman - Number: 1968 - Prize name: Lightning - Ship type: MV - How taken: HM Frigate Medusa - When taken: 2 Apr 1813 - Where taken: Bay of Biscay - Date received: 15 Jul 1813 - From what ship: Plymouth - Born: Messina - Age: 31 - Discharged on 17 Jun 1814 and sent to Dartmoor on HMS Redbreast.

Joseph, Lewis - Seaman - Number: 3297 - Prize name: Montgomery - Ship type: P - How taken: HM Frigate Nymphe - When taken: 5 May 1813 - Where taken: off Cape Cod - Date received: 23 Feb 1814 - From what ship: Halifax via HMT Malabar - Born: Guadeloupe - Age: 18 - Race: Black - Discharged on 22 Jun 1814 and sent to Calais, France on the Simon & Mary.

Joseph, Michael - Cook - Number: 938 - Prize name: Argus - Ship type: MV - How taken: HM Cutter Fancy - When taken: 19 Dec 1812 - Where taken: Bay of Biscay - Date received: 10 Mar 1813 - From what ship: HMS Tigress - Born: New York - Age: 24 - Race: Negro - Discharged on 2 Jul 1813 and released to Cartel Moses Brown.

Joseph, Nicholas - Boy - Number: 2690 - Prize name: Growler - Ship type: P - How taken: HM Brig Electra - When taken: 7 Jul 1813 - Where taken: off St. Johns - Date received: 7 Jan 1814 - From what ship: Portsmouth - Born: Marblehead - Age: 14 - Discharged on 22 Oct 1814 and sent to Dartmoor on HMS Leyden.

Jourdan, John - Seaman - Number: 2913 - Prize name: Pomona, prize of Privateer Prince de Neuchatel - Ship type: P - How taken: HM Frigate Ethalion - When taken: 14 Dec 1813 - Where taken: at sea - Date received: 7 Jan 1814 - From what ship: Portsmouth - Born: New Orleans - Age: 24 - Released on 6 Aug 1814.

Jupiter, James - Seaman - Number: 3216 - Prize name: Volunteer - Ship type: MV - How taken: Vittoria, British privateer from Guernsey - When taken: 26 Dec 1813 - Where taken: Bay of Biscay - Date received: 13 Jan 1814 - From what ship: Portsmouth via HMS Poictiers - Born: Philadelphia - Age: 24 - Race: Black - Discharged on 25 Sep 1814 and sent to Dartmoor on HMS Leyden.

Kain, Peter - Seaman - Number: 820 - Prize name: Columbia - Ship type: MV - How taken: HM Frigate Briton - When taken: 17 Dec 1812 - Where taken: off Bordeaux, France - Date received: 27 Feb 1813 - From what ship: Plymouth via HMS Namur - Born: Naveau, France - Age: 39 - Discharged in Jul 1813 and released to Cartel Moses Brown.

Kane, William - Seaman - Number: 3618 - Prize name: Liberty - Ship type: MV - How taken: Surrendered at Stromness, Scotland - When taken: 30 Dec 1813 - Date received: 29 Mar 1814 - From what ship: Hired tender Anna - Born: New York - Age: 24 - Discharged on 25 Sep 1814 and sent to Dartmoor on HMS Leyden.

Kay, James - Seaman - Number: 2043 - How taken: Impressed at Gravesend, England - When taken: 4 Jul 1813 - Date received: 4 Aug 1813 - From what ship: HMS Christian VII - Born: Jersey - Age: 27 - Discharged on 25

Sep 1814 and sent to Dartmoor on HMS Niobe.

Keen, Benjamin - Seaman - Number: 2931 - Prize name: Governor Plumer - Ship type: P - How taken: HM Brig Shamrock - When taken: 26 May 1813 - Where taken: at sea - Date received: 7 Jan 1814 - From what ship: Halifax - Born: Massachusetts - Age: 24 - Discharged on 25 Sep 1814 and sent to Dartmoor on HMS Leyden.

Keen, Joseph - Seaman - Number: 3557 - Prize name: Zephyr, prize of Privateer Rattlesnake - Ship type: P - How taken: HM Frigate Surveillante - When taken: 6 Jan 1814 - Where taken: Bay of Biscay - Date received: 7 May 1814 - From what ship: Portsmouth via HMS Favorite - Born: Massachusetts - Age: 25 - Discharged on 25 Sep 1814 and sent to Dartmoor on HMS Niobe.

Keen, Robert - Seaman - Number: 71 - Prize name: Elson - Ship type: MV - How taken: HM Frigate Ethalion - When taken: 12 Aug 1812 - Where taken: Baltic - Date received: 4 Nov 1812 - From what ship: HMS Namur - Born: Massachusetts - Age: 23 - Discharged on 10 May 1813 and released to Cartel Admittance.

Keen, Stewart - Seaman - Number: 3610 - Prize name: Liberty - Ship type: MV - How taken: Surrendered at Stromness, Scotland - When taken: 30 Dec 1813 - Date received: 29 Mar 1814 - From what ship: Hired tender Anna - Born: New Haven - Age: 21 - Discharged on 25 Sep 1814 and sent to Dartmoor on HMS Niobe.

Kegs, Zenas - Seaman - Number: 2719 - Prize name: Growler - Ship type: P - How taken: HM Brig Electra - When taken: 7 Jul 1813 - Where taken: off St. Johns - Date received: 7 Jan 1814 - From what ship: Portsmouth - Born: Massachusetts - Age: 22 - Discharged on 25 Sep 1814 and sent to Dartmoor on HMS Leyden.

Keith, James - Seaman - Number: 813 - Prize name: Leader - Ship type: MV - How taken: HM Frigate Andromach - When taken: 10 Dec 1812 - Where taken: off Bordeaux, France - Date received: 27 Feb 1813 - From what ship: Plymouth via HMS Namur - Born: Waring, MA - Age: 20 - Discharged in Jul 1813 and released to Cartel Moses Brown.

Kellam, John - Seaman - Number: 3896 - How taken: Gave himself up from HM Frigate Leda - When taken: 6 Jul 1813 - Date received: 30 Aug 1814 - From what ship: Transport Office - Born: Salem - Age: 30 - Discharged on 2 Sep 1814 and sent to Dartmoor on HMS Leyden.

Kelley, William - Private - Number: 2643 - Prize name: 14th U.S. Infantry - Ship type: LF - How taken: British forces - When taken: 24 Jun 1813 - Where taken: Beaver Dams, Upper Canada - Date received: 5 Nov 1813 - From what ship: HMS Hindostan - Born: North Ireland - Age: 59 - Discharged on 10 Oct 1814 and sent to U.S. on Cartel St. Philip.

Kellum, Smith - Seaman - Number: 2097 - How taken: Gave himself up from HM Ship-of-the-Line Barfleur - When taken: 27 May 1813 - Date received: 9 Aug 1813 - From what ship: HMS Thames - Born: Virginia - Age: 31 - Discharged on 12 Aug 1814 and sent to Dartmoor on HMS Alpheus.

Kellogg, Asa - Private - Number: 3063 - Prize name: 14th U.S. Infantry - Ship type: LF - How taken: British forces - When taken: 24 Jun 1813 - Where taken: Beaver Dams, Upper Canada - Date received: 7 Jan 1814 - From what ship: Halifax - Born: Connecticut - Age: 37 - Discharged on 10 Oct 1814 and sent to U.S. on Cartel St. Philip.

Kelly, Charles - Private - Number: 2625 - Prize name: 14th U.S. Infantry - Ship type: LF - How taken: British forces - When taken: 24 Jun 1813 - Where taken: Beaver Dams, Upper Canada - Date received: 5 Nov 1813 - From what ship: HMS Hindostan - Born: North Ireland - Age: 28 - Discharged on 10 Oct 1814 and sent to U.S. on Cartel St. Philip.

Kelly, Henry - Private - Number: 1630 - Prize name: 13th U.S. Infantry - Ship type: LF - How taken: British forces - When taken: 13 Oct 1812 - Where taken: Upper Canada - Date received: 9 May 1813 - From what ship: HMS Raisonnable - Born: County Antrim, Ireland - Age: 30 - Discharged on 22 Oct 1814 and sent to Dartmoor on HMS Leyden.

Kelly, John - Seaman - Number: 2050 - How taken: Gave himself up from HM Ship-of-the-Line Fame - When taken: 4 May 1813 - Date received: 4 Aug 1813 - From what ship: HMS Christian VII - Born: Newburgh, NY - Age: 19 - Discharged on 4 Aug 1814 and sent to Dartmoor on HMS Liverpool.

Kelly, John - Seaman - Number: 2970 - Prize name: Enterprise - Ship type: P - How taken: HM Frigate Tenedos -

When taken: 21 May 1813 - Where taken: off Cape Cod - Date received: 7 Jan 1814 - From what ship: Halifax - Born: Delaware - Age: 33 - Discharged on 25 Sep 1814 and sent to Dartmoor on HMS Leyden.

Kelly, Samuel - Seaman - Number: 3638 - Prize name: Bunker Hill - Ship type: P - How taken: HM Frigate Pomone & HM Frigate Cydnus - When taken: 4 Mar 1814 - Where taken: Bay of Biscay - Date received: 31 Mar 1814 - From what ship: HMS Raisonnable - Born: New York - Age: 33 - Race: Black - Discharged on 25 Sep 1814 and sent to Dartmoor on HMS Niobe.

Kemble, John - Sailmaker - Number: 3830 - Prize name: Rambler - Ship type: MV - How taken: HM Transport Morley - When taken: 10 Feb 1813 - Where taken: off Isle de France (Mauritius) - Date received: 16 Aug 1814 - From what ship: London - Born: Ipswich - Age: 25 - Discharged on 22 Oct 1814 and sent to Dartmoor on HMS Leyden.

Kemble, Samuel - Seaman - Number: 3807 - How taken: Given up from HM Frigate Indefatigable at Cape of Good Hope - When taken: 12 Aug 1813 - Date received: 5 Jun 1814 - From what ship: HMS Raisonnable - Born: Pawtucket - Age: 28 - Discharged on 22 Oct 1814 and sent to Dartmoor on HMS Leyden.

Kennard, Joseph - Seaman - Number: 800 - Prize name: Dolphin - Ship type: MV - How taken: HM Ship-of-the-Line Colossus - When taken: 5 Jan 1813 - Where taken: off the Western Isles, Scotland - Date received: 27 Feb 1813 - From what ship: Plymouth via HMS Namur - Born: Maryland - Age: 22 - Race: Black - Died on 1 Aug 1813 from phthisis (tuberculosis).

Kennedy, Dennis - Seaman - Number: 3206 - Prize name: Volunteer - Ship type: MV - How taken: Vittoria, British privateer from Guernsey - When taken: 26 Dec 1813 - Where taken: Bay of Biscay - Date received: 13 Jan 1814 - From what ship: Portsmouth via HMS Poictiers - Born: South Carolina - Age: 31 - Discharged on 25 Sep 1814 and sent to Dartmoor on HMS Leyden.

Kennedy, Henry - 2nd Mate - Number: 723 - Prize name: Eos - Ship type: MV - How taken: Detained at Portsmouth harbor - When taken: 31 Jul 1812 - Date received: 24 Feb 1813 - From what ship: Portsmouth via HMS Ulysses - Born: Boston - Age: 27 - Discharged on 23 Mar 1813 and released to the Cartel Robinson Potter.

Kennedy, John - Seaman - Number: 408 - Prize name: Hope - Ship type: MV - How taken: HM Sloop Pheasant - When taken: 13 Dec 1812 - Where taken: off Azores - Date received: 19 Feb 1813 - From what ship: HMS Modeste - Born: Newburgh - Age: 24 - Discharged on 2 Jul 1813 and released to Cartel Moses Brown.

Kennedy, Peter - Seaman - Number: 1441 - Prize name: Orbit - Ship type: MV - How taken: HM Brig Achates - When taken: 29 Jan 1813 - Where taken: Lat 49 N Long 13 W - Date received: 6 Apr 1813 - From what ship: Plymouth via HMS Decoy - Born: New Jersey - Age: 20 - Discharged on 24 Jul 1814 and sent to Dartmoor.

Kennedy, William (alias William Freeman) - Seaman - Number: 1986 - How taken: Gave himself up from HM Ship-of-the-Line Ajax - Date received: 15 Jul 1813 - From what ship: Plymouth - Born: Boston - Age: 29 - Discharged on 17 Jun 1814 and sent to Dartmoor on HMS Pincher.

Kenner, John Downing - Seaman - Number: 1183 - Prize name: William - Ship type: MV - How taken: HM Brig Recruit - When taken: 29 Aug 1812 - Where taken: at sea - Date received: 16 Mar 1813 - From what ship: Portsmouth, via HMS Abundance - Born: Northumberland, VA - Age: 24 - Discharged on 10 May 1813 and released to Cartel Admittance.

Kenny, George - Boy - Number: 1169 - Prize name: Sword Fish - Ship type: P - How taken: HM Ship-of-the-Line Elephant - When taken: 28 Dec 1812 - Where taken: off Azores - Date received: 16 Mar 1813 - From what ship: Portsmouth, via HMS Abundance - Born: Salem - Age: 14 - Discharged on 24 Jul 1813 and released to Cartel Hoffminy.

Kent, James - Seaman - Number: 1503 - How taken: Impressed at Cork - When taken: 19 Mar 1813 - Date received: 8 Apr 1813 - From what ship: Portsmouth, via an admiral's tender - Born: Waterbury - Age: 24 - Discharged on 14 Aug 1814 and sent to Dartmoor.

Kent, Wilson - Seaman - Number: 2994 - Prize name: America - Ship type: P - How taken: HM Frigate Shannon - When taken: 25 May 1813 - Where taken: off Cape Cod - Date received: 7 Jan 1814 - From what ship: Halifax - Born: Rhode Island - Age: 36 - Discharged on 25 Sep 1814 and sent to Dartmoor on HMS Leyden.

Kerhow, Samuel - Seaman - Number: 1271 - Prize name: Sword Fish - Ship type: P - How taken: HM Ship-of-the-Line Elephant - When taken: 28 Dec 1812 - Where taken: off Azores - Date received: 16 Mar 1813 - From what ship: Portsmouth, via HMS Abundance - Born: Salem - Age: 44 - Discharged on 24 Jul 1813 and released to Cartel Hoffminy.

Kerry, Isaac - Seaman - Number: 3241 - How taken: Gave himself up from HM Transport Bruisor - When taken: 3 Feb 1814 - Date received: 10 Feb 1814 - From what ship: HMS Cadmus - Born: Fredricka - Age: 25 - Race: Black - Discharged on 25 Sep 1814 and sent to Dartmoor on HMS Leyden.

Kershon, Abraham - Seaman - Number: 1874 - Prize name: Tiger - Ship type: MV - How taken: HM Brig Scylla - When taken: 22 Mar 1813 - Where taken: Bay of Biscay - Date received: 7 Jul 1813 - From what ship: Portsmouth via HMS Tribune - Born: Long Island - Age: 32 - Released on 11 Jul 1814.

Kile, George - Seaman - Number: 1151 - Prize name: Sword Fish - Ship type: P - How taken: HM Ship-of-the-Line Elephant - When taken: 28 Dec 1812 - Where taken: off Azores - Date received: 16 Mar 1813 - From what ship: Portsmouth, Mundane - Born: Philadelphia - Age: 23 - Discharged on 24 Jul 1813 and released to Cartel Hoffminy.

Killerman, Maxwell - Seaman - Number: 3381 - Prize name: Yorktown - Ship type: P - How taken: HM Frigate Maidstone - When taken: 17 Jul 1813 - Where taken: Grand Banks - Date received: 23 Feb 1814 - From what ship: Halifax via HMT Malabar - Born: New Orleans - Age: 38 - Race: Black - Discharged on 22 Oct 1814 and sent to Dartmoor on HMS Leyden.

Killingsworth, John - Seaman - Number: 3534 - Prize name: Commodore Perry - Ship type: MV - How taken: Sent into custody from a cutter - When taken: 25 Feb 1814 - Where taken: off Bordeaux, France - Date received: 5 Mar 1814 - From what ship: HMS Raisonnable - Born: Sussex, MA - Age: 20 - Discharged on 26 Sep 1814 and sent to Dartmoor on HMS Leyden.

Kimberly, Elisha - Seaman - Number: 745 - Prize name: Quebec of London, prize of the Privateer Paul Jones - Ship type: P - How taken: HM Brig Derwent - When taken: 29 Jan 1813 - Where taken: off Lisbon - Date received: 25 Feb 1813 - From what ship: HMS Brazen - Born: New Haven, CT - Age: 21 - Discharged on 23 Jul 1814 and sent to Dartmoor on HMS Acasta.

Kinder, Ephraim G. - Seaman - Number: 2974 - Prize name: Enterprise - Ship type: P - How taken: HM Frigate Tenedos - When taken: 21 May 1813 - Where taken: off Cape Cod - Date received: 7 Jan 1814 - From what ship: Halifax - Born: Massachusetts - Age: 25 - Discharged on 25 Sep 1814 and sent to Dartmoor on HMS Leyden.

King, John - Seaman - Number: 1905 - Prize name: Weasel - Ship type: MV - How taken: HM Brig Foxhound - When taken: 25 Mar 1813 - Where taken: Bay of Biscay - Date received: 7 Jul 1813 - From what ship: Portsmouth via HMS Tribune - Born: New York - Age: 20 - Discharged on 4 Aug 1814 and sent to Dartmoor on HMS Liverpool.

King, Peter - Seaman - Number: 3499 - How taken: Gave himself up from HM Ship-of-the-Line Bulwark - Date received: 23 Feb 1814 - From what ship: Portsmouth via HMT Malabar - Born: Boston - Age: 40 - Discharged on 22 Oct 1814 and sent to Dartmoor on HMS Leyden.

King, Solomon - Prize Master - Number: 2824 - Prize name: Portsmouth Packet - Ship type: P - How taken: HM Brig Fantome - When taken: 5 Oct 1813 - Where taken: off Portland - Date received: 7 Jan 1814 - From what ship: Halifax - Born: New York - Age: 27 - Discharged on 25 Sep 1814 and sent to Dartmoor on HMS Leyden.

King, William - Private - Number: 3104 - Prize name: 14th U.S. Infantry - Ship type: LF - How taken: British forces - When taken: 24 Jun 1813 - Where taken: Beaver Dams, Upper Canada - Date received: 7 Jan 1814 - From what ship: Halifax - Born: Maryland - Age: 27 - Discharged on 10 Oct 1814 and sent to U.S. on Cartel St. Philip.

Kingbutton, John - Seaman - Number: 2882 - Prize name: Taken off an English whaler - How taken: HM Ship-of-the-Line Illustrious - When taken: 22 Oct 1813 - Where taken: at sea - Date received: 7 Jan 1814 - From what ship: Portsmouth - Born: Providence - Age: 26 - Discharged on 25 Sep 1814 and sent to Dartmoor on HMS Leyden.

Kingley, Benjamin - Seaman - Number: 1427 - How taken: Taken off the HM Frigate Andromache - When taken: 24 Dec 1812 - Date received: 6 Apr 1813 - From what ship: Plymouth via HMS Decoy - Born: Nobleboro -

Age: 35 - Discharged on 24 Jul 1814 and sent to Dartmoor.

Kinlay, Joseph - Seaman - Number: 1409 - Prize name: Porcupine - Ship type: MV - How taken: HM Frigate Dryand - When taken: 8 Jan 1813 - Where taken: off Bordeaux, France - Date received: 5 Apr 1813 - From what ship: Plymouth via HMS Dwarf - Born: New Haven - Age: 19 - Discharged on 24 Jul 1813 and released to Cartel Hoffminy.

Kinnard, Charles - Carpenter - Number: 2896 - Prize name: Dart - Ship type: P - How taken: HM Frigate Niger & HMS Fortunee - When taken: 10 Nov 1813 - Where taken: off Cape Finisterre, Spain - Date received: 7 Jan 1814 - From what ship: Portsmouth - Born: New Orleans - Age: 27 - Discharged on 22 Jun 1814 and sent to Calais, France on the Simon & Mary.

Kinnard, George - Seaman - Number: 2933 - Prize name: Governor Plumer - Ship type: P - How taken: HM Brig Shamrock - When taken: 26 May 1813 - Where taken: at sea - Date received: 7 Jan 1814 - From what ship: Halifax - Born: New Hampshire - Age: 21 - Discharged on 25 Sep 1814 and sent to Dartmoor on HMS Leyden.

Kinot, Robert - Captain - Number: 3478 - Prize name: Volunteer - Ship type: MV - How taken: Vittoria, British privateer from Guernsey - When taken: 28 Dec 1813 - Where taken: Bay of Biscay - Date received: 23 Feb 1814 - From what ship: Halifax via HMT Malabar - Born: Nantucket - Age: 49 - Discharged on 28 Feb 1814 and sent to Reading on parole.

Kirby, Benjamin - 2nd Mate - Number: 1457 - Prize name: Union - Ship type: MV - How taken: HM Frigate Iris - When taken: 17 Jan 1813 - Where taken: at sea - Date received: 6 Apr 1813 - From what ship: Plymouth via HMS Decoy - Born: Philadelphia - Age: 24 - Discharged on 24 Jul 1813 and released to Cartel Hoffminy.

Kirkpatrick, William - Seaman - Number: 2452 - Prize name: Wiley Reynard - Ship type: P - How taken: HM Frigate Shannon - When taken: 16 Aug 1812 - Where taken: off Halifax - Date received: 21 Oct 1813 - From what ship: Portsmouth via HMT Malabar - Born: Wilmington - Age: 28 - Discharged on 4 Sep 1814 and sent to Dartmoor on HMS Freya.

Kitchen, Daniel - Mate - Number: 3729 - Prize name: Argus - Ship type: MV - How taken: HM Ship-of-the-Line San Domingo - When taken: 1 Mar 1814 - Where taken: off Savannah - Date received: 26 May 1814 - From what ship: HMS Hindostan - Born: West Chester - Age: 31 - Discharged on 25 Sep 1814 and sent to Dartmoor on HMS Niobe.

Knapp, Ezekiel - Seaman - Number: 266 - Prize name: Mandrel - Ship type: MV - How taken: Apprehended at London - When taken: 7 Dec 1812 - Date received: 7 Dec 1812 - From what ship: HMS Raisonnable - Born: Greenwich, CT - Age: 41 - Discharged on 24 Jul 1813 and released to Cartel Hoffminy.

Knapp, Samuel - Seaman - Number: 3181 - Prize name: Wolf Cove - Ship type: MV - How taken: HM Frigate Briton - When taken: 1 Dec 1813 - Where taken: off Brest, France - Date received: 7 Jan 1813 - From what ship: Halifax - Born: Massachusetts - Age: 24 - Discharged on 25 Sep 1814 and sent to Dartmoor on HMS Leyden.

Knapp, Walker - Seaman - Number: 638 - Prize name: Rhode & Betsey - Ship type: MV - How taken: HM Sloop Talbot - When taken: 12 Aug 1812 - Where taken: off Cape Clear, Ireland - Date received: 23 Feb 1813 - From what ship: Portsmouth via HMS Dromedary - Born: Stanford - Age: 21 - Discharged on 2 Jul 1813 and released to Cartel Moses Brown.

Knight, Daniel - Seaman - Number: 2772 - Prize name: Thomas - Ship type: P - How taken: HM Frigate Nymphe - When taken: 24 Jun 1813 - Where taken: off Halifax - Date received: 7 Jan 1814 - From what ship: Halifax - Born: Massachusetts - Age: 28 - Discharged on 8 Sep 1814 and sent to Dartmoor on HMS Niobe.

Knight, George - Seaman - Number: 884 - Prize name: Print of Boston - Ship type: MV - How taken: HM Ship-of-the-Line Colossus - When taken: 21 Jan 1813 - Where taken: at sea - Date received: 1 Mar 1813 - From what ship: Plymouth via HMS Namur - Born: Marblehead, MA - Age: 25 - Discharged on 17 Jun 1814 and sent to Dartmoor on HMS Redbreast.

Knight, Isaac D. - Boy - Number: 1501 - Prize name: Union - Ship type: MV - How taken: HM Frigate Iris - When taken: 17 Jan 1813 - Where taken: at sea - Date received: 6 Apr 1813 - From what ship: Plymouth via an admiral's tender - Born: Philadelphia - Age: 10 - Discharged on 27 Jul 1813 and released to Cartel Hoffminy.

Knight, William - Seaman - Number: 886 - Prize name: Print of Boston - Ship type: MV - How taken: HM Ship-of-the-Line Colossus - When taken: 21 Jan 1813 - Where taken: at sea - Date received: 1 Mar 1813 - From what ship: Plymouth via HMS Namur - Born: Marblehead, MA - Age: 19 - Discharged on 17 Jun 1814 and sent to Dartmoor on HMS Redbreast.

Knight, Zachariah - Seaman - Number: 579 - How taken: Gave himself up from HM Ship-of-the-Line Victory - When taken: 18 Dec 1812 - Date received: 23 Feb 1813 - From what ship: Portsmouth via HMS Dromedary - Born: Portland - Age: 26 - Discharged on 26 Jul 1814 and sent to Dartmoor on HMS Raven.

Knox, Thomas - Seaman - Number: 444 - Prize name: Hunter - Ship type: P - How taken: HM Frigate Phoebe - When taken: 23 Dec 1812 - Where taken: off Azores - Date received: 19 Feb 1813 - From what ship: HMS Modeste - Born: Boston - Age: 52 - Discharged on 2 Jul 1813 and released to Cartel Moses Brown.

Kraft, Michael - Seaman - Number: 2717 - Prize name: Growler - Ship type: P - How taken: HM Brig Electra - When taken: 7 Jul 1813 - Where taken: off St. Johns - Date received: 7 Jan 1814 - From what ship: Portsmouth - Born: Pennsylvania - Age: 21 - Discharged on 25 Sep 1814 and sent to Dartmoor on HMS Leyden.

Kylor, John - Seaman - Number: 3949 - How taken: Impressed at London - When taken: 13 Oct 1814 - Date received: 21 Oct 1813 - From what ship: Quebec - Born: Bollington - Age: 36 - Discharged on 22 Oct 1814 and sent to Dartmoor on HMS Leyden.

La Roche, Jean - Seaman - Number: 2914 - Prize name: Pomona, prize of Privateer Prince de Neuchatel - Ship type: P - How taken: HM Frigate Ethalion - When taken: 14 Dec 1813 - Where taken: at sea - Date received: 7 Jan 1814 - From what ship: Portsmouth - Born: New Orleans - Age: 24 - Discharged on 23 Oct 1814 and sent to Dartmoor on HMS Leyden.

Labbas, John - Seaman - Number: 1249 - Prize name: Industry - Ship type: MV - How taken: HM Frigate Dryand - When taken: 7 Jan 1813 - Where taken: at sea - Date received: 16 Mar 1813 - From what ship: Portsmouth, via HMS Abundance - Born: New Orleans - Age: 25 - Discharged on 2 Jul 1813 and released to Cartel Moses Brown.

Lackey, Joseph - Seaman - Number: 2962 - Prize name: Enterprise - Ship type: P - How taken: HM Frigate Tenedos - When taken: 21 May 1813 - Where taken: off Cape Cod - Date received: 7 Jan 1814 - From what ship: Halifax - Born: Massachusetts - Age: 30 - Discharged on 25 Sep 1814 and sent to Dartmoor on HMS Leyden.

Lake, George - Seaman - Number: 3421 - Prize name: Thomas - Ship type: P - How taken: HM Frigate Nymphe - When taken: 27 Jun 1813 - Where taken: at sea - Date received: 23 Feb 1814 - From what ship: Halifax via HMT Malabar - Born: Cumberland - Age: 22 - Race: Black - Discharged on 21 Jul 1814 and sent to Dartmoor on HMS Portia.

Lake, Noah - Seaman - Number: 1115 - How taken: Gave himself up from the Gosport Rendezvous - Date received: 14 Mar 1813 - From what ship: Portsmouth via HMS Beagle - Born: Rhode Island - Age: 26 - Discharged on 17 Jun 1813 and released to HMS Ceres.

Lakeman, Samuel - Seaman - Number: 698 - Prize name: Deanna, recaptured British vessel - Ship type: P - How taken: HM Ship-of-the-Line Polyphemus - When taken: 14 Sep 1812 - Where taken: at sea - Date received: 24 Feb 1813 - From what ship: Portsmouth via HMS Ulysses - Born: Ipswich, MA - Age: 24 - Discharged on 8 Jun 1813 and released to Cartel Rodrigo.

Lalan, John - Seaman - Number: 781 - Prize name: Eliza - Ship type: MV - How taken: HM Sloop Hyacinth - When taken: 27 Aug 1812 - Where taken: off Gibraltar - Date received: 27 Feb 1813 - From what ship: Plymouth via HMS Namur - Born: St. Johns, SC - Age: 23 - Discharged on 10 May 1813 and released to Cartel Admittance.

Lamb, Jack - Cook - Number: 2344 - Prize name: Hindostan - Ship type: MV - How taken: HM Brig Zenobia - When taken: 25 Jun 1813 - Where taken: off Lisbon - Date received: 20 Oct 1813 - From what ship: Portsmouth, via an admiral's tender - Born: Africa - Age: 20 - Race: Black - Discharged on 4 Sep 1814 and sent to Dartmoor on HMS Freya.

Lambert, Calvin - Seaman - Number: 3474 - Prize name: Yankee - Ship type: P - How taken: HM Frigate Shannon -

When taken: 20 Aug 1813 - Where taken: at sea - Date received: 23 Feb 1814 - From what ship: Halifax via HMT Malabar - Born: Manchester - Age: 18 - Discharged on 22 Oct 1814 and sent to Dartmoor on HMS Leyden.

Lambert, Ephraim - Seaman - Number: 3287 - Prize name: Vivid - Ship type: P - How taken: HM Frigate Nymphe - When taken: 20 Apr 1813 - Where taken: off Cape Cod - Date received: 23 Feb 1814 - From what ship: Halifax via HMT Malabar - Born: Truro - Age: 19 - Discharged on 10 Oct 1814 and sent to Dartmoor on the Mermaid.

Lambert, John - Seaman - Number: 1143 - Prize name: Sword Fish - Ship type: P - How taken: HM Ship-of-the-Line Elephant - When taken: 28 Dec 1812 - Where taken: off Azores - Date received: 16 Mar 1813 - From what ship: Portsmouth, Mundane - Born: Woolwich, MA - Age: 22 - Discharged on 24 Jul 1813 and released to Cartel Hoffminy.

Lamboard, Thomas - Seaman - Number: 2324 - How taken: Gave himself up from HM Ship-of-the-Line Ville de Paris - When taken: 1 Jun 1813 - Date received: 8 Oct 1813 - From what ship: Portsmouth, via an admiral's tender - Born: Massachusetts - Age: 39 - Race: Black - Discharged on 25 Sep 1814 and sent to Dartmoor on HMS Leyden.

Lamon, James - Seaman - Number: 1241 - Prize name: Rossie - Ship type: MV - How taken: HM Frigate Dryand - When taken: 7 Jan 1813 - Where taken: at sea - Date received: 16 Mar 1813 - From what ship: Portsmouth, via HMS Abundance - Born: Wilmington - Age: 36 - Race: Black - Discharged on 24 Jul 1813 and released to Cartel Hoffminy.

Lamon, John - Seaman - Number: 199 - Prize name: Iris - Ship type: MV - How taken: Impressed at Great Belt, Denmark - When taken: 26 Jul 1812 - Date received: 12 Nov 1812 - From what ship: HMS Raisonnable - Born: Elizabeth, NJ - Age: 22 - Discharged on 24 Feb 1813 and released to HMS Ceres.

Lamson, Amos - Seaman - Number: 2959 - Prize name: Enterprise - Ship type: P - How taken: HM Frigate Tenedos - When taken: 21 May 1813 - Where taken: off Cape Cod - Date received: 7 Jan 1814 - From what ship: Halifax - Born: Massachusetts - Age: 20 - Discharged on 25 Sep 1814 and sent to Dartmoor on HMS Leyden.

Lamson, Noah - Seaman - Number: 3276 - Prize name: Cossack - Ship type: MV - How taken: HM Brig Curlew - When taken: 22 Apr 1813 - Where taken: Indian Island - Date received: 23 Feb 1814 - From what ship: Halifax via HMT Malabar - Born: Plymouth - Age: 17 - Discharged on 10 Oct 1814 and sent to Dartmoor on the Mermaid.

Lanigan, Daniel - Seaman - Number: 3923 - How taken: Gave himself up from HM Ship-of-the-Line Revenge - When taken: 23 Sep 1814 - Date received: 24 Sep 1814 - From what ship: HMS Namur - Born: Beverly - Age: 47 - Discharged on 29 Sep 1814 and sent to Dartmoor on HMS Freya.

Landback, Rich - Seaman - Number: 1177 - Prize name: Sword Fish - Ship type: P - How taken: HM Ship-of-the-Line Elephant - When taken: 28 Dec 1812 - Where taken: off Azores - Date received: 16 Mar 1813 - From what ship: Portsmouth, via HMS Abundance - Born: New Hampshire - Age: 25 - Discharged on 24 Jul 1813 and released to Cartel Hoffminy.

Lane, James - Prize Master - Number: 2911 - Prize name: Pomona, prize of Privateer Prince de Neuchatel - Ship type: P - How taken: HM Frigate Ethalion - When taken: 14 Dec 1813 - Where taken: at sea - Date received: 7 Jan 1814 - From what ship: Portsmouth - Born: Massachusetts - Age: 39 - Discharged on 25 Sep 1814 and sent to Dartmoor on HMS Leyden.

Lane, John - Boy - Number: 752 - Prize name: Quebec of London, prize of the Privateer Paul Jones - Ship type: P - How taken: HM Brig Derwent - When taken: 29 Jan 1813 - Where taken: off Lisbon - Date received: 25 Feb 1813 - From what ship: HMS Brazen - Born: New York - Age: 18 - Discharged on 23 Jul 1814 and sent to Dartmoor on HMS Acasta.

Lane, William - Seaman - Number: 3493 - How taken: Gave himself up from HM Sloop Comet - When taken: 2 Feb 1814 - Date received: 23 Feb 1814 - From what ship: Portsmouth via HMT Malabar - Born: New York - Age: 32 - Discharged on 21 Jul 1814 and sent to Dartmoor on HMS Portia.

Lane, William - Seaman - Number: 2916 - Prize name: Wiley Reynard - Ship type: P - How taken: HM Frigate

Shannon - When taken: 14 Oct 1812 - Where taken: off Halifax - Date received: 7 Jan 1814 - From what ship: Halifax - Born: Boston - Age: 30 - Discharged on 25 Sep 1814 and sent to Dartmoor on HMS Leyden.

Langford, Samuel - Seaman - Number: 2765 - Prize name: Thomas - Ship type: P - How taken: HM Frigate Nymphe - When taken: 24 Jun 1813 - Where taken: off Halifax - Date received: 7 Jan 1814 - From what ship: Halifax - Born: Massachusetts - Age: 18 - Discharged on 8 Sep 1814 and sent to Dartmoor on HMS Niobe.

Langroth, Francis - Seaman - Number: 1422 - How taken: Gave himself up from MV Martial - When taken: 7 Jan 1813 - Date received: 5 Apr 1813 - From what ship: Plymouth via HMS Dwarf - Born: Hungary - Age: 33 - Discharged on 25 Sep 1814 and sent to Dartmoor.

Lant, Henry - Seaman - Number: 3458 - Prize name: Elbridge Gerry - Ship type: P - How taken: HM Frigate Crescent - When taken: 16 Sep 1813 - Where taken: at sea - Date received: 23 Feb 1814 - From what ship: Halifax via HMT Malabar - Born: Bath - Age: 18 - Died on 14 Apr 1814 from fever.

Lapham, Cushion - Prize Master - Number: 1119 - Prize name: Quebec of London, prize of the Privateer Paul Jones - Ship type: P - How taken: HM Brig Derwent - When taken: 29 Jan 1813 - Where taken: off Lisbon - Date received: 14 Mar 1813 - From what ship: Portsmouth via HMS Beagle - Born: Ring - Age: 32 - Discharged on 11 Aug 1814 and sent to Dartmoor on HMS Freya.

Lappish, Andrew - Sergeant - Number: 2818 - Prize name: Portsmouth Packet - Ship type: P - How taken: HM Brig Fantome - When taken: 5 Oct 1813 - Where taken: off Portland - Date received: 7 Jan 1814 - From what ship: Halifax - Born: Hampshire - Age: 24 - Discharged on 25 Sep 1814 and sent to Dartmoor on HMS Leyden.

Larrabee, Thomas - Seaman - Number: 2837 - Prize name: Portsmouth Packet - Ship type: P - How taken: HM Brig Fantome - When taken: 5 Oct 1813 - Where taken: off Portland - Date received: 7 Jan 1814 - From what ship: Halifax - Born: Massachusetts - Age: 21 - Discharged on 25 Sep 1814 and sent to Dartmoor on HMS Leyden.

Larey, Henry - Seaman - Number: 3945 - How taken: Impressed at St. Johns - When taken: 1 May 1814 - Date received: 10 Oct 1814 - From what ship: Quebec - Born: New York - Age: 25 - Discharged on 22 Oct 1814 and sent to Dartmoor on HMS Leyden.

Larkins, Thomas - Seaman - Number: 275 - How taken: Apprehended at London - When taken: 10 Dec 1812 - Date received: 23 Dec 1812 - From what ship: HMS Raisonnable - Born: Baltimore - Age: 20 - Discharged on 24 Jul 1813 and released to Cartel Hoffminy.

Laskey, Benjamin - Seaman - Number: 2814 - Prize name: Industry - Ship type: P - How taken: HM Brig Heron - When taken: 3 Nov 1813 - Where taken: off Halifax - Date received: 7 Jan 1814 - From what ship: Halifax - Born: Marblehead - Age: 18 - Discharged on 8 Sep 1814 and sent to Dartmoor on HMS Niobe.

Latham, John - Seaman - Number: 2113 - How taken: Gave himself up from HM Brig Shearwater - When taken: 27 May 1813 - Date received: 9 Aug 1813 - From what ship: HMS Thames - Born: New York - Age: 25 - Discharged on 12 Aug 1814 and sent to Dartmoor on HMS Alpheus.

Lathrope, Gurdon - Master - Number: 1707 - Prize name: Decatur - Ship type: MV - How taken: HM Frigate Desiree - When taken: 7 May 1813 - Where taken: off Nantes, France - Date received: 25 May 1813 - From what ship: Portsmouth via HMS Impetius - Born: New Castle - Age: 27 - Discharged on 3 Jun 1813 and sent to Reading on parole.

Lathrum, William - Private - Number: 3111 - Prize name: 14th U.S. Infantry - Ship type: LF - How taken: British forces - When taken: 24 Jun 1813 - Where taken: Beaver Dams, Upper Canada - Date received: 7 Jan 1814 - From what ship: Halifax - Born: Marblehead - Age: 30 - Died on 1 May 1814 from fever.

Latimer, John - Seaman - Number: 769 - Prize name: Margarethe - Ship type: MV - How taken: HM Ship-of-the-Line San Juan - When taken: 8 May 1812 - Where taken: Gibraltar - Date received: 25 Feb 1813 - From what ship: HMS Brazen - Born: Philadelphia - Age: 19 - Discharged on 10 May 1813 and released to Cartel Admittance.

Latish, Joseph - Boy - Number: 643 - Prize name: Purse - Ship type: MV - How taken: HM Frigate Armide - When taken: 20 May 1812 - Where taken: off Bordeaux, France - Date received: 24 Feb 1813 - From what ship: Portsmouth via HMS Ulysses - Born: Philadelphia - Age: 10 - Discharged on 17 Nov 1813 to the Cartel

Robinson Potter.

Lauson, Isaac - Seaman - Number: 276 - Prize name: Messenger - Ship type: MV - How taken: Apprehended at London - When taken: 14 Dec 1812 - Date received: 23 Dec 1812 - From what ship: HMS Raisonnable - Born: Virginia - Age: 29 - Race: Mulatto - Discharged on 24 Jul 1813 and released to Cartel Hoffminy.

Law, John - Seaman - Number: 843 - Prize name: Vengeance - Ship type: LM - How taken: HM Frigate Phoebe - When taken: 1 Jan 1813 - Where taken: Lat 44.4 Long 23 - Date received: 1 Mar 1813 - From what ship: Plymouth via HMS Namur - Born: Robinstown - Age: 23 - Discharged on 24 Jul 1813 and released to Cartel Hoffminy.

Lawdy, Benjamin - 2nd Mate - Number: 281 - Prize name: Francis Ann - Ship type: MV - How taken: Apprehended at Leight, Scotland - When taken: 5 Aug 1812 - Date received: 23 Dec 1812 - From what ship: Greenlaw Depot - Born: Long Island - Age: 20 - Discharged on 23 Mar 1813 and released to the Cartel Robinson Potter.

Lawrence, David - Seaman - Number: 1550 - Prize name: Industry, prize to Privateer Decatur - Ship type: P - How taken: Channel fleet - When taken: 7 Dec 1812 - Where taken: Channel - Date received: 8 Apr 1813 - From what ship: Plymouth via HMS Olympia - Born: Newburyport - Age: 18 - Discharged on 2 Jul 1813 and released to Cartel Moses Brown.

Lawrence, George - Seaman - Number: 2477 - Prize name: Juliana Smith - Ship type: P - How taken: HM Frigate Nymphe - When taken: 12 May 1813 - Where taken: off Cape Sable, Florida - Date received: 22 Oct 1813 - From what ship: Portsmouth via HMT Malabar - Born: Alexandria - Age: 20 - Discharged on 8 Sep 1814 and sent to Dartmoor on HMS Niobe.

Lawrence, Peter - Seaman - Number: 1140 - Prize name: Sword Fish - Ship type: P - How taken: HM Ship-of-the-Line Elephant - When taken: 28 Dec 1812 - Where taken: off Azores - Date received: 16 Mar 1813 - From what ship: Portsmouth, Mundane - Born: Petersburg - Age: 21 - Race: Black - Discharged on 24 Jul 1813 and released to Cartel Hoffminy.

Lawrence, Robert - Seaman - Number: 2019 - How taken: Gave himself up from HMS Decoy - Date received: 15 Jul 1813 - From what ship: Plymouth - Born: Boston - Age: 27 - Discharged on 17 Jun 1814 and sent to Dartmoor on HMS Pincher.

Laws, Peter - Seaman - Number: 2279 - How taken: Impressed at London - When taken: 3 Sep 1813 - Date received: 17 Sep 1813 - From what ship: HMS Raisonnable - Born: New York - Age: 30 - Race: Black - Discharged on 4 Sep 1814 and sent to Dartmoor on HMS Freya.

Lawson, James - Seaman - Number: 1818 - Prize name: tender to the Privateer True Blooded Yankee - Ship type: P - How taken: HM Ship-of-the-Line Fame - When taken: 24 Jun 1813 - Where taken: off Brest, France - Date received: 7 Jul 1813 - From what ship: Portsmouth via HMS Scorpion - Born: New York - Age: 48 - Released on 11 Jul 1814.

Lawson, Lawrence - Seaman - Number: 1836 - Prize name: tender to the Privateer True Blooded Yankee - Ship type: P - How taken: HM Ship-of-the-Line Fame - When taken: 24 Jun 1813 - Where taken: off Brest, France - Date received: 7 Jul 1813 - From what ship: Portsmouth via HMS Scorpion - Born: Old York - Age: 26 - Discharged on 7 Jun 1813 and released to HMS Ceres.

Lawson, Mathew - Seaman - Number: 588 - Prize name: Antelope - Ship type: P - How taken: HM Brig Zephyr - When taken: 10 Dec 1812 - Where taken: at sea - Date received: 23 Feb 1813 - From what ship: Portsmouth via HMS Dromedary - Born: Baltimore - Age: 31 - Discharged on 2 Jul 1813 and released to Cartel Moses Brown.

Lawson, Peter - Seaman - Number: 373 - Prize name: Navigator - Ship type: MV - How taken: HM Ship-of-the-Line Cressy - When taken: 11 Aug 1812 - Where taken: Baltic - Date received: 21 Jan 1813 - From what ship: HMS Raisonnable - Born: Fronham, Norway - Age: 36 - Released on 19 Mar 1813 to HMS Navigator.

Lawson, Thomas - Seaman - Number: 2773 - Prize name: Thomas - Ship type: P - How taken: HM Frigate Nymphe - When taken: 24 Jun 1813 - Where taken: off Halifax - Date received: 7 Jan 1814 - From what ship: Halifax - Born: Massachusetts - Age: 27 - Discharged on 25 Sep 1814 and sent to Dartmoor on HMS Leyden.

Lawton, William - Seaman - Number: 3649 - Prize name: Bunker Hill - Ship type: P - How taken: HM Frigate

Pomone & HM Frigate Cydnus - When taken: 4 Mar 1814 - Where taken: Bay of Biscay - Date received: 31 Mar 1814 - From what ship: HMS Raisonnable - Born: Portsmouth - Age: 28 - Discharged on 25 Sep 1814 and sent to Dartmoor on HMS Niobe.

Laycock, Thomas - Seaman - Number: 116 - Prize name: Urbana - Ship type: MV - How taken: Stopped at London - When taken: 26 Oct 1812 - Date received: 4 Nov 1812 - From what ship: HMS Namur - Born: Norfolk, VA - Age: 26 - Discharged in Jul 1813 and released to Cartel Moses Brown.

Layton, William - Boy - Number: 1950 - Prize name: Gleamer - Ship type: MV - How taken: Brothers, British privateer - When taken: 16 Mar 1813 - Where taken: Bay of Biscay - Date received: 15 Jul 1813 - From what ship: Plymouth - Born: Castine - Age: 18 - Discharged on 17 Jun 1814 and sent to Dartmoor on HMS Redbreast.

Le Goff, Herve - Boy - Number: 3687 - Prize name: Bunker Hill - Ship type: P - How taken: HM Frigate Pomone & HM Frigate Cydnus - When taken: 4 Mar 1814 - Where taken: Bay of Biscay - Date received: 4 May 1814 - From what ship: Portsmouth - Born: Brest, France - Age: 10 - Discharged on 22 Jun 1814 and sent to Calais, France on the Simon & Mary.

Le Moor, John - Seaman - Number: 2756 - Prize name: Globe - Ship type: P - How taken: HM Frigate Spartan - When taken: 13 Jun 1813 - Where taken: off Delaware - Date received: 7 Jan 1814 - From what ship: Halifax - Born: New York - Age: 23 - Race: Black - Discharged on 25 Sep 1814 and sent to Dartmoor on HMS Leyden.

Le Petit, John Baptiste - Boy - Number: 3688 - Prize name: Bunker Hill - Ship type: P - How taken: HM Frigate Pomone & HM Frigate Cydnus - When taken: 4 Mar 1814 - Where taken: Bay of Biscay - Date received: 4 May 1814 - From what ship: Portsmouth - Born: Caen, France - Age: 18 - Escaped on 20 May 1814 from HM Prison Ship Glory.

Leach, Benjamin - Seaman - Number: 799 - Prize name: Dolphin - Ship type: MV - How taken: HM Ship-of-the-Line Colossus - When taken: 5 Jan 1813 - Where taken: off the Western Isles, Scotland - Date received: 27 Feb 1813 - From what ship: Plymouth via HMS Namur - Born: Virginia - Age: 24 - Discharged on 24 Jul 1813 and released to Cartel Hoffminy.

Leach, Charles - Seaman - Number: 3653 - Prize name: prize to the Privateer Blockade - Ship type: P - How taken: HM Sloop Sapphire - When taken: 24 Feb 1814 - Where taken: coast of America - Date received: 31 Mar 1814 - From what ship: HMS Raisonnable - Born: Salem - Age: 27 - Discharged on 22 Oct 1814 and sent to Dartmoor on HMS Leyden.

Leach, Charles - Sailing Master - Number: 411 - Prize name: Hunter - Ship type: P - How taken: HM Frigate Phoebe - When taken: 23 Dec 1812 - Where taken: off Azores - Date received: 19 Feb 1813 - From what ship: HMS Modeste - Born: Salem - Age: 26 - Discharged on 2 Jul 1813 and released to Cartel Moses Brown.

Leach, Daniel - Seaman - Number: 2836 - Prize name: Portsmouth Packet - Ship type: P - How taken: HM Brig Fantome - When taken: 5 Oct 1813 - Where taken: off Portland - Date received: 7 Jan 1814 - From what ship: Halifax - Born: Massachusetts - Age: 52 - Discharged on 25 Sep 1814 and sent to Dartmoor on HMS Leyden.

Leach, James - Seaman - Number: 302 - Prize name: Cygnet - Ship type: MV - How taken: HM Brig Sarpedon - When taken: 12 Aug 1812 - Date received: 23 Dec 1812 - From what ship: Greenlaw Depot - Born: Thornton - Age: 47 - Discharged on 10 May 1813 and released to Cartel Admittance.

Lear, Alexander - Seaman - Number: 1136 - Prize name: Sword Fish - Ship type: P - How taken: HM Ship-of-the-Line Elephant - When taken: 28 Dec 1812 - Where taken: off Azores - Date received: 16 Mar 1813 - From what ship: Portsmouth, Mundane - Born: Portsmouth - Age: 47 - Discharged on 24 Jul 1813 and released to Cartel Hoffminy.

LeBaron, Peter - Seaman - Number: 2190 - Prize name: True Blooded Yankee - Ship type: P - How taken: HM Frigate Hamadryad - When taken: 24 Jul 1813 - Where taken: off Norway - Date received: 17 Aug 1813 - From what ship: HMS Raisonnable - Born: Cape Ann - Age: 28 - Discharged on 11 Aug 1814 and sent to Dartmoor on HMS Freya.

Lebon, Philip - Seaman - Number: 620 - Prize name: King of Rome - Ship type: P - How taken: HM Brig Wolverine

- When taken: 13 Dec 1812 - Where taken: at sea - Date received: 23 Feb 1813 - From what ship: Portsmouth via HMS Dromedary - Born: New Orleans - Age: 25 - Discharged on 2 Jul 1813 and released to Cartel Moses Brown.

Lebour, Francois - Seaman - Number: 3685 - Prize name: Bunker Hill - Ship type: P - How taken: HM Frigate Pomone & HM Frigate Cydnus - When taken: 4 Mar 1814 - Where taken: Bay of Biscay - Date received: 4 May 1814 - From what ship: Portsmouth - Born: Brest, France - Age: 29 - Discharged on 22 Jun 1814 and sent to Calais, France on the Simon & Mary.

Ledlowe, John - Seaman - Number: 635 - How taken: Gave himself up from HM Ship-of-the-Line Vigo - When taken: 31 Dec 1812 - Date received: 23 Feb 1813 - From what ship: Portsmouth via HMS Dromedary - Born: New Bedford - Age: 36 - Race: Black man - Died on 23 Mar 1813.

Lee, Edward - Seaman - Number: 1658 - How taken: Gave himself up from HM Ship-of-the-Line Scepter - Date received: 9 May 1813 - From what ship: HMS Raisonnable - Born: Maryland - Age: 25 - Race: Mulatto - Discharged on 13 Aug 1814 and sent to Dartmoor.

Lee, George - Cook - Number: 98 - Prize name: Frederick - Ship type: MV - How taken: Stopped at London - When taken: 26 Oct 1812 - Date received: 4 Nov 1812 - From what ship: HMS Namur - Born: Salem, MA - Age: 23 - Discharged in Jul 1813 and released to Cartel Moses Brown.

Lee, George - Seaman - Number: 1953 - Prize name: Ferox - Ship type: MV - How taken: HM Frigate Medusa & HM Brig Lyra - When taken: 28 Mar 1813 - Where taken: off Cape Ortegal, Spain - Date received: 15 Jul 1813 - From what ship: Plymouth - Born: New York - Age: 37 - Discharged on 17 Jun 1814 and sent to Dartmoor on HMS Redbreast.

Lee, Isaac - Seaman - Number: 2270 - Prize name: Eliza - Ship type: MV - How taken: HMS Charles - When taken: 20 Jul 1813 - Where taken: off Petershead, Scotland - Date received: 14 Sep 1813 - From what ship: HMS Raisonnable - Born: New York - Age: 19 - Discharged on 20 Aug 1814 and sent to Dartmoor on HMS Shamrock.

Lee, John - Seaman - Number: 3754 - Prize name: Argus - Ship type: MV - How taken: HM Ship-of-the-Line San Domingo - When taken: 1 Mar 1814 - Where taken: off Savannah - Date received: 26 May 1814 - From what ship: HMS Hindostan - Born: Providence - Age: 25 - Discharged on 25 Sep 1814 and sent to Dartmoor on HMS Niobe.

Lee, John - Seaman - Number: 3027 - How taken: Gave himself up from HMS Spectrum - When taken: 29 Oct 1813 - Date received: 7 Jan 1814 - From what ship: Portsmouth - Born: New Orleans - Age: 40 - Discharged on 11 Aug 1814 and sent to Dartmoor on HMS Freya.

Lee, Joseph - Seaman - Number: 1778 - How taken: Gave himself up at Chatham - When taken: 25 Jun 1813 - Date received: 21 Jun 1813 - From what ship: Chatham - Born: New York - Age: 25 - Discharged on 24 Jul 1814 and sent to Dartmoor on HMS Liffey.

Lee, Michael - Seaman - Number: 3446 - Prize name: Elbridge Gerry - Ship type: P - How taken: HM Frigate Crescent - When taken: 16 Sep 1813 - Where taken: at sea - Date received: 23 Feb 1814 - From what ship: Halifax via HMT Malabar - Born: North Carolina - Age: 22 - Discharged on 21 Jul 1814 and sent to Dartmoor on HMS Portia.

Lee, Nathaniel - Seaman - Number: 453 - Prize name: Hunter - Ship type: P - How taken: HM Frigate Phoebe - When taken: 23 Dec 1812 - Where taken: off Azores - Date received: 19 Feb 1813 - From what ship: HMS Modeste - Born: Manchester - Age: 48 - Discharged on 24 Jul 1813 and released to Cartel Hoffminy.

Lee, Nathaniel - Boy - Number: 2216 - Prize name: Growler - Ship type: P - How taken: HM Brig Electra - When taken: 7 Jul 1813 - Where taken: off St. Johns - Date received: 18 Aug 1813 - From what ship: Portsmouth, via an admiral's tender - Born: Marblehead - Age: 12 - Discharged on 11 Aug 1814 and sent to Dartmoor on HMS Freya.

Lee, Richard - Seaman - Number: 1154 - Prize name: Sword Fish - Ship type: P - How taken: HM Ship-of-the-Line Elephant - When taken: 28 Dec 1812 - Where taken: off Azores - Date received: 16 Mar 1813 - From what ship: Portsmouth, via HMS Abundance - Born: Marblehead - Age: 57 - Discharged on 24 Jul 1813 and released to Cartel Hoffminy.

Lee, Samuel - Seaman - Number: 1232 - Prize name: Rossie - Ship type: MV - How taken: HM Frigate Dryand - When taken: 7 Jan 1813 - Where taken: at sea - Date received: 16 Mar 1813 - From what ship: Portsmouth, via HMS Abundance - Born: Maryland - Age: 25 - Race: Black - Discharged on 24 Jul 1813 and released to Cartel Hoffminy.

Lee, Williams - Seaman - Number: 78 - Prize name: Cup - Ship type: MV - How taken: HM Brig Sarpedon - When taken: 12 Aug 1812 - Where taken: Great Belt, Denmark - Date received: 4 Nov 1812 - From what ship: HMS Namur - Born: Baltimore, MD - Age: 31 - Discharged on 10 May 1813 and released to Cartel Admittance.

Legere, Joseph - Seaman - Number: 628 - Prize name: King of Rome - Ship type: P - How taken: HM Brig Wolverine - When taken: 13 Dec 1812 - Where taken: at sea - Date received: 23 Feb 1813 - From what ship: Portsmouth via HMS Dromedary - Born: Tohe, Spain - Age: 34 - Discharged on 2 Jul 1813 and released to Cartel Moses Brown.

Legos, Philip - Seaman - Number: 2142 - Prize name: Matilda, prize of the U.S. Brig Argus - Ship type: War - How taken: HM Frigate Revolutionnaire - When taken: 25 Jul 1813 - Where taken: off Lorient, France - Date received: 9 Aug 1813 - From what ship: HMS Thames - Born: Massachusetts - Age: 31 - Discharged on 4 Aug 1814 and sent to Dartmoor on HMS Alpheus.

Leighton, Otis - Seaman - Number: 505 - How taken: Gave himself up from HM Ship-of-the-Line Ruby - When taken: 15 Aug 1812 - Date received: 23 Feb 1813 - From what ship: Portsmouth via HMS Dromedary - Born: Columbia - Age: 19 - Discharged on 19 May 1813 and released to HMS Ceres.

Leion, Alexander - Seaman - Number: 2001 - How taken: Gave himself up from HM Ship-of-the-Line Clarence - Date received: 15 Jul 1813 - From what ship: Plymouth - Born: Boston - Age: 20 - Discharged on 11 Aug 1814 and sent to Dartmoor on HMS Freya.

Lemeeker, Barner - Seaman - Number: 141 - Prize name: Davy Dearborn - Ship type: MV - How taken: Stopped at London - When taken: 26 Oct 1812 - Date received: 5 Nov 1812 - From what ship: HMS Namur - Born: Reading, CT - Age: 35 - Discharged in Jul 1813 and released to Cartel Moses Brown.

Lemmon, Henry - Seaman - Number: 1899 - Prize name: Weasel - Ship type: MV - How taken: HM Brig Foxhound - When taken: 25 Mar 1813 - Where taken: Bay of Biscay - Date received: 7 Jul 1813 - From what ship: Portsmouth via HMS Tribune - Born: Savannah - Age: 22 - Discharged on 1 Aug 1813 and released to HMS Ceres.

Lemon, Nicholas, C. - 2nd Lieutenant - Number: 2312 - Prize name: John - Ship type: P - How taken: HM Brig Peruvian - When taken: 6 Feb 1813 - Where taken: West Indies - Date received: 8 Oct 1813 - From what ship: Portsmouth, via an admiral's tender - Born: Marblehead - Age: 33 - Discharged on 13 Aug 1814 and sent to Dartmoor on HMS Freya.

Lenderson, Henry - Seaman - Number: 1052 - How taken: Taken off the HM Battery Princess at Liverpool - When taken: 26 Oct 1812 - Date received: 11 Mar 1813 - From what ship: Yarmouth via HMS Tenders - Born: New York - Age: 30 - Race: Black - Discharged on 19 May 1813 and released to HMS Ceres.

Lent, Joseph - Seaman - Number: 1369 - How taken: Gave himself up from HM Frigate Niobe - When taken: 13 Mar 1813 - Date received: 3 Apr 1813 - From what ship: Portsmouth, via an admiral's tender - Born: Salem - Age: 39 - Discharged on 24 Jul 1814 and sent to Dartmoor.

Lent, Samuel - Seaman - Number: 3940 - Prize name: Perseverance - Ship type: MV - How taken: HM Frigate Barbadoes - When taken: 29 Jan 1814 - Where taken: off St. Bartholomew, WI - Date received: 10 Oct 1814 - From what ship: Quebec - Born: Cumberland - Age: 27 - Discharged on 22 Oct 1814 and sent to Dartmoor on HMS Leyden.

Leonard, John - Seaman - Number: 2153 - How taken: Gave himself up at London - When taken: 4 Aug 1813 - Date received: 14 Aug 1813 - From what ship: HMS Raisonnable - Born: Sandwich - Age: 30 - Race: Mulatto - Discharged on 12 Aug 1814 and sent to Dartmoor on HMS Alpheus.

Leonard, Robert - Seaman - Number: 2418 - Prize name: Sampson - Ship type: MV - How taken: HM Brig Rebuff - When taken: 12 May 1813 - Where taken: off Cape St. Vincent, Portugal - Date received: 21 Oct 1813 - From what ship: Portsmouth via HMT Malabar - Born: New York - Age: 29 - Discharged on 4 Sep 1814 and sent to Dartmoor on HMS Freya.

Lerocque, Olivier (alias Peter Rock) - Seaman - Number: 3697 - Prize name: Bunker Hill - Ship type: P - How taken: HM Frigate Pomone & HM Frigate Cydnus - When taken: 4 Mar 1814 - Where taken: Bay of Biscay - Date received: 4 May 1814 - From what ship: Portsmouth - Born: New York - Age: 32 - Escaped on 20 May 1814 from HM Prison Ship Glory.

Lesaut, Jacques - Marine Private - Number: 3698 - Prize name: Bunker Hill - Ship type: P - How taken: HM Frigate Pomone & HM Frigate Cydnus - When taken: 4 Mar 1814 - Where taken: Bay of Biscay - Date received: 4 May 1814 - From what ship: Portsmouth - Born: Saint Pollion, France - Age: 22 - Escaped on 20 May 1814 from HM Prison Ship Glory.

Leserver, Florence - Seaman - Number: 1215 - Prize name: Leader - Ship type: MV - How taken: HM Frigate Briton - When taken: 10 Dec 1812 - Where taken: off Bordeaux, France - Date received: 16 Mar 1813 - From what ship: Portsmouth, via HMS Abundance - Born: Pembroke - Age: 20 - Discharged on 2 Jul 1813 and released to Cartel Moses Brown.

Levan, Thomas - Seaman - Number: 3021 - How taken: Gave himself up from HM Ship-of-the-Line Invincible - When taken: 14 Jan 1813 - Date received: 7 Jan 1814 - From what ship: Portsmouth - Born: New York - Age: 24 - Discharged on 26 Sep 1814 and sent to Dartmoor on HMS Leyden.

Lewis, Francis - Boy - Number: 267 - How taken: Apprehended at London - When taken: 1 Oct 1812 - Date received: 7 Dec 1812 - From what ship: HMS Raisonnable - Born: New York - Age: 16 - Discharged in Jul 1813 and released to Cartel Moses Brown.

Lewis, Gabriel - Seaman - Number: 1711 - Prize name: Decatur - Ship type: MV - How taken: HM Frigate Desiree - When taken: 7 May 1813 - Where taken: off Nantes, France - Date received: 25 May 1813 - From what ship: Portsmouth via HMS Impetius - Born: Virginia - Age: 23 - Discharged on 24 Jul 1814 and sent to Dartmoor on HMS Liffey.

Lewis, George - Seaman - Number: 1451 - Prize name: Orbit - Ship type: MV - How taken: HM Brig Achates - When taken: 29 Jan 1813 - Where taken: Lat 49 N Long 13 W - Date received: 6 Apr 1813 - From what ship: Plymouth via HMS Decoy - Born: Delaware - Age: 22 - Race: Negro - Discharged on 4 Jul 1813 and released to HMS Ceres.

Lewis, Henry - Seaman - Number: 3744 - Prize name: Argus - Ship type: MV - How taken: HM Ship-of-the-Line San Domingo - When taken: 1 Mar 1814 - Where taken: off Savannah - Date received: 26 May 1814 - From what ship: HMS Hindostan - Born: Barnstable - Age: 17 - Discharged on 25 Sep 1814 and sent to Dartmoor on HMS Niobe.

Lewis, Job - Seaman - Number: 3215 - Prize name: Volunteer - Ship type: MV - How taken: Vittoria, British privateer from Guernsey - When taken: 26 Dec 1813 - Where taken: Bay of Biscay - Date received: 13 Jan 1814 - From what ship: Portsmouth via HMS Poictiers - Born: New York - Age: 23 - Died on 19 Mar 1814 from fever.

Lewis, John - Seaman - Number: 3857 - How taken: Gave himself up from HM Frigate Theban - When taken: 24 Jun 1813 - Date received: 24 Aug 1814 - From what ship: London - Born: Annapolis - Age: 28 - Race: Black - Discharged on 26 Sep 1814 and sent to Dartmoor on HMS Leyden.

Lewis, John - Seaman - Number: 3536 - Prize name: Commodore Perry - Ship type: MV - How taken: Sent into custody from a cutter - When taken: 25 Feb 1814 - Where taken: off Bordeaux, France - Date received: 5 Mar 1814 - From what ship: HMS Raisonnable - Born: Amsterdam - Age: 26 - Released on 16 Jun 1814.

Lewis, John - Cook - Number: 856 - Prize name: Brutus - Ship type: MV - How taken: Briton, letter of marque - When taken: 13 Jan 1813 - Where taken: Bay of Biscay - Date received: 1 Mar 1813 - From what ship: Plymouth via HMS Namur - Born: New Orleans - Age: 45 - Race: Blackman - Discharged on 24 Jul 1813 and released to Cartel Hoffminy.

Lewis, John - Seaman - Number: 1058 - Prize name: Independence - Ship type: MV - How taken: HM Frigate Medusa - When taken: 9 Nov 1812 - Where taken: off San Sebastian, Spain - Date received: 11 Mar 1813 - From what ship: Yarmouth via HMS Tenders - Born: Maryland - Age: 25 - Race: Black - Discharged on 8 Jun 1813 and released to Cartel Rodrigo.

Lewis, John - Seaman - Number: 1361 - Prize name: Dart - Ship type: MV - How taken: HM Brig Doterel - When taken: 5 Mar 1813 - Where taken: at sea - Date received: 3 Apr 1813 - From what ship: Portsmouth, via an admiral's tender - Born: Natchez - Age: 27 - Race: Black - Discharged on 22 Oct 1814 and sent to Dartmoor on HMS Leyden.

Lewis, John - Seaman - Number: 621 - Prize name: King of Rome - Ship type: P - How taken: HM Brig Wolverine - When taken: 13 Dec 1812 - Where taken: at sea - Date received: 23 Feb 1813 - From what ship: Portsmouth via HMS Dromedary - Born: New Orleans - Age: 34 - Discharged on 2 Jul 1813 and released to Cartel Moses Brown.

Lewis, John - Seaman - Number: 3430 - Prize name: Juliana Smith - Ship type: P - How taken: HM Frigate Nymphe - When taken: 12 May 1813 - Where taken: off Cape Sable, Florida - Date received: 23 Feb 1814 - From what ship: Halifax via HMT Malabar - Born: Dundee - Age: 56 - Race: Black - Discharged on 22 Oct 1814 and sent to Dartmoor on HMS Leyden.

Lewis, Peter - Seaman - Number: 2728 - Prize name: Mary, prize to the Privateer True Blooded Yankee - Ship type: P - How taken: HM Ship of-the-Line Bellerophon - When taken: 16 Dec 1813 - Where taken: off Land's End, England - Date received: 7 Jan 1814 - From what ship: Portsmouth - Born: Charleston - Age: 34 - Discharged on 8 Sep 1814 and sent to Dartmoor on HMS Niobe.

Lewis, Raymond - Seaman - Number: 450 - Prize name: Hunter - Ship type: P - How taken: HM Frigate Phoebe - When taken: 23 Dec 1812 - Where taken: off Azores - Date received: 19 Feb 1813 - From what ship: HMS Modeste - Born: Earthorn - Age: 20 - Discharged on 24 Jul 1813 and released to Cartel Hoffminy.

Lewis, Solomon - Seaman - Number: 1805 - How taken: Impressed at London - When taken: 23 Jun 1813 - Date received: 3 Jul 1813 - From what ship: HMS Raisonnable - Born: Stratford - Age: 22 - Race: Blackman - Discharged on 25 Jul 1814 and sent to Dartmoor on HMS Bittern.

Lewis, Thomas - Seaman - Number: 3944 - How taken: Impressed at Trinidad - When taken: 9 Mar 1814 - Date received: 10 Oct 1814 - From what ship: Quebec - Born: Calais, France - Age: 31 - Race: Black - Discharged on 22 Oct 1814 and sent to Dartmoor on HMS Leyden.

Lewis, William - Seaman - Number: 3380 - Prize name: Yorktown - Ship type: P - How taken: HM Frigate Maidstone - When taken: 17 Jul 1813 - Where taken: Grand Banks - Date received: 23 Feb 1814 - From what ship: Halifax via HMT Malabar - Born: Leghorn - Age: 17 - Discharged on 10 Oct 1814 and sent to Dartmoor on the Mermaid.

Lexious, Peter - Seaman - Number: 46 - Prize name: General Blake - Ship type: MV - How taken: HM Brig Recruit - When taken: 11 Jun 1812 - Where taken: off Rhode Island - Date received: 3 Nov 1812 - From what ship: HMS Plover - Born: Rhode Island - Age: 30 - Discharged on 23 Mar 1813 and released to the Cartel Robinson Potter.

Liddle, John - Seaman - Number: 600 - Prize name: Antelope - Ship type: P - How taken: HM Brig Zephyr - When taken: 10 Dec 1812 - Where taken: at sea - Date received: 23 Feb 1813 - From what ship: Portsmouth via HMS Dromedary - Born: Dorchester - Age: 17 - Discharged on 2 Jul 1813 and released to Cartel Moses Brown.

Liddle, Morris - Seaman - Number: 1070 - How taken: Gave himself up from HM Frigate Ulysses - When taken: 13 Jan 1813 - Date received: 14 Mar 1813 - From what ship: Portsmouth via HMS Cornwell - Born: Philadelphia - Age: 24 - Discharged on 10 Jun 1813 and released to HMS Ceres.

Liemo, Frederick - Seaman - Number: 3696 - Prize name: Bunker Hill - Ship type: P - How taken: HM Frigate Pomone & HM Frigate Cydnus - When taken: 4 Mar 1814 - Where taken: Bay of Biscay - Date received: 4 May 1814 - From what ship: Portsmouth - Born: Stralsund, Sweden - Age: 28 - Discharged on 25 Sep 1814 and sent to Dartmoor on HMS Niobe.

Light, John - Lieutenant - Number: 2918 - Prize name: Juliana Smith - Ship type: P - How taken: HM Frigate Nymphe - When taken: 12 May 1813 - Where taken: off Cape Sable, Florida - Date received: 7 Jan 1814 - From what ship: Halifax - Born: New York - Age: 28 - Died on 10 Mar 1814 from fever.

Lilsle, Richard - Seaman - Number: 1740 - How taken: Gave himself up from HM Ship-of-the-Line Cornwall - When taken: 14 May 1813 - Date received: 25 May 1813 - From what ship: Portsmouth via HMS Impetius -

Born: New York - Age: 36 - Discharged on 24 Jul 1814 and sent to Dartmoor on HMS Liffey.

Limon, Andrew - Seaman - Number: 2545 - Prize name: Prize to the U.S. Frigate President - Ship type: War - How taken: HM Transport Regulus - When taken: 4 Sep 1812 - Where taken: Newfoundland Bank - Date received: 22 Oct 1813 - From what ship: Portsmouth via HMT Malabar - Born: Norway - Age: 33 - Died on 7 Nov 1813 from pneumonia.

Lincoln, Ephraim - Seaman - Number: 3746 - Prize name: Argus - Ship type: MV - How taken: HM Ship-of-the-Line San Domingo - When taken: 1 Mar 1814 - Where taken: off Savannah - Date received: 26 May 1814 - From what ship: HMS Hindostan - Born: Boston - Age: 18 - Discharged on 25 Sep 1814 and sent to Dartmoor on HMS Niobe.

Lind, Andrew - Seaman - Number: 966 - Prize name: Empress - Ship type: MV - How taken: HM Brig Rover - When taken: 30 Nov 1812 - Where taken: St. Andrew - Date received: 10 Mar 1813 - From what ship: HMS Tigress - Born: Nuremberg, Germany - Age: 49 - Discharged on 8 Jun 1813 and released to Cartel Rodrigo.

Lindholm, Nicholas - Seaman - Number: 547 - Prize name: Baltimore - Ship type: P - How taken: HM Transport Diadem - When taken: 7 Oct 1812 - Where taken: S. Andres - Date received: 23 Feb 1813 - From what ship: Portsmouth via HMS Dromedary - Born: Karlskrona, Sweden - Age: 33 - Released on 20 May 1813.

Lindsay, Nathaniel - Captain - Number: 2215 - Prize name: Growler - Ship type: P - How taken: HM Brig Electra - When taken: 7 Jul 1813 - Where taken: off St. Johns - Date received: 18 Aug 1813 - From what ship: Portsmouth, via an admiral's tender - Born: Salem - Age: 42 - Discharged on 11 Aug 1814 and sent to Dartmoor on HMS Freya.

Lindsey, Samuel - Seaman - Number: 2102 - How taken: Gave himself up from HM Frigate Bombay - When taken: 27 May 1813 - Date received: 9 Aug 1813 - From what ship: HMS Thames - Born: Virginia - Age: 33 - Discharged on 12 Aug 1814 and sent to Dartmoor on HMS Alpheus.

Lindsey, William - Seaman - Number: 2454 - Prize name: Wiley Reynard - Ship type: P - How taken: HM Frigate Shannon - When taken: 16 Aug 1812 - Where taken: off Halifax - Date received: 21 Oct 1813 - From what ship: Portsmouth via HMT Malabar - Born: Philadelphia - Age: 21 - Discharged on 4 Sep 1814 and sent to Dartmoor on HMS Freya.

Ling, Thomas - 2nd Mate - Number: 168 - Prize name: Forester - Ship type: MV - How taken: Detained at Sheerness, England - When taken: 1 Aug 1812 - Date received: 5 Nov 1812 - From what ship: HMS Namur - Born: New York - Age: 22 - Discharged on 4 Mar 1813 to the Wailey.

Lingard, Ludwig - Cook - Number: 192 - Prize name: Mary Ann - Ship type: MV - How taken: HM Brig Castilian - When taken: 14 Aug 1812 - Where taken: Downs - Date received: 6 Nov 1812 - From what ship: HMS Echo - Born: Altona - Age: 48 - Discharged in Jul 1813 and released to Cartel Moses Brown.

Linnard, Alfred - Private - Number: 3145 - Prize name: U.S. Artillery - Ship type: LF - How taken: British forces - When taken: 24 Jun 1813 - Where taken: Beaver Dams, Upper Canada - Date received: 7 Jan 1814 - From what ship: Halifax - Born: Massachusetts - Age: 33 - Discharged on 10 Oct 1814 and sent to U.S. on Cartel St. Philip.

Linnel, Jonathan - Seaman - Number: 57 - Prize name: Gossypium - Ship type: MV - How taken: HM Sloop Goree - When taken: 15 Aug 1812 - Where taken: off Bermuda - Date received: 3 Nov 1812 - From what ship: HMS Plover - Born: Orleans, MA - Age: 24 - Discharged on 10 May 1813 and released to Cartel Admittance.

Lippen, Stephen - Seaman - Number: 616 - Prize name: King of Rome - Ship type: P - How taken: HM Brig Wolverine - When taken: 13 Dec 1812 - Where taken: at sea - Date received: 23 Feb 1813 - From what ship: Portsmouth via HMS Dromedary - Born: New Orleans - Age: 29 - Discharged on 2 Jul 1813 and released to Cartel Moses Brown.

Lipscomb, William - Seaman - Number: 3619 - Prize name: Liberty - Ship type: MV - How taken: Surrendered at Stromness, Scotland - When taken: 30 Dec 1813 - Date received: 29 Mar 1814 - From what ship: Hired tender Anna - Born: New York - Age: 25 - Discharged on 25 Sep 1814 and sent to Dartmoor on HMS Niobe.

Liscomb, John - Seaman - Number: 948 - Prize name: Mariner - Ship type: MV - How taken: HM Brig Lyra - When taken: 15 Dec 1812 - Where taken: off Bilboa, Spain - Date received: 10 Mar 1813 - From what ship: HMS Tigress - Born: Portsmouth, NH - Age: 26 - Discharged on 2 Jul 1813 and released to Cartel Moses Brown.

Lisconet, Francis - Seaman - Number: 3650 - Prize name: Bunker Hill - Ship type: P - How taken: HM Frigate Pomone & HM Frigate Cydnus - When taken: 4 Mar 1814 - Where taken: Bay of Biscay - Date received: 31 Mar 1814 - From what ship: HMS Raisonnable - Born: Morlaix, France - Age: 20 - Discharged on 22 Jun 1814 and sent to Calais, France on the Simon & Mary.

Lissel, Joseph - Seaman - Number: 260 - How taken: Gave himself up at London - When taken: 28 Nov 1812 - Date received: 7 Dec 1812 - From what ship: HMS Raisonnable - Born: St. Marys, MD - Age: 32 - Discharged on 24 Jul 1813 and released to Cartel Hoffminy.

Lister, Louis - Seaman - Number: 1067 - How taken: Gave himself up from HM Frigate Ulysses - When taken: 13 Jan 1813 - Date received: 14 Mar 1813 - From what ship: Portsmouth via HMS Cornwell - Born: New York - Age: 25 - Discharged on 11 Aug 1814 and sent to Dartmoor.

Litchfield, Enoch - Seaman - Number: 1745 - How taken: Taken up at London - When taken: 24 May 1813 - Date received: 28 May 1813 - From what ship: HMS Raisonnable - Born: Cohasset, MA - Age: 31 - Discharged on 24 Jul 1814 and sent to Dartmoor on HMS Liffey.

Litnay, Peter - Seaman - Number: 3338 - Prize name: Porcupine - Ship type: LM - How taken: HM Frigate Acasta - When taken: 18 Jul 1813 - Where taken: off Cape Sable, Florida - Date received: 23 Feb 1814 - From what ship: Halifax via HMT Malabar - Born: St. Malo - Age: 25 - Discharged on 22 Jun 1814 and sent to Calais, France on the Simon & Mary.

Little, Silas W. - Seaman - Number: 305 - Prize name: Cygnet - Ship type: MV - How taken: HM Brig Sarpedon - When taken: 12 Aug 1812 - Date received: 23 Dec 1812 - From what ship: Greenlaw Depot - Born: Plainfield - Age: 32 - Race: Black man - Discharged on 10 May 1813 and released to Cartel Admittance.

Little, Thomas - Seaman - Number: 3841 - How taken: Gave himself up from HM Frigate Theban at Madras, India - When taken: 21 Jul 1814 - Date received: 21 Aug 1814 - From what ship: Gravesend - Born: Philadelphia - Age: 25 - Discharged on 20 Sep 1814 and sent to Dartmoor on HMS Leyden.

Littlefield, Samuel - Seaman - Number: 3828 - Prize name: Rattlesnake - Ship type: LM - How taken: HM Frigate Rhin - When taken: 12 Mar 1814 - Where taken: off Bermuda - Date received: 16 Aug 1814 - From what ship: London - Born: Frankfort - Age: 21 - Discharged on 22 Oct 1814 and sent to Dartmoor on HMS Leyden.

Livesley, Thomas - Seaman - Number: 3642 - Prize name: Bunker Hill - Ship type: P - How taken: HM Frigate Pomone & HM Frigate Cydnus - When taken: 4 Mar 1814 - Where taken: Bay of Biscay - Date received: 31 Mar 1814 - From what ship: HMS Raisonnable - Born: New York - Age: 34 - Discharged on 25 Sep 1814 and sent to Dartmoor on HMS Niobe.

Livingston, Henry - Seaman - Number: 3512 - Prize name: Pilot - Ship type: LM - How taken: Vittoria, British privateer from Guernsey - When taken: 28 Jan 1814 - Where taken: off Bordeaux, France - Date received: 23 Feb 1814 - From what ship: Portsmouth via HMT Malabar - Born: New York - Age: 25 - Race: Black - Discharged on 26 Sep 1814 and sent to Dartmoor on HMS Leyden.

Lock, Nathaniel - Seaman - Number: 525 - Prize name: Diamond - Ship type: MV - How taken: Detained at Bermuda - When taken: 17 Sep 1812 - Date received: 23 Feb 1813 - From what ship: Portsmouth via HMS Dromedary - Born: Falmouth, MA - Age: 24 - Discharged on 23 Mar 1813 and released to the Cartel Robinson Potter.

Locker, Michael - Seaman - Number: 3875 - How taken: Gave himself up from HM Brig Hecate - When taken: 26 Aug 1814 - Date received: 28 Aug 1814 - From what ship: London - Born: Saint Marys, MD - Age: 21 - Discharged on 26 Sep 1814 and sent to Dartmoor on HMS Leyden.

Lockerby, William - 1st Mate - Number: 1487 - Prize name: Pallas - Ship type: MV - How taken: HM Brig Rebuff - When taken: 23 Nov 1812 - Where taken: off Cadiz, Spain - Date received: 6 Apr 1813 - From what ship: Plymouth via HMS Decoy - Born: New York - Age: 29 - Discharged on 21 Apr 1813 and sent to Reading on parole.

Lockett, Thomas R. - Seaman - Number: 1250 - Prize name: Industry - Ship type: MV - How taken: HM Frigate Dryand - When taken: 7 Jan 1813 - Where taken: at sea - Date received: 16 Mar 1813 - From what ship: Portsmouth, via HMS Abundance - Born: Virginia - Age: 19 - Race: Black - Discharged on 2 Jul 1813 and released to Cartel Moses Brown.

Lockwood, Benjamin - Seaman - Number: 3724 - Prize name: Valentine - Ship type: MV - How taken: HM Ship-of-the-Line Minden - When taken: 17 Nov 1812 - Where taken: off Cape of Good Hope - Date received: 23 May 1814 - From what ship: London - Born: Baltimore - Age: 39 - Discharged on 22 Oct 1814 and released to HMS Argonaut.

Lockwood, Caleb - Seaman - Number: 753 - Prize name: Quebec of London, prize of the Privateer Paul Jones - Ship type: P - How taken: HM Brig Derwent - When taken: 29 Jan 1813 - Where taken: off Lisbon - Date received: 25 Feb 1813 - From what ship: HMS Brazen - Born: Rhode Island - Age: 21 - Discharged on 23 Jul 1814 and sent to Dartmoor on HMS Acasta.

Lockwood, Charles - Seaman - Number: 144 - Prize name: Harmak & Sally - Ship type: MV - How taken: Detained in the London docks - When taken: 3 Aug 1812 - Date received: 5 Nov 1812 - From what ship: HMS Namur - Born: New York - Age: 19 - Discharged on 24 Feb 1813 and released to HMS Ceres.

Lockwood, Charles - Seaman - Number: 83 - Prize name: Anna & Lilley - Ship type: MV - How taken: Stopped at London - When taken: 26 Oct 1812 - Date received: 4 Nov 1812 - From what ship: HMS Namur - Born: New York - Age: 19 - Discharged in Jul 1813 and released to Cartel Moses Brown.

Lodge, Ebenezer - Seaman - Number: 147 - Prize name: Country Square - Ship type: MV - How taken: Stopped at London - When taken: 27 Oct 1812 - Date received: 5 Nov 1812 - From what ship: HMS Namur - Born: Rowley, MA - Age: 25 - Discharged in Jul 1813 and released to Cartel Moses Brown.

Logan, Timothy - Private - Number: 3154 - Prize name: 14th U.S. Infantry - Ship type: LF - How taken: British forces - When taken: 24 Jun 1813 - Where taken: Beaver Dams, Upper Canada - Date received: 7 Jan 1814 - From what ship: Halifax - Born: New York - Age: 30 - Discharged on 10 Oct 1814 and sent to U.S. on Cartel St. Philip.

Loggett, Gilbert - Seaman - Number: 751 - Prize name: Quebec of London, prize of the Privateer Paul Jones - Ship type: P - How taken: HM Brig Derwent - When taken: 29 Jan 1813 - Where taken: off Lisbon - Date received: 25 Feb 1813 - From what ship: HMS Brazen - Born: New York - Age: 21 - Escaped on 22 May 1814 from HM Prison Ship Nassau.

Loland, Levi - Seaman - Number: 330 - Prize name: Mountaineer - Ship type: MV - How taken: Apprehended at London - When taken: 3 Jan 1813 - Date received: 11 Jan 1813 - From what ship: HMS Raisonnable - Born: North Yarmouth, MA - Age: 26 - Race: Mulatto - Discharged on 24 Jul 1813 and released to Cartel Hoffminy.

Lomondy, Joseph - Seaman - Number: 51 - How taken: Discharged from HM Frigate Shannon - When taken: 24 Jun 1812 - Date received: 3 Nov 1812 - From what ship: HMS Plover - Born: New York - Age: 24 - Discharged on 7 Jun 1813 and released to the HMS Ceres.

Long, Joseph - Seaman - Number: 2927 - Prize name: Fame - Ship type: P - How taken: HMS Pratteo - When taken: 3 May 1813 - Where taken: Bay of Biscay - Date received: 7 Jan 1814 - From what ship: Halifax - Born: Massachusetts - Age: 21 - Discharged on 25 Sep 1814 and sent to Dartmoor on HMS Leyden.

Longreen, Andrew - Seaman - Number: 36 - Prize name: Mary - Ship type: MV - How taken: From a cutter's boat off Bermuda - When taken: 8 Aug 1812 - Date received: 3 Nov 1812 - From what ship: HMS Plover - Born: Karlskrona, Sweden - Age: 31 - Released on 6 Mar 1813.

Longwheel, Amos - Seaman - Number: 1227 - Prize name: Rossie - Ship type: MV - How taken: HM Frigate Dryand - When taken: 7 Jan 1813 - Where taken: at sea - Date received: 16 Mar 1813 - From what ship: Portsmouth, via HMS Abundance - Born: Maryland - Age: 24 - Discharged on 24 Jul 1813 and released to Cartel Hoffminy.

Lopans, William - Seaman - Number: 1893 - Prize name: Prompt - Ship type: MV - How taken: Chance, British privateer - When taken: 28 Mar 1813 - Where taken: Bay of Biscay - Date received: 7 Jul 1813 - From what ship: Portsmouth via HMS Tribune - Born: Boston - Age: 21 - Discharged on 12 Aug 1814 and sent to Dartmoor on HMS Alpheus.

Lord, John - Seaman - Number: 301 - Prize name: Cygnet - Ship type: MV - How taken: HM Brig Sarpedon - When taken: 12 Aug 1812 - Date received: 23 Dec 1812 - From what ship: Greenlaw Depot - Born: Ipswich - Age:

20 - Discharged on 10 May 1813 and released to Cartel Admittance.

Lorenden, George - Seaman - Number: 359 - Prize name: Postsea, prize to the Privateer Thrasher - Ship type: P - How taken: HM Sloop Helena - When taken: 31 Dec 1813 - Where taken: off Azores - Date received: 19 Jan 1813 - From what ship: HMS Raisonnable - Born: Stettin, Prussia - Age: 22 - Discharged on 24 Jul 1813 and released to Cartel Hoffminy.

Loring, Samuel - Seaman - Number: 3749 - Prize name: Argus - Ship type: MV - How taken: HM Ship-of-the-Line San Domingo - When taken: 1 Mar 1814 - Where taken: off Savannah - Date received: 26 May 1814 - From what ship: HMS Hindostan - Born: Boston - Age: 18 - Discharged on 26 Sep 1814 and sent to Dartmoor on HMS Leyden.

Lothrop, James - Seaman - Number: 1321 - How taken: Gave himself up from HM Guardship Royal William - When taken: 3 Feb 1813 - Date received: 16 Mar 1813 - From what ship: Portsmouth, via HMS Abundance - Born: Boston - Age: 28 - Discharged on 23 Jul 1814 and sent to Dartmoor.

Lotton, John - Seaman - Number: 1611 - How taken: Gave himself up from HM Frigate President at Chatham - When taken: 27 Apr 1813 - Date received: 1 May 1813 - From what ship: HMS President - Born: Boston - Age: 24 - Discharged on 28 Aug 1813 and released to HMS Ceres.

Love, Peter - Seaman - Number: 760 - Prize name: Margarethe - Ship type: MV - How taken: HM Ship-of-the-Line San Juan - When taken: 8 May 1812 - Where taken: Gibraltar - Date received: 25 Feb 1813 - From what ship: HMS Brazen - Born: New Orleans - Age: 48 - Discharged on 23 Mar 1813 and released to the Cartel Robinson Potter.

Loveitson, John - Private - Number: 3102 - Prize name: 14th U.S. Infantry - Ship type: LF - How taken: British forces - When taken: 24 Jun 1813 - Where taken: Beaver Dams, Upper Canada - Date received: 7 Jan 1814 - From what ship: Halifax - Born: Maryland - Age: 29 - Discharged on 10 Oct 1814 and sent to U.S. on Cartel St. Philip.

Lovelin, Abussha - Seaman - Number: 351 - Prize name: Postsea, prize to the Privateer Thrasher - Ship type: P - How taken: HM Sloop Helena - When taken: 31 Dec 1813 - Where taken: off Azores - Date received: 19 Jan 1813 - From what ship: HMS Raisonnable - Born: Portland - Age: 17 - Discharged on 24 Jul 1813 and released to Cartel Hoffminy.

Lovell, William - Seaman - Number: 3853 - How taken: Gave himself up from HM Frigate Owen Glendower - When taken: 20 Jun 1813 - Date received: 24 Aug 1814 - From what ship: London - Born: Spitsburg - Age: 35 - Discharged on 26 Sep 1814 and sent to Dartmoor on HMS Leyden.

Lovering, William - Seaman - Number: 1568 - Prize name: Dolphin - Ship type: LM - How taken: HM Ship-of-the-Line Colossus - When taken: 5 Jan 1813 - Where taken: off the Western Isles, Scotland - Date received: 8 Apr 1813 - From what ship: Plymouth via HMS Olympia - Born: Pennsylvania - Age: 21 - Discharged on 27 Jul 1813 and released to Cartel Hoffminy.

Lovet, Robert - Seaman - Number: 2271 - Prize name: prize to the Privateer Blockade - Ship type: P - How taken: HM Frigate Brazen - When taken: 29 Jun 1813 - Where taken: coast of Scotland - Date received: 14 Sep 1813 - From what ship: HMS Raisonnable - Born: Rhode Island - Age: 20 - Discharged on 4 Sep 1814 and sent to Dartmoor on HMS Freya.

Low, Thomas - Seaman - Number: 1556 - Prize name: Dolphin - Ship type: LM - How taken: HM Ship-of-the-Line Colossus - When taken: 5 Jan 1813 - Where taken: off the Western Isles, Scotland - Date received: 8 Apr 1813 - From what ship: Plymouth via HMS Olympia - Born: Delaware - Age: 29 - Discharged on 27 Jul 1813 and released to Cartel Hoffminy.

Lowder, Henry - Cook - Number: 435 - Prize name: Hunter - Ship type: P - How taken: HM Frigate Phoebe - When taken: 23 Dec 1812 - Where taken: off Azores - Date received: 19 Feb 1813 - From what ship: HMS Modeste - Born: Georgetown - Age: 38 - Discharged on 2 Jul 1813 and released to Cartel Moses Brown.

Lowdie, Samuel - Seaman - Number: 1841 - How taken: Gave himself up from HM Frigate Hyperion - Date received: 7 Jul 1813 - From what ship: Portsmouth via HMS Tribune - Born: New York - Age: 25 - Race: Black - Discharged on 12 Aug 1814 and sent to Dartmoor on HMS Alpheus.

Lowe, George - Prize Master - Number: 3349 - Prize name: Thomas - Ship type: P - How taken: HM Frigate

Nymphe - When taken: 26 Jun 1813 - Where taken: off Halifax - Date received: 23 Feb 1814 - From what ship: Halifax via HMT Malabar - Born: Portsmouth - Age: 23 - Discharged on 10 Oct 1814 and sent to Dartmoor on the Mermaid.

Lowe, Thomas - Seaman - Number: 2561 - How taken: Gave himself up from HM Battery Gorgon - When taken: 1 Nov 1812 - Date received: 23 Oct 1813 - From what ship: Portsmouth via HMS Raisonnable - Born: Massachusetts - Age: 28 - Discharged on 8 Sep 1814 and sent to Dartmoor on HMS Niobe.

Lownsburg, Carpenter - Carpenter - Number: 1465 - Prize name: Union - Ship type: MV - How taken: HM Frigate Iris - When taken: 17 Jan 1813 - Where taken: at sea - Date received: 6 Apr 1813 - From what ship: Portsmouth via Tender Eliza - Born: Delaware - Age: 45 - Discharged on 24 Jul 1813 and released to Cartel Hoffminy.

Lowry, James - Private - Number: 2660 - Prize name: 2nd U.S. Artillery - Ship type: LF - How taken: British forces - When taken: 6 Jun 1813 - Where taken: Stoney Creek, Upper Canada - Date received: 5 Nov 1813 - From what ship: HMS Hindostan - Born: Tirone, Ireland - Age: 30 - Discharged on 17 Jun 1814 and sent to Dartmoor.

Luburg, John C. - Seaman - Number: 3539 - Prize name: Commodore Perry - Ship type: MV - How taken: Sent into custody from a cutter - When taken: 25 Feb 1814 - Where taken: off Bordeaux, France - Date received: 5 Mar 1814 - From what ship: HMS Raisonnable - Born: Pilllau, Prussia - Age: 28 - Discharged on 25 Sep 1814 and sent to Dartmoor on HMS Niobe.

Lucas, Benjamin - Seaman - Number: 548 - Prize name: Baltimore - Ship type: P - How taken: HM Transport Diadem - When taken: 7 Oct 1812 - Where taken: S. Andres - Date received: 23 Feb 1813 - From what ship: Portsmouth via HMS Dromedary - Born: Baltimore - Age: 21 - Discharged on 8 Jun 1813 and released to Cartel Rodrigo.

Lucas, Daniel - Seaman - Number: 2497 - Prize name: Porcupine - Ship type: LM - How taken: HM Frigate Acasta - When taken: 3 Jun 1813 - Where taken: off Cape Sable, Florida - Date received: 22 Oct 1813 - From what ship: Portsmouth via HMT Malabar - Born: Virginia - Age: 23 - Race: Blackman - Discharged on 8 Sep 1814 and sent to Dartmoor on HMS Niobe.

Lucas, Francois Rene - Marine Private - Number: 3690 - Prize name: Bunker Hill - Ship type: P - How taken: HM Frigate Pomone & HM Frigate Cydnus - When taken: 4 Mar 1814 - Where taken: Bay of Biscay - Date received: 4 May 1814 - From what ship: Portsmouth - Born: Brest, France - Age: 36 - Escaped on 20 May 1814 from HM Prison Ship Glory.

Lucas, Martin - Seaman - Number: 2366 - How taken: Gave himself up from HM Ship-of-the-Line Swiftsure - When taken: 25 Jun 1813 - Date received: 20 Oct 1813 - From what ship: Portsmouth, via an admiral's tender - Born: New York - Age: 50 - Race: Black - Discharged on 4 Sep 1814 and sent to Dartmoor on HMS Freya.

Luce, Charles - Seaman - Number: 3477 - Prize name: Yankee - Ship type: P - How taken: HM Frigate Shannon - When taken: 20 Aug 1813 - Where taken: at sea - Date received: 23 Feb 1814 - From what ship: Halifax via HMT Malabar - Born: Martha's Vineyard - Age: 21 - Discharged on 22 Oct 1814 and sent to Dartmoor on HMS Leyden.

Ludlow, Reuben - Seaman - Number: 1877 - Prize name: Tiger - Ship type: MV - How taken: HM Brig Scylla - When taken: 22 Mar 1813 - Where taken: Bay of Biscay - Date received: 7 Jul 1813 - From what ship: Portsmouth via HMS Tribune - Born: Philadelphia - Age: 33 - Died on 24 Mar 1814 from fever.

Luffie, Warren - Seaman - Number: 3455 - Prize name: Elbridge Gerry - Ship type: P - How taken: HM Frigate Crescent - When taken: 16 Sep 1813 - Where taken: at sea - Date received: 23 Feb 1814 - From what ship: Halifax via HMT Malabar - Born: New York - Age: 31 - Escaped on 20 May 1814 by acting as a Frenchman.

Lufkin, William - Seaman - Number: 2975 - Prize name: Enterprise - Ship type: P - How taken: HM Frigate Tenedos - When taken: 21 May 1813 - Where taken: off Cape Cod - Date received: 7 Jan 1814 - From what ship: Halifax - Born: Massachusetts - Age: 22 - Discharged on 25 Sep 1814 and sent to Dartmoor on HMS Leyden.

Lumburger, Jacob - Prize Master - Number: 2159 - Prize name: tender to the Privateer True Blooded Yankee - Ship type: P - How taken: HM Ship-of-the-Line Fame - When taken: 24 Jun 1813 - Where taken: at sea - Date received: 16 Aug 1813 - From what ship: Portsmouth, via an admiral's tender - Born: Sweden - Age: 28 - Discharged on 2 Dec 1813 for passage to Yarmouth.

Lunes, Charles - Mate - Number: 163 - Prize name: Elson - Ship type: MV - How taken: HM Frigate Ethalion - When taken: 12 Aug 1812 - Where taken: Baltic - Date received: 5 Nov 1812 - From what ship: HMS Namur - Born: Boston - Age: 28 - Discharged on 23 Mar 1813 and released to the Cartel Robinson Potter.

Lunt, Daniel - Seaman - Number: 3747 - Prize name: Argus - Ship type: MV - How taken: HM Ship-of-the-Line San Domingo - When taken: 1 Mar 1814 - Where taken: off Savannah - Date received: 26 May 1814 - From what ship: HMS Hindostan - Born: Newbury - Age: 23 - Discharged on 22 Oct 1814 and sent to Dartmoor on HMS Leyden.

Lupy, Marcus - Seaman - Number: 2915 - Prize name: Pomona, prize of Privateer Prince de Neuchatel - Ship type: P - How taken: HM Frigate Ethalion - When taken: 14 Dec 1813 - Where taken: at sea - Date received: 7 Jan 1814 - From what ship: Portsmouth - Born: Isle of France - Age: 20 - Discharged on 22 Jun 1814 and sent to Calais, France on the Simon & Mary.

Luther, Cromwell - Seaman - Number: 3791 - Prize name: Valentine - Ship type: MV - How taken: HM Ship-of-the-Line Minden - When taken: 16 Nov 1812 - Where taken: off Cape of Good Hope - Date received: 26 May 1814 - From what ship: HMS Hindostan - Born: Warren - Age: 23 - Discharged on 29 Sep 1814 and sent to Dartmoor on HMS Freya.

Luther, Jeremiah - Seaman - Number: 1798 - Prize name: Henry - Ship type: MV - How taken: Impressed at Shields - When taken: 18 May 1813 - Date received: 3 Jul 1813 - From what ship: HMS Raisonnable - Born: Swansea - Age: 25 - Released on 11 Jul 1814.

Lynch, Elias - Seaman - Number: 1755 - How taken: Gave himself up from HMS Impeteux - When taken: 2 Dec 1812 - Date received: 30 May 1813 - From what ship: HMS Impetius - Born: Dorchester - Age: 27 - Race: Mulatto - Discharged on 24 Jul 1814 and sent to Dartmoor on HMS Liffey.

Lynch, John - Private - Number: 2655 - Prize name: 16th U.S. Infantry - Ship type: LF - How taken: British forces - When taken: 6 Jun 1813 - Where taken: Stoney Creek, Upper Canada - Date received: 5 Nov 1813 - From what ship: HMS Hindostan - Born: Leinster, Ireland - Age: 49 - Discharged on 17 Jun 1814 and sent to Dartmoor.

Lynch, Joseph - Seaman - Number: 481 - Prize name: Vengeance - Ship type: LM - How taken: HM Frigate Phoebe - When taken: 1 Jan 1813 - Where taken: Lat 44.4 Long 23 - Date received: 19 Feb 1813 - From what ship: HMS Modeste - Born: Philadelphia - Age: 26 - Discharged on 24 Jul 1813 and released to Cartel Hoffminy.

Lynch, Thomas - Seaman - Number: 2400 - How taken: Gave himself up from HM Frigate Orpheus - When taken: 26 Dec 1812 - Date received: 21 Oct 1813 - From what ship: Portsmouth via HMT Malabar - Born: Maryland - Age: 38 - Escaped on 10 Jun 1814 from HM Prison Ship Crown Prince.

Lynch, William - Seaman - Number: 3542 - Prize name: Commodore Perry - Ship type: MV - How taken: Sent into custody from a cutter - When taken: 25 Feb 1814 - Where taken: off Bordeaux, France - Date received: 5 Mar 1814 - From what ship: HMS Raisonnable - Born: Philadelphia - Age: 35 - Discharged on 25 Sep 1814 and sent to Dartmoor on HMS Niobe.

Lynch, William - Seaman - Number: 928 - Prize name: Experiment - Ship type: MV - How taken: HM Brig Rover - When taken: 10 Nov 1812 - Where taken: off Bordeaux, France - Date received: 10 Mar 1813 - From what ship: HMS Tigress - Born: Maryland - Age: 21 - Discharged on 8 Jun 1813 and released to Cartel Rodrigo.

Lyon, Ezekiel - 1st Mate - Number: 1329 - Prize name: Sea Nymph - Ship type: MV - How taken: HM Brig Thrasher - When taken: 4 Mar 1813 - Where taken: off River Jade (Germany) - Date received: 22 Mar 1813 - From what ship: HMS Thrasher - Born: Connecticut - Age: 27 - Discharged on 3 Jun 1813 and sent to Reading on parole.

Lyons, Charles - Seaman - Number: 3175 - Prize name: Wolf Cove - Ship type: MV - How taken: HM Frigate Briton - When taken: 1 Dec 1813 - Where taken: off Brest, France - Date received: 7 Jan 1814 - From what ship: Halifax - Born: Massachusetts - Age: 20 - Discharged on 25 Sep 1814 and sent to Dartmoor on HMS

Leyden.

Lyons, Henry - Seaman - Number: 849 - Prize name: Ocean, prized to the Privateer Diligent - Ship type: P - How taken: HM Frigate Surveillante - When taken: 20 Dec 1812 - Where taken: Lat 44 N, Long 6 W - Date received: 1 Mar 1813 - From what ship: Plymouth via HMS Namur - Born: New Jersey - Age: 18 - Discharged on 20 Aug 1814 and sent to Dartmoor on HMS Shamrock.

Lyons, Peter - Seaman - Number: 1402 - Prize name: Porcupine - Ship type: MV - How taken: HM Frigate Dryand - When taken: 8 Jan 1813 - Where taken: off Bordeaux, France - Date received: 5 Apr 1813 - From what ship: Plymouth via HMS Dwarf - Born: Baltimore - Age: 37 - Discharged on 24 Jul 1813 and released to Cartel Hoffminy.

Lyons, Samuel - Seaman - Number: 1414 - Prize name: Porcupine - Ship type: MV - How taken: HM Frigate Dryand - When taken: 8 Jan 1813 - Where taken: off Bordeaux, France - Date received: 5 Apr 1813 - From what ship: Plymouth via HMS Dwarf - Born: Connecticut - Age: 32 - Discharged on 24 Jul 1813 and released to Cartel Hoffminy.

Macceaming, James - Seaman - Number: 336 - How taken: Impressed at London off British MV Study - When taken: 8 Jan 1813 - Date received: 18 Jan 1813 - From what ship: HMS Raisonnable - Born: Blackbush, Long Island - Age: 41 - Discharged on 24 Feb 1813 and released to HMS Ceres.

Macconahay, Benjamin - Private - Number: 2611 - Prize name: 14th U.S. Infantry - Ship type: LF - How taken: British forces - When taken: 24 Jun 1813 - Where taken: Beaver Dams, Upper Canada - Date received: 5 Nov 1813 - From what ship: HMS Hindostan - Born: County Antrim, Ireland - Age: 25 - Discharged on 17 Jun 1814 and sent to Dartmoor.

Macintoie, Alexander - Seaman - Number: 528 - Prize name: Leonidas - Ship type: MV - How taken: Detained at Portsmouth harbor - When taken: 31 Jul 1812 - Date received: 23 Feb 1813 - From what ship: Portsmouth via HMS Dromedary - Born: New York - Age: 21 - Discharged on 23 Mar 1813 and released to the Cartel Robinson Potter.

Mack, John - Seaman - Number: 2334 - How taken: Impressed at Nore, England - When taken: 2 Sep 1813 - Date received: 12 Oct 1813 - From what ship: HMS Raisonnable - Born: Virginia - Age: 27 - Discharged on 4 Sep 1814 and sent to Dartmoor on HMS Freya.

Mackay, John - Private - Number: 2617 - Prize name: 14th U.S. Infantry - Ship type: LF - How taken: British forces - When taken: 24 Jun 1813 - Where taken: Beaver Dams, Upper Canada - Date received: 5 Nov 1813 - From what ship: HMS Hindostan - Born: North Ireland - Age: 51 - Discharged on 10 Oct 1814 and sent to U.S. on Cartel St. Philip.

Mackensey, John - Seaman - Number: 2100 - How taken: Gave himself up from HM Ship-of-the-Line Barfleur - When taken: 27 May 1813 - Date received: 9 Aug 1813 - From what ship: HMS Thames - Born: Baltimore - Age: 36 - Race: Black - Discharged on 12 Aug 1814 and sent to Dartmoor on HMS Alpheus.

Mackenwick, George - Private - Number: 2609 - Prize name: U.S. Light Artillery - Ship type: LF - How taken: British forces - When taken: 1 Jun 1813 - Where taken: Upper Canada - Date received: 5 Nov 1813 - From what ship: HMS Hindostan - Born: Ireland - Age: 31 - Discharged on 17 Jun 1814 and sent to Dartmoor.

Mackey, Charles - Seaman - Number: 3395 - Prize name: Centurion, prize - Ship type: P - How taken: HM Frigate Maidstone - When taken: 18 Jul 1813 - Where taken: Grand Banks - Date received: 23 Feb 1814 - From what ship: Halifax via HMT Malabar - Born: Amsterdam - Age: 42 - Discharged on 22 Oct 1814 and sent to Dartmoor on HMS Leyden.

Mackey, James - Seaman - Number: 2096 - How taken: Gave himself up from HM Ship-of-the-Line Barfleur - When taken: 27 May 1813 - Date received: 9 Aug 1813 - From what ship: HMS Thames - Born: Massachusetts - Age: 24 - Discharged on 12 Aug 1814 and sent to Dartmoor on HMS Alpheus.

Mackey, John - Seaman - Number: 2530 - Prize name: Yorktown - Ship type: P - How taken: HM Brig Nimrod - When taken: 17 Jul 1813 - Where taken: Grand Banks - Date received: 22 Oct 1813 - From what ship: Portsmouth via HMT Malabar - Born: New York - Age: 36 - Discharged on 8 Sep 1814 and sent to Dartmoor on HMS Niobe.

Macquillon, Hugh - Seaman - Number: 788 - Prize name: Dolphin - Ship type: MV - How taken: HM Ship-of-the-

Line Colossus - When taken: 5 Jan 1813 - Where taken: off the Western Isles, Scotland - Date received: 27 Feb 1813 - From what ship: Plymouth via HMS Namur - Born: Philadelphia - Age: 21 - Discharged on 24 Jul 1813 and released to Cartel Hoffminy.

Macrombie, Elijah - Seaman - Number: 569 - Prize name: Perseverance - Ship type: MV - How taken: HM Sloop Atalante - When taken: 31 Jul 1812 - Where taken: at sea - Date received: 23 Feb 1813 - From what ship: Portsmouth via HMS Dromedary - Born: Taunton, MA - Age: 25 - Discharged on 23 Mar 1813 and released to the Cartel Robinson Potter.

Macure, Angelo - Seaman - Number: 402 - How taken: Gave himself up from HM Gunpowder Hulk Alexander - When taken: 1 Feb 1813 - Date received: 13 Feb 1813 - From what ship: HMS Raisonnable - Born: New Orleans - Age: 22 - Discharged on 26 Jul 1814 and sent to Dartmoor on HMS Raven.

Madden, Peter - Seaman - Number: 2679 - How taken: Gave himself up from HM Bomb Vessel Thunder - When taken: 29 Oct 1812 - Date received: 2 Dec 1813 - From what ship: HMS Raisonnable - Born: Saxony, Germany - Age: 23 - Discharged on 29 Dec 1813 and sent to France.

Madillion, Peter - Seaman - Number: 394 - Prize name: Dolphin - Ship type: MV - How taken: HM Ship-of-the-Line Invincible - When taken: 24 Aug 1812 - Where taken: Mediterranean - Date received: 13 Feb 1813 - From what ship: HMS Raisonnable - Born: New Orleans - Age: 28 - Discharged on 8 Jun 1813 and released to Cartel Rodrigo.

Magee, Robert - Private - Number: 3076 - Prize name: 14th U.S. Infantry - Ship type: LF - How taken: British forces - When taken: 24 Jun 1813 - Where taken: Beaver Dams, Upper Canada - Date received: 7 Jan 1814 - From what ship: Halifax - Born: Pennsylvania - Age: 26 - Discharged on 10 Oct 1814 and sent to U.S. on Cartel St. Philip.

Magrath, James - Seaman - Number: 576 - How taken: Gave himself up from HM Prison Ship Minerve - When taken: 5 Dec 1812 - Date received: 23 Feb 1813 - From what ship: Portsmouth via HMS Dromedary - Born: Philadelphia - Age: 30 - Discharged on 26 Jul 1814 and sent to Dartmoor on HMS Raven.

Main, Henry - Boy - Number: 476 - Prize name: Hunter - Ship type: P - How taken: HM Frigate Phoebe - When taken: 23 Dec 1812 - Where taken: off Azores - Date received: 19 Feb 1813 - From what ship: HMS Modeste - Born: Boston - Age: 18 - Race: Negro - Discharged on 24 Jul 1813 and released to Cartel Hoffminy.

Mains, Henry - Seaman - Number: 3764 - Prize name: Argus - Ship type: MV - How taken: HM Ship-of-the-Line San Domingo - When taken: 1 Mar 1814 - Where taken: off Savannah - Date received: 26 May 1814 - From what ship: HMS Hindostan - Born: Boston - Age: 19 - Race: Black - Discharged on 25 Sep 1814 and sent to Dartmoor on HMS Niobe.

Mains, John - Seaman - Number: 3582 - How taken: Gave himself up from HM Schooner Whiting - When taken: 14 Jan 1814 - Date received: 26 Mar 1814 - From what ship: Plymouth via HMS Raleigh - Born: Shrewsbury - Age: 39 - Discharged on 26 Sep 1814 and sent to Dartmoor on HMS Leyden.

Mains, John - Seaman - Number: 1420 - How taken: Impressed at Falmouth - When taken: 7 Jan 1813 - Date received: 5 Apr 1813 - From what ship: Plymouth via HMS Dwarf - Born: Rhinebeck - Age: 26 - Discharged on 27 Jul 1813 and released to Cartel Hoffminy.

Makeniney, George - Seaman - Number: 2064 - How taken: Gave himself up from HM Ship-of-the-Line Berwick - When taken: 29 Oct 1812 - Date received: 9 Aug 1813 - From what ship: HMS Thames - Born: Georgetown - Age: 37 - Discharged on 12 Aug 1814 and sent to Dartmoor on HMS Alpheus.

Malbrough, Francis - Seaman - Number: 3229 - How taken: Gave himself up from HM Ship-of-the-Line Dannemark - When taken: 12 Dec 1813 - Date received: 13 Jan 1814 - From what ship: Portsmouth via HMS Poictiers - Born: Hartford - Age: 47 - Race: Black - Discharged on 25 Sep 1814 and sent to Dartmoor on HMS Leyden.

Malcomb, Alexander - Seaman - Number: 2721 - Prize name: Growler - Ship type: P - How taken: HM Brig Electra - When taken: 7 Jul 1813 - Where taken: off St. Johns - Date received: 7 Jan 1814 - From what ship: Portsmouth - Born: Massachusetts - Age: 23 - Discharged on 25 Sep 1814 and sent to Dartmoor on HMS Leyden.

Malis, John - Seaman - Number: 1300 - How taken: Gave himself up from HM Guardship Royal William - When taken: 3 Feb 1813 - Date received: 16 Mar 1813 - From what ship: Portsmouth, via HMS Abundance - Born:

New Jersey - Age: 26 - Discharged on 23 Jul 1814 and sent to Dartmoor.

Mallack, Joseph - Private - Number: 3125 - Prize name: 14th U.S. Infantry - Ship type: LF - How taken: British forces - When taken: 24 Jun 1813 - Where taken: Beaver Dams, Upper Canada - Date received: 7 Jan 1814 - From what ship: Halifax - Born: Pennsylvania - Age: 20 - Discharged on 10 Oct 1814 and sent to U.S. on Cartel St. Philip.

Mallan, James - Seaman - Number: 1519 - How taken: Gave himself up from HM Frigate Brune - When taken: 19 Jan 1813 - Date received: 8 Apr 1813 - From what ship: Portsmouth, via an admiral's tender - Born: New Jersey - Age: 37 - Discharged on 4 Aug 1814 and sent to Dartmoor on HMS Alpheus.

Mallard, James - Seaman - Number: 2784 - Prize name: Thomas - Ship type: P - How taken: HM Frigate Nymphe - When taken: 24 Jun 1813 - Where taken: off Halifax - Date received: 7 Jan 1814 - From what ship: Halifax - Born: Canterbury - Age: 24 - Discharged on 8 Sep 1814 and sent to Dartmoor on HMS Niobe.

Mallet, William - Seaman - Number: 2723 - Prize name: U.S. Schooner Growler - Ship type: War - How taken: HM Schooner Lord Melvin - When taken: 11 Aug 1813 - Where taken: Lake Ontario - Date received: 7 Jan 1814 - From what ship: Portsmouth - Born: New York - Age: 23 - Discharged on 10 Oct 1814 and sent to U.S. on Cartel St. Philip.

Mallison, Jacob - Seaman - Number: 3237 - How taken: Impressed off HM Frigate Surveillante - When taken: 6 Dec 1813 - Date received: 8 Feb 1814 - From what ship: HMS Raisonnable - Born: Princeton - Age: 46 - Discharged on 23 Feb 1814 and released to HMS Ceres.

Malony, Hughey - Seaman - Number: 792 - Prize name: Dolphin - Ship type: MV - How taken: HM Ship-of-the-Line Colossus - When taken: 5 Jan 1813 - Where taken: off the Western Isles, Scotland - Date received: 27 Feb 1813 - From what ship: Plymouth via HMS Namur - Born: Philadelphia - Age: 37 - Discharged on 24 Jul 1813 and released to Cartel Hoffminy.

Malony, Robert - Seaman - Number: 3454 - Prize name: Elbridge Gerry - Ship type: P - How taken: HM Frigate Crescent - When taken: 16 Sep 1813 - Where taken: at sea - Date received: 23 Feb 1814 - From what ship: Halifax via HMT Malabar - Born: New York - Age: 42 - Race: Black - Died on 31 Mar 1814 from fever.

Malvern, Landis - Seaman - Number: 952 - How taken: Gave himself up from HM Sloop Comet - When taken: 25 Nov 1812 - Date received: 10 Mar 1813 - From what ship: HMS Tigress - Born: Norfolk, VA - Age: 22 - Race: Negro - Died on 28 Apr 1814 from phthisis (tuberculosis).

Manaham, David - Private - Number: 3079 - Prize name: 14th U.S. Infantry - Ship type: LF - How taken: British forces - When taken: 24 Jun 1813 - Where taken: Beaver Dams, Upper Canada - Date received: 7 Jan 1814 - From what ship: Halifax - Born: Maryland - Age: 28 - Discharged on 10 Oct 1814 and sent to U.S. on Cartel St. Philip.

Manion, John - Seaman - Number: 2441 - How taken: Taken off of the Russian MV Neptune at Cork - When taken: 28 Sep 1812 - Date received: 21 Oct 1813 - From what ship: Portsmouth via HMT Malabar - Born: New Orleans - Age: 33 - Discharged on 22 Jun 1814 and sent to Calais, France on the Simon & Mary.

Manley, David - Seaman - Number: 3670 - Prize name: Pilot - Ship type: LM - How taken: Vittoria, British privateer from Guernsey - When taken: 28 Jan 1813 - Where taken: off Bordeaux, France - Date received: 4 May 1814 - From what ship: Portsmouth - Born: Portsmouth - Age: 30 - Race: Mulatto - Discharged on 25 Sep 1814 and sent to Dartmoor on HMS Niobe.

Manley, Randolph - Seaman - Number: 2420 - Prize name: Sampson - Ship type: MV - How taken: HM Brig Rebuff - When taken: 12 May 1813 - Where taken: off Cape St. Vincent, Portugal - Date received: 21 Oct 1813 - From what ship: Portsmouth via HMT Malabar - Born: Maryland - Age: 27 - Died on 25 May 1814 from fever.

Mann, John - 2nd Mate - Number: 1948 - Prize name: Cannoniere - Ship type: P - How taken: HM Ship-of-the-Line Warspite - When taken: 14 Mar 1813 - Where taken: Bay of Biscay - Date received: 15 Jul 1813 - From what ship: Plymouth - Born: Philadelphia - Age: 27 - Discharged on 17 Jun 1814 and sent to Dartmoor on HMS Redbreast.

Manning, Burrell - Boy - Number: 2689 - Prize name: Growler - Ship type: P - How taken: HM Brig Electra - When taken: 7 Jul 1813 - Where taken: off St. Johns - Date received: 7 Jan 1814 - From what ship: Portsmouth -

Born: Salem - Age: 11 - Released on 15 Jun 1814.

Manning, Enoch - Captain's Clerk - Number: 1011 - Prize name: Sword Fish - Ship type: P - How taken: HM Ship-of-the-Line Elephant - When taken: 28 Dec 1812 - Where taken: off Azores - Date received: 10 Mar 1813 - From what ship: HMS Furious - Born: Amherst - Age: 28 - Discharged on 10 May 1813 and released to Cartel Admittance.

Manning, George - Seaman - Number: 3847 - How taken: Gave himself up from HM Frigate Africanus at Madeira, Portugal - When taken: 4 Oct 1813 - Date received: 21 Aug 1814 - From what ship: Gravesend - Born: New Brunswick - Age: 36 - Discharged on 10 Oct 1814 and sent to Dartmoor on the Mermaid.

Manning, Thomas - Seaman - Number: 708 - Prize name: Leonidas - Ship type: MV - How taken: Detained at Portsmouth harbor - When taken: 31 Jul 1812 - Date received: 24 Feb 1813 - From what ship: Portsmouth via HMS Ulysses - Born: Salem, MA - Age: 23 - Discharged on 23 Mar 1813 and released to the Cartel Robinson Potter.

Mansfield, Elijah - Mate - Number: 173 - Prize name: Wasp - Ship type: MV - How taken: Earl Spencer, East Indianman - When taken: 28 Oct 1812 - Where taken: off Cape Clear, Ireland - Date received: 5 Nov 1812 - From what ship: HMS Namur - Born: New Haven, CT - Age: 29 - Died on 11 Apr 1813 from pneumonia.

Manson, James - 2nd Lieutenant - Number: 1010 - Prize name: Sword Fish - Ship type: P - How taken: HM Ship-of-the-Line Elephant - When taken: 28 Dec 1812 - Where taken: off Azores - Date received: 10 Mar 1813 - From what ship: HMS Furious - Born: Salem - Age: 31 - Discharged on 8 Jun 1813 and released to Cartel Rodrigo.

Manuel, Anthony - Seaman - Number: 1759 - Prize name: Pallas - Ship type: MV - How taken: HM Brig Rebuff - When taken: 23 Dec 1812 - Where taken: off Cadiz, Spain - Date received: 11 Jun 1813 - From what ship: HMS Raisonnable - Born: St. Andres - Age: 33 - Discharged on 16 Jun 1813 and released to HMS Ceres.

Manuel, John - Seaman - Number: 1061 - Prize name: Independence - Ship type: MV - How taken: HM Frigate Medusa - When taken: 9 Nov 1812 - Where taken: off San Sebastian, Spain - Date received: 11 Mar 1813 - From what ship: Yarmouth via HMS Tenders - Born: New Orleans - Age: 37 - Race: Black - Discharged on 8 Jun 1813 and released to Cartel Rodrigo.

Manuel, Josef - Seaman - Number: 350 - Prize name: Postsea, prize to the Privateer Thrasher - Ship type: P - How taken: HM Sloop Helena - When taken: 31 Dec 1813 - Where taken: off Azores - Date received: 19 Jan 1813 - From what ship: HMS Raisonnable - Born: Portland - Age: 17 - Discharged on 24 Jul 1813 and released to Cartel Hoffminy.

Manuel, Joseph - Seaman - Number: 1044 - Prize name: Warren - Ship type: MV - How taken: HM Frigate Sybille & HMS Fortunee - When taken: 3 Sep 1812 - Where taken: Lat 41.4 Long 33 - Date received: 11 Mar 1813 - From what ship: Yarmouth via HMS Tenders - Born: Oporto, Portugal - Age: 25 - Discharged on 8 Jun 1813 and released to Cartel Rodrigo.

Manuel, Peter - Seaman - Number: 2144 - Prize name: Matilda, prize of the U.S. Brig Argus - Ship type: War - How taken: HM Frigate Revolutionnaire - When taken: 25 Jul 1813 - Where taken: off Lorient, France - Date received: 9 Aug 1813 - From what ship: HMS Thames - Born: New Orleans - Age: 18 - Discharged on 22 Jun 1814 and sent to Calais, France on the Simon & Mary.

Marble, Samuel - Seaman - Number: 2781 - Prize name: Thomas - Ship type: P - How taken: HM Frigate Nymphe - When taken: 24 Jun 1813 - Where taken: off Halifax - Date received: 7 Jan 1814 - From what ship: Halifax - Born: Hampshire - Age: 46 - Discharged on 8 Sep 1814 and sent to Dartmoor on HMS Niobe.

Marcel, James - Seaman - Number: 1981 - How taken: Gave himself up from HM Ship-of-the-Line Malta - Date received: 15 Jul 1813 - From what ship: Plymouth - Born: Norristown - Age: 20 - Discharged on 17 Jun 1814 and sent to Dartmoor on HMS Pincher.

Mark, James - Seaman - Number: 3623 - Prize name: Liberty - Ship type: MV - How taken: Surrendered at Stromness, Scotland - When taken: 30 Dec 1813 - Date received: 29 Mar 1814 - From what ship: Hired tender Anna - Born: New York - Age: 17 - Discharged on 25 Sep 1814 and sent to Dartmoor on HMS Niobe.

Marks, Peter - Seaman - Number: 1195 - How taken: Gave himself up from HM Ship-of-the-Line Tigre - When taken: 15 Aug 1812 - Date received: 16 Mar 1813 - From what ship: Portsmouth, via HMS Abundance -

Born: New Orleans - Age: 31 - Discharged on 11 Aug 1814 and sent to Dartmoor on HMS Freya.

Marlow, Owen - Seaman - Number: 3207 - Prize name: Volunteer - Ship type: MV - How taken: Vittoria, British privateer from Guernsey - When taken: 26 Dec 1813 - Where taken: Bay of Biscay - Date received: 13 Jan 1814 - From what ship: Portsmouth via HMS Poictiers - Born: Massachusetts - Age: 32 - Discharged on 25 Sep 1814 and sent to Dartmoor on HMS Leyden.

Mars, George - Seaman - Number: 1875 - Prize name: Tiger - Ship type: MV - How taken: HM Brig Scylla - When taken: 22 Mar 1813 - Where taken: Bay of Biscay - Date received: 7 Jul 1813 - From what ship: Portsmouth via HMS Tribune - Born: Massachusetts - Age: 39 - Discharged on 4 Aug 1814 and sent to Dartmoor on HMS Liverpool.

Marsh, Hercules - Seaman - Number: 2319 - Prize name: Fame - Ship type: MV - How taken: HM Ship of-the-Line Cressy - When taken: 20 Jul 1813 - Where taken: at sea - Date received: 8 Oct 1813 - From what ship: Portsmouth, via an admiral's tender - Born: Rhode Island - Age: 58 - Discharged on 4 Sep 1814 and sent to Dartmoor on HMS Freya.

Marshall, Benjamin - Seaman - Number: 3892 - How taken: Gave himself up from HM Ship-of-the-Line Minden - When taken: 17 Jul 1813 - Date received: 30 Aug 1814 - From what ship: Transport Office - Born: Islesboro - Age: 23 - Discharged on 10 Oct 1814 and sent to Dartmoor on the Mermaid.

Marshall, Francis - Seaman - Number: 1069 - How taken: Gave himself up from HM Frigate Ulysses - When taken: 13 Jan 1813 - Date received: 14 Mar 1813 - From what ship: Portsmouth via HMS Cornwell - Born: Virginia - Age: 29 - Discharged on 11 Aug 1814 and sent to Dartmoor.

Marshall, John - Seaman - Number: 18 - Prize name: Lucky - Ship type: MV - How taken: Detained at Hanoi Bay - When taken: 11 Aug 1812 - Date received: 29 Oct 1812 - From what ship: HMS Raisonnable - Born: Beverly - Age: 19 - Discharged on 10 May 1813 and released to Cartel Admittance.

Marshall, John - Seaman - Number: 2504 - Prize name: Thomas - Ship type: P - How taken: HM Frigate Nymphe - When taken: 28 Jun 1813 - Where taken: off Halifax - Date received: 22 Oct 1813 - From what ship: Portsmouth via HMT Malabar - Born: New York - Age: 21 - Discharged on 8 Sep 1814 and sent to Dartmoor on HMS Niobe.

Marshall, Levi - Seaman - Number: 1783 - How taken: Taken out of the St. Vincent - When taken: May 1813 - Date received: 1 Jul 1813 - From what ship: HMS Raisonnable - Born: Maryland - Age: 39 - Discharged on 22 Oct 1814 and released to HMS Argonaut.

Marshall, William - Seaman - Number: 1929 - Prize name: Edward - Ship type: MV - How taken: Seringapatam, British letter of marque - When taken: 6 Jan 1813 - Where taken: South America - Date received: 11 Jul 1813 - From what ship: HMS Raisonnable - Born: Nantucket - Age: 34 - Discharged on 24 Jul 1813 and released to Cartel Hoffminy.

Martin, Ephraim - Seaman - Number: 833 - Prize name: John Barnes - Ship type: MV - How taken: Gave himself up at Liverpool - When taken: 7 Nov 1813 - Date received: 1 Mar 1813 - From what ship: Plymouth via HMS Namur - Born: Wiscasset - Age: 40 - Discharged in Jul 1813 and released to Cartel Moses Brown.

Martin, Henry - Seaman - Number: 1373 - How taken: Gave himself up from HM Ship-of-the-Line Christian VII - When taken: 19 Mar 1813 - Date received: 3 Apr 1813 - From what ship: Portsmouth, via an admiral's tender - Born: Albany - Age: 28 - Discharged on 24 Jul 1814 and sent to Dartmoor.

Martin, John - Seaman - Number: 804 - Prize name: Bell - Ship type: MV - How taken: Phillis - When taken: 18 Dec 1812 - Where taken: off Cadiz, Spain - Date received: 27 Feb 1813 - From what ship: Plymouth via HMS Namur - Born: New Orleans - Age: 27 - Discharged on 8 Jun 1813 and released to Cartel Rodrigo.

Martin, John - Seaman - Number: 2138 - Prize name: Matilda, prize of the U.S. Brig Argus - Ship type: War - How taken: HM Frigate Revolutionnaire - When taken: 25 Jul 1813 - Where taken: off Lorient, France - Date received: 9 Aug 1813 - From what ship: HMS Thames - Born: Curacao - Age: 27 - Race: Mulatto - Discharged on 2 Dec 1813 for passage to Yarmouth.

Martin, John J. - Seaman - Number: 1315 - How taken: Gave himself up from HM Guardship Royal William - When taken: 3 Feb 1813 - Date received: 16 Mar 1813 - From what ship: Portsmouth, via HMS Abundance - Born: New York - Age: 32 - Released on 20 Jul 1814.

Martin, Jonathan - Seaman - Number: 667 - Prize name: U.S.R.M. Cutter James Madison - Ship type: War - How taken: HM Frigate Barbadoes - When taken: 22 Aug 1812 - Where taken: at sea - Date received: 24 Feb 1813 - From what ship: Portsmouth via HMS Ulysses - Born: Baltimore - Age: 37 - Discharged on 10 May 1813 and released to Cartel Admittance.

Martin, William - Private - Number: 3164 - Prize name: 14th U.S. Infantry - Ship type: LF - How taken: British forces - When taken: 24 Jun 1813 - Where taken: Beaver Dams, Upper Canada - Date received: 7 Jan 1814 - From what ship: Halifax - Born: Baltimore - Age: 21 - Discharged on 10 Oct 1814 and sent to U.S. on Cartel St. Philip.

Martin, William - Seaman - Number: 2240 - Prize name: Orders in Council - Ship type: LM - How taken: HM Frigate Surveillante - When taken: 1 Jan 1813 - Where taken: off Cape Ortegal, Spain - Date received: 7 Sep 1813 - From what ship: HMS Raisonnable - Born: Norfolk - Age: 25 - Race: Mulatto - Discharged on 11 Aug 1814 and sent to Dartmoor on HMS Freya.

Martini, Francis - Seaman - Number: 3222 - Prize name: Volunteer - Ship type: MV - How taken: Vittoria, British privateer from Guernsey - When taken: 26 Dec 1813 - Where taken: Bay of Biscay - Date received: 13 Jan 1814 - From what ship: Portsmouth via HMS Poictiers - Born: Galicia, Spain - Age: 24 - Discharged on 25 Sep 1814 and sent to Dartmoor on HMS Leyden.

Marvell, David - Seaman - Number: 3897 - How taken: Gave himself up from HM Brig Hecate - When taken: 6 Jul 1813 - Date received: 30 Aug 1814 - From what ship: Transport Office - Born: Rhode Island - Age: 36 - Discharged on 2 Sep 1814 and sent to Dartmoor on HMS Leyden.

Mason, Aaron - Mate - Number: 3009 - Prize name: Yankee - Ship type: P - How taken: HM Frigate Shannon - When taken: 20 Aug 1813 - Where taken: at sea - Date received: 7 Jan 1814 - From what ship: Halifax - Born: Rhode Island - Age: 21 - Discharged on 25 Sep 1814 and sent to Dartmoor on HMS Leyden.

Mason, Daniel - Seaman - Number: 3412 - Prize name: Stark (General Stark) - Ship type: P - How taken: HM Frigate Maidstone - When taken: 15 Jul 1813 - Where taken: Halifax - Date received: 23 Feb 1814 - From what ship: Halifax via HMT Malabar - Born: Rosebay - Age: 26 - Discharged on 22 Oct 1814 and sent to Dartmoor on HMS Leyden.

Mason, Francis - Seaman - Number: 1491 - Prize name: Union - Ship type: MV - How taken: HM Frigate Iris - When taken: 17 Jan 1813 - Where taken: at sea - Date received: 6 Apr 1813 - From what ship: Plymouth via an admiral's tender - Born: Philadelphia - Age: 15 - Discharged on 26 Jul 1813 and released to Cartel Hoffminy.

Mason, Hiram - Seaman - Number: 3387 - Prize name: Polly - Ship type: P - How taken: HM Frigate Maidstone - When taken: 18 Jul 1813 - Where taken: Grand Banks - Date received: 23 Feb 1814 - From what ship: Halifax via HMT Malabar - Born: Salem - Age: 20 - Discharged on 10 Oct 1814 and sent to Dartmoor on the Mermaid.

Mason, James - Seaman - Number: 3390 - Prize name: Fox - Ship type: P - How taken: HM Frigate Maidstone - When taken: 18 Jul 1813 - Where taken: Grand Banks - Date received: 23 Feb 1814 - From what ship: Halifax via HMT Malabar - Born: Portsmouth - Age: 26 - Discharged on 22 Oct 1814 and sent to Dartmoor on HMS Leyden.

Mason, John - Seaman - Number: 1079 - How taken: Gave himself up from HM Sloop Ariel - When taken: 21 Oct 1812 - Date received: 14 Mar 1813 - From what ship: Portsmouth via HMS Cornwell - Born: New Haven - Age: 32 - Discharged on 11 Aug 1814 and sent to Dartmoor.

Mason, John (alias Manson) - Seaman - Number: 2225 - Prize name: Eliza - Ship type: MV - How taken: HM Frigate Tenedos - When taken: 29 Jun 1813 - Where taken: coast of America - Date received: 22 Aug 1813 - From what ship: HMS Raisonnable - Born: Jacobstown - Age: 34 - Discharged on 11 Aug 1814 and sent to Dartmoor on HMS Freya.

Mason, Joseph J. - Master - Number: 2313 - Prize name: John - Ship type: P - How taken: HM Brig Peruvian - When taken: 6 Feb 1813 - Where taken: West Indies - Date received: 8 Oct 1813 - From what ship: Portsmouth, via an admiral's tender - Born: Marblehead - Age: 26 - Discharged on 8 Sep 1814 and sent to Dartmoor on HMS Niobe.

Mason, Richard - Seaman - Number: 3364 - Prize name: York - Ship type: MV - How taken: Briton, letter of marque - When taken: 3 Jul 1813 - Where taken: Franklin - Date received: 23 Feb 1814 - From what ship: Halifax via HMT Malabar - Born: Caiosso, Africa - Age: 47 - Race: Mulatto - Discharged on 21 Jul 1814 and sent to Dartmoor on HMS Portia.

Maston, John - Seaman - Number: 899 - Prize name: John - Ship type: MV - How taken: HM Sloop Blossom - When taken: 15 Aug 1812 - Where taken: off Gibraltar - Date received: 1 Mar 1813 - From what ship: Plymouth via HMS Namur - Born: Averhill, MA - Age: 29 - Discharged on 10 May 1813 and released to Cartel Admittance.

Mathew, Lewis - Seaman - Number: 1821 - Prize name: tender to the Privateer True Blooded Yankee - Ship type: P - How taken: HM Brig Hope - When taken: 24 Jun 1813 - Where taken: off Brest, France - Date received: 7 Jul 1813 - From what ship: Portsmouth via HMS Scorpion - Born: Dover, DE - Age: 35 - Race: Black - Discharged on 25 Jul 1814 and sent to Dartmoor on HMS Bittern.

Mathews, Cornelius - Seaman - Number: 3866 - Prize name: Harriett - Ship type: MV - How taken: HM Brig Thistle - When taken: 24 Feb 1813 - Where taken: off St. Bartholomew, WI - Date received: 25 Aug 1814 - From what ship: London - Born: Baltimore - Age: 25 - Race: Black - Discharged on 22 Oct 1814 and sent to Dartmoor on HMS Leyden.

Mathews, Edward - Seaman - Number: 133 - Prize name: Leander - Ship type: MV - How taken: Stopped at London - When taken: 26 Oct 1812 - Date received: 5 Nov 1812 - From what ship: HMS Namur - Born: Philadelphia - Age: 27 - Discharged on 19 Jan 1813 to the HMS Scipion.

Mathews, John - Seaman - Number: 2565 - How taken: Gave himself up from HM Frigate Undaunted - When taken: 19 Nov 1812 - Date received: 23 Oct 1813 - From what ship: Portsmouth via HMS Raisonnable - Born: Delaware - Age: 37 - Discharged on 25 Sep 1814 and sent to Dartmoor on HMS Leyden.

Mathews, John - Private - Number: 3167 - Prize name: 14th U.S. Infantry - Ship type: LF - How taken: British forces - When taken: 24 Jun 1813 - Where taken: Beaver Dams, Upper Canada - Date received: 7 Jan 1814 - From what ship: Halifax - Born: New York - Age: 19 - Discharged on 10 Oct 1814 and sent to U.S. on Cartel St. Philip.

Mathewson, Andrew - Seaman - Number: 602 - Prize name: Antelope - Ship type: P - How taken: HM Brig Zephyr - When taken: 10 Dec 1812 - Where taken: at sea - Date received: 23 Feb 1813 - From what ship: Portsmouth via HMS Dromedary - Born: New York - Age: 26 - Discharged on 2 Jul 1813 and released to Cartel Moses Brown.

Maxwell, Robert - Private - Number: 2631 - Prize name: 14th U.S. Infantry - Ship type: LF - How taken: British forces - When taken: 24 Jun 1813 - Where taken: Beaver Dams, Upper Canada - Date received: 5 Nov 1813 - From what ship: HMS Hindostan - Born: County Tyrone, Ireland - Age: 27 - Discharged on 10 Oct 1814 and sent to U.S. on Cartel St. Philip.

May, William - Seaman - Number: 3611 - Prize name: Liberty - Ship type: MV - How taken: Surrendered at Stromness, Scotland - When taken: 30 Dec 1813 - Date received: 29 Mar 1814 - From what ship: Hired tender Anna - Born: Richmond - Age: 28 - Discharged on 15 Oct 1814 and sent to Dartmoor on HMS Argonaut.

Maybank, John - Seaman - Number: 3525 - How taken: Not legible - Date received: 26 Feb 1814 - From what ship: HMS Raisonnable - Born: New Orleans - Age: 32 - Discharged on 22 Jun 1814 and sent to Calais, France on the Simon & Mary.

Mayeau, Morris - Seaman - Number: 1709 - Prize name: Decatur - Ship type: MV - How taken: HM Frigate Desiree - When taken: 7 May 1813 - Where taken: off Nantes, France - Date received: 25 May 1813 - From what ship: Portsmouth via HMS Impetius - Born: Kipsey - Age: 19 - Discharged on 25 Sep 1814 and sent to Dartmoor on HMS Leyden.

Mayo, Nathaniel - Seaman - Number: 2192 - Prize name: True Blooded Yankee - Ship type: P - How taken: HM Frigate Hamadryad - When taken: 24 Jul 1813 - Where taken: off Norway - Date received: 17 Aug 1813 - From what ship: HMS Raisonnable - Born: Cape Cod - Age: 26 - Discharged on 11 Aug 1814 and sent to Dartmoor on HMS Freya.

McAlpin, Cornelius - Seaman - Number: 2413 - How taken: Gave himself up from HM Brig Hope - When taken: 18 Oct 1813 - Date received: 21 Oct 1813 - From what ship: Portsmouth via HMT Malabar - Born: Philadelphia - Age: 28 - Discharged on 4 Sep 1814 and sent to Dartmoor on HMS Freya.

McAvory, Lewis - Seaman - Number: 3340 - Prize name: Porcupine - Ship type: LM - How taken: HM Frigate Acasta - When taken: 18 Jul 1813 - Where taken: off Cape Sable, Florida - Date received: 23 Feb 1814 - From what ship: Halifax via HMT Malabar - Born: Bayonne - Age: 20 - Discharged on 22 Jun 1814 and sent to Calais, France on the Simon & Mary.

McBrearthy, Patrick - Private - Number: 1618 - Prize name: 13th U.S. Infantry - Ship type: LF - How taken: British forces - When taken: 13 Oct 1812 - Where taken: Upper Canada - Date received: 9 May 1813 - From what ship: HMS Raisonnable - Born: County Donegal, Ireland - Age: 40 - Discharged on 22 Oct 1814 and sent to Dartmoor on HMS Leyden.

McBride, James - Seaman - Number: 2000 - How taken: Gave himself up from HM Ship-of-the-Line Clarence - Date received: 15 Jul 1813 - From what ship: Plymouth - Born: Baltimore - Age: 27 - Discharged on 17 Jun 1814 and sent to Dartmoor on HMS Pincher.

McCannon, Dominique - Private - Number: 2639 - Prize name: 14th U.S. Infantry - Ship type: LF - How taken: British forces - When taken: 24 Jun 1813 - Where taken: Beaver Dams, Upper Canada - Date received: 5 Nov 1813 - From what ship: HMS Hindostan - Born: North Ireland - Age: 25 - Discharged on 10 Oct 1814 and sent to U.S. on Cartel St. Philip.

McCannon, Thomas - Private - Number: 1616 - Prize name: 13th U.S. Infantry - Ship type: LF - How taken: British forces - When taken: 13 Oct 1812 - Where taken: Upper Canada - Date received: 9 May 1813 - From what ship: HMS Raisonnable - Born: County Waterford, Ireland - Age: 39 - Discharged on 22 Oct 1814 and sent to Dartmoor on HMS Leyden.

McCoates, Samuel - Seaman - Number: 551 - Prize name: Baltimore - Ship type: P - How taken: HM Transport Diadem - When taken: 7 Oct 1812 - Where taken: S. Andres - Date received: 23 Feb 1813 - From what ship: Portsmouth via HMS Dromedary - Born: Harford - Age: 30 - Discharged on 8 Jun 1813 and released to Cartel Rodrigo.

McCormac, William - Carpenter - Number: 246 - How taken: Gave himself up from HM Ship-of-the-Line Dublin - When taken: 1 Nov 1812 - Date received: 1 Dec 1812 - From what ship: HMS Raisonnable - Born: Philadelphia - Age: 45 - Discharged on 25 Jul 1814 and sent to Dartmoor on HMS Bittern.

McCumber, Job - Seaman - Number: 2401 - How taken: Gave himself up from HM Frigate Orpheus - When taken: 26 Dec 1812 - Date received: 21 Oct 1813 - From what ship: Portsmouth via HMT Malabar - Born: Dartmouth - Age: 27 - Discharged on 11 Aug 1814 and sent to Dartmoor on HMS Freya.

McDermont, James - Seaman - Number: 123 - Prize name: Forester - Ship type: MV - How taken: Detained at London - When taken: 26 Oct 1812 - Date received: 4 Nov 1812 - From what ship: HMS Namur - Born: New York - Age: 21 - Discharged in Jul 1813 and released to Cartel Moses Brown.

McDonald, John - Seaman - Number: 1283 - How taken: Gave himself up from HM Guardship Royal William - When taken: 3 Feb 1813 - Date received: 16 Mar 1813 - From what ship: Portsmouth, via HMS Abundance - Born: New York - Age: 44 - Discharged on 23 Jul 1814 and sent to Dartmoor.

McDonald, John - Seaman - Number: 1473 - Prize name: Union - Ship type: MV - How taken: HM Frigate Iris - When taken: 17 Jan 1813 - Where taken: at sea - Date received: 6 Apr 1813 - From what ship: Portsmouth via Tender Eliza - Born: Philadelphia - Age: 24 - Discharged on 26 Jul 1813 and released to Cartel Hoffminy.

McDowell, Andrew - Captain - Number: 3091 - Prize name: U.S. Artillery - Ship type: LF - How taken: British forces - When taken: 24 Jun 1813 - Where taken: Beaver Dams, Upper Canada - Date received: 7 Jan 1814 - From what ship: Halifax - Born: New York - Age: 30 - Discharged on 14 Jan 1814 and sent to Reading on parole.

McElroy, William - Cooper - Number: 1463 - Prize name: Union - Ship type: MV - How taken: HM Frigate Iris - When taken: 17 Jan 1813 - Where taken: at sea - Date received: 6 Apr 1813 - From what ship: Portsmouth via Tender Eliza - Born: Philadelphia - Age: 24 - Discharged on 24 Jul 1813 and released to Cartel

Hoffminy.

McEver, William - Private - Number: 2624 - Prize name: 14th U.S. Infantry - Ship type: LF - How taken: British forces - When taken: 24 Jun 1813 - Where taken: Beaver Dams, Upper Canada - Date received: 5 Nov 1813 - From what ship: HMS Hindostan - Born: North Ireland - Age: 31 - Died on 28 Jul 1814 from fever.

McFarlan, Daniel - Seaman - Number: 3639 - Prize name: Bunker Hill - Ship type: P - How taken: HM Frigate Pomone & HM Frigate Cydnus - When taken: 4 Mar 1814 - Where taken: Bay of Biscay - Date received: 31 Mar 1814 - From what ship: HMS Raisonnable - Born: Philadelphia - Age: 17 - Race: Mulatto - Discharged on 25 Sep 1814 and sent to Dartmoor on HMS Niobe.

McFee, John - Seaman - Number: 1577 - How taken: Gave himself up from HM Ship-of-the-Line Braham - When taken: 10 Dec 1812 - Date received: 16 Apr 1813 - From what ship: HMS Namur, admiral's tender - Born: Alexandria - Age: 21 - Discharged on 24 Jul 1814 and sent to Dartmoor.

McGee, Robert - Seaman - Number: 2166 - How taken: Gave himself up from HM Ship-of-the-Line Swiftsure - When taken: 26 Dec 1812 - Date received: 16 Aug 1813 - From what ship: Portsmouth, via an admiral's tender - Born: Pennsylvania - Age: 35 - Discharged on 25 Sep 1814 and sent to Dartmoor on HMS Leyden.

McGill, Robert - Seaman - Number: 2782 - Prize name: Thomas - Ship type: P - How taken: HM Frigate Nymphe - When taken: 24 Jun 1813 - Where taken: off Halifax - Date received: 7 Jan 1814 - From what ship: Halifax - Born: Portsmouth - Age: 32 - Discharged on 8 Sep 1814 and sent to Dartmoor on HMS Niobe.

McGinnis, B. S. - Seaman - Number: 2393 - How taken: Gave himself up from HM Frigate Cerberus - When taken: 26 Dec 1812 - Date received: 20 Oct 1813 - From what ship: Portsmouth, via an admiral's tender - Born: Pennsylvania - Age: 22 - Discharged on 4 Sep 1814 and sent to Dartmoor on HMS Freya.

McGinnis, Patrick - Private - Number: 2612 - Prize name: 14th U.S. Infantry - Ship type: LF - How taken: British forces - When taken: 24 Jun 1813 - Where taken: Beaver Dams, Upper Canada - Date received: 5 Nov 1813 - From what ship: HMS Hindostan - Born: Ireland - Age: 23 - Discharged on 10 Oct 1814 and sent to U.S. on Cartel St. Philip.

McGowan, John - Private - Number: 2632 - Prize name: 14th U.S. Infantry - Ship type: LF - How taken: British forces - When taken: 24 Jun 1813 - Where taken: Beaver Dams, Upper Canada - Date received: 5 Nov 1813 - From what ship: HMS Hindostan - Born: County Donegal, Ireland - Age: 29 - Discharged on 10 Oct 1814 and sent to U.S. on Cartel St. Philip.

McInley, James - Seaman - Number: 3231 - How taken: Gave himself up from HM Ship-of-the-Line Dannemark - When taken: 12 Dec 1813 - Date received: 13 Jan 1814 - From what ship: Portsmouth via HMS Poictiers - Born: New York - Age: 33 - Discharged on 11 Aug 1814 and sent to Dartmoor on HMS Freya.

McIntire, John - Seaman - Number: 2973 - Prize name: Enterprise - Ship type: P - How taken: HM Frigate Tenedos - When taken: 21 May 1813 - Where taken: off Cape Cod - Date received: 7 Jan 1814 - From what ship: Halifax - Born: Massachusetts - Age: 22 - Discharged on 25 Sep 1814 and sent to Dartmoor on HMS Leyden.

McIntire, Petty - Seaman - Number: 2505 - Prize name: Thomas - Ship type: P - How taken: HM Frigate Nymphe - When taken: 28 Jun 1813 - Where taken: off Halifax - Date received: 22 Oct 1813 - From what ship: Portsmouth via HMT Malabar - Born: New York - Age: 29 - Discharged on 8 Sep 1814 and sent to Dartmoor on HMS Niobe.

McIntyre, William - Seaman - Number: 2214 - Prize name: Jane, prize of the Privateer Snap Dragon - Ship type: P - How taken: HM Frigate Crescent & HM Ship of-the-Line Bellerophon - When taken: 28 Jun 1813 - Where taken: Newfoundland Bank - Date received: 18 Aug 1813 - From what ship: Portsmouth, via an admiral's tender - Born: Ireland - Age: 56 - Discharged on 11 Aug 1814 and sent to Dartmoor on HMS Freya.

McIver, John - Seaman - Number: 2201 - How taken: Gave himself up from HM Ship-of-the-Line Kent - When taken: 26 Oct 1812 - Date received: 18 Aug 1813 - From what ship: Portsmouth, via an admiral's tender - Born: Massachusetts - Age: 20 - Discharged on 11 Aug 1814 and sent to Dartmoor on HMS Freya.

McKenzie, John - Seaman - Number: 1042 - Prize name: Wasp - Ship type: MV - How taken: Earl Spencer, East Indianman - When taken: 4 Aug 1812 - Where taken: off Cape Clear, Ireland - Date received: 11 Mar 1813 - From what ship: Yarmouth via HMS Tenders - Born: Massachusetts - Age: 25 - Race: Black - Discharged on

8 Jun 1813 and released to Cartel Rodrigo.

McKenzie, Kenneth - Captain - Number: 3092 - Prize name: 14th U.S. Infantry - Ship type: LF - How taken: British forces - When taken: 24 Jun 1813 - Where taken: Beaver Dams, Upper Canada - Date received: 7 Jan 1814 - From what ship: Halifax - Born: New York - Age: 25 - Discharged on 14 Jan 1814 and sent to Reading on parole.

McKenzie, William - Seaman - Number: 2434 - Prize name: Hepsey - Ship type: MV - How taken: HM Brig Zenobia - When taken: 22 Jun 1813 - Where taken: off Lisbon - Date received: 21 Oct 1813 - From what ship: Portsmouth via HMT Malabar - Born: New York - Age: 23 - Discharged on 4 Sep 1814 and sent to Dartmoor on HMS Freya.

McKever, Charles - Private - Number: 2618 - Prize name: 14th U.S. Infantry - Ship type: LF - How taken: British forces - When taken: 24 Jun 1813 - Where taken: Beaver Dams, Upper Canada - Date received: 5 Nov 1813 - From what ship: HMS Hindostan - Born: North Ireland - Age: 36 - Discharged on 10 Oct 1814 and sent to U.S. on Cartel St. Philip.

McKinney, Isaac - Seaman - Number: 2492 - Prize name: Governor Plumer - Ship type: P - How taken: Sent into custody from a privateer - When taken: 1 Jun 1813 - Where taken: off Cape Ann - Date received: 22 Oct 1813 - From what ship: Portsmouth via HMT Malabar - Born: Massachusetts - Age: 20 - Discharged on 8 Sep 1814 and sent to Dartmoor on HMS Niobe.

McKinney, Isaac - Seaman - Number: 2936 - Prize name: Governor Plumer - Ship type: P - How taken: HM Brig Shamrock - When taken: 26 May 1813 - Where taken: at sea - Date received: 7 Jan 1814 - From what ship: Halifax - Born: New Hampshire - Age: 24 - Discharged on 25 Sep 1814 and sent to Dartmoor on HMS Leyden.

McKinney, Isaac - Seaman - Number: 2932 - Prize name: Governor Plumer - Ship type: P - How taken: HM Brig Shamrock - When taken: 26 May 1813 - Where taken: at sea - Date received: 7 Jan 1814 - From what ship: Halifax - Born: Massachusetts - Age: 24 - Discharged on 25 Sep 1814 and sent to Dartmoor on HMS Leyden.

McKinnon, John - Seaman - Number: 2450 - Prize name: Wiley Reynard - Ship type: P - How taken: HM Frigate Shannon - When taken: 16 Aug 1812 - Where taken: off Halifax - Date received: 21 Oct 1813 - From what ship: Portsmouth via HMT Malabar - Born: Chester - Age: 23 - Discharged on 4 Sep 1814 and sent to Dartmoor on HMS Freya.

McLane, George - Seaman - Number: 3443 - Prize name: Frolic - Ship type: P - How taken: HM Frigate Maidstone - When taken: 16 Jul 1813 - Where taken: Grand Banks - Date received: 23 Feb 1814 - From what ship: Halifax via HMT Malabar - Born: Amsterdam - Age: 20 - Discharged on 22 Oct 1814 and sent to Dartmoor on HMS Leyden.

McLean, John - Seaman - Number: 3264 - Prize name: Volante - Ship type: P - How taken: HM Brig Curlew - When taken: 25 Mar 1813 - Where taken: off Boston - Date received: 23 Feb 1814 - From what ship: Halifax via HMT Malabar - Born: Providence - Age: 25 - Discharged on 10 Oct 1814 and sent to Dartmoor on the Mermaid.

McMiller, Andrew - Seaman - Number: 2040 - Prize name: Kitty, prize of the U.S. Frigate President - Ship type: War - How taken: Dart, British privateer from Guernsey - When taken: 20 Jun 1813 - Where taken: off the Western Isles, Scotland - Date received: 4 Aug 1813 - From what ship: HMS Christian VII - Born: Salem - Age: 45 - Discharged on 4 Aug 1814 and sent to Dartmoor on HMS Liverpool.

McNeal, Alexander - Seaman - Number: 608 - Prize name: Antelope - Ship type: P - How taken: HM Brig Zephyr - When taken: 10 Dec 1812 - Where taken: at sea - Date received: 23 Feb 1813 - From what ship: Portsmouth via HMS Dromedary - Born: Chester - Age: 31 - Race: Man of color - Discharged on 10 May 1813 and released to Cartel Admittance.

McPhee, Alexander - Seaman - Number: 76 - Prize name: Antelope - Ship type: MV - How taken: HMS Horato - When taken: 2 Aug 1812 - Where taken: off Norway - Date received: 4 Nov 1812 - From what ship: HMS Namur - Born: New York - Age: 18 - Discharged on 23 Mar 1813 and released to the Cartel Robinson Potter.

McGuire, Hugh - Private - Number: 2610 - Prize name: 14th U.S. Infantry - Ship type: LF - How taken: British forces - When taken: 24 Jun 1813 - Where taken: Beaver Dams, Upper Canada - Date received: 5 Nov 1813 - From what ship: HMS Hindostan - Born: Ireland - Age: 23 - Discharged on 17 Jun 1814 and sent to Dartmoor.

McWarren, Nathaniel - Seaman - Number: 1859 - How taken: Gave himself up from HM Frigate Leonidas - Date received: 7 Jul 1813 - From what ship: Portsmouth via HMS Tribune - Born: Durham, MA - Age: 33 - Discharged on 25 Jul 1814 and sent to Dartmoor on HMS Bittern.

Mead, Ezekiel - Seaman - Number: 3620 - Prize name: Liberty - Ship type: MV - How taken: Surrendered at Stromness, Scotland - When taken: 30 Dec 1813 - Date received: 29 Mar 1814 - From what ship: Hired tender Anna - Born: New York - Age: 26 - Discharged on 20 Aug 1814 and sent to Dartmoor on HMS Shamrock.

Mead, James - Carpenter - Number: 183 - How taken: Stopped at London - When taken: 29 Oct 1812 - Date received: 5 Nov 1812 - From what ship: HMS Namur - Born: New York - Age: 26 - Discharged in Jul 1813 and released to Cartel Moses Brown.

Mead, Lewis - Seaman - Number: 3331 - Prize name: Porcupine - Ship type: LM - How taken: HM Frigate Acasta - When taken: 18 Jul 1813 - Where taken: off Cape Sable, Florida - Date received: 23 Feb 1814 - From what ship: Halifax via HMT Malabar - Born: New York - Age: 30 - Discharged on 11 Mar 1814 and released to Cartel Thomas, an Indianman.

Meath, Solomon - Seaman - Number: 3023 - How taken: Gave himself up from HM Ship-of-the-Line Invincible - When taken: 14 Jan 1813 - Date received: 7 Jan 1814 - From what ship: Portsmouth - Born: Maryland - Age: 25 - Race: Black - Discharged on 26 Sep 1814 and sent to Dartmoor on HMS Leyden.

Meeker, James - Seaman - Number: 1789 - How taken: Taken up at London - When taken: 12 Jun 1813 - Date received: 1 Jul 1813 - From what ship: HMS Raisonnable - Born: New Jersey - Age: 30 - Race: Mulatto - Discharged on 25 Jul 1814 and sent to Dartmoor on HMS Bittern.

Melcher, John - Seaman - Number: 191 - Prize name: Mary Ann - Ship type: MV - How taken: HM Brig Castilian - When taken: 14 Aug 1812 - Where taken: Downs - Date received: 6 Nov 1812 - From what ship: HMS Echo - Born: Bremen - Age: 32 - Discharged in Jul 1813 and released to Cartel Moses Brown.

Melcher, John - Seaman - Number: 3256 - Prize name: Revenge - Ship type: MV - How taken: HM Frigate Shannon - When taken: 5 Nov 1813 - Where taken: off Halifax - Date received: 23 Feb 1814 - From what ship: Halifax via HMT Malabar - Born: Wilmington - Age: 24 - Discharged on 10 Oct 1814 and sent to Dartmoor on the Mermaid.

Melville, Charles - Seaman - Number: 1728 - Prize name: Powhattan - Ship type: MV - How taken: HMS Horatio - When taken: 13 Dec 1812 - Where taken: Bay of Biscay - Date received: 25 May 1813 - From what ship: Portsmouth via HMS Impetius - Born: Memel - Age: 38 - Discharged on 24 Jul 1813 and released to Cartel Hoffminy.

Melville, John - Seaman - Number: 1408 - Prize name: Porcupine - Ship type: MV - How taken: HM Frigate Dryand - When taken: 8 Jan 1813 - Where taken: off Bordeaux, France - Date received: 5 Apr 1813 - From what ship: Plymouth via HMS Dwarf - Born: Baltimore - Age: 19 - Discharged on 24 Jul 1813 and released to Cartel Hoffminy.

Melvin, John - Seaman - Number: 3033 - How taken: Gave himself up from HMS Minstrel - When taken: 28 Jul 1813 - Date received: 7 Jan 1814 - From what ship: Portsmouth - Born: Boston - Age: 22 - Discharged on 11 Aug 1814 and sent to Dartmoor on HMS Freya.

Melvin, William - Private - Number: 2662 - Prize name: 2nd U.S. Artillery - Ship type: LF - How taken: British forces - When taken: 6 Jun 1813 - Where taken: Stoney Creek, Upper Canada - Date received: 5 Nov 1813 - From what ship: HMS Hindostan - Born: County Sligo, Ireland - Age: 30 - Discharged on 17 Jun 1814 and sent to Dartmoor.

Melzard, Peter - Seaman - Number: 2482 - Prize name: Enterprise - Ship type: P - How taken: HM Frigate Tenedos - When taken: 21 May 1813 - Where taken: off Cape Cod - Date received: 22 Oct 1813 - From what ship: Portsmouth via HMT Malabar - Born: Marblehead - Age: 20 - Discharged on 8 Sep 1814 and sent to Dartmoor on HMS Niobe.

Mercer, Chaumont - Steward - Number: 1466 - Prize name: Union - Ship type: MV - How taken: HM Frigate Iris - When taken: 17 Jan 1813 - Where taken: at sea - Date received: 6 Apr 1813 - From what ship: Portsmouth via Tender Eliza - Born: Prince George's County, MD - Age: 25 - Discharged on 24 Jul 1813 and released to Cartel Hoffminy.

Merkell, John - Seaman - Number: 1668 - How taken: Gave himself up from HM Schooner Pigmy - Date received: 9 May 1813 - From what ship: HMS Raisonnable - Born: Boston - Age: 23 - Discharged on 11 Aug 1814 and sent to Dartmoor on HMS Freya.

Merle, John - Seaman - Number: 1372 - How taken: Gave himself up from HM Ship-of-the-Line Christian VII - When taken: 19 Mar 1813 - Date received: 3 Apr 1813 - From what ship: Portsmouth, via an admiral's tender - Born: New York - Age: 24 - Discharged on 24 Jul 1814 and sent to Dartmoor.

Merrel, Enoch - Seaman - Number: 3806 - How taken: Impressed at Philos - When taken: 20 Mar 1814 - Date received: 5 Jun 1814 - From what ship: HMS Raisonnable - Born: Salisbury - Age: 22 - Discharged on 29 Sep 1814 and sent to Dartmoor on HMS Freya.

Merriday, John - Seaman - Number: 1160 - Prize name: Sword Fish - Ship type: P - How taken: HM Ship-of-the-Line Elephant - When taken: 28 Dec 1812 - Where taken: off Azores - Date received: 16 Mar 1813 - From what ship: Portsmouth, via HMS Abundance - Born: Kent Island - Age: 30 - Race: Mulatto - Discharged on 24 Jul 1813 and released to Cartel Hoffminy.

Merrish, Joseph - Seaman - Number: 3382 - Prize name: Teazer - Ship type: P - How taken: HM Frigate Boreas - When taken: 15 Jun 1813 - Where taken: off Halifax - Date received: 23 Feb 1814 - From what ship: Halifax via HMT Malabar - Born: Bremen - Age: 25 - Discharged on 10 Oct 1814 and sent to Dartmoor on the Mermaid.

Merritt, Enoch - Seaman - Number: 3564 - Prize name: Minerva - Ship type: MV - How taken: HM Ship-of-the-Line Conquestador - When taken: 19 Jan 1814 - Where taken: Bay of Biscay - Date received: 7 May 1814 - From what ship: Portsmouth via HMS Favorite - Born: Falmouth - Age: 19 - Discharged on 25 Sep 1814 and sent to Dartmoor on HMS Niobe.

Mesniers, Benjamin - Seaman - Number: 1497 - Prize name: Union - Ship type: MV - How taken: HM Frigate Iris - When taken: 17 Jan 1813 - Where taken: at sea - Date received: 6 Apr 1813 - From what ship: Plymouth via an admiral's tender - Born: New London - Age: 22 - Discharged on 11 Aug 1814 and sent to Dartmoor.

Metcalf, William - Seaman - Number: 544 - Prize name: Baltimore - Ship type: P - How taken: HM Transport Diadem - When taken: 7 Oct 1812 - Where taken: S. Andres - Date received: 23 Feb 1813 - From what ship: Portsmouth via HMS Dromedary - Born: New York - Age: 21 - Discharged on 8 Jun 1813 and released to Cartel Rodrigo.

Metrash, Ezekiel - Seaman - Number: 514 - Prize name: William - Ship type: MV - How taken: HM Brig Recruit - When taken: 29 Aug 1812 - Where taken: at sea - Date received: 23 Feb 1813 - From what ship: Portsmouth via HMS Dromedary - Born: Norwalk - Age: 19 - Race: Man of color - Discharged on 10 May 1813 and released to Cartel Admittance.

Meyer, John - Seaman - Number: 541 - Prize name: Baltimore - Ship type: P - How taken: HM Transport Diadem - When taken: 7 Oct 1812 - Where taken: S. Andres - Date received: 23 Feb 1813 - From what ship: Portsmouth via HMS Dromedary - Born: Bremen - Age: 24 - Discharged on 8 Jun 1813 and released to Cartel Rodrigo.

Meyers, James - Seaman - Number: 2386 - How taken: Gave himself up from HM Frigate Ganymede - When taken: 26 Dec 1812 - Date received: 20 Oct 1813 - From what ship: Portsmouth, via an admiral's tender - Born: Philadelphia - Age: 23 - Discharged on 4 Sep 1814 and sent to Dartmoor on HMS Freya.

Miars, Michael - Private - Number: 3071 - Prize name: 14th U.S. Infantry - Ship type: LF - How taken: British forces - When taken: 24 Jun 1813 - Where taken: Beaver Dams, Upper Canada - Date received: 7 Jan 1814 - From what ship: Halifax - Born: Pennsylvania - Age: 21 - Discharged on 10 Oct 1814 and sent to U.S. on Cartel St. Philip.

Michael, Peter - Seaman - Number: 981 - Prize name: Hope - Ship type: MV - How taken: HM Sloop Pheasant - When taken: 13 Dec 1812 - Where taken: off Azores - Date received: 10 Mar 1813 - From what ship: HMS

Tigress - Born: Greece - Age: 24 - Released on 23 Apr 1813.

Michel, John William - Seaman - Number: 101 - Prize name: Liberty - Ship type: MV - How taken: Stopped at London - When taken: 26 Oct 1812 - Date received: 4 Nov 1812 - From what ship: HMS Namur - Born: Norfolk, VA - Age: 25 - Discharged in Jul 1813 and released to Cartel Moses Brown.

Middleton, John - Seaman - Number: 3487 - How taken: Gave himself up from HMS Muros & HM Frigate Rosamund - When taken: 28 Dec 1813 - Date received: 23 Feb 1814 - From what ship: Portsmouth via HMT Malabar - Born: Maryland - Age: 24 - Race: Black - Discharged on 26 Sep 1814 and sent to Dartmoor on HMS Leyden.

Middleton, Reuben - Seaman - Number: 1135 - Prize name: Sword Fish - Ship type: P - How taken: HM Ship-of-the-Line Elephant - When taken: 28 Dec 1812 - Where taken: off Azores - Date received: 16 Mar 1813 - From what ship: Portsmouth, Mundane - Born: Salem - Age: 22 - Discharged on 24 Jul 1813 and released to Cartel Hoffminy.

Middleton, Reuben - Seaman - Number: 2062 - Prize name: Sword Fish - Ship type: P - How taken: HM Ship-of-the-Line Elephant - When taken: 28 Dec 1812 - Where taken: off Azores - Date received: 2 Aug 1813 - From what ship: Cartel Hoffminy - Born: Salem - Age: 22 - Discharged on 20 Aug 1814 and sent to Dartmoor on HMS Shamrock.

Mids, Michael - Seaman - Number: 3518 - Prize name: Pilot - Ship type: LM - How taken: Vittoria, British privateer from Guernsey - When taken: 28 Jan 1814 - Where taken: off Bordeaux, France - Date received: 23 Feb 1814 - From what ship: Portsmouth via HMT Malabar - Born: Baltimore - Age: 21 - Discharged on 26 Sep 1814 and sent to Dartmoor on HMS Leyden.

Milborne, William - Seaman - Number: 3679 - Prize name: Sally - Ship type: MV - How taken: HM Brig Derwent - When taken: 21 Jul 1814 - Where taken: at sea - Date received: 4 May 1814 - From what ship: Portsmouth - Born: Salem - Age: 39 - Discharged on 25 Sep 1814 and sent to Dartmoor on HMS Niobe.

Miles, John - Seaman - Number: 2892 - Prize name: Dart - Ship type: P - How taken: HM Frigate Niger & HMS Fortunee - When taken: 10 Nov 1813 - Where taken: off Cape Finisterre, Spain - Date received: 7 Jan 1814 - From what ship: Portsmouth - Born: Whitehall - Age: 18 - Died on 10 Jun 1814 from fever.

Miller, Ezekiel - Seaman - Number: 47 - Prize name: General Blake - Ship type: MV - How taken: HM Brig Recruit - When taken: 11 Jun 1812 - Where taken: off Rhode Island - Date received: 3 Nov 1812 - From what ship: HMS Plover - Born: Norfolk, VA - Age: 21 - Died on 1 Mar 1813 from spasmodic affection.

Miller, George - Carpenter - Number: 1094 - Prize name: Calcutta, East Indian Ship - Ship type: MV - How taken: Two Brothers, British privateer from Guernsey - When taken: 30 Nov 1812 - Where taken: off St. Helena - Date received: 14 Mar 1813 - From what ship: Portsmouth via HMS Beagle - Born: New York - Age: 24 - Discharged on 8 Jun 1813 and released to Cartel Rodrigo.

Miller, George - Seaman - Number: 2148 - Prize name: Matilda, prize of the U.S. Brig Argus - Ship type: War - How taken: HM Frigate Revolutionnaire - When taken: 25 Jul 1813 - Where taken: off Lorient, France - Date received: 9 Aug 1813 - From what ship: HMS Thames - Born: Rhode Island - Age: 24 - Race: Black - Discharged on 12 Aug 1814 and sent to Dartmoor on HMS Alpheus.

Miller, George M. - Private - Number: 2638 - Prize name: 14th U.S. Infantry - Ship type: LF - How taken: British forces - When taken: 24 Jun 1813 - Where taken: Beaver Dams, Upper Canada - Date received: 5 Nov 1813 - From what ship: HMS Hindostan - Born: County Antrim, Ireland - Age: 24 - Discharged on 10 Oct 1814 and sent to U.S. on Cartel St. Philip.

Miller, Henry - Seaman - Number: 338 - Prize name: Postsea, prize to the Privateer Thrasher - Ship type: P - How taken: HM Sloop Helena - When taken: 31 Dec 1813 - Where taken: off Azores - Date received: 19 Jan 1813 - From what ship: HMS Raisonnable - Born: Waldarbrough - Age: 23 - Discharged on 24 Jul 1813 and released to Cartel Hoffminy.

Miller, James - Seaman - Number: 8 - Prize name: Eliza Ann - Ship type: MV - How taken: HM Ship-of-the-Line Vigo - When taken: 11 Aug 1812 - Where taken: Hanoi Bay - Date received: 29 Oct 1812 - From what ship: HMS Raisonnable - Born: Beverly - Age: 17 - Discharged on 10 May 1813 and released to Cartel Admittance.

Miller, James - Seaman - Number: 3403 - Prize name: Elbridge Gerry - Ship type: P - How taken: HM Frigate Tenedos - When taken: 21 May 1813 - Where taken: off Cape Cod - Date received: 23 Feb 1814 - From what ship: Halifax via HMT Malabar - Born: Portsmouth - Age: 19 - Discharged on 22 Oct 1814 and sent to Dartmoor on HMS Leyden.

Miller, James - Private - Number: 2644 - Prize name: 14th U.S. Infantry - Ship type: LF - How taken: British forces - When taken: 24 Jun 1813 - Where taken: Beaver Dams, Upper Canada - Date received: 5 Nov 1813 - From what ship: HMS Hindostan - Born: North Ireland - Age: 42 - Discharged on 10 Oct 1814 and sent to U.S. on Cartel St. Philip.

Miller, James - Seaman - Number: 2902 - Prize name: Dart - Ship type: P - How taken: HM Frigate Niger & HMS Fortunee - When taken: 10 Nov 1813 - Where taken: off Cape Finisterre, Spain - Date received: 7 Jan 1814 - From what ship: Portsmouth - Born: Charleston - Age: 27 - Discharged on 25 Sep 1814 and sent to Dartmoor on HMS Leyden.

Miller, Jeremiah - Seaman - Number: 2091 - How taken: Gave himself up from HM Ship-of-the-Line Scipion - When taken: 27 May 1813 - Date received: 9 Aug 1813 - From what ship: HMS Thames - Born: Kennebunk, MA - Age: 32 - Discharged on 16 Sep 1814 and released to HMS Ceres.

Miller, John - Seaman - Number: 1835 - Prize name: tender to the Privateer True Blooded Yankee - Ship type: P - How taken: HM Ship-of-the-Line Fame - When taken: 24 Jun 1813 - Where taken: off Brest, France - Date received: 7 Jul 1813 - From what ship: Portsmouth via HMS Scorpion - Born: New York - Age: 28 - Discharged on 25 Jul 1814 and sent to Dartmoor on HMS Bittern.

Miller, John - Seaman - Number: 2284 - How taken: Gave himself up from HM Ship-of-the-Line Royal George - When taken: 29 Oct 1812 - Date received: 17 Sep 1813 - From what ship: HMS Raisonnable - Born: New Jersey - Age: 37 - Discharged on 4 Sep 1814 and sent to Dartmoor on HMS Freya.

Miller, John Jacob - Seaman - Number: 549 - Prize name: Baltimore - Ship type: P - How taken: HM Transport Diadem - When taken: 7 Oct 1812 - Where taken: S. Andres - Date received: 23 Feb 1813 - From what ship: Portsmouth via HMS Dromedary - Born: Germantown - Age: 29 - Discharged on 8 Jun 1813 and released to Cartel Rodrigo.

Miller, Samuel - Seaman - Number: 343 - Prize name: Postsea, prize to the Privateer Thrasher - Ship type: P - How taken: HM Sloop Helena - When taken: 31 Dec 1813 - Where taken: off Azores - Date received: 19 Jan 1813 - From what ship: HMS Raisonnable - Born: Polervan, NH - Age: 26 - Discharged on 24 Jul 1813 and released to Cartel Hoffminy.

Millett, John - Seaman - Number: 2978 - Prize name: Enterprise - Ship type: P - How taken: HM Frigate Tenedos - When taken: 21 May 1813 - Where taken: off Cape Cod - Date received: 7 Jan 1814 - From what ship: Halifax - Born: Massachusetts - Age: 19 - Discharged on 25 Sep 1814 and sent to Dartmoor on HMS Leyden.

Millett, Joseph - Seaman - Number: 2855 - Prize name: Fire Fly - Ship type: LM - How taken: HM Frigate Revolutionnaire - When taken: 19 Oct 1813 - Where taken: off Cape Ortegal, Spain - Date received: 7 Jan 1814 - From what ship: Portsmouth - Born: Massachusetts - Age: 39 - Discharged on 26 Sep 1814 and sent to Dartmoor on HMS Leyden.

Millikan, William - Seaman - Number: 114 - Prize name: Urbana - Ship type: MV - How taken: Stopped at London - When taken: 26 Oct 1812 - Date received: 4 Nov 1812 - From what ship: HMS Namur - Born: East Town, MD - Age: 24 - Discharged on 11 Jan 1813 and released to the Rebecca.

Mills, Henry - Seaman - Number: 1146 - Prize name: Sword Fish - Ship type: P - How taken: HM Ship-of-the-Line Elephant - When taken: 28 Dec 1812 - Where taken: off Azores - Date received: 16 Mar 1813 - From what ship: Portsmouth, Mundane - Born: Kittery - Age: 40 - Race: Black - Discharged on 24 Jul 1813 and released to Cartel Hoffminy.

Mills, John - Seaman - Number: 919 - How taken: Gave himself up from HM Frigate Belle Poule - When taken: 5 Sep 1812 - Date received: 10 Mar 1813 - From what ship: HMS Tigress - Born: Portsmouth - Age: 21 - Discharged on 25 Sep 1814 and sent to Dartmoor on HMS Niobe.

Mills, Samuel - 2nd Mate - Number: 212 - How taken: Gave himself up from MV Perverance - When taken: 2 Nov

1812 - Date received: 15 Nov 1812 - From what ship: HMS Raisonnable - Born: Fairfield, CT - Age: 28 - Died on 21 Mar 1813 from pneumonia.

Mills, Stephen - Private - Number: 3132 - Prize name: 14th U.S. Infantry - Ship type: LF - How taken: British forces - When taken: 24 Jun 1813 - Where taken: Beaver Dams, Upper Canada - Date received: 7 Jan 1814 - From what ship: Halifax - Born: Dover - Age: 19 - Discharged on 10 Oct 1814 and sent to U.S. on Cartel St. Philip.

Miner, Benjamin F. - Seaman - Number: 1096 - Prize name: Calcutta, East Indian Ship - Ship type: MV - How taken: Two Brothers, British privateer from Guernsey - When taken: 30 Nov 1812 - Where taken: off St. Helena - Date received: 14 Mar 1813 - From what ship: Portsmouth via HMS Beagle - Born: Northfield - Age: 22 - Discharged on 8 Jun 1813 and released to Cartel Rodrigo.

Minor, David - Seaman - Number: 1681 - How taken: Gave himself up from MV Quebec - When taken: 23 Mar 1813 - Date received: 15 May 1813 - From what ship: HMS Raisonnable - Born: New London - Age: 27 - Discharged on 25 Sep 1814 and sent to Dartmoor on HMS Niobe.

Minor, John - Seaman - Number: 3597 - Prize name: Liberty - Ship type: MV - How taken: Surrendered at Stromness, Scotland - When taken: 30 Dec 1813 - Date received: 29 Mar 1814 - From what ship: Hired tender Anna - Born: New London - Age: 14 - Discharged on 25 Sep 1814 and sent to Dartmoor on HMS Niobe.

Minor, Pedro - Seaman - Number: 908 - How taken: Impressed off the Tessie - When taken: 17 Jan 1813 - Date received: 9 Mar 1813 - From what ship: HMS Raisonnable - Born: New Orleans - Age: 29 - Discharged on 24 Jul 1813 and released to Cartel Hoffminy.

Miramon, Roch - Merchant & Passenger - Number: 2900 - Prize name: Dart - Ship type: P - How taken: HM Frigate Niger & HMS Fortunee - When taken: 10 Nov 1813 - Where taken: off Cape Finisterre, Spain - Date received: 7 Jan 1814 - From what ship: Portsmouth - Born: New Orleans - Age: 45 - Released on 15 Jun 1814.

Mirpaine, Bruce - Seaman - Number: 552 - Prize name: Baltimore - Ship type: P - How taken: HM Transport Diadem - When taken: 7 Oct 1812 - Where taken: S. Andres - Date received: 23 Feb 1813 - From what ship: Portsmouth via HMS Dromedary - Born: New York - Age: 22 - Discharged on 8 Jun 1813 and released to Cartel Rodrigo.

Mirrel, Samuel B. - Surgeon - Number: 2699 - Prize name: Growler - Ship type: P - How taken: HM Brig Electra - When taken: 7 Jul 1813 - Where taken: off St. Johns - Date received: 7 Jan 1814 - From what ship: Portsmouth - Born: Massachusetts - Age: 24 - Released on 15 Jun 1814.

Mista, William - Seaman - Number: 3916 - Prize name: Atlantic - Ship type: MV - How taken: HM Frigate Barbadoes - When taken: 18 Jan 1814 - Where taken: off St. Bartholomew, WI - Date received: 11 Sep 1814 - From what ship: London - Born: Virginia - Age: 36 - Discharged on 10 Oct 1814 and sent to Dartmoor on the Mermaid.

Mitch, Thomas - Seaman - Number: 2083 - How taken: Gave himself up from HM Ship-of-the-Line Scipion - When taken: 27 May 1813 - Date received: 9 Aug 1813 - From what ship: HMS Thames - Born: Philadelphia - Age: 28 - Discharged on 24 Jul 1814 and sent to Dartmoor on HMS Liffey.

Mitchell, Carr - Seaman - Number: 2254 - Prize name: Joseph - Ship type: MV - How taken: HM Frigate Iris - When taken: 8 Jun 1813 - Where taken: off Spain - Date received: 7 Sep 1813 - From what ship: HMS Raisonnable - Born: Virginia - Age: 18 - Race: Mulatto - Discharged on 11 Aug 1814 and sent to Dartmoor on HMS Freya.

Mitchell, Charles - Private - Number: 3160 - Prize name: 14th U.S. Infantry - Ship type: LF - How taken: British forces - When taken: 24 Jun 1813 - Where taken: Beaver Dams, Upper Canada - Date received: 7 Jan 1814 - From what ship: Halifax - Born: New York - Age: 26 - Discharged on 10 Oct 1814 and sent to U.S. on Cartel St. Philip.

Mitchell, Francis - Seaman - Number: 1221 - Prize name: Rossie - Ship type: MV - How taken: HM Frigate Dryand - When taken: 7 Jan 1813 - Where taken: at sea - Date received: 16 Mar 1813 - From what ship: Portsmouth, via HMS Abundance - Born: Alexandria - Age: 21 - Discharged on 24 Jul 1813 and released to Cartel Hoffminy.

Mitchell, James - Seaman - Number: 470 - Prize name: Hunter - Ship type: P - How taken: HM Frigate Phoebe - When taken: 23 Dec 1812 - Where taken: off Azores - Date received: 19 Feb 1813 - From what ship: HMS Modeste - Born: Warrington - Age: 20 - Discharged on 24 Jul 1813 and released to Cartel Hoffminy.

Mitchell, James M. - Seaman - Number: 1108 - Prize name: Tom Thumb - Ship type: MV - How taken: Lion, British privateer - When taken: 15 Feb 1813 - Where taken: Bay of Biscay - Date received: 14 Mar 1813 - From what ship: Portsmouth via HMS Beagle - Born: New York - Age: 19 - Race: Man of Color - Discharged on 11 Aug 1814 and sent to Dartmoor on HMS Freya.

Mitchell, John - Seaman - Number: 460 - Prize name: Hunter - Ship type: P - How taken: HM Frigate Phoebe - When taken: 23 Dec 1812 - Where taken: off Azores - Date received: 19 Feb 1813 - From what ship: HMS Modeste - Born: Baltimore - Age: 18 - Discharged on 24 Jul 1813 and released to Cartel Hoffminy.

Mitchell, John - Seaman - Number: 531 - Prize name: Baltimore - Ship type: P - How taken: HM Transport Diadem - When taken: 7 Oct 1812 - Where taken: S. Andres - Date received: 23 Feb 1813 - From what ship: Portsmouth via HMS Dromedary - Born: Baltimore - Age: 23 - Discharged on 8 Jun 1813 and released to Cartel Rodrigo.

Mitchell, John - Seaman - Number: 3348 - Prize name: Teazer - Ship type: P - How taken: HM Frigate Boreas - When taken: 26 Jul 1813 - Where taken: off Halifax - Date received: 23 Feb 1814 - From what ship: Halifax via HMT Malabar - Born: Bordeaux, France - Age: 41 - Discharged on 10 Oct 1814 and sent to Dartmoor on the Mermaid.

Mitchell, Thomas - Seaman - Number: 1307 - How taken: Gave himself up from HM Guardship Royal William - When taken: 3 Feb 1813 - Date received: 16 Mar 1813 - From what ship: Portsmouth, via HMS Abundance - Born: Marblehead - Age: 34 - Discharged on 23 Jul 1814 and sent to Dartmoor.

Mitchell, William - Seaman - Number: 3315 - Prize name: Yorktown - Ship type: P - How taken: HM Ship-of-the-Line La Hogue - When taken: 17 Jul 1813 - Where taken: Grand Banks - Date received: 12 Apr 1814 - From what ship: HMS Glory - Born: Salem - Age: 26 - Discharged on 8 Sep 1814 and sent to Dartmoor on HMS Niobe.

Moaton, Bryant - Seaman - Number: 2686 - How taken: Impressed at London - When taken: 26 Dec 1813 - Date received: 28 Dec 1813 - From what ship: HMS Raisonnable - Born: Portland - Age: 22 - Discharged on 8 Sep 1814 and sent to Dartmoor on HMS Niobe.

Modre, John - Seaman - Number: 3555 - Prize name: Zephyr, prize of Privateer Rattlesnake - Ship type: P - How taken: HM Frigate Surveillante - When taken: 6 Jan 1814 - Where taken: Bay of Biscay - Date received: 7 May 1814 - From what ship: Portsmouth via HMS Favorite - Born: Madeira, Portugal - Age: 26 - Discharged on 25 Sep 1814 and sent to Dartmoor on HMS Niobe.

Moffett, Hugh - Seaman - Number: 3385 - Prize name: Teazer - Ship type: P - How taken: HM Frigate Boreas - When taken: 15 Jun 1813 - Where taken: off Halifax - Date received: 23 Feb 1814 - From what ship: Halifax via HMT Malabar - Born: Moose Island - Age: 24 - Discharged on 10 Oct 1814 and sent to Dartmoor on the Mermaid.

Moffett, John - Steward - Number: 1962 - Prize name: Napoleon - Ship type: MV - How taken: HM Frigate Belle Poule - When taken: 3 Apr 1813 - Where taken: off Cape Ortegal, Spain - Date received: 15 Jul 1813 - From what ship: Plymouth - Born: New York - Age: 33 - Discharged on 17 Jun 1814 and sent to Dartmoor on HMS Redbreast.

Molbin, Benjamin - Seaman - Number: 1931 - Prize name: Edward - Ship type: MV - How taken: Seringapatam, British letter of marque - When taken: 6 Jan 1813 - Where taken: South America - Date received: 11 Jul 1813 - From what ship: HMS Raisonnable - Born: Newport, RI - Age: 19 - Race: Black - Discharged on 19 Jul 1813 and released to HMS Ceres.

Molloy, Peter - Seaman - Number: 3484 - How taken: Gave himself up from HMS Muros - When taken: 27 Jan 1813 - Date received: 23 Feb 1814 - From what ship: Portsmouth via HMT Malabar - Born: New York - Age: 44 - Discharged on 26 Sep 1814 and sent to Dartmoor on HMS Leyden.

Molton, Nathaniel - Seaman - Number: 2283 - Prize name: Yankee - Ship type: P - How taken: HM Frigate Pyramus - When taken: 15 Oct 1812 - Where taken: off the Western Isles, Scotland - Date received: 17 Sep 1813 -

From what ship: HMS Raisonnable - Born: Newburyport - Age: 18 - Discharged on 22 Oct 1813 and released to HMS Ceres.

Monk, Joseph - Seaman - Number: 3804 - Prize name: James - Ship type: MV - How taken: HM Brig Harpy - When taken: 13 Dec 1812 - Where taken: off Isle de France (Mauritius) - Date received: 5 Jun 1814 - From what ship: HMS Raisonnable - Born: Philadelphia - Age: 18 - Discharged on 29 Sep 1814 and sent to Dartmoor on HMS Freya.

Monnett, Samuel - Seaman - Number: 472 - Prize name: Hunter - Ship type: P - How taken: HM Frigate Phoebe - When taken: 23 Dec 1812 - Where taken: off Azores - Date received: 19 Feb 1813 - From what ship: HMS Modeste - Born: Salem - Age: 19 - Discharged on 24 Jul 1813 and released to Cartel Hoffminy.

Monroe, James - Seaman - Number: 3906 - How taken: Gave himself up from HM Frigate Freya - When taken: 31 Aug 1812 - Date received: 1 Sep 1814 - From what ship: HMS Namur - Born: New York - Age: 34 - Discharged on 8 Sep 1814 and sent to Dartmoor on HMS Niobe.

Monroe, William - Seaman - Number: 3818 - How taken: Apprehended at London - When taken: 29 Jan 1814 - Date received: 5 Jul 1814 - From what ship: Transport Office - Born: New York - Age: 23 - Race: Black - Released on 10 Jul 1814.

Montgomery, William - Seaman - Number: 3820 - Prize name: Vengeance - Ship type: LM - How taken: HM Frigate Herald - When taken: 26 Jun 1813 - Where taken: Mississippi - Date received: 23 Jun 1814 - From what ship: Quebec - Born: New York - Age: 41 - Discharged on 22 Oct 1814 and sent to Dartmoor on HMS Leyden.

Moody, Samuel - Mate - Number: 383 - Prize name: Draper - Ship type: MV - How taken: HM Brig Fearless - When taken: 18 Sep 1812 - Where taken: off Cadiz, Spain - Date received: 13 Feb 1813 - From what ship: HMS Raisonnable - Born: Philadelphia - Age: 25 - Discharged on 8 Jun 1813 and released to Cartel Rodrigo.

Moon, Joseph - Private - Number: 3053 - Prize name: U.S. Light Dragoons - Ship type: LF - How taken: British forces - When taken: 24 Jun 1813 - Where taken: Beaver Dams, Upper Canada - Date received: 7 Jan 1814 - From what ship: Halifax - Born: Virginia - Age: 29 - Discharged on 10 Oct 1814 and sent to U.S. on Cartel St. Philip.

Mooney, Mathew - Private - Number: 1622 - Prize name: 13th U.S. Infantry - Ship type: LF - How taken: British forces - When taken: 13 Oct 1812 - Where taken: Upper Canada - Date received: 9 May 1813 - From what ship: HMS Raisonnable - Born: Londonderry, Ireland - Age: 43 - Discharged on 22 Oct 1814 and sent to Dartmoor on HMS Leyden.

Moor, John - Seaman - Number: 798 - Prize name: Dolphin - Ship type: MV - How taken: HM Ship-of-the-Line Colossus - When taken: 5 Jan 1813 - Where taken: off the Western Isles, Scotland - Date received: 27 Feb 1813 - From what ship: Plymouth via HMS Namur - Born: New York - Age: 19 - Discharged on 24 Jul 1813 and released to Cartel Hoffminy.

Moor, Thomas - Cook's Mate - Number: 436 - Prize name: Hunter - Ship type: P - How taken: HM Frigate Phoebe - When taken: 23 Dec 1812 - Where taken: off Azores - Date received: 19 Feb 1813 - From what ship: HMS Modeste - Born: Long Island - Age: 25 - Race: Negro - Discharged on 2 Jul 1813 and released to Cartel Moses Brown.

Moore, Abraham - Seaman - Number: 3575 - How taken: Impressed at Gravesend, England - When taken: 29 Jan 1814 - Date received: 11 Mar 1814 - From what ship: HMS Raisonnable - Born: Chester - Age: 38 - Race: Black - Discharged on 10 Oct 1814 and sent to Dartmoor on the Mermaid.

Moore, Benjamin - Seaman - Number: 1447 - Prize name: Orbit - Ship type: MV - How taken: HM Brig Achates - When taken: 29 Jan 1813 - Where taken: Lat 49 N Long 13 W - Date received: 6 Apr 1813 - From what ship: Plymouth via HMS Decoy - Born: Staten Island - Age: 20 - Discharged on 24 Jul 1814 and sent to Dartmoor.

Moore, Benjamin - Seaman - Number: 1107 - Prize name: Tom Thumb - Ship type: MV - How taken: Lion, British privateer - When taken: 15 Feb 1813 - Where taken: Bay of Biscay - Date received: 14 Mar 1813 - From what ship: Portsmouth via HMS Beagle - Born: Brattleboro - Age: 30 - Died on 21 Mar 1813 from pneumonia.

Moore, Daniel - Seaman - Number: 735 - Prize name: Nancy - Ship type: MV - How taken: HM Brig Parthian -

When taken: 1 Aug 1812 - Where taken: off the Needles, Isle of Wight - Date received: 24 Feb 1813 - From what ship: Portsmouth via HMS Ulysses - Born: York, MA - Age: 21 - Discharged on 23 Mar 1813 and released to the Cartel Robinson Potter.

Moore, Edward - Seaman - Number: 3640 - Prize name: Bunker Hill - Ship type: P - How taken: HM Frigate Pomone & HM Frigate Cydnus - When taken: 4 Mar 1814 - Where taken: Bay of Biscay - Date received: 31 Mar 1814 - From what ship: HMS Raisonnable - Born: New York - Age: 22 - Race: Mulatto - Discharged on 25 Sep 1814 and sent to Dartmoor on HMS Niobe.

Moore, Henry - Seaman - Number: 277 - How taken: Apprehended at London - When taken: 14 Dec 1812 - Date received: 23 Dec 1812 - From what ship: HMS Raisonnable - Born: Baltimore - Age: 29 - Discharged on 24 Jul 1813 and released to Cartel Hoffminy.

Moore, Jacob - Seaman - Number: 963 - Prize name: Empress - Ship type: MV - How taken: HM Brig Rover - When taken: 30 Nov 1812 - Where taken: St. Andrew - Date received: 10 Mar 1813 - From what ship: HMS Tigress - Born: New York - Age: 21 - Discharged on 8 Jun 1813 and released to Cartel Rodrigo.

Moore, James - Seaman - Number: 2361 - How taken: Gave himself up from HM Brig Rapid - When taken: 25 Jun 1813 - Date received: 20 Oct 1813 - From what ship: Portsmouth, via an admiral's tender - Born: New York - Age: 32 - Race: Mulatto - Discharged on 21 Jan 1814 and released to HMS Ceres.

Moore, John - Seaman - Number: 1825 - Prize name: tender to the Privateer True Blooded Yankee - Ship type: P - How taken: HM Brig Hope - When taken: 24 Jun 1813 - Where taken: off Brest, France - Date received: 7 Jul 1813 - From what ship: Portsmouth via HMS Scorpion - Born: Norwich, CT - Age: 26 - Discharged on 25 Jul 1814 and sent to Dartmoor on HMS Bittern.

Moore, John - Seaman - Number: 2035 - How taken: Impressed at London - When taken: 26 Jul 1813 - Date received: 1 Aug 1813 - From what ship: HMS Raisonnable - Born: Baltimore - Age: 30 - Discharged on 4 Aug 1814 and sent to Dartmoor on HMS Liverpool.

Moore, Michael - Seaman - Number: 976 - Prize name: Empress - Ship type: MV - How taken: HM Brig Rover - When taken: 30 Nov 1812 - Where taken: St. Andrew - Date received: 10 Mar 1813 - From what ship: HMS Tigress - Born: New York - Age: 23 - Discharged on 8 Jun 1813 and released to Cartel Rodrigo.

Moore, Samuel - Seaman - Number: 2494 - Prize name: Governor Plumer - Ship type: P - How taken: Sent into custody from a privateer - When taken: 1 Jun 1813 - Where taken: off Cape Ann - Date received: 22 Oct 1813 - From what ship: Portsmouth via HMT Malabar - Born: New Hampshire - Age: 24 - Discharged on 8 Sep 1814 and sent to Dartmoor on HMS Niobe.

Morell, John - Seaman - Number: 1524 - How taken: Gave himself up from HM Frigate Mermaid - When taken: 30 Nov 1812 - Date received: 8 Apr 1813 - From what ship: Portsmouth, via an admiral's tender - Born: Haven - Age: 31 - Discharged on 4 Aug 1814 and sent to Dartmoor on HMS Alpheus.

Morelly, Samuel - 1st Lieutenant - Number: 3480 - Prize name: Volunteer - Ship type: MV - How taken: Vittoria, British privateer from Guernsey - When taken: 28 Dec 1813 - Where taken: Bay of Biscay - Date received: 23 Feb 1814 - From what ship: Halifax via HMT Malabar - Born: Connecticut - Age: 27 - Discharged on 28 Feb 1814 and sent to Reading on parole.

Morgan, James - Seaman - Number: 155 - How taken: Gave himself up at London - When taken: 27 Oct 1812 - Date received: 5 Nov 1812 - From what ship: HMS Namur - Born: Baltimore - Age: 35 - Discharged in Jul 1813 and released to Cartel Moses Brown.

Morgan, James - Seaman - Number: 3212 - Prize name: Volunteer - Ship type: MV - How taken: Vittoria, British privateer from Guernsey - When taken: 26 Dec 1813 - Where taken: Bay of Biscay - Date received: 13 Jan 1814 - From what ship: Portsmouth via HMS Poictiers - Born: Pilau, Prussia - Age: 24 - Discharged on 25 Sep 1814 and sent to Dartmoor on HMS Leyden.

Morgan, John R. - Captain - Number: 2941 - Prize name: Enterprise - Ship type: P - How taken: HM Frigate Tenedos - When taken: 21 May 1813 - Where taken: off Cape Cod - Date received: 7 Jan 1814 - From what ship: Halifax - Born: Philadelphia - Age: 43 - Died on 14 Mar 1814 from fever.

Morgan, William - Seaman - Number: 795 - Prize name: Dolphin - Ship type: MV - How taken: HM Ship-of-the-Line Colossus - When taken: 5 Jan 1813 - Where taken: off the Western Isles, Scotland - Date received: 27

Feb 1813 - From what ship: Plymouth via HMS Namur - Born: Washington, MD - Age: 24 - Discharged on 24 Jul 1813 and released to Cartel Hoffminy.

Moriarty, Thomas - Master - Number: 3797 - Prize name: Alligator - Ship type: MV - How taken: HM Ship-of-the-Line San Domingo - When taken: 16 May 1813 - Where taken: off Bengal - Date received: 5 Jun 1814 - From what ship: HMS Raisonnable - Born: Salem - Age: 27 - Released from Chatham on 10 Jun 1814 and sent to Ashburton on parole.

Morrell, Francis - Seaman - Number: 3261 - Prize name: Volante - Ship type: P - How taken: HM Brig Curlew - When taken: 25 Mar 1813 - Where taken: off Boston - Date received: 23 Feb 1814 - From what ship: Halifax via HMT Malabar - Born: Marblehead - Age: 22 - Discharged on 10 Oct 1814 and sent to Dartmoor on the Mermaid.

Morris, Andrew - Seaman - Number: 3775 - Prize name: Argus - Ship type: MV - How taken: HM Ship-of-the-Line San Domingo - When taken: 1 Mar 1814 - Where taken: off Savannah - Date received: 26 May 1814 - From what ship: HMS Hindostan - Born: Maryland - Age: 18 - Race: Black - Discharged on 25 Sep 1814 and sent to Dartmoor on HMS Niobe.

Morris, George - Seaman - Number: 1113 - Prize name: Tom Thumb - Ship type: MV - How taken: Lion, British privateer - When taken: 15 Feb 1813 - Where taken: Bay of Biscay - Date received: 14 Mar 1813 - From what ship: Portsmouth via HMS Beagle - Born: Worcester, MA - Age: 17 - Race: Mulatto - Discharged on 19 May 1813 and released to HMS Ceres.

Morris, Isaac - Seaman - Number: 1840 - Prize name: tender to the Privateer True Blooded Yankee - Ship type: P - How taken: HM Ship-of-the-Line Fame - When taken: 24 Jun 1813 - Where taken: off Brest, France - Date received: 7 Jul 1813 - From what ship: Portsmouth via HMS Scorpion - Born: New Orleans - Age: 12 - Discharged on 24 Oct 1813 and released to HMS Ceres.

Morris, Jacob - Seaman - Number: 2805 - Prize name: Industry - Ship type: P - How taken: HM Brig Heron - When taken: 3 Nov 1813 - Where taken: off Halifax - Date received: 7 Jan 1814 - From what ship: Halifax - Born: Pennsylvania - Age: 29 - Race: Black - Discharged on 8 Sep 1814 and sent to Dartmoor on HMS Niobe.

Morris, James - Steward - Number: 1886 - Prize name: Tiger - Ship type: MV - How taken: HM Brig Scylla - When taken: 22 Mar 1813 - Where taken: Bay of Biscay - Date received: 7 Jul 1813 - From what ship: Portsmouth via HMS Tribune - Born: New York - Age: 29 - Discharged on 22 Jun 1814 and sent to Calais, France on the Simon & Mary.

Morris, John - Seaman - Number: 1475 - Prize name: Union - Ship type: MV - How taken: HM Frigate Iris - When taken: 17 Jan 1813 - Where taken: at sea - Date received: 6 Apr 1813 - From what ship: Portsmouth via Tender Eliza - Born: Delaware - Age: 24 - Discharged on 26 Jul 1813 and released to Cartel Hoffminy.

Morris, Louis - Seaman - Number: 1371 - How taken: Gave himself up from HM Ship-of-the-Line Christian VII - When taken: 19 Mar 1813 - Date received: 3 Apr 1813 - From what ship: Portsmouth, via an admiral's tender - Born: New Haven - Age: 23 - Discharged on 24 Jul 1814 and sent to Dartmoor.

Morris, S. - Seaman - Number: 161 - Prize name: Galen - Ship type: MV - How taken: HM Battery Gorgon - When taken: 12 Aug 1812 - Where taken: Great Belt, Denmark - Date received: 5 Nov 1812 - From what ship: HMS Namur - Born: New York - Age: 25 - Discharged on 10 May 1813 and released to Cartel Admittance.

Morris, Samuel - Seaman - Number: 3870 - How taken: Gave himself up from HM Ship-of-the-Line Africa - When taken: 4 Oct 1813 - Date received: 24 Aug 1814 - From what ship: London - Born: New York - Age: 25 - Race: Black - Discharged on 22 Oct 1814 and sent to Dartmoor on HMS Leyden.

Morris, Thomas - Seaman - Number: 1492 - Prize name: Union - Ship type: MV - How taken: HM Frigate Iris - When taken: 17 Jan 1813 - Where taken: at sea - Date received: 6 Apr 1813 - From what ship: Plymouth via an admiral's tender - Born: Maryland - Age: 22 - Discharged on 26 Jul 1813 and released to Cartel Hoffminy.

Morris, Thomas - Cook - Number: 137 - Prize name: Frederick - Ship type: MV - How taken: Stopped at London - When taken: 23 Oct 1812 - Date received: 5 Nov 1812 - From what ship: HMS Namur - Born: Lancaster, PA - Age: 51 - Race: Mulatto - Discharged on 7 Apr 1813 and released to the HMS Raisonnable.

Morris, William - Seaman - Number: 826 - How taken: Gave himself up for being an American - When taken: 4 Jan 1813 - Date received: 1 Mar 1813 - From what ship: Plymouth via HMS Namur - Born: Charlestown - Age:

30 - Discharged on 24 Jul 1813 and released to Cartel Hoffminy.

Morris, William - Seaman - Number: 254 - How taken: Gave himself up at London - When taken: 29 Nov 1812 - Date received: 7 Dec 1812 - From what ship: HMS Raisonnable - Born: Nantucket - Age: 23 - Discharged on 24 Jul 1813 and released to Cartel Hoffminy.

Morrison, John - Seaman - Number: 1526 - How taken: Gave himself up from HM Frigate Mermaid - When taken: 30 Nov 1812 - Date received: 8 Apr 1813 - From what ship: Portsmouth, via an admiral's tender - Born: Philadelphia - Age: 22 - Discharged on 4 Nov 1813 and released to HMS Ceres.

Morrison, Thomas - Seaman - Number: 3632 - Prize name: Bunker Hill - Ship type: P - How taken: HM Frigate Pomone & HM Frigate Cydnus - When taken: 4 Mar 1814 - Where taken: Bay of Biscay - Date received: 31 Mar 1814 - From what ship: HMS Raisonnable - Born: Galloway, Scotland - Age: 24 - Discharged on 25 Sep 1814 and sent to Dartmoor on HMS Niobe.

Morrison, William - Boy - Number: 2186 - How taken: Gave himself up from HM Ship-of-the-Line Leviathan - When taken: 28 Oct 1812 - Date received: 16 Aug 1813 - From what ship: Portsmouth, via an admiral's tender - Born: New York - Age: 17 - Discharged on 11 Aug 1814 and sent to Dartmoor on HMS Freya.

Morrow, Joseph - Marine Private - Number: 1164 - Prize name: Sword Fish - Ship type: P - How taken: HM Ship-of-the-Line Elephant - When taken: 28 Dec 1812 - Where taken: off Azores - Date received: 16 Mar 1813 - From what ship: Portsmouth, via HMS Abundance - Born: Brookfield - Age: 19 - Discharged on 24 Jul 1813 and released to Cartel Hoffminy.

Morton, Seth - Mate - Number: 388 - Prize name: John - Ship type: MV - How taken: HM Sloop Blossom - When taken: 16 Aug 1812 - Where taken: off Gibraltar - Date received: 13 Feb 1813 - From what ship: HMS Raisonnable - Born: Plymouth, MA - Age: 37 - Discharged on 23 Mar 1813 and released to the Cartel Robinson Potter.

Moses, James - Seaman - Number: 2023 - How taken: Impressed at London - When taken: 9 Jul 1813 - Date received: 16 Jul 1813 - From what ship: HMS Raisonnable - Born: Standish, MA - Age: 21 - Discharged on 4 Aug 1814 and sent to Dartmoor on HMS Liverpool.

Moss, William - Seaman - Number: 832 - Prize name: John Barnes - Ship type: MV - How taken: Gave himself up at Liverpool - When taken: 7 Nov 1813 - Date received: 1 Mar 1813 - From what ship: Plymouth via HMS Namur - Born: Norfolk - Age: 29 - Discharged in Jul 1813 and released to Cartel Moses Brown.

Mossland, Reuben - Seaman - Number: 1872 - Prize name: Tiger - Ship type: MV - How taken: HM Brig Scylla - When taken: 22 Mar 1813 - Where taken: Bay of Biscay - Date received: 7 Jul 1813 - From what ship: Portsmouth via HMS Tribune - Born: Nantucket - Age: 22 - Died on 26 Nov 1813 from hydrocephalus.

Mott, Thomas - Seaman - Number: 3367 - Prize name: Yorktown - Ship type: P - How taken: HM Frigate Maidstone - When taken: 17 Jul 1813 - Where taken: Grand Banks - Date received: 23 Feb 1814 - From what ship: Halifax via HMT Malabar - Born: Philadelphia - Age: 17 - Discharged on 26 Sep 1814 and sent to Dartmoor on HMS Leyden.

Moulden, William - Seaman - Number: 1513 - How taken: Gave himself up from HM Ship-of-the-Line Blake - When taken: 10 Dec 1812 - Date received: 8 Apr 1813 - From what ship: Portsmouth, via an admiral's tender - Born: Andover - Age: 41 - Discharged on 25 Sep 1814 and sent to Dartmoor.

Mountain, Emanuel - Seaman - Number: 1208 - Prize name: Expectation - Ship type: MV - How taken: HM Frigate Briton - When taken: 17 Dec 1812 - Where taken: at sea - Date received: 16 Mar 1813 - From what ship: Portsmouth, via HMS Abundance - Born: Massachusetts - Age: 23 - Discharged on 2 Jul 1813 and released to Cartel Moses Brown.

Mourin, James - Seaman - Number: 791 - Prize name: Dolphin - Ship type: MV - How taken: HM Ship-of-the-Line Colossus - When taken: 5 Jan 1813 - Where taken: off the Western Isles, Scotland - Date received: 27 Feb 1813 - From what ship: Plymouth via HMS Namur - Born: Ipswich, MA - Age: 37 - Discharged on 24 Jul 1813 and released to Cartel Hoffminy.

Muckleroy, Samuel - Seaman - Number: 1771 - How taken: Gave himself up from HM Frigate Menelaus - When taken: 6 Jun 1813 - Date received: 14 Jun 1813 - From what ship: HMS Arethusa - Born: Philadelphia - Age: 40 - Discharged on 24 Jul 1814 and sent to Dartmoor on HMS Liffey.

Muckleroy, William - Private - Number: 2661 - Prize name: 2nd U.S. Artillery - Ship type: LF - How taken: British forces - When taken: 6 Jun 1813 - Where taken: Stoney Creek, Upper Canada - Date received: 5 Nov 1813 - From what ship: HMS Hindostan - Born: County Armagh, Ireland - Age: 29 - Discharged on 17 Jun 1814 and sent to Dartmoor.

Muller, William - Seaman - Number: 1843 - How taken: Given up from HM Frigate Hyperion - Date received: 7 Jul 1813 - From what ship: Portsmouth via HMS Tribune - Born: Boston - Age: 22 - Discharged on 11 Aug 1814 and sent to Dartmoor on HMS Freya.

Mullett, Joseph - Seaman - Number: 3310 - Prize name: Enterprise - Ship type: P - How taken: HM Frigate Tenedos - When taken: 21 May 1813 - Where taken: off Cape Cod - Date received: 23 Feb 1814 - From what ship: Halifax via HMT Malabar - Born: Marblehead - Age: 19 - Discharged on 10 Oct 1814 and sent to Dartmoor on the Mermaid.

Mullins, Joseph - Mate - Number: 758 - Prize name: Margarethe - Ship type: MV - How taken: HM Ship-of-the-Line San Juan - When taken: 8 May 1812 - Where taken: Gibraltar - Date received: 25 Feb 1813 - From what ship: HMS Brazen - Born: Philadelphia - Age: 37 - Discharged on 23 Mar 1813 and released to the Cartel Robinson Potter.

Mulloy, William - Seaman - Number: 3312 - Prize name: Enterprise - Ship type: P - How taken: HM Frigate Tenedos - When taken: 21 May 1813 - Where taken: off Cape Cod - Date received: 23 Feb 1814 - From what ship: Halifax via HMT Malabar - Born: Salem - Age: 16 - Discharged on 10 Oct 1814 and sent to Dartmoor on the Mermaid.

Mulloy, William - Seaman - Number: 2999 - Prize name: Grand Turk - Ship type: P - How taken: HM Frigate Tenedos - When taken: 26 May 1813 - Where taken: off Cape Sable, Florida - Date received: 7 Jan 1814 - From what ship: Halifax - Born: Massachusetts - Age: 30 - Discharged on 25 Sep 1814 and sent to Dartmoor on HMS Leyden.

Mumery, James - Seaman - Number: 671 - Prize name: U.S.R.M. Cutter James Madison - Ship type: War - How taken: HM Frigate Barbadoes - When taken: 22 Aug 1812 - Where taken: at sea - Date received: 24 Feb 1813 - From what ship: Portsmouth via HMS Ulysses - Born: New York - Age: 33 - Discharged on 10 May 1813 and released to Cartel Admittance.

Muncy, Daniel - Seaman - Number: 1082 - Prize name: Hope - Ship type: MV - How taken: HM Schooner Bramble - When taken: 9 Dec 1812 - Where taken: at sea - Date received: 14 Mar 1813 - From what ship: Portsmouth via HMS Cornwell - Born: Cumberland - Age: 23 - Released on 10 Apr 1813.

Munro, John - Seaman - Number: 1314 - How taken: Gave himself up from HM Guardship Royal William - When taken: 3 Feb 1813 - Date received: 16 Mar 1813 - From what ship: Portsmouth, via HMS Abundance - Born: New York - Age: 31 - Discharged on 23 Jul 1814 and sent to Dartmoor.

Munroe, Henry - Seaman - Number: 3317 - Prize name: Yankee - Ship type: P - How taken: HM Frigate Shannon - When taken: 13 Jul 1813 - Date received: 23 Feb 1814 - From what ship: Halifax via HMT Malabar - Born: Bristol - Age: 15 - Race: Black - Discharged on 10 Oct 1814 and sent to Dartmoor on the Mermaid.

Murphy, George - Private - Number: 3163 - Prize name: U.S. Light Dragoons - Ship type: LF - How taken: British forces - When taken: 24 Jun 1813 - Where taken: Beaver Dams, Upper Canada - Date received: 7 Jan 1814 - From what ship: Halifax - Born: Virginia - Age: 22 - Discharged on 10 Oct 1814 and sent to U.S. on Cartel St. Philip.

Murray, Charles - Passenger - Number: 2898 - Prize name: Dart - Ship type: P - How taken: HM Frigate Niger & HMS Fortunee - When taken: 10 Nov 1813 - Where taken: off Cape Finisterre, Spain - Date received: 7 Jan 1814 - From what ship: Portsmouth - Born: Philadelphia - Age: 45 - Discharged on 10 Oct 1814 and sent to U.S. on Cartel St. Philip.

Murray, David - Seaman - Number: 3663 - Prize name: Vivid - Ship type: P - How taken: HM Frigate Nymphe - When taken: 20 Apr 1813 - Where taken: off Cape Cod - Date received: 4 May 1814 - From what ship: Portsmouth - Born: Boston - Age: 20 - Discharged on 26 Sep 1814 and sent to Dartmoor on HMS Leyden.

Murray, James - Seaman - Number: 2092 - How taken: Gave himself up from HM Ship-of-the-Line Scipion - When taken: 27 May 1813 - Date received: 9 Aug 1813 - From what ship: HMS Thames - Born: Salem, MA - Age:

38 - Discharged on 12 Aug 1814 and sent to Dartmoor on HMS Alpheus.

Murray, John - Cook - Number: 3572 - Prize name: Commodore Perry - Ship type: MV - How taken: Sent into custody from a cutter - When taken: 25 Feb 1814 - Where taken: off Bordeaux, France - Date received: 7 May 1814 - From what ship: HM Sloop (not readable) - Born: Maryland - Age: 40 - Race: Black - Discharged on 25 Sep 1814 and sent to Dartmoor on HMS Niobe.

Murray, John - Seaman - Number: 918 - Prize name: Experiment - Ship type: MV - How taken: HM Transport Deptford - When taken: 2 Nov 1812 - Where taken: Dublin - Date received: 10 Mar 1813 - From what ship: HMS Tigress - Born: New Castle - Age: 22 - Discharged on 2 Jul 1813 and released to Cartel Moses Brown.

Murray, Nathaniel - Seaman - Number: 567 - Prize name: Rising States - Ship type: MV - How taken: HM Frigate Fortunee - When taken: 28 Aug 1812 - Where taken: off the Western Isles, Scotland - Date received: 23 Feb 1813 - From what ship: Portsmouth via HMS Dromedary - Born: Long Island - Age: 27 - Race: Man of color - Discharged on 8 Jun 1813 and released to Cartel Rodrigo.

Murray, Peter - Seaman - Number: 2125 - How taken: Gave himself up from HM Ship-of-the-Line Ocean - When taken: 28 May 1813 - Date received: 9 Aug 1813 - From what ship: HMS Thames - Born: Harlem - Age: 28 - Discharged on 12 Aug 1814 and sent to Dartmoor on HMS Alpheus.

Murray, Richard - Seaman - Number: 138 - Prize name: Frederick - Ship type: MV - How taken: Stopped at Harwich, England - When taken: Sep 1812 - Date received: 5 Nov 1812 - From what ship: HMS Namur - Born: Philadelphia - Age: 34 - Race: Mulatto - Discharged in Jul 1813 and released to Cartel Moses Brown.

Murray, Richard - Steward - Number: 3300 - Prize name: Montgomery - Ship type: P - How taken: HM Frigate Nymphe - When taken: 5 May 1813 - Where taken: off Cape Cod - Date received: 23 Feb 1814 - From what ship: Halifax via HMT Malabar - Born: Salem - Age: 16 - Discharged on 10 Oct 1814 and sent to Dartmoor on the Mermaid.

Mutch, James - Seaman - Number: 2111 - How taken: Gave himself up from HM Brig Shearwater - When taken: 27 May 1813 - Date received: 9 Aug 1813 - From what ship: HMS Thames - Born: Philadelphia - Age: 35 - Discharged on 12 Aug 1814 and sent to Dartmoor on HMS Alpheus.

Myer, John - Cooper - Number: 1554 - Prize name: Dolphin - Ship type: LM - How taken: HM Ship-of-the-Line Colossus - When taken: 5 Jan 1813 - Where taken: off the Western Isles, Scotland - Date received: 8 Apr 1813 - From what ship: Plymouth via HMS Olympia - Born: Philadelphia - Age: 24 - Discharged on 27 Jul 1813 and released to Cartel Hoffminy.

Myer, Peter - Seaman - Number: 535 - Prize name: Baltimore - Ship type: P - How taken: HM Transport Diadem - When taken: 7 Oct 1812 - Where taken: S. Andres - Date received: 23 Feb 1813 - From what ship: Portsmouth via HMS Dromedary - Born: New Orleans - Age: 26 - Discharged on 8 Jun 1813 and released to Cartel Rodrigo.

Myers, David - Seaman - Number: 1954 - Prize name: Ferox - Ship type: MV - How taken: HM Frigate Medusa & HM Brig Lyra - When taken: 28 Mar 1813 - Where taken: off Cape Ortegal, Spain - Date received: 15 Jul 1813 - From what ship: Plymouth - Born: Thomastown - Age: 20 - Discharged on 17 Jun 1814 and sent to Dartmoor on HMS Redbreast.

Myers, Frederick - Seaman - Number: 1406 - Prize name: Porcupine - Ship type: MV - How taken: HM Frigate Dryand - When taken: 8 Jan 1813 - Where taken: off Bordeaux, France - Date received: 5 Apr 1813 - From what ship: Plymouth via HMS Dwarf - Born: Baltimore - Age: 37 - Discharged on 24 Jul 1813 and released to Cartel Hoffminy.

Myers, Jacob - Seaman - Number: 618 - Prize name: King of Rome - Ship type: P - How taken: HM Brig Wolverine - When taken: 13 Dec 1812 - Where taken: at sea - Date received: 23 Feb 1813 - From what ship: Portsmouth via HMS Dromedary - Born: Philadelphia - Age: 24 - Discharged on 2 Jul 1813 and released to Cartel Moses Brown.

Myers, John - Private - Number: 3064 - Prize name: 14th U.S. Infantry - Ship type: LF - How taken: British forces - When taken: 24 Jun 1813 - Where taken: Beaver Dams, Upper Canada - Date received: 7 Jan 1814 - From what ship: Halifax - Born: Pennsylvania - Age: 19 - Discharged on 10 Oct 1814 and sent to U.S. on Cartel St. Philip.

Myrick, William - Seaman - Number: 945 - Prize name: Mariner - Ship type: MV - How taken: HM Brig Lyra - When taken: 15 Dec 1812 - Where taken: off Bilboa, Spain - Date received: 10 Mar 1813 - From what ship: HMS Tigress - Born: Massachusetts - Age: 23 - Discharged on 2 Jul 1813 and released to Cartel Moses Brown.

Nald, John - Seaman - Number: 955 - How taken: Gave himself up from HM Frigate Pomone - When taken: 9 Jan 1813 - Date received: 10 Mar 1813 - From what ship: HMS Tigress - Born: New York - Age: 30 - Discharged on 4 Aug 1814 and sent to Dartmoor on HMS Liverpool.

Napperknac, John - Private - Number: 2656 - Prize name: 22nd U.S. Infantry - Ship type: LF - How taken: British forces - When taken: 6 Jun 1813 - Where taken: Stoney Creek, Upper Canada - Date received: 5 Nov 1813 - From what ship: HMS Hindostan - Born: Dublin, Ireland - Age: 49 - Discharged on 17 Jun 1814 and sent to Dartmoor.

Narbone, Nicholas - Seaman - Number: 2272 - Prize name: prize to the Privateer Blockade - Ship type: P - How taken: HM Frigate Brazen - When taken: 29 Jun 1813 - Where taken: coast of Scotland - Date received: 14 Sep 1813 - From what ship: HMS Raisonnable - Born: Rhode Island - Age: 17 - Discharged on 4 Sep 1814 and sent to Dartmoor on HMS Freya.

Nargney, James - Seaman - Number: 1563 - Prize name: Dolphin - Ship type: LM - How taken: HM Ship-of-the-Line Colossus - When taken: 5 Jan 1813 - Where taken: off the Western Isles, Scotland - Date received: 8 Apr 1813 - From what ship: Plymouth via HMS Olympia - Born: Pennsylvania - Age: 28 - Discharged on 27 Jul 1813 and released to Cartel Hoffminy.

Nartique, John - 2nd Mate - Number: 852 - Prize name: Brutus - Ship type: MV - How taken: Briton, letter of marque - When taken: 13 Jan 1813 - Where taken: Bay of Biscay - Date received: 1 Mar 1813 - From what ship: Plymouth via HMS Namur - Born: Georgia - Age: 24 - Discharged on 24 Jul 1813 and released to Cartel Hoffminy.

Nash, William - Seaman - Number: 1691 - Prize name: Governor Middleton - Ship type: MV - How taken: Thetis, British privateer - When taken: 2 May 1813 - Where taken: Bay of Biscay - Date received: 15 May 1813 - From what ship: HMS Viper - Born: Baltimore - Age: 40 - Died on 30 Sep 1813 from phthisis (tuberculosis).

Nason, William - Seaman - Number: 80 - Prize name: Edward - Ship type: MV - How taken: HM Frigate Ethalion - When taken: 12 Aug 1812 - Where taken: Great Belt, Denmark - Date received: 4 Nov 1812 - From what ship: HMS Namur - Born: Marblehead - Age: 44 - Discharged on 10 May 1813 and released to Cartel Admittance.

Nassan, Joseph - Boy - Number: 1934 - Prize name: Lepo (Leo) - Ship type: LM - How taken: HM Frigate Magiciene - When taken: 4 Jun 1813 - Where taken: coast of France - Date received: 11 Jul 1813 - From what ship: HMS Raisonnable - Born: Limerick, MA - Age: 18 - Discharged on 4 Aug 1814 and sent to Dartmoor on HMS Liverpool.

Neal, Henry - Seaman - Number: 465 - Prize name: Hunter - Ship type: P - How taken: HM Frigate Phoebe - When taken: 23 Dec 1812 - Where taken: off Azores - Date received: 19 Feb 1813 - From what ship: HMS Modeste - Born: Boston - Age: 18 - Discharged on 24 Jul 1813 and released to Cartel Hoffminy.

Neal, John - Seaman - Number: 3495 - How taken: Gave himself up from HM Ship-of-the-Line Saturn - When taken: 2 Feb 1814 - Date received: 23 Feb 1814 - From what ship: Portsmouth via HMT Malabar - Born: Gloucester - Age: 30 - Discharged on 20 Aug 1814 and sent to Dartmoor on HMS Shamrock.

Ned, Deaf - Seaman - Number: 3609 - Prize name: Liberty - Ship type: MV - How taken: Surrendered at Stromness, Scotland - When taken: 30 Dec 1813 - Date received: 29 Mar 1814 - From what ship: Hired tender Anna - Born: Norfolk - Age: 28 - Race: Black - Discharged on 25 Sep 1814 and sent to Dartmoor on HMS Niobe.

Nellim, George - Seaman - Number: 575 - How taken: Gave himself up from HM Sloop Cherub - When taken: 5 Dec 1812 - Date received: 23 Feb 1813 - From what ship: Portsmouth via HMS Dromedary - Born: New York - Age: 25 - Discharged on 4 Aug 1814 and sent to Dartmoor on HMS Liverpool.

Nelson, Richard - Seaman - Number: 1988 - How taken: Gave himself up from HM Ship-of-the-Line Ajax - Date received: 15 Jul 1813 - From what ship: Plymouth - Born: New York - Age: 28 - Discharged on 17 Jun 1814 and sent to Dartmoor on HMS Pincher.

Nelson, Samuel A. - Seaman - Number: 720 - Prize name: James - Ship type: MV - How taken: Detained at Portsmouth harbor - When taken: 31 Jul 1812 - Date received: 24 Feb 1813 - From what ship: Portsmouth via HMS Ulysses - Born: Portsmouth, NH - Age: 28 - Died on 8 Mar 1813 from fever.

Nelson, Thomas - Seaman - Number: 3281 - Prize name: Vivid - Ship type: P - How taken: HM Frigate Nymphe - When taken: 20 Apr 1813 - Where taken: off Cape Cod - Date received: 23 Feb 1814 - From what ship: Halifax via HMT Malabar - Born: Truro - Age: 17 - Discharged on 10 Oct 1814 and sent to Dartmoor on the Mermaid.

Newby, John - Seaman - Number: 693 - Prize name: Fame, prize of Privateer Decatur - Ship type: P - How taken: HM Ship-of-the-Line Polyphemus - When taken: 13 Sep 1812 - Where taken: at sea - Date received: 24 Feb 1813 - From what ship: Portsmouth via HMS Ulysses - Born: Isle of Wight - Age: 27 - Race: Black man - Died on 3 May 1813 from fever.

Newel, George - Seaman - Number: 1708 - Prize name: Decatur - Ship type: MV - How taken: HM Frigate Desiree - When taken: 7 May 1813 - Where taken: off Nantes, France - Date received: 25 May 1813 - From what ship: Portsmouth via HMS Impetius - Born: Newburyport - Age: 23 - Discharged on 24 Jul 1814 and sent to Dartmoor on HMS Liffey.

Newell, Benjamin (2) - Mate - Number: 2860 - Prize name: Fire Fly - Ship type: LM - How taken: HM Frigate Revolutionnaire - When taken: 19 Oct 1813 - Where taken: off Cape Ortegal, Spain - Date received: 7 Jan 1814 - From what ship: Portsmouth - Born: Boston - Age: 25 - Died on 18 Apr 1814 from fever.

Newell, Paul - Seaman - Number: 2415 - How taken: Gave himself up from HM Frigate Astrea - When taken: 18 Oct 1813 - Date received: 21 Oct 1813 - From what ship: Portsmouth via HMT Malabar - Born: Marblehead - Age: 22 - Discharged on 8 Sep 1814 and sent to Dartmoor on HMS Niobe.

Newell, Stephen C. - Seaman - Number: 2436 - Prize name: Hepsey - Ship type: MV - How taken: HM Brig Zenobia - When taken: 22 Jun 1813 - Where taken: off Lisbon - Date received: 21 Oct 1813 - From what ship: Portsmouth via HMT Malabar - Born: Newburyport - Age: 23 - Discharged on 4 Sep 1814 and sent to Dartmoor on HMS Freya.

Newland, Thomas L. - Sergeant - Number: 2606 - Prize name: U.S. Light Artillery - Ship type: LF - How taken: British forces - When taken: 1 Jun 1813 - Where taken: Upper Canada - Date received: 5 Nov 1813 - From what ship: HMS Hindostan - Born: Ireland - Age: 40 - Discharged on 17 Jun 1814 and sent to Dartmoor.

Newman, Henry - Seaman - Number: 3882 - How taken: Gave himself up from HM Frigate Clorinde - When taken: 24 Aug 1814 - Date received: 28 Aug 1814 - From what ship: London - Born: Washington - Age: 30 - Discharged on 8 Sep 1814 and sent to Dartmoor on HMS Niobe.

Newry, Peter - Seaman - Number: 764 - Prize name: Margarethe - Ship type: MV - How taken: HM Ship-of-the-Line San Juan - When taken: 8 May 1812 - Where taken: Gibraltar - Date received: 25 Feb 1813 - From what ship: HMS Brazen - Born: New Orleans - Age: 22 - Discharged on 10 May 1813 and released to Cartel Admittance.

Newton, John - Pilot - Number: 3578 - Prize name: Commodore Perry - Ship type: MV - How taken: Sent into custody from a cutter - When taken: 25 Feb 1814 - Where taken: off Bordeaux, France - Date received: 16 Mar 1814 - From what ship: Transport Office - Born: New Jersey - Age: 25 - Discharged on 25 Sep 1814 and sent to Dartmoor on HMS Niobe.

Nicholas, Henry - Seaman - Number: 1596 - How taken: Impressed at Gravesend, England - When taken: 5 Jan 1813 - Date received: 19 Apr 1813 - From what ship: HMS Raisonnable - Born: Connecticut - Age: 22 - Discharged on 24 Jul 1813 and released to Cartel Hoffminy.

Nicholas, John - Seaman - Number: 1882 - Prize name: Tiger - Ship type: MV - How taken: HM Brig Scylla - When taken: 22 Mar 1813 - Where taken: Bay of Biscay - Date received: 7 Jul 1813 - From what ship: Portsmouth via HMS Tribune - Born: New York - Age: 18 - Discharged on 4 Aug 1814 and sent to Dartmoor on HMS Liverpool.

Nicholas, John - Cook - Number: 1935 - Prize name: Lepo (Leo) - Ship type: LM - How taken: HM Frigate Magiciene - When taken: 4 Jun 1813 - Where taken: coast of France - Date received: 11 Jul 1813 - From what ship: HMS Raisonnable - Born: New Orleans - Age: 30 - Race: Black - Discharged on 22 Jun 1814 and sent to Calais, France on the Simon & Mary.

Nicholls, Thomas - Seaman - Number: 2316 - Prize name: Fame - Ship type: MV - How taken: HM Ship of-the-Line Cressy - When taken: 20 Jul 1813 - Where taken: at sea - Date received: 8 Oct 1813 - From what ship: Portsmouth, via an admiral's tender - Born: Rhode Island - Age: 22 - Discharged on 4 Sep 1814 and sent to Dartmoor on HMS Freya.

Nichols, Henry - Clerk - Number: 3802 - Prize name: Rambler - Ship type: MV - How taken: HM Transport Morley - When taken: 10 Feb 1813 - Date received: 5 Jun 1814 - From what ship: HMS Raisonnable - Born: Salem - Age: 20 - Discharged on 10 Jun 1814 and sent to Plymouth for embarkation.

Nichols, John - Seaman - Number: 3602 - Prize name: Liberty - Ship type: MV - How taken: Surrendered at Stromness, Scotland - When taken: 30 Dec 1813 - Date received: 29 Mar 1814 - From what ship: Hired tender Anna - Born: Plymouth - Age: 23 - Discharged on 25 Sep 1814 and sent to Dartmoor on HMS Niobe.

Nichols, John - Seaman - Number: 584 - How taken: Gave himself up from HM Ship-of-the-Line Aboukir - When taken: 26 Dec 1812 - Date received: 23 Feb 1813 - From what ship: Portsmouth via HMS Dromedary - Born: Dartmouth - Age: 22 - Discharged on 26 Jul 1814 and sent to Dartmoor on HMS Raven.

Nichols, John - Seaman - Number: 2108 - How taken: Gave himself up from HM Ship-of-the-Line Repulse - When taken: 27 May 1813 - Date received: 9 Aug 1813 - From what ship: HMS Thames - Born: New York - Age: 30 - Discharged on 23 Feb 1813 and released to HMS Ceres.

Nichols, William - Captain - Number: 1809 - Prize name: Decatur - Ship type: P - How taken: HM Frigate Surprise - When taken: 14 Jan 1813 - Where taken: at sea - Date received: 7 Jul 1813 - From what ship: Portsmouth via HMS Scorpion - Born: Newbury - Age: 31 - Released on 23 Jan 1814 and exchanged.

Nicholson, Charles - Seaman - Number: 2170 - How taken: Gave himself up from HM Ship-of-the-Line Swiftsure - When taken: 26 Dec 1812 - Date received: 16 Aug 1813 - From what ship: Portsmouth, via an admiral's tender - Born: Baltimore - Age: 22 - Race: Blackman - Discharged on 15 Oct 1813 and released to HMS Ceres.

Nicholson, James - Seaman - Number: 2720 - Prize name: Growler - Ship type: P - How taken: HM Brig Electra - When taken: 7 Jul 1813 - Where taken: off St. Johns - Date received: 7 Jan 1814 - From what ship: Portsmouth - Born: Marblehead - Age: 21 - Discharged on 25 Sep 1814 and sent to Dartmoor on HMS Leyden.

Nicholson, Jesse - Seaman - Number: 490 - How taken: Gave himself up at London - When taken: 4 Jan 1813 - Date received: 19 Feb 1813 - From what ship: HMS Raisonnable - Born: Beverly - Age: 37 - Discharged on 26 Jul 1813 and released to Cartel Hoffminy.

Nicholson, Jonas - Seaman - Number: 2696 - Prize name: Growler - Ship type: P - How taken: HM Brig Electra - When taken: 7 Jul 1813 - Where taken: off St. Johns - Date received: 7 Jan 1814 - From what ship: Portsmouth - Born: Marblehead - Age: 23 - Discharged on 25 Sep 1814 and sent to Dartmoor on HMS Leyden.

Nicholson, Thomas - Seaman - Number: 1332 - Prize name: Sea Nymph - Ship type: MV - How taken: HM Brig Thrasher - When taken: 4 Mar 1813 - Where taken: off River Jade (Germany) - Date received: 22 Mar 1813 - From what ship: HMS Thrasher - Born: Stralsund, Sweden - Age: 39 - Discharged on 23 Jul 1814 and sent to Dartmoor.

Nicholson, William - Seaman - Number: 3396 - Prize name: Centurion, prize - Ship type: P - How taken: HM Frigate Maidstone - When taken: 18 Jul 1813 - Where taken: Grand Banks - Date received: 23 Feb 1814 - From what ship: Halifax via HMT Malabar - Born: Marblehead - Age: 22 - Discharged on 10 Oct 1814 and sent to U.S. on Cartel St. Philip.

Nickels, Hugh - Prize Master - Number: 2209 - Prize name: Jane, prize of the Privateer Snap Dragon - Ship type: P - How taken: HM Frigate Crescent & HM Ship of-the-Line Bellerophon - When taken: 28 Jun 1813 - Where taken: Newfoundland Bank - Date received: 18 Aug 1813 - From what ship: Portsmouth, via an admiral's tender - Born: North Carolina - Age: 28 - Died on 6 Jan 1814 from debility (feeble).

Nicolls, Herold - Seaman - Number: 213 - How taken: Gave himself up from MV Perverance - When taken: 2 Nov 1812 - Date received: 15 Nov 1812 - From what ship: HMS Raisonnable - Born: Talbot, MA - Age: 28 -

Race: Mulatto - Discharged on 12 Apr 1813 and released to HMS Carnatic.

Nicolson, Benjamin - Seaman - Number: 1598 - How taken: Impressed at Gravesend, England - When taken: 12 Nov 1812 - Date received: 19 Apr 1813 - From what ship: HMS Raisonnable - Born: Falmouth, MA - Age: 28 - Discharged on 24 Jul 1813 and released to Cartel Hoffminy.

Niel, E. C. - Private - Number: 2641 - Prize name: 14th U.S. Infantry - Ship type: LF - How taken: British forces - When taken: 24 Jun 1813 - Where taken: Beaver Dams, Upper Canada - Date received: 5 Nov 1813 - From what ship: HMS Hindostan - Born: North Ireland - Age: 54 - Discharged on 10 Oct 1814 and sent to U.S. on Cartel St. Philip.

Niles, Nathaniel - Private - Number: 3090 - Prize name: 23rd U.S. Infantry - Ship type: LF - How taken: British forces - When taken: 24 Jun 1813 - Where taken: Beaver Dams, Upper Canada - Date received: 7 Jan 1814 - From what ship: Halifax - Born: Connecticut - Age: 23 - Discharged on 10 Oct 1814 and sent to U.S. on Cartel St. Philip.

Nilodas, M. - Seaman - Number: 626 - Prize name: King of Rome - Ship type: P - How taken: HM Brig Wolverine - When taken: 13Dec 1812 - Where taken: at sea - Date received: 23 Feb 1813 - From what ship: Portsmouth via HMS Dromedary - Born: Havana - Age: 25 - Race: Black - Discharged on 2 Jul 1813 and released to Cartel Moses Brown.

Nixon, Charles - Seaman - Number: 2594 - How taken: Gave himself up from HM Frigate Bombay - When taken: 27 May 1813 - Date received: 5 Nov 1813 - From what ship: HMS Hindostan - Born: Boston - Age: 43 - Race: Blackman - Discharged on 12 Aug 1814 and sent to Dartmoor on HMS Alpheus.

Noble, Charles - Seaman - Number: 2552 - How taken: Gave himself up from HM Ship-of-the-Line Scipion - When taken: 2 Dec 1812 - Date received: 23 Oct 1813 - From what ship: Portsmouth via HMS Raisonnable - Born: Cape Ann - Age: 22 - Discharged on 8 Sep 1814 and sent to Dartmoor on HMS Niobe.

Noble, Daniel - Seaman - Number: 3942 - How taken: Gave himself up from MV Martha - When taken: 2 Apr 1814 - Date received: 10 Oct 1814 - From what ship: Quebec - Born: Calais, France - Age: 24 - Discharged on 22 Oct 1814 and sent to Dartmoor on HMS Leyden.

Noble, Isaac - Seaman - Number: 334 - How taken: Apprehended at Leight, Scotland - When taken: 14 Dec 1812 - Date received: 11 Jan 1813 - From what ship: HMS Raisonnable - Born: Providence, RI - Age: 29 - Discharged on 24 Jul 1813 and released to Cartel Hoffminy.

Nolton, John - Seaman - Number: 1386 - How taken: Impressed at Sunderland, England - When taken: 6 Mar 1813 - Date received: 5 Apr 1813 - From what ship: HMS Raisonnable - Born: Boston - Age: 22 - Discharged on 24 Jul 1814 and sent to Dartmoor.

Noonan, William - Prize Master - Number: 1015 - Prize name: Sword Fish - Ship type: P - How taken: HM Ship-of-the-Line Elephant - When taken: 28 Dec 1812 - Where taken: off Azores - Date received: 10 Mar 1813 - From what ship: HMS Furious - Born: Marblehead - Age: 28 - Discharged on 24 Jul 1813 and released to Cartel Hoffminy.

Noonan, William - Seaman - Number: 1270 - Prize name: Sword Fish - Ship type: P - How taken: HM Ship-of-the-Line Elephant - When taken: 28 Dec 1812 - Where taken: off Azores - Date received: 16 Mar 1813 - From what ship: Portsmouth, via HMS Abundance - Born: Boston - Age: 15 - Discharged on 24 Jul 1813 and released to Cartel Hoffminy.

Norcross, Abel - Seaman - Number: 3529 - How taken: Impressed at London - When taken: 11 Feb 1814 - Date received: 26 Feb 1814 - From what ship: HMS Raisonnable - Born: Nantucket - Age: 23 - Race: Black - Discharged on 21 Jul 1814 and sent to Dartmoor on HMS Portia.

Norcross, Archibald - Seaman - Number: 2833 - Prize name: Portsmouth Packet - Ship type: P - How taken: HM Brig Fantome - When taken: 5 Oct 1813 - Where taken: off Portland - Date received: 7 Jan 1814 - From what ship: Halifax - Born: Massachusetts - Age: 35 - Discharged on 25 Sep 1814 and sent to Dartmoor on HMS Leyden.

Norcross, Thomas - Seaman - Number: 3750 - Prize name: Argus - Ship type: MV - How taken: HM Ship-of-the-Line San Domingo - When taken: 1 Mar 1814 - Where taken: off Savannah - Date received: 26 May 1814 - From what ship: HMS Hindostan - Born: Boston - Age: 19 - Discharged on 25 Sep 1814 and sent to

Dartmoor on HMS Niobe.

Norkett, George - Seaman - Number: 2237 - Prize name: Marianna - Ship type: MV - How taken: Impressed at London - When taken: 27 Aug 1813 - Date received: 7 Sep 1813 - From what ship: HMS Raisonnable - Born: Berkshire - Age: 20 - Discharged on 11 Aug 1814 and sent to Dartmoor on HMS Freya.

Norman, Edward - Private - Number: 2652 - Prize name: 6th U.S. Infantry - Ship type: LF - How taken: British forces - When taken: 24 Jun 1813 - Where taken: Beaver Dams, Upper Canada - Date received: 5 Nov 1813 - From what ship: HMS Hindostan - Born: County Cork, Ireland - Age: 34 - Discharged on 10 Oct 1814 and sent to U.S. on Cartel St. Philip.

Norris, George - 2nd Lieutenant - Number: 3186 - Prize name: U.S. Light Artillery - Ship type: LF - How taken: British forces - When taken: 24 Jun 1813 - Where taken: Beaver Dams, Upper Canada - Date received: 7 Jan 1813 - From what ship: Halifax - Born: Not listed - Age: 0 - Discharged on 14 Jan 1814.

Northey, Joseph - Seaman - Number: 3890 - How taken: Gave himself up from HM Frigate Hussar - When taken: 26 Jul 1813 - Date received: 30 Aug 1814 - From what ship: Transport Office - Born: Massachusetts - Age: 25 - Discharged on 25 Sep 1814 and sent to Dartmoor on HMS Leyden.

Norton, David - Seaman - Number: 3504 - Prize name: Elbridge Gerry - Ship type: P - How taken: HM Frigate Crescent - When taken: 16 Sep 1813 - Where taken: at sea - Date received: 23 Feb 1814 - From what ship: Portsmouth via HMT Malabar - Born: Massachusetts - Age: 24 - Died on 19 May 1814 from palsy.

Norton, Josiah - Seaman - Number: 2769 - Prize name: Thomas - Ship type: P - How taken: HM Frigate Nymphe - When taken: 24 Jun 1813 - Where taken: off Halifax - Date received: 7 Jan 1814 - From what ship: Halifax - Born: Massachusetts - Age: 17 - Discharged on 8 Sep 1814 and sent to Dartmoor on HMS Niobe.

Norton, Richard - Seaman - Number: 2238 - Prize name: Heartless - Ship type: MV - How taken: Impressed at London - When taken: 31 Aug 1813 - Date received: 7 Sep 1813 - From what ship: HMS Raisonnable - Born: Massachusetts - Age: 27 - Discharged on 11 Aug 1814 and sent to Dartmoor on HMS Freya.

Norton, Robert - Private - Number: 2648 - Prize name: 6th U.S. Infantry - Ship type: LF - How taken: British forces - When taken: 24 Jun 1813 - Where taken: Beaver Dams, Upper Canada - Date received: 5 Nov 1813 - From what ship: HMS Hindostan - Born: County Antrim, Ireland - Age: 24 - Discharged on 10 Oct 1814 and sent to U.S. on Cartel St. Philip.

Norton, Solomon - Seaman - Number: 2925 - Prize name: Juliana Smith - Ship type: P - How taken: HM Frigate Nymphe - When taken: 12 May 1813 - Where taken: off Cape Sable, Florida - Date received: 7 Jan 1814 - From what ship: Halifax - Born: Massachusetts - Age: 32 - Discharged on 25 Sep 1814 and sent to Dartmoor on HMS Leyden.

Nowland, Andrew - Seaman - Number: 1180 - Prize name: Sword Fish - Ship type: P - How taken: HM Ship-of-the-Line Elephant - When taken: 28 Dec 1812 - Where taken: off Azores - Date received: 16 Mar 1813 - From what ship: Portsmouth, via HMS Abundance - Born: Marblehead - Age: 15 - Discharged on 24 Jul 1813 and released to Cartel Hoffminy.

Nowland, Andrew - Seaman - Number: 1157 - Prize name: Sword Fish - Ship type: P - How taken: HM Ship-of-the-Line Elephant - When taken: 28 Dec 1812 - Where taken: off Azores - Date received: 16 Mar 1813 - From what ship: Portsmouth, via HMS Abundance - Born: Marblehead - Age: 44 - Discharged on 24 Jul 1813 and released to Cartel Hoffminy.

Nunns, William - Seaman - Number: 1251 - How taken: Gave himself up from HM Guardship Royal William - When taken: 25 Jan 1813 - Date received: 16 Mar 1813 - From what ship: Portsmouth, via HMS Abundance - Born: Philadelphia - Age: 34 - Discharged on 23 Jul 1814 and sent to Dartmoor.

Nuting, Charles - Seaman - Number: 679 - Prize name: U.S.R.M. Cutter James Madison - Ship type: War - How taken: HM Frigate Barbadoes - When taken: 22 Aug 1812 - Where taken: at sea - Date received: 24 Feb 1813 - From what ship: Portsmouth via HMS Ulysses - Born: Gloucester - Age: 29 - Discharged on 10 May 1813 and released to Cartel Admittance.

Nybro, Godfrey - Private - Number: 3142 - Prize name: 14th U.S. Infantry - Ship type: LF - How taken: British forces - When taken: 24 Jun 1813 - Where taken: Beaver Dams, Upper Canada - Date received: 7 Jan 1814 - From what ship: Halifax - Born: Copenhagen - Age: 34 - Discharged on 10 Oct 1814 and sent to U.S. on

Cartel St. Philip.

Nye, Charles N. - Boatswain - Number: 434 - Prize name: Hunter - Ship type: P - How taken: HM Frigate Phoebe - When taken: 23 Dec 1812 - Where taken: off Azores - Date received: 19 Feb 1813 - From what ship: HMS Modeste - Born: Halliwell - Age: 24 - Discharged on 2 Jul 1813 and released to Cartel Moses Brown.

Nye, William - Seaman - Number: 3719 - How taken: English forces off Bordeaux - When taken: 26 Mar 1814 - Date received: 18 May 1814 - From what ship: HMS Raisonnable - Born: Boston - Age: 20 - Discharged on 26 Sep 1814 and sent to Dartmoor on HMS Leyden.

Nye, William - Seaman - Number: 1688 - Prize name: Governor Middleton - Ship type: MV - How taken: Thetis, British privateer - When taken: 2 May 1813 - Where taken: Bay of Biscay - Date received: 15 May 1813 - From what ship: HMS Viper - Born: Philadelphia - Age: 30 - Discharged on 24 Jul 1814 and sent to Dartmoor on HMS Liffey.

Oakes, George - Seaman - Number: 2980 - Prize name: Enterprise - Ship type: P - How taken: HM Frigate Tenedos - When taken: 21 May 1813 - Where taken: off Cape Cod - Date received: 7 Jan 1814 - From what ship: Halifax - Born: Massachusetts - Age: 19 - Discharged on 25 Sep 1814 and sent to Dartmoor on HMS Leyden.

Oberville, Michael - Seaman - Number: 1234 - Prize name: Rossie - Ship type: MV - How taken: HM Frigate Dryand - When taken: 7 Jan 1813 - Where taken: at sea - Date received: 16 Mar 1813 - From what ship: Portsmouth, via HMS Abundance - Born: New Orleans - Age: 28 - Discharged on 24 Jul 1813 and released to Cartel Hoffminy.

Obrion, John - Marine Officer - Number: 412 - Prize name: Hunter - Ship type: P - How taken: HM Frigate Phoebe - When taken: 23 Dec 1812 - Where taken: off Azores - Date received: 19 Feb 1813 - From what ship: HMS Modeste - Born: Newburgh - Age: 22 - Discharged on 2 Jul 1813 and released to Cartel Moses Brown.

Odium, Joseph H. - Seaman - Number: 2714 - Prize name: Growler - Ship type: P - How taken: HM Brig Electra - When taken: 7 Jul 1813 - Where taken: off St. Johns - Date received: 7 Jan 1814 - From what ship: Portsmouth - Born: New Hampshire - Age: 21 - Discharged on 25 Sep 1814 and sent to Dartmoor on HMS Leyden.

Oilson, Andrew - Seaman - Number: 572 - How taken: Gave himself up from HM Schooner Antelope - When taken: 3 Dec 1812 - Date received: 23 Feb 1813 - From what ship: Portsmouth via HMS Dromedary - Born: Postcrown, Norway - Age: 24 - Discharged on 9 Jul 1813 and released to HMS Ceres.

Okes, George - Seaman - Number: 699 - Prize name: Deanna, recaptured British vessel - Ship type: P - How taken: HM Ship-of-the-Line Polyphemus - When taken: 14 Sep 1812 - Where taken: at sea - Date received: 24 Feb 1813 - From what ship: Portsmouth via HMS Ulysses - Born: Marblehead, MA - Age: 18 - Discharged on 8 Jun 1813 and released to Cartel Rodrigo.

Oliver, Anthony - Seaman - Number: 3365 - Prize name: Yorktown - Ship type: P - How taken: HM Frigate Maidstone - When taken: 17 Jul 1813 - Where taken: Grand Banks - Date received: 23 Feb 1814 - From what ship: Halifax via HMT Malabar - Born: Hackensack, NJ - Age: 47 - Race: Black - Discharged on 10 Oct 1814 and sent to Dartmoor on the Mermaid.

Oliver, Joseph - Seaman - Number: 3652 - Prize name: Bunker Hill - Ship type: P - How taken: HM Frigate Pomone & HM Frigate Cydnus - When taken: 4 Mar 1814 - Where taken: Bay of Biscay - Date received: 31 Mar 1814 - From what ship: HMS Raisonnable - Born: Portugal - Age: 33 - Discharged on 25 Sep 1814 and sent to Dartmoor on HMS Niobe.

Orne, Israel - Prize Master - Number: 2701 - Prize name: Growler - Ship type: P - How taken: HM Brig Electra - When taken: 7 Jul 1813 - Where taken: off St. Johns - Date received: 7 Jan 1814 - From what ship: Portsmouth - Born: Salem - Age: 25 - Discharged on 8 Sep 1814 and sent to Dartmoor on HMS Leyden.

Orne, W. B. - Seaman - Number: 1326 - How taken: Gave himself up from HMS Endeavour at Portsmouth - When taken: 9 Feb 1812 - Date received: 16 Mar 1813 - From what ship: Portsmouth, via HMS Abundance - Born: Marblehead - Age: 28 - Discharged on 10 May 1813 and released to Cartel Admittance.

Orphan, John - Seaman - Number: 762 - Prize name: Margarethe - Ship type: MV - How taken: HM Ship-of-the-Line San Juan - When taken: 8 May 1812 - Where taken: Gibraltar - Date received: 25 Feb 1813 - From what ship: HMS Brazen - Born: Stralsund, Sweden - Age: 29 - Discharged on 23 Mar 1813 and released to the Cartel Robinson Potter.

Orr, Levi - Seaman - Number: 499 - How taken: Gave himself up from HM Ship-of-the-Line Ruby - When taken: 15 Aug 1812 - Date received: 23 Feb 1813 - From what ship: Portsmouth via HMS Dromedary - Born: New York - Age: 45 - Discharged on 19 May 1813 and released to HMS Ceres.

Osborn, Stephen - Seaman - Number: 3411 - Prize name: Stark (General Stark) - Ship type: P - How taken: HM Frigate Maidstone - When taken: 15 Jul 1813 - Where taken: Halifax - Date received: 23 Feb 1814 - From what ship: Halifax via HMT Malabar - Born: New York - Age: 30 - Discharged on 21 Jul 1814 and sent to Dartmoor on HMS Portia.

Osborne, Lewis - Seaman - Number: 2577 - How taken: Gave himself up from HM Ship-of-the-Line Scipion - When taken: 10 Dec 1812 - Date received: 23 Oct 1813 - From what ship: Portsmouth via HMS Raisonnable - Born: New York - Age: 30 - Discharged on 8 Sep 1814 and sent to Dartmoor on HMS Niobe.

Osborne, Peter - Seaman - Number: 1024 - Prize name: Rising Sun - Ship type: MV - How taken: Taken up at Liverpool - When taken: 18 Oct 1812 - Date received: 11 Mar 1813 - From what ship: Yarmouth via HMS Tenders - Born: Long Island - Age: 23 - Race: Black - Discharged in Jul 1813 and released to Cartel Moses Brown.

Osborne, Samuel - Seaman - Number: 3646 - Prize name: Bunker Hill - Ship type: P - How taken: HM Frigate Pomone & HM Frigate Cydnus - When taken: 4 Mar 1814 - Where taken: Bay of Biscay - Date received: 31 Mar 1814 - From what ship: HMS Raisonnable - Born: Sussex, DE - Age: 30 - Race: Black - Discharged on 25 Sep 1814 and sent to Dartmoor on HMS Niobe.

Osborne, Thomas - Seaman - Number: 649 - Prize name: U.S.R.M. Cutter James Madison - Ship type: War - How taken: HM Frigate Barbadoes - When taken: 22 Aug 1812 - Where taken: at sea - Date received: 24 Feb 1813 - From what ship: Portsmouth via HMS Ulysses - Born: Connecticut - Age: 26 - Discharged on 10 May 1813 and released to Cartel Admittance.

Osgood, David - Seaman - Number: 1065 - How taken: Impressed at the Cowles Rendezvous - When taken: 5 Feb 1813 - Date received: 14 Mar 1813 - From what ship: Portsmouth via HMS Cornwell - Born: Baltimore - Age: 26 - Discharged on 11 Aug 1814 and sent to Dartmoor.

Osmond, David - Seaman - Number: 2321 - Prize name: Fame - Ship type: MV - How taken: HM Ship of-the-Line Cressy - When taken: 20 Jul 1813 - Where taken: at sea - Date received: 8 Oct 1813 - From what ship: Portsmouth, via an admiral's tender - Born: Connecticut - Age: 20 - Discharged on 4 Sep 1814 and sent to Dartmoor on HMS Freya.

Otis, Ezekiel - Seaman - Number: 259 - How taken: Gave himself up at London - When taken: 25 Nov 1812 - Date received: 7 Dec 1812 - From what ship: HMS Raisonnable - Born: New Haven, CT - Age: 26 - Discharged on 24 Jul 1813 and released to Cartel Hoffminy.

Oulson, Frederick - Mate - Number: 1639 - Prize name: Henryettos - Ship type: MV - How taken: HMS Castilian - When taken: 12 Mar 1813 - Where taken: off Cape Ortegal, Spain - Date received: 9 May 1813 - From what ship: HMS Raisonnable - Born: Konigsberg, Germany - Age: 32 - Released on 20 Jul 1813.

Owen, Burden - Seaman - Number: 2556 - How taken: Gave himself up from HM Ship-of-the-Line Ocean - When taken: 29 Oct 1812 - Date received: 23 Oct 1813 - From what ship: Portsmouth via HMS Raisonnable - Born: New York - Age: 47 - Discharged on 8 Sep 1814 and sent to Dartmoor on HMS Niobe.

Owen, John - Mate - Number: 325 - Prize name: Sidney - Ship type: MV - How taken: Apprehended at London - When taken: 23 Nov 1812 - Date received: 11 Jan 1813 - From what ship: HMS Raisonnable - Born: Northumberland, VA - Age: 29 - Released on 11 Mar 1813.

Owen, Zachariah - Seaman - Number: 2463 - Prize name: prize to the Privateer Hunter - Ship type: P - How taken: Distress - When taken: 14 Jan 1813 - Where taken: off Halifax - Date received: 21 Oct 1813 - From what ship: Portsmouth via HMT Malabar - Born: Massachusetts - Age: 19 - Discharged on 25 Sep 1814 and sent to Dartmoor on HMS Leyden.

Owens, Eugene - Seaman - Number: 1683 - How taken: Gave up from HM Ship-of-the-Line Indus - When taken: 23 Jul 1813 - Date received: 15 May 1813 - From what ship: HMS Raisonnable - Born: Portsmouth, NH - Age:

30 - Discharged on 4 Jul 1813 and released to HMS Ceres.

Oxford, James - Seaman - Number: 38 - Prize name: Mary - Ship type: MV - How taken: From a cutter's boat off Bermuda - When taken: 8 Aug 1812 - Date received: 3 Nov 1812 - From what ship: HMS Plover - Born: Medford, MA - Age: 23 - Discharged on 23 Mar 1813 and released to the Cartel Robinson Potter.

Packard, William - Seaman - Number: 920 - How taken: Gave himself up from HM Frigate Belle Poule - When taken: 5 Sep 1812 - Date received: 10 Mar 1813 - From what ship: HMS Tigress - Born: Bridgewater - Age: 23 - Discharged on 25 Sep 1814 and sent to Dartmoor on HMS Liverpool.

Packman, George - Seaman - Number: 1054 - Prize name: Independence - Ship type: MV - How taken: HM Frigate Medusa - When taken: 9 Nov 1812 - Where taken: off San Sebastian, Spain - Date received: 11 Mar 1813 - From what ship: Yarmouth via HMS Tenders - Born: Baltimore - Age: 32 - Discharged on 8 Jun 1813 and released to Cartel Rodrigo.

Paddock, Benjamin Mead - Seaman - Number: 1423 - Prize name: Argus - Ship type: MV - How taken: HM Cutter Fancy - When taken: 19 Dec 1812 - Where taken: Bay of Biscay - Date received: 5 Apr 1813 - From what ship: Plymouth via HMS Dwarf - Born: Rhinebeck - Age: 24 - Discharged on 2 Jul 1813 and released to Cartel Moses Brown.

Page, John - Seaman - Number: 564 - Prize name: Rising States - Ship type: MV - How taken: HM Frigate Fortunee - When taken: 28 Aug 1812 - Where taken: off the Western Isles, Scotland - Date received: 23 Feb 1813 - From what ship: Portsmouth via HMS Dromedary - Born: New York - Age: 21 - Discharged on 8 Jun 1813 and released to Cartel Rodrigo.

Pain, James - Seaman - Number: 1842 - How taken: Given up from HM Frigate Hyperion - Date received: 7 Jul 1813 - From what ship: Portsmouth via HMS Tribune - Born: Block Island - Age: 32 - Discharged on 25 Jul 1814 and sent to Dartmoor on HMS Bittern.

Paine, Clement - Clerk - Number: 2866 - Prize name: Elbridge Gerry - Ship type: P - How taken: HM Frigate Crescent - When taken: 16 Sep 1813 - Where taken: at sea - Date received: 7 Jan 1814 - From what ship: Portsmouth - Born: Massachusetts - Age: 20 - Died on 20 Apr 1814 from fever.

Paine, Joshua - Seaman - Number: 640 - Prize name: Perseverance - Ship type: MV - How taken: HM Sloop Atalante - When taken: 31 Jul 1812 - Where taken: at sea - Date received: 24 Feb 1813 - From what ship: Portsmouth via HMS Ulysses - Born: Bath - Age: 35 - Discharged on 17 Nov 1813 to the Cartel Robinson Potter.

Paine, R. B. - Seaman - Number: 1603 - How taken: Gave up from a West Indian Vessel - Date received: 19 Apr 1813 - From what ship: HMS Raisonnable - Born: New York - Age: 31 - Discharged on 24 Jul 1814 and sent to Dartmoor.

Paline, William - Seaman - Number: 674 - Prize name: U.S.R.M. Cutter James Madison - Ship type: War - How taken: HM Frigate Barbadoes - When taken: 22 Aug 1812 - Where taken: at sea - Date received: 24 Feb 1813 - From what ship: Portsmouth via HMS Ulysses - Born: Philadelphia - Age: 28 - Discharged on 10 May 1813 and released to Cartel Admittance.

Palmer, George H. - Seaman - Number: 2685 - Prize name: reef boat - How taken: Impressed at Hull - When taken: 31 Oct 1813 - Date received: 25 Dec 1813 - From what ship: HMS Raisonnable - Born: Massachusetts - Age: 24 - Discharged on 8 Sep 1814 and sent to Dartmoor on HMS Niobe.

Palmer, Peter - Seaman - Number: 1110 - Prize name: Tom Thumb - Ship type: MV - How taken: Lion, British privateer - When taken: 15 Feb 1813 - Where taken: Bay of Biscay - Date received: 14 Mar 1813 - From what ship: Portsmouth via HMS Beagle - Born: Branford - Age: 22 - Discharged on 11 Aug 1814 and sent to Dartmoor on HMS Freya.

Palmer, William - Seaman - Number: 1847 - How taken: Given up from HMS Horatio - Date received: 7 Jul 1813 - From what ship: Portsmouth via HMS Tribune - Born: Portsmouth, NH - Age: 21 - Discharged on 25 Jul 1814 and sent to Dartmoor on HMS Bittern.

Pannell, Hugh - Seaman - Number: 1557 - Prize name: Dolphin - Ship type: LM - How taken: HM Ship-of-the-Line Colossus - When taken: 5 Jan 1813 - Where taken: off the Western Isles, Scotland - Date received: 8 Apr 1813 - From what ship: Plymouth via HMS Olympia - Born: Baltimore - Age: 28 - Discharged on 27 Jul

1813 and released to Cartel Hoffminy.

Pardell, Charles - Seaman - Number: 555 - How taken: Gave himself up from HM Ship-of-the-Line Ocean - When taken: 15 Aug 1812 - Date received: 23 Feb 1813 - From what ship: Portsmouth via HMS Dromedary - Born: New Orleans - Age: 28 - Discharged on 12 Aug 1814 and sent to Dartmoor on HMS Alpheus.

Paris, Peter - Seaman - Number: 3889 - How taken: Gave himself up from HM Frigate Hussar - When taken: 26 Jul 1813 - Date received: 30 Aug 1814 - From what ship: Transport Office - Born: Philadelphia - Age: 23 - Discharged on 25 Sep 1814 and sent to Dartmoor on HMS Leyden.

Parish, Samuel - Seaman - Number: 491 - How taken: Impressed out of HM Transport Simpson - When taken: Oct 1812 - Date received: 23 Feb 1813 - From what ship: Portsmouth via HMS Dromedary - Born: Gosport, VA - Age: 27 - Discharged on 2 Jul 1813 and released to Cartel Moses Brown.

Parker, David - Seaman - Number: 1495 - Prize name: Union - Ship type: MV - How taken: HM Frigate Iris - When taken: 17 Jan 1813 - Where taken: at sea - Date received: 6 Apr 1813 - From what ship: Plymouth via an admiral's tender - Born: Massachsetts - Age: 18 - Discharged on 27 Jul 1813 and released to Cartel Hoffminy.

Parker, George - Seaman - Number: 1770 - How taken: Gave himself up from HM Frigate Menelaus - When taken: 6 Jun 1813 - Date received: 14 Jun 1813 - From what ship: HMS Arethusa - Born: Cambridge - Age: 26 - Discharged on 10 Oct 1814 and sent to Dartmoor on the Mermaid.

Parker, John - Seaman - Number: 789 - Prize name: Dolphin - Ship type: MV - How taken: HM Ship-of-the-Line Colossus - When taken: 5 Jan 1813 - Where taken: off the Western Isles, Scotland - Date received: 27 Feb 1813 - From what ship: Plymouth via HMS Namur - Born: Philadelphia - Age: 21 - Discharged on 24 Jul 1813 and released to Cartel Hoffminy.

Parker, Robert - Seaman - Number: 2461 - Prize name: Thorn - Ship type: P - How taken: Shannon, Nova Scotia privateer - When taken: 2 Oct 1812 - Where taken: off Newfoundland - Date received: 21 Oct 1813 - From what ship: Portsmouth via HMT Malabar - Born: Boston - Age: 51 - Race: Blackman - Discharged on 4 Sep 1814 and sent to Dartmoor on HMS Freya.

Parker, Samuel - Seaman - Number: 857 - Prize name: Brutus - Ship type: MV - How taken: Briton, letter of marque - When taken: 13 Jan 1813 - Where taken: Bay of Biscay - Date received: 1 Mar 1813 - From what ship: Plymouth via HMS Namur - Born: New Orleans - Age: 23 - Race: Black - Discharged on 24 Jul 1813 and released to Cartel Hoffminy.

Parker, William - Seaman - Number: 3859 - Prize name: Derby - Ship type: MV - How taken: HM Frigate Nereus - When taken: 4 Feb 1813 - Where taken: off Cape of Good Hope - Date received: 24 Aug 1814 - From what ship: London - Born: Barnstable - Age: 20 - Discharged on 22 Oct 1814 and sent to Dartmoor on HMS Leyden.

Parks, Richard - Seaman - Number: 779 - Prize name: Eliza - Ship type: MV - How taken: HM Sloop Hyacinth - When taken: 27 Aug 1812 - Where taken: off Gibraltar - Date received: 27 Feb 1813 - From what ship: Plymouth via HMS Namur - Born: Baltimore - Age: 44 - Discharged on 10 May 1813 and released to Cartel Admittance.

Parr, James - Seaman - Number: 1410 - Prize name: Porcupine - Ship type: MV - How taken: HM Frigate Dryand - When taken: 8 Jan 1813 - Where taken: off Bordeaux, France - Date received: 5 Apr 1813 - From what ship: Plymouth via HMS Dwarf - Born: Philadelphia - Age: 20 - Discharged on 24 Jul 1813 and released to Cartel Hoffminy.

Parrish, William - Seaman - Number: 3457 - Prize name: Elbridge Gerry - Ship type: P - How taken: HM Frigate Crescent - When taken: 16 Sep 1813 - Where taken: at sea - Date received: 23 Feb 1814 - From what ship: Halifax via HMT Malabar - Born: Newbury - Age: 26 - Discharged on 22 Oct 1814 and sent to Dartmoor on HMS Leyden.

Parrott, Ebenezer - Seaman - Number: 3448 - Prize name: Elbridge Gerry - Ship type: P - How taken: HM Frigate Crescent - When taken: 16 Sep 1813 - Where taken: at sea - Date received: 23 Feb 1814 - From what ship: Halifax via HMT Malabar - Born: North Yarmouth - Age: 27 - Discharged on 22 Oct 1814 and sent to Dartmoor on HMS Leyden.

Parsons, Andrew - Seaman - Number: 1175 - Prize name: Sword Fish - Ship type: P - How taken: HM Ship-of-the-Line Elephant - When taken: 28 Dec 1812 - Where taken: off Azores - Date received: 16 Mar 1813 - From what ship: Portsmouth, via HMS Abundance - Born: Salem - Age: 24 - Discharged on 24 Jul 1813 and released to Cartel Hoffminy.

Parsons, Daniel - Seaman - Number: 2248 - Prize name: Joseph - Ship type: MV - How taken: HM Frigate Iris - When taken: 8 Jun 1813 - Where taken: off Spain - Date received: 7 Sep 1813 - From what ship: HMS Raisonnable - Born: Gloucester - Age: 28 - Discharged on 11 Aug 1814 and sent to Dartmoor on HMS Freya.

Parsons, David - Seaman - Number: 117 - Prize name: Urbana - Ship type: MV - How taken: Stopped at London - When taken: 26 Oct 1812 - Date received: 4 Nov 1812 - From what ship: HMS Namur - Born: Durham, CT - Age: 21 - Discharged in Jul 1813 and released to Cartel Moses Brown.

Parsons, George - Seaman - Number: 345 - Prize name: Postsea, prize to the Privateer Thrasher - Ship type: P - How taken: HM Sloop Helena - When taken: 31 Dec 1813 - Where taken: off Azores - Date received: 19 Jan 1813 - From what ship: HMS Raisonnable - Born: Cape Ann - Age: 21 - Discharged on 24 Jul 1813 and released to Cartel Hoffminy.

Parsons, Ignatius - Seaman - Number: 2007 - How taken: Gave himself up from HM Brig Foxhound - Date received: 15 Jul 1813 - From what ship: Plymouth - Born: Gloucester - Age: 24 - Discharged on 17 Jun 1814 and sent to Dartmoor on HMS Pincher.

Parsons, John - Armorer - Number: 2869 - Prize name: Elbridge Gerry - Ship type: P - How taken: HM Frigate Crescent - When taken: 16 Sep 1813 - Where taken: at sea - Date received: 7 Jan 1814 - From what ship: Portsmouth - Born: Massachusetts - Age: 25 - Discharged on 25 Sep 1814 and sent to Dartmoor on HMS Leyden.

Parsons, Joseph - Seaman - Number: 1084 - Prize name: Hope - Ship type: MV - How taken: HM Schooner Bramble - When taken: 9 Dec 1812 - Where taken: at sea - Date received: 14 Mar 1813 - From what ship: Portsmouth via HMS Cornwell - Born: Sussex - Age: 21 - Released on 10 Apr 1813.

Parsons, Rufus - Seaman - Number: 1354 - Prize name: Dart - Ship type: MV - How taken: HM Brig Doterel - When taken: 5 Mar 1813 - Where taken: at sea - Date received: 3 Apr 1813 - From what ship: Portsmouth, via an admiral's tender - Born: York - Age: 22 - Discharged on 25 Jul 1814 and sent to Dartmoor on HMS Bittern.

Parsons, Samuel - Seaman - Number: 438 - Prize name: Hunter - Ship type: P - How taken: HM Frigate Phoebe - When taken: 23 Dec 1812 - Where taken: off Azores - Date received: 19 Feb 1813 - From what ship: HMS Modeste - Born: Virginia - Age: 32 - Discharged on 8 Jun 1813 and released to Cartel Rodrigo.

Parsons, Thomas - Seaman - Number: 1127 - Prize name: Sword Fish - Ship type: P - How taken: HM Ship-of-the-Line Elephant - When taken: 28 Dec 1812 - Where taken: off Azores - Date received: 14 Mar 1813 - From what ship: Portsmouth via HMS Beagle - Born: Old York - Age: 51 - Discharged on 24 Jul 1813 and released to Cartel Hoffminy.

Parsons, Wanery - Seaman - Number: 878 - Prize name: Hero - Ship type: MV - How taken: Cornet - When taken: 10 Feb 1813 - Where taken: off Lisbon - Date received: 1 Mar 1813 - From what ship: Plymouth via HMS Namur - Born: Copetown, MA - Age: 22 - Released on 27 Mar 1813.

Patrick, John - Seaman - Number: 252 - How taken: Gave himself up at London - When taken: 15 Nov 1812 - Date received: 7 Dec 1812 - From what ship: HMS Raisonnable - Born: Stockbridge, CT - Age: 30 - Discharged in Jul 1813 and released to Cartel Moses Brown.

Patrick, John F. - Private - Number: 2663 - Prize name: 2nd U.S. Artillery - Ship type: LF - How taken: British forces - When taken: 6 Jun 1813 - Where taken: Stoney Creek, Upper Canada - Date received: 5 Nov 1813 - From what ship: HMS Hindostan - Born: County Kilkenny, Ireland - Age: 30 - Discharged on 17 Jun 1814 and sent to Dartmoor.

Patten, David - Private - Number: 3143 - Prize name: 14th U.S. Infantry - Ship type: LF - How taken: British forces - When taken: 24 Jun 1813 - Where taken: Beaver Dams, Upper Canada - Date received: 7 Jan 1814 - From what ship: Halifax - Born: Pennsylvania - Age: 25 - Discharged on 10 Oct 1814 and sent to U.S. on Cartel St.

Philip.

Patten, John - Seaman - Number: 1353 - Prize name: Dart - Ship type: MV - How taken: HM Brig Doterel - When taken: 5 Mar 1813 - Where taken: at sea - Date received: 3 Apr 1813 - From what ship: Portsmouth, via an admiral's tender - Born: Durham - Age: 23 - Discharged on 25 Jul 1814 and sent to Dartmoor on HMS Bittern.

Patterson, Archibald - Private - Number: 2645 - Prize name: 14th U.S. Infantry - Ship type: LF - How taken: British forces - When taken: 24 Jun 1813 - Where taken: Beaver Dams, Upper Canada - Date received: 5 Nov 1813 - From what ship: HMS Hindostan - Born: North Ireland - Age: 34 - Discharged on 10 Oct 1814 and sent to U.S. on Cartel St. Philip.

Patterson, John - Seaman - Number: 1368 - How taken: Gave himself up from HM Frigate Niobe - When taken: 13 Mar 1813 - Date received: 3 Apr 1813 - From what ship: Portsmouth, via an admiral's tender - Born: New York - Age: 26 - Discharged on 24 Jul 1814 and sent to Dartmoor.

Patterson, Peter - Seaman - Number: 1284 - How taken: Gave himself up from HM Guardship Royal William - When taken: 3 Feb 1813 - Date received: 16 Mar 1813 - From what ship: Portsmouth, via HMS Abundance - Born: Philadelphia - Age: 40 - Discharged on 23 Jul 1814 and sent to Dartmoor.

Patterson, William - Seaman - Number: 3030 - How taken: Gave himself up from HM Brig Racehorse - When taken: 25 Oct 1813 - Date received: 7 Jan 1814 - From what ship: Portsmouth - Born: Brewbury Port - Age: 26 - Discharged on 10 Oct 1814 and sent to Dartmoor on the Mermaid.

Pattingale, Enoch - Seaman - Number: 1032 - Prize name: Phillipsburg - Ship type: MV - How taken: Taken up at Liverpool - When taken: 9 Nov 1812 - Date received: 11 Mar 1813 - From what ship: Yarmouth via HMS Tenders - Born: Boston - Age: 24 - Discharged in Jul 1813 and released to Cartel Moses Brown.

Patton, Robert - Seaman - Number: 1996 - How taken: Gave himself up from HM Ship-of-the-Line Dublin - Date received: 15 Jul 1813 - From what ship: Plymouth - Born: Charlestown - Age: 34 - Discharged on 17 Jun 1814 and sent to Dartmoor on HMS Pincher.

Paul, Dempie - Mate - Number: 392 - Prize name: Dolphin - Ship type: MV - How taken: HM Ship-of-the-Line Invincible - When taken: 24 Aug 1812 - Where taken: Mediterranean - Date received: 13 Feb 1813 - From what ship: HMS Raisonnable - Born: Martha's Vineyard, MA - Age: 26 - Discharged on 23 Mar 1813 and released to the Cartel Robinson Potter.

Paul, Jacob - Seaman - Number: 1358 - Prize name: Dart - Ship type: MV - How taken: HM Brig Doterel - When taken: 5 Mar 1813 - Where taken: at sea - Date received: 3 Apr 1813 - From what ship: Portsmouth, via an admiral's tender - Born: Elliott - Age: 21 - Discharged on 4 Aug 1814 and sent to Dartmoor on HMS Alpheus.

Paul, Jonathan - Seaman - Number: 1682 - How taken: Impressed at Hind - When taken: 17 Mar 1813 - Date received: 15 May 1813 - From what ship: HMS Raisonnable - Born: Charleston - Age: 30 - Discharged on 24 Jul 1814 and sent to Dartmoor on HMS Liffey.

Paulfrey, Richard - Seaman - Number: 1272 - Prize name: Sword Fish - Ship type: P - How taken: HM Ship-of-the-Line Elephant - When taken: 28 Dec 1812 - Where taken: off Azores - Date received: 16 Mar 1813 - From what ship: Portsmouth, via HMS Abundance - Born: Salem - Age: 12 - Discharged on 24 Jul 1813 and released to Cartel Hoffminy.

Pault, Beloner - Seaman - Number: 681 - Prize name: U.S.R.M. Cutter James Madison - Ship type: War - How taken: HM Frigate Barbadoes - When taken: 22 Aug 1812 - Where taken: at sea - Date received: 24 Feb 1813 - From what ship: Portsmouth via HMS Ulysses - Born: Savannah - Age: 15 - Discharged on 10 May 1813 and released to Cartel Admittance.

Payne, Ransom - Seaman - Number: 1381 - How taken: Gave himself up from HM Ship-of-the-Line Sterling Castle - When taken: 26 Mar 1813 - Date received: 3 Apr 1813 - From what ship: Portsmouth, via an admiral's tender - Born: Huntingdon - Age: 21 - Discharged on 24 Jul 1814 and sent to Dartmoor.

Payne, Walter - Seaman - Number: 3011 - Prize name: Yankee - Ship type: P - How taken: HM Frigate Shannon - When taken: 20 Aug 1813 - Where taken: at sea - Date received: 7 Jan 1814 - From what ship: Halifax - Born: Massachusetts - Age: 22 - Discharged on 22 Oct 1814 and sent to Dartmoor on HMS Leyden.

Peach, John - Seaman - Number: 3434 - Prize name: Enterprise - Ship type: P - How taken: HM Frigate Tenedos - When taken: 21 May 1813 - Where taken: off Cape Cod - Date received: 23 Feb 1814 - From what ship: Halifax via HMT Malabar - Born: Salem - Age: 16 - Discharged on 22 Oct 1814 and sent to Dartmoor on HMS Leyden.

Peadon, William - Seaman - Number: 3028 - How taken: Gave himself up from HM Transport Dictator - When taken: 3 Nov 1813 - Date received: 7 Jan 1814 - From what ship: Portsmouth - Born: Philadelphia - Age: 34 - Discharged on 26 Sep 1814 and sent to Dartmoor on HMS Leyden.

Peak, John W. - Seaman - Number: 1370 - How taken: Gave himself up from HM Ship-of-the-Line Christian VII - When taken: 19 Mar 1813 - Date received: 3 Apr 1813 - From what ship: Portsmouth, via an admiral's tender - Born: Albany - Age: 26 - Discharged on 8 Sep 1814 and sent to Dartmoor on HMS Niobe.

Pearce, David - Seaman - Number: 3185 - Prize name: Wolf Cove - Ship type: MV - How taken: HM Frigate Briton - When taken: 1 Dec 1813 - Where taken: off Brest, France - Date received: 7 Jan 1813 - From what ship: Halifax - Born: Massachusetts - Age: 24 - Discharged on 25 Sep 1814 and sent to Dartmoor on HMS Leyden.

Pearce, David - Seaman - Number: 3180 - Prize name: Wolf Cove - Ship type: MV - How taken: HM Frigate Briton - When taken: 1 Dec 1813 - Where taken: off Brest, France - Date received: 7 Jan 1813 - From what ship: Halifax - Born: Massachusetts - Age: 19 - Discharged on 25 Sep 1814 and sent to Dartmoor on HMS Leyden.

Pearce, Emanuel - Seaman - Number: 1236 - Prize name: Rossie - Ship type: MV - How taken: HM Frigate Dryand - When taken: 7 Jan 1813 - Where taken: at sea - Date received: 16 Mar 1813 - From what ship: Portsmouth, via HMS Abundance - Born: New Orleans - Age: 20 - Discharged on 24 Jul 1813 and released to Cartel Hoffminy.

Pearson, Benjamin - Seaman - Number: 244 - How taken: Gave himself up from HM Ship-of-the-Line Mulgrave - When taken: 17 Nov 1812 - Date received: 1 Dec 1812 - From what ship: HMS Raisonnable - Born: Baltimore - Age: 35 - Discharged on 25 Jul 1814 and sent to Dartmoor on HMS Bittern.

Pearson, Samuel - Seaman - Number: 637 - Prize name: Charles - Ship type: MV - How taken: HM Brig Intelligent - When taken: 1 Aug 1812 - Where taken: Channel - Date received: 23 Feb 1813 - From what ship: Portsmouth via HMS Dromedary - Born: Gloucester - Age: 22 - Discharged on 17 Nov 1813 to the Cartel Robinson Potter.

Pearson, Samuel - Seaman - Number: 2853 - Prize name: Fire Fly - Ship type: LM - How taken: HM Frigate Revolutionnaire - When taken: 19 Oct 1813 - Where taken: off Cape Ortegal, Spain - Date received: 7 Jan 1814 - From what ship: Portsmouth - Born: Massachusetts - Age: 24 - Discharged on 25 Sep 1814 and sent to Dartmoor on HMS Leyden.

Pearson, Thomas - Mate - Number: 1093 - Prize name: Calcutta, East Indian Ship - Ship type: MV - How taken: Two Brothers, British privateer from Guernsey - When taken: 30 Nov 1812 - Where taken: off St. Helena - Date received: 14 Mar 1813 - From what ship: Portsmouth via HMS Beagle - Born: Philadelphia - Age: 38 - Discharged on 23 Mar 1813 and released to the Cartel Robinson Potter.

Peck, Elisha - Mate - Number: 165 - Prize name: Ann - Ship type: MV - How taken: Detained at London - When taken: 1 Aug 1812 - Date received: 5 Nov 1812 - From what ship: HMS Namur - Born: New Haven, CT - Age: 23 - Discharged on 23 Mar 1813 and released to the Cartel Robinson Potter.

Peckham, Hazard - Seaman - Number: 1828 - Prize name: tender to the Privateer True Blooded Yankee - Ship type: P - How taken: HM Ship-of-the-Line Fame - When taken: 24 Jun 1813 - Where taken: off Brest, France - Date received: 7 Jul 1813 - From what ship: Portsmouth via HMS Scorpion - Born: Newburyport - Age: 25 - Discharged on 25 Jul 1814 and sent to Dartmoor on HMS Bittern.

Peckham, Isaac - Seaman - Number: 2425 - Prize name: Maydock - Ship type: MV - How taken: HM Brig Rebuff - When taken: 16 Jun 1813 - Where taken: off Cape St. Marys, Newfoundland - Date received: 21 Oct 1813 - From what ship: Portsmouth via HMT Malabar - Born: Portsmouth - Age: 23 - Discharged on 4 Sep 1814 and sent to Dartmoor on HMS Freya.

Pedersen, John - Seaman - Number: 1802 - Prize name: Spencer - Ship type: MV - How taken: Impressed at London

- When taken: 28 May 1813 - Date received: 3 Jul 1813 - From what ship: HMS Raisonnable - Born: Baltimore - Age: 33 - Discharged on 25 Jul 1814 and sent to Dartmoor on HMS Bittern.

Peek, David - Seaman - Number: 794 - Prize name: Dolphin - Ship type: MV - How taken: HM Ship-of-the-Line Colossus - When taken: 5 Jan 1813 - Where taken: off the Western Isles, Scotland - Date received: 27 Feb 1813 - From what ship: Plymouth via HMS Namur - Born: Salem, NJ - Age: 20 - Discharged on 24 Jul 1813 and released to Cartel Hoffminy.

Peirce, Edward - Seaman - Number: 1048 - How taken: Gave himself up from HM Frigate Circe - When taken: 13 Nov 1812 - Date received: 11 Mar 1813 - From what ship: Yarmouth via HMS Tenders - Born: Baltimore - Age: 26 - Discharged on 4 Aug 1814 and sent to Dartmoor on HMS Liverpool.

Peirson, Robert - Seaman - Number: 2 - Prize name: Cato - Ship type: MV - How taken: Detained on the Baltic - When taken: 11 Aug 1812 - Date received: 29 Oct 1812 - From what ship: HMS Raisonnable - Born: Marblehead - Age: 23 - Discharged on 10 May 1813 and released to Cartel Admittance.

Pendergrass, Morris - Seaman - Number: 1782 - How taken: Taken out of the MV William Bentley, Indianman - When taken: 16 May 1813 - Date received: 1 Jul 1813 - From what ship: HMS Raisonnable - Born: Boston - Age: 27 - Discharged on 24 Jul 1814 and sent to Dartmoor on HMS Liffey.

Pendleton, Asa - Seaman - Number: 583 - How taken: Gave himself up from HM Ship-of-the-Line Aboukir - When taken: 28 Oct 1812 - Date received: 23 Feb 1813 - From what ship: Portsmouth via HMS Dromedary - Born: Salisbury - Age: 21 - Discharged on 4 Aug 1814 and sent to Dartmoor on HMS Liverpool.

Penfield, John - Seaman - Number: 3494 - How taken: Gave himself up from HM Brig Swinger - When taken: 2 Feb 1814 - Date received: 23 Feb 1814 - From what ship: Portsmouth via HMT Malabar - Born: Baltimore - Age: 26 - Discharged on 26 Sep 1814 and sent to Dartmoor on HMS Leyden.

Penn, William - Seaman - Number: 2760 - Prize name: Thomas - Ship type: P - How taken: HM Frigate Nymphe - When taken: 24 Jun 1813 - Where taken: off Halifax - Date received: 7 Jan 1814 - From what ship: Halifax - Born: Eastport - Age: 28 - Discharged on 8 Sep 1814 and sent to Dartmoor on HMS Niobe.

Penny, James - Seaman - Number: 2212 - Prize name: Jane, prize of the Privateer Snap Dragon - Ship type: P - How taken: HM Frigate Crescent & HM Ship of-the-Line Bellerophon - When taken: 28 Jun 1813 - Where taken: Newfoundland Bank - Date received: 18 Aug 1813 - From what ship: Portsmouth, via an admiral's tender - Born: Newbury - Age: 21 - Discharged on 25 Sep 1814 and sent to Dartmoor on HMS Leyden.

Penny, Richard - Seaman - Number: 2085 - How taken: Gave himself up from HM Ship-of-the-Line Scipion - When taken: 27 May 1813 - Date received: 9 Aug 1813 - From what ship: HMS Thames - Born: New Jersey - Age: 36 - Discharged on 12 Aug 1814 and sent to Dartmoor on HMS Alpheus.

Penrose, Abraham - Seaman - Number: 2129 - How taken: Gave himself up from HM Ship-of-the-Line Ocean - When taken: 28 May 1813 - Date received: 9 Aug 1813 - From what ship: HMS Thames - Born: Albany - Age: 32 - Race: Black - Discharged on 12 Aug 1814 and sent to Dartmoor on HMS Alpheus.

Percival, John - Seaman - Number: 3938 - Prize name: Hawk - Ship type: P - How taken: HM Frigate Piqua - When taken: 26 Apr 1814 - Where taken: West Indies - Date received: 3 Oct 1814 - From what ship: London - Born: Sandwich - Age: 25 - Discharged on 22 Oct 1814 and sent to Dartmoor on HMS Leyden.

Perez, Joseph - Seaman - Number: 854 - Prize name: Brutus - Ship type: MV - How taken: Briton, letter of marque - When taken: 13 Jan 1813 - Where taken: Bay of Biscay - Date received: 1 Mar 1813 - From what ship: Plymouth via HMS Namur - Born: Figueroa, Portugal - Age: 22 - Released on 20 May 1813 to Rising Sun.

Perham, Ezekiel - Seaman - Number: 3848 - How taken: Gave himself up from HM Frigate Theban at Madras, India - When taken: 13 Aug 1813 - Date received: 22 Aug 1814 - From what ship: Gravesend - Born: Newburyport - Age: 31 - Discharged on 26 Sep 1814 and sent to Dartmoor on HMS Leyden.

Perkins, Benjamin - Seaman - Number: 2838 - Prize name: Portsmouth Packet - Ship type: P - How taken: HM Brig Fantome - When taken: 5 Oct 1813 - Where taken: off Portland - Date received: 7 Jan 1814 - From what ship: Halifax - Born: Massachusetts - Age: 22 - Discharged on 25 Sep 1814 and sent to Dartmoor on HMS Leyden.

Perkins, Henry - Seaman - Number: 1006 - How taken: Gave himself up from HM Ship of-the-Line Cressy - When taken: 20 Dec 1812 - Date received: 10 Mar 1813 - From what ship: HMS Furious - Born: Boston - Age: 26 - Discharged on 4 Aug 1814 and sent to Dartmoor on HMS Liverpool.

Perkins, James - Seaman - Number: 2842 - Prize name: Portsmouth Packet - Ship type: P - How taken: HM Brig Fantome - When taken: 5 Oct 1813 - Where taken: off Portland - Date received: 7 Jan 1814 - From what ship: Halifax - Born: Massachusetts - Age: 19 - Discharged on 25 Sep 1814 and sent to Dartmoor on HMS Leyden.

Perkins, John - Commander - Number: 2831 - Prize name: Portsmouth Packet - Ship type: P - How taken: HM Brig Fantome - When taken: 5 Oct 1813 - Where taken: off Portland - Date received: 7 Jan 1814 - From what ship: Halifax - Born: Massachusetts - Age: 30 - Discharged on 25 Sep 1814 and sent to Dartmoor on HMS Leyden.

Perkins, John - Seaman - Number: 2761 - Prize name: Thomas - Ship type: P - How taken: HM Frigate Nymphe - When taken: 24 Jun 1813 - Where taken: off Halifax - Date received: 7 Jan 1814 - From what ship: Halifax - Born: Massachusetts - Age: 21 - Discharged on 8 Sep 1814 and sent to Dartmoor on HMS Niobe.

Perkins, Nicholas - Seaman - Number: 3375 - Prize name: U.S.R.M. Cutter Surveyor - Ship type: War - How taken: HM Frigate Narcissus - When taken: 12 Jun 1813 - Where taken: York River, Virginia - Date received: 23 Feb 1814 - From what ship: Halifax via HMT Malabar - Born: Hampton - Age: 50 - Discharged on 10 Oct 1814 and sent to Dartmoor on the Mermaid.

Perkins, Rufus - Private - Number: 3166 - Prize name: U.S. Light Dragoons - Ship type: LF - How taken: British forces - When taken: 24 Jun 1813 - Where taken: Beaver Dams, Upper Canada - Date received: 7 Jan 1814 - From what ship: Halifax - Born: New Haven - Age: 25 - Discharged on 10 Oct 1814 and sent to U.S. on Cartel St. Philip.

Perkins, William - Seaman - Number: 1669 - How taken: Gave himself up from HM Ship-of-the-Line Pembroke - Date received: 9 May 1813 - From what ship: HMS Raisonnable - Born: New Hampshire - Age: 33 - Discharged on 11 Aug 1814 and sent to Dartmoor on HMS Shamrock.

Perkinson, James - Seaman - Number: 2834 - Prize name: Portsmouth Packet - Ship type: P - How taken: HM Brig Fantome - When taken: 5 Oct 1813 - Where taken: off Portland - Date received: 7 Jan 1814 - From what ship: Halifax - Born: Massachusetts - Age: 20 - Discharged on 25 Sep 1814 and sent to Dartmoor on HMS Leyden.

Perott, Jean Francois - Seaman - Number: 3571 - Prize name: Devon, prize to the Privateer Bunker Hill - Ship type: P - How taken: HM Brig Fly - When taken: 21 Jan 1814 - Where taken: at sea - Date received: 7 May 1814 - From what ship: Portsmouth via HMS Favorite - Born: Isle de France - Age: 21 - Race: Black - Escaped from HM Prison Ship Glory.

Perry, Daniel - Lieutenant - Number: 2917 - Prize name: Wiley Reynard - Ship type: P - How taken: HM Frigate Shannon - When taken: 14 Oct 1812 - Where taken: off Halifax - Date received: 7 Jan 1814 - From what ship: Halifax - Born: New York - Age: 30 - Escaped on 8 Sep 1814 from HM Prison Ship Bahama.

Perry, John (alias D. Wilson) - Seaman - Number: 1764 - How taken: Gave up from HM Ship-of-the-Line Tigre - When taken: 19 May 1813 - Date received: 14 Jun 1813 - From what ship: HMS Arethusa - Born: North Yarmouth - Age: 20 - Discharged on 24 Jul 1814 and sent to Dartmoor on HMS Shamrock.

Perry, Samuel - Seaman - Number: 2385 - How taken: Gave himself up from HM Ship-of-the-Line America - When taken: 26 Dec 1812 - Date received: 20 Oct 1813 - From what ship: Portsmouth, via an admiral's tender - Born: Salem - Age: 25 - Race: Mulatto - Discharged on 4 Sep 1814 and sent to Dartmoor on HMS Freya.

Perry, William - Seaman - Number: 2409 - How taken: Gave himself up from HM Ship-of-the-Line America - Date received: 21 Oct 1813 - From what ship: Portsmouth via HMT Malabar - Born: Massachusetts - Age: 31 - Discharged on 4 Sep 1814 and sent to Dartmoor on HMS Freya.

Peters, Benjamin - Boatswain - Number: 3734 - Prize name: Argus - Ship type: MV - How taken: HM Ship-of-the-Line San Domingo - When taken: 1 Mar 1814 - Where taken: off Savannah - Date received: 26 May 1814 - From what ship: HMS Hindostan - Born: Providence - Age: 28 - Discharged on 25 Sep 1814 and sent to Dartmoor on HMS Niobe.

Peters, Jacob - Seaman - Number: 466 - Prize name: Hunter - Ship type: P - How taken: HM Frigate Phoebe - When taken: 23 Dec 1812 - Where taken: off Azores - Date received: 19 Feb 1813 - From what ship: HMS Modeste - Born: Holland - Age: 26 - Discharged on 24 Jul 1813 and released to Cartel Hoffminy.

Peters, John - Seaman - Number: 3598 - Prize name: Liberty - Ship type: MV - How taken: Surrendered at Stromness, Scotland - When taken: 30 Dec 1813 - Date received: 29 Mar 1814 - From what ship: Hired tender Anna - Born: Tennessee - Age: 45 - Discharged on 22 Oct 1814 and sent to Dartmoor on HMS Leyden.

Peters, John - Seaman - Number: 406 - Prize name: Hope - Ship type: MV - How taken: HM Schooner Bramble - When taken: 3 Dec 1812 - Where taken: Coruna, Spain - Date received: 19 Feb 1813 - From what ship: HMS Modeste - Born: Wilmington - Age: 32 - Race: Negro - Discharged on 2 Jul 1813 and released to Cartel Moses Brown.

Peters, John - Cook - Number: 122 - Prize name: Lucky - Ship type: MV - How taken: Detained at Hanoi Bay - When taken: 11 Aug 1812 - Date received: 4 Nov 1812 - From what ship: HMS Namur - Born: Sumatra, East Indies - Age: 28 - Race: Black - Discharged on 10 May 1813 and released to Cartel Admittance.

Peters, John - Seaman - Number: 513 - Prize name: William - Ship type: MV - How taken: HM Brig Recruit - When taken: 29 Aug 1812 - Where taken: at sea - Date received: 23 Feb 1813 - From what ship: Portsmouth via HMS Dromedary - Born: Philadelphia - Age: 24 - Discharged on 10 May 1813 and released to Cartel Admittance.

Peters, John - Seaman - Number: 3319 - Prize name: Porcupine - Ship type: LM - How taken: HM Frigate Acasta - When taken: 18 Jul 1813 - Where taken: off Cape Sable, Florida - Date received: 23 Feb 1814 - From what ship: Halifax via HMT Malabar - Born: New Orleans - Age: 42 - Race: Black - Discharged on 10 Oct 1814 and sent to Dartmoor on the Mermaid.

Peters, John - Seaman - Number: 2184 - How taken: Gave himself up from HM Ship-of-the-Line Leviathan - When taken: 28 Oct 1812 - Date received: 16 Aug 1813 - From what ship: Portsmouth, via an admiral's tender - Born: Pennsylvania - Age: 29 - Discharged on 25 Sep 1814 and sent to Dartmoor on HMS Leyden.

Peters, Thomas - Seaman - Number: 2363 - How taken: Gave himself up from HM Ship-of-the-Line Berwick - When taken: 25 Jun 1813 - Date received: 20 Oct 1813 - From what ship: Portsmouth, via an admiral's tender - Born: Baltimore - Age: 39 - Race: Black - Discharged on 25 Sep 1814 and sent to Dartmoor on HMS Leyden.

Peters, William - Seaman - Number: 1515 - How taken: Gave himself up from HM Transport Minerva - When taken: 14 Oct 1812 - Date received: 8 Apr 1813 - From what ship: Portsmouth, via an admiral's tender - Born: New Orleans - Age: 27 - Race: Mulatto - Discharged on 2 Jul 1813 and released to Cartel Moses Brown.

Peterson, James - Boatswain's Mate - Number: 430 - Prize name: Hunter - Ship type: P - How taken: HM Frigate Phoebe - When taken: 23 Dec 1812 - Where taken: off Azores - Date received: 19 Feb 1813 - From what ship: HMS Modeste - Born: Tarlborough - Age: 28 - Discharged on 2 Jul 1813 and released to Cartel Moses Brown.

Peterson, John - Seaman - Number: 825 - How taken: Gave himself up from HM Hospital Ship Prince Frederick - When taken: 4 Jan 1813 - Date received: 1 Mar 1813 - From what ship: Plymouth via HMS Namur - Born: New York - Age: 34 - Race: Blackman - Discharged on 7 Apr 1813 and released to the HMS Raisonnable.

Peterson, M. - Seaman - Number: 2127 - How taken: Gave himself up from HM Ship-of-the-Line Ocean - When taken: 28 May 1813 - Date received: 9 Aug 1813 - From what ship: HMS Thames - Born: Long Island - Age: 28 - Race: Black - Discharged on 12 Aug 1814 and sent to Dartmoor on HMS Alpheus.

Peterson, Nicholas - Seaman - Number: 445 - Prize name: Hunter - Ship type: P - How taken: HM Frigate Phoebe - When taken: 23 Dec 1812 - Where taken: off Azores - Date received: 19 Feb 1813 - From what ship: HMS Modeste - Born: New Orleans - Age: 38 - Discharged on 24 Jul 1813 and released to Cartel Hoffminy.

Peterson, Peter - Seaman - Number: 739 - How taken: Sent to prison off the HM Guardship Royal William - When taken: 20 Dec 1812 - Date received: 24 Feb 1813 - From what ship: Portsmouth via HMS Ulysses - Born: Copenhagen - Age: 35 - Discharged on 9 Jul 1813 and released to HMS Ceres.

Petterson, Andrew - Seaman - Number: 3666 - Prize name: open boat - How taken: HM Brig Nautilus - When taken:

10 Jun 1813 - Where taken: Chesapeake Bay - Date received: 4 May 1814 - From what ship: Portsmouth - Born: Gothenburg, Sweden - Age: 70 - Discharged on 10 Oct 1814 and sent to U.S. on Cartel St. Philip.

Petterson, John - Seaman - Number: 665 - Prize name: U.S.R.M. Cutter James Madison - Ship type: War - How taken: HM Frigate Barbadoes - When taken: 22 Aug 1812 - Where taken: at sea - Date received: 24 Feb 1813 - From what ship: Portsmouth via HMS Ulysses - Born: Sweden - Age: 24 - Released on 7 Apr 1813 for being a Sweden citizen.

Pettigrew, William - Seaman - Number: 2763 - Prize name: Thomas - Ship type: P - How taken: HM Frigate Nymphe - When taken: 24 Jun 1813 - Where taken: off Halifax - Date received: 7 Jan 1814 - From what ship: Halifax - Born: Massachusetts - Age: 16 - Discharged on 8 Sep 1814 and sent to Dartmoor on HMS Niobe.

Pettingale, John - Seaman - Number: 664 - Prize name: U.S.R.M. Cutter James Madison - Ship type: War - How taken: HM Frigate Barbadoes - When taken: 22 Aug 1812 - Where taken: at sea - Date received: 24 Feb 1813 - From what ship: Portsmouth via HMS Ulysses - Born: Haverhill - Age: 46 - Discharged on 10 May 1813 and released to Cartel Admittance.

Pettingall, Joseph - Seaman - Number: 2490 - Prize name: Enterprise - Ship type: P - How taken: HM Frigate Tenedos - When taken: 21 May 1813 - Where taken: off Cape Cod - Date received: 22 Oct 1813 - From what ship: Portsmouth via HMT Malabar - Born: Salem - Age: 18 - Discharged on 8 Sep 1814 and sent to Dartmoor on HMS Niobe.

Peverley, Henry - Seaman - Number: 2104 - How taken: Gave himself up from HM Frigate Bombay - When taken: 27 May 1813 - Date received: 9 Aug 1813 - From what ship: HMS Thames - Born: New Hampshire - Age: 33 - Discharged on 26 Sep 1814 and sent to Dartmoor on HMS Leyden.

Peverly, Richard - Seaman - Number: 2768 - Prize name: Thomas - Ship type: P - How taken: HM Frigate Nymphe - When taken: 24 Jun 1813 - Where taken: off Halifax - Date received: 7 Jan 1814 - From what ship: Halifax - Born: Portsmouth - Age: 20 - Discharged on 8 Sep 1814 and sent to Dartmoor on HMS Niobe.

Pleasanton, Robert - Seaman - Number: 902 - Prize name: Pallas - Ship type: MV - How taken: HM Brig Papillon - When taken: 17 Aug 1812 - Where taken: off Cadiz, Spain - Date received: 1 Mar 1813 - From what ship: Plymouth via HMS Namur - Born: Sandwich, MA - Age: 24 - Discharged on 23 Mar 1813 and released to the Cartel Robinson Potter.

Philbrook, Bartholomew - Seaman - Number: 1078 - How taken: Gave himself up from HM Brig Forester - When taken: 29 Dec 1812 - Date received: 14 Mar 1813 - From what ship: Portsmouth via HMS Cornwell - Born: Portsmouth - Age: 29 - Discharged on 11 Aug 1814 and sent to Dartmoor.

Phillips, Benjamin - Carpenter - Number: 2395 - How taken: Gave himself up from HM Frigate Castor - When taken: 26 Dec 1812 - Date received: 21 Oct 1813 - From what ship: Portsmouth via HMT Malabar - Born: Charlestown - Age: 29 - Discharged on 4 Sep 1814 and sent to Dartmoor on HMS Freya.

Phillips, Edward - Seaman - Number: 2534 - Prize name: Yorktown - Ship type: P - How taken: HM Brig Nimrod - When taken: 17 Jul 1813 - Where taken: Grand Banks - Date received: 22 Oct 1813 - From what ship: Portsmouth via HMT Malabar - Born: New York - Age: 22 - Discharged on 14 Sep 1813 and released to HMS Ceres.

Phillips, George - Seaman - Number: 3803 - Prize name: Rambler - Ship type: MV - How taken: HM Transport Morley - When taken: 10 Feb 1813 - Date received: 5 Jun 1814 - From what ship: HMS Raisonnable - Born: Salem - Age: 28 - Discharged on 29 Sep 1814 and sent to Dartmoor on HMS Freya.

Phillips, George W. - Prize Master - Number: 2273 - Prize name: prize to the Privateer Blockade - Ship type: P - How taken: HM Frigate Brazen - When taken: 29 Jun 1813 - Where taken: coast of Scotland - Date received: 14 Sep 1813 - From what ship: HMS Raisonnable - Born: Providence - Age: 27 - Discharged on 4 Sep 1814 and sent to Dartmoor on HMS Freya.

Phillips, Jackson - Seaman - Number: 166 - Prize name: Antelope - Ship type: MV - How taken: HMS Horato - When taken: 2 Aug 1812 - Where taken: off Norway - Date received: 5 Nov 1812 - From what ship: HMS Namur - Born: Eastern Shore, VA - Age: 27 - Discharged on 23 Mar 1813 and released to the Cartel Robinson Potter.

Phillips, John - Seaman - Number: 3813 - How taken: Gave himself up from HM Frigate Hussar - When taken: 26 Jul 1813 - Date received: 13 Jun 1814 - From what ship: Quebec - Born: New York - Age: 40 - Race: Black - Discharged on 25 Sep 1814 and sent to Dartmoor on HMS Leyden.

Phillips, Joseph - Seaman - Number: 3320 - Prize name: Porcupine - Ship type: LM - How taken: HM Frigate Acasta - When taken: 18 Jul 1813 - Where taken: off Cape Sable, Florida - Date received: 23 Feb 1814 - From what ship: Halifax via HMT Malabar - Born: Port of Spain, Trinidad - Age: 20 - Race: Black - Discharged on 10 Oct 1814 and sent to Dartmoor on the Mermaid.

Phillips, Thomas - Seaman - Number: 1355 - Prize name: Dart - Ship type: MV - How taken: HM Brig Doterel - When taken: 5 Mar 1813 - Where taken: at sea - Date received: 3 Apr 1813 - From what ship: Portsmouth, via an admiral's tender - Born: York - Age: 29 - Discharged on 25 Jul 1814 and sent to Dartmoor on HMS Bittern.

Phillips, Timothy - Seaman - Number: 2996 - Prize name: Grand Turk - Ship type: P - How taken: HM Frigate Tenedos - When taken: 26 May 1813 - Where taken: off Cape Sable, Florida - Date received: 7 Jan 1814 - From what ship: Halifax - Born: Massachusetts - Age: 26 - Discharged on 25 Sep 1814 and sent to Dartmoor on HMS Leyden.

Phillips, William - Seaman - Number: 2285 - How taken: Gave himself up from HM Ship-of-the-Line Scipion - When taken: 20 Oct 1812 - Date received: 17 Sep 1813 - From what ship: HMS Raisonnable - Born: Baltimore - Age: 29 - Race: Black - Discharged on 4 Sep 1814 and sent to Dartmoor on HMS Freya.

Phinney, John - Seaman - Number: 2475 - Prize name: Juliana Smith - Ship type: P - How taken: HM Frigate Nymphe - When taken: 12 May 1813 - Where taken: off Cape Sable, Florida - Date received: 22 Oct 1813 - From what ship: Portsmouth via HMT Malabar - Born: Sandwich - Age: 25 - Discharged on 8 Sep 1814 and sent to Dartmoor on HMS Niobe.

Pichon, John - Seaman - Number: 3336 - Prize name: Porcupine - Ship type: LM - How taken: HM Frigate Acasta - When taken: 18 Jul 1813 - Where taken: off Cape Sable, Florida - Date received: 23 Feb 1814 - From what ship: Halifax via HMT Malabar - Born: Nantes, France - Age: 22 - Discharged on 22 Jun 1814 and sent to Calais, France on the Simon & Mary.

Picket, Richard - Prize Master - Number: 694 - Prize name: Deanna, recaptured British vessel - Ship type: P - How taken: HM Ship-of-the-Line Polyphemus - When taken: 14 Sep 1812 - Where taken: at sea - Date received: 24 Feb 1813 - From what ship: Portsmouth via HMS Ulysses - Born: Marblehead, MA - Age: 24 - Discharged on 8 Jun 1813 and released to Cartel Rodrigo.

Pickens, Benjamin - Seaman - Number: 113 - Prize name: Urbana - Ship type: MV - How taken: Stopped at London - When taken: 26 Oct 1812 - Date received: 4 Nov 1812 - From what ship: HMS Namur - Born: Rochester, MA - Age: 23 - Race: Mulatto - Discharged in Jul 1813 and released to Cartel Moses Brown.

Pierce, Joseph - Seaman - Number: 2991 - Prize name: America - Ship type: P - How taken: HM Frigate Shannon - When taken: 25 May 1813 - Where taken: off Cape Cod - Date received: 7 Jan 1814 - From what ship: Halifax - Born: Massachusetts - Age: 22 - Discharged on 25 Sep 1814 and sent to Dartmoor on HMS Leyden.

Pierce, Thomas - Seaman - Number: 1772 - How taken: Gave up from HM Frigate Amelia - When taken: 1 Jun 1813 - Date received: 14 Jun 1813 - From what ship: HMS Arethusa - Born: Boston - Age: 36 - Discharged on 24 Jul 1814 and sent to Dartmoor on HMS Liffey.

Pierce, William - Seaman - Number: 1118 - How taken: Gave himself up from HMS Muros - Date received: 14 Mar 1813 - From what ship: Portsmouth via HMS Beagle - Born: Providence - Age: 18 - Discharged on 11 Aug 1814 and sent to Dartmoor on HMS Freya.

Piers, Nathaniel - Seaman - Number: 60 - Prize name: York - Ship type: MV - How taken: HM Sloop Rattler - When taken: 11 Jul 1812 - Where taken: off Bermuda - Date received: 3 Nov 1812 - From what ship: HMS Plover - Born: Middleburg, MA - Age: 30 - Discharged on 23 Mar 1813 and released to the Cartel Robinson Potter.

Pigott, James - Seaman - Number: 851 - Prize name: Ocean, prized to the Privateer Diligent - Ship type: P - How taken: HM Frigate Surveillante - When taken: 20 Dec 1812 - Where taken: Lat 44 N, Long 6 W - Date received: 1 Mar 1813 - From what ship: Plymouth via HMS Namur - Born: New Jersey - Age: 20 -

Discharged on 8 Sep 1814 and sent to Dartmoor on HMS Niobe.

Pike, Jeremiah - Boatswain's Mate - Number: 2822 - Prize name: Portsmouth Packet - Ship type: P - How taken: HM Brig Fantome - When taken: 5 Oct 1813 - Where taken: off Portland - Date received: 7 Jan 1814 - From what ship: Halifax - Born: Portsmouth - Age: 21 - Discharged on 25 Sep 1814 and sent to Dartmoor on HMS Leyden.

Piles, James - Seaman - Number: 3914 - How taken: Gave himself up - When taken: 10 Sep 1814 - Date received: 10 Sep 1814 - From what ship: Chatham - Born: Philadelphia - Age: 37 - Discharged on 22 Oct 1814 and sent to Dartmoor on HMS Leyden.

Piles, John - Seaman - Number: 2742 - Prize name: Teazer - Ship type: P - How taken: HM Frigate Boreas - When taken: 15 Jun 1813 - Where taken: off Halifax - Date received: 7 Jan 1814 - From what ship: Halifax - Born: New York - Age: 27 - Discharged on 25 Sep 1814 and sent to Dartmoor on HMS Leyden.

Pinder, George - Seaman - Number: 2464 - Prize name: Cossack - Ship type: P - How taken: HM Frigate Amelia - When taken: 11 Apr 1813 - Where taken: off St. Johns - Date received: 21 Oct 1813 - From what ship: Portsmouth via HMT Malabar - Born: Ipswich - Age: 21 - Discharged on 8 Sep 1814 and sent to Dartmoor on HMS Niobe.

Pines, Isaac - Seaman - Number: 3617 - Prize name: Liberty - Ship type: MV - How taken: Surrendered at Stromness, Scotland - When taken: 30 Dec 1813 - Date received: 29 Mar 1814 - From what ship: Hired tender Anna - Born: Swedesboro - Age: 35 - Discharged on 25 Sep 1814 and sent to Dartmoor on HMS Leyden.

Pinkham, Allen - Seaman - Number: 1532 - How taken: Gave himself up from HM Frigate Franchise - When taken: 20 Sep 1812 - Date received: 8 Apr 1813 - From what ship: Portsmouth, via an admiral's tender - Born: Bristol - Age: 25 - Discharged on 4 Aug 1814 and sent to Dartmoor on HMS Alpheus.

Pinkham, Daniel - 2nd Mate - Number: 2881 - Prize name: Taken off an English whaler - How taken: HM Ship-of-the-Line Illustrious - When taken: 22 Oct 1813 - Where taken: at sea - Date received: 7 Jan 1814 - From what ship: Portsmouth - Born: Nantucket - Age: 30 - Died on 6 Jun 1814 from fever.

Pinne, John - Seaman - Number: 2391 - How taken: Gave himself up from HM Ship-of-the-Line Achille - When taken: 26 Dec 1812 - Date received: 20 Oct 1813 - From what ship: Portsmouth, via an admiral's tender - Born: Long Island - Age: 26 - Race: Black - Discharged on 4 Sep 1814 and sent to Dartmoor on HMS Freya.

Pippin, Isaac - Seaman - Number: 3188 - Prize name: Growler - Ship type: P - How taken: HM Brig Electra - When taken: 7 Jul 1813 - Where taken: off St. Johns - Date received: 7 Jan 1813 - From what ship: Portsmouth - Born: Marblehead - Age: 28 - Discharged on 25 Sep 1814 and sent to Dartmoor on HMS Leyden.

Pippin, Isaac - Seaman - Number: 2731 - Prize name: Growler - Ship type: P - How taken: HM Brig Electra - When taken: 7 Jul 1813 - Where taken: off St. Johns - Date received: 7 Jan 1814 - From what ship: Halifax - Born: New York - Age: 30 - Discharged on 25 Sep 1814 and sent to Dartmoor on HMS Leyden.

Pitt, William - Seaman - Number: 3018 - How taken: Gave himself up from HM Ship-of-the-Line Invincible - When taken: 14 Jan 1813 - Date received: 7 Jan 1814 - From what ship: Portsmouth - Born: Salem - Age: 26 - Discharged on 4 Sep 1814 and sent to Dartmoor on HMS Freya.

Pittman, Henry - Seaman - Number: 2503 - Prize name: Thomas - Ship type: P - How taken: HM Frigate Nymphe - When taken: 28 Jun 1813 - Where taken: off Halifax - Date received: 22 Oct 1813 - From what ship: Portsmouth via HMT Malabar - Born: Baltimore - Age: 23 - Discharged on 8 Sep 1814 and sent to Dartmoor on HMS Niobe.

Pitts, Charles - Seaman - Number: 2424 - Prize name: Maydock - Ship type: MV - How taken: HM Brig Rebuff - When taken: 16 Jun 1813 - Where taken: off Cape St. Marys, Newfoundland - Date received: 21 Oct 1813 - From what ship: Portsmouth via HMT Malabar - Born: Massachusetts - Age: 20 - Discharged on 4 Sep 1814 and sent to Dartmoor on HMS Freya.

Pitts, George - Lieutenant - Number: 3003 - Prize name: Yankee - Ship type: P - How taken: HM Frigate Shannon - When taken: 20 Aug 1813 - Where taken: at sea - Date received: 7 Jan 1814 - From what ship: Halifax - Born: Massachusetts - Age: 31 - Discharged on 25 Sep 1814 and sent to Dartmoor on HMS Leyden.

Place, Thomas - Seaman - Number: 2934 - Prize name: Governor Plumer - Ship type: P - How taken: HM Brig Shamrock - When taken: 26 May 1813 - Where taken: at sea - Date received: 7 Jan 1814 - From what ship: Halifax - Born: Massachusetts - Age: 30 - Discharged on 25 Sep 1814 and sent to Dartmoor on HMS Leyden.

Plair, John - Seaman - Number: 360 - Prize name: Postsea, prize to the Privateer Thrasher - Ship type: P - How taken: HM Sloop Helena - When taken: 31 Dec 1813 - Where taken: off Azores - Date received: 19 Jan 1813 - From what ship: HMS Raisonnable - Born: Monet, Prussia - Age: 26 - Discharged on 28 Apr 1813 and released to the David Scott.

Platt, Daniel - Seaman - Number: 3515 - Prize name: Pilot - Ship type: LM - How taken: Vittoria, British privateer from Guernsey - When taken: 28 Jan 1814 - Where taken: off Bordeaux, France - Date received: 23 Feb 1814 - From what ship: Portsmouth via HMT Malabar - Born: Long Island - Age: 21 - Race: Black - Discharged on 21 Jul 1814 and sent to Dartmoor on HMS Portia.

Platt, John Henry - Seaman - Number: 617 - Prize name: King of Rome - Ship type: P - How taken: HM Brig Wolverine - When taken: 13 Dec 1812 - Where taken: at sea - Date received: 23 Feb 1813 - From what ship: Portsmouth via HMS Dromedary - Born: Bedford - Age: 25 - Discharged on 2 Jul 1813 and released to Cartel Moses Brown.

Ploughman, Joseph - Seaman - Number: 1867 - How taken: Given up from HM Ship-of-the-Line Vigo - Date received: 7 Jul 1813 - From what ship: Monmouth, Tribune - Born: Connecticut - Age: 32 - Discharged on 4 Aug 1814 and sent to Dartmoor on HMS Liverpool.

Plumber, William Reed - Seaman - Number: 3554 - Prize name: Zephyr, prize of Privateer Rattlesnake - Ship type: P - How taken: HM Frigate Surveillante - When taken: 6 Jan 1814 - Where taken: Bay of Biscay - Date received: 7 May 1814 - From what ship: Portsmouth via HMS Favorite - Born: Connecticut - Age: 32 - Discharged on 25 Sep 1814 and sent to Dartmoor on HMS Niobe.

Plummer, William - Seaman - Number: 3461 - Prize name: Elbridge Gerry - Ship type: P - How taken: HM Frigate Crescent - When taken: 16 Sep 1813 - Where taken: at sea - Date received: 23 Feb 1814 - From what ship: Halifax via HMT Malabar - Born: Gray - Age: 21 - Discharged on 21 Jul 1814 and sent to Dartmoor on HMS Portia.

Poland, Abraham - Seaman - Number: 2929 - Prize name: Lark - Ship type: MV - How taken: HM Schooner Bream - When taken: 17 Apr 1813 - Where taken: off Cape Sable, Florida - Date received: 7 Jan 1814 - From what ship: Halifax - Born: Salem - Age: 27 - Discharged on 25 Sep 1814 and sent to Dartmoor on HMS Leyden.

Poland, David - Prize Master - Number: 417 - Prize name: Hunter - Ship type: P - How taken: HM Frigate Phoebe - When taken: 23 Dec 1812 - Where taken: off Azores - Date received: 19 Feb 1813 - From what ship: HMS Modeste - Born: Ipswich - Age: 22 - Discharged on 2 Jul 1813 and released to Cartel Moses Brown.

Pollard, Charles - Cook - Number: 100 - Prize name: Fair Play - Ship type: MV - How taken: Stopped at London - When taken: 26 Oct 1812 - Date received: 4 Nov 1812 - From what ship: HMS Namur - Born: Norfolk, VA - Age: 27 - Discharged in Jul 1813 and released to Cartel Moses Brown.

Pollet, William - Seaman - Number: 3177 - Prize name: Wolf Cove - Ship type: MV - How taken: HM Frigate Briton - When taken: 1 Dec 1813 - Where taken: off Brest, France - Date received: 7 Jan 1814 - From what ship: Halifax - Born: Massachusetts - Age: 20 - Died on 27 Jan 1814 from phthisis (tuberculosis).

Pollett, Edward - Seaman - Number: 2904 - Prize name: Dart - Ship type: P - How taken: HM Frigate Niger & HMS Fortunee - When taken: 10 Nov 1813 - Where taken: off Cape Finisterre, Spain - Date received: 7 Jan 1814 - From what ship: Portsmouth - Born: Baltimore - Age: 22 - Died on 21 Apr 1814 from fever.

Pool, John - Seaman - Number: 2080 - How taken: Gave himself up from HM Ship-of-the-Line Armada - When taken: 8 Jun 1813 - Date received: 9 Aug 1813 - From what ship: HMS Thames - Born: Maryland - Age: 22 - Discharged on 4 Aug 1814 and sent to Dartmoor on HMS Liverpool.

Pool, Richard - Seaman - Number: 1715 - Prize name: Recaptured British MV - Ship type: P - How taken: HM Frigate Revolutionnaire - When taken: 10 Apr 1813 - Where taken: off the Western Isles, Scotland - Date received: 25 May 1813 - From what ship: Portsmouth via HMS Impetius - Born: Bristol, MA - Age: 23 - Discharged on 1 Oct 1813 and released to HMS Ceres.

Poole, John - Seaman - Number: 1282 - How taken: Gave himself up from HM Guardship Royal William - When taken: 3 Feb 1813 - Date received: 16 Mar 1813 - From what ship: Portsmouth, via HMS Abundance - Born: Baltimore - Age: 27 - Race: Black – Discharge not listed.

Pope, William - Seaman - Number: 1529 - How taken: Gave himself up from HM Frigate Franchise - When taken: 20 Sep 1812 - Date received: 8 Apr 1813 - From what ship: Portsmouth, via an admiral's tender - Born: Blemham, NY - Age: 30 - Discharged on 14 May 1813 and released to HMS Ceres.

Porgan, Theodore - Seaman - Number: 1391 - Prize name: Stephen - Ship type: MV - How taken: Briton, letter of marque - When taken: 1 Jan 1813 - Where taken: off Bordeaux, France - Date received: 5 Apr 1813 - From what ship: Plymouth via HMS Dwarf - Born: Stralsund, Sweden - Age: 16 - Discharged on 24 Jul 1813 and released to Cartel Hoffminy.

Port, John - Seaman - Number: 3592 - Prize name: Harvest, prize of the Privateer Bunker Hill - Ship type: P - How taken: HM Brig Orestes - When taken: 21 Jan 1814 - Where taken: Bay of Biscay - Date received: 26 Mar 1814 - From what ship: Plymouth via HMS Raleigh - Born: Rhode Island - Age: 21 - Race: Black - Discharged on 25 Sep 1814 and sent to Dartmoor on HMS Niobe.

Porter, Calvin - Seaman - Number: 3781 - Prize name: Argus - Ship type: MV - How taken: HM Ship-of-the-Line San Domingo - When taken: 1 Mar 1814 - Where taken: off Savannah - Date received: 26 May 1814 - From what ship: HMS Hindostan - Born: Boston - Age: 16 - Race: Black - Discharged on 25 Sep 1814 and sent to Dartmoor on HMS Niobe.

Porter, Charles - Seaman - Number: 2884 - Prize name: Taken off an English whaler - How taken: HM Ship-of-the-Line Illustrious - When taken: 22 Oct 1813 - Where taken: at sea - Date received: 7 Jan 1814 - From what ship: Portsmouth - Born: Massachusetts - Age: 28 - Discharged on 25 Sep 1814 and sent to Dartmoor on HMS Leyden.

Porter, Edward - Seaman - Number: 2928 - Prize name: Fame - Ship type: P - How taken: HMS Pratteo - When taken: 3 May 1813 - Where taken: Bay of Biscay - Date received: 7 Jan 1814 - From what ship: Halifax - Born: Salem - Age: 27 - Discharged on 25 Sep 1814 and sent to Dartmoor on HMS Leyden.

Porter, Ephraim - Seaman - Number: 3843 - How taken: Gave himself up from HM Frigate Theban at Madras, India - When taken: 21 Jul 1814 - Date received: 21 Aug 1814 - From what ship: Gravesend - Born: Bethlehem - Age: 25 - Discharged on 20 Sep 1814 and sent to Dartmoor on HMS Leyden.

Porter, Gideon - Seaman - Number: 3707 - How taken: Gave himself up from HM Brig Acteon - When taken: 9 May 1814 - Date received: 15 May 1815 - From what ship: Eagle - Born: Newport - Age: 32 - Discharged on 26 Sep 1814 and sent to Dartmoor on HMS Leyden.

Porter, Josiah - Seaman - Number: 2115 - How taken: Gave himself up from HM Ship-of-the-Line Tremendous - When taken: 15 Oct 1812 - Date received: 9 Aug 1813 - From what ship: HMS Thames - Born: Boston - Age: 25 - Discharged on 12 Aug 1814 and sent to Dartmoor on HMS Alpheus.

Porter, Louis - Seaman - Number: 3006 - Prize name: Yankee - Ship type: P - How taken: HM Frigate Shannon - When taken: 20 Aug 1813 - Where taken: at sea - Date received: 7 Jan 1814 - From what ship: Halifax - Born: South Carolina - Age: 24 - Discharged on 25 Sep 1814 and sent to Dartmoor on HMS Leyden.

Porter, Nathaniel - Seaman - Number: 607 - Prize name: Antelope - Ship type: P - How taken: HM Brig Zephyr - When taken: 10 Dec 1812 - Where taken: at sea - Date received: 23 Feb 1813 - From what ship: Portsmouth via HMS Dromedary - Born: Middlesex - Age: 32 - Discharged on 2 Jul 1813 and released to Cartel Moses Brown.

Porter, Samuel - Seaman - Number: 2182 - How taken: Gave himself up from HM Ship-of-the-Line Leviathan - When taken: 28 Oct 1812 - Date received: 16 Aug 1813 - From what ship: Portsmouth, via an admiral's tender - Born: Boston - Age: 23 - Discharged on 11 Aug 1814 and sent to Dartmoor on HMS Freya.

Porter, Stephen - Clerk - Number: 174 - How taken: Stopped at London - When taken: 28 Oct 1812 - Date received: 5 Nov 1812 - From what ship: HMS Namur - Born: New Orleans - Age: 25 - Discharged on 23 Mar 1813 and released to the Cartel Robinson Potter.

Porter, William - Seaman - Number: 2736 - Prize name: Growler - Ship type: P - How taken: HM Brig Electra - When taken: 7 Jul 1813 - Where taken: off St. Johns - Date received: 7 Jan 1814 - From what ship: Halifax - Born: Massachusetts - Age: 28 - Died on 23 May 1814 from fever.

Posey, Valentine - Acting Mate & Passenger - Number: 1733 - Prize name: Messenger - Ship type: MV - How taken: HM Frigate Iris - When taken: 10 Mar 1813 - Where taken: Bay of Biscay - Date received: 25 May 1813 - From what ship: Portsmouth via HMS Impetius - Born: Charles County, MD - Age: 24 - Discharged on 24 Jul 1814 and sent to Dartmoor on HMS Liffey.

Potter, Henry - Seaman - Number: 132 - Prize name: Leander - Ship type: MV - How taken: Stopped at London - When taken: 24 Oct 1812 - Date received: 5 Nov 1812 - From what ship: HMS Namur - Born: Providence, RI - Age: 22 - Race: Mulatto - Discharged in Jul 1813 and released to Cartel Moses Brown.

Potter, Jacob - Seaman - Number: 1667 - How taken: Gave himself up from HM Schooner Antelope - Date received: 9 May 1813 - From what ship: HMS Raisonnable - Born: Lewistown - Age: 30 - Race: Mulatto - Discharged on 11 Aug 1814 and sent to Dartmoor on HMS Shamrock.

Potter, John - Seaman - Number: 1594 - How taken: Impressed at Gravesend, England - When taken: 13 Mar 1813 - Date received: 19 Apr 1813 - From what ship: HMS Raisonnable - Born: Philadelphia - Age: 32 - Discharged on 12 Aug 1814 and sent to Dartmoor on HMS Alpheus.

Potter, John - Seaman - Number: 2352 - How taken: Gave himself up from HM Ship-of-the-Line Pompee - When taken: 25 Jun 1813 - Date received: 20 Oct 1813 - From what ship: Portsmouth, via an admiral's tender - Born: New York - Age: 27 - Discharged on 4 Sep 1814 and sent to Dartmoor on HMS Freya.

Pousland, William - Seaman - Number: 3240 - How taken: Gave himself up from HM Transport Bruisor - When taken: 3 Feb 1814 - Date received: 10 Feb 1814 - From what ship: HMS Cadmus - Born: Marblehead - Age: 27 - Died on 2 Apr 1814 from fever.

Powell, Elijah - Seaman - Number: 1245 - Prize name: Rossie - Ship type: MV - How taken: HM Frigate Dryand - When taken: 7 Jan 1813 - Where taken: at sea - Date received: 16 Mar 1813 - From what ship: Portsmouth, via HMS Abundance - Born: Maryland - Age: 34 - Discharged on 24 Jul 1813 and released to Cartel Hoffminy.

Powell, John - Seaman - Number: 262 - Prize name: Benjamin Franklin - Ship type: P - How taken: HM Frigate Rosamund - When taken: 8 Aug 1812 - Where taken: off Newfoundland - Date received: 7 Dec 1812 - From what ship: HMS Raisonnable - Born: Norfolk, VA - Age: 25 - Discharged on 23 Mar 1813 and released to the Cartel Robinson Potter.

Powell, Joseph - Seaman - Number: 2876 - Prize name: Falcon, prize of the U.S. Frigate President - Ship type: War - How taken: Spanish army - When taken: 2 Jul 1813 - Where taken: off Passage Harbor - Date received: 7 Jan 1814 - From what ship: Portsmouth - Born: Pennsylvania - Age: 43 - Race: Black - Discharged on 10 Oct 1814 and sent to U.S. on Cartel St. Philip.

Powell, Joseph - Seaman - Number: 2567 - How taken: Gave himself up from HM Ship-of-the-Line Berwick - When taken: 30 Oct 1812 - Date received: 23 Oct 1813 - From what ship: Portsmouth via HMS Raisonnable - Born: Philadelphia - Age: 32 - Discharged on 8 Sep 1814 and sent to Dartmoor on HMS Niobe.

Powell, Richard - Seaman - Number: 593 - Prize name: Antelope - Ship type: P - How taken: HM Brig Zephyr - When taken: 10 Dec 1812 - Where taken: at sea - Date received: 23 Feb 1813 - From what ship: Portsmouth via HMS Dromedary - Born: New York - Age: 37 - Discharged on 2 Jul 1813 and released to Cartel Moses Brown.

Powers, John - Private - Number: 3112 - Prize name: 14th U.S. Infantry - Ship type: LF - How taken: British forces - When taken: 24 Jun 1813 - Where taken: Beaver Dams, Upper Canada - Date received: 7 Jan 1814 - From what ship: Halifax - Born: Baltimore - Age: 22 - Discharged on 10 Oct 1814 and sent to U.S. on Cartel St. Philip.

Powers, William - Seaman - Number: 519 - Prize name: William - Ship type: MV - How taken: HM Brig Recruit - When taken: 29 Aug 1812 - Where taken: at sea - Date received: 23 Feb 1813 - From what ship: Portsmouth via HMS Dromedary - Born: Georgetown - Age: 18 - Discharged on 8 Jun 1813 and released to Cartel Rodrigo.

Pratt, Asa - Seaman - Number: 734 - Prize name: Nancy - Ship type: MV - How taken: HM Brig Parthian - When taken: 1 Aug 1812 - Where taken: off the Needles, Isle of Wight - Date received: 24 Feb 1813 - From what ship: Portsmouth via HMS Ulysses - Born: Weymouth, MA - Age: 19 - Discharged on 23 Mar 1813 and released to the Cartel Robinson Potter.

Pratt, Daniel - Seaman - Number: 3633 - Prize name: Bunker Hill - Ship type: P - How taken: HM Frigate Pomone & HM Frigate Cydnus - When taken: 4 Mar 1814 - Where taken: Bay of Biscay - Date received: 31 Mar 1814 - From what ship: HMS Raisonnable - Born: Maidenhead, England - Age: 32 - Escaped on 20 May 1814 from HM Prison Ship Glory.

Pratt, Lester - Seaman - Number: 2264 - Prize name: Eliza - Ship type: MV - How taken: HMS Charles - When taken: 20 Jul 1813 - Where taken: off Petershead, Scotland - Date received: 14 Sep 1813 - From what ship: HMS Raisonnable - Born: Connecticut - Age: 22 - Discharged on 20 Aug 1814 and sent to Dartmoor on HMS Shamrock.

Pratt, Philip - Seaman - Number: 2750 - Prize name: Wasp - Ship type: P - How taken: HM Schooner Bream - When taken: 9 Jun 1813 - Where taken: off Halifax - Date received: 7 Jan 1814 - From what ship: Halifax - Born: Massachusetts - Age: 20 - Discharged on 25 Sep 1814 and sent to Dartmoor on HMS Leyden.

Prendwelle, James - Seaman - Number: 537 - Prize name: Baltimore - Ship type: P - How taken: HM Transport Diadem - When taken: 7 Oct 1812 - Where taken: S. Andres - Date received: 23 Feb 1813 - From what ship: Portsmouth via HMS Dromedary - Born: Baltimore - Age: 20 - Discharged on 8 Jun 1813 and released to Cartel Rodrigo.

Prentiss, James - Seaman - Number: 744 - Prize name: Swift of Hull - Ship type: MV - How taken: Gave himself up at London - When taken: 10 Feb 1813 - Date received: 25 Feb 1813 - From what ship: HMS Raisonnable - Born: Boston - Age: 27 - Discharged on 23 Jul 1814 and sent to Dartmoor on HMS Acasta.

Prescot, John - Master - Number: 3594 - Prize name: Liberty - Ship type: MV - How taken: Surrendered at Stromness, Scotland - When taken: 30 Dec 1813 - Date received: 29 Mar 1814 - From what ship: Hired tender Anna - Born: Old York - Age: 37 - Released from Chatham on 10 Jun 1814 and sent to Ashburton on parole.

Preston, Isaac - Seaman - Number: 9 - Prize name: Eliza Ann - Ship type: MV - How taken: HM Ship-of-the-Line Vigo - When taken: 11 Aug 1812 - Where taken: Hanoi Bay - Date received: 29 Oct 1812 - From what ship: HMS Raisonnable - Born: Nantucket - Age: 18 - Discharged on 10 May 1813 and released to Cartel Admittance.

Preston, John - Prize Master - Number: 2747 - Prize name: Wasp - Ship type: P - How taken: HM Schooner Bream - When taken: 9 Jun 1813 - Where taken: off Halifax - Date received: 7 Jan 1814 - From what ship: Halifax - Born: Salem - Age: 26 - Discharged on 8 Sep 1814 and sent to Dartmoor on HMS Niobe.

Preston, William - Seaman - Number: 731 - Prize name: Richmond - Ship type: MV - How taken: Detained at Portsmouth harbor - When taken: 31 Jul 1812 - Date received: 24 Feb 1813 - From what ship: Portsmouth via HMS Ulysses - Born: Philadelphia - Age: 27 - Race: Black man - Discharged on 23 Mar 1813 and released to the Cartel Robinson Potter.

Price, Carlton - Seaman - Number: 2414 - How taken: Gave himself up from HM Frigate Laurel - When taken: 18 Oct 1813 - Date received: 21 Oct 1813 - From what ship: Portsmouth via HMT Malabar - Born: Concord - Age: 21 - Discharged on 4 Sep 1814 and sent to Dartmoor on HMS Freya.

Price, John - Seaman - Number: 2945 - Prize name: Enterprise - Ship type: P - How taken: HM Frigate Tenedos - When taken: 21 May 1813 - Where taken: off Cape Cod - Date received: 7 Jan 1814 - From what ship: Halifax - Born: Massachusetts - Age: 33 - Discharged on 25 Sep 1814 and sent to Dartmoor on HMS Leyden.

Prico, Job - Private - Number: 3158 - Prize name: 14th U.S. Infantry - Ship type: LF - How taken: British forces - When taken: 24 Jun 1813 - Where taken: Beaver Dams, Upper Canada - Date received: 7 Jan 1814 - From what ship: Halifax - Born: Maryland - Age: 24 - Discharged on 10 Oct 1814 and sent to U.S. on Cartel St. Philip.

Priest, William - Seaman - Number: 3361 - Prize name: U.S.R.M. Cutter Surveyor - Ship type: War - How taken:

HM Frigate Narcissus - When taken: 12 Jun 1813 - Where taken: York River, Virginia - Date received: 23 Feb 1814 - From what ship: Halifax via HMT Malabar - Born: Norfolk - Age: 22 - Race: Black - Discharged on 10 Oct 1814 and sent to U.S. on Cartel St. Philip.

Primas, James - Seaman - Number: 2878 - Prize name: Baroness Longueville, British South Sea Whaler - Ship type: MV - How taken: HM Ship-of-the-Line Illustrious - When taken: 5 Aug 1813 - Where taken: off St. Helena - Date received: 7 Jan 1814 - From what ship: Portsmouth - Born: Long Island - Age: 28 - Race: Black - Discharged on 25 Sep 1814 and sent to Dartmoor on HMS Leyden.

Primis, George - Cook - Number: 164 - Prize name: Elson - Ship type: MV - How taken: HM Frigate Ethalion - When taken: 12 Aug 1812 - Where taken: Baltic - Date received: 5 Nov 1812 - From what ship: HMS Namur - Born: Winchester, NH - Age: 32 - Discharged on 10 May 1813 and released to Cartel Admittance.

Prince, Jeffry - Seaman - Number: 245 - How taken: Gave himself up from HM Ship-of-the-Line Dublin - When taken: 24 Oct 1812 - Date received: 1 Dec 1812 - From what ship: HMS Raisonnable - Born: South Hold, NY - Age: 30 - Discharged on 25 Jul 1814 and sent to Dartmoor on HMS Bittern.

Prince, William - Seaman - Number: 574 - How taken: Gave himself up from HM Sloop Cherub - When taken: 5 Dec 1812 - Date received: 23 Feb 1813 - From what ship: Portsmouth via HMS Dromedary - Born: New York - Age: 26 - Discharged on 24 Jul 1814 and sent to Dartmoor on HMS Liffey.

Prio, Peter - Seaman - Number: 2141 - Prize name: Matilda, prize of the U.S. Brig Argus - Ship type: War - How taken: HM Frigate Revolutionnaire - When taken: 25 Jul 1813 - Where taken: off Lorient, France - Date received: 9 Aug 1813 - From what ship: HMS Thames - Born: New Orleans - Age: 22 - Discharged on 22 Jun 1814 and released to HMS Ceres.

Prissey, John - Seaman - Number: 3325 - Prize name: Porcupine - Ship type: LM - How taken: HM Frigate Acasta - When taken: 18 Jul 1813 - Where taken: off Cape Sable, Florida - Date received: 23 Feb 1814 - From what ship: Halifax via HMT Malabar - Born: Salem - Age: 19 - Discharged on 10 Oct 1814 and sent to Dartmoor on the Mermaid.

Pritchard, Israel - Seaman - Number: 3559 - Prize name: Hannah - Ship type: MV - How taken: HM Ship-of-the-Line Conquestador - When taken: 15 Jan 1814 - Where taken: at sea - Date received: 7 May 1814 - From what ship: Portsmouth via HMS Favorite - Born: Marblehead - Age: 22 - Discharged on 25 Sep 1814 and sent to Dartmoor on HMS Niobe.

Prout, Henry - Seaman - Number: 349 - Prize name: Postsea, prize to the Privateer Thrasher - Ship type: P - How taken: HM Sloop Helena - When taken: 31 Dec 1813 - Where taken: off Azores - Date received: 19 Jan 1813 - From what ship: HMS Raisonnable - Born: Philadelphia - Age: 29 - Discharged on 4 May 1813 and sent to London.

Prutty, Henry - Seaman - Number: 1401 - Prize name: Porcupine - Ship type: MV - How taken: HM Frigate Dryand - When taken: 8 Jan 1813 - Where taken: off Bordeaux, France - Date received: 5 Apr 1813 - From what ship: Plymouth via HMS Dwarf - Born: Plymouth, England - Age: 35 - Discharged on 12 Apr 1813 and released to HMS Carnatic.

Pudober, Jonathan - Mate - Number: 14 - Prize name: Lucky - Ship type: MV - How taken: Detained at Hanoi Bay - When taken: 11 Aug 1812 - Date received: 29 Oct 1812 - From what ship: HMS Raisonnable - Born: Beverly - Age: 44 - Discharged on 23 Mar 1813 and released to the Cartel Robinson Potter.

Puffer, John - Seaman - Number: 2791 - Prize name: Yorktown - Ship type: P - How taken: British squadron - When taken: 17 Jul 1813 - Where taken: Grand Banks - Date received: 7 Jan 1814 - From what ship: Halifax - Born: Canton - Age: 30 - Discharged on 8 Sep 1814 and sent to Dartmoor on HMS Niobe.

Purnal, Elisha - Seaman - Number: 2522 - Prize name: Yorktown - Ship type: P - How taken: HM Brig Nimrod - When taken: 17 Jul 1813 - Where taken: Grand Banks - Date received: 22 Oct 1813 - From what ship: Portsmouth via HMT Malabar - Born: Maryland - Age: 24 - Released in Oct 1814.

Purrington, John - Seaman - Number: 341 - Prize name: Postsea, prize to the Privateer Thrasher - Ship type: P - How taken: HM Sloop Helena - When taken: 31 Dec 1813 - Where taken: off Azores - Date received: 19 Jan 1813 - From what ship: HMS Raisonnable - Born: Bath, MA - Age: 20 - Discharged on 24 Jul 1813 and released to Cartel Hoffminy.

Putnam, Allen - Mate & passenger - Number: 2439 - How taken: Taken off of the Russian MV Neptune at Cork - When taken: 28 Sep 1812 - Date received: 21 Oct 1813 - From what ship: Portsmouth via HMT Malabar - Born: Danvers - Age: 20 - Discharged on 20 Aug 1814 and sent to Dartmoor on HMS Shamrock.

Quaan, George - Seaman - Number: 1390 - Prize name: Stephen - Ship type: MV - How taken: Briton, letter of marque - When taken: 1 Jan 1813 - Where taken: off Bordeaux, France - Date received: 5 Apr 1813 - From what ship: Plymouth via HMS Dwarf - Born: New Jersey - Age: 25 - Discharged on 24 Jul 1813 and released to Cartel Hoffminy.

Quackenbush, William - Seaman - Number: 1873 - Prize name: Tiger - Ship type: MV - How taken: HM Brig Scylla - When taken: 22 Mar 1813 - Where taken: Bay of Biscay - Date received: 7 Jul 1813 - From what ship: Portsmouth via HMS Tribune - Born: New York - Age: 33 - Released on 11 Jul 1814.

Quarterman, William - Seaman - Number: 2353 - How taken: Gave himself up from HM Ship-of-the-Line Ocean - When taken: 25 Jun 1813 - Date received: 20 Oct 1813 - From what ship: Portsmouth, via an admiral's tender - Born: Charlestown - Age: 23 - Discharged on 4 Sep 1814 and sent to Dartmoor on HMS Freya.

Queen, Daniel - Seaman - Number: 3951 - How taken: Gave himself up from HM Ship-of-the-Line Blenheim - When taken: 27 Aug 1814 - Date received: 21 Oct 1813 - From what ship: Quebec - Born: Prince George's County, MD - Age: 31 - Race: Black - Discharged on 22 Oct 1814 and sent to Dartmoor on HMS Leyden.

Quenichet, Joseph - Seaman - Number: 2034 - How taken: Impressed at London - When taken: 23 Jul 1813 - Date received: 1 Aug 1813 - From what ship: HMS Raisonnable - Born: Portland, MA - Age: 30 - Discharged on 4 Aug 1814 and sent to Dartmoor on HMS Liverpool.

Quince, Peter - Seaman - Number: 3250 - Prize name: Thorn - Ship type: P - How taken: Shannon, Nova Scotia privateer - When taken: 7 Nov 1813 - Where taken: off Newfoundland - Date received: 23 Feb 1814 - From what ship: Halifax via HMT Malabar - Born: Marblehead - Age: 17 - Discharged on 21 Jul 1814 and sent to Dartmoor on HMS Portia.

Quiner, Stephen - Seaman - Number: 3182 - Prize name: Wolf Cove - Ship type: MV - How taken: HM Frigate Briton - When taken: 1 Dec 1813 - Where taken: off Brest, France - Date received: 7 Jan 1813 - From what ship: Halifax - Born: Massachusetts - Age: 18 - Discharged on 25 Sep 1814 and sent to Dartmoor on HMS Leyden.

Quinton, James - Seaman - Number: 3627 - How taken: Impressed at London - When taken: 20 Mar 1814 - Date received: 31 Mar 1814 - From what ship: HMS Raisonnable - Born: Massachusetts - Age: 29 - Discharged on 1 Apr 1814 and released to the William Hastings.

Raddick, Ebenezer - Seaman - Number: 3528 - How taken: Impressed at Harwich, England - When taken: 21 Feb 1814 - Date received: 26 Feb 1814 - From what ship: HMS Raisonnable - Born: Cambridge - Age: 36 - Discharged on 22 Oct 1814 and sent to Dartmoor on HMS Leyden.

Rahabe, William - Seaman - Number: 1453 - Prize name: Orbit - Ship type: MV - How taken: HM Brig Achates - When taken: 29 Jan 1813 - Where taken: Lat 49 N Long 13 W - Date received: 6 Apr 1813 - From what ship: Plymouth via HMS Decoy - Born: Portland - Age: 44 - Discharged on 24 Jul 1814 and sent to Dartmoor.

Rainy, Thomas - Seaman - Number: 489 - How taken: Gave himself up at Sunderland off the Collier Argo - When taken: 7 Jan 1813 - Date received: 19 Feb 1813 - From what ship: HMS Raisonnable - Born: Charlestown - Age: 21 - Discharged on 26 Jul 1813 and released to Cartel Hoffminy.

Ramady, James - Seaman - Number: 1117 - How taken: Gave himself up from HM Frigate Hamadryad - Date received: 14 Mar 1813 - From what ship: Portsmouth via HMS Beagle - Born: Baltimore - Age: 20 - Discharged on 11 Aug 1814 and sent to Dartmoor on HMS Freya.

Ramans, Nicholas - Seaman - Number: 701 - Prize name: Deanna, recaptured British vessel - Ship type: P - How taken: HM Ship-of-the-Line Polyphemus - When taken: 14 Sep 1812 - Where taken: at sea - Date received: 24 Feb 1813 - From what ship: Portsmouth via HMS Ulysses - Born: Holland - Age: 18 - Discharged on 28 Apr 1813 and released to the David Scott.

Ramsey, John - Seaman - Number: 3628 - Prize name: Bunker Hill - Ship type: P - How taken: HM Frigate Pomone & HM Frigate Cydnus - When taken: 4 Mar 1814 - Where taken: Bay of Biscay - Date received: 31 Mar 1814 - From what ship: HMS Raisonnable - Born: New York - Age: 30 - Discharged on 1 Apr 1814 and released to the William Hastings.

Randal, Benjamin - Seaman - Number: 86 - Prize name: Bellville - Ship type: MV - How taken: Stopped at Portsmouth - When taken: 5 Aug 1812 - Date received: 4 Nov 1812 - From what ship: HMS Namur - Born: New York - Age: 26 - Discharged on 23 Mar 1813 and released to the Cartel Robinson Potter.

Randal, Frederick - Seaman - Number: 1489 - Prize name: Union - Ship type: MV - How taken: HM Frigate Iris - When taken: 17 Jan 1813 - Where taken: at sea - Date received: 6 Apr 1813 - From what ship: Plymouth via an admiral's tender - Born: Maryland - Age: 30 - Discharged on 26 Jul 1813 and released to Cartel Hoffminy.

Randall, Forest - Seaman - Number: 2109 - How taken: Gave himself up from HM Frigate Undaunted - When taken: 28 May 1813 - Date received: 9 Aug 1813 - From what ship: HMS Thames - Born: New Hampshire - Age: 19 - Released on 8 Oct 1814.

Randall, Jacob - Seaman - Number: 3771 - Prize name: Argus - Ship type: MV - How taken: HM Ship-of-the-Line San Domingo - When taken: 1 Mar 1814 - Where taken: off Savannah - Date received: 26 May 1814 - From what ship: HMS Hindostan - Born: Norfolk - Age: 19 - Discharged on 25 Sep 1814 and sent to Dartmoor on HMS Niobe.

Randolph, Exum - Seaman - Number: 1647 - Prize name: Nancy - Ship type: MV - How taken: HM Brig Parthian - When taken: 1 Aug 1812 - Where taken: off the Needles, Isle of Wight - Date received: 9 May 1813 - From what ship: HMS Raisonnable - Born: Virginia - Age: 26 - Race: Black - Discharged on 24 Jul 1813 and released to Cartel Hoffminy.

Randolph, George - Seaman - Number: 3376 - Prize name: U.S.R.M. Cutter Surveyor - Ship type: War - How taken: HM Frigate Narcissus - When taken: 12 Jun 1813 - Where taken: York River, Virginia - Date received: 23 Feb 1814 - From what ship: Halifax via HMT Malabar - Born: Williamsburg - Age: 17 - Discharged on 10 Oct 1814 and sent to U.S. on Cartel St. Philip.

Randson, John - Seaman - Number: 595 - Prize name: Antelope - Ship type: P - How taken: HM Brig Zephyr - When taken: 10 Dec 1812 - Where taken: at sea - Date received: 23 Feb 1813 - From what ship: Portsmouth via HMS Dromedary - Born: Portsmouth, NH - Age: 35 - Died on 7 May 1813 from pneumonia.

Rankins, William - Caulker - Number: 2396 - How taken: Gave himself up from HM Frigate Castor - When taken: 26 Dec 1812 - Date received: 21 Oct 1813 - From what ship: Portsmouth via HMT Malabar - Born: Delaware - Age: 32 - Discharged on 4 Sep 1814 and sent to Dartmoor on HMS Freya.

Ranlot, John - Seaman - Number: 2402 - How taken: Gave himself up from HM Frigate Castor - When taken: 26 Dec 1812 - Date received: 21 Oct 1813 - From what ship: Portsmouth via HMT Malabar - Born: Newport - Age: 27 - Discharged on 4 Sep 1814 and sent to Dartmoor on HMS Freya.

Rape, Nicholas - Seaman - Number: 1440 - Prize name: Orbit - Ship type: MV - How taken: HM Brig Achates - When taken: 29 Jan 1813 - Where taken: Lat 49 N Long 13 W - Date received: 6 Apr 1813 - From what ship: Plymouth via HMS Decoy - Born: Philadelphia - Age: 40 - Discharged on 24 Jul 1814 and sent to Dartmoor.

Ratuse, Peter - Seaman - Number: 906 - Prize name: Dolphin - Ship type: MV - How taken: HM Ship-of-the-Line Colossus - When taken: 5 Jan 1813 - Where taken: off the Western Isles, Scotland - Date received: 1 Mar 1813 - From what ship: Plymouth via HMS Namur - Born: Philadelphia - Age: 23 - Discharged on 24 Jul 1813 and released to Cartel Hoffminy.

Ray, Charles - Seaman - Number: 1738 - How taken: Gave himself up from HM Transport Chatham - When taken: 5 May 1813 - Date received: 25 May 1813 - From what ship: Portsmouth via HMS Impetius - Born: New London - Age: 30 - Discharged on 24 Jul 1814 and sent to Dartmoor on HMS Liffey.

Ray, Christian - Seaman - Number: 485 - How taken: Gave himself up from British MV Pelican - When taken: 20 Dec 1812 - Date received: 19 Feb 1813 - From what ship: HMS Raisonnable - Born: Barnstable - Age: 43 - Discharged on 26 Jul 1813 and released to Cartel Hoffminy.

Ray, William - Seaman - Number: 3790 - Prize name: Ocean, south seaman - Ship type: MV - How taken: HM Sloop Atalante - When taken: 16 Nov 1812 - Where taken: off Cape of Good Hope - Date received: 26 May 1814 - From what ship: HMS Hindostan - Born: Baltimore - Age: 20 - Discharged on 22 Oct 1814 and sent to Dartmoor on HMS Leyden.

Raymond, George - Seaman - Number: 956 - How taken: Gave himself up from HM Schooner Arrow - When taken: 4 Jan 1813 - Date received: 10 Mar 1813 - From what ship: HMS Tigress - Born: Newburgh - Age: 26 - Discharged on 4 Aug 1814 and sent to Dartmoor on HMS Liverpool.

Rea, William J. - Seaman - Number: 1785 - How taken: Taken up at London - When taken: 13 Jun 1813 - Date received: 1 Jul 1813 - From what ship: HMS Raisonnable - Born: Boston - Age: 46 - Discharged on 24 Jul 1814 and sent to Dartmoor on HMS Liffey.

Read, Hugh - Seaman - Number: 1587 - How taken: Gave himself up from HM Ship-of-the-Line Christian VII - When taken: 21 Dec 1812 - Date received: 18 Apr 1813 - From what ship: HMS Rosario - Born: Topsal - Age: 26 - Escaped on 16 May 1814 from the HM Prison Ship Crown Prince.

Read, Major - Seaman - Number: 90 - Prize name: Orpheus - Ship type: MV - How taken: Stopped at London - When taken: 26 Oct 1812 - Date received: 4 Nov 1812 - From what ship: HMS Namur - Born: Philadelphia - Age: 26 - Died on 20 Nov 1812 from fever.

Read, William - Seaman - Number: 220 - How taken: Apprehended at London - When taken: 3 Nov 1812 - Date received: 15 Nov 1812 - From what ship: HMS Raisonnable - Born: Philadelphia - Age: 32 - Discharged in Jul 1813 and released to Cartel Moses Brown.

Reans, John - Seaman - Number: 1588 - How taken: Gave himself up from HM Ship-of-the-Line Christian VII - When taken: 21 Dec 1812 - Date received: 18 Apr 1813 - From what ship: HMS Rosario - Born: Baltimore - Age: 19 - Discharged on 31 Aug 1813 and released to HMS Ceres.

Record, Frederick - Seaman - Number: 586 - Prize name: Antelope - Ship type: P - How taken: HM Brig Zephyr - When taken: 10 Dec 1812 - Where taken: at sea - Date received: 23 Feb 1813 - From what ship: Portsmouth via HMS Dromedary - Born: Rhyne, Germany - Age: 38 - Discharged on 2 Jul 1813 and released to Cartel Moses Brown.

Rectout, John J. - Seaman - Number: 2163 - How taken: Gave himself up from HM Frigate Unicorn - When taken: 17 Jun 1813 - Date received: 16 Aug 1813 - From what ship: Portsmouth, via an admiral's tender - Born: Baltimore - Age: 28 - Discharged on 17 Jun 1814 and sent to Dartmoor on the Penebar.

Redman, David - Seaman - Number: 2399 - How taken: Gave himself up from HM Ship-of-the-Line Scepter - When taken: 26 Dec 1812 - Date received: 21 Oct 1813 - From what ship: Portsmouth via HMT Malabar - Born: Maryland - Age: 21 - Discharged on 4 Sep 1814 and sent to Dartmoor on HMS Freya.

Reed, Abraham - Seaman - Number: 3543 - Prize name: Commodore Perry - Ship type: MV - How taken: Sent into custody from a cutter - When taken: 25 Feb 1814 - Where taken: off Bordeaux, France - Date received: 5 Mar 1814 - From what ship: HMS Raisonnable - Born: New York - Age: 19 - Discharged on 25 Sep 1814 and sent to Dartmoor on HMS Niobe.

Reed, Charles - Prize Master - Number: 3865 - Prize name: Harriett - Ship type: MV - How taken: HM Brig Thistle - When taken: 24 Feb 1813 - Where taken: off St. Bartholomew, WI - Date received: 25 Aug 1814 - From what ship: London - Born: Reading - Age: 32 - Discharged on 22 Oct 1814 and sent to Dartmoor on HMS Leyden.

Reed, George - Seaman - Number: 2993 - Prize name: America - Ship type: P - How taken: HM Frigate Shannon - When taken: 25 May 1813 - Where taken: off Cape Cod - Date received: 7 Jan 1814 - From what ship: Halifax - Born: Rhode Island - Age: 22 - Discharged on 25 Sep 1814 and sent to Dartmoor on HMS Leyden.

Reed, H. W. - Prize Master - Number: 1018 - Prize name: Sword Fish - Ship type: P - How taken: HM Ship-of-the-Line Elephant - When taken: 28 Dec 1812 - Where taken: off Azores - Date received: 10 Mar 1813 - From what ship: HMS Furious - Born: Salem - Age: 32 - Discharged on 24 Jul 1813 and released to Cartel Hoffminy.

Reed, James - Seaman - Number: 1773 - How taken: Gave himself up from HM Frigate Arethusa - When taken: 5 Jun 1813 - Date received: 14 Jun 1813 - From what ship: HMS Arethusa - Born: New York - Age: 40 - Discharged on 24 Jul 1814 and sent to Dartmoor on HMS Liffey.

Reed, John - Boatswain - Number: 1813 - Prize name: Benjamin Franklin - Ship type: P - How taken: Row boat out of Martinique - When taken: 11 Oct 1812 - Date received: 7 Jul 1813 - From what ship: Portsmouth via HMS Scorpion - Born: Newcastle - Age: 28 - Discharged on 26 Jul 1813 and released to Cartel Hoffminy.

Reed, John - Seaman - Number: 689 - Prize name: Fame, prize of Privateer Decatur - Ship type: P - How taken: HM Ship-of-the-Line Polyphemus - When taken: 13 Sep 1812 - Where taken: at sea - Date received: 24 Feb 1813 - From what ship: Portsmouth via HMS Ulysses - Born: Marblehead, MA - Age: 19 - Discharged on 8 Jun 1813 and released to Cartel Rodrigo.

Reed, John - Seaman - Number: 880 - Prize name: Hero - Ship type: MV - How taken: Cornet - When taken: 10 Feb 1813 - Where taken: off Lisbon - Date received: 1 Mar 1813 - From what ship: Plymouth via HMS Namur - Born: New Bedford - Age: 25 - Race: Black - Released on 27 Mar 1813.

Reed, Joseph - Seaman - Number: 2206 - Prize name: Jane, prize of the Privateer Snap Dragon - Ship type: P - How taken: HM Frigate Crescent & HM Ship of-the-Line Bellerophon - When taken: 28 Jun 1813 - Where taken: Newfoundland Bank - Date received: 18 Aug 1813 - From what ship: Portsmouth, via an admiral's tender - Born: Plymouth - Age: 27 - Discharged on 26 Sep 1814 and sent to Dartmoor on HMS Leyden.

Reed, Thomas - Seaman - Number: 1384 - Prize name: Saragossa - Ship type: MV - How taken: Impressed at Gravesend, England - When taken: 10 Mar 1813 - Date received: 3 Apr 1813 - From what ship: HMS Namur - Born: Philadelphia - Age: 46 - Discharged on 24 Jul 1814 and sent to Dartmoor.

Rees, William - Steward - Number: 182 - Prize name: Echo - Ship type: MV - How taken: Stopped at London - When taken: 29 Oct 1812 - Date received: 5 Nov 1812 - From what ship: HMS Namur - Born: Baltimore - Age: 26 - Discharged on 7 Jun 1813 and released to the HMS Ceres.

Reeves, Essex - Seaman - Number: 3533 - Prize name: Commodore Perry - Ship type: MV - How taken: Sent into custody from a cutter - When taken: 25 Feb 1814 - Where taken: off Bordeaux, France - Date received: 5 Mar 1814 - From what ship: HMS Raisonnable - Born: Salem - Age: 45 - Discharged on 26 Sep 1814 and sent to Dartmoor on HMS Leyden.

Reeves, Joseph - Seaman - Number: 1470 - Prize name: Union - Ship type: MV - How taken: HM Frigate Iris - When taken: 17 Jan 1813 - Where taken: at sea - Date received: 6 Apr 1813 - From what ship: Portsmouth via Tender Eliza - Born: New Jersey - Age: 33 - Discharged on 26 Jul 1813 and released to Cartel Hoffminy.

Reid, John - Seaman - Number: 2570 - How taken: Gave himself up from HM Frigate Undaunted - When taken: 15 Oct 1812 - Date received: 23 Oct 1813 - From what ship: Portsmouth via HMS Raisonnable - Born: Virginia - Age: 49 - Discharged on 25 Sep 1814 and sent to Dartmoor on HMS Leyden.

Reid, John - Seaman - Number: 2670 - Prize name: Hamlett - Ship type: MV - How taken: Impressed at London - When taken: 11 Nov 1813 - Date received: 21 Nov 1813 - From what ship: HMS Raisonnable - Born: Virginia - Age: 37 - Escaped on 10 Jun 1814 from HM Prison Ship Crown Prince.

Reid, John - Seaman - Number: 2569 - How taken: Gave himself up from HM Schooner Charlotte - When taken: 15 Oct 1812 - Date received: 23 Oct 1813 - From what ship: Portsmouth via HMS Raisonnable - Born: Philadelphia - Age: 24 - Race: Black - Discharged on 25 Sep 1814 and sent to Dartmoor on HMS Leyden.

Reid, Joseph - Seaman - Number: 1570 - How taken: Impressed at Greenock, Scotland - When taken: 27 Nov 1812 - Date received: 8 Apr 1813 - From what ship: Plymouth via HMS Olympia - Born: Alexandria - Age: 19 - Discharged on 27 Jul 1813 and released to Cartel Hoffminy.

Reid, William - Seaman - Number: 3230 - How taken: Gave himself up from HM Ship-of-the-Line Dannemark - When taken: 12 Dec 1813 - Date received: 13 Jan 1814 - From what ship: Portsmouth via HMS Poictiers - Born: Philadelphia - Age: 44 - Race: Mulatto - Discharged on 11 Aug 1814 and sent to Dartmoor on HMS Freya.

Reid, William - Seaman - Number: 3029 - How taken: Gave himself up from HM Brig Racehorse - When taken: 25 Oct 1813 - Date received: 7 Jan 1814 - From what ship: Portsmouth - Born: Portsmouth, NH - Age: 25 - Discharged on 11 Aug 1814 and sent to Dartmoor on HMS Freya.

Renelds, Amos - Seaman - Number: 1579 - How taken: Gave himself up from HM Ship-of-the-Line Colossus - When taken: 10 Dec 1812 - Date received: 16 Apr 1813 - From what ship: HMS Namur, admiral's tender - Born: Connecticut - Age: 24 - Discharged on 24 Jul 1814 and sent to Dartmoor.

Rennell, States William - Seaman - Number: 1072 - How taken: Gave himself up from HM Frigate Freya - When taken: 2 Aug 1812 - Date received: 14 Mar 1813 - From what ship: Portsmouth via HMS Cornwell - Born: Charlestown - Age: 30 - Discharged on 25 Sep 1814 and sent to Dartmoor.

Rest, Zebulon - Seaman - Number: 778 - Prize name: Eliza - Ship type: MV - How taken: HM Sloop Hyacinth - When taken: 27 Aug 1812 - Where taken: off Gibraltar - Date received: 27 Feb 1813 - From what ship: Plymouth via HMS Namur - Born: Gloucester - Age: 28 - Discharged on 10 May 1813 and released to Cartel Admittance.

Reymond, Caleb - Seaman - Number: 2341 - Prize name: Hindostan - Ship type: MV - How taken: HM Brig Zenobia - When taken: 25 Jun 1813 - Where taken: off Lisbon - Date received: 20 Oct 1813 - From what ship: Portsmouth, via an admiral's tender - Born: Portsmouth - Age: 33 - Discharged on 20 May 1814 and released to HMS Ceres.

Reynolds, Frederick - Boy - Number: 1963 - Prize name: Napoleon - Ship type: MV - How taken: HM Frigate Belle Poule - When taken: 3 Apr 1813 - Where taken: off Cape Ortegal, Spain - Date received: 15 Jul 1813 - From what ship: Plymouth - Born: New York - Age: 18 - Discharged on 17 Jun 1814 and sent to Dartmoor on HMS Redbreast.

Reynolds, Stephen - Seaman - Number: 2220 - How taken: Apprehended at London - When taken: 17 Aug 1813 - Date received: 22 Aug 1813 - From what ship: HMS Raisonnable - Born: New York - Age: 24 - Discharged on 11 Aug 1814 and sent to Dartmoor on HMS Freya.

Rhea, John - Private - Number: 3121 - Prize name: 14th U.S. Infantry - Ship type: LF - How taken: British forces - When taken: 24 Jun 1813 - Where taken: Beaver Dams, Upper Canada - Date received: 7 Jan 1814 - From what ship: Halifax - Born: Wilmington - Age: 26 - Discharged on 10 Oct 1814 and sent to U.S. on Cartel St. Philip.

Rice, George - Master - Number: 200 - Prize name: Lucy - Ship type: MV - How taken: Apprehended at London - When taken: 2 Nov 1812 - Date received: 15 Nov 1812 - From what ship: HMS Raisonnable - Born: Teaborough, MA - Age: 20 - Discharged in Jul 1813 and released to Cartel Moses Brown.

Rice, John - Seaman - Number: 1308 - How taken: Gave himself up from HM Guardship Royal William - When taken: 3 Feb 1813 - Date received: 16 Mar 1813 - From what ship: Portsmouth, via HMS Abundance - Born: Wilmington - Age: 23 - Discharged on 22 Jul 1813 and released to HMS Ceres.

Rice, John - Seaman - Number: 1544 - Prize name: Industry - Ship type: P - How taken: Caroline, recaptured by the crew - Date received: 8 Apr 1813 - From what ship: Plymouth via HMS Olympia - Born: Boston - Age: 23 - Discharged on 8 Jun 1813 and released to Cartel Rodrigo.

Rice, Thomas - Seaman - Number: 1543 - Prize name: Industry - Ship type: P - How taken: Caroline, recaptured by the crew - Date received: 8 Apr 1813 - From what ship: Plymouth via HMS Olympia - Born: Boston - Age: 25 - Discharged on 8 Jun 1813 and released to Cartel Rodrigo.

Rice, Thomas - Commander - Number: 2797 - Prize name: Industry - Ship type: P - How taken: HM Brig Heron - When taken: 3 Nov 1813 - Where taken: off Halifax - Date received: 7 Jan 1814 - From what ship: Halifax - Born: Boston - Age: 26 - Discharged on 8 Sep 1814 and sent to Dartmoor on HMS Niobe.

Rich, Elisha - Seaman - Number: 2021 - How taken: Gave himself up rom HM Sloop-Brig Rosario - Date received: 15 Jul 1813 - From what ship: Plymouth - Born: Baltimore - Age: 29 - Discharged on 17 Jun 1814 and sent to Dartmoor on HMS Pincher.

Rich, Francis - Seaman - Number: 970 - Prize name: Brutus - Ship type: MV - How taken: Briton, letter of marque - When taken: 6 Jan 1813 - Where taken: off Bordeaux, France - Date received: 10 Mar 1813 - From what ship: HMS Tigress - Born: New Orleans - Age: 27 - Discharged on 24 Jul 1813 and released to Cartel Hoffminy.

Rich, William - Seaman - Number: 1980 - How taken: Gave himself up from HM Ship-of-the-Line Malta - Date received: 15 Jul 1813 - From what ship: Plymouth - Born: Maryland - Age: 23 - Race: Black - Discharged on 23 Feb 1814 and released to HMS Ceres.

Richards, Edward - Seaman - Number: 1857 - How taken: Gave himself up from HM Bomb Vessel Strombolo - Date received: 7 Jul 1813 - From what ship: Portsmouth via HMS Tribune - Born: Portland, MA - Age: 46 - Discharged on 25 Jul 1814 and sent to Dartmoor on HMS Bittern.

Richards, George - Seaman - Number: 565 - Prize name: Rising States - Ship type: MV - How taken: HM Frigate Fortunee - When taken: 28 Aug 1812 - Where taken: off the Western Isles, Scotland - Date received: 23 Feb

1813 - From what ship: Portsmouth via HMS Dromedary - Born: New York - Age: 27 - Race: Man of color - Died on 28 Mar 1813 at Portsmouth from pneumonia.

Richards, Henry - Seaman - Number: 2123 - How taken: Gave himself up from HM Ship-of-the-Line Ocean - When taken: 28 May 1813 - Date received: 9 Aug 1813 - From what ship: HMS Thames - Born: Massachusetts - Age: 32 - Discharged on 12 Aug 1814 and sent to Dartmoor on HMS Alpheus.

Richards, James - Seaman - Number: 3634 - Prize name: Bunker Hill - Ship type: P - How taken: HM Frigate Pomone & HM Frigate Cydnus - When taken: 4 Mar 1814 - Where taken: Bay of Biscay - Date received: 31 Mar 1814 - From what ship: HMS Raisonnable - Born: Charlestown - Age: 34 - Race: Black - Discharged on 25 Sep 1814 and sent to Dartmoor on HMS Niobe.

Richards, James - Seaman - Number: 2003 - How taken: Gave himself up from HM Hospital Ship Trent - Date received: 15 Jul 1813 - From what ship: Plymouth - Born: Newburyport - Age: 44 - Discharged on 17 Jun 1814 and sent to Dartmoor on HMS Pincher.

Richards, John - Seaman - Number: 1829 - Prize name: tender to the Privateer True Blooded Yankee - Ship type: P - How taken: HM Ship-of-the-Line Fame - When taken: 24 Jun 1813 - Where taken: off Brest, France - Date received: 7 Jul 1813 - From what ship: Portsmouth via HMS Scorpion - Born: Boston - Age: 22 - Discharged on 25 Jul 1814 and sent to Dartmoor on HMS Bittern.

Richards, Sandy - Seaman - Number: 3408 - Prize name: Elbridge Gerry - Ship type: P - How taken: HM Frigate Tenedos - When taken: 21 May 1813 - Where taken: off Cape Cod - Date received: 23 Feb 1814 - From what ship: Halifax via HMT Malabar - Born: Baltimore - Age: 44 - Discharged on 22 Oct 1814 and sent to Dartmoor on HMS Leyden.

Richardson, Allen - Seaman - Number: 184 - How taken: Stopped at London - When taken: 23 Oct 1812 - Date received: 5 Nov 1812 - From what ship: HMS Namur - Born: Wilmington, NC - Age: 23 - Discharged in Jul 1813 and released to Cartel Moses Brown.

Richardson, Daniel - Seaman - Number: 808 - Prize name: Leader - Ship type: MV - How taken: HM Frigate Andromach - When taken: 10 Dec 1812 - Where taken: off Bordeaux, France - Date received: 27 Feb 1813 - From what ship: Plymouth via HMS Namur - Born: Maryland - Age: 25 - Discharged in Jul 1813 and released to Cartel Moses Brown.

Richardson, James - Seaman - Number: 1080 - How taken: Gave himself up from HM Ship-of-the-Line Dannemark - When taken: 21 Oct 1812 - Date received: 14 Mar 1813 - From what ship: Portsmouth via HMS Cornwell - Born: Massachusetts - Age: 30 - Discharged on 23 Jul 1814 and sent to Dartmoor.

Richardson, James - Seaman - Number: 2513 - Prize name: Wasp - Ship type: P - How taken: HM Schooner Bream - When taken: 9 Jun 1813 - Where taken: off Halifax - Date received: 22 Oct 1813 - From what ship: Portsmouth via HMT Malabar - Born: Salem - Age: 60 - Discharged on 25 Sep 1814 and sent to Dartmoor on HMS Leyden.

Richardson, John - Seaman - Number: 1425 - How taken: Taken off the HM Frigate Andromache - When taken: 24 Dec 1812 - Date received: 5 Apr 1813 - From what ship: Plymouth via HMS Dwarf - Born: Dresden - Age: 25 - Discharged on 25 Sep 1814 and sent to Dartmoor.

Richardson, John - Seaman - Number: 2175 - How taken: Gave himself up from HM Ship-of-the-Line Leviathan - When taken: 28 Oct 1812 - Date received: 16 Aug 1813 - From what ship: Portsmouth, via an admiral's tender - Born: Jersey - Age: 42 - Race: Blackman - Discharged on 11 Aug 1814 and sent to Dartmoor on HMS Freya.

Richardson, Perry - Seaman - Number: 1277 - Prize name: Sword Fish - Ship type: P - How taken: HM Ship-of-the-Line Elephant - When taken: 28 Dec 1812 - Where taken: off Azores - Date received: 16 Mar 1813 - From what ship: Portsmouth, via HMS Abundance - Born: Maryland - Age: 21 - Race: Black - Discharged on 24 Jul 1813 and released to Cartel Hoffminy.

Richardson, Randolph - Seaman - Number: 54 - Prize name: Trim - Ship type: MV - How taken: From a cutter off Bermuda - When taken: 26 Jul 1812 - Date received: 3 Nov 1812 - From what ship: HMS Plover - Born: Hobern, MA - Age: 18 - Discharged on 23 Mar 1813 and released to the Cartel Robinson Potter.

Richardson, Robert - Seaman - Number: 2371 - How taken: Gave himself up from HM Ship-of-the-Line Swiftsure -

When taken: 26 Dec 1812 - Date received: 20 Oct 1813 - From what ship: Portsmouth, via an admiral's tender - Born: Philadelphia - Age: 43 - Race: Mulatto - Discharged on 4 Sep 1814 and sent to Dartmoor on HMS Freya.

Richardson, Samuel - Sailmaker - Number: 1553 - Prize name: Dolphin - Ship type: LM - How taken: HM Ship-of-the-Line Colossus - When taken: 5 Jan 1813 - Where taken: off the Western Isles, Scotland - Date received: 8 Apr 1813 - From what ship: Plymouth via HMS Olympia - Born: Philadelphia - Age: 23 - Discharged on 27 Jul 1813 and released to Cartel Hoffminy.

Richardson, Samuel - Seaman - Number: 2193 - How taken: Impressed off British MV Atlas at Shields - When taken: 3 Aug 1812 - Date received: 18 Aug 1813 - From what ship: French Account - Born: Lewistown - Age: 39 - Race: Blackman - Discharged on 12 Aug 1814 and sent to Dartmoor on HMS Alpheus.

Richardson, William - Seaman - Number: 2946 - Prize name: Enterprise - Ship type: P - How taken: HM Frigate Tenedos - When taken: 21 May 1813 - Where taken: off Cape Cod - Date received: 7 Jan 1814 - From what ship: Halifax - Born: Massachusetts - Age: 27 - Discharged on 25 Sep 1814 and sent to Dartmoor on HMS Leyden.

Richardson, William - Seaman - Number: 2990 - Prize name: America - Ship type: P - How taken: HM Frigate Shannon - When taken: 25 May 1813 - Where taken: off Cape Cod - Date received: 7 Jan 1814 - From what ship: Halifax - Born: Massachusetts - Age: 18 - Discharged on 25 Sep 1814 and sent to Dartmoor on HMS Leyden.

Richmond, Caleb - Seaman - Number: 111 - Prize name: Phoenix - Ship type: MV - How taken: Stopped at London - When taken: 26 Oct 1812 - Date received: 4 Nov 1812 - From what ship: HMS Namur - Born: Dighton, MA - Age: 23 - Discharged in Jul 1813 and released to Cartel Moses Brown.

Rick, William - Seaman - Number: 3392 - Prize name: Fox - Ship type: P - How taken: HM Frigate Maidstone - When taken: 18 Jul 1813 - Where taken: Grand Banks - Date received: 23 Feb 1814 - From what ship: Halifax via HMT Malabar - Born: Portsmouth - Age: 16 - Discharged on 21 Jul 1814 and sent to Dartmoor on HMS Portia.

Ricks, Thomas - Seaman - Number: 613 - Prize name: King of Rome - Ship type: P - How taken: HM Brig Wolverine - When taken: 13 Dec 1812 - Where taken: at sea - Date received: 23 Feb 1813 - From what ship: Portsmouth via HMS Dromedary - Born: New York - Age: 36 - Discharged on 2 Jul 1813 and released to Cartel Moses Brown.

Riggins, Laban - Private - Number: 3066 - Prize name: 14th U.S. Infantry - Ship type: LF - How taken: British forces - When taken: 24 Jun 1813 - Where taken: Beaver Dams, Upper Canada - Date received: 7 Jan 1814 - From what ship: Halifax - Born: Maryland - Age: 26 - Discharged on 10 Oct 1814 and sent to U.S. on Cartel St. Philip.

Rightman, John - Seaman - Number: 2041 - Prize name: Kitty, prize of the U.S. Frigate President - Ship type: War - How taken: Dart, British privateer from Guernsey - When taken: 20 Jun 1813 - Where taken: off the Western Isles, Scotland - Date received: 4 Aug 1813 - From what ship: HMS Christian VII - Born: Canaan, CT - Age: 24 - Discharged on 4 Aug 1814 and sent to Dartmoor on HMS Liverpool.

Riker, Samuel - Seaman - Number: 727 - Prize name: Eos - Ship type: MV - How taken: Detained at Portsmouth harbor - When taken: 31 Jul 1812 - Date received: 24 Feb 1813 - From what ship: Portsmouth via HMS Ulysses - Born: Wells, York County - Age: 24 - Discharged on 23 Mar 1813 and released to the Cartel Robinson Potter.

Riley, Jonathan - Seaman - Number: 573 - Prize name: Felix - Ship type: MV - How taken: HM Frigate Gladiator - When taken: 5 Dec 1812 - Where taken: Portsmouth harbor - Date received: 23 Feb 1813 - From what ship: Portsmouth via HMS Dromedary - Born: New York - Age: 35 - Released on 25 Mar 1813.

Riley, William - Seaman - Number: 1047 - How taken: Gave himself up from HM Frigate Circe - When taken: 13 Nov 1812 - Date received: 11 Mar 1813 - From what ship: Yarmouth via HMS Tenders - Born: New Jersey - Age: 22 - Released on 26 Sep 1814.

Ring, Andrew - Seaman - Number: 3460 - Prize name: Elbridge Gerry - Ship type: P - How taken: HM Frigate Crescent - When taken: 16 Sep 1813 - Where taken: at sea - Date received: 23 Feb 1814 - From what ship:

Halifax via HMT Malabar - Born: Yarmouth - Age: 20 - Discharged on 22 Oct 1814 and sent to Dartmoor on HMS Leyden.

Ringgold, Thomas - Seaman - Number: 3743 - Prize name: Argus - Ship type: MV - How taken: HM Ship-of-the-Line San Domingo - When taken: 1 Mar 1814 - Where taken: off Savannah - Date received: 26 May 1814 - From what ship: HMS Hindostan - Born: Baltimore - Age: 32 - Race: Black - Discharged on 25 Sep 1814 and sent to Dartmoor on HMS Niobe.

Ringman, Charles - Seaman - Number: 2460 - Prize name: Wiley Reynard - Ship type: P - How taken: HM Frigate Shannon - When taken: 16 Aug 1812 - Where taken: off Halifax - Date received: 21 Oct 1813 - From what ship: Portsmouth via HMT Malabar - Born: Boston - Age: 16 - Discharged on 4 Sep 1814 and sent to Dartmoor on HMS Freya.

Ringold, Thomas B. - Seaman - Number: 358 - Prize name: Postsea, prize to the Privateer Thrasher - Ship type: P - How taken: HM Sloop Helena - When taken: 31 Dec 1813 - Where taken: off Azores - Date received: 19 Jan 1813 - From what ship: HMS Raisonnable - Born: Prince George's County, MD - Age: 34 - Discharged on 24 Jul 1813 and released to Cartel Hoffminy.

Rippaviere, John - Seaman - Number: 940 - Prize name: Three Brothers - Ship type: MV - How taken: HM Brig Bermuda - When taken: 9 Dec 1812 - Where taken: off St. Valery - Date received: 10 Mar 1813 - From what ship: HMS Tigress - Born: Basel, Switzerland - Age: 28 - Discharged on 2 Jul 1813 and released to Cartel Moses Brown.

Riswell, Palmer - Seaman - Number: 3296 - Prize name: Montgomery - Ship type: P - How taken: HM Frigate Nymphe - When taken: 5 May 1813 - Where taken: off Cape Cod - Date received: 23 Feb 1814 - From what ship: Halifax via HMT Malabar - Born: Old Georges - Age: 35 - Discharged on 10 Oct 1814 and sent to Dartmoor on the Mermaid.

Ritchie, Allan - Private - Number: 3157 - Prize name: 14th U.S. Infantry - Ship type: LF - How taken: British forces - When taken: 24 Jun 1813 - Where taken: Beaver Dams, Upper Canada - Date received: 7 Jan 1814 - From what ship: Halifax - Born: Pennsylvania - Age: 21 - Discharged on 10 Oct 1814 and sent to U.S. on Cartel St. Philip.

Roach, Nicholas - 2nd Mate - Number: 815 - Prize name: Columbia - Ship type: MV - How taken: HM Frigate Briton - When taken: 17 Dec 1812 - Where taken: off Bordeaux, France - Date received: 27 Feb 1813 - From what ship: Plymouth via HMS Namur - Born: Philadelphia - Age: 36 - Discharged in Jul 1813 and released to Cartel Moses Brown.

Roach, Reuben - Seaman - Number: 1995 - How taken: Gave himself up from HM Ship-of-the-Line Dublin - Date received: 15 Jul 1813 - From what ship: Plymouth - Born: Maryland - Age: 29 - Discharged on 17 Jun 1814 and sent to Dartmoor on HMS Pincher.

Roath, James - Seaman - Number: 3658 - Prize name: Mary - Ship type: MV - How taken: HM Schooner Racer - When taken: 17 Dec 1813 - Where taken: off Cape Florida (Haida) - Date received: 23 Apr 1814 - From what ship: HMS Raisonnable - Born: Norwich - Age: 25 - Discharged on 10 Oct 1814 and sent to Dartmoor on the Mermaid.

Roberson, James - Seaman - Number: 143 - Prize name: Harmak & Sally - Ship type: MV - How taken: Detained in the London docks - When taken: 3 Aug 1812 - Date received: 5 Nov 1812 - From what ship: HMS Namur - Born: Philadelphia - Age: 31 - Discharged on 23 Mar 1813 and released to the Cartel Robinson Potter.

Robert, Nicholas - Seaman - Number: 27 - Prize name: Arial - Ship type: MV - How taken: HM Brig Recruit - When taken: 2 Jun 1812 - Where taken: coast of America - Date received: 3 Nov 1812 - From what ship: HMS Plover - Born: Lancaster, PA - Age: 26 - Discharged on 23 Mar 1813 and released to the Cartel Robinson Potter.

Roberts, David - Seaman - Number: 1754 - How taken: Gave himself up from HMS Impeteux - When taken: 2 Dec 1812 - Date received: 30 May 1813 - From what ship: HMS Impetius - Born: King & Queen County, VA - Age: 24 - Race: Blackman - Discharged on 24 Jul 1814 and sent to Dartmoor on HMS Liffey.

Roberts, George - Seaman - Number: 1144 - Prize name: Sword Fish - Ship type: P - How taken: HM Ship-of-the-Line Elephant - When taken: 28 Dec 1812 - Where taken: off Azores - Date received: 16 Mar 1813 - From what ship: Portsmouth, Mundane - Born: Marblehead - Age: 24 - Discharged on 24 Jul 1813 and released to Cartel Hoffminy.

Roberts, James - Seaman - Number: 1514 - How taken: Gave himself up from HM Ship-of-the-Line Blake - When taken: 10 Dec 1812 - Date received: 8 Apr 1813 - From what ship: Portsmouth, via an admiral's tender - Born: Philadelphia - Age: 35 - Race: Black - Discharged on 5 Nov 1813 and released to HMS Ceres.

Roberts, Josiah - Seaman - Number: 977 - Prize name: Empress - Ship type: MV - How taken: HM Brig Rover - When taken: 30 Nov 1812 - Where taken: St. Andrew - Date received: 10 Mar 1813 - From what ship: HMS Tigress - Born: New Jersey - Age: 21 - Discharged on 8 Jun 1813 and released to Cartel Rodrigo.

Roberts, Nathaniel - Seaman - Number: 3786 - Prize name: Adaline - Ship type: LM - How taken: HM Frigate Magiciene - When taken: 14 Mar 1814 - Where taken: off Cape Ortegal, Spain - Date received: 26 May 1814 - From what ship: HMS Hindostan - Born: Beverly - Age: 19 - Discharged on 29 Sep 1814 and sent to Dartmoor on HMS Freya.

Roberts, Robert - Seaman - Number: 1189 - How taken: Gave himself up from HM Brig Zephyr - When taken: 12 Sep 1812 - Date received: 16 Mar 1813 - From what ship: Portsmouth, via HMS Abundance - Born: New York - Age: 27 - Discharged on 11 Aug 1814 and sent to Dartmoor on HMS Freya.

Roberts, William - Seaman - Number: 326 - Prize name: Eliza - Ship type: MV - How taken: Apprehended at London - When taken: 3 Jan 1813 - Date received: 11 Jan 1813 - From what ship: HMS Raisonnable - Born: Maryland - Age: 31 - Discharged on 28 Apr 1813 and released to the David Scott.

Roberts, William - Seaman - Number: 2038 - How taken: Impressed at London - When taken: 24 Jul 1813 - Date received: 1 Aug 1813 - From what ship: HMS Raisonnable - Born: Baltimore - Age: 36 - Race: Black - Discharged on 4 Dec 1813 and released to HMS Ceres.

Robertson, Thomas - Seaman - Number: 3867 - Prize name: Rattlesnake - Ship type: LM - How taken: HM Frigate Rhin - When taken: 17 Mar 1814 - Where taken: off Bermuda - Date received: 25 Aug 1814 - From what ship: London - Born: Boston - Age: 21 - Race: Black - Discharged on 22 Oct 1814 and sent to Dartmoor on HMS Leyden.

Robertson, William - Seaman - Number: 2883 - Prize name: Taken off an English whaler - How taken: HM Ship-of-the-Line Illustrious - When taken: 22 Oct 1813 - Where taken: at sea - Date received: 7 Jan 1814 - From what ship: Portsmouth - Born: Philadelphia - Age: 26 - Discharged on 25 Sep 1814 and sent to Dartmoor on HMS Leyden.

Robes, Edward - Boy - Number: 2815 - Prize name: Industry - Ship type: P - How taken: HM Brig Heron - When taken: 3 Nov 1813 - Where taken: off Halifax - Date received: 7 Jan 1814 - From what ship: Halifax - Born: Marblehead - Age: 15 - Discharged on 25 Sep 1814 and sent to Dartmoor on HMS Leyden.

Robinet, Samuel - Seaman - Number: 23 - How taken: Discharged from HM Ship Sarpedo - When taken: 22 Oct 1812 - Date received: 29 Oct 1812 - From what ship: HMS Raisonnable - Born: Philadelphia - Age: 46 - Discharged on 24 Jul 1814 and sent to Dartmoor on HMS Raven.

Robins, Jeremiah - Seaman - Number: 463 - Prize name: Hunter - Ship type: P - How taken: HM Frigate Phoebe - When taken: 23 Dec 1812 - Where taken: off Azores - Date received: 19 Feb 1813 - From what ship: HMS Modeste - Born: Sudbury - Age: 28 - Discharged on 24 Jul 1813 and released to Cartel Hoffminy.

Robins, John - Seaman - Number: 1383 - Prize name: Saragossa - Ship type: MV - How taken: Impressed at Gravesend, England - When taken: 10 Mar 1813 - Date received: 3 Apr 1813 - From what ship: HMS Namur - Born: Philadelphia - Age: 34 - Race: Mulatto - Discharged on 12 Aug 1814 and sent to Dartmoor on HMS Alpheus.

Robins, Thomas - Seaman - Number: 1860 - How taken: Gave himself up from HM Frigate Leonidas - Date received: 7 Jul 1813 - From what ship: Portsmouth via HMS Tribune - Born: Plymouth - Age: 28 - Discharged on 5 Oct 1813 and released to HMS Ceres.

Robins, William - Steward - Number: 3573 - Prize name: Commodore Perry - Ship type: MV - How taken: Sent into custody from a cutter - When taken: 25 Feb 1814 - Where taken: off Bordeaux, France - Date received: 7 May 1814 - From what ship: HMS Peruvian - Born: Eddington - Age: 27 - Race: Mulatto - Discharged on 25 Sep 1814 and sent to Dartmoor on HMS Niobe.

Robins, Willis - Seaman - Number: 218 - Prize name: Elizabeth - Ship type: MV - How taken: Impressed at Gravesend, England - When taken: 25 Aug 1812 - Date received: 15 Nov 1812 - From what ship: HMS Raisonnable - Born: Edington - Age: 24 - Discharged in Jul 1813 and released to Cartel Moses Brown.

Robinson, Benjamin - Seaman - Number: 1312 - How taken: Gave himself up from HM Guardship Royal William - When taken: 3 Feb 1813 - Date received: 16 Mar 1813 - From what ship: Portsmouth, via HMS Abundance - Born: Boston - Age: 31 - Discharged on 23 Jul 1814 and sent to Dartmoor.

Robinson, Benjamin - Seaman - Number: 818 - Prize name: Columbia - Ship type: MV - How taken: HM Frigate Briton - When taken: 17 Dec 1812 - Where taken: off Bordeaux, France - Date received: 27 Feb 1813 - From what ship: Plymouth via HMS Namur - Born: Philadelphia - Age: 24 - Discharged in Jul 1813 and released to Cartel Moses Brown.

Robinson, Charles - Seaman - Number: 557 - Prize name: Felix - Ship type: MV - How taken: HM Frigate Indefatigable - When taken: 13 Nov 1812 - Where taken: Portsmouth harbor - Date received: 23 Feb 1813 - From what ship: Portsmouth via HMS Dromedary - Born: Nantucket - Age: 24 - Discharged on 8 Jun 1813 and released to Cartel Rodrigo.

Robinson, David - Seaman - Number: 1494 - Prize name: Union - Ship type: MV - How taken: HM Frigate Iris - When taken: 17 Jan 1813 - Where taken: at sea - Date received: 6 Apr 1813 - From what ship: Plymouth via an admiral's tender - Born: Massachsetts - Age: 28 - Discharged on 27 Jun 1813 and released to HMS Ceres.

Robinson, Edward - Seaman - Number: 1252 - How taken: Gave himself up from HM Ship-of-the-Line Elephant - Date received: 16 Mar 1813 - From what ship: Portsmouth, via HMS Abundance - Born: Bath - Age: 27 - Discharged on 23 Jul 1814 and sent to Dartmoor.

Robinson, Edward - Seaman - Number: 560 - How taken: Gave himself up from HM Guardship Royal William - When taken: 18 Nov 1812 - Date received: 23 Feb 1813 - From what ship: Portsmouth via HMS Dromedary - Born: Talbot - Age: 24 - Discharged on 4 Aug 1814 and sent to Dartmoor on HMS Liverpool.

Robinson, Henry - Seaman - Number: 2597 - How taken: Gave himself up from HM Ship-of-the-Line Berwick - When taken: 27 May 1813 - Date received: 5 Nov 1813 - From what ship: HMS Hindostan - Born: Philadelphia - Age: 33 - Race: Blackman - Discharged on 12 Aug 1814 and sent to Dartmoor on HMS Alpheus.

Robinson, Jacob - Seaman - Number: 318 - Prize name: Joseph Ricketsen - Ship type: MV - How taken: HM Brig Rifleman - When taken: 22 Aug 1812 - Where taken: off Scotland - Date received: 23 Dec 1812 - From what ship: Greenlaw Depot - Born: New London - Age: 21 - Race: Black man - Discharged on 10 May 1813 and released to Cartel Admittance.

Robinson, James - Seaman - Number: 1389 - Prize name: Stephen - Ship type: MV - How taken: Briton, letter of marque - When taken: 1 Jan 1813 - Where taken: off Bordeaux, France - Date received: 5 Apr 1813 - From what ship: Plymouth via HMS Dwarf - Born: Philadelphia - Age: 22 - Discharged on 24 Jul 1813 and released to Cartel Hoffminy.

Robinson, James - Seaman - Number: 2297 - How taken: Apprehended at London - When taken: 23 Sep 1813 - Date received: 29 Sep 1813 - From what ship: HMS Raisonnable - Born: Rhode Island - Age: 22 - Discharged on 4 Sep 1814 and sent to Dartmoor on HMS Freya.

Robinson, John - Seaman - Number: 3881 - How taken: Gave himself up from HM Frigate Clorinde - When taken: 10 Feb 1814 - Date received: 28 Aug 1814 - From what ship: London - Born: Pennsylvania - Age: 32 - Race: Black - Discharged on 4 Sep 1814 and sent to Dartmoor on HMS Freya.

Robinson, John - Seaman - Number: 1567 - Prize name: Dolphin - Ship type: LM - How taken: HM Ship-of-the-Line Colossus - When taken: 5 Jan 1813 - Where taken: off the Western Isles, Scotland - Date received: 8 Apr 1813 - From what ship: Plymouth via HMS Olympia - Born: Delaware - Age: 21 - Discharged on 10 May 1813 and released to HMS Ceres.

Robinson, John - 2nd Lieutenant - Number: 2746 - Prize name: Wasp - Ship type: P - How taken: HM Schooner Bream - When taken: 9 Jun 1813 - Where taken: off Halifax - Date received: 7 Jan 1814 - From what ship: Halifax - Born: Nantucket - Age: 28 - Discharged on 8 Sep 1814 and sent to Dartmoor on HMS Niobe.

Robinson, John - Seaman - Number: 2379 - How taken: Gave himself up from HM Ship-of-the-Line America -

When taken: 26 Dec 1812 - Date received: 20 Oct 1813 - From what ship: Portsmouth, via an admiral's tender - Born: Massachusetts - Age: 26 - Discharged on 4 Sep 1814 and sent to Dartmoor on HMS Freya.

Robinson, Michael - Seaman - Number: 842 - Prize name: Vengeance - Ship type: LM - How taken: HM Frigate Phoebe - When taken: 1 Jan 1813 - Where taken: Lat 44.4 Long 23 - Date received: 1 Mar 1813 - From what ship: Plymouth via HMS Namur - Born: Bristol - Age: 18 - Discharged on 24 Jul 1813 and released to Cartel Hoffminy.

Robinson, Robert - Seaman - Number: 3394 - Prize name: Polly - Ship type: P - How taken: HM Brig Borer - When taken: 25 Jun 1813 - Where taken: off Halifax - Date received: 23 Feb 1814 - From what ship: Halifax via HMT Malabar - Born: Boston - Age: 26 - Discharged on 22 Oct 1814 and sent to Dartmoor on HMS Leyden.

Robinson, Stephen - Seaman - Number: 3772 - Prize name: Argus - Ship type: MV - How taken: HM Ship-of-the-Line San Domingo - When taken: 1 Mar 1814 - Where taken: off Savannah - Date received: 26 May 1814 - From what ship: HMS Hindostan - Born: Boston - Age: 25 - Race: Black - Discharged on 25 Sep 1814 and sent to Dartmoor on HMS Niobe.

Robinson, Thomas - Seaman - Number: 2825 - Prize name: Portsmouth Packet - Ship type: P - How taken: HM Brig Fantome - When taken: 5 Oct 1813 - Where taken: off Portland - Date received: 7 Jan 1814 - From what ship: Halifax - Born: Pennsylvania - Age: 27 - Discharged on 25 Sep 1814 and sent to Dartmoor on HMS Leyden.

Robinson, William - Seaman - Number: 3924 - How taken: Gave himself up from HM Ship-of-the-Line Revenge - When taken: 23 Sep 1814 - Date received: 24 Sep 1814 - From what ship: HMS Namur - Born: Baltimore - Age: 21 - Race: Mulatto - Discharged on 29 Sep 1814 and sent to Dartmoor on HMS Freya.

Robinson, William - Seaman - Number: 2976 - Prize name: Enterprise - Ship type: P - How taken: HM Frigate Tenedos - When taken: 21 May 1813 - Where taken: off Cape Cod - Date received: 7 Jan 1814 - From what ship: Halifax - Born: Massachusetts - Age: 27 - Discharged on 25 Sep 1814 and sent to Dartmoor on HMS Leyden.

Robson, Robert - Seaman - Number: 587 - Prize name: Antelope - Ship type: P - How taken: HM Brig Zephyr - When taken: 10 Dec 1812 - Where taken: at sea - Date received: 23 Feb 1813 - From what ship: Portsmouth via HMS Dromedary - Born: Salem - Age: 32 - Discharged on 2 Jul 1813 and released to Cartel Moses Brown.

Roderick, Frank - Seaman - Number: 1810 - Prize name: Decatur - Ship type: P - How taken: HM Frigate Surprise - When taken: 14 Jan 1813 - Where taken: at sea - Date received: 7 Jul 1813 - From what ship: Portsmouth via HMS Scorpion - Born: Eastport - Age: 26 - Discharged on 26 Jul 1813 and released to Cartel Hoffminy.

Rodgers, Abraham - Seaman - Number: 2889 - Prize name: Dart - Ship type: P - How taken: HM Frigate Niger & HMS Fortunee - When taken: 10 Nov 1813 - Where taken: off Cape Finisterre, Spain - Date received: 7 Jan 1814 - From what ship: Portsmouth - Born: Delaware - Age: 21 - Discharged on 25 Sep 1814 and sent to Dartmoor on HMS Leyden.

Rodgers, Samuel - Seaman - Number: 2309 - Prize name: Kitty, prize of the U.S. Frigate President - Ship type: War - How taken: Dart, British privateer from Guernsey - When taken: 20 Jun 1813 - Where taken: off the Western Isles, Scotland - Date received: 8 Oct 1813 - From what ship: Portsmouth, via an admiral's tender - Born: Boston - Age: 18 - Discharged on 8 Sep 1814 and sent to Dartmoor on HMS Niobe.

Rodgers, William - Seaman - Number: 2528 - Prize name: Yorktown - Ship type: P - How taken: HM Brig Nimrod - When taken: 17 Jul 1813 - Where taken: Grand Banks - Date received: 22 Oct 1813 - From what ship: Portsmouth via HMT Malabar - Born: Boston - Age: 27 - Discharged on 8 Sep 1814 and sent to Dartmoor on HMS Niobe.

Roe, Johnman - Seaman - Number: 112 - Prize name: Phoenix - Ship type: MV - How taken: Stopped at London - When taken: 26 Oct 1812 - Date received: 4 Nov 1812 - From what ship: HMS Namur - Born: Rhode Island - Age: 24 - Race: Mulatto - Discharged in Jul 1813 and released to Cartel Moses Brown.

Roffe, Isaac - Seaman - Number: 3819 - How taken: Apprehended at London - When taken: 29 Jan 1814 - Date received: 5 Jul 1814 - From what ship: Transport Office - Born: New Jersey - Age: 23 - Discharged on 22 Oct 1814 and sent to Dartmoor on HMS Leyden.

Roger, Christopher - Seaman - Number: 3686 - Prize name: Bunker Hill - Ship type: P - How taken: HM Frigate Pomone & HM Frigate Cydnus - When taken: 4 Mar 1814 - Where taken: Bay of Biscay - Date received: 4 May 1814 - From what ship: Portsmouth - Born: Brest, France - Age: 46 - Escaped on 20 May 1814 from HM Prison Ship Glory.

Rogers, Edward - Seaman - Number: 1721 - Prize name: Powhattan - Ship type: MV - How taken: HMS Horatio - When taken: 13 Dec 1812 - Where taken: Bay of Biscay - Date received: 25 May 1813 - From what ship: Portsmouth via HMS Impetius - Born: New York - Age: 26 - Discharged on 24 Jul 1813 and released to Cartel Hoffminy.

Rogers, Edward - Seaman - Number: 2329 - How taken: Impressed at Gravesend, England - When taken: 7 Jul 1813 - Date received: 12 Oct 1813 - From what ship: HMS Raisonnable - Born: Boston - Age: 29 - Discharged on 4 Sep 1814 and sent to Dartmoor on HMS Freya.

Rogers, Epinetos - Seaman - Number: 2208 - Prize name: Jane, prize of the Privateer Snap Dragon - Ship type: P - How taken: HM Frigate Crescent & HM Ship-of-the-Line Bellerophon - When taken: 28 Jun 1813 - Where taken: Newfoundland Bank - Date received: 18 Aug 1813 - From what ship: Portsmouth, via an admiral's tender - Born: Long Island - Age: 22 - Discharged on 11 Aug 1814 and sent to Dartmoor on HMS Freya.

Rogers, Francis - Seaman - Number: 1833 - Prize name: tender to the Privateer True Blooded Yankee - Ship type: P - How taken: HM Ship-of-the-Line Fame - When taken: 24 Jun 1813 - Where taken: off Brest, France - Date received: 7 Jul 1813 - From what ship: Portsmouth via HMS Scorpion - Born: Philadelphia - Age: 33 - Discharged on 22 Jun 1814 and sent to Calais, France on the Simon & Mary.

Rogers, Gorham - Seaman - Number: 2252 - Prize name: Joseph - Ship type: MV - How taken: HM Frigate Iris - When taken: 8 Jun 1813 - Where taken: off Spain - Date received: 7 Sep 1813 - From what ship: HMS Raisonnable - Born: Gloucester - Age: 22 - Discharged on 11 Aug 1814 and sent to Dartmoor on HMS Freya.

Rogers, James - Seaman - Number: 52 - Prize name: Trim - Ship type: MV - How taken: From a cutter off Bermuda - When taken: 26 Jul 1812 - Date received: 3 Nov 1812 - From what ship: HMS Plover - Born: New York - Age: 43 - Discharged on 23 Mar 1813 and released to the Cartel Robinson Potter.

Rogers, James - Seaman - Number: 1278 - Prize name: Sword Fish - Ship type: P - How taken: HM Ship-of-the-Line Elephant - When taken: 28 Dec 1812 - Where taken: off Azores - Date received: 16 Mar 1813 - From what ship: Portsmouth, via HMS Abundance - Born: Newport - Age: 29 - Race: Black - Discharged on 24 Jul 1813 and released to Cartel Hoffminy.

Rogers, John - Seaman - Number: 1749 - How taken: Gave himself up from HMS Nigo - When taken: 18 Dec 1812 - Date received: 29 May 1813 - From what ship: HMS Raven - Born: Virginia - Age: 35 - Discharged on 24 Jul 1814 and sent to Dartmoor on HMS Liffey.

Rogers, John - Seaman - Number: 84 - Prize name: Eliza - Ship type: MV - How taken: Stopped at London - When taken: 24 Oct 1812 - Date received: 4 Nov 1812 - From what ship: HMS Namur - Born: Massachusetts - Age: 31 - Discharged in Jul 1813 and released to Cartel Moses Brown.

Rogers, Nathaniel - Seaman - Number: 1975 - Prize name: Polly - Ship type: MV - How taken: HM Frigate Surveillante - When taken: 23 Mar 1813 - Where taken: Bay of Biscay - Date received: 15 Jul 1813 - From what ship: Plymouth - Born: Marblehead - Age: 23 - Discharged on 17 Jun 1814 and sent to Dartmoor on HMS Pincher.

Rogers, Piley - Seaman - Number: 3468 - Prize name: Yankee - Ship type: P - How taken: HM Frigate Shannon - When taken: 20 Aug 1813 - Where taken: at sea - Date received: 23 Feb 1814 - From what ship: Halifax via HMT Malabar - Born: Warren - Age: 22 - Discharged on 22 Oct 1814 and sent to Dartmoor on HMS Leyden.

Rogers, Samuel - Mate - Number: 1 - Prize name: Cato - Ship type: MV - How taken: Detained on the Baltic - When taken: 11 Aug 1812 - Date received: 29 Oct 1812 - From what ship: HMS Raisonnable - Born: Marblehead - Age: 29 - Discharged on 23 Mar 1813 and released to the Cartel Robinson Potter.

Rogers, Samuel - Prize Master - Number: 2188 - Prize name: True Blooded Yankee - Ship type: P - How taken: HM Frigate Hamadryad - When taken: 24 Jul 1813 - Where taken: off Norway - Date received: 17 Aug 1813 - From what ship: HMS Raisonnable - Born: New York - Age: 20 - Discharged on 11 Aug 1814 and sent to

Dartmoor on HMS Freya.

Rogers, William - Seaman - Number: 538 - Prize name: Baltimore - Ship type: P - How taken: HM Transport Diadem - When taken: 7 Oct 1812 - Where taken: S. Andres - Date received: 23 Feb 1813 - From what ship: Portsmouth via HMS Dromedary - Born: Washington - Age: 21 - Discharged on 8 Jun 1813 and released to Cartel Rodrigo.

Rogers, William - Mate - Number: 375 - Prize name: Union American - Ship type: MV - How taken: Impressed at London - When taken: 22 Jan 1813 - Date received: 31 Jan 1813 - From what ship: HMS Raisonnable - Born: Georgetown - Age: 26 - Discharged on 23 Mar 1813 and released to the Cartel Robinson Potter.

Rollo, William - Seaman - Number: 1365 - How taken: Gave himself up from HM Guardship Royal William - When taken: 12 Mar 1813 - Date received: 3 Apr 1813 - From what ship: Portsmouth, via an admiral's tender - Born: Gloucester - Age: 33 - Discharged on 8 Sep 1814 and sent to Dartmoor on HMS Niobe.

Rooter, John - Seaman - Number: 3234 - Prize name: Calmar - Ship type: MV - How taken: Friends, British privateer from Antigua - When taken: 1 Mar 1813 - Where taken: off St. Bartholomew, WI - Date received: 13 Jan 1814 - From what ship: Portsmouth via HMS Poictiers - Born: Maryland - Age: 26 - Died on 9 May 1814 from fever.

Roper, John - Seaman - Number: 1149 - Prize name: Sword Fish - Ship type: P - How taken: HM Ship-of-the-Line Elephant - When taken: 28 Dec 1812 - Where taken: off Azores - Date received: 16 Mar 1813 - From what ship: Portsmouth, Mundane - Born: Gloucester - Age: 17 - Discharged on 24 Jul 1813 and released to Cartel Hoffminy.

Ropes, Daniel - Seaman - Number: 2469 - Prize name: Montgomery - Ship type: P - How taken: HM Frigate Nymphe - When taken: 5 May 1813 - Where taken: off Cape Cod - Date received: 21 Oct 1813 - From what ship: Portsmouth via HMT Malabar - Born: Salem - Age: 18 - Died on 9 Feb 1814 from phthisis (tuberculosis).

Ropes, David - Seaman - Number: 3275 - Prize name: Cossack - Ship type: MV - How taken: HM Brig Curlew - When taken: 22 Apr 1813 - Where taken: Indian Island - Date received: 23 Feb 1814 - From what ship: Halifax via HMT Malabar - Born: Salem - Age: 16 - Discharged on 10 Oct 1814 and sent to Dartmoor on the Mermaid.

Rose, Francis - Seaman - Number: 209 - Prize name: Raymond - Ship type: MV - How taken: Impressed at Gravesend, England - When taken: 22 Oct 1812 - Date received: 15 Nov 1812 - From what ship: HMS Raisonnable - Born: Nantucket, MA - Age: 21 - Discharged on 12 Apr 1813 and released to HMS Carnatic.

Rose, William - Seaman - Number: 1606 - How taken: Gave himself up from HM Ship-of-the-Line Raisonnable - When taken: 19 Apr 1813 - Date received: 19 Apr 1813 - From what ship: HMS Raisonnable - Born: Virginia - Age: 36 - Escaped on 28 Sep 1814.

Rosecrans, Philip - Cook - Number: 1645 - Prize name: Henryettos - Ship type: MV - How taken: HMS Castilian - When taken: 12 Mar 1813 - Where taken: off Cape Ortegal, Spain - Date received: 9 May 1813 - From what ship: HMS Raisonnable - Born: New York - Age: 27 - Race: Black - Discharged on 24 Jul 1814 and sent to Dartmoor.

Rosell, John (alias Jose Maria Gavrero - Seaman - Number: 3233 - How taken: Impressed at Dublin - When taken: Aug 1813 - Date received: 13 Jan 1814 - From what ship: Portsmouth via HMS Poictiers - Born: Not listed - Discharged on 25 Sep 1814 and sent to Dartmoor on HMS Leyden.

Roselof, Thomas - Seaman - Number: 893 - Prize name: Poor Sailor - Ship type: P - How taken: HM Frigate Garland - When taken: 5 Aug 1812 - Where taken: off Cuba - Date received: 1 Mar 1813 - From what ship: Plymouth via HMS Namur - Born: Easthamer, Sweden - Age: 25 - Discharged on 23 Mar 1813 and released to the Cartel Robinson Potter.

Rosignol, James - 1st Mate - Number: 1105 - Prize name: Tom Thumb - Ship type: MV - How taken: Lion, British privateer - When taken: 15 Feb 1813 - Where taken: Bay of Biscay - Date received: 14 Mar 1813 - From what ship: Portsmouth via HMS Beagle - Born: Maryland - Age: 34 - Discharged on 23 Mar 1813 and released to the Cartel Robinson Potter.

Ross, Benjamin T. - Seaman - Number: 367 - How taken: Impressed at Gravesend, England - When taken: 3 Jan

1813 - Date received: 21 Jan 1813 - From what ship: HMS Raisonnable - Born: Cumberland, RI - Age: 25 - Discharged on 28 Apr 1813 and released to the David Scott.

Ross, David - Seaman - Number: 2813 - Prize name: Industry - Ship type: P - How taken: HM Brig Heron - When taken: 3 Nov 1813 - Where taken: off Halifax - Date received: 7 Jan 1814 - From what ship: Halifax - Born: Marblehead - Age: 37 - Discharged on 25 Sep 1814 and sent to Dartmoor on HMS Leyden.

Ross, George - Seaman - Number: 3937 - How taken: Gave himself up from HM Ship-of-the-Line Fame - When taken: 20 Sep 1814 - Date received: 28 Sep 1814 - From what ship: Fame - Born: Hanover - Age: 33 - Discharged on 29 Sep 1814 and sent to Dartmoor on HMS Freya.

Ross, George - Seaman - Number: 443 - Prize name: Hunter - Ship type: P - How taken: HM Frigate Phoebe - When taken: 23 Dec 1812 - Where taken: off Azores - Date received: 19 Feb 1813 - From what ship: HMS Modeste - Born: Boston - Age: 56 - Discharged on 2 Jul 1813 and released to Cartel Moses Brown.

Ross, John - Seaman - Number: 1539 - How taken: Impressed at Belfast - When taken: Nov 1812 - Date received: 8 Apr 1813 - From what ship: Plymouth via HMS Olympia - Born: Not readable - Age: 22 - Discharged on 2 Jul 1813 and released to Cartel Moses Brown.

Ross, John - Seaman - Number: 2397 - How taken: Gave himself up from HM Ship-of-the-Line Majestic - When taken: 26 Dec 1812 - Date received: 21 Oct 1813 - From what ship: Portsmouth via HMT Malabar - Born: New York - Age: 51 - Discharged on 4 Sep 1814 and sent to Dartmoor on HMS Freya.

Ross, Peter - Seaman - Number: 3322 - Prize name: Porcupine - Ship type: LM - How taken: HM Frigate Acasta - When taken: 18 Jul 1813 - Where taken: off Cape Sable, Florida - Date received: 23 Feb 1814 - From what ship: Halifax via HMT Malabar - Born: Bayonne - Age: 24 - Discharged on 22 Jun 1814 and sent to Calais, France on the Simon & Mary.

Ross, Richard - Steward - Number: 1424 - Prize name: Friendship - Ship type: MV - How taken: HM Frigate Rosamund - When taken: 12 Aug 1812 - Where taken: off Halifax - Date received: 5 Apr 1813 - From what ship: Plymouth via HMS Dwarf - Born: Savannah - Age: 19 - Discharged on 8 Jun 1813 and released to Cartel Rodrigo.

Rotch, David - Seaman - Number: 2031 - Prize name: Clive - Ship type: MV - How taken: Impressed at London - When taken: 14 Jul 1812 - Date received: 24 Jul 1813 - From what ship: HMS Raisonnable - Born: Baltimore - Age: 22 - Discharged on 21 Jan 1814 and released to HMS Ceres.

Roundy, Jeremiah - Boy - Number: 3196 - Prize name: Growler - Ship type: P - How taken: HM Brig Electra - When taken: 7 Jul 1813 - Where taken: off St. Johns - Date received: 7 Jan 1813 - From what ship: Portsmouth - Born: Marblehead - Age: 17 - Discharged on 25 Sep 1814 and sent to Dartmoor on HMS Leyden.

Roundy, Jonathan - Seaman - Number: 972 - Prize name: Empress - Ship type: MV - How taken: HM Brig Rover - When taken: 30 Nov 1812 - Where taken: St. Andrew - Date received: 10 Mar 1813 - From what ship: HMS Tigress - Born: Lynn - Age: 35 - Discharged on 8 Jun 1813 and released to Cartel Rodrigo.

Roundy, Thomas - Boatswain - Number: 2705 - Prize name: Growler - Ship type: P - How taken: HM Brig Electra - When taken: 7 Jul 1813 - Where taken: off St. Johns - Date received: 7 Jan 1814 - From what ship: Portsmouth - Born: Marblehead - Age: 26 - Discharged on 8 Sep 1814 and sent to Dartmoor on HMS Leyden.

Rowe, Daniel - Seaman - Number: 297 - Prize name: America - Ship type: MV - How taken: HM Brig Cracker - When taken: 1 Aug 1812 - Date received: 23 Dec 1812 - From what ship: Greenlaw Depot - Born: Gloucester, VA - Age: 27 - Discharged on 23 Mar 1813 and released to the Cartel Robinson Potter.

Rowe, Isaac - Boatswain's Mate - Number: 339 - Prize name: Postsea, prize to the Privateer Thrasher - Ship type: P - How taken: HM Sloop Helena - When taken: 31 Dec 1813 - Where taken: off Azores - Date received: 19 Jan 1813 - From what ship: HMS Raisonnable - Born: Cape Ann - Age: 25 - Discharged on 24 Jul 1813 and released to Cartel Hoffminy.

Rowe, John - Seaman - Number: 960 - How taken: Gave himself up from HM Ship-of-the-Line Salvador del Mundo - Date received: 10 Mar 1813 - From what ship: HMS Tigress - Born: Cape Ann - Age: 22 - Discharged on 28 Nov 1813 and released to HMS Ceres.

Rowe, Richard - Seaman - Number: 1769 - How taken: Gave up from HM Frigate North Star - When taken: 26 May 1813 - Date received: 14 Jun 1813 - From what ship: HMS Arethusa - Born: Philadelphia - Age: 43 - Discharged on 24 Jul 1814 and sent to Dartmoor on HMS Liffey.

Rowe, Simon - Seaman - Number: 1849 - How taken: Given up from HM Ship-of-the-Line Malta - Date received: 7 Jul 1813 - From what ship: Portsmouth via HMS Tribune - Born: New Hampshire - Age: 25 - Discharged on 16 Sep 1813 and released to HMS Ceres.

Rowe, Stephen - Seaman - Number: 469 - Prize name: Hunter - Ship type: P - How taken: HM Frigate Phoebe - When taken: 23 Dec 1812 - Where taken: off Azores - Date received: 19 Feb 1813 - From what ship: HMS Modeste - Born: Virginia - Age: 30 - Discharged on 24 Jul 1813 and released to Cartel Hoffminy.

Rowe, William - Seaman - Number: 340 - Prize name: Postsea, prize to the Privateer Thrasher - Ship type: P - How taken: HM Sloop Helena - When taken: 31 Dec 1813 - Where taken: off Azores - Date received: 19 Jan 1813 - From what ship: HMS Raisonnable - Born: Gloucester, MA - Age: 26 - Discharged on 24 Jul 1813 and released to Cartel Hoffminy.

Rowe, William - Seaman - Number: 2851 - Prize name: Fire Fly - Ship type: LM - How taken: HM Frigate Revolutionnaire - When taken: 19 Oct 1813 - Where taken: off Cape Ortegal, Spain - Date received: 7 Jan 1814 - From what ship: Portsmouth - Born: Boston - Age: 27 - Discharged on 25 Sep 1814 and sent to Dartmoor on HMS Leyden.

Rowel, Mathew - Seaman - Number: 2984 - Prize name: Enterprise - Ship type: P - How taken: HM Frigate Tenedos - When taken: 21 May 1813 - Where taken: off Cape Cod - Date received: 7 Jan 1814 - From what ship: Halifax - Born: Portsmouth - Age: 23 - Discharged on 25 Sep 1814 and sent to Dartmoor on HMS Leyden.

Rowell, James - Carpenter's Mate - Number: 425 - Prize name: Hunter - Ship type: P - How taken: HM Frigate Phoebe - When taken: 23 Dec 1812 - Where taken: off Azores - Date received: 19 Feb 1813 - From what ship: HMS Modeste - Born: Salem - Age: 22 - Discharged on 2 Jul 1813 and released to Cartel Moses Brown.

Roweth, William - Seaman - Number: 3032 - How taken: Gave himself up from HM Brig Racehorse - When taken: 25 Oct 1813 - Date received: 7 Jan 1814 - From what ship: Portsmouth - Born: New Jersey - Age: 37 - Discharged on 26 Sep 1814 and sent to Dartmoor on HMS Leyden.

Roy, Charles - Seaman - Number: 861 - Prize name: Brutus - Ship type: MV - How taken: Briton, letter of marque - When taken: 13 Jan 1813 - Where taken: Bay of Biscay - Date received: 1 Mar 1813 - From what ship: Plymouth via HMS Namur - Born: Nantucket - Age: 19 - Discharged on 24 Jul 1813 and released to Cartel Hoffminy.

Ruddick, William - 2nd Mate - Number: 1967 - Prize name: Lightning - Ship type: MV - How taken: HM Frigate Medusa - When taken: 2 Apr 1813 - Where taken: Bay of Biscay - Date received: 15 Jul 1813 - From what ship: Plymouth - Born: Philadelphia - Age: 25 - Discharged on 17 Jun 1814 and sent to Dartmoor on HMS Redbreast.

Ruliff, London - Cook - Number: 1548 - Prize name: Hunter - Ship type: P - How taken: HM Frigate Phoebe - When taken: 23 Dec 1812 - Where taken: off Azores - Date received: 8 Apr 1813 - From what ship: Plymouth via HMS Olympia - Born: Salem - Age: 22 - Race: Negro - Discharged on 27 Jul 1813 and released to Cartel Hoffminy.

Rumsey, Joseph - Private - Number: 3134 - Prize name: 14th U.S. Infantry - Ship type: LF - How taken: British forces - When taken: 24 Jun 1813 - Where taken: Beaver Dams, Upper Canada - Date received: 7 Jan 1814 - From what ship: Halifax - Born: New Jersey - Age: 20 - Discharged on 10 Oct 1814 and sent to U.S. on Cartel St. Philip.

Runlet, Ebenezer - Seaman - Number: 1765 - How taken: Gave up from HM Ship-of-the-Line Jupiter - When taken: 22 May 1813 - Date received: 14 Jun 1813 - From what ship: HMS Arethusa - Born: Wiscasset - Age: 30 - Discharged on 24 Jul 1814 and sent to Dartmoor on HMS Liffey.

Russell, John - Seaman - Number: 3343 - Prize name: Porcupine - Ship type: LM - How taken: HM Frigate Acasta - When taken: 18 Jul 1813 - Where taken: off Cape Sable, Florida - Date received: 23 Feb 1814 - From what ship: Halifax via HMT Malabar - Born: Dieppe - Age: 28 - Discharged on 22 Jun 1814 and sent to Calais,

France on the Simon & Mary.

Russell, Joseph (alias Joseph Wood) - Seaman - Number: 1650 - How taken: Gave himself up from HM Ship-of-the-Line Sterling Castle - Date received: 9 May 1813 - From what ship: HMS Raisonnable - Born: Philadelphia - Age: 28 - Race: Black - Discharged on 28 Nov 1813 and released to HMS Ceres.

Russell, Louis - Seaman - Number: 2804 - Prize name: Industry - Ship type: P - How taken: HM Brig Heron - When taken: 3 Nov 1813 - Where taken: off Halifax - Date received: 7 Jan 1814 - From what ship: Halifax - Born: Marblehead - Age: 21 - Discharged on 8 Sep 1814 and sent to Dartmoor on HMS Niobe.

Russell, M. - Seaman - Number: 2011 - How taken: Gave himself up from HM Brig Royalist - Date received: 15 Jul 1813 - From what ship: Plymouth - Born: Savannah - Age: 22 - Race: Black - Discharged on 16 Feb 1814 and released to HMS Ceres.

Russell, Moses - Boatswain's Mate - Number: 2823 - Prize name: Portsmouth Packet - Ship type: P - How taken: HM Brig Fantome - When taken: 5 Oct 1813 - Where taken: off Portland - Date received: 7 Jan 1814 - From what ship: Halifax - Born: Virginia - Age: 38 - Discharged on 25 Sep 1814 and sent to Dartmoor on HMS Leyden.

Russell, Robert - Seaman - Number: 2486 - Prize name: Enterprise - Ship type: P - How taken: HM Frigate Tenedos - When taken: 21 May 1813 - Where taken: off Cape Cod - Date received: 22 Oct 1813 - From what ship: Portsmouth via HMT Malabar - Born: Marblehead - Age: 38 - Discharged on 8 Sep 1814 and sent to Dartmoor on HMS Niobe.

Russell, Samuel - Seaman - Number: 176 - How taken: Gave himself up at London - When taken: 31 Oct 1812 - Date received: 5 Nov 1812 - From what ship: HMS Namur - Born: East Hampton, Long Island - Age: 42 - Discharged in Jul 1813 and released to Cartel Moses Brown.

Russell, William - Seaman - Number: 949 - Prize name: Castor - Ship type: MV - How taken: HM Schooner Antelope - When taken: 31 Jul 1813 - Where taken: at sea - Date received: 10 Mar 1813 - From what ship: HMS Tigress - Born: New York - Age: 21 - Discharged on 8 Jun 1813 and released to Cartel Rodrigo.

Russell, William - Seaman - Number: 2694 - Prize name: Growler - Ship type: P - How taken: HM Brig Electra - When taken: 7 Jul 1813 - Where taken: off St. Johns - Date received: 7 Jan 1814 - From what ship: Portsmouth - Born: Marblehead - Age: 19 - Discharged on 8 Sep 1814 and sent to Dartmoor on HMS Niobe.

Rust, John - Mate - Number: 3678 - Prize name: Sally - Ship type: MV - How taken: HM Brig Derwent - When taken: 21 Jul 1814 - Where taken: at sea - Date received: 4 May 1814 - From what ship: Portsmouth - Born: Salem - Age: 27 - Discharged on 26 Sep 1814 and sent to Dartmoor on HMS Niobe.

Rust, John - Seaman - Number: 523 - Prize name: Lydia - Ship type: MV - How taken: HM Frigate Orpheus - When taken: 3 Sep 1812 - Where taken: at sea - Date received: 23 Feb 1813 - From what ship: Portsmouth via HMS Dromedary - Born: Baltimore - Age: 29 - Discharged on 10 May 1813 and released to Cartel Admittance.

Rust, John - 1st Lieutenant - Number: 2709 - Prize name: Growler - Ship type: P - How taken: HM Brig Electra - When taken: 7 Jul 1813 - Where taken: off St. Johns - Date received: 7 Jan 1814 - From what ship: Portsmouth - Born: Salem - Age: 51 - Discharged on 25 Sep 1814 and sent to Dartmoor on HMS Leyden.

Rust, John - Seaman - Number: 3197 - Prize name: Growler - Ship type: P - How taken: HM Brig Electra - When taken: 7 Jul 1813 - Where taken: off St. Johns - Date received: 7 Jan 1813 - From what ship: Portsmouth - Born: Massachusetts - Age: 33 - Discharged on 25 Sep 1814 and sent to Dartmoor on HMS Leyden.

Ryan, Thomas - Seaman - Number: 1989 - How taken: Gave himself up from HM Sloop Favorite - Date received: 15 Jul 1813 - From what ship: Plymouth - Born: Philadelphia - Age: 34 - Race: Black - Died on 15 Oct 1813 from dysentery.

Safford, Roger - Seaman - Number: 3418 - Prize name: Thomas - Ship type: P - How taken: HM Frigate Nymphe - When taken: 27 Jun 1813 - Where taken: at sea - Date received: 23 Feb 1814 - From what ship: Halifax via HMT Malabar - Born: Kittery - Age: 19 - Discharged on 15 Oct 1814 and released to HMS Argonaut.

Sait, Gasper - Seaman - Number: 395 - Prize name: Dolphin - Ship type: MV - How taken: HM Ship-of-the-Line Invincible - When taken: 24 Aug 1812 - Where taken: Mediterranean - Date received: 13 Feb 1813 - From what ship: HMS Raisonnable - Born: Palermo - Age: 26 - Discharged on 28 Apr 1813 and released to the

David Scott.

- Salkins, Nathaniel - Seaman - Number: 696 - Prize name: Deanna, recaptured British vessel - Ship type: P - How taken: HM Ship-of-the-Line Polyphemus - When taken: 14 Sep 1812 - Where taken: at sea - Date received: 24 Feb 1813 - From what ship: Portsmouth via HMS Ulysses - Born: Marblehead, MA - Age: 20 - Discharged on 8 Jun 1813 and released to Cartel Rodrigo.

- Salmon, Archibald - Seaman - Number: 2988 - Prize name: America - Ship type: P - How taken: HM Frigate Shannon - When taken: 25 May 1813 - Where taken: off Cape Cod - Date received: 7 Jan 1814 - From what ship: Halifax - Born: Massachusetts - Age: 21 - Discharged on 25 Sep 1814 and sent to Dartmoor on HMS Leyden.

- Salyear, John - Seaman - Number: 624 - Prize name: King of Rome - Ship type: P - How taken: HM Brig Wolverine - When taken: 13 Dec 1812 - Where taken: at sea - Date received: 23 Feb 1813 - From what ship: Portsmouth via HMS Dromedary - Born: North Carolina - Age: 26 - Discharged on 2 Jul 1813 and released to Cartel Moses Brown.

- Samblasen, Edward - Seaman - Number: 539 - Prize name: Baltimore - Ship type: P - How taken: HM Transport Diadem - When taken: 7 Oct 1812 - Where taken: S. Andres - Date received: 23 Feb 1813 - From what ship: Portsmouth via HMS Dromedary - Born: Philadelphia - Age: 23 - Race: Mulatto - Discharged on 8 Jun 1813 and released to Cartel Rodrigo.

- Samerton, George - Seaman - Number: 2739 - Prize name: Teazer - Ship type: P - How taken: HM Frigate Boreas - When taken: 15 Jun 1813 - Where taken: off Halifax - Date received: 7 Jan 1814 - From what ship: Halifax - Born: Salem - Age: 17 - Discharged on 25 Sep 1814 and sent to Dartmoor on HMS Leyden.

- Sampson, David - Seaman - Number: 877 - Prize name: Hero - Ship type: MV - How taken: Cornet - When taken: 10 Feb 1813 - Where taken: off Lisbon - Date received: 1 Mar 1813 - From what ship: Plymouth via HMS Namur - Born: Frog, MA - Age: 35 - Released on 27 Mar 1813.

- Sampson, Jacob - Seaman - Number: 1883 - Prize name: Tiger - Ship type: MV - How taken: HM Brig Scylla - When taken: 22 Mar 1813 - Where taken: Bay of Biscay - Date received: 7 Jul 1813 - From what ship: Portsmouth via HMS Tribune - Born: New York - Age: 24 - Race: Black - Discharged on 4 Aug 1814 and sent to Dartmoor on HMS Liverpool.

- Sampson, William - Seaman - Number: 3333 - Prize name: Porcupine - Ship type: LM - How taken: HM Frigate Acasta - When taken: 18 Jul 1813 - Where taken: off Cape Sable, Florida - Date received: 23 Feb 1814 - From what ship: Halifax via HMT Malabar - Born: Charlestown - Age: 18 - Discharged on 21 Jul 1814 and sent to Dartmoor on HMS Portia.

- Samson, Thomas - Seaman - Number: 17 - Prize name: Lucky - Ship type: MV - How taken: Detained at Hanoi Bay - When taken: 11 Aug 1812 - Date received: 29 Oct 1812 - From what ship: HMS Raisonnable - Born: Virginia - Age: 23 - Discharged on 10 May 1813 and released to Cartel Admittance.

- Sanburn, James - Seaman - Number: 3314 - Prize name: Enterprise - Ship type: P - How taken: HM Frigate Tenedos - When taken: 21 May 1813 - Where taken: off Cape Cod - Date received: 23 Feb 1814 - From what ship: Halifax via HMT Malabar - Born: Pennsylvania - Age: 25 - Discharged on 21 Jul 1814 and sent to Dartmoor on HMS Portia.

- Sanderson, John - Cook - Number: 978 - Prize name: Empress - Ship type: MV - How taken: HM Brig Rover - When taken: 30 Nov 1812 - Where taken: St. Andrew - Date received: 10 Mar 1813 - From what ship: HMS Tigress - Born: Bombay - Age: 54 - Race: Black - Discharged on 8 Jun 1813 and released to Cartel Rodrigo.

- Sands, Thomas - Seaman - Number: 1083 - Prize name: Hope - Ship type: MV - How taken: HM Schooner Bramble - When taken: 9 Dec 1812 - Where taken: at sea - Date received: 14 Mar 1813 - From what ship: Portsmouth via HMS Cornwell - Born: Gloucester - Age: 21 - Released on 10 Apr 1813.

- Sanford, James - Seaman - Number: 2566 - How taken: Gave himself up from HM Ship-of-the-Line Berwick - When taken: 30 Oct 1812 - Date received: 23 Oct 1813 - From what ship: Portsmouth via HMS Raisonnable - Born: Philadelphia - Age: 31 - Race: Mulatto - Discharged on 4 Sep 1814 and sent to Dartmoor on HMS Freya.

- Sankey, Caesar - Seaman - Number: 3834 - How taken: Gave himself up from HM Frigate Africanus at Madeira,

Portugal - When taken: 4 Oct 1813 - Date received: 19 Aug 1814 - From what ship: London - Born: New Hampshire - Age: 32 - Discharged on 22 Oct 1814 and sent to Dartmoor on HMS Leyden.

Sanssuillon, John - Seaman - Number: 1809a - How taken: Unknown - Date received: 4 Jul 1813 - From what ship: HMS Raisonnable - Born: Bordeaux, France - Age: 0 - Released on 28 Jan 1814 and sent to Calais, France.

Saucry, John - Seaman - Number: 70 - Prize name: Elson - Ship type: MV - How taken: HM Frigate Ethalion - When taken: 12 Aug 1812 - Where taken: Baltic - Date received: 4 Nov 1812 - From what ship: HMS Namur - Born: Boston - Age: 18 - Discharged on 10 May 1813 and released to Cartel Admittance.

Saul, Francis - Seaman - Number: 365 - How taken: Gave himself up from HMS Mercurious - When taken: 5 Dec 1812 - Date received: 21 Jan 1813 - From what ship: HMS Raisonnable - Born: Wiscasset, MA - Age: 32 - Discharged on 26 Jul 1814 and sent to Dartmoor on HMS Raven.

Saunders, Charles - Seaman - Number: 2325 - How taken: Impressed at Gravesend, England - When taken: 10 Aug 1813 - Date received: 12 Oct 1813 - From what ship: HMS Raisonnable - Born: Virginia - Age: 20 - Died on 26 Mar 1814 from fever.

Saunders, James - Mate - Number: 2210 - Prize name: Jane, prize of the Privateer Snap Dragon - Ship type: P - How taken: HM Frigate Crescent & HM Ship-of-the-Line Bellerophon - When taken: 28 Jun 1813 - Where taken: Newfoundland Bank - Date received: 18 Aug 1813 - From what ship: Portsmouth, via an admiral's tender - Born: North Carolina - Age: 23 - Discharged on 11 Aug 1814 and sent to Dartmoor on HMS Freya.

Saunders, Joseph - Seaman - Number: 28 - Prize name: Arial - Ship type: MV - How taken: HM Brig Recruit - When taken: 2 Jun 1812 - Where taken: coast of America - Date received: 3 Nov 1812 - From what ship: HMS Plover - Born: Delaware - Age: 39 - Discharged on 23 Mar 1813 and released to the Cartel Robinson Potter.

Saunders, Peter - Seaman - Number: 2588 - How taken: Gave himself up from HM Ship-of-the-Line Union - When taken: 27 May 1813 - Date received: 5 Nov 1813 - From what ship: HMS Hindostan - Born: Salem - Age: 32 - Discharged on 12 Aug 1814 and sent to Dartmoor on HMS Alpheus.

Saunders, Richard - Seaman - Number: 3254 - Prize name: Thorn - Ship type: P - How taken: Shannon, Nova Scotia privateer - When taken: 7 Nov 1813 - Where taken: off Newfoundland - Date received: 23 Feb 1814 - From what ship: Halifax via HMT Malabar - Born: Boston - Age: 17 - Discharged on 10 Oct 1814 and sent to Dartmoor on the Mermaid.

Saunders, Thomas - Seaman - Number: 1150 - Prize name: Sword Fish - Ship type: P - How taken: HM Ship-of-the-Line Elephant - When taken: 28 Dec 1812 - Where taken: off Azores - Date received: 16 Mar 1813 - From what ship: Portsmouth, Mundane - Born: Boston - Age: 29 - Discharged on 24 Jul 1813 and released to Cartel Hoffminy.

Saunders, Thomas - Seaman - Number: 1259 - How taken: Gave himself up from HM Ship-of-the-Line Mars - When taken: 9 Dec 1812 - Date received: 16 Mar 1813 - From what ship: Portsmouth, via HMS Abundance - Born: Norfolk - Age: 28 - Discharged on 23 Jul 1814 and sent to Dartmoor.

Saunders, Thomas - Seaman - Number: 967 - Prize name: Empress - Ship type: MV - How taken: HM Brig Rover - When taken: 30 Nov 1812 - Where taken: St. Andrew - Date received: 10 Mar 1813 - From what ship: HMS Tigress - Born: Baileyfield, Germany - Age: 30 - Discharged on 8 Jun 1813 and released to Cartel Rodrigo.

Saunders, William - Seaman - Number: 2674 - How taken: Gave himself up from HM Ship-of-the-Line Warrior - When taken: 15 Nov 1813 - Date received: 2 Dec 1813 - From what ship: HMS Raisonnable - Born: Norway - Age: 30 - Discharged on 29 Dec 1813 and sent to France.

Saunderson, William - Seaman - Number: 1311 - How taken: Gave himself up from HM Guardship Royal William - When taken: 3 Feb 1813 - Date received: 16 Mar 1813 - From what ship: Portsmouth, via HMS Abundance - Born: Baltimore - Age: 25 - Discharged on 4 Aug 1814 and sent to Dartmoor on HMS Alpheus.

Saundry, Nathaniel - Seaman - Number: 3311 - Prize name: Enterprise - Ship type: P - How taken: HM Frigate Tenedos - When taken: 21 May 1813 - Where taken: off Cape Cod - Date received: 23 Feb 1814 - From what ship: Halifax via HMT Malabar - Born: Boston - Age: 19 - Discharged on 10 Oct 1814 and sent to Dartmoor on the Mermaid.

Sawyer, Jacob - Seaman - Number: 3932 - How taken: Impressed at London - When taken: 14 Sep 1814 - Date received: 24 Sep 1814 - From what ship: HMS Namur - Born: Providence - Age: 27 - Race: Mulatto - Discharged on 29 Sep 1814 and sent to Dartmoor on HMS Freya.

Sawyer, James - Seaman - Number: 2740 - Prize name: Teazer - Ship type: P - How taken: HM Frigate Boreas - When taken: 15 Jun 1813 - Where taken: off Halifax - Date received: 7 Jan 1814 - From what ship: Halifax - Born: Portland - Age: 50 - Discharged on 25 Sep 1814 and sent to Dartmoor on HMS Leyden.

Sawyer, Jonathan - Gunner - Number: 2867 - Prize name: Elbridge Gerry - Ship type: P - How taken: HM Frigate Crescent - When taken: 16 Sep 1813 - Where taken: at sea - Date received: 7 Jan 1814 - From what ship: Portsmouth - Born: Massachusetts - Age: 29 - Died on 26 Mar 1814 from fever.

Sawyer, Peter - Seaman - Number: 2795 - Prize name: Fox - Ship type: P - How taken: HM Brig Manly - When taken: 1 Aug 1813 - Where taken: off Halifax - Date received: 7 Jan 1814 - From what ship: Halifax - Born: Portland - Age: 31 - Discharged on 8 Sep 1814 and sent to Dartmoor on HMS Niobe.

Scaff, Nicholas - Seaman - Number: 609 - Prize name: Antelope - Ship type: P - How taken: HM Brig Zephyr - When taken: 10 Dec 1812 - Where taken: at sea - Date received: 23 Feb 1813 - From what ship: Portsmouth via HMS Dromedary - Born: Richmond, VA - Age: 24 - Discharged on 2 Jul 1813 and released to Cartel Moses Brown.

Scanck, William - Seaman - Number: 2101 - How taken: Gave himself up from HM Frigate Bombay - When taken: 27 May 1813 - Date received: 9 Aug 1813 - From what ship: HMS Thames - Born: Philadelphia - Age: 33 - Discharged on 12 Aug 1814 and sent to Dartmoor on HMS Alpheus.

Scanel, Cornelius - Seaman - Number: 1026 - Prize name: John - Ship type: MV - How taken: Taken up at Liverpool - When taken: 18 Oct 1812 - Date received: 11 Mar 1813 - From what ship: Yarmouth via HMS Tenders - Born: Darby - Age: 27 - Discharged in Jul 1813 and released to Cartel Moses Brown.

Schiffky, Jacobus Orgen - Marine Private - Number: 3695 - Prize name: Bunker Hill - Ship type: P - How taken: HM Frigate Pomone & HM Frigate Cydnus - When taken: 4 Mar 1814 - Where taken: Bay of Biscay - Date received: 4 May 1814 - From what ship: Portsmouth - Born: Danzig, East Prussia - Age: 42 - Discharged on 25 Sep 1814 and sent to Dartmoor on HMS Niobe.

Schuetzer, Peter - Seaman - Number: 381 - How taken: Impressed at Gravesend off MV Fortune of London - When taken: 3 Jan 1813 - Date received: 31 Jan 1813 - From what ship: HMS Raisonnable - Born: Oldenburg - Age: 35 - Discharged on 18 Jul 1813 and released to HMS Ceres.

Schyder, Jacob Knapp - Seaman - Number: 1476 - Prize name: Union - Ship type: MV - How taken: HM Frigate Iris - When taken: 17 Jan 1813 - Where taken: at sea - Date received: 6 Apr 1813 - From what ship: Portsmouth via Tender Eliza - Born: Philadelphia - Age: 20 - Discharged on 26 Jul 1813 and released to Cartel Hoffminy.

Scofield, Wells - Captain - Number: 1106 - Prize name: Tom Thumb - Ship type: MV - How taken: Lion, British privateer - When taken: 15 Feb 1813 - Where taken: Bay of Biscay - Date received: 14 Mar 1813 - From what ship: Portsmouth via HMS Beagle - Born: East Haddam, MA - Age: 25 - Discharged on 18 Oct 1813 and released to HMS Ceres.

Scols, William - Seaman - Number: 2683 - Prize name: Alexander - Ship type: MV - How taken: Impressed at Hull - When taken: 20 Nov 1813 - Date received: 21 Dec 1813 - From what ship: HMS Raisonnable - Born: New York - Age: 29 - Escaped on 10 May 1814 from HM Prison Ship Crown Prince.

Scott, Abraham - Seaman - Number: 1575 - How taken: Gave himself up from HM Ship-of-the-Line Braham - When taken: 10 Dec 1812 - Date received: 16 Apr 1813 - From what ship: HMS Namur, admiral's tender - Born: Philadelphia - Age: 29 - Discharged on 24 Jul 1814 and sent to Dartmoor.

Scott, Andrew - Seaman - Number: 969 - Prize name: Brutus - Ship type: MV - How taken: Briton, letter of marque - When taken: 6 Jan 1813 - Where taken: off Bordeaux, France - Date received: 10 Mar 1813 - From what ship: HMS Tigress - Born: New Orleans - Age: 28 - Discharged on 24 Jul 1813 and released to Cartel Hoffminy.

Scott, Anthony - Seaman - Number: 3842 - How taken: Gave himself up from HM Frigate Theban at Madras, India - When taken: 21 Jul 1814 - Date received: 21 Aug 1814 - From what ship: Gravesend - Born: New Orleans -

Age: 31 - Discharged on 20 Sep 1814 and sent to Dartmoor on HMS Leyden.

Scott, Benjamin - Seaman - Number: 829 - Prize name: John Barnes - Ship type: MV - How taken: Gave himself up at Liverpool - When taken: 7 Nov 1813 - Date received: 1 Mar 1813 - From what ship: Plymouth via HMS Namur - Born: Virginia - Age: 24 - Discharged in Jul 1813 and released to Cartel Moses Brown.

Scott, Ezekiel - Seaman - Number: 1541 - How taken: Impressed at Greenock, Scotland - When taken: 2 Dec 1812 - Date received: 8 Apr 1813 - From what ship: Plymouth via HMS Olympia - Born: Virginia - Age: 45 - Race: Black - Discharged on 27 Jul 1813 and released to Cartel Hoffminy.

Scott, Henry - Seaman - Number: 3668 - Prize name: Volunteer - Ship type: P - How taken: HM Brig Curlew - Where taken: at sea - Date received: 4 May 1814 - From what ship: Portsmouth - Born: Boston - Age: 43 - Discharged on 25 Sep 1814 and sent to Dartmoor on HMS Niobe.

Scott, Henry - Seaman - Number: 3015 - Prize name: Go' On - Ship type: MV - How taken: HM Frigate Barrosa - When taken: 1 Jul 1813 - Where taken: off Cape Virginia - Date received: 7 Jan 1814 - From what ship: Halifax - Born: New York - Age: 28 - Died on 3 Apr 1814 from fever.

Scott, Henry - 2nd Mate - Number: 2256 - Prize name: Hannah & Eliza - Ship type: MV - How taken: HM Brig Lyra - When taken: 29 May 1813 - Where taken: off Spain - Date received: 7 Sep 1813 - From what ship: HMS Raisonnable - Born: Providence - Age: 21 - Discharged on 11 Aug 1814 and sent to Dartmoor on HMS Freya.

Scott, James - Steward - Number: 715 - How taken: Taken up at Liverpool - When taken: 18 Oct 1812 - Date received: 24 Feb 1813 - From what ship: Portsmouth via HMS Ulysses - Born: Boston - Age: 27 - Discharged in Jul 1813 and released to Cartel Moses Brown.

Scott, James - Private - Number: 2621 - Prize name: 14th U.S. Infantry - Ship type: LF - How taken: British forces - When taken: 24 Jun 1813 - Where taken: Beaver Dams, Upper Canada - Date received: 5 Nov 1813 - From what ship: HMS Hindostan - Born: North Ireland - Age: 34 - Discharged on 10 Oct 1814 and sent to U.S. on Cartel St. Philip.

Scott, John - Seaman - Number: 187 - Prize name: Calaban - Ship type: MV - How taken: HM Battery Gorgon - When taken: 12 Aug 1812 - Where taken: Great Belt, Denmark - Date received: 5 Nov 1812 - From what ship: HMS Namur - Born: Catskill, MA - Age: 27 - Discharged on 10 May 1813 and released to Cartel Admittance.

Scott, John - Seaman - Number: 1985 - How taken: Gave himself up from HM Ship-of-the-Line Ajax - Date received: 15 Jul 1813 - From what ship: Plymouth - Born: Essex - Age: 35 - Discharged on 17 Jun 1814 and sent to Dartmoor on HMS Pincher.

Scott, John - Private - Number: 3115 - Prize name: 14th U.S. Infantry - Ship type: LF - How taken: British forces - When taken: 24 Jun 1813 - Where taken: Beaver Dams, Upper Canada - Date received: 7 Jan 1814 - From what ship: Halifax - Born: Maryland - Age: 34 - Discharged on 10 Oct 1814 and sent to U.S. on Cartel St. Philip.

Scott, Samuel - Seaman - Number: 1385 - How taken: Discharged from HM Schooner Caroline - When taken: 26 Mar 1813 - Date received: 5 Apr 1813 - From what ship: HMS Raisonnable - Born: Alexandria - Age: 20 - Discharged on 10 Oct 1814 and sent to Dartmoor on the Mermaid.

Scott, William - Carpenter's Mate - Number: 2114 - How taken: Gave himself up from HM Ship-of-the-Line Tremendous - When taken: 15 Oct 1812 - Date received: 9 Aug 1813 - From what ship: HMS Thames - Born: South Carolina - Age: 32 - Discharged on 12 Aug 1814 and sent to Dartmoor on HMS Alpheus.

Scribner, Elijah - Prize Master - Number: 416 - Prize name: Hunter - Ship type: P - How taken: HM Frigate Phoebe - When taken: 23 Dec 1812 - Where taken: off Azores - Date received: 19 Feb 1813 - From what ship: HMS Modeste - Born: Westford - Age: 29 - Discharged on 2 Jul 1813 and released to Cartel Moses Brown.

Scribner, William - Seaman - Number: 1303 - How taken: Gave himself up from HM Guardship Royal William - When taken: 3 Feb 1813 - Date received: 16 Mar 1813 - From what ship: Portsmouth, via HMS Abundance - Born: New Haven - Age: 35 - Discharged on 23 Jul 1814 and sent to Dartmoor.

Scriver, Richard - Private - Number: 3128 - Prize name: U.S. Artillery - Ship type: LF - How taken: British forces -

When taken: 24 Jun 1813 - Where taken: Beaver Dams, Upper Canada - Date received: 7 Jan 1814 - From what ship: Halifax - Born: Boston - Age: 28 - Discharged on 10 Oct 1814 and sent to U.S. on Cartel St. Philip.

Seabold, John - Seaman - Number: 1480 - Prize name: Union - Ship type: MV - How taken: HM Frigate Iris - When taken: 17 Jan 1813 - Where taken: at sea - Date received: 6 Apr 1813 - From what ship: Portsmouth via Tender Eliza - Born: Philadelphia - Age: 24 - Discharged on 26 Jul 1813 and released to Cartel Hoffminy.

Sears, Abraham - Private - Number: 3085 - Prize name: 14th U.S. Infantry - Ship type: LF - How taken: British forces - When taken: 24 Jun 1813 - Where taken: Beaver Dams, Upper Canada - Date received: 7 Jan 1814 - From what ship: Halifax - Born: New York - Age: 23 - Discharged on 10 Oct 1814 and sent to U.S. on Cartel St. Philip.

Sears, Bartlett - Master - Number: 387 - Prize name: John - Ship type: MV - How taken: HM Sloop Blossom - When taken: 16 Aug 1812 - Where taken: off Gibraltar - Date received: 13 Feb 1813 - From what ship: HMS Raisonnable - Born: Plymouth, MA - Age: 34 - Discharged on 23 Mar 1813 and released to the Cartel Robinson Potter.

Seawell, George - Seaman - Number: 1720 - Prize name: Powhattan - Ship type: MV - How taken: HMS Horatio - When taken: 13 Dec 1812 - Where taken: Bay of Biscay - Date received: 25 May 1813 - From what ship: Portsmouth via HMS Impetius - Born: Greenwich, NY - Age: 27 - Discharged on 24 Jul 1813 and released to Cartel Hoffminy.

Seely, James - Seaman - Number: 492 - Prize name: Hannibal - Ship type: MV - How taken: MV Potent - When taken: 24 Sep 1812 - Where taken: off Bermuda - Date received: 23 Feb 1813 - From what ship: Portsmouth via HMS Dromedary - Born: New York - Age: 26 - Discharged on 8 Jun 1813 and released to Cartel Rodrigo.

Seely, Truman - Seaman - Number: 169 - Prize name: Forester - Ship type: MV - How taken: Detained at Sheerness, England - When taken: 1 Aug 1812 - Date received: 5 Nov 1812 - From what ship: HMS Namur - Born: Litchfield - Age: 26 - Discharged on 23 Mar 1813 and released to the Cartel Robinson Potter.

Selby, Hans - Seaman - Number: 2531 - Prize name: Yorktown - Ship type: P - How taken: HM Brig Nimrod - When taken: 17 Jul 1813 - Where taken: Grand Banks - Date received: 22 Oct 1813 - From what ship: Portsmouth via HMT Malabar - Born: Galicia, Spain - Age: 33 - Died on 14 ?? 1814 from fever.

Selby, James - Captain - Number: 759 - Prize name: Margarethe - Ship type: MV - How taken: HM Ship-of-the-Line San Juan - When taken: 8 May 1812 - Where taken: Gibraltar - Date received: 25 Feb 1813 - From what ship: HMS Brazen - Born: Maryland - Age: 39 - Discharged on 23 Mar 1813 and released to the Cartel Robinson Potter.

Self, Thomas M. - Seaman - Number: 3660 - How taken: Impressed at London - When taken: 2 Mar 1814 - Date received: 4 May 1814 - From what ship: HMS Raisonnable - Born: Charlestown - Age: 20 - Discharged on 10 Oct 1814 and sent to Dartmoor on the Mermaid.

Selman, Francis G. - 2nd Lieutenant - Number: 2711 - Prize name: Growler - Ship type: P - How taken: HM Brig Electra - When taken: 7 Jul 1813 - Where taken: off St. Johns - Date received: 7 Jan 1814 - From what ship: Portsmouth - Born: Marblehead - Age: 28 - Discharged on 25 Sep 1814 and sent to Dartmoor on HMS Leyden.

Selman, John - Seaman - Number: 3560 - Prize name: Hannah - Ship type: MV - How taken: HM Ship-of-the-Line Conquestador - When taken: 15 Jan 1814 - Where taken: at sea - Date received: 7 May 1814 - From what ship: Portsmouth via HMS Favorite - Born: Marblehead - Age: 19 - Discharged on 25 Sep 1814 and sent to Dartmoor on HMS Niobe.

Senholm, Jacob - Seaman - Number: 662 - Prize name: U.S.R.M. Cutter James Madison - Ship type: War - How taken: HM Frigate Barbadoes - When taken: 22 Aug 1812 - Where taken: at sea - Date received: 24 Feb 1813 - From what ship: Portsmouth via HMS Ulysses - Born: Niland, Finland - Age: 33 - Discharged on 10 May 1813 and released to Cartel Admittance.

Senter, Noah - Seaman - Number: 3785 - Prize name: Adaline - Ship type: LM - How taken: HM Frigate Magiciene - When taken: 14 Mar 1814 - Where taken: off Cape Ortegal, Spain - Date received: 26 May 1814 - From what ship: HMS Hindostan - Born: New Hampshire - Age: 27 - Discharged on 29 Sep 1814 and sent to Dartmoor on HMS Freya.

Sergeant, William - Seaman - Number: 3352 - Prize name: Thomas - Ship type: P - How taken: HM Frigate Nymphe - When taken: 26 Jun 1813 - Where taken: off Halifax - Date received: 23 Feb 1814 - From what ship: Halifax via HMT Malabar - Born: Old York - Age: 53 - Discharged on 10 Oct 1814 and sent to Dartmoor on the Mermaid.

Sargant, Phillip - 2nd Mate - Number: 289 - Prize name: Dido - Ship type: MV - How taken: Detained off Faco - When taken: 12 Aug 1812 - Date received: 23 Dec 1812 - From what ship: Greenlaw Depot - Born: Mendith - Age: 28 - Discharged on 10 May 1813 and released to Cartel Admittance.

Setchell, Samuel - Master's Mate - Number: 1131 - Prize name: Sword Fish - Ship type: P - How taken: HM Ship-of-the-Line Elephant - When taken: 28 Dec 1812 - Where taken: off Azores - Date received: 16 Mar 1813 - From what ship: Portsmouth, Mundane - Born: Gloucester - Age: 26 - Discharged on 24 Jul 1813 and released to Cartel Hoffminy.

Seth, John - Seaman - Number: 2755 - Prize name: Globe - Ship type: P - How taken: HM Frigate Spartan - When taken: 13 Jun 1813 - Where taken: off Delaware - Date received: 7 Jan 1814 - From what ship: Halifax - Born: Maryland - Age: 25 - Discharged on 25 Sep 1814 and sent to Dartmoor on HMS Leyden.

Severence, Gideon - Seaman - Number: 1085 - Prize name: Benjamin - Ship type: MV - How taken: HM Frigate Medusa - When taken: 31 Dec 1812 - Where taken: at sea - Date received: 14 Mar 1813 - From what ship: Portsmouth via HMS Cornwell - Born: Chester - Age: 28 - Discharged on 24 Jul 1813 and released to Cartel Hoffminy.

Sevratt, William - Surgeon's Mate - Number: 422 - Prize name: Hunter - Ship type: P - How taken: HM Frigate Phoebe - When taken: 23 Dec 1812 - Where taken: off Azores - Date received: 19 Feb 1813 - From what ship: HMS Modeste - Born: Salisbury - Age: 21 - Discharged on 23 Mar 1813 and released to the Cartel Robinson Potter.

Seyman, Paul - Seaman - Number: 224 - How taken: Apprehended at London - When taken: 13 Nov 1812 - Date received: 25 Nov 1812 - From what ship: HMS Raisonnable - Born: Philadelphia - Age: 23 - Discharged on 4 Mar 1813 to the Wailey.

Shade, Joseph - Seaman - Number: 3400 - Prize name: Yankee - Ship type: P - How taken: HM Brig Ringdove - When taken: 17 Oct 1813 - Where taken: at sea - Date received: 23 Feb 1814 - From what ship: Halifax via HMT Malabar - Born: Boston - Age: 53 - Discharged on 22 Oct 1814 and sent to Dartmoor on HMS Leyden.

Sharp, Peter - Seaman - Number: 32 - Prize name: Arial - Ship type: MV - How taken: HM Brig Recruit - When taken: 2 Jun 1812 - Where taken: coast of America - Date received: 3 Nov 1812 - From what ship: HMS Plover - Born: New Jersey - Age: 21 - Discharged on 23 Mar 1813 and released to the Cartel Robinson Potter.

Shaw, Andrew - Seaman - Number: 2682 - Prize name: Liveoak - Ship type: MV - How taken: Impressed at Leight, Scotland - When taken: 4 Dec 1813 - Date received: 16 Dec 1813 - From what ship: HMS Raisonnable - Born: Newburyport - Age: 24 - Discharged on 8 Sep 1814 and sent to Dartmoor on HMS Niobe.

Shaw, Henry - Cook - Number: 2861 - Prize name: Fire Fly - Ship type: LM - How taken: HM Frigate Revolutionnaire - When taken: 19 Oct 1813 - Where taken: off Cape Ortegal, Spain - Date received: 7 Jan 1814 - From what ship: Portsmouth - Born: Boston - Age: 23 - Race: Black - Discharged on 25 Sep 1814 and sent to Dartmoor on HMS Leyden.

Shaw, John - Seaman - Number: 1698 - Prize name: Governor Middleton - Ship type: MV - How taken: Thetis, British privateer - When taken: 2 May 1813 - Where taken: Bay of Biscay - Date received: 15 May 1813 - From what ship: HMS Viper - Born: Bath, MA - Age: 20 - Discharged on 12 Aug 1814 and sent to Dartmoor on HMS Alpheus.

Shaw, Samuel - Prize Master - Number: 3200 - Prize name: Elbridge Gerry - Ship type: P - How taken: HM Frigate Crescent - When taken: 16 Sep 1813 - Where taken: at sea - Date received: 7 Jan 1813 - From what ship: Portsmouth - Born: Massachusetts - Age: 48 - Discharged on 25 Sep 1814 and sent to Dartmoor on HMS Leyden.

Shaw, William - Seaman - Number: 3635 - Prize name: Bunker Hill - Ship type: P - How taken: HM Frigate Pomone & HM Frigate Cydnus - When taken: 4 Mar 1814 - Where taken: Bay of Biscay - Date received: 31 Mar 1814 - From what ship: HMS Raisonnable - Born: Beverly - Age: 19 - Discharged on 25 Sep 1814 and sent to Dartmoor on HMS Niobe.

Shechford, John - Seaman - Number: 3947 - How taken: Impressed at London - When taken: 6 Oct 1814 - Date received: 12 Oct 1813 - From what ship: Quebec - Born: Salem - Age: 23 - Discharged on 22 Oct 1814 and sent to Dartmoor on HMS Leyden.

Shed, William - Seaman - Number: 1274 - Prize name: Sword Fish - Ship type: P - How taken: HM Ship-of-the-Line Elephant - When taken: 28 Dec 1812 - Where taken: off Azores - Date received: 16 Mar 1813 - From what ship: Portsmouth, via HMS Abundance - Born: Salem - Age: 20 - Discharged on 24 Jul 1813 and released to Cartel Hoffminy.

Shepherd, Henry - Seaman - Number: 3852 - Prize name: James - Ship type: MV - How taken: HM Brig Harpy - When taken: 16 Dec 1812 - Where taken: off Isle de France (Mauritius) - Date received: 22 Aug 1814 - From what ship: Gravesend - Born: Maryland - Age: 28 - Discharged on 22 Oct 1814 and sent to Dartmoor on HMS Leyden.

Shepherd, Samuel - Gunner - Number: 3733 - Prize name: Argus - Ship type: MV - How taken: HM Ship-of-the-Line San Domingo - When taken: 1 Mar 1814 - Where taken: off Savannah - Date received: 26 May 1814 - From what ship: HMS Hindostan - Born: Salem - Age: 29 - Discharged on 25 Sep 1814 and sent to Dartmoor on HMS Niobe.

Sheppard, Daniel - Seaman - Number: 985 - Prize name: Otter - Ship type: MV - How taken: HM Ship-Sloop Jalouse - When taken: 1 Dec 1812 - Where taken: off Cape St. Vincent, Portugal - Date received: 10 Mar 1813 - From what ship: HMS Tigress - Born: Morton - Age: 24 - Released on 20 Mar 1813 to HMS Otter.

Sheppard, David - Seaman - Number: 283 - Prize name: Francis Ann - Ship type: MV - How taken: Apprehended at Leight, Scotland - When taken: 5 Aug 1812 - Date received: 23 Dec 1812 - From what ship: Greenlaw Depot - Born: Dartmouth - Age: 23 - Discharged on 23 Mar 1813 and released to the Cartel Robinson Potter.

Sheppard, Henry - Seaman - Number: 1696 - Prize name: Governor Middleton - Ship type: MV - How taken: Thetis, British privateer - When taken: 2 May 1813 - Where taken: Bay of Biscay - Date received: 15 May 1813 - From what ship: HMS Viper - Born: Charleston, SC - Age: 35 - Discharged on 30 Sep 1814 and released to HMS Argonaut.

Sheppard, James - Seaman - Number: 2287 - How taken: Gave himself up from HM Ship-of-the-Line Royal George - When taken: 29 Oct 1812 - Date received: 17 Sep 1813 - From what ship: HMS Raisonnable - Born: New Hampshire - Age: 29 - Discharged on 11 Aug 1814 and sent to Dartmoor on HMS Freya.

Sheppard, Joseph - Seaman - Number: 1267 - Prize name: Sword Fish - Ship type: P - How taken: HM Ship-of-the-Line Elephant - When taken: 28 Dec 1812 - Where taken: off Azores - Date received: 16 Mar 1813 - From what ship: Portsmouth, via HMS Abundance - Born: Dartmouth, MA - Age: 35 - Discharged on 24 Jul 1813 and released to Cartel Hoffminy.

Sheridan, Henry - Seaman - Number: 2362 - How taken: Gave himself up from HM Ship-of-the-Line Scipion - When taken: 25 Jun 1813 - Date received: 20 Oct 1813 - From what ship: Portsmouth, via an admiral's tender - Born: New York - Age: 22 - Race: Mulatto - Discharged on 4 Sep 1814 and sent to Dartmoor on HMS Freya.

Sherman, Riley - Seaman - Number: 1924 - Prize name: Rowe of Liverpool, prize of the Privateer Bone - Ship type: P - How taken: HM Sloop Lightning - When taken: 29 Nov 1812 - Where taken: Barbados - Date received: 11 Jul 1813 - From what ship: HMS Raisonnable - Born: Newport, RI - Age: 28 - Discharged on 24 Jul 1813 and released to Cartel Hoffminy.

Sherriff, Benjamin P. - Seaman - Number: 2348 - How taken: Gave himself up from HM Ship-of-the-Line Implacable - When taken: 25 Jun 1813 - Date received: 20 Oct 1813 - From what ship: Portsmouth, via an admiral's tender - Born: Exeter - Age: 22 - Discharged on 4 Sep 1814 and sent to Dartmoor on HMS Freya.

Shields, Mathew - Private - Number: 1635 - Prize name: U.S. Light Artillery - Ship type: LF - How taken: British forces - When taken: 13 Oct 1812 - Where taken: Upper Canada - Date received: 9 May 1813 - From what ship: HMS Raisonnable - Born: County Donegal, Ireland - Age: 21 - Discharged on 22 Oct 1814 and sent to Dartmoor on HMS Leyden.

Shillings, Morris - Seaman - Number: 3039 - How taken: Gave himself up from HM Brig Echo - When taken: 3 Nov 1812 - Date received: 7 Jan 1814 - From what ship: Portsmouth - Born: Connecticut - Age: 24 - Discharged on 11 Aug 1814 and sent to Dartmoor on HMS Freya.

Shipley, Charles - Seaman - Number: 1071 - How taken: Gave himself up from HM Frigate Gladiator - When taken: 7 Feb 1813 - Date received: 14 Mar 1813 - From what ship: Portsmouth via HMS Cornwell - Born: Boston - Age: 32 - Discharged on 11 Aug 1814 and sent to Dartmoor.

Shippard, James - Seaman - Number: 3645 - Prize name: Bunker Hill - Ship type: P - How taken: HM Frigate Pomone & HM Frigate Cydnus - When taken: 4 Mar 1814 - Where taken: Bay of Biscay - Date received: 31 Mar 1814 - From what ship: HMS Raisonnable - Born: New York - Age: 35 - Discharged on 25 Sep 1814 and sent to Dartmoor on HMS Niobe.

Shirly, Pharos - Master - Number: 1325 - Prize name: Rachael - Ship type: MV - How taken: HM Schooner Herring - When taken: 9 Feb 1812 - Where taken: at sea - Date received: 16 Mar 1813 - From what ship: Portsmouth, via HMS Abundance - Born: Marblehead - Age: 29 - Discharged on 2 Jul 1813 and released to Cartel Moses Brown.

Shoe, Bernard - Sailmaker - Number: 3675 - Prize name: Lord Ponsonby, prize of the Privateer Diomede - Ship type: P - How taken: HM Brig Sappho - When taken: 27 Feb 1814 - Where taken: at sea - Date received: 4 May 1814 - From what ship: Portsmouth - Born: Holland - Age: 53 - Discharged on 25 Sep 1814 and sent to Dartmoor on HMS Niobe.

Sholes, Giles - Seaman - Number: 615 - Prize name: King of Rome - Ship type: P - How taken: HM Brig Wolverine - When taken: 13 Dec 1812 - Where taken: at sea - Date received: 23 Feb 1813 - From what ship: Portsmouth via HMS Dromedary - Born: Connecticut - Age: 22 - Discharged on 2 Jul 1813 and released to Cartel Moses Brown.

Shorne, H. - Seaman - Number: 270 - Prize name: Albion - Ship type: MV - How taken: Impressed at Sunderland, England - When taken: 26 Oct 1812 - Date received: 7 Dec 1812 - From what ship: HMS Raisonnable - Born: Dresden - Age: 26 - Discharged in Jul 1813 and released to Cartel Moses Brown.

Short, James - Seaman - Number: 1933 - Prize name: John - Ship type: P - How taken: HM Brig Peruvian - When taken: 6 Feb 1813 - Where taken: West Indies - Date received: 11 Jul 1813 - From what ship: HMS Raisonnable - Born: Salem - Age: 46 - Discharged on 24 Jul 1813 and released to Cartel Hoffminy.

Short, Samuel - Seaman - Number: 2544 - Prize name: Prize to the U.S. Frigate President - Ship type: War - How taken: HM Transport Regulus - When taken: 4 Sep 1812 - Where taken: Newfoundland Bank - Date received: 22 Oct 1813 - From what ship: Portsmouth via HMT Malabar - Born: Rhode Island - Age: 32 - Discharged on 25 Sep 1814 and sent to Dartmoor on HMS Leyden.

Shot, John - Boy - Number: 1162 - Prize name: Sword Fish - Ship type: P - How taken: HM Ship-of-the-Line Elephant - When taken: 28 Dec 1812 - Where taken: off Azores - Date received: 16 Mar 1813 - From what ship: Portsmouth, via HMS Abundance - Born: Salem - Age: 13 - Discharged on 24 Jul 1813 and released to Cartel Hoffminy.

Shroudy, William - Seaman - Number: 3706 - How taken: Gave himself up from HM Brig Acteon - When taken: 9 May 1814 - Date received: 15 May 1815 - From what ship: Eagle - Born: Philadelphia - Age: 30 - Discharged on 26 Sep 1814 and sent to Dartmoor on HMS Leyden.

Sibert, Frederick - Seaman - Number: 1099 - Prize name: Calcutta, East Indian Ship - Ship type: MV - How taken: Two Brothers, British privateer from Guernsey - When taken: 30 Nov 1812 - Where taken: off St. Helena - Date received: 14 Mar 1813 - From what ship: Portsmouth via HMS Beagle - Born: Philadelphia - Age: 22 - Discharged on 8 Jun 1813 and released to Cartel Rodrigo.

Sidebottom, John - Seaman - Number: 1281 - How taken: Gave himself up from HM Guardship Royal William - When taken: 3 Feb 1813 - Date received: 16 Mar 1813 - From what ship: Portsmouth, via HMS Abundance - Born: Virginia - Age: 25 - Discharged on 23 Jul 1814 and sent to Dartmoor.

Sides, Samuel - Seaman - Number: 2939 - Prize name: Governor Plumer - Ship type: P - How taken: HM Brig

Shamrock - When taken: 26 May 1813 - Where taken: at sea - Date received: 7 Jan 1814 - From what ship: Halifax - Born: Portsmouth - Age: 34 - Discharged on 25 Sep 1814 and sent to Dartmoor on HMS Leyden.

Siers, Uriah - Seaman - Number: 308 - Prize name: Cuba - Ship type: MV - How taken: HM Brig Sarpedon - When taken: 12 Aug 1812 - Date received: 23 Dec 1812 - From what ship: Greenlaw Depot - Born: Barnstable - Age: 21 - Discharged on 10 May 1813 and released to Cartel Admittance.

Sieway, Peter - Seaman - Number: 1075 - How taken: Gave himself up from HM Brig Electra - When taken: 20 Sep 1812 - Date received: 14 Mar 1813 - From what ship: Portsmouth via HMS Cornwell - Born: Boston - Age: 28 - Discharged on 11 Aug 1814 and sent to Dartmoor.

Signard, Samuel Francis - Seaman - Number: 447 - Prize name: Hunter - Ship type: P - How taken: HM Frigate Phoebe - When taken: 23 Dec 1812 - Where taken: off Azores - Date received: 19 Feb 1813 - From what ship: HMS Modeste - Born: New Orleans - Age: 29 - Race: Negro - Discharged on 24 Jul 1813 and released to Cartel Hoffminy.

Sikes, Charles - Seaman - Number: 369 - Prize name: Charlotte - Ship type: MV - How taken: Impressed at Gravesend, England - When taken: 22 Dec 1812 - Date received: 21 Jan 1813 - From what ship: HMS Raisonnable - Born: Philadelphia - Age: 17 - Discharged on 24 Jul 1813 and released to Cartel Hoffminy.

Sillock, Amos - Seaman - Number: 1844 - How taken: Given up from HM Frigate Hyperion - Date received: 7 Jul 1813 - From what ship: Portsmouth via HMS Tribune - Born: Sheffield - Age: 30 - Discharged on 25 Jul 1814 and sent to Dartmoor on HMS Bittern.

Silsby, Nathaniel - Seaman - Number: 1265 - How taken: Gave himself up from HMS Dapper - When taken: 9 Dec 1812 - Date received: 16 Mar 1813 - From what ship: Portsmouth, via HMS Abundance - Born: Salem - Age: 19 – Discharge not listed.

Silver, Samuel - Seaman - Number: 3435 - Prize name: Enterprise - Ship type: P - How taken: HM Frigate Tenedos - When taken: 21 May 1813 - Where taken: off Cape Cod - Date received: 23 Feb 1814 - From what ship: Halifax via HMT Malabar - Born: Salem - Age: 16 - Race: Black - Died on 11 Aug 1814 from phthisis (tuberculosis).

Silverthorn, James - Seaman - Number: 2847 - Prize name: Blockade - Ship type: P - How taken: HM Brig Recruit - When taken: 17 Aug 1813 - Where taken: coast of America - Date received: 7 Jan 1814 - From what ship: Halifax - Born: Virginia - Age: 19 - Discharged on 25 Sep 1814 and sent to Dartmoor on HMS Leyden.

Silvey, John - Seaman - Number: 3826 - Prize name: Penn, whaler - Ship type: MV - How taken: HM Sloop Acorn - When taken: 27 Oct 1813 - Where taken: South Seas - Date received: 14 Aug 1814 - From what ship: Deptford - Born: Nantucket - Age: 20 - Discharged on 22 Oct 1814 and sent to Dartmoor on HMS Leyden.

Simmik, John - Seaman - Number: 2678 - How taken: Gave himself up from HM Bomb Vessel Thunder - When taken: 29 Oct 1812 - Date received: 2 Dec 1813 - From what ship: HMS Raisonnable - Born: Rotterdam - Age: 23 - Discharged on 17 Dec 1813.

Simmonds, David - Seaman - Number: 2951 - Prize name: Enterprise - Ship type: P - How taken: HM Frigate Tenedos - When taken: 21 May 1813 - Where taken: off Cape Cod - Date received: 7 Jan 1814 - From what ship: Halifax - Born: Massachusetts - Age: 18 - Discharged on 25 Sep 1814 and sent to Dartmoor on HMS Leyden.

Simmonds, Henry - Seaman - Number: 3517 - Prize name: Pilot - Ship type: LM - How taken: Vittoria, British privateer from Guernsey - When taken: 28 Jan 1814 - Where taken: off Bordeaux, France - Date received: 23 Feb 1814 - From what ship: Portsmouth via HMT Malabar - Born: Staten Island - Age: 23 - Race: Black - Discharged on 26 Sep 1814 and sent to Dartmoor on HMS Leyden.

Simmons, Charles - Seaman - Number: 3753 - Prize name: Argus - Ship type: MV - How taken: HM Ship-of-the-Line San Domingo - When taken: 1 Mar 1814 - Where taken: off Savannah - Date received: 26 May 1814 - From what ship: HMS Hindostan - Born: Barnstable - Age: 21 - Discharged on 25 Sep 1814 and sent to Dartmoor on HMS Niobe.

Simmons, Daniel - Seaman - Number: 1310 - How taken: Gave himself up from HM Guardship Royal William - When taken: 3 Feb 1813 - Date received: 16 Mar 1813 - From what ship: Portsmouth, via HMS Abundance - Born: Pennsylvania - Age: 49 - Race: Black - Discharged on 38 Jun 1813 and released to HMS Ceres.

Simmons, Joel - Seaman - Number: 3756 - Prize name: Argus - Ship type: MV - How taken: HM Ship-of-the-Line San Domingo - When taken: 1 Mar 1814 - Where taken: off Savannah - Date received: 26 May 1814 - From what ship: HMS Hindostan - Born: Barnstable - Age: 19 - Discharged on 25 Sep 1814 and sent to Dartmoor on HMS Niobe.

Simmons, William - Seaman - Number: 2051 - How taken: Gave himself up from HM Ship-of-the-Line Fame - When taken: 4 May 1813 - Date received: 4 Aug 1813 - From what ship: HMS Christian VII - Born: Charleston - Age: 29 - Race: Blackman - Discharged on 22 Feb 1814 and released to HMS Ceres.

Simonds, Joseph - Seaman - Number: 1220 - Prize name: Rossie - Ship type: MV - How taken: HM Frigate Dryand - When taken: 7 Jan 1813 - Where taken: at sea - Date received: 16 Mar 1813 - From what ship: Portsmouth, via HMS Abundance - Born: Alexandria - Age: 21 - Discharged on 24 Jul 1813 and released to Cartel Hoffminy.

Simonds, Proctor - Seaman - Number: 3183 - Prize name: Wolf Cove - Ship type: MV - How taken: HM Frigate Briton - When taken: 1 Dec 1813 - Where taken: off Brest, France - Date received: 7 Jan 1813 - From what ship: Halifax - Born: Massachusetts - Age: 20 - Died on 15 Mar 1814 from fever.

Simoni, John - Seaman - Number: 2985 - Prize name: Enterprise - Ship type: P - How taken: HM Frigate Tenedos - When taken: 21 May 1813 - Where taken: off Cape Cod - Date received: 7 Jan 1814 - From what ship: Halifax - Born: Portsmouth - Age: 30 - Released on 6 Aug 1814.

Simons, John - Seaman - Number: 1643 - Prize name: Henryettos - Ship type: MV - How taken: HMS Castilian - When taken: 12 Mar 1813 - Where taken: off Cape Ortegal, Spain - Date received: 9 May 1813 - From what ship: HMS Raisonnable - Born: Washington - Age: 18 - Discharged on 24 Jul 1814 and sent to Dartmoor.

Simpson, James - Seaman - Number: 1211 - Prize name: Expectation - Ship type: MV - How taken: HM Frigate Briton - When taken: 17 Dec 1812 - Where taken: at sea - Date received: 16 Mar 1813 - From what ship: Portsmouth, via HMS Abundance - Born: Sweetland - Age: 36 - Discharged on 2 Jul 1813 and released to Cartel Moses Brown.

Simpson, John - Steward - Number: 741 - Prize name: Ferret - Ship type: MV - How taken: Apprehended at London - When taken: 10 Feb 1813 - Date received: 25 Feb 1813 - From what ship: HMS Raisonnable - Born: Boston - Age: 32 - Race: Mulatto - Discharged on 19 Sep 1813 and released to HMS Ceres.

Simpson, John - Seaman - Number: 2204 - How taken: Gave himself up from HM Brig Swallow - When taken: 25 Mar 1813 - Date received: 18 Aug 1813 - From what ship: Portsmouth, via an admiral's tender - Born: New York - Age: 33 - Discharged on 11 Aug 1814 and sent to Dartmoor on HMS Freya.

Simpson, Mark - Private - Number: 3129 - Prize name: 14th U.S. Infantry - Ship type: LF - How taken: British forces - When taken: 24 Jun 1813 - Where taken: Beaver Dams, Upper Canada - Date received: 7 Jan 1814 - From what ship: Halifax - Born: Philadelphia - Age: 25 - Discharged on 10 Oct 1814 and sent to U.S. on Cartel St. Philip.

Simpson, Martin - Seaman - Number: 22 - Prize name: Navigator - Ship type: MV - How taken: HM Ship-of-the-Line Cressy - When taken: 11 Aug 1812 - Where taken: Baltic - Date received: 29 Oct 1812 - From what ship: HMS Raisonnable - Born: Austria - Age: 27 - Discharged on 19 Mar 1813 and released to the Navigator.

Simpson, William - Seaman - Number: 483 - Prize name: Vengeance - Ship type: LM - How taken: HM Frigate Phoebe - When taken: 1 Jan 1813 - Where taken: Lat 44.4 Long 23 - Date received: 19 Feb 1813 - From what ship: HMS Modeste - Born: New York - Age: 24 - Discharged on 24 Jul 1813 and released to Cartel Hoffminy.

Simpson, William - Seaman - Number: 2267 - Prize name: Eliza - Ship type: MV - How taken: HMS Charles - When taken: 20 Jul 1813 - Where taken: off Petershead, Scotland - Date received: 14 Sep 1813 - From what ship: HMS Raisonnable - Born: North Carolina - Age: 18 - Discharged on 31 Oct 1813 and released to HMS Ceres.

Simpson, William - Seaman - Number: 2069 - How taken: Gave himself up from HM Frigate Resistance - When taken: Aug 1813 - Date received: 9 Aug 1813 - From what ship: HMS Thames - Born: Sutton, MA - Age: 24 - Escaped on 17 Aug 1814 from HMS Betelgeuse.

Sims, Clement - Seaman - Number: 1525 - How taken: Gave himself up from HM Frigate Mermaid - When taken: 30 Nov 1812 - Date received: 8 Apr 1813 - From what ship: Portsmouth, via an admiral's tender - Born: Baltimore - Age: 30 - Race: Black - Discharged on 4 Aug 1814 and sent to Dartmoor on HMS Alpheus.

Sims, Joseph - Seaman - Number: 2266 - Prize name: Eliza - Ship type: MV - How taken: HMS Charles - When taken: 20 Jul 1813 - Where taken: off Petershead, Scotland - Date received: 14 Sep 1813 - From what ship: HMS Raisonnable - Born: Africa - Age: 30 - Race: Black - Discharged on 20 Aug 1814 and sent to Dartmoor on HMS Shamrock.

Sims, Oliver - Seaman - Number: 1965 - How taken: Impressed at Dublin - When taken: 12 Feb 1813 - Date received: 15 Jul 1813 - From what ship: Plymouth - Born: Rhode Island - Age: 19 - Discharged on 17 Jun 1814 and sent to Dartmoor on HMS Redbreast.

Sims, William - Seaman - Number: 2599 - How taken: Gave himself up from HM Ship-of-the-Line Berwick - When taken: 27 May 1813 - Date received: 5 Nov 1813 - From what ship: HMS Hindostan - Born: Norfolk, VA - Age: 21 - Discharged on 12 Aug 1814 and sent to Dartmoor on HMS Alpheus.

Simson, Smith - Seaman - Number: 3925 - How taken: Gave himself up from HM Ship-of-the-Line Blenheim - When taken: 2 Sep 1814 - Date received: 24 Sep 1814 - From what ship: HMS Namur - Born: North Carolina - Age: 20 - Discharged on 29 Sep 1814 and sent to Dartmoor on HMS Freya.

Sinclair, Solomon - Seaman - Number: 3824 - How taken: Gave himself up from HM Frigate Andromache - When taken: 20 Jul 1814 - Date received: 23 Jun 1814 - From what ship: Quebec - Born: New Jersey - Age: 35 - Race: Black - Discharged on 20 Aug 1814 and sent to Dartmoor on HMS Shamrock.

Sinnett, William - Seaman - Number: 3414 - Prize name: Yankee - Ship type: P - How taken: HM Brig Ringdove - When taken: 17 Oct 1813 - Where taken: at sea - Date received: 23 Feb 1814 - From what ship: Halifax via HMT Malabar - Born: Barnstable - Age: 25 - Discharged on 22 Oct 1814 and sent to Dartmoor on HMS Leyden.

Skilling, James - Seaman - Number: 3463 - Prize name: Elbridge Gerry - Ship type: P - How taken: HM Frigate Crescent - When taken: 16 Sep 1813 - Where taken: at sea - Date received: 23 Feb 1814 - From what ship: Halifax via HMT Malabar - Born: Freeport - Age: 19 - Discharged on 22 Oct 1814 and sent to Dartmoor on HMS Leyden.

Skinner, Ebenezer - 1st Mate - Number: 2880 - Prize name: Taken off an English whaler - How taken: HM Ship-of-the-Line Illustrious - When taken: 22 Oct 1813 - Where taken: at sea - Date received: 7 Jan 1814 - From what ship: Portsmouth - Born: Nantucket - Age: 33 - Died on 2 Mar 1814 from fever.

Skinner, Johnson - Master - Number: 391 - Prize name: Dolphin - Ship type: MV - How taken: HM Ship-of-the-Line Invincible - When taken: 24 Aug 1812 - Where taken: Mediterranean - Date received: 13 Feb 1813 - From what ship: HMS Raisonnable - Born: New York - Age: 29 - Discharged on 23 Mar 1813 and released to the Cartel Robinson Potter.

Skudder, Alexander - Boatswain's Mate - Number: 3731 - Prize name: Argus - Ship type: MV - How taken: HM Ship-of-the-Line San Domingo - When taken: 1 Mar 1814 - Where taken: off Savannah - Date received: 26 May 1814 - From what ship: HMS Hindostan - Born: Philadelphia - Age: 30 - Discharged on 25 Sep 1814 and sent to Dartmoor on HMS Niobe.

Slackpole, John - Seaman - Number: 323 - Prize name: Catherine Charlotte - Ship type: MV - How taken: Thracian - When taken: 16 Dec 1812 - Where taken: off Norway - Date received: 5 Jan 1813 - From what ship: HMS Sheldrake - Born: Somersworth, NH - Age: 24 - Discharged in Jul 1813 and released to Cartel Moses Brown.

Slaiter, John - Boatswain's Mate - Number: 3915 - Prize name: Union - Ship type: MV - How taken: HM Transport Malabar No. 352 - When taken: 17 Jan 1813 - Where taken: Calcutta - Date received: 10 Sep 1814 - From what ship: Censor - Born: Philadelphia - Age: 32 - Discharged on 26 Sep 1814 and sent to Dartmoor on HMS Leyden.

Slate, Henry V. - Pilot - Number: 855 - Prize name: Brutus - Ship type: MV - How taken: Briton, letter of marque - When taken: 13 Jan 1813 - Where taken: Bay of Biscay - Date received: 1 Mar 1813 - From what ship: Plymouth via HMS Namur - Born: New York - Age: 24 - Discharged on 24 Jul 1813 and released to Cartel Hoffminy.

Slaughter, George - Sergeant - Number: 3150 - Prize name: U.S. Light Dragoons - Ship type: LF - How taken: British forces - When taken: 24 Jun 1813 - Where taken: Beaver Dams, Upper Canada - Date received: 7 Jan 1814 - From what ship: Halifax - Born: Virginia - Age: 27 - Discharged on 10 Oct 1814 and sent to U.S. on Cartel St. Philip.

Slebar, Samuel - Seaman - Number: 1734 - How taken: Taken up at Cork - When taken: 7 Apr 1813 - Date received: 25 May 1813 - From what ship: Portsmouth via HMS Impetius - Born: Christian Bridge - Age: 22 - Discharged on 24 Jul 1814 and sent to Dartmoor on HMS Liffey.

Sloan, William - Private - Number: 2616 - Prize name: 14th U.S. Infantry - Ship type: LF - How taken: British forces - When taken: 24 Jun 1813 - Where taken: Beaver Dams, Upper Canada - Date received: 5 Nov 1813 - From what ship: HMS Hindostan - Born: County Antrim, Ireland - Age: 48 - Discharged on 10 Oct 1814 and sent to U.S. on Cartel St. Philip.

Sloane, William - Seaman - Number: 3577 - How taken: Impressed at London - When taken: 5 Mar 1814 - Date received: 15 Mar 1814 - From what ship: HMS Raisonnable - Born: East Hartford - Age: 28 - Discharged on 20 Aug 1814 and sent to Dartmoor on HMS Shamrock.

Slocum, William - Seaman - Number: 2239 - Prize name: Orders in Council - Ship type: LM - How taken: HM Frigate Surveillante - When taken: 1 Jan 1813 - Where taken: off Cape Ortegal, Spain - Date received: 7 Sep 1813 - From what ship: HMS Raisonnable - Born: Rhode Island - Age: 23 - Discharged on 11 Aug 1814 and sent to Dartmoor on HMS Freya.

Sluckley, Richard - Seaman - Number: 2326 - How taken: Impressed at Gravesend, England - When taken: 10 Aug 1813 - Date received: 12 Oct 1813 - From what ship: HMS Raisonnable - Born: Massachusetts - Age: 26 - Discharged on 4 Sep 1814 and sent to Dartmoor on HMS Freya.

Small, George D. - Seaman - Number: 1881 - Prize name: Tiger - Ship type: MV - How taken: HM Brig Scylla - When taken: 22 Mar 1813 - Where taken: Bay of Biscay - Date received: 7 Jul 1813 - From what ship: Portsmouth via HMS Tribune - Born: New York - Age: 24 - Discharged on 25 Sep 1814 and sent to Dartmoor on HMS Niobe.

Small, Joseph - Seaman - Number: 115 - Prize name: Urbana - Ship type: MV - How taken: Stopped at London - When taken: 26 Oct 1812 - Date received: 4 Nov 1812 - From what ship: HMS Namur - Born: Massachusetts - Age: 24 - Discharged on 4 Mar 1813 to the Wailey.

Small, Thomas - Seaman - Number: 1148 - Prize name: Sword Fish - Ship type: P - How taken: HM Ship-of-the-Line Elephant - When taken: 28 Dec 1812 - Where taken: off Azores - Date received: 16 Mar 1813 - From what ship: Portsmouth, Mundane - Born: Portsmouth - Age: 16 - Discharged on 19 May 1813 and released to HMS Ceres.

Smasher, Allen - Seaman - Number: 1561 - Prize name: Dolphin - Ship type: LM - How taken: HM Ship-of-the-Line Colossus - When taken: 5 Jan 1813 - Where taken: off the Western Isles, Scotland - Date received: 8 Apr 1813 - From what ship: Plymouth via HMS Olympia - Born: Philadelphia - Age: 32 - Race: Negro - Discharged on 27 Jul 1813 and released to Cartel Hoffminy.

Smiley, John - Private - Number: 2629 - Prize name: 14th U.S. Infantry - Ship type: LF - How taken: British forces - When taken: 24 Jun 1813 - Where taken: Beaver Dams, Upper Canada - Date received: 5 Nov 1813 - From what ship: HMS Hindostan - Born: Londonderry, Ireland - Age: 33 - Discharged on 10 Oct 1814 and sent to U.S. on Cartel St. Philip.

Smith, Thomas - Seaman - Number: 2943 - Prize name: Enterprise - Ship type: P - How taken: HM Frigate Tenedos - When taken: 21 May 1813 - Where taken: off Cape Cod - Date received: 7 Jan 1814 - From what ship: Halifax - Born: Massachusetts - Age: 37 - Discharged on 25 Sep 1814 and sent to Dartmoor on HMS Leyden.

Smith, Aesop - Seaman - Number: 2145 - Prize name: Matilda, prize of the U.S. Brig Argus - Ship type: War - How taken: HM Frigate Revolutionnaire - When taken: 25 Jul 1813 - Where taken: off Lorient, France - Date received: 9 Aug 1813 - From what ship: HMS Thames - Born: Cape Cod - Age: 30 - Discharged on 12 Aug 1814 and sent to Dartmoor on HMS Alpheus.

Smith, Benjamin - Seaman - Number: 2695 - Prize name: Growler - Ship type: P - How taken: HM Brig Electra -

When taken: 7 Jul 1813 - Where taken: off St. Johns - Date received: 7 Jan 1814 - From what ship: Portsmouth - Born: Salem - Age: 19 - Discharged on 8 Sep 1814 and sent to Dartmoor on HMS Niobe.

Smith, Buphus - Seaman - Number: 310 - Prize name: Cuba - Ship type: MV - How taken: HM Brig Sarpedon - When taken: 12 Aug 1812 - Date received: 23 Dec 1812 - From what ship: Greenlaw Depot - Born: Thomastown - Age: 19 - Discharged on 10 May 1813 and released to Cartel Admittance.

Smith, Caesar - Seaman - Number: 1302 - How taken: Gave himself up from HM Guardship Royal William - When taken: 3 Feb 1813 - Date received: 16 Mar 1813 - From what ship: Portsmouth, via HMS Abundance - Born: Long Island - Age: 32 - Race: Black - Discharged on 23 Jul 1814 and sent to Dartmoor.

Smith, Charles - Seaman - Number: 3329 - Prize name: Porcupine - Ship type: LM - How taken: HM Frigate Acasta - When taken: 18 Jul 1813 - Where taken: off Cape Sable, Florida - Date received: 23 Feb 1814 - From what ship: Halifax via HMT Malabar - Born: Baltimore - Age: 34 - Race: Black - Discharged on 10 Oct 1814 and sent to Dartmoor on the Mermaid.

Smith, Chester - Seaman - Number: 844 - Prize name: Vengeance - Ship type: LM - How taken: HM Frigate Phoebe - When taken: 1 Jan 1813 - Where taken: Lat 44.4 Long 23 - Date received: 1 Mar 1813 - From what ship: Plymouth via HMS Namur - Born: Cohenger - Age: 24 - Discharged on 24 Jul 1813 and released to Cartel Hoffminy.

Smith, Elisha - Seaman - Number: 2926 - Prize name: Juliana Smith - Ship type: P - How taken: HM Frigate Nymphe - When taken: 12 May 1813 - Where taken: off Cape Sable, Florida - Date received: 7 Jan 1814 - From what ship: Halifax - Born: Salem - Age: 28 - Discharged on 25 Sep 1814 and sent to Dartmoor on HMS Leyden.

Smith, Elisha - Seaman - Number: 2514 - Prize name: Wasp - Ship type: P - How taken: HM Schooner Bream - When taken: 9 Jun 1813 - Where taken: off Halifax - Date received: 22 Oct 1813 - From what ship: Portsmouth via HMT Malabar - Born: Hampshire - Age: 36 - Discharged on 30 Sep 1814 and released to HMS Argonaut.

Smith, George M. - Seaman - Number: 3739 - Prize name: Argus - Ship type: MV - How taken: HM Ship-of-the-Line San Domingo - When taken: 1 Mar 1814 - Where taken: off Savannah - Date received: 26 May 1814 - From what ship: HMS Hindostan - Born: South Carolina - Age: 20 - Discharged on 10 Oct 1814 and sent to Dartmoor on the Mermaid.

Smith, Henry - Seaman - Number: 3451 - Prize name: Elbridge Gerry - Ship type: P - How taken: HM Frigate Crescent - When taken: 16 Sep 1813 - Where taken: at sea - Date received: 23 Feb 1814 - From what ship: Halifax via HMT Malabar - Born: Durham - Age: 30 - Discharged on 22 Oct 1814 and sent to Dartmoor on HMS Leyden.

Smith, Henry - Seaman - Number: 1095 - Prize name: Calcutta, East Indian Ship - Ship type: MV - How taken: Two Brothers, British privateer from Guernsey - When taken: 30 Nov 1812 - Where taken: off St. Helena - Date received: 14 Mar 1813 - From what ship: Portsmouth via HMS Beagle - Born: Carolina - Age: 25 - Discharged on 8 Jun 1813 and released to Cartel Rodrigo.

Smith, Henry - Seaman - Number: 683 - Prize name: U.S.R.M. Cutter James Madison - Ship type: War - How taken: HM Frigate Barbadoes - When taken: 22 Aug 1812 - Where taken: at sea - Date received: 24 Feb 1813 - From what ship: Portsmouth via HMS Ulysses - Born: Berkshire, MA - Age: 26 - Discharged on 10 May 1813 and released to Cartel Admittance.

Smith, Henry - Seaman - Number: 2780 - Prize name: Thomas - Ship type: P - How taken: HM Frigate Nymphe - When taken: 24 Jun 1813 - Where taken: off Halifax - Date received: 7 Jan 1814 - From what ship: Halifax - Born: Portsmouth - Age: 21 - Discharged on 8 Sep 1814 and sent to Dartmoor on HMS Niobe.

Smith, Henry - Seaman - Number: 2372 - How taken: Gave himself up from HM Ship-of-the-Line Swiftsure - When taken: 26 Dec 1812 - Date received: 20 Oct 1813 - From what ship: Portsmouth, via an admiral's tender - Born: New Hampshire - Age: 32 - Discharged on 4 Sep 1814 and sent to Dartmoor on HMS Freya.

Smith, J. W. - Seaman - Number: 3511 - Prize name: Pilot - Ship type: LM - How taken: Vittoria, British privateer from Guernsey - When taken: 28 Jan 1814 - Where taken: off Bordeaux, France - Date received: 23 Feb 1814 - From what ship: Portsmouth via HMT Malabar - Born: New York - Age: 23 - Race: Black - Discharged on

26 Sep 1814 and sent to Dartmoor on HMS Leyden.

Smith, Jacob - Seaman - Number: 921 - Prize name: Experiment - Ship type: MV - How taken: HM Brig Rover - When taken: 10 Nov 1812 - Where taken: off Bordeaux, France - Date received: 10 Mar 1813 - From what ship: HMS Tigress - Born: Prussia - Age: 36 - Discharged on 8 Jun 1813 and released to Cartel Rodrigo.

Smith, James - Seaman - Number: 300 - Prize name: America - Ship type: MV - How taken: HM Brig Cracker - When taken: 1 Aug 1812 - Date received: 23 Dec 1812 - From what ship: Greenlaw Depot - Born: Marblehead - Age: 16 - Discharged on 23 Mar 1813 and released to the Cartel Robinson Potter.

Smith, James - Carpenter - Number: 240 - How taken: Gave himself up from HM Ship-of-the-Line Dublin - When taken: 1 Nov 1812 - Date received: 1 Dec 1812 - From what ship: HMS Raisonnable - Born: Cakiott, NY - Age: 39 - Discharged on 26 Jul 1814 and sent to Dartmoor on HMS Raven.

Smith, James - Seaman - Number: 2130 - How taken: Gave himself up from HM Ship-of-the-Line Kent - When taken: 28 May 1813 - Date received: 9 Aug 1813 - From what ship: HMS Thames - Born: Virginia - Age: 51 - Discharged on 15 Sep 1813 and released to HMS Ceres.

Smith, Jeremiah - Prize Master - Number: 2700 - Prize name: Growler - Ship type: P - How taken: HM Brig Electra - When taken: 7 Jul 1813 - Where taken: off St. Johns - Date received: 7 Jan 1814 - From what ship: Portsmouth - Born: Marblehead - Age: 35 - Discharged on 25 Sep 1814 and sent to Dartmoor on HMS Leyden.

Smith, John - Seaman - Number: 3877 - How taken: Gave himself up from HM Frigate Clorinde - When taken: 18 Dec 1813 - Date received: 28 Aug 1814 - From what ship: London - Born: Philadelphia - Age: 30 - Race: Black - Discharged on 8 Sep 1814 and sent to Dartmoor on HMS Niobe.

Smith, John - Seaman - Number: 41 - Prize name: Suwarrow - Ship type: MV - How taken: HM Brig Recruit - When taken: 20 Jul 1812 - Where taken: off New York - Date received: 3 Nov 1812 - From what ship: HMS Plover - Born: Providence - Age: 49 - Discharged on 23 Mar 1813 and released to the Cartel Robinson Potter.

Smith, John - Seaman - Number: 1292 - How taken: Gave himself up from HM Guardship Royal William - When taken: 3 Feb 1813 - Date received: 16 Mar 1813 - From what ship: Portsmouth, via HMS Abundance - Born: Philadelphia - Age: 29 - Race: Black - Discharged on 23 Jul 1814 and sent to Dartmoor.

Smith, John - Seaman - Number: 770 - Prize name: Alagana - Ship type: MV - How taken: HM Ship-of-the-Line San Juan - When taken: 8 May 1812 - Where taken: Gibraltar - Date received: 25 Feb 1813 - From what ship: HMS Brazen - Born: Norfolk, VA - Age: 26 - Discharged on 10 May 1813 and released to Cartel Admittance.

Smith, John - Seaman - Number: 372 - How taken: Impressed at Gravesend, England - When taken: 28 Dec 1812 - Date received: 21 Jan 1813 - From what ship: HMS Raisonnable - Born: New York - Age: 22 - Discharged on 24 Jul 1813 and released to Cartel Hoffminy.

Smith, John - Boy - Number: 1334 - Prize name: Sea Nymph - Ship type: MV - How taken: HM Brig Thrasher - When taken: 4 Mar 1813 - Where taken: off River Jade (Germany) - Date received: 22 Mar 1813 - From what ship: HMS Thrasher - Born: New York - Age: 18 - Discharged on 12 Aug 1814 and sent to Dartmoor on HMS Alpheus.

Smith, John - Seaman - Number: 2359 - How taken: Gave himself up from HM Ship-of-the-Line Hibernia - When taken: 25 Jun 1813 - Date received: 20 Oct 1813 - From what ship: Portsmouth, via an admiral's tender - Born: Boston - Age: 43 - Discharged on 4 Sep 1814 and sent to Dartmoor on HMS Freya.

Smith, John - Seaman - Number: 2692 - Prize name: Growler - Ship type: P - How taken: HM Brig Electra - When taken: 7 Jul 1813 - Where taken: off St. Johns - Date received: 7 Jan 1814 - From what ship: Portsmouth - Born: Marblehead - Age: 25 - Discharged on 25 Sep 1814 and sent to Dartmoor on HMS Leyden.

Smith, John - Master - Number: 1918 - Prize name: Flora, a Spanish brig - Ship type: MV - How taken: Impressed at London - When taken: 28 Jun 1813 - Date received: 7 Jul 1813 - From what ship: HMS Raisonnable - Born: New York - Age: 22 - Discharged on 13 May 1814 and sent to Reading on parole.

Smith, John - Seaman - Number: 2037 - How taken: Impressed at London - When taken: 24 Jul 1813 - Date received: 1 Aug 1813 - From what ship: HMS Raisonnable - Born: New York - Age: 27 - Race: Black - Discharged on 12 Aug 1814 and sent to Dartmoor on HMS Liverpool.

Smith, John - Seaman - Number: 2012 - How taken: Gave himself up from HM Ship-of-the-Line Ville de Paris - Date received: 15 Jul 1813 - From what ship: Plymouth - Born: Massachsetts - Age: 28 - Discharged on 11 Aug 1814 and sent to Dartmoor on HMS Freya.

Smith, John - Seaman - Number: 2906 - Prize name: U.S. Schooner Julia - Ship type: War - How taken: HM Schooner Earl Moria - When taken: 11 Aug 1813 - Where taken: Lake Ontario - Date received: 7 Jan 1814 - From what ship: Portsmouth - Born: New York - Age: 21 - Discharged on 10 Oct 1814 and sent to U.S. on Cartel St. Philip.

Smith, John - Private - Number: 2614 - Prize name: 14th U.S. Infantry - Ship type: LF - How taken: British forces - When taken: 24 Jun 1813 - Where taken: Beaver Dams, Upper Canada - Date received: 5 Nov 1813 - From what ship: HMS Hindostan - Born: Ireland - Age: 30 - Discharged on 10 Oct 1814 and sent to U.S. on Cartel St. Philip.

Smith, John - Mate - Number: 3205 - Prize name: Isabella - Ship type: MV - How taken: Impressed at London - When taken: 3 Jan 1814 - Date received: 10 Jan 1814 - From what ship: HMS Raisonnable - Born: New York - Age: 44 - Discharged on 25 Sep 1814 and sent to Dartmoor on HMS Leyden.

Smith, John - Seaman - Number: 3038 - How taken: Gave himself up from HM Ship-of-the-Line Illustrious - When taken: 7 Sep 1813 - Date received: 7 Jan 1814 - From what ship: Portsmouth - Born: Delaware - Age: 36 - Discharged on 8 Sep 1814 and sent to Dartmoor.

Smith, John - Seaman - Number: 2117 - How taken: Gave himself up from HM Ship-of-the-Line Union - When taken: 27 May 1813 - Date received: 9 Aug 1813 - From what ship: HMS Thames - Born: Connecticut - Age: 34 - Discharged on 12 Aug 1814 and sent to Dartmoor on HMS Alpheus.

Smith, John - Seaman - Number: 3189 - Prize name: Growler - Ship type: P - How taken: HM Brig Electra - When taken: 7 Jul 1813 - Where taken: off St. Johns - Date received: 7 Jan 1813 - From what ship: Portsmouth - Born: Marblehead - Age: 27 - Died on 22 Apr 1814 from fever.

Smith, Kilby - 2nd Mate - Number: 3838 - Prize name: Derby - Ship type: MV - How taken: HM Frigate Nereus - When taken: 4 Feb 1813 - Where taken: off Cape of Good Hope - Date received: 21 Aug 1814 - From what ship: London - Born: Boston - Age: 27 - Discharged on 4 Sep 1814 and sent to Dartmoor on HMS Freya.

Smith, Mark - Seaman - Number: 121 - Prize name: Anna & Lilley - Ship type: MV - How taken: Detained at London - When taken: 26 Oct 1812 - Date received: 4 Nov 1812 - From what ship: HMS Namur - Born: Africa - Age: 18 - Race: Black - Released on 15 Mar 1813.

Smith, Monday - Seaman - Number: 3456 - Prize name: Elbridge Gerry - Ship type: P - How taken: HM Frigate Crescent - When taken: 16 Sep 1813 - Where taken: at sea - Date received: 23 Feb 1814 - From what ship: Halifax via HMT Malabar - Born: Richmond - Age: 21 - Race: Black - Discharged on 22 Oct 1814 and sent to Dartmoor on HMS Leyden.

Smith, Noble (alias James Smith) - Seaman - Number: 1679 - How taken: Gave himself up at Chatham - When taken: 13 May 1813 - Date received: 13 May 1813 - From what ship: Chatham - Born: New York - Age: 26 - Discharged on 2 Jul 1813 and released to Cartel Moses Brown.

Smith, Obadiah - Seaman - Number: 773 - Prize name: Alagana - Ship type: MV - How taken: HM Ship-of-the-Line San Juan - When taken: 8 May 1812 - Where taken: Gibraltar - Date received: 25 Feb 1813 - From what ship: HMS Brazen - Born: Belfast, MA - Age: 24 - Discharged on 10 May 1813 and released to Cartel Admittance.

Smith, Paul - Seaman - Number: 2077 - How taken: Gave himself up from HM Ship-of-the-Line Armada - When taken: 8 Jun 1813 - Date received: 9 Aug 1813 - From what ship: HMS Thames - Born: Charlestown - Age: 28 - Race: Black - Discharged on 4 Aug 1814 and sent to Dartmoor on HMS Liverpool.

Smith, Peter - Seaman - Number: 1582 - How taken: Gave himself up from HM Ship-of-the-Line Christian VII - When taken: 21 Dec 1812 - Date received: 18 Apr 1813 - From what ship: HMS Rosario - Born: Red Hook, NJ - Age: 23 - Race: Black - Discharged on 11 Apr 1814 and sent to Dartmoor.

Smith, Richard - Seaman - Number: 3550 - Prize name: General Kempt, prize of the Privateer Grand Turk - Ship type: P - How taken: HM Brig Foxhound - When taken: 18 Dec 1813 - Where taken: Lat 48.4 Long 6 - Date received: 7 May 1814 - From what ship: Portsmouth via HMS Favorite - Born: Salem - Age: 24 - Discharged on 25 Sep 1814 and sent to Dartmoor on HMS Niobe.

Smith, Samuel - Seaman - Number: 344 - Prize name: Postsea, prize to the Privateer Thrasher - Ship type: P - How taken: HM Sloop Helena - When taken: 31 Dec 1813 - Where taken: off Azores - Date received: 19 Jan 1813 - From what ship: HMS Raisonnable - Born: Cape Ann - Age: 17 - Discharged on 24 Jul 1813 and released to Cartel Hoffminy.

Smith, Thomas - Seaman - Number: 3683 - How taken: Gave himself up from HM Frigate Rota - Date received: 4 May 1814 - From what ship: Portsmouth - Born: Virginia - Age: 26 - Race: Black - Discharged on 26 Sep 1814 and sent to Dartmoor on HMS Leyden.

Smith, Thomas - Seaman - Number: 487 - How taken: Gave himself up from HM Brig Persian - When taken: 13 Dec 1812 - Date received: 19 Feb 1813 - From what ship: HMS Raisonnable - Born: Somerset, MD - Age: 23 - Discharged on 25 Sep 1814 and sent to Dartmoor on HMS Leyden.

Smith, Thomas - Seaman - Number: 994 - Prize name: Rising - Ship type: MV - How taken: HM Ship-Sloop Jalouse - When taken: 6 Dec 1812 - Where taken: at sea - Date received: 10 Mar 1813 - From what ship: HMS Tigress - Born: Charlestown - Age: 25 - Released on 20 Mar 1813 to the Rising Sun.

Smith, Thomas - Seaman - Number: 1512 - How taken: Gave himself up from HM Ship-of-the-Line Blake - When taken: 10 Dec 1812 - Date received: 8 Apr 1813 - From what ship: Portsmouth, via an admiral's tender - Born: New York - Age: 38 - Race: Black - Discharged on 12 Aug 1814 and sent to Dartmoor on HMS Alpheus.

Smith, Thomas - Seaman - Number: 2905 - Prize name: Dart - Ship type: P - How taken: HM Frigate Niger & HMS Fortunee - When taken: 10 Nov 1813 - Where taken: off Cape Finisterre, Spain - Date received: 7 Jan 1814 - From what ship: Portsmouth - Born: Massachusetts - Age: 25 - Discharged on 25 Sep 1814 and sent to Dartmoor on HMS Leyden.

Smith, Thomas - Seaman - Number: 1664 - How taken: Gave himself up from HM Ship-of-the-Line Blake - Date received: 9 May 1813 - From what ship: HMS Raisonnable - Born: New York - Age: 18 - Discharged on 13 Aug 1814 and sent to Dartmoor.

Smith, Thomas R. - Seaman - Number: 517 - Prize name: William - Ship type: MV - How taken: HM Brig Recruit - When taken: 29 Aug 1812 - Where taken: at sea - Date received: 23 Feb 1813 - From what ship: Portsmouth via HMS Dromedary - Born: Altona - Age: 25 - Discharged on 8 Mar 1813 and released to HMS Ceres.

Smith, William - Seaman - Number: 968 - Prize name: Empress - Ship type: MV - How taken: HM Brig Rover - When taken: 30 Nov 1812 - Where taken: St. Andrew - Date received: 10 Mar 1813 - From what ship: HMS Tigress - Born: New York - Age: 22 - Discharged on 8 Jun 1813 and released to Cartel Rodrigo.

Smith, William - Seaman - Number: 974 - Prize name: Empress - Ship type: MV - How taken: HM Brig Rover - When taken: 30 Nov 1812 - Where taken: St. Andrew - Date received: 10 Mar 1813 - From what ship: HMS Tigress - Born: New Haven - Age: 30 - Discharged on 8 Jun 1813 and released to Cartel Rodrigo.

Smith, William - Seaman - Number: 230 - How taken: Apprehended at London - When taken: 16 Nov 1812 - Date received: 25 Nov 1812 - From what ship: HMS Raisonnable - Born: Rhode Island - Age: 31 - Discharged on 24 Jul 1813 and released to Cartel Hoffminy.

Smith, William - Seaman - Number: 509 - Prize name: Josephine - Ship type: MV - How taken: HM Sloop Goree - When taken: 15 Aug 1812 - Where taken: off Bermuda - Date received: 23 Feb 1813 - From what ship: Portsmouth via HMS Dromedary - Born: Columbo - Age: 21 - Discharged on 10 May 1813 and released to Cartel Admittance.

Smith, William - Seaman - Number: 160 - Prize name: Galen - Ship type: MV - How taken: HM Battery Gorgon - When taken: 12 Aug 1812 - Where taken: Great Belt, Denmark - Date received: 5 Nov 1812 - From what ship: HMS Namur - Born: New York - Age: 29 - Discharged on 23 Mar 1813 and released to the Cartel Robinson Potter.

Smith, William B. - Cook - Number: 3681 - Prize name: Sally - Ship type: MV - How taken: HM Brig Derwent - When taken: 21 Jul 1814 - Where taken: at sea - Date received: 4 May 1814 - From what ship: Portsmouth -

Born: Salem - Age: 17 - Discharged on 25 Sep 1814 and sent to Dartmoor on HMS Niobe.

Smith, William Pitt - Seaman - Number: 554 - How taken: Sent into custody - When taken: 1 Oct 1812 - Date received: 23 Feb 1813 - From what ship: Portsmouth via HMS Dromedary - Born: Georgetown - Age: 30 - Discharged on 2 Jul 1813 and released to Cartel Moses Brown.

Smith, William S. - 1st Mate - Number: 2278 - Prize name: Maria - Ship type: MV - How taken: HM Sloop Thais - When taken: 20 Jan 1813 - Where taken: coast of Guinea - Date received: 17 Sep 1813 - From what ship: HMS Raisonnable - Born: New York - Age: 49 - Discharged on 13 Aug 1814 and sent to Dartmoor on HMS Freya.

Smithers, Thomas - Seaman - Number: 3379 - Prize name: Polly - Ship type: MV - How taken: Prize - When taken: 20 Jul 1813 - Where taken: Georges Bank - Date received: 23 Feb 1814 - From what ship: Halifax via HMT Malabar - Born: Boston - Age: 28 - Escaped on 19 May 1814.

Snider, Lewis - 1st Mate - Number: 998 - Prize name: Brunswick - Ship type: MV - How taken: HM Frigate Iris - When taken: 17 Dec 1812 - Where taken: off Spain - Date received: 10 Mar 1813 - From what ship: HMS Tigress - Born: New York - Age: 25 - Discharged on 23 Mar 1813 and released to the Cartel Robinson Potter.

Snow, Collyer - Seaman - Number: 3903 - How taken: Gave himself up from the MV Shannon - When taken: 28 Aug 1814 - Date received: 31 Aug 1814 - From what ship: Transport Office - Born: Massachusetts - Age: 23 - Discharged on 25 Sep 1814 and sent to Dartmoor on HMS Leyden.

Snow, Daniel - Seaman - Number: 3283 - Prize name: Vivid - Ship type: P - How taken: HM Frigate Nymphe - When taken: 20 Apr 1813 - Where taken: off Cape Cod - Date received: 23 Feb 1814 - From what ship: Halifax via HMT Malabar - Born: San Domingo (Haiti) - Age: 19 - Discharged on 10 Oct 1814 and sent to Dartmoor on the Mermaid.

Snow, James - Seaman - Number: 2806 - Prize name: Industry - Ship type: P - How taken: HM Brig Heron - When taken: 3 Nov 1813 - Where taken: off Halifax - Date received: 7 Jan 1814 - From what ship: Halifax - Born: Salem - Age: 24 - Discharged on 8 Sep 1814 and sent to Dartmoor on HMS Niobe.

Snow, Thomas - Seaman - Number: 2479 - Prize name: Juliana Smith - Ship type: P - How taken: HM Frigate Nymphe - When taken: 12 May 1813 - Where taken: off Cape Sable, Florida - Date received: 22 Oct 1813 - From what ship: Portsmouth via HMT Malabar - Born: Massachusetts - Age: 25 - Discharged on 8 Sep 1814 and sent to Dartmoor on HMS Niobe.

Snowden, Joshua L. - Seaman - Number: 120 - Prize name: Anna & Lilley - Ship type: MV - How taken: Detained at London - When taken: 26 Oct 1812 - Date received: 4 Nov 1812 - From what ship: HMS Namur - Born: Charleston, SC - Age: 17 - Discharged in Jul 1813 and released to Cartel Moses Brown.

Soder, Bastion D. - Seaman - Number: 721 - Prize name: James - Ship type: MV - How taken: Detained at Portsmouth harbor - When taken: 31 Jul 1812 - Date received: 24 Feb 1813 - From what ship: Portsmouth via HMS Ulysses - Born: St. Michaels, Portugal - Age: 28 - Discharged on 23 Mar 1813 and released to the Cartel Robinson Potter.

Soder, Jacob - Private - Number: 3056 - Prize name: 14th U.S. Infantry - Ship type: LF - How taken: British forces - When taken: 9 Jun 1813 - Where taken: Canada - Date received: 7 Jan 1814 - From what ship: Halifax - Born: Swiss - Age: 24 - Released on 17 Jun 1814.

Sodoburgh, John - Boy - Number: 477 - Prize name: Hunter - Ship type: P - How taken: HM Frigate Phoebe - When taken: 23 Dec 1812 - Where taken: off Azores - Date received: 19 Feb 1813 - From what ship: HMS Modeste - Born: Boston - Age: 13 - Discharged on 24 Jul 1813 and released to Cartel Hoffminy.

Soley, Nathaniel - Seaman - Number: 3358 - Prize name: York - Ship type: MV - How taken: HM Frigate Tenedos - When taken: 26 May 1813 - Where taken: off Cape Sable, Florida - Date received: 23 Feb 1814 - From what ship: Halifax via HMT Malabar - Born: Haverhill - Age: 28 - Discharged on 10 Oct 1814 and sent to Dartmoor on the Mermaid.

Sourivier, Daniel - Boy - Number: 2230 - Prize name: Porcupine - Ship type: LM - How taken: HM Frigate Acasta - When taken: 29 Jun 1813 - Where taken: off Cape Sable, Florida - Date received: 22 Aug 1813 - From what ship: HMS Raisonnable - Born: Not readable - Age: 15 - Released on 9 Feb 1814.

Southward, Samuel W. - Seaman - Number: 1214 - Prize name: Leader - Ship type: MV - How taken: HM Frigate Briton - When taken: 10 Dec 1812 - Where taken: off Bordeaux, France - Date received: 16 Mar 1813 - From what ship: Portsmouth, via HMS Abundance - Born: Stratford - Age: 25 - Discharged on 2 Jul 1813 and released to Cartel Moses Brown.

Southwich, James - Seaman - Number: 2169 - How taken: Gave himself up from HM Ship-of-the-Line Swiftsure - When taken: 26 Dec 1812 - Date received: 16 Aug 1813 - From what ship: Portsmouth, via an admiral's tender - Born: Boston - Age: 22 - Discharged on 17 Jun 1814 and sent to Dartmoor on the Penebar.

Spalding, William - Private - Number: 3118 - Prize name: 14th U.S. Infantry - Ship type: LF - How taken: British forces - When taken: 24 Jun 1813 - Where taken: Beaver Dams, Upper Canada - Date received: 7 Jan 1814 - From what ship: Halifax - Born: Maryland - Age: 22 - Discharged on 10 Oct 1814 and sent to U.S. on Cartel St. Philip.

Sparkes, Thomas - Seaman - Number: 2474 - Prize name: Montgomery - Ship type: P - How taken: HM Frigate Nymphe - When taken: 5 May 1813 - Where taken: off Cape Cod - Date received: 22 Oct 1813 - From what ship: Portsmouth via HMT Malabar - Born: Salem - Age: 38 - Discharged on 8 Sep 1814 and sent to Dartmoor on HMS Niobe.

Sparks, Henry - 3rd Mate - Number: 1458 - Prize name: Union - Ship type: MV - How taken: HM Frigate Iris - When taken: 17 Jan 1813 - Where taken: at sea - Date received: 6 Apr 1813 - From what ship: Plymouth via HMS Decoy - Born: Philadelphia - Age: 20 - Discharged on 24 Jul 1813 and released to Cartel Hoffminy.

Sparling, William - Seaman - Number: 702 - Prize name: Deanna, recaptured British vessel - Ship type: P - How taken: HM Ship-of-the-Line Polyphemus - When taken: 14 Sep 1812 - Where taken: at sea - Date received: 24 Feb 1813 - From what ship: Portsmouth via HMS Ulysses - Born: Monmouth - Age: 19 - Discharged on 8 Jun 1813 and released to Cartel Rodrigo.

Sparrow, John - Seaman - Number: 1374 - How taken: Gave himself up from HM Ship-of-the-Line Christian VII - When taken: 19 Mar 1813 - Date received: 3 Apr 1813 - From what ship: Portsmouth, via an admiral's tender - Born: Norfolk - Age: 22 - Discharged on 24 Jul 1814 and sent to Dartmoor.

Sparrow, Joseph - Cook - Number: 2134 - How taken: Gave himself up from HMS Montrell - When taken: 5 Jul 1813 - Date received: 9 Aug 1813 - From what ship: HMS Thames - Born: Virginia - Age: 43 - Race: Black - Discharged on 12 Aug 1814 and sent to Dartmoor on HMS Alpheus.

Spear, Joseph - Seaman - Number: 1703 - How taken: Taken up at London - When taken: 12 May 1813 - Date received: 22 May 1813 - From what ship: HMS Raisonnable - Born: Boston - Age: 22 - Discharged on 12 Aug 1814 and sent to Dartmoor on HMS Alpheus.

Spencer, John - Seaman - Number: 2568 - Prize name: Sampson - Ship type: MV - How taken: Impressed at Portsmouth - When taken: 1 Oct 1813 - Date received: 23 Oct 1813 - From what ship: Portsmouth via HMS Raisonnable - Born: Exeter - Age: 24 - Discharged on 25 Sep 1814 and sent to Dartmoor on HMS Leyden.

Spencer, Leonard - Seaman - Number: 1868 - Prize name: Tiger - Ship type: MV - How taken: HM Brig Scylla - When taken: 22 Mar 1813 - Where taken: Bay of Biscay - Date received: 7 Jul 1813 - From what ship: Portsmouth via HMS Tribune - Born: East Harford, CT - Age: 32 - Discharged on 4 Aug 1814 and sent to Dartmoor on HMS Liverpool.

Spencer, Samuel - Seaman - Number: 1559 - Prize name: Dolphin - Ship type: LM - How taken: HM Ship-of-the-Line Colossus - When taken: 5 Jan 1813 - Where taken: off the Western Isles, Scotland - Date received: 8 Apr 1813 - From what ship: Plymouth via HMS Olympia - Born: Delaware - Age: 22 - Discharged on 27 Jul 1813 and released to Cartel Hoffminy.

Spenny, Nathaniel - Seaman - Number: 2841 - Prize name: Portsmouth Packet - Ship type: P - How taken: HM Brig Fantome - When taken: 5 Oct 1813 - Where taken: off Portland - Date received: 7 Jan 1814 - From what ship: Halifax - Born: Massachusetts - Age: 19 - Discharged on 25 Sep 1814 and sent to Dartmoor on HMS Leyden.

Spice, Alexander - Seaman - Number: 3704 - How taken: Gave himself up from the Earl Falk - When taken: 9 May 1814 - Date received: 10 May 1814 - From what ship: Eagle - Born: Dover - Age: 35 - Race: Mulatto - Discharged on 25 Sep 1814 and sent to Dartmoor on HMS Leyden.

Spick, John - Passenger - Number: 3353 - Prize name: Rolla - Ship type: P - How taken: HM Ship-of-the-Line Victorious - When taken: 8 Jan 1813 - Where taken: off Halifax - Date received: 23 Feb 1814 - From what ship: Halifax via HMT Malabar - Born: Baltimore - Age: 18 - Discharged on 10 Oct 1814 and sent to Dartmoor on the Mermaid.

Spiers, Nathaniel - Seaman - Number: 3631 - Prize name: Bunker Hill - Ship type: P - How taken: HM Frigate Pomone & HM Frigate Cydnus - When taken: 4 Mar 1814 - Where taken: Bay of Biscay - Date received: 31 Mar 1814 - From what ship: HMS Raisonnable - Born: Providence - Age: 23 - Race: Black - Discharged on 25 Sep 1814 and sent to Dartmoor on HMS Niobe.

Spiney, Nathaniel - Seaman - Number: 722 - Prize name: James - Ship type: MV - How taken: Detained at Portsmouth harbor - When taken: 31 Jul 1812 - Date received: 24 Feb 1813 - From what ship: Portsmouth via HMS Ulysses - Born: Comsbark, MA - Age: 17 - Discharged on 23 Mar 1813 and released to the Cartel Robinson Potter.

Spouding, Joseph - Seaman - Number: 2515 - Prize name: Wasp - Ship type: P - How taken: HM Schooner Bream - When taken: 9 Jun 1813 - Where taken: off Halifax - Date received: 22 Oct 1813 - From what ship: Portsmouth via HMT Malabar - Born: Massachusetts - Age: 21 - Discharged on 8 Sep 1814 and sent to Dartmoor on HMS Niobe.

Spratt, Thomas - Seaman - Number: 1064 - How taken: Gave himself up from HM Frigate Ethalion - When taken: 5 Feb 1813 - Date received: 14 Mar 1813 - From what ship: Portsmouth via HMS Cornwell - Born: Virginia - Age: 32 - Discharged on 11 Aug 1814 and sent to Dartmoor.

Sprismo, John - Seaman - Number: 3943 - How taken: Gave himself up from MV Martha - When taken: 2 Apr 1814 - Date received: 10 Oct 1814 - From what ship: Quebec - Born: Calais, France - Age: 21 - Discharged on 22 Oct 1814 and sent to Dartmoor on HMS Leyden.

Spryon, John - Seaman - Number: 1397 - Prize name: Blue Bird - Ship type: MV - How taken: HM Frigate Briton - When taken: 1 Jan 1813 - Where taken: off Bordeaux, France - Date received: 5 Apr 1813 - From what ship: Plymouth via HMS Dwarf - Born: New Orleans - Age: 30 - Discharged on 24 Jul 1813 and released to Cartel Hoffminy.

Spurr, Elijah - Seaman - Number: 3548 - Prize name: General Kempt, prize of the Privateer Grand Turk - Ship type: P - How taken: HM Brig Foxhound - When taken: 18 Dec 1813 - Where taken: Lat 48.4 Long 6 - Date received: 7 May 1814 - From what ship: Portsmouth via HMS Favorite - Born: Boston - Age: 18 - Discharged on 25 Sep 1814 and sent to Dartmoor on HMS Niobe.

Squires, Prince - Seaman - Number: 1601 - How taken: Impressed at London - When taken: 22 Mar 1813 - Date received: 19 Apr 1813 - From what ship: HMS Raisonnable - Born: Montfort - Age: 34 - Race: Black - Discharged on 24 Jul 1814 and sent to Dartmoor.

Stables, James - Seaman - Number: 2886 - Prize name: Taken off an English whaler - How taken: HM Ship-of-the-Line Illustrious - When taken: 22 Oct 1813 - Where taken: at sea - Date received: 7 Jan 1814 - From what ship: Portsmouth - Born: Boston - Age: 21 - Discharged on 25 Sep 1814 and sent to Dartmoor on HMS Leyden.

Stacey, Benjamin - Seaman - Number: 68 - Prize name: Elson - Ship type: MV - How taken: HM Frigate Ethalion - When taken: 12 Aug 1812 - Where taken: Baltic - Date received: 4 Nov 1812 - From what ship: HMS Namur - Born: Massachusetts - Age: 18 - Discharged on 10 May 1813 and released to Cartel Admittance.

Stacey, Benjamin - Seaman - Number: 3170 - Prize name: Wolf Cove - Ship type: MV - How taken: HM Frigate Briton - When taken: 1 Dec 1813 - Where taken: off Brest, France - Date received: 7 Jan 1814 - From what ship: Halifax - Born: Massachusetts - Age: 19 - Discharged on 25 Sep 1814 and sent to Dartmoor on HMS Leyden.

Stacey, John - Seaman - Number: 2808 - Prize name: Industry - Ship type: P - How taken: HM Brig Heron - When taken: 3 Nov 1813 - Where taken: off Halifax - Date received: 7 Jan 1814 - From what ship: Halifax - Born: Marblehead - Age: 37 - Discharged on 11 Aug 1814 and sent to Dartmoor on HMS Freya.

Stacey, Samuel - Seaman - Number: 3174 - Prize name: Wolf Cove - Ship type: MV - How taken: HM Frigate Briton - When taken: 1 Dec 1813 - Where taken: off Brest, France - Date received: 7 Jan 1814 - From what ship: Halifax - Born: Massachusetts - Age: 24 - Discharged on 25 Sep 1814 and sent to Dartmoor on HMS Leyden.

Stacy, Perry - Seaman - Number: 1507 - How taken: Gave himself up from HM Ship-of-the-Line Blake - When taken: 10 Dec 1812 - Date received: 8 Apr 1813 - From what ship: Portsmouth, via an admiral's tender - Born: Baltimore - Age: 28 - Race: Mulatto - Discharged on 4 Aug 1814 and sent to Dartmoor on HMS Alpheus.

Stacy, William - Seaman - Number: 692 - Prize name: Fame, prize of Privateer Decatur - Ship type: P - How taken: HM Ship-of-the-Line Polyphemus - When taken: 13 Sep 1812 - Where taken: at sea - Date received: 24 Feb 1813 - From what ship: Portsmouth via HMS Ulysses - Born: Marblehead, MA - Age: 22 - Discharged on 8 Jun 1813 and released to Cartel Rodrigo.

Stafford, John - Apprentice - Number: 3520 - Prize name: Pilot - Ship type: LM - How taken: Vittoria, British privateer from Guernsey - When taken: 28 Jan 1814 - Where taken: off Bordeaux, France - Date received: 23 Feb 1814 - From what ship: Portsmouth via HMT Malabar - Born: Virginia - Age: 30 - Race: Black - Discharged on 26 Sep 1814 and sent to Dartmoor on HMS Leyden.

Stafford, William J. - Captain - Number: 3479 - Prize name: Pilot - Ship type: LM - How taken: Vittoria, British privateer from Guernsey - When taken: 1 Jan 1814 - Where taken: off Bordeaux, France - Date received: 23 Feb 1814 - From what ship: Halifax via HMT Malabar - Born: Winchester - Age: 31 - Discharged on 28 Feb 1814 and sent to Reading on parole.

Stage, William - Seaman - Number: 2339 - Prize name: Hindostan - Ship type: MV - How taken: HM Brig Zenobia - When taken: 25 Jun 1813 - Where taken: off Lisbon - Date received: 20 Oct 1813 - From what ship: Portsmouth, via an admiral's tender - Born: Charlestown - Age: 26 - Discharged on 4 Sep 1814 and sent to Dartmoor on HMS Freya.

Staggs, Henry - Seaman - Number: 1193 - How taken: Gave himself up from HM Transport Romulus - When taken: 11 Aug 1812 - Date received: 16 Mar 1813 - From what ship: Portsmouth, via HMS Abundance - Born: Harford - Age: 32 - Discharged on 11 Aug 1814 and sent to Dartmoor on HMS Freya.

Staley, John - Private - Number: 3073 - Prize name: 14th U.S. Infantry - Ship type: LF - How taken: British forces - When taken: 24 Jun 1813 - Where taken: Beaver Dams, Upper Canada - Date received: 7 Jan 1814 - From what ship: Halifax - Born: Maryland - Age: 21 - Discharged on 10 Oct 1814 and sent to U.S. on Cartel St. Philip.

Stanfield, George - Seaman - Number: 2753 - Prize name: Globe - Ship type: P - How taken: HM Frigate Spartan - When taken: 13 Jun 1813 - Where taken: off Delaware - Date received: 7 Jan 1814 - From what ship: Halifax - Born: Philadelphia - Age: 22 - Discharged on 25 Sep 1814 and sent to Dartmoor on HMS Leyden.

Stanley, Joseph - Steward - Number: 1437 - Prize name: Orbit - Ship type: MV - How taken: HM Brig Achates - When taken: 29 Jan 1813 - Where taken: Lat 49 N Long 13 W - Date received: 6 Apr 1813 - From what ship: Plymouth via HMS Decoy - Born: New Orleans - Age: 25 - Discharged on 19 Jul 1813 and released to HMS Ceres.

Stanley, Peter - Seaman - Number: 49 - Prize name: White Oak - Ship type: MV - How taken: HM Brig Recruit - When taken: 22 Jul 1812 - Where taken: off Bermuda - Date received: 3 Nov 1812 - From what ship: HMS Plover - Born: Beverly, MA - Age: 44 - Discharged on 23 Mar 1813 and released to the Cartel Robinson Potter.

Stanly, Benjamin - Master - Number: 1613 - Prize name: Dick - Ship type: MV - How taken: Detained at London - When taken: 24 Apr 1813 - Date received: 3 May 1813 - From what ship: HMS Raisonnable - Born: Salem - Age: 28 - Discharged on 24 Jul 1814 and sent to Dartmoor.

Stanton, Gideon A. - Seaman - Number: 1097 - Prize name: Calcutta, East Indian Ship - Ship type: MV - How taken: Two Brothers, British privateer from Guernsey - When taken: 30 Nov 1812 - Where taken: off St. Helena - Date received: 14 Mar 1813 - From what ship: Portsmouth via HMS Beagle - Born: Westbury - Age: 20 - Discharged on 8 Jun 1813 and released to Cartel Rodrigo.

Stanton, James - Seaman - Number: 2392 - How taken: Gave himself up from HM Ship-of-the-Line Achille - When taken: 26 Dec 1812 - Date received: 20 Oct 1813 - From what ship: Portsmouth, via an admiral's tender -

Born: Baltimore - Age: 24 - Discharged on 4 Sep 1814 and sent to Dartmoor on HMS Freya.

Stanwood, Timothy - Seaman - Number: 581 - How taken: Gave himself up from HM Ship-of-the-Line Aboukir - When taken: 28 Oct 1812 - Date received: 23 Feb 1813 - From what ship: Portsmouth via HMS Dromedary - Born: Newburyport - Age: 23 - Discharged on 26 Jul 1814 and sent to Dartmoor on HMS Raven.

Starbourg, W. G. - Seaman - Number: 1746 - How taken: Taken up at London - When taken: 24 May 1813 - Date received: 28 May 1813 - From what ship: HMS Raisonnable - Born: Portland, MA - Age: 23 - Discharged on 24 Jul 1814 and sent to Dartmoor on HMS Liffey.

Starkweather, James - Seaman - Number: 3894 - How taken: Gave himself up from HM Frigate Phoenix - When taken: 17 Jul 1813 - Date received: 30 Aug 1814 - From what ship: Transport Office - Born: Connecticut - Age: 33 - Discharged on 2 Sep 1814 and sent to Dartmoor on HMS Leyden.

Starr, G. C. - 2nd Mate - Number: 1398 - Prize name: Porcupine - Ship type: MV - How taken: HM Frigate Dryand - When taken: 8 Jan 1813 - Where taken: off Bordeaux, France - Date received: 5 Apr 1813 - From what ship: Plymouth via HMS Dwarf - Born: Connecticut - Age: 25 - Discharged on 24 Jul 1813 and released to Cartel Hoffminy.

Steele, Thomas - Seaman - Number: 3833 - Prize name: Rattlesnake - Ship type: LM - How taken: HM Frigate Rhin - When taken: 12 Mar 1814 - Where taken: off Bermuda - Date received: 19 Aug 1814 - From what ship: London - Born: Boston - Age: 21 - Discharged on 22 Oct 1814 and sent to Dartmoor on HMS Leyden.

Stegman, Christian - Seaman - Number: 2345 - Prize name: Hindostan - Ship type: MV - How taken: HM Brig Zenobia - When taken: 25 Jun 1813 - Where taken: off Lisbon - Date received: 20 Oct 1813 - From what ship: Portsmouth, via an admiral's tender - Born: Stockholm - Age: 40 - Released on 10 Feb 1814.

Stephens, David - Seaman - Number: 1167 - Prize name: Sword Fish - Ship type: P - How taken: HM Ship-of-the-Line Elephant - When taken: 28 Dec 1812 - Where taken: off Azores - Date received: 16 Mar 1813 - From what ship: Portsmouth, via HMS Abundance - Born: Gloucester - Age: 49 - Discharged on 24 Jul 1813 and released to Cartel Hoffminy.

Stephens, Henry - Seaman - Number: 92 - Prize name: Rising Stars - Ship type: MV - How taken: Stopped at London - When taken: 26 Nov 1812 - Date received: 4 Nov 1812 - From what ship: HMS Namur - Born: Massachusetts - Age: 26 - Discharged on 4 Mar 1813 to the Wailey.

Stephens, Michael - Seaman - Number: 597 - Prize name: Antelope - Ship type: P - How taken: HM Brig Zephyr - When taken: 10 Dec 1812 - Where taken: at sea - Date received: 23 Feb 1813 - From what ship: Portsmouth via HMS Dromedary - Born: Prussia - Age: 30 - Discharged on 2 Jul 1813 and released to Cartel Moses Brown.

Stephens, Thomas - Seaman - Number: 498 - Prize name: Nancy - Ship type: MV - How taken: HM Brig Parthian - When taken: 1 Aug 1812 - Where taken: off the Needles, Isle of Wight - Date received: 23 Feb 1813 - From what ship: Portsmouth via HMS Dromedary - Born: Marblehead - Age: 26 - Discharged on 17 Nov 1813 to the Cartel Robinson Potter.

Stephens, Trey - Seaman - Number: 1273 - Prize name: Sword Fish - Ship type: P - How taken: HM Ship-of-the-Line Elephant - When taken: 28 Dec 1812 - Where taken: off Azores - Date received: 16 Mar 1813 - From what ship: Portsmouth, via HMS Abundance - Born: Marshfield - Age: 15 - Discharged on 18 Oct 1813 and released to HMS Ceres.

Stephens, William - Seaman - Number: 2260 - Prize name: Eliza - Ship type: MV - How taken: HMS Charles - When taken: 20 Jul 1813 - Where taken: off Petershead, Scotland - Date received: 14 Sep 1813 - From what ship: HMS Raisonnable - Born: Portsmouth - Age: 21 - Discharged on 21 Jan 1814 and released to HMS Ceres.

Sterns, Henry - Seaman - Number: 1098 - Prize name: Calcutta, East Indian Ship - Ship type: MV - How taken: Two Brothers, British privateer from Guernsey - When taken: 30 Nov 1812 - Where taken: off St. Helena - Date received: 14 Mar 1813 - From what ship: Portsmouth via HMS Beagle - Born: Boston - Age: 19 - Discharged on 8 Jun 1813 and released to Cartel Rodrigo.

Sterns, Joseph - Seaman - Number: 3665 - Prize name: Elbridge Gerry - Ship type: P - How taken: HM Frigate Crescent - When taken: 13 Nov 1813 - Where taken: off St. Johns - Date received: 4 May 1814 - From what ship: Portsmouth - Born: Portland - Age: 24 - Discharged on 25 Sep 1814 and sent to Dartmoor on HMS Niobe.

Stetson, Hiram - Seaman - Number: 3745 - Prize name: Argus - Ship type: MV - How taken: HM Ship-of-the-Line San Domingo - When taken: 1 Mar 1814 - Where taken: off Savannah - Date received: 26 May 1814 - From what ship: HMS Hindostan - Born: Boston - Age: 17 - Discharged on 25 Sep 1814 and sent to Dartmoor on HMS Niobe.

Stevens, James - Seaman - Number: 2673 - Prize name: Rambler - Ship type: P - How taken: HM Frigate Thais - When taken: 31 Mar 1813 - Where taken: off Liberia, Africa - Date received: 2 Dec 1813 - From what ship: HMS Raisonnable - Born: Boston - Age: 32 - Race: Blackman - Discharged on 8 Sep 1814 and sent to Dartmoor on HMS Niobe.

Stevens, John - Seaman - Number: 1757 - How taken: Gave himself up from HMS Decoy - When taken: 12 Nov 1812 - Date received: 11 Jun 1813 - From what ship: HMS Raisonnable - Born: Philadelphia - Age: 38 - Discharged on 24 Jul 1814 and sent to Dartmoor on HMS Liffey.

Stevens, Joseph - Mate - Number: 1419 - Prize name: Postsea, prize to the Privateer Thrasher - Ship type: P - How taken: HM Sloop Helena - When taken: 31 Dec 1813 - Where taken: off Azores - Date received: 5 Apr 1813 - From what ship: Plymouth via HMS Dwarf - Born: Gloucester - Age: 24 - Discharged on 24 Jul 1813 and released to Cartel Hoffminy.

Stevens, William - Seaman - Number: 3885 - How taken: Gave himself up from HM Frigate Hussar - When taken: 26 Jul 1813 - Date received: 30 Aug 1814 - From what ship: Transport Office - Born: Virginia - Age: 39 - Discharged on 25 Sep 1814 and sent to Dartmoor on HMS Leyden.

Stevens, William - Seaman - Number: 2582 - How taken: Impressed at London - When taken: 15 Oct 1813 - Date received: 1 Nov 1813 - From what ship: HMS Raisonnable - Born: Boston - Age: 22 - Race: Black - Discharged on 25 Sep 1814 and sent to Dartmoor on HMS Leyden.

Stevenson, George - Prize Master - Number: 1714 - Prize name: Recaptured British MV - Ship type: P - How taken: HM Frigate Revolutionnaire - When taken: 10 Apr 1813 - Where taken: off the Western Isles, Scotland - Date received: 25 May 1813 - From what ship: Portsmouth via HMS Impetius - Born: New York - Age: 34 - Discharged on 24 Jul 1814 and sent to Dartmoor on HMS Liffey.

Stevenson, Levi - Seaman - Number: 2122 - How taken: Gave himself up from HM Ship-of-the-Line Prince of Wales - When taken: 28 May 1813 - Date received: 9 Aug 1813 - From what ship: HMS Thames - Born: Virginia - Age: 22 - Race: Black - Discharged on 12 Aug 1814 and sent to Dartmoor on HMS Alpheus.

Stevenson, Thaddeus - Seaman - Number: 1238 - Prize name: Rossie - Ship type: MV - How taken: HM Frigate Dryand - When taken: 7 Jan 1813 - Where taken: at sea - Date received: 16 Mar 1813 - From what ship: Portsmouth, via HMS Abundance - Born: Baltimore - Age: 30 - Discharged on 24 Jul 1813 and released to Cartel Hoffminy.

Stevenson, Thomas - Seaman - Number: 533 - Prize name: Baltimore - Ship type: P - How taken: HM Transport Diadem - When taken: 7 Oct 1812 - Where taken: S. Andres - Date received: 23 Feb 1813 - From what ship: Portsmouth via HMS Dromedary - Born: Havre de Grace - Age: 19 - Discharged on 8 Jun 1813 and released to Cartel Rodrigo.

Steward, Alexander - Seaman - Number: 944 - Prize name: Mariner - Ship type: MV - How taken: HM Brig Lyra - When taken: 15 Dec 1812 - Where taken: off Bilboa, Spain - Date received: 10 Mar 1813 - From what ship: HMS Tigress - Born: Massachusetts - Age: 28 - Discharged on 2 Jul 1813 and released to Cartel Moses Brown.

Steward, James - Steward - Number: 331 - Prize name: Jane - Ship type: MV - How taken: Apprehended at London - When taken: 26 Dec 1812 - Date received: 11 Jan 1813 - From what ship: HMS Raisonnable - Born: New York - Age: 28 - Race: Mulatto - Discharged on 26 Jul 1814 and sent to Dartmoor on HMS Raven.

Steward, John - Seaman - Number: 1850 - How taken: Gave himself up from HM Ship-of-the-Line Malta - Date received: 7 Jul 1813 - From what ship: Portsmouth via HMS Tribune - Born: Virginia - Age: 26 - Discharged on 25 Jul 1814 and sent to Dartmoor on HMS Bittern.

Steward, John - Seaman - Number: 2195 - How taken: Gave himself up from HM Ship-of-the-Line Caledonia -

When taken: 5 Dec 1812 - Date received: 18 Aug 1813 - From what ship: French Account - Born: Philadelphia - Age: 35 - Discharged on 11 Aug 1814 and sent to Dartmoor on HMS Freya.

Steward, Thomas - Private - Number: 2628 - Prize name: 14th U.S. Infantry - Ship type: LF - How taken: British forces - When taken: 24 Jun 1813 - Where taken: Beaver Dams, Upper Canada - Date received: 5 Nov 1813 - From what ship: HMS Hindostan - Born: County Tyrone, Ireland - Age: 27 - Discharged on 10 Oct 1814 and sent to U.S. on Cartel St. Philip.

Stewart, William - Steward - Number: 93 - Prize name: Rising Stars - Ship type: MV - How taken: Stopped at London - When taken: 26 Nov 1812 - Date received: 4 Nov 1812 - From what ship: HMS Namur - Born: Isle of Wight - Age: 23 - Race: Mulatto - Discharged on 24 Feb 1813 and released to HMS Ceres.

Stibbens, Thomas - Steward - Number: 2042 - How taken: Impressed at Dover off British West Indiaman William - When taken: 10 Jul 1813 - Date received: 4 Aug 1813 - From what ship: HMS Christian VII - Born: Chatham, St. Georges - Age: 27 - Race: Blackman - Discharged on 4 Aug 1814 and sent to Dartmoor on HMS Liverpool.

Stickney, Abraham - Carpenter - Number: 3735 - Prize name: Argus - Ship type: MV - How taken: HM Ship-of-the-Line San Domingo - When taken: 1 Mar 1814 - Where taken: off Savannah - Date received: 26 May 1814 - From what ship: HMS Hindostan - Born: Newburyport - Age: 24 - Discharged on 25 Sep 1814 and sent to Dartmoor on HMS Niobe.

Stiles, Jurich - Seaman - Number: 3328 - Prize name: Porcupine - Ship type: LM - How taken: HM Frigate Acasta - When taken: 18 Jul 1813 - Where taken: off Cape Sable, Florida - Date received: 23 Feb 1814 - From what ship: Halifax via HMT Malabar - Born: Boxford - Age: 28 - Discharged on 10 Oct 1814 and sent to Dartmoor on the Mermaid.

Stilman, Elijah - Seaman - Number: 321 - Prize name: Amphion - Ship type: MV - How taken: Thracian - When taken: 16 Dec 1812 - Where taken: off Norway - Date received: 5 Jan 1813 - From what ship: HMS Sheldrake - Born: Gloucester - Age: 36 - Discharged in Jul 1813 and released to Cartel Moses Brown.

Stilman, William A. - Boatswain's Mate - Number: 3732 - Prize name: Argus - Ship type: MV - How taken: HM Ship-of-the-Line San Domingo - When taken: 1 Mar 1814 - Where taken: off Savannah - Date received: 26 May 1814 - From what ship: HMS Hindostan - Born: Barnstable - Age: 21 - Discharged on 20 Aug 1814 and sent to Dartmoor on HMS Shamrock.

Stilwell, William - Seaman - Number: 3922 - How taken: Gave himself up from HM Ship-of-the-Line Revenge - When taken: 23 Sep 1814 - Date received: 24 Sep 1814 - From what ship: HMS Namur - Born: Middletown - Age: 25 - Discharged on 29 Sep 1814 and sent to Dartmoor on HMS Freya.

Stinchcombe, George - Mate - Number: 1719 - Prize name: Price - Ship type: LM - How taken: HM Frigate Iris - When taken: 13 Apr 1813 - Where taken: Bay of Biscay - Date received: 25 May 1813 - From what ship: Portsmouth via HMS Impetius - Born: Baltimore - Age: 24 - Discharged on 24 Jul 1814 and sent to Dartmoor on HMS Liffey.

Stiver, David - Seaman - Number: 2296 - How taken: Impressed at London - When taken: 14 Sep 1813 - Date received: 20 Sep 1813 - From what ship: HMS Raisonnable - Born: New York - Age: 27 - Discharged on 19 Oct 1813 and released to HMS Ceres.

Stockhouse, Charles - Seaman - Number: 907 - How taken: Impressed at London - When taken: 12 Jan 1813 - Date received: 9 Mar 1813 - From what ship: HMS Raisonnable - Born: New Orleans - Age: 43 - Discharged on 24 Jul 1813 and released to Cartel Hoffminy.

Stockley, W. D. - Seaman - Number: 263 - Prize name: Xenophon - Ship type: MV - How taken: Impressed at Gravesend, England - When taken: 18 Oct 1812 - Date received: 7 Dec 1812 - From what ship: HMS Raisonnable - Born: Accomack County, VA - Age: 37 - Discharged in Jul 1813 and released to Cartel Moses Brown.

Stoddard, Conrad - Seaman - Number: 3383 - Prize name: Teazer - Ship type: P - How taken: HM Frigate Boreas - When taken: 15 Jun 1813 - Where taken: off Halifax - Date received: 23 Feb 1814 - From what ship: Halifax via HMT Malabar - Born: Newport - Age: 25 - Discharged on 10 Oct 1814 and sent to Dartmoor on the Mermaid.

Stoff, Samuel - Seaman - Number: 736 - Prize name: Leonidas - Ship type: MV - How taken: Detained at Portsmouth harbor - When taken: 31 Jul 1812 - Date received: 24 Feb 1813 - From what ship: Portsmouth via HMS Ulysses - Born: York, MA - Age: 24 - Race: Man of color - Discharged on 23 Mar 1813 and released to the Cartel Robinson Potter.

Stoltenberg, Manuel - Seaman - Number: 3720 - How taken: English forces off Bordeaux - When taken: 26 Mar 1814 - Date received: 18 May 1814 - From what ship: HMS Raisonnable - Born: Boston - Age: 30 - Discharged on 10 Oct 1814 and sent to Dartmoor on the Mermaid.

Stone, Henry - Seaman - Number: 2560 - How taken: Gave himself up from HM Battery Gorgon - When taken: 1 Nov 1812 - Date received: 23 Oct 1813 - From what ship: Portsmouth via HMS Raisonnable - Born: Connecticut - Age: 26 - Discharged on 8 Sep 1814 and sent to Dartmoor on HMS Niobe.

Stone, Isaac - Passenger - Number: 3625 - How taken: Taken off a Swedish ship bound for America - Date received: 29 Mar 1814 - From what ship: Hired tender Anna - Born: Danvers - Age: 25 - Race: Mulatto - Discharged on 25 Sep 1814 and sent to Dartmoor on HMS Niobe.

Stone, John - Seaman - Number: 676 - Prize name: U.S.R.M. Cutter James Madison - Ship type: War - How taken: HM Frigate Barbadoes - When taken: 22 Aug 1812 - Where taken: at sea - Date received: 24 Feb 1813 - From what ship: Portsmouth via HMS Ulysses - Born: Levant - Age: 22 - Discharged on 10 May 1813 and released to Cartel Admittance.

Stone, Robert - Seaman - Number: 2832 - Prize name: Portsmouth Packet - Ship type: P - How taken: HM Brig Fantome - When taken: 5 Oct 1813 - Where taken: off Portland - Date received: 7 Jan 1814 - From what ship: Halifax - Born: Massachusetts - Age: 32 - Discharged on 25 Sep 1814 and sent to Dartmoor on HMS Leyden.

Stone, Samuel - Seaman - Number: 324 - Prize name: Catherine Charlotte - Ship type: MV - How taken: Thracian - When taken: 16 Dec 1812 - Where taken: off Norway - Date received: 5 Jan 1813 - From what ship: HMS Sheldrake - Born: Ipswich, MA - Age: 23 - Discharged in Jul 1813 and released to Cartel Moses Brown.

Stone, William - Seaman - Number: 1488 - Prize name: Union - Ship type: MV - How taken: HM Frigate Iris - When taken: 17 Jan 1813 - Where taken: at sea - Date received: 6 Apr 1813 - From what ship: Plymouth via an admiral's tender - Born: New Jersey - Age: 19 - Discharged on 26 Jul 1813 and released to Cartel Hoffminy.

Storer, John (alias James Tarlton) - Private - Number: 3100 - Prize name: 14th U.S. Infantry - Ship type: LF - How taken: British forces - When taken: 24 Jun 1813 - Where taken: Beaver Dams, Upper Canada - Date received: 7 Jan 1814 - From what ship: Halifax - Born: Not listed - Age: 0 - Discharged on 25 Sep 1814 and sent to Dartmoor on HMS Leyden.

Storm, Daniel - Seaman - Number: 2533 - Prize name: Yorktown - Ship type: P - How taken: HM Brig Nimrod - When taken: 17 Jul 1813 - Where taken: Grand Banks - Date received: 22 Oct 1813 - From what ship: Portsmouth via HMT Malabar - Born: New York - Age: 28 - Discharged on 8 Sep 1814 and sent to Dartmoor on HMS Niobe.

Story, William - Prize Master - Number: 2187 - Prize name: True Blooded Yankee - Ship type: P - How taken: HM Frigate Hamadryad - When taken: 24 Jul 1813 - Where taken: off Norway - Date received: 17 Aug 1813 - From what ship: HMS Raisonnable - Born: Philadelphia - Age: 40 - Discharged on 11 Aug 1814 and sent to Dartmoor on HMS Freya.

Stout, Sairer - Seaman - Number: 39 - Prize name: Mary - Ship type: MV - How taken: From a cutter's boat off Bermuda - When taken: 8 Aug 1812 - Date received: 3 Nov 1812 - From what ship: HMS Plover - Born: Huntingdon, NJ - Age: 28 - Discharged on 23 Mar 1813 and released to the Cartel Robinson Potter.

Stow, Jeremiah - Seaman - Number: 1946 - How taken: Gave himself up from HM Ship-of-the-Line Leyden - Date received: 15 Jul 1813 - From what ship: Plymouth - Born: Philadelphia - Age: 44 - Discharged on 17 Jun 1814 and sent to Dartmoor on HMS Redbreast.

Strand, Peter - Seaman - Number: 3954 - How taken: Gave himself up from HM Sloop Indian - When taken: 20 Aug 1814 - Date received: 21 Oct 1813 - From what ship: HMS Namur - Born: Long Island - Age: 28 - Race: Black - Discharged on 22 Oct 1814 and sent to Dartmoor on HMS Leyden.

Strayer, George L. - Seaman - Number: 3912 - Prize name: Sister - Ship type: MV - How taken: HM Frigate Unicorn - When taken: 3 Jul 1814 - Where taken: off Christian Land - Date received: 9 Sep 1814 - From what ship: HMS Namur - Born: Philadelphia - Age: 28 - Discharged on 22 Oct 1814 and sent to Dartmoor on HMS Leyden.

Stretton, Samuel - Seaman - Number: 2754 - Prize name: Globe - Ship type: P - How taken: HM Frigate Spartan - When taken: 13 Jun 1813 - Where taken: off Delaware - Date received: 7 Jan 1814 - From what ship: Halifax - Born: Norfolk - Age: 27 - Discharged on 25 Sep 1814 and sent to Dartmoor on HMS Leyden.

Strong, William - Seaman - Number: 1137 - Prize name: Sword Fish - Ship type: P - How taken: HM Ship-of-the-Line Elephant - When taken: 28 Dec 1812 - Where taken: off Azores - Date received: 16 Mar 1813 - From what ship: Portsmouth, Mundane - Born: Marblehead - Age: 22 - Discharged on 24 Jul 1813 and released to Cartel Hoffminy.

Strong, William - Seaman - Number: 2063 - Prize name: Sword Fish - Ship type: P - How taken: HM Ship-of-the-Line Elephant - When taken: 28 Dec 1812 - Where taken: off Azores - Date received: 2 Aug 1813 - From what ship: Cartel Hoffminy - Born: Marblehead - Age: 22 - Discharged on 22 Oct 1814 and sent to Dartmoor on HMS Leyden.

Strordvant, David - Seaman - Number: 1748 - How taken: Taken up at London - When taken: 21 May 1813 - Date received: 28 May 1813 - From what ship: HMS Raisonnable - Born: Summer, MA - Age: 23 - Discharged on 24 Jul 1814 and sent to Dartmoor on HMS Liffey.

Stroud, John - Private - Number: 3095 - Prize name: 14th U.S. Infantry - Ship type: LF - How taken: British forces - When taken: 24 Jun 1813 - Where taken: Beaver Dams, Upper Canada - Date received: 7 Jan 1814 - From what ship: Halifax - Born: Massachusetts - Age: 35 - Discharged on 10 Oct 1814 and sent to U.S. on Cartel St. Philip.

Sturges, John - Seaman - Number: 1724 - Prize name: Powhattan - Ship type: MV - How taken: HMS Horatio - When taken: 13 Dec 1812 - Where taken: Bay of Biscay - Date received: 25 May 1813 - From what ship: Portsmouth via HMS Impetius - Born: Baltimore - Age: 34 - Discharged on 24 Jul 1813 and released to Cartel Hoffminy.

Sultan, John - Seaman - Number: 215 - How taken: Gave himself up from Triton at Gravesend - When taken: 29 Sep 1812 - Date received: 15 Nov 1812 - From what ship: HMS Raisonnable - Born: Boston - Age: 34 - Discharged in Jul 1813 and released to Cartel Moses Brown.

Sumerg, Benjamin - Seaman - Number: 3330 - Prize name: Porcupine - Ship type: LM - How taken: HM Frigate Acasta - When taken: 18 Jul 1813 - Where taken: off Cape Sable, Florida - Date received: 23 Feb 1814 - From what ship: Halifax via HMT Malabar - Born: New Haven - Age: 33 - Race: Black - Discharged on 10 Oct 1814 and sent to Dartmoor on the Mermaid.

Sunonton, John - Seaman - Number: 151 - Prize name: Country Square - Ship type: MV - How taken: Stopped at London - When taken: 28 Oct 1812 - Date received: 5 Nov 1812 - From what ship: HMS Namur - Born: Cape Elizabeth - Age: 23 - Discharged in Jul 1813 and released to Cartel Moses Brown.

Sutton, John - Seaman - Number: 3201 - How taken: Gave himself up from HM Transport Leopard - When taken: 25 Dec 1813 - Date received: 7 Jan 1813 - From what ship: Portsmouth - Born: Washington - Age: 39 - Discharged on 11 Aug 1814 and sent to Dartmoor on HMS Freya.

Sutton, John - Seaman - Number: 1871 - Prize name: Tiger - Ship type: MV - How taken: HM Brig Scylla - When taken: 22 Mar 1813 - Where taken: Bay of Biscay - Date received: 7 Jul 1813 - From what ship: Portsmouth via HMS Tribune - Born: Nantucket - Age: 26 - Discharged on 4 Aug 1814 and sent to Dartmoor on HMS Liverpool.

Sutton, Prince - Seaman - Number: 1377 - How taken: Gave himself up from HM Ship of-the-Line Bellerophon - When taken: 18 Mar 1813 - Date received: 3 Apr 1813 - From what ship: Portsmouth, via an admiral's tender - Born: Rhode Island - Age: 45 - Race: Mulatto - Discharged on 24 Jul 1814 and sent to Dartmoor.

Swain, David - 1st Mate - Number: 2677 - Prize name: Walker - Ship type: MV - How taken: HM Brig Nimrod - When taken: 29 Mar 1813 - Where taken: Pacific Ocean - Date received: 2 Dec 1813 - From what ship: HMS Raisonnable - Born: Nantucket - Age: 27 - Discharged on 8 Sep 1814 and sent to Dartmoor on HMS Niobe.

Swain, James - Seaman - Number: 2315 - Prize name: Fame - Ship type: MV - How taken: HM Ship of-the-Line Cressy - When taken: 20 Jul 1813 - Where taken: at sea - Date received: 8 Oct 1813 - From what ship: Portsmouth, via an admiral's tender - Born: Nantucket - Age: 49 - Discharged on 4 Sep 1814 and sent to Dartmoor on HMS Freya.

Swain, Obadiah - Seaman - Number: 3864 - Prize name: William Penn - Ship type: MV - How taken: HM Sloop Acorn - When taken: 27 Oct 1812 - Where taken: Lat 14 - Date received: 24 Aug 1814 - From what ship: London - Born: Nantucket - Age: 21 - Discharged on 29 Sep 1814 and sent to Dartmoor on HMS Freya.

Swain, Thomas - Prize Master - Number: 1248 - Prize name: Industry - Ship type: MV - How taken: HM Frigate Dryand - When taken: 7 Jan 1813 - Where taken: at sea - Date received: 16 Mar 1813 - From what ship: Portsmouth, via HMS Abundance - Born: Newburyport - Age: 29 - Discharged on 2 Jul 1813 and released to Cartel Moses Brown.

Swanston, Jacob - Seaman - Number: 1478 - Prize name: Union - Ship type: MV - How taken: HM Frigate Iris - When taken: 17 Jan 1813 - Where taken: at sea - Date received: 6 Apr 1813 - From what ship: Portsmouth via Tender Eliza - Born: Christiana - Age: 29 - Discharged on 26 Jul 1813 and released to Cartel Hoffminy.

Swanton, John - Seaman - Number: 1031 - Prize name: Phillipsburg - Ship type: MV - How taken: Taken up at Liverpool - When taken: 9 Nov 1812 - Date received: 11 Mar 1813 - From what ship: Yarmouth via HMS Tenders - Born: Pennsylvania - Age: 24 - Discharged in Jul 1813 and released to Cartel Moses Brown.

Swasey, Alexander - Mate - Number: 322 - Prize name: Catherine Charlotte - Ship type: MV - How taken: Thracian - When taken: 16 Dec 1812 - Where taken: off Norway - Date received: 5 Jan 1813 - From what ship: HMS Sheldrake - Born: Somerset - Age: 27 - Discharged in Jul 1813 and released to Cartel Moses Brown.

Swatwood, Jacob - Private - Number: 3068 - Prize name: 14th U.S. Infantry - Ship type: LF - How taken: British forces - When taken: 24 Jun 1813 - Where taken: Beaver Dams, Upper Canada - Date received: 7 Jan 1814 - From what ship: Halifax - Born: Jersey - Age: 25 - Discharged on 19 Jan 1814 and released to HMS Ceres.

Sweet, Moses - Seaman - Number: 526 - Prize name: Diamond - Ship type: MV - How taken: Detained at Bermuda - When taken: 17 Sep 1812 - Date received: 23 Feb 1813 - From what ship: Portsmouth via HMS Dromedary - Born: Falmouth, MA - Age: 21 - Discharged on 23 Mar 1813 and released to the Cartel Robinson Potter.

Sweetman, Samuel - Seaman - Number: 1454 - Prize name: Orbit - Ship type: MV - How taken: HM Brig Achates - When taken: 29 Jan 1813 - Where taken: Lat 49 N Long 13 W - Date received: 6 Apr 1813 - From what ship: Plymouth via HMS Decoy - Born: New York - Age: 25 - Discharged on 24 Jul 1814 and sent to Dartmoor.

Swett, Francis - Seaman - Number: 888 - Prize name: Print of Boston - Ship type: MV - How taken: HM Ship-of-the-Line Colossus - When taken: 21 Jan 1813 - Where taken: at sea - Date received: 1 Mar 1813 - From what ship: Plymouth via HMS Namur - Born: Marblehead, MA - Age: 24 - Discharged on 17 Jun 1814 and sent to Dartmoor on HMS Redbreast.

Swier, Louis - Seaman - Number: 1732 - Prize name: Powhattan - Ship type: MV - How taken: HMS Horatio - When taken: 13 Dec 1812 - Where taken: Bay of Biscay - Date received: 25 May 1813 - From what ship: Portsmouth via HMS Impetius - Born: Blays, France - Age: 27 - Discharged on 24 Jul 1813 and released to Cartel Hoffminy.

Swinny, Edward - Seaman - Number: 1392 - Prize name: Blue Bird - Ship type: MV - How taken: HM Frigate Briton - When taken: 1 Jan 1813 - Where taken: off Bordeaux, France - Date received: 5 Apr 1813 - From what ship: Plymouth via HMS Dwarf - Born: Maryland - Age: 21 - Discharged on 24 Jul 1813 and released to Cartel Hoffminy.

Swise, Carl - Seaman - Number: 2224 - Prize name: Hiram - Ship type: MV - How taken: HM Frigate Tenedos - When taken: 29 Jun 1813 - Where taken: coast of America - Date received: 22 Aug 1813 - From what ship: HMS Raisonnable - Born: Stettin, Prussia - Age: 40 - Released on 9 Feb 1814.

Syder, John - Seaman - Number: 1725 - Prize name: Powhattan - Ship type: MV - How taken: HMS Horatio - When taken: 13 Dec 1812 - Where taken: Bay of Biscay - Date received: 25 May 1813 - From what ship: Portsmouth via HMS Impetius - Born: Baltimore - Age: 32 - Discharged on 24 Jul 1813 and released to Cartel Hoffminy.

Symonds, Israel - Seaman - Number: 892 - Prize name: Print of Boston - Ship type: MV - How taken: HM Ship-of-the-Line Colossus - When taken: 21 Jan 1813 - Where taken: at sea - Date received: 1 Mar 1813 - From what ship: Plymouth via HMS Namur - Born: Ipswich, MA - Age: 21 - Discharged on 17 Jun 1814 and sent to Dartmoor on HMS Redbreast.

Syphon, Lewis - Seaman - Number: 3616 - Prize name: Liberty - Ship type: MV - How taken: Surrendered at Stromness, Scotland - When taken: 30 Dec 1813 - Date received: 29 Mar 1814 - From what ship: Hired tender Anna - Born: Glastonbury - Age: 16 - Race: Black - Discharged on 25 Sep 1814 and sent to Dartmoor on HMS Leyden.

Tafe, Henry - Seaman - Number: 1104 - Prize name: Calcutta, East Indian Ship - Ship type: MV - How taken: Two Brothers, British privateer from Guernsey - When taken: 30 Nov 1812 - Where taken: off St. Helena - Date received: 14 Mar 1813 - From what ship: Portsmouth via HMS Beagle - Born: Long Island - Age: 38 - Race: Mulatto - Discharged on 8 Jun 1813 and released to Cartel Rodrigo.

Taggart, Archibald - Private - Number: 3080 - Prize name: 14th U.S. Infantry - Ship type: LF - How taken: British forces - When taken: 24 Jun 1813 - Where taken: Beaver Dams, Upper Canada - Date received: 7 Jan 1814 - From what ship: Halifax - Born: Pennsylvania - Age: 37 - Discharged on 10 Oct 1814 and sent to U.S. on Cartel St. Philip.

Taggart, John - Seaman - Number: 271 - How taken: Gave himself up from HM Frigate Inconstant - When taken: 1 Dec 1812 - Date received: 19 Dec 1812 - From what ship: HMS Raisonnable - Born: Philadelphia - Age: 25 - Discharged on 25 Jul 1814 and sent to Dartmoor on HMS Bittern.

Taggart, Thomas - Private - Number: 2630 - Prize name: 14th U.S. Infantry - Ship type: LF - How taken: British forces - When taken: 24 Jun 1813 - Where taken: Beaver Dams, Upper Canada - Date received: 5 Nov 1813 - From what ship: HMS Hindostan - Born: County Antrim, Ireland - Age: 28 - Discharged on 10 Oct 1814 and sent to U.S. on Cartel St. Philip.

Tagle, Amos - Seaman - Number: 657 - Prize name: U.S.R.M. Cutter James Madison - Ship type: War - How taken: HM Frigate Barbadoes - When taken: 22 Aug 1812 - Where taken: at sea - Date received: 24 Feb 1813 - From what ship: Portsmouth via HMS Ulysses - Born: Gilmanton, NH - Age: 24 - Discharged on 10 May 1813 and released to Cartel Admittance.

Tahyor, Ebenezer - Seaman - Number: 1673 - How taken: Gave himself up from HM Ship-of-the-Line Gloucester - When taken: 26 Dec 1812 - Date received: 9 May 1813 - From what ship: HMS Raisonnable - Born: Boston - Age: 21 - Discharged on 20 Aug 1814 and sent to Dartmoor on HMS Shamrock.

Tamblen, John - Seaman - Number: 3821 - Prize name: Viper - Ship type: P - How taken: HM Frigate Brilliant - When taken: 25 Dec 1813 - Where taken: Hole in the Wall, England - Date received: 23 Jun 1814 - From what ship: Quebec - Born: Salem - Age: 45 - Race: Mulatto - Discharged on 20 Aug 1814 and sent to Dartmoor on HMS Shamrock.

Tanner, John - Seaman - Number: 559 - Prize name: Felix - Ship type: MV - How taken: HM Frigate Indefatigable - When taken: 13 Nov 1812 - Where taken: Portsmouth harbor - Date received: 23 Feb 1813 - From what ship: Portsmouth via HMS Dromedary - Born: New York - Age: 22 - Discharged on 8 Jun 1813 and released to Cartel Rodrigo.

Tapley, Isaac - Seaman - Number: 3335 - Prize name: Porcupine - Ship type: LM - How taken: HM Frigate Acasta - When taken: 18 Jul 1813 - Where taken: off Cape Sable, Florida - Date received: 23 Feb 1814 - From what ship: Halifax via HMT Malabar - Born: Cambridge - Age: 16 - Discharged on 10 Oct 1814 and sent to Dartmoor on the Mermaid.

Tardy, Anthony - Mate - Number: 2895 - Prize name: Dart - Ship type: P - How taken: HM Frigate Niger & HMS Fortunee - When taken: 10 Nov 1813 - Where taken: off Cape Finisterre, Spain - Date received: 7 Jan 1814 - From what ship: Portsmouth - Born: New York - Age: 22 - Died on 27 Mar 1814 from fever.

Tardy, Edward - Seaman - Number: 2894 - Prize name: Dart - Ship type: P - How taken: HM Frigate Niger & HMS Fortunee - When taken: 10 Nov 1813 - Where taken: off Cape Finisterre, Spain - Date received: 7 Jan 1814 - From what ship: Portsmouth - Born: New York - Age: 16 - Released on 6 Aug 1814.

Tarlton, George - Seaman - Number: 2829 - Prize name: Portsmouth Packet - Ship type: P - How taken: HM Brig Fantome - When taken: 5 Oct 1813 - Where taken: off Portland - Date received: 7 Jan 1814 - From what ship: Halifax - Born: Hampshire - Age: 23 - Discharged on 26 Sep 1814 and sent to Dartmoor on HMS Leyden.

Tarlton, John - Seaman - Number: 2491 - Prize name: Governor Plumer - Ship type: P - How taken: Sent into custody from a privateer - When taken: 1 Jun 1813 - Where taken: off Cape Ann - Date received: 22 Oct 1813 - From what ship: Portsmouth via HMT Malabar - Born: New Castle - Age: 29 - Discharged on 8 Sep 1814 and sent to Dartmoor on HMS Niobe.

Tarlton, Thomas P. - Seaman - Number: 1360 - Prize name: Dart - Ship type: MV - How taken: HM Brig Doterel - When taken: 5 Mar 1813 - Where taken: at sea - Date received: 3 Apr 1813 - From what ship: Portsmouth, via an admiral's tender - Born: Greenland - Age: 21 - Discharged on 4 Aug 1814 and sent to Dartmoor on HMS Alpheus.

Tarr, Caleb - Seaman - Number: 2852 - Prize name: Fire Fly - Ship type: LM - How taken: HM Frigate Revolutionnaire - When taken: 19 Oct 1813 - Where taken: off Cape Ortegal, Spain - Date received: 7 Jan 1814 - From what ship: Portsmouth - Born: Massachusetts - Age: 29 - Discharged on 25 Sep 1814 and sent to Dartmoor on HMS Leyden.

Tarr, James - Seaman - Number: 3921 - How taken: Gave himself up from MV John at Chatham - When taken: 22 Sep 1814 - Date received: 22 Sep 1814 - From what ship: London - Born: Virginia - Age: 22 - Discharged on 29 Sep 1814 and sent to Dartmoor on HMS Freya.

Tatem, George W. - 1st Lieutenant - Number: 3784 - Prize name: Adaline - Ship type: LM - How taken: HM Frigate Magiciene - When taken: 14 Mar 1814 - Where taken: off Cape Ortegal, Spain - Date received: 26 May 1814 - From what ship: HMS Hindostan - Born: Philadelphia - Age: 26 - Released from Chatham on 27 Jun 1814 and sent to Ashburton on parole.

Taugherty, M. - Private - Number: 2640 - Prize name: 14th U.S. Infantry - Ship type: LF - How taken: British forces - When taken: 24 Jun 1813 - Where taken: Beaver Dams, Upper Canada - Date received: 5 Nov 1813 - From what ship: HMS Hindostan - Born: County Mayo, Ireland - Age: 35 - Discharged on 10 Oct 1814 and sent to U.S. on Cartel St. Philip.

Taylor, George - Seaman - Number: 3522 - Prize name: Pilot - Ship type: LM - How taken: Vittoria, British privateer from Guernsey - When taken: 28 Jan 1814 - Where taken: off Bordeaux, France - Date received: 23 Feb 1814 - From what ship: Portsmouth via HMT Malabar - Born: Rhode Island - Age: 26 - Race: Black - Discharged on 26 Sep 1814 and sent to Dartmoor on HMS Leyden.

Taylor, Godfrey - Seaman - Number: 1331 - Prize name: Sea Nymph - Ship type: MV - How taken: HM Brig Thrasher - When taken: 4 Mar 1813 - Where taken: off River Jade (Germany) - Date received: 22 Mar 1813 - From what ship: HMS Thrasher - Born: Cobourg - Age: 40 - Released on 20 Jul 1813.

Taylor, James - Mate - Number: 319 - Prize name: Amphion - Ship type: MV - How taken: Thracian - When taken: 16 Dec 1812 - Where taken: off Norway - Date received: 5 Jan 1813 - From what ship: HMS Sheldrake - Born: New York - Age: 32 - Discharged in Jul 1813 and released to Cartel Moses Brown.

Taylor, James - Seaman - Number: 1845 - How taken: Given up from HM Frigate Hyperion - Date received: 7 Jul 1813 - From what ship: Portsmouth via HMS Tribune - Born: Philadelphia - Age: 27 - Discharged on 25 Jul 1814 and sent to Dartmoor on HMS Bittern.

Taylor, John - Seaman - Number: 835 - Prize name: Vengeance - Ship type: LM - How taken: HM Frigate Phoebe - When taken: 1 Jan 1813 - Where taken: Lat 44.4 Long 23 - Date received: 1 Mar 1813 - From what ship: Plymouth via HMS Namur - Born: Africa - Age: 30 - Race: Blackman - Discharged on 24 Jul 1813 and released to Cartel Hoffminy.

Taylor, Joseph - Seaman - Number: 2203 - How taken: Gave himself up from HM Ship-of-the-Line Fame - When taken: 31 Dec 1812 - Date received: 18 Aug 1813 - From what ship: Portsmouth, via an admiral's tender - Born: Philadelphia - Age: 24 - Discharged on 11 Aug 1814 and sent to Dartmoor on HMS Freya.

Taylor, Peter - Seaman - Number: 1823 - Prize name: tender to the Privateer True Blooded Yankee - Ship type: P - How taken: HM Brig Hope - When taken: 24 Jun 1813 - Where taken: off Brest, France - Date received: 7 Jul 1813 - From what ship: Portsmouth via HMS Scorpion - Born: New York - Age: 22 - Discharged on 25 Jul 1814 and sent to Dartmoor on HMS Bittern.

Taylor, Thomas - Seaman - Number: 2301 - Prize name: Volante - Ship type: P - How taken: HM Brig Curlew - When taken: 28 Mar 1813 - Where taken: coast of America - Date received: 29 Sep 1813 - From what ship: HMS Raisonnable - Born: New York - Age: 21 - Discharged on 4 Sep 1814 and sent to Dartmoor on HMS Freya.

Taylor, William - Seaman - Number: 1086 - Prize name: Benjamin - Ship type: MV - How taken: HM Frigate Medusa - When taken: 31 Dec 1812 - Where taken: at sea - Date received: 14 Mar 1813 - From what ship: Portsmouth via HMS Cornwell - Born: Billica - Age: 21 - Discharged on 24 Jul 1813 and released to Cartel Hoffminy.

Taylor, William - Seaman - Number: 2595 - How taken: Gave himself up from HM Frigate Bombay - When taken: 27 May 1813 - Date received: 5 Nov 1813 - From what ship: HMS Hindostan - Born: Long Island - Age: 34 - Discharged on 12 Aug 1814 and sent to Dartmoor on HMS Alpheus.

Tedrick, Joseph - Seaman - Number: 497 - Prize name: Nancy - Ship type: MV - How taken: HM Brig Parthian - When taken: 1 Aug 1812 - Where taken: off the Needles, Isle of Wight - Date received: 23 Feb 1813 - From what ship: Portsmouth via HMS Dromedary - Born: Marblehead - Age: 27 - Discharged on 17 Nov 1813 to the Cartel Robinson Potter.

Teilman, John - Seaman - Number: 3805 - Prize name: James - Ship type: MV - How taken: HM Brig Harpy - When taken: 13 Dec 1812 - Where taken: off Isle de France (Mauritius) - Date received: 5 Jun 1814 - From what ship: HMS Raisonnable - Born: Boston - Age: 26 - Discharged on 29 Sep 1814 and sent to Dartmoor on HMS Freya.

Tellebrown, William - Seaman - Number: 1007 - How taken: Gave himself up from HM Frigate Ceres - When taken: 20 Dec 1812 - Date received: 10 Mar 1813 - From what ship: HMS Furious - Born: Boston - Age: 25 - Discharged on 4 Aug 1814 and sent to Dartmoor on HMS Liverpool.

Telley, Edward - Seaman - Number: 2328 - How taken: Impressed at Gravesend, England - When taken: 7 Jul 1813 - Date received: 12 Oct 1813 - From what ship: HMS Raisonnable - Born: New London - Age: 21 - Discharged on 14 Dec 1813 and released to HMS Ceres.

Terry, Joseph - Seaman - Number: 3345 - Prize name: Porcupine - Ship type: LM - How taken: HM Frigate Acasta - When taken: 18 Jul 1813 - Where taken: off Cape Sable, Florida - Date received: 23 Feb 1814 - From what ship: Halifax via HMT Malabar - Born: Dorchester - Age: 18 - Discharged on 10 Oct 1814 and sent to Dartmoor on the Mermaid.

Tethery, Robert - Seaman - Number: 2935 - Prize name: Governor Plumer - Ship type: P - How taken: HM Brig Shamrock - When taken: 26 May 1813 - Where taken: at sea - Date received: 7 Jan 1814 - From what ship: Halifax - Born: Massachusetts - Age: 22 - Discharged on 25 Sep 1814 and sent to Dartmoor on HMS Leyden.

Thaley, Abraham - Seaman - Number: 2354 - How taken: Gave himself up from HM Ship-of-the-Line Hibernia - When taken: 25 Jun 1813 - Date received: 20 Oct 1813 - From what ship: Portsmouth, via an admiral's tender - Born: New York - Age: 32 - Race: Black - Discharged on 4 Sep 1814 and sent to Dartmoor on HMS Freya.

Thatcher, Samuel G. - Seaman - Number: 185 - Prize name: Calaban - Ship type: MV - How taken: HM Battery Gorgon - When taken: 12 Aug 1812 - Where taken: Great Belt, Denmark - Date received: 5 Nov 1812 - From what ship: HMS Namur - Born: Massachusetts - Age: 22 - Discharged on 10 May 1813 and released to Cartel Admittance.

Thayer, James - Seaman - Number: 2562 - How taken: Gave himself up from HM Battery Gorgon - When taken: 1 Nov 1812 - Date received: 23 Oct 1813 - From what ship: Portsmouth via HMS Raisonnable - Born: Massachusetts - Age: 23 - Discharged on 8 Sep 1814 and sent to Dartmoor on HMS Niobe.

Thayer, Laban - Prize Master - Number: 3503 - Prize name: Elbridge Gerry - Ship type: P - How taken: HM Frigate Crescent - When taken: 16 Sep 1813 - Where taken: at sea - Date received: 23 Feb 1814 - From what ship: Portsmouth via HMT Malabar - Born: Taunton - Age: 30 - Discharged on 22 Oct 1814 and sent to Dartmoor on HMS Leyden.

Thimonier, Peter - Seaman - Number: 206 - How taken: Gave himself up from HM Ship of the Line Adamant - When taken: 11 Oct 1812 - Date received: 15 Nov 1812 - From what ship: HMS Raisonnable - Born: New

Orleans - Age: 25 - Discharged on 26 Jul 1814 and sent to Dartmoor on HMS Raven.

Thinney, Alvin - Seaman - Number: 3757 - Prize name: Argus - Ship type: MV - How taken: HM Ship-of-the-Line San Domingo - When taken: 1 Mar 1814 - Where taken: off Savannah - Date received: 26 May 1814 - From what ship: HMS Hindostan - Born: Barnstable - Age: 20 - Discharged on 25 Sep 1814 and sent to Dartmoor on HMS Niobe.

Thistlewood, Charles - Private - Number: 3136 - Prize name: 14th U.S. Infantry - Ship type: LF - How taken: British forces - When taken: 24 Jun 1813 - Where taken: Beaver Dams, Upper Canada - Date received: 7 Jan 1814 - From what ship: Halifax - Born: Delaware - Age: 24 - Discharged on 10 Oct 1814 and sent to U.S. on Cartel St. Philip.

Thomas, Alexander - Seaman - Number: 1547 - Prize name: Hunter - Ship type: P - How taken: HM Frigate Phoebe - When taken: 23 Dec 1812 - Where taken: off Azores - Date received: 8 Apr 1813 - From what ship: Plymouth via HMS Olympia - Born: Portland - Age: 30 - Discharged on 19 May 1813 and released to HMS Ceres.

Thomas, Charles - Seaman - Number: 1528 - How taken: Gave himself up from HM Frigate Franchise - When taken: 20 Sep 1812 - Date received: 8 Apr 1813 - From what ship: Portsmouth, via an admiral's tender - Born: Boston - Age: 24 - Discharged on 4 Aug 1814 and sent to Dartmoor on HMS Alpheus.

Thomas, Charles - Steward - Number: 1936 - Prize name: Tickler of Nantes - Ship type: MV - How taken: HM Frigate Magiciene - When taken: 5 Jun 1813 - Where taken: Bay of Biscay - Date received: 11 Jul 1813 - From what ship: HMS Raisonnable - Born: Philadelphia - Age: 37 - Race: Black - Discharged on 29 Sep 1814 and sent to Dartmoor on HMS Freya.

Thomas, Elisha - Seaman - Number: 2840 - Prize name: Portsmouth Packet - Ship type: P - How taken: HM Brig Fantome - When taken: 5 Oct 1813 - Where taken: off Portland - Date received: 7 Jan 1814 - From what ship: Halifax - Born: Newmarket - Age: 21 - Discharged on 25 Sep 1814 and sent to Dartmoor on HMS Leyden.

Thomas, Francis - Seaman - Number: 1376 - How taken: Gave himself up from HM Ship of-the-Line Bellerophon - When taken: 18 Mar 1813 - Date received: 3 Apr 1813 - From what ship: Portsmouth, via an admiral's tender - Born: Salem - Age: 32 - Race: Black - Discharged on 24 Jul 1814 and sent to Dartmoor.

Thomas, George - Seaman - Number: 458 - Prize name: Hunter - Ship type: P - How taken: HM Frigate Phoebe - When taken: 23 Dec 1812 - Where taken: off Azores - Date received: 19 Feb 1813 - From what ship: HMS Modeste - Born: Georgetown - Age: 24 - Race: Black - Discharged on 24 Jul 1813 and released to Cartel Hoffminy.

Thomas, Henry - Seaman - Number: 1564 - Prize name: Dolphin - Ship type: LM - How taken: HM Ship-of-the-Line Colossus - When taken: 5 Jan 1813 - Where taken: off the Western Isles, Scotland - Date received: 8 Apr 1813 - From what ship: Plymouth via HMS Olympia - Born: Baltimore - Age: 25 - Race: Negro - Discharged on 18 Oct 1813 and released to HMS Ceres.

Thomas, Henry - Seaman - Number: 1343 - How taken: Gave himself up from HM Ship-of-the-Line Cornwall - When taken: 21 Mar 1813 - Date received: 26 Mar 1813 - From what ship: HMS Raisonnable - Born: Blockley - Age: 21 - Race: Blackman - Discharged on 25 Jul 1814 and sent to Dartmoor on HMS Bittern.

Thomas, James - Seaman - Number: 3500 - How taken: Gave himself up from HM Ship-of-the-Line Bulwark - Date received: 23 Feb 1814 - From what ship: Portsmouth via HMT Malabar - Born: Salem - Age: 23 - Race: Black - Discharged on 25 Sep 1814 and sent to Dartmoor on HMS Leyden.

Thomas, John - Seaman - Number: 3546 - Prize name: Pilot - Ship type: LM - How taken: Vittoria, British privateer from Guernsey - When taken: 28 Jan 1814 - Where taken: off Bordeaux, France - Date received: 7 May 1814 - From what ship: Portsmouth via HMS Favorite - Born: Long Island - Age: 22 - Race: Black - Discharged on 26 Sep 1814 and sent to Dartmoor on HMS Leyden.

Thomas, John - Steward - Number: 3516 - Prize name: Pilot - Ship type: LM - How taken: Vittoria, British privateer from Guernsey - When taken: 28 Jan 1814 - Where taken: off Bordeaux, France - Date received: 23 Feb 1814 - From what ship: Portsmouth via HMT Malabar - Born: Maryland - Age: 29 - Race: Black - Discharged on 25 Sep 1814 and sent to Dartmoor on HMS Niobe.

Thomas, John - Cook - Number: 1212 - Prize name: Expectation - Ship type: MV - How taken: HM Frigate Briton - When taken: 17 Dec 1812 - Where taken: at sea - Date received: 16 Mar 1813 - From what ship: Portsmouth, via HMS Abundance - Born: Boston - Age: 26 - Race: Black - Discharged on 2 Jul 1813 and released to Cartel Moses Brown.

Thomas, John - Boy - Number: 3293 - Prize name: Montgomery - Ship type: P - How taken: HM Frigate Nymphe - When taken: 5 May 1813 - Where taken: off Cape Cod - Date received: 23 Feb 1814 - From what ship: Halifax via HMT Malabar - Born: Boston - Age: 19 - Race: Black - Discharged on 10 Oct 1814 and sent to Dartmoor on the Mermaid.

Thomas, John - Seaman - Number: 2280 - How taken: Impressed at London - When taken: 3 Sep 1813 - Date received: 17 Sep 1813 - From what ship: HMS Raisonnable - Born: Long Island - Age: 30 - Race: Black - Discharged on 24 Nov 1813 and released to HMS Ceres.

Thomas, John - Seaman - Number: 3359 - Prize name: York - Ship type: MV - How taken: HM Frigate Tenedos - When taken: 26 May 1813 - Where taken: off Cape Sable, Florida - Date received: 23 Feb 1814 - From what ship: Halifax via HMT Malabar - Born: Charleston - Age: 18 - Discharged on 11 Mar 1814 and released to HMS Thames.

Thomas, John (1) - Seaman - Number: 2089 - How taken: Gave himself up from HM Ship-of-the-Line Scipion - When taken: 27 May 1813 - Date received: 9 Aug 1813 - From what ship: HMS Thames - Born: Bristol, PA - Age: 26 - Discharged on 12 Aug 1814 and sent to Dartmoor on HMS Alpheus.

Thomas, John (2) - Seaman - Number: 2090 - How taken: Gave himself up from HM Ship-of-the-Line Scipion - When taken: 27 May 1813 - Date received: 9 Aug 1813 - From what ship: HMS Thames - Born: New York - Age: 24 - Race: Black - Discharged on 12 Aug 1814 and sent to Dartmoor on HMS Alpheus.

Thomas, John L. - Seaman - Number: 957 - How taken: Gave himself up from HM Schooner Arrow - When taken: 4 Jan 1813 - Date received: 10 Mar 1813 - From what ship: HMS Tigress - Born: North Carolina - Age: 40 - Race: Black - Discharged on 14 May 1813 and released to HMS Ceres.

Thomas, John L. - Seaman - Number: 442 - Prize name: Hunter - Ship type: P - How taken: HM Frigate Phoebe - When taken: 23 Dec 1812 - Where taken: off Azores - Date received: 19 Feb 1813 - From what ship: HMS Modeste - Born: New Orleans - Age: 32 - Discharged on 2 Jul 1813 and released to Cartel Moses Brown.

Thomas, Moses - Seaman - Number: 2367 - How taken: Gave himself up from HM Ship-of-the-Line Swiftsure - When taken: 25 Jun 1813 - Date received: 20 Oct 1813 - From what ship: Portsmouth, via an admiral's tender - Born: Norfolk - Age: 21 - Race: Black - Discharged on 4 Sep 1814 and sent to Dartmoor on HMS Freya.

Thomas, Samuel - Private - Number: 3086 - Prize name: 14th U.S. Infantry - Ship type: LF - How taken: British forces - When taken: 15 Jun 1813 - Where taken: Canada - Date received: 7 Jan 1814 - From what ship: Halifax - Born: Jersey - Age: 22 - Discharged on 10 Oct 1814 and sent to U.S. on Cartel St. Philip.

Thomas, Spencer - Seaman - Number: 2251 - Prize name: Joseph - Ship type: MV - How taken: HM Frigate Iris - When taken: 8 Jun 1813 - Where taken: off Spain - Date received: 7 Sep 1813 - From what ship: HMS Raisonnable - Born: Gloucester - Age: 20 - Discharged on 11 Aug 1814 and sent to Dartmoor on HMS Freya.

Thomas, Terry - Seaman - Number: 274 - How taken: Apprehended at London - When taken: 10 Dec 1812 - Date received: 23 Dec 1812 - From what ship: HMS Raisonnable - Born: Talbot County, MD - Age: 31 - Discharged on 24 Jul 1813 and released to Cartel Hoffminy.

Thomas, Thomas - Seaman - Number: 1585 - How taken: Gave himself up from HM Ship of-the-Line Bellerophon - When taken: 7 Nov 1812 - Date received: 18 Apr 1813 - From what ship: HMS Rosario - Born: Long Island - Age: 32 - Race: Black - Discharged on 11 Apr 1814 and sent to Dartmoor.

Thomas, Thomas - Seaman - Number: 2603 - How taken: Gave himself up from HM Ship-of-the-Line Prince of Wales - When taken: 27 May 1813 - Date received: 5 Nov 1813 - From what ship: HMS Hindostan - Born: New York - Age: 23 - Race: Blackman - Discharged on 12 Aug 1814 and sent to Dartmoor on HMS Alpheus.

Thomas, William - Seaman - Number: 3530 - How taken: Impressed at London - When taken: 17 Jan 1814 - Date received: 5 Mar 1814 - From what ship: HMS Raisonnable - Born: Boston - Age: 30 - Race: Black -

Discharged on 22 Oct 1814 and sent to Dartmoor on HMS Leyden.

Thomas, William - Seaman - Number: 405 - Prize name: Hope - Ship type: MV - How taken: HM Schooner Bramble - When taken: 3 Dec 1812 - Where taken: Coruna, Spain - Date received: 19 Feb 1813 - From what ship: HMS Modeste - Born: New Orleans - Age: 32 - Race: Negro - Released on 10 Apr 1813.

Thomas, William - Seaman - Number: 1581 - How taken: Gave himself up from HM Ship-of-the-Line Colossus - When taken: 10 Dec 1812 - Date received: 16 Apr 1813 - From what ship: HMS Namur, admiral's tender - Born: Philadelphia - Age: 23 - Race: Black - Discharged on 24 Jul 1814 and sent to Dartmoor.

Thomas, William - Seaman - Number: 2200 - How taken: Gave himself up from HM Ship-of-the-Line Malta - When taken: 20 Oct 1812 - Date received: 18 Aug 1813 - From what ship: Portsmouth, via an admiral's tender - Born: North Carolina - Age: 26 - Discharged on 25 Sep 1814 and sent to Dartmoor on HMS Leyden.

Thomodice, John - Seaman - Number: 2281 - How taken: Impressed at London - When taken: 8 Sep 1813 - Date received: 17 Sep 1813 - From what ship: HMS Raisonnable - Born: New London - Age: 25 - Discharged on 4 Sep 1814 and sent to Dartmoor on HMS Freya.

Thompson, Courtney - Seaman - Number: 1448 - Prize name: Orbit - Ship type: MV - How taken: HM Brig Achates - When taken: 29 Jan 1813 - Where taken: Lat 49 N Long 13 W - Date received: 6 Apr 1813 - From what ship: Plymouth via HMS Decoy - Born: New York - Age: 19 - Discharged on 24 Jul 1814 and sent to Dartmoor.

Thompson, George - Cook - Number: 222 - How taken: Apprehended at London - When taken: 18 Nov 1812 - Date received: 25 Nov 1812 - From what ship: HMS Raisonnable - Born: Beverly, MA - Age: 30 - Race: Mulatto - Died on 21 Dec 1812 for ulcerated throat.

Thompson, George - Seaman - Number: 2358 - How taken: Gave himself up from HM Ship-of-the-Line Hibernia - When taken: 25 Jun 1813 - Date received: 20 Oct 1813 - From what ship: Portsmouth, via an admiral's tender - Born: New York - Age: 27 - Discharged on 4 Sep 1814 and sent to Dartmoor on HMS Freya.

Thompson, Henry - Seaman - Number: 352 - Prize name: Postsea, prize to the Privateer Thrasher - Ship type: P - How taken: HM Sloop Helena - When taken: 31 Dec 1813 - Where taken: off Azores - Date received: 19 Jan 1813 - From what ship: HMS Raisonnable - Born: Tunsbug, MD - Age: 27 - Discharged on 28 Apr 1813 and released to the David Scott.

Thompson, Isaac - Seaman - Number: 303 - Prize name: Cygnet - Ship type: MV - How taken: HM Brig Sarpedon - When taken: 12 Aug 1812 - Date received: 23 Dec 1812 - From what ship: Greenlaw Depot - Born: Pennsylvania - Age: 31 - Discharged on 10 May 1813 and released to Cartel Admittance.

Thompson, James - Seaman - Number: 1438 - Prize name: Orbit - Ship type: MV - How taken: HM Brig Achates - When taken: 29 Jan 1813 - Where taken: Lat 49 N Long 13 W - Date received: 6 Apr 1813 - From what ship: Plymouth via HMS Decoy - Born: Brooklyn - Age: 36 - Discharged on 24 Jul 1814 and sent to Dartmoor.

Thompson, James - Seaman - Number: 2171 - How taken: Gave himself up from HM Ship-of-the-Line Swiftsure - When taken: 26 Dec 1812 - Date received: 16 Aug 1813 - From what ship: Portsmouth, via an admiral's tender - Born: Hudson - Age: 32 - Discharged on 17 Jun 1814 and sent to Dartmoor on the Penebar.

Thompson, James - Seaman - Number: 3202 - How taken: Gave himself up from HM Transport Leopard - When taken: 25 Dec 1813 - Date received: 7 Jan 1813 - From what ship: Portsmouth - Born: Boston - Age: 34 - Escaped on 13 May 1814 from HM Prison Ship Crown Prince.

Thompson, James - Seaman - Number: 2112 - How taken: Gave himself up from HM Brig Shearwater - When taken: 27 May 1813 - Date received: 9 Aug 1813 - From what ship: HMS Thames - Born: Salem - Age: 36 - Discharged on 12 Aug 1814 and sent to Dartmoor on HMS Alpheus.

Thompson, John - Seaman - Number: 1222 - Prize name: Rossie - Ship type: MV - How taken: HM Frigate Dryand - When taken: 7 Jan 1813 - Where taken: at sea - Date received: 16 Mar 1813 - From what ship: Portsmouth, via HMS Abundance - Born: New Orleans - Age: 40 - Discharged on 24 Jul 1813 and released to Cartel Hoffminy.

Thompson, John - Seaman - Number: 950 - Prize name: Enterprise - Ship type: P - How taken: HM Sloop Hazard - When taken: 30 Sep 1812 - Where taken: at sea - Date received: 10 Mar 1813 - From what ship: HMS

Tigress - Born: Long Island - Age: 22 - Discharged on 8 Jun 1813 and released to Cartel Rodrigo.

Thompson, John - Seaman - Number: 2500 - Prize name: Porcupine - Ship type: LM - How taken: HM Frigate Acasta - When taken: 3 Jun 1813 - Where taken: off Cape Sable, Florida - Date received: 22 Oct 1813 - From what ship: Portsmouth via HMT Malabar - Born: Massachusetts - Age: 28 - Discharged on 8 Sep 1814 and sent to Dartmoor on HMS Niobe.

Thompson, John - Seaman - Number: 2966 - Prize name: Enterprise - Ship type: P - How taken: HM Frigate Tenedos - When taken: 21 May 1813 - Where taken: off Cape Cod - Date received: 7 Jan 1814 - From what ship: Halifax - Born: Massachusetts - Age: 22 - Discharged on 25 Sep 1814 and sent to Dartmoor on HMS Leyden.

Thompson, John - Seaman - Number: 2684 - Prize name: Dorset - Ship type: MV - How taken: Impressed at London - When taken: 31 Oct 1813 - Date received: 25 Dec 1813 - From what ship: HMS Raisonnable - Born: Virginia - Age: 24 - Discharged on 8 Sep 1814 and sent to Dartmoor on HMS Niobe.

Thompson, Joseph - Seaman - Number: 1194 - How taken: Gave himself up from HM Transport Romulus - When taken: 11 Aug 1812 - Date received: 16 Mar 1813 - From what ship: Portsmouth, via HMS Abundance - Born: Newcastle - Age: 28 - Discharged on 11 Aug 1814 and sent to Dartmoor on HMS Freya.

Thompson, Lamon - Seaman - Number: 64 - Prize name: Laurel - Ship type: MV - How taken: From a cutter off Bermuda - When taken: 24 Jul 1812 - Date received: 3 Nov 1812 - From what ship: HMS Plover - Born: Connecticut - Age: 18 - Discharged on 23 Mar 1813 and released to the Cartel Robinson Potter.

Thompson, Lawrence - Seaman - Number: 3699 - Prize name: Bunker Hill - Ship type: P - How taken: HM Frigate Pomone & HM Frigate Cydnus - When taken: 4 Mar 1814 - Where taken: Bay of Biscay - Date received: 4 May 1814 - From what ship: Portsmouth - Born: Sweden - Age: 25 - Discharged on 26 Sep 1814 and sent to Dartmoor on HMS Leyden.

Thompson, Michael - Seaman - Number: 3263 - Prize name: Volante - Ship type: P - How taken: HM Brig Curlew - When taken: 25 Mar 1813 - Where taken: off Boston - Date received: 23 Feb 1814 - From what ship: Halifax via HMT Malabar - Born: Abingdon - Age: 23 - Discharged on 10 Oct 1814 and sent to Dartmoor on the Mermaid.

Thompson, Nathaniel - Seaman - Number: 1892 - Prize name: Prompt - Ship type: MV - How taken: Chance, British privateer - When taken: 28 Mar 1813 - Where taken: Bay of Biscay - Date received: 7 Jul 1813 - From what ship: Portsmouth via HMS Tribune - Born: Virginia - Age: 31 - Discharged on 4 Aug 1814 and sent to Dartmoor on HMS Liverpool.

Thompson, Owen - Seaman - Number: 1393 - Prize name: Blue Bird - Ship type: MV - How taken: HM Frigate Briton - When taken: 1 Jan 1813 - Where taken: off Bordeaux, France - Date received: 5 Apr 1813 - From what ship: Plymouth via HMS Dwarf - Born: Little York - Age: 31 - Discharged on 24 Jul 1813 and released to Cartel Hoffminy.

Thompson, Robert - Seaman - Number: 2605 - How taken: Gave himself up from HM Ship-of-the-Line Aboukir - When taken: 27 May 1813 - Date received: 5 Nov 1813 - From what ship: HMS Hindostan - Born: Pennsylvania - Age: 25 - Discharged on 12 Aug 1814 and sent to Dartmoor on HMS Alpheus.

Thompson, Samuel - Seaman - Number: 1404 - Prize name: Porcupine - Ship type: MV - How taken: HM Frigate Dryand - When taken: 8 Jan 1813 - Where taken: off Bordeaux, France - Date received: 5 Apr 1813 - From what ship: Plymouth via HMS Dwarf - Born: New York - Age: 18 - Discharged on 24 Jul 1813 and released to Cartel Hoffminy.

Thompson, Thomas - Seaman - Number: 3422 - Prize name: Thomas - Ship type: P - How taken: HM Frigate Nymphe - When taken: 27 Jun 1813 - Where taken: at sea - Date received: 23 Feb 1814 - From what ship: Halifax via HMT Malabar - Born: Brooklyn - Age: 32 - Race: Black - Discharged on 22 Oct 1814 and sent to Dartmoor on HMS Leyden.

Thompson, William - Seaman - Number: 1589 - How taken: Gave himself up from HM Frigate Freya - When taken: 1 Nov 1812 - Date received: 18 Apr 1813 - From what ship: HMS Rosario - Born: Pittsfield - Age: 29 - Discharged on 11 Apr 1814 and sent to Dartmoor.

Thompson, William - Seaman - Number: 1477 - Prize name: Union - Ship type: MV - How taken: HM Frigate Iris -

When taken: 17 Jan 1813 - Where taken: at sea - Date received: 6 Apr 1813 - From what ship: Portsmouth via Tender Eliza - Born: New York - Age: 19 - Discharged on 26 Jul 1813 and released to Cartel Hoffminy.

Thompson, William - Seaman - Number: 1533 - How taken: Gave himself up from HM Frigate Franchise - When taken: 20 Sep 1812 - Date received: 8 Apr 1813 - From what ship: Portsmouth, via an admiral's tender - Born: Copenhagen - Age: 29 - Released on 14 Aug 1814.

Thompson, William - Cook - Number: 396 - Prize name: Dolphin - Ship type: MV - How taken: HM Ship-of-the-Line Invincible - When taken: 24 Aug 1812 - Where taken: Mediterranean - Date received: 13 Feb 1813 - From what ship: HMS Raisonnable - Born: New Orleans - Age: 26 - Race: Black man - Discharged on 8 Jun 1813 and released to Cartel Rodrigo.

Thompson, William - Seaman - Number: 3278 - Prize name: Cossack - Ship type: MV - How taken: HM Brig Curlew - When taken: 22 Apr 1813 - Where taken: Indian Island - Date received: 23 Feb 1814 - From what ship: Halifax via HMT Malabar - Born: Hancock - Age: 21 - Discharged on 10 Oct 1814 and sent to Dartmoor on the Mermaid.

Thorndike, Robert - Seaman - Number: 150 - Prize name: Country Square - Ship type: MV - How taken: Stopped at London - When taken: 28 Oct 1812 - Date received: 5 Nov 1812 - From what ship: HMS Namur - Born: Cape Elizabeth - Age: 27 - Discharged in Jul 1813 and released to Cartel Moses Brown.

Thornning, Thomas - Seaman - Number: 2724 - Prize name: U.S. Schooner Growler - Ship type: War - How taken: HM Schooner Lord Melvin - When taken: 11 Aug 1813 - Where taken: Lake Ontario - Date received: 7 Jan 1814 - From what ship: Portsmouth - Born: New York - Age: 19 - Discharged on 10 Oct 1814 and sent to U.S. on Cartel St. Philip.

Thornton, David - Seaman - Number: 2421 - Prize name: Sampson - Ship type: MV - How taken: HM Brig Rebuff - When taken: 12 May 1813 - Where taken: off Cape St. Vincent, Portugal - Date received: 21 Oct 1813 - From what ship: Portsmouth via HMT Malabar - Born: Virginia - Age: 24 - Discharged on 4 Sep 1814 and sent to Dartmoor on HMS Freya.

Thornton, John - Seaman - Number: 2972 - Prize name: Enterprise - Ship type: P - How taken: HM Frigate Tenedos - When taken: 21 May 1813 - Where taken: off Cape Cod - Date received: 7 Jan 1814 - From what ship: Halifax - Born: Massachusetts - Age: 19 - Discharged on 25 Sep 1814 and sent to Dartmoor on HMS Leyden.

Thrasher, John - Seaman - Number: 2749 - Prize name: Wasp - Ship type: P - How taken: HM Schooner Bream - When taken: 9 Jun 1813 - Where taken: off Halifax - Date received: 7 Jan 1814 - From what ship: Halifax - Born: Maryland - Age: 24 - Discharged on 8 Sep 1814 and sent to Dartmoor on HMS Niobe.

Thuel, Bristow - Seaman - Number: 2320 - Prize name: Fame - Ship type: MV - How taken: HM Ship of-the-Line Cressy - When taken: 20 Jul 1813 - Where taken: at sea - Date received: 8 Oct 1813 - From what ship: Portsmouth, via an admiral's tender - Born: Nantucket - Age: 38 - Discharged on 4 Sep 1814 and sent to Dartmoor on HMS Freya.

Ticham, Jeremiah - Seaman - Number: 284 - Prize name: Francis Ann - Ship type: MV - How taken: Apprehended at Leight, Scotland - When taken: 5 Aug 1812 - Date received: 23 Dec 1812 - From what ship: Greenlaw Depot - Born: Middleburg - Age: 22 - Discharged on 23 Mar 1813 and released to the Cartel Robinson Potter.

Tiffs, Joseph - Seaman - Number: 1909 - Prize name: Weasel - Ship type: MV - How taken: HM Brig Foxhound - When taken: 25 Mar 1813 - Where taken: Bay of Biscay - Date received: 7 Jul 1813 - From what ship: Portsmouth via HMS Tribune - Born: Gloucester - Age: 22 - Discharged on 4 Aug 1814 and sent to Dartmoor on HMS Liverpool.

Tightham, Peter - Carpenter - Number: 823 - Prize name: Columbia - Ship type: MV - How taken: HM Frigate Briton - When taken: 17 Dec 1812 - Where taken: off Bordeaux, France - Date received: 27 Feb 1813 - From what ship: Plymouth via HMS Namur - Born: Philadelphia - Age: 22 - Discharged in Jul 1813 and released to Cartel Moses Brown.

Tildon, Robert - Seaman - Number: 2967 - Prize name: Enterprise - Ship type: P - How taken: HM Frigate Tenedos - When taken: 21 May 1813 - Where taken: off Cape Cod - Date received: 7 Jan 1814 - From what ship:

Halifax - Born: Massachusetts - Age: 21 - Discharged on 25 Sep 1814 and sent to Dartmoor on HMS Leyden.

Tillman, John - Seaman - Number: 3547 - Prize name: Agnes, prize of the Privateer Rambler - Ship type: P - How taken: Jane, British privateer from London - When taken: 29 Nov 1813 - Where taken: Bay of Biscay - Date received: 7 May 1814 - From what ship: Portsmouth via HMS Favorite - Born: Boston - Age: 17 - Discharged on 20 Aug 1814 and sent to Dartmoor on HMS Shamrock.

Tink, Henry - Seaman - Number: 1327 - How taken: Gave himself up from HM Ship-of-the-Line Pembroke - When taken: 9 Feb 1812 - Date received: 16 Mar 1813 - From what ship: Portsmouth, via HMS Abundance - Born: Salem - Age: 23 - Discharged on 23 Jul 1814 and sent to Dartmoor.

Tinkham, John - Seaman - Number: 3410 - Prize name: Stark (General Stark) - Ship type: P - How taken: HM Frigate Maidstone - When taken: 15 Jul 1813 - Where taken: Halifax - Date received: 23 Feb 1814 - From what ship: Halifax via HMT Malabar - Born: Duxbury - Age: 21 - Discharged on 26 Sep 1814 and sent to Dartmoor on HMS Leyden.

Tinkham, Seth - 2nd Mate - Number: 711 - Prize name: Ganges - Ship type: MV - How taken: Detained at Portsmouth harbor - When taken: 31 Jul 1812 - Date received: 24 Feb 1813 - From what ship: Portsmouth via HMS Ulysses - Born: Wiscasset - Age: 23 - Discharged on 23 Mar 1813 and released to the Cartel Robinson Potter.

Tipp, Nicholas - Seaman - Number: 2903 - Prize name: Dart - Ship type: P - How taken: HM Frigate Niger & HMS Fortunee - When taken: 10 Nov 1813 - Where taken: off Cape Finisterre, Spain - Date received: 7 Jan 1814 - From what ship: Portsmouth - Born: New Orleans - Age: 19 - Discharged on 25 Sep 1814 and sent to Dartmoor on HMS Leyden.

Tippet, Joseph - Seaman - Number: 180 - How taken: Stopped at London - When taken: 27 Oct 1812 - Date received: 5 Nov 1812 - From what ship: HMS Namur - Born: New York - Age: 20 - Discharged in Jul 1813 and released to Cartel Moses Brown.

Tipton, Solomon - Seaman - Number: 1446 - Prize name: Orbit - Ship type: MV - How taken: HM Brig Achates - When taken: 29 Jan 1813 - Where taken: Lat 49 N Long 13 W - Date received: 6 Apr 1813 - From what ship: Plymouth via HMS Decoy - Born: Baltimore - Age: 53 - Discharged on 24 Jul 1814 and sent to Dartmoor.

Tishure, Samuel - Master's Mate - Number: 2704 - Prize name: Growler - Ship type: P - How taken: HM Brig Electra - When taken: 7 Jul 1813 - Where taken: off St. Johns - Date received: 7 Jan 1814 - From what ship: Portsmouth - Born: Marblehead - Age: 26 - Discharged on 8 Sep 1814 and sent to Dartmoor on HMS Leyden.

Todd, John - Private - Number: 2619 - Prize name: 14th U.S. Infantry - Ship type: LF - How taken: British forces - When taken: 24 Jun 1813 - Where taken: Beaver Dams, Upper Canada - Date received: 5 Nov 1813 - From what ship: HMS Hindostan - Born: Maryland - Age: 40 - Discharged on 10 Oct 1814 and sent to U.S. on Cartel St. Philip.

Todd, Samuel - Sailing Master - Number: 2759 - Prize name: Thomas - Ship type: P - How taken: HM Frigate Nymphe - When taken: 24 Jun 1813 - Where taken: off Halifax - Date received: 7 Jan 1814 - From what ship: Halifax - Born: Massachusetts - Age: 32 - Discharged on 8 Sep 1814 and sent to Dartmoor on HMS Niobe.

Todd, William - Seaman - Number: 869 - Prize name: Columbia - Ship type: MV - How taken: HM Frigate Briton - When taken: 17 Dec 1812 - Where taken: off Bordeaux, France - Date received: 1 Mar 1813 - From what ship: Plymouth via HMS Namur - Born: Massachusetts - Age: 33 - Discharged in Jul 1813 and released to Cartel Moses Brown.

Tois, Manuel - Seaman - Number: 2456 - Prize name: Wiley Reynard - Ship type: P - How taken: HM Frigate Shannon - When taken: 16 Aug 1812 - Where taken: off Halifax - Date received: 21 Oct 1813 - From what ship: Portsmouth via HMT Malabar - Born: Massachusetts - Age: 19 - Race: Mulatto - Discharged on 3 Nov 1813 and released to HMS Ceres.

Tolpie, Jonathan - Seaman - Number: 3291 - Prize name: Vivid - Ship type: P - How taken: HM Frigate Nymphe - When taken: 20 Apr 1813 - Where taken: off Cape Cod - Date received: 23 Feb 1814 - From what ship:

Halifax via HMT Malabar - Born: York - Age: 25 - Discharged on 10 Oct 1814 and sent to Dartmoor on the Mermaid.

Tolson, Jeremy - Seaman - Number: 916 - Prize name: Elk - Ship type: MV - How taken: Rose, tender - When taken: 27 Sep 1812 - Where taken: Greenock, Scotland - Date received: 10 Mar 1813 - From what ship: HMS Tigress - Born: Richmond, VA - Age: 22 - Race: Black - Discharged on 2 Jul 1813 and released to Cartel Moses Brown.

Tomas, Andrew - Seaman - Number: 3776 - Prize name: Argus - Ship type: MV - How taken: HM Ship-of-the-Line San Domingo - When taken: 1 Mar 1814 - Where taken: off Savannah - Date received: 26 May 1814 - From what ship: HMS Hindostan - Born: Newport - Age: 22 - Race: Black - Discharged on 25 Sep 1814 and sent to Dartmoor on HMS Niobe.

Tombinson, George William - Marine Private - Number: 2405 - How taken: Gave himself up from HM Ship-of-the-Line Plantagenet (Royal Marines) - Date received: 21 Oct 1813 - From what ship: Portsmouth via HMT Malabar - Born: New York - Age: 25 - Discharged on 11 Aug 1814 and sent to Dartmoor on HMS Freya.

Tomkins, Ephraim - Seaman - Number: 1796 - Prize name: Mars - Ship type: MV - How taken: Impressed at Shields - When taken: 1 Jun 1813 - Date received: 3 Jul 1813 - From what ship: HMS Raisonnable - Born: Rhode Island - Age: 27 - Discharged on 25 Jul 1814 and sent to Dartmoor on HMS Bittern.

Tomlinson, John - Private - Number: 3048 - Prize name: U.S. Light Dragoons - Ship type: LF - How taken: British forces - When taken: 24 Jun 1813 - Where taken: Beaver Dams, Upper Canada - Date received: 7 Jan 1814 - From what ship: Halifax - Born: Virginia - Age: 23 - Discharged on 10 Oct 1814 and sent to U.S. on Cartel St. Philip.

Toole, Gannet - Seaman - Number: 2378 - How taken: Gave himself up from HM Ship-of-the-Line America - When taken: 26 Dec 1812 - Date received: 20 Oct 1813 - From what ship: Portsmouth, via an admiral's tender - Born: Virginia - Age: 42 - Discharged on 4 Sep 1814 and sent to Dartmoor on HMS Freya.

Torry, Henry - Seaman - Number: 2485 - Prize name: Enterprise - Ship type: P - How taken: HM Frigate Tenedos - When taken: 21 May 1813 - Where taken: off Cape Cod - Date received: 22 Oct 1813 - From what ship: Portsmouth via HMT Malabar - Born: Massachusetts - Age: 21 - Discharged on 25 Sep 1814 and sent to Dartmoor on HMS Leyden.

Towe, Seth - Lieutenant - Number: 2745 - Prize name: Wasp - Ship type: P - How taken: HM Schooner Bream - When taken: 9 Jun 1813 - Where taken: off Halifax - Date received: 7 Jan 1814 - From what ship: Halifax - Born: Massachusetts - Age: 41 - Discharged on 8 Sep 1814 and sent to Dartmoor on HMS Niobe.

Towns, Asa - Seaman - Number: 3601 - Prize name: Liberty - Ship type: MV - How taken: Surrendered at Stromness, Scotland - When taken: 30 Dec 1813 - Date received: 29 Mar 1814 - From what ship: Hired tender Anna - Born: New Hampshire - Age: 25 - Discharged on 25 Sep 1814 and sent to Dartmoor on HMS Niobe.

Towns, Daniel - Seaman - Number: 467 - Prize name: Hunter - Ship type: P - How taken: HM Frigate Phoebe - When taken: 23 Dec 1812 - Where taken: off Azores - Date received: 19 Feb 1813 - From what ship: HMS Modeste - Born: Danbury - Age: 18 - Discharged on 24 Jul 1813 and released to Cartel Hoffminy.

Towns, Nicholas - Seaman - Number: 786 - Prize name: Dolphin - Ship type: MV - How taken: HM Ship-of-the-Line Colossus - When taken: 5 Jan 1813 - Where taken: off the Western Isles, Scotland - Date received: 27 Feb 1813 - From what ship: Plymouth via HMS Namur - Born: Philadelphia - Age: 23 - Discharged on 24 Jul 1813 and released to Cartel Hoffminy.

Townsend, Melby - Seaman - Number: 971 - How taken: Impressed at Dover - When taken: 19 Aug 1812 - Date received: 10 Mar 1813 - From what ship: HMS Tigress - Born: Mouland - Age: 25 - Discharged on 24 Jul 1813 and released to Cartel Hoffminy.

Townsend, Solomon - Seaman - Number: 1204 - Prize name: Expectation - Ship type: MV - How taken: HM Frigate Briton - When taken: 17 Dec 1812 - Where taken: at sea - Date received: 16 Mar 1813 - From what ship: Portsmouth, via HMS Abundance - Born: Philadelphia - Age: 24 - Discharged on 2 Jul 1813 and released to Cartel Moses Brown.

Trank, Abraham - Private - Number: 3046 - Prize name: U.S. Light Dragoons - Ship type: LF - How taken: British forces - When taken: 24 Jun 1813 - Where taken: Beaver Dams, Upper Canada - Date received: 7 Jan 1814 - From what ship: Halifax - Born: Pennsylvania - Age: 26 - Discharged on 10 Oct 1814 and sent to U.S. on Cartel St. Philip.

Traphagan, Peter - Seaman - Number: 2082 - How taken: Gave himself up from HM Ship-of-the-Line Scipion - When taken: 27 May 1813 - Date received: 9 Aug 1813 - From what ship: HMS Thames - Born: New Jersey - Age: 26 - Discharged on 25 Sep 1814 and sent to Dartmoor on HMS Leyden.

Trask, Osmond - Seaman - Number: 2668 - Prize name: Diana - Ship type: MV - How taken: Impressed at Hull - When taken: 18 Oct 1813 - Date received: 20 Nov 1813 - From what ship: HMS Raisonnable - Born: Beverly - Age: 29 - Discharged on 8 Sep 1814 and sent to Dartmoor on HMS Niobe.

Trask, William - Seaman - Number: 1521 - How taken: Gave himself up from HM Frigate Brune - When taken: 19 Jan 1813 - Date received: 8 Apr 1813 - From what ship: Portsmouth, via an admiral's tender - Born: Boston - Age: 25 - Discharged on 4 Aug 1814 and sent to Dartmoor on HMS Alpheus.

Travers, Thomas - Seaman - Number: 3244 - How taken: Impressed from HMS Conqueror - When taken: 26 Dec 1813 - Date received: 14 Feb 1814 - From what ship: HMS Raisonnable - Born: Maryland - Age: 28 - Race: Black - Discharged on 26 Sep 1814 and sent to Dartmoor on HMS Leyden.

Treadwell, Alphecca - Seaman - Number: 510 - Prize name: Josephine - Ship type: MV - How taken: HM Sloop Goree - When taken: 15 Aug 1812 - Where taken: off Bermuda - Date received: 23 Feb 1813 - From what ship: Portsmouth via HMS Dromedary - Born: Bridgeport - Age: 27 - Discharged on 10 May 1813 and released to Cartel Admittance.

Treadwell, Nathaniel - Seaman - Number: 2963 - Prize name: Enterprise - Ship type: P - How taken: HM Frigate Tenedos - When taken: 21 May 1813 - Where taken: off Cape Cod - Date received: 7 Jan 1814 - From what ship: Halifax - Born: Massachusetts - Age: 28 - Discharged on 25 Sep 1814 and sent to Dartmoor on HMS Leyden.

Tremus, Fit - Seaman - Number: 264 - How taken: Apprehended at London - When taken: 23 Oct 1812 - Date received: 7 Dec 1812 - From what ship: HMS Raisonnable - Born: Sag Harbor, NY - Age: 35 - Discharged in Jul 1813 and released to Cartel Moses Brown.

Tresroy, Thomas - Seaman - Number: 69 - Prize name: Elson - Ship type: MV - How taken: HM Frigate Ethalion - When taken: 12 Aug 1812 - Where taken: Baltic - Date received: 4 Nov 1812 - From what ship: HMS Namur - Born: Massachusetts - Age: 18 - Discharged on 10 May 1813 and released to Cartel Admittance.

Treyer, John - Gunner - Number: 1551 - Prize name: Dolphin - Ship type: LM - How taken: HM Ship-of-the-Line Colossus - When taken: 5 Jan 1813 - Where taken: off the Western Isles, Scotland - Date received: 8 Apr 1813 - From what ship: Plymouth via HMS Olympia - Born: Pennsylvania - Age: 29 - Discharged on 27 Jul 1813 and released to Cartel Hoffminy.

Tripper, Robert - Seaman - Number: 2775 - Prize name: Thomas - Ship type: P - How taken: HM Frigate Nymphe - When taken: 24 Jun 1813 - Where taken: off Halifax - Date received: 7 Jan 1814 - From what ship: Halifax - Born: Portsmouth - Age: 24 - Discharged on 8 Sep 1814 and sent to Dartmoor on HMS Niobe.

Tristram, Joseph - Seaman - Number: 684 - Prize name: U.S.R.M. Cutter James Madison - Ship type: War - How taken: HM Frigate Barbadoes - When taken: 22 Aug 1812 - Where taken: at sea - Date received: 24 Feb 1813 - From what ship: Portsmouth via HMS Ulysses - Born: Warrington, MA - Age: 25 - Discharged on 28 Apr 1813 and released to the David Scott.

Trought, Joseph - Seaman - Number: 631 - Prize name: King of Rome - Ship type: P - How taken: HM Brig Wolverine - When taken: 13 Dec 1812 - Where taken: at sea - Date received: 23 Feb 1813 - From what ship: Portsmouth via HMS Dromedary - Born: New Jersey - Age: 22 - Discharged on 2 Jul 1813 and released to Cartel Moses Brown.

Truman, Isaac - Seaman - Number: 3280 - Prize name: Vivid - Ship type: P - How taken: HM Frigate Nymphe - When taken: 20 Apr 1813 - Where taken: off Cape Cod - Date received: 23 Feb 1814 - From what ship: Halifax via HMT Malabar - Born: Wellfleet - Age: 27 - Discharged on 10 Oct 1814 and sent to Dartmoor on the Mermaid.

Trundy, Thomas - Seaman - Number: 1925 - Prize name: May (Newburyport) - Ship type: MV - How taken: HM

Brig Surinam - When taken: 14 Jun 1813 - Where taken: Surinam - Date received: 11 Jul 1813 - From what ship: HMS Raisonnable - Born: Dervish, MA - Age: 24 - Discharged on 24 Jul 1813 and released to Cartel Hoffminy.

Trusty, Henry - 2nd Mate - Number: 1951 - Prize name: Ferox - Ship type: MV - How taken: HM Frigate Medusa & HM Brig Lyra - When taken: 28 Mar 1813 - Where taken: off Cape Ortegal, Spain - Date received: 15 Jul 1813 - From what ship: Plymouth - Born: Philadelphia - Age: 29 - Discharged on 17 Jun 1814 and sent to Dartmoor on HMS Redbreast.

Tuck, James - 2nd Mate - Number: 2246 - Prize name: Joseph - Ship type: MV - How taken: HM Frigate Iris - When taken: 8 Jun 1813 - Where taken: off Spain - Date received: 7 Sep 1813 - From what ship: HMS Raisonnable - Born: Manchester - Age: 22 - Escaped on 16 May 1814 from HM Prison Ship Crown Prince.

Tucker, Andrew - Prize Master - Number: 3187 - Prize name: Growler - Ship type: P - How taken: HM Brig Electra - When taken: 7 Jul 1813 - Where taken: off St. Johns - Date received: 7 Jan 1813 - From what ship: Portsmouth - Born: Marblehead - Age: 36 - Discharged on 25 Sep 1814 and sent to Dartmoor on HMS Leyden.

Tucker, Edward - Seaman - Number: 471 - Prize name: Hunter - Ship type: P - How taken: HM Frigate Phoebe - When taken: 23 Dec 1812 - Where taken: off Azores - Date received: 19 Feb 1813 - From what ship: HMS Modeste - Born: Salem - Age: 18 - Discharged on 24 Jul 1813 and released to Cartel Hoffminy.

Tucker, Henry - Mate - Number: 3709 - Prize name: Requin - Ship type: LM - How taken: HM Frigate Venus - When taken: 5 Mar 1814 - Where taken: off Bordeaux, France - Date received: 18 May 1814 - From what ship: HMS Raisonnable - Born: Charleston - Age: 21 - Discharged on 25 Sep 1814 and sent to Dartmoor on HMS Leyden.

Tucker, James - Seaman - Number: 3599 - Prize name: Liberty - Ship type: MV - How taken: Surrendered at Stromness, Scotland - When taken: 30 Dec 1813 - Date received: 29 Mar 1814 - From what ship: Hired tender Anna - Born: Long Island - Age: 24 - Race: Black - Discharged on 25 Sep 1814 and sent to Dartmoor on HMS Niobe.

Tucker, Nathaniel - Seaman - Number: 3192 - Prize name: Growler - Ship type: P - How taken: HM Brig Electra - When taken: 7 Jul 1813 - Where taken: off St. Johns - Date received: 7 Jan 1813 - From what ship: Portsmouth - Born: Marblehead - Age: 22 - Discharged on 25 Sep 1814 and sent to Dartmoor on HMS Leyden.

Tucker, Nathaniel - Seaman - Number: 2422 - Prize name: Sampson - Ship type: MV - How taken: HM Brig Rebuff - When taken: 12 May 1813 - Where taken: off Cape St. Vincent, Portugal - Date received: 21 Oct 1813 - From what ship: Portsmouth via HMT Malabar - Born: New Hampshire - Age: 20 - Discharged on 4 Sep 1814 and sent to Dartmoor on HMS Freya.

Tucker, Samuel - 1st Mate - Number: 1114 - Prize name: Endeavour - Ship type: MV - How taken: Lion, British privateer - When taken: 27 Dec 1812 - Where taken: at sea - Date received: 14 Mar 1813 - From what ship: Portsmouth via HMS Beagle - Born: Marblehead - Age: 21 - Discharged on 24 Jul 1813 and released to Cartel Hoffminy.

Tucker, Samuel - Master - Number: 2799 - Prize name: Industry - Ship type: P - How taken: HM Brig Heron - When taken: 3 Nov 1813 - Where taken: off Halifax - Date received: 7 Jan 1814 - From what ship: Halifax - Born: Marblehead - Age: 21 - Discharged on 8 Sep 1814 and sent to Dartmoor on HMS Niobe.

Tucker, William - Seaman - Number: 2982 - Prize name: Enterprise - Ship type: P - How taken: HM Frigate Tenedos - When taken: 21 May 1813 - Where taken: off Cape Cod - Date received: 7 Jan 1814 - From what ship: Halifax - Born: Portsmouth - Age: 17 - Discharged on 25 Sep 1814 and sent to Dartmoor on HMS Leyden.

Tuckerman, Nathaniel - Seaman - Number: 2940 - Prize name: Governor Plumer - Ship type: P - How taken: HM Brig Shamrock - When taken: 26 May 1813 - Where taken: at sea - Date received: 7 Jan 1814 - From what ship: Halifax - Born: New Hampshire - Age: 27 - Discharged on 22 Oct 1814 and sent to Dartmoor on HMS Leyden.

Tufts, Eleazer - Seaman - Number: 646 - Prize name: U.S.R.M. Cutter James Madison - Ship type: War - How taken: HM Frigate Barbadoes - When taken: 22 Aug 1812 - Where taken: at sea - Date received: 24 Feb 1813 - From what ship: Portsmouth via HMS Ulysses - Born: Medford - Age: 26 - Discharged on 10 May 1813 and released to Cartel Admittance.

Tull, John - Seaman - Number: 546 - Prize name: Baltimore - Ship type: P - How taken: HM Transport Diadem - When taken: 7 Oct 1812 - Where taken: S. Andres - Date received: 23 Feb 1813 - From what ship: Portsmouth via HMS Dromedary - Born: St. Michaels - Age: 27 - Discharged on 8 Jun 1813 and released to Cartel Rodrigo.

Turnbull, James - Seaman - Number: 3466 - Prize name: Elbridge Gerry - Ship type: P - How taken: HM Frigate Crescent - When taken: 16 Sep 1813 - Where taken: at sea - Date received: 23 Feb 1814 - From what ship: Halifax via HMT Malabar - Born: Boston - Age: 15 - Discharged on 21 Jul 1814 and sent to Dartmoor on HMS Portia.

Turnbull, James - Seaman - Number: 1191 - How taken: Gave himself up from HM Transport Romulus - When taken: 14 Aug 1812 - Date received: 16 Mar 1813 - From what ship: Portsmouth, via HMS Abundance - Born: Charlestown - Age: 33 - Discharged on 11 Aug 1814 and sent to Dartmoor on HMS Freya.

Turner, David - Seaman - Number: 3860 - Prize name: Derby - Ship type: MV - How taken: HM Frigate Nereus - When taken: 4 Feb 1813 - Where taken: off Cape of Good Hope - Date received: 24 Aug 1814 - From what ship: London - Born: Boston - Age: 23 - Discharged on 22 Oct 1814 and sent to Dartmoor on HMS Leyden.

Turner, Gardner - Seaman - Number: 3793 - Prize name: Valentine - Ship type: MV - How taken: HM Ship-of-the-Line Minden - When taken: 16 Nov 1812 - Where taken: off Cape of Good Hope - Date received: 26 May 1814 - From what ship: HMS Hindostan - Born: Tiverton - Age: 20 - Discharged on 29 Sep 1814 and sent to Dartmoor on HMS Freya.

Turner, Henry B. - Seaman - Number: 37 - Prize name: Mary - Ship type: MV - How taken: From a cutter's boat off Bermuda - When taken: 8 Aug 1812 - Date received: 3 Nov 1812 - From what ship: HMS Plover - Born: Wilmington, NC - Age: 23 - Discharged on 23 Mar 1813 and released to the Cartel Robinson Potter.

Turner, James - Seaman - Number: 3469 - Prize name: Yankee - Ship type: P - How taken: HM Frigate Shannon - When taken: 20 Aug 1813 - Where taken: at sea - Date received: 23 Feb 1814 - From what ship: Halifax via HMT Malabar - Born: Charleston - Age: 22 - Discharged on 22 Oct 1814 and sent to Dartmoor on HMS Leyden.

Turner, John - Seaman - Number: 678 - Prize name: U.S.R.M. Cutter James Madison - Ship type: War - How taken: HM Frigate Barbadoes - When taken: 22 Aug 1812 - Where taken: at sea - Date received: 24 Feb 1813 - From what ship: Portsmouth via HMS Ulysses - Born: Randolph, MA - Age: 23 - Discharged on 10 May 1813 and released to Cartel Admittance.

Turner, Leonard - Seaman - Number: 356 - Prize name: Postsea, prize to the Privateer Thrasher - Ship type: P - How taken: HM Sloop Helena - When taken: 31 Dec 1813 - Where taken: off Azores - Date received: 19 Jan 1813 - From what ship: HMS Raisonnable - Born: Cape Ann - Age: 25 - Discharged on 24 Jul 1813 and released to Cartel Hoffminy.

Turner, Samuel - Seaman - Number: 1266 - How taken: Impressed at the Rude Rendezvous - When taken: 9 Dec 1812 - Date received: 16 Mar 1813 - From what ship: Portsmouth, via HMS Abundance - Born: Newburgh - Age: 26 - Discharged on 24 Jul 1813 and released to Cartel Hoffminy.

Turner, Samuel - Seaman - Number: 641 - Prize name: Purse - Ship type: MV - How taken: HM Frigate Armide - When taken: 20 May 1812 - Where taken: off Bordeaux, France - Date received: 24 Feb 1813 - From what ship: Portsmouth via HMS Ulysses - Born: New York - Age: 24 - Discharged on 13 May 1813 and released the Cartel Admittance.

Turner, Samuel - Seaman - Number: 171 - How taken: Stopped at London - When taken: 28 Oct 1812 - Date received: 5 Nov 1812 - From what ship: HMS Namur - Born: Newburgh, NY - Age: 36 - Discharged on 14 Dec 1812 and released to HMS Suffolk.

Turner, Samuel - Captain - Number: 2864 - Prize name: Elbridge Gerry - Ship type: P - How taken: HM Frigate Crescent - When taken: 16 Sep 1813 - Where taken: at sea - Date received: 7 Jan 1814 - From what ship: Portsmouth - Born: New York - Age: 26 - Discharged on 25 Sep 1814 and sent to Dartmoor on HMS

Leyden.

Turner, Silas - Seaman - Number: 3347 - Prize name: Porcupine - Ship type: LM - How taken: HM Frigate Acasta - When taken: 18 Jul 1813 - Where taken: off Cape Sable, Florida - Date received: 23 Feb 1814 - From what ship: Halifax via HMT Malabar - Born: Montville - Age: 24 - Discharged on 22 Oct 1814 and sent to Dartmoor on HMS Leyden.

Turner, Thomas - Seaman - Number: 830 - Prize name: John Barnes - Ship type: MV - How taken: Gave himself up at Liverpool - When taken: 7 Nov 1813 - Date received: 1 Mar 1813 - From what ship: Plymouth via HMS Namur - Born: Charlestown - Age: 28 - Discharged in Jul 1813 and released to Cartel Moses Brown.

Turner, William - Seaman - Number: 257 - How taken: Gave himself up at London - When taken: 28 Nov 1812 - Date received: 7 Dec 1812 - From what ship: HMS Raisonnable - Born: New York - Age: 21 - Discharged on 24 Jul 1813 and released to Cartel Hoffminy.

Turpin, Francis - Seaman - Number: 858 - Prize name: Brutus - Ship type: MV - How taken: Briton, letter of marque - When taken: 13 Jan 1813 - Where taken: Bay of Biscay - Date received: 1 Mar 1813 - From what ship: Plymouth via HMS Namur - Born: New Orleans - Age: 28 - Discharged on 24 Jul 1813 and released to Cartel Hoffminy.

Tuttle, Joseph - Seaman - Number: 3587 - Prize name: Devon, prize to the Privateer Bunker Hill - Ship type: P - How taken: HM Brig Fly - When taken: 21 Jan 1814 - Where taken: at sea - Date received: 26 Mar 1814 - From what ship: Plymouth via HMS Raleigh - Born: Freeport - Age: 27 - Discharged on 25 Sep 1814 and sent to Dartmoor on HMS Niobe.

Twikes, Samuel - Seaman - Number: 3277 - Prize name: Cossack - Ship type: MV - How taken: HM Brig Curlew - When taken: 22 Apr 1813 - Where taken: Indian Island - Date received: 23 Feb 1814 - From what ship: Halifax via HMT Malabar - Born: Salem - Age: 16 - Discharged on 10 Oct 1814 and sent to Dartmoor on the Mermaid.

Twycross, Samuel - Mate - Number: 335 - How taken: Impressed at London off British MV Three Brothers - When taken: 13 Jan 1813 - Date received: 18 Jan 1813 - From what ship: HMS Raisonnable - Born: Dresden, MA - Age: 35 - Discharged on 26 Jul 1814 and sent to Dartmoor on HMS Raven.

Tyler, Joseph - Seaman - Number: 3752 - Prize name: Argus - Ship type: MV - How taken: HM Ship-of-the-Line San Domingo - When taken: 1 Mar 1814 - Where taken: off Savannah - Date received: 26 May 1814 - From what ship: HMS Hindostan - Born: Newburyport - Age: 19 - Discharged on 25 Sep 1814 and sent to Dartmoor on HMS Niobe.

Tyler, Lewis - Seaman - Number: 1866 - How taken: Gave himself up from HM Ship-of-the-Line Puissant - Date received: 7 Jul 1813 - From what ship: Portsmouth via HMS Tribune - Born: Bedford, NY - Age: 23 - Discharged on 4 Aug 1814 and sent to Dartmoor on HMS Liverpool.

Underwood, Benjamin - Boatswain - Number: 1460 - Prize name: Union - Ship type: MV - How taken: HM Frigate Iris - When taken: 17 Jan 1813 - Where taken: at sea - Date received: 6 Apr 1813 - From what ship: Portsmouth via Tender Eliza - Born: Not readable - Age: 24 - Discharged on 24 Jul 1813 and released to Cartel Hoffminy.

Underwood, John Francis - Seaman - Number: 1036 - Prize name: Catharine - Ship type: MV - How taken: HM Frigate Leonidas - When taken: 31 Jul 1812 - Where taken: off Ireland - Date received: 11 Mar 1813 - From what ship: Yarmouth via HMS Tenders - Born: Westport - Age: 21 - Discharged on 26 Jul 1813 and released to Cartel Hoffminy.

Upham, Timothy - 2nd Mate - Number: 1927 - Prize name: Edward - Ship type: MV - How taken: Seringapatam, British letter of marque - When taken: 6 Jan 1813 - Where taken: South America - Date received: 11 Jul 1813 - From what ship: HMS Raisonnable - Born: Nantucket - Age: 26 - Discharged on 24 Jul 1813 and released to Cartel Hoffminy.

Upton, Jeduthun - Captain - Number: 1416 - Prize name: Hunter - Ship type: P - How taken: HM Frigate Phoebe - When taken: 23 Dec 1812 - Where taken: off Azores - Date received: 5 Apr 1813 - From what ship: Plymouth via HMS Dwarf - Born: Salem - Age: 27 - Discharged on 16 May 1813 and released to Cartel Admittance.

Upton, John B. - Seaman - Number: 89 - Prize name: Calaban - Ship type: MV - How taken: HM Battery Gorgon - When taken: 12 Aug 1812 - Where taken: Great Belt, Denmark - Date received: 4 Nov 1812 - From what ship: HMS Namur - Born: Massachusetts - Age: 22 - Discharged on 10 May 1813 and released to Cartel Admittance.

Upton, Samuel - Master's Mate - Number: 420 - Prize name: Hunter - Ship type: P - How taken: HM Frigate Phoebe - When taken: 23 Dec 1812 - Where taken: off Azores - Date received: 19 Feb 1813 - From what ship: HMS Modeste - Born: Salem - Age: 21 - Discharged on 2 Jul 1813 and released to Cartel Moses Brown.

Urey, Peter - Seaman - Number: 1258 - How taken: Gave himself up from HM Ship-of-the-Line Mars - When taken: 9 Dec 1812 - Date received: 16 Mar 1813 - From what ship: Portsmouth, via HMS Abundance - Born: New York - Age: 22 - Discharged on 23 Jul 1814 and sent to Dartmoor.

Vail, Jeremiah - Seaman - Number: 2060 - How taken: Gave up from HMS Dwarf - When taken: 28 Jul 1813 - Date received: 4 Aug 1813 - From what ship: HMS Raisonnable - Born: Long Island - Age: 32 - Discharged on 12 Aug 1814 and sent to Dartmoor on HMS Alpheus.

Valentine, Andrew - Seaman - Number: 688 - Prize name: Fame, prize of Privateer Decatur - Ship type: P - How taken: HM Ship-of-the-Line Polyphemus - When taken: 13 Sep 1812 - Where taken: at sea - Date received: 24 Feb 1813 - From what ship: Portsmouth via HMS Ulysses - Born: Marblehead, MA - Age: 26 - Discharged on 8 Jun 1813 and released to Cartel Rodrigo.

Valentine, James - Seaman - Number: 765 - Prize name: Margarethe - Ship type: MV - How taken: HM Ship-of-the-Line San Juan - When taken: 8 May 1812 - Where taken: Gibraltar - Date received: 25 Feb 1813 - From what ship: HMS Brazen - Born: Wilmington - Age: 24 - Discharged on 10 May 1813 and released to Cartel Admittance.

Valentine, John - Seaman - Number: 2383 - How taken: Gave himself up from HM Ship-of-the-Line America - When taken: 26 Dec 1812 - Date received: 20 Oct 1813 - From what ship: Portsmouth, via an admiral's tender - Born: Boston - Age: 37 - Race: Black - Discharged on 4 Sep 1814 and sent to Dartmoor on HMS Freya.

Van Donveer, Peter - Seaman - Number: 1060 - Prize name: Independence - Ship type: MV - How taken: HM Frigate Medusa - When taken: 9 Nov 1812 - Where taken: off San Sebastian, Spain - Date received: 11 Mar 1813 - From what ship: Yarmouth via HMS Tenders - Born: New Jersey - Age: 24 - Discharged on 8 Jun 1813 and released to Cartel Rodrigo.

Vanderhovan, John - Seaman - Number: 755 - Prize name: Quebec of London, prize of the Privateer Paul Jones - Ship type: P - How taken: HM Brig Derwent - When taken: 29 Jan 1813 - Where taken: off Lisbon - Date received: 25 Feb 1813 - From what ship: HMS Brazen - Born: New Jersey - Age: 29 - Discharged on 2 Jul 1813 and released to HMS Ceres.

Vanderhovan, Mathew - Seaman - Number: 756 - Prize name: Quebec of London, prize of the Privateer Paul Jones - Ship type: P - How taken: HM Brig Derwent - When taken: 29 Jan 1813 - Where taken: off Lisbon - Date received: 25 Feb 1813 - From what ship: HMS Brazen - Born: New Jersey - Age: 21 - Discharged on 23 Jul 1814 and sent to Dartmoor on HMS Acasta.

Vanderwenter, John - Seaman - Number: 2592 - How taken: Gave himself up from HM Ship-of-the-Line Scipion - When taken: 27 May 1813 - Date received: 5 Nov 1813 - From what ship: HMS Hindostan - Born: Southernbay - Age: 22 - Discharged on 12 Aug 1814 and sent to Dartmoor on HMS Alpheus.

Vangorbet, Cato - Seaman - Number: 1908 - Prize name: Weasel - Ship type: MV - How taken: HM Brig Foxhound - When taken: 25 Mar 1813 - Where taken: Bay of Biscay - Date received: 7 Jul 1813 - From what ship: Portsmouth via HMS Tribune - Born: New Jersey - Age: 22 - Race: Black - Discharged on 4 Aug 1814 and sent to Dartmoor on HMS Liverpool.

Vannog, John P. - Steward - Number: 749 - Prize name: Quebec of London, prize of the Privateer Paul Jones - Ship type: P - How taken: HM Brig Derwent - When taken: 29 Jan 1813 - Where taken: off Lisbon - Date received: 25 Feb 1813 - From what ship: HMS Brazen - Born: New Orleans - Age: 40 - Race: Mulatto - Discharged on 22 Jun 1814 and sent to Calais, France on the Simon & Mary.

Vanrant, John - Seaman - Number: 3370 - Prize name: Yorktown - Ship type: P - How taken: HM Frigate Maidstone

- When taken: 17 Jul 1813 - Where taken: Grand Banks - Date received: 23 Feb 1814 - From what ship: Halifax via HMT Malabar - Born: Savannah - Age: 25 - Race: Black - Discharged on 10 Oct 1814 and sent to Dartmoor on the Mermaid.

Varney, John - Seaman - Number: 2493 - Prize name: Governor Plumer - Ship type: P - How taken: Sent into custody from a privateer - When taken: 1 Jun 1813 - Where taken: off Cape Ann - Date received: 22 Oct 1813 - From what ship: Portsmouth via HMT Malabar - Born: Massachusetts - Age: 21 - Discharged on 8 Sep 1814 and sent to Dartmoor on HMS Niobe.

Veney, George - Seaman - Number: 1351 - Prize name: Tom Thumb - Ship type: MV - How taken: Lion, British privateer - When taken: 15 Feb 1813 - Where taken: Bay of Biscay - Date received: 3 Apr 1813 - From what ship: Portsmouth, via an admiral's tender - Born: Philadelphia - Age: 22 - Race: Mulatto - Discharged on 25 Jul 1814 and sent to Dartmoor on HMS Bittern.

Verplasts, Nicholas - Seaman - Number: 2478 - Prize name: Juliana Smith - Ship type: P - How taken: HM Frigate Nymphe - When taken: 12 May 1813 - Where taken: off Cape Sable, Florida - Date received: 22 Oct 1813 - From what ship: Portsmouth via HMT Malabar - Born: Massachusetts - Age: 27 - Discharged on 22 Jun 1814 and sent to Calais, France on the Simon & Mary.

Very, Samuel - Prize Master - Number: 747 - Prize name: Quebec of London, prize of the Privateer Paul Jones - Ship type: P - How taken: HM Brig Derwent - When taken: 29 Jan 1813 - Where taken: off Lisbon - Date received: 25 Feb 1813 - From what ship: HMS Brazen - Born: Salem - Age: 28 - Discharged on 23 Jul 1814 and sent to Dartmoor on HMS Acasta.

Vicary, Richard - Seaman - Number: 1976 - Prize name: Polly - Ship type: MV - How taken: HM Frigate Surveillante - When taken: 23 Mar 1813 - Where taken: Bay of Biscay - Date received: 15 Jul 1813 - From what ship: Plymouth - Born: Beverly - Age: 17 - Discharged on 17 Jun 1814 and sent to Dartmoor on HMS Pincher.

Vincent, Henry - Seaman - Number: 2423 - Prize name: Sampson - Ship type: MV - How taken: HM Brig Rebuff - When taken: 12 May 1813 - Where taken: off Cape St. Vincent, Portugal - Date received: 21 Oct 1813 - From what ship: Portsmouth via HMT Malabar - Born: Massachusetts - Age: 23 - Discharged on 31 Oct 1813 and released to HMS Ceres.

Vincent, John - Seaman - Number: 1574 - How taken: Gave himself up from HM Ship-of-the-Line Braham - When taken: 10 Dec 1812 - Date received: 16 Apr 1813 - From what ship: HMS Namur, admiral's tender - Born: Philadelphia - Age: 29 - Discharged on 24 Jul 1814 and sent to Dartmoor.

Vincent, Stephen Stiles - Seaman - Number: 3662 - Prize name: Pilot - Ship type: LM - How taken: Vittoria, British privateer from Guernsey - When taken: 28 Jan 1814 - Where taken: off Bordeaux, France - Date received: 4 May 1814 - From what ship: Portsmouth - Born: New Jersey - Age: 20 - Discharged on 26 Sep 1814 and sent to Dartmoor on HMS Leyden.

Vine, William - Seaman - Number: 973 - Prize name: Empress - Ship type: MV - How taken: HM Brig Rover - When taken: 30 Nov 1812 - Where taken: St. Andrew - Date received: 10 Mar 1813 - From what ship: HMS Tigress - Born: Charlestown - Age: 21 - Discharged on 8 Jun 1813 and released to Cartel Rodrigo.

Vingen, Nicholas - Seaman - Number: 311 - Prize name: Cuba - Ship type: MV - How taken: HM Brig Sarpedon - When taken: 12 Aug 1812 - Date received: 23 Dec 1812 - From what ship: Greenlaw Depot - Born: New York - Age: 32 - Race: Black man - Discharged on 10 May 1813 and released to Cartel Admittance.

Voight, Henry - Seaman - Number: 2167 - How taken: Gave himself up from HM Ship-of-the-Line Swiftsure - When taken: 26 Dec 1812 - Date received: 16 Aug 1813 - From what ship: Portsmouth, via an admiral's tender - Born: Pennsylvania - Age: 31 - Discharged on 17 Jun 1814 and sent to Dartmoor on the Penebar.

Vorge, James - Seaman - Number: 1240 - Prize name: Rossie - Ship type: MV - How taken: HM Frigate Dryand - When taken: 7 Jan 1813 - Where taken: at sea - Date received: 16 Mar 1813 - From what ship: Portsmouth, via HMS Abundance - Born: Maryland - Age: 24 - Race: Black - Discharged on 24 Jul 1813 and released to Cartel Hoffminy.

Voughon, Robert - Seaman - Number: 1604 - How taken: Gave himself up from HM Brig Peruvian - When taken: 26 Aug 1813 - Date received: 19 Apr 1813 - From what ship: HMS Raisonnable - Born: Boston - Age: 24 -

Discharged on 24 Jul 1814 and sent to Dartmoor.

Wade, Otis - Seaman - Number: 989 - Prize name: Otter - Ship type: MV - How taken: HM Ship-Sloop Jalouse - When taken: 1 Dec 1812 - Where taken: off Cape St. Vincent, Portugal - Date received: 10 Mar 1813 - From what ship: HMS Tigress - Born: Scituate - Age: 28 - Released on 20 Mar 1813 to HMS Otter.

Wadsworth, Daniel - Passenger - Number: 3208 - Prize name: Volunteer - Ship type: MV - How taken: Vittoria, British privateer from Guernsey - When taken: 26 Dec 1813 - Where taken: Bay of Biscay - Date received: 13 Jan 1814 - From what ship: Portsmouth via HMS Poictiers - Born: Connecticut - Age: 22 - Discharged on 17 Feb 1814 and sent to Reading on parole.

Wain, Benjamin - 1st Lieutenant - Number: 1545 - Prize name: Hunter - Ship type: P - How taken: HM Frigate Phoebe - When taken: 23 Dec 1812 - Where taken: off Azores - Date received: 8 Apr 1813 - From what ship: Plymouth via HMS Olympia - Born: Boston - Age: 45 - Discharged on 23 Jul 1813 and released to the Transport Office.

Wair, Francis - 2nd Mate - Number: 709 - Prize name: Bellville - Ship type: MV - How taken: Detained at Portsmouth harbor - When taken: 31 Jul 1812 - Date received: 24 Feb 1813 - From what ship: Portsmouth via HMS Ulysses - Born: Oldenburg, Germany - Age: 27 - Discharged on 23 Mar 1813 and released to the Cartel Robinson Potter.

Wait, Philip - Seaman - Number: 21 - Prize name: Navigator - Ship type: MV - How taken: HM Ship-of-the-Line Cressy - When taken: 11 Aug 1812 - Where taken: Baltic - Date received: 29 Oct 1812 - From what ship: HMS Raisonnable - Born: New York - Age: 36 - Discharged on 19 Mar 1813 and released to the Navigator.

Walden, James - Seaman - Number: 409 - Prize name: Hope - Ship type: MV - How taken: HM Sloop Pheasant - When taken: 13 Dec 1812 - Where taken: off Azores - Date received: 19 Feb 1813 - From what ship: HMS Modeste - Born: Virginia - Age: 21 - Discharged on 2 Jul 1813 and released to Cartel Moses Brown.

Walden, James - Seaman - Number: 2177 - How taken: Gave himself up from HM Ship-of-the-Line Leviathan - When taken: 28 Oct 1812 - Date received: 16 Aug 1813 - From what ship: Portsmouth, via an admiral's tender - Born: New London - Age: 32 - Discharged on 11 Aug 1814 and sent to Dartmoor on HMS Freya.

Walker, Benjamin - Seaman - Number: 2404 - How taken: Gave himself up from HM Store Ship Woolwich - Date received: 21 Oct 1813 - From what ship: Portsmouth via HMT Malabar - Born: Maryland - Age: 27 - Race: Mulatto - Discharged on 4 Sep 1814 and sent to Dartmoor on HMS Freya.

Walker, James - Seaman - Number: 639 - Prize name: Friendship - Ship type: MV - How taken: HM Frigate Rosamund - When taken: 12 Aug 1812 - Where taken: off Halifax - Date received: 23 Feb 1813 - From what ship: Portsmouth via HMS Dromedary - Born: Boston - Age: 33 - Race: Black man - Discharged on 17 Nov 1813 to the Cartel Robinson Potter.

Walker, John - Seaman - Number: 82 - Prize name: Edward - Ship type: MV - How taken: HM Frigate Ethalion - When taken: 12 Aug 1812 - Where taken: Great Belt, Denmark - Date received: 4 Nov 1812 - From what ship: HMS Namur - Born: Africa - Age: 22 - Race: Mulatto - Discharged on 10 May 1813 and released to Cartel Admittance.

Walker, John - Seaman - Number: 2071 - How taken: Gave himself up from HM Ship-of-the-Line Royal George - When taken: 29 Oct 1812 - Date received: 9 Aug 1813 - From what ship: HMS Thames - Born: Virginia - Age: 19 - Discharged on 4 Aug 1814 and sent to Dartmoor on HMS Liverpool.

Walker, Samuel - Seaman - Number: 2969 - Prize name: Enterprise - Ship type: P - How taken: HM Frigate Tenedos - When taken: 21 May 1813 - Where taken: off Cape Cod - Date received: 7 Jan 1814 - From what ship: Halifax - Born: Massachusetts - Age: 20 - Discharged on 25 Sep 1814 and sent to Dartmoor on HMS Leyden.

Walker, Seth - Prize Master - Number: 3553 - Prize name: Zephyr, prize of Privateer Rattlesnake - Ship type: P - How taken: HM Frigate Surveillante - When taken: 6 Jan 1814 - Where taken: Bay of Biscay - Date received: 7 May 1814 - From what ship: Portsmouth via HMS Favorite - Born: Portsmouth - Age: 35 - Discharged on 26 Sep 1814 and sent to Dartmoor on HMS Leyden.

Walker, William - Seaman - Number: 802 - Prize name: Eliza - Ship type: MV - How taken: HM Sloop Hyacinth - When taken: 27 Aug 1812 - Where taken: off Gibraltar - Date received: 27 Feb 1813 - From what ship:

Plymouth via HMS Namur - Born: Charlestown - Age: 28 - Discharged on 10 May 1813 and released to Cartel Admittance.

Walker, William - Seaman - Number: 2407 - How taken: Gave himself up from HM Ship-Sloop Jalouse - Date received: 21 Oct 1813 - From what ship: Portsmouth via HMT Malabar - Born: New Hampshire - Age: 36 - Race: Black - Discharged on 23 Nov 1813 and released to HMS Ceres.

Walkington, George - Mate - Number: 384 - Prize name: Eliza - Ship type: MV - How taken: HM Sloop Hyacinth - When taken: 27 Aug 1812 - Where taken: Straits of Gibraltar - Date received: 13 Feb 1813 - From what ship: HMS Raisonnable - Born: Georgetown - Age: 29 - Discharged on 10 May 1813 and released to Cartel Admittance.

Wall, William - Seaman - Number: 3840 - How taken: Gave himself up from HM Ship-of-the-Line Leader - When taken: 18 Jul 1813 - Date received: 21 Aug 1814 - From what ship: Gravesend - Born: Boston - Age: 23 - Discharged on 20 Sep 1814 and sent to Dartmoor on HMS Leyden.

Wallace, James - Seaman - Number: 1972 - Prize name: Lightning - Ship type: MV - How taken: HM Frigate Medusa - When taken: 2 Apr 1813 - Where taken: Bay of Biscay - Date received: 15 Jul 1813 - From what ship: Plymouth - Born: St. Michaels - Age: 31 - Discharged on 17 Jun 1814 and sent to Dartmoor on HMS Redbreast.

Wallace, Thomas - Master - Number: 3728 - Prize name: Argus - Ship type: MV - How taken: HM Ship-of-the-Line San Domingo - When taken: 1 Mar 1814 - Where taken: off Savannah - Date received: 26 May 1814 - From what ship: HMS Hindostan - Born: Boston - Age: 52 - Discharged on 25 Sep 1814 and sent to Dartmoor on HMS Niobe.

Wallace, William - Seaman - Number: 983 - Prize name: Brunswick - Ship type: MV - How taken: HM Frigate Iris - When taken: 17 Dec 1812 - Where taken: off Spain - Date received: 10 Mar 1813 - From what ship: HMS Tigress - Born: New Jersey - Age: 31 - Discharged on 2 Jul 1813 and released to Cartel Moses Brown.

Wallace, William - Caulker - Number: 401 - How taken: Gave himself up from HM Gunpowder Hulk Alexander - When taken: 1 Feb 1813 - Date received: 13 Feb 1813 - From what ship: HMS Raisonnable - Born: Baltimore - Age: 38 - Discharged on 25 Sep 1814 and sent to Dartmoor on HMS Freya.

Waller, George - Seaman - Number: 529 - Prize name: Baltimore - Ship type: P - How taken: HM Transport Diadem - When taken: 7 Oct 1812 - Where taken: S. Andres - Date received: 23 Feb 1813 - From what ship: Portsmouth via HMS Dromedary - Born: River Neek, MD - Age: 24 - Discharged on 8 Jun 1813 and released to Cartel Rodrigo.

Walling, James - Seaman - Number: 2543 - How taken: Gave himself up from HM Brig Bold - When taken: 12 Jul 1813 - Date received: 22 Oct 1813 - From what ship: Portsmouth via HMT Malabar - Born: New Jersey - Age: 32 - Discharged on 25 Sep 1814 and sent to Dartmoor on HMS Leyden.

Walton, Christopher - Seaman - Number: 1697 - Prize name: Governor Middleton - Ship type: MV - How taken: Thetis, British privateer - When taken: 2 May 1813 - Where taken: Bay of Biscay - Date received: 15 May 1813 - From what ship: HMS Viper - Born: Danzig, East Prussia - Age: 30 - Discharged on 12 Aug 1814 and sent to Dartmoor on HMS Alpheus.

Walton, John - Seaman - Number: 296 - Prize name: America - Ship type: MV - How taken: HM Brig Cracker - When taken: 1 Aug 1812 - Date received: 23 Dec 1812 - From what ship: Greenlaw Depot - Born: Newburgh - Age: 34 - Discharged on 23 Mar 1813 and released to the Cartel Robinson Potter.

Wane, Michael - Private - Number: 2659 - Prize name: 2nd U.S. Artillery - Ship type: LF - How taken: British forces - When taken: 6 Jun 1813 - Where taken: Stoney Creek, Upper Canada - Date received: 5 Nov 1813 - From what ship: HMS Hindostan - Born: North Ireland - Age: 32 - Discharged on 17 Jun 1814 and sent to Dartmoor.

Wanton, William - Seaman - Number: 2472 - Prize name: Montgomery - Ship type: P - How taken: HM Frigate Nymphe - When taken: 5 May 1813 - Where taken: off Cape Cod - Date received: 21 Oct 1813 - From what ship: Portsmouth via HMT Malabar - Born: Marblehead - Age: 32 - Discharged on 8 Sep 1814 and sent to Dartmoor on HMS Niobe.

Ward, Alfred - Seaman - Number: 3899 - How taken: Gave himself up from HM Frigate Owen Glendower - When taken: 28 Jun 1813 - Date received: 30 Aug 1814 - From what ship: Transport Office - Born: Middlesex - Age: 28 - Discharged on 25 Sep 1814 and sent to Dartmoor on HMS Leyden.

Ward, Benjamin - Seaman - Number: 2467 - Prize name: Cossack - Ship type: P - How taken: HM Frigate Amelia - When taken: 11 Apr 1813 - Where taken: off St. Johns - Date received: 21 Oct 1813 - From what ship: Portsmouth via HMT Malabar - Born: Hancock - Age: 21 - Discharged on 8 Sep 1814 and sent to Dartmoor on HMS Niobe.

Ward, James - Seaman - Number: 719 - Prize name: James - Ship type: MV - How taken: Detained at Portsmouth harbor - When taken: 31 Jul 1812 - Date received: 24 Feb 1813 - From what ship: Portsmouth via HMS Ulysses - Born: Newmarket, NH - Age: 24 - Discharged on 23 Mar 1813 and released to the Cartel Robinson Potter.

Ward, Mason - Seaman - Number: 767 - Prize name: Margarethe - Ship type: MV - How taken: HM Ship-of-the-Line San Juan - When taken: 8 May 1812 - Where taken: Gibraltar - Date received: 25 Feb 1813 - From what ship: HMS Brazen - Born: Hanfield, NJ - Age: 25 - Discharged on 10 May 1813 and released to Cartel Admittance.

Ward, Peter - Seaman - Number: 2665 - Prize name: Henryettos - Ship type: MV - How taken: Impressed at London - When taken: 21 Oct 1813 - Date received: 11 Nov 1813 - From what ship: HMS Namur, admiral's tender - Born: Hudson - Age: 20 - Discharged on 8 Sep 1814 and sent to Dartmoor on HMS Niobe.

Ward, Thomas - Prize Master - Number: 2910 - Prize name: Pomona, prize of Privateer Prince de Neuchatel - Ship type: P - How taken: HM Frigate Ethalion - When taken: 14 Dec 1813 - Where taken: at sea - Date received: 7 Jan 1814 - From what ship: Portsmouth - Born: Baltimore - Age: 39 - Discharged on 25 Sep 1814 and sent to Dartmoor on HMS Leyden.

Warmsley, Samuel - Seaman - Number: 1382 - Prize name: Melville - Ship type: MV - How taken: Impressed at London - When taken: 28 Mar 1813 - Date received: 3 Apr 1813 - From what ship: HMS Namur - Born: Nantucket - Age: 29 - Race: Mulatto - Discharged on 4 Nov 1813 and released to HMS Ceres.

Warner, Charles - Steward's Mate - Number: 427 - Prize name: Hunter - Ship type: P - How taken: HM Frigate Phoebe - When taken: 23 Dec 1812 - Where taken: off Azores - Date received: 19 Feb 1813 - From what ship: HMS Modeste - Born: Bicksford - Age: 26 - Discharged on 2 Jul 1813 and released to Cartel Moses Brown.

Warner, George - Seaman - Number: 448 - Prize name: Hunter - Ship type: P - How taken: HM Frigate Phoebe - When taken: 23 Dec 1812 - Where taken: off Azores - Date received: 19 Feb 1813 - From what ship: HMS Modeste - Born: Salem - Age: 22 - Discharged on 24 Jul 1813 and released to Cartel Hoffminy.

Warner, John - Seaman - Number: 2121 - How taken: Gave himself up from HM Ship-of-the-Line Prince of Wales - When taken: 28 May 1813 - Date received: 9 Aug 1813 - From what ship: HMS Thames - Born: Connecticut - Age: 23 - Discharged on 26 Sep 814 and sent to Dartmoor on HMS Leyden.

Warner, John - Seaman - Number: 2433 - Prize name: Hepsey - Ship type: MV - How taken: HM Brig Zenobia - When taken: 22 Jun 1813 - Where taken: off Lisbon - Date received: 21 Oct 1813 - From what ship: Portsmouth via HMT Malabar - Born: Gothenburg, Sweden - Age: 29 - Released on 10 Feb 1814.

Warner, Thomas - Seaman - Number: 2018 - How taken: Gave himself up from HM Brig Cordelia - When taken: 28 May 1813 - Date received: 15 Jul 1813 - From what ship: Plymouth - Born: Boston - Age: 28 - Discharged on 17 Jun 1814 and sent to Dartmoor on HMS Pincher.

Warrance, John - Seaman - Number: 1970 - Prize name: Lightning - Ship type: MV - How taken: HM Frigate Medusa - When taken: 2 Apr 1813 - Where taken: Bay of Biscay - Date received: 15 Jul 1813 - From what ship: Plymouth - Born: Philadelphia - Age: 19 - Discharged on 17 Jun 1814 and sent to Dartmoor on HMS Redbreast.

Warren, David - Seaman - Number: 2998 - Prize name: Grand Turk - Ship type: P - How taken: HM Frigate Tenedos - When taken: 26 May 1813 - Where taken: off Cape Sable, Florida - Date received: 7 Jan 1814 - From what ship: Halifax - Born: Massachusetts - Age: 18 - Discharged on 25 Sep 1814 and sent to Dartmoor on HMS Leyden.

Warren, James - Seaman - Number: 1915 - Prize name: Regulator - Ship type: MV - How taken: Impressed at

London - When taken: 5 Jul 1813 - Date received: 7 Jul 1813 - From what ship: HMS Raisonnable - Born: Philadelphia - Age: 39 - Died on 30 Jan 1814 from debility (feeble).

Warren, John - Seaman - Number: 1421 - How taken: Impressed at Plymouth - When taken: 25 Jan 1813 - Date received: 5 Apr 1813 - From what ship: Plymouth via HMS Dwarf - Born: Baltimore - Age: 40 - Race: Negro - Discharged on 27 Jul 1813 and released to Cartel Hoffminy.

Warwick, Robert - Seaman - Number: 2072 - How taken: Gave himself up from HM Ship-of-the-Line Royal George - When taken: 29 Oct 1812 - Date received: 9 Aug 1813 - From what ship: HMS Thames - Born: Willis Town, PA - Age: 34 - Discharged on 4 Aug 1814 and sent to Dartmoor on HMS Liverpool.

Washy, George - Seaman - Number: 879 - Prize name: Hero - Ship type: MV - How taken: Cornet - When taken: 10 Feb 1813 - Where taken: off Lisbon - Date received: 1 Mar 1813 - From what ship: Plymouth via HMS Namur - Born: Salem - Age: 16 - Released on 27 Mar 1813.

Waterhouse, Joseph - Seaman - Number: 3855 - How taken: Gave himself up from HM Ship-of-the-Line Africa - When taken: 4 Oct 1813 - Date received: 24 Aug 1814 - From what ship: London - Born: Havana - Age: 24 - Race: Mulatto - Discharged on 26 Sep 1814 and sent to Dartmoor on HMS Leyden.

Waterhouse, Moses - Seaman - Number: 2495 - Prize name: Theresa - Ship type: P - How taken: Moor - When taken: 14 Jun 1813 - Where taken: off Cape Ann - Date received: 22 Oct 1813 - From what ship: Portsmouth via HMT Malabar - Born: Massachusetts - Age: 23 - Discharged on 8 Sep 1814 and sent to Dartmoor on HMS Niobe.

Waterman, John - 2nd Mate - Number: 1887 - Prize name: Tiger - Ship type: MV - How taken: HM Brig Scylla - When taken: 22 Mar 1813 - Where taken: Bay of Biscay - Date received: 7 Jul 1813 - From what ship: Portsmouth via HMS Tribune - Born: Nantucket - Age: 21 - Discharged on 25 Sep 1814 and sent to Dartmoor on HMS Niobe.

Waterman, Thomas - Master - Number: 1614 - How taken: Detained from British MV Robert Ann at London - When taken: 24 Apr 1813 - Date received: 3 May 1813 - From what ship: HMS Raisonnable - Born: New York - Age: 23 - Discharged on 25 Sep 1814 and sent to Dartmoor.

Waterman, William - Seaman - Number: 591 - Prize name: Antelope - Ship type: P - How taken: HM Brig Zephyr - When taken: 10 Dec 1812 - Where taken: at sea - Date received: 23 Feb 1813 - From what ship: Portsmouth via HMS Dromedary - Born: Nantucket - Age: 17 - Discharged on 2 Jul 1813 and released to Cartel Moses Brown.

Waters, Philip - Seaman - Number: 1572 - How taken: Impressed at Greenock, Scotland - When taken: 27 Nov 1812 - Date received: 8 Apr 1813 - From what ship: Plymouth via HMS Olympia - Born: Baltimore - Age: 29 - Race: Negro - Discharged on 27 Jul 1813 and released to Cartel Hoffminy.

Watkins, Fredrick - Seaman - Number: 1029 - Prize name: Washington - Ship type: MV - How taken: Taken up at Liverpool - When taken: 18 Oct 1812 - Date received: 11 Mar 1813 - From what ship: Yarmouth via HMS Tenders - Born: New York - Age: 22 - Discharged in Jul 1813 and released to Cartel Moses Brown.

Watkins, George - Seaman - Number: 1506 - How taken: Gave himself up from HM Ship-of-the-Line Blake - When taken: 10 Dec 1812 - Date received: 8 Apr 1813 - From what ship: Portsmouth, via an admiral's tender - Born: Newport, RI - Age: 43 - Race: Black - Discharged on 4 Aug 1814 and sent to Dartmoor on HMS Alpheus.

Watson, Daniel - Seaman - Number: 2370 - How taken: Gave himself up from HM Ship-of-the-Line Swiftsure - When taken: 26 Dec 1812 - Date received: 20 Oct 1813 - From what ship: Portsmouth, via an admiral's tender - Born: Rhode Island - Age: 24 - Race: Mulatto - Discharged on 4 Sep 1814 and sent to Dartmoor on HMS Freya.

Watson, David - Seaman - Number: 2909 - Prize name: U.S. Schooner Julia - Ship type: War - How taken: HM Schooner Earl Moria - When taken: 11 Aug 1813 - Where taken: Lake Ontario - Date received: 7 Jan 1814 - From what ship: Portsmouth - Born: New York - Age: 22 - Discharged on 10 Oct 1814 and sent to U.S. on Cartel St. Philip.

Watson, James - Seaman - Number: 2307 - Prize name: Kitty, prize of the U.S. Frigate President - Ship type: War - How taken: Dart, British privateer from Guernsey - When taken: 20 Jun 1813 - Where taken: off the Western

Isles, Scotland - Date received: 8 Oct 1813 - From what ship: Portsmouth, via an admiral's tender - Born: Boston - Age: 18 - Discharged on 8 Sep 1814 and sent to Dartmoor on HMS Niobe.

Watson, John - Seaman - Number: 3787 - Prize name: Adaline - Ship type: LM - How taken: HM Frigate Magiciene - When taken: 14 Mar 1814 - Where taken: off Cape Ortegal, Spain - Date received: 26 May 1814 - From what ship: HMS Hindostan - Born: New Haven - Age: 35 - Race: Black - Died on 8 Oct 1814 from pneumonia.

Watson, Macy - Private - Number: 2658 - Prize name: Benedict's Regiment - Ship type: LF - How taken: British forces - When taken: 22 Jun 1813 - Where taken: Upper Canada - Date received: 5 Nov 1813 - From what ship: HMS Hindostan - Born: North Ireland - Age: 62 - Discharged on 10 Oct 1814 and sent to U.S. on Cartel St. Philip.

Watson, Stephen - Seaman - Number: 2288 - How taken: Gave himself up from HM Ship-of-the-Line Royal George - When taken: 29 Oct 1812 - Date received: 17 Sep 1813 - From what ship: HMS Raisonnable - Born: New Hampshire - Age: 35 - Discharged on 27 Mar 1814 and sent to Calais, France.

Watson, William - Seaman - Number: 3566 - Prize name: Minerva - Ship type: MV - How taken: HM Ship-of-the-Line Conquestador - When taken: 19 Jan 1814 - Where taken: Bay of Biscay - Date received: 7 May 1814 - From what ship: Portsmouth via HMS Favorite - Born: Scarboro - Age: 20 - Discharged on 25 Sep 1814 and sent to Dartmoor on HMS Niobe.

Watson, William - Seaman - Number: 2593 - How taken: Gave himself up from HM Frigate Bombay - When taken: 27 May 1813 - Date received: 5 Nov 1813 - From what ship: HMS Hindostan - Born: Charleston - Age: 30 - Race: Blackman - Discharged on 31 Mar 1814 and released to HMS Ceres.

Watson, William - Private - Number: 3067 - Prize name: 14th U.S. Infantry - Ship type: LF - How taken: British forces - When taken: 24 Jun 1813 - Where taken: Beaver Dams, Upper Canada - Date received: 7 Jan 1814 - From what ship: Halifax - Born: Baltimore - Age: 27 - Discharged on 10 Oct 1814 and sent to U.S. on Cartel St. Philip.

Watts, Anthony - Seaman - Number: 66 - Prize name: Meon - Ship type: MV - How taken: Hospital in London - When taken: 26 Oct 1812 - Date received: 4 Nov 1812 - From what ship: HMS Namur - Born: Boston - Age: 45 - Discharged on 12 Apr 1813 and released to HMS Carnatic.

Watts, James - Seaman - Number: 1592 - Prize name: Dick - Ship type: MV - How taken: HM Brig Dispatch - When taken: 15 Mar 1813 - Where taken: off Bordeaux, France - Date received: 18 Apr 1813 - From what ship: HMS Rosario - Born: New York - Age: 24 - Discharged on 13 Apr 1814 and sent to Dartmoor.

Weare, Ebenezer - Seaman - Number: 2751 - Prize name: Wasp - Ship type: P - How taken: HM Schooner Bream - When taken: 9 Jun 1813 - Where taken: off Halifax - Date received: 7 Jan 1814 - From what ship: Halifax - Born: York - Age: 18 - Discharged on 8 Sep 1814 and sent to Dartmoor on HMS Niobe.

Weaver, Thomas - Seaman - Number: 822 - Prize name: Columbia - Ship type: MV - How taken: HM Frigate Briton - When taken: 17 Dec 1812 - Where taken: off Bordeaux, France - Date received: 27 Feb 1813 - From what ship: Plymouth via HMS Namur - Born: Philadelphia - Age: 28 - Discharged in Jul 1813 and released to Cartel Moses Brown.

Webb, John - Boy - Number: 1456 - Prize name: Orbit - Ship type: MV - How taken: HM Brig Achates - When taken: 29 Jan 1813 - Where taken: Lat 49 N Long 13 W - Date received: 6 Apr 1813 - From what ship: Plymouth via HMS Decoy - Born: New York - Age: 16 - Discharged on 24 Jul 1814 and sent to Dartmoor.

Webb, John - Seaman - Number: 2977 - Prize name: Enterprise - Ship type: P - How taken: HM Frigate Tenedos - When taken: 21 May 1813 - Where taken: off Cape Cod - Date received: 7 Jan 1814 - From what ship: Halifax - Born: Massachusetts - Age: 27 - Discharged on 25 Sep 1814 and sent to Dartmoor on HMS Leyden.

Webb, Nathaniel - Quarter Gunner - Number: 2873 - Prize name: Elbridge Gerry - Ship type: P - How taken: HM Frigate Crescent - When taken: 16 Sep 1813 - Where taken: at sea - Date received: 7 Jan 1814 - From what ship: Portsmouth - Born: Massachusetts - Age: 26 - Discharged on 25 Sep 1814 and sent to Dartmoor on HMS Leyden.

Webb, Stephen - Seaman - Number: 534 - Prize name: Baltimore - Ship type: P - How taken: HM Transport Diadem - When taken: 7 Oct 1812 - Where taken: S. Andres - Date received: 23 Feb 1813 - From what ship: Portsmouth via HMS Dromedary - Born: Baltimore - Age: 31 - Discharged on 11 Aug 1814 and sent to Dartmoor on HMS Freya.

Webb, William - Seaman - Number: 1474 - Prize name: Union - Ship type: MV - How taken: HM Frigate Iris - When taken: 17 Jan 1813 - Where taken: at sea - Date received: 6 Apr 1813 - From what ship: Portsmouth via Tender Eliza - Born: Philadelphia - Age: 19 - Discharged on 26 Jul 1813 and released to Cartel Hoffminy.

Webber, Stephen - Seaman - Number: 2741 - Prize name: Teazer - Ship type: P - How taken: HM Frigate Boreas - When taken: 15 Jun 1813 - Where taken: off Halifax - Date received: 7 Jan 1814 - From what ship: Halifax - Born: Bath - Age: 19 - Died on 3 May 1814 from fever.

Webster, Asa - Seaman - Number: 2960 - Prize name: Enterprise - Ship type: P - How taken: HM Frigate Tenedos - When taken: 21 May 1813 - Where taken: off Cape Cod - Date received: 7 Jan 1814 - From what ship: Halifax - Born: Massachusetts - Age: 23 - Discharged on 25 Sep 1814 and sent to Dartmoor on HMS Leyden.

Webster, David - Seaman - Number: 3253 - Prize name: Thorn - Ship type: P - How taken: Shannon, Nova Scotia privateer - When taken: 7 Nov 1813 - Where taken: off Newfoundland - Date received: 23 Feb 1814 - From what ship: Halifax via HMT Malabar - Born: Salisbury - Age: 19 - Discharged on 10 Oct 1814 and sent to Dartmoor on the Mermaid.

Webster, William - Seaman - Number: 2176 - How taken: Gave himself up from HM Ship-of-the-Line Leviathan - When taken: 28 Oct 1812 - Date received: 16 Aug 1813 - From what ship: Portsmouth, via an admiral's tender - Born: New York - Age: 28 - Discharged on 11 Aug 1814 and sent to Dartmoor on HMS Freya.

Wedgewood, James - Seaman - Number: 1359 - Prize name: Dart - Ship type: MV - How taken: HM Brig Doterel - When taken: 5 Mar 1813 - Where taken: at sea - Date received: 3 Apr 1813 - From what ship: Portsmouth, via an admiral's tender - Born: Massachusetts - Age: 29 - Discharged on 4 Aug 1814 and sent to Dartmoor on HMS Alpheus.

Wedmore, Charles - Seaman - Number: 2029 - How taken: Impressed at London off Russian MV Augnona - When taken: 11 Jul 1812 - Date received: 24 Jul 1813 - From what ship: HMS Raisonnable - Born: New Haven, CT - Age: 27 - Discharged on 28 Sep 1813 and released to HMS Ceres.

Weeden, Richard - Cook - Number: 2323 - Prize name: Fame - Ship type: MV - How taken: HM Ship of-the-Line Cressy - When taken: 20 Jul 1813 - Where taken: at sea - Date received: 8 Oct 1813 - From what ship: Portsmouth, via an admiral's tender - Born: Rhode Island - Age: 30 - Race: Black - Discharged on 4 Sep 1814 and sent to Dartmoor on HMS Freya.

Weeks, George - Seaman - Number: 619 - Prize name: King of Rome - Ship type: P - How taken: HM Brig Wolverine - When taken: 13 Dec 1812 - Where taken: at sea - Date received: 23 Feb 1813 - From what ship: Portsmouth via HMS Dromedary - Born: New York - Age: 16 - Discharged on 2 Jul 1813 and released to Cartel Moses Brown.

Weeks, Lewis - Seaman - Number: 2584 - How taken: Impressed at London - When taken: 21 Oct 1813 - Date received: 1 Nov 1813 - From what ship: HMS Raisonnable - Born: New York - Age: 36 - Race: Black - Discharged on 8 Sep 1814 and sent to Dartmoor on HMS Niobe.

Weilwright, Joseph - Seaman - Number: 704 - Prize name: Deanna, recaptured British vessel - Ship type: P - How taken: HM Ship-of-the-Line Polyphemus - When taken: 14 Sep 1812 - Where taken: at sea - Date received: 24 Feb 1813 - From what ship: Portsmouth via HMS Ulysses - Born: Boston - Age: 20 - Discharged on 8 Jun 1813 and released to Cartel Rodrigo.

Weinberg, John - Seaman - Number: 712 - Prize name: Ganges - Ship type: MV - How taken: Detained at Portsmouth harbor - When taken: 31 Jul 1812 - Date received: 24 Feb 1813 - From what ship: Portsmouth via HMS Ulysses - Born: Edenton, NC - Age: 32 - Discharged on 23 Mar 1813 and released to the Cartel Robinson Potter.

Weisser, Philip - Seaman - Number: 3718 - How taken: English forces off Bordeaux - When taken: 26 Mar 1814 -

Date received: 18 May 1814 - From what ship: HMS Raisonnable - Born: Boston - Age: 27 - Discharged on 25 Sep 1814 and sent to Dartmoor on HMS Leyden.

Welch, John - Seaman - Number: 1863 - How taken: Gave himself up from HM Frigate Leonidas - Date received: 7 Jul 1813 - From what ship: Portsmouth via HMS Tribune - Born: Virginia - Age: 28 - Discharged on 12 Aug 1814 and sent to Dartmoor on HMS Alpheus.

Welch, Samuel - Seaman - Number: 1333 - Prize name: Sea Nymph - Ship type: MV - How taken: HM Brig Thrasher - When taken: 4 Mar 1813 - Where taken: off River Jade (Germany) - Date received: 22 Mar 1813 - From what ship: HMS Thrasher - Born: Baltimore - Age: 24 - Discharged on 23 Jul 1814 and sent to Dartmoor.

Welch, William - Seaman - Number: 566 - Prize name: Rising States - Ship type: MV - How taken: HM Frigate Fortunee - When taken: 28 Aug 1812 - Where taken: off the Western Isles, Scotland - Date received: 23 Feb 1813 - From what ship: Portsmouth via HMS Dromedary - Born: New York - Age: 25 - Discharged on 8 Jun 1813 and released to Cartel Rodrigo.

Wells, Moses - Boy - Number: 1166 - Prize name: Sword Fish - Ship type: P - How taken: HM Ship-of-the-Line Elephant - When taken: 28 Dec 1812 - Where taken: off Azores - Date received: 16 Mar 1813 - From what ship: Portsmouth, via HMS Abundance - Born: Newburyport - Age: 13 - Discharged on 24 Jul 1813 and released to Cartel Hoffminy.

Wells, Thomas - Cook - Number: 728 - Prize name: Eos - Ship type: MV - How taken: Detained at Portsmouth harbor - When taken: 31 Jul 1812 - Date received: 24 Feb 1813 - From what ship: Portsmouth via HMS Ulysses - Born: New York - Age: 29 - Race: Man of color - Discharged on 23 Mar 1813 and released to the Cartel Robinson Potter.

Wells, William - Seaman - Number: 153 - Prize name: Country Square - Ship type: MV - How taken: Stopped at London - When taken: 26 Oct 1812 - Date received: 5 Nov 1812 - From what ship: HMS Namur - Born: Wethersfield, CT - Age: 25 - Race: Mulatto - Discharged in Jul 1813 and released to Cartel Moses Brown.

Welsh, Henry - Private - Number: 3162 - Prize name: U.S. Light Dragoons - Ship type: LF - How taken: British forces - When taken: 24 Jun 1813 - Where taken: Beaver Dams, Upper Canada - Date received: 7 Jan 1814 - From what ship: Halifax - Born: Harford, MD - Age: 24 - Discharged on 10 Oct 1814 and sent to U.S. on Cartel St. Philip.

Welsh, Richard H. - Seaman - Number: 272 - How taken: Apprehended at London - When taken: 7 Dec 1812 - Date received: 19 Dec 1812 - From what ship: HMS Raisonnable - Born: Roxbury, MA - Age: 30 - Discharged on 24 Jul 1813 and released to Cartel Hoffminy.

Welsh, William - Seaman - Number: 1751 - How taken: Gave himself up from HMS Impeteux - When taken: 2 Dec 1812 - Date received: 30 May 1813 - From what ship: HMS Impetius - Born: New York - Age: 22 - Discharged on 24 Jul 1814 and sent to Dartmoor on HMS Liffey.

Welsh, William - Seaman - Number: 2094 - How taken: Gave himself up from HM Ship-of-the-Line Scipion - When taken: 27 May 1813 - Date received: 9 Aug 1813 - From what ship: HMS Thames - Born: Providence, RI - Age: 26 - Discharged on 3 Nov 1813 and released to HMS Ceres.

Wepple, Joseph - Seaman - Number: 3939 - Prize name: Perfect - Ship type: P - How taken: HM Gunboat Grinder - When taken: 6 Jul 1814 - Where taken: off St. Bartholomew, WI - Date received: 3 Oct 1814 - From what ship: London - Born: Providence - Age: 27 - Discharged on 22 Oct 1814 and sent to Dartmoor on HMS Leyden.

Werman, John - Seaman - Number: 3538 - Prize name: Commodore Perry - Ship type: MV - How taken: Sent into custody from a cutter - When taken: 25 Feb 1814 - Where taken: off Bordeaux, France - Date received: 5 Mar 1814 - From what ship: HMS Raisonnable - Born: Philadelphia - Age: 18 - Discharged on 22 Oct 1814 and sent to Dartmoor on HMS Leyden.

Werner, John - Seaman - Number: 1341 - How taken: Gave himself up from HM Ship-of-the-Line Cornwall - When taken: 21 Mar 1813 - Date received: 26 Mar 1813 - From what ship: HMS Raisonnable - Born: Boston - Age: 23 - Discharged on 23 Jul 1814 and sent to Dartmoor.

Weslemyer, John - Seaman - Number: 3782 - Prize name: Argus - Ship type: MV - How taken: HM Ship-of-the-

Line San Domingo - When taken: 1 Mar 1814 - Where taken: off Savannah - Date received: 26 May 1814 - From what ship: HMS Hindostan - Born: Charlestown - Age: 27 - Discharged on 25 Sep 1814 and sent to Dartmoor on HMS Niobe.

Wessels, William - Seaman - Number: 201 - How taken: Gave himself up from HM Hulk Prince William - When taken: 13 Oct 1812 - Date received: 15 Nov 1812 - From what ship: HMS Raisonnable - Born: New York - Age: 23 - Discharged on 26 Jul 1814 and sent to Dartmoor on HMS Raven.

West, Abiah - Private - Number: 3156 - Prize name: 14th U.S. Infantry - Ship type: LF - How taken: British forces - When taken: 24 Jun 1813 - Where taken: Beaver Dams, Upper Canada - Date received: 7 Jan 1814 - From what ship: Halifax - Born: New York - Age: 25 - Discharged on 10 Oct 1814 and sent to U.S. on Cartel St. Philip.

West, George - Seaman - Number: 1851 - How taken: Gave himself up from HM Ship-of-the-Line Malta - Date received: 7 Jul 1813 - From what ship: Portsmouth via HMS Tribune - Born: Baltimore - Age: 24 - Discharged on 25 Jul 1814 and sent to Dartmoor on HMS Bittern.

West, Henry - Prize Master - Number: 1812 - Prize name: Blockade - Ship type: P - How taken: HM Brig Charybdis - When taken: 31 Oct 1812 - Where taken: off Virgin Islands, WI - Date received: 7 Jul 1813 - From what ship: Portsmouth via HMS Scorpion - Born: Newport - Age: 27 - Discharged on 26 Jul 1813 and released to Cartel Hoffminy.

West, John - Seaman - Number: 3919 - Prize name: Gotham - Ship type: MV - How taken: HM Frigate Barbadoes - When taken: 31 Jan 1814 - Where taken: off St. Bartholomew, WI - Date received: 15 Sep 1814 - From what ship: London - Born: Virginia - Age: 19 - Discharged on 22 Oct 1814 and sent to Dartmoor on HMS Leyden.

West, John - Seaman - Number: 1027 - Prize name: Martin - Ship type: MV - How taken: Taken up at Liverpool - When taken: 18 Oct 1812 - Date received: 11 Mar 1813 - From what ship: Yarmouth via HMS Tenders - Born: New Orleans - Age: 20 - Discharged in Jul 1813 and released to Cartel Moses Brown.

West, Nathaniel - Seaman - Number: 1428 - How taken: Gave himself up from HM Frigate Andromache - When taken: 24 Dec 1812 - Date received: 6 Apr 1813 - From what ship: Plymouth via HMS Decoy - Born: Greenfield - Age: 21 - Released on 26 Sep 1814.

West, Silas - Mate - Number: 1926 - Prize name: Edward - Ship type: MV - How taken: Seringapatam, British letter of marque - When taken: 6 Jan 1813 - Where taken: South America - Date received: 11 Jul 1813 - From what ship: HMS Raisonnable - Born: Nantucket - Age: 32 - Discharged on 4 Apr 1814 and sent to Ready on parole.

Westerbest, William - Seaman - Number: 1949 - Prize name: Tiger - Ship type: MV - How taken: HM Brig Scylla - When taken: 22 Mar 1813 - Where taken: Bay of Biscay - Date received: 15 Jul 1813 - From what ship: Plymouth - Born: New York - Age: 22 - Discharged on 17 Jun 1814 and sent to Dartmoor on HMS Redbreast.

Westler, John - Seaman - Number: 2139 - Prize name: Matilda, prize of the U.S. Brig Argus - Ship type: War - How taken: HM Frigate Revolutionnaire - When taken: 25 Jul 1813 - Where taken: off Lorient, France - Date received: 9 Aug 1813 - From what ship: HMS Thames - Born: New Jersey - Age: 18 - Discharged on 4 Aug 1814 and sent to Dartmoor on HMS Alpheus.

Weston, Nathaniel - Seaman - Number: 2465 - Prize name: Cossack - Ship type: P - How taken: HM Frigate Amelia - When taken: 11 Apr 1813 - Where taken: off St. Johns - Date received: 21 Oct 1813 - From what ship: Portsmouth via HMT Malabar - Born: Woban - Age: 20 - Discharged on 8 Sep 1814 and sent to Dartmoor on HMS Niobe.

Wetou, William (alias Andrew Quicken) - Seaman - Number: 1655 - How taken: Gave himself up from HM Ship-of-the-Line Ajax - Date received: 9 May 1813 - From what ship: HMS Raisonnable - Born: New York - Age: 21 - Discharged on 13 Aug 1814 and sent to Dartmoor.

Wettey, Philip - Seaman - Number: 2964 - Prize name: Enterprise - Ship type: P - How taken: HM Frigate Tenedos - When taken: 21 May 1813 - Where taken: off Cape Cod - Date received: 7 Jan 1814 - From what ship: Halifax - Born: Waysel, Prussia - Age: 31 - Discharged on 22 Jun 1814 and sent to Calais, France on the Simon & Mary.

Whagerman, Joseph - Private - Number: 3138 - Prize name: 14th U.S. Infantry - Ship type: LF - How taken: British forces - When taken: 24 Jun 1813 - Where taken: Beaver Dams, Upper Canada - Date received: 7 Jan 1814 - From what ship: Halifax - Born: Delaware - Age: 26 - Discharged on 10 Oct 1814 and sent to U.S. on Cartel St. Philip.

Wheebell, Robert - Seaman - Number: 1675 - How taken: Gave himself up from HM Ship-of-the-Line Warrior - When taken: 21 Apr 1813 - Date received: 9 May 1813 - From what ship: HMS Raisonnable - Born: Newbury - Age: 33 - Discharged on 20 Aug 1814 and sent to Dartmoor on HMS Shamrock.

Wheeler, Anthony - Private - Number: 3147 - Prize name: 14th U.S. Infantry - Ship type: LF - How taken: British forces - When taken: 24 Jun 1813 - Where taken: Beaver Dams, Upper Canada - Date received: 7 Jan 1814 - From what ship: Halifax - Born: Maryland - Age: 23 - Discharged on 10 Oct 1814 and sent to U.S. on Cartel St. Philip.

Wheeler, Michael - Seaman - Number: 3388 - Prize name: Fox - Ship type: P - How taken: HM Frigate Maidstone - When taken: 18 Jul 1813 - Where taken: Grand Banks - Date received: 23 Feb 1814 - From what ship: Halifax via HMT Malabar - Born: Boston - Age: 27 - Discharged on 20 Aug 1814 and sent to Dartmoor on HMS Shamrock.

Wheeler, William - Seaman - Number: 1445 - Prize name: Orbit - Ship type: MV - How taken: HM Brig Achates - When taken: 29 Jan 1813 - Where taken: Lat 49 N Long 13 W - Date received: 6 Apr 1813 - From what ship: Plymouth via HMS Decoy - Born: Newburyport - Age: 20 - Discharged on 24 Jul 1814 and sent to Dartmoor.

Wheelock, Abel - Lieutenant - Number: 3043 - Prize name: U.S. Light Dragoons - Ship type: LF - How taken: British forces - When taken: 28 May 1813 - Where taken: Sackets Harbor - Date received: 7 Jan 1814 - From what ship: Halifax - Born: Lancaster - Age: 45 - Discharged on 14 Jan 1814 and sent to Reading on parole.

Wherry, Daniel - Passenger - Number: 3355 - Prize name: Rolla - Ship type: P - How taken: HM Ship-of-the-Line Victorious - When taken: 8 Jan 1813 - Where taken: off Halifax - Date received: 23 Feb 1814 - From what ship: Halifax via HMT Malabar - Born: Philadelphia - Age: 18 - Discharged on 10 Oct 1814 and sent to Dartmoor on the Mermaid.

Whipple, Samuel - Seaman - Number: 449 - Prize name: Hunter - Ship type: P - How taken: HM Frigate Phoebe - When taken: 23 Dec 1812 - Where taken: off Azores - Date received: 19 Feb 1813 - From what ship: HMS Modeste - Born: Newport - Age: 26 - Discharged on 24 Jul 1813 and released to Cartel Hoffminy.

Whitchouse, Lewis - Marine Private - Number: 1172 - Prize name: Sword Fish - Ship type: P - How taken: HM Ship-of-the-Line Elephant - When taken: 28 Dec 1812 - Where taken: off Azores - Date received: 16 Mar 1813 - From what ship: Portsmouth, via HMS Abundance - Born: Brookfield - Age: 19 - Discharged on 24 Jul 1813 and released to Cartel Hoffminy.

White, Alden - Seaman - Number: 1035 - Prize name: Catharine - Ship type: MV - How taken: HM Frigate Leonidas - When taken: 31 Jul 1812 - Where taken: off Ireland - Date received: 11 Mar 1813 - From what ship: Yarmouth via HMS Tenders - Born: New Bedford - Age: 20 - Discharged on 26 Jul 1813 and released to Cartel Hoffminy.

White, Benjamin - Prize Master - Number: 1017 - Prize name: Sword Fish - Ship type: P - How taken: HM Ship-of-the-Line Elephant - When taken: 28 Dec 1812 - Where taken: off Azores - Date received: 10 Mar 1813 - From what ship: HMS Furious - Born: Salem - Age: 27 - Discharged on 24 Jul 1813 and released to Cartel Hoffminy.

White, Charles - Seaman - Number: 1576 - How taken: Gave himself up from HM Ship-of-the-Line Braham - When taken: 10 Dec 1812 - Date received: 16 Apr 1813 - From what ship: HMS Namur, admiral's tender - Born: Virginia - Age: 25 - Race: Black - Discharged on 20 Sep 1813 and released to HMS Ceres.

White, Charles - Seaman - Number: 2180 - How taken: Gave himself up from HM Ship-of-the-Line Leviathan - When taken: 28 Oct 1812 - Date received: 16 Aug 1813 - From what ship: Portsmouth, via an admiral's tender - Born: New York - Age: 38 - Race: Mulatto - Discharged on 11 Aug 1814 and sent to Dartmoor on HMS Freya.

White, Edward - Seaman - Number: 2793 - Prize name: Yorktown - Ship type: P - How taken: British squadron - When taken: 17 Jul 1813 - Where taken: Grand Banks - Date received: 7 Jan 1814 - From what ship: Halifax

- Born: New York - Age: 30 - Discharged on 26 Sep 1814 and sent to Dartmoor on HMS Leyden.

White, George - Seaman - Number: 3765 - Prize name: Argus - Ship type: MV - How taken: HM Ship-of-the-Line San Domingo - When taken: 1 Mar 1814 - Where taken: off Savannah - Date received: 26 May 1814 - From what ship: HMS Hindostan - Born: Boston - Age: 19 - Discharged on 25 Sep 1814 and sent to Dartmoor on HMS Niobe.

White, Henry - Shipwright - Number: 243 - How taken: Gave himself up from HM Ship-of-the-Line Mulgrave - When taken: 28 Nov 1812 - Date received: 1 Dec 1812 - From what ship: HMS Raisonnable - Born: New Hampshire - Age: 43 - Discharged on 25 Jul 1814 and sent to Dartmoor on HMS Bittern.

White, J. William - Seaman - Number: 716 - Prize name: James - Ship type: MV - How taken: Detained at Portsmouth harbor - When taken: 31 Jul 1812 - Date received: 24 Feb 1813 - From what ship: Portsmouth via HMS Ulysses - Born: Providence - Age: 29 - Discharged on 23 Mar 1813 and released to the Cartel Robinson Potter.

White, James - Seaman - Number: 3946 - How taken: Impressed at London - When taken: 6 Oct 1814 - Date received: 12 Oct 1813 - From what ship: Quebec - Born: Hartford - Age: 26 - Discharged on 22 Oct 1814 and sent to Dartmoor on HMS Leyden.

White, John - Seaman - Number: 807 - Prize name: Bell - Ship type: MV - How taken: Phillis - When taken: 18 Dec 1812 - Where taken: off Cadiz, Spain - Date received: 27 Feb 1813 - From what ship: Plymouth via HMS Namur - Born: New Orleans - Age: 23 - Discharged on 8 Jun 1813 and released to Cartel Rodrigo.

White, John - Prize Master - Number: 1814 - Prize name: tender to the Privateer True Blooded Yankee - Ship type: P - How taken: HM Ship-of-the-Line Fame - When taken: 24 Jun 1813 - Where taken: off Brest, France - Date received: 7 Jul 1813 - From what ship: Portsmouth via HMS Scorpion - Born: Portsmouth, NH - Age: 29 - Discharged on 25 Jul 1814 and sent to Dartmoor on HMS Bittern.

White, John - Private - Number: 3103 - Prize name: 14th U.S. Infantry - Ship type: LF - How taken: British forces - When taken: 24 Jun 1813 - Where taken: Beaver Dams, Upper Canada - Date received: 7 Jan 1814 - From what ship: Halifax - Born: Baltimore - Age: 24 - Discharged on 10 Oct 1814 and sent to U.S. on Cartel St. Philip.

White, John W. - Seaman - Number: 1263 - How taken: Gave himself up from HM Ship-of-the-Line Mars - When taken: 9 Dec 1812 - Date received: 16 Mar 1813 - From what ship: Portsmouth, via HMS Abundance - Born: Petersburg - Age: 23 - Race: Black - Discharged on 18 Oct 1813 and released to HMS Ceres.

White, John W. - Prize Master - Number: 1016 - Prize name: Sword Fish - Ship type: P - How taken: HM Ship-of-the-Line Elephant - When taken: 28 Dec 1812 - Where taken: off Azores - Date received: 10 Mar 1813 - From what ship: HMS Furious - Born: Marblehead - Age: 23 - Discharged on 24 Jul 1813 and released to Cartel Hoffminy.

White, Robert - Cook - Number: 2131 - How taken: Gave himself up from HM Brig Confounder - When taken: 10 Jun 1813 - Date received: 9 Aug 1813 - From what ship: HMS Thames - Born: Salem - Age: 27 - Discharged on 12 Aug 1814 and sent to Dartmoor on HMS Alpheus.

White, Sampson - Reserve Officer - Number: 418 - Prize name: Hunter - Ship type: P - How taken: HM Frigate Phoebe - When taken: 23 Dec 1812 - Where taken: off Azores - Date received: 19 Feb 1813 - From what ship: HMS Modeste - Born: Boston - Age: 24 - Discharged on 2 Jul 1813 and released to Cartel Moses Brown.

White, Thomas - Sailmaker - Number: 1777 - Prize name: Antelope - Ship type: P - How taken: HM Brig Zephyr - When taken: 10 Dec 1812 - Where taken: at sea - Date received: 14 Jun 1813 - From what ship: HMS Arethusa - Born: Burlington - Age: 21 - Released on 24 Jul 1814.

White, William - Seaman - Number: 2165 - How taken: Gave himself up from HM Transport Malabar - When taken: 22 Sep 1812 - Date received: 16 Aug 1813 - From what ship: Portsmouth, via an admiral's tender - Born: Philadelphia - Age: 21 - Escaped on 16 May 1814 from HM Prison Ship Crown Prince.

White, William - Seaman - Number: 1726 - Prize name: Powhattan - Ship type: MV - How taken: HMS Horatio - When taken: 13 Dec 1812 - Where taken: Bay of Biscay - Date received: 25 May 1813 - From what ship: Portsmouth via HMS Impetius - Born: New York - Age: 21 - Discharged on 24 Jul 1813 and released to

Cartel Hoffminy.

White, William - Seaman - Number: 3419 - Prize name: Thomas - Ship type: P - How taken: HM Frigate Nymphe - When taken: 27 Jun 1813 - Where taken: at sea - Date received: 23 Feb 1814 - From what ship: Halifax via HMT Malabar - Born: Portsmouth - Age: 19 - Discharged on 22 Oct 1814 and sent to Dartmoor on HMS Leyden.

White, William (1) - Seaman - Number: 1992 - How taken: Gave himself up from HM Ship-of-the-Line Clarence - Date received: 15 Jul 1813 - From what ship: Plymouth - Born: New York - Age: 25 - Discharged on 17 Jun 1814 and sent to Dartmoor on HMS Pincher.

White, William (2) - Seaman - Number: 1993 - How taken: Gave himself up from HM Ship-of-the-Line Clarence - Date received: 15 Jul 1813 - From what ship: Plymouth - Born: Boston - Age: 23 - Discharged on 17 Jun 1814 and sent to Dartmoor on HMS Pincher.

Whitlock, Sidney B. - 2nd Mate - Number: 979 - Prize name: Empress - Ship type: MV - How taken: HM Brig Rover - When taken: 30 Nov 1812 - Where taken: St. Andrew - Date received: 10 Mar 1813 - From what ship: HMS Tigress - Born: New York - Age: 19 - Discharged on 8 Jun 1813 and released to Cartel Rodrigo.

Whitman, Joseph - Seaman - Number: 3360 - Prize name: York - Ship type: MV - How taken: HM Frigate Tenedos - When taken: 26 May 1813 - Where taken: off Cape Sable, Florida - Date received: 23 Feb 1814 - From what ship: Halifax via HMT Malabar - Born: Little York - Age: 25 - Race: Black - Discharged on 11 Mar 1814 and released to HMS Thames.

Whitman, Samuel - Private - Number: 3146 - Prize name: 14th U.S. Infantry - Ship type: LF - How taken: British forces - When taken: 24 Jun 1813 - Where taken: Beaver Dams, Upper Canada - Date received: 7 Jan 1814 - From what ship: Halifax - Born: Massachusetts - Age: 18 - Discharged on 10 Oct 1814 and sent to U.S. on Cartel St. Philip.

Whitmore, John - Seaman - Number: 1612 - How taken: Gave himself up from HM Frigate President at Chatham - When taken: 27 Apr 1813 - Date received: 1 May 1813 - From what ship: HMS President - Born: Portsmouth, VA - Age: 25 - Discharged on 24 Jul 1814 and sent to Dartmoor.

Whitney, Joseph - Seaman - Number: 838 - Prize name: Vengeance - Ship type: LM - How taken: HM Frigate Phoebe - When taken: 1 Jan 1813 - Where taken: Lat 44.4 Long 23 - Date received: 1 Mar 1813 - From what ship: Plymouth via HMS Namur - Born: Northampton - Age: 20 - Discharged on 24 Jul 1813 and released to Cartel Hoffminy.

Whitow, Miles - Seaman - Number: 3917 - Prize name: Union - Ship type: MV - How taken: HM Transport Malabar No. 352 - When taken: 17 Jan 1814 - Where taken: Calcutta - Date received: 12 Sep 1814 - From what ship: London - Born: Richmond - Age: 27 - Discharged on 22 Oct 1814 and sent to Dartmoor on HMS Leyden.

Whittington, George - Seaman - Number: 3440 - Prize name: Portsmouth Packet - Ship type: P - How taken: HM Brig Fantome - When taken: 5 Oct 1813 - Where taken: Grand Banks - Date received: 23 Feb 1814 - From what ship: Halifax via HMT Malabar - Born: Gloucester - Age: 25 - Discharged on 21 Jul 1814 and sent to Dartmoor on HMS Portia.

Whittlebank, Edward - Seaman - Number: 738 - How taken: Sent to prison off the HM Brig Parthian - Date received: 24 Feb 1813 - From what ship: Portsmouth via HMS Ulysses - Born: Portsmouth, NH - Age: 21 - Discharged on 26 Jul 1814 and sent to Dartmoor on HMS Raven.

Whitton, John - Private - Number: 3049 - Prize name: U.S. Light Dragoons - Ship type: LF - How taken: British forces - When taken: 24 Jun 1813 - Where taken: Beaver Dams, Upper Canada - Date received: 7 Jan 1814 - From what ship: Halifax - Born: Delaware - Age: 23 - Discharged on 10 Oct 1814 and sent to U.S. on Cartel St. Philip.

Wickham, Ezekiel - Seaman - Number: 2205 - How taken: Gave himself up from HM Ship-of-the-Line Goliath - When taken: 8 Aug 1813 - Date received: 18 Aug 1813 - From what ship: Portsmouth, via an admiral's tender - Born: Connecticut - Age: 25 - Discharged on 10 Oct 1813 and released to HMS Ceres.

Wickham, Thaddeus - Seaman - Number: 1518 - How taken: Gave himself up from HM Frigate Brune - When taken: 19 Jan 1813 - Date received: 8 Apr 1813 - From what ship: Portsmouth, via an admiral's tender - Born: Bridgetown - Age: 28 - Race: Mulatto - Discharged on 4 Aug 1814 and sent to Dartmoor on HMS Alpheus.

Wicks, James - Seaman - Number: 119 - How taken: Impressed at London off MV Henry - When taken: 26 Oct 1812 - Date received: 4 Nov 1812 - From what ship: HMS Namur - Born: Providence, RI - Age: 30 - Died on 14 Apr 1813 from phthisis (tuberculosis).

Wicks, Littleton - Seaman - Number: 1022 - Prize name: Hannah - Ship type: MV - How taken: Taken up at Liverpool - When taken: 18 Oct 1812 - Date received: 11 Mar 1813 - From what ship: Yarmouth via HMS Tenders - Born: Virginia - Age: 27 - Race: Black - Discharged in Jul 1813 and released to Cartel Moses Brown.

Wickwall, Joseph - Seaman - Number: 1005 - How taken: Gave himself up from HM Ship-of-the-Line Cressy - When taken: 20 Dec 1812 - Date received: 10 Mar 1813 - From what ship: HMS Furious - Born: Bennington - Age: 25 - Discharged on 4 Aug 1814 and sent to Dartmoor on HMS Liverpool.

Widger, John - Seaman - Number: 2481 - Prize name: Enterprise - Ship type: P - How taken: HM Frigate Tenedos - When taken: 21 May 1813 - Where taken: off Cape Cod - Date received: 22 Oct 1813 - From what ship: Portsmouth via HMT Malabar - Born: Marblehead - Age: 27 - Discharged on 8 Sep 1814 and sent to Dartmoor on HMS Niobe.

Widger, Joseph - Seaman - Number: 2693 - Prize name: Growler - Ship type: P - How taken: HM Brig Electra - When taken: 7 Jul 1813 - Where taken: off St. Johns - Date received: 7 Jan 1814 - From what ship: Portsmouth - Born: Marblehead - Age: 21 - Discharged on 8 Sep 1814 and sent to Dartmoor on HMS Niobe.

Widger, Thomas - Seaman - Number: 3 - Prize name: Cato - Ship type: MV - How taken: Detained on the Baltic - When taken: 11 Aug 1812 - Date received: 29 Oct 1812 - From what ship: HMS Raisonnable - Born: Marblehead - Age: 22 - Discharged on 10 May 1813 and released to Cartel Admittance.

Wiggins, Richard - Seaman - Number: 3307 - Prize name: Lark - Ship type: MV - How taken: HM Schooner Bream - When taken: 12 Apr 1813 - Where taken: off Cape Sable, Florida - Date received: 23 Feb 1814 - From what ship: Halifax via HMT Malabar - Born: Salem - Age: 30 - Discharged on 10 Oct 1814 and sent to Dartmoor on the Mermaid.

Wiggins, Samuel - 2nd Mate - Number: 3849 - Prize name: Rose - Ship type: MV - How taken: HM Brig Racehorse - When taken: 6 Feb 1813 - Where taken: Madras, India - Date received: 22 Aug 1814 - From what ship: Gravesend - Born: Salem - Age: 29 - Discharged on 10 Oct 1814 and sent to Dartmoor on the Mermaid.

Wilcox, Caesar - Seaman - Number: 457 - Prize name: Hunter - Ship type: P - How taken: HM Frigate Phoebe - When taken: 23 Dec 1812 - Where taken: off Azores - Date received: 19 Feb 1813 - From what ship: HMS Modeste - Born: Connecticut - Age: 41 - Race: Negro - Discharged on 24 Jul 1813 and released to Cartel Hoffminy.

Wilcox, Ephraim - Seaman - Number: 1605 - How taken: Gave himself up from HM Brig Acteon - When taken: 2 Apr 1813 - Date received: 19 Apr 1813 - From what ship: HMS Raisonnable - Born: Hantan, CT - Age: 23 - Discharged on 4 Nov 1813 and released to HMS Ceres.

Wilcox, William - Seaman - Number: 3927 - How taken: Gave himself up from HM Frigate Quebec - When taken: 1 Sep 1814 - Date received: 24 Sep 1814 - From what ship: HMS Namur - Born: Connecticut - Age: 43 - Discharged on 29 Sep 1814 and sent to Dartmoor on HMS Freya.

Wilder, Titus - Private - Number: 3088 - Prize name: 23rd U.S. Infantry - Ship type: LF - How taken: British forces - When taken: 24 Jun 1813 - Where taken: Beaver Dams, Upper Canada - Date received: 7 Jan 1814 - From what ship: Halifax - Born: York - Age: 20 - Discharged on 10 Oct 1814 and sent to U.S. on Cartel St. Philip.

Wiley, David - Seaman - Number: 1648 - How taken: Gave himself up from HM Frigate Unicorn - When taken: 17 Jun 1813 - Date received: 9 May 1813 - From what ship: HMS Raisonnable - Born: Wellfleet - Age: 37 - Discharged on 13 Aug 1814 and sent to Dartmoor.

Wiley, John - Private - Number: 1626 - Prize name: 13th U.S. Infantry - Ship type: LF - How taken: British forces - When taken: 13 Oct 1812 - Where taken: Upper Canada - Date received: 9 May 1813 - From what ship: HMS Raisonnable - Born: Downs, Ireland - Age: 41 - Discharged on 22 Oct 1814 and sent to Dartmoor on HMS Leyden.

Wilkey, Timothy - Seaman - Number: 2426 - Prize name: Maydock - Ship type: MV - How taken: HM Brig Rebuff - When taken: 16 Jun 1813 - Where taken: off Cape St. Marys, Newfoundland - Date received: 21 Oct 1813 -

From what ship: Portsmouth via HMT Malabar - Born: Dartmouth - Age: 18 - Discharged on 4 Sep 1814 and sent to Dartmoor on HMS Freya.

Willet, Jonathan - Seaman - Number: 167 - Prize name: Antelope - Ship type: MV - How taken: HMS Horato - When taken: 2 Aug 1812 - Where taken: off Norway - Date received: 5 Nov 1812 - From what ship: HMS Namur - Born: Eastern Shore, VA - Age: 26 - Discharged on 23 Mar 1813 and released to the Cartel Robinson Potter.

Willett, John - Seaman - Number: 2020 - How taken: Gave himself up rom HM Sloop-Brig Rosario - Date received: 15 Jul 1813 - From what ship: Plymouth - Born: Baltimore - Age: 28 - Discharged on 17 Jun 1814 and sent to Dartmoor on HMS Pincher.

Williams, Abraham - Mate - Number: 1762 - How taken: Given up from HM Brig Acteon - When taken: 12 Jun 1813 - Date received: 14 Jun 1813 - From what ship: HMS Raisonnable - Born: Philadelphia - Age: 44 - Race: Blackman - Discharged on 24 Jul 1814 and sent to Dartmoor on HMS Liffey.

Williams, Alexander - Seaman - Number: 1030 - Prize name: Industry - Ship type: MV - How taken: Taken up at Liverpool - When taken: 18 Oct 1812 - Date received: 11 Mar 1813 - From what ship: Yarmouth via HMS Tenders - Born: Long Island - Age: 21 - Race: Black - Discharged in Jul 1813 and released to Cartel Moses Brown.

Williams, Andrew - Private - Number: 3131 - Prize name: 14th U.S. Infantry - Ship type: LF - How taken: British forces - When taken: 24 Jun 1813 - Where taken: Beaver Dams, Upper Canada - Date received: 7 Jan 1814 - From what ship: Halifax - Born: New York - Age: 35 - Discharged on 10 Oct 1814 and sent to U.S. on Cartel St. Philip.

Williams, Benjamin - Seaman - Number: 3900 - How taken: Gave himself up from the MV Emily - When taken: 28 Aug 1814 - Date received: 31 Aug 1814 - From what ship: Transport Office - Born: Boston - Age: 24 - Discharged on 25 Sep 1814 and sent to Dartmoor on HMS Leyden.

Williams, Benjamin - Seaman - Number: 1233 - Prize name: Rossie - Ship type: MV - How taken: HM Frigate Dryand - When taken: 7 Jan 1813 - Where taken: at sea - Date received: 16 Mar 1813 - From what ship: Portsmouth, via HMS Abundance - Born: Baltimore - Age: 14 - Discharged on 24 Jul 1813 and released to Cartel Hoffminy.

Williams, Charles - Seaman - Number: 3672 - Prize name: Pilot - Ship type: LM - How taken: Vittoria, British privateer from Guernsey - When taken: 28 Jan 1813 - Where taken: off Bordeaux, France - Date received: 4 May 1814 - From what ship: Portsmouth - Born: New London - Age: 22 - Race: Black - Discharged on 25 Sep 1814 and sent to Dartmoor on HMS Niobe.

Williams, Charles - Seaman - Number: 3258 - Prize name: Volante - Ship type: P - How taken: HM Brig Curlew - When taken: 25 Mar 1813 - Where taken: off Boston - Date received: 23 Feb 1814 - From what ship: Halifax via HMT Malabar - Born: Marblehead - Age: 21 - Discharged on 21 Jul 1814 and sent to Dartmoor on HMS Portia.

Williams, Darius - Seaman - Number: 500 - How taken: Gave himself up from HM Ship-of-the-Line Ruby - When taken: 15 Aug 1812 - Date received: 23 Feb 1813 - From what ship: Portsmouth via HMS Dromedary - Born: Seabrook - Age: 27 - Race: Man of color - Discharged on 26 Jul 1814 and sent to Dartmoor on HMS Raven.

Williams, David - Seaman - Number: 3608 - Prize name: Liberty - Ship type: MV - How taken: Surrendered at Stromness, Scotland - When taken: 30 Dec 1813 - Date received: 29 Mar 1814 - From what ship: Hired tender Anna - Born: Not readable - Age: 21 - Escaped on 20 May 1814 from HM Prison Ship Glory.

Williams, David - Seaman - Number: 571 - Prize name: Castor - Ship type: MV - How taken: HM Schooner Antelope - When taken: 30 Jul 1812 - Where taken: at sea - Date received: 23 Feb 1813 - From what ship: Portsmouth via HMS Dromedary - Born: Wiscasset, MA - Age: 30 - Discharged on 23 Mar 1813 and released to the Cartel Robinson Potter.

Williams, Edward - Seaman - Number: 210 - How taken: Gave himself up from MV Expedition - When taken: 16 Nov 1812 - Date received: 15 Nov 1812 - From what ship: HMS Raisonnable - Born: Greenwich, NJ - Age: 32 - Died on 12 Feb 1813 from debility (feeble).

Williams, Frederick (1) - Seaman - Number: 2487 - Prize name: Enterprise - Ship type: P - How taken: HM Frigate

Tenedos - When taken: 21 May 1813 - Where taken: off Cape Cod - Date received: 22 Oct 1813 - From what ship: Portsmouth via HMT Malabar - Born: Marblehead - Age: 21 - Discharged on 8 Sep 1814 and sent to Dartmoor on HMS Niobe.

Williams, Frederick (2) - Seaman - Number: 2952 - Prize name: Enterprise - Ship type: P - How taken: HM Frigate Tenedos - When taken: 21 May 1813 - Where taken: off Cape Cod - Date received: 7 Jan 1814 - From what ship: Halifax - Born: Massachusetts - Age: 21 - Died on 3 Oct 1814 from phthisis (tuberculosis).

Williams, Gaspar - Seaman - Number: 644 - Prize name: U.S.R.M. Cutter James Madison - Ship type: War - How taken: HM Frigate Barbadoes - When taken: 22 Aug 1812 - Where taken: at sea - Date received: 24 Feb 1813 - From what ship: Portsmouth via HMS Ulysses - Born: Dunkirk, France - Age: 42 - Discharged on 8 Jun 1813 and released to Cartel Rodrigo.

Williams, George - Seaman - Number: 3714 - Prize name: Requin - Ship type: LM - How taken: HM Frigate Venus - When taken: 5 Mar 1814 - Where taken: off Bordeaux, France - Date received: 18 May 1814 - From what ship: HMS Raisonnable - Born: Charlestown - Age: 32 - Race: Black - Discharged on 26 Sep 1814 and sent to Dartmoor on HMS Leyden.

Williams, George - Seaman - Number: 1299 - How taken: Gave himself up from HM Guardship Royal William - When taken: 3 Feb 1813 - Date received: 16 Mar 1813 - From what ship: Portsmouth, via HMS Abundance - Born: New Jersey - Age: 32 - Died on 10 Jan 1814 from fever.

Williams, George - Seaman - Number: 2194 - How taken: Gave himself up from HM Ship-of-the-Line Caledonia - When taken: 5 Dec 1812 - Date received: 18 Aug 1813 - From what ship: French Account - Born: Massachusetts - Age: 39 - Race: Mulatto - Discharged on 11 Aug 1814 and sent to Dartmoor on HMS Freya.

Williams, George (1) - Seaman - Number: 1037 - Prize name: Catharine - Ship type: MV - How taken: HM Frigate Leonidas - When taken: 31 Jul 1812 - Where taken: off Ireland - Date received: 11 Mar 1813 - From what ship: Yarmouth via HMS Tenders - Born: Queen Anne's County - Age: 23 - Race: Black - Discharged on 26 Jul 1813 and released to Cartel Hoffminy.

Williams, George (2) - Seaman - Number: 1038 - Prize name: Catharine - Ship type: MV - How taken: HM Frigate Leonidas - When taken: 31 Jul 1812 - Where taken: off Ireland - Date received: 11 Mar 1813 - From what ship: Yarmouth via HMS Tenders - Born: Baltimore - Age: 26 - Race: Black - Discharged on 26 Jul 1813 and released to Cartel Hoffminy.

Williams, George F. - 2nd Lieutenant - Number: 3726 - Prize name: Argus - Ship type: MV - How taken: HM Ship-of-the-Line San Domingo - When taken: 1 Mar 1814 - Where taken: off Savannah - Date received: 26 May 1814 - From what ship: London - Born: Nottingham - Age: 29 - Discharged on 20 Aug 1814 and sent to Dartmoor on HMS Shamrock.

Williams, Henry - 2nd Mate - Number: 611 - Prize name: King of Rome - Ship type: P - How taken: HM Brig Wolverine - When taken: 13 Dec 1812 - Where taken: at sea - Date received: 23 Feb 1813 - From what ship: Portsmouth via HMS Dromedary - Born: Seabrook - Age: 24 - Discharged on 2 Jul 1813 and released to Cartel Moses Brown.

Williams, James - Seaman - Number: 3773 - Prize name: Argus - Ship type: MV - How taken: HM Ship-of-the-Line San Domingo - When taken: 1 Mar 1814 - Where taken: off Savannah - Date received: 26 May 1814 - From what ship: HMS Hindostan - Born: Baltimore - Age: 21 - Race: Black - Discharged on 25 Sep 1814 and sent to Dartmoor on HMS Niobe.

Williams, James - Seaman - Number: 3808 - How taken: Gave himself up from HM Ship-of-the-Line Leader - When taken: 6 Jul 1813 - Date received: 13 Jun 1814 - From what ship: Quebec - Born: Boston - Age: 27 - Discharged on 12 Aug 1814 and sent to Dartmoor on HMS Alpheus.

Williams, James - Seaman - Number: 1405 - Prize name: Porcupine - Ship type: MV - How taken: HM Frigate Dryand - When taken: 8 Jan 1813 - Where taken: off Bordeaux, France - Date received: 5 Apr 1813 - From what ship: Plymouth via HMS Dwarf - Born: Norfolk - Age: 28 - Discharged on 24 Jul 1813 and released to Cartel Hoffminy.

Williams, James - Seaman - Number: 1656 - How taken: Gave himself up from HM Frigate Loire - Date received: 9 May 1813 - From what ship: HMS Raisonnable - Born: Taunton - Age: 26 - Discharged on 13 Aug 1814 and sent to Dartmoor.

Williams, John - Seaman - Number: 3643 - Prize name: Bunker Hill - Ship type: P - How taken: HM Frigate Pomone & HM Frigate Cydnus - When taken: 4 Mar 1814 - Where taken: Bay of Biscay - Date received: 31 Mar 1814 - From what ship: HMS Raisonnable - Born: New York - Age: 21 - Discharged on 25 Sep 1814 and sent to Dartmoor on HMS Niobe.

Williams, John - Seaman - Number: 1597 - How taken: Impressed at Gravesend, England - When taken: 13 Jan 1813 - Date received: 19 Apr 1813 - From what ship: HMS Raisonnable - Born: Salem - Age: 29 - Discharged on 24 Jul 1813 and released to Cartel Hoffminy.

Williams, John - Seaman - Number: 74 - Prize name: Gulliver - Ship type: MV - How taken: Impressed off Alafase - When taken: 20 May 1812 - Date received: 4 Nov 1812 - From what ship: HMS Namur - Born: Salem, MA - Age: 27 - Discharged on 23 Mar 1813 and released to the Cartel Robinson Potter.

Williams, John - Seaman - Number: 1178 - Prize name: Sword Fish - Ship type: P - How taken: HM Ship-of-the-Line Elephant - When taken: 28 Dec 1812 - Where taken: off Azores - Date received: 16 Mar 1813 - From what ship: Portsmouth, via HMS Abundance - Born: Portland - Age: 31 - Discharged on 19 May 1813 and released to HMS Ceres.

Williams, John - Seaman - Number: 1837 - Prize name: tender to the Privateer True Blooded Yankee - Ship type: P - How taken: HM Ship-of-the-Line Fame - When taken: 24 Jun 1813 - Where taken: off Brest, France - Date received: 7 Jul 1813 - From what ship: Portsmouth via HMS Scorpion - Born: Staten Island - Age: 42 - Race: Mulatto - Released on 11 Jul 1814.

Williams, John - Seaman - Number: 1826 - Prize name: tender to the Privateer True Blooded Yankee - Ship type: P - How taken: HM Brig Hope - When taken: 24 Jun 1813 - Where taken: off Brest, France - Date received: 7 Jul 1813 - From what ship: Portsmouth via HMS Scorpion - Born: Virginia - Age: 27 - Discharged on 5 Aug 1813 and released to HMS Ceres.

Williams, John - Seaman - Number: 2554 - How taken: Gave himself up from HM Ship-of-the-Line Prince of Wales - When taken: 21 May 1813 - Date received: 23 Oct 1813 - From what ship: Portsmouth via HMS Raisonnable - Born: New Jersey - Age: 26 - Discharged on 11 Aug 1814 and sent to Dartmoor on HMS Freya.

Williams, John - Seaman - Number: 2067 - How taken: Gave himself up from HM Brig Eclair - When taken: 26 May 1813 - Date received: 9 Aug 1813 - From what ship: HMS Thames - Born: Worcester, MA - Age: 32 - Discharged on 4 Aug 1814 and sent to Dartmoor on HMS Liverpool.

Williams, John - Seaman - Number: 2059 - How taken: Gave up from HM Ship-of-the-Line Monmouth - When taken: 28 Jul 1813 - Date received: 4 Aug 1813 - From what ship: HMS Raisonnable - Born: Kennebunk - Age: 33 - Discharged on 4 Aug 1814 and sent to Dartmoor on HMS Liverpool.

Williams, Joseph - Seaman - Number: 3880 - How taken: Gave himself up from HM Frigate Clorinde - When taken: 18 Dec 1813 - Date received: 28 Aug 1814 - From what ship: London - Born: Martha's Vineyard - Age: 26 - Race: Black - Discharged on 8 Sep 1814 and sent to Dartmoor on HMS Niobe.

Williams, Joseph - Seaman - Number: 366 - How taken: Gave himself up from HM Frigate Frederichsteen - When taken: 14 Oct 1812 - Date received: 21 Jan 1813 - From what ship: HMS Raisonnable - Born: Peekskill, NY - Age: 29 - Discharged on 26 Jul 1814 and sent to Dartmoor on HMS Raven.

Williams, Joseph - Seaman - Number: 2777 - Prize name: Thomas - Ship type: P - How taken: HM Frigate Nymphe - When taken: 24 Jun 1813 - Where taken: off Halifax - Date received: 7 Jan 1814 - From what ship: Halifax - Born: Massachusetts - Age: 23 - Discharged on 8 Sep 1814 and sent to Dartmoor on HMS Niobe.

Williams, Joseph - Seaman - Number: 1712 - Prize name: Decatur - Ship type: MV - How taken: HM Frigate Desiree - When taken: 7 May 1813 - Where taken: off Nantes, France - Date received: 25 May 1813 - From what ship: Portsmouth via HMS Impetius - Born: Philadelphia - Age: 24 - Released on 11 Jul 1814.

Williams, Joseph - Seaman - Number: 2257 - Prize name: Hannah & Eliza - Ship type: MV - How taken: HM Brig Lyra - When taken: 29 May 1813 - Where taken: off Spain - Date received: 7 Sep 1813 - From what ship: HMS Raisonnable - Born: New London - Age: 20 - Discharged on 11 Aug 1814 and sent to Dartmoor on HMS Freya.

Williams, Josiah - Seaman - Number: 951 - How taken: Gave himself up from HM Sloop Comet - When taken: 25 Nov 1812 - Date received: 10 Mar 1813 - From what ship: HMS Tigress - Born: Boston - Age: 36 - Race: Black - Discharged on 4 Aug 1814 and sent to Dartmoor on HMS Liverpool.

Williams, Jotham - Seaman - Number: 488 - How taken: Gave himself up from HM Brig Raleigh - When taken: 7 Jan 1813 - Date received: 19 Feb 1813 - From what ship: HMS Raisonnable - Born: Boston - Age: 33 - Discharged on 26 Jul 1814 and sent to Dartmoor on HMS Raven.

Williams, Michael - Seaman - Number: 882 - Prize name: George & Mary - Ship type: P - How taken: HM Frigate Narcissus - When taken: 24 Nov 1812 - Where taken: off San Domingo (Haiti) - Date received: 1 Mar 1813 - From what ship: Plymouth via HMS Namur - Born: North Carolina - Age: 26 - Discharged on 8 Jun 1813 and released to Cartel Rodrigo.

Williams, Moses - Seaman - Number: 3677 - Prize name: Lord Ponsonby, prize of the Privateer Diomede - Ship type: P - How taken: HM Brig Sappho - When taken: 27 Feb 1814 - Where taken: at sea - Date received: 4 May 1814 - From what ship: Portsmouth - Born: Middleton - Age: 25 - Race: Black - Discharged on 25 Sep 1814 and sent to Dartmoor on HMS Niobe.

Williams, Noble - Seaman - Number: 3366 - Prize name: Yorktown - Ship type: P - How taken: HM Frigate Maidstone - When taken: 17 Jul 1813 - Where taken: Grand Banks - Date received: 23 Feb 1814 - From what ship: Halifax via HMT Malabar - Born: New York - Age: 27 - Discharged on 10 Oct 1814 and sent to Dartmoor on the Mermaid.

Williams, Peter - Seaman - Number: 1496 - Prize name: Union - Ship type: MV - How taken: HM Frigate Iris - When taken: 17 Jan 1813 - Where taken: at sea - Date received: 6 Apr 1813 - From what ship: Plymouth via an admiral's tender - Born: Philadelphia - Age: 24 - Race: Negro - Discharged on 27 Jul 1813 and released to Cartel Hoffminy.

Williams, Richard - Seaman - Number: 1806 - How taken: Impressed at London - When taken: 24 Jun 1813 - Date received: 3 Jul 1813 - From what ship: HMS Raisonnable - Born: Elizabethtown - Age: 21 - Race: Blackman - Discharged on 25 Jul 1814 and sent to Dartmoor on HMS Bittern.

Williams, Robert - Seaman - Number: 2578 - How taken: Gave himself up from HM Ship-of-the-Line Union - When taken: 9 Dec 1812 - Date received: 23 Oct 1813 - From what ship: Portsmouth via HMS Raisonnable - Born: New York - Age: 23 - Discharged on 8 Sep 1814 and sent to Dartmoor on HMS Niobe.

Williams, Robert - Seaman - Number: 2572 - How taken: Gave himself up from HM Ship-of-the-Line Scipion - When taken: 2 Dec 1812 - Date received: 23 Oct 1813 - From what ship: Portsmouth via HMS Raisonnable - Born: New York - Age: 24 - Race: Black - Discharged on 8 Sep 1814 and sent to Dartmoor on HMS Niobe.

Williams, Stephen - Seaman - Number: 2322 - Prize name: Fame - Ship type: MV - How taken: HM Ship of-the-Line Cressy - When taken: 20 Jul 1813 - Where taken: at sea - Date received: 8 Oct 1813 - From what ship: Portsmouth, via an admiral's tender - Born: Albany - Age: 27 - Discharged on 4 Sep 1814 and sent to Dartmoor on HMS Freya.

Williams, Thomas - Private - Number: 1632 - Prize name: 6th U.S. Infantry - Ship type: LF - How taken: British forces - When taken: 13 Oct 1812 - Where taken: Upper Canada - Date received: 9 May 1813 - From what ship: HMS Raisonnable - Born: North Wales - Age: 40 - Discharged on 22 Oct 1814 and sent to Dartmoor on HMS Leyden.

Williams, Thomas - Seaman - Number: 2164 - How taken: Gave himself up from HM Frigate Unicorn - When taken: 17 Jun 1813 - Date received: 16 Aug 1813 - From what ship: Portsmouth, via an admiral's tender - Born: Connecticut - Age: 23 - Discharged on 17 Jun 1814 and sent to Dartmoor on the Penebar.

Williams, Thomas - Seaman - Number: 2431 - Prize name: Hepsey - Ship type: MV - How taken: HM Brig Zenobia - When taken: 22 Jun 1813 - Where taken: off Lisbon - Date received: 21 Oct 1813 - From what ship: Portsmouth via HMT Malabar - Born: Baltimore - Age: 40 - Discharged on 4 Sep 1814 and sent to Dartmoor on HMS Freya.

Williams, Thomas - Seaman - Number: 2185 - How taken: Gave himself up from HM Ship-of-the-Line Leviathan - When taken: 28 Oct 1812 - Date received: 16 Aug 1813 - From what ship: Portsmouth, via an admiral's tender - Born: Maryland - Age: 27 - Race: Mulatto - Discharged on 11 Aug 1814 and sent to Dartmoor on

HMS Freya.

Williams, William - Seaman - Number: 3850 - Prize name: James - Ship type: MV - How taken: HM Brig Harpy - When taken: 16 Dec 1812 - Where taken: off Isle de France (Mauritius) - Date received: 22 Aug 1814 - From what ship: Gravesend - Born: Eastport - Age: 28 - Discharged on 22 Oct 1814 and sent to Dartmoor on HMS Leyden.

Williams, William - Seaman - Number: 1335 - How taken: Gave himself up from HM Ship-of-the-Line Sultan - When taken: 1 Nov 1812 - Date received: 22 Mar 1813 - From what ship: HMS Raisonnable - Born: Wilmington - Age: 30 - Race: Blackman - Discharged on 23 Jul 1814 and sent to Dartmoor.

Williams, William - Boy - Number: 2858 - Prize name: Fire Fly - Ship type: LM - How taken: HM Frigate Revolutionnaire - When taken: 19 Oct 1813 - Where taken: off Cape Ortegal, Spain - Date received: 7 Jan 1814 - From what ship: Portsmouth - Born: Massachusetts - Age: 14 - Discharged on 26 Sep 1814 and sent to Dartmoor on HMS Leyden.

Williams, William - Seaman - Number: 2299 - Prize name: Maria - Ship type: MV - How taken: Apprehended at London - When taken: 22 Sep 1813 - Date received: 29 Sep 1813 - From what ship: HMS Raisonnable - Born: Georgetown - Age: 22 - Discharged on 4 Sep 1814 and sent to Dartmoor on HMS Freya.

Williamson, Charles - Seaman - Number: 924 - Prize name: Experiment - Ship type: MV - How taken: HM Brig Rover - When taken: 10 Nov 1812 - Where taken: off Bordeaux, France - Date received: 10 Mar 1813 - From what ship: HMS Tigress - Born: Maryland - Age: 27 - Discharged on 8 Jun 1813 and released to Cartel Rodrigo.

Williamson, Charles - Seaman - Number: 605 - Prize name: Antelope - Ship type: P - How taken: HM Brig Zephyr - When taken: 10 Dec 1812 - Where taken: at sea - Date received: 23 Feb 1813 - From what ship: Portsmouth via HMS Dromedary - Born: Germany - Age: 28 - Discharged on 2 Jul 1813 and released to Cartel Moses Brown.

Williamson, David - Seaman - Number: 3556 - Prize name: Zephyr, prize of Privateer Rattlesnake - Ship type: P - How taken: HM Frigate Surveillante - When taken: 6 Jan 1814 - Where taken: Bay of Biscay - Date received: 7 May 1814 - From what ship: Portsmouth via HMS Favorite - Born: Philadelphia - Age: 25 - Discharged on 25 Sep 1814 and sent to Dartmoor on HMS Niobe.

Williamson, George J. - Seaman - Number: 1254 - How taken: Impressed at the Farhan Rendezvous - When taken: 23 Dec 1812 - Date received: 16 Mar 1813 - From what ship: Portsmouth, via HMS Abundance - Born: Philadelphia - Age: 24 - Discharged on 24 Jul 1813 and released to Cartel Hoffminy.

Williamson, John - Seaman - Number: 1305 - How taken: Gave himself up from HM Guardship Royal William - When taken: 3 Feb 1813 - Date received: 16 Mar 1813 - From what ship: Portsmouth, via HMS Abundance - Born: Philadelphia - Age: 29 - Race: Black - Discharged on 23 Jul 1814 and sent to Dartmoor.

Williamson, John - Seaman - Number: 1077 - How taken: Gave himself up from HM Brig Electra - When taken: 20 Sep 1812 - Date received: 14 Mar 1813 - From what ship: Portsmouth via HMS Cornwell - Born: New Haven - Age: 28 - Discharged on 11 Aug 1814 and sent to Dartmoor.

Williamson, John - Seaman - Number: 1987 - How taken: Gave himself up from HM Ship-of-the-Line Ajax - Date received: 15 Jul 1813 - From what ship: Plymouth - Born: Germantown - Age: 30 - Escaped on 16 May 1814 from the HM Prison Ship Crown Prince.

Williamson, John - Seaman - Number: 2901 - Prize name: Dart - Ship type: P - How taken: HM Frigate Niger & HMS Fortunee - When taken: 10 Nov 1813 - Where taken: off Cape Finisterre, Spain - Date received: 7 Jan 1814 - From what ship: Portsmouth - Born: Boston - Age: 37 - Discharged on 25 Sep 1814 and sent to Dartmoor on HMS Leyden.

Willingsworth, Jeffery - Seaman - Number: 926 - Prize name: Experiment - Ship type: MV - How taken: HM Brig Rover - When taken: 10 Nov 1812 - Where taken: off Bordeaux, France - Date received: 10 Mar 1813 - From what ship: HMS Tigress - Born: Somerset - Age: 48 - Discharged on 8 Jun 1813 and released to Cartel Rodrigo.

Willis, Alfred - Private - Number: 3159 - Prize name: 14th U.S. Infantry - Ship type: LF - How taken: British forces - When taken: 24 Jun 1813 - Where taken: Beaver Dams, Upper Canada - Date received: 7 Jan 1814 - From what ship: Halifax - Born: Massachusetts - Age: 30 - Discharged on 10 Oct 1814 and sent to U.S. on Cartel St. Philip.

Willis, Charles - Seaman - Number: 73 - Prize name: Llan Romney - Ship type: MV - How taken: Stopped at London - When taken: 26 Oct 1812 - Date received: 4 Nov 1812 - From what ship: HMS Namur - Born: New York - Age: 25 - Discharged in Jul 1813 and released to Cartel Moses Brown.

Willy, John - Seaman - Number: 3272 - Prize name: Volante - Ship type: P - How taken: HM Brig Curlew - When taken: 25 Mar 1813 - Where taken: off Boston - Date received: 23 Feb 1814 - From what ship: Halifax via HMT Malabar - Born: Baltimore - Age: 25 - Discharged on 21 Jul 1814 and sent to Dartmoor on HMS Portia.

Wilmer, Isaac - Seaman - Number: 536 - Prize name: Baltimore - Ship type: P - How taken: HM Transport Diadem - When taken: 7 Oct 1812 - Where taken: S. Andres - Date received: 23 Feb 1813 - From what ship: Portsmouth via HMS Dromedary - Born: Rockhall, MD - Age: 27 - Race: Mulatto - Discharged on 8 Jun 1813 and released to Cartel Rodrigo.

Willot, Robert - Seaman - Number: 1429 - How taken: Gave himself up from HM Frigate Andromache - When taken: 24 Dec 1812 - Date received: 6 Apr 1813 - From what ship: Plymouth via HMS Decoy - Born: Newburyport - Age: 21 - Discharged on 24 Jul 1814 and sent to Dartmoor.

Willson, Henry - Seaman - Number: 2221 - How taken: Gave himself up from HMS Fortune - When taken: 16 Jan 1813 - Date received: 22 Aug 1813 - From what ship: HMS Raisonnable - Born: Beverly - Age: 43 - Race: Blackman - Discharged on 11 Aug 1814 and sent to Dartmoor on HMS Freya.

Willson, James - Seaman - Number: 2197 - How taken: Gave himself up from HM Ship-of-the-Line Caledonia - When taken: 5 Dec 1812 - Date received: 18 Aug 1813 - From what ship: Portsmouth, via an admiral's tender - Born: Rhode Island - Age: 46 - Race: Mulatto - Discharged on 17 Dec 1813 and released to HMS Ceres.

Willson, John - Seaman - Number: 900 - Prize name: Pallas - Ship type: MV - How taken: HM Brig Papillon - When taken: 17 Aug 1812 - Where taken: off Cadiz, Spain - Date received: 1 Mar 1813 - From what ship: Plymouth via HMS Namur - Born: Maryland - Age: 30 - Discharged on 23 Mar 1813 and released to the Cartel Robinson Potter.

Willson, John - Seaman - Number: 1701 - Prize name: Governor Middleton - Ship type: MV - How taken: Thetis, British privateer - When taken: 2 May 1813 - Where taken: Bay of Biscay - Date received: 15 May 1813 - From what ship: HMS Viper - Born: New York - Age: 36 - Discharged on 24 Jul 1814 and sent to Dartmoor on HMS Liffey.

Willson, John - Seaman - Number: 2243 - Prize name: Orders in Council - Ship type: LM - How taken: HM Frigate Surveillante - When taken: 1 Jan 1813 - Where taken: off Cape Ortegal, Spain - Date received: 7 Sep 1813 - From what ship: HMS Raisonnable - Born: Charlestown - Age: 23 - Discharged on 11 Aug 1814 and sent to Dartmoor on HMS Freya.

Willson, William - Seaman - Number: 669 - Prize name: U.S.R.M. Cutter James Madison - Ship type: War - How taken: HM Frigate Barbadoes - When taken: 22 Aug 1812 - Where taken: at sea - Date received: 24 Feb 1813 - From what ship: Portsmouth via HMS Ulysses - Born: Providence - Age: 30 - Discharged on 10 May 1813 and released to Cartel Admittance.

Wilson, Charles - Passenger - Number: 253 - How taken: Gave himself up from MV Venus - When taken: 23 Nov 1812 - Date received: 7 Dec 1812 - From what ship: HMS Raisonnable - Born: Taunton, MA - Age: 29 - Released from Chatham on 27 Jun 1814 and sent to Ashburton on parole.

Wilson, Daniel - Seaman - Number: 1364 - How taken: Gave himself up from HM Guardship Royal William - When taken: 12 Mar 1813 - Date received: 3 Apr 1813 - From what ship: Portsmouth, via an admiral's tender - Born: Boston - Age: 39 - Discharged on 25 Sep 1814 and sent to Dartmoor on HMS Niobe.

Wilson, Francis - Seaman - Number: 3492 - How taken: Gave himself up from HM Transport Dover - Date received: 23 Feb 1814 - From what ship: Portsmouth via HMT Malabar - Born: New York - Age: 31 - Discharged on 22 Oct 1814 and sent to Dartmoor on HMS Leyden.

Wilson, George - Seaman - Number: 3901 - How taken: Gave himself up from the MV Blenheim - When taken: 28 Aug 1814 - Date received: 31 Aug 1814 - From what ship: Transport Office - Born: Hollis - Age: 25 -

Discharged on 25 Sep 1814 and sent to Dartmoor on HMS Leyden.

Wilson, Hezekiel - Seaman - Number: 2455 - Prize name: Wiley Reynard - Ship type: P - How taken: HM Frigate Shannon - When taken: 16 Aug 1812 - Where taken: off Halifax - Date received: 21 Oct 1813 - From what ship: Portsmouth via HMT Malabar - Born: Philadelphia - Age: 23 - Race: Blackman - Discharged on 10 Oct 1813 and released to HMS Ceres.

Wilson, James - Seaman - Number: 2527 - Prize name: Yorktown - Ship type: P - How taken: HM Brig Nimrod - When taken: 17 Jul 1813 - Where taken: Grand Banks - Date received: 22 Oct 1813 - From what ship: Portsmouth via HMT Malabar - Born: Portsmouth - Age: 31 - Discharged on 8 Sep 1814 and sent to Dartmoor on HMS Niobe.

Wilson, James - Seaman - Number: 2579 - How taken: Gave himself up from HM Ship-of-the-Line Colossus - When taken: 17 Oct 1812 - Date received: 23 Oct 1813 - From what ship: Portsmouth via HMS Raisonnable - Born: Hampshire - Age: 37 - Discharged on 25 Sep 1814 and sent to Dartmoor on HMS Leyden.

Wilson, James - Seaman - Number: 2600 - How taken: Gave himself up from HM Ship-of-the-Line Berwick - When taken: 27 May 1813 - Date received: 5 Nov 1813 - From what ship: HMS Hindostan - Born: Maryland - Age: 38 - Race: Blackman - Discharged on 12 Aug 1814 and sent to Dartmoor on HMS Alpheus.

Wilson, John - Seaman - Number: 1101 - Prize name: Calcutta, East Indian Ship - Ship type: MV - How taken: Two Brothers, British privateer from Guernsey - When taken: 30 Nov 1812 - Where taken: off St. Helena - Date received: 14 Mar 1813 - From what ship: Portsmouth via HMS Beagle - Born: Newburn, NY - Age: 31 - Discharged on 8 Jun 1813 and released to Cartel Rodrigo.

Wilson, John - Seaman - Number: 3384 - Prize name: Teazer - Ship type: P - How taken: HM Frigate Boreas - When taken: 15 Jun 1813 - Where taken: off Halifax - Date received: 23 Feb 1814 - From what ship: Halifax via HMT Malabar - Born: Philadelphia - Age: 28 - Discharged on 10 Oct 1814 and sent to Dartmoor on the Mermaid.

Wilson, John - Seaman - Number: 2748 - Prize name: Wasp - Ship type: P - How taken: HM Schooner Bream - When taken: 9 Jun 1813 - Where taken: off Halifax - Date received: 7 Jan 1814 - From what ship: Halifax - Born: Massachusetts - Age: 50 - Discharged on 8 Sep 1814 and sent to Dartmoor on HMS Niobe.

Wilson, John (alias Andrew Joseph) - Seaman - Number: 1602 - How taken: Gave up from a West Indian Vessel - Date received: 19 Apr 1813 - From what ship: HMS Raisonnable - Born: New York - Age: 25 - Discharged on 24 Jul 1814 and sent to Dartmoor.

Wilson, Nathaniel - Passenger - Number: 2199 - Prize name: unknown MV - Ship type: MV - How taken: HM Sloop Volentaire - When taken: 15 Nov 1812 - Where taken: off Sardinia - Date received: 18 Aug 1813 - From what ship: Portsmouth, via an admiral's tender - Born: Bristol - Age: 24 - Discharged on 10 Oct 1813 and released to HMS Ceres.

Wilson, Peter - Seaman - Number: 910 - Prize name: Independence - Ship type: MV - How taken: HM Frigate Medusa - When taken: 9 Nov 1812 - Where taken: off San Sebastian, Spain - Date received: 10 Mar 1813 - From what ship: HMS Tigress - Born: New York - Age: 42 - Discharged on 8 Jun 1813 and released to Cartel Rodrigo.

Wilson, R. G. - Passenger - Number: 3501 - Prize name: Atlantic, recaptured prize - Ship type: P - How taken: HM Ship-of-the-Line Swiftsure - Date received: 23 Feb 1814 - From what ship: Portsmouth via HMT Malabar - Born: New York - Age: 25 - Discharged on 22 Oct 1814 and sent to Dartmoor on HMS Leyden.

Wilson, Robert - Seaman - Number: 2381 - How taken: Gave himself up from HM Ship-of-the-Line America - When taken: 26 Dec 1812 - Date received: 20 Oct 1813 - From what ship: Portsmouth, via an admiral's tender - Born: Connecticut - Age: 45 - Discharged on 4 Sep 1814 and sent to Dartmoor on HMS Freya.

Wilson, Thomas - Seaman - Number: 1846 - How taken: Given up from HM Frigate Hyperion - Date received: 7 Jul 1813 - From what ship: Portsmouth via HMS Tribune - Born: Alexandria - Age: 34 - Discharged on 25 Jul 1814 and sent to Dartmoor on HMS Bittern.

Wilson, William - Seaman - Number: 3485 - How taken: Gave himself up from HMS Muros - When taken: 27 Jan 1813 - Date received: 23 Feb 1814 - From what ship: Portsmouth via HMT Malabar - Born: Boston - Age: 32 - Discharged on 26 Sep 1814 and sent to Dartmoor on HMS Leyden.

Wilson, William - Seaman - Number: 43 - Prize name: General Blake - Ship type: MV - How taken: HM Brig Recruit - When taken: 11 Jun 1812 - Where taken: off Rhode Island - Date received: 3 Nov 1812 - From what ship: HMS Plover - Born: Baltimore, MD - Age: 26 - Discharged on 23 Mar 1813 and released to the Cartel Robinson Potter.

Wilson, William - Seaman - Number: 1056 - Prize name: Independence - Ship type: MV - How taken: HM Frigate Medusa - When taken: 9 Nov 1812 - Where taken: off San Sebastian, Spain - Date received: 11 Mar 1813 - From what ship: Yarmouth via HMS Tenders - Born: Richmond - Age: 28 - Discharged on 8 Jun 1813 and released to Cartel Rodrigo.

Wilson, William - Seaman - Number: 238 - Prize name: Venus - Ship type: MV - How taken: Impressed off Beachy Head - When taken: 24 Jul 1812 - Date received: 1 Dec 1812 - From what ship: HMS Raisonnable - Born: Taunton, MA - Age: 28 - Discharged on 23 Mar 1813 and released to the Cartel Robinson Potter.

Wilson, William - Seaman - Number: 1511 - How taken: Gave himself up from HM Ship-of-the-Line Blake - When taken: 10 Dec 1812 - Date received: 8 Apr 1813 - From what ship: Portsmouth, via an admiral's tender - Born: Acton - Age: 28 - Discharged on 25 Sep 1814 and sent to Dartmoor.

Wilson, William - Seaman - Number: 2211 - Prize name: Jane, prize of the Privateer Snap Dragon - Ship type: P - How taken: HM Frigate Crescent & HM Ship of-the-Line Bellerophon - When taken: 28 Jun 1813 - Where taken: Newfoundland Bank - Date received: 18 Aug 1813 - From what ship: Portsmouth, via an admiral's tender - Born: Philadelphia - Age: 31 - Discharged on 11 Aug 1814 and sent to Dartmoor on HMS Freya.

Winchester, Ebenezer - Seaman - Number: 3766 - Prize name: Argus - Ship type: MV - How taken: HM Ship-of-the-Line San Domingo - When taken: 1 Mar 1814 - Where taken: off Savannah - Date received: 26 May 1814 - From what ship: HMS Hindostan - Born: Boston - Age: 21 - Discharged on 25 Sep 1814 and sent to Dartmoor on HMS Niobe.

Winchester, Richard - Seaman - Number: 2857 - Prize name: Fire Fly - Ship type: LM - How taken: HM Frigate Revolutionnaire - When taken: 19 Oct 1813 - Where taken: off Cape Ortegal, Spain - Date received: 7 Jan 1814 - From what ship: Portsmouth - Born: Salem - Age: 22 - Died on 9 Mar 1814 from fever.

Winckley, John - 2nd Lieutenant - Number: 1417 - Prize name: Postsea, prize to the Privateer Thrasher - Ship type: P - How taken: HM Sloop Helena - When taken: 31 Dec 1813 - Where taken: off Azores - Date received: 5 Apr 1813 - From what ship: Plymouth via HMS Dwarf - Born: Kittery - Age: 21 - Discharged on 24 Jul 1813 and released to Cartel Hoffminy.

Windford, Charles - Seaman - Number: 1380 - How taken: Gave himself up from HM Ship-of-the-Line Sterling Castle - When taken: 26 Mar 1813 - Date received: 3 Apr 1813 - From what ship: Portsmouth, via an admiral's tender - Born: New York - Age: 31 - Discharged on 17 Jul 1813 and released to HMS Ceres.

Wing, Nathaniel - Seaman - Number: 2255 - Prize name: Hannah & Eliza - Ship type: MV - How taken: HM Brig Lyra - When taken: 29 May 1813 - Where taken: off Spain - Date received: 7 Sep 1813 - From what ship: HMS Raisonnable - Born: Massachusetts - Age: 26 - Discharged on 11 Aug 1814 and sent to Dartmoor on HMS Freya.

Wingate, David - Seaman - Number: 2559 - How taken: Gave himself up from HM Battery Gorgon - When taken: 1 Nov 1812 - Date received: 23 Oct 1813 - From what ship: Portsmouth via HMS Raisonnable - Born: New Hampshire - Age: 23 - Discharged on 25 Sep 1814 and sent to Dartmoor on HMS Leyden.

Winn, Clement - Private - Number: 3114 - Prize name: 14th U.S. Infantry - Ship type: LF - How taken: British forces - When taken: 24 Jun 1813 - Where taken: Beaver Dams, Upper Canada - Date received: 7 Jan 1814 - From what ship: Halifax - Born: Maryland - Age: 21 - Discharged on 10 Oct 1814 and sent to U.S. on Cartel St. Philip.

Winner, Michael - Private - Number: 3148 - Prize name: 16th U.S. Infantry - Ship type: LF - How taken: British forces - When taken: 24 Jun 1813 - Where taken: Beaver Dams, Upper Canada - Date received: 7 Jan 1814 - From what ship: Halifax - Born: Pennsylvania - Age: 25 - Discharged on 10 Oct 1814 and sent to U.S. on Cartel St. Philip.

Winslow, William - Carpenter's Mate - Number: 1134 - Prize name: Sword Fish - Ship type: P - How taken: HM Ship-of-the-Line Elephant - When taken: 28 Dec 1812 - Where taken: off Azores - Date received: 16 Mar

1813 - From what ship: Portsmouth, Mundane - Born: Salem - Age: 26 - Discharged on 24 Jul 1813 and released to Cartel Hoffminy.

Winston, William - Seaman - Number: 3464 - Prize name: Elbridge Gerry - Ship type: P - How taken: HM Frigate Crescent - When taken: 16 Sep 1813 - Where taken: at sea - Date received: 23 Feb 1814 - From what ship: Halifax via HMT Malabar - Born: Treport, France - Age: 19 - Discharged on 11 Mar 1814 and released to HMS Thames.

Wise, John - Seaman - Number: 543 - Prize name: Baltimore - Ship type: P - How taken: HM Transport Diadem - When taken: 7 Oct 1812 - Where taken: S. Andres - Date received: 23 Feb 1813 - From what ship: Portsmouth via HMS Dromedary - Born: Altona - Age: 35 - Discharged on 8 Jun 1813 and released to Cartel Rodrigo.

Wise, John - Seaman - Number: 2347 - How taken: Gave himself up from HM Ship-of-the-Line Implacable - When taken: 25 Jun 1813 - Date received: 20 Oct 1813 - From what ship: Portsmouth, via an admiral's tender - Born: New York - Age: 26 - Race: Mulatto - Discharged on 4 Sep 1814 and sent to Dartmoor on HMS Freya.

Witherell, Charles - Seaman - Number: 3552 - Prize name: Amity, prize of the Privateer Prince de Neufchatel - Ship type: P - How taken: HM Brig Achates - When taken: 22 Nov 1813 - Where taken: Bay of Biscay - Date received: 7 May 1814 - From what ship: Portsmouth via HMS Favorite - Born: Massachusetts - Age: 28 - Discharged on 22 Oct 1814 and sent to Dartmoor on HMS Leyden.

Withers, Edward - Seaman - Number: 1121 - Prize name: U.S.R.M. Cutter James Madison - Ship type: War - How taken: HM Frigate Barbadoes - When taken: 22 Aug 1812 - Where taken: at sea - Date received: 14 Mar 1813 - From what ship: Portsmouth via HMS Beagle - Born: Berke, GA - Age: 23 - Discharged on 10 May 1813 and released to Cartel Admittance.

Withiem, Burrell - Quartermaster - Number: 2706 - Prize name: Growler - Ship type: P - How taken: HM Brig Electra - When taken: 7 Jul 1813 - Where taken: off St. Johns - Date received: 7 Jan 1814 - From what ship: Portsmouth - Born: Marblehead - Age: 23 - Discharged on 4 Sep 1814 and sent to Dartmoor on HMS Freya.

Withman, William - Seaman - Number: 982 - Prize name: Hazard - Ship type: MV - How taken: Detained at Greenock, Scotland - When taken: 20 Sep 1812 - Date received: 10 Mar 1813 - From what ship: HMS Tigress - Born: Bath - Age: 25 - Discharged on 2 Jul 1813 and released to Cartel Moses Brown.

Witney, Samuel - Seaman - Number: 379 - Prize name: Union American - Ship type: MV - How taken: Taken up at London - When taken: 25 Jan 1813 - Date received: 31 Jan 1813 - From what ship: HMS Raisonnable - Born: Boston - Age: 27 - Died on 26 Apr 1813 from pneumonia.

Wolfe, Andre - Seaman - Number: 1260 - How taken: Gave himself up from HM Ship-of-the-Line Mars - When taken: 9 Dec 1812 - Date received: 16 Mar 1813 - From what ship: Portsmouth, via HMS Abundance - Born: Baltimore - Age: 28 - Discharged on 23 Jul 1814 and sent to Dartmoor.

Wood, Alexander - Seaman - Number: 486 - How taken: Gave himself up from HM Brig Persian - When taken: 13 Dec 1812 - Date received: 19 Feb 1813 - From what ship: HMS Raisonnable - Born: Chatham, CT - Age: 27 - Discharged on 17 Nov 1813 to the Cartel Robinson Potter.

Wood, Benjamin - Seaman - Number: 3398 - Prize name: Yankee - Ship type: P - How taken: HM Brig Ringdove - When taken: 17 Oct 1813 - Where taken: at sea - Date received: 23 Feb 1814 - From what ship: Halifax via HMT Malabar - Born: New Orleans - Age: 18 - Discharged on 22 Oct 1814 and sent to Dartmoor on HMS Leyden.

Wood, George - Steward - Number: 1130 - Prize name: Sword Fish - Ship type: P - How taken: HM Ship-of-the-Line Elephant - When taken: 28 Dec 1812 - Where taken: off Azores - Date received: 16 Mar 1813 - From what ship: Portsmouth, Mundane - Born: Beverly - Age: 23 - Discharged on 24 Jul 1813 and released to Cartel Hoffminy.

Wood, John - Seaman - Number: 58 - Prize name: Amiable - Ship type: MV - How taken: From a cutter off Bermuda - When taken: Jun 1812 - Date received: 3 Nov 1812 - From what ship: HMS Plover - Born: New Haven, CT - Age: 21 - Discharged on 23 Mar 1813 and released to the Cartel Robinson Potter.

Wood, Joseph - Seaman - Number: 2457 - Prize name: Wiley Reynard - Ship type: P - How taken: HM Frigate Shannon - When taken: 16 Aug 1812 - Where taken: off Halifax - Date received: 21 Oct 1813 - From what ship: Portsmouth via HMT Malabar - Born: Baltimore - Age: 27 - Discharged on 4 Sep 1814 and sent to Dartmoor on HMS Freya.

Wood, Richard - Seaman - Number: 124 - Prize name: Edward - Ship type: MV - How taken: Detained at Deptford - When taken: 26 Oct 1812 - Date received: 4 Nov 1812 - From what ship: HMS Namur - Born: Noble Port, MA - Age: 24 - Discharged in Jul 1813 and released to Cartel Moses Brown.

Wood, William - Seaman - Number: 290 - Prize name: Dido - Ship type: MV - How taken: Detained off Faco - When taken: 12 Aug 1812 - Date received: 23 Dec 1812 - From what ship: Greenlaw Depot - Born: Beverly - Age: 25 - Discharged on 10 May 1813 and released to Cartel Admittance.

Wood, William - Seaman - Number: 2151 - How taken: Gave himself up at London - When taken: 22 Jul 1813 - Date received: 14 Aug 1813 - From what ship: HMS Raisonnable - Born: Marblehead - Age: 25 - Escaped on 2 Nov 1813.Woodard, Elijah - Seaman - Number: 933 - Prize name: Argus - Ship type: MV - How taken: HM Cutter Fancy - When taken: 17 Dec 1812 - Where taken: Bay of Biscay - Date received: 10 Mar 1813 - From what ship: HMS Tigress - Born: Massachusetts - Age: 24 - Discharged on 2 Jul 1813 and released to Cartel Moses Brown.

Woodberry, Caleb - Prize Master - Number: 1430 - Prize name: Louisa, prize of the Privateer Decatur - Ship type: P - How taken: HM Frigate Andromache - When taken: 11 Jan 1813 - Where taken: off Bordeaux, France - Date received: 6 Apr 1813 - From what ship: Plymouth via HMS Decoy - Born: Gloucester - Age: 38 - Discharged on 24 Jul 1813 and released to Cartel Hoffminy.

Woodborne, John - Seaman - Number: 1689 - Prize name: Governor Middleton - Ship type: MV - How taken: Thetis, British privateer - When taken: 2 May 1813 - Where taken: Bay of Biscay - Date received: 15 May 1813 - From what ship: HMS Viper - Born: Wilmington - Age: 30 - Discharged on 24 Jul 1814 and sent to Dartmoor on HMS Liffey.

Woodbury, Dixie - Seaman - Number: 3535 - Prize name: Commodore Perry - Ship type: MV - How taken: Sent into custody from a cutter - When taken: 25 Feb 1814 - Where taken: off Bordeaux, France - Date received: 5 Mar 1814 - From what ship: HMS Raisonnable - Born: Beverly - Age: 25 - Discharged on 26 Sep 1814 and sent to Dartmoor on HMS Leyden.

Woodbury, John - Seaman - Number: 2249 - Prize name: Joseph - Ship type: MV - How taken: HM Frigate Iris - When taken: 8 Jun 1813 - Where taken: off Spain - Date received: 7 Sep 1813 - From what ship: HMS Raisonnable - Born: Gloucester - Age: 24 - Discharged on 11 Aug 1814 and sent to Dartmoor on HMS Freya.

Woodford, James - Seaman - Number: 2848 - Prize name: Blockade - Ship type: P - How taken: HM Brig Recruit - When taken: 17 Aug 1813 - Where taken: coast of America - Date received: 7 Jan 1814 - From what ship: Halifax - Born: Baltimore - Age: 19 - Discharged on 26 Sep 1814 and sent to Dartmoor on HMS Leyden.

Woodford, William - Seaman - Number: 2923 - Prize name: Juliana Smith - Ship type: P - How taken: HM Frigate Nymphe - When taken: 12 May 1813 - Where taken: off Cape Sable, Florida - Date received: 7 Jan 1814 - From what ship: Halifax - Born: New York - Age: 23 - Discharged on 25 Sep 1814 and sent to Dartmoor on HMS Leyden.

Woods, Charles - Seaman - Number: 1179 - Prize name: Sword Fish - Ship type: P - How taken: HM Ship-of-the-Line Elephant - When taken: 28 Dec 1812 - Where taken: off Azores - Date received: 16 Mar 1813 - From what ship: Portsmouth, via HMS Abundance - Born: Gloucester - Age: 44 - Discharged on 24 Jul 1813 and released to Cartel Hoffminy.

Woods, Jeremiah - Seaman - Number: 2771 - Prize name: Thomas - Ship type: P - How taken: HM Frigate Nymphe - When taken: 24 Jun 1813 - Where taken: off Halifax - Date received: 7 Jan 1814 - From what ship: Halifax - Born: Portsmouth - Age: 23 - Discharged on 22 Oct 1814 and sent to Dartmoor on HMS Leyden.

Woods, Merrill - Seaman - Number: 1737 - How taken: Gave himself up from HM Transport Chatham - When taken: 5 May 1813 - Date received: 25 May 1813 - From what ship: Portsmouth via HMS Impetius - Born: Eaton, NH - Age: 30 - Discharged on 24 Jul 1814 and sent to Dartmoor on HMS Liffey.

Woods, William - Seaman - Number: 1161 - Prize name: Sword Fish - Ship type: P - How taken: HM Ship-of-the-Line Elephant - When taken: 28 Dec 1812 - Where taken: off Azores - Date received: 16 Mar 1813 - From what ship: Portsmouth, via HMS Abundance - Born: New York - Age: 26 - Discharged on 24 Jul 1813 and released to Cartel Hoffminy.

Woods, William - Seaman - Number: 2564 - How taken: Gave himself up from HM Ship-of-the-Line Ocean - When taken: 29 Oct 1812 - Date received: 23 Oct 1813 - From what ship: Portsmouth via HMS Raisonnable - Born: Philadelphia - Age: 22 - Discharged on 26 Dec 1813 and released to HMS Ceres.

Wooldridge, William - Seaman - Number: 1590 - How taken: Gave himself up from HM Brig Banterer - When taken: 1 Apr 1813 - Date received: 18 Apr 1813 - From what ship: HMS Rosario - Born: Preston - Age: 38 - Discharged on 13 Apr 1814 and sent to Dartmoor.

Worthing, Isaac - Seaman - Number: 1685 - How taken: Impressed from Russian MV Moscow - When taken: 27 Apr 1813 - Date received: 15 May 1813 - From what ship: HMS Raisonnable - Born: Brenham, NH - Age: 21 - Died on 7 Jun 1814 from phthisis (tuberculosis).

Worthy, James - Seaman - Number: 3449 - Prize name: Elbridge Gerry - Ship type: P - How taken: HM Frigate Crescent - When taken: 16 Sep 1813 - Where taken: at sea - Date received: 23 Feb 1814 - From what ship: Halifax via HMT Malabar - Born: Greenwich - Age: 24 - Discharged on 21 Jul 1814 and sent to Dartmoor on HMS Portia.

Wright, Edward - Seaman - Number: 2387 - How taken: Gave himself up from HM Ship-of-the-Line Achille - When taken: 26 Dec 1812 - Date received: 20 Oct 1813 - From what ship: Portsmouth, via an admiral's tender - Born: New Jersey - Age: 25 - Race: Black - Discharged on 4 Sep 1814 and sent to Dartmoor on HMS Freya.

Wright, Isaac - Seaman - Number: 1983 - How taken: Gave himself up from HM Ship-of-the-Line Ajax - Date received: 15 Jul 1813 - From what ship: Plymouth - Born: Philadelphia - Age: 33 - Discharged on 25 Sep 1814 and sent to Dartmoor on HMS Leyden.

Wright, John - Seaman - Number: 3839 - How taken: Gave himself up from HM Ship-of-the-Line Leader - When taken: 18 Jul 1813 - Date received: 21 Aug 1814 - From what ship: Gravesend - Born: Rhode Island - Age: 23 - Discharged on 20 Sep 1814 and sent to Dartmoor on HMS Leyden.

Wright, John - Seaman - Number: 1188 - How taken: Gave himself up from HM Frigate Stag - When taken: 17 Jan 1813 - Date received: 16 Mar 1813 - From what ship: Portsmouth, via HMS Abundance - Born: Virginia - Age: 32 - Race: Man of Color - Discharged on 1 Dec 1813 and released to HMS Ceres.

Wright, Samuel - Seaman - Number: 953 - How taken: Gave himself up from HM Sloop Comet - When taken: 25 Nov 1812 - Date received: 10 Mar 1813 - From what ship: HMS Tigress - Born: Rhode Island - Age: 23 - Race: Negro - Discharged on 19 May 1813 and released to HMS Ceres.

Wright, Thomas - Seaman - Number: 1695 - Prize name: Governor Middleton - Ship type: MV - How taken: Thetis, British privateer - When taken: 2 May 1813 - Where taken: Bay of Biscay - Date received: 15 May 1813 - From what ship: HMS Viper - Born: Wilmington, NC - Age: 29 - Discharged on 24 Jul 1814 and sent to Dartmoor on HMS Liffey.

Wyatt, Jesse - Seaman - Number: 2827 - Prize name: Portsmouth Packet - Ship type: P - How taken: HM Brig Fantome - When taken: 5 Oct 1813 - Where taken: off Portland - Date received: 7 Jan 1814 - From what ship: Halifax - Born: New York - Age: 20 - Discharged on 25 Sep 1814 and sent to Dartmoor on HMS Leyden.

Wyatt, Joseph - Seaman - Number: 691 - Prize name: Fame, prize of Privateer Decatur - Ship type: P - How taken: HM Ship-of-the-Line Polyphemus - When taken: 13 Sep 1812 - Where taken: at sea - Date received: 24 Feb 1813 - From what ship: Portsmouth via HMS Ulysses - Born: Ipswich, MA - Age: 18 - Discharged on 8 Jun 1813 and released to Cartel Rodrigo.

Wyman, William - Seaman - Number: 3740 - Prize name: Argus - Ship type: MV - How taken: HM Ship-of-the-Line San Domingo - When taken: 1 Mar 1814 - Where taken: off Savannah - Date received: 26 May 1814 - From what ship: HMS Hindostan - Born: Boston - Age: 16 - Discharged on 26 Sep 1814 and sent to Dartmoor on HMS Leyden.

Wynn, John - seaman - Number: 3920 - How taken: Gave himself up from HM Brig Amaranthe - When taken: 17 Jan 1814 - Date received: 16 Sep 1814 - From what ship: London - Born: Boston - Age: 28 - Discharged on

29 Sep 1814 and sent to Dartmoor on HMS Freya.

Yale, Nathaniel - Cook - Number: 1125 - Prize name: Hope - Ship type: MV - How taken: HM Sloop Pheasant - When taken: 13 Dec 1812 - Where taken: at sea - Date received: 14 Mar 1813 - From what ship: Portsmouth via HMS Beagle - Born: Prince George's County, MD - Age: 27 - Discharged on 2 Jul 1813 and released to Cartel Moses Brown.

Yatton, James - Seaman - Number: 2394 - How taken: Gave himself up from HM Frigate Cerberus - When taken: 26 Dec 1812 - Date received: 20 Oct 1813 - From what ship: Portsmouth, via an admiral's tender - Born: New Hampshire - Age: 30 - Discharged on 4 Sep 1814 and sent to Dartmoor on HMS Freya.

Yeaton, Charles - Seaman - Number: 2778 - Prize name: Thomas - Ship type: P - How taken: HM Frigate Nymphe - When taken: 24 Jun 1813 - Where taken: off Halifax - Date received: 7 Jan 1814 - From what ship: Halifax - Born: Massachusetts - Age: 22 - Discharged on 8 Sep 1814 and sent to Dartmoor on HMS Niobe.

Yenno, William - Seaman - Number: 995 - Prize name: Rising - Ship type: MV - How taken: HM Ship-Sloop Jalouse - When taken: 6 Dec 1812 - Where taken: at sea - Date received: 10 Mar 1813 - From what ship: HMS Tigress - Born: Richmond - Age: 23 - Released on 20 Mar 1813 to the Rising Sun.

York, Nathaniel - Seaman - Number: 1176 - Prize name: Sword Fish - Ship type: P - How taken: HM Ship-of-the-Line Elephant - When taken: 28 Dec 1812 - Where taken: off Azores - Date received: 16 Mar 1813 - From what ship: Portsmouth, via HMS Abundance - Born: Exeter - Age: 50 - Discharged on 24 Jul 1813 and released to Cartel Hoffminy.

Young, Ebenezer R. - Seaman - Number: 558 - Prize name: Felix - Ship type: MV - How taken: HM Frigate Indefatigable - When taken: 13 Nov 1812 - Where taken: Portsmouth harbor - Date received: 23 Feb 1813 - From what ship: Portsmouth via HMS Dromedary - Born: Nantucket - Age: 32 - Discharged on 8 Jun 1813 and released to Cartel Rodrigo.

Young, Ebenezer - 2nd Mate - Number: 2235 - Prize name: Confidence - Ship type: MV - How taken: HM Sloop Erebus - When taken: 25 Jun 1813 - Where taken: off Gothenburg, Sweden - Date received: 7 Sep 1813 - From what ship: HMS Raisonnable - Born: Chatham - Age: 21 - Discharged on 11 Aug 1814 and sent to Dartmoor on HMS Freya.

Young, John - Seaman - Number: 85 - Prize name: Bee - Ship type: MV - How taken: Stopped at London - When taken: 26 Oct 1812 - Date received: 4 Nov 1812 - From what ship: HMS Namur - Born: Philadelphia - Age: 32 - Discharged in Jul 1813 and released to Cartel Moses Brown.

Young, John - Seaman - Number: 3346 - Prize name: Porcupine - Ship type: LM - How taken: HM Frigate Acasta - When taken: 18 Jul 1813 - Where taken: off Cape Sable, Florida - Date received: 23 Feb 1814 - From what ship: Halifax via HMT Malabar - Born: Milford - Age: 21 - Discharged on 22 Oct 1814 and sent to Dartmoor on HMS Leyden.

Young, John - Marine Private - Number: 3350 - Prize name: Thomas - Ship type: P - How taken: HM Frigate Nymphe - When taken: 26 Jun 1813 - Where taken: off Halifax - Date received: 23 Feb 1814 - From what ship: Halifax via HMT Malabar - Born: Barrington - Age: 44 - Discharged on 10 Oct 1814 and sent to Dartmoor on the Mermaid.

Young, Moses - Seaman - Number: 502 - How taken: Gave himself up from HM Ship-of-the-Line Ruby - When taken: 15 Aug 1812 - Date received: 23 Feb 1813 - From what ship: Portsmouth via HMS Dromedary - Born: Chatham, MA - Age: 32 - Discharged on 26 Jul 1814 and sent to Dartmoor on HMS Raven.

Young, Nathaniel - Seaman - Number: 2277 - Prize name: Garter Wester - Ship type: MV - How taken: HM Ship-of-the-Line Elizabeth - When taken: 25 Jan 1813 - Where taken: off St. Bartholomew, WI - Date received: 17 Sep 1813 - From what ship: HMS Raisonnable - Born: Baltimore - Age: 30 - Race: Black - Discharged on 4 Sep 1814 and sent to Dartmoor on HMS Freya.

Young, Thomas - Seaman - Number: 2098 - How taken: Gave himself up from HM Ship-of-the-Line Barfleur - When taken: 27 May 1813 - Date received: 9 Aug 1813 - From what ship: HMS Thames - Born: Salem, MA - Age: 45 - Discharged on 12 Aug 1814 and sent to Dartmoor on HMS Alpheus.

Younger, Lewis - Seaman - Number: 2351 - How taken: Gave himself up from HM Ship-of-the-Line Pompee - When taken: 25 Jun 1813 - Date received: 20 Oct 1813 - From what ship: Portsmouth, via an admiral's tender

- Born: Massachusetts - Age: 27 - Discharged on 4 Sep 1814 and sent to Dartmoor on HMS Freya.

Zelluck, Thomas - Prize Master - Number: 2792 - Prize name: Yorktown - Ship type: P - How taken: British squadron - When taken: 17 Jul 1813 - Where taken: Grand Banks - Date received: 7 Jan 1814 - From what ship: Halifax - Born: New York - Age: 29 - Discharged on 26 Sep 1814 and sent to Dartmoor on HMS Leyden.

Numeric listing by prisoner number

1	Rogers, Samuel	47	Miller, Ezekiel	93	Stewart, William
2	Peirson, Robert	48	Fernald, Tobias	94	Crafts, William
3	Widger, Thomas	49	Stanley, Peter	95	Ellen, Nathaniel
4	Hammond, William	50	Caley, Henry	96	Hopkins, Samuel
5	Andrew, Joseph	51	Lomondy, Joseph	97	Campbell, John
6	Currin, Andrew	52	Rogers, James	98	Lee, George
7	Doe, Thomas	53	Freeman, John	99	Hand, Wilson
8	Miller, James	54	Richardson, Randolph	100	Pollard, Charles
9	Preston, Isaac	55	Carso, John	101	Michel, John William
10	Fowler, Timothy	56	Hale, Robert	102	Howell, Sullivan
11	Cooper, Eleazer	57	Linnell, Jonathan	103	Dickson, Enos
12	English, James	58	Wood, John	104	Hoy, Philip
13	Ayers, John	59	Hammond, Stephen	105	Brown, William
14	Pudober, Jonathan	60	Piers, Nathaniel	106	Anderson, Joseph
15	Hill, Charles	61	Burk, John	107	Ball, Erastus
16	Drew, Samuel	62	Allyn, David	108	Colwell, John
17	Samson, Thomas	63	Bradbury, Nathan	109	Johnson, Samuel
18	Marshall, John	64	Thompson, Lamon	110	Brooks, Oliver
19	Fresk, Joshua	65	Johnson, Robert	111	Richmond, Caleb
20	Ellis, John	66	Watts, Anthony	112	Roe, Johnman
21	Wait, Philip	67	Atkin, Robert G.	113	Pickens, Benjamin
22	Simpson, Martin	68	Stacey, Benjamin	114	Millican, William
23	Robinet, Samuel	69	Tresroy, Thomas	115	Small, Joseph
24	Bugs, Abram	70	Saucry, John	116	Laycock, Thomas
25	Chapman, John	71	Keen, Robert	117	Parsons, David
26	Brown, James	72	Grant, John	118	Cook, Jacob
27	Robert, Nicholas	73	Willis, Charles	119	Wicks, James
28	Saunders, Joseph	74	Williams, John	120	Snowden, Joshua L.
29	Barnes, Isaac	75	Funk, Samuel	121	Smith, Mark
30	Hall, George	76	McPhee, Alexander	122	Peters, John
31	Durant, John	77	Barlett, N.	123	McDermont, James
32	Sharp, Peter	78	Lee, Williams	124	Wood, Richard
33	Beers, James	79	Greenleaf, James	125	Brickall, William
34	Gregous, William	80	Nason, William	126	Jackson, John
35	Bowman, John	81	Callec, Samuel	127	Hunter, John
36	Longreen, Andrew	82	Walker, John	128	Coffin, Charles
37	Turner, Henry B.	83	Lockwood, Charles	129	Bailey, Charles
38	Oxford, James	84	Rogers, John	130	Barchant, George
39	Stout, Sairer	85	Young, John	131	Allen, Daniel
40	Hoyt, James M.	86	Randal, Benjamin	132	Potter, Henry
41	Smith, John	87	Holston, John	133	Mathews, Edward
42	Barber, Henry	88	Eaton, Benjamin	134	Cainmel, Jeremiah
43	Wilson, William	89	Upton, John B.	135	Green, James
44	Blackbourn, William	90	Read, Major	136	Coaner, Peter
45	Bennet, Andrew	91	Collier, Thomas	137	Morris, Thomas
46	Lexious, Peter	92	Stephens, Henry	138	Murray, Richard

139	Fitch, Henry	188	Butler, John	237	Bourns, Solomon
140	Herdru, Charles	189	Fisher, Francis	238	Wilson, William
141	Lemeeker, Barner	190	Case, Barns	239	Canada, William
142	Hallman, Anthony	191	Melcher, John	240	Smith, James
143	Roberson, James	192	Lingard, Ludwig	241	Hoffman, Joseph
144	Lockwood, Charles	193	Herts, John Edward	242	Hutchinson, Thomas
145	Gilbert, William A.	194	Baxter, Alexander	243	White, Henry
146	Griffin, James	195	Coats, John	244	Pearson, Benjamin
147	Lodge, Ebenezer	196	Delosia, Samuel	245	Prince, Jeffry
148	Hart, William	197	Ballard, John	246	McCormack, William
149	Chappell, John	198	Clerk, Robert	247	Fargo, Elijah
150	Thorndike, Robert	199	Lamon, John	248	Homes, Thomas
151	Sunonton, John	200	Rice, George	249	Hardward, Isaac
152	Davis, Benjamin	201	Wessels, William	250	Doboll, William
153	Wells, William	202	Johnson, Joseph	251	Davis, Nicholas
154	Alexander, John	203	Davis, George	252	Patrick, John
155	Morgan, James	204	Caliban, Ambrose	253	Wilson, Charles
156	Gibbs, Perry	205	Carr, Joseph	254	Morris, William
157	Jacobs, George	206	Thimonier, Peter	255	Johnson, William
158	Felt, John	207	Darran, Duncan	256	Adams, Robert
159	Cooper, William	208	Caen, John	257	Turner, William
160	Smith, William	209	Rose, Francis	258	Brimhall, Cornelius
161	Morris, S.	210	Williams, Edward	259	Otis, Ezekiel
162	Evans, Jonathan	211	Broughton, John	260	Lissel, Joseph
163	Lunes, Charles	212	Mills, Samuel	261	Fameroy, Ashley
164	Primis, George	213	Nicolls, Herold	262	Powell, John
165	Peck, Elisha	214	Henwood, Eliza	263	Stockley, W. D.
166	Phillips, Jackson	215	Sultan, John	264	Tremus, Fit
167	Willet, Jonathan	216	Clough, Isaac	265	Davis, John
168	Ling, Thomas	217	Baptist, Michael	266	Knapp, Ezekiel
169	Seely, Truman	218	Robins, Willis	267	Lewis, Francis
170	Bourn, James	219	Jones, Samuel	268	Johnson, Stephen
171	Turner, Samuel	220	Read, William	269	Dieson, Abraham
172	Jones, Henry	221	Chandler, Ezekiel	270	Shorne, H.
173	Mansfield, Elijah	222	Thompson, George	271	Taggart, John
174	Porter, Stephen	223	Boger, James	272	Welsh, Richard H.
175	Jones, David	224	Seyman, Paul	273	Hoyt, Robert
176	Russell, Samuel	225	Evans, John	274	Thomas, Terry
177	Adams, Thomas	226	Bounty, Charles	275	Larkins, Thomas
178	Erskine, George	227	Barrett, Bias	276	Lauson, Isaac
179	Halbrook, Benjamin	228	Edwards, Price	277	Moore, Henry
180	Tippet, Joseph	229	Johnson, George	278	Chonard, Jack
181	Basset, Edward S.	230	Smith, William	279	Bendionan, Vincent
182	Rees, William	231	Hamlet, John	280	Hood, Daniel
183	Mead, James	232	Anderson, Niels	281	Lawdy, Benjamin
184	Richardson, Allen	233	Jefferies, David	282	Hammond, Benjamin
185	Thatcher, Samuel G.	234	Emlin, Edward	283	Sheppard, David
186	Blood, Simon	235	Courtney, John	284	Ticham, Jeremiah
187	Scott, John	236	James, Isaac	285	Cook, Tarden

Numeric listing by prisoner number

286	Grinnell, William	335	Twycross, Samuel	384	Walkington, George
287	Howland, William	336	Macceaming, James	385	Hall, Spencer
288	Bicketson, John	337	Fowler, John	386	Chapman, Josiah F.
289	Sargent, Phillip	338	Miller, Henry	387	Sears, Bartlett
290	Wood, William	339	Rowe, Isaac	388	Morton, Seth
291	Andrews, Asa	340	Rowe, William	389	Brassier, William
292	Crane, Andrew	341	Purrington, John	390	Homes, Zachariah
293	Allen, Andrew	342	Galt, Robert	391	Skinner, Johnson
294	Allen, John	343	Miller, Samuel	392	Paul, Dempie
295	Elwell, James	344	Smith, Samuel	393	De Young, Richard
296	Walton, John	345	Parsons, George	394	Madillion, Peter
297	Rowe, Daniel	346	Goday, W.	395	Sait, Gasper
298	Green, John	347	Bennet, William	396	Thompson, William
299	Hopkins, Robert	348	Far, William	397	Harding, John G.
300	Smith, James	349	Prout, Henry	398	Craig, William
301	Lord, John	350	Manuel, Josef	399	Brant, Solomon
302	Leach, James	351	Lovelin, Abussha	400	Evans, Robert
303	Thompson, Isaac	352	Thompson, Henry	401	Wallace, William
304	Foxwell, George	353	Abbot, William F.	402	Macure, Angelo
305	Little, Silas W.	354	Elwell, Abraham	403	Burel, Angelo
306	Holland, William	355	Davis, William	404	Dominic, John
307	Hewitt, James	356	Turner, Leonard	405	Thomas, William
308	Siers, Uriah	357	Donaway, Daniel	406	Peters, John
309	Cartwright, Philip	358	Ringold, Thomas B.	407	Glenn, Robert
310	Smith, Buphus	359	Lorenden, George	408	Kennedy, John
311	Vingen, Nicholas	360	Plair, John	409	Walden, James
312	Johnston, Benjamin	361	Gravelin, Jesse	410	Hotchkiss, Levi
313	Jacobson, William	362	Holm, Andre	411	Leach, Charles
314	Clark, Peleg	363	Calentine, Samuel	412	Obrion, John
315	Brinkman, Jan	364	Edmunds, Francis	413	Carter, Moses
316	Bishop, James	365	Saul, Francis	414	Flushman, H. P.
317	Deny, James	366	Williams, Joseph	415	Hall, William
318	Robinson, Jacob	367	Ross, Benjamin T.	416	Scribner, Elijah
319	Taylor, James	368	Burham, Benjamin	417	Poland, David
320	Jackson, C. L.	369	Sikes, Charles	418	White, Sampson
321	Stilman, Elijah	370	Bircham, Joseph	419	Barchman, John
322	Swasey, Alexander	371	Eccleston, Gardner	420	Upton, Samuel
323	Slackpole, John	372	Smith, John	421	Bickford, Ebenezer
324	Stone, Samuel	373	Lawson, Peter	422	Sevratt, William
325	Owen, John	374	Carpenter, William	423	Dean, Daniel
326	Roberts, William	375	Rogers, William	424	Holden, Charles
327	Craig, James	376	Irvin, John	425	Rowell, James
328	Boyle, James	377	Bray, George	426	Cogswell, Edward
329	Booth, Joseph	378	Alexander, James	427	Warner, Charles
330	Loland, Levi	379	Witney, Samuel	428	Hosmer, Joseph
331	Steward, James	380	Bovey, Jesse	429	Fletcher, Henry
332	Hunter, Isaac	381	Schuetzer, Peter	430	Peterson, James
333	Gran, Abraham	382	Freeborn, John	431	Card, Nathaniel
334	Noble, Isaac	383	Moody, Samuel	432	Gardner, Samuel

433	Cloutman, Samuel	482	Couet, John	531	Mitchell, John
434	Nye, Charles N.	483	Simpson, William	532	Allen, Barnes
435	Lowder, Henry	484	Cole, Peter	533	Stevenson, Thomas
436	Moor, Thomas	485	Ray, Christian	534	Webb, Stephen
437	Grunlief, Timothy	486	Wood, Alexander	535	Myer, Peter
438	Parsons, Samuel	487	Smith, Thomas	536	Wilmer, Isaac
439	Jenkins, Richard	488	Williams, Jotham	537	Prendwelle, James
440	Anthony, Abraham	489	Rainy, Thomas	538	Rogers, William
441	Hammet, John	490	Nicholson, Jesse	539	Samblasen, Edward
442	Thomas, John L.	491	Parish, Samuel	540	Chattels, John
443	Ross, George	492	Seely, James	541	Meyer, John
444	Knox, Thomas	493	Barton, Elijah	542	Johnson, Andre
445	Peterson, Nicholas	494	Clark, William	543	Wise, John
446	Hobert, George	495	Hastings, Johnson	544	Metcalf, William
447	Signard, Samuel Francis	496	Chapel, Samuel	545	Hansen, William
448	Warner, George	497	Tedrick, Joseph	546	Tull, John
449	Whipple, Samuel	498	Stephens, Thomas	547	Lindholm, Nicholas
450	Lewis, Raymond	499	Orr, Levi	548	Lucas, Benjamin
451	Dolorer, John	500	Williams, Darius	549	Miller, John Jacob
452	Carves, John	501	Cummings, Edward	550	Cunningham, John
453	Lee, Nathaniel	502	Young, Moses	551	McCoates, Samuel
454	Boyd, Edward	503	Jeffreys, Philip	552	Mirpaine, Bruce
455	Ingells, Edward	504	Dowling, Peter	553	Andrey, Alexander
456	Foster, Isaiah	505	Leighton, Otis	554	Smith, William Pitt
457	Wilcox, Caesar	506	Haywood, John	555	Pardell, Charles
458	Thomas, George	507	Hurst, Dudley	556	Dobbs, Jeremiah
459	Glascow, John	508	George, Peter	557	Robinson, Charles
460	Mitchell, John	509	Smith, William	558	Young, Ebenezer R.
461	Fannol, Augustus	510	Treadwell, Alphecca	559	Tanner, John
462	Carrol, Robert	511	Awe, Joseph	560	Robinson, Edward
463	Robins, Jeremiah	512	Brooks, Edward	561	Barnett, John
464	Andersen, James	513	Peters, John	562	de Park, John
465	Neal, Henry	514	Metrash, Ezekiel	563	Ball, John
466	Peters, Jacob	515	Gibson, William	564	Page, John
467	Towns, Daniel	516	Chidsey, Abraham	565	Richards, George
468	Childs, Samuel	517	Smith, Thomas R.	566	Welch, William
469	Rowe, Stephen	518	Cooper, James	567	Murray, Nathaniel
470	Mitchell, James	519	Powers, William	568	Gall, William
471	Tucker, Edward	520	Barry, John	569	Macrombie, Elijah
472	Monnett, Samuel	521	Dennis, Thomas	570	Armstrong, Thomas
473	Brown, John	522	Clarke, Clarence	571	Williams, David
474	Bowdley, Thomas	523	Rust, John	572	Oilson, Andrew
475	Burroth, Mansfield	524	Davis, Michael	573	Riley, Jonathan
476	Main, Henry	525	Lock, Nathaniel	574	Prince, William
477	Sodoburgh, John	526	Sweet, Moses	575	Nellim, George
478	Henry, Edward	527	Dyer, Ezekiel	576	Magrath, James
479	Brown, Jesse	528	Macintoie, Alexander	577	Boyd, John
480	Bowen, Lewis	529	Waller, George	578	Armstrong, Elijah
481	Lynch, Joseph	530	Anthony, Luke	579	Knight, Zachariah

580	Godsoe, William	629	Bowie, Henry	678	Turner, John
581	Stanwood, Timothy	630	Cox, Isaac	679	Nuting, Charles
582	Davis, Daniel	631	Trought, Joseph	680	Gale, Oliver
583	Pendleton, Asa	632	Fuster, Peter	681	Pault, Beloner
584	Nichols, John	633	Johnson, Samuel	682	Gasseyr, Zephier
585	David, Michael	634	Golever, William	683	Smith, Henry
586	Record, Frederick	635	Ledlowe, John	684	Tristram, Joseph
587	Robson, Robert	636	Bramblecome, David	685	Dorr, Edward
588	Lawson, Mathew	637	Pearson, Samuel	686	Harris, Abraham Harris
589	Branham, Stephen	638	Knapp, Walker	687	Cruff, William
590	Couley, Andrew	639	Walker, James	688	Valentine, Andrew
591	Waterman, William	640	Paine, Joshua	689	Reed, John
592	Cornelius, John	641	Turner, Samuel	690	Hackett, Theophilus
593	Powell, Richard	642	Dussing, Caesar	691	Wyatt, Joseph
594	Greenfield, William	643	Latish, Joseph	692	Stacy, William
595	Randson, John	644	Williams, Gaspar	693	Newby, John
596	Giles, John	645	James, John	694	Picket, Richard
597	Stephens, Michael	646	Tufts, Eleazer	695	Homan, Joseph
598	Jones, William	647	Even, Peter	696	Salkins, Nathaniel
599	Cowen, William	648	Ellis, John	697	Harris, David
600	Liddle, John	649	Osborne, Thomas	698	Lakeman, Samuel
601	Cross, John	650	Dagman, Caleb	699	Okes, George
602	Mathewson, Andrew	651	Hutchins, William	700	Antonie, John
603	Evans, John	652	Clements, Henry	701	Ramans, Nicholas
604	Delancey, William	653	Harding, Joseph	702	Sparling, William
605	Williamson, Charles	654	Helman, John	703	Hecox, George
606	Gifford, Francis	655	Drinkwater, Andrew	704	Weilwright, Joseph
607	Porter, Nathaniel	656	Blankenship, Charles	705	Dominico, Joseph
608	McNeal, Alexander	657	Tagle, Amos	706	Geely, Joseph
609	Scaff, Nicholas	658	Alley, Jacob	707	Christie, William
610	Beckner, Henry	659	Anderson, Andrew	708	Manning, Thomas
611	Williams, Henry	660	Anderson, Oliver	709	Wair, Francis
612	Allen, Peter	661	Gard, Gulab	710	Dennis, Thomas
613	Ricks, Thomas	662	Senholm, Jacob	711	Tinkham, Seth
614	Dennis, John	663	Davis, Nathan	712	Weinberg, John
615	Sholes, Giles	664	Pettingale, John	713	Gase, Zachariah
616	Lippen, Stephen	665	Petterson, John	714	Harlow, Sylvanus
617	Platt, John Henry	666	Johnson, Andrew	715	Scott, James
618	Myers, Jacob	667	Martin, Jonathan	716	White, J. William
619	Weeks, George	668	Baker, Henry	717	Boston, Robert
620	Lebon, Philip	669	Willson, William	718	Eldridge, Samuel
621	Lewis, John	670	Henricks, Jeremiah	719	Ward, James
622	Hill, George	671	Mumery, James	720	Nelson, Samuel A.
623	Burke, Samuel	672	Chase, Samuel	721	Soder, Bastion D.
624	Salyear, John	673	Coleman, Daniel	722	Spiney, Nathaniel
625	Inberg, Gabriel	674	Paline, William	723	Kennedy, Henry
626	Nilodas, M.	675	Gebers, Henry	724	Henderson, Benjamin
627	Hyatt, William	676	Stone, John	725	Chase, Eliphalet
628	Legere, Joseph	677	Carebo, Henry	726	Jackson, John

727	Riker, Samuel	776	Hardwick, James	825	Peterson, John
728	Wells, Thomas	777	Daniels, Bradley	826	Morris, William
729	Berry, John	778	Rest, Zebulon	827	Geline, John
730	Holt, Simeon	779	Parks, Richard	828	Brandy, Francis
731	Preston, William	780	Hutchinson, James	829	Scott, Benjamin
732	Clark, Alexander	781	Lalan, John	830	Turner, Thomas
733	Hoyt, Ichabod	782	Cunningham, Silas	831	Gibey, John
734	Pratt, Asa	783	Jenkins, Peter	832	Moss, William
735	Moore, Daniel	784	Condon, John	833	Martin, Ephraim
736	Stoff, Samuel	785	Hera, John A.	834	Coffin, Frederick H.
737	Coggins, George	786	Towns, Nicholas	835	Taylor, John
738	Whittlebank, Edward	787	Jones, Thomas	836	Bienent, Edward
739	Peterson, Peter	788	Macquillon, Hugh	837	Aulajo, Thomas
740	Dunn, Henry G.	789	Parker, John	838	Whitney, Joseph
741	Simpson, John	790	Gill, James	839	Green, Horace
742	Hall, Charles	791	Mourin, James	840	Cochran, Stephen
743	Burlugh, Henry	792	Malony, Hughey	841	Bevers, Clement
744	Prentiss, James	793	Crow, Jonathan	842	Robinson, Michael
745	Kimberly, Elisha	794	Peek, David	843	Law, John
746	Chalk, John	795	Morgan, William	844	Smith, Chester
747	Very, Samuel	796	Brown, Zeth	845	Davis, John
748	Johnson, Alexander	797	Hart, Frederick	846	Godson, John
749	Vannog, John P.	798	Moor, John	847	Haywood, Simon
750	Adams, Leonard	799	Leach, Benjamin	848	Dowling, Anthony
751	Loggett, Gilbert	800	Kennard, Joseph	849	Lyons, Henry
752	Lane, John	801	Baptist, John	850	Anderson, William
753	Lockwood, Caleb	802	Walker, William	851	Pigott, James
754	Bovey, Benjamin	803	Bain, John	852	Nartique, John
755	Vanderhovan, John	804	Martin, John	853	Gomez, Manuel
756	Vanderhovan, Mathew	805	Bellas, John	854	Perez, Joseph
757	Beatty, James	806	Jones, Urigh	855	Slate, Henry V.
758	Mullins, Joseph	807	White, John	856	Lewis, John
759	Selby, James	808	Richardson, Daniel	857	Parker, Samuel
760	Love, Peter	809	Hatch, Abraham	858	Turpin, Francis
761	Coomes, Richard	810	Anderson, William	859	Johns, Bellona
762	Orphan, John	811	Brewer, James	860	Cooperies, Nicholas
763	Chase, Mathew	812	Bell, George	861	Roy, Charles
764	Newry, Peter	813	Keith, James	862	Capron, William
765	Valentine, James	814	Gardner, James	863	Calkins, Zera
766	Carlander, John	815	Roach, Nicholas	864	Douchney, Hiram
767	Ward, Mason	816	Garthon, Willey	865	Hartford, John
768	Davies, Charles	817	Cousor, Adam	866	Canada, Prince
769	Latimer, John	818	Robinson, Benjamin	867	Barton, Nathan
770	Smith, John	819	Henderson, David	868	Belford, Isaac
771	Bourn, John	820	Kain, Peter	869	Todd, William
772	Gore, John	821	Dickinson, Francis	870	Helm, Charles
773	Smith, Obadiah	822	Weaver, Thomas	871	Jackson, John
774	Allen, William	823	Tightham, Peter	872	Harris, William
775	Harrison, Joseph	824	Carson, Robert	873	Gardner, Anthony

874	Benny, Malloc	923	Anthony, John	972	Roundy, Jonathan
875	Bailey, Joseph	924	Williamson, Charles	973	Vine, William
876	Bickford, William	925	Benner, Lewis	974	Smith, William
877	Sampson, David	926	Willingsworth, Jeffery	975	Jameson, George
878	Parsons, Wanery	927	Ellis, John	976	Moore, Michael
879	Washy, George	928	Lynch, William	977	Roberts, Josiah
880	Reed, John	929	Jewell, Samuel	978	Sanderson, John
881	Fortune, John	930	Harris, James	979	Whitlock, Sidney B.
882	Williams, Michael	931	Dunn, Hezekiah	980	Haley, Thomas
883	Jackson, George	932	Drybourgh, James	981	Michael, Peter
884	Knight, George	933	Woodard, Elijah	982	Withman, William
885	Dolabar, John	934	Flower, Artemas	983	Wallace, William
886	Knight, William	935	Green, Samuel	984	Brown, John
887	Chine, Samuel	936	Gibbons, Andrew	985	Sheppard, Daniel
888	Swett, Francis	937	Arthur, Alexander	986	Hitching, John
889	Ireson, Robert B.	938	Joseph, Michael	987	Jerry, Daniel
890	Greaves, Samuel	939	Howland, William	988	Hook, Aaron
891	Brooks, Edward	940	Rippaviere, John	989	Wade, Otis
892	Symonds, Israel	941	Jacobson, Jacob	990	Howlen, Samuel
893	Roselof, Thomas	942	Caroline, Tobias	991	Benster, John
894	Barton, Peter	943	Coleman, Jonathan	992	Carr, Samuel
895	Bachelor, Nathaniel	944	Steward, Alexander	993	Evans, Thomas
896	Daniels, John	945	Myrick, William	994	Smith, Thomas
897	Dorrick, James	946	Allen, William	995	Yenno, William
898	Dodick, Mathew	947	DeBock, Cornelius	996	Dawson, John
899	Maston, John	948	Liscomb, John	997	Hartford, James
900	Willson, John	949	Russell, William	998	Snider, Lewis
901	Davis, Andrew	950	Thompson, John	999	Chambers, Charles
902	Pleasanton, Robert	951	Williams, Josiah	1000	Black, William
903	Butterfield, Edward	952	Malvern, Lanis	1001	Grose, Daniel
904	Hatch, Walter	953	Wright, Samuel	1002	Baptiste, John
905	Jennings, John	954	Gunnell, William	1003	Douglas, Thomas
906	Ratuse, Peter	955	Nald, John	1004	Cobb, Samuel
907	Stockhouse, Charles	956	Raymond, George	1005	Wickwall, Joseph
908	Minor, Pedro	957	Thomas, John L.	1006	Perkins, Henry
909	Fountain, Isaac	958	Gray, Charles	1007	Tellebrown, William
910	Wilson, Peter	959	Bocatt, John	1008	Butler, George
911	Francoise, James	960	Rowe, John	1009	Cloutman, Robert
912	Davis, John	961	Chult, David	1010	Manson, James
913	Brown, John	962	Burns, George	1011	Manning, Enoch
914	Carr, Richard	963	Moore, Jacob	1012	Anderton, Samuel
915	Carban, Thomas	964	Fron, Frederick	1013	Badsse, Philip
916	Tolson, Jeremy	965	Chandler, Henry	1014	Carney, Thomas
917	Johnson, Robert	966	Lind, Andrew	1015	Noonan, William
918	Murray, John	967	Saunders, Thomas	1016	White, John W.
919	Mills, John	968	Smith, William	1017	White, Benjamin
920	Packard, William	969	Scott, Andrew	1018	Reed, H. W.
921	Smith, Jacob	970	Rich, Francis	1019	Ingalls, Samuel
922	Fate, Thomas	971	Townsend, Milby	1020	Cloutman, George

1021	Cole, Hutchinson A.	1070	Liddle, Morris	1119	Lapham, Cushion
1022	Wicks, Littleton	1071	Shipley, Charles	1120	Dennison, Laurence
1023	Beckett, William	1072	Rennell, States William	1121	Withers, Edward
1024	Osborne, Peter	1073	Johnson, William	1122	George, Thomas
1025	Johnson, Henry	1074	Conway, Andrew	1123	Hutchins, Josiah
1026	Scanel, Cornelius	1075	Sieway, Peter	1124	Johnson, David
1027	West, John	1076	Johnson, John	1125	Yale, Nathaniel
1028	Higgins, William	1077	Williamson, John	1126	Castor, Charles
1029	Watkins, Fredrick	1078	Philbrook, Bartholomew	1127	Parsons, Thomas
1030	Williams, Alexander	1079	Mason, John	1128	Benjamin, Joseph
1031	Swanton, John	1080	Richardson, James	1129	Bagley, Moses
1032	Pattingale, Enoch	1081	Burnham, John	1130	Wood, George
1033	Brightman, Joseph	1082	Muncy, Daniel	1131	Setchell, Samuel
1034	Gifford, Barry	1083	Sands, Thomas	1132	Doevall, Francis
1035	White, Alden	1084	Parsons, Joseph	1133	Dixey, Peter
1036	Underwood, John Francis	1085	Severence, Gideon	1134	Winslow, William
1037	Williams, George (1)	1086	Taylor, William	1135	Middleton, Reuben
1038	Williams, George (2)	1087	Goodwin, Jonas B.	1136	Lear, Alexander
1039	Allen, Elijah	1088	Doliber, Joseph	1137	Strong, William
1040	Freeman, Alexander	1089	Broden, Norman	1138	Booder, Jacob
1041	Green, John	1090	Homan, John	1139	Elwell, Jonathan
1042	McKenzie, John	1091	Homan, Jonas	1140	Lawrence, Peter
1043	Jane, Joseph	1092	George, William W.	1141	Black, John
1044	Manuel, Joseph	1093	Pearson, Thomas	1142	Francis, Frederick
1045	Hazard, Thomas	1094	Miller, George	1143	Lambert, John
1046	Hathaway, William N.	1095	Smith, Henry	1144	Roberts, George
1047	Riley, William	1096	Miner, Benjamin F.	1145	Fernandes, Anthony
1048	Peirce, Edward	1097	Stanton, Gideon A.	1146	Mills, Henry
1049	Cunningham, John	1098	Sterns, Henry	1147	Cox, Daniel
1050	Floyd, James	1099	Sibert, Frederick	1148	Small, Thomas
1051	Bardoe, John	1100	Brower, Frederick	1149	Roper, John
1052	Lenderson, Henry	1101	Wilson, John	1150	Saunders, Thomas
1053	Conway, Samuel	1102	Anderson, Aaron	1151	Kile, George
1054	Packman, George	1103	Caban, Samuel	1152	Jeremy, Stephen
1055	Francis, Peter	1104	Tafe, Henry	1153	Griffin, Samuel
1056	Wilson, William	1105	Rosignol, James	1154	Lee, Richard
1057	Farrell, John	1106	Scofield, Wells	1155	Grant, Christian
1058	Lewis, John	1107	Moore, Benjamin	1156	Anderton, Thomas
1059	Garrison, John	1108	Mitchell, James M.	1157	Nowland, Andrew
1060	Van Donveer, Peter	1109	Blazon, Stephen	1158	Brimmer, John
1061	Manuel, John	1110	Palmer, Peter	1159	Johnson, Andrew
1062	Carney, William	1111	Arnold, William	1160	Merriday, John
1063	Hedley, John	1112	Cooper, Alfred	1161	Woods, William
1064	Spratt, Thomas	1113	Morris, George	1162	Shot, John
1065	Osgood, David	1114	Tucker, Samuel	1163	Hanson, Henry
1066	Church, Richard	1115	Lake, Noah	1164	Morrow, Joseph
1067	Lister, Louis	1116	Cain, Enoch	1165	Bessom, Nicholas
1068	Brown, William	1117	Ramady, James	1166	Wells, Moses
1069	Marshall, Francis	1118	Pierce, William	1167	Stephens, David

1168	Innis, John	1217	Brady, James	1266	Turner, Samuel
1169	Kenny, George	1218	Hill, William	1267	Sheppard, Joseph
1170	Asten, John	1219	Barber, John	1268	Blake, Charles
1171	Dalliber, James	1220	Simonds, Joseph	1269	Gudlers, George
1172	Whitchouse, Lewis	1221	Mitchell, Francis	1270	Noonan, William
1173	Dudley, Ephraim	1222	Thompson, John	1271	Kerhow, Samuel
1174	Carrel, Michael	1223	Ellis, William	1272	Paulfrey, Richard
1175	Parsons, Andrew	1224	Eaton, John	1273	Stephens, Trey
1176	York, Nathaniel	1225	Hall, Thomas	1274	Shed, William
1177	Landback, Rich	1226	Boyd, John	1275	Bisbee, Asaph
1178	Williams, John	1227	Longwheel, Amos	1276	Bray, Zacharias
1179	Woods, Charles	1228	Copasses, Matthew	1277	Richardson, Perry
1180	Nowland, Andrew	1229	Ford, M. Benjamin	1278	Rogers, James
1181	Evans, John	1230	Berry, Joseph	1279	Green, Henry
1182	Bartlett, George B.	1231	Hill, Pompey	1280	Deistel, John
1183	Kenner, John Downing	1232	Lee, Samuel	1281	Sidebottom, John
1184	Anderson, Joseph	1233	Williams, Benjamin	1282	Poole, John
1185	Corban, Daniel	1234	Oberville, Michael	1283	McDonald, John
1186	Conner, Jesse	1235	Combs, Thomas	1284	Patterson, Peter
1187	Buddington, Asa	1236	Pearce, Emanuel	1285	Johnson, William
1188	Wright, John	1237	Hurt, Samuel	1286	Gilbert, Thomas
1189	Roberts, Robert	1238	Stevenson, Thaddeus	1287	Babb, Benjamin
1190	Branton, Samuel	1239	Hobdyke, John	1288	Church, Benjamin
1191	Turnbull, James	1240	Vorge, James	1289	Covelle, Ephraim
1192	Johnson, Oliver	1241	Lamon, James	1290	Hooseman, John
1193	Staggs, Henry	1242	Bayman, James	1291	Brainard, Richard
1194	Thompson, Joseph	1243	Howard, Henry	1292	Smith, John
1195	Marks, Peter	1244	Douglas, Charles	1293	Atwood, Edward
1196	Clarke, Arnold	1245	Powell, Elijah	1294	Brenton, York
1197	Fingersen, John F.	1246	Chambers, Joseph	1295	Albert, John
1198	George, Isaac	1247	Duhard, Thomas	1296	Bark, David
1199	Baker, John	1248	Swain, Thomas	1297	Booth, Thomas
1200	Earl, Maris	1249	Labbas, John	1298	Denham, William
1201	Beasley, Edward	1250	Lockett, Thomas R.	1299	Williams, George
1202	Benjamin, James	1251	Nunns, William	1300	Malis, John
1203	Bitters, John	1252	Robinson, Edward	1301	Johnson, Frederick
1204	Townsend, Solomon	1253	Carman, James	1302	Smith, Caesar
1205	Colwell, John	1254	Williamson, George J.	1303	Scribner, William
1206	Beans, James	1255	Dunstan, John	1304	Dairs, William
1207	Esperaza, Jacob	1256	Courtis, Thomas	1305	Williamson, John
1208	Mountain, Emanuel	1257	Dildure, Samuel	1306	Beck, William
1209	John, Richard J.	1258	Urey, Peter	1307	Mitchell, Thomas
1210	Ingraham, Peter	1259	Saunders, Thomas	1308	Rice, John
1211	Simpson, James	1260	Wolfe, Andre	1309	Hawley, Frederick
1212	Thomas, John	1261	Ferris, Jacob	1310	Simmons, Daniel
1213	Hardy, John	1262	Connoway, James	1311	Saunderson, William
1214	Southward, Samuel W.	1263	White, John W.	1312	Robinson, Benjamin
1215	Leserver, Florence	1264	Bean, Amos	1313	Davis, George
1216	Jones, Cabell	1265	Silsby, Nathaniel	1314	Munro, John

1315	Martin, John J.	1364	Wilson, Daniel	1413	Harris, William
1316	Best, John	1365	Rollo, William	1414	Lyons, Samuel
1317	Francis, Prince	1366	Davis, Daniel	1415	Abraham, William
1318	Barrett, James	1367	Deverter, William	1416	Upton, Jeduthun
1319	Burnham, David	1368	Patterson, John	1417	Winckley, John
1320	Ferriere, George	1369	Lent, Joseph	1418	Davidson, Thomas
1321	Lothrop, James	1370	Peak, John W.	1419	Stevens, Joseph
1322	Hogan, William	1371	Morris, Louis	1420	Mains, John
1323	Gammell, Samuel	1372	Merle, John	1421	Warren, John
1324	Allen, Henry	1373	Martin, Henry	1422	Langroth, Francis
1325	Shirly, Phares	1374	Sparrow, John	1423	Paddock, Benjamin Mead
1326	Orne, W. B.	1375	Hutchinson, Townsend	1424	Ross, Richard
1327	Tink, Henry	1376	Thomas, Francis	1425	Richardson, John
1328	Downing, Henry	1377	Sutton, Prince	1426	Clark, Elisha
1329	Lyon, Ezekiel	1378	Hayden, William	1427	Kingley, Benjamin
1330	Allen, Edward	1379	George, William Main	1428	West, Nathaniel
1331	Taylor, Godfrey	1380	Winford, Charles	1429	Willot, Robert
1332	Nicholson, Thomas	1381	Payne, Ransom	1430	Woodberry, Caleb
1333	Welch, Samuel	1382	Warmsley, Samuel	1431	Jones, John
1334	Smith, John	1383	Robins, John	1432	Boss, Thomas
1335	Williams, William	1384	Reed, Thomas	1433	Jennings, Samuel
1336	Amos, Isaac	1385	Scott, Samuel	1434	Chestly, Amos
1337	Conklin, Enoch	1386	Nolton, John	1435	Huntress, Robert
1338	Hall, Henry	1387	Graham, George	1436	Brown, Wheeler
1339	Forrest, William	1388	Dickson, Richard	1437	Stanley, Joseph
1340	Allen, John	1389	Robinson, James	1438	Thompson, James
1341	Werner, John	1390	Quaan, George	1439	Frees, James
1342	Green, John	1391	Porgan, Theodore	1440	Rape, Nicholas
1343	Thomas, Henry	1392	Swinny, Edward	1441	Kennedy, Peter
1344	Fitch, John	1393	Thompson, Owen	1442	Albert, Hezekiah
1345	Gale, Sam	1394	Dishele, Alexander	1443	Cleveland, Davis
1346	Burrell, Rial	1395	Jones, John	1444	Dow, John
1347	Harris, William	1396	Fuller, Zachariah	1445	Wheeler, William
1348	Coleman, John	1397	Spryon, John	1446	Tipton, Solomon
1349	Gardiner, Amboy	1398	Starr, G. C.	1447	Moore, Benjamin
1350	Huff, Charles	1399	Cochran, Peter	1448	Thompson, Courtney
1351	Veney, George	1400	Henry, John	1449	Greenleaf, Thomas
1352	Delenne, John	1401	Prutty, Henry	1450	Johnson, James
1353	Patten, John	1402	Lyons, Peter	1451	Lewis, George
1354	Parsons, Rufus	1403	Bunker, Peter	1452	Johnson, Jacob
1355	Phillips, Thomas	1404	Thompson, Samuel	1453	Rahabe, William
1356	Clark, Samuel	1405	Williams, James	1454	Sweetman, Samuel
1357	Gould, John	1406	Myers, Frederick	1455	Jackson, Thomas
1358	Paul, Jacob	1407	Duffy, Nathaniel	1456	Webb, John
1359	Wedgewood, James	1408	Melville, John	1457	Kirby, Benjamin
1360	Tarlton, Thomas P.	1409	Kinlay, Joseph	1458	Sparks, Henry
1361	Lewis, John	1410	Parr, James	1459	Fairweather, Robert
1362	Deselva, Manuel	1411	Carver, Abraham	1460	Underwood, Benjamin
1363	Coon, John	1412	Evans, Hale	1461	Johnston, Samuel

1462	Crofts, William	1511	Wilson, William	1560	Hamilton, John
1463	McElroy, William	1512	Smith, Thomas	1561	Smasher, Allen
1464	Hasem, John	1513	Moulden, William	1562	Coffin, George
1465	Lownsburg, Carpenter	1514	Roberts, James	1563	Nargney, James
1466	Mercer, Chaumont	1515	Peters, William	1564	Thomas, Henry
1467	Johnstone, William	1516	Fredericks, John	1565	James, John
1468	Harrison, John	1517	Campbell, John	1566	Chew, Joseph
1469	Elliott, Francis	1518	Wickham, Thaddeus	1567	Robinson, John
1470	Reeves, Joseph	1519	Mallan, James	1568	Lovering, William
1471	Allen, Jacob	1520	Johnson, Edward	1569	Forbes, James
1472	Gilligan, William	1521	Trask, William	1570	Reid, Joseph
1473	McDonald, John	1522	Clifford, S. L.	1571	Jackson, Thomas
1474	Webb, William	1523	Edwards, John	1572	Waters, Philip
1475	Morris, John	1524	Morell, John	1573	Conklin, Enoch
1476	Schyder, Jacob Knapp	1525	Sims, Clement	1574	Vincent, John
1477	Thompson, William	1526	Morrison, John	1575	Scott, Abraham
1478	Swanston, Jacob	1527	Gilpin, John	1576	White, Charles
1479	Carns, Richard	1528	Thomas, Charles	1577	McFee, John
1480	Seabold, John	1529	Pope, William	1578	Atkinson, John
1481	Jones, John	1530	Brown, Elisha	1579	Renelds, Amos
1482	Hill, William	1531	Hall, William	1580	Benson, George
1483	Armstrong, Nicholas	1532	Pinkham, Allen	1581	Thomas, William
1484	Chapell, William	1533	Thompson, William	1582	Smith, Peter
1485	Jordan, David	1534	Bennyman, John	1583	Colquhoun, William
1486	de Colville, Laurence	1535	Hughes, Peter	1584	Cromwell, Glacio
1487	Lockerby, William	1536	Chip, Charles	1585	Thomas, Thomas
1488	Stone, William	1537	Busson, John	1586	Conelly, James
1489	Randale, Frederick	1538	Gibbs, James	1587	Read, Hugh
1490	Godshall, John	1539	Ross, John	1588	Reans, John
1491	Mason, Francis	1540	Hudson, William	1589	Thompson, William
1492	Morris, Thomas	1541	Scott, Ezekiel	1590	Wooldridge, William
1493	Graham, William	1542	Crowell, Uriel	1591	Fangall, William
1494	Robinson, David	1543	Rice, Thomas	1592	Watts, James
1495	Parker, David	1544	Rice, John	1593	Jeffreys, Henry
1496	Williams, Peter	1545	Wain, Benjamin	1594	Potter, John
1497	Mesniers, Benjamin	1546	Johnston, Samuel	1595	Gilles, St. Clair
1498	Irwin, Magnus	1547	Thomas, Alexander	1596	Nicholas, Henry
1499	Douglas, Thomas	1548	Ruliff, London	1597	Williams, John
1500	Curtis, George	1549	Johnston, Edward	1598	Nicolson, Benjamin
1501	Knight, Isaac D.	1550	Lawrence, David	1599	Barnett, John
1502	Burch, James	1551	Treyer, John	1600	Cannon, William
1503	Kent, James	1552	Fisher, Richard D.	1601	Squires, Prince
1504	Benjamin, Polasskie	1553	Richardson, Samuel	1602	Wilson, John
1505	Fitch, William	1554	Myer, John	1603	Paine, R. B.
1506	Watkins, George	1555	Carney, Edward	1604	Voughon, Robert
1507	Stacy, Perry	1556	Low, Thomas	1605	Wilcox, Ephraim
1508	Hitchcock, Edward	1557	Pannell, Hugh	1606	Rose, William
1509	Albro, George	1558	Carman, Francis	1607	Hool, Salmon
1510	Burton, William	1559	Spencer, Samuel	1608	Garrison, Christian

1609	Irwin, Andrew	1658	Lee, Edward	1707	Lathrope, Gurdon
1610	Brown, George	1659	Heywood, John	1708	Newel, George
1611	Lotton, John	1660	Edwards, Isaac	1709	Mayeau, Morris
1612	Whitmore, John	1661	Howell, John	1710	Burns, John
1613	Stanly, Benjamin	1662	Clay, John	1711	Lewis, Gabriel
1614	Waterman, Thomas	1663	Butler, Thomas	1712	Williams, Joseph
1615	Conklin, Enoch	1664	Smith, Thomas	1713	Ears, Ludwig
1616	McCannon, Thomas	1665	Bumpus, Asa	1714	Stevenson, George
1617	Bin, Peter	1666	Jackson, Allison	1715	Pool, Richard
1618	McBrearthy, Patrick	1667	Potter, Jacob	1716	Ingrain, John
1619	Gill, John	1668	Merkell, John	1717	Istill, James
1620	Cowgan, John	1669	Perkins, William	1718	Anderson, Henry
1621	Dalton, John	1670	Hinton, John	1719	Stinchcombe, George
1622	Mooney, Mathew	1671	Barrett, George	1720	Seawell, George
1623	Doniner, John	1672	Brown, John	1721	Rogers, Edward
1624	Blaney, Henry	1673	Thayer, Ebenezer	1722	Bontrous, John
1625	Condon, Michael	1674	Hopkins, Samuel	1723	Drake, John
1626	Wiley, John	1675	Wheebell, Robert	1724	Sturges, John
1627	Donnally, Anthony	1676	Basstisto, John	1725	Syder, John
1628	Fitzgerald, John	1677	Davis, James	1726	White, William
1629	Clarke, John	1678	Bachelor, Nathaniel	1727	Hronias, Henry
1630	Kelly, Henry	1679	Smith, Noble	1728	Melville, Charles
1631	Ganagon, Edward	1680	Gould, Nicholas	1729	Hazel, Thomas
1632	Williams, Thomas	1681	Minor, David	1730	Gamslo, Carl
1633	Johnson, George	1682	Paul, Jonathan	1731	Capilo, Francis
1634	Hearins, Patrick	1683	Owens, Eugene	1732	Swier, Louis
1635	Shields, Mathew	1684	Horsey, Thomas W.	1733	Posey, Valentine
1636	Dole, Anthony	1685	Worthing, Isaac	1734	Slebar, Samuel
1637	Folsom, Abraham	1686	Cushman, Orson	1735	Briant, Moses
1638	Davis, Joseph	1687	Dodge, Joseph	1736	Francis, John
1639	Oulson, Frederick	1688	Nye, William	1737	Woods, Merrill
1640	Haller, Joseph	1689	Woodborne, John	1738	Ray, Charles
1641	Butler, William	1690	Brown, Peter	1739	Grey, James
1642	Groves, Pierce	1691	Nash, William	1740	Lilsle, Richard
1643	Simons, John	1692	Doer, James	1741	Gilbert, Thomas
1644	Hendrickson, Michael	1693	Driver, Thomas	1742	Fogerty, Archibald
1645	Rosecrens, Philip	1694	Fry, Peter	1743	Bailey, John
1646	Foloson, Christopher	1695	Wright, Thomas	1744	Bowins, George
1647	Randolph, Exum	1696	Sheppard, Henry	1745	Litchfield, Enoch
1648	Wiley, David	1697	Walton, Christopher	1746	Starbourg, W. G.
1649	Gray, Thomas	1698	Shaw, John	1747	Carter, Ebenezer
1650	Russell, Joseph	1699	Johnson, John	1748	Strordvant, David
1651	Banta, John	1700	Jackson, J. K.	1749	Rogers, John
1652	Flood, John	1701	Willson, John	1750	Allen, Isaac
1653	Jackson, William	1702	Dean, Samuel	1751	Welsh, William
1654	Harris, James	1703	Spear, Joseph	1752	Haushaw, George
1655	Wetou, William	1704	Brown, Abijah	1753	Cooper, James
1656	Williams, James	1705	Hale, William	1754	Roberts, David
1657	Corvet, Isaac	1706	Jarrat, Abraham	1755	Lynch, Elias

1756	Hart, Marquis	1805	Lewis, Solomon	1853	Forrest, James
1757	Stevens, John	1806	Williams, Richard	1854	Eaton, James
1758	Goswick, William	1807	Foster, Joseph	1855	Bean, William
1759	Manuel, Anthony	1808	Elisha, Thomas	1856	Johnson, Thomas
1760	Degars, Pedro	1809	Nichols, William	1857	Richards, Edward
1761	Johnson, Thomas	1809 a	Sanssuillon, John	1858	Avery, Charles
1762	Williams, Abraham	1810	Roderick, Frank	1859	McWarren, Nathaniel
1763	Bergen, Leven	1811	Cole, Stephen	1860	Robins, Thomas
1764	Perry, John	1812	West, Henry	1861	Hemp, James
1765	Runlet, Ebenezer	1813	Reed, John	1862	Frazier, John
1766	Hubbard, George	1814	White, John	1863	Welch, John
1767	Clarke, William	1815	Boterol, John	1864	Cody, James
1768	Benson, Jonas	1816	Dennis, Thomas	1865	Anderson, James
1769	Rowe, Richard	1817	Ingersoll, Abraham	1866	Tyler, Lewis
1770	Parker, George	1818	Lawson, James	1867	Ploughman, Joseph
1771	Muckleroy, Samuel	1819	Briggs, Boileau	1868	Spencer, Leonard
1772	Pierce, Thomas	1820	Fuller, John	1869	Calder, John H.
1773	Reed, James	1821	Mathew, Lewis	1870	Churchill, Henry
1774	Dews, William	1822	Christie, John	1871	Sutton, John
1775	Hughes, John	1823	Taylor, Peter	1872	Mossland, Reuben
1776	Alexander, Robert	1824	Fyans, Joseph	1873	Quackenbush, William
1777	White, Thomas	1825	Moore, John	1874	Kershon, Abraham
1778	Lee, Joseph	1826	Williams, John	1875	Mars, George
1779	Gardner, Jonathan	1827	Allen, William	1876	Hill, Josiah
1780	Babcock, Clark	1828	Peckham, Hazard	1877	Ludlow, Reuben
1781	Chappell, Edward	1829	Richards, John	1878	Byer, Peter
1782	Pendergrast, Morris	1830	Hardiman, John	1879	Cadwell, Samuel
1783	Marshall, Levi	1831	Follinsbe, William	1880	Bartholf, Nicholas
1784	Charles, Thomas	1832	Howater, Henry	1881	Small, George D.
1785	Rea, William J.	1833	Rogers, Francis	1882	Nicholas, John
1786	Jones, Charles	1834	Brown, Seth	1883	Sampson, Jacob
1787	Hebius, Jeremiah	1835	Miller, John	1884	Hill, Ephraim
1788	Adivoe, Henry	1836	Lawson, Lawrence	1885	Jones, James
1789	Meeker, James	1837	Williams, John	1886	Morris, James
1790	Church, Jeremiah	1838	Cole, William	1887	Waterman, John
1791	Dalton, Joseph	1839	Baurs, Francis	1888	Donaldson, Joseph
1792	Harway, Samuel	1840	Morris, Isaac	1889	Bishop, Edward
1793	Gray, Thomas	1841	Lowdie, Samuel	1890	Hubbard, Alfred
1794	Jackson, John	1842	Pain, James	1891	Cole, William
1795	Brown, James	1843	Muller, William	1892	Thompson, Nathaniel
1796	Tomkins, Ephraim	1844	Sillock, Amos	1893	Lopans, William
1797	Carpenter, Nathaniel	1845	Taylor, James	1894	Bartis, John
1798	Luther, Jeremiah	1846	Wilson, Thomas	1895	Chase, Nathaniel
1799	Butcher, James	1847	Palmer, William	1896	Atwood, Thomas
1800	Clements, William	1848	Estey, William	1897	Beecher, William Palmer
1801	Hosstidler, Jesse	1849	Rowe, Simon	1898	Allen, John
1802	Pedersen, John	1850	Steward, John	1899	Lemmon, Henry
1803	Gordon, William	1851	West, George	1900	Gibbs, Daniel
1804	Fogg, Noel	1852	Harris, William	1901	Hull, Edward

1902	Fohis, James	1951	Trusty, Henry	2000	McBride, James
1903	Ashfield, Henry	1952	Bailey, Samuel	2001	Leion, Alexander
1904	Cappel, John	1953	Lee, George	2002	Cotterell, James
1905	King, John	1954	Myers, David	2003	Richards, James
1906	Blackman, Moses	1955	Durham, Charles	2004	Freeman, Prince
1907	Bailey, John	1956	Deal, John	2005	Anderson, Robert
1908	Vangorbet, Cato	1957	Crandell, John	2006	Evans, James
1909	Tiffs, Joseph	1958	Aurel, Leonard	2007	Parsons, Ignatius
1910	Brill, John	1959	Freeman, Charles	2008	Harvey, John
1911	Carter, John	1960	Cadwell, James	2009	Edgerly, William
1912	Dunn, David	1961	Gilbert, George	2010	Gardner, Peter
1913	Cole, John	1962	Moffett, John	2011	Russell, M.
1914	Davis, Francis	1963	Reynolds, Frederick	2012	Smith, John
1915	Warren, James	1964	Endersen, James	2013	Claw, Morris
1916	Hussey, Thomas	1965	Sims, Oliver	2014	Harwill, William
1917	Dennis, Thomas	1966	Jones, Benjamin	2015	Bryant, James
1918	Smith, John	1967	Ruddick, William	2016	Goss, Joshua
1919	Holms, John	1968	Jordan, Peter	2017	Dunchellier, Isaac
1920	Hunter, Isaac	1969	Garthy, James	2018	Warner, Thomas
1921	Brown, George	1970	Warrance, John	2019	Lawrence, Robert
1922	Bliss, Frederick	1971	Crawford, Nelson	2020	Willett, John
1923	Allen, John D.	1972	Wallace, James	2021	Rich, Elisha
1924	Sherman, Riley	1973	Bustin, John	2022	Ingersen, James B.
1925	Trundy, Thomas	1974	Harris, William	2023	Moses, James
1926	West, Silas	1975	Rogers, Nathaniel	2024	Hitch, Joshua
1927	Upham, Timothy	1976	Vicary, Richard	2025	Braley, George
1928	Derrick, John	1977	Hunt, David	2026	Baley, J. K.
1929	Marshall, William	1978	Eldridge, Nicholas	2027	Crapsey, James
1930	Boston, Peter	1979	Delaney, Mathew	2028	French, Dudley
1931	Molbin, Benjamin	1980	Rich, William	2029	Wedmore, Charles
1932	Burke, J. C.	1981	Marcel, James	2030	Carlton, William N.
1933	Short, James	1982	James, Sacket	2031	Rotch, David
1934	Nassan, Joseph	1983	Wright, Isaac	2032	Boyd, Peter
1935	Nicholas, John	1984	Jackson, Daniel	2033	Codshell, Joseph
1936	Thomas, Charles	1985	Scott, John	2034	Quenichet, Joseph
1937	Hudson, Peter	1986	Kennedy, William	2035	Moore, John
1938	Arnold, James	1987	Williamson, John	2036	Farmer, Joseph
1939	Blue, Peter	1988	Nelson, Richard	2037	Smith, John
1940	Johnston, Thomas	1989	Ryan, Thomas	2038	Roberts, William
1941	Anderson, Alexander	1990	Jones, Peter	2039	Babbitt, Edward B.
1942	Hall, James	1991	Barnsall, Lewis	2040	McMiller, Andrew
1943	Harrens, William	1992	White, William (1)	2041	Rightman, John
1944	Gault, William	1993	White, William (2)	2042	Stibbens, Thomas
1945	Hawkins, John	1994	Jones, William	2043	Kay, James
1946	Stow, Jeremiah	1995	Roach, Reuben	2044	Jackson, Thomas
1947	Fernald, John	1996	Patton, Robert	2045	Bell, Robert L.
1948	Mann, John	1997	Farrell, Andrew	2046	Brown, Samuel
1949	Westerbest, William	1998	Austin, Jonathan	2047	Hurstley, Charles
1950	Layton, William	1999	Ferley, John	2048	Johnson, Mathew

Numeric listing by prisoner number 309

2049	Butler, John	2098	Young, Thomas	2147	Jasmine, Paul
2050	Kelly, John	2099	Bordley, George	2148	Miller, George
2051	Simmons, William	2100	Mackensey, John	2149	Andersen, John
2052	Davies, John	2101	Scanck, William	2150	Jones, William
2053	Bird, James	2102	Lindsey, Samuel	2151	Wood, William
2054	Harrison, Henry	2103	Hallbrook, D.	2152	Boyd, John
2055	Jeurnuseu, John	2104	Peverley, Henry	2153	Leonard, John
2056	Chase, Joseph	2105	Brown, Thomas	2154	Cuff, Charles
2057	Brown, Jacob	2106	Handley, Thomas	2155	House, Snow
2058	Blumbhouser, Samuel	2107	Blake, William	2156	Chapley, John
2059	Williams, John	2108	Nichols, John	2157	Clark, Abraham D.
2060	Vail, Jeremiah	2109	Randall, Forest	2158	Hearl, Hiram
2061	Berry, George	2110	Jilson, Samuel	2159	Lumburger, Jacob
2062	Middleton, Reuben	2111	Mutch, James	2160	Carter, Thomas
2063	Strong, William	2112	Thompson, James	2161	Dunn, James
2064	Makeniney, George	2113	Latham, John	2162	Fields, Alexander
2065	Flood, John	2114	Scott, William	2163	Rectout, John J.
2066	Brown, Reuben	2115	Porter, Josiah	2164	Williams, Thomas
2067	Williams, John	2116	Austin, James	2165	White, William
2068	Hill, Timothy	2117	Smith, John	2166	McGee, Robert
2069	Simpson, William	2118	Bailey, William	2167	Voight, Henry
2070	Gray, John	2119	Baker, Daniel	2168	Armstrong, Thomas
2071	Walker, John	2120	Hutson, John	2169	Southwich, James
2072	Warwick, Robert	2121	Warner, John	2170	Nicholson, Charles
2073	Augustus, Benjamin	2122	Stevenson, Levi	2171	Thompson, James
2074	Elliott, Robert	2123	Richards, Henry	2172	Codding, Caleb
2075	Jackson, Sidney	2124	Brice, John	2173	Brown, Joseph
2076	Emming, Thomas	2125	Murray, Peter	2174	Brooks, John
2077	Smith, Paul	2126	Bond, Samuel	2175	Richardson, John
2078	Butler, William	2127	Peterson, M.	2176	Webster, William
2079	Awker, Edward	2128	Brown, John	2177	Walden, James
2080	Pool, John	2129	Penrose, Abraham	2178	Brown, Mark
2081	Calanan, John	2130	Smith, James	2179	Guire, Andrew
2082	Traphagan, Peter	2131	White, Robert	2180	White, Charles
2083	Mitch, Thomas	2132	Filch, Jonathan	2181	Gourley, William
2084	Alexander, George	2133	Daggett, Hansel	2182	Porter, Samuel
2085	Penny, Richard	2134	Sparrow, Joseph	2183	Forbes, Robert
2086	Gordon, James	2135	Jackson, William	2184	Peters, John
2087	Howland, William	2136	Groves, Richard	2185	Williams, Thomas
2088	Fogust, Able	2137	Handerson, Hans	2186	Morrison, William
2089	Thomas, John (1)	2138	Martin, John	2187	Story, William
2090	Thomas, John (2)	2139	Westler, John	2188	Rogers, Samuel
2091	Miller, Jeremiah	2140	Hatch, William	2189	Cornille, Jacques
2092	Murray, James	2141	Prio, Peter	2190	LeBaron, Peter
2093	Cook, John	2142	Legos, Philip	2191	Hamilton, Richard
2094	Welsh, William	2143	Hanson, Peter	2192	Mayo, Nathaniel
2095	Crawford, James	2144	Manuel, Peter	2193	Richardson, Samuel
2096	Mackey, James	2145	Smith, Aesop	2194	Williams, George
2097	Kellum, Smith	2146	Hanscon, Thomas	2195	Steward, John

2196	Brown, James	2245	Davis, Moses	2294	Eldridge, William
2197	Willson, James	2246	Tuck, James	2295	Brown, David
2198	Henney, Peter	2247	Bartelett, John	2296	Stiver, David
2199	Wilson, Nathaniel	2248	Parsons, Daniel	2297	Robinson, James
2200	Thomas, William	2249	Woodbury, John	2298	Freeman, Asa
2201	McIver, John	2250	Doliver, Joseph	2299	Williams, William
2202	Campbell, James	2251	Thomas, Spencer	2300	Deagle, James
2203	Taylor, Joseph	2252	Rogers, Gorham	2301	Taylor, Thomas
2204	Simpson, John	2253	Covell, John	2302	Ayres, Henry
2205	Wickham, Ezekiel	2254	Mitchell, Carr	2303	Ferguson, John
2206	Reed, Joseph	2255	Wing, Nathaniel	2304	Jackson, Isaac
2207	Bunker, Nicholas	2256	Scott, Henry	2305	Davis, George
2208	Rogers, Epinetos	2257	Williams, Joseph	2306	Aldor, Robert
2209	Nickels, Hugh	2258	Boggs, James	2307	Watson, James
2210	Saunders, James	2259	Holdridge, Hector	2308	Huse, Ebenezer
2211	Wilson, William	2260	Stephens, William	2309	Rodgers, Samuel
2212	Penny, James	2261	Clark, Titus	2310	Chase, Nathaniel
2213	Eastlake, James	2262	Huston, James	2311	Griswold, Josiah
2214	McIntyre, William	2263	Fredericks, John	2312	Lemon, Nicholas, C.
2215	Lindsay, Nathaniel	2264	Pratt, Lester	2313	Mason, Joseph J.
2216	Lee, Nathaniel	2265	Atkins, Francis	2314	Dunham, David
2217	Hitchcock, Moses	2266	Sims, Joseph	2315	Swain, James
2218	Grush, Joseph	2267	Simpson, William	2316	Nicholls, Thomas
2219	Davis, Andrew	2268	Burrow, Charles	2317	Hussy, Edward
2220	Reynolds, Stephen	2269	Crumpton, William	2318	Bunker, Thomas
2221	Willson, Henry	2270	Lee, Isaac	2319	Marsh, Hercules
2222	Fadden, Charles	2271	Lovet, Robert	2320	Thuel, Bristo
2223	Jennings, Luther	2272	Narbone, Nicholas	2321	Osmond, David
2224	Swise, Carl	2273	Phillips, George W.	2322	Williams, Stephen
2225	Mason, John	2274	Dayley, G. W.	2323	Weeden, Richard
2226	Garmindia, Stephen	2275	Clements, William	2324	Lamboard, Thomas
2227	Diseveriere, Cosnery	2276	Boillet, John	2325	Saunders, Charles
2228	Iriarty, Ignacio	2277	Young, Nathaniel	2326	Sluckley, Richard
2229	Idiarty, Francois	2278	Smith, William S.	2327	Billings, Thomas
2230	Sourivier, Daniel	2279	Laws, Peter	2328	Telley, Edward
2231	Gannet, Mathew	2280	Thomas, John	2329	Rogers, Edward
2232	Dunn, Thomas	2281	Thomodice, John	2330	Abraham, Joseph
2233	Burk, William	2282	Ely, Abraham	2331	Burdock, Enos
2234	Devine, John	2283	Molton, Nathaniel	2332	Gordon, John
2235	Young, Ebenezer	2284	Miller, John	2333	Jackson, William
2236	Allen, E. T.	2285	Phillips, William	2334	Mack, John
2237	Norkett, George	2286	Haywood, John	2335	Church, Ezekiel
2238	Norton, Richard	2287	Sheppard, James	2336	Henry, Henry
2239	Slocum, William	2288	Watson, Stephen	2337	Hadley, George
2240	Martin, William	2289	Hall, John	2338	Horner, John
2241	Gardner, William	2290	Howell, John	2339	Stage, William
2242	Baptieste, John	2291	Douglass, John	2340	Boyd, Stephen
2243	Willson, John	2292	Anderson, James	2341	Reymond, Caleb
2244	Allen, John	2293	Adams, Thomas	2342	Davidson, John

2343	Duvall, N. D.	2392	Stanton, James	2441	Manion, John
2344	Lamb, Jack	2393	McGinnie, B. S.	2442	Frazier, William
2345	Stegman, Christian	2394	Yatton, James	2443	Brown, Francis
2346	Elfe, James	2395	Phillips, Benjamin	2444	Coston, Thomas
2347	Wise, John	2396	Rankins, William	2445	Jones, John
2348	Sherriff, Benjamin P.	2397	Ross, John	2446	Jackson, John
2349	Branch, Anthony	2398	Cotterell, Henry	2447	Butler, Henry
2350	Clawson, John	2399	Redman, David	2448	Carlos, John
2351	Younger, Lewis	2400	Lynch, Thomas	2449	Brisk, John
2352	Potter, John	2401	McCumber, Job	2450	McKinnon, John
2353	Quarterman, William	2402	Ranlot, John	2451	Boyer, John
2354	Thaley, Abraham	2403	Brown, Thomas	2452	Kirkpatrick, William
2355	Jameson, George	2404	Walker, Benjamin	2453	Hall, Perry
2356	Duncan, Edward	2405	Tombinson, George W.	2454	Lindsey, William
2357	Baker, Robert	2406	Barry, Peter	2455	Wilson, Hezekiah
2358	Thompson, George	2407	Walker, William	2456	Tois, Manuel
2359	Smith, John	2408	Caesar, James	2457	Wood, Joseph
2360	Gardner, James	2409	Perry, William	2458	Brown, Joseph
2361	Moore, James	2410	Hurd, Abel	2459	Holden, Nathaniel
2362	Sheridan, Henry	2411	Haskins, John	2460	Ringman, Charles
2363	Peters, Thomas	2412	Darrow, Aaron	2461	Parker, Robert
2364	Hazard, Thomas	2413	McAlpin, Cornelius	2462	Forester, Joseph
2365	Hubbard, William	2414	Price, Carlton	2463	Owen, Zachariah
2366	Lucas, Martin	2415	Newell, Paul	2464	Pinder, George
2367	Thomas, Moses	2416	Jones, Anthony	2465	Weston, Nathaniel
2368	Folger, Frederick	2417	Gibbs, Valentine	2466	Green, Charles
2369	Glower, Samuel	2418	Leonard, Robert	2467	Ward, Benjamin
2370	Watson, Daniel	2419	Coffin, James	2468	Hill, Benjamin
2371	Richardson, Robert	2420	Manley, Randolph	2469	Ropes, Daniel
2372	Smith, Henry	2421	Thornton, David	2470	Hanfield, Enos
2373	Bates, Joseph	2422	Tucker, Nathaniel	2471	Clarke, William
2374	Hubart, Joseph	2423	Vincent, Henry	2472	Wanton, William
2375	Davis, Osborn	2424	Pitts, Charles	2473	Forbes, John
2376	Heaton, Henry	2425	Peckham, Isaac	2474	Sparkes, Thomas
2377	Harvey, Peter	2426	Wilkey, Timothy	2475	Phinney, John
2378	Toole, Gannet	2427	Barber, Major	2476	Higgins, Asa
2379	Robinson, John	2428	Fleming, Alexander	2477	Lawrence, George
2380	Andrews, John (1)	2429	Harwood, William	2478	Verplasts, Nicholas
2381	Wilson, Robert	2430	Boyd, Andrew	2479	Snow, Thomas
2382	Green, George	2431	Williams, Thomas	2480	Cloutman, Joseph
2383	Valentine, John	2432	Bakeman, Ely	2481	Widger, John
2384	Andrews, John (2)	2433	Warner, John	2482	Melzard, Peter
2385	Perry, Samuel	2434	McKenzie, William	2483	Fuller, Nathaniel
2386	Meyers, James	2435	Bissell, Samuel W.	2484	Clothy, John
2387	Wright, Edward	2436	Newell, Stephen C.	2485	Torry, Henry
2388	Fry, Thomas	2437	Anderson, John	2486	Russell, Robert
2389	Gardner, George	2438	Buffington, James	2487	Williams, Frederick (1)
2390	Copland, Thomas	2439	Putnam, Allen	2488	Goss, Jesse
2391	Pinne, John	2440	Johnston, Henry	2489	Clothy, William

2490	Pettingall, Joseph	2539	Birmingham, Thomas	2588	Saunders, Peter
2491	Tarlton, John	2540	Brown, Thomas	2589	Gordon, William
2492	McKinney, Isaac	2541	Hull, Thomas	2590	Cox, Abraham
2493	Varney, John	2542	Evert, John	2591	Allen, William
2494	Moore, Samuel	2543	Walling, James	2592	Vanderwenter, John
2495	Waterhouse, Moses	2544	Short, Samuel	2593	Watson, William
2496	Francis, Abraham	2545	Limon, Andrew	2594	Nixon, Charles
2497	Lucas, Daniel	2546	Colborne, John L.	2595	Taylor, William
2498	Johnson, Jacob	2547	Gardner, John	2596	Hall, James
2499	Andrews, John	2548	Clark, John	2597	Robinson, Henry
2500	Thompson, John	2549	Johnson, Richard	2598	Graves, John
2501	Card, Thomas	2550	Dunham, Joseph	2599	Sims, William
2502	Holbrook, Robert	2551	Cadwell, Abraham	2600	Wilson, James
2503	Pittman, Henry	2552	Noble, Charles	2601	Adams, Thomas
2504	Marshall, John	2553	James, John	2602	Backman, Charles
2505	McIntire, Petty	2554	Williams, John	2603	Thomas, Thomas
2506	Driscol, Jeremiah	2555	Cook, Isaac	2604	Johnson, Richard
2507	Cross, Ephraim	2556	Owen, Burden	2605	Thompson, Robert
2508	Brown, Robert	2557	Boyd, John	2606	Newland, Thomas L.
2509	Ferguson, Thomas	2558	Campbell, Nicholas	2607	Eagin, John
2510	Hunter, James	2559	Wingate, David	2608	Clayton, Thomas
2511	Forsyth, Robert	2560	Stone, Henry	2609	Mackenwick, George
2512	Cooper, Edward	2561	Lowe, Thomas	2610	McGuire, Hugh
2513	Richardson, James	2562	Thayer, James	2611	Macconahay, Benjamin
2514	Smith, Elisha	2563	Jordan, Artemas	2612	McGinnis, Patrick
2515	Spouding, Joseph	2564	Woods, William	2613	Brown, James
2516	Haddart, Robert	2565	Mathews, John	2614	Smith, John
2517	Hamilton, G. W.	2566	Sanford, James	2615	Gray, Samuel
2518	Anderson, Goodman	2567	Powell, Joseph	2616	Sloan, William
2519	Jessamine, John	2568	Spencer, John	2617	Mackay, John
2520	Davis, John	2569	Reid, John	2618	McKever, Charles
2521	Blake, Charles	2570	Reid, John	2619	Todd, John
2522	Purnal, Elisha	2571	Butts, Joseph W.	2620	Caughan, Patrick
2523	Bump, Henry	2572	Williams, Robert	2621	Scott, James
2524	Johnson, Charles	2573	Brown, Isaac	2622	Brown, John
2525	Gilbert, Isaac	2574	Heady, Linsey	2623	Dibbins, Edward
2526	Goulding, Samuel	2575	Brown, George	2624	McEver, William
2527	Wilson, James	2576	Foster, Thomas	2625	Kelly, Charles
2528	Rodgers, William	2577	Osborne, Lewis	2626	Courtney, George
2529	Eddy, Richard	2578	Williams, Robert	2627	Denvon, Charles
2530	Mackey, John	2579	Wilson, James	2628	Steward, Thomas
2531	Selby, Hans	2580	Bale, Charles	2629	Smiley, John
2532	Brown, Charles	2581	Horsefall, William	2630	Taggart, Thomas
2533	Storm, Daniel	2582	Stevens, William	2631	Maxwell, Robert
2534	Phillips, Edward	2583	Abbott, Samuel	2632	McGowan, John
2535	Burne, John	2584	Weeks, Lewis	2633	Henry, James
2536	Brown, William	2585	Fell, William	2634	Anderson, Andre
2537	Cook, John	2586	Cunning, James	2635	Daumied, Edward
2538	Hawkins, Isaac	2587	Chasses, Jacob	2636	Carbody, Darby

2637	Doud, John	2686	Moaton, Bryant	2735	Day, Frederick
2638	Miller, George M.	2687	Bartlett, Robert	2736	Porter, William
2639	McCannon, Dominique	2688	Jones, Thomas	2737	Brown, John
2640	Taugherty, M.	2689	Manning, Burrell	2738	Chandler, Enoch
2641	Niel, E. C.	2690	Joseph, Nicholas	2739	Samerton, George
2642	Givin, James	2691	Bowden, William	2740	Sawyer, James
2643	Kelley, William	2692	Smith, John	2741	Webber, Stephen
2644	Miller, James	2693	Widger, Joseph	2742	Piles, John
2645	Patterson, Archibald	2694	Russell, William	2743	Fortune, John
2646	Hoy, Barney	2695	Smith, Benjamin	2744	Bridges, John
2647	Evans, James	2696	Nicholson, Jonas	2745	Towe, Seth
2648	Norton, Robert	2697	Derring, William F.	2746	Robinson, John
2649	Finey, John	2698	Crocker, Sylvester	2747	Preston, John
2650	Hunter, James	2699	Mirrel, Samuel B.	2748	Wilson, John
2651	Craney, Edward	2700	Smith, Jeremiah	2749	Thrasher, John
2652	Norman, Edward	2701	Orne, Israel	2750	Pratt, Philip
2653	Cole, Andrew	2702	Bowden, Benjamin	2751	Weare, Ebenezer
2654	Barlow, John	2703	Garrett, Simon T.	2752	Dew, Frederick
2655	Lynch, John	2704	Tishure, Samuel	2753	Stanfield, George
2656	Napperknac, John	2705	Roundy, Thomas	2754	Stretton, Samuel
2657	Carey, James	2706	Withiem, Burrell	2755	Seth, John
2658	Watson, Macy	2707	Florence, Charles	2756	Le Moor, John
2659	Wane, Michael	2708	Hooper, Joseph A.	2757	Bacchus, John
2660	Lowry, James	2709	Rust, John	2758	Caufield, Arthur
2661	Muckleroy, William	2710	Devereux, Benjamin	2759	Todd, Samuel
2662	Melvin, William	2711	Selman, Francis G.	2760	Penn, William
2663	Patrick, John F.	2712	Brown, Joseph	2761	Perkins, John
2664	Hall, George	2713	Gatchell, John G.	2762	Billings, Richard
2665	Ward, Peter	2714	Odiam, Joseph H.	2763	Pettigrew, William
2666	Berry, George	2715	Euston, Ephraim	2764	Bailey, Daniel
2667	Bane, Charles	2716	Emerson, David	2765	Langford, Samuel
2668	Trask, Osmond	2717	Kraft, Michael	2766	Holmes, Elisha
2669	Brown, Thomas	2718	Hart, William	2767	Brown, Samuel
2670	Reid, John	2719	Kegs, Zenas	2768	Peverly, Richard
2671	Hules, Cyrus	2720	Nicholson, James	2769	Norton, Josiah
2672	Cullett, William	2721	Malcomb, Alexander	2770	Davis, William
2673	Stevens, James	2722	Buell, Jeremiah	2771	Woods, Jeremiah
2674	Saunders, William	2723	Mallet, William	2772	Knight, Daniel
2675	Bernard, Zacharias	2724	Thornning, Thomas	2773	Lawson, Thomas
2676	Brightman, Isaac	2725	Christie, John	2774	Johnson, Thomas
2677	Swain, David	2726	Aldrigde, Richard	2775	Tripper, Robert
2678	Simmik, John	2727	Griffen, William	2776	Jones, James
2679	Madden, Peter	2728	Lewis, Peter	2777	Williams, Joseph
2680	Hinkle, Henry	2729	Benjamin, Edward	2778	Yeaton, Charles
2681	Dole, Henry	2730	Davis, William	2779	Harbrook, Richard
2682	Shaw, Andrew	2731	Pippin, Isaac	2780	Smith, Henry
2683	Scols, William	2732	Cash, John	2781	Marble, Samuel
2684	Thompson, John	2733	Foster, Samuel	2782	McGill, Robert
2685	Palmer, George H.	2734	Dodge, John	2783	Bailey, Peter

2784	Mallard, James	2833	Norcross, Archibald	2882	Kingbutton, John
2785	Dooley, James	2834	Perkinson, James	2883	Robertson, William
2786	Hart, Samuel	2835	Gordon, Sperrin	2884	Porter, Charles
2787	Cameron, Daniel	2836	Leach, Daniel	2885	Claby, Martin L.
2788	Black, Philip	2837	Larabee, Thomas	2886	Stables, James
2789	Davis, John	2838	Perkins, Benjamin	2887	Johnstone, Robert
2790	Handy, Levi	2839	Dennison, Andrew	2888	Hill, John
2791	Puffer, John	2840	Thomas, Elisha	2889	Rodgers, Abraham
2792	Zelluck, Thomas	2841	Spenny, Nathaniel	2890	Fredericks, John
2793	White, Edward	2842	Perkins, James	2891	Johnson, John
2794	Brown, Thomas	2843	Grant, Samuel	2892	Miles, John
2795	Sawyer, Peter	2844	Baddrige, Charles	2893	Harding, J. Christian
2796	Hovey, Joseph	2845	Hussey, Ebenezer	2894	Tardy, Edward
2797	Rice, Thomas	2846	Evans, John	2895	Tardy, Anthony
2798	Eaton, Israel	2847	Silverthorn, James	2896	Kinnard, Charles
2799	Tucker, Samuel	2848	Woodford, James	2897	Green, James Beckwith
2800	Burridge, Robert	2849	Anthony, James	2898	Murray, Charles
2801	Inglas, John	2850	Hazard, Prince	2899	Camsure, Dominick
2802	Gowalter, John	2851	Rowe, William	2900	Miramon, Roch
2803	Bartell, William	2852	Tarr, Caleb	2901	Williamson, John
2804	Russell, Louis	2853	Pearson, Samuel	2902	Miller, James
2805	Morris, Jacob	2854	Allen, David	2903	Tipp, Nicholas
2806	Snow, James	2855	Millett, Joseph	2904	Pollett, Edward
2807	Brush, Thomas	2856	Jones, Stephen	2905	Smith, Thomas
2808	Stacey, John	2857	Winchester, Richard	2906	Smith, John
2809	Blair, Robert	2858	Williams, William	2907	Clawson, Henry
2810	Cheslie, Amos	2859	Day, John	2908	Harvey, Peter
2811	Burrell, Jesse	2860	Newell, Benjamin (2)	2909	Watson, David
2812	Gowalter, John	2861	Shaw, Henry	2910	Ward, Thomas
2813	Ross, David	2862	Dempsey, Daniel	2911	Lane, James
2814	Laskey, Benjamin	2863	Jefferys, Henry	2912	Baron, Peter
2815	Robes, Edward	2864	Turner, Samuel	2913	Jourdan, John
2816	Glover, John	2865	Head, James	2914	La Roche, Jean
2817	Chace, Nathaniel	2866	Paine, Clement	2915	Lupy, Marcus
2818	Lapish, Andrew	2867	Sawyer, Jonathan	2916	Lane, William
2819	Appleton, John	2868	Cook, Silvanus	2917	Perry, Daniel
2820	Goff, Peter	2869	Parsons, John	2918	Light, John
2821	Jackson, Samuel	2870	Harman, Isaac	2919	Holmes, Abraham
2822	Pike, Jeremiah	2871	Hitchins, William	2920	Denishaw, Henry
2823	Russell, Moses	2872	Brown, John	2921	Behon, Simon
2824	King, Solomon	2873	Webb, Nathaniel	2922	Atwood, Nathaniel
2825	Robinson, Thomas	2874	Freeman, John	2923	Woodford, William
2826	Anderson, David	2875	Davis, John	2924	Briggs, Thomas
2827	Wyatt, Jesse	2876	Powell, Joseph	2925	Norton, Solomon
2828	Hanson, William	2877	Holstien, Richard	2926	Smith, Elisha
2829	Tarlton, George	2878	Primas, James	2927	Long, Joseph
2830	Johnson, Francis	2879	Jackson, William	2928	Porter, Edward
2831	Perkins, John	2880	Skinner, Ebenezer	2929	Poland, Abraham
2832	Stone, Robert	2881	Pinkham, Daniel	2930	Fall, James

2931	Keen, Benjamin	2980	Oakes, George	3029	Reid, William
2932	McKinney, Isaac	2981	Johnson, George	3030	Patterson, William
2933	Kinnard, George	2982	Tucker, William	3031	Chase, Oliver
2934	Place, Thomas	2983	Blaney, Stephen	3032	Roweth, William
2935	Tethery, Robert	2984	Rowel, Mathew	3033	Melvin, John
2936	McKinney, Isaac	2985	Simoni, John	3034	Heater, William
2937	Ducat, William	2986	Brown, Jesse	3035	James, John
2938	Fernald, William	2987	Carswell, William	3036	Francis, John
2939	Sides, Samuel	2988	Salmon, Archibald	3037	Johnson, Easton
2940	Tuckerman, Nathaniel	2989	Blanchard, John	3038	Smith, John
2941	Morgan, John R.	2990	Richardson, William	3039	Shillings, Morris
2942	Harris, Joseph	2991	Pierce, Joseph	3040	Davis, Nicholas
2943	Smith, Thomas	2992	Hubbard, William	3041	Day, Thomas
2944	Downey, John	2993	Reed, George	3042	Collins, George
2945	Price, John	2994	Kent, Wilson	3043	Wheelock, Abel
2946	Richardson, William	2995	Jones, John	3044	Bird, Benjamin E.
2947	Hanson, William	2996	Phillips, Timothy	3045	Dodson, Thomas
2948	Holt, Jacob L.	2997	Curry, William	3046	Trank, Abraham
2949	Battes, John	2998	Warren, David	3047	Cashinan, William
2950	Bassett, John	2999	Mulloy, William	3048	Tomlinson, John
2951	Simmonds, David	3000	Devereux, John	3049	Whitton, John
2952	Williams, Frederick (2)	3001	Hall, James	3050	Henry, George
2953	Gibbins, Hiram	3002	Beatty, John	3051	Drummond, John
2954	Cone, John	3003	Pitts, George	3052	Childers, Joshua
2955	Duncan, Thomas	3004	Elburn, John	3053	Moon, Joseph
2956	Gomerson, James	3005	Hall, John	3054	House, Frederick
2957	Grandy, Amos	3006	Porter, Louis	3055	Goodwin, Joseph
2958	Hanson, John	3007	Dunningberg, Henry	3056	Soder, Jacob
2959	Lamson, Amos	3008	Allen, Edward D.	3057	Cord, Jacob
2960	Webster, Asa	3009	Mason, Aaron	3058	Hill, Stephen
2961	Gage, Thomas	3010	Devol, Alexander	3059	Hargood, George
2962	Lackey, Joseph	3011	Payne, Walter	3060	Carr, John
2963	Treadwell, Nathaniel	3012	Forstman, John	3061	Hunderville, John
2964	Wettey, Philip	3013	Hathaway, Philip	3062	Andrews, Edward
2965	Christian, John	3014	Hall, Sylvester	3063	Kellogg, Asa
2966	Thompson, John	3015	Scott, Henry	3064	Myers, John
2967	Tildon, Robert	3016	Coffin, Joseph	3065	Farman, Joseph
2968	Clarke, Isaac	3017	Brown, Sawyer	3066	Riggins, Laban
2969	Walker, Samuel	3018	Pitt, William	3067	Watson, William
2970	Kelly, John	3019	Hill, James	3068	Swatwood, Jacob
2971	Findley, Thomas	3020	Connor, John	3069	County, David
2972	Thornton, John	3021	Levan, Thomas	3070	Chambers, Henry
2973	McIntire, John	3022	Jones, Thomas	3071	Miars, Michael
2974	Kinder, Ephraim G.	3023	Meath, Solomon	3072	Avis, Jervis
2975	Lufkin, William	3024	Ferris, James	3073	Staley, John
2976	Robinson, William	3025	Johnson, John	3074	Cook, John
2977	Webb, John	3026	Cooper, Thomas	3075	Huff, Michael
2978	Millett, John	3027	Lee, John	3076	Magee, Robert
2979	Brown, Edward	3028	Peadon, William	3077	Gray, John

3078	Delignay, George	3127	Ballard, Martin	3176	Grant, William
3079	Manaham, David	3128	Scriver, Richard	3177	Pollet, William
3080	Taggart, Archibald	3129	Simpson, Mark	3178	Alexander, Richard
3081	Hedden, Amos	3130	Grimes, Nicholas	3179	Chivers, Joseph
3082	Berlew, Gibeon	3131	Williams, Andrew	3180	Pearce, David
3083	Brown, Michael	3132	Mills, Stephen	3181	Knapp, Samuel
3084	Goodrich, H. C.	3133	Halloo, John	3182	Quiner, Stephen
3085	Sears, Abraham	3134	Rumsey, Joseph	3183	Simonds, Proctor
3086	Thomas, Samuel	3135	Hurd, John	3184	Carnes, John
3087	Herrington, Ezekiel	3136	Thistlewood, Charles	3185	Pearce, David
3088	Wilder, Titus	3137	Ireland, John	3186	Norris, George
3089	Gilbert, Elijah	3138	Whagerman, Joseph	3187	Tucker, Andrew
3090	Niles, Nathaniel	3139	Cook, William	3188	Pippin, Isaac
3091	McDowell, Andrew	3140	Fullerton, John	3189	Smith, John
3092	McKenzie, Kenneth	3141	Hunter, James	3190	Coombe, Michael
3093	Cummins, David	3142	Nybro, Godfrey	3191	Foster, George
3094	Bowen, Artemas	3143	Patten, David	3192	Tucker, Nathaniel
3095	Stroud, John	3144	Cunningham, Caleb	3193	Ellingwood, William H.
3096	Bowen, William	3145	Linnard, Alfred	3194	Grush, Nathaniel
3097	Brison, James	3146	Whitman, Samuel	3195	Harvey, Anthony
3098	Beard, Richard	3147	Wheeler, Anthony	3196	Roundy, Jeremiah
3099	Frazer, Hulbert	3148	Winner, Michael	3197	Rust, John
3100	Storer, John	3149	Jacobs, John	3198	Forman, William
3101	Broadest, Moses	3150	Slaughter, George	3199	Bradford, George
3102	Loveitson, John	3151	Jones, William M.	3200	Shaw, Samuel
3103	White, John	3152	Cook, Hazard	3201	Sutton, John
3104	King, William	3153	Forrester, Arthur	3202	Thompson, James
3105	Andrews, David (1)	3154	Logan, Timothy	3203	Beckwith, James
3106	Duganeu, Charles	3155	Johnson, Hugh	3204	Hatton, Peter
3107	Jenny, John	3156	West, Abiah	3205	Smith, John
3108	Clark, Stephen	3157	Ritchie, Allan	3206	Kennedy, Dennis
3109	Beals, John	3158	Prico, Job	3207	Marlow, Owen
3110	Andrews, David (2)	3159	Willis, Alfred	3208	Wadsworth, Daniel
3111	Lathrum, William	3160	Mitchell, Charles	3209	Coursis, Frederick
3112	Powers, John	3161	Elsworth, John	3210	Anderson, George
3113	Davis, Thomas	3162	Welsch, Henry	3211	Hunter, John
3114	Winn, Clement	3163	Murphy, George	3212	Morgan, James
3115	Scott, John	3164	Martin, William	3213	Johnson, Peter
3116	Griffin, John	3165	Dandridge, Richard	3214	Caverena, Jose Maria
3117	Booth, George	3166	Perkins, Rufus	3215	Lewis, Job
3118	Spaldings, William	3167	Mathews, John	3216	Jupiter, James
3119	Davis, John	3168	Cloutman, Robert	3217	Doyle, John
3120	Cane, Thomas	3169	Fippen, John	3218	Campbell, John
3121	Rhea, John	3170	Stacey, Benjamin	3219	Cusser, John Charles
3122	Dougherty, Hamilton	3171	Clough, Isaac	3220	Harms, John
3123	Black, John	3172	Andrews, Joseph	3221	Antonio, Francis
3124	Beard, John	3173	Eaton, Joseph	3222	Martini, Francis
3125	Mallack, Joseph	3174	Stacey, Samuel	3223	Bushfield, James
3126	Crosy, S. M.	3175	Lyons, Charles	3224	Jones, William

3225	Chase, John	3274	Dupre, John	3323	Hagen, Joel
3226	Hill, Jeremiah	3275	Ropes, David	3324	Dudes, J. B.
3227	Cooper, Thomas	3276	Lamson, Noah	3325	Prissey, John
3228	Angel, Sylvester	3277	Twikes, Samuel	3326	Cleveland, Ebenezer
3229	Malbrough, Francis	3278	Thompson, William	3327	Allen, George
3230	Reid, William	3279	Collins, Sylvester	3328	Stiles, Jurich
3231	McInley, James	3280	Truman, Isaac	3329	Smith, Charles
3232	Hubbard, Christian	3281	Nelson, Thomas	3330	Sumerg, Benjamin
3233	Rosell, John	3282	Howe, William	3331	Mead, Lewis
3234	Rooter, John	3283	Snow, Daniel	3332	Davis, John
3235	Grendy, Edward	3284	Fiels, Jacob	3333	Sampson, William
3236	Forseyth, Alexander	3285	Jacobs, William	3334	Brown, Benjamin
3237	Mallison, Jacob	3286	Bateman, Michael	3335	Tapley, Isaac
3238	Antoine, John	3287	Lambert, Ephraim	3336	Pichon, John
3239	Gibson, Samuel	3288	Avory, John	3337	Hill, Manuel
3240	Pousland, William	3289	Higgins, John	3338	Litnay, Peter
3241	Kerry, Isaac	3290	Abbott, Daniel	3339	Christo, Peter
3242	Gibson, Samuel	3291	Tolpie, Jonathan	3340	McAvory, Lewis
3243	Brown, James	3292	Bragden, James	3341	Deambo, Dom
3244	Travers, Thomas	3293	Thomas, John	3342	Girdler, James
3245	Brown, Michael	3294	Briggs, William	3343	Russell, John
3246	Hammon, William	3295	Brooks, John	3344	Giria, John
3247	Burgess, Francis	3296	Riswell, Palmer	3345	Terry, Joseph
3248	Archer, James	3297	Joseph, Lewis	3346	Young, John
3249	Hammon, John	3298	Callam, John	3347	Turner, Silas
3250	Quince, Peter	3299	Henley, John	3348	Mitchell, John
3251	Gross, James	3300	Murray, Richard	3349	Lowe, George
3252	Holden, John	3301	Goodwin, John	3350	Young, John
3253	Webster, David	3302	Barker, George	3351	Bodkin, William
3254	Saunders, Richard	3303	Hay, John	3352	Sergeant, William
3255	Green, John	3304	Harding, Joseph	3353	Spick, John
3256	Melcher, John	3305	Brown, John	3354	Chaplin, Thomas
3257	Brackett, John	3306	Bids, Thomas	3355	Wherry, Daniel
3258	Williams, Charles	3307	Wiggins, Richard	3356	Adams, Henry
3259	Alston, Richard	3308	Butler, George	3357	Dealing, Elisha
3260	Dotto, Cornelius	3309	Drisco, James	3358	Soley, Nathaniel
3261	Morrell, Francis	3310	Mullett, Joseph	3359	Thomas, John
3262	Conley, Cornelius	3311	Saundry, Nathaniel	3360	Whitman, Joseph
3263	Thompson, Michael	3312	Mulloy, William	3361	Priest, William
3264	McLean, John	3313	Abbott, William	3362	Cole, Zachariah
3265	Bean, John	3314	Sanburn, James	3363	Berry, Samuel
3266	Didler, Henry	3315	Mitchell, William	3364	Mason, Richard
3267	James, George	3316	Digereas, William	3365	Oliver, Anthony
3268	Jacob, Lewis	3317	Munroe, Henry	3366	Williams, Noble
3269	Bailey, Isaac	3318	Henday, Thomas	3367	Mott, Thomas
3270	Dow, Henry	3319	Peters, John	3368	Crosby, Andrew
3271	Boyle, Joseph	3320	Phillips, Joseph	3369	Goodman, James
3272	Willly, John	3321	Cross, Stephen	3370	Vanrant, John
3273	Anthony, John	3322	Ross, Peter	3371	Davis, James

3372	Berry, William	3421	Lake, George	3470	Briggs, Frank
3373	Brush, Abel	3422	Thompson, Thomas	3471	Dennison, Nathaniel
3374	Fray, James	3423	Bell, Richard	3472	Atwood, John
3375	Perkins, Nicholas	3424	Diamond, George	3473	Hicks, Ogershill
3376	Randolph, George	3425	Edmond, John	3474	Lambert, Calvin
3377	Bowden, John	3426	Ellis, John	3475	Black, Ruddick
3378	Darrison, William	3427	Fulton, James	3476	Bissun, Thomas
3379	Smithers, Thomas	3428	Dullivan, James	3477	Luce, Charles
3380	Lewis, William	3429	Jarvis, Thomas	3478	Kinot, Robert
3381	Killerman, Maxwell	3430	Lewis, John	3479	Stafford, William J.
3382	Merrish, Joseph	3431	Artis, William	3480	Morelly, Samuel
3383	Stoddard, Conrad	3432	Blair, David	3481	Hall, Ezekiel
3384	Wilson, John	3433	Blair, Benjamin	3482	Gyer, Henry
3385	Moffett, Hugh	3434	Peach, John	3483	Curtis, Enoch
3386	Brown, Thomas	3435	Silver, Samuel	3484	Molloy, Peter
3387	Mason, Hiram	3436	Jackson, James	3485	Wilson, William
3388	Wheeler, Michael	3437	Hooper, Samuel	3486	James, John
3389	Black, James	3438	Childs, William	3487	Middleton, John
3390	Mason, James	3439	Bull, James	3488	Cannon, Thomas
3391	Dannell, Edward	3440	Whittington, George	3489	Jones, Theodore
3392	Rick, William	3441	Card, Samuel	3490	Burke, John
3393	Elliott, Andrew	3442	Byron, Ebenezer	3491	Butler, Thomas
3394	Robinson, Robert	3443	McLane, George	3492	Wilson, Francis
3395	Mackey, Charles	3444	Homer, Henry	3493	Lane, William
3396	Nicholson, William	3445	Clark, Joseph	3494	Penfield, John
3397	Fletcher, John	3446	Lee, Michael	3495	Neal, John
3398	Wood, Benjamin	3447	Douglass, Samuel	3496	Dixon, Peter
3399	Boswell, Samuel	3448	Parrott, Ebenezer	3497	Dibble, Zachariah
3400	Shade, Joseph	3449	Worthy, James	3498	Fiske, Cyrus
3401	Allen, William	3450	Boyd, Andrew	3499	King, Peter
3402	Baptiste, John	3451	Smith, Henry	3500	Thomas, James
3403	Miller, James	3452	Eagerly, Elijah	3501	Wilson, R. G.
3404	Donnell, Samuel	3453	Cree, William	3502	Hunt, Samuel
3405	Drake, Daniel	3454	Malony, Robert	3503	Thayer, Laban
3406	Barton, James	3455	Luffie, Warren	3504	Norton, David
3407	Brown, Thomas	3456	Smith, Monday	3505	Dean, Jeremiah B.
3408	Richards, Sandy	3457	Parrish, William	3506	Barnes, William Smith
3409	Blossom, Seth	3458	Lant, Henry	3507	Green, William
3410	Tinkham, John	3459	Foot, Benjamin	3508	Howell, William
3411	Osborn, Stephen	3460	Ring, Andrew	3509	Downs, William
3412	Mason, Daniel	3461	Plummer, William	3510	Downs, John
3413	Giles, John	3462	Humphrey, Asa	3511	Smith, J. W.
3414	Sinnett, William	3463	Skilling, James	3512	Livingston, Henry
3415	Bourn, Oliver	3464	Winston, William	3513	Anderson, John
3416	Cosse, Francis D.	3465	Davis, Lot	3514	Coffin, Edward
3417	Brower, John	3466	Turnbull, James	3515	Platt, Daniel
3418	Safford, Roger	3467	Bowen, Sylvester	3516	Thomas, John
3419	White, William	3468	Rogers, Piley	3517	Simmonds, Henry
3420	Cotton, Edward	3469	Turner, James	3518	Mids, Michael

3519	Demarlow, Francis	3568	Hill, Daniel	3617	Pines, Isaac
3520	Stafford, John	3569	Campbell, William	3618	Kane, William
3521	Jackson, Frederick	3570	Debaize, Francois Jean	3619	Lipscomb, William
3522	Taylor, George	3571	Perott, Jean Francois	3620	Mead, Ezekiel
3523	Brickman, John	3572	Murray, John	3621	Burris, M.
3524	Crow, John	3573	Robins, William	3622	Jackson, Henry
3525	Maybank, John	3574	Fethien, Thomas	3623	Mark, James
3526	Duncan, George	3575	Moore, Abraham	3624	Hazard, Robert
3527	Grey, William	3576	Devine, John	3625	Stone, Isaac
3528	Raddick, Ebenezer	3577	Sloane, William	3626	Hall, Richard
3529	Norcross, Abel	3578	Newton, John	3627	Quinton, James
3530	Thomas, William	3579	Gardener, Jerry	3628	Ramsey, John
3531	Hogg, Jacob	3580	Conklin, Smith	3629	Black, Thomas
3532	Carman, George	3581	Harris, John	3630	Beauty, Edmund
3533	Reeves, Essex	3582	Mains, John	3631	Spiers, Nathaniel
3534	Killingsworth, John	3583	Gravely, Joseph	3632	Morrison, Thomas
3535	Woodbury, Dixie	3584	Chauvel, Thomas	3633	Pratt, Daniel
3536	Lewis, John	3585	Demerie, Etienne	3634	Richards, James
3537	Edwards, William	3586	Grosette, Jean Maurice	3635	Shaw, William
3538	Werman, John	3587	Tuttle, Joseph	3636	Hazard, Charles
3539	Luburg, John C.	3588	Carter, Enoch	3637	Arnold, Obadiah
3540	Henzeman, Christopher	3589	Bloomdale, John	3638	Kelly, Samuel
3541	Hamilton, Robert	3590	Hubble, James	3639	McFarlan, Daniel
3542	Lynch, William	3591	Ewell, Edward	3640	Moore, Edward
3543	Reed, Abraham	3592	Port, John	3641	Dean, Peter
3544	Gosling, Joseph	3593	Johnson, Samuel B.	3642	Livesley, Thomas
3545	Heimer, Daniel	3594	Prescot, John	3643	Williams, John
3546	Thomas, John	3595	Cilby, Thomas	3644	Brown, Frederick
3547	Tillman, John	3596	Defray, Edward	3645	Shippard, James
3548	Spurr, Elijah	3597	Minor, John	3646	Osborne, Samuel
3549	Dieman, John	3598	Peters, John	3647	Butler, William
3550	Smith, Richard	3599	Tucker, James	3648	Brisons, John
3551	Gregory, George	3600	Douglass, William	3649	Lawton, William
3552	Witherell, Charles	3601	Towns, Asa	3650	Lisconet, Francis
3553	Walker, Seth	3602	Nichols, John	3651	Gordon, Richard
3554	Plumber, William Reed	3603	Beach, John	3652	Oliver, Joseph
3555	Modre, John	3604	Hamilton, John	3653	Leach, Charles
3556	Williamson, David	3605	Hall, David	3654	Allison, William R.
3557	Keen, Joseph	3606	Creiger, John	3655	Coffin, Abel
3558	Harris, Simon	3607	Chase, Welcome	3656	Baxter, David
3559	Pritchard, Israel	3608	Williams, David	3657	Jones, Lewis
3560	Selman, John	3609	Ned, Deaf	3658	Roath, James
3561	Blaird, David	3610	Keen, Stewart	3659	Golding, Abijah
3562	Harvey, Joseph	3611	May, William	3660	Self, Thomas M.
3563	Carter, Henry	3612	Hill, Justice	3661	Gotier, Charles J.
3564	Merritt, Enoch	3613	Francis, John	3662	Vincent, Stephen Stiles
3565	Harris, Ebenezer	3614	Curtis, Ephraim	3663	Murray, David
3566	Watson, William	3615	Jackson, Charles	3664	Bartlett, John
3567	Conner, Michael	3616	Syphon, Lewis	3665	Sterns, Joseph

3666	Petterson, Andrew	3715	Bartlett, Scipio	3764	Mains, Henry
3667	Baisley, Abraham	3716	Henry, William	3765	White, George
3668	Scott, Henry	3717	Griffin, John	3766	Winchester, Ebenezer
3669	Bassett, William	3718	Weisser, Philip	3767	Hodges, Hercules
3670	Manley, David	3719	Nye, William	3768	Davis, Solomon
3671	Harding, William	3720	Stolsenberg, Manuel	3769	Dill, William
3672	Williams, Charles	3721	Green, John	3770	Gale, William
3673	Caleb, Lewis	3722	Hellen, John P.	3771	Randall, Jacob
3674	Arnold, Benjamin	3723	Davis, Henry	3772	Robinson, Stephen
3675	Shoe, Bernard	3724	Lockwood, Benjamin	3773	Williams, James
3676	Doosenberry, Richard	3725	Johnson, James	3774	Edwards, John
3677	Williams, Moses	3726	Williams, George F.	3775	Morris, Andrew
3678	Rust, John	3727	Collins, John	3776	Tomas, Andrew
3679	Milborne, William	3728	Wallace, Thomas	3777	Francis, John
3680	Boston, John	3729	Kitchen, Daniel	3778	Freeman, Plim
3681	Smith, William B.	3730	Chase, Constant	3779	Hendrick, John
3682	Jardine, Samuel	3731	Skudder, Alexander	3780	Hendrick, Thomas
3683	Smith, Thomas	3732	Stilman, William A.	3781	Porter, Calvin
3684	Hemonder, Peter	3733	Shepherd, Samuel	3782	Weslemyer, John
3685	Lebour, Francois	3734	Peters, Benjamin	3783	Harris, Alpheus
3686	Roger, Christopher	3735	Stickney, Abraham	3784	Tatem, George W.
3687	Le Goff, Herve	3736	Jones, William	3785	Senter, Noah
3688	Le Petit, John Baptiste	3737	Gavet, James	3786	Roberts, Nathaniel
3689	Gavot, Henry	3738	Brower, John	3787	Watson, John
3690	Lucas, Francois Rene	3739	Smith, George M.	3788	Hughes, John
3691	Boite, Julius Pierre	3740	Wyman, William	3789	Coffin, Valentine
3692	Hubi, Pierre M.	3741	Bisbee, J. D.	3790	Ray, William
3693	Ferlecque, Augustine	3742	Crosby, John	3791	Luther, Cromwell
3694	D'Emery, Adrian	3743	Ringgold, Thomas	3792	Crapon, George
3695	Schiffky, Jacobus Orgen	3744	Lewis, Henry	3793	Turner, Gardner
3696	Liemo, Frederick	3745	Stetson, Hiram	3794	Johnson, James
3697	Lerocque, Olivier	3746	Lincoln, Ephraim	3795	Jones, Samuel B.
3698	Lesaut, Jacques	3747	Lunt, Daniel	3796	Griffiths, Joseph
3699	Thompson, Lawrence	3748	Dixon, John	3797	Moriarty, Thomas
3700	Cutler, Thomas	3749	Loring, Samuel	3798	Higby, James
3701	Edwards, Thomas	3750	Norcross, Thomas	3799	Ingersoll, John
3702	Hammond, Isaac	3751	Bridges, Jeremiah	3800	Fell, George
3703	Bennet, John	3752	Tyler, Joseph	3801	Bryan, Timothy
3704	Spice, Alexander	3753	Simmons, Charles	3802	Nichols, Henry
3705	Johnson, George	3754	Lee, John	3803	Phillips, George
3706	Shroudy, William	3755	Gage, Lot	3804	Monk, Joseph
3707	Porter, Gideon	3756	Simmons, Joel	3805	Teilman, John
3708	Black, William	3757	Thinney, Alvin	3806	Merrill, Enoch
3709	Tucker, Henry	3758	Howe, Jacob	3807	Kemble, Samuel
3710	Haley, John	3759	Choete, Thomas	3808	Williams, James
3711	Crosus, Richard	3760	Bisbee, Elijah	3809	Conway, James
3712	Caldwell, Charles	3761	Harding, John	3810	Baxter, Franklin
3713	Finn, John	3762	Furness, Jesse	3811	Barnard, John
3714	Williams, George	3763	Hallet, William	3812	Cooper, Thomas

Numeric listing by prisoner number 321

3813	Phillips, John	3861	Evans, Williams	3909	Gaskin, William
3814	Bradie, John	3862	Fife, Thomas	3910	Collier, Thomas
3815	Elvyn, Laurence	3863	Bennett, Robert	3911	Franklin, William
3816	Fitzpatrick, John	3864	Swain, Obadiah	3912	Strayer, George L.
3817	Evans, James	3865	Reed, Charles	3913	Bates, Josiah
3818	Monroe, William	3866	Mathews, Cornelius	3914	Piles, James
3819	Roffe, Isaac	3867	Robertson, Thomas	3915	Slaiter, John
3820	Montgomery, William	3868	Groves, Thomas	3916	Mista, William
3821	Tamblen, John	3869	Buskell, William	3917	Whitow, Miles
3822	Jarvis, George	3870	Morris, Samuel	3918	Clover, Louis
3823	Chivers, Cantab	3871	Gorton, John	3919	West, John
3824	Sinclair, Solomon	3872	Gould, Henry	3920	Wynn, John
3825	Harris, George	3873	Jones, John	3921	Tarr, James
3826	Silvey, John	3874	Cooper, William	3922	Stilwell, William
3827	Arnold, James	3875	Locker, Michael	3923	Lanagan, Daniel
3828	Littlefield, Samuel	3876	Hunn, John	3924	Robinson, William
3829	Averill, Samuel	3877	Smith, John	3925	Simson, Smith
3830	Kemble, John	3878	Clark, Samuel	3926	Jones, Thomas
3831	Atkinson, Charles	3879	Austin, William	3927	Wilcox, William
3832	Cowen, William	3880	Williams, Joseph	3928	Griffen, John
3833	Steele, Thomas	3881	Robinson, John	3929	Green, Thomas
3834	Sankey, Caesar	3882	Newman, Henry	3930	Drayton, John
3835	Davis, Samuel	3883	Dyer, Thomas	3931	Graves, Thomas
3836	Dexter, Philip	3884	Dissmore, Abraham	3932	Sawyer, Jacob
3837	Dexter, George W.	3885	Stevens, William	3933	Catley, William
3838	Smith, Kilby	3886	Jones, James	3934	Dame, John
3839	Wright, John	3887	Bussey, Charles	3935	Davis, John
3840	Wall, William	3888	Johnson, Henry	3936	Hubbard, John G.
3841	Little, Thomas	3889	Paris, Peter	3937	Ross, George
3842	Scott, Anthony	3890	Northey, Joseph	3938	Percival, John
3843	Porter, Ephraim	3891	Jones, Isaac	3939	Wepple, Joseph
3844	Jonathan, Jonathan	3892	Marshall, Benjamin	3940	Lent, Samuel
3845	Christian, Tyrel	3893	Allen, John	3941	Dodge, Joseph
3846	Ayres, William	3894	Starkweather, James	3942	Noble, Daniel
3847	Manning, George	3895	Evans, Hezekiah	3943	Sprismo, John
3848	Perham, Ezekiel	3896	Kellam, John	3944	Lewis, Thomas
3849	Wiggins, Samuel	3897	Marvell, David	3945	Larey, Henry
3850	Williams, William	3898	Card, Israel	3946	White, James
3851	Hartford, William	3899	Ward, Alfred	3947	Shechford, John
3852	Shepherd, Henry	3900	Williams, Benjamin	3948	Adams, Abijah
3853	Lovell, William	3901	Wilson, George	3949	Kylor, John
3854	Bordage, Raymond	3902	Ellis, Cornelius	3950	Anan, John
3855	Waterhouse, Joseph	3903	Snow, Collyer	3951	Queen, Daniel
3856	Adams, William	3904	Jewett, Jasper	3952	Canada, James
3857	Lewis, John	3905	Glover, Benjamin	3953	Fosset, Robert
3858	Dixey, Walston	3906	Monroe, James	3954	Strand, Peter
3859	Parker, William	3907	Brown, Abraham	3955	Hicks, James
3860	Turner, David	3908	Fowler, Joshua		

Prisoner listing by ship or regiment

13th U.S. Infantry
- Bin, Peter
- Blaney, Henry
- Clarke, John
- Condon, Michael
- Cowgan, John
- Dalton, John
- Doniner, John
- Donnally, Anthony
- Fitzgerald, John
- Gill, John
- Kelly, Henry
- McBrearthy, Patrick
- McCannon, Thomas
- Mooney, Mathew
- Wiley, John

14th U.S. Infantry
- Anderson, Andre
- Andrews, David (1)
- Andrews, David (2)
- Andrews, Edward
- Avis, Jervis
- Ballard, Martin
- Beals, John
- Beard, John
- Beard, Richard
- Berlew, Gibeon
- Black, John
- Booth, George
- Bowen, Artemas
- Bowen, William
- Brison, James
- Broadest, Moses
- Brown, James
- Brown, John
- Brown, Michael
- Cane, Thomas
- Carbody, Darby
- Carey, James
- Carr, John
- Caughan, Patrick
- Chambers, Henry
- Clark, Stephen
- Cook, Hazard
- Cook, John
- Cord, Jacob
- County, David

14th U.S. Infantry
- Courtney, George
- Crosy, S. M.
- Cummins, David
- Cunningham, Caleb
- Daumied, Edward
- Davis, John
- Davis, Thomas
- Delignay, George
- Denvon, Charles
- Dibbins, Edward
- Doud, John
- Dougherty, Hamilton
- Duganeu, Charles
- Elsworth, John
- Farman, Joseph
- Frazer, Hulbert
- Given, James
- Goodrich, H. C.
- Goodwin, Joseph
- Gray, John
- Gray, Samuel
- Griffin, John
- Grimes, Nicholas
- Halloo, John
- Hargood, George
- Hedden, Amos
- Henry, James
- Herrington, Ezekiel
- Hill, Stephen
- Huff, Michael
- Hunderville, John
- Hunter, James
- Hurd, John
- Jacobs, John
- Jenny, John
- Johnson, Hugh
- Jones, William M.
- Kelley, William
- Kellogg, Asa
- Kelly, Charles
- King, William
- Lathrum, William
- Logan, Timothy
- Loveitson, John
- Macconahay, Benjamin
- Mackay, John

14th U.S. Infantry	Magee, Robert	14th U.S. Infantry	Watson, William
	Mallack, Joseph		West, Abiah
	Manaham, David		Whagerman, Joseph
	Martin, William		Wheeler, Anthony
	Mathews, John		White, John
	Maxwell, Robert		Whitman, Samuel
	McCannon, Dominique		Williams, Andrew
	McEver, William		Willis, Alfred
	McGinnis, Patrick		Winn, Clement
	McGowan, John		
	McKenzie, Kenneth	16th U.S. Infantry	Lynch, John
	McKever, Charles		Winner, Michael
	McGuire, Hugh		
	Miars, Michael	22nd U.S. Infantry	Napperknac, John
	Miller, George M.		
	Miller, James	23rd U.S. Infantry	Evans, James
	Mills, Stephen		Gilbert, Elijah
	Mitchell, Charles		Hoy, Barney
	Myers, John		Niles, Nathaniel
	Niel, E. C.		Wilder, Titus
	Nybro, Godfrey		
	Patten, David	2nd U.S. Artillery	Lowry, James
	Patterson, Archibald		Melvin, William
	Powers, John		Muckleroy, William
	Prico, Job		Patrick, John F.
	Rhea, John		Wane, Michael
	Riggins, Laban		
	Ritchie, Allan	4th U.S. Infantry	Folsom, Abraham
	Rumsey, Joseph		
	Scott, James	5th U.S. Infantry	Barlow, John
	Scott, John		
	Sears, Abraham	6th U.S. Infantry	Cole, Andrew
	Simpson, Mark		Craney, Edward
	Sloan, William		Finney, John
	Smiley, John		Ganagon, Edward
	Smith, John		Hunter, James
	Soder, Jacob		Ireland, John
	Spaldings, William		Johnson, George
	Staley, John		Norman, Edward
	Steward, Thomas		Norton, Robert
	Storer, John		Williams, Thomas
	Stroud, John		
	Swatwood, Jacob	Abraham Newland	Horsey, Thomas W.
	Taggart, Archibald		
	Taggart, Thomas	Adaline	Hughes, John
	Taugherty, M.		Roberts, Nathaniel
	Thistlewood, Charles		Senter, Noah
	Thomas, Samuel		Tatem, George W.
	Todd, John		Watson, John

Agnes	Tillman, John	Anna & Lilley	Lockwood, Charles
prize of the Privateer Rambler			Smith, Mark
			Snowden, Joshua L.
Ajax,	Cole, John		
prize to the Privateer Governor Tomkins		Antelope	Bartlett, N.
	Davis, Francis		Beckner, Henry
			Bowie, Henry
Alagana	Allen, William		Branham, Stephen
	Bourn, John		Conklin, Enoch
	Gore, John		Cornelius, John
	Smith, John		Couley, Andrew
	Smith, Obadiah		Cowen, William
			Cox, Isaac
Albion	Shorne, H.		Cross, John
			Delancey, William
Alexander	Scols, William		Gifford, Francis
			Giles, John
Alligator	Higby, James		Greenfield, William
	Ingersoll, John		Jones, William
	Moriarty, Thomas		Lawson, Mathew
			Liddle, John
America	Blanchard, John		Mathewson, Andrew
	Brown, Jesse		McNeal, Alexander
	Carswell, William		MacPhie, Alexander
	Digereas, William		Phillips, Jackson
	Elwell, James		Porter, Nathaniel
	Green, John		Powell, Richard
	Hopkins, Robert		Randson, John
	Hubbard, William		Record, Frederick
	Jones, John		Robson, Robert
	Kent, Wilson		Scaff, Nicholas
	Pierce, Joseph		Stephens, Michael
	Reed, George		Waterman, William
	Richardson, William		White, Thomas
	Rowe, Daniel		Willet, Jonathan
	Salmon, Archibald		Williamson, Charles
	Smith, James		
	Walton, John	Arabella	Butler, John
Amiable	Wood, John	Argus	Arthur, Alexander
			Bisbee, Elijah
Amity	Witherell, Charles		Bisbee, J. D.
prize of the Privateer Prince de Neufchatel			Bridges, Jeremiah
			Brower, John
Amphion	Jackson, C. L.		Chase, Constant
	Stilman, Elijah		Choete, Thomas
	Taylor, James		Collins, John
			Crosby, John
Ann	Dunn, Thomas		Davis, Solomon
	Peck, Elisha		

Argus
- Dill, William
- Dixon, John
- Drybourgh, James
- Edwards, John
- Flower, Artemas
- Francis, John
- Freeman, Plim
- Furness, Jesse
- Gage, Lot
- Gale, William
- Gavet, James
- Gibbons, Andrew
- Green, Samuel
- Griffiths, Joseph
- Hallet, William
- Harding, John
- Harris, Alpheus
- Hendrick, John
- Hendrick, Thomas
- Hodges, Hercules
- Howe, Jacob
- Jones, William
- Joseph, Michael
- Kitchen, Daniel
- Lee, John
- Lewis, Henry
- Lincoln, Ephraim
- Loring, Samuel
- Lunt, Daniel
- Mains, Henry
- Morris, Andrew
- Norcross, Thomas
- Paddock, Benjamin M.
- Peters, Benjamin
- Porter, Calvin
- Randall, Jacob
- Ringgold, Thomas
- Robinson, Stephen
- Shepherd, Samuel
- Simmons, Charles
- Simmons, Joel
- Skudder, Alexander
- Smith, George M.
- Stetson, Hiram
- Stickney, Abraham
- Stilman, William A.
- Thinney, Alvin
- Tomas, Andrew
- Tyler, Joseph

Argus
- Wallace, Thomas
- Weslemyer, John
- White, George
- Williams, George F.
- Williams, James
- Winchester, Ebenezer
- Woodard, Elijah
- Wyman, William

Arial
- Barnes, Isaac
- Beers, James
- Durant, John
- Gregous, William
- Hall, George
- Robert, Nicholas
- Saunders, Joseph
- Sharp, Peter

Atlantic
- Mista, William

Atlantic, recaptured prize
- Wilson, R. G.

Baltimore
- Allen, Barnes
- Andrey, Alexander
- Anthony, Luke
- Chattels, John
- Cunningham, John
- Hansen, William
- Johnson, Andre
- Lindholm, Nicholas
- Lucas, Benjamin
- McCoates, Samuel
- Metcalf, William
- Meyer, John
- Miller, John Jacob
- Mirpaine, Bruce
- Mitchell, John
- Myer, Peter
- Prendwelle, James
- Rogers, William
- Samblasen, Edward
- Stevenson, Thomas
- Tull, John
- Waller, George
- Webb, Stephen
- Wilmer, Isaac
- Wise, John

Baroness Longueville
- Holstien, Richard

British South Sea Whaler	Jackson, William	Brutus	Bailey, Charles
	Primas, James		Barchant, George
			Calkings, Zera
Bee	Young, John		Capron, William
			Cooperies, Nicholas
Bell	Bellas, John		Gomez, Manuel
	Jones, Urigh		Jackson, John
	Martin, John		Johns, Bellona
	White, John		Lewis, John
			Nartique, John
Bellville	Dennis, Thomas		Parker, Samuel
	Randal, Benjamin		Perez, Joseph
	Wair, Francis		Rich, Francis
			Roy, Charles
Benedict's Regiment	Watson, Macy		Scott, Andrew
			Slate, Henry V.
Benjamin	Goodwin, Jonas B.		Turpin, Francis
	Severence, Gideon		
	Taylor, William	Bunker Hill	Arnold, Obadiah
			Beauty, Edmund
Benjamin Franklin	Powell, John		Black, Thomas
	Reed, John		Boite, Julius Pierre
			Brisons, John
Blockade	Anthony, James		Brown, Frederick
	Evans, John		Butler, William
	Griswold, Josiah		Dean, Peter
	Hazard, Prince		D'Emery, Adrian
	Hussey, Ebenezer		Ferlecque, Augustine
	Silverthorn, James		Gavot, Henry
	West, Henry		Gordon, Richard
	Woodford, James		Hazard, Charles
			Hemonder, Peter
Blue Bird	Dishelle, Alexander		Hubi, Pierre M.
	Fuller, Zachariah		Kelly, Samuel
	Jones, John		Lawton, William
	Spryon, John		Le Goff, Herve
	Swinny, Edward		Le Petit, John Baptiste
	Thompson, Owen		Lebour, Francois
			Lerocque, Olivier
Bonne Citoyenne	Basstisto, John		Lesaut, Jacques
			Liemo, Frederick
Bows (British MV)	Crapsey, James		Lisconet, Francis
			Livesley, Thomas
Brunswick	Baptiste, John		Lucas, Francois Rene
	Black, William		McFarlan, Daniel
	Chambers, Charles		Moore, Edward
	Grose, Daniel		Morrison, Thomas
	Snider, Lewis		Oliver, Joseph
	Wallace, William		Osborne, Samuel

Bunker Hill	Pratt, Daniel	Catharine	Freeman, Alexander
	Ramsey, John		Gifford, Barry
	Richards, James		Underwood, John F.
	Roger, Christopher		White, Alden
	Schiffky, Jacobus Orgen		Williams, George (1)
	Shaw, William		Williams, George (2)
	Shippard, James		Barker, George
	Spiers, Nathaniel		Goodwin, John
	Thompson, Lawrence		
	Williams, John	Cato	Andrew, Joseph
			Chapman, John
Caliban	Blood, Simon		Clough, Isaac
	Eaton, Benjamin		Hammond, William
	Scott, John		Peirson, Robert
	Thatcher, Samuel G.		Rogers, Samuel
	Upton, John B.		Widger, Thomas
Calcutta, East Indian Ship	Anderson, Aaron	Centurion, prize	Mackey, Charles
	Brower, Frederick		Nicholson, William
	Caban, Samuel		
	Cole, Hutchinson A.	Ceres	Johnson, Robert
	Miller, George		
	Miner, Benjamin F.	Charles	Forbes, James
	Pearson, Thomas		Higgins, William
	Sibert, Frederick		Pearson, Samuel
	Smith, Henry		
	Stanton, Gideon A.	Charlotte	Sikes, Charles
	Sterns, Henry		
	Tafe, Henry	Clive	Rotch, David
	Wilson, John		
		Columbia	Barton, Nathan
Calmar	Rooter, John		Belford, Isaac
			Canada, Prince
Caneware	Johnson, Robert		Carson, Robert
			Castor, Charles
Cannoniere	Gault, William		Cousor, Adam
	Mann, John		Dickinson, Francis
			Douchney, Hiram
Caroline	Baxter, David		Douglas, Thomas
	Jones, Lewis		Garthon, Willey
			George, Isaac
Catharine Charlotte	Slackpole, John		Hartford, John
	Stone, Samuel		Hawkins, Isaac
	Swasey, Alexander		Helm, Charles
			Henderson, David
Castor	Russell, William		Jackson, John
	Williams, David		Kain, Peter
			Roach, Nicholas
Catharine	Allen, Elijah		Robinson, Benjamin

Columbia	Tightham, Peter	Cuba	Cartwright, Philip
	Todd, William		Hewitt, James
	Weaver, Thomas		Holland, William
			Johnston, Benjamin
Commodore Perry	Carman, George		Siers, Uriah
	Edwards, William		Smith, Buphus
	Gosling, Joseph		Vingen, Nicholas
	Hamilton, Robert		
	Heimer, Daniel	Cup	Lee, Williams
	Henzeman, Christopher		
	Hogg, Jacob	Cygnet	Foxwell, George
	Killingsworth, John		Leach, James
	Lewis, John		Little, Silas W.
	Luburg, John C.		Lord, John
	Lynch, William		Thompson, Isaac
	Murray, John		
	Newton, John	Darby	Hale, William
	Reed, Abraham		Jarratt, Abraham
	Reeves, Essex		
	Robins, William	Dart	Camsure, Dominick
	Werman, John		Clark, Samuel
	Woodbury, Dixie		Delenne, John
			Deselva, Manuel
Confidence	Devine, John		Fredericks, John
	Young, Ebenezer		Gould, John
			Green, James Beckwith
Cornelia	Bramblecome, David		Harding, J. Christian
			Johnson, John
Cossack	Green, Charles		Kinnard, Charles
	Hill, Benjamin		Lewis, John
	Lamson, Noah		Miles, John
	Pinder, George		Miller, James
	Ropes, David		Miramon, Roch
	Thompson, William		Murray, Charles
	Twikes, Samuel		Parsons, Rufus
	Ward, Benjamin		Patten, John
	Weston, Nathaniel		Paul, Jacob
			Phillips, Thomas
Country Square	Chappell, John		Pollett, Edward
	Davis, Benjamin		Rodgers, Abraham
	Griffin, James		Smith, Thomas
	Hart, William		Tardy, Anthony
	Lodge, Ebenezer		Tardy, Edward
	Sunonton, John		Tarlton, Thomas P.
	Thorndike, Robert		Tipp, Nicholas
	Wells, William		Wedgewood, James
			Williamson, John
Criterion	Anderson, Alexander		
	Johnston, Thomas	Davy Dearborn	Herdru, Charles

Davy Dearborn	Lemeeker, Barner	Diana	Trask, Osmond
Deanna recaptured British vessel	Antonie, John Dominico, Joseph Geely, Joseph Harris, David Hecox, George Homan, Joseph Lakeman, Samuel Okes, George Picket, Richard Ramans, Nicholas Salkins, Nathaniel Sparling, William Weilwright, Joseph	Dick Dido	Bishop, Edward Busson, John Chip, Charles Donaldson, Joseph Fangall, William Jeffreys, Henry Stanly, Benjamin Watts, James Allen, Andrew Allen, John Andrews, Asa Crane, Andrew Sargent, Phillip Wood, William
Decatur	Burns, John Ears, Ludwig Lathrope, Gurdon Lewis, Gabriel Mayeau, Morris Newel, George Nichols, William Roderick, Frank Williams, Joseph	Dolphin	Ayres, Henry Bain, John Baptist, John Brown, Zeth Carman, Francis Carney, Edward Chew, Joseph Coffin, George
Derby	Dexter, George W. Dexter, Philip Dixey, Walston Dyer, Thomas Parker, William Smith, Kilby Turner, David		Condon, John Crow, Jonathan De Young, Richard Fisher, Richard D. Gill, James Hamilton, John Hart, Frederick Hera, John A.
Devon prize to the Privateer Bunker Hill	Bloomdale, John Carter, Enoch Chauvel, Thomas Debaize, Francois Jean Demerie, Etienne Ewell, Edward Gravely, Joseph Grosette, Jean Maurice Hubble, James Perott, Jean Francois Tuttle, Joseph		James, John Jenkins, Peter Jones, Thomas Kennard, Joseph Leach, Benjamin Lovering, William Low, Thomas Macquillon, Hugh Madillion, Peter Malony, Hughey Moor, John Morgan, William Mourin, James
Diamond	Dyer, Ezekiel Lock, Nathaniel Sweet, Moses		Myer, John Nargney, James

Dolphin	Pannell, Hugh	Elbridge Gerry	Clark, Joseph
	Parker, John		Cook, Silvanus
	Paul, Dempie		Cree, William
	Peek, David		Davis, John
	Ratuse, Peter		Davis, Lot
	Richardson, Samuel		Dean, Jeremiah B.
	Robinson, John		Donnell, Samuel
	Sait, Gasper		Douglass, Samuel
	Skinner, Johnson		Drake, Daniel
	Smasher, Allen		Eagerly, Elijah
	Spencer, Samuel		Foot, Benjamin
	Thomas, Henry		Freeman, John
	Thompson, William		Green, William
	Towns, Nicholas		Harman, Isaac
	Treyer, John		Head, James
			Hitchens, William
Dominick	Hoy, Philip		Homer, Henry
			Humphrey, Asa
Dorset	Thompson, John		Lant, Henry
			Lee, Michael
Draper	Moody, Samuel		Luffie, Warren
			Malony, Robert
Earl St. Vincent	Brown, William		Miller, James
			Norton, David
Echo	Rees, William		Paine, Clement
			Parrish, William
Edward	Boston, Peter		Parrott, Ebenezer
	Callec, Samuel		Parsons, John
	Derrick, John		Plummer, William
	Gilbert, William A.		Richards, Sandy
	Greenleaf, James		Ring, Andrew
	Marshall, William		Sawyer, Jonathan
	Molbin, Benjamin		Shaw, Samuel
	Nason, William		Skilling, James
	Upham, Timothy		Smith, Henry
	Walker, John		Smith, Monday
	West, Silas		Sterns, Joseph
	Wood, Richard		Thayer, Laban
			Turnbull, James
Elbridge Gerry	Allen, William		Turner, Samuel
	Baptiste, John		Webb, Nathaniel
	Barnes, William Smith		Winston, William
	Bartlett, John		Worthy, James
	Barton, James		
	Blossom, Seth	Eliza	Atkins, Francis
	Boyd, Andrew		Burrow, Charles
	Bradford, George		Clark, Titus
	Brown, John		Crumpton, William
	Brown, Thomas		Cunningham, Silas

Eliza	Daniels, Bradley	Emeline	Dunn, Henry G.
	Dunchellier, Isaac		
	Fredericks, John	Empress	Burns, George
	Hardwick, James		Chandler, Henry
	Harrison, Joseph		Fron, Frederick
	Holdridge, Hector		Jameson, George
	Hunter, John		Johnson, David
	Huston, James		Lind, Andrew
	Hutchinson, James		Moore, Jacob
	Lalan, John		Moore, Michael
	Lee, Isaac		Roberts, Josiah
	Mason, John		Roundy, Jonathan
	Parks, Richard		Sanderson, John
	Pratt, Lester		Saunders, Thomas
	Rest, Zebulon		Smith, William
	Roberts, William		Vine, William
	Rogers, John		Whitlock, Sidney B.
	Simpson, William		
	Sims, Joseph	Endeavour	Tucker, Samuel
	Stephens, William		
	Walker, William	Enterprise	Abbott, William
	Walkington, George		Bassett, John
			Battes, John
Eliza Ann	Allen, Daniel		Blair, Benjamin
	Ayers, John		Blaney, Stephen
	Ball, Erastus		Brown, Edward
	Colwell, John		Christian, John
	Cooper, Eleazer		Clarke, Isaac
	Crafts, William		Clothy, John
	Currin, Andrew		Clothy, William
	Doe, Thomas		Cloutman, Joseph
	Ellen, Nathaniel		Cone, John
	English, James		Downey, John
	Fowler, Timothy		Duncan, Thomas
	Miller, James		Findley, Thomas
	Preston, Isaac		Fuller, Nathaniel
			Gage, Thomas
Elizabeth	Robins, Willis		Gibbins, Hiram
			Gomerson, James
Elk	Tolson, Jeremy		Goss, Jesse
			Grandy, Amos
Elson	Atkin, Robert G.		Hamson, John
	Grant, John		Hamson, William
	Keen, Robert		Harris, Joseph
	Lunes, Charles		Holt, Jacob L.
	Primis, George		Jackson, James
	Saucry, John		Johnson, George
	Stacey, Benjamin		Kelly, John
	Tresroy, Thomas		Kinder, Ephraim G.

Enterprise	Lackey, Joseph	Expectation	Beans, James
	Lamson, Amos		Beasley, Edward
	Lufkin, William		Benjamin, James
	McIntire, John		Bitters, John
	Melzard, Peter		Colwell, John
	Millett, John		Earl, Maris
	Morgan, John R.		Esperaza, Jacob
	Mullett, Joseph		Hardy, John
	Mulloy, William		Ingraham, Peter
	Oakes, George		John, Richard J.
	Peach, John		Mountain, Emanuel
	Pettingill, Joseph		Simpson, James
	Price, John		Thomas, John
	Richardson, William		Townsend, Solomon
	Robinson, William		
	Rowel, Mathew	Experiment	Anthony, John
	Russell, Robert		Benner, Lewis
	Sanburn, James		Cobb, Samuel
	Saundry, Nathaniel		Dunn, Hezekiah
	Silver, Samuel		Ellis, John
	Simmonds, David		Fate, Thomas
	Simoni, John		Harris, James
	Smith, Thomas		Jewell, Samuel
	Thompson, John		Lynch, William
	Thornton, John		Murray, John
	Tildon, Robert		Smith, Jacob
	Torry, Henry		Williamson, Charles
	Treadwell, Nathaniel		Willingsworth, Jeffery
	Tucker, William		
	Walker, Samuel	Fair Play	Pollard, Charles
	Webb, John		
	Webster, Asa	Falcon	Hadley, George
	Wettey, Philip	prize of the U.S. Frigate President	
	Widger, John		Henry, Henry
	Williams, Frederick (1)		Horner, John
	Williams, Frederick (2)		Powell, Joseph
Eos	Berry, John	Fame	Bunker, Thomas
	Chase, Eliphalet		Dunham, David
	Henderson, Benjamin		Hussy, Edward
	Holt, Simeon		Johnson, Richard
	Jackson, John		Long, Joseph
	Kennedy, Henry		Marsh, Hercules
	Riker, Samuel		Nicholls, Thomas
	Wells, Thomas		Osmond, David
			Porter, Edward
Eunice	Brandy, Francis		Swain, James
			Thuel, Bristo
Expectation	Baker, John		Weeden, Richard
			Williams, Stephen

Fame prize of Privateer Decatur	Cruff, William Dorr, Edward Hackett, Theophilus Harris, Abraham Harris Newby, John Reed, John Stacy, William Valentine, Andrew Wyatt, Joseph	Fly prize of the U.S. Frigate President Forester Fox	Hatton, Peter Hood, Daniel Ling, Thomas McDermont, James Seely, Truman Black, James Brown, Thomas
Felix	Dobbs, Jeremiah Riley, Jonathan Robinson, Charles Tanner, John Young, Ebenezer R.		Dannell, Edward Elliott, Andrew Green, John Hovey, Joseph Mason, James Rick, William
Ferox	Aurel, Leonard Bailey, Samuel Cadwell, James Crandell, John Deal, John Durham, Charles Freeman, Charles Gilbert, George Lee, George Myers, David Trusty, Henry	Frances Ann	Sawyer, Peter Wheeler, Michael Ferguson, John Bicketson, John Cook, Tarden Grinnell, William Hammond, Benjamin Howland, William Lawdy, Benjamin Sheppard, David Ticham, Jeremiah
Ferret	Simpson, John	Frederick	Baptist, Michael
Fire Fly	Allen, David Day, John Dempsey, Daniel Jefferys, Henry Jones, Stephen Millett, Joseph Newell, Benjamin (2) Pearson, Samuel Rowe, William Shaw, Henry Tarr, Caleb Williams, William Winchester, Richard	 Friendship Frolic Galen	Coaner, Peter Lee, George Morris, Thomas Murray, Richard Ross, Richard Walker, James McLane, George Evans, Jonathan Morris, S. Smith, William
Fleetwood	Hopkins, Samuel	Ganges	Gase, Zachariah Harlow, Sylvanus
Flora, a Spanish brig	Smith, John		Hutchins, Josiah Tinkham, Seth
Fly	Dealing, Elisha	 Garter Wester	Weinbarg, John Young, Nathaniel

Gartlen	Holston, John	Governor Middleton	Nash, William
			Nye, William
General Blake	Bennet, Andrew		Shaw, John
	Blackburn, William		Sheppard, Henry
	Lexious, Peter		Walton, Christopher
	Miller, Ezekiel		Willson, John
	Wilson, William		Woodborne, John
			Wright, Thomas
General Kempt prize of the Privateer Grand Turk	Dieman, John	Governor Plumer	Butler, George
	Smith, Richard		Drisco, James
	Spurr, Elijah		Ducat, William
			Fall, James
George & Mary	Williams, Michael		Fernald, William
			Keen, Benjamin
George Carming	Fitch, Henry		Kinnard, George
			McKinney, Isaac
Gleamer	Layton, William		Moore, Samuel
			Place, Thomas
Globe	Brower, John		Sides, Samuel
	Brown, Robert		Tarlton, John
	Dew, Frederick		Tethery, Robert
	Ferguson, Thomas		Tuckerman, Nathaniel
	Forsyth, Robert		Varney, John
	Hunter, James		
	Le Moor, John	Grand Turk	Beatty, John
	Seth, John		Curry, William
	Stanfield, George		Devereux, John
	Stretton, Samuel		Hall, James
			Mulloy, William
Gloucester	Davis, John		Phillips, Timothy
			Warren, David
Go' On	Scott, Henry		
		Growler	Bartlett, Robert
Gossypium	Linnel, Jonathan		Bowden, Benjamin
			Bowden, William
Gothans	West, John		Brown, John
			Brown, Joseph
Governor Gerry	Braley, George		Cash, John
	Hitch, Joshua		Chandler, Enoch
			Coombe, Michael
Governor McKane	Boggs, James		Crocker, Sylvester
			Davis, William
Governor Middleton	Brown, Peter		Day, Frederick
	Dodge, Joseph		Derring, William F.
	Doer, James		Devereux, Benjamin
	Driver, Thomas		Dodge, John
	Fry, Peter		Ellingwood, William H.
	Jackson, J. K.		Emerson, David
	Johnson, John		

Growler	Euston, Ephraim	Hannah	Pritchard, Israel
	Fletcher, John		Selman, John
	Florence, Charles		Wicks, Littleton
	Forman, William		
	Foster, George	Hannah & Eliza	Scott, Henry
	Foster, Samuel		Williams, Joseph
	Garrett, Simon T.		Wing, Nathaniel
	Gatchell, John G.		
	Grush, Nathaniel	Hannah of New York	Barton, Peter
	Hart, William		
	Harvey, Anthony	Hannibal	Barton, Elijah
	Hooper, Joseph A.		Clark, William
	Jones, Thomas		Hastings, Johnson
	Joseph, Nicholas		Seely, James
	Kegs, Zenas		
	Kraft, Michael	Harmak & Sally	Hallman, Anthony
	Lee, Nathaniel		Lockwood, Charles
	Lindsay, Nathaniel		Roberson, James
	Malcomb, Alexander		
	Manning, Burrell	Harriett	Mathews, Cornelius
	Mirrel, Samuel B.		Reed, Charles
	Nicholson, James		
	Nicholson, Jonas	Harvest	Carter, Henry
	Odiam, Joseph H.	prize of the Privateer Bunker Hill	
	Orne, Israel		Port, John
	Pippin, Isaac		
	Porter, William	Hawk	Catley, William
	Roundy, Jeremiah		Dame, John
	Roundy, Thomas		Dodge, Joseph
	Russell, William		Percival, John
	Rust, John		
	Selman, Francis G.	Hazard	Withman, William
	Smith, Benjamin		
	Smith, Jeremiah	Heartless	Norton, Richard
	Smith, John		
	Tishure, Samuel	Hebe	Hand, Wilson
	Tucker, Andrew		
	Tucker, Nathaniel	Henry	Carpenter, Nathaniel
	Widger, Joseph		Eculeston, Gardner
	Withiem, Burrell		Hosstidler, Jesse
	Williams, John		Luther, Jeremiah
Hamlett	Brown, Thomas	Henryettos	Butler, William
	Hules, Cyrus		Davis, Joseph
	Reid, John		Foloson, Christopher
			Groves, Pierce
Hannah	Blaird, David		Haller, Joseph
	Harvey, Joseph		Hendrickson, Michael
	Johnson, Henry		Oulson, Frederick
			Rosecrans, Philip

Henryettos	Simons, John	Hunter	Andersen, James
	Ward, Peter		Anthony, Abraham
			Barchman, John
Hepsey	Bakeman, Ely		Bickford, Ebenezer
	Bissell, Samuel W.		Bowdley, Thomas
	Boyd, Andrew		Boyd, Edward
	McKenzie, William		Brown, Jesse
	Newell, Stephen C.		Brown, John
	Warner, John		Burroth, Mansfield
	Williams, Thomas		Card, Nathaniel
			Carrol, Robert
Hero	Bickford, William		Carter, Moses
	Fortune, John		Carves, John
	Parsons, Wanery		Childs, Samuel
	Reed, John		Cloutman, Samuel
	Sampson, David		Cogswell, Edward
	Washy, George		Dean, Daniel
			Dolorer, John
Hibernia	Beckett, William		Fannol, Augustus
			Fletcher, Henry
Hickerson	Barrett, Bias		Flushman, H. P.
			Foster, Isaiah
Hindostan	Boyd, Stephen		Gardner, Samuel
	Davidson, John		Glascow, John
	Duvall, N. D.		Grunlief, Timothy
	Elfe, James		Hall, William
	Lamb, Jack		Hammet, John
	Reymond, Caleb		Henry, Edward
	Stage, William		Hobert, George
	Stegman, Christian		Holden, Charles
			Hosmer, Joseph
Hiram	Swise, Carl		Hotchkiss, Levi
			Ingells, Edward
Hope	Anderson, Joseph		Jenkins, Richard
	Blue, Peter		Johnston, Samuel
	Dominic, John		Knox, Thomas
	Glenn, Robert		Leach, Charles
	Haley, Thomas		Lee, Nathaniel
	Kennedy, John		Lewis, Raymond
	Michael, Peter		Lowder, Henry
	Muncy, Daniel		Main, Henry
	Parsons, Joseph		Mitchell, James
	Peters, John		Mitchell, John
	Sands, Thomas		Monnett, Samuel
	Thomas, William		Moor, Thomas
	Walden, James		Neal, Henry
	Yale, Nathaniel		Nye, Charles N.
			Obrion, John
Hope & Anchor (Danish sloop)	Codshell, Joseph		Parsons, Samuel

Hunter	Peters, Jacob	Industry	Fulton, James
	Peterson, James		Gardiner, Amboy
	Peterson, Nicholas		Glover, John
	Poland, David		Gowalter, John
	Robins, Jeremiah		Ingles, John
	Ross, George		Jarvis, Thomas
	Rowe, Stephen		Labbas, John
	Rowell, James		Laskey, Benjamin
	Ruliff, London		Lockett, Thomas R.
	Scribner, Elijah		Morris, Jacob
	Sevratt, William		Rice, John
	Signard, Samuel Francis		Rice, Thomas
	Sodoburgh, John		Robes, Edward
	Thomas, Alexander		Ross, David
	Thomas, George		Russell, Louis
	Thomas, John L.		Snow, James
	Towns, Daniel		Stacey, John
	Tucker, Edward		Swain, Thomas
	Upton, Jeduthun		Tucker, Samuel
	Upton, Samuel		Williams, Alexander
	Wain, Benjamin		
	Warner, Charles	Industry	Lawrence, David
	Warner, George	prize to Privateer Decatur	
	Whipple, Samuel		
	White, Sampson	Iris	Lamon, John
	Wilcox, Caesar		
		Isabella	Courtney, John
Independence	Davis, John		Smith, John
	Farrell, John		
	Fountain, Isaac	James	Boston, Robert
	Francis, Peter		Eldridge, Samuel
	Francoise, James		Evans, Williams
	Garrison, John		Fife, Thomas
	Lewis, John		Hartford, William
	Manuel, John		Monk, Joseph
	Packman, George		Nelson, Samuel A.
	Van Donveer, Peter		Shepherd, Henry
	Wilson, Peter		Soder, Bastion D.
	Wilson, William		Spiney, Nathaniel
			Teilman, John
Industry	Bartell, William		Ward, James
	Blair, Robert		White, J. William
	Brush, Thomas		Williams, William
	Burrell, Jesse		
	Burridge, Robert	Jane	Steward, James
	Cheslie, Amos		
	Dullivan, James	Jane	Bunker, Nicholas
	Eaton, Israel	prize of the Privateer Snap Dragon	
	Ellis, John		Eastlake, James

Ship/Regiment	Prisoner
Jane *prize of the Privateer Snap Dragon*	McIntyre, William
	Nickels, Hugh
	Penny, James
	Reed, Joseph
	Rogers, Epinetos
	Saunders, James
	Wilson, William
Javen	Bourn, James
John	Brassier, William
	Burke, J. C.
	Dodick, Mathew
	Dorrick, James
	Homes, Zachariah
	Lemon, Nicholas, C.
	Mason, Joseph J.
	Maston, John
	Morton, Seth
	Scanel, Cornelius
	Sears, Bartlett
	Short, James
John Barnes	Coffin, Frederick H.
	Gibey, John
	Martin, Ephraim
	Moss, William
	Scott, Benjamin
	Turner, Thomas
Joseph	Bartelett, John
	Covell, John
	Davis, Moses
	Doliver, Joseph
	Mitchell, Carr
	Parsons, Daniel
	Rogers, Gorham
	Thomas, Spencer
	Tuck, James
	Woodbury, John
Joseph Ricketson	Bishop, James
	Brinkman, Jan
	Clark, Peleg
	Deny, James
	Jacobson, William
	Robinson, Jacob
Josephine	Awe, Joseph
Josephine	Brooks, Edward
	George, Peter
	Haywood, John
	Hurst, Dudley
	Smith, William
	Treadwell, Alphecca
Juliana Smith	Artis, William
	Atwood, Nathaniel
	Behon, Simon
	Blair, David
	Briggs, Thomas
	Denishaw, Henry
	Eldridge, William
	Harding, Joseph
	Hay, John
	Higgins, Asa
	Holmes, Abraham
	Lawrence, George
	Lewis, John
	Light, John
	Norton, Solomon
	Phinney, John
	Smith, Elisha
	Snow, Thomas
	Verplasts, Nicholas
	Woodford, William
Julius Caesar	Campbell, John
Jupiter	Brown, James
King of Rome	Allen, Peter
	Burke, Samuel
	Dennis, John
	Fuster, Peter
	Hill, George
	Hyatt, William
	Inberg, Gabriel
	Lebon, Philip
	Legere, Joseph
	Lewis, John
	Lippen, Stephen
	Myers, Jacob
	Nilodas, M.
	Platt, John Henry
	Ricks, Thomas
	Salyear, John
	Sholes, Giles

Ship	Prisoner
King of Rome	Trought, Joseph
	Weeks, George
	Williams, Henry
Kitty *prize of the U.S. Frigate President*	Babbitt, Edward B.
	Chase, Nathaniel
	Huse, Ebenezer
	McMiller, Andrew
	Rightman, John
	Rodgers, Samuel
	Watson, James
Lark	Bids, Thomas
	Brown, John
	Poland, Abraham
	Wiggins, Richard
Laurel	Allyn, David
	Bradbury, Nathan
	Thompson, Lamon
Leader	Anderson, William
	Bell, George
	Brewer, James
	Gardner, James
	Hatch, Abraham
	Keith, James
	Leserver, Florence
	Richardson, Daniel
	Southward, Samuel W.
Leander	Cainmel, Jeremiah
	Green, James
	Mathews, Edward
	Potter, Henry
Leonidas	Christie, William
	Macintoie, Alexander
	Manning, Thomas
	Stoff, Samuel
Lepo (or Leo)	Nassan, Joseph
	Nicholas, John
Liberty	Beach, John
	Burris, M.
	Chase, Welcome
	Cilby, Thomas
Liberty	Creiger, John
	Curtis, Ephraim
	Defray, Edward
	Dickson, Enos
	Douglass, William
	Francis, John
	Hall, David
	Hamilton, John
	Hill, Justice
	Howell, Sullivan
	Jackson, Charles
	Jackson, Henry
	Kane, William
	Keen, Stewart
	Lipscomb, William
	Mark, James
	May, William
	Mead, Ezekiel
	Michel, John William
	Minor, John
	Ned, Deaf
	Nichols, John
	Peters, John
	Pines, Isaac
	Prescot, John
	Syphon, Lewis
	Towns, Asa
	Tucker, James
	Williams, David
Lightning	Bustin, John
	Crawford, Nelson
	Garthy, James
	Jordan, Peter
	Ruddick, William
	Wallace, James
	Warrance, John
Liveoak	Dole, Henry
	Shaw, Andrew
Llan Romney	Willis, Charles
Lord Hebes	Baxter, Alexander
Lord Ponsonbe *prize of the Privateer Diomede*	Arnold, Benjamin
	Doosenberry, Richard
	Shoe, Bernard
	Williams, Moses

Ship	Prisoner
Louisa prize of the Privateer Decatur	Boss, Thomas Chestly, Amos Jennings, Samuel Jones, John Woodbery, Caleb
Lucian prize of the Privateer Armstrong	Davis, John Godson, John Haywood, Simon
Lucky	Drew, Samuel Fresk, Joshua Hill, Charles Marshall, John Peters, John Pudober, Jonathan Samson, Thomas
Lucy	Rice, George
Lydia	Clarke, Clarence Davis, Michael Rust, John
Lyon	Jones, William
Madelina	Hool, Salmon
Madisonia	Jackson, George
Marchion of Ely	Gannet, Mathew
Mardriel	Davis, John Knapp, Ezekiel
Margaret prize of the Privateer True Blooded Yankee	Brown, George
Margarith	Carlander, John Chase, Mathew Coomes, Richard Davies, Charles Latimer, John Love, Peter Mullins, Joseph Newry, Peter Orphan, John Selby, James
Margarith	Valentine, James Ward, Mason
Maria	Brant, Solomon Craigg, William Deagle, James Evans, Robert Harding, John G. Smith, William S. Williams, William
Marianna	Norkett, George
Mariner	Abraham, William Allen, William DeBock, Cornelius Liscomb, John Myrick, William Steward, Alexander
Marquis of Huntley East Indianman	Jackson, Thomas
Mars	Tomkins, Ephraim
Martin	West, John
Mary	Bowman, John French, Dudley Longreen, Andrew Oxford, James Roath, James Stout, Sairer Turner, Henry B.
Mary Ann	Herts, John Edward Lingard, Ludwig Melcher, John
Mary Ann (Transport)	Halbrook, Benjamin
Mary prize to the Privateer True Blooded Yankee	Aldrigde, Richard Benjamin, Edward Griffen, William Lewis, Peter
Matilda prize of the U.S. Brig Argus	Andersen, John Groves, Richard

Ship	Prisoner
Matilda prize of the U.S. Brig Argus	Handerson, Hans
	Hanscon, Thomas
	Hanson, Peter
	Hatch, William
	Jasmine, Paul
	Legos, Philip
	Manuel, Peter
	Martin, John
	Miller, George
	Prio, Peter
	Smith, Aesop
	Westler, John
May	Trundy, Thomas
Maydock	Barber, Major
	Fleming, Alexander
	Harwood, William
	Peckham, Isaac
	Pitts, Charles
	Wilkey, Timothy
Melville	Warmsley, Samuel
Meon	Watts, Anthony
Messenger	Lauson, Isaac
	Posey, Valentine
Minerva	Campbell, William
	Conner, Michael
	Harris, Ebenezer
	Hill, Daniel
	Merritt, Enoch
	Watson, William
Montgomery	Bragden, James
	Briggs, William
	Brooks, John
	Callam, John
	Clarke, William
	Forbes, John
	Hanfield, Enos
	Hart, Samuel
	Henley, John
	Joseph, Lewis
	Murray, Richard
	Riswell, Palmer
	Ropes, Daniel
Montgomery	Sparkes, Thomas
	Thomas, John
	Wanton, William
Moscow	Babcock, Clark
	Chappell, Edward
	Gardner, Jonathan
Moses Brown	Jefferies, David
Mountaineer	Hunter, Isaac
	Loland, Levi
Namur	Calentine, Samuel
	Edmunds, Francis
Nancy	Chapel, Samuel
	Coggins, George
	Hoyt, Ichabod
	Moore, Daniel
	Pratt, Asa
	Randolph, Exum
	Stephens, Thomas
	Tedrick, Joseph
Napoleon	Moffett, John
	Reynolds, Frederick
Navigator	Anderson, Niels
	Brown, James
	Caliban, Ambrose
	Davis, George
	Ellis, John
	Lawson, Peter
	Simpson, Martin
	Wait, Philip
New Zealand	Coats, John
Norfolk, prize to the Globe	Bacchus, John
	Caufield, Arthur
Oaks	David, Michael
Ocean prized to the Privateer Diligent	Anderson, William
	Lyons, Henry
	Pigott, James
Ocean	Coffin, Valentine

Ocean	Ray, William	Pallas	Degars, Pedro
			Fitch, William
open boat	Petterson, Andrew		Lockerby, William
			Manuel, Anthony
Orbit	Albert, Hezekiah		Pheasonton, Robert
	Brown, Wheeler		Willson, John
	Cleveland, Davis		
	Dow, John	Patent	Fameroy, Ashley
	Frees, James		Hardward, Isaac
	Greenleaf, Thomas		
	Huntress, Robert	Penn (a whaler)	Harris, George
	Jackson, Thomas		Silvey, John
	Johnson, Jacob		
	Johnson, James	Perfect	Wepple, Joseph
	Kennedy, Peter		
	Lewis, George	Perseverance	Armstrong, Thomas
	Moore, Benjamin		Godsoe, William
	Rahabe, William		Hataway, William N.
	Rape, Nicholas		Lent, Samuel
	Stanley, Joseph		Macrombie, Elijah
	Sweetman, Samuel		Paine, Joshua
	Thompson, Courtney		
	Thompson, James	Phillipsburg	Pattingale, Enoch
	Tipton, Solomon		Swanton, John
	Webb, John		
	Wheeler, William	Phoenix	Bachelor, Nathaniel
			Brooks, Oliver
Orders in Council	Allen, John		Daniels, John
	Baptieste, John		Johnson, Samuel
	Gardner, William		Richmond, Caleb
	Martin, William		Roe, Johnman
	Slocum, William		
	Willson, John	Pigmy	Davis, Nicholas
			Doboll, William
Orpheus	Read, Major		
		Pilot	Anderson, John
Otter	Benster, John		Brickman, John
	Brown, John		Coffin, Edward
	Carr, Samuel		Demarlow, Francis
	Hitchin, John		Downs, John
	Hook, Aaron		Downs, William
	Howlen, Samuel		Gotier, Charles J.
	Jerry, Daniel		Hall, Ezekiel
	Sheppard, Daniel		Harding, William
	Wade, Otis		Howell, William
			Jackson, Frederick
Pallas	Benjamin, Polasskie		Livingston, Henry
	Butterfield, Edward		Manley, David
	Davis, Andrew		Mids, Michael

Pilot	Platt, Daniel	Porcupine	Garmindia, Stephen
	Simmonds, Henry		Girdler, James
	Smith, J. W.		Giria, John
	Stafford, John		Hagen, Joel
	Stafford, William J.		Harris, William
	Taylor, George		Henday, Thomas
	Thomas, John		Henry, John
	Vincent, Stephen Stiles		Hill, Manuel
	Williams, Charles		Idiarty, Francois
			Iriarty, Ignacio
Polly	Baddrige, Charles		Johnson, Jacob
	Brown, Thomas		Kinlay, Joseph
	Brown, William		Litnay, Peter
	Bryant, James		Lucas, Daniel
	Cook, John		Lyons, Peter
	Darrison, William		Lyons, Samuel
	Goss, Joshua		McAvory, Lewis
	Harris, William		Mead, Lewis
	Mason, Hiram		Melville, John
	Robinson, Robert		Myers, Frederick
	Rogers, Nathaniel		Parr, James
	Smithers, Thomas		Peters, John
	Vicary, Richard		Phillips, Joseph
			Pichon, John
Pomona	Baron, Peter		Prissey, John
prize of Privateer Prince de Neuchatel			Prutty, Henry
	Jourdan, John		Ross, Peter
	La Roche, Jean		Russell, John
	Lane, James		Sampson, William
	Lupy, Marcus		Smith, Charles
	Ward, Thomas		Sourivier, Daniel
			Starr, G. C.
Poor Sailor	Roselof, Thomas		Stiles, Jodich
			Sumerg, Benjamin
Porcupine	Allen, George		Tapley, Isaac
	Andrews, John		Terry, Joseph
	Brown, Benjamin		Thompson, John
	Bunker, Peter		Thompson, Samuel
	Carver, Abraham		Turner, Silas
	Christo, Peter		Williams, James
	Cleveland, Ebenezer		Young, John
	Cochran, Peter		
	Cross, Stephen	Portsmouth Packet	Anderson, David
	Davis, John		Appleton, John
	Deambo, Dom		Bourn, Oliver
	Diseveriere, Cosnery		Bull, James
	Dudes, J. B.		Byron, Ebenezer
	Duffy, Nathaniel		Card, Samuel
	Evans, Hale		Chace, Nathaniel
	Francis, Abraham		

Portsmouth Packet	Childs, William	Postsea	Ringold, Thomas B.
	Dennison, Andrew	prize to the Privateer Thrasher	
	Goff, Peter		Rowe, Isaac
	Gordon, Sperrin		Rowe, William
	Grant, Samuel		Smith, Samuel
	Hanson, William		Stevens, Joseph
	Hooper, Samuel		Thompson, Henry
	Jackson, Samuel		Turner, Leonard
	Johnson, Francis		Winckley, John
	King, Solomon		
	Lapish, Andrew	Powhattan	Bontrous, John
	Larabee, Thomas		Capilo, Francis
	Leach, Daniel		Drake, John
	Norcross, Archibald		Gamslo, Carl
	Perkins, Benjamin		Hazel, Thomas
	Perkins, James		Hronias, Henry
	Perkins, John		Melville, Charles
	Perkinson, James		Rogers, Edward
	Pike, Jeremiah		Seawell, George
	Robinson, Thomas		Sturges, John
	Russell, Moses		Swier, Louis
	Spenny, Nathaniel		Syder, John
	Stone, Robert		White, William
	Tarlton, George		
	Thomas, Elisha	Price	Stinchcombe, George
	Whittington, George		
	Wyatt, Jesse	Print of Boston	Brooks, Edward
			Chine, Samuel
Postsea	Abbot, William F.		Dolabar, John
prize to the Privateer Thrasher			Greaves, Samuel
	Bennet, William		Ireson, Robert B.
	Davidson, Thomas		Knight, George
	Davis, William		Knight, William
	Donaway, Daniel		Swett, Francis
	Elwell, Abraham		Symonds, Israel
	Far, William		
	Fowler, John	Prompt	Allen, John
	Galt, Robert		Atwood, Thomas
	Goday, W.		Bartis, John
	Gravelin, Jesse		Beecher, William P.
	Holm, Andre		Chase, Nathaniel
	Lorenden, George		Cole, William
	Lovelin, Abussha		Hubbard, Alfred
	Manuel, Josef		Lopans, William
	Miller, Henry		Thompson, Nathaniel
	Miller, Samuel		
	Parsons, George	Purse	Dussing, Caesar
	Plair, John		Latish, Joseph
	Prout, Henry		Turner, Samuel
	Purrington, John		

Ship	Name
Quebec of London *prize of the Privateer Paul Jones*	Adams, Leonard
	Beaty, James
	Bovey, Benjamin
	Chalk, John
	Johnson, Alexander
	Kimberly, Elisha
	Lane, John
	Lapham, Cushion
	Lockwood, Caleb
	Loggett, Gilbert
	Vanderhovan, John
	Vanderhovan, Mathew
	Vannog, John P.
	Very, Samuel
Rachael	Broden, Norman
	Doliber, Joseph
	George, William W.
	Homan, John
	Homan, Jonas
	Shirly, Pharos
Rachel & Ann	Funk, Samuel
Rambler	Atkinson, Charles
	Bryan, Timothy
	Dissmore, Abraham
	Fell, George
	Kemble, John
	Nichols, Henry
	Phillips, George
	Stevens, James
Rattlesnake	Adams, Abijah
	Arnold, James
	Averill, Samuel
	Buskell, William
	Groves, Thomas
	Littlefield, Samuel
	Robertson, Thomas
	Steele, Thomas
Raymond	Rose, Francis
Rebecca	Freeman, Asa
A recaptured British MV	Anderson, Henry
	Ingrain, John
	Istill, James
A recaptured British MV	Pool, Richard
	Stevenson, George
reef boat	Palmer, George H.
Regulator	Hussey, Thomas
	Warren, James
Renown (a whaler)	Bernard, Zacharias
	Brightman, Isaac
Requin	Bartlett, Scipio
	Caldwell, Charles
	Crosus, Richard
	Finn, John
	Green, John
	Griffin, John
	Haley, John
	Henry, William
	Tucker, Henry
	Williams, George
Resolution	Burch, James
	Chapell, William
	Johnston, Edward
	Jordan, David
Revenge	Brackett, John
	Johnson, Thomas
	Melcher, John
Rhode & Betsey	Knapp, Walker
Richmond	Clark, Alexander
	Preston, William
Rising	Evans, Thomas
	Smith, Thomas
	Yenno, William
Rising Stars	Collier, Thomas
	Stephens, Henry
	Stewart, William
Rising States	Gall, William
	Murray, Nathaniel
	Page, John
	Richards, George
	Welch, William

Rising Sun	Dowling, Anthony	Salley	Burk, John
	Osborne, Peter		
		Sally	Boston, John
Roberson	Case, Barns		Chapman, Josiah F.
	Fisher, Francis		Hall, Spencer
			Milborne, William
Rolla	Adams, Henry		Rust, John
	Chaplin, Thomas		Smith, William B.
	Dooley, James		
	Spick, John	Sampson	Coffin, James
	Wherry, Daniel		Leonard, Robert
			Manley, Randolph
Rose	Bennett, Robert		Spencer, John
	Wiggins, Samuel		Thornton, David
			Tucker, Nathaniel
Rossie	Barber, John		Vincent, Henry
	Bayman, James		
	Berry, Joseph	Saragossa	Reed, Thomas
	Boyd, John		Robins, John
	Brady, James		
	Chambers, Joseph	Savannah	Anderson, John
	Combs, Thomas		
	Copasses, Matthew	Sea Nymph	Allen, Edward
	Douglas, Charles		Downing, Henry
	Duhard, Thomas		Lyon, Ezekiel
	Eaton, John		Nicholson, Thomas
	Ellis, William		Smith, John
	Ford, M. Benjamin		Taylor, Godfrey
	Hall, Thomas		Welch, Samuel
	Hill, Pompey		
	Hill, William	Sidney	Owen, John
	Hobdyke, John		
	Howard, Henry	Sister	Bates, Josiah
	Hurt, Samuel		Strayer, George L.
	Jones, Cabel		
	Lamon, James	Snap Dragon	Burne, John
	Lee, Samuel		
	Longwheel, Amos	Spencer	Pedersen, John
	Mitchell, Francis		
	Oberville, Michael	Squirrel	Gregory, George
	Pearce, Emanuel		
	Powell, Elijah	Stark (General Stark)	Giles, John
	Simonds, Joseph		Mason, Daniel
	Stevenson, Thaddeus		Osborn, Stephen
	Thompson, John		Tinkham, John
	Vorge, James		
	Williams, Benjamin	Stephen	Bailey, Joseph
			Benny, Mallock
Rowe of Liverpool	Sherman, Riley		Dickson, Richard
prize of the Privateer Bone			

Ship	Name
Stephen	Gardner, Anthony
	Graham, George
	Harris, William
	Porgan, Theodore
	Quaan, George
	Robinson, James
Suwarrow	Barber, Henry
	Hoyt, James M.
	Smith, John
Swift of Hull	Prentiss, James
Sword Fish	Allen, Henry
	Anderton, Samuel
	Anderton, Thomas
	Asten, John
	Badsse, Philip
	Bagley, Moses
	Bartlett, George B.
	Bessom, Nicholas
	Bisbee, Asaph
	Black, John
	Blake, Charles
	Booder, Jacob
	Bray, Zacharias
	Brimmer, John
	Carney, Thomas
	Carrel, Michael
	Cloutman, George
	Cloutman, Robert
	Cox, Daniel
	Dalliber, James
	Deistel, John
	Dixey, Peter
	Doevall, Francis
	Dudley, Ephraim
	Ellwell, Jonathan
	Evans, John
	Fernandes, Anthony
	Francis, Frederick
	Grant, Christian
	Green, Henry
	Griffin, Samuel
	Gudlers, George
	Hamson, Henry
	Huff, Charles
	Ingalls, Samuel
	Innis, John
Sword Fish	Jeremy, Stephen
	Johnson, Andrew
	Kenny, George
	Kerhow, Samuel
	Kile, George
	Lambert, John
	Landback, Rich
	Lawrence, Peter
	Lear, Alexander
	Lee, Richard
	Manning, Enoch
	Manson, James
	Merriday, John
	Middleton, Reuben
	Mills, Henry
	Morrow, Joseph
	Noonan, William
	Nowland, Andrew
	Parsons, Andrew
	Parsons, Thomas
	Paulfrey, Richard
	Reed, H. W.
	Richardson, Perry
	Roberts, George
	Rogers, James
	Roper, John
	Saunders, Thomas
	Setchell, Samuel
	Shed, William
	Sheppard, Joseph
	Shot, John
	Small, Thomas
	Stephens, David
	Stephens, Trey
	Strong, William
	Wells, Moses
	Whitchouse, Lewis
	White, Benjamin
	White, John W.
	Williams, John
	Winslow, William
	Wood, George
	Woods, Charles
	Woods, William
	York, Nathaniel
Teazer	Bassett, William
	Cosse, Francis D.
	Fortune, John

Teazer	Merrish, Joseph	Thomas	Pittman, Henry
	Mitchell, John		Safford, Roger
	Moffett, Hugh		Sergeant, William
	Piles, John		Smith, Henry
	Samerton, George		Thompson, Thomas
	Sawyer, James		Todd, Samuel
	Stoddard, Conrad		Tripper, Robert
	Webber, Stephen		White, William
	Wilson, John		Williams, Joseph
			Woods, Jeremiah
Theresa	Waterhouse, Moses		Yeaton, Charles
			Young, John
Thomas	Bailey, Daniel		
	Bailey, Peter	Thorn	Archer, James
	Bell, Richard		Burgess, Francis
	Billings, Richard		Forester, Joseph
	Bodkin, William		Gross, James
	Booth, Joseph		Hammon, John
	Brown, Samuel		Hammon, William
	Card, Thomas		Holden, John
	Cooper, William		Parker, Robert
	Cotton, Edward		Quince, Peter
	Cross, Ephraim		Saunders, Richard
	Davis, William		Webster, David
	Diamond, George		
	Driscol, Jeremiah	Three Brothers	Howland, William
	Fadden, Charles		Jacobson, Jacob
	Harbrook, Richard		Rippaviere, John
	Holbrook, Robert		
	Holmes, Elisha	Tickler of Nantes	Hudson, Peter
	Hull, Thomas		Thomas, Charles
	Jennings, Luther		
	Johnson, Thomas	Tiger	Bartholf, Nicholas
	Jones, James		Byer, Peter
	Knight, Daniel		Cadwell, Samuel
	Lake, George		Calder, John H.
	Langford, Samuel		Churchill, Henry
	Lawson, Thomas		Hill, Ephraim
	Lowe, George		Hill, Josiah
	Mallard, James		Jones, James
	Marble, Samuel		Kershon, Abraham
	Marshall, John		Ludlow, Reuben
	McGill, Robert		Mars, George
	McIntire, Petty		Morris, James
	Norton, Josiah		Mossland, Reuben
	Penn, William		Nicholas, John
	Perkins, John		Quackenbush, William
	Pettigrew, William		Sampson, Jacob
	Peverly, Richard		Small, George D.

Unit/Ship	Names	Unit/Ship	Names
Tiger	Spencer, Leonard Sutton, John Waterman, John Westerbest, William	U.S. Light Dragoons	Childers, Joshua Dandridge, Richard Dodson, Thomas Drummond, John Henry, George
Tom Thumb	Arnold, William Blazon, Stephen Cooper, Alfred Mitchell, James M. Moore, Benjamin Morris, George Palmer, Peter Rosignol, James Scofield, Wells Veney, George		Moon, Joseph Murphy, George Perkins, Rufus Slaughter, George Tomlinson, John Trank, Abraham Welch, Henry Wheelock, Abel Whitton, John
		U.S. Schooner Growler	Buell, Jeremiah Christie, John Mallet, William Thornning, Thomas
Trim	Carso, John Freeman, John Hale, Robert Richardson, Randolph Rogers, James	U.S. Schooner Julia	Clawson, Henry Harvey, Peter Smith, John Watson, David
True Blooded Yankee	Cornille, Jacques Hamilton, Richard LeBaron, Peter Mayo, Nathaniel Rogers, Samuel Story, William	U.S.R.M. Cutter James Madison	Alley, Jacob Anderson, Andrew Anderson, Oliver
U.S. Artillery	Cook, William Forrester, Arthur Fullerton, John Linnard, Alfred McDowell, Andrew Scriver, Richard		Baker, Henry Blankenship, Charles Carebo, Henry Chase, Samuel Clements, Henry Coleman, Daniel Dagman, Caleb
U.S. Heavy Artillery	House, Frederick		Davis, Nathan Drinkwater, Andrew
U.S. Light Artillery	Clayton, Thomas Dole, Anthony Eagan, John Hearins, Patrick Mackenwick, George Newland, Thomas L. Norris, George Shields, Mathew		Ellis, John Even, Peter Gale, Oliver Gard, Gelab Gasseyr, Zepher Gebers, Henry George, Thomas Harding, Joseph Harris, William
U.S. Light Dragoons	Bird, Benjamin E. Cashinan, William		Helman, John Henricks, Jeremiah

Ship/Regiment	Prisoners	Ship/Regiment	Prisoners
U.S.R.M. Cutter James Madison	Hughes, Peter	Union	Hill, William
	Hutchins, William		Irwin, Magnus
	James, John		Johnston, Samuel
	Johnson, Andrew		Johnstone, William
	Martin, Jonathan		Jones, John
	Mumery, James		Kirby, Benjamin
	Nuting, Charles		Knight, Isaac D.
	Osborne, Thomas		Lownsburg, Carpenter
	Paline, William		Mason, Francis
	Pault, Beloner		McDonald, John
	Petterson, John		McElroy, William
	Pettingale, John		Mercer, Chaumont
	Senholm, Jacob		Mesniers, Benjamin
	Smith, Henry		Morris, John
	Stone, John		Morris, Thomas
	Tagle, Amos		Parker, David
	Tristram, Joseph		Randale, Frederick
	Tufts, Eleazer		Reeves, Joseph
	Turner, John		Robinson, David
	Williams, Gaspar		Schyder, Jacob Knapp
	Willson, William		Seabold, John
	Withers, Edward		Slaiter, John
			Sparks, Henry
			Stone, William
U.S.R.M. Cutter Surveyor	Berry, Samuel		Swanston, Jacob
	Bowden, John		Thompson, William
	Cole, Zachariah		Underwood, Benjamin
	Perkins, Nicholas		Webb, William
	Priest, William		Whitow, Miles
	Randolph, George		Williams, Peter
Ulysses	Birmingham, Thomas	Union American	Alexander, James
			Bovey, Jesse
Union	Allen, Jacob		Bray, George
	Armstrong, Nicholas		Irvin, John
	Carns, Richard		Rogers, William
	Clerk, Robert		Witney, Samuel
	Clover, Louis		
	Cooper, Thomas	Urbana	Alexander, John
	Crofts, William		Cook, Jacob
	Curtis, George		Laycock, Thomas
	Douglas, Thomas		Millican, William
	Elliott, Francis		Parsons, David
	Fairweather, Robert		Pickins, Benjamin
	Gilligan, William		Small, Joseph
	Godshall, John		
	Graham, William	Valentine	Crapon, George
	Harrison, John		Davis, Henry
	Hasem, John		Hellen, John P.

Valentine	Johnson, James	Volante	Didler, Henry
	Jones, Samuel B.		Dotto, Cornelius
	Lockwood, Benjamin		Dow, Henry
	Luther, Cromwell		Dupre, John
	Turner, Gardner		Jacob, Lewis
			James, George
Vengeance	Aulajo, Thomas		McLean, John
	Bevers, Clement		Morrell, Francis
	Bienent, Edward		Taylor, Thomas
	Bowen, Lewis		Thompson, Michael
	Cochran, Stephen		Williams, Charles
	Couet, John		Willy, John
	Green, Horace		
	Law, John	Volunteer	Anderson, George
	Lynch, Joseph		Antonio, Francis
	Montgomery, William		Bushfield, James
	Robinson, Michael		Campbell, John
	Simpson, William		Caverena, Jose Maria
	Smith, Chester		Chase, John
	Taylor, John		Coursis, Frederick
	Whitney, Joseph		Cusser, John Charles
			Doyle, John
Venus	Jones, John		Harms, John
	Wilson, William		Hunt, Samuel
			Hunter, John
Viper	Tamblen, John		Johnson, Peter
			Jones, William
Vivid	Abbott, Daniel		Jupiter, James
	Avory, John		Kennedy, Dennis
	Bateman, Michael		Kinot, Robert
	Collins, Sylvester		Lewis, Job
	Fields, Jacob		Marlow, Owen
	Higgins, John		Martini, Francis
	Howe, William		Morelly, Samuel
	Jacobs, William		Morgan, James
	Lambert, Ephraim		Scott, Henry
	Murray, David		Wadsworth, Daniel
	Nelson, Thomas		
	Snow, Daniel	Walker	Swain, David
	Tolpie, Jonathan		
	Truman, Isaac	Warren	Hazard, Thomas
			Jane, Joseph
Volante	Alston, Richard		Manuel, Joseph
	Anthony, John		
	Bailey, Isaac	Washington	Watkins, Fredrick
	Bean, John		
	Boyle, Joseph	Wasp	Bridges, John
	Brown, Thomas		Cooper, Edward
	Conley, Cornelius		Edmond, John

Ship/Regiment	Prisoner	Ship/Regiment	Prisoner
Wasp	Green, John	Wiley Reynard	Lane, William
	Haddart, Robert		Lindsey, William
	Mansfield, Elijah		McKinnon, John
	McKenzie, John		Perry, Daniel
	Pratt, Philip		Ringman, Charles
	Preston, John		Tois, Manuel
	Richardson, James		Wilson, Hezekiel
	Robinson, John		Wood, Joseph
	Smith, Elisha		
	Spouding, Joseph	William	Barry, John
	Thrasher, John		Chidsey, Abraham
	Towe, Seth		Cooper, James
	Weare, Ebenezer		Dennis, Thomas
	Wilson, John		Gibson, William
			Kenner, John Downing
Watson	Hill, Jeremiah		Metrash, Ezekiel
prize of the Privateer True Blooded Yankee			Peters, John
			Powers, William
Watts	Delosia, Samuel		Smith, Thomas R.
Weasel	Ashfield, Henry	William Bayard	Hall, James
	Bailey, John		Harrens, William
	Blackman, Moses		Jones, Benjamin
	Brill, John		
	Cappel, John	William Penn	Swain, Obadiah
	Carter, John		
	Dunn, David	William Rathbourn	Cole, Stephen
	Fohis, James	prize of the Privateer Jack	
	Gibbs, Daniel		
	Hull, Edward	Wolf Cove	Alexander, Richard
	King, John		Andrews, Joseph
	Lemmon, Henry		Carnes, John
	Tiffs, Joseph		Chivers, Joseph
	Vangorbet, Cato		Clough, Isaac
			Cloutman, Robert
White Oak	Caley, Henry		Eaton, Joseph
	Fernald, Tobias		Fippen, John
	Stanley, Peter		Grant, William
			Knapp, Samuel
Wiley Reynard	Boyer, John		Lyons, Charles
	Brisk, John		Pearce, David
	Brown, Joseph		Pollet, William
	Butler, Henry		Quiner, Stephen
	Carlos, John		Simonds, Proctor
	Coston, Thomas		Stacey, Benjamin
	Hall, Perry		Stacey, Samuel
	Holden, Nathaniel		
	Jackson, John	Xenophon	Stockley, W. D.
	Jones, John		
	Kirkpatrick, William	Yankee	Allen, Edward D.

354   American Prisoners of War Held at Chatham During the War of 1812

Ship	Prisoners
Yankee	Atwood, John
	Bissun, Thomas
	Black, Ruddick
	Boswell, Samuel
	Bowen, Sylvester
	Briggs, Frank
	Dennison, Nathaniel
	Devol, Alexander
	Dunningberg, Henry
	Elburn, John
	Forstman, John
	Hall, John
	Hall, Sylvester
	Hathaway, Philip
	Hicks, Ogershill
	Lambert, Calvin
	Luce, Charles
	Mason, Aaron
	Molton, Nathaniel
	Munroe, Henry
	Payne, Walter
	Pitts, George
	Porter, Louis
	Rogers, Piley
	Shade, Joseph
	Sinnett, William
	Turner, James
	Wood, Benjamin
York	Hammond, Stephen
	Mason, Richard
	Piers, Nathaniel
	Soley, Nathaniel
	Thomas, John
	Whitman, Joseph
Yorktown	Anderson, Goodman
	Baisley, Abraham
	Berry, William
	Black, Philip
	Blake, Charles
	Brown, Charles
	Brush, Abel
	Bump, Henry
	Cameron, Daniel
	Crosby, Andrew
	Davis, James
	Davis, John
	Eddy, Richard
Yorktown	Evert, John
	Fray, James
	Gilbert, Isaac
	Goodman, James
	Goulding, Samuel
	Hamilton, G. W.
	Handy, Levi
	Jessamine, John
	Johnson, Charles
	Killerman, Maxwell
	Lewis, William
	Mackey, John
	Mitchell, William
	Mott, Thomas
	Oliver, Anthony
	Phillips, Edward
	Puffer, John
	Purnal, Elisha
	Rodgers, William
	Selby, Hans
	Storm, Daniel
	Vanrant, John
	White, Edward
	Williams, Noble
	Wilson, James
	Zelluck, Thomas
Zephyr prize of Privateer Rattlesnake	Harris, Simon
	Keen, Joseph
	Modre, John
	Plumber, William Reed
	Walker, Seth
	Williamson, David
Unknown	Abbott, Samuel
	Abraham, Joseph
	Adams, Robert
	Adams, Thomas
	Adams, William
	Adivoe, Henry
	Albert, John
	Albro, George
	Aldor, Robert
	Alexander, George
	Alexander, Robert
	Allen, E. T.
	Allen, Isaac
	Allen, John
	Allen, John D.

Prisoner listing by ship or regiment 355

Unknown

Allen, William
Amos, Isaac
Anan, John
Anderson, James
Anderson, Joseph
Anderson, Robert
Andrews, John (1)
Andrews, John (2)
Angel, Sylvester
Antoine, John
Armstrong, Elijah
Armstrong, Thomas
Arnold, James
Atkinson, John
Atwood, Edward
Augustus, Benjamin
Austin, James
Austin, Jonathan
Austin, William
Avery, Charles
Awker, Edward
Ayres, William
Babb, Benjamin
Backman, Charles
Bailey, John
Bailey, William
Baker, Daniel
Baker, Robert
Bale, Charles
Baley, J. K.
Ball, John
Ballard, John
Bane, Charles
Banta, John
Bardoe, John
Bark, David
Barnard, John
Barnett, John
Barnsall, Lewis
Barrett, George
Barrett, James
Barry, Peter
Basset, Edward S.
Bates, Joseph
Baxter, Franklin
Bean, Amos
Bean, William
Beck, William
Beckwith, James

Unknown

Bell, Robert L.
Bendionan, Vincent
Benjamin, Joseph
Bennet, John
Bennyman, John
Benson, George
Benson, Jonas
Bergen, Leven
Berry, George
Best, John
Billings, Thomas
Bircham, Joseph
Bird, James
Black, William
Blake, William
Bliss, Frederick
Blumbhouser, Samuel
Bocatt, John
Boger, James
Boillet, John
Bond, Samuel
Booth, Thomas
Bordage, Raymond
Bordley, George
Bounty, Charles
Bourns, Solomon
Bowens, George
Boyd, John
Boyd, Peter
Boyle, James
Bradie, John
Brainard, Richard
Branch, Anthony
Branton, Samuel
Brenton, York
Briant, Moses
Brice, John
Brickell, William
Brightman, Joseph
Brimhall, Cornelius
Brooks, John
Broughton, John
Brown, Abijah
Brown, Abraham
Brown, David
Brown, Elisha
Brown, Francis
Brown, George
Brown, Isaac

Unknown

Brown, Jacob
Brown, James
Brown, John
Brown, Joseph
Brown, Mark
Brown, Michael
Brown, Reuben
Brown, Samuel
Brown, Sawyer
Brown, Thomas
Brown, William
Buddington, Asa
Buffington, James
Bugs, Abram
Bumpus, Asa
Burdock, Enos
Burrell, Angelo
Burham, Benjamin
Burk, William
Burke, John
Burlugh, Henry
Burnham, David
Burnham, John
Burrell, Rial
Burton, William
Bussey, Charles
Butcher, James
Butler, George
Butler, John
Butler, Thomas
Butler, William
Butts, Joseph W.
Cadwell, Abraham
Caen, John
Cain, Enoch
Callanan, John
Caleb, Lewis
Campbell, James
Campbell, John
Campbell, Nicholas
Canada, James
Canada, William
Cannon, Thomas
Cannon, William
Carban, Thomas
Card, Israel
Carlton, William N.
Carman, James
Carney, William

Unknown

Caroline, Tobias
Carpenter, William
Carr, Joseph
Carr, Richard
Carter, Ebenezer
Caesar, James
Chandler, Ezekiel
Chapley, John
Charles, Thomas
Chase, Joseph
Chase, Oliver
Chasses, Jacob
Chivers, Cantab
Chonard, Jack
Christian, Tyrel
Chult, David
Church, Benjamin
Church, Ezekiel
Church, Jeremiah
Church, Richard
Clark, Elisha
Clark, John
Clark, Samuel
Clarke, Arnold
Clarke, William
Claw, Morris
Clawson, John
Clay, John
Clements, William
Clifford, S. L.
Codding, Caleb
Cody, James
Coffin, Charles
Coffin, Joseph
Cole, Peter
Coleman, John
Coleman, Jonathan
Collier, Thomas
Collins, George
Colquhoun, William
Connelly, James
Conklin, Smith
Conner, Jesse
Connor, John
Connoway, James
Conway, Andrew
Conway, James
Conway, Samuel
Cook, Isaac

Unknown	Cook, John	Unknown	Deverter, William
	Coon, John		Dews, William
	Cooper, James		Dibble, Zachariah
	Cooper, Thomas		Dieson, Abraham
	Cooper, William		Dildure, Samuel
	Copland, Thomas		Dixon, Peter
	Corban, Daniel		Douglass, John
	Corvet, Isaac		Dowling, Peter
	Cotterill, Henry		Drayton, John
	Cotterill, James		Duncan, Edward
	Courtis, Thomas		Duncan, George
	Covelle, Ephraim		Dunham, Joseph
	Cowen, William		Dunn, James
	Cox, Abraham		Dunstan, John
	Craig, James		Eaton, James
	Crawford, James		Edgerly, William
	Cromwell, Glacio		Edwards, Isaac
	Crow, John		Edwards, John
	Crowell, Uriel		Edwards, Price
	Cuff, Charles		Edwards, Thomas
	Cullett, William		Eldridge, Nicholas
	Cummings, Edward		Elisha, Thomas
	Cunning, James		Elliott, Robert
	Cunningham, John		Ellis, Cornelius
	Curtis, Enoch		Elvyn, Laurence
	Cushman, Orson		Ely, Abraham
	Cutler, Thomas		Emlin, Edward
	Daggett, Hansel		Emming, Thomas
	Dairs, William		Endersen, James
	Dalton, Joseph		Erskine, George
	Darren, Duncan		Estey, William
	Darrow, Aaron		Evans, Hezekiel
	Davies, John		Evans, James
	Davis, Andrew		Evans, John
	Davis, Daniel		Fargo, Elijah
	Davis, George		Farmer, Joseph
	Davis, James		Farrell, Andrew
	Davis, Nicholas		Fell, William
	Davis, Osborn		Felt, John
	Davis, Samuel		Ferley, John
	Dawson, John		Fernald, John
	Day, Thomas		Ferriere, George
	de Colville, Laurence		Ferris, Jacob
	de Park, John		Ferris, James
	Dean, Samuel		Fethien, Thomas
	Delaney, Mathew		Fields, Alexander
	Denham, William		Filch, Jonathan
	Dennis, Thomas		Fingersen, John F.
	Dennison, Laurence		Fiske, Cyrus

Unknown

Fitch, John
Fitzpatrick, John
Flood, John
Floyd, James
Fogerty, Archibald
Fogg, Noel
Fogust, Able
Folger, Frederick
Forbes, Robert
Forrest, James
Forrest, William
Forsyth, Alexander
Fosset, Robert
Foster, Joseph
Foster, Thomas
Fowler, Joshua
Francis, John
Francis, Prince
Franklin, William
Frazier, John
Frazier, William
Fredericks, John
Freeborn, John
Freeman, Prince
Fry, Thomas
Gale, Sam
Gammell, Samuel
Gardener, Jerry
Gardner, George
Gardner, James
Gardner, Peter
Garrison, Christian
Gaskin, William
Geline, John
George, William Main
Gibbs, James
Gibbs, Perry
Gibbs, Valentine
Gibson, Samuel
Gilbert, Thomas
Gilles, St. Clair
Gilpin, John
Glover, Benjamin
Glower, Samuel
Golding, Abijah
Golever, William
Gordon, James
Gordon, John
Gordon, William

Unknown

Gorton, John
Goswick, William
Gould, Henry
Gould, Nicholas
Gourley, William
Gran, Abraham
Graves, John
Graves, Thomas
Gray, Charles
Gray, John
Gray, Thomas
Green, George
Green, John
Green, Thomas
Grendy, Edward
Grey, James
Grey, William
Griffen, John
Grush, Joseph
Guire, Andrew
Gunnell, William
Gyer, Henry
Hall, Charles
Hall, George
Hall, Henry
Hall, James
Hall, John
Hall, Richard
Hall, William
Halbrook, D.
Hamlet, John
Hammond, Isaac
Handley, Thomas
Harris, James
Harris, John
Harris, William
Harrison, Henry
Hart, Marquis
Hartford, James
Harvey, John
Harvey, Peter
Harway, Samuel
Harwill, William
Haskins, John
Hatch, Walter
Haushaw, George
Hawkins, John
Hawley, Frederick
Haywood, John

Unknown	Hazard, Robert	Unknown	Jackson, Isaac
	Hazard, Thomas		Jackson, John
	Heady, Linsey		Jackson, Sidney
	Heater, William		Jackson, Thomas
	Heaton, Henry		Jackson, William
	Hebius, Jeremiah		Jacobs, George
	Hedley, John		James, Isaac
	Hemp, James		James, John
	Henney, Peter		James, Sacket
	Henwood, Eliza		Jameson, George
	Heyden, William		Jardine, Samuel
	Heywood, John		Jarvis, George
	Hicks, James		Jeffreys, Philip
	Hill, James		Jennings, John
	Hill, Timothy		Jeurnuseu, John
	Hinkle, Henry		Jewett, Jasper
	Hinton, John		Jilson, Samuel
	Hitchcock, Edward		Johnson, Easton
	Hitchcock, Moses		Johnson, Edward
	Hoffman, Joseph		Johnson, Frederick
	Hogan, William		Johnson, George
	Holms, John		Johnson, Henry
	Homes, Thomas		Johnson, John
	Hooseman, John		Johnson, Joseph
	Hopkins, Samuel		Johnson, Mathew
	Horsefall, William		Johnson, Oliver
	House, Snow		Johnson, Richard
	Howell, John		Johnson, Samuel
	Howland, William		Johnson, Samuel B.
	Hoyt, Robert		Johnson, Stephen
	Hubart, Joseph		Johnson, Thomas
	Hubbard, Christian		Johnson, William
	Hubbard, George		Johnston, Henry
	Hubbard, John G.		Jonathan, Jonathan
	Hubbard, William		Jones, Anthony
	Hudson, William		Jones, Charles
	Hughes, John		Jones, David
	Hunn, John		Jones, Henry
	Hunt, David		Jones, Isaac
	Hunter, Isaac		Jones, James
	Hurd, Abel		Jones, Peter
	Hurstley, Charles		Jones, Samuel
	Hutchinson, Thomas		Jones, Theodore
	Hutchinson, Townsend		Jones, Thomas
	Hutson, John		Jones, William
	Ingersen, James B.		Jordan, Artemas
	Irwin, Andrew		Kay, James
	Jackson, Allison		Kellam, John
	Jackson, Daniel		Kellum, Smith

Unknown

Kelly, John
Kemble, Samuel
Kennedy, William
Kent, James
Kerry, Isaac
King, Peter
Kingley, Benjamin
Knight, Zachariah
Kylor, John
Lake, Noah
Lamboard, Thomas
Lanigan, Daniel
Lane, William
Langroth, Francis
Larey, Henry
Larkins, Thomas
Latham, John
Lawrence, Robert
Laws, Peter
Ledlowe, John
Lee, Edward
Lee, John
Lee, Joseph
Leighton, Otis
Leion, Alexander
Lenderson, Henry
Lent, Joseph
Leonard, John
Levan, Thomas
Lewis, Francis
Lewis, John
Lewis, Solomon
Lewis, Thomas
Liddle, Morris
Lilsle, Richard
Lindsey, Samuel
Lissel, Joseph
Lister, Louis
Litchfield, Enoch
Little, Thomas
Locker, Michael
Lomondy, Joseph
Lothrop, James
Lotton, John
Lovell, William
Lowdie, Samuel
Lowe, Thomas
Lucas, Martin
Lynch, Elias

Unknown

Lynch, Thomas
Macceaming, James
Mack, John
Mackensey, John
Mackey, James
Macure, Angelo
Madden, Peter
Magrath, James
Mains, John
Makeniney, George
Marlborough, Francis
Malis, John
Mallan, James
Mallison, Jacob
Malvern, Lanis
Manion, John
Manning, George
Marcel, James
Marks, Peter
Marshall, Benjamin
Marshall, Francis
Marshall, Levi
Martin, Henry
Martin, John J.
Marvell, David
Mason, John
Mathews, John
Maybank, John
McAlpin, Cornelius
McBride, James
McCormack, William
McCumbers, Job
McDonald, John
McFee, John
McGee, Robert
McGinnis, B. S.
McInley, James
McIver, John
McWarren, Nathaniel
Mead, James
Meath, Solomon
Meeker, James
Melvin, John
Merkell, John
Merle, John
Merrel, Enoch
Meyers, James
Middleton, John
Miller, Jeremiah

Unknown

Miller, John
Mills, John
Mills, Samuel
Minor, David
Minor, Pedro
Mitch, Thomas
Mitchell, Thomas
Moaton, Bryant
Molloy, Peter
Monroe, James
Monroe, William
Moore, Abraham
Moore, Henry
Moore, James
Moore, John
Morell, John
Morgan, James
Morris, Louis
Morris, Samuel
Morris, William
Morrison, John
Morrison, William
Moses, James
Moulden, William
Muckleroy, Samuel
Muller, William
Munro, John
Murray, James
Murray, Peter
Mutch, James
Nald, John
Neal, John
Nellim, George
Nelson, Richard
Newell, Paul
Newman, Henry
Nicholas, Henry
Nichols, John
Nicholson, Charles
Nicholson, Jesse
Nicolls, Herold
Nicolson, Benjamin
Nixon, Charles
Noble, Charles
Noble, Daniel
Noble, Isaac
Nolton, John
Norcross, Abel
Northey, Joseph

Unknown

Nunns, William
Nye, William
Oilson, Andrew
Orne, W. B.
Orr, Levi
Osborne, Lewis
Osgood, David
Otis, Ezekiel
Owen, Burden
Owens, Eugene
Packard, William
Pain, James
Paine, R. B.
Palmer, William
Pardell, Charles
Paris, Peter
Parish, Samuel
Parker, George
Parsons, Ignatius
Patrick, John
Patterson, John
Patterson, Peter
Patterson, William
Patton, Robert
Paul, Jonathan
Payne, Ransom
Peadon, William
Peak, John W.
Pearson, Benjamin
Peirce, Edward
Pendergrass, Morris
Pendleton, Asa
Penfield, John
Penny, Richard
Penrose, Abraham
Perham, Ezekiel
Perkins, Henry
Perkins, William
Perry, John
Perry, Samuel
Perry, William
Peters, John
Peters, Thomas
Peters, William
Peterson, John
Peterson, M.
Peterson, Peter
Peverley, Henry
Philbrook, Bartholomew

Unknown		Unknown	
	Phillips, Benjamin		Renelds, Amos
	Phillips, John		Rennell, States William
	Phillips, William		Reynolds, Stephen
	Pierce, Thomas		Rice, John
	Pierce, William		Rich, Elisha
	Piles, James		Rich, William
	Pinkham, Allen		Richards, Edward
	Pinne, John		Richards, Henry
	Pitt, William		Richards, James
	Ploughman, Joseph		Richardson, Allen
	Pool, John		Richardson, James
	Poole, John		Richardson, John
	Pope, William		Richardson, Robert
	Porter, Ephraim		Richardson, Samuel
	Porter, Gideon		Riley, William
	Porter, Josiah		Roach, Reuben
	Porter, Samuel		Roberts, David
	Porter, Stephen		Roberts, James
	Potter, Jacob		Roberts, Robert
	Potter, John		Roberts, William
	Pousland, William		Robinet, Samuel
	Powell, Joseph		Robins, Thomas
	Price, Carlton		Robinson, Benjamin
	Prince, Jeffry		Robinson, Edward
	Prince, William		Robinson, Henry
	Putnam, Allen		Robinson, James
	Quarterman, William		Robinson, John
	Queen, Daniel		Robinson, William
	Quenichet, Joseph		Roffe, Isaac
	Quinton, James		Rogers, Edward
	Raddick, Ebenezer		Rogers, John
	Rainy, Thomas		Rollo, William
	Ramady, James		Rose, William
	Randall, Forest		Rosell, John
	Rankins, William		Ross, Benjamin T.
	Ranlot, John		Ross, George
	Ray, Charles		Ross, John
	Ray, Christian		Rowe, John
	Raymond, George		Rowe, Richard
	Rea, William J.		Rowe, Simon
	Read, Hugh		Roweth, William
	Read, William		Runlet, Ebenezer
	Reans, John		Russell, Joseph
	Rectout, John J.		Russell, M.
	Redman, David		Russell, Samuel
	Reed, James		Ryan, Thomas
	Reid, John		Sanford, James
	Reid, Joseph		Sankey, Caesar
	Reid, William		Sanssuillon, John

Unknown

Saul, Francis
Saunders, Charles
Saunders, Peter
Saunders, Thomas
Saunders, William
Saunderson, William
Sawyer, Jacob
Scanck, William
Schuetzer, Peter
Scott, Abraham
Scott, Anthony
Scott, Ezekiel
Scott, James
Scott, John
Scott, Samuel
Scott, William
Scribner, William
Self, Thomas M.
Seyman, Paul
Shechford, John
Sheppard, James
Sheridan, Henry
Sherriff, Benjamin P.
Shillings, Morris
Shipley, Charles
Shroudy, William
Sidebottom, John
Sieway, Peter
Sillock, Amos
Silsby, Nathaniel
Simmik, John
Simmons, Daniel
Simmons, William
Simpson, John
Simpson, William
Sims, Clement
Sims, Oliver
Sims, William
Simson, Smith
Sinclair, Solomon
Slebar, Samuel
Sloane, William
Sluckley, Richard
Smith, Caesar
Smith, Henry
Smith, James
Smith, John
Smith, Noble
Smith, Paul

Unknown

Smith, Peter
Smith, Thomas
Smith, William
Smith, William Pitt
Snow, Collyer
Southwich, James
Sparrow, John
Sparrow, Joseph
Spear, Joseph
Spice, Alexander
Spratt, Thomas
Sprismo, John
Squires, Prince
Stacy, Perry
Staggs, Henry
Stanton, James
Stanwood, Timothy
Starbourg, W. G.
Starkweather, James
Stevens, John
Stevens, William
Stevenson, Levi
Steward, John
Stibbens, Thomas
Stilwell, William
Stiver, David
Stockhouse, Charles
Stolsenberg, Manuel
Stone, Henry
Stone, Isaac
Stow, Jeremiah
Strand, Peter
Strordvant, David
Sultan, John
Sutton, John
Sutton, Prince
Taggart, John
Thayer, Ebenezer
Tarr, James
Taylor, James
Taylor, Joseph
Taylor, William
Tellebrown, William
Telley, Edward
Thaley, Abraham
Thayer, James
Thimonier, Peter
Thomas, Charles
Thomas, Francis

Unknown	Thomas, Henry	Unknown	Waterhouse, Joseph
	Thomas, James		Waterman, Thomas
	Thomas, John		Waters, Philip
	Thomas, John (1)		Watkins, George
	Thomas, John (2)		Watson, Daniel
	Thomas, John L.		Watson, Stephen
	Thomas, Moses		Watson, William
	Thomas, Terry		Webster, William
	Thomas, Thomas		Wedmore, Charles
	Thomas, William		Weeks, Lewis
	Thomodice, John		Weisser, Philip
	Thompson, George		Welch, John
	Thompson, James		Welsh, Richard H.
	Thompson, Joseph		Welsh, William
	Thompson, Robert		Werner, John
	Thompson, William		Wessels, William
	Tink, Henry		West, George
	Tippet, Joseph		West, Nathaniel
	Tombinson, George W.		Wetou, William
	Toole, Gannet		Wheebell, Robert
	Townsend, Milby		White, Charles
	Traphagan, Peter		White, Henry
	Trask, William		White, James
	Travers, Thomas		White, John W.
	Tremus, Fit		White, Robert
	Turnbull, James		White, William
	Turner, Samuel		White, William (1)
	Turner, William		White, William (2)
	Twycross, Samuel		Whitmore, John
	Tyler, Lewis		Whittlebank, Edward
	Urey, Peter		Wickham, Ezekiel
	Vail, Jeremiah		Wickham, Thaddeus
	Valentine, John		Wicks, James
	Vanderwenter, John		Wickwall, Joseph
	Vincent, John		Wilcox, Ephraim
	Voight, Henry		Wilcox, William
	Voughon, Robert		Wiley, David
	Walden, James		Willett, John
	Walker, Benjamin		Williams, Abraham
	Walker, John		Williams, Benjamin
	Walker, William		Williams, Darius
	Wall, William		Williams, Edward
	Wallace, William		Williams, George
	Walling, James		Williams, James
	Ward, Alfred		Williams, John
	Warner, John		Williams, Joseph
	Warner, Thomas		Williams, Josiah
	Warren, John		Williams, Jotham
	Warwick, Robert		Williams, Richard

Unknown	Williams, Robert	Unknown	Colborne, John L.
	Williams, Thomas	*prize to the U.S. Frigate President*	
	Williams, William		Gardner, John
	Williamson, George J.		Limon, Andrew
	Williamson, John		Short, Samuel
	Willot, Robert		
	Willson, Henry	Unknown	Claby, Martin L.
	Willson, James	*taken off an English whaler*	Hill, John
	Wilson, Charles		Johnstone, Robert
	Wilson, Daniel		Kingbutton, John
	Wilson, Francis		Pinkham, Daniel
	Wilson, George		Porter, Charles
	Wilson, James		Robertson, William
	Wilson, John		Skinner, Ebenezer
	Wilson, Robert		Stables, James
	Wilson, Thomas		
	Wilson, William	Unknown	Allen, William
	Windford, Charles	*tender to the Privateer True Blooded Yankee*	
	Wingate, David		Baurs, Francis
	Wise, John		Boterol, John
	Wolfe, Andre		Briggs, Boileau
	Wood, Alexander		Brown, Seth
	Wood, William		Carter, Thomas
	Woods, Merrill		Christie, John
	Woods, William		Clark, Abraham D.
	Wooldridge, William		Cole, William
	Worthing, Isaac		Dennis, Thomas
	Wright, Edward		Follinsbe, William
	Wright, Isaac		Fuller, John
	Wright, John		Fyans, Joseph
	Wright, Samuel		Hardiman, John
	Wynn, John		Hearl, Hiram
	Yatton, James		Howater, Henry
	Young, Moses		Ingersoll, Abraham
	Young, Thomas		Lawson, James
	Younger, Lewis		Lawson, Lawrence
			Lumburger, Jacob
Unknown	Allison, William R.		Mathew, Lewis
prize to the Privateer Blockade			Miller, John
	Coffin, Abel		Moore, John
	Dayley, G. W.		Morris, Isaac
	Leach, Charles		
	Lovet, Robert	Unknown	Peckham, Hazard
	Narbone, Nicholas	*tender to the Privateer True Blooded Yankee*	
	Phillips, George W.		Richards, John
			Rogers, Francis
Unknown	Owen, Zachariah		Taylor, Peter
prize to the Privateer Hunter			White, John

Unknown
  tender to the Privateer True Blooded Yankee

Williams, John

Unknown MV

Wilson, Nathaniel

Definitions

Prisoner of War Terms

Barracks
A permanent structure for housing or quartering prisoners of war within a prison depot.

Cartel
A cartel is a military agreement between hostile powers, which regulates the conduct of warfare.

Cartel Ship
A vessel chartered to carry prisoners or impressed to carry prisoners taken by a vessel of war to the nearest port; also, formerly a vessel which carried proposals between belligerent powers. A chartered cartel must carry no arms, and is liable to seizure by the enemy if she attempts to trade.

Depot
Depot is a British term for a prisoner of war camp. Depots were actually forts, which contained up to seven prisons within their walls.

Goal
Goal is the British word for 'jail.'

Letter of Marque (or Letter of Marque and Reprisal)
A Letter of Marque is a license granted by a nation to a private citizen which permits that person to arm a ship and seize merchant vessels from an enemy nation.

Non-Combatants
Non-combatants were military surgeons, surgeons' mates, pursers, secretaries, chaplains and schoolmasters. All passengers on warships and merchant vessels were classified as non-combatants, which included women and girls, and all boys under the age of twelve.

Parole
Prisoners of war who were on parole status were given permission to return to their homes if they signed an agreement not to take up arms until they were exchanged. Enemy officers were granted another type parole in which they agreed not to escape and in turn they were permitted to walk freely around a town or a given area.

Parole Station
A village or city in which prisoners of war were housed.

Prison Ship
Prison ships were obsolete warships and transports, ranging in size from ships-of-the-line to frigates and cargo ships used to house prisoners of war and convicts.

Prisoner of War
Soldiers or sailors who had been captured by an enemy and confined until either exchanged or paroled.

Transport Board
His Majesty's Transport Board of the Royal Navy was responsible for transporting Royal Army regiments and their supplies throughout the British Empire. The board was also responsible for handling the prisoner of war facilities and the transportation of these prisoners.

Naval Terms

Armourer
An armourer repairs the ship's small arms.

Boatswain
A warrant officer who has charge of the work of the seamen, the general oversight of the cleanliness of the ship, and of the work pertaining to the boats, spars, rigging, etc., anchoring and the mooring and unmooring of the ship.

Boatswain's Mate
Assists the boatswain in his duties.

Boy
A male minor who is in naval training to become an officer. Also called a cabin boy, a powder monkey and ship's boy.

Brig
A brig is a two-mast vessel with square sails.

Captain
The highest commissioned officer rank in the U.S. Navy during the War of 1812. The captain's rank was above a master commandant.

Captain's Clerk
The commanding officer of a vessel of war was formerly allowed a civilian clerk who was frequently a male member of his own family.

Carpenter
A carpenter is responsible for maintenance of the ship's hull and masts.

Carpenter's Mate
Assists the carpenter in his duties.

Chaplain
A chaplain provides pastoral, spiritual and emotional support for the ship's personnel

Clerk – see Captain's Clerk

Commandant
The officer in command of a navy yard or station.

Commodore
A title in the U.S. Navy given by the Navy Secretary for certain commissioned officers who were in command of a naval base, a squadron or a flotilla. The rank of commodore would not be created in the navy until 1862.

Cook
A cook handles the preparation of food for the ship's personnel.

Coxswain
A coxswain is in charge of the crew of a small boat from a vessel of war.

Frigate
A three-mast sailing ship with square sails which had a gun deck. The number of guns varied from 28 to 44 and sometimes more guns. Guns were also placed on the spar deck.

Gunboat
A gunboat was the smallest warship in the U.S. Navy. They could be propelled by oars or sails, and were usually designed for coastal waters or the Great Lakes. Many gunboats carried only one or two guns on swivel mounts.

Gunner
A gunner was responsible for the care and maintenance of the ship's guns and gunpowder.

Gunner's Mate
Assists the gunner in his duties.

Landsman
A recruit with no sea experience.

Lieutenant
A commissioned officer who was below the rank of master commandant and above a warrant officer.

Marines
Naval soldiers who were used as guards aboard ships and provided musket support during naval battles. They also assisted in shore actions.

Master (Naval)
The master was the senior warrant officer on board a ship who was a qualified navigator and experienced seaman who set the sails, maintained the ship's log and advised the captain on the seaworthiness of the ship and crew.

Master (Merchant Vessel)
The commander of a merchant vessel was called a master. Other terms used were sea captain, captain and shipmaster.

Masters-at-Arms
Masters-at-Arms were in charge of keeping the swords, pistols, carbines and muskets in good working order.

Master Commandant
A commissioned officer's rank which was below a captain and above a lieutenant. The name of this rank was changed to 'commander' in 1838.

Mate
The assistant or subordinate of a warrant officer.

Merchant Vessel or Merchantman
A ship that transports cargo and/or passengers.

Midshipman
The lowest commissioned officer's rank in the U.S. Navy was a midshipman. The rank was below a lieutenant. This rank was abolished in 1845 and term was then used to describe cadets at the U.S. Naval Academy.

Privateer
An armed vessel, owned by private parties, licensed to prey on an enemy's commerce in time of war. In the War of 1812 a number of the merchant vessels of the United States, which were debarred from their usual trade, were fitted out as armed cruisers and created much havoc among British shipping.

Prize
A captured vessel or other property taken by a naval vessel in war. The circumstances of the capture and of the ownership of the property are taken under consideration by a court which awards the proportionate share of the money accruing from the sale of a prize. Provision is made by statute for distribution of prize money from the Treasury in cases of destruction of the vessels of an enemy.

Provincial Marine
A naval force operated by the Canadian provinces to man the warships on the Great Lakes, Lake Champlain and the St. Lawrence River. The naval force was established in 1778 and lasted until the Royal Navy absorbed the Provincial Marine in May 1813. It was also the main transport service for the government in western Upper Canada.

Purser
The financial officer responsible for supplies, provisions, and pay for the crew.

Sailmaker
A sailmaker makes and repairs the ship's sails.

Sailmaker's Mate
Assists the sailmaker in his duties.

Sailing Master – see Master
Another term for master.

Schoolmaster
Schoolmasters were involved in the education of boys, midshipmen and others aboard ship.

Schooner
A two-mast vessel with triangular sails before and after the mast is called a schooner.

Seamen
The lowest skilled enlisted rank in the navy.

Ship
A sailing vessel with three masts and rigged with square sails. A captain normally commanded a ship. The ship did not have a gun deck and it was rated between a frigate and a brig.

Sloop
A small vessel with one mast equipped with triangular sails before and after the mast.

Steward
A steward organizes the mess (meals) aboard ship working with the cook and the purser.

Store Ship
A vessel attached to a navy and used to transport supplies to distant naval depots.

Supercargo
A supercargo is a person employed on board a vessel by the owner of cargo carried on the ship. The duties of a supercargo include managing the cargo owner's trade, selling the merchandise in ports to which the vessel is sailing, and buying and receiving goods to be carried on the return voyage.

Surgeon

A surgeon was a warrant officer in charge of the medical department. On larger ships, the surgeon had one or more assistant surgeons, also called a surgeon's mate.

Warrant Officer

Warrant officers were ship officers who had a warrant and not a commission. Warrants were issued for a specific trade, that is, a purser, a carpenter, a sailmaker, etc. These men were not line officers and could not command a ship. However, masters (sailing masters) could and did command small vessels for the navy.

Bibliography

American Vessels Captured by the British during the Revolution and War of 1812, (The Essex Institute: Salem, MA 1911).

Coggeshall, George, *History of the American Privateers, and Letters-of-Marque, during our War with England in the Years 1812, 1813 and 1814*, (New York, 1856).

General Entry Book of American Prisoners of War, British Admiralty, Public Record Office, London, Great Britain (Series ADM 103 / Ledgers 56 through 59), General Entry Book of American prisoners of war at Dartmoor Prison and American alphabetical book.

General Entry Book of American Prisoners of War, British Admiralty, Public Record Office, London, Great Britain (Series ADM 103 / Ledgers 465 and 640), Miscellaneous Lists and Records (Certificates of Death).

Lewis, Lt. Col. George C., and Capt. John Mewha, *History of Prisoner of War Utilization by the United States Army 1776-1945*, Department of the Army Pamphlet number 20-213, (Washington, DC: Department of the Army, 1955), Part One – the Early Wars, Chapter 2 – Prisoners of War as Instruments of Retaliation and Parole, The War of 1812, pp. 22-25.

Maclay, Edgar Stanton, *A History of American Privateers*, (D. Appleton and Company: New York 1900).

Records Relating to American Prisoners of War, 1812-1815, British Records Relating to America Microform (BRRAM) Series, (Microform Academic Publishers: Wakefield, West Yorkshire, United Kingdom, 1980).

Scott, Colonel H. L., *Military Dictionary comprising Technical Definitions; information of raising and keeping troops, including makeshifts and improved materiel; and law, government, regulation, and administration relating to land forces*, (D. Van Nostrand, New York, New York: 1861).

Heritage Books by the Society of the War of 1812
in the State of Ohio:

Transcribed by Harrison Scott Baker

*American Prisoners of War Held at Bermuda,
Cape of Good Hope and Jamaica During the War of 1812*

*American Prisoners of War Held at Barbados,
Newfoundland and New Providence During the War of 1812*

*American Prisoners of War Held at Halifax
During the War of 1812, Volume I and II*

Transcribed by Eric Eugene Johnson

American Prisoners of War Held at Chatham During the War of 1812

American Prisoners of War Held at Dartmoor During the War of 1812

*American Prisoners of War Held in Montreal
and Quebec During the War of 1812*

*American Prisoners of War Held at Plymouth
During the War of 1812*

*American Prisoners of War Held at Quebec
During the War of 1812, 8 June 1813–11 December 1814*

*American Prisoners of War Paroled at Dartmouth,
Halifax, Jamaica and Odiham During the War of 1812*

*American Sea Fencibles in the War of 1812:
United States Sea Fencibles, State Sea Fencibles*

Black Regulars in the War of 1812

Black Regulars and Militiamen in the War of 1812

Forgotten Americans Who Served in the War of 1812

Ohio and the War of 1812: A Collection of Lists, Musters and Essays

Ohio's Regulars in the War of 1812

Heritage Books by the Society of the War of 1812
in the State of Maryland:

Maryland Regulars in the War of 1812
Transcribed by Eric Eugene Johnson; Foreword by Christos Christou

www.ingramcontent.com/pod-product-compliance
Lightning Source LLC
Chambersburg PA
CBHW081143230426
43664CB00018B/2789